Lecture Notes in Computer Science 13510

More information about this series at https://link.springer.com/bookseries/558

Yevgeniy Dodis · Thomas Shrimpton (Eds.)

Advances in Cryptology – CRYPTO 2022

42nd Annual International Cryptology Conference, CRYPTO 2022
Santa Barbara, CA, USA, August 15–18, 2022
Proceedings, Part IV

Editors
Yevgeniy Dodis
New York University
New York, NY, USA

Thomas Shrimpton
University of Florida
Gainesville, FL, USA

ISSN 0302-9743 ISSN 1611-3349 (electronic)
Lecture Notes in Computer Science
ISBN 978-3-031-15984-8 ISBN 978-3-031-15985-5 (eBook)
https://doi.org/10.1007/978-3-031-15985-5

This Springer imprint is published by the registered company Springer Nature Switzerland AG
The registered company address is: Gewerbestrasse 11, 6330 Cham, Switzerland

Preface

The 42nd International Cryptology Conference (CRYPTO 2022) was held at the University of California, Santa Barbara, California, USA, during August 15–18, 2022. The conference had a hybrid format, with some presentations made in person, and some delivered virtually. CRYPTO 2022 was sponsored by the International Association for Cryptologic Research (IACR). The conference was preceded by two days of workshops on various topics.

The conference set new records for both submissions and publications: 455 papers were submitted, and 100 were accepted. Two papers were merged into a single joint paper. Three pairs of papers were soft-merged, meaning that they were written separately, but only one paper in each pair was given a presentation slot at the conference. This resulted in 96 presentations, a record by some margin for a non-virtual edition of Crypto. It took a Program Committee of 72 cryptography experts working with 435 external reviewers almost three months to select the accepted papers. We Chairs extend our heartfelt gratitude for the effort and professionalism displayed by the Program Committee; it was our pleasure to be your Chairs.

We experimented with some new policies and mechanisms this year. The most important had to do with the quality of reviewing, author feedback and interaction with the authors.

Shortly after the standard doubly-blind reviewing stage, we assigned a unique discussion leader (DL) to every paper. The DL's job was to make sure the paper received a thorough and fair treatment, and to moderate interactive communication between the reviewers and authors (described below). The DL also prepared a "Reviewers' consensus summary", which provided the authors with a concise summary of the discussion, the decision, and overall trajectory of the paper throughout the process. Many authors expressed gratitude for receiving the Reviewers' consensus summary, in addition to the usual reviews and scores. Overall, feedback on our DL experiment was quite positive, and we recommend it to future chairs to adopt this process as well.

We also experimented with an "interactive rebuttal" process. Traditionally, the rebuttal process has consisted of a single round: the authors were provided with the initial reviews, and had one opportunity to respond prior to the final decision. While better than no opportunity to rebut, our opinion is that the traditional process suffers from several important flaws. First, the authors were left to respond in (say) 750 words to multiple reviews that are, each, much longer. Too often, the authors are left to divine what are the *crucial* points to address; getting this wrong can lead to reviewers feeling that the rebuttal has missed (or dismissed) what mattered to them. In any case, the authors had no idea if their rebuttal was correctly focused, let alone convincing, until the decisions and final reviews were released. In many instances, the final reviews gave no signal that the rebuttal had been thoughtfully considered. In our view, and personal experience, the traditional rebuttal process led to frustration on both sides, with reviewers and authors feeling that their time had been wasted. Moreover, it had unclear benefits in terms of helping the PC to pick the best possible program.

To address this, we created a review form that required reviewers to make explicit what were their core concerns and criticisms; and we allowed for multiple, DL-moderated, rounds of communication between the reviewers and the authors.

Our review form had *exactly one* field visible to the authors during the initial rebuttal round. The field was called "Question/Clarifications for Authors", and reviewers were instructed to include *only* those things that had significant bearing upon the reviewer's accept/reject stance. We gave all reviewers detailed guidance on things that *must* be included. For example, any claimed errors, crucial prior work that was not cited, or other objective weaknesses that appeared in the detailed review comments. In addition, the reviewers were instructed to clearly state less objective concerns that factored into their initial score and disposition towards the paper. Thus, the authors should know exactly what to focus upon in their response. While not perfect, the new rebuttal format was a resounding success. Very strong/weak papers typically had very short rebuttals, allowing the PC to focus their time and energy on papers in need of extensive discussion or additional reviews.

In concert with the new review form and detailed review instructions, we also implemented *interactive discussions* between the reviewers and authors. The traditional rebuttal round became the first round of the interactive discussion. One round was enough for a fraction of the papers (primarily papers that were very strong or very weak), but the evaluation of most submissions benefited from numerous rounds: reviewers were able to sharpen their questions, authors were able to address points directly and in greater detail. The whole review process shifted more towards a collegial technical exchange. We did not encounter any problems that we initially feared, e.g., authors spamming the PC with comment. We believe that having the DLs moderate these interactions was important for keeping emotions and egos in check, and for encouraging reviewers to share any significant new concerns with the authors.

A few minor hiccups notwithstanding, the focused review forms and the "interactive rebuttal" mechanism received a lot of positive feedback, and we strongly encourage future chairs to adopt this tradition.

We also mention several smaller details which worked well. First, our review form included a "Brief Score Justification" field that remained reviewer-visible (only) for the entire process. This was a space for reviewers to speak freely, but concisely, about how they came to their scores. As Chairs, we found this extremely useful for getting a quick view of each paper's reviews. Second, we had an early rejection round roughly in the middle of our reviewing process. This allowed us to reject roughly half of submissions, i.e., those that clearly had no chance of being accepted to the final program. The process generally worked, and we tried to err on the side of caution, keeping papers alive if the PC was unsure of their seemingly negative views. For example, we allowed PC members to tag papers that they wanted to keep alive, even to the point of overturning a preliminary decision to early reject. However, we did feel slightly rushed in finalizing the early reject decisions, as we made them after less than two weeks after the initial reviewing round, and less than a week after the initial rebuttal round. Part of this rush was due to late reviews. Thus, we recommend that future chairs give themselves a bit more slack in the schedule, and perhaps add a second (less) early rejection round. Third, we experimented with allowing PC members to have a variable number of submissions, rather than the usual hard limits (e.g., at most one or two). Concretely, at most 4 papers could be submitted; the first paper was "free", but every subsequent paper submitted by the PC member resulted in this PC member getting roughly three more papers to review, and one additional DL appointment. We adopted this policy to make it easier for experts to accept our invitation to join the PC. (As always, the chairs were not allowed to submit papers.) Despite some unexpected difficulties and complaints about this system, most having to do with the logistic difficulty of assigning DLs to PC members with late initial reviews, many PC members told us that they appreciated the flexibility to submit more papers, especially when students were involved. We found no evidence that our system resulted in more accepted papers that were co-authored by the PC members, or any other biases and irregularities. Hence, we found it to be positive, overall.

The Program Committee recognized three papers and their authors for particularly outstanding work

- "Batch Arguments for NP and More from Standard Bilinear Group Assumptions," by Brent Waters and David Wu
- "Breaking Rainbow Takes a Weekend on a Laptop", by Ward Beullens
- "Some Easy Instances of Ideal-SVP and Implications to the Partial Vandermonde Knapsack Problem", by Katharina Boudgoust, Erell Gachon, and Alice Pellet-Mary

We were very pleased to have Yehuda Lindell as the Invited Speaker at CRYPTO 2022, who spoke about "The MPC journey from theoretical foundations to commercial success: a story of science and business".

We would like to express our sincere gratitude to all the reviewers for volunteering their time and knowledge in order to select a great program for 2022. Additionally, we are grateful to the following people for helping to make CRYPTO 2022 a success: Allison Bishop (General Chair, CRYPTO 2022), Kevin McCurley and Kay McKelly (IACR IT experts), Carmit Hazay (Workshops Chair), and Whitney Morris and her staff at UCSB conference services.

We would also like to thank the generous sponsors, all of the authors of the submissions, the rump session chair, the regular session chairs, and the speakers.

August 2022

Yevgeniy Dodis
Thomas Shrimpton

Organization

General Chair

Allison Bishop	Proof Trading and City College, CUNY, USA

Program Committee Chairs

Yevgeniy Dodis	New York University, USA
Thomas Shrimpton	University of Florida, USA

Steering Committee

Helena Handschuh	Rambus Inc., USA
Anna Lysyanskaya	Brown University, USA

Program Committee

Shweta Agarwal	IIT Madras, India
Prabhanjan Ananth	University of California Santa Barbara, USA
Saikrishna Badrinarayanan	Visa Research, USA
Lejla Batina	Radboud University, Netherlands
Carsten Baum	Aarhus University, Denmark
Jeremiah Blocki	Purdue University, USA
Alexandra Boldyreva	Georgia Tech, USA
Elette Boyle	IDC Herzliya and NTT Research, Israel
David Cash	University of Chicago, USA
Itai Dinur	Ben-Gurion University, Israel
François Dupressoir	University of Bristol, UK
Nico Döttling	Helmholtz Center for Information Security (CISPA), Germany
Dario Fiore	IMDEA Software Institute, Spain
Ben Fisch	Stanford, USA
Marc Fischlin	TU Darmstadt, Germany
Rosario Gennaro	City College of New York, USA
Divya Gupta	Microsoft Research, India
Felix Günther	ETH Zurich, Switzerland
Mohammad Hajiabadi	University of Waterloo, Canada
Helena Handschuh	Rambus Inc., USA

Nadia Heninger	University of California San Diego, USA
Viet Hoang	Florida State University, USA
Susan Hohenberger	Johns Hopkins University, USA
Joseph Jaeger	Georgia Tech, USA
Tibor Jager	Bergische Universität Wuppertal, Germany
Daniel Jost	New York University, USA
Seny Kamara	Brown University, USA
Aggelos Kiayias	University of Edinburgh and IOHK, UK
Markulf Kohlweiss	University of Edinburgh, UK
Vladimir Kolesnikov	Georgia Tech, USA
Gregor Leander	University Bochum, Germany
Benoît Libert	CNRS and ENS Lyon, France
Feng-Hao Liu	Florida Atlantic University, USA
Anna Lysyanskaya	Brown University, USA
Vadim Lyubashevsky	IBM Research Europe Zurich, Switzerland
Fermi Ma	Simons Institute and UC Berkeley, USA
Bernardo Magri	The University of Manchester, UK
Mohammad Mahmoody	University of Virginia, USA
Hemanta Maji	Purdue University, USA
Alex Malozemoff	Galois Inc., USA
Antonio Marcedone	Zoom, USA
Bart Mennink	Radboud University, Netherlands
Daniele Micciancio	University of California San Diego, USA
Kazuhiko Minematsu	NEC and Yokohama National University, Japan
María Naya-Plasencia	Inria, France
Ryo Nishimaki	NTT Corporation, Japan
Rafael Pass	Cornell Tech, USA
Thomas Peyrin	Nanyang Technological University, Singapore
Antigoni Polychroniadou	J.P. Morgan AI Research, USA
Mariana Raykova	Google, USA
Christian Rechberger	TU Graz, Austria
Leonid Reyzin	Boston University, USA
Lior Rotem	Hebrew University, Israel
Paul Rösler	New York University, USA
Alessandra Scafuro	North Carolina State University, USA
Christian Schaffner	University of Amsterdam and QuSoft, Netherlands
Mark Simkin	Ethereum Foundation, USA
Naomi Sirkin	Cornell Tech, USA
Akshayaram Srinivasan	Tata Institute of Fundamental Research, India
Noah Stephens-Davidowitz	Cornell University, USA
Marc Stevens	CWI, Netherlands

Ni Trieu	Arizona State University, USA
Yiannis Tselekounis	Carnegie Mellon University, USA
Mayank Varia	Boston University, USA
Xiao Wang	Northwestern University, USA
Daniel Wichs	Northeastern University and NTT Research, USA
David Wu	UT Austin, USA
Shota Yamada	AIST, Japan
Kan Yasuda	NTT Labs, Japan
Kevin Yeo	Google and Columbia University, USA
Eylon Yogev	Bar-Ilan University, Israel
Vassilis Zikas	Purdue University, USA

Additional Reviewers

Masayuki Abe
Calvin Abou Haidar
Anasuya Acharya
Divesh Aggarwal
Shashank Agrawal
Gorjan Alagic
Navid Alamati
Martin R. Albrecht
Nicolas Alhaddad
Bar Alon
Estuardo Alpirez Bock
Jacob Alprerin-Shreiff
Joel Alwen
Ghous Amjad
Kazumaro Aoki
Gal Arnon
Rotem Arnon-Friedman
Arasu Arun
Thomas Attema
Benedikt Auerbach
Christian Badertscher
David Balbás
Marco Baldi
Gustavo Banegas
Fabio Banfi
Laaysa Bangalore
James Bartusek
Andrea Basso
Christof Beierle
Amos Beimel
Mihir Bellare
Adrien Benamira
Fabrice Benhamouda
Huck Bennett
Ward Beullens
Tim Beyne
Rishabh Bhadauria
Amit Singh Bhati
Ritam Bhaumik
Sai Lakshmi Bhavana Obbattu
Jean-Francois Biasse
Alexander Bienstock
Nina Bindel
Nir Bitansky
Olivier Blazy
Alexander Block
Xavier Bonnetain
Jonathan Bootle
Katharina Boudgoust
Christina Boura
Pedro Branco
Konstantinos Brazitikos
Jacqueline Brendel
Marek Broll
Chris Brzuska
Ileana Buhan
Benedikt Bunz
Bin-Bin Cai
Federico Canale
Ran Canetti

Ignacio Cascudo
Gaëtan Cassiers
Dario Catalano
Pyrros Chaidos
Suvradip Chakraborty
Jeff Champion
Benjamin Chan
Alishah Chator
Shan Chen
Weikeng Chen
Yilei Chen
Yu Long Chen
Nai-Hui Chia
Lukasz Chmielewski
Chongwon Cho
Arka Rai Choudhuri
Miranda Christ
Chitchanok Chuengsatiansup
Peter Chvojka
Michele Ciampi
Benoît Cogliati
Ran Cohen
Alex Cojocaru
Sandro Coretti-Drayton
Arjan Cornelissen
Henry Corrigan-Gibbs
Geoffroy Couteau
Elizabeth Crites
Jan Czajkwoski
Joan Daemen
Quang Dao
Pratish Datta
Bernardo David
Nicolas David
Hannah Davis
Koen de Boer
Leo de Castro
Luca De Feo
Gabrielle De Micheli
Jean Paul Degabriele
Patrick Derbez
Jesus Diaz
Jack Doerner
Jelle Don
Jesko Dujmovic
Sebastien Duval
Ted Eaton
Nadia El Mrabet
Reo Eriguchi
Llorenç Escolà Farràs
Daniel Escudero
Saba Eskandarian
Thomas Espitau
Antonio Faonio
Pooya Farshim
Serge Fehr
Peter Fenteany
Rex Fernando
Rune Fiedler
Matthias Fitzi
Nils Fleischhacker
Danilo Francati
Cody Freitag
Tommaso Gagliardoni
Chaya Ganesh
Rachit Garg
Lydia Garms
Luke Garratt
Adria Gascon
Romain Gay
Peter Gaži
Nicholas Genise
Marios Georgiou
Koustabh Ghosh
Ashrujit Ghoshal
Barbara Gigerl
Niv Gilboa
Emanuele Giunta
Aarushi Goel
Eli Goldin
Junqing Gong
Jesse Goodman
Lorenzo Grassi
Alex Grilo
Alex Bredariol Grilo
Aditya Gulati
Sam Gunn
Aldo Gunsing
Siyao Guo
Yue Guo

Chun Guo
Julie Ha
Ben Hamlin
Ariel Hamlin
Abida Haque
Patrick Harasser
Ben Harsha
Eduard Hauck
Julia Hesse
Clemens Hlauschek
Justin Holmgren
Alexander Hoover
Kai Hu
Yuval Ishai
Muhammad Ishaq
Takanori Isobe
Tetsu Iwata
Hakon Jacobsen
Aayush Jain
Ashwin Jha
Dingding Jia
Zhengzhong Jin
Nathan Ju
Fatih Kaleoglu
Daniel Kales
Simon Kamp
Daniel M. Kane
Dimitris Karakostas
Harish Karthikeyan
Shuichi Katsumata
Marcel Keller
Thomas Kerber
Mustafa Khairallah
Hamidreza Amini Khorasgani
Hamidreza Khoshakhlagh
Dakshita Khurana
Elena Kirshanova
Fuyuki Kitagawa
Susumu Kiyoshima
Dima Kogan
Lisa Kohl
Stefan Kolbl
Dimitris Kolonelos
Ilan Komargodski
Chelsea Komlo
Yashvanth Kondi
Venkata Koppula
Daniel Kuijsters
Mukul Kulkarni
Nishant Kumar
Fukang Liu
Norman Lahr
Russell W. F. Lai
Qiqi Lai
Baptiste Lambin
David Lanzenberger
Philip Lazos
Seunghoon Lee
Jooyoung Lee
Julia Len
Tancrède Lepoint
Gaëtan Leurent
Hanjun Li
Songsong Li
Baiyu Li
Xiao Liang
Yao-Ting Lin
Han-Hsuan Lin
Huijia Lin
Xiaoyuan Liu
Meicheng Liu
Jiahui Liu
Qipeng Liu
Zeyu Liu
Yanyi Liu
Chen-Da Liu-Zhang
Alex Lombardi
Sébastien Lord
Paul Lou
Donghang Lu
George Lu
Yun Lu
Reinhard Lüftenegger
Varun Madathil
Monosij Maitra
Giulio Malavolta
Mary Maller
Jasleen Malvai
Nathan Manohar
Deepak Maram

Lorenzo Martinico
Christian Matt
Sahar Mazloom
Kelsey Melissaris
Nicolas Meloni
Florian Mendel
Rebekah Mercer
Pierre Meyer
Charles Meyer-Hilfiger
Peihan Miao
Brice Minaud
Pratyush Mishra
Tarik Moataz
Victor Mollimard
Andrew Morgan
Tomoyuki Morimae
Travis Morrison
Fabrice Mouhartem
Tamer Mour
Pratyay Mukherjee
Marta Mularczyk
Marcel Nageler
Yusuke Naito
Kohei Nakagawa
Mridul Nandi
Varun Narayanan
Patrick Neumann
Gregory Neven
Samuel Neves
Ngoc Khanh Nguyen
Hai Nguyen
Luca Nizzardo
Ariel Nof
Adam O'Neill
Maciej Obremski
Kazuma Ohara
Miyako Ohkubo
Claudio Orlandi
Michele Orrù
Elisabeth Oswald
Morten Øygarden
Alex Ozdemir
Elena Pagnin
Tapas Pal
Jiaxin Pan
Giorgos Panagiotakos
Omer Paneth
Udaya Parampalli
Anat Paskin-Cherniavsky
Alain Passelègue
Sikhar Patranabis
Chris Peikert
Alice Pellet-Mary
Zachary Pepin
Leo Perrin
Giuseppe Persiano
Edoardo Persichetti
Peter Pessl
Thomas Peters
Stjepan Picek
Maxime Plancon
Bertram Poettering
Christian Porter
Eamonn Postlethwaite
Thomas Prest
Robert Primas
Luowen Qian
Willy Quach
Srinivasan Raghuraman
Samuel Ranellucci
Shahram Rasoolzadeh
Deevashwer Rathee
Mayank Rathee
Divya Ravi
Krijn Reijnders
Doreen Riepel
Peter Rindal
Guilherme Rito
Bhaskar Roberts
Felix Rohrbach
Leah Rosenbloom
Mike Rosulek
Adeline Roux-Langlois
Joe Rowell
Lawrence Roy
Tim Ruffing
Keegan Ryan
Yusuke Sakai
Louis Salvail
Simona Samardjiska

Katerina Samari
Olga Sanina
Amirreza Sarencheh
Pratik Sarkar
Yu Sasaki
Tobias Schmalz
Markus Schofnegger
Peter Scholl
Jan Schoone
Phillipp Schoppmann
André Schrottenloher
Jacob Schuldt
Sven Schäge
Gregor Seiler
Joon Young Seo
Karn Seth
Srinath Setty
Aria Shahverdi
Laura Shea
Yaobin Shen
Emily Shen
Sina Shiehian
Omri Shmueli
Ferdinand Sibleyras
Janno Siim
Jad Silbak
Luisa Siniscalchi
Daniel Slamanig
Yifan Song
Min Jae Song
Fang Song
Nicholas Spooner
Lukas Stennes
Igors Stepanovs
Christoph Striecks
Sathya Subramanian
Adam Suhl
George Sullivan
Mehrdad Tahmasbi
Akira Takahashi
Atsushi Takayasu
Abdul Rahman Taleb
Quan Quan Tan
Ewin Tang
Tianxin Tang
Stefano Tessaro
Justin Thaler
Emmanuel Thome
Søren Eller Thomsen
Mehdi Tibouchi
Radu Titiu
Yosuke Todo
Junichi Tomida
Monika Trimoska
Daniel Tschudi
Ida Tucker
Nirvan Tyagi
Rei Ueno
Dominique Unruh
David Urbanik
Wessel van Woerden
Prashant Vasudevan
Serge Vaudenay
Muthu Venkitasubramaniam
Damien Vergnaud
Thomas Vidick
Mikhail Volkhov
Satyanarayana Vusirikala
Riad Wahby
Roman Walch
Hendrik Waldner
Michael Walter
Qingju Wang
Han Wang
Haoyang Wang
Mingyuan Wang
Zhedong Wang
Geng Wang
Hoeteck Wee
Shiyi Wei
Mor Weiss
Chenkai Weng
Benjamin Wesolowski
Lichao Wu
Keita Xagawa
Jiayu Xu
Anshu Yadav
Sophia Yakoubov
Takashi Yamakawa
Trevor Yap Hong Eng

Xiuyu Ye
Albert Yu
Thomas Zacharias
Michal Zajac
Hadas Zeilberger
Mark Zhandry
Yupeng Zhang
Cong Zhang
Bingsheng Zhang
Dionysis Zindros

Sponsor Logos

JPMorgan Chase & Co.

SUNSCREEN

Western Digital.

Contents – Part IV

Zero Knowledge

Secure Multiparty Computation III

Threshold Signatures

Secret Sharing and Secure Multiparty Computation

Sharing Transformation and Dishonest Majority MPC with Packed Secret Sharing

Vipul Goyal[1,2](✉), Antigoni Polychroniadou[3], and Yifan Song[1]

[1] Carnegie Mellon University, Pittsburgh, PA, USA
goyal@cs.cmu.edu, yifans2@andrew.cmu.edu
[2] NTT Research, Sunnyvale, CA, USA
[3] J.P. Morgan AI Research, New York, NY, USA

Abstract. In the last few years, the efficiency of secure multi-party computation (MPC) in the dishonest majority setting has increased by several orders of magnitudes starting with the SPDZ protocol family which offers a speedy information-theoretic online phase in the prepossessing model. However, state-of-the-art n-party MPC protocols in the dishonest majority setting incur online communication complexity per multiplication gate which is linear in the number of parties, i.e. $O(n)$, per gate across all parties. In this work, we construct the first MPC protocols in the preprocessing model for dishonest majority with sub-linear communication complexity per gate in the number of parties n. To achieve our results, we extend the use of packed secret sharing to the dishonest majority setting. For a constant fraction of corrupted parties (i.e. if 99 percent of the parties are corrupt), we can achieve a communication complexity of $O(1)$ field elements per multiplication gate across all parties.

At the crux of our techniques lies a new technique called *sharing transformation*. The sharing transformation technique allows us to transform shares under one type of linear secret sharing scheme into another, and even perform arbitrary linear maps on the secrets of (packed) secret sharing schemes with optimal communication complexity. This technique can be of independent interest since transferring shares from one type of scheme into another (e.g., for degree reduction) is ubiquitous in MPC. Furthermore, we introduce what we call *sparsely packed Shamir sharing* which allows us to address the issue of network routing efficiently, and *packed Beaver triples* which is an extension of the widely used technique of Beaver triples for packed secret sharing (for dishonest majority).

1 Introduction

In this work we initiate the study of *sharing transformations* which allow us to perform *arbitrary* linear maps on the secrets of (possibly packed) secret-sharing schemes. More specifically, suppose Σ and Σ' are two linear secret sharing schemes over a finite field $\mathbb{F}$. A set of n parties $\{P_1, P_2, \ldots, P_n\}$ start with holding a Σ-sharing $\boldsymbol{X}$. Here $\boldsymbol{X}$ could be the sharing of a single field element or

Y. Dodis and T. Shrimpton (Eds.): CRYPTO 2022, LNCS 13510, pp. 3–32, 2022.
https://doi.org/10.1007/978-3-031-15985-5_1

a vector of field elements (e.g., as in packed secret sharing where multiple secrets are stored within a single sharing). The parties wish to compute a Σ'-sharing $\boldsymbol{Y}$ whose secret is a *linear map* of the secret of $\boldsymbol{X}$. Here a linear map means that each output secret is a linear combination of the input secrets (recall that the secret can be a vector in $\mathbb{F}$). We refer to this problem as *sharing transformation.*

Restricted cases of sharing transformations occur frequently in the construction of secure computation protocols based on secret sharing. For example,

- In the well-known BGW protocol [BOGW88] and DN protocol [DN07] and their followups (see [CGH+18, BGIN20, GLO+21] and the citations therein), when evaluating a multiplication gate, all parties first locally compute a Shamir secret sharing of the result with a larger degree. To proceed the computation, all parties wish to transform it to a Shamir secret sharing of the result with a smaller degree. Here the two linear secret sharing schemes Σ, Σ' are both the Shamir secret sharing schemes but with different degrees.
- A recent line of works [CCXY18, PS21, CRX21] use the notion of reverse multiplication-friendly embeddings (RMFE) to construct efficient information-theoretic MPC protocols over small fields or rings $\mathbb{Z}/p^\ell\mathbb{Z}$. This technique requires all parties to transform a secret sharing of a vector of secrets that are encoded by an encoding scheme to another secret sharing of the same secrets that are encoded by a different encoding scheme.
- A line of works [DIK10, GIP15, GSY21, BGJK21, GPS21] focus on the strong honest majority setting (i.e., $t = (1/2 - \epsilon) \cdot n$) and use the packed secret-sharing technique [FY92] to construct MPC protocols with sub-linear communication complexity in the number of parties. The main technical difficulty is to perform a linear map on the secrets of a single packed secret sharing (e.g., permutation or fan-out). In particular, depending on the circuit, each time the linear map we need to perform can be different.

Unlike the above results, our sharing transformation protocol (1) can perform arbitrary linear maps (2) is not restricted to a specific secret-sharing scheme and (3) can achieve optimal communication complexity[1]. Our transformation can find applications to different protocols based on different secret sharing schemes. In this work we focus on applications to information-theoretic (IT) MPC protocols. Furthermore, since we can handle any linear secret sharing scheme, our sharing transformation works for an arbitrary packing factor k as long as $t \leq n-2k+1$ where n is the number of participants and t is the number of corrupted parties by the adversary. This allows us to present the first IT MPC protocols with online communication complexity per gate sub-linear in the number of parties in

[1] To be more precise, our protocol achieves linear communication complexity in the summation of the sharing sizes of the two secret sharing schemes in the transformation. This is optimal (up to a constant factor) since it matches the communication complexity of using an ideal functionality to do sharing transformation: the size of the input is the sharing size of the first secret sharing scheme, the size of the output is the sharing size of the second secret sharing scheme, and the communication complexity is the size of the input and output.

the circuit-independent prepossessing model for a variety of corruption thresholds based on packed secret sharing. That said, we are able to extend the use of packed secret sharing beyond the strong honest majority setting.

For the case where $t = n-1$, any function can be computed with IT security in the preprocessing model with online communication complexity of $O(n)$ field elements per gate across all parties [DPSZ12]. Existing protocols in the literature even for $t \in [(n-1)/2, n-1]$ still required communication complexity of $O(n)$ elements per gate. We note that most of these protocols follow the "gate-by-gate" design pattern described in [DNPR16]. In particular, the work [DNPR16] shows that any information-theoretic protocol that works in this design pattern must communicate $\Omega(n)$ for every multiplication gate. However, recent protocols in the strong honest majority setting, based on packed secret-sharing [FY92], where the number of corrupted parties $t = (1/2-\epsilon) \cdot n$ and $\epsilon \in (0, 1/2)$ [GPS21] do achieve $O(1/\epsilon)$ communication complexity per gate among all parties. Note that the packed secret sharing technique evaluates a batch of multiplication gates in parallel, which differs from the above "gate-by-gate" design pattern in [DNPR16], and therefore does not contradict with the result in [DNPR16]. Our result closes the gap in achieving sub-linear communication complexity per gate in the number of parties for the more popular settings of standard honest majority and dishonest majority.

1.1 Our Contributions

Sharing Transformation. For our arbitrary linear-map transformation on (packed) linear secret sharing schemes we obtain the following informal result focusing on share size 1 (i.e., each share is a single field element).

Theorem 1 (Informal). *Let $k = (n-t+1)/2$. For all k tuples of $\{(\Sigma_i, \Sigma'_i, f_i)\}_{i=1}^{k}$ linear secret sharing schemes with injective sharing functions and for all Σ_i-sharings $\{\boldsymbol{X}_i\}_{i=1}^{k}$, there is an information-theoretic MPC protocol with semi-honest security against t corrupted parties that transforms $\boldsymbol{X}_i$ to a Σ'_i-sharing $\boldsymbol{Y}_i$ such that the secret of $\boldsymbol{Y}_i$ is equal to the result of applying a linear map f_i on the secret of $\boldsymbol{X}_i$ for all $i \in \{1, \ldots, k\}$ (Here the secrets of $\boldsymbol{X}_i$ and $\boldsymbol{Y}_i$ can be vectors). The cost of the protocol is $O(n^3/k^2)$ elements of communication per sharing in a (sharing independent) preprocessing stage leading to preprocessed data of size $O(n^2/k)$, and $O(n^2/k)$ elements of communication per sharing in the online phase. When $t = (1-\epsilon) \cdot n$ for a positive constant ϵ, the overall communication complexity is $O(n)$ elements per sharing transformation.*

The formal theorem is stated in the full version of this paper [GPS22]. In Sect. 4, we show that our sharing transformation works for any share size ℓ (with an increase in the communication complexity by a factor ℓ), and in the full version of this paper [GPS22], we show that it is naturally extended to any finite fields and rings $\mathbb{Z}/p^{\ell}\mathbb{Z}$. The main application of our sharing transformation technique is to construct MPC protocols. And we achieve malicious security by directly compiling our semi-honest MPC protocol instead of relying on a maliciously secure sharing transformation protocol. Therefore, in this work, we do not attempt to achieve malicious security for our sharing transformation technique.

We now turn our attention to constructing general MPC using our sharing transformation technique.

Dishonest Majority. In the setting of dishonest majority where the number of corrupted parties $t = (1 - \epsilon) \cdot n$ for a positive constant ϵ, our MPC protocol achieves the cost of $O(1/\epsilon^2)$ elements of (the size of) preprocessing data, and $O(1/\epsilon)$ elements of communication per gate among all parties. Thus when ϵ is a constant (e.g., up to 99 percent of all parties may be corrupted), the achieved communication complexity in the online phase is $O(1)$ elements per gate.

Honest Majority. As a corollary of our results in the dishonest majority setting, we can achieve $O(1)$ elements per gate of online communication and $O(1)$ elements of preprocessing data per gate across all parties in the standard honest majority setting (i.e., where the number of corrupted parties t is $(n-1)/2$).

Our main results are summarized below. Note that we have omitted the additive terms of the overhead of the communication complexity in the informal theorems below. The additive terms are dependent on n and the depth of the evaluated circuit. Our first theorem is for the semi-honest setting:

Theorem 2 (Informal). *For an arithmetic circuit C over a finite field $\mathbb{F}$ of size $|\mathbb{F}| \geq |C|+n$, there exists an information-theoretic MPC protocol in the preprocessing model which securely computes the arithmetic circuit C in the presence of a semi-honest adversary controlling up to t parties. The cost of the protocol is $O(|C| \cdot n^2/k^2)$ elements of preprocessing data, and $O(|C| \cdot n/k)$ elements of communication where $k = \frac{n-t+1}{2}$ is the packing parameter. For the case where $k = O(n)$, the achieved communication complexity in the online phase is $O(1)$ elements per gate.*

Our theorem also holds in the presence of a malicious adversary for all $1 \leq k \leq [\frac{n+2}{3}]$. The formal theorem for semi-honest security is stated in Theorem 3. We refer the readers to the full version of this paper [GPS22] for the formal theorem for malicious security. Moreover, using our sharing transformation based on the construction of [GPS21], we can also achieve online communication complexity of $O(1)$ elements per gate for small finite fields of size $|\mathbb{F}| \geq 2n$. We refer the readers to the full version of this paper [GPS22] for more details.

2 Technical Overview

In this section, we give an overview of our techniques. We use bold letters to represent vectors.

Reducing Sharing Transformation to Random Sharing Preparation. Usually, sharing transformation is solved by using a pair of random sharings $(\boldsymbol{R}, \boldsymbol{R}')$ such that $\boldsymbol{R}$ is a random Σ-sharing and $\boldsymbol{R}'$ is a random Σ'-sharing which satisfies that the secret of $\boldsymbol{R}'$ is equal to the result of applying f on the secret of $\boldsymbol{R}$, where f is the desired linear map. Then all parties can run the following steps to efficiently transform $\boldsymbol{X}$ to $\boldsymbol{Y}$.

1. All parties locally compute $\boldsymbol{X} + \boldsymbol{R}$ and send their shares to the first party P_1.
2. P_1 reconstructs the secret of $\boldsymbol{X} + \boldsymbol{R}$, denoted by $\boldsymbol{w}$. Then P_1 computes $f(\boldsymbol{w})$ and generates a Σ'-sharing of $f(\boldsymbol{w})$, denoted by $\boldsymbol{W}$. Finally, P_1 distributes the shares of $\boldsymbol{W}$ to all parties.
3. All parties locally compute $\boldsymbol{Y} = \boldsymbol{W} - \boldsymbol{R}'$.

If we use $\mathtt{rec}, \mathtt{rec}'$ to denote the reconstruction maps of Σ and Σ' (which are linear by definition) respectively, the correctness follows from that

$$\mathtt{rec}'(\boldsymbol{Y}) = \mathtt{rec}'(\boldsymbol{W}) - \mathtt{rec}'(\boldsymbol{R}') = f(\boldsymbol{w}) - f(\mathtt{rec}(\boldsymbol{R})) = f(\mathtt{rec}(\boldsymbol{X}+\boldsymbol{R}) - \mathtt{rec}(\boldsymbol{R})) = f(\mathtt{rec}(\boldsymbol{X})).$$

And the security follows from the fact that $\boldsymbol{X}+\boldsymbol{R}$ is a random Σ-sharing and thus reveals no information about the secret of $\boldsymbol{X}$. Therefore, the problem of sharing transformation is reduced to preparing a pair of random sharings $(\boldsymbol{R}, \boldsymbol{R}')$. Let $\widetilde{\Sigma} = \widetilde{\Sigma}(\Sigma, \Sigma', f)$ be the secret sharing scheme which satisfies that a $\widetilde{\Sigma}$-sharing of a secret $\boldsymbol{x}$ consists of $\boldsymbol{X}$ which is a Σ-sharing of $\boldsymbol{x}$, and $\boldsymbol{Y}$ which is a Σ'-sharing of $f(\boldsymbol{x})$. Then, the goal becomes to prepare a random $\widetilde{\Sigma}$-sharing.

The generic approach of preparing random sharings of a linear secret sharing scheme over $\mathbb{F}$ is as follows:

1. Each party P_i first samples a random sharing $\boldsymbol{R}_i$ and distributes the shares to all other parties.
2. All parties use a linear randomness extractor over $\mathbb{F}$ to extract a batch of random sharings such that they remain uniformly random even given the random sharings sampled by corrupted parties. For a large finite field, we can use the transpose of a Vandermonde matrix [DN07] as a linear randomness extractor. The use of a randomness extractor is to reduce the communication complexity per random sharing. Alternatively, we can simply add all random sharings $\{\boldsymbol{R}_i\}_{i=1}^n$ and output a single random sharing, which results in quadratic communication complexity in the number of parties.

If t is the number of corrupted parties, all parties can extract $n - t$ random sharings when using a large finite field. Then, the amortized communication cost per sharing is $n^2/(n-t)$ field elements (assuming each share is a single field element). When $n - t = O(n)$, e.g., the honest majority setting, the amortized cost becomes $n^2/(n-t) = O(n)$, which is generally good enough since it matches the communication complexity of delivering a random sharing by a trusted party, which seems like the best we can hope, up to a constant factor.

Thus when we need to prepare many random sharings for the same linear secret sharing scheme, the generic approach is already good enough. And in particular, it is good enough for random $\widetilde{\Sigma}$-sharings which are used for the *same* sharing transformation defined by $\widetilde{\Sigma} = \widetilde{\Sigma}(\Sigma, \Sigma', f)$, since $\widetilde{\Sigma}$ is also a linear secret sharing scheme. This is exactly the case when we need to do degree reduction in [BOGW88,DN07] and change the encoding of the secrets in [CCXY18,PS21, CRX21]. However, it is a different story if we need to prepare random sharings for different linear secret sharing schemes: If only a constant number of random sharings are needed for each linear secret sharing scheme, the amortized cost per sharing becomes $O(n^2)$ field elements. This is exactly the case when we need to perform permutation on the secrets of a packed secret sharing in [DIK10, GIP15,BGJK21,GPS21]. In their setting, the permutations are determined by the circuit structure. In particular, these permutations can all be distinct in the worst case. As a result, the cost of preparing random sharings becomes the dominating term in the communication complexity in the MPC protocols. To avoid it, previous works either restrict the number of different secret sharing schemes they need to prepare random sharings for [DIK10,GIP15,GPS21] or restrict the types of circuits [BGJK21].

This leads to the following fundamental question: *Can we prepare random sharings (used for sharing transformations) for different linear secret sharing schemes with amortized communication complexity $O(n)$?*

2.1 Preparing Random Sharings for Different Linear Secret Sharing Schemes

To better expose our idea, we focus on a large finite field $\mathbb{F}$. In the following, we use n for the number of parties, and t for the number of corrupted parties. We assume semi-honest security in the technical overview.

Linear Secret Sharing Scheme over $\mathbb{F}$. For a linear secret sharing scheme Σ over $\mathbb{F}$, we use $Z = \mathbb{F}^{\tilde{k}}$ to denote the secret space. $\tilde{k}$ is also referred to as the secret size of Σ. For simplicity, we focus on the linear secret sharing schemes that have share size 1 (i.e., each share is a single field element even though the secret is a vector of $\tilde{k}$ elements). Let $\texttt{share} : Z \times \mathbb{F}^{\tilde{r}} \to \mathbb{F}^n$ be the deterministic sharing map which takes as input a secret $\boldsymbol{x}$ and $\tilde{r}$ random field elements, and outputs a Σ-sharing of $\boldsymbol{x}$. We focus on linear secret sharing schemes whose sharing maps are injective, which implies that $\tilde{k} + \tilde{r} \leq n$. Let $\texttt{rec} : \mathbb{F}^n \to Z$ be the reconstruction map which takes as input a Σ-sharing and outputs the secret of the input sharing. As discussed above, we have shown that preparing many random sharings for the same linear secret sharing scheme can be efficiently achieved.

We use the standard Shamir secret sharing scheme over $\mathbb{F}$, and use $[x]_t$ to denote a degree-t Shamir sharing of x. A degree-t Shamir sharing requires $t+1$ shares to reconstruct the secret. And any t shares of a degree-t Shamir sharing are independent of the secret.

Starting Point - Preparing a Random Sharing for a Single Linear Secret Sharing Scheme. Let Σ be an arbitrary linear secret sharing scheme.

Although we have already shown how to prepare a random sharing for a single linear secret sharing scheme Σ, we consider the following process which is easy to be extended (discussed later).

1. All parties prepare $\tilde{k} + \tilde{r}$ random degree-t Shamir sharings. Let $\boldsymbol{\tau}$ be the secrets of the first $\tilde{k}$ sharings, and $\boldsymbol{\rho}$ be the secrets of the last $\tilde{r}$ sharings. Our goal is to compute a random Σ-sharing of $\boldsymbol{\tau}$ with random tape $\boldsymbol{\rho}$, i.e., $\mathtt{share}(\boldsymbol{\tau}, \boldsymbol{\rho})$.
2. Since $\mathtt{share}$ is $\mathbb{F}$-linear, for all $j \in \{1, 2, \ldots, n\}$, the j-th share of $\mathtt{share}(\boldsymbol{\tau}, \boldsymbol{\rho})$ is a linear combination of the values in $\boldsymbol{\tau}$ and $\boldsymbol{\rho}$. Thus, all parties can locally compute a degree-t Shamir sharing of the j-th share of $\mathtt{share}(\boldsymbol{\tau}, \boldsymbol{\rho})$ by using the degree-t Shamir sharings of the values in $\boldsymbol{\tau}$ and $\boldsymbol{\rho}$ prepared in Step 1 and applying linear combinations on their local shares. Let $[X_j]_t$ denote the resulting sharing.
3. For all $j \in \{1, 2, \ldots, n\}$, all parties send their shares of $[X_j]_t$ to P_j to let P_j reconstruct X_j. All parties take $\boldsymbol{X} = (X_1, \ldots, X_n)$ as output.

Note that $\boldsymbol{\tau}$ and $\boldsymbol{\rho}$ are all uniform field elements, and $\boldsymbol{X} = \mathtt{share}(\boldsymbol{\tau}, \boldsymbol{\rho})$. Therefore, the output $\boldsymbol{X}$ is a random Σ-sharing.

We note that this approach requires to prepare $\tilde{k}+\tilde{r} = O(n)$ random degree-t Shamir sharings and communicate n^2 field elements in order to prepare a random Σ-sharing, which is far from $O(n)$. To improve the efficiency, we try to prepare random sharings for a batch of (potentially different) secret sharing schemes each time.

Preparing Random Sharings for a Batch of Different Linear Secret Sharing Schemes. We note that the above vanilla process can be viewed as all parties securely evaluating a circuit for the sharing map $\mathtt{share}$ of Σ. In particular, (1) the circuit only involves linear operations, and (2) circuits for different secret sharing schemes (i.e., $\mathtt{share}_1, \mathtt{share}_2, \ldots, \mathtt{share}_k$) all satisfy that each output value is a linear combination of all input values with different coefficients. When we want to prepare random sharings for a batch of different secret sharing schemes, the joint circuit is very similar to a SIMD circuit (which is a circuit that contains many copies of the same sub-circuit). The only difference is that, in our case, each sub-circuit corresponds to a different secret sharing scheme, and therefore the coefficients used in different sub-circuits are distinct. On the other hand, a SIMD circuit would use the same coefficients in all sub-circuits. Thus, it motivates us to explore the packed secret-sharing technique in [FY92], which is originally used to evaluate a SIMD circuit.

Starting Idea. Suppose $\Sigma_1, \Sigma_2, \ldots, \Sigma_k$ are k arbitrary linear secret sharing schemes (Recall that we want to prepare random sharings for different sharing transformations, and every different sharing transformation requires to prepare a random sharing of a different secret sharing scheme). We assume that they all have share size 1 (i.e., each share is a single field element) for simplicity. We consider to use a packed secret sharing scheme that can store k secrets in each sharing. Our attempt is as follows:

1. All parties first prepare n random packed secret sharings (Our construction will use the packed Shamir secret sharings introduced below). The secrets are denoted by $\boldsymbol{r}_1, \boldsymbol{r}_2, \ldots, \boldsymbol{r}_n$, where each secret $\boldsymbol{r}_j$ is a vector of k random elements in $\mathbb{F}$.
2. For all $i \in \{1, 2, \ldots, k\}$, we want to use the i-th values of all secret vectors to prepare a random sharing of Σ_i. With more details, suppose Σ_i has secret space $Z_i = \mathbb{F}^{\tilde{k}_i}$, and the sharing map of Σ_i is $\mathtt{share}_i : Z_i \times \mathbb{F}^{\tilde{r}_i} \rightarrow \mathbb{F}^n$. Consider the vector $(r_{1,i}, r_{2,i}, \ldots, r_{n,i})$ which contains the i-th values of all secret vectors. We plan to use the first $\tilde{k}_i$ values as the secret $\boldsymbol{\tau}_i$, and the next $\tilde{r}_i$ values as the random tape $\boldsymbol{\rho}_i$. Recall that we require $\mathtt{share}_i$ to be injective. We have $\tilde{k}_i + \tilde{r}_i \leq n$. Therefore, there are enough values for $\boldsymbol{\tau}_i$ and $\boldsymbol{\rho}_i$. The goal is to compute a random Σ_i-sharing $\boldsymbol{X}_i$ of the secret $\boldsymbol{\tau}_i$ with random tape $\boldsymbol{\rho}_i$, i.e., $\boldsymbol{X}_i = \mathtt{share}_i(\boldsymbol{\tau}_i, \boldsymbol{\rho}_i)$.
3. For each party P_j, let $\boldsymbol{u}_j$ denote the j-th shares of $\boldsymbol{X}_1, \ldots, \boldsymbol{X}_k$. We want to use the packed secret sharings of $\boldsymbol{r}_1, \ldots, \boldsymbol{r}_n$ to compute a single packed secret sharing of $\boldsymbol{u}_j$.
4. After obtaining a packed secret sharing of $\boldsymbol{u}_j$, we can reconstruct the sharing to P_j so that he learns the j-th share of each of $\boldsymbol{X}_1, \ldots, \boldsymbol{X}_k$. Thus, we start with n packed secret sharings (of $\boldsymbol{r}_1, \ldots, \boldsymbol{r}_n$) of the same secret sharing scheme and end with k sharings $\boldsymbol{X}_1, \ldots, \boldsymbol{X}_k$ of k potentially different secret sharing schemes.

Clearly, the main question is how to realize Step 3. We observe that, since Σ_i is a linear secret sharing scheme, the j-th share of $\boldsymbol{X}_i$ can be written as a linear combination of the values in $\boldsymbol{\tau}_i$ and $\boldsymbol{\rho}_i$. Therefore, the j-th share of $\boldsymbol{X}_i$ is a linear combination of the values $(r_{1,i}, r_{2,i}, \ldots, r_{n,i})$. Since it holds for all $i \in \{1, 2, \ldots, k\}$, there exists constant vectors $\boldsymbol{c}_1, \ldots, \boldsymbol{c}_n \in \mathbb{F}^k$ such that

$$\boldsymbol{u}_j := \boldsymbol{c}_1 * \boldsymbol{r}_1 + \ldots + \boldsymbol{c}_n * \boldsymbol{r}_n,$$

where $*$ denotes the coordinate-wise multiplication operation. Thus, *what we need is a packed secret sharing scheme that supports efficient coordinate-wise multiplication with a constant vector.* We note that the packed Shamir secret sharing scheme fits our need as we show next.

Packed Shamir Secret Sharing Scheme and Multiplication-Friendliness. The packed Shamir secret sharing scheme [FY92] is a natural generalization of the standard Shamir secret sharing scheme [Sha79]. It allows to secret-share a batch of secrets within a single Shamir sharing. For a vector $\boldsymbol{x} \in \mathbb{F}^k$, we use $[\boldsymbol{x}]_d$ to denote a degree-d packed Shamir sharing, where $k - 1 \leq d \leq n - 1$. It requires $d + 1$ shares to reconstruct the whole sharing, and any $d - k + 1$ shares are independent of the secrets. The packed Shamir secret sharing scheme has the following nice properties:

- Linear Homomorphism: For all $d \geq k - 1$ and $\boldsymbol{x}, \boldsymbol{y} \in \mathbb{F}^k$, $[\boldsymbol{x} + \boldsymbol{y}]_d = [\boldsymbol{x}]_d + [\boldsymbol{y}]_d$.
- Multiplicative: For all $d_1, d_2 \geq k - 1$ subject to $d_1 + d_2 < n$, and for all $\boldsymbol{x}, \boldsymbol{y} \in \mathbb{F}^k$, $[\boldsymbol{x} * \boldsymbol{y}]_{d_1 + d_2} = [\boldsymbol{x}]_{d_1} \cdot [\boldsymbol{y}]_{d_2}$, where the multiplications are performed on the corresponding shares.

Note that when $d \le n-k$, all parties can locally multiply a public vector $\boldsymbol{c} \in \mathbb{F}^k$ with a degree-d packed Shamir sharing $[\boldsymbol{x}]_d$:

1. All parties first locally compute a degree-$(k-1)$ packed Shamir sharing of $\boldsymbol{c}$, denoted by $[\boldsymbol{c}]_{k-1}$. Note that for a degree-$(k-1)$ packed Shamir sharing, all shares are determined by the secret $\boldsymbol{c}$.
2. All parties then locally compute $[\boldsymbol{c} * \boldsymbol{x}]_{n-1} = [\boldsymbol{c}]_{k-1} \cdot [\boldsymbol{x}]_{n-k}$.

We simply write $[\boldsymbol{c} * \boldsymbol{x}]_{n-1} = \boldsymbol{c} \cdot [\boldsymbol{x}]_{n-k}$ to denote the above process. We refer to this property as multiplication-friendliness.

To make sure that the packed Shamir secret sharing scheme is secure against t corrupted parties, we also require $d \ge t+k-1$. When $d = n-k$ and $k = (n-t+1)/2$, the degree-$(n-k)$ packed Shamir secret sharing scheme is both multiplication-friendly and secure against t corrupted parties.

Observe that when we use the degree-$(n-k)$ packed Shamir secret sharing scheme in our attempt, all parties can locally compute a degree-$(n-1)$ packed Shamir sharing of $\boldsymbol{u}_j$ by

$$[\boldsymbol{u}_j]_{n-1} = \boldsymbol{c}_1 \cdot [\boldsymbol{r}_1]_{n-k} + \ldots + \boldsymbol{c}_n \cdot [\boldsymbol{r}_n]_{n-k},$$

which solves the problem.

Summary of Our Construction. In summary, all parties run the following steps to prepare random sharings for k different linear secret sharing schemes $\Sigma_1, \Sigma_2, \ldots, \Sigma_k$.

1. Prepare Packed Shamir Sharings: All parties prepare n random degree-$(n-k)$ packed Shamir sharings, denoted by $[\boldsymbol{r}_1]_{n-k}, \ldots, [\boldsymbol{r}_n]_{n-k}$.
2. Use Packed Secrets as Randomness for Target LSSS: For all $i \in \{1, 2, \ldots, k\}$, let $\boldsymbol{\tau}_i = (r_{1,i}, \ldots, r_{\tilde{k}_i,i})$ and $\boldsymbol{\rho}_i = (r_{\tilde{k}_i+1,i}, \ldots, r_{\tilde{k}_i+\tilde{r}_i,i})$. Let $\boldsymbol{X}_i = \mathtt{share}_i(\boldsymbol{\tau}_i, \boldsymbol{\rho}_i)$.
3. Compute a Single Packed Shamir Sharing for All j-th Shares of Target LSSS via Local Operations: For all $j \in \{1, 2, \ldots, n\}$, let $\boldsymbol{u}_j$ be the j-th shares of $(\boldsymbol{X}_1, \ldots, \boldsymbol{X}_k)$. All parties locally compute a degree-$(n-1)$ packed Shamir sharing of $\boldsymbol{u}_j$ by using $[\boldsymbol{r}_1]_{n-k}, \ldots, [\boldsymbol{r}_n]_{n-k}$. The resulting sharing is denoted by $[\boldsymbol{u}_j]_{n-1}$.
4. Reconstruct the Single Packed Shamir Sharing of All j-th Shares to P_j: For all $j \in \{1, 2, \ldots, n\}$, all parties reconstruct the sharing $[\boldsymbol{u}_j]_{n-1}$ to P_j to let him learn $\boldsymbol{u}_j = (u_j^{(1)}, \ldots, u_j^{(k)})$. Then all parties take $\{\boldsymbol{X}_i = (u_1^{(i)}, \ldots, u_n^{(i)})\}_{i=1}^k$ as output.

We note that in Step 4, $[\boldsymbol{u}_j]_{n-1}$ is not a random degree-$(n-1)$ packed Shamir sharing of $\boldsymbol{u}_j$. *Directly sending the shares of $[\boldsymbol{u}_j]_{n-1}$ to P_j may leak the information about honest parties' shares.* To solve it, all parties also prepare n random degree-$(n-1)$ packed Shamir sharings of $\boldsymbol{0} \in \mathbb{F}^k$, denoted by $[\boldsymbol{o}_1]_{n-1}, \ldots, [\boldsymbol{o}_n]_{n-1}$. Then all parties use $[\boldsymbol{o}_j]_{n-1}$ to refresh the shares of $[\boldsymbol{u}_j]_{n-1}$ by computing $[\boldsymbol{u}_j]_{n-1} := [\boldsymbol{u}_j]_{n-1} + [\boldsymbol{o}_j]_{n-1}$. Now $[\boldsymbol{u}_j]_{n-1}$ is a random degree-$(n-1)$ packed Shamir sharing of $\boldsymbol{u}_j$. All parties send their shares of $[\boldsymbol{u}_j]_{n-1}$ to P_j to let him reconstruct $\boldsymbol{u}_j$.

Communication Complexity. Thus, to prepare random sharings for k linear secret sharing schemes, our construction requires to prepare n random degree-$(n-k)$ packed Shamir sharings and n random degree-$(n-1)$ packed Shamir sharings of $\mathbf{0} \in \mathbb{F}^k$. And the communication complexity is n^2 field elements. On average, each random sharing costs $2n/k$ packed Shamir sharings and n^2/k elements of communication. When we use the generic approach to prepare random packed Shamir sharings, the total communication complexity per random sharing is $O(n^2/k)$ elements.

Recall that $k = (n-t+1)/2$. When $t = (1-\epsilon)\cdot n$ for a positive constant ϵ, the communication complexity per random sharing is $O(n)$ elements, which matches the communication complexity of delivering a random sharing by a trusted party up to a constant factor. In Sect. 4, we show that our technique works for any share size ℓ (with an increase in the communication complexity by a factor ℓ), and is naturally extended to any finite fields and rings $\mathbb{Z}/p^\ell\mathbb{Z}$.

Efficient Sharing Transformation. Recall that in the problem of sharing transformation, all parties start with holding a sharing $\boldsymbol{X}$ of a linear secret sharing scheme Σ. They want to compute a sharing $\boldsymbol{Y}$ of another linear secret sharing scheme Σ' such that the secret of $\boldsymbol{Y}$ is a linear map of the secret of $\boldsymbol{X}$.

As we discussed above, sharing transformation can be achieved efficiently with the help of a pair of random sharings $(\boldsymbol{R}, \boldsymbol{R}')$ such that $\boldsymbol{R}$ is a random Σ-sharing and $\boldsymbol{R}'$ is a random Σ'-sharing which satisfies that the secret of $\boldsymbol{R}'$ is equal to the result of applying the desired linear map on the secret of $\boldsymbol{R}$. *A key insight is that $(\boldsymbol{R}, \boldsymbol{R}')$ can just be seen as a linear secret sharing on its own.* With our technique of preparing random sharings for different linear secret sharing schemes, we can efficiently prepare a pair of random sharings $(\boldsymbol{R}, \boldsymbol{R}')$, allowing efficient sharing transformation from $\boldsymbol{X}$ to $\boldsymbol{Y}$.

When $t = (1-\epsilon)\cdot n$ for a positive constant ϵ, each sharing transformation only requires $O(n)$ field elements of communication.

2.2 Application: MPC via Packed Shamir Secret Sharing Schemes

In this section, we show that our technique for sharing transformation allows us to design an efficient MPC protocol via packed Shamir secret sharing schemes. We focus on the *dishonest majority setting* and information-theoretic setting in the circuit-independent preprocessing model. In the preprocessing model, all parties receive correlated randomness from a trusted party before the computation. The preprocessing model enables the possibility of an information-theoretic protocol in the dishonest majority setting, which otherwise cannot exist in the plain model. The cost of a protocol in the preprocessing model is measured by both the amount of preprocessing data prepared in the preprocessing phase and the amount of communication in the online phase [Cou19,BGIN21].

Let n be the number of parties, and t be the number of corrupted parties. For any positive constant ϵ, we show that there is an information-theoretic MPC protocol in the circuit-independent preprocessing model with semi-honest security (or malicious security) that computes an arithmetic circuit C over a large finite field $\mathbb{F}$ (with $|\mathbb{F}| \geq |C| + n$) against $t = (1 - \epsilon) \cdot n$ corrupted parties with $O(|C|)$ field elements of preprocessing data and $O(|C|)$ field elements of communication. Compared with the recent work [GPS21] that achieves $O(|C|)$ communication complexity in the strong honest majority setting (i.e., $t = (1/2 - \epsilon) \cdot n$), our construction has the following advantages:

1. Our protocol works in the dishonest majority setting.
2. With our new technique for sharing transformation, we avoid the heavy machinery in [GPS21] for the network routing (see more discussion in the full version of this paper [GPS22]).

On the other hand, we note that the protocol in [GPS21] works for a finite field of size $2n$ while our protocol requires the field size to be $|C| + n$. We discuss how our technique for sharing transformation can be used to simplify the protocol in [GPS21] and how to extend their protocol to the dishonest majority setting using our techniques in the full version of this paper [GPS22]. We also refer the readers to the full version of this paper [GPS22] for a more detailed comparison with [GPS21] and other related works.

Review the Packed Shamir Secret Sharing Scheme. We recall the notion of the packed Shamir secret sharing scheme. Let $\alpha_1, \ldots, \alpha_n$ be n distinct elements in $\mathbb{F}$ and $\mathsf{pos} = (p_1, p_2, \ldots, p_k)$ be another k distinct elements in $\mathbb{F}$. A *degree-d ($d \geq k - 1$)* packed Shamir sharing of $\boldsymbol{x} = (x_1, \ldots, x_k) \in \mathbb{F}^k$ is a vector $(w_1, \ldots, w_n)$ for which there exists a polynomial $f(\cdot) \in \mathbb{F}[X]$ of degree at most d such that $f(p_i) = x_i$ for all $i \in \{1, 2, \ldots, k\}$, and $f(\alpha_i) = w_i$ for all $i \in \{1, 2, \ldots, n\}$. The i-th share w_i is held by party P_i.

In our protocol, we will always use the same elements $\alpha_1, \ldots, \alpha_n$ for the positions of the shares of all parties. However, we may use different elements pos for the secrets. We will use $[\boldsymbol{x} \| \mathsf{pos}]_d$ to denote a degree-d packed Shamir sharing of $\boldsymbol{x} \in \mathbb{F}^k$ stored at positions pos. Let $\boldsymbol{\beta} = (\beta_1, \ldots, \beta_k)$ be distinct field elements in $\mathbb{F}$ that are different from $\alpha_1, \ldots, \alpha_n$. We will use $\boldsymbol{\beta}$ as the default positions for the secrets, and simply write $[\boldsymbol{x}]_d = [\boldsymbol{x} \| \boldsymbol{\beta}]_d$.

Recall that t is the number of corrupted parties. Let $k = (n - t + 1)/2$ and $d = n - k$. As we have shown in Sect. 2.1, all parties can locally multiply a public vector with a degree-$(n - k)$ packed Shamir sharing, and a degree-$(n - k)$ packed Shamir sharing is secure against t corrupted parties.

An Overview of Our Construction. At a high-level,

1. All parties start with sharing their input values by using packed Shamir sharings.
2. In each layer, addition gates and multiplication gates are divided into groups of size k. Each time we will evaluate a group of k gates:
   (a) For each group of k gates, all parties prepare two packed Shamir sharings, one for the first inputs of all gates, and the other one for the second inputs of all gates. Note that the secrets we want to be in a single sharing can be scattered in different output sharings from previous layers. This step

is referred to as *network routing*. Relying on our technique of sharing transformation, we can use a much simpler approach to handle network routing than that in [GPS21].

(b) After preparing the two input sharings, all parties evaluate these k gates. Addition gates can be locally computed since the packed Shamir secret sharing scheme is linearly homomorphic. For multiplication gates, we extend the technique of Beaver triples [Bea91] to our setting, which we refer to as *packed Beaver triples*. All parties need to prepare packed Beaver triples in the preprocessing phase.

3. After evaluating the whole circuit, all parties reconstruct the sharings they hold to the parties who should receive the result.

Sparsely Packed Shamir Sharings. Our idea is to use a different position to store the output value of each gate. Recall that $|\mathbb{F}| \geq |C| + n$. Let $\beta_1, \beta_2, \ldots, \beta_{|C|}$ be $|C|$ distinct field elements that are different from $\alpha_1, \alpha_2, \ldots, \alpha_n$. (Recall that we have already defined $\boldsymbol{\beta} = (\beta_1, \ldots, \beta_k)$, which are used as the default positions for a packed Shamir sharing.) We associate the field element β_i with the i-th gate in C. We will use β_i as the position to store the output value of the i-th gate in a degree-$(n-k)$ packed Shamir sharing (see an example below).

Concretely, for each group of k gates, all parties will compute a degree-$(n-k)$ packed Shamir sharing such that the results are stored at the positions associated with these k gates respectively. For example, when $k = 3$, for a batch of 3 gates which are associated with the positions $\beta_1, \beta_3, \beta_6$ respectively, all parties will compute a degree-$(n-k)$ packed Shamir sharing $[(z_1, z_3, z_6)\|(\beta_1, \beta_3, \beta_6)]_{n-k}$ for this batch of gates, where z_1, z_3, z_6 are the output wires of these 3 gates.

As we will see later, it greatly simplifies the protocol for network routing.

Network Routing. In each intermediate layer, for every group of k gates, suppose $\boldsymbol{x}$ are the first inputs of these k gates, and $\boldsymbol{y}$ are the second inputs of these k gates. All parties will prepare two degree-$(n-k)$ packed Shamir sharings $[\boldsymbol{x}]_{n-k}$ and $[\boldsymbol{y}]_{n-k}$ stored at the default positions using the following approach. The reason of choosing the default positions is to use the packed Beaver triples, which use the default positions since the preprocessing phase is circuit-independent (discussed later). We focus on how to obtain $[\boldsymbol{x}]_{n-k}$.

Let $\boldsymbol{x} = (x_1, x_2, \ldots, x_k)$. For simplicity, we assume that $x_1, x_2, \ldots, x_k$ are output wires from k distinct gates. Later on, we will show how to handle the scenario where the same output wire is used multiple times by using fan-out operations. Since we use a different position to store the output of each gate, the positions of these k gates are all different. Let $p_1, \ldots, p_k$ denote the positions of these k gates and $\mathsf{pos} = (p_1, \ldots, p_k)$. We first show that all parties can locally compute a degree-$(n-1)$ packed Shamir sharing $[\boldsymbol{x}\|\mathsf{pos}]_{n-1}$.

Selecting the Correct Secrets. For all $i \in \{1, 2, \ldots, k\}$, let $[\boldsymbol{x}^{(i)}\|\mathsf{pos}^{(i)}]_{n-k}$ be the degree-$(n-k)$ packed Shamir sharing that contains the secret x_i at position p_i from some previous layer. Let $\boldsymbol{e}_i$ be the i-th unit vector in $\mathbb{F}^k$ (i.e., only the i-th term is 1 and all other terms are 0). All parties locally compute a degree-$(k-1)$ packed Shamir sharing $[\mathbf{e}_i\|\mathsf{pos}]_{k-1}$. Consider the following degree-$(n-1)$ packed Shamir sharing:

$$[\mathbf{e}_i\|\mathsf{pos}]_{k-1}\cdot[\boldsymbol{x}^{(i)}\|\mathsf{pos}^{(i)}]_{n-k}.$$

We claim that, the resulting sharing satisfies that the value stored at position p_i is x_i and the values stored at other positions in pos are all 0. To see this, recall that each packed Shamir sharing corresponds to a polynomial. Let f be the polynomial corresponding to $[\mathbf{e}_i\|\mathsf{pos}]_{k-1}$, and g be the polynomial corresponding to $[\boldsymbol{x}^{(i)}\|\mathsf{pos}^{(i)}]_{n-k}$. Then f satisfies that $f(p_i)=1$ and $f(p_j)=0$ for all $j\neq i$, and g satisfies that $g(p_i)=x_i$. Note that $h=f\cdot g$ is the polynomial corresponding to the resulting sharing $[\mathbf{e}_i\|\mathsf{pos}]_{k-1}\cdot[\boldsymbol{x}^{(i)}\|\mathsf{pos}^{(i)}]_{n-k}$, which satisfies that $h(p_i)=f(p_i)\cdot g(p_i)=1\cdot x_i=x_i$, and $h(p_j)=f(p_j)\cdot g(p_j)=0\cdot g(p_j)=0$ for all $j\neq i$. Thus, the resulting sharing has value x_i in the position p_i and 0 in all other positions in pos. Effectively, we select the secret x_i from $[\boldsymbol{x}^{(i)}\|\mathsf{pos}^{(i)}]_{n-k}$ at position p_i and zero-out the values stored at other positions in pos.

Getting all Secrets into a Single Packed Shamir Sharing. Thus, for the following degree-$(n-1)$ packed Shamir sharing

$$\sum_{i=1}^{k}[\mathbf{e}_i\|\mathsf{pos}]_{k-1}\cdot[\boldsymbol{x}^{(i)}\|\mathsf{pos}^{(i)}]_{n-k},$$

it has value x_i stored in the position p_i for all $i\in\{1,2,\ldots,k\}$, which means that it is a degree-$(n-1)$ packed Shamir sharing $[\boldsymbol{x}\|\mathsf{pos}]_{n-1}$. Therefore, all parties can locally compute $[\boldsymbol{x}\|\mathsf{pos}]_{n-1}=\sum_{i=1}^{k}[\mathbf{e}_i\|\mathsf{pos}]_{k-1}\cdot[\boldsymbol{x}^{(i)}\|\mathsf{pos}^{(i)}]_{n-k}$.

Applying Sharing Transformation. Finally, to obtain $[\boldsymbol{x}]_{n-k}=[\boldsymbol{x}\|\boldsymbol{\beta}]_{n-k}$, all parties only need to do a sharing transformation from $[\boldsymbol{x}\|\mathsf{pos}]_{n-1}$ to $[\boldsymbol{x}]_{n-k}$. Relying on our technique for sharing transformation, we can achieve this step with $O(n)$ field elements of communication.

Therefore, our protocol for network routing only requires a local computation for $[\boldsymbol{x}\|\mathsf{pos}]_{n-1}$ and an efficient sharing transformation for $[\boldsymbol{x}]_{n-k}$ with $O(n)$ field elements of communication.

Handling Fan-Out Operations. The above solution only works when all the wire values of $\boldsymbol{x}$ come from different gates. In a general case, $\boldsymbol{x}$ may contain many wire values from the same gate. We modify the above protocol as follows:

1. Suppose $x'_1,\ldots,x'_{k'}$ are the different values in $\boldsymbol{x}$. Let $\boldsymbol{x}'=(x'_1,\ldots,x'_{k'},0,\ldots,0)\in\mathbb{F}^k$. For all $i\in\{1,2,\ldots,k'\}$, let p_i be the position associated with the gate that outputs x'_i. We choose $p_{k'+1},\ldots,p_k$ to be the first $(k-k')$ unused positions and set $\mathsf{pos}=(p_1,\ldots,p_k)$. Then, all parties follow a similar approach to locally compute a degree-$(n-1)$ packed Shamir sharing of $[\boldsymbol{x}'\|\mathsf{pos}]_{n-1}$.
2. Note that $\boldsymbol{x}'$ contains all different values in $\boldsymbol{x}$. Thus, there is a linear map $f:\mathbb{F}^k\to\mathbb{F}^k$ such that $\boldsymbol{x}=f(\boldsymbol{x}')$. Therefore, relying on our technique for sharing transformation, all parties transform $[\boldsymbol{x}'\|\mathsf{pos}]_{n-1}$ to $[\boldsymbol{x}]_{n-k}$.

The communication complexity remains $O(n)$ field elements.

Evaluating Multiplication Gates Using Packed Beaver Triples. For a group of k multiplication gates, suppose all parties have prepared two degree-$(n-k)$ packed Shamir sharings $[\boldsymbol{x}]_{n-k}$ and $[\boldsymbol{y}]_{n-k}$. Let pos be the positions associated with these k gates. The goal is to compute a degree-$(n-k)$ packed Shamir sharing of $\boldsymbol{x} * \boldsymbol{y}$ stored at positions pos. To this end, we extend the technique of Beaver triples [Bea91] to our setting, which we refer to as *packed Beaver triples*. We make use of a random packed Beaver triple $([\boldsymbol{a}]_{n-k}, [\boldsymbol{b}]_{n-k}, [\boldsymbol{c}]_{n-k})$, where $\boldsymbol{a}, \boldsymbol{b}$ are random vectors in $\mathbb{F}^k$ and $\boldsymbol{c} = \boldsymbol{a} * \boldsymbol{b}$. All parties run the following steps:

1. All parties locally compute $[\boldsymbol{x} + \boldsymbol{a}]_{n-k} = [\boldsymbol{x}]_{n-k} + [\boldsymbol{a}]_{n-k}$ and $[\boldsymbol{y} + \boldsymbol{b}]_{n-k} = [\boldsymbol{y}]_{n-k} + [\boldsymbol{b}]_{n-k}$.
2. The first party P_1 collects the whole sharings $[\boldsymbol{x} + \boldsymbol{a}]_{n-k}, [\boldsymbol{y} + \boldsymbol{b}]_{n-k}$ and reconstructs the secrets $\boldsymbol{x} + \boldsymbol{a}, \boldsymbol{y} + \boldsymbol{b}$. Recall that $\boldsymbol{x} = (x_1, \ldots, x_k)$ and $\boldsymbol{a} = (a_1, \ldots, a_k)$ are vectors in $\mathbb{F}^k$, and $\boldsymbol{x} + \boldsymbol{a} = (x_1 + a_1, \ldots, x_k + a_k)$. Similarly, $\boldsymbol{y} + \boldsymbol{b} = (y_1 + b_1, \ldots, y_k + b_k)$. P_1 computes the sharings $[\boldsymbol{x} + \boldsymbol{a}]_{k-1}, [\boldsymbol{y} + \boldsymbol{b}]_{k-1}$ and distributes the shares to other parties.
3. All parties locally compute
$$[\boldsymbol{z}]_{n-1} := [\boldsymbol{x}+\boldsymbol{a}]_{k-1} \cdot [\boldsymbol{y}+\boldsymbol{b}]_{k-1} - [\boldsymbol{x}+\boldsymbol{a}]_{k-1} \cdot [\boldsymbol{b}]_{n-k} - [\boldsymbol{y}+\boldsymbol{b}]_{k-1} \cdot [\boldsymbol{a}]_{n-k} + [\boldsymbol{c}]_{n-k}.$$
Here the resulting sharing $[\boldsymbol{z}]_{n-1}$ has degree $n-1$ due to the second term and the third term.
4. Finally, all parties transform the sharing $[\boldsymbol{z}]_{n-1}$ to $[\boldsymbol{z}\|\mathsf{pos}]_{n-k}$. Relying on our technique of sharing transformation, this can be done with $O(n)$ field elements of communication.

Note that in the above steps, all parties only reveal $[\boldsymbol{x} + \boldsymbol{a}]_{n-k}$ and $[\boldsymbol{y} + \boldsymbol{b}]_{n-k}$ to P_1. Recall that $[\boldsymbol{a}]_{n-k}$ and $[\boldsymbol{b}]_{n-k}$ are random degree-$(n-k)$ packed Shamir sharings. Therefore, $[\boldsymbol{x} + \boldsymbol{a}]_{n-k}$ and $[\boldsymbol{y} + \boldsymbol{b}]_{n-k}$ are also random degree-$(n-k)$ packed Shamir sharings, which leak no information about $\boldsymbol{x}$ and $\boldsymbol{y}$ to P_1. Thus, the security follows.

Therefore, to evaluate a group of k multiplication gates, all parties need to prepare a random packed Beaver triple $([\boldsymbol{a}]_{n-k}, [\boldsymbol{b}]_{n-k}, [\boldsymbol{c}]_{n-k})$, which is of size $O(n)$ field elements. The communication complexity is $O(n)$ field elements.

Summary. In summary, our protocol works as follows. All parties first prepare enough packed Beaver triples stored at the default positions in the preprocessing phase. Then in the online phase, all parties evaluate the circuit layer by layer. For each layer, all parties first use the protocol for network routing to prepare degree-$(n-k)$ packed Shamir sharings for the inputs of this layer. Then, for every group of addition gates, all parties can compute them locally due to the linear homomorhpism of the packed Shamir secret sharing scheme. For every group of multiplication gates, we use the technique of packed Beaver triple to evaluate these gates. In particular, evaluating each group of multiplication gates will consume one fresh packed Beaver triple prepared in the preprocessing phase.

When $t = (1-\epsilon) \cdot n$ for a positive constant ϵ, we have $k = (n-t+1)/2 = O(n)$. For the amount of preprocessing data, we need to prepare a packed Beaver triple for each group of k multiplication gates. Thus, the amount of preprocessing data is bounded by $O(\frac{|C|}{k} \cdot n) = O(|C|)$. For the amount of communication, note that all parties need to communicate during the network routing and the evaluation of multiplication gates. Both protocols require $O(n)$ elements of communication to process k secrets. Thus, the amount of communication complexity is also bounded by $O(\frac{|C|}{k} \cdot n) = O(|C|)$.

Therefore, we obtain an information-theoretic MPC protocol in the circuit-independent preprocessing model with semi-honest security that computes an arithmetic circuit C over a large finite field $\mathbb{F}$ (with $|\mathbb{F}| \geq |C| + n$) against $t = (1 - \epsilon) \cdot n$ corrupted parties with $O(|C|)$ field elements of preprocessing data and $O(|C|)$ field elements of communication.

Other Results

Malicious Security of the Online Protocol. To achieve malicious security, we extend the idea of using information-theoretic MACs introduced in [BDOZ11, DPSZ12] to authenticate packed Shamir sharings. Concretely, at the beginning of the computation, all parties will prepare a random degree-$(n-k)$ packed Shamir sharing $[\boldsymbol{\gamma}]_{n-k}$, where $\boldsymbol{\gamma} = (\gamma, \gamma, \ldots, \gamma) \in \mathbb{F}^k$ and γ is a random field element. The secrets $\boldsymbol{\gamma}$ serve as the MAC key. To authenticate the secrets of a degree-$(n-k)$ packed Shamir sharing $[\boldsymbol{x}]_{n-k}$, all parties will compute a degree-$(n-k)$ packed Shamir sharing $[\boldsymbol{\gamma} * \boldsymbol{x}]_{n-k}$. We will show that almost all malicious behaviors of corrupted parties can be transformed to additive attacks, i.e., adding errors to the secrets of degree-$(n-k)$ packed Shamir sharings.

Note that if the corrupted parties change the secrets $\boldsymbol{x}$ to $\boldsymbol{x} + \boldsymbol{\delta}_1$, they also need to change the secrets $\boldsymbol{\gamma} * \boldsymbol{x}$ to $\boldsymbol{\gamma} * \boldsymbol{x} + \boldsymbol{\delta}_2$ such that $\boldsymbol{\delta}_2 = \boldsymbol{\gamma} * \boldsymbol{\delta}_1$. However, since γ is a uniform value in $\mathbb{F}$, the probability of a success attack is at most $1/|\mathbb{F}|$. When the field size is large enough, we can detect such an attack with overwhelming probability. See more details in the full version of this paper [GPS22].

Using the Result of [GPS21] *for Small Finite Fields.* Recall that our protocol requires the field size to be at least $|C| + n$. On the other hand, the protocol in [GPS21] can use a finite field of size $2n$. This is due to the use of different approaches to handle network routing.

When using a small finite field, we can use the technique in [GPS21] to handle network routing. Our technique for sharing transformation also improves the concrete efficiency of computing fan-out gates and performing permutations in [GPS21]. More details can be found in the full version of this paper [GPS22].

3 Preliminaries

In this work, we use the *client-server* model for the secure multi-party computation. In the client-server model, clients provide inputs to the functionality and receive outputs, and servers can participate in the computation but do not have inputs nor get outputs. Each party may have different roles in the computation.

Note that, if every party plays a single client and a single server, this corresponds to a protocol in the standard MPC model. Let c denote the number of clients and n denote the number of servers. For all clients and servers, we assume that every two of them are connected via a secure (private and authentic) synchronous channel so that they can directly send messages to each other.

We focus on functions that can be represented as arithmetic circuits over a finite field $\mathbb{F}$ with input, addition, multiplication, and output gates.[2] We use κ to denote the security parameter, C to denote the circuit, and $|C|$ for the size of the circuit. In this work, we assume that the field size is $|\mathbb{F}| \geq 2^\kappa$. Note that it implies $|\mathbb{F}| \geq |C| + n$ since both the number of parties and the circuit size are bounded by $\text{poly}(\kappa)$.

We are interested in the information-theoretic setting in the (circuit-independent) preprocessing model. The preprocessing model assumes that there is an ideal functionality which can prepare circuit-independent correlated randomness before the computation. Then the correlated randomness is used in a lightweight and fast online protocol. In particular, the preprocessing model enables the possibility of an information-theoretic protocol in the *dishonest majority setting*, which otherwise cannot exist in the plain model. The cost of a protocol in the preprocessing model is measured by both the amount of communication via private channels in the online phase and the amount of preprocessing data prepared in the preprocessing phase [Cou19, BGIN21].

An adversary $\mathcal{A}$ can corrupt at most c clients and t servers, provide inputs to corrupted clients, and receive all messages sent to corrupted clients and servers. Corrupted clients and servers can deviate from the protocol arbitrarily. One benefit of the client-server model is that it is sufficient to only consider maximum adversaries, i.e., adversaries which corrupt exactly t parties. We refer the readers to the full version of this paper [GPS22] for more details about the security definition and the benefit of the client-server model. In the following, we assume that there are exactly t corrupted parties.

4 Preparing Random Sharings for Different Arithmetic Secret Sharing Schemes

4.1 Arithmetic Secret Sharing Schemes

Let $\mathcal{R}$ be a finite commutative ring. In this work, we consider the following arithmetic secret sharing schemes from [ACD+20] (with slight modifications).

Definition 1 (Arithmetic Secret Sharing Schemes). *The syntax of an $\mathcal{R}$-arithmetic secret sharing scheme Σ consists of the following data:*

- *A set of parties $\mathcal{I} = \{1, \ldots, n\}$.*

[2] In this work, we only focus on deterministic functions. A randomized function can be transformed to a deterministic function by taking as input an additional random tape from each party. The XOR of the input random tapes of all parties is used as the randomness of the randomized function.

- *A secret space* $Z = \mathcal{R}^k$. *k is also denoted as the number of secrets packed within* Σ.
- *A share space* $U = \mathcal{R}^\ell$. ℓ *is also denoted as the share size.*
- *A sharing space* $C \subset U^{\mathcal{I}}$, *where* $U^{\mathcal{I}}$ *denotes the indexed Cartesian product* $\prod_{i \in \mathcal{I}} U$.
- *An injective* $\mathcal{R}$*-module homomorphism:* $\mathtt{share} : Z \times \mathcal{R}^r \to C$, *which maps a secret* $\boldsymbol{x} \in Z$ *and a random tape* $\boldsymbol{\rho} \in \mathcal{R}^r$, *to a sharing* $\boldsymbol{X} \in C$. share *is also denoted as the sharing map of* Σ.
- *A surjective* $\mathcal{R}$*-module homomorphism:* $\mathtt{rec} : C \to Z$, *which takes as input a sharing* $\boldsymbol{X} \in C$ *and outputs a secret* $\boldsymbol{x} \in Z$. rec *is also denoted as the reconstruction map of* Σ.

The scheme Σ *satisfies that for all* $\boldsymbol{x} \in Z$ *and* $\boldsymbol{\rho} \in \mathcal{R}^r$, $\mathtt{rec}(\mathtt{share}(\boldsymbol{x}, \boldsymbol{\rho})) = \boldsymbol{x}$. *We may refer to* Σ *as the 6-tuple* $(n, Z, U, C, \mathtt{share}, \mathtt{rec})$.

For a non-empty set $A \subset \mathcal{I}$, the natural projection π_A maps a tuple $u = (u_i)_{i \in \mathcal{I}} \in U^{\mathcal{I}}$ to the tuple $(u_i)_{i \in A} \in U^A$.

Definition 2 (Privacy Set and Reconstruction Set). *Suppose* $A \subset \mathcal{I}$ *is nonempty. We say A is a privacy set if for all* $\boldsymbol{x}_0, \boldsymbol{x}_1 \in Z$, *and for all vector* $\boldsymbol{v} \in U^A$,

$$\Pr_{\boldsymbol{\rho}}[\pi_A(\mathtt{share}(\boldsymbol{x}_0, \boldsymbol{\rho})) = \boldsymbol{v}] \;=\; \Pr_{\boldsymbol{\rho}}[\pi_A(\mathtt{share}(\boldsymbol{x}_1, \boldsymbol{\rho})) = \boldsymbol{v}].$$

We say A is a reconstruction set if there is an $\mathcal{R}$*-module homomorphism* $\mathtt{rec}_A : \pi_A(C) \to Z$, *such that for all* $\boldsymbol{X} \in C$,

$$\mathtt{rec}_A(\pi_A(\boldsymbol{X})) = \mathtt{rec}(\boldsymbol{X}).$$

Intuitively, for a privacy set A, the shares of parties in A are independent of the secret. For a reconstruction set A, the shares of parties in A fully determine the secret.

Threshold Linear Secret Sharing Schemes and Multiplication-friendly Property. In this work, we are interested in threshold arithmetic secret sharing schemes. Concretely, for a positive integer $t < n$, a threshold-t arithmetic secret sharing scheme satisfies that for all $A \subset \mathcal{I}$ with $|A| \leq t$, A is a privacy set.

We are interested in the following property.

Property 1 (Multiplication-Friendliness). We say $\Sigma = (n, Z = \mathcal{R}^k, U, C, \mathtt{share}, \mathtt{rec})$ is multiplication-friendly if there is an $\mathcal{R}$-arithmetic secret sharing scheme $\Sigma' = (n, Z = \mathcal{R}^k, U', C', \mathtt{share}', \mathtt{rec}')$ and n functions $\{f_i : \mathcal{R}^k \times U \to U'\}_{i=1}^n$ such that for all $\boldsymbol{c} \in \mathcal{R}^k$ and for all $\boldsymbol{X} \in C$,

- $\boldsymbol{Y} = (f_1(\boldsymbol{c}, X_1), f_2(\boldsymbol{c}, X_2), \ldots, f_n(\boldsymbol{c}, X_n))$ is in C', i.e., a sharing in Σ'. We will use $\boldsymbol{Y} = \boldsymbol{c} \cdot \boldsymbol{X}$ to represent the computation process from $\boldsymbol{c}$ and $\boldsymbol{X}$ to $\boldsymbol{Y}$.

- $\texttt{rec}'(\boldsymbol{Y}) = \boldsymbol{c} * \texttt{rec}(\boldsymbol{X})$, where $*$ is the coordinate-wise multiplication operation.

Intuitively, for a multiplication-friendly scheme Σ, if all parties hold a Σ-sharing of a secret $\boldsymbol{x} \in Z$ and a public vector $\boldsymbol{c} \in \mathcal{R}^k$, they can locally compute a Σ'-sharing of the secret $\boldsymbol{c}*\boldsymbol{x}$, where $*$ denotes the coordinate-wise multiplication operation. We prove Lemma 1 in the full version of this paper [GPS22].

Lemma 1. *If Σ is a multiplication-friendly threshold-t $\mathcal{R}$-arithmetic secret sharing scheme, and Σ' be the $\mathcal{R}$-arithmetic secret sharing scheme defined in Property 1, then Σ' has threshold t.*

4.2 Packed Shamir Secret Sharing Scheme

In our work, we are interested in the packed Shamir secret sharing scheme. We use the packed secret-sharing technique introduced by Franklin and Yung [FY92]. This is a generalization of the standard Shamir secret sharing scheme [Sha79]. Let $\mathbb{F}$ be a finite field of size $|\mathbb{F}| \geq 2n$. Let n be the number of parties and k be the number of secrets that are packed in one sharing. Let $\alpha_1, \dots, \alpha_n$ be n distinct elements in $\mathbb{F}$ and $\mathsf{pos} = (p_1, p_2, \dots, p_k)$ be another k distinct elements in $\mathbb{F}$. A *degree-d* ($d \geq k-1$) packed Shamir sharing of $\boldsymbol{x} = (x_1, \dots, x_k) \in \mathbb{F}^k$ is a vector $(w_1, \dots, w_n)$ for which there exists a polynomial $f(\cdot) \in \mathbb{F}[X]$ of degree at most d such that $f(p_i) = x_i$ for all $i \in \{1, 2, \dots, k\}$, and $f(\alpha_i) = w_i$ for all $i \in \{1, 2, \dots, n\}$. The i-th share w_i is held by party P_i. Reconstructing a degree-d packed Shamir sharing requires $d+1$ shares and can be done by Lagrange interpolation. For a random degree-d packed Shamir sharing of $\boldsymbol{x}$, any $d-k+1$ shares are independent of the secret $\boldsymbol{x}$.

In our work, we will always use the same elements $\alpha_1, \dots, \alpha_n$ for the shares of all parties. However, we may use different elements pos for the secrets. We will use $[\boldsymbol{x}\|\mathsf{pos}]_d$ to denote a degree-d packed Shamir sharing of $\boldsymbol{x} \in \mathbb{F}^k$ stored at positions pos. In the following, operations (addition and multiplication) between two packed Shamir sharings are coordinate-wise. We recall two properties of the packed Shamir sharing scheme:

- Linear Homomorphism: For all $d \geq k-1$ and $\boldsymbol{x}, \boldsymbol{y} \in \mathbb{F}^k$, $[\boldsymbol{x}+\boldsymbol{y}\|\mathsf{pos}]_d = [\boldsymbol{x}\|\mathsf{pos}]_d + [\boldsymbol{y}\|\mathsf{pos}]_d$.
- Multiplicative: Let $*$ denote the coordinate-wise multiplication operation. For all $d_1, d_2 \geq k-1$ subject to $d_1 + d_2 < n$, and for all $\boldsymbol{x}, \boldsymbol{y} \in \mathbb{F}^k$, $[\boldsymbol{x} * \boldsymbol{y}\|\mathsf{pos}]_{d_1+d_2} = [\boldsymbol{x}\|\mathsf{pos}]_{d_1} \cdot [\boldsymbol{y}\|\mathsf{pos}]_{d_2}$.

These two properties directly follow from the computation of the underlying polynomials.

Note that the second property implies that, for all $k-1 \leq d \leq n-k$, a degree-d packed Shamir secret sharing scheme is multiplication-friendly (defined in Property 1). Concretely, for all $\boldsymbol{x}, \boldsymbol{c} \in \mathbb{F}^k$, all parties can locally compute $[\boldsymbol{c} * \boldsymbol{x}\|\mathsf{pos}]_{d+k-1}$ from $[\boldsymbol{x}\|\mathsf{pos}]_d$ and the public vector $\boldsymbol{c}$. To see this, all parties can locally transform $\boldsymbol{c}$ to a degree-$(k-1)$ packed Shamir sharing $[\boldsymbol{c}\|\mathsf{pos}]_{k-1}$.

Then, they can use the property of the packed Shamir sharing scheme to compute $[\boldsymbol{c} * \boldsymbol{x} \| \texttt{pos}]_{d+k-1} = [\boldsymbol{c} \| \texttt{pos}]_{k-1} \cdot [\boldsymbol{x} \| \texttt{pos}]_d$.

Recall that t is the number of corrupted parties. Also recall that a degree-d packed Shamir secret sharing scheme is of threshold $d - k + 1$. To ensure that the packed Shamir secret sharing scheme has threshold t and is multiplication-friendly, we choose k such that $t \leq d - k + 1$ and $d \leq n - k$. When $d = n - k$ and $k = (n - t + 1)/2$, both requirements hold and k is maximal.

4.3 Preparing Random Sharings for Different Arithmetic Secret Sharing Schemes

In this part, we introduce our main contribution: an efficient protocol that prepares random sharings for a batch of different arithmetic secret sharing schemes. Let $\mathcal{R}$ be a finite commutative ring. Let $\Pi = (n, \tilde{Z}, \tilde{U}, \tilde{C}, \texttt{share}_\Pi, \texttt{rec}_\Pi)$ be an $\mathcal{R}$-arithmetic secret sharing scheme. Our goal is to realize the functionality $\mathcal{F}_{\text{rand-sharing}}$ presented in Functionality 1.

Functionality 1: $\mathcal{F}_{\text{rand-sharing}}(\Pi)$

1. $\mathcal{F}_{\text{rand-sharing}}$ receives the set of corrupted parties, denoted by $\mathcal{C}orr$.
2. $\mathcal{F}_{\text{rand-sharing}}$ receives from the adversary a set of shares $\{\boldsymbol{u}_j\}_{j \in \mathcal{C}orr}$ where $\boldsymbol{u}_j \in \tilde{U}$ for all $j \in \mathcal{C}orr$.
3. $\mathcal{F}_{\text{rand-sharing}}$ samples a random Π-sharing $\boldsymbol{X}$ such that the shares of $\boldsymbol{X}$ held by corrupted parties are identical to those received from the adversary, i.e., $\pi_{\mathcal{C}orr}(\boldsymbol{X}) = (\boldsymbol{u}_j)_{j \in \mathcal{C}orr}$. If such a sharing does not exist, $\mathcal{F}_{\text{rand-sharing}}$ sends $\texttt{abort}$ to all honest parties and halts.
4. Otherwise, $\mathcal{F}_{\text{rand-sharing}}$ distributes the shares of $\boldsymbol{X}$ to honest parties.

Initialization. Let $\Sigma = (n, Z = \mathcal{R}^k, U, C, \texttt{share}, \texttt{rec})$ be a multiplication-friendly threshold-t $\mathcal{R}$-arithmetic secret sharing scheme. In the following, we will use $[\boldsymbol{x}]$ to denote a Σ-sharing of $\boldsymbol{x} \in \mathcal{R}^k$. Let $\Sigma' = (n, Z' = \mathcal{R}^k, U', C', \texttt{share}', \texttt{rec}')$ be the $\mathcal{R}$-arithmetic secret sharing scheme in Property 1. By Lemma 1, Σ' has threshold t. We use $\langle \boldsymbol{y} \rangle$ to denote a Σ'-sharing of $\boldsymbol{y} \in \mathcal{R}^k$. For all $\boldsymbol{c} \in \mathcal{R}^k$, we will write

$$\langle \boldsymbol{c} * \boldsymbol{x} \rangle = \boldsymbol{c} \cdot [\boldsymbol{x}]$$

to represent the computation process from $\boldsymbol{c}$ and $[\boldsymbol{x}]$ to $\langle \boldsymbol{c} * \boldsymbol{x} \rangle$ in Property 1.

Our construction will use the ideal functionality $\mathcal{F}_{\text{rand}} = \mathcal{F}_{\text{rand-sharing}}(\Sigma)$ that prepares a random Σ-sharing, and the ideal functionality $\mathcal{F}_{\text{randZero}}$ (Functionality 2) that prepares a random Σ'-sharing of $\boldsymbol{0} \in \mathcal{R}^k$.

Let $\Pi_1, \Pi_2, \ldots, \Pi_k$ be k arbitrary $\mathcal{R}$-arithmetic secret sharing schemes with the restriction that all schemes have the same share size, i.e., the share space

Functionality 2: $\mathcal{F}_{\text{randZero}}$

1. Let $\Sigma' = (n, Z' = \mathcal{R}^k, U', C', \mathtt{share}', \mathtt{rec}')$. $\mathcal{F}_{\text{randZero}}$ receives the set of corrupted parties, denoted by $\mathcal{C}orr$.
2. $\mathcal{F}_{\text{randZero}}$ receives from the adversary a set of shares $\{\boldsymbol{u}'_j\}_{j\in\mathcal{C}orr}$, where $\boldsymbol{u}'_j \in U'$ for all $P_j \in \mathcal{C}orr$.
3. $\mathcal{F}_{\text{randZero}}$ samples a random Σ'-sharing of $\mathbf{0} \in \mathcal{R}^k$, $\langle\mathbf{0}\rangle$, such that the shares of corrupted parties are identical to those received from the adversary, i.e., $\pi_{\mathcal{C}orr}(\langle\mathbf{0}\rangle) = (\boldsymbol{u}'_j)_{j\in\mathcal{C}orr}$. If such a sharing does not exist, $\mathcal{F}_{\text{randZero}}$ sends `abort` to all honest parties and halts.
4. Otherwise, $\mathcal{F}_{\text{randZero}}$ distributes the shares of $\langle\mathbf{0}\rangle$ to honest parties.

$\tilde{U} = \mathcal{R}^{\tilde{\ell}}$. Let $\tilde{Z}_i = \mathcal{R}^{\tilde{k}_i}$ be the secret space of Π_i and $\mathtt{share}_i : \tilde{Z}_i \times \mathcal{R}^{\tilde{r}_i} \to \tilde{C}_i$ be the sharing map. Since $\mathtt{share}_i$ is injective, and $\tilde{C}_i \subset \tilde{U}^{\mathcal{I}}$, we have $\tilde{k}_i + \tilde{r}_i \leq n \cdot \tilde{\ell}$.

The goal is to prepare k random sharings $\boldsymbol{X}_1, \boldsymbol{X}_2, \ldots, \boldsymbol{X}_k$ such that $\boldsymbol{X}_i$ is a random Π_i-sharing, i.e., realizing $\{\mathcal{F}_{\text{rand-sharing}}(\Pi_i)\}_{i=1}^k$.

Protocol Description. The construction of our protocol RAND-SHARING appears in Protocol 3. We prove Lemma 2 in the full version of this paper [GPS22]. Protocol RAND-SHARING requires $n^2 \cdot \tilde{\ell} \cdot (\ell + \ell')$ ring elements of preprocessing data and $n^2 \cdot \tilde{\ell} \cdot \ell'$ ring elements of communication to prepare k random sharings for $\Pi_1, \Pi_2, \ldots, \Pi_k$, one for each secret sharing scheme. The detailed cost analysis can also be found in the full version of this paper [GPS22].

Lemma 2. *For any k $\mathcal{R}$-arithmetic secret sharing schemes $\{\Pi_i\}_{i=1}^k$ such that they have the same share size, Protocol* RAND-SHARING *securely computes $\{\mathcal{F}_{\textit{rand-sharing}}(\Pi_i)\}_{i=1}^k$ in the $\{\mathcal{F}_{\textit{rand}}, \mathcal{F}_{\textit{randZero}}\}$-hybrid model against a semi-honest adversary who controls t parties.*

4.4 Instantiating Protocol RAND-SHARING via Packed Shamir Secret Sharing Scheme

Recall that when $k = (n - t + 1)/2$, a degree-$(n - k)$ packed Shamir secret sharing has threshold t and is multiplication-friendly. Therefore, we use a degree-$(n-k)$ packed Shamir secret sharing scheme to instantiate Σ in Protocol RAND-SHARING. Then Σ' is a degree-$(n-1)$ packed Shamir secret sharing scheme. For Σ and Σ',

- The secret space is $\mathbb{F}^k$, where $k = (n - t + 1)/2$.
- The share space is $\mathbb{F}$, i.e., each share is a single field element. Therefore $\ell = \ell' = 1$.

Thus, we obtain a protocol that prepares random sharings for $\Pi_1, \Pi_2, \ldots, \Pi_k$ with $2 \cdot n^2 \cdot \tilde{\ell} = O(n^2 \cdot \tilde{\ell})$ field elements of preprocessing data and $n^2 \cdot \tilde{\ell}$ field elements

Protocol 3: RAND-SHARING

1. Let $\Pi_1, \Pi_2, \ldots, \Pi_k$ be k arbitrary $\mathcal{R}$-arithmetic secret sharing schemes such that they have the same share size. Let $\tilde{U} = \mathcal{R}^{\tilde{\ell}}$ denote the share space. For all $i \in \{1, 2, \ldots, k\}$, let $\tilde{Z}_i = \mathcal{R}^{\tilde{k}_i}$ be the secret space of Π_i, and $\mathtt{share}_i : \tilde{Z}_i \times \mathcal{R}^{\tilde{r}_i} \to \tilde{C}_i$ be the sharing map of Π_i. We have $\tilde{k}_i + \tilde{r}_i \leq n \cdot \tilde{\ell}$.
2. All parties invoke $\mathcal{F}_{\text{rand}}$ $n \cdot \tilde{\ell}$ times and obtain $n \cdot \tilde{\ell}$ random Σ-sharings, denoted by $[\boldsymbol{r}_1], [\boldsymbol{r}_2], \ldots, [\boldsymbol{r}_{n \cdot \tilde{\ell}}]$. For all $i \in \{1, 2, \ldots, k\}$, let $\boldsymbol{\tau}_i = (r_{1,i}, r_{2,i}, \ldots, r_{\tilde{k}_i,i}) \in \mathcal{R}^{\tilde{k}_i}$, and $\boldsymbol{\rho}_i = (r_{\tilde{k}_i+1,i}, r_{\tilde{k}_i+2,i}, \ldots, r_{\tilde{k}_i+\tilde{r}_i,i}) \in \mathcal{R}^{\tilde{r}_i}$. The goal of this protocol is to compute the Π_i-sharing $\boldsymbol{X}_i = \mathtt{share}_i(\boldsymbol{\tau}_i, \boldsymbol{\rho}_i)$.
3. All parties invoke $\mathcal{F}_{\text{randZero}}$ $n \cdot \tilde{\ell}$ times and obtain $n \cdot \tilde{\ell}$ random Σ'-sharings of $\boldsymbol{0} \in \mathcal{R}^k$, denoted by $\{\langle \boldsymbol{o}_j^{(1)} \rangle, \langle \boldsymbol{o}_j^{(2)} \rangle, \ldots, \langle \boldsymbol{o}_j^{(\tilde{\ell})} \rangle\}_{j=1}^n$.
4. For all $i \in \{1, 2, \ldots, k\}$, $j \in \{1, 2, \ldots, n\}$, and $m \in \{1, 2, \ldots, \tilde{\ell}\}$, let $\mathcal{L}_j^{(i,m)} : \tilde{Z}_i \times \mathcal{R}^{\tilde{r}_i} \to \mathcal{R}$ denote the $\mathcal{R}$-module homomorphism such that for all $\boldsymbol{\tau} \in \tilde{Z}_i$ and $\boldsymbol{\rho} \in \mathcal{R}^{\tilde{r}_i}$, $\mathcal{L}_j^{(i,m)}(\boldsymbol{\tau}, \boldsymbol{\rho})$ outputs the m-th element of the j-th share of the Π_i-sharing $\mathtt{share}_i(\boldsymbol{\tau}, \boldsymbol{\rho})$. Then there exist $c_{j,1}^{(i,m)}, \ldots, c_{j,\tilde{k}_i+\tilde{r}_i}^{(i,m)} \in \mathcal{R}$ such that
$$\mathcal{L}_j^{(i,m)}(\boldsymbol{\tau}, \boldsymbol{\rho}) = \sum_{v=1}^{\tilde{k}_i} c_{j,v}^{(i,m)} \cdot \tau_v + \sum_{v=1}^{\tilde{r}_i} c_{j,\tilde{k}_i+v}^{(i,m)} \cdot \rho_v.$$
For all $j \in \{1, 2, \ldots, n\}$, $m \in \{1, 2, \ldots, \tilde{\ell}\}$, and $v \in \{1, \ldots, n \cdot \tilde{\ell}\}$, let
$$\boldsymbol{c}_{j,v}^{(*,m)} = (c_{j,v}^{(1,m)}, c_{j,v}^{(2,m)}, \ldots, c_{j,v}^{(k,m)}) \in \mathcal{R}^k,$$
where $c_{j,v}^{(i,m)} = 0$ for all $v > \tilde{k}_i + \tilde{r}_i$.
5. For all $i \in \{1, 2, \ldots, k\}$, $j \in \{1, 2, \ldots, n\}$, and $m \in \{1, 2, \ldots, \tilde{\ell}\}$, let $u_j^{(i,m)} = \mathcal{L}_j^{(i,m)}(\boldsymbol{\tau}_i, \boldsymbol{\rho}_i)$. Let $\boldsymbol{u}_j^{(*,m)} = (u_j^{(1,m)}, u_j^{(2,m)}, \ldots, u_j^{(k,m)})$. For all $j \in \{1, 2, \ldots, n\}$ and $m \in \{1, 2, \ldots, \tilde{\ell}\}$, all parties locally compute a Σ'-sharing
$$\langle \boldsymbol{u}_j^{(*,m)} \rangle = \langle \boldsymbol{o}_j^{(m)} \rangle + \sum_{v=1}^{n \cdot \tilde{\ell}} \boldsymbol{c}_{j,v}^{(*,m)} \cdot [\boldsymbol{r}_v].$$
Then, all parties send their shares of $\langle \boldsymbol{u}_j^{(*,m)} \rangle$ to P_j.
6. For all $j \in \{1, 2, \ldots, n\}$ and $m \in \{1, 2, \ldots, \tilde{\ell}\}$, P_j reconstructs the Σ'-sharing $\langle \boldsymbol{u}_j^{(*,m)} \rangle$ and learns $\boldsymbol{u}_j^{(*,m)} = (u_j^{(1,m)}, u_j^{(2,m)}, \ldots, u_j^{(k,m)})$. Then for all $i \in \{1, 2, \ldots, k\}$, P_j sets his share of the Π_i-sharing, $\boldsymbol{X}_i$, to be $\boldsymbol{u}_j^{(i)} = (u_j^{(i,1)}, u_j^{(i,2)}, \ldots, u_j^{(i,\tilde{\ell})})$. All parties take $\boldsymbol{X}_1, \boldsymbol{X}_2, \ldots, \boldsymbol{X}_k$ as output.

of communication. On average, the cost per random sharing is $O(\frac{n^2}{n-t+1} \cdot \tilde{\ell})$ field elements of both preprocessing data and communication. Note that when $t = (1 - \epsilon) \cdot n$ for a positive constant ϵ, the achieved amortized cost per sharing is $O(n \cdot \tilde{\ell})$ field elements. In particular, $n \cdot \tilde{\ell}$ is the sharing size of Π_i for all $i \in \{1, 2, \dots, k\}$. Essentially, it costs the same as letting a trusted party generate a random Π_i-sharing and distribute to all parties.

In the full version of this paper [GPS22], we discuss how to instantiate Protocol RAND-SHARING for small fields $\mathbb{F}_q$ and rings $\mathbb{Z}/p^\ell\mathbb{Z}$.

4.5 Application of $\mathcal{F}_{\text{rand-sharing}}$

Let Σ and Σ' be two threshold-t $\mathcal{R}$-arithmetic secret sharing schemes. Let $f : Z \to Z'$ be an $\mathcal{R}$-module homomorphism, where Z and Z' are the secret spaces of Σ and Σ' respectively. Suppose given a Σ-sharing, $\boldsymbol{X}$, all parties want to compute a Σ'-sharing, $\boldsymbol{Y}$, subject to $\texttt{rec}'(\boldsymbol{Y}) = f(\texttt{rec}(\boldsymbol{X}))$, where $\texttt{rec}$ and $\texttt{rec}'$ are reconstruction maps of Σ and Σ', respectively. We refer to this problem as sharing transformation.

As discussed in Sect. 2, sharing transformation can be efficiently solved with the help of a pair of random sharings $(\boldsymbol{R}, \boldsymbol{R}')$, where $\boldsymbol{R}$ is a Σ-sharing, and $\boldsymbol{R}'$ is a Σ'-sharing subject to $\texttt{rec}'(\boldsymbol{R}') = f(\texttt{rec}(\boldsymbol{R}))$. Consider the following $\mathcal{R}$-arithmetic secret sharing scheme $\widetilde{\Sigma} = \widetilde{\Sigma}(\Sigma, \Sigma', f)$:

- The secret space is Z, the same as that of Σ.
- The share space is $U \times U'$, where U is the share space of Σ and U' is the share space of Σ'.
- For a secret $\boldsymbol{x} \in Z$, the sharing of $\boldsymbol{x}$ is the concatenation of a Σ-sharing of $\boldsymbol{x}$ and a Σ'-sharing of $f(\boldsymbol{x})$.
- For a sharing $\boldsymbol{X}$, recall that each share of $\widetilde{\Sigma}$ consists of one share of Σ and one share of Σ'. The secret of $\boldsymbol{X}$ can be recovered by applying $\texttt{rec}$ of Σ on the sharing which consists of the shares of Σ in $\boldsymbol{X}$.

Then, $(\boldsymbol{R}, \boldsymbol{R}')$ is a random $\widetilde{\Sigma}$-sharing. The problem is reduced to prepare a random $\widetilde{\Sigma}$-sharing, which can be done by $\mathcal{F}_{\text{rand-sharing}}(\widetilde{\Sigma})$.

We summarize the functionality $\mathcal{F}_{\text{tran}}$ in Functionality 4 and the protocol TRAN for $\mathcal{F}_{\text{tran}}$ in Protocol 5.

Lemma 3. *For all threshold-t $\mathcal{R}$-arithmetic secret sharing schemes Σ, Σ' and for all $\mathcal{R}$-module homomorphism $f : Z \to Z'$, Protocol* TRAN *securely computes $\mathcal{F}_{\text{tran}}$ in the $\mathcal{F}_{\text{rand-sharing}}$-hybrid model against a semi-honest adversary who controls t parties.*

A formal theorem of Theorem 1 can be found in the full version of this paper [GPS22].

5 Semi-honest Protocol

In this section, we focus on the semi-honest security. We show how to use packed Shamir sharing schemes and $\mathcal{F}_{\text{tran}}$ (introduced in Sect. 4.5) to evaluate a circuit against a semi-honest adversary who controls t parties. Let $k = (n - t + 1)/2$.

Functionality 4: $\mathcal{F}_{\text{tran}}$

1. $\mathcal{F}_{\text{tran}}$ receives the set of corrupted parties, denoted by $\mathcal{C}orr$. $\mathcal{F}_{\text{tran}}$ also receives two threshold-t $\mathcal{R}$-arithmetic secret sharing schemes Σ, Σ' and an $\mathcal{R}$-module homomorphism $f : Z \to Z'$.
2. $\mathcal{F}_{\text{tran}}$ receives a Σ-sharing $\boldsymbol{X}$ from all parties and computes $f(\texttt{rec}(\boldsymbol{X}))$.
3. $\mathcal{F}_{\text{tran}}$ receives from the adversary a set of shares $\{\boldsymbol{u}'_j\}_{j\in\mathcal{C}orr}$, where $\boldsymbol{u}'_j \in U'$ for all $P_j \in \mathcal{C}orr$.
4. $\mathcal{F}_{\text{tran}}$ samples a random Σ'-sharing, $\boldsymbol{Y}$, such that $\texttt{rec}'(\boldsymbol{Y}) = f(\texttt{rec}(\boldsymbol{X}))$ and the shares of corrupted parties are identical to those received from the adversary, i.e., $\pi_{\mathcal{C}orr}(\boldsymbol{Y}) = (\boldsymbol{u}'_j)_{j\in\mathcal{C}orr}$. If such a sharing does not exist, $\mathcal{F}_{\text{tran}}$ sends `abort` to honest parties and halts.
5. Otherwise, $\mathcal{F}_{\text{tran}}$ distributes the shares of $\boldsymbol{Y}$ to honest parties.

Protocol 5: TRAN

1. Let Σ, Σ' be two threhsold-t $\mathcal{R}$-arithmetic secret sharing schemes and $f : Z \to Z'$ be an $\mathcal{R}$-module homomorphism. All parties hold a Σ-sharing, $\boldsymbol{X}$, at the beginning of the protocol.
2. Let $\widetilde{\Sigma} = \widetilde{\Sigma}(\Sigma, \Sigma', f)$ be the threshold-t $\mathcal{R}$-arithmetic secret sharing scheme defined above. All parties invoke $\mathcal{F}_{\text{rand-sharing}}(\widetilde{\Sigma})$ and obtain a $\widetilde{\Sigma}$-sharing $(\boldsymbol{R}, \boldsymbol{R}')$.
3. All parties locally compute $\boldsymbol{X} + \boldsymbol{R}$ and send their shares to the first party P_1.
4. P_1 reconstructs the secret of $\boldsymbol{X} + \boldsymbol{R}$, denoted by $\boldsymbol{w}$. Then P_1 computes $f(\boldsymbol{w})$ and generates a Σ'-sharing of $f(\boldsymbol{w})$, denoted by $\boldsymbol{W}$. Finally, P_1 distributes the shares of $\boldsymbol{W}$ to all parties.
5. All parties locally compute $\boldsymbol{Y} = \boldsymbol{W} - \boldsymbol{R}'$.

Recall that we use $[\boldsymbol{x}\|\mathbf{pos}]_d$ to represent a degree-d packed Shamir sharing of $\boldsymbol{x} \in \mathbb{F}^k$ stored at positions $\mathbf{pos} = (p_1, p_2, \ldots, p_k)$. Also recall that the shares of a degree-d packed Shamir sharing are at evaluation points $\alpha_1, \alpha_2, \ldots, \alpha_n$. Let $\boldsymbol{\beta} = (\beta_1, \beta_2, \ldots, \beta_k)$ be k distinct elements in $\mathbb{F}$ that are different from $(\alpha_1, \alpha_2, \ldots, \alpha_n)$. We use $\boldsymbol{\beta}$ as the default positions for a degree-d packed Shamir sharing, and simply write $[\boldsymbol{x}]_d = [\boldsymbol{x}\|\boldsymbol{\beta}]_d$.

5.1 Circuit-Independent Preprocessing Phase

In the circuit-independent preprocessing phase, all parties need to prepare packed Beaver triples. For every group of k multiplication gates, all parties prepare a packed Beaver triple $([\boldsymbol{a}]_{n-k}, [\boldsymbol{b}]_{n-k}, [\boldsymbol{c}]_{n-k})$ where $\boldsymbol{a}, \boldsymbol{b}$ are random vectors in $\mathbb{F}^k$ and $\boldsymbol{c} = \boldsymbol{a} * \boldsymbol{b}$. We will use the technique of packed Beaver triples to compute multiplication gates in the online phase. The functionality $\mathcal{F}_{\text{prep}}$ for the circuit independent preprocessing phase appears in Functionality 6.

Functionality 6: $\mathcal{F}_{\text{prep}}$

For every group of k multiplication gates:

1. $\mathcal{F}_{\text{prep}}$ receives the set of corrupted parties, denoted by $\mathcal{C}orr$.
2. $\mathcal{F}_{\text{prep}}$ receives from the adversary a set of shares $\{(a_j, b_j, c_j)\}_{j \in \mathcal{C}orr}$. $\mathcal{F}_{\text{prep}}$ samples two random vectors $\boldsymbol{a}, \boldsymbol{b} \in \mathbb{F}^k$ and computes $\boldsymbol{c} = \boldsymbol{a} * \boldsymbol{b}$. Then $\mathcal{F}_{\text{prep}}$ computes three degree-$(n-k)$ packed Shamir sharings $[\boldsymbol{a}]_{n-k}, [\boldsymbol{b}]_{n-k}, [\boldsymbol{c}]_{n-k}$ such that for all $P_j \in \mathcal{C}orr$, the j-th share of $([\boldsymbol{a}]_{n-k}, [\boldsymbol{b}]_{n-k}, [\boldsymbol{c}]_{n-k})$ is (a_j, b_j, c_j).
3. $\mathcal{F}_{\text{prep}}$ distributes the shares of $([\boldsymbol{a}]_{n-k}, [\boldsymbol{b}]_{n-k}, [\boldsymbol{c}]_{n-k})$ to honest parties.

5.2 Online Computation Phase

Recall that for the field size it holds that $|\mathbb{F}| \geq |C| + n$, where $|C|$ is the circuit size. Let $\beta_1, \beta_2, \ldots, \beta_{|C|}$ be $|C|$ distinct field elements that are different from $\alpha_1, \alpha_2, \ldots, \alpha_n$. (Recall that we have already defined $\boldsymbol{\beta} = (\beta_1, \ldots, \beta_k)$, which are used as the default positions for a packed Shamir sharing.) We associate the field element β_i with the i-th gate in C. We will use β_i as the position to store the output value of the i-th gate in a degree-$(n-k)$ packed Shamir sharing.

Concretely, for each layer, gates that have the same type are divided into groups of size k. For each group of k gates, all parties will compute a degree-$(n-k)$ packed Shamir sharing such that the results are stored at the positions associated with these k gates respectively.

Input Layer. In the input layer, input gates are divided into groups of size k based on the input holders. For a group of k input gates belonging to the same client, suppose $\boldsymbol{x}$ are the inputs, and $\mathsf{pos} = (p_1, p_2, \ldots, p_k)$ are the positions associated with these k gates. The client generates a random degree-$(n-k)$ packed Shamir sharing $[\boldsymbol{x}\|\mathsf{pos}]_{n-k}$ and distributes the shares to all parties.

Network Routing. In each intermediate layer, all gates are divided into groups of size k based on their types (i.e., multiplication gates or addition gates). For a group of k gates, all parties prepare two degree-$(n-k)$ packed Shamir sharings, one for the first inputs of all gates, and the other one for the second inputs of all gates.

Concretely, for a group k gates in the current layer, suppose $\boldsymbol{x}$ are the first inputs of these k gates, and $\boldsymbol{y}$ are the second inputs of these k gates. All parties will prepare two degree-$(n-k)$ packed Shamir sharings $[\boldsymbol{x}]_{n-k}$ and $[\boldsymbol{y}]_{n-k}$ stored at the default positions. The reason of choosing the default positions is to use the packed Beaver triples all parties have prepared in the preprocessing phase. Recall that the packed Beaver triples all use the default positions. In the following, we focus on inputs $\boldsymbol{x}$.

Collecting Secrets from Previous Layers. Let $x'_1, x'_2, \ldots, x'_{\ell_1}$ be the different values in $\boldsymbol{x}$ from previous layers. Let $c_1, c_2, \ldots, c_{\ell_2}$ be the constant values in $\boldsymbol{x}$. Then $\ell_1 + \ell_2 \leq k$. For each of the rest of $k - \ell_1 - \ell_2$ values in $\boldsymbol{x}$, it is the same as x'_i for some $i \in \{1, 2, \ldots, \ell_1\}$. In this step, we will prepare a degree-$(n-1)$ packed Shamir sharing that contains the secrets $x'_1, x'_2, \ldots, x'_{\ell_1}$ and $c_1, c_2, \ldots, c_{\ell_2}$.

Note that $\{x'_i\}_{i=1}^{\ell_1}$ are the output values of ℓ_1 different gates in previous layers. Let $p_1, p_2, \ldots, p_{\ell_1}$ be the positions associated with these ℓ_1 gates. We choose another arbitrary $k - \ell_1$ different positions $p_{\ell_1+1}, \ldots, p_k$ which are also different from $\alpha_1, \alpha_2, \ldots, \alpha_n$, and set $\mathsf{pos} = (p_1, p_2, \ldots, p_k)$. Suppose for all $1 \leq i \leq \ell_1$, $[\boldsymbol{x}^{(i)} \| \mathsf{pos}^{(i)}]_{n-k}$ is the degree-$(n-k)$ packed Shamir sharing from some previous layer that contains the secret x'_i stored at position p_i.

Let $\boldsymbol{e}_i$ be the i-th unit vector in $\mathbb{F}^k$ (i.e., only the i-th term is 1 and all other terms are 0). All parties locally compute a degree-$(k-1)$ packed Shamir sharing $[\boldsymbol{e}_i \| \mathsf{pos}]_{k-1}$. Let $\boldsymbol{x}' = (x'_1, \ldots, x'_{\ell_1}, c_1, \ldots, c_{\ell_2}, 0, \ldots, 0)$ be a vector in $\mathbb{F}^k$. Then all parties locally compute

$$\sum_{i=1}^{\ell_1} [\boldsymbol{e}_i \| \mathsf{pos}]_{k-1} \cdot [\boldsymbol{x}^{(i)} \| \mathsf{pos}^{(i)}]_{n-k} + \sum_{i=1}^{\ell_2} c_i \cdot [\boldsymbol{e}_{\ell_1+i} \| \mathsf{pos}]_{k-1}.$$

We show that this is a degree-$(n-1)$ packed Shamir sharing of $\boldsymbol{x}'$ stored at positions pos. It is clear that the resulting sharing has degree $n-1$. We only need to show the following three points:

- For all $1 \leq j \leq \ell_1$, the secret stored at position p_j is equal to x'_j.
- For all $\ell_1 + 1 \leq j \leq \ell_1 + \ell_2$, the secret stored at position p_j is equal to $c_{j-\ell_1}$.
- For all $\ell_1 + \ell_2 + 1 \leq j \leq k$, the secret stored at position p_j is equal to 0.

For all $1 \leq i \leq \ell_1 + \ell_2$, let f_i be the polynomial corresponding to $[\boldsymbol{e}_i \| \mathsf{pos}]_{k-1}$. For all $1 \leq i \leq \ell_1$, let g_i be the polynomial corresponding to $[\boldsymbol{x}^{(i)} \| \mathsf{pos}^{(i)}]_{n-k}$. Then the polynomial corresponding to the resulting sharing is $h = \sum_{i=1}^{\ell_1} f_i \cdot g_i + \sum_{i=1}^{\ell_2} c_i \cdot f_{\ell_1+i}$.

Note that f_i satisfies that $f_i(p_i) = 1$ and $f_i(p_j) = 0$ for all $j \neq i$. And g_i satisfies that $g_i(p_i) = x'_i$. Therefore, for all $1 \leq j \leq \ell_1$,

$$h(p_j) = \sum_{i=1}^{\ell_1} f_i(p_j) \cdot g_i(p_j) + \sum_{i=1}^{\ell_2} c_i \cdot f_{\ell_1+i}(p_j) = f_j(p_j) \cdot g_j(p_j) = x'_j.$$

For all $\ell_1 + 1 \leq j \leq \ell_2$,

$$h(p_j) = \sum_{i=1}^{\ell_1} f_i(p_j) \cdot g_i(p_j) + \sum_{i=1}^{\ell_2} c_i \cdot f_{\ell_1+i}(p_j) = c_{j-\ell_1} \cdot f_j(p_j) = c_{j-\ell_1}.$$

For all $\ell_1 + \ell_2 + 1 \leq j \leq k$,

$$h(p_j) = \sum_{i=1}^{\ell_1} f_i(p_j) \cdot g_i(p_j) + \sum_{i=1}^{\ell_2} c_i \cdot f_{\ell_1+i}(p_j) = 0.$$

Thus, the resulting sharing is a degree-$(n-1)$ packed Shamir sharing of $\boldsymbol{x}'$ stored at positions pos, denoted by $[\boldsymbol{x}'\|\mathsf{pos}]_{n-1}$.

Transforming to the Desired Sharing. Now all parties hold a degree-$(n-1)$ packed Shamir sharing $[\boldsymbol{x}'\|\mathsf{pos}]_{n-1}$. Recall that $\boldsymbol{x}'$ contains all different values in $\boldsymbol{x}$ from previous layers and all constant values. For each of the rest of values in $\boldsymbol{x}$, it is the same as x'_i for some $i \in \{1, 2, \ldots, \ell_1\}$. Then there is a linear map $f : \mathbb{F}^k \to \mathbb{F}^k$ such that $\boldsymbol{x} = f(\boldsymbol{x}')$. Recall that $\boldsymbol{\beta} = (\beta_1, \ldots, \beta_k)$ are the default positions. Let Σ be the degree-$(n-1)$ packed Shamir secret sharing scheme that stores secrets at positions pos. Let Σ' be the degree-$(n-k)$ packed Shamir secret sharing scheme that stores secrets at positions $\boldsymbol{\beta}$. Then $[\boldsymbol{x}'\|\mathsf{pos}]_{n-1}$ is a Σ-sharing, and the sharing we want to prepare, $[\boldsymbol{x}]_{n-k} = [\boldsymbol{x}\|\boldsymbol{\beta}]_{n-k}$, is a Σ'-sharing with $\boldsymbol{x} = f(\boldsymbol{x}')$.

All parties invoke $\mathcal{F}_{\text{tran}}$ with (Σ, Σ', f) and $[\boldsymbol{x}'\|\mathsf{pos}]_{n-1}$, and obtain $[\boldsymbol{x}]_{n-k}$.

Summary of Network Routing. We describe the protocol Network of preparing an input degree-$(n-k)$ packed Shamir sharing $[\boldsymbol{x}]_{n-k}$ in Protocol 7.

Evaluating Addition Gates and Multiplication Gates

Addition Gates. For a group of k addition gates, recall that all parties have prepared two degree-$(n-k)$ packed Shamir sharings $[\boldsymbol{x}]_{n-k}, [\boldsymbol{y}]_{n-k}$ where $\boldsymbol{x}$ are the first inputs of these k gates, and $\boldsymbol{y}$ are the second inputs of these k gates. The description of Add appears in Protocol 8. Note that in Step 3 of Protocol Add, we use the fact that a degree-$(n-k)$ packed Shamir sharing can be viewed as a degree-$(n-1)$ packed Shamir sharing.

Multiplication Gates. For a group of k multiplication gates, recall that all parties have prepared two degree-$(n-k)$ packed Shamir sharings $[\boldsymbol{x}]_{n-k}, [\boldsymbol{y}]_{n-k}$ where $\boldsymbol{x}$ are the first inputs of these k gates, and $\boldsymbol{y}$ are the second inputs of these k gates. Let $([\boldsymbol{a}]_{n-k}, [\boldsymbol{b}]_{n-k}, [\boldsymbol{c}]_{n-k})$ be the packed Beaver triple prepared in the preprocessing phase. We will use the technique of packed Beaver triples to evaluate multiplication gates. The description of Mult appears in Protocol 9.

Output Layer. In the output layer, output gates are divided into groups of size k based on the output receivers. For a group of k output gates belonging to the same client, suppose $\boldsymbol{x}$ are the inputs. All parties invoke the protocol Network to prepare $[\boldsymbol{x}]_{n-k}$. Then, all parties send their shares to the client to allow him to reconstruct the output.

Protocol 7: NETWORK

1. Suppose all parties want to prepare a degree-$(n-k)$ packed Shamir sharing of $\boldsymbol{x}$ stored at the default positions $\boldsymbol{\beta}$.
2. Let $x'_1, x'_2, \ldots, x'_{\ell_1}$ be the different wire values in $\boldsymbol{x}$ from previous layers. Let $c_1, c_2, \ldots, c_{\ell_2}$ be the constant values in $\boldsymbol{x}$. Let $\boldsymbol{x}' = (x'_1, \ldots, x'_{\ell_1}, c_1, \ldots, c_{\ell_2}, 0, \ldots, 0) \in \mathbb{F}^k$.
3. For all $1 \le i \le \ell_1$, let $[\boldsymbol{x}^{(i)} \| \mathsf{pos}^{(i)}]_{n-k}$ be the degree-$(n-k)$ packed Shamir sharing from some previous layer that contains the secret x'_i stored at position p_i. Let $p_{\ell_1+1}, \ldots, p_k$ be the first $k-\ell_1$ distinct positions that are different from $p_1, \ldots, p_{\ell_1}$ and $\alpha_1, \ldots, \alpha_n$. Let $\mathsf{pos} = (p_1, \ldots, p_k)$.
4. Let $\boldsymbol{e}_i$ be the i-th unit vector in $\mathbb{F}^k$ (i.e., only the i-th term is 1 and all other terms are 0). All parties locally compute a degree-$(k-1)$ packed Shamir sharing $[\boldsymbol{e}_i \| \mathsf{pos}]_{k-1}$.
5. All parties locally compute
$$[\boldsymbol{x}' \| \mathsf{pos}]_{n-1} = \sum_{i=1}^{\ell_1} [\boldsymbol{e}_i \| \mathsf{pos}]_{k-1} \cdot [\boldsymbol{x}^{(i)} \| \mathsf{pos}^{(i)}]_{n-k} + \sum_{i=1}^{\ell_2} c_i \cdot [\boldsymbol{e}_{\ell_1+i} \| \mathsf{pos}]_{k-1}.$$
6. Let $f : \mathbb{F}^k \to \mathbb{F}^k$ be a linear map such that $\boldsymbol{x} = f(\boldsymbol{x}')$. Let Σ be the degree-$(n-1)$ packed Shamir secret sharing scheme that stores secrets at positions pos. Let Σ' be the degree-$(n-k)$ packed Shamir secret sharing scheme that stores secrets at positions $\boldsymbol{\beta}$.
All parties invoke $\mathcal{F}_{\text{tran}}$ with (Σ, Σ', f) and $[\boldsymbol{x}' \| \mathsf{pos}]_{n-1}$, and output $[\boldsymbol{x}]_{n-k}$.

Protocol 8: ADD

1. Suppose $[\boldsymbol{x}]_{n-k}, [\boldsymbol{y}]_{n-k}$ are the input packed Shamir sharings of the addition gates.
2. All parties locally compute $[\boldsymbol{z}]_{n-k} = [\boldsymbol{x}]_{n-k} + [\boldsymbol{y}]_{n-k}$.
3. Suppose $\mathsf{pos} = (p_1, p_2, \ldots, p_k)$ are the positions associated with these k addition gates. Recall that $\boldsymbol{\beta} = (\beta_1, \ldots, \beta_k)$ are the default positions. Let Σ be the degree-$(n-1)$ packed Shamir secret sharing scheme that stores secrets at positions $\boldsymbol{\beta}$. Let Σ' be the degree-$(n-k)$ packed Shamir secret sharing scheme that stores secrets at positions pos. Let $I : \mathbb{F}^k \to \mathbb{F}^k$ be the identity map.
All parties invoke $\mathcal{F}_{\text{tran}}$ with (Σ, Σ', I) and $[\boldsymbol{z}]_{n-k}$, and output $[\boldsymbol{z} \| \mathsf{pos}]_{n-k}$.

Main Protocol. Given the above protocols the main semi-honest protocol follows in a straightforward way. We refer the readers to the full version of this paper [GPS22] for the description of our main protocol, the security proof, and the analysis of the cost. Overall we obtain the following theorem.

Protocol 9: MULT

1. Suppose $[\boldsymbol{x}]_{n-k}, [\boldsymbol{y}]_{n-k}$ are the input packed Shamir sharings of the multiplication gates. All parties will use a fresh random packed Beaver triple $([\boldsymbol{a}]_{n-k}, [\boldsymbol{b}]_{n-k}, [\boldsymbol{c}]_{n-k})$ prepared in the preprocessing phase.
2. All parties locally compute $[\boldsymbol{x}+\boldsymbol{a}]_{n-k} = [\boldsymbol{x}]_{n-k} + [\boldsymbol{a}]_{n-k}$ and $[\boldsymbol{y}+\boldsymbol{b}]_{n-k} = [\boldsymbol{y}]_{n-k} + [\boldsymbol{b}]_{n-k}$.
3. The first party P_1 collects the whole sharings $[\boldsymbol{x}+\boldsymbol{a}]_{n-k}, [\boldsymbol{y}+\boldsymbol{b}]_{n-k}$ and reconstructs the secrets $\boldsymbol{x}+\boldsymbol{a}, \boldsymbol{y}+\boldsymbol{b}$. Then, P_1 computes the sharings $[\boldsymbol{x}+\boldsymbol{a}]_{k-1}, [\boldsymbol{y}+\boldsymbol{b}]_{k-1}$ and distributes the shares to other parties.
4. All parties locally compute
$$[\boldsymbol{z}]_{n-1} := [\boldsymbol{x}+\boldsymbol{a}]_{k-1} \cdot [\boldsymbol{y}+\boldsymbol{b}]_{k-1} - [\boldsymbol{x}+\boldsymbol{a}]_{k-1} \cdot [\boldsymbol{b}]_{n-k} - [\boldsymbol{y}+\boldsymbol{b}]_{k-1} \cdot [\boldsymbol{a}]_{n-k} + [\boldsymbol{c}]_{n-k}.$$
5. Suppose $\mathsf{pos} = (p_1, p_2, \ldots, p_k)$ are the positions associated with these k multiplication gates. Recall that $\boldsymbol{\beta} = (\beta_1, \ldots, \beta_k)$ are the default positions. Let Σ be the degree-$(n-1)$ packed Shamir secret sharing scheme that stores secrets at positions $\boldsymbol{\beta}$. Let Σ' be the degree-$(n-k)$ packed Shamir secret sharing scheme that stores secrets at positions pos. Let $I : \mathbb{F}^k \to \mathbb{F}^k$ be the identity map.
All parties invoke $\mathcal{F}_{\text{tran}}$ with (Σ, Σ', I) and $[\boldsymbol{z}]_{n-1}$, and output $[\boldsymbol{z}\|\mathsf{pos}]_{n-k}$.

Theorem 3. *In the client-server model, let* c *denote the number of clients,* n *denote the number of parties (servers), and* t *denote the number of corrupted parties (servers). Let* $\mathbb{F}$ *be a finite field of size* $|\mathbb{F}| \geq |C| + n$. *For an arithmetic circuit* C *over* $\mathbb{F}$, *there exists an information-theoretic MPC protocol in the preprocessing model which securely computes the arithmetic circuit* C *in the presence of a semi-honest adversary controlling up to* c *clients and* t *parties. The cost of the protocol is* $O(|C| \cdot \frac{n^2}{k^2} + (\mathsf{Depth} + \mathsf{c}) \cdot \frac{n^2}{k})$ *field elements of preprocessing data and* $O(|C| \cdot \frac{n}{k} + (\mathsf{Depth} + \mathsf{c}) \cdot n)$ *field elements of communication, where* $k = \frac{n-t+1}{2}$ *and* Depth *is the circuit depth.*

Acknowledgement. V. Goyal, Y. Song—Supported by the NSF award 1916939, DARPA SIEVE program under Agreement No. HR00112020025, a gift from Ripple, a DoE NETL award, a JP Morgan Faculty Fellowship, a PNC center for financial services innovation award, and a Cylab seed funding award. Y. Song was also supported by a Cylab Presidential Fellowship.

A. Polychroniadou—This paper was prepared in part for information purposes by the Artificial Intelligence Research group of JPMorgan Chase & Co and its affiliates ("JP Morgan"), and is not a product of the Research Department of JP Morgan. JP Morgan makes no representation and warranty whatsoever and disclaims all liability, for the completeness, accuracy or reliability of the information contained herein. This document is not intended as investment research or investment advice, or a recommendation, offer or solicitation for the purchase or sale of any security, financial instrument, financial product or service, or to be used in any way for evaluating the merits of

References

[ACD+20] Abspoel, M., et al.: Asymptotically good multiplicative LSSS over galois rings and applications to MPC over $\mathbb{Z}/p^k\mathbb{Z}$. In: Moriai, S., Wang, H. (eds.) ASIACRYPT 2020. LNCS, vol. 12493, pp. 151–180. Springer, Cham (2020). https://doi.org/10.1007/978-3-030-64840-4_6

[BDOZ11] Bendlin, R., Damgård, I., Orlandi, C., Zakarias, S.: Semi-homomorphic encryption and multiparty computation. In: Paterson, K.G. (ed.) EUROCRYPT 2011. LNCS, vol. 6632, pp. 169–188. Springer, Heidelberg (2011). https://doi.org/10.1007/978-3-642-20465-4_11

[Bea91] Beaver, D.: Efficient multiparty protocols using circuit randomization. In: Feigenbaum, J. (ed.) CRYPTO 1991. LNCS, vol. 576, pp. 420–432. Springer, Heidelberg (1992). https://doi.org/10.1007/3-540-46766-1_34

[BGIN20] Boyle, E., Gilboa, N., Ishai, Y., Nof, A.: Efficient fully secure computation via distributed zero-knowledge proofs. In: Moriai, S., Wang, H. (eds.) ASIACRYPT 2020. LNCS, vol. 12493, pp. 244–276. Springer, Cham (2020). https://doi.org/10.1007/978-3-030-64840-4_9

[BGIN21] Boyle, E., Gilboa, N., Ishai, Y., Nof, A.: Sublinear GMW-style compiler for MPC with preprocessing. In: Malkin, T., Peikert, C. (eds.) CRYPTO 2021. LNCS, vol. 12826, pp. 457–485. Springer, Cham (2021). https://doi.org/10.1007/978-3-030-84245-1_16

[BGJK21] Beck, G., Goel, A., Jain, A., Kaptchuk, G.: Order-C secure multiparty computation for highly repetitive circuits. In: Canteaut, A., Standaert, F.-X. (eds.) EUROCRYPT 2021. LNCS, vol. 12697, pp. 663–693. Springer, Cham (2021). https://doi.org/10.1007/978-3-030-77886-6_23

[BOGW88] Ben-Or, M., Goldwasser, S., Wigderson, A.: Completeness theorems for non-cryptographic fault-tolerant distributed computation. In: Proceedings of the Twentieth Annual ACM Symposium on Theory of Computing, pp. 1–10. ACM (1988)

[CCXY18] Cascudo, I., Cramer, R., Xing, C., Yuan, C.: Amortized complexity of information-theoretically secure MPC revisited. In: Shacham, H., Boldyreva, A. (eds.) CRYPTO 2018. LNCS, vol. 10993, pp. 395–426. Springer, Cham (2018). https://doi.org/10.1007/978-3-319-96878-0_14

[CGH+18] Chida, K., et al.: Fast large-scale honest-majority MPC for malicious adversaries. In: Shacham, H., Boldyreva, A. (eds.) CRYPTO 2018. LNCS, vol. 10993, pp. 34–64. Springer, Cham (2018). https://doi.org/10.1007/978-3-319-96878-0_2

[Cou19] Couteau, G.: A note on the communication complexity of multiparty computation in the correlated randomness model. In: Ishai, Y., Rijmen, V. (eds.) EUROCRYPT 2019. LNCS, vol. 11477, pp. 473–503. Springer, Cham (2019). https://doi.org/10.1007/978-3-030-17656-3_17

[CRX21] Cramer, R., Rambaud, M., Xing, C.: Asymptotically-good arithmetic secret sharing over $\mathbb{Z}/p^\ell\mathbb{Z}$ with strong multiplication and its applications to efficient MPC. In: Malkin, T., Peikert, C. (eds.) CRYPTO 2021. LNCS, vol. 12827, pp. 656–686. Springer, Cham (2021). https://doi.org/10.1007/978-3-030-84252-9_22

[DIK10] Damgård, I., Ishai, Y., Krøigaard, M.: Perfectly secure multiparty computation and the computational overhead of cryptography. In: Gilbert, H. (ed.) EUROCRYPT 2010. LNCS, vol. 6110, pp. 445–465. Springer, Heidelberg (2010). https://doi.org/10.1007/978-3-642-13190-5_23

[DN07] Damgård, I., Nielsen, J.B.: Scalable and unconditionally secure multiparty computation. In: Menezes, A. (ed.) CRYPTO 2007. LNCS, vol. 4622, pp. 572–590. Springer, Heidelberg (2007). https://doi.org/10.1007/978-3-540-74143-5_32

[DNPR16] Damgård, I., Nielsen, J.B., Polychroniadou, A., Raskin, M.: On the communication required for unconditionally secure multiplication. In: Robshaw, M., Katz, J. (eds.) CRYPTO 2016. LNCS, vol. 9815, pp. 459–488. Springer, Heidelberg (2016). https://doi.org/10.1007/978-3-662-53008-5_16

[DPSZ12] Damgård, I., Pastro, V., Smart, N., Zakarias, S.: Multiparty computation from somewhat homomorphic encryption. In: Safavi-Naini, R., Canetti, R. (eds.) CRYPTO 2012. LNCS, vol. 7417, pp. 643–662. Springer, Heidelberg (2012). https://doi.org/10.1007/978-3-642-32009-5_38

[FY92] Franklin, M., Yung, M.: Communication complexity of secure computation (Extended Abstract). In: Proceedings of the Twenty-Fourth Annual ACM Symposium on Theory of Computing, STOC 1992, pp. 699–710. Association for Computing Machinery, New York (1992)

[GIP15] Genkin, D., Ishai, Y., Polychroniadou, A.: Efficient multi-party computation: from passive to active security via secure SIMD circuits. In: Gennaro, R., Robshaw, M. (eds.) CRYPTO 2015. LNCS, vol. 9216, pp. 721–741. Springer, Heidelberg (2015). https://doi.org/10.1007/978-3-662-48000-7_35

[GLO+21] Goyal, V., Li, H., Ostrovsky, R., Polychroniadou, A., Song, Y.: ATLAS: efficient and scalable MPC in the honest majority setting. In: Malkin, T., Peikert, C. (eds.) CRYPTO 2021. LNCS, vol. 12826, pp. 244–274. Springer, Cham (2021). https://doi.org/10.1007/978-3-030-84245-1_9

[GPS21] Goyal, V., Polychroniadou, A., Song, Y.: Unconditional communication-efficient MPC via hall's marriage theorem. In: Malkin, T., Peikert, C. (eds.) CRYPTO 2021. LNCS, vol. 12826, pp. 275–304. Springer, Cham (2021). https://doi.org/10.1007/978-3-030-84245-1_10

[GPS22] Goyal, V., Polychroniadou, A., Song, Y.: Sharing transformation and dishonest majority MPC with packed secret sharing. Cryptology ePrint Archive (2022)

[GSY21] Gordon, S.D., Starin, D., Yerukhimovich, A.: The more the merrier: reducing the cost of large scale MPC. In: Canteaut, A., Standaert, F.-X. (eds.) EUROCRYPT 2021. LNCS, vol. 12697, pp. 694–723. Springer, Cham (2021). https://doi.org/10.1007/978-3-030-77886-6_24

[PS21] Polychroniadou, A., Song, Y.: Constant-overhead unconditionally secure multiparty computation over binary fields. In: Canteaut, A., Standaert, F.-X. (eds.) EUROCRYPT 2021. LNCS, vol. 12697, pp. 812–841. Springer, Cham (2021). https://doi.org/10.1007/978-3-030-77886-6_28

[Sha79] Shamir, A.: How to share a secret. Commun. ACM **22**(11), 612–613 (1979)

Verifiable Relation Sharing and Multi-verifier Zero-Knowledge in Two Rounds: Trading NIZKs with Honest Majority
(Extended Abstract)

Benny Applebaum[1(✉)], Eliran Kachlon[1], and Arpita Patra[2]

[1] Tel-Aviv University, Tel-Aviv, Israel
benny.applebaum@gmail.com
[2] Indian Institute of Science, Bangalore, India
arpita@iisc.ac.in

Abstract. We introduce the problem of *Verifiable Relation Sharing* (VRS) where a client (prover) wishes to share a vector of secret data items among k servers (the verifiers) while proving in zero-knowledge that the shared data satisfies some properties. This combined task of sharing and proving generalizes notions like verifiable secret sharing and zero-knowledge proofs over secret-shared data. We study VRS from a theoretical perspective and focus on its round complexity.

As our main contribution, we show that every efficiently-computable relation can be realized by a VRS with an optimal round complexity of two rounds where the first round is input-independent (offline round). The protocol achieves full UC-security against an active adversary that is allowed to corrupt any t-subset of the parties that may include the client together with some of the verifiers. For a small (logarithmic) number of parties, we achieve an optimal resiliency threshold of $t < 0.5(k + 1)$, and for a large (polynomial) number of parties, we achieve an almost-optimal resiliency threshold of $t < 0.5(k+1)(1-\epsilon)$ for an arbitrarily small constant $\epsilon > 0$. Both protocols can be based on sub-exponentially hard injective one-way functions. If the parties have an access to a collision resistance hash function, we can derive *statistical everlasting security*, i.e., the protocols are secure against adversaries that are computationally bounded during the protocol execution and become computationally unbounded after the protocol execution.

Previous 2-round solutions achieve smaller resiliency thresholds and weaker security notions regardless of the underlying assumptions. As a special case, our protocols give rise to 2-round offline/online constructions of multi-verifier zero-knowledge proofs (MVZK). Such constructions were previously obtained under the same type of assumptions that are needed for NIZK, i.e., public-key assumptions or random-oracle type assumptions (Abe et al., Asiacrypt 2002; Groth and Ostrovsky, Crypto 2007; Boneh et al., Crypto 2019; Yang, and Wang, Eprint 2022). Our work shows, for the first time, that in the presence of an honest majority

A full version of this paper appears in [6].

Y. Dodis and T. Shrimpton (Eds.): CRYPTO 2022, LNCS 13510, pp. 33–56, 2022.
https://doi.org/10.1007/978-3-031-15985-5_2

these assumptions can be replaced with more conservative "Minicrypt"-type assumptions like injective one-way functions and collision-resistance hash functions. Indeed, our MVZK protocols provide a round-efficient substitute for NIZK in settings where honest-majority is present. Additional applications are also presented.

1 Introduction

In recent years, a large amount of research was dedicated to the study of zero-knowledge proofs in *distributed settings*, such as zero-knowledge proofs with multiple verifiers [9,37,51] and zero-knowledge proofs over secret-shared data [16,17,24,25]. Those variants of zero-knowledge proofs have applications both in theory and practice, in round-optimal multiparty computation [2], private data aggregation [24], and anonymous communication [25].

A typical scenario of interest consists of a client $\mathcal{P}$ (the prover) that holds a vector of secret data items $\mathbf{s}$, together with several servers $\mathcal{V}_1, \ldots, \mathcal{V}_k$ (the verifiers). The client wishes to share $\mathbf{s}$ among the servers, and also prove in zero-knowledge that the shared data satisfies some properties. Previous works usually let $\mathcal{P}$ send each $\mathcal{V}_i$ its share, and then perform a zero-knowledge proof on the shared data. A natural question is whether considering the sharing and the proving as a single task could result in a protocol with better round-complexity and better security guarantees. To capture this joint task of sharing-and-proving, we present the notion of *verifiable relation sharing* (VRS).

Verifiable Relation Sharing. The VRS functionality of a public relation R receives from the prover an input $\mathbf{x} = (x_0, x_1, \ldots, x_k)$, where we think of x_0 as a private information of the prover, and of x_i as the share of $\mathcal{V}_i$. The functionality verifies that $R(\mathbf{x}) = 1$, and if the verification fails, then it returns a failure-symbol $\perp$ to all the verifiers. If the verification succeeds, the functionality returns x_i to $\mathcal{V}_i$. Observe that the VRS functionality captures the typical scenario discussed above, as well as several cryptographic primitives, including verifiable secret sharing [23], verifiable function secret sharing [17], secure multicast [33], and zero-knowledge proofs with multiple verifiers.

We formalize the VRS functionality under the definitions of secure multiparty computation (MPC) in the universal-composability (UC) framework of [21]. We strive for full-security, including guaranteed output delivery, at the presence of an honest majority in the plain model. We note that honest-majority is necessary due to impossibility of UC-secure Zero-knowledge proofs in the plain model [22]. The active (aka Byzantine or malicious) adversary is allowed to corrupt any minority subset of the $k+1$ parties $\{\mathcal{P}, \mathcal{V}_1, \ldots, \mathcal{V}_k\}$ that may include the prover together with some of the verifiers. The use of MPC-based "full-security" definitions provides strong guarantees that are not supported by related notions of distributed zero-knowledge. Specifically, when the prover $\mathcal{P}$ is honest, we get *correctness*, i.e., every honest $\mathcal{V}_i$ outputs x_i even in the presence of corrupt active verifiers, as well as simulation-based *privacy*, which implies that the adversary only learns the outputs of the corrupt verifiers. For a corrupt $\mathcal{P}$, we get *soundness* and *knowledge extraction* even when $\mathcal{P}$ colludes with some of the verifiers. In contrast, previous works on weaker notions, such as zero-knowledge proofs over secret-shared data, achieve correctness only for semi-honest verifiers [16,17,24,25], and in some cases (e.g., [24,25]) provide soundness only when all the verifiers are honest. Further discussion of related works and a comparison of known results appear in Sect. 1.2 and Table 1.

We study the VRS problem from a theoretical perspective while focusing on the best-achievable *round complexity*. It is known that VRS cannot be realized in 1 round even for relatively simple relations (e.g., VSS [7]). Looking for the second best, we ask:

> **Q1:** Can VRS be realized by a 2-round protocol? Moreover, can we make the first round input-independent ("offline round")? If so, under what assumptions?

The question of obtaining a 2-round protocol in the plain model is open even for weaker notions like distributed zero-knowledge over secret-shared data.

Multi-verifier Zero-Knowledge. It is useful to consider the somewhat degenerate version of VRS in which all the verifiers get the same information except for some private witness that is kept by $\mathcal{P}$. This variant essentially corresponds to *multi-verifier zero-knowledge* proofs (MVZK) [20]. When modeled as an ideal functionality, MVZK is parameterized by a public relation R, it receives from $\mathcal{P}$ a statement x and a witness w, and verifies that $R(x, w) = 1$. If the verification fails, then the functionality returns a failure-symbol $\perp$ to all the verifiers $\mathcal{V}_1, \ldots, \mathcal{V}_k$, and if the verification succeeds, the functionality returns x to all the verifiers. Again, we strive for a 2-round offline/online solution in the plain model.

Observe that the single verifier case (where the adversary can either corrupt the verifier or the prover) corresponds to the standard notion of zero-knowledge proofs. Classical impossibility results [36] show that a plain-model protocol that consists of a single message from the prover to the verifier, also known as *non-interactive zero-knowledge* (NIZK), exist only for languages in BPP, even when one considers only stand-alone security. Assuming a minimal trusted setup in the form of a common reference string (CRS), one can achieve NIZK for every language in **NP** from public-key assumptions [13,15,30,38,48,50], or, alternatively, in the random oracle model [11,31]. In a related notion, called *Zaps* [28], the CRS is replaced with a preprocessing round in which only the verifier communicates by broadcasting its random coins, at the expense of downgrading zero-knowledge to witness-indistinguishability. Assuming the existence of one-way functions, it is known that Zaps are equivalent to NIZK [28].

Let us move back to the setting of multiple verifiers. Striving for a 2-round simulation-based zero-knowledge, we make the necessary assumption of an honest majority among the set of all parties (including the prover).[1] To the best

[1] Without an honest majority, a 2-round plain-model MVZK protocol (where in each round both the verifiers and prover can talk simultaneously) implies a 2-step ZK protocol (where the verifier sends a message and gets a response from the prover) which is ruled-out by [36] for non-trivial languages outside BPP.

of our knowledge, the only known solution in this setting follows from the work of Groth and Ostrovsky on Multi-string NIZK Proofs [37]. Specifically, their work implicitly give rise to a 2-round offline/online honest-majority MVZK that achieves simulation-based security based on Zaps and public-key encryption [37, Theorem 3]. These assumptions are as strong (or even stronger) than the ones needed for NIZK protocols in the seemingly "harder" 2-party settings. We therefore ask:

> **Q2:** Are NIZK/Zaps assumptions inherently needed for an MVZK protocol with 1-offline and 1-online round in the honest-majority setting? Is it possible to replace these assumptions with weaker assumptions?

1.1 Our Contribution

1.1.1 Round-Optimal VRS and MVZK in Minicrypt

We answer Questions 1 and 2 in the affirmative. Our main result is a protocol with 1-offline round and 1-online round for VRS in the UC-framework, assuming the existence of perfectly-binding non-interactive commitment scheme (NICOM) with sub-exponential privacy. Such a NICOM scheme can be based on injective one-way functions with sub-exponential hardness or even on standard one-way function with sub-exponential hardness assuming worst-case complexity-theoretic derandomization assumptions [8,45].[2] Throughout, we assume that the parties communicate over pairwise secure and authenticated point-to-point channels, as well as over a common broadcast channel, which allows each party to send a message to all parties and ensures that the received message is identical.

Theorem 1. *Assuming the existence of injective one-way functions with sub-exponential hardness, for every $\epsilon > 0$ the VRS functionality of every efficiently computable relation R can be realized in 1-offline round and 1-online round, with full security against an active rushing adversary, in any of the following settings.*

- (Optimal resiliency for small number of verifiers) *The number of verifiers k is at most logarithmic in the security parameter, and the adversary corrupts less than $(k + 1)/2$ parties.*
- (Almost-optimal resiliency for polynomially-many verifiers) *The number of verifiers k grows polynomially with the security parameter and the adversary corrupts less than $(k + 1) \cdot (\frac{1}{2} - \epsilon)$ parties.*

Since MVZK is a special case of VRS, we obtain the following corollary.

Corollary 1. *Assuming the existence of injective one-way functions with sub-exponential hardness, the MVZK functionality of every efficiently computable relation R can be realized in 1-offline round and 1-online round, with full security against an active rushing adversary, in the same settings of Theorem 1.*

[2] For technical reasons, the NICOM should satisfy some level of security against selective opening that, by "complexity leveraging", follows from the assumption that the underlying one-way function (or injective one-way function) cannot be inverted in polynomial-time with more than sub-exponential probability. This seems to be a relatively mild assumption; See Remark 2.

For optimal resiliency, we obtain a protocol with complexity polynomial in the security parameter, but exponential in the number of verifiers k. On the other hand, for every $\epsilon > 0$ we obtain a protocol with resiliency $(k+1) \cdot (\frac{1}{2} - \epsilon)$, whose complexity is polynomial both in the security parameter and in k. (In fact, we can push ϵ to be as small as $\epsilon = \Omega(\frac{1}{\sqrt{\log k}})$; see the full version [6] for full details.)

The difference between optimal resiliency and "almost-optimal resiliency" is mostly relevant when the number of verifiers is small, e.g., constant. In this setting, the first protocol provides an efficient solution. Specifically, we highlight the case of 3-party computation, with a single prover and two verifiers, and we note that by adding just a single verifier to the standard zero-knowledge settings, we can obtain a protocol with 1-offline round and 1-online round for the case of a single corruption from Minicrypt-type assumptions. (In contrast, general-purpose 3-party MPC for honest majority requires 3 rounds [47].)

Still, the existence of a strict-honest-majority 2-round VRS protocol whose complexity scales polynomially with the number of parties, remains an interesting open problem. We show that such a protocol can be constructed if one is willing to make stronger assumptions (e.g., random oracle or correlation-intractable functions) or if the adversary is non-rushing. In fact, we note that a weak limitation of the rushing capabilities of the adversary suffices, and present a new notion of *semi-rushing* adversary to model such a behavior.[3]

1.1.2 VRS and MVZK with Everlasting Security in Minicrypt

It is known that if we do not put restriction on the round complexity, then, in the setting of honest-majority, one can obtain *unconditional* results and no assumptions are needed at all! Specifically, as shown by Rabin and Ben-Or [49], every efficiently computable function can be securely computed with statistical security against computationally-unbounded adversaries. While we do not know whether it is possible to achieve statistical security in 2 rounds, we show that VRS and MVZK can be implemented by a protocol that achieves *statistical everlasting security* assuming an access to a collision-resistant hash function h. The notion of statistical everlasting security [44] can be viewed as a hybrid version of statistical and computational security. During the run-time, the adversary is assumed to be computationally-bounded (e.g., cannot find collisions in the hash function) but after the protocol terminates, the adversary hands its view to a computationally-unbounded analyst who can apply arbitrary computations in

3 The difference between rushing and non-rushing adversary boils down to the scheduling of the messages within a single round of a protocol. A *non-rushing* adversary must send the messages of the corrupt parties in a given round before receiving the messages of the honest parties in that round, whereas a *rushing* adversary may delay sending the messages of the corrupt parties until receiving the messages from the honest parties. Thus, the messages of the corrupt parties may depend on the messages of the honest parties in the same round. Our notion of *semi-rushing* adversary allows the adversary to see all the messages of the honest parties, except for one. For more about this model and its relevance, see the full version [6].

order to extract information on the inputs of the honest parties (e.g., finding collisions or even reading the whole truth table of h).[4] This feature is one of the main advantages of information-theoretic protocols: after-the-fact secrecy holds regardless of technological advances and the time invested by the adversary.

Theorem 2. *Given an access to a collision-resistant hash function, the VRS and MVZK functionalities of efficiently computable relations can be realized in 1-offline round and 1-online round, with full security and* everlasting security *against an active rushing adversary, in the same settings (honest-majority with few verifiers or almost-honest majority with many verifiers) of Theorem 1.*

Remark 1 (On the use of hash function). Our protocol assumes that all parties are given an access to a collision resistance hash function h. Theoretically speaking, such a function should be chosen from a family of functions $\mathcal{H}$ in order to defeat non-uniform adversaries. One may assume that h is chosen once and for all by some simple set-up mechanism. In particular, by using the standard concatenation-based combiner for hash functions [41], this set-up mechanism may be realized distributively by a single round of public random coins where security holds against an active rushing adversary that may corrupt all the participants except for a single one. The choice of the hash function can be abstracted by a CRS functionality, or even, using the multi-string model of [37] with a single honestly-generated string. However, it should be emphasized that this CRS is being used in a very *weak* way: It is "non-programmable" (the simulator receives h as an input) and it can be sampled once and for all by using the above trivial public-coin mechanism. Even if one counts this extra set-up step as an additional round, to the best of our knowledge, everlasting security was not known to be achievable regardless of the underlying assumptions.

The difference between everlasting and computational security is *fundamental* and is analogous to the difference between statistical commitments and computational commitments or statistical ZK vs. computational ZK (see, e.g., the discussions in [19,46]). Indeed, Theorem 2 provides (UC-secure) MVZK with a *statistical zero-knowledge* property. As a side bonus, Theorem 2 does not require sub-exponential hardness assumptions.

1.1.3 Round-Optimal Linear Function Computation in Minicrypt

Using the machinery we develop for VRS and MVZK, we obtain a 3-round protocol for linear function computation. By the lower-bound of [34] our protocol has optimal round complexity. Like in previous results, we assume the existence of injective one-way functions with sub-exponential hardness in order to obtain a protocol with computational security in the plain model, or an access to a collision resistance hash-function in order to obtain a protocol with everlasting security. In contrast, previous works achieve only computational security by assuming public-key encryption and Zaps [2]. We emphasize that in Theorem 3

[4] Technically, in the UC-framework we allow the environment to output its view and require statistical indistinguishability between the real and ideal experiments.

we obtain *optimal resiliency* even when the number of parties is polynomial in the security parameter.

Theorem 3. *Assuming the existence of injective one-way functions with sub-exponential hardness, every efficiently computable linear function can be realized in 3 rounds, with full security against an active rushing adversary, that corrupts a minority of the parties. If we replace the one-way function with an access to a collision resistance hash-function, we also obtain everlasting security.*

1.1.4 Applications

We present some applications of our protocols. For full details, see the full version [6].

MVZK as a NIZK-Substitute for Honest Majority. We notice that our MVZK protocol captures an important aspect of NIZK, its *minimal round complexity*, while using only Minicrypt-type assumptions. Indeed, our MVZK protocol implies that the CRS for NIZK is not required, and can be replaced with only a *single* offline-round of communication. Similar to NIZK, the proof itself requires only *one online round.* However, unlike NIZK, in our protocol all the parties have to communicate in the online round.

Round-Efficient Manipulation of Non-homomorphic Commitments. In a common scenario in multiparty computation, a party $\mathcal{P}$ holds openings to public commitments $C_1, \ldots, C_\ell$. $\mathcal{P}$ wishes to apply some function f on the committed values $z_1, \ldots, z_\ell$ and let the rest of the parties learn $y := f(z_1, \ldots, z_\ell)$, while proving in zero-knowledge that she used the committed values in the computation of f. Alternatively, $\mathcal{P}$ may want to generate another commitment C, that hides y, while proving in zero-knowledge that C was honestly generated. Both the tasks can be solved in 1-offline round and 1-online round by using our MVZK. Since the offline round can be executed in parallel to the generation of $C_1, \ldots, C_\ell$, both tasks require only one additional round!

Round-Efficient GMW-Type Compilers in Minicrypt. Using VRS one can obtain round-efficient GMW-type compilers in Minicrypt, for the case of honest majority. Given a protocol π which is secure against a semi-malicious adversary,[5] we obtain a protocol π' with unanimous abort against an active adversary at the expense of adding a single offline round. If π is secure against a passive (aka semi-honest) adversary, the overhead grows to 4 rounds. Notably, unlike the GMW compiler, our transformation avoids the use of public-key encryption.

Round-Optimal Honest-Majority MPC in Minicrypt. A followup work by the same authors [5] shows that general secure multiparty computation with *full-security* (including guaranteed output delivery) in the presence of an honest

[5] A *semi-malicious* adversary is allowed to choose its input and randomness but otherwise follows the protocol. Many passively secure protocols (e.g., [12]) actually offer semi-malicious security.

majority can be achieved in an optimal number of 3 rounds based on Minicrypt-type assumptions (e.g., NICOMs). A main building block of the protocol is our 2-round offline/online VRS protocol.

Bibliographic Note. Previous unpublished version of [5] contained a weak form of some of the current results based on the Fiat-Shamir heuristic. These results were removed from the new version of [5], and are fully subsumed by the current paper.

1.2 Related Works and Comparison

The VRS functionality was implicitly studied by Gennaro *et al.* [34], in the context of single input functionalities. Gennaro *et al.* provided a two-round perfect protocol with resiliency $(k+1)/6$. The resiliency was improved to $(k+1)/3$ by Applebaum et al. [3], at the cost of degrading the perfect security to computational security, assuming the existence of NICOMs.

Boneh et al. [16] initiated the formal study of zero-knowledge proofs over secret-shared data. They considered information-theoretic security in the following models of corruptions: (1) the adversary corrupts the prover *or* up to $k-1$ verifiers, and (2) the adversary corrupts the prover *and* less than $k/2$ verifiers. In both corruption models, they only provide *security with abort.* Their protocols exploit PCP machinery to achieve low communication complexity (sub-linear in the description of the relation), but have a super-constant number of rounds. Based on a random oracle, the number of rounds can be collapsed to 2, assuming that the data is already secret-shared among the verifiers.

MVZKs were first introduced in [20]. The most relevant MVZK for us can be derived from [37] which provides a construction of NIZK in the *multi-string model* assuming the existence of Zaps. In the multi-string model, the CRS is replaced with several authorities, each providing the protocol with a public random string, and the protocol is secure as long as a majority of those authorities are honest (that is, if a majority of the strings are uniformly distributed). An MVZK protocol with an honest majority of parties can be obtained in the plain model by letting each party broadcast a random string in the offline round, so that a majority of the strings are uniformly distributed. Simulation-based security can be obtained via the additional help of public-key encryption [37, Theorem 3].

Other non-interactive variants of MVZK were presented in [1]. Translated to our model, their work yield 2-round MVZK for $t < k/3$ and a 3-round protocol for $t < n/2$. Both results hold under public-key (discrete-log) hardness assumptions. Recently, [51] and [9] constructed MVZK with practical real-world efficiency in honest and super-honest majority settings. However, their low round (2 or 3) variants rely on random oracle and achieve either selective or identifiable abort.

Comparison. We compare our results with the relevant existing results in Table 1. Except for this work and [37], none of the works achieves an offline/online construction.

Table 1. Comparison of our work with the state-of-the-art relevant results

Ref.	Primitive	Rounds	Threshold	Assumptions	Security†
[34]	VRS	2	$t < (k+1)/6$	-	it and full security
[3]	VRS	2	$t < (k+1)/3$	NICOM	cs and full security
[16]	ZK over shared data	2*	$t < (k+1)/2^{\ddagger}$	Random Oracle	it and abort
[37]	MVZK	2	$t < (k+1)/2$	PKE	cs and full security
[1]	MVZK	3	$t < (k+1)/2$	Discrete-log	cs and full security
[51]	MVZK	2	$t < (k+1)/2$	Random Oracle	it and abort
[9]	MVZK	2	$t < (k+1)/3$	Random Oracle	it and identifiable abort
This paper	VRS	2	$t < (k+1)(\frac{1}{2} - \epsilon)^{\S}$	NICOM**	cs/es and full security

† it: information-theoretic, es: everlasting security, cs: computational security,

‡ They assume the adversary corrupts (1) the prover *or* up to $k-1$ verifiers, and (2) the prover *and* less than $k/2$ verifiers

* The round complexity does not include the rounds needed for data sharing.

** Perfectly-binding and sub-exponentially hiding NICOM for cs security and Computationally-binding and statistically-hiding NICOM for es security.

§ We achieve $t < (k+1)/2$ when k is logarithmic in the security parameter.

2 Preliminaries

Single-Input Functionalities. We adopt an MPC-based notation and replace VRS with the following notion of *single-input functionalities* (SIF). We assume that there are n parties, $\mathsf{P} = \{P_1, \ldots, P_n\}$, where one party (e.g., P_n) takes the role of a *Dealer* D. The SIF functionality $\mathcal{F}$ is parameterized with a function $f : \{0,1\}^* \to (\{0,1\}^*)^n$, it takes an input string $\mathbf{z}$ from the dealer, computes the outputs $(\mathbf{y}_1, \ldots, \mathbf{y}_n) = f(\mathbf{z})$ and delivers $\mathbf{y}_i$ to the ith party P_i. It is not hard to see that VRS is a special case of SIF, and that VRS implies SIF in a round-preserving way. (Indeed, to realize $\mathcal{F}$ define the relation R that accepts a vector $(x_0, x_1, \ldots, x_{n-1})$ if $x_i = f_i(x_0)$ for $i \in [n-1]$, and let D invoke a VRS for R with the input $(z, f_1(z), \ldots, f_{n-1}(z))$.) We will mostly focus on the special case of *public-SIF* that delivers the same output to all the parties. In the full version [6] we show that a 2-round offline/online general-SIF reduces to 2-round offline/online public-SIF via the aid of NICOMs.

Security Model. We consider an active static, rushing adversary that may corrupt up to t parties. We consider two main settings: the optimal resiliency setting where $n = 2t + 1$ and the almost-optimal resiliency setting where $n = (2 + \epsilon)t$ for some arbitrarily small constant $\epsilon > 0$. The parties are connected by pairwise secure channels and additionally a broadcast channel is available. We prove security of our protocols in the UC-framework [21]. We identify the set of parties P with $\{1, \ldots, n\}$, and denote the set of honest parties by $\mathsf{H} \subseteq \mathsf{P}$, and the set of corrupt parties by $\mathsf{C} \subseteq \mathsf{P}$. In our protocols, we follow the convention that the honest parties can "disqualify" the dealer whenever it is clear from broadcast messages that the dealer misbehaves. This does not violate "guaranteed output delivery" since in case of disqualification, the honest parties can always apply f on some predetermined default value and output the result. We denote by κ the security parameter and implicitly assume that all other parameters (e.g., the number of parties, and the complexity of the functionalities and protocols) depend in κ.

NICOM. A NICOM consists of two PPT algorithms $(\mathsf{commit}, \mathsf{open})$ where commit takes a security parameter κ, message x and random coins r, and outputs a commitment C and a corresponding opening information o. The open algorithm takes κ, and a commitment/opening pair (C, o) and outputs the message x or a failure message $\perp$. The algorithms should satisfy the standard properties of correctness, binding (i.e., it must be hard for an adversary to come up with two different openings of any C) and hiding (a commitment must not leak information about the underlying message) properties. NICOM comes in 2 main flavors: (1) with computational hiding and perfect binding, and (2) with statistical hiding and computational binding. Type (1) commitments can be based on injective one-way functions [14,35,52], and type (2) commitments can be based on collision resistance hash functions [27,39]. In the latter case, a description of a collision resistance hash function h (that is sampled from a family $\mathcal{H}$) is given to the algorithms $(\mathsf{commit}, \mathsf{open})$ as an auxiliary public parameter. Our protocols make use of NICOM in a modular way such that a type (1) instantiation (with sub-exponential computational hiding) yield computational protocols and type (2) instantiation yield protocols with everlasting security.

Remark 2 (Sub-exponential hiding). Assuming injective OWF over m-bit inputs that cannot be inverted by a PPT adversary with probability better than $2^{-m^{\delta}}$, it is possible to construct [14,35,52] a plain-model (with no public parameters) perfectly-binding NICOM whose computational hiding property holds for $\epsilon \leq 2^{-\kappa}$. We refer to such a commitment as *perfectly binding sub-exponentially hiding* NICOM. Moreover, under worst-case derandomization assumptions [8], such NICOMs can be based on general (not necessarily injective) sub-exponentially hard OWFs. Similar sub-exponential hardness assumptions are quite common in the literature and typical candidate one-way functions seem to achieve sub-exponential hardness. In fact, our variant of sub-exponential hardness is relatively mild compared to other notions, since we do not allow the adversary to run in sub-exponential time, but only allow it to succeed with sub-exponentially small probability.

3 Technical Overview

In this section we provide a high level overview of our SIF protocol. Full details of the protocol appear in the full version [6]. Intuitively, a SIF protocol consists of the following sequential parts: (1) The dealer presents a statement; (2) The other parties challenge it via a random challenge; (3) The dealer sends a respond; and (4) The other parties decide whether to accept or reject. Compressing these steps into 2 rounds is highly challenging. For comparison, even the task of verifiable secret sharing (without revealing it) takes at least 2 rounds [7,33]. To bypass this problem, we are forced to run sub-protocols in parallel and with some overlap. Specifically, we make an extensive use of (1) *tentative-output* protocols that prepare a tentative version of the output in an early round and only later, at the end, approve/reject/correct the tentative output; and (2) *offline-phase* protocols that begin with an *offline*, input-independent, round and only later receive the inputs. This allows us to save some rounds by allowing partial overlap between sub-protocols.

Our protocol makes an extensive use of *verifiable secret sharing* (VSS) [23]. For now, let us think about a VSS protocol as an actively-secure realization of the ideal functionality that takes as an input a secret $s \in \mathbb{F}$ and randomness r from a dealer, and delivers to each party P_i a share s_i that is generated from s and r by using some threshold secret sharing scheme with threshold t. Here and throughout the paper, $\mathbb{F}$ is a finite field whose size is assumed to be exponential in the security parameter κ, by default, $\mathbb{F} = \mathrm{GF}(2^\kappa)$. The underlying secret sharing scheme should be *binding* in the sense that a corrupted party cannot "lie" about its share. (This property implies that correct reconstruction is achievable even at the presence of an active adversary as long as we have $n - t$ honest parties.) To simplify the exposition, let us assume for now that the underlying secret sharing is *linearly homomorphic* and that the VSS protocol takes a *single round*. We emphasize that both features are unrealistic and even impossible to achieve when $t > n/3$, let alone when t is close to $n/2$.[6] Jumping ahead, a considerable part of this work will be devoted to the removal of these assumption while preserving the round complexity; see Sect. 3.3.

3.1 SIF for Few Parties

Let us restrict our attention to the case where the number of parties n is small, i.e., $n = O(\log \kappa)$. Recall that our goal is to construct a 2-round protocol for a general SIF functionality whose first round is an offline round that does not depend on the input of the dealer. We will use standard techniques to reduce this problem to the problem of constructing a 2-round protocol for a specific SIF functionality known as *triple secret sharing* (TSS) where the dealer wishes to share a triple (a, b, c) such that $c = ab$. For TSS, let us strive for a "standard" 2 round protocol whose first round is allowed to depend on the input.

2-Round TSS Against Non-rushing Adversary. Our starting point is the following 2 round protocol that assumes that a corrupted dealer is non-rushing. In the

[6] Even without homomorphism, computational VSS requires 2 rounds [7] when $n < 3t$. Moreover, even for such a large resiliency threshold, linear homomorphism is non-trivial to achieve. Specifically, for 2-round VSS, it is unknown how to achieve linear homomorphism without relying on strong primitives such as *homomorphic* NICOMs. The latter are typically constructed based on "structured" (public-key type) assumptions and are not known to follow from standard NICOMs.

first round, the dealer D, that holds a triple (a, b, c) with $c = ab$, picks three polynomials $A(x), B(x)$ and $C(x)$ of degree n, n and $2n$, respectively, such that $A(0) = a$, $B(0) = b$, $C(0) = c$ and $C(x) = A(x) \cdot B(x)$. Let A^i, B^i and C^i be the ith coefficient of $A(x), B(x)$ and $C(x)$, and note that $A^0 = a, B^0 = b$ and $C^0 = c$. The dealer shares all the coefficients $\{A^i, B^i\}_{i \in \{0,\dots,n\}}$, and $\{C^i\}_{i \in \{0,\dots,2n\}}$ via VSS. The parties now hold the shares of $a = A^0, b = B^0$ and $c = C^0$.

In order to ensure that $c = ab$, it suffices to verify that the polynomial $C(x)$ is equal to the polynomial $A(x) \cdot B(x)$. To this end, we want to compute $A(\alpha), B(\alpha)$ and $C(\alpha)$ for a random non-zero field element α, and verify that $C(\alpha) = A(\alpha)B(\alpha)$. Indeed, if $C(x) = A(x) \cdot B(x)$ then equality always holds, while if $C(x) \neq A(x) \cdot B(x)$ then the probability that the verification succeeds is at most $2n/(|\mathbb{F}| - 1) = \mathsf{negl}(\kappa)$. Therefore, in the first round, concurrently to the sharing of the dealer, we let every party P_i broadcast a random non-zero field element α_i.

In the second round, our goal is to compute $A(\alpha_i), B(\alpha_i), C(\alpha_i)$ for all $i \in \{1, \dots, n\}$ and "disqualify the dealer" if for some α_i the test $A(\alpha_i) \cdot B(\alpha_i) = C(\alpha_i)$ fails. Recall that $A(x)$ and $B(x)$ are random polynomials of degree n conditioned on $A(0) = a$ and $B(0) = b$, and therefore one can safely release all these α_i evaluations without revealing any information on a, b and c. The actual computation of $A(\alpha_i), B(\alpha_i), C(\alpha_i)$ makes use of the linear-homomorphism of the secret-sharing. Specifically, observe that $A(\alpha)$ is just a linear function of $A^0, \dots, A^n$ with coefficients $(\alpha^0, \dots, \alpha^n)$ (and similarly for $B(\alpha)$ and $C(\alpha)$), and therefore each party can reveal in the second round its share of $A(\alpha_i)$ (resp., $B(\alpha_i), C(\alpha_i)$). The binding property of the VSS guarantees that a corrupted party cannot lie about its shares and the existence of $t + 1$ honest parties guarantees successful reconstruction. The protocol follows the standard commit-challenge-response template with a minor tweak: many challenges are generated (one for each "verifier") concurrently to the commitment stage, and each of the responses is being computed collectively by the "verifiers".

Coping with a Rushing Adversary. The above protocol is insecure against a rushing adversary since such an adversary can wait to see the selected challenges and then share triples that do not satisfy the product relation and yet pass the tests. We solve this problem by hiding at least some of the challenges from the adversary while revealing them to enough parties so that the response (via reconstruction) can be computed in the second round. Details follow.

Consider all the possible $(t + 1)$-subsets of the parties, $Q_1, \dots, Q_N$ where $N = \binom{n}{t+1}$. In the first round, we let each subset Q_i generate a secret challenge α_i that is known only to the members of Q_i. Specifically, we define some canonical "leader" for Q_i (e.g., the party with the smallest index) and let her sample a random non-zero α_i and send it to the other members of Q_i over private channels. Concurrently, the dealer shares the coefficients of the polynomials A, B, C among the n parties as before, except that now the degree of A and B is taken to be $d = N(t + 1)$ and the degree of C is taken to be $2d$. In the second round, each party P_j in Q_i broadcasts the value α_i and uses local linear operations to reveal to all the parties the jth share of $A(\alpha_i), B(\alpha_i)$ and $C(\alpha_i)$. After the second round, for each i, each party P (possibly outside Q_i) verifies that all the parties in Q_i broadcast the same point α_i and that their shares are valid. If one of these checks fail, we refer to the ith test as *bad* and ignore it; Otherwise, the i-th test is called *good*, and P can recover the points $A(\alpha_i), B(\alpha_i)$ and $C(\alpha_i)$. If these values satisfy the product relation, we say that the (good) test *passes*. Finally, P accepts the triple if all the good tests pass, and disqualifies the dealer otherwise.

The analysis is fairly simple. For a corrupt D, we note that there exists (at least) one set Q_i in which all the parties are honest, and that a corrupt dealer has no information about α_i in the first round. The parties in Q_i provide in the second round $t+1$ shares of $A(\alpha_i), B(\alpha_i)$ and $C(\alpha_i)$ and so these values can be publicly recovered, and the probability that $C(x) \neq A(x) \cdot B(x)$ and $C(\alpha_i) = A(\alpha_i) \cdot B(\alpha_i)$ is at most $2d/(|\mathbb{F}|-1) = 2N(t+1)/(|\mathbb{F}|-1) = \mathsf{negl}(\kappa)$. Thus, except with negligible probability, there will be at least one good test that fails to pass. On the other hand, an honest dealer will never be disqualified since, by the binding property of the secret sharing, even a fully corrupted set of verifiers Q_i cannot reveal incorrect shares. As for privacy, there are N sets, and from each set the adversary can learn information about at most $(t+1)$ points of $A(x), B(x)$ and $C(x)$ (a corrupt leader in a set Q can send different evaluation points to the parties in Q). Since the degree of $A(x)$ and $B(x)$ is d, and the adversary can learn information about at most $N(t+1) = d$ points, we conclude that the adversary learns no information about $A(0), B(0)$ and $C(0)$, as required. The complexity of the protocol is exponential in $t = \lceil n/2 \rceil - 1$ and so the protocol is efficient (polynomial in the security parameter κ) only when the number of parties n is logarithmic in κ. Indeed, this is the only place where the assumption $n = O(\log \kappa)$ is really necessary.

From TSS to Public SIF. By the standard NP-completeness of quadratic equations, public SIF non-interactively reduces to public SIF where f computes a vector of degree-2 polynomials over an arbitrary finite field [34] and the same output is given to all the parties. One can easily adopt the TSS protocol to the case of general degree-2 SIF functionality (e.g., share the input vector $\mathbf{z}$ and the output vector $\mathbf{y}$, prove that they satisfy a degree-2 relation and ask the parties to publicly reconstruct $\mathbf{y}$.) However, this will not lead to an offline/online protocol. Instead, we use Beaver's trick [10] to transform random triple sharing (realized by TSS) into a degree-2 SIF. The standard transformation has an overhead of 2 additional rounds, and we avoid it by exploiting the SIF setting, i.e., the fact that a single dealer knows *all* the secrets. A reduction from general SIF to public SIF appears in the full version [6].

3.2 SIF for Any Number of Parties

We move on to the case where the number of parties, n, is large (polynomial in κ) and the resiliency threshold t is almost optimal, i.e., $n = (2+\epsilon)t$ for some constant $\epsilon > 0$. Our goal is to construct a 2-round offline/online protocol Π for some public SIF functionality $\mathcal{F}$ that takes an input $\mathbf{z}$ from the dealer D and delivers the same output $\mathbf{y} = f(\mathbf{z})$ to all the parties.

We will handle this case by composing two protocols: (1) The aforementioned 2-round SIF protocol Π_s ("s" for small) that achieves an optimal resiliency for a small (logarithmic) number of parties; and (2) a perfectly-secure SIF protocol Π_b ("b" for big) with constant resiliency of, say 1/3, that works efficiently for polynomially many parties. The latter protocol can have many rounds and can be instantiated, for example, by the classical protocol of Ben-Or, Goldwasser and Wigderson (BGW) [12]. We will combine the 2 protocols into a single SIF protocol with almost-optimal threshold and poly(n) complexity via *player virtualization* technique. This idea goes back to the work of Bracha [18] in the context of Byzantine Agreement, and since then has been used several times in the MPC literature [26,32,40] culminating in the celebrated MPC-in-the head paradigm [42,43]. Here we show how to apply this idea in the context of SIF. Unlike other contexts, we show that the combined protocol inherits the round complexity of the first ("internal") protocol, and therefore can be executed in 2 rounds! Details follow.

Let us partition the n parties to $M = \text{poly}(n)$ committees $A_1, \ldots, A_M$ each of size n' for some constant n' that depends on the constant ϵ. Call a committee *good* if it contains at least $(n'+1)/2$ honest parties, and *bad* otherwise. We will make sure that the fraction of bad sets is at most $M/10$ no matter which subset of t parties the adversary decides to corrupt. Such a property can be guaranteed by taking all n' multisets or, more efficiently, based on expander graphs (see, e.g., [26, Lemma 5]).[7] Let Π_b be the BGW protocol that realizes the SIF f among the dealer D and M "virtual" parties $Q_1, \ldots, Q_M$.

In our new protocol, Π, the dealer D executes the BGW protocol Π_b in her "head" with the input $\mathbf{z}$ and then broadcasts a commitment to the transcript. That is, D samples random tapes $r_1, \ldots, r_M$ for the virtual parties $Q_1, \ldots, Q_M$ and computes all the messages that are sent in Π_b, both over private channels and over broadcast channels. Then, D commits to each of these messages and to the randomness r_i of each party Q_i, and broadcasts the tuple of commitments G. We emphasize that every message from Q_i to Q_j has only *one* commitment, that belongs both to the view of Q_i and the view of Q_j. In addition, D broadcasts the value $\mathbf{y} = f(\mathbf{z})$. Now, we let each committee A_i verify, with the aid of the small protocol Π_s, that the view of Q_i is *self-consistent*, i.e., that the (committed) randomness and incoming messages of Q_i yield the (committed) outgoing messages of Q_i and that the final output is indeed $\mathbf{y}$. More precisely, the committee A_i together with D, compute the following public-SIF functionality $\mathcal{G}_{\mathsf{zk}}$:

- (Dealer's input:) An index $i \in \{1, \ldots, M\}$, a vector of commitments G_i, supposedly to the randomness of Q_i and his incoming and outgoing messages, and the corresponding openings.

[7] In principle, n' should be taken to be $\Omega(1/\epsilon^2)$. Thus, in order to keep n' small (e.g., logarithmic in the security parameter), one has to assume that ϵ is not too small, e.g., at least $\Omega(1/\sqrt{\log \kappa})$. We limit the discussion to a constant ϵ only for the sake of simplicity.

- (Public output:) the tuple $(v_i, \mathbf{y}_i, G_i, i)$ where v_i is a consistency bit that indicates whether the committed values are self-consistent, and the value $\mathbf{y}_i$ is the output that the virtual party Q_i outputs given the committed view.[8]

We realize this sub-computation by running the small SIF protocol Π_s among D and the sub-committee A_i while making sure that the final output is available to all parties including ones that do not belong to A_i. This can be done (without an extra round of communication) by passing all the broadcast messages of the small protocol Π_s over the external n-party broadcast channel. Indeed, we note that, for public-output SIF, the public output of our protocol Π_s can be fully recovered based on its broadcast messages. Getting back to Π, we conclude the protocol, by letting each party P_i accept the output $\mathbf{y}$ if at least $0.9M$ of the committees approve this output (i.e., if the output of the ith committee is $(1, \mathbf{y}, G_i, i)$ where G_i is consistent with G), and disqualify the dealer otherwise.

The protocol Π can be executed in 2 rounds where the first round is devoted to the offline round of all the instances of the Π_s protocol, and the second round is devoted to the commitment generation and to the second online-round of the Π_s instances. Note that the first round of Π remains input-independent. Let us briefly analyze the security of Π.

For an honest dealer, the verification Π_s succeeds for every good committee Q_i that contains an honest majority, and may fail for a bad committee Q_i that contains a dishonest majority. We conclude that at most $M/10$ of the verifications fail, and so an honest dealer will never be disqualified. As for privacy, a bad committee Q_i may completely learn the input of the dealer D in the corresponding SIF $\mathcal{G}_{\mathsf{zk}}$. This leakage is equivalent to learning the internal state of the virtual party Q_i in the external protocol Π_b. Since there are at most $M/10$ bad committees, the adversary can learn the state of at most $M/10$ parties of Π_b. The privacy of Π_b therefore protects us against such a leakage. (In fact, for this part we only use the privacy of Π_b against a passive corruption.)

A corrupt dealer can commit to an illegal transcript while being approved by all bad committees. So, in order to be approved, such a dealer must still get the votes of at least $0.8M$ good committees. Hence, cheating in Π reduces to cheating in Π_b while actively controlling at most $0.2M$ of the virtual parties, and while controlling the randomness of the honest virtual parties. Since Π_b is *perfectly correct* against $0.2M$ active corruptions, a cheating dealer will always be caught. (For this part, no privacy is needed and Π_b is only required to achieve "perfect correctness with abort" against an active adversary.)

Remark 3 (Comparison to the MPC-to-ZK transformation of [42]*).* It is instructive to consider the following variant of the protocol. First, the dealer secret-shares its input $\mathbf{z}$ to $(\mathbf{z}_1, \ldots, \mathbf{z}_M)$ via some robust $M/3$-out-of-M secret sharing then it virtually runs an MPC protocol among the parties $Q_1, \ldots, Q_M$ for the public SIF $\mathcal{F}'$ that takes $(\mathbf{z}_1, \ldots, \mathbf{z}_M)$ from the parties, recovers $\mathbf{z}$ via robust reconstruction, and delivers the output $f(\mathbf{z})$. The dealer commits to the views

[8] The circuit that realizes $\mathcal{G}_{\mathsf{zk}}$ depends on the code of the NICOM, consequently, our final construction makes a non-black-box use of the NICOM.

and transcript and the committees $A_1, \ldots, A_M$ use the small SIF protocol to verify consistency for each virtual party. This description be can viewed as a special case of the protocol Π in which Π_b is realized by sharing $\mathbf{z}$ and computing $\mathcal{F}'$.

Under this choice, our transformation can be viewed as a multi-verifier version of the MPC-to-ZK transformation of [42]. The two versions differ with respect to the underlying secret sharing (M-out-of-M in [42] vs. $M/3$-out-of-M in our case), and, more importantly, with respect to the verification part. In [42] a single verifier opens few views (for soundness) while keeping other views unopened (for zero-knowledge), whereas in our case multiple verifiers distributively open (all) the views in a way that preserves soundness "globally", and secrecy for bounded-size coalitions. Furthermore, we show that verification can be realized with low round complexity based on an "internal" SIF protocol.

3.3 Replacing the Idealised VSS with 1.5-Round Protocols

In the previous section, TSS and public SIF for logarithmic number of parties are the direct consumers of the idealized VSS. In both, the scenario is as follows: D has m inputs $s_1, \ldots, s_m$ and the parties want to compute a linear combination of the inputs. The coefficients of the linear combination may be chosen by some other party, and the output should be delivered by the end of second round. For simplicity, we consider the somewhat degenerate case where the goal is to compute $z := s_1 + \ldots + s_m$. As mentioned earlier, two challenges arise: (a) VSS sharing itself requires 2 rounds, whereas our requirement is to complete sharing and reconstruction within 2 rounds and (b) the known 2-round VSS from Minicrypt-like assumptions is not homomorphic. In a nutshell, we solve the first issue by noting that the VSS of [7] is a "1.5-round" VSS in the sense that "tentative shares" are distributed already in the first round, and any update that may occur in the second round is *publicly known* to all parties. To solve the second issue, we construct a novel protocol that allows a party to reveal a "certified" linear combination of its shares. This protocol, glinear, has 2 rounds where the first round is an offline round. Since our protocols employ linear homomorphism during their second round, glinear forms a viable substitute. Related tools have been developed in [4] for a smaller resiliency threshold (e.g., $n \geq 3t+1$), and we extend them to the challenging setting of $n = 2t+1$ while maintaining efficiency for polynomially many parties $n = \text{poly}(\kappa)$. Before describing our solutions in more detail, we present some background on the underlying secret sharing scheme.

The Underlying Secret Sharing Scheme. The secret sharing scheme is essentially the classical t-out-of-n Shamir-like scheme (extended to bivariate polynomials as in [12]) accompanied with public commitments to all the shares. To (honestly) share a secret $s \in \mathbb{F}$, one samples a random symmetric bivariate polynomial $F(x, y)$ of degree at most t in each variable conditioned on $F(0,0) = s$, and hands to each party P_i the vector $(F(i,0), \ldots, F(i,n))$ which fully defines the degree-t univariate polynomial $f_i(x) = F(i,x)$. We embed these elements in an $(n+1)$-by-$(n+1)$ matrix $\mathbf{F} = (F(i,j))_{i,j \in \{0,\ldots,n\}}$, and note that this matrix is symmetric since $F(i, j) = F(j, i)$. The 0th row of this matrix is referred to as the *main* row and its ith entry $F(0, i) = F(i, 0)$ is referred to as the main share of party P_i. (The main row corresponds to the univariate polynomial $f_0(x) = F(0, x)$ which forms a standard Shamir sharing of s.) As part of the secret sharing, we publish a symmetric matrix, $\mathbf{C} = (C_{ij})_{i,j \in \{0,\ldots,n\}}$ of commitments to each entry of $\mathbf{F}$, and hand the openings, $\mathbf{O}_i = (o_{ij})_{j \in \{0,\ldots,n\}}$, of the ith row to party P_i. We let $\mathbf{O}$ denote the matrix of openings $(o_{ij})_{i,j \in \{0,\ldots,n\}}$. It is well-known that this scheme is t-out-of-n secret sharing scheme. The commitment layer makes it impossible for a corrupted party to lie about its share (the scheme is "binding"), and so it enables robust reconstruction.[9] We point out that a statistically-hiding computationally-binding commitment leads to a secret sharing scheme with statistical privacy whose robustness holds only against computationally-bounded adversaries whereas a computationally-hiding statistically-binding commitment scheme yields a secret sharing scheme with computational privacy and robustness against computationally-unbounded adversaries. Let us record the fact that the "polynomial part" of the secret sharing is linearly homomorphic but the "commitment part" is not.

1.5-Round VSS. Backes et al. [7] describe a 2-round protocol for securely distributing a secret according to the above secret sharing scheme. We note that this protocol has the following structure. After the first ("sharing") round, the commitment matrix $\mathbf{C}$ is delivered to all the parties and each party holds a private *tentative share* that may be invalid. During the second ("verification") round of the protocol, each party P_i who may be "unhappy" for some reason, can form a "complaint" against the dealer D. At the end of this round, either some complaint turns to be "justified", or all the complaints are rejected as being "unjustified". In the former case, the dealer is being publicly disqualified, and in the latter case, the private shares of all unhappy parties are publicly revealed. (That is, all parties learn the openings $(\mathbf{O}_i)_{i \in \mathsf{W}}$ where W is the set of all unhappy parties.) By design, an honest party never complains about an honest dealer. We will make use of the fact that a tentative share either remains unchanged during the second round, or becomes publicly available to all parties.

We formalize these properties via a new 2-phase functionality $\mathcal{F}_{\mathsf{vss}}$ (a refined version of VSS), and prove that the protocol UC-realizes it. The choice of being unhappy is captured by an input $\mathsf{flag}_i \in \{0, 1\}$ that is given to P_i at the beginning of the verification phase. As a result P_i can ask to publicly reveal $\mathbf{O}_i$ even it is unhappy with D due to some external reason, that does not depend on the VSS execution (say, P_i thinks that D is corrupt in the outer-protocol).

[9] We, in fact, consider a weak variant of this sharing in which for a pair of corrupted parties, (P_i, P_j), the share $f_i(j)$ may be inconsistent with the commitment C_{ij}. Still, it can be shown that P_i and P_j cannot lie about their *main shares* and so this scheme still allows robust reconstruction. For details, refer to the full version of this paper [6].

3.3.1 Supporting Linear Operations

Let us now go back to our goal of computing $z := s_1 + \ldots + s_m$ in two rounds where the secrets $s_1, \ldots, s_m$ are given to D as inputs. We start by running the first round of the VSS to distribute tentative shares for $s_1, \ldots, s_m$ via the polynomials $F^1, \ldots, F^m$ and the commitments $\mathbf{C}^1, \ldots, \mathbf{C}^m$. Our goal now is to publicly reveal the value $z := s_1 + \ldots + s_m$ by using a single round of communication that will be carried in parallel to the verification phase of the VSS. Denote by $F^z(x, y)$ the bivariate polynomial $F^1(x, y) + \ldots + F^m(x, y)$. Observe that it suffices to design a single-round protocol that allows to each party P_i to publish the univariate polynomial $F^z(i, \cdot)$ while providing a certificate for correctness (and while hiding the original shares). Formally, for every "guide" P_i the parties engage in a subprotocol glinear ("guided linear computation") so that (1) if P_i is honest then all parties output $F^z(i, x)$, and (2) if P_i is corrupt then all parties output either $F^z(i, x)$ or an erasure $\perp$. Since there are $n - t \geq t + 1$ honest parties, and all non-$\perp$ shares are consistent with $F^z(x, y)$, the parties can recover the polynomial $F^z(x, y)$ and output $z = F^z(0, 0)$. Observe that we can restrict our attention to the case where the guide is "happy" with the dealer D, since the shares of a non-happy guide will be publicly released anyway in the end of the second round by the verification phase of the secret sharing.

Guided Linear Computation from SCG. To explain how glinear is implemented, let us focus, for concreteness, on the case where the guide is P_1. After the input sharing, the guide P_1 holds all the information regarding the first rows $F^1(1, x), \ldots, F^m(1, x)$, including the openings to the corresponding commitments. In addition, every P_j holds all the information regarding the j-th share of each first-row, $F^1(1, j), \ldots, F^m(1, j)$. The idea now is to let the guide P_1 and every P_j engage in a subprotocol for the computation of $F^z(1, j)$ where the role of P_j is to *guard* the computation, i.e., to make sure that P_1 uses the "correct" values as inputs. Formally, we construct such a subprotocol, called *secure computation with a guard* and denoted scg, that has essentially the following "patrial security" guarantees:

- If both, P_1 and P_j, are honest then the value $F^z(1, j)$ is given to all parties while the values, $\boldsymbol{F}(1, j) := (F^1(1, j), \ldots, F^m(1, j))$, remain hidden.
- If P_1 and P_j are both corrupt, there are no correctness or privacy guarantees.
- If exactly one party is corrupt (either P_1 or P_j) then there are no privacy guarantees and the public output is either $F^z(1, j)$ or an identifiable abort (i.e., $\perp$ symbol accompanied with the identity of the corrupt party).

We postpone the description of the scg protocol. For now, let us mention that the protocol is *publicly decodable* (all honest parties receive the same output that is computed based on broadcasted values), and has 2 rounds in the offline/online model. Since the first round is input-independent we can execute it in parallel to the first round of VSS. Now glinear can be reduced to n executions of scg between P_1 and each of the parties $P_1, \ldots, P_n$, where each P_j acts as the guard of the computation of $F^z(1, j)$. Given the scg outputs, we output a degree-t polynomial $f_1(\cdot)$ if and only if (1) P_1 was not disqualified by any of the scg calls, and (2)

$f_1(\cdot)$ is consistent with all the revealed points. Otherwise, we disqualify P_1. The analysis is straightforward. If P_1 is honest, for every honest guard P_j all the parties learn $F^z(1,j)$ (without leaking information on $\boldsymbol{F}(1,j)$), while for every corrupt P_j the parties either learn $F^z(1,j)$ or an erasure $\perp$ (since the adversary already knows $\boldsymbol{F}(1,j)$ we do not care about leakage in this case). Since there are $n-t \geq t+1$ honest parties, the parties recover uniquely the polynomial $F^z(1,x)$. If P_1 is corrupt, then it is either being disqualified by one of the honest guards, or release at least $n-t \geq t+1$ points that are consistent with $F^z(1,\cdot)$. This means that the final outcome is either $F^z(1,\cdot)$ or $\perp$. Before delving into the scg construction, we mention that the VSS together with the guided linear computation lead to a protocol for general linear function evaluation in 3 rounds which is optimal by [34].

Realizing scg. Roughly speaking, in an scg protocol, the guide Alice is given as an input a vector b^A and the guard Bob receives a copy, b^B, of this vector that supposedly agrees with b^A. Alice wishes to publicly reveal the value $f(b^A)$, for some public function f, and the guard Bob should make sure that f is computed consistently with respect to his input. This notion was introduced by [3] who constructed a 2-round offline/online protocol that statistically realizes the partial security properties defined above. However, their protocol works with a designated receiver, and so multiple invocations of this protocol (with different receivers) may lead to inconsistent outputs. (Such inconsistencies were tolerated in [3] by leveraging the existence of a strong honest majority, i.e., $t < n/3$.) We present a publicly decodable scg by exploiting the fact that all parties are given *external commitments* C to the input b^A and that the corresponding openings, o, are given to Alice as certificates. Moreover, we make use of NICOM internally in the scg itself, and so get only computational security. Details follow.

Thanks to the external commitments, it suffices to securely compute the functionality $\mathcal{F}$ that takes $x = (b^A, o)$ from Alice and $y = b^B$ from Bob, and outputs

$$y = \begin{cases} f(b^A), & \text{if } b^A = b^B, \\ (b^A, o) & \text{otherwise.} \end{cases}$$

Indeed, if Alice and Bob are honest the output will be $f(b^A)$. If the parties disagree (due to a single cheater) then the output reveals Alice's certified input, and one can check whether the released values (b^A, o) are consistent with the external commitments or not. In the former case, we can decode the output $f(b^A)$, and in the latter case, we conclude that Alice aborted the computation. While we will not be able to realize $\mathcal{F}$ with full security, we provide an instantiation that suffices for "partial security".

Our starting point is the following variant of private simultaneous message (PSM) protocol of [29]. Bob samples a random string r and sends it to Alice privately during the offline phase. Then, in the online phase, given the inputs, x and y, Alice and Bob publish messages, $A(x, r)$ and $B(y, r)$, that publicly reveal $\mathcal{F}$ and nothing else. Unfortunately, the standard PSM realization only works when both parties are honest, and a dishonest party, say Alice, can violate correctness by sending an invalid message a' that does not correspond to any input x (with respect to the chosen r).

Focusing on the case of corrupt Alice, we modify the protocol as follows. At the offline round, Bob broadcasts *internal commitments* to all the possible PSM online-messages. That is, for every possible Alice-input x (resp., every possible Bob-input y), Bob computes a commitment C'_x to the PSM message $A(x, r)$ (resp., C'_y to the PSM message $B(y, r)$). At the offline round, Bob broadcasts the (randomly permuted) list of commitments $(C'_x)_x$ and $(C'_y)_y$ and privately sends to Alice all the information: the PSM randomness r together with the corresponding openings $(o'_x)_x$ and $(o'_y)_y$. At the online round, Alice and Bob compute the PSM messages that correspond to their inputs, and certify them by opening the corresponding internal commitments. Now, assuming that Bob is honest, Alice is forced to behave honestly in the PSM and must send a "valid" PSM message that corresponds to an actual input x. This protocol achieves a similar guarantee against a cheating Bob and honest Alice, provided that Bob behaves *honestly* in the offline round. We handle the case where Bob misbehaves in the offline round (e.g., by committing to bad values or sending to Alice bad openings) by letting Alice fully expose her certified input. That is, if Alice sees that Bob misbehaved in the offline round, she simply broadcasts her inputs together with the external openings as certificates while ignoring the PSM execution. Here we exploit the fact that no privacy is required at the presence of a cheating Bob.

The above description is somewhat simplified and yields a solution whose complexity is linear in the domain of $\mathcal{F}$ which is too expensive. Moreover, when scg is modelled as a reactive functionality, simulation becomes somewhat subtle and the commitments should satisfy some level of security under a selective-opening attack. More details (including an efficient version based on multiparty PSM protocols and a refined definition of scg) appear in the full version [6].

Acknowledgements. B. Applebaum and E. Kachlon are supported by the Israel Science Foundation grant no. 2805/21. A. Patra is supported by DST National Mission on Interdisciplinary Cyber-Physical Systems (NM-CPS) 2020–2025 and SERB MATRICS (Theoretical Sciences) Grant 2020–2023.

References

1. Abe, M., Cramer, R., Fehr, S.: Non-interactive distributed-verifier proofs and proving relations among commitments. In: Zheng, Y. (ed.) ASIACRYPT 2002. LNCS, vol. 2501, pp. 206–224. Springer, Heidelberg (2002). https://doi.org/10.1007/3-540-36178-2_13
2. Ananth, P., Choudhuri, A.R., Goel, A., Jain, A.: Round-optimal secure multiparty computation with honest majority. In: Shacham, H., Boldyreva, A. (eds.) CRYPTO 2018, Part II. LNCS, vol. 10992, pp. 395–424. Springer, Cham (2018). https://doi.org/10.1007/978-3-319-96881-0_14

3. Applebaum, B., Kachlon, E., Patra, A.: The resiliency of MPC with low interaction: the benefit of making errors (extended abstract). In: Pass, R., Pietrzak, K. (eds.) TCC 2020, Part II. LNCS, vol. 12551, pp. 562–594. Springer, Cham (2020). https://doi.org/10.1007/978-3-030-64378-2_20
4. Applebaum, B., Kachlon, E., Patra, A.: The round complexity of perfect MPC with active security and optimal resiliency. In: 61st IEEE Annual Symposium on Foundations of Computer Science, FOCS 2020, Durham, NC, USA, 16–19 November 2020, pp. 1277–1284 (2020)
5. Applebaum, B., Kachlon, E., Patra, A.: Round-optimal honest-majority MPC in minicrypt and with everlasting security. Cryptology ePrint Archive **2021**, 346 (2021)
6. Applebaum, B., Kachlon, E., Patra, A.: Verifiable relation sharing and multi-verifier zero-knowledge in two rounds: trading NIZKs with honest majority. Cryptology ePrint Archive (2022). https://eprint.iacr.org/2022/167
7. Backes, M., Kate, A., Patra, A.: Computational verifiable secret sharing revisited. In: Lee, D.H., Wang, X. (eds.) ASIACRYPT 2011. LNCS, vol. 7073, pp. 590–609. Springer, Heidelberg (2011). https://doi.org/10.1007/978-3-642-25385-0_32
8. Barak, B., Ong, S.J., Vadhan, S.: Derandomization in cryptography. In: Boneh, D. (ed.) CRYPTO 2003. LNCS, vol. 2729, pp. 299–315. Springer, Heidelberg (2003). https://doi.org/10.1007/978-3-540-45146-4_18
9. Baum, C., Jadoul, R., Orsini, E., Scholl, P., Smart, N.P.: Feta: efficient threshold designated-verifier zero-knowledge proofs. Cryptology ePrint Archive (2022)
10. Beaver, D.: Efficient multiparty protocols using circuit randomization. In: Feigenbaum, J. (ed.) CRYPTO 1991. LNCS, vol. 576, pp. 420–432. Springer, Heidelberg (1992). https://doi.org/10.1007/3-540-46766-1_34
11. Bellare, M., Rogaway, P.: Random oracles are practical: a paradigm for designing efficient protocols. In: ACM Conference on Computer and Communications Security, pp. 62–73 (1993)
12. Ben-Or, M., Goldwasser, S., Wigderson, A.: Completeness theorems for non-cryptographic fault-tolerant distributed computation (extended abstract). In: Proceedings of the 20th Annual ACM Symposium on Theory of Computing, Chicago, Illinois, USA, 2–4 May 1988, pp. 1–10 (1988)
13. Bitansky, N., Paneth, O.: ZAPs and non-interactive witness indistinguishability from indistinguishability obfuscation. In: Dodis, Y., Nielsen, J.B. (eds.) TCC 2015, Part II. LNCS, vol. 9015, pp. 401–427. Springer, Heidelberg (2015). https://doi.org/10.1007/978-3-662-46497-7_16
14. Blum, M.: Coin flipping by telephone. In: Advances in Cryptology: A Report on CRYPTO 1981, CRYPTO 1981, IEEE Workshop on Communications Security, Santa Barbara, California, USA, 24–26 August 1981, pp. 11–15 (1981)
15. Blum, M., Feldman, P., Micali, S.: Non-interactive zero-knowledge and its applications (extended abstract). In: Proceedings of the 20th Annual ACM Symposium on Theory of Computing, Chicago, Illinois, USA, 2–4 May 1988, pp. 103–112 (1988)
16. Boneh, D., Boyle, E., Corrigan-Gibbs, H., Gilboa, N., Ishai, Y.: Zero-knowledge proofs on secret-shared data via fully linear PCPs. In: Boldyreva, A., Micciancio, D. (eds.) CRYPTO 2019. LNCS, vol. 11694, pp. 67–97. Springer, Cham (2019). https://doi.org/10.1007/978-3-030-26954-8_3
17. Boyle, E., Gilboa, N., Ishai, Y.: Function secret sharing: improvements and extensions. In: Proceedings of the 2016 ACM SIGSAC Conference on Computer and Communications Security, pp. 1292–1303 (2016)

18. Bracha, G.: An o(log n) expected rounds randomized Byzantine generals protocol. J. ACM **34**(4), 910–920 (1987)
19. Brassard, G., Chaum, D., Crépeau, C.: Minimum disclosure proofs of knowledge. J. Comput. Syst. Sci. **37**(2), 156–189 (1988)
20. Burmester, M., Desmedt, Y.: Broadcast interactive proofs. In: Davies, D.W. (ed.) EUROCRYPT 1991. LNCS, vol. 547, pp. 81–95. Springer, Heidelberg (1991). https://doi.org/10.1007/3-540-46416-6_7
21. Canetti, R.: Universally composable security: a new paradigm for cryptographic protocols. In: 42nd Annual Symposium on Foundations of Computer Science, FOCS 2001, Las Vegas, Nevada, USA, 14–17 October 2001, pp. 136–145 (2001)
22. Canetti, R., Kushilevitz, E., Lindell, Y.: On the limitations of universally composable two-party computation without set-up assumptions. In: Biham, E. (ed.) EUROCRYPT 2003. LNCS, vol. 2656, pp. 68–86. Springer, Heidelberg (2003). https://doi.org/10.1007/3-540-39200-9_5
23. Chor, B., Goldwasser, S., Micali, S., Awerbuch, B.: Verifiable secret sharing and achieving simultaneity in the presence of faults (extended abstract). In: 26th Annual Symposium on Foundations of Computer Science, Portland, Oregon, USA, 21–23 October 1985, pp. 383–395 (1985)
24. Corrigan-Gibbs, H., Boneh, D.: Prio: private, robust, and scalable computation of aggregate statistics. In: 14th USENIX Symposium on Networked Systems Design and Implementation (NSDI 2017), pp. 259–282 (2017)
25. Corrigan-Gibbs, H., Boneh, D., Mazières, D.: Riposte: an anonymous messaging system handling millions of users. In: Proceedings of the 2015 IEEE Symposium on Security and Privacy, pp. 321–338 (2015)
26. Damgård, I., Ishai, Y., Krøigaard, M., Nielsen, J.B., Smith, A.: Scalable multiparty computation with nearly optimal work and resilience. In: Wagner, D. (ed.) CRYPTO 2008. LNCS, vol. 5157, pp. 241–261. Springer, Heidelberg (2008). https://doi.org/10.1007/978-3-540-85174-5_14
27. Damgård, I., Pedersen, T.P., Pfitzmann, B.: Statistical secrecy and multibit commitments. IEEE Trans. Inf. Theory **44**(3), 1143–1151 (1998)
28. Dwork, C., Naor, M.: Zaps and their applications. SIAM J. Comput. **36**(6), 1513–1543 (2007)
29. Feige, U., Kilian, J., Naor, M.: A minimal model for secure computation (extended abstract). In: Proceedings of the Twenty-Sixth Annual ACM Symposium on Theory of Computing, Montréal, Québec, Canada, 23–25 May 1994, pp. 554–563 (1994)
30. Feige, U., Lapidot, D., Shamir, A.: Multiple noninteractive zero knowledge proofs under general assumptions. SIAM J. Comput. **29**(1), 1–28 (1999)
31. Fiat, A., Shamir, A.: How to prove yourself: practical solutions to identification and signature problems. In: Odlyzko, A.M. (ed.) CRYPTO 1986. LNCS, vol. 263, pp. 186–194. Springer, Heidelberg (1987). https://doi.org/10.1007/3-540-47721-7_12
32. Fitzi, M., Franklin, M., Garay, J., Vardhan, S.H.: Towards optimal and efficient perfectly secure message transmission. In: Vadhan, S.P. (ed.) TCC 2007. LNCS, vol. 4392, pp. 311–322. Springer, Heidelberg (2007). https://doi.org/10.1007/978-3-540-70936-7_17
33. Gennaro, R., Ishai, Y., Kushilevitz, E., Rabin, T.: The round complexity of verifiable secret sharing and secure multicast. In: Proceedings of the Thirty-Third Annual ACM Symposium on Theory of Computing, pp. 580–589 (2001)

34. Gennaro, R., Ishai, Y., Kushilevitz, E., Rabin, T.: On 2-round secure multiparty computation. In: Yung, M. (ed.) CRYPTO 2002. LNCS, vol. 2442, pp. 178–193. Springer, Heidelberg (2002). https://doi.org/10.1007/3-540-45708-9_12
35. Goldreich, O., Levin, L.A.: A hard-core predicate for all one-way functions. In: Proceedings of the 21st Annual ACM Symposium on Theory of Computing, Seattle, Washigton, USA, 14–17 May 1989, pp. 25–32 (1989)
36. Goldreich, O., Oren, Y.: Definitions and properties of zero-knowledge proof systems. J. Cryptol. **7**(1), 1–32 (1994). https://doi.org/10.1007/BF00195207
37. Groth, J., Ostrovsky, R.: Cryptography in the multi-string model. J. Cryptol. **27**(3), 506–543 (2014). https://doi.org/10.1007/s00145-013-9152-y
38. Groth, J., Ostrovsky, R., Sahai, A.: New techniques for noninteractive zero-knowledge. J. ACM (JACM) **59**(3), 1–35 (2012)
39. Halevi, S., Micali, S.: Practical and provably-secure commitment schemes from collision-free hashing. In: Koblitz, N. (ed.) CRYPTO 1996. LNCS, vol. 1109, pp. 201–215. Springer, Heidelberg (1996). https://doi.org/10.1007/3-540-68697-5_16
40. Harnik, D., Ishai, Y., Kushilevitz, E.: How many oblivious transfers are needed for secure multiparty computation? In: Menezes, A. (ed.) CRYPTO 2007. LNCS, vol. 4622, pp. 284–302. Springer, Heidelberg (2007). https://doi.org/10.1007/978-3-540-74143-5_16
41. Herzberg, A.: Folklore, practice and theory of robust combiners. J. Comput. Secur. **17**(2), 159–189 (2009)
42. Ishai, Y., Kushilevitz, E., Ostrovsky, R., Sahai, A.: Zero-knowledge from secure multiparty computation. In: Proceedings of the 39th Annual ACM Symposium on Theory of Computing, San Diego, California, USA, 11–13 June 2007, pp. 21–30 (2007)
43. Ishai, Y., Prabhakaran, M., Sahai, A.: Founding cryptography on oblivious transfer – efficiently. In: Wagner, D. (ed.) CRYPTO 2008. LNCS, vol. 5157, pp. 572–591. Springer, Heidelberg (2008). https://doi.org/10.1007/978-3-540-85174-5_32
44. Müller-Quade, J., Unruh, D.: Long-term security and universal composability. J. Cryptol. **23**(4), 594–671 (2010). https://doi.org/10.1007/978-3-540-70936-7_3
45. Naor, M.: Bit commitment using pseudorandomness. J. Cryptol. **4**(2), 151–158 (1991). https://doi.org/10.1007/BF00196774
46. Naor, M., Ostrovsky, R., Venkatesan, R., Yung, M.: Perfect zero-knowledge arguments for NP using any one-way permutation. J. Cryptol. **11**(2), 87–108 (1998). https://doi.org/10.1007/s001459900037
47. Patra, A., Ravi, D.: On the exact round complexity of secure three-party computation. In: Shacham, H., Boldyreva, A. (eds.) CRYPTO 2018, Part II. LNCS, vol. 10992, pp. 425–458. Springer, Cham (2018). https://doi.org/10.1007/978-3-319-96881-0_15
48. Peikert, C., Shiehian, S.: Noninteractive zero knowledge for NP from (Plain) learning with errors. In: Boldyreva, A., Micciancio, D. (eds.) CRYPTO 2019. LNCS, vol. 11692, pp. 89–114. Springer, Cham (2019). https://doi.org/10.1007/978-3-030-26948-7_4
49. Rabin, T., Ben-Or, M.: Verifiable secret sharing and multiparty protocols with honest majority (extended abstract). In: Proceedings of the 21st Annual ACM Symposium on Theory of Computing, Seattle, Washington, USA, 14–17 May 1989, pp. 73–85 (1989)
50. Sahai, A., Waters, B.: How to use indistinguishability obfuscation: deniable encryption, and more. In: Proceedings of the Forty-Sixth Annual ACM Symposium on Theory of Computing, pp. 475–484 (2014)

51. Yang, K., Wang, X.: Non-interactive zero-knowledge proofs to multiple verifiers. Cryptology ePrint Archive (2022)
52. Yao, A.C.: Theory and applications of trapdoor functions (extended abstract). In: 23rd Annual Symposium on Foundations of Computer Science, Chicago, Illinois, USA, 3–5 November 1982, pp. 80–91 (1982)

Authenticated Garbling from Simple Correlations

Samuel Dittmer[1(✉)], Yuval Ishai[2], Steve Lu[1], and Rafail Ostrovsky[1,3]

[1] Stealth Software Technologies, Inc., Los Angeles, USA
{samdittmer,steve,rafail}@stealthsoftwareinc.com

[2] Technion - Israel Institute of Technology, Haifa, Israel
yuval@cs.technion.ac.il

[3] University of California, Los Angeles, Los Angeles, USA
rafail@cs.ucla.edu

Abstract. We revisit the problem of constant-round malicious secure two-party computation by considering the use of *simple correlations*, namely sources of correlated randomness that can be securely generated with sublinear communication complexity and good concrete efficiency. The current state-of-the-art protocol of Katz et al. (Crypto 2018) achieves malicious security by realizing a variant of the *authenticated garbling* functionality of Wang et al. (CCS 2017). Given oblivious transfer correlations, the communication cost of this protocol (with 40 bits of statistical security) is comparable to roughly 10 garbled circuits (GCs). This protocol inherently requires more than 2 rounds of interaction.

In this work, we use other kinds of simple correlations to realize the authenticated garbling functionality with better efficiency. Concretely, we get the following reduced costs in the random oracle model:

- Using variants of both vector oblivious linear evaluation (VOLE) and multiplication triples (MT), we reduce the cost to 1.31 GCs.
- Using only variants of VOLE, we reduce the cost to 2.25 GCs.
- Using only variants of MT, we obtain a *non-interactive* (i.e., 2-message) protocol with cost comparable to 8 GCs.

Finally, we show that by using recent constructions of pseudorandom correlation generators (Boyle et al., CCS 2018, Crypto 2019, 2020), the simple correlations consumed by our protocols can be securely realized without forming an efficiency bottleneck.

1 Introduction

Practical protocols for low-latency secure 2-party computation typically rely on Garbled Circuits (GC) [24]. Such protocols have constant round complexity, online communication proportional to the input size, total communication proportional to the circuit size, and good computational cost. We revisit the question of concretely efficient GC-based protocols with malicious security, which has been the topic of a long line of work originating from [16,17]. The authenticated garbling approach of Wang et al. [21] and Katz et al. [15] gives the state-of-the-art protocols along this line. This approach relies on oblivious transfers for a cut-and-choose based implementation of a preprocessing functionality made up of a collection of authenticated wire labels.

Y. Dodis and T. Shrimpton (Eds.): CRYPTO 2022, LNCS 13510, pp. 57–87, 2022.
https://doi.org/10.1007/978-3-031-15985-5_3

This work is motivated by recent techniques for securely generating simple forms of correlated randomness [3–7,19,23], which make it feasible to explore practical alternatives to constructions based only on OTs. In this work, we give three new constructions, including a non-interactive secure computation (NISC) protocol [14], which use simple correlations that can be securely generated with sublinear communication complexity and good concrete efficiency.

Table 1. Communication complexity for evaluating a large circuit after a "silent" randomness generation step, as a ratio to the cost of a semi-honest garbled circuit, with $\kappa = 128$ bits of computational security and $\rho = 40$ bits of statistical security. The bucket size for KRRW is set to $B = 3$, which is a lower bound for circuits of size less than 2^ρ. Dep. + online communication refers to the higher of the two party's one-way *circuit-dependent* communication cost, including online and offline phase costs. The total column adds in the cost of circuit-independent offline communication.

Protocol	**Correlation**	**Cost (garbled circuits)**	
		Dep. + online	Total
WRK [21]	OT	2.5	11.0
KRRW [15] v1	OT	1.5	7.75
KRRW [15] v2	OT	1	9.7
KRRW [15] with VOLE	$\mathcal{F}_{\mathsf{VOLE}}$	1	2.5
KRRW [15] with SPDZ	MT	1	7
KRRW [15] with SPDZ and cert. VOLE	MT-$\mathcal{F}_{\mathsf{VOLE}}$-$\mathcal{F}_{\mathsf{subVOLE}}$	1	2.9
Ours, v1 (KRRW with $\mathcal{F}_{\mathsf{DAMT}}$ compiler to $\mathcal{F}_{\mathsf{pre}(\kappa)}$)	$\mathcal{F}_{\mathsf{DAMT}}$-$\mathcal{F}_{\mathsf{subVOLE}}$-$\mathcal{F}_{\mathsf{VOLE}}$	1	1.31
Ours, v2	$\mathcal{F}_{\mathsf{bVOLE}}$-$\mathcal{F}_{\mathsf{subVOLE}}$-$\mathcal{F}_{\mathsf{VOLE}}$	1.47	2.25
NISC in the single-execution setting			
Ours, v3	$\mathcal{F}_{\mathsf{OLE}}$	8	8
AMPR14 [1]	CRS	40	40

Our approach achieves significant savings over the approach of [15], reducing the total communication cost from around 10 semi-honest GCs to 1.31 GCs in our first protocol (comparing to the size of half-gates garbled circuits in both cases). Our second protocol uses a compressed preprocessing functionality that is expensive to generate for small circuits, but outperforms [15] in the large circuit setting, requiring only 2.25 GCs and using only simple "VOLE-type" correlations (see Sect. 1.1).

Our third protocol is non-interactive (NISC) and achieves comparable communication complexity (8 GCs) than the variant of [15] with round complexity proportional to the circuit depth, and roughly 5× the communication efficiency of the best NISC protocols [1] in the single execution setting.

Part of our advantage comes from swapping out less efficient ways of generating correlated randomness with recent advantages. For example, a large part of the cost of [15] comes from their methods of generating an *authenticated bits functionality*, which can be realized without any communication given two instances of vector oblivious linear evaluation (VOLE), defined in Sect. 1.1. But our main advantage comes from novel compilers from new forms of simple correlated randomness to authenticated garbling functionality, including the use of efficient generalizations of *certified VOLE* protocols (see Sect. 3.2) that allow verification across more of the verification work to be done under statistical security instead of computational security (see Sect. 4.2). As we show in Table 1, our most efficient protocol still uses roughly 2× less communication than [15] would use, even if we replaced their authenticated bits generation procedure with VOLE.

Alternatively, the SPDZ protocol [10] could be used to realize the preprocessing functionality of [15] with authenticated multiplication triples (MTs) in a black box way. Doing this would require 7 GCs. Applying our certified randomness optimization of Sect. 4.2 to this SPDZ approach would reduce communication to 2.9 GCs, which is still more than both our non-NISC variants.

As we further discuss below, the secure generation of the correlated randomness required by our protocols is typically cheaper than the protocol that consumes it, especially for VOLE-type correlations or when using multiple cores. Moreover, this secure generation is circuit-independent and only involves local computation without any interaction.

1.1 Simple Correlations

Our informal definition of a *simple correlation* is one that can be securely generated with sublinear communication complexity and good concrete efficiency. The cost of sending a GC in the semi-honest setting is already linear in the circuit size, and so will dominate the communication cost of setting up the randomness, and any reasonably efficient randomness protocol can be run on multiple cores in the background faster than the communication of the main protocol.

We note that all of the flavors of simple correlations discussed here can be realized with a one-time setup step that generates randomness seeds. These seeds can then be expanded into the full correlated randomness locally by each party. This property facilitates running these protocols in a streaming mode, where the randomness is unpacked as needed. To draw attention to this, and to simplify the presentation, we write $\mathsf{Extend}(\mathcal{F})$ to denote unpacking additional entries from the correlated randomness seeds. Additionally, this one-time setup can be performed non-interactively, which we need to make step 2 of Fig. 12 non-interactive for our NISC protocol. We describe the correlation calculus more formally in the full version of this paper [12].

We rely on two main flavors of simple correlations: vector oblivious linear evaluation (VOLE)-type correlations, and multiplication triple (MT)-type correlations. In VOLE, a receiving party learns $\mathbf{v} := \mathbf{a}\beta + \mathbf{c}$ along with the scalar β, while the sending party learns $\mathbf{a}, \mathbf{c}$. VOLE with sublinear communication complexity was introduced by Boyle et al. [3] in 2019 and has been improved since then, see [7] for the most efficient current variant.

In MT, parties learn shares of vectors $\mathbf{x}, \mathbf{y}$ along with shares of the piecewise product $\mathbf{z}$, $z_i = x_i \cdot y_i$. MT have been studied as an important primitive for

Table 2. Correlated randomness used throughout the paper. For programmable OLE, the set Q is an arbitrary set of ordered pairs of indices. Cost comparison is given with reference to the "base" randomness protocol, either VOLE or MT. Generating 1 million entries of VOLE costs roughly 0.05 s on standard computers. Generating 1 million entries of MT costs roughly 10 s.

Functionality	$\mathcal{F}$-notation	Mathematical relation	Cost comparison
		VOLE-type correlations	
Vector OLE	$\mathcal{F}_{\mathsf{VOLE}}$	$\mathbf{v} = \mathbf{a}\beta + \mathbf{c}$, for $\mathbf{a}, \mathbf{c} \in \mathbb{F}_{2^\rho}$	1 VOLE
Subfield Vector OLE	$\mathcal{F}_{\mathsf{subVOLE}}$	$\mathbf{v} = \mathbf{a}\beta + \mathbf{c}$, for $\mathbf{a} \in \mathbb{F}_2, \mathbf{c} \in \mathbb{F}_{2^\rho}$	≈ 0.6 VOLE
Block Vector OLE	$\mathcal{F}_{\mathsf{bVOLE}}$	$\mathbf{v}_i = \mathbf{a}\beta_i + \mathbf{c}_i$, for $i = 1 \ldots, L$	L VOLE
		MT-type correlations	
Two-sided authenticated multiplication triples	$\mathcal{F}_{\mathsf{DAMT}}$	Choose $x \cdot y = z$, then share $[x], [y], [z], [\alpha z], [\beta z]$	2 MT
Programmable OLE	$\mathcal{F}_{\mathsf{OLE}}$	$\mathbf{v}_{i,j} = \mathbf{a}_i \cdot \boldsymbol{\beta}_j + \mathbf{c}_{i,j}$ for $(i,j) \in Q$	$\lvert Q \rvert$ MT

years, e.g. [10] but only recently have been able to be generated efficiently and silently [6].

We require several variants of these two types of randomness, as summarized in Table 2. We define all non-standard correlations as functionalities where they arise in the presentation. Crucially, both flavors of randomness generation allow for "programmability" in such a way that each new variant does not require an entirely new protocol, see e.g. [4,6].

Indeed, we can think of VOLE-type and MT-type correlations in terms of simple atomic operations under a "correlation calculus". For VOLE, atomic operations consist of choosing a vector $\mathbf{v} \in F^n$, for some field F, multiplying $\mathbf{v}$ by a scalar β (possibly in an extension field E), sending a vector to a party, and secret-sharing a vector between parties. Taking $F = E = \mathbb{F}_{2^\rho}$ or $\mathbb{F}_{2^\kappa}$ gives standard VOLE, taking $F = \mathbb{F}$ and $E = \mathbb{F}_{2^\rho}$ gives subfield VOLE. Reusing the vector $\mathbf{v}$ with a set of scalars β_i gives block VOLE and block subfield VOLE.

For MT-type correlations, atomic operations consist of picking a random vector $\mathbf{x} \in F^n$, computing the scalar product $\beta\mathbf{x}$, computing the point-wise product $\mathbf{x} \cdot \mathbf{y}$, sending a vector to a party, and sharing a vector between parties. Standard authenticated triples come from computing $\mathbf{z} := \mathbf{x} \cdot \mathbf{y}$ and $\beta\mathbf{z}$ and sharing all four vectors. Our *two-sided authentication triples* come from additionally computing $\alpha\mathbf{z}$, and sharing this as well.

Finally, programmable OLE consists of a family of OLE vectors $\mathbf{v}_{i,j} = \mathbf{a}_i\boldsymbol{\beta}_j + \mathbf{c}_{i,j}$, where the parties agree to re-use certain vectors $\mathbf{a}_i$ and $\boldsymbol{\beta}_j$ on certain entries. The generation time and seed size of programmable OLE scales linearly with the number of pairs (i,j) for which we generate a vector of OLE entries.

The VOLE protocol of [7] can generate a million entries of VOLE correlations in roughly 0.05 s, or a million entries of subfield VOLE in roughly 0.03 s. The OLE protocol of [6] can generate a million OLE correlations in roughly 10 s. For each of these protocols, the dominant cost is the secret sharing of vectors. We therefore expect that block VOLE over L instances costs roughly L times as much computation as a single VOLE, that standard authenticated triples costs two times as much communication as OLE, and two-sided authenticated triples cost three times as much.

We remark here that the Ring-LPN approach only allows silent generation of authenticated multiplication triples over large fields of characteristic 2 such as $\mathbb{F}_{2^\rho}$. If authenticated triples could be silently generated over $\mathbb{F}_2$, then the preprocessing functionality of [15] could be generated with only 2 bits of communication per gate, via a procedure similar to that given in Lemma 3. It is precisely because there is no simple correlation that can generate the preprocessing functionality directly that the question of the most efficient compiler from simple correlations to that functionality arises.

1.2 Notation

We let f be a function realized by a circuit C, where C is made up of input gates $\mathcal{I}$, boolean gates $\mathcal{G}$, and output gates $\mathcal{O}$. Let the input $\mathcal{I} = \mathcal{I}_A \cup \mathcal{I}_B$ be held by two parties A and B, and define n to be the number of AND gates in $\mathcal{G}$, and $m = |\mathcal{I}| + |\mathcal{G}|$, including all gates in m.

We use κ and ρ as a computational and statistical security parameter, respectively, and take $\kappa = 128$ and $\rho = 40$ for our concrete communication metrics.

During the evaluation of a garbled circuit, we write z_i for the true value of a wire, λ_i for the wire mask, and share λ_i among A and B as $\lambda_i = a_i \oplus b_i$. We use $(\oplus, \wedge)$ for field addition and multiplication over $\mathbb{F}_2$, any of $(\oplus, +, -)$ for field addition over larger fields of characteristic 2, and $\cdot$ or concatenation for field multiplication over larger fields of characteristic 2.

We use α, β for VOLE receiver inputs over $\mathbb{F}_{2^\rho}$ held by A, B respectively, and Δ_A for a VOLE receiver input held by A over $\mathbb{F}_{2^\kappa}$.

When discussing randomness certification in Sect. 3.2, we need to distinguish between an instance of $\mathcal{F}_{\mathsf{VOLE}}$ where party A is the receiver and party B the sender with another instance of $\mathcal{F}_{\mathsf{VOLE}}$ with the roles reversed. In this instance, we refer to the latter functionality as $\mathcal{F}_{\mathsf{ELOV}}$.

1.3 Our Contribution

Our first protocol relies on both VOLE-type and MT-type correlations. It employs the same authenticated garbling technique as that in [15], but uses authenticated triples over $\mathbb{F}_{2^\rho}$, rather than cut-and-choose techniques, to generated authenticated wire labels. This construction relies on a new compiler from a special flavor of authenticated triples to the desired preprocessing functionality given in Sect. 4.1, as well as a lightweight compiler from preprocessing with statistical security to preprocessing with computational security, given in Sect. 4.2.

Theorem 1. *There is a protocol that securely computes f against malicious adversaries in the RO$-\mathcal{F}_{\mathsf{DAMT}}-\mathcal{F}_{\mathsf{VOLE}}-\mathcal{F}_{\mathsf{subVOLE}}$-hybrid model with the following features:*

- **Online Communication:** $O(\kappa(|\mathcal{I}| + |\mathcal{O}|))$.
- **Circuit Dependent Communication:** $(2\kappa + 2)n$ *bits of communication.*
- **Total Communication:** $(2\kappa+2\rho+2)n$ *(one-way) or* $(2\kappa+4\rho+2)n$ *(two-way) plus terms sublinear in* n.
- **Computation:** $O(\kappa n)$.

Our second protocol relies only on VOLE-type correlations, and a modification of the authenticated garbling protocol that, approximately, uses a garbling approach from [21] to replace the authentication procedure in [15]. We give this modified garbling protocol and prove its correctness in Sect. 5.1.

This modified approach increases the communication cost of the online plus circuit dependent step, but allows the use of a simple *block VOLE* functionality instead of one of the more computationally intensive PCGs used to build authenticated triples. As written, the protocol uses quasi-linear work instead of linear work, but this can be reduced to linear work by dividing the gates into blocks of some large fixed size, and running the compressed preprocessing functionality $\mathcal{F}_{\mathsf{cp}}$ on each block in parallel.

This approach is best suited to the large circuit setting, since it requires $L \approx \rho \log |C|$ instances of VOLE (or for sufficiently large N and $|C| > N$, $L = |C| \frac{\rho \log N}{N}$), in order to construct the compressed functionality $\mathcal{F}_{\mathsf{cp}}$. Because VOLE-type correlations are so much more efficient, the computation of the randomness generation for this protocol is roughly comparable to that of the first protocol, but the communication of the VOLE seeds is much larger.

Theorem 2. *There is a protocol that securely computes* f *against malicious adversaries in the* $RO-\mathcal{F}_{\mathsf{VOLE}}-\mathcal{F}_{\mathsf{subVOLE}}-\mathcal{F}_{\mathsf{bVOLE}}$*-hybrid model with the following features:*

- **Online Communication:** $O(\kappa(|\mathcal{I}| + |\mathcal{O}|))$.
- **Circuit Dependent Communication:** $(2\kappa + 3\rho)n$ *bits of communication.*
- **Total Communication:** $(2\kappa + 8\rho + 1)n + o(n)$.
- **Computation:** $O(\kappa n \log n)$ *or* $O(\kappa n)$ *with running* $\mathcal{F}_{\mathsf{cp}}$ *on blocks.*

Our third protocol relies only on MT-type correlations. It uses a similar preprocessing functionality and authenticated garbling protocol as our first protocol, but combines them into a (single-use) NISC protocol. These protocols require certain modifications in order to make them non-interactive. In particular, we require a conditional disclosure of secrets (CDS) functionality to allow the receiver to authenticate their inputs without communication to the prover. We give the details in Sect. 6.1.

Theorem 3. *There is a NISC protocol that securely computes* f *against malicious adversaries in the* $RO - \mathcal{F}_{\mathsf{OLE}}$*-hybrid model with the following features:*

- **Online Communication:** $O(\kappa(|\mathcal{I}| + |\mathcal{O}|))$.
- **Circuit Dependent Communication:** $(2\kappa + 3\rho)n$ *bits of communication.*
- **Total Communication:** $16\kappa n + o(n)$ *(one-way) or* $(29\kappa + 3\rho)n + o(1)$ *(two-way).*

- **Computation:** $O(\kappa n)$.

We expect the first and third protocols to be dominant in the secure 2PC and NISC settings, respectively, in the million gate setting and the second protocol to be competitive around ten million gates.

1.4 Structure of Paper

In Sect. 2, we give an overview of the construction of [15], and explain how this construction can be treated as a blueprint pattern for a family of authenticated garbling constructions. We then describe, at a high-level, how each level of the blueprint is modified for each of our three protocols. In Sect. 3 we describe a series of technical results about certified VOLE, combining correlated randomness functionalities, and conditional disclosure of secrets. Each of these results serve the same general purpose of allowing one party to authenticate that their inputs are well-formed to the other party. We give some additional protocols and proofs in the full version of this paper [12]. We then give our three protocols $\mathbf{\Pi}_{\mathsf{2pc}}^{\mathsf{DAMT}}$, $\mathbf{\Pi}_{\mathsf{2pc}}^{\mathsf{VOLE}}$ and $\mathbf{\Pi}_{\mathsf{2pc}}^{\mathsf{NISC}}$ in Sects. 4, 5, 6, respectively.

2 Authenticated Garbling: Blueprints and Variations

We will present the authenticated garbling protocols in this paper as three different constructions following the same general blueprint design. The protocols can be pictured as a series of structures built side-by-side with the same number of *levels*, and corresponding levels play a similar role in each protocol. We begin by reviewing the approach of [15] through this framework, and then go into more detail about how our approaches differ.

2.1 Review: The Authenticated Garbling Blueprint of KRRW [15]

Authenticated Shared Bits. The first level of the construction is an authenticated shared bits functionality. In [15], this functionality is presented through the language of IT-MACs. We offer an equivalent definition in the language of simple correlations: The authenticated shared bits functionality is a pair of implementations of $\mathcal{F}_{\mathsf{subVOLE}}$, the first instance is over $\mathbb{F}_{2^\rho}$, with party A acting as sender and B acting as receiver, so that B receives $\beta \in \mathbb{F}_{2^\rho}$, A receives $\mathbf{a} \in \mathbb{F}_2^m$ and $\mathbf{c} \in \mathbb{F}_{2^\rho}^m$, and B receives $\mathbf{v} := \mathbf{a}\beta + \mathbf{c}$. In the second instance, the roles reversed and the $\mathcal{F}_{\mathsf{subVOLE}}$ is given over $\mathbb{F}_{2^\kappa}$, so that A receives $\alpha \in \mathbb{F}_{2^\kappa}$, B receives $\mathbf{b} \in \mathbb{F}_2^m$ and $\mathbf{d} \in \mathbb{F}_{2^\kappa}^m$, and A receives $\mathbf{w} := \mathbf{b}\alpha + \mathbf{d}$.

These shares will play the role of the wire masks in Yao's garbled circuits. For the i-th wire, party B will learn the value $a_i \oplus b_i \oplus z_i$, where z_i is the true wire value under a plaintext evaluation of the circuit. Because the value a_i is unknown to B, B learns nothing from this value. Because the value b_i is unknown to A, A is unable to employ a selective-failure attack to deduce which row of the garbled table B is attempting to read.

Authenticated Parallel AND. To make the protocol secure against a malicious A, party B needs to be able to verify that the row of the garbled table B is reading from was constructed correctly. In order to do this, the parties augment the authenticated bit randomness above with authenticated shares of the bits $(a_i \oplus b_i) \wedge (a_j \oplus b_j)$, for every AND gate $\mathcal{G}_k := (i, j, k, \wedge)$, as shown in Fig. 1.

This construction requires two stages. The first stage we call *authenticated parallel AND*. Let $\mathsf{PAnd}(n)$ be a circuit consisting of n AND gates executed in parallel, so that the kth gate has input wires $(2k-1, 2k)$ and output wire $2n+k$. To simplify notation, we write $\mathcal{F}_{\mathsf{pre}(\kappa)}$ for $\mathcal{F}_{\mathsf{pre}}^{(\mathsf{PAnd}(n),\kappa,\rho)}$ and $\mathcal{F}_{\mathsf{pre}(\rho)}$ for $\mathcal{F}_{\mathsf{pre}}^{(\mathsf{PAnd}(n),\rho,\rho)}$ where n is clear from context. In [15], the parties realize the preprocessing functionality in the special case of $\mathcal{F}_{\mathsf{pre}(\kappa)}$. Equivalently, they construct authenticated multiplication triples with entries in $\mathbb{F}_2$; as remarked above, there is no simple correlation that can generate these triples silently.

In [15], these triples are generated using cut-and-choose techniques, which makes up the lion's share of the *circuit-independent* communication cost of that protocol.

Remark 1. We note that, as well as translating the language of $\mathcal{F}_{\mathsf{pre}}$ in [15] from IT-MACs to VOLE, we now require that if A holds an input bit, B's share of that input bit's wire mask is 0, and vice versa. This does not alter the security of the protocol but it simplifies some of the proofs.

Functionality $\mathcal{F}_{\mathsf{pre}}^{(C,\rho,\kappa)}$: Pre-processing of wire labels for authenticated garbling.

Parametrized by values ρ, κ, and a circuit C consisting of $\mathcal{W}$ wires, $\mathcal{I}$ input wires, $\mathcal{O}$ output wires, and gates $\mathcal{G}$ of the form (i, j, k, T), for $T \in \{\wedge, \oplus\}$, $i, j \in \mathcal{I} \cup \mathcal{W}$, and $k \in \mathcal{W} \cup \mathcal{O}$. Recall that $m := |\mathcal{I}| + |\mathcal{G}|$.

- A chooses $\alpha \in \mathbb{F}_{2^\kappa}$ and wire labels $\mathbf{a} \in \mathbb{F}_2^m$, $\mathbf{c} \in \mathbb{F}_{2^\rho}^m$ and sends them to $\mathcal{F}_{\mathsf{pre}}$.
- B chooses $\beta \in \mathbb{F}_{2^\rho}$ and wire labels $\mathbf{b} \in \mathbb{F}_2^m$, $\mathbf{d} \in \mathbb{F}_{2^\kappa}^m$ and sends them to $\mathcal{F}_{\mathsf{pre}}$.
- For each input wire $i \in \mathcal{I}$, if $i \in \mathcal{I}_A$, set $b_i := 0$, and if $i \in \mathcal{I}_B$, set $a_i := 0$.
- For each gate $\mathcal{G} = (i, j, k, T)$, in topological order:
  - If $T = \oplus$, $\mathcal{F}_{\mathsf{pre}}$ sets the values $a_k = a_i + a_j$, $b_k = b_i + b_j$, $c_k = c_i + c_j$, and $d_k = d_i + d_j$, where the addition is performed in the appropriate field of characteristic 2.
  - If $T = \wedge$, $\mathcal{F}_{\mathsf{pre}}$ chooses values $\hat{a}_k$ uniformly at random from $\mathbb{F}_{2^\rho}$, $\hat{c}_k$ uniformly at random from $\mathbb{F}$, $\hat{d}_k$ uniformly at random from $\mathbb{F}_{2^\kappa}$, and $\hat{b}_k = (a_i + b_i) \cdot (a_j + b_j) + \hat{a}_k$.
- $\mathcal{F}_{\mathsf{pre}}$ computes

$$(\mathbf{v}, \hat{\mathbf{v}}, \mathbf{w}, \hat{\mathbf{w}}) = (\mathbf{a}\beta + \mathbf{c}, \hat{\mathbf{a}}\beta + \hat{\mathbf{c}}, \mathbf{b}\alpha + \mathbf{d}, \hat{\mathbf{b}}\alpha + \hat{\mathbf{d}}).$$

- $\mathcal{F}_{\mathsf{pre}}$ sends $(\mathbf{v}, \hat{\mathbf{v}}, \hat{\mathbf{b}}, \hat{\mathbf{d}})$ to B and $(\mathbf{w}, \hat{\mathbf{w}}, \hat{\mathbf{a}}, \hat{\mathbf{c}})$ to A.

Fig. 1. Authenticated wire labels

Authenticated Circuit Wires. The second step is to convert this generic preprocessing $\mathcal{F}_{\mathsf{pre}(\kappa)}$, which serves the parallel AND gate circuit only, to the circuit-dependent preprocessing $\mathcal{F}_{\mathsf{pre}}^{(C,\rho,\kappa)}$. In other words, we now want shares of the bit $(a_i \oplus b_i) \wedge (a_j \oplus b_j)$ for arbitrary pairs of indices (i, j), and $a_i \oplus b_i$, $a_j \oplus b_j$ may in turn represent the XOR of several prior bits.

This conversion is done using standard Beaver triple techniques [2], as we show below in Sect. 4.2. In one variant of [15] the triples are instead constructed "in-place", which gives a modified construction with less total communication, but some additional communication in the circuit-dependent phase. The main result of [15] can now be re-stated as follows:

Theorem 4 ([15]). *The KRRW protocol [15] securely computes a functionality f against malicious adversaries in the RO-$\mathcal{F}_{\mathsf{pre}}$-hybrid model, with $2\kappa+2$ bits of communication per AND gate, $\kappa+1$ bits of communication per input gate, and 1 bit of communication per output gate.*

Authenticated Garbling. The authenticated garbling protocols of both [21] and the follow-up work [15] are both instructive here. After the authenticated circuit wire labels are completed, party A plays the role of the sender in a semi-honest evaluation of Yao's garbled circuit, and some additional interaction allows B to verify the correctness of the opened entry of each AND gate.

For an AND gate $\mathcal{G}_k := (i, j, k, \wedge)$, let $\hat{a}_k, \hat{b}_k$ be the authenticated bit shares of $(a_i \oplus b_i) \wedge (a_j \oplus b_j)$, and let $\lambda_k := a_k \oplus b_k$, with $\hat{\lambda}_k$ defined similarly. If both parties know the value $(\lambda_i \oplus z_i)$, where z_i is the true value of the wire, then they can locally construct authenticated bit shares of

$$z_i \wedge z_j \oplus \lambda_k = \lambda_k \oplus \hat{\lambda}_k \oplus (z_i \oplus \lambda_i)\lambda_j \oplus (z_j \oplus \lambda_j)\lambda_i \oplus (z_i \oplus \lambda_i) \wedge (z_j \oplus \lambda_j).$$

From there, B evaluates the garbled circuit, A securely opens their bit share of $z_i \wedge z_j \oplus \lambda_k$, and B verifies that the value $z_i \wedge z_j \oplus \lambda_k$ is equal to the wire label $z_k \wedge \lambda_k$ computed from garbled circuit evaluation.

The primary distinction between [21] and [15] is how the value of $\lambda_i \oplus z_i$ is computed. In [21], party A computes all four possibilities of $(\lambda_i \oplus z_i, \lambda_j \oplus z_j)$, with the accompanying shares of $z_i \wedge z_j \oplus \lambda_k$. They then construct what are essentially two garbled circuits. The first garbled circuit, used for evaluation, uses computational security to hide gate labels from B. The second garbled circuit, used for authentication, hides only the masked wire labels $z_i \oplus \lambda_i$ and the accompanying share of $z_i \wedge z_j \oplus \lambda_k$, and uses statistical security to stop A from flipping a bit of the masked wire label. In [21], the first garbled circuit requires 3κ communication per gate, and the second requires 4ρ bits of communication.

In the [15] protocol, the first circuit is improved to 2κ bits of communication by applying the half-gate technique of Zahur et al. [25], and the second circuit is replaced with one more round of communication wherein B opens all masked wire labels to A, and A then batches together the proof of correct garbling on the traveled path.

Remark 2. A recent advance due to Rosulek and Roy [18] reduces the cost of semi-honest garbled circuits to $1.5\kappa+5$ bits per AND gate and is compatible with free XOR. A natural question is whether the approach of [15] can be extended to this new "three-halves" garbled circuit construction. We hope the answer is yes, although there are some obstacles to overcome.

In the [18] construction, the gates and wire labels are "sliced and diced" into half labels, but there is no canonical way for the evaluator to perform a linear combination of these half labels and compute the output wire's half labels. Instead, the desired linear combination is *garbling-dependent*, and randomized and encrypted in such a way that the evaluator learns the desired linear combination without learning anything about the garbling. In the [15] paradigm, the garbler cannot know the garbling, and naturally, it is harder to randomize and encrypt something you do not know. We leave the study of this question to future work.

2.2 New Ideas: Authenticated Shared Bits

We now go through the levels of this blueprint again, this time explaining the changes that each of our three protocols make to the pattern laid out above. First, for authenticated shared bits, as mentioned above, two instances of $\mathcal{F}_{\mathsf{subVOLE}}$ are sufficient to generate this randomness, and we use exactly this for our first protocol, $\mathbf{\Pi}_{\mathsf{2pc}}^{\mathsf{DAMT}}$.

For the protocol using only VOLE-type correlations, $\mathbf{\Pi}_{\mathsf{2pc}}^{\mathsf{VOLE}}$, we introduce a complication. We now generate all wire tags b_i as a (public) linear combination of entries of a vector $\widetilde{b}$ of wire tags. The length of $\widetilde{b}$ is $O(\rho \log n)$. This allows us to generate shares of values $a_i \wedge b_j$ as a linear combination of values $a_i \wedge \widetilde{b}_{j'}$, which can in turn be represented as entries of VOLE.

To ensure that security against a malicious A remains, we have to verify that we are still protected against selective failure attacks. Following the protocol of [21], we do not allow A to learn the values $z_i \oplus \lambda_i$, and instead send a second garbled circuit that allows B to learn $z_i \oplus \lambda_i$ and the accompanying share of $z_i \wedge z_j \oplus \lambda_k$. If A corrupts only a single gate, then by the randomness of $\widetilde{b}$, A will learn nothing from an abort. However, if A corrupts more gates, the values b_i may be linearly related, and so A could learn something from whether or not B aborts. However, with an appropriate choice of parameters, the values b_i will only be linearly related if A has corrupted so many gates that an abort is inevitable.

We note that a similar approach that generates the vector $\mathbf{a}$ as a linear transformation of a shorter vector $\widetilde{a}$ (i.e. $\mathbf{a} = M_H \widetilde{a}$) would be insecure. Indeed, any vector $\mathbf{w}$ in the (non-empty) left kernel of M_H is orthogonal to $\mathbf{a}$. B must learn the values $z_i \oplus \lambda_i$ in order to evaluate the circuit, and can then subtract their share to obtain $z_i \oplus a_i$. Taking the dot product of $\mathbf{a} \oplus \mathbf{z}$ with $\mathbf{w}$ gives $\mathbf{w} \cdot \mathbf{z}$, and B has broken the zero-knowledge property of the secure computation.

Finally, for the NISC protocol $\mathbf{\Pi}_{\mathsf{2pc}}^{\mathsf{NISC}}$, we can not realize an instance of $\mathcal{F}_{\mathsf{subVOLE}}$ where B is the sender and A is the receiver non-interactively. Instead, we let one of A's inputs to programmable OLE be the vector $\overline{\boldsymbol{\alpha}} := (\alpha, \alpha, \dots, \alpha)$, and then B's input $\mathbf{b}$ intended for $\mathcal{F}_{\mathsf{subVOLE}}$ can instead be given to $\mathcal{F}_{\mathsf{OLE}}$.

2.3 Authenticated Parallel AND

For our first protocol, $\mathbf{\Pi}_{\mathsf{2pc}}^{\mathsf{DAMT}}$, we construct authenticated parallel AND gates from doubly authenticated multiplication triples in two steps. First, we convert from $\mathcal{F}_{\mathsf{DAMT}}^{(\rho,n)}$ to $\mathcal{F}_{\mathsf{pre}(\rho)}$ using a construction inspired by Beaver triples, see Sect. 4.2. This conversion requires 2ρ bits of communication per AND gate.

We then convert from $\mathcal{F}_{\mathsf{pre}(\rho)}$ to $\mathcal{F}_{\mathsf{pre}(\kappa)}$, that is, from preprocessing for parallel AND gates over $\mathbb{F}_{2^\rho}$ to parallel AND gates where bits held by party B are authenticated over $\mathbb{F}_{2^\kappa}$ instead of $\mathbb{F}_{2^\rho}$, using a lightweight protocol that requires only $3 + o(1)$ bits per AND gate. This can be done with semi-honest security using the usual compiler from random to fixed subfield VOLE (see e.g. [3]). To make this secure against malicious B, B must convince A that the bits used for this instance of fixed $\mathcal{F}_{\mathsf{subVOLE}}$ match the authenticated bits generated by $\mathcal{F}_{\mathsf{pre}(\rho)}$. We give a lightweight protocol for this authentication in Sect. 4.2.

For our VOLE-only protocol, we instead use the block VOLE construction ($\mathcal{F}_{\mathsf{bVOLE}}$) to obtain bit shares of the product $(a_{2i-1} \oplus b_{2i-1}) \wedge (a_{2i} \oplus b_{2i})$ term by term. Party A holds the bit $a_{2i-1} \wedge a_{2i}$ locally, and can use this value as an entry of its authenticated bits constructed above, and verify its correctness under LPZK. Likewise party B holds the bit $b_{2i-1} \wedge b_{2i}$ locally and can authenticate and verify under LPZK. The cross terms $a_{2i-1} \wedge b_{2i}$ and $a_{2i} \wedge b_{2i-1}$ are linear combinations of terms of the form $a_{2i-1} \wedge \widetilde{b}_j$ and $a_{2i} \wedge \widetilde{b}_j$, respectively, and so bit shares of these terms can be obtained from the block VOLE.

In order to obtain *authenticated* shares, we also need to generate shares of $(a_i \wedge \widetilde{b}_j)\beta$. To do this, we double the size of B's input to the block VOLE, so that B's inputs are $\widetilde{b}_j, \widetilde{b}_j\beta$. (For security reasons, we need to shift all of B's inputs by a random value γ, which is an additional input. We give the details in Sect. 5.2 and additional details in the full version of this paper [12]. To verify that B's inputs satisfy the correct relation, B passes their inputs to an instance of $\mathcal{F}_{\mathsf{VOLE}}$, playing the role of Sender, and proves correctness under LPZK.

For technical reasons, our protocol does not guarantee that a cheating A is detected immediately, but instead ensures that, if A cheats, A corrupts their own share of $\hat{b}_i\alpha$, which will then be detected during the evaluation of the garbled circuit with overwhelming probability.

Because of the linear dependence on B's bits, this is no longer a realization of $\mathcal{F}_{\mathsf{pre}(\rho)}$. We define a modified functionality $\mathcal{F}_{\mathsf{cp}}$ and show that the converter from $\mathcal{F}_{\mathsf{pre}(\rho)}$ to $\mathcal{F}_{\mathsf{pre}(\kappa)}$ can likewise convert from $\mathcal{F}_{\mathsf{cp}}^{(\rho)}$ to $\mathcal{F}_{\mathsf{cp}}^{(\kappa)}$.

For our NISC protocol, we follow the same approach as in the VOLE-only protocol to produce shares of $(a_{2i-1} \oplus b_{2i-1}) \wedge (a_{2i} \oplus b_{2i})$ and $(a_{2i-1} \oplus b_{2i-1}) \wedge (a_{2i} \oplus b_{2i})\beta$, term by term. As discussed above, the parties have to generate authenticated bits through a call to $\mathcal{F}_{\mathsf{OLE}}$ instead of $\mathcal{F}_{\mathsf{subVOLE}}$. To generate the pairwise products $b_{2i} \wedge a_{2i-1}$ and $b_{2i-1} \wedge a_{2i}$, and so-on, we re-use A's input $\mathbf{a}$ to the $\mathcal{F}_{\mathsf{OLE}}$ functionality, and pair it with a new vector $\mathbf{b}'$, which reverses the order of every pair (b_{2i-1}, b_{2i}).

Because the protocol is non-interactive, B cannot prove anything about their inputs to A (in the CRS model, this would require a CRS generated by A and a message from B to A before A's final message from A to B for the secure computation, giving a 3 round protocol). Instead, A and B use a lightweight conditional disclosure of secrets protocol (CDS) which ensures that either B's inputs are well-formed or A's message to B in the NISC protocol appears uniformly random to B. We sketch the protocol briefly here, and describe it in more detail in Sect. 6.1.

For the CDS protocol, parties A and B generate an instance of $\mathcal{F}_{\mathsf{OLE}}$ with A's input the vector $\overline{\boldsymbol{\alpha}} := (\alpha, \alpha, \ldots, \alpha)$, and B's input the vector $\overline{\boldsymbol{\beta}} := (\beta, \beta, \ldots, \beta)$. Call the resulting shares $(\mathbf{v}, \mathbf{c})$, so that if both parties are honest, we have $v_i + c_i = \alpha\beta$ for all i. Then likewise $v_1 - v_i = c_1 - c_i$ for all i if both parties are honest, and are otherwise offset by a term unknown to the cheating party.

Let the vector $\mathbf{s} := (c_i - c_i)$ be held by A and the vector $\mathbf{t} := (v_1 - v_i)$ be held by B. Then A adds $H(\mathbf{s})$ to all future messages, B subtracts $H(\mathbf{t})$ from all future messages. if B cheats, B will be unable to construct $\mathbf{s}$, and so A's messages will appear random.

Similar protocols are used to guarantee that the vector $\mathbf{b}'$ really holds the desired re-ordering of $\mathbf{b}$, and that all necessary polynomial relations on $\mathbf{b}$ hold. We give more detail in Sect. 6.1.

We note that our converters from authenticated gates over ρ to authenticated gates over κ (i.e. the conversion from $\mathcal{F}_{\mathsf{pre}(\rho)}$ to $\mathcal{F}_{\mathsf{pre}(\kappa)}$, and related protocols) can no longer be applied in the NISC setting because this protocol requires opening certain shared values publicly, and thus is interactive. This is one of the reasons that our NISC protocol requires more communication than our other two protocols.

2.4 Authenticated Circuit Wires

For our first interactive protocol, $\mathbf{\Pi}_{\mathsf{2pc}}^{\mathsf{DAMT}}$, the converter from $\mathcal{F}_{\mathsf{pre}(\kappa)}$ to $\mathcal{F}_{\mathsf{pre}}^{(C,\kappa,\rho)}$ follows the approach of [15]. We give the protocol converting from $\mathcal{F}_{\mathsf{pre}(\kappa)}$ to $\mathcal{F}_{\mathsf{pre}}^{(C,\kappa,\rho)}$ in Sect. 4.2. For our VOLE-based protocol $\mathbf{\Pi}_{\mathsf{2pc}}^{\mathsf{VOLE}}$, we give instead build $\mathcal{F}_{\mathsf{cp}}^{(C,\rho,\rho)}$ directly and convert from that functionality to $\mathcal{F}_{\mathsf{cp}}^{(C,\kappa,\rho)}$. We describe these conversions in Sect. 5.2.

For our NISC protocol, we define a modified functionality $\mathcal{F}_{\mathsf{pre-wbc}}^{(C,\rho,\kappa)}$ which is similar to the functionality $\mathcal{F}_{\mathsf{pre}}$, but has the property from $\mathcal{F}_{\mathsf{cp}}$ that a cheating A is not immediately detected but corrupts their own shares. We observe that the protocol sketched above for obtaining authenticated parallel AND gates from authenticated bits can be used to obtain authenticated wires for an arbitrary circuit. Instead of swapping b_{2i-1} and b_{2i} in a second input vector to $\mathcal{F}_{\mathsf{OLE}}$, we have one input vector $\mathbf{b}_L$ to the $\mathcal{F}_{\mathsf{OLE}}$ of all left inputs b_i to gates $\mathcal{G}_k = (i, j, k, \wedge)$, and a second input vector $\mathbf{b}_R$ of all right inputs b_j. The same techniques are used to ensure that $\mathbf{b}_L$ and $\mathbf{b}_R$ hold the correct linear transformations of $\mathbf{b}$.

2.5 Authenticated Garbling

For our first protocol, we can use the authenticated garbling protocol of [15] directly, once the functionality $\mathcal{F}_{\mathsf{pre}}^{(C,\rho,\kappa)}$ has been realized, with a small modification to the step where the initial gate labels are determined to account for our small modification to $\mathcal{F}_{\mathsf{pre}}^{(C,\rho,\kappa)}$ where we allow a party's wire mask zero when the other party knows the true wire value. The protocol still requires, as in [15], $2\kappa + 2$ bits of offline circuit dependent communication per AND gate.

For our VOLE-only protocol, we can no longer use the authentication approach of [15] where B reveals to A the masked wire labels $z_i \oplus \lambda_i = z_i \oplus a_i \oplus b_i$. Of course, A can XOR these shares by the values a_i that A holds, leaving $z_i \oplus b_i$, and, because the values b_i are computed as linear combinations of some shorter vector $\widetilde{b}$, there is some linear combination of the $z_i \oplus b_i$ terms that causes the b_i terms to cancel identically, and A would learn some linear relation on the vector $\mathbf{z}$ of true wire values.

Instead, we combine the techniques of [21] with Zahur's half-gate techniques, so that B can open exactly one authenticated bit, corresponding to $(z_i \wedge z_j) \oplus \lambda_k$, for the k-th multiplication gate. This requires only statistical security, since the output is only used for verification, and does not play the role of a gate label for an output wire. On the other hand, since the output is being used for verification, we can no longer allow a term $H(L_{i,0}, k) \oplus H(L_{j,0}, k)$ to be added to the output, so we need to send an additional element of $\mathbb{F}_{2^\rho}$ as part of the garbled table. In total, the authenticated garbling requires $2\kappa + 3\rho$ bits of offline circuit dependent communication per AND gate.

In our NISC protocol, we also cannot have party B revealing masked wire labels to A, because that would require additional rounds of communication. We use the same approach as in our VOLE-only protocol, but need to show additional care to verify that the protocol can be made non-interactive. We give the details in Sect. 6.2 and additional details in the full version of this paper [12].

3 Authenticating Correlated Randomness

Before we proceed with a technical description of our main protocols, we give an overview of the techniques related to correlated randomness we use throughout the rest of the paper.

3.1 Compilers from "Random" to "Fixed" Randomness Variants

There is a standard compiler from random VOLE to fixed VOLE (see e.g. [3]) that allows parties to replace a randomly selected vector $\mathbf{v} := \mathbf{a}\beta + \mathbf{c}$, where all entries are chosen randomly, with a new vector $\mathbf{v}' := \mathbf{a}'\beta' + \mathbf{c}'$, where $\mathbf{a}', \mathbf{c}'$ are chosen by the sender, β' is chosen by the receiver, and the receiver additionally learns $\mathbf{v}'$ given above. The conversion protocol can be stated simply: the receiver sends $\beta' - \beta$ to the sender, the sender sends $\mathbf{a}' - \mathbf{a}$ and $\mathbf{c}' - \mathbf{c} + (\beta' - \beta) \cdot \mathbf{a}'$ to the receiver, and both parties adjust their shares locally. In cases where the sender does not need to control the value of $\mathbf{c}'$, the sender sends only $\mathbf{a}' - \mathbf{a}$, and sets their pair of vectors to $(\mathbf{a}', \mathbf{c} - (\beta' - \beta) \cdot \mathbf{a})$.

We can use this same compiler with block VOLE, where a vector $\mathbf{a}$ is used across several instances of VOLE. To replace a random $\mathbf{a}$ with a fixed vector $\mathbf{a}'$, party A only needs to send the message $\mathbf{a}' - \mathbf{a}$ once across all instances.

A similar compiler exists for a batch of OLE correlations $\mathbf{v} := \mathbf{ab} + \mathbf{c}$, where one party sends $\mathbf{a}' - \mathbf{a}$, the other sends $\mathbf{b}' - \mathbf{b}$, and both parties compute locally to obtain $\mathbf{v}' := \mathbf{a}'\mathbf{b}' + \mathbf{c}'$. As with block VOLE, if the random vector $\mathbf{a}$ is used in multiple instances of programmable OLE, a single message suffices to convert this vector to $\mathbf{a}'$ across all instances.

For a careful accounting of round complexity, we note that, when the value of $\mathbf{c}$ can be chosen randomly, these messages can be sent concurrently or in sequence, in either order. If one party does not require fixed inputs, that party does not need to send a message at all.

3.2 Certification Between Varieties of Correlated Randomness

Recall the "correlation calculus" introduced in Sect. 1.1, that allows us to express each of our randomness functionalities in terms of a short list of atomic operations. This same "correlation calculus" allows us to re-use vectors and scalars across distinct flavors of correlated randomness as long as they are of the same type (that is, VOLE-type or MT-type).

For example, if we wish to have an instance of $\mathcal{F}_{\mathsf{VOLE}}$ and an instance of $\mathcal{F}_{\mathsf{subVOLE}}$ using the same value β but different vectors $\mathbf{a}, \mathbf{a}'$, then we generate $\mathbf{a}, \mathbf{a}'$ randomly, multiple each vector by β, and share each of the results over the desired field. Similar approaches allow us to use the same vector and different values β, β', and can also be applied to use the same vectors or values between instances of $\mathcal{F}_{\mathsf{subVOLE}}$ or $\mathcal{F}_{\mathsf{VOLE}}$ over different (top-level) fields.

By combining this with the previous observation about compilers from random to fixed VOLE and OLE, we can allow any vector or scalar to be used as an input to any instance of $\mathcal{F}_{\mathsf{VOLE}}$, $\mathcal{F}_{\mathsf{subVOLE}}$, or $\mathcal{F}_{\mathsf{bVOLE}}$.

There are three situations that are not covered by this approach, for which we require bespoke protocols. Each of them work by extending the randomness instances with fresh randomness and evaluating some short polynomial expression on the outputs, which will produce equal outputs for both parties if and only if the desired equality condition holds. A random oracle is applied to the outputs and then the results are compared; any number of certifications of this form can be batched together by applying the random oracle to the collection of outputs.

First, in Sect. 4 we wish to authenticate that the same value α is used in a call to $\mathcal{F}_{\mathsf{VOLE}}$ and a call to $\mathcal{F}_{\mathsf{DAMT}}$. These are generated by different "correlation calculuses", and it would be a massive efficiency hit to generate $\mathcal{F}_{\mathsf{VOLE}}$ as MT-type randomness. We give a lightweight protocol $\mathbf{\Pi}_{\mathsf{cert}}^{\mathsf{DAMT} \wedge \mathsf{VOLE}}$ in the full version of this paper [12].

Second, in Sect. 5, we wish to show that, for two calls to VOLE with the parties switching between the role of receiver and sender, the constant value β used by one party in their role as receiver matches another value b used by the same party while playing the role of the sender. We give a lightweight protocol $\mathbf{\Pi}_{\mathsf{cert}}^{\mathsf{VOLE} \wedge \mathsf{ELOV}}$ in the full version of this paper [12].

Third, in Sects. 4 and 5, we wish to certify that two instances of subfield VOLE with different receiver inputs α, Δ_A over different fields $\mathbb{F}_{2^\rho}$, $\mathbb{F}_{2^\kappa}$ have the same vector inputs $\mathbf{b}$, even if one vector is generated via the compiler from random to fixed VOLE, and another is generated using an unspecified possibly interactive protocol. We give a lightweight protocol $\mathbf{\Pi}_{\mathsf{cert}}^{\rho\wedge\kappa}$ in the full version of this paper [12].

3.3 Line Point Zero Knowledge

In [11], Dittmer, Ishai and Ostrovsky introduced *Line Point Zero Knowledge*, or LPZK, a protocol for building a NIZK for general circuits using a single instance of VOLE. When working in the random oracle model on circuits corresponding to low degree polynomials, LPZK is especially powerful, because many verifications can be batched together. As shown in [22], any number of polynomials on a total of n inputs of degree at most d can be verified with communication of $(n+d)\kappa$ bits communication. For completeness, and because we use similar arguments elsewhere in this paper, we sketch the argument here.

A prover P wishes to convince a verifier V that P holds inputs $\mathbf{a} = (a_i)$ such that $g(\mathbf{a}) = 0$. Each input a_i becomes the entry of a VOLE $v_i = a_i\beta + c_i$, and V evaluates $g(\mathbf{v})$, which will be a polynomial in β of degree at most $d-1$ if P is telling the truth. After masking these values with an oblivious polynomial evaluation of degree $d-1$, P opens the coefficients and V confirms the desired equality. In the ROM, many such checks can be batched together, with V computing $\sum g(\mathbf{v})H(\mathbf{m};i)$ and P computing the coefficients of $\sum g(\mathbf{a}t + \mathbf{c})H(\mathbf{m};i)$, where $\mathbf{m}$ represents some message transcript committing P to the values $\mathbf{a}$, and i is the index representing the number of times we've evoked this batch check.

This construction includes the cost of the compiler from random VOLE to fixed VOLE. In our case, where we wish to prove relations on an already set fixed VOLE, we can omit the $n\kappa$ bits of communication, and send only $d\kappa$ bits. In this paper, we exclusively apply LPZK to the setting where we wish to prove that already set VOLE inputs satisfy some collection of polynomials of degree d, and take $d \leq 3$ throughout. We write $\mathbf{\Pi}_{\mathsf{LPZK}}(\mathbf{a}, \mathbf{c}, \beta, \mathbf{v}, \mathcal{R})$ for the protocol that proves that $\mathbf{a}$ satisfies the set of relations $\mathcal{R}$, when one party holds $(\mathbf{a}, \mathbf{c})$ and the other party holds β and $\mathbf{v} := \mathbf{a}\beta + \mathbf{c}$.

4 Authenticated Garbling from Authenticated Garbled Triples

We follow the blueprint laid out in Sect. 2, giving the full protocol description and proofs. Recall that in Fig. 1, we gave the a preprocessing functionality $\mathcal{F}_{\mathsf{pre}}^{(C,\rho,\kappa)}$ used in the constructions of [21] and [15]. Let $\mathsf{PAnd}(n)$ be a circuit consisting of n AND gates executed in parallel, so that the kth gate has input wires $(2k-1, 2k)$ and output wire $2n+k$. Recall that we write $\mathcal{F}_{\mathsf{pre}(\kappa)}$ for $\mathcal{F}_{\mathsf{pre}}^{(\mathsf{PAnd}(n),\kappa,\rho)}$ and $\mathcal{F}_{\mathsf{pre}(\rho)}$ for $\mathcal{F}_{\mathsf{pre}}^{(\mathsf{PAnd}(n),\rho,\rho)}$.

4.1 From Authenticated Bits to Parallel and with Authenticated Triples

The underlying correlated randomness we need for our protocol is subfield VOLE for generating authenticated bits, VOLE, for running proofs of input correctness under LPZK, and doubly authenticated multiplication triples, for converting from authenticated bits to authenticated parallel AND.

Doubly authenticated multiplication triples can be generated from Ring-LPN under the "correlation calculus" discussed in Sect. 1.1. This correlated randomness is nonstandard, although it can be viewed as a modified form of the authenticated triples of SPDZ [10]. We give the functionality formally in Fig. 2. We then prove the following lemma, which shows how to generate authenticated bits and how to convert these bits to authenticated parallel AND gates.

Functionality $\mathcal{F}_{\mathsf{DAMT}}^{(\rho,n)}$: Two-sided authenticated triple generation

Parametrized by values $\rho, n \in \mathbb{N}$.

- A chooses $\alpha \in \mathbb{F}_{2^\rho}$ and sends α to $\mathcal{F}_{\mathsf{DAMT}}$.
- B chooses $\beta \in \mathbb{F}_{2^\rho}$ and sends β to $\mathcal{F}_{\mathsf{DAMT}}$.
- $\mathcal{F}_{\mathsf{DAMT}}$ samples vectors $(\mathbf{x}, \mathbf{y})$ uniformly at random from $\mathbb{F}_{2^\rho}^n$.
- $\mathcal{F}_{\mathsf{DAMT}}$ sets $\mathbf{z} := \mathbf{x} \cdot \mathbf{y}$, where the multiplication is done element-wise.
- $\mathcal{F}_{\mathsf{DAMT}}$ generates random shares $(\mathbf{x}_{A,1}, \mathbf{y}_{A,1}, \mathbf{z}_{A,1})$ and $(\mathbf{x}_{B,1}, \mathbf{y}_{B,1}, \mathbf{z}_{B,1})$ of the vectors $(\mathbf{x}, \mathbf{y}, \mathbf{z})$, with random shares chosen in $\mathbb{F}_{2^\rho}$.
- $\mathcal{F}_{\mathsf{DAMT}}$ generates random shares $(\mathbf{x}_{A,2}, \mathbf{y}_{A,2}, \mathbf{z}_{A,2})$ and $(\mathbf{x}_{B,2}, \mathbf{y}_{B,2}, \mathbf{z}_{B,2})$ of the vectors $(\alpha\mathbf{x}, \alpha\mathbf{y}, \alpha\mathbf{z})$, with random shares chosen in $\mathbb{F}_{2^\rho}$.
- $\mathcal{F}_{\mathsf{DAMT}}$ generates random shares $(\mathbf{x}_{A,3}, \mathbf{y}_{A,3}, \mathbf{z}_{A,3})$ and $(\mathbf{x}_{B,3}, \mathbf{y}_{B,3}, \mathbf{z}_{B,3})$ of the vectors $(\beta\mathbf{x}, \beta\mathbf{y}, \beta\mathbf{z})$, with random shares chosen in $\mathbb{F}_{2^\rho}$.
- For $i \in \{1, 2, 3\}$, $\mathcal{F}_{\mathsf{DAMT}}$ sends $(\mathbf{x}_{A,i}, \mathbf{y}_{A,i}, \mathbf{z}_{A,i})$ to A and $(\mathbf{x}_{B,i}, \mathbf{y}_{B,i}, \mathbf{z}_{B,i})$ to B.

Fig. 2. Two-sided authenticated triples

Lemma 1. *The protocol in Fig. 3 securely computes $\mathcal{F}_{\mathsf{pre}(\rho)}$ against malicious adversaries in the $\mathcal{F}_{\mathsf{DAMT}} - \mathcal{F}_{\mathsf{subVOLE}} - \mathcal{F}_{\mathsf{VOLE}}$-hybrid model with 2ρ bits of communication from B to A and 2ρ bits of communication from A to B per AND gate.*

Completeness. Expanding as in the standard Beaver triple approach, we have

$$\hat{a}_k + \hat{b}_k = ef + ey + fx + z = (a_i + b_i)(a_j + b_j),$$

as desired. Then note that

$$\hat{w}_k + \hat{d}_k = (a_i + b_i)(a_j + b_j)\alpha + \hat{a}_k\alpha = \hat{b}_k\alpha,$$

Protocol $\Pi^{\mathsf{pre}(\rho)}_{\mathsf{DAMT}}$: Circuit dependent pre-processing of wire labels from authenticated parallel AND gates.

Parametrized by values ρ, κ, and a circuit C consisting of $\mathcal{W}$ wires, $\mathcal{I}$ input wires, $\mathcal{O}$ output wires, and gates $\mathcal{G}$ of the form (i, j, k, T), for $T \in \{\wedge, \oplus\}$, $i, j \in \mathcal{I} \cup \mathcal{W}$, and $k \in \mathcal{W} \cup \mathcal{O}$.

1. A and B invoke $\mathcal{F}_{\mathsf{subVOLE}}$ with A as sender and B as receiver so that A receives $\alpha \in \mathbb{F}_{2^\kappa}$, B receives $\mathbf{b} \in \mathbb{F}_2^m$ and $\mathbf{d} \in \mathbb{F}_{2^\kappa}^m$, and A receives $\mathbf{w} := \mathbf{b}\alpha + \mathbf{d}$.
2. A and B invoke $\mathcal{F}_{\mathsf{subVOLE}}$ with B as sender and A as receiver, so that B receives $\beta \in \mathbb{F}_{2^\rho}$, A receives $\mathbf{a} \in \mathbb{F}_2^m$ and $\mathbf{c} \in \mathbb{F}_{2^\rho}^m$, and B receives $\mathbf{v} := \mathbf{a}\beta + \mathbf{c}$.
3. A and B invoke $\mathcal{F}_{\mathsf{DAMT}}$ with A's input α, B's input β, so that party P receives $(x_{P,\ell,i}, y_{P,\ell,i}, z_{P,\ell,i})$ for $\ell \in \{1, 2, 3\}$ and $1 \leq i \leq n$.
4. A and B compute the authentication messages $(\mathbf{m}_A, \mathbf{m}_B)$ using $\Pi^{\mathsf{DAMT} \wedge \mathsf{subVOLE}}_{\mathsf{cert}}$. A sends $H(\mathbf{m}_A)$ to B, who verifies that this equals $H(\mathbf{m}_B)$, and otherwise aborts.
5. Initialize a counter $t \leftarrow 1$.
6. For each gate $\mathcal{G} = (i, j, k, T)$, in topological order:
   - If $T = \oplus$:
     - A sets the values $a_k = a_i + a_j$, $c_k = c_i + c_j$, and $w_k = w_i + w_j$.
     - B sets the values $b_k = b_i + b_j$, $d_k = d_i + d_j$ and $v_k = v_i + v_j$.
   - If $T = \wedge$:
     - A sends to B the messages
$$(m_1^A, m_2^A, m_3^A, m_4^A) := (a_i + x_{A,1,t}, a_j + y_{A,1,t}, c_i + x_{A,3,t}, c_j + y_{A,3,t}).$$
     - B sends to A the messages
$$(m_1^B, m_2^B, m_3^B, m_4^B) := (b_i + x_{B,1,t}, b_j + y_{B,1,t}, d_i + x_{B,2,t}, d_j + y_{B,2,t}).$$
     - A locally verifies that $(w_i + \alpha x_{A,1,t} + x_{A,2,t} + m_3^B, w_j + y_{A,2,t} + \alpha y_{A,1,t} + m_4^B) = (m_1^B \alpha, m_2^B \alpha)$ and aborts if not.
     - B locally verifies that $(v_i + \beta x_{B,1} + x_{B,3} + m_3^A, v_j + y_{B,3,t} + \beta y_{B,1,t} + m_4^A) = (m_1^A \beta, m_2^A \beta)$ and aborts if not.
     - Both parties locally compute $e := m_1^A + m_1^B$ and $f := m_2^A + m_2^B$.
     - A locally computes
$$\begin{aligned}\hat{a}_k &= ef + ey_{A,1,t} + fx_{A,1,t} + z_{A,1,t}\\ \hat{c}_k &= ey_{A,3,t} + fx_{A,3,t} + z_{A,3,t}\\ \hat{w}_k &= (ef + \hat{a}_k)\alpha + ey_{A,2,t} + fx_{A,2,t} + z_{A,2,t}.\end{aligned}$$
     - B locally computes
$$\begin{aligned}\hat{b}_k &= ey_{B,1,t} + fx_{B,1,t} + z_{B,1,t}\\ \hat{d}_k &= ey_{B,2,t} + fx_{B,2,t} + z_{B,2,t}\\ \hat{v}_k &= (ef + \hat{b}_k)\beta + ey_{B,3,t} + fx_{B,3,t} + z_{B,3,t}.\end{aligned}$$
     - $t \leftarrow t + 1$.
7. Party A performs
$$\hat{\mathbf{w}} \rightarrow \hat{\mathbf{w}} + (\mathbf{a} + \mathsf{lsb}(\hat{\mathbf{a}}))\alpha, \hat{\mathbf{a}} \rightarrow \mathsf{lsb}(\hat{\mathbf{a}})$$
8. Party B performs
$$\hat{\mathbf{v}} \rightarrow \hat{\mathbf{v}} + (\mathbf{b} + \mathsf{lsb}(\hat{\mathbf{b}}))\beta, \hat{\mathbf{b}} \rightarrow \mathsf{lsb}(\hat{\mathbf{b}}),$$

Fig. 3. Authenticated parallel AND gates from $\mathcal{F}_{\mathsf{DAMT}}$

as desired. Similarly, we have $\hat{a}_k\beta + \hat{c}_k = \hat{v}_k$, as desired.

At the end of the protocol, parties A and B locally adjust these shares so that $\hat{\mathbf{a}}$ and $\hat{\mathbf{b}}$ become vectors of bits. Since $\hat{\mathbf{a}}+\hat{\mathbf{b}} \in \{0,1\}^n$, we have $(\mathbf{a}+\mathsf{lsb}(\hat{\mathbf{a}})) = (\mathbf{b}+\mathsf{lsb}(\hat{\mathbf{b}}))$, so this adjustment preserves the desired relations.

Security. By the symmetry of the protocol, it is sufficient to consider the case of a malicious A. Let $\mathcal{A}$ be an adversary corrupting A. First, we show that if $\mathcal{A}$ sends incorrect values in a message, B will abort with overwhelming probability. Indeed, if A sends $a_i + x_{A,1} + \phi_1$ instead of $a_i + x_{A,1}$ and $c_i + x_{A,3} + \phi_2$ instead of $c_i + x_{A,3}$, B will verify whether

$$(a_i + x_{A,1} + \phi_1)\beta = (a_i + x_{A,1})\beta + \phi_2,$$

i.e. whether $\beta\phi_1 = \phi_2$.

We can then construct a simple simulator $\mathcal{S}$ that runs $\mathcal{A}$ as a subroutine and plays the role of A in the ideal world. The simulator generates B's last two messages uniformly at random, and the first two messages so that they satisfy the desired check. By the uniform randomness of $y_{B,1}$ and $y_{B,2}$, the distribution of B's messages $d_i + y_{B,1}, d_j + y_{B,2}$ in the real world are identical to the distribution of $\mathcal{S}$'s simulation of B in the ideal world. Since $b_i + x_{B,1}$ and $b_j + x_{B,2}$ can be computed from A's data and the message $d_i + y_{B,1}, d_j + y_{B,2}$, the distribution of these values are identical as well.

$\mathcal{S}$ then sends B's messages to $\mathcal{A}$, and aborts if $\mathcal{A}$ responds with anything besides $(a_i + x_{A,1}, a_j + y_{B,1}, c_i + x_{A,3}, c_j + y_{A,3})$. Otherwise, $\mathcal{S}$ outputs whatever $\mathcal{A}$ outputs. As discussed above, with overwhelming probability an honest B aborts in the real world whenever $\mathcal{S}$ aborts, so the joint distribution of the outputs of $\mathcal{A}$ and an honest B in the real world are indistinguishable from the joint distribution of the outputs of $\mathcal{A}$ and $\mathcal{S}$ in the ideal world.

4.2 Circuit-Dependent Preprocessing from Parallel and Gates

We now go from authenticated parallel AND gates over ρ to authenticated parallel AND gates over κ, and then to authenticated circuit wires. We begin with the conversion from $\mathcal{F}_{\mathsf{pre}(\rho)}$ to $\mathcal{F}_{\mathsf{pre}(\kappa)}$.

Lemma 2. *The protocol in Fig. 4 realizes $\mathcal{F}_{\mathsf{pre}}^{(C,\rho,\kappa)}$ securely in the $\mathcal{F}_{\mathsf{pre}}^{(C,\rho,\rho)} - \mathcal{F}_{\mathsf{subVOLE}}$-RO hybrid model, at the cost of an additional $3n+O(\kappa)$ bits of communication. In particular, $\mathcal{F}_{\mathsf{pre}(\kappa)}$ is securely realizable in the $\mathcal{F}_{\mathsf{pre}(\rho)} - \mathcal{F}_{\mathsf{subVOLE}}$-RO hybrid model.*

Proof. **Completeness.** We have $\mathbf{w}' = \mathbf{b}'\Delta_A + \mathbf{d}'$ and $\hat{\mathbf{w}}' = \hat{\mathbf{b}}'\Delta_A + \hat{\mathbf{d}}'$ both immediately before Step 4 and immediately after Step 5. The desired relations on the vectors $\mathbf{a}+\mathbf{b}$, $\hat{\mathbf{a}}+\hat{\mathbf{b}}$ follow from the correctness of the $\mathcal{F}_{\mathsf{pre}}^{(C,\rho,\rho)}$ functionality.
Security. Security of steps 1,2, and 6 follow from the security of the underlying protocols. Security against a malicious B follows from the correctness of $\mathbf{\Pi}_{\mathsf{cert}}^{\rho\wedge\kappa}$, shown in the full version of this paper [12], which guarantees that A (or a simulator $\mathcal{S}$) will detect an incorrect message with high probability.

For security against a malicious A, note that A sends no message in steps 3 through 5, and that the messages $\mathbf{m}_1$, $\mathbf{m}_2$ can be simulated by sampling uniformly random sequences of bits, by the security of $\mathcal{F}_{\mathsf{subVOLE}}$.

Complexity. We have $|\mathbf{w}| = 2n$ and $|\hat{\mathbf{w}}| = n$, so the messages $\mathbf{m}_1, \mathbf{m}_2$ take $2n + n = 3n$ bits. The certification step calling $\mathbf{\Pi}_{\mathsf{cert}}^{\rho \wedge \kappa}$ costs $O(\kappa)$ bits, as shown in the full version of this paper [12]. See Sect. 3.2 for an overview of this certified functionality notation.

Protocol $\mathbf{\Pi}_{\mathsf{pre}(\rho)}^{\mathsf{pre}(\kappa)}$: Circuit dependent pre-processing of wire labels from authenticated parallel ρ-AND gates.

Parametrized by values ρ, κ, and a circuit C consisting of $\mathcal{W}$ wires, $\mathcal{I}$ input wires, $\mathcal{O}$ output wires, and gates $\mathcal{G}$ of the form (i, j, k, T), for $T \in \{\wedge, \oplus\}$, $i, j \in \mathcal{I} \cup \mathcal{W}$, and $k \in \mathcal{W} \cup \mathcal{O}$.

1. A and B invoke $\mathcal{F}_{\mathsf{pre}}^{(C,\rho,\rho)}$, generating vectors $\mathbf{a}, \mathbf{c}, \mathbf{w}, \hat{\mathbf{a}}, \hat{\mathbf{c}}, \hat{\mathbf{w}}$ and a value α for A and vectors $\mathbf{b}, \mathbf{d}, \mathbf{v}, \hat{\mathbf{b}}, \hat{\mathbf{d}}, \hat{\mathbf{v}}$ and a value β for B.
2. A and B invoke $\mathcal{F}_{\mathsf{subVOLE}}$ with B as sender and A as receiver for the fields $(\mathbb{F}_2, \mathbb{F}_{2^\kappa})$, so that B learns $\mathbf{b}', \mathbf{d}', \hat{\mathbf{b}}', \hat{\mathbf{d}}'$, and A learns $\Delta_A \in \mathbb{F}_{2^\kappa}$ and vectors $\mathbf{w}' := \mathbf{b}'\Delta_A + \mathbf{d}'$ and $\hat{\mathbf{w}}' := \hat{\mathbf{b}}'\Delta_A + \hat{\mathbf{d}}'$.
3. B sends to A the vectors $\mathbf{m}_1 := \mathbf{b} + \mathbf{b}'$ and $\mathbf{m}_2 := \hat{\mathbf{b}} + \hat{\mathbf{b}}'$.
4. A adds to obtain $\mathbf{w}' \leftarrow \mathbf{w}' + \mathbf{m}_1\Delta_A$ and $\hat{\mathbf{w}}' \leftarrow \hat{\mathbf{w}}' + \mathbf{m}_2\Delta_A$.
5. B adds to obtain $\mathbf{b}' \leftarrow \mathbf{b}' + \mathbf{m}_1$, $\hat{\mathbf{b}}' \leftarrow \hat{\mathbf{b}}' + \mathbf{m}_2$.
6. A and B invoke $\mathbf{\Pi}_{\mathsf{cert}}^{\rho \wedge \kappa}$ to certify that the new values of $\mathbf{b}, \hat{\mathbf{b}}$ match their original values.
7. A and B return $\mathbf{a}, \mathbf{c}, \mathbf{w}', \hat{\mathbf{a}}, \hat{\mathbf{c}}, \hat{\mathbf{w}}', \Delta_A$ and $\mathbf{b}', \mathbf{d}', \mathbf{v}, \hat{\mathbf{b}}', \hat{\mathbf{d}}', \hat{\mathbf{v}}, \beta$ respectively.

Fig. 4. Authenticated wire labels over κ from wire labels over ρ

Next, for completeness, we give a protocol for converting from $\mathcal{F}_{\mathsf{pre}(\kappa)}$ to $\mathcal{F}_{\mathsf{pre}}^{(C,\rho,\kappa)}$. The following result is implicit in [15] and [21].

Lemma 3. *Let C be a circuit with n AND gates. Then the protocol in Fig. 5 securely computes $\mathcal{F}_{\mathsf{pre}}^{(C,\kappa,\rho)}$ against malicious adversaries in the RO-subVOLE-$\mathcal{F}_{\mathsf{pre}(\kappa)}$ hybrid model, with an additional $2n$ bits of communication.*

Proof. The security of the first three steps follows from the security of the underlying protocols.

Correctness is immediate, and the proof of security against malicious parties is similar to the proof of Lemma 1.

Protocol $\Pi^{\mathsf{pre}(C)}_{\mathsf{pre}(\kappa)}$: Circuit dependent pre-processing of wire labels from authenticated parallel AND gates.

Parametrized by values ρ, κ, and a circuit C consisting of $\mathcal{W}$ wires, $\mathcal{I}$ input wires, $\mathcal{O}$ output wires, and gates $\mathcal{G}$ of the form (i, j, k, T), for $T \in \{\wedge, \oplus\}$, $i, j \in \mathcal{I} \cup \mathcal{W}$, and $k \in \mathcal{W} \cup \mathcal{O}$.

1. A and B invoke $\mathcal{F}_{\mathsf{subVOLE}}$ with A as sender and B as receiver, so that A receives $\alpha \in \mathbb{F}_{2^\kappa}$, B receives $\mathbf{b} \in \mathbb{F}_2^m$ and $\mathbf{d} \in \mathbb{F}_{2^\kappa}^m$, and A receives $\mathbf{w} := \mathbf{b}\alpha + \mathbf{d}$.
2. A and B invoke $\mathcal{F}_{\mathsf{subVOLE}}$ with B as sender and A as receiver, so that B receives $\beta \in \mathbb{F}_{2^\rho}$, A receives $\mathbf{a} \in \mathbb{F}_2^m$ and $\mathbf{c} \in \mathbb{F}_{2^\rho}^m$, and B receives $\mathbf{v} := \mathbf{a}\beta + \mathbf{c}$.
3. A and B invoke $\mathcal{F}^{(\mathsf{PAnd}(n), \kappa, \rho)}_{\mathsf{pre}(\rho)}$ so that A obtains $(\mathbf{w}', \hat{\mathbf{w}}', \hat{\mathbf{a}}', \hat{\mathbf{c}}')$ and B obtains $(\mathbf{v}', \hat{\mathbf{v}}', \hat{\mathbf{a}}', \hat{\mathbf{c}}')$.
4. For each gate $\mathcal{G} = (i, j, k, T)$, in topological order:
   - If $T = \oplus$:
     - A sets the values $a_k = a_i + a_j$, $c_k = c_i + c_j$, and $w_k = w_i + w_j$. B sets the values $b_k = b_i + b_j$, $d_k = d_i + d_j$ and $v_k = v_i + v_j$.
   - If $T = \wedge$ is the t-th AND gate:
     - A sends $(a_i + a'_{2t-1}, a_j + a'_{2t})$ to B
     - B sends $(b_i + b'_{2t-1}, b_j + b'_{2t})$ to A
     - A and B locally compute $e_k := a_i + b_i + a'_{2t-1} + b'_{2t-1}$ and $f_k := a_j + b_j + a'_{2t} + b'_{2t}$.
     - A locally computes

$$\begin{aligned}\hat{a}_k &= e_k f_k + e_k a_j + f_k a_i + \hat{a}'_t\\ \hat{c}_k &= e_k c_j + f_k c_i + \hat{c}'_t\\ \hat{w}_k &= e_k w_j + f_k w_i + \hat{w}'_t.\end{aligned}$$

     - B locally computes

$$\begin{aligned}\hat{b}_k &= e_k b_j + f_k b_i + \hat{b}'_t\\ \hat{d}_k &= e_k d_j + f_k d_i + \hat{d}'_t\\ \hat{v}_k &= e_k f_k \beta + e_k v_j + f_k v_i + \hat{v}'_t.\end{aligned}$$

Fig. 5. Authenticated wire labels from authenticated parallel AND gates

Remark 3. As discussed in Sect. 2.1, Katz et al. in [15] realize $\mathcal{F}_{\mathsf{pre}(\kappa)}$ using an optimized version of the TinyOT protocol. Their protocol, in addition to the cost of producing authenticated bits, which could be done with sublinear communication under VOLE, requires $B\kappa$ bits of communication per gate, with $B \approx \rho/\log|C|$. In particular, $B \geq 3$ for $|C| < 2^\rho$. Adding back in the 2κ bits required in the online phase, the cost of [15] is at least 2.5x the cost of a semi-honest garbled circuit for circuits with size $|C| < 2^\rho$. Unfortunately, Lemma 2 does not offer any improvements the approach of [15], since their compiler to

$\mathcal{F}_{\mathsf{pre}(\kappa)}$ requires computational security, and so replacing it with a compiler to $\mathcal{F}_{\mathsf{pre}(\rho)}$ would still require $B\kappa$ bits per gate.

An alternative realization of the $\mathcal{F}_{\mathsf{pre}(\kappa)}$ functionality could be accomplished by the SPDZ protocol [10]. This would consume 6 authenticated multiplication triples per AND gate and require 12κ additional communication under a naive implementation. Applying Lemma 2 to the naive SPDZ-style approach gives a compiler to $\mathcal{F}_{\mathsf{pre}(\kappa)}$ by way of $\mathcal{F}_{\mathsf{pre}(\rho)}$ that costs $12\rho+3$ bits of communication per gate, and thus $2\kappa + 12\rho + 3$ bits per gate for the entire protocol, approximately 3x the cost of a semi-honest garbled circuit.

4.3 Authenticated Garbling

The only changes we make to the authenticated garbling protocol of [15] are after-effects of our decision to alter the preprocessing functionality so that A does not hold a mask for a wire value that is one of B's inputs, and vice versa. The only steps that change materially therefore are steps 3 and 4. Step 3 in [15], after translating into the language of VOLE, reads:

- For each $i \in \mathcal{I}_B$, A sends a_i to B and invoke $\mathbf{\Pi}_{\mathsf{LPZK}}$ to prove that this a_i matches the value in $\mathcal{F}_{\mathsf{pre}}$. B then sends $y_i \oplus \lambda_i = y_i \oplus a_i \oplus b_i$ to A. Finally, A sends $L_{i,y_i \oplus \lambda_i}$ to B.

We replace this step with the following:

- For each $i \in \mathcal{I}_B$, B sends $y_i \oplus b_i$ to A. Then A sends $L_{i,y_i \oplus \mathbf{b}_i}$ to B.

It is possible to simulate the previous protocol from this version by having B generate A's messages a_i uniformly at random for $i \in \mathcal{I}_A$, and adjusting their value b_i to keep the sum $a_i \oplus b_i$ constant, and having A set $a_i = 0$. These adjustments can occur without any communication, since the values a_i, b_i are never used again by A, B respectively. Therefore the security of one protocol implies the security of the other. We make similar adjustments to Step 4.

Proof of Theorem 1. Combining the three lemmas in this section gives a realization of $\mathcal{F}_{\mathsf{pre}}^{(C,\rho,\kappa)}$ in the $\mathcal{F}_{\mathsf{DAMT}} - \mathcal{F}_{\mathsf{VOLE}} - \mathcal{F}_{\mathsf{subVOLE}}$ model. Applying Theorem 4 and incorporating the minor changes to the authenticated garbling protocol outlined above gives that the desired $\mathbf{\Pi}_{\mathsf{2pc}}^{\mathsf{DAMT}}$ protocol.

5 Authenticated Garbling from Block VOLE

5.1 Compressed Authenticated Bits from Block VOLE

We begin by stating formally the compressed preprocessing functionality and the block (subfield) VOLE functionality.

The compressed preprocessing functionality *compresses* B's wire labels belonging to AND gates in $\mathbf{b}$ to a much shorter vector $\widetilde{b}$ of length

$$L := \frac{\rho \log n - \rho \log \rho}{\log 2} + 2\rho.$$

Write $\mathbf{b}_{\mathcal{I}}$ for input wires, and $\mathbf{b}'$ for AND gate wires. Then the vector $\mathbf{b}$ is determined from $\mathbf{b}_{\mathcal{I}} \cup \mathbf{b}'$ in the obvious way, and $\mathbf{b}'$ is determined from $\widetilde{b}$ by some public linear transformation M_H. Similarly B's wire masks $\mathbf{d}'$ are computed as $M_H \widetilde{d}$, where $\widetilde{d} \in \mathbb{F}_{2^\kappa}^L$ (Fig. 6).

Functionality $\mathcal{F}_{\mathsf{cp}}^{(C,\rho)}$: Compressed pre-processing of wire labels for authenticated garbling.

Parametrized by the value ρ, and a circuit C consisting of $\mathcal{W}$ wires, $\mathcal{I}$ input wires, $\mathcal{O}$ output wires, and gates $\mathcal{G}$ of the form (i, j, k, T), for $T \in \{\wedge, \oplus\}$, $i, j \in \mathcal{I} \cup \mathcal{W}$, and $k \in \mathcal{W} \cup \mathcal{O}$. Let n be the number of AND gates. Where clear from context, we omit the parameters C, ρ, κ and write $\mathcal{F}_{\mathsf{cp}}$ for $\mathcal{F}_{\mathsf{cp}}^{(C,\rho,\kappa)}$.

- All parties compute
$$L = \frac{\rho \log n - \rho \log \rho}{\log 2} + 2\rho.$$
- A chooses $\alpha \in \mathbb{F}_{2^\rho}$ and wire labels $\mathbf{a} \in \mathbb{F}_2^n$, $\mathbf{c} \in \mathbb{F}_{2^\rho}^n$ and sends them to $\mathcal{F}_{\mathsf{cp}}$.
- B chooses $\beta \in \mathbb{F}_{2^\rho}$ and wire labels $\mathbf{b}_{\mathcal{I}} \in \mathbb{F}^{|\mathcal{I}|}, \widetilde{b} \in \mathbb{F}_2^L$, $\mathbf{d}_{\mathcal{I}} \in \mathbb{F}_{2^\rho}^{|\mathcal{I}|}, \widetilde{d} \in \mathbb{F}_{2^\rho}^L$ and sends them to $\mathcal{F}_{\mathsf{cp}}$.
- $\mathcal{F}_{\mathsf{cp}}$ chooses a random $n \times L$ matrix M_H over $\mathbb{F}_2$ and sends M_H to A and B.
- $\mathcal{F}_{\mathsf{cp}}$ computes the vectors $\mathbf{b}', \mathbf{d}'$ via $\mathbf{b}, = M_H \widetilde{b}$ and $\mathbf{d}' = M_H \widetilde{d}$, and computes $\mathbf{b}, \mathbf{d}$ from $\mathbf{b}', \mathbf{d}'$.
- As a sub-protocol, $\mathcal{F}_{\mathsf{cp}}$ runs a simulation of the interaction of A, B, and $\mathcal{F}_{\mathsf{pre}}^{(C,\rho,\kappa)}$ using $\alpha, \beta, \mathbf{a}, \mathbf{b}, \mathbf{c}, \mathbf{d}$ as the various parties' inputs, and stores the output.
- $\mathcal{F}_{\mathsf{cp}}$ sends $(\mathbf{v}, \hat{\mathbf{v}}, \hat{\mathbf{b}}, \hat{\mathbf{d}})$ to B and $(\mathbf{w}, \hat{\mathbf{a}}, \hat{\mathbf{c}})$ to A.
- A sends either Honest or $(\mathsf{Cheat}, \mathbf{m}^*)$ to $\mathcal{F}_{\mathsf{cp}}$.
- If A sent Honest, then $\mathcal{F}_{\mathsf{cp}}$ sends $(\hat{\mathbf{w}})$ to A.
- If A sent $(\mathsf{Cheat}, \mathbf{m}^*)$, then $\mathcal{F}_{\mathsf{cp}}$ sends $(\hat{\mathbf{w}} + \mathbf{m}^* \beta^{-1})$ to A.

Fig. 6. Compressed authenticated wire labels

The other change made in this pre-processing functionality is that we allow party A to cheat in such a way that is not immediately detected, but corrupts its own output. Specifically, if A sends faulty messages, A can ensure both parties hold shares of $\hat{b}_i \alpha + m^* \beta^{-1}$, rather than $\hat{b}_i \alpha$. Since A does not know β, A cannot use these corrupted shares, and B will discover the error and abort during the execution of the authenticated garbling, as we show in Sect. 5.3.

Functionality $\mathcal{F}_{\mathsf{bVOLE}}^{(F,E,k,n)}$: Block VOLE

Parametrized by a pair of fields $F \subseteq E$ and integers k and n. In this paper, we have $F \in \{\mathbb{F}_2, \mathbb{F}_{2^\rho}\}$ and $E = \mathbb{F}_{2^\rho}$. We refer colloquially to the first variant as block subfield VOLE and the second as block VOLE.

- B chooses parameters $\beta_1, \ldots, \beta_k \in E$ and sends them to $\mathcal{F}_{\mathsf{bVOLE}}$.
- $\mathcal{F}_{\mathsf{bVOLE}}$ chooses a collection of vectors $\mathbf{b}_1, \ldots, \mathbf{b}_k \in E^n$ and sends the vectors to A.
- A chooses a vector $\mathbf{a} \in F^n$ and sends $\mathbf{a}$ to $\mathcal{F}_{\mathsf{bVOLE}}$.
- For $i = 1, \ldots, k$, the functionality $\mathcal{F}_{\mathsf{bVOLE}}$ computes $\mathbf{v}_i = \mathbf{a}\beta_i + \mathbf{b}_i$ and sends the result to B.

Fig. 7. Block subfield VOLE

5.2 From Block VOLE to Compressed Authenticated Wire Labels

We realize this preprocessing functionality using block VOLE, a collection of VOLE or subfield VOLE instances where one party A uses the same inputs across the VOLE calls. We define this protocol formally in Fig. 7, and give the converter from block VOLE to $\mathcal{F}_{\mathsf{cp}}$ in Fig. 8. We note that, in Step 12, if $\overline{a}$ is one of A's input to a block VOLE, and $\overline{b} + \gamma$ and γ are two of B's inputs to that block VOLE, then A and B can produce shares of the value $\overline{a}\overline{b}$ by subtracting their respective shares of $\overline{a}(\overline{b} + \gamma)$ and $\overline{a}\gamma$. All monomial terms in Step 12 can be shared in this fashion. We defer the proof of the following lemma to the full version of this paper [12].

Lemma 4. *The protocol in Fig. 8 can securely compute $\mathcal{F}_{\mathsf{cp}}^{(C,\rho,\rho)}$ against malicious adversaries in the $\mathcal{F}_{\mathsf{bVOLE}} - \mathcal{F}_{\mathsf{VOLE}} - \mathcal{F}_{\mathsf{subVOLE}}$ model with $1 + O(\frac{L}{n})$ bits of communication per gate from B to A and $5\rho + 1$ bits of communication per gate from A to B.*

To convert from $\mathcal{F}_{\mathsf{cp}}^{(C,\rho,\rho)}$ to $\mathcal{F}_{\mathsf{cp}}^{(C,\rho,\kappa)}$, we used almost the identical protocol to that used to convert from $\mathcal{F}_{\mathsf{pre}(\rho)}$ to $\mathcal{F}_{\mathsf{pre}(\kappa)}$.

Lemma 5. *The protocol in Fig. 4 realizes $\mathcal{F}_{\mathsf{cp}}^{(C,\rho,\kappa)}$ in the $\mathcal{F}_{\mathsf{cp}}^{(C,\rho,\rho)} - \mathcal{F}_{\mathsf{subVOLE}}$-hybrid model, replacing $\mathcal{F}_{\mathsf{pre}}^{(C,\rho,\rho)}$ with $\mathcal{F}_{\mathsf{cp}}^{(C,\rho,\rho)}$ in Step 1.*

Proof. The argument is identical to the argument in Lemma 2. We need only note that the messages $\mathbf{m}_1, \mathbf{m}_2$ are still uniformly random in A's view, in spite of the linear relations on $\mathbf{b}$ allowed by $\mathcal{F}_{\mathsf{cp}}$, because of the masks $\mathbf{b}', \hat{\mathbf{b}}'$.

5.3 Authenticated Garbling

In Fig. 9, we give our modified authenticated garbled circuit protocol. The wire labels are computed as in [15], but in the authentication step we apply the half

Protocol $\mathbf{\Pi}_{\mathsf{cp}}(C, \rho)$: Compressed pre-processing of wire labels for authenticated garbling.

Parametrized by the value ρ, and a circuit C consisting of $\mathcal{W}$ wires, $\mathcal{I}$ input wires, $\mathcal{O}$ output wires, and gates $\mathcal{G}$ of the form (i, j, k, T), for $T \in \{\wedge, \oplus\}$, $i, j \in \mathcal{I} \cup \mathcal{W}$, and $k \in \mathcal{W} \cup \mathcal{O}$. Let n be the number of AND gates.

1. All parties compute
$$L = \frac{\rho \log n - \rho \log \rho}{\log 2} + 2\rho$$
and choose a public $n \times L$ matrix M_H over $\mathbb{F}_2$.
2. A and B invoke $\mathcal{F}_{\mathsf{subVOLE}}$ with B as sender and A as receiver, so that B learns $(\widetilde{b}, \widetilde{d})$ and A holds $\widetilde{w}$, with length of the VOLE equal to L.
3. The parties extend the VOLE by length n, with additional entries $(w_{i,j}, b_{i,j}, d_{i,j})$ where $b_{i,j}$ is the (i,j)-th entry of $(M_H\widetilde{b})^T \cdot (M_H\widetilde{b})$.
4. Party A locally computes $w = M_H\widetilde{w}$.
5. B constructs the vector $\overline{\mathbf{b}} = \widetilde{b}_i\beta + \gamma, \beta + \gamma, \gamma$ with $\gamma \in \mathbb{F}_{2^\rho}$ chosen randomly.
6. Party A constructs the vector $\overline{\mathbf{a}} := \mathbf{a} \cup (a_i a_j) \cup (\hat{a}_i)$. The first vector is A's input to $\mathcal{F}_{\mathsf{cp}}$, the second vector is the the values $a_i \wedge a_j$, for every multiplication gate $\mathcal{G}_k = (\wedge, i, j)$, and the third vector is a string of random bits which will be part of A's output.
7. The parties call $\mathsf{Extend}(\mathcal{F}_{\mathsf{subVOLE}})$, adding $\overline{\mathbf{b}}$ as an additional $L + 2$ entries.
8. A and B perform $\mathcal{F}_{\mathsf{bVOLE}}^{(\mathbb{F}_{2^\rho}, \mathbb{F}_2, L+2, n)}$, the subfield variant of block VOLE, with B's inputs the vector $\overline{\mathbf{b}}$ and A's inputs the vector $\overline{\mathbf{a}}$.
9. A and B invoke $\mathcal{F}_{\mathsf{bVOLE}}^{(\mathbb{F}_{2^\rho}, \mathbb{F}_{2^\rho}, L+2, n)}$. B's input to the block VOLE is again the vector $\overline{\mathbf{b}}$ with γ as above, and A's input is the vector $\alpha \cdot \overline{\mathbf{a}} \cup (\hat{a}_{i,2}) \cup \{\alpha\}$, that is, A's input above multiplied by α, along with a vector of masks $\hat{a}_{i,2} \in \mathbb{F}_{2^\rho}$ and the additional input α.
10. Both parties call $\mathbf{\Pi}_{\mathsf{LPZK}}$ to prove correctness of the values $a_i \wedge a_j$, $b_{i,j}$, and $\widetilde{b}_i\beta$ under LPZK.
11. B certifies that their inputs to the block VOLE match their inputs to the VOLE with A as receiver, with the $\mathbf{\Pi}_{\mathsf{cert}}^{\mathsf{VOLE} \wedge \mathsf{ELOV}}$ protocol discussed in §3.2.
12. B locally computes:
$$\hat{v}_i := \hat{a}_i\beta + \hat{c}_i$$
$$v_{i,2} := \hat{a}_{i,2}\beta + c_{i,2}$$
$$v_{i,3} := \hat{a}_i\alpha\beta + c_{i,3}$$
$$v_{i,4} := (a_i a_j + a_i b_j + a_j b_i)\beta + c_{i,4}$$
$$v_{i,5} := (a_i a_j + a_i b_j + a_j b_i)\alpha\beta + c_{i,5}$$
where all terms $\hat{c}_i, c_{i,j}$ can be computed locally by A.
13. A sends to B the terms $(m_{i,1}, m_{i,2}) := (\hat{c}_i + c_{i,4}, c_{i,2} + c_{i,3} + c_{i,5})$, and B defines
$$\hat{b}_i := (\hat{v}_i + v_{i,4} + m_{i,1})\beta^{-1} + b_i b_j$$
and
$$\hat{d}_i := (v_{i,2} + v_{i,3} + v_{i,5} + m_{i,2})\beta^{-1} + d_{i,j},$$
respectively.
14. A adds locally to hold $\hat{w}_i := \hat{a}_{i,2} + w_{i,j}$.

Fig. 8. Compressed authenticated wire labels from block VOLE

gate technique of Zahur et al. [25] to the secondary garbled circuit approach of [21]. We also replace $\mathcal{F}_{\mathsf{pre}}$ with $\mathcal{F}_{\mathsf{cp}}$, and modify Steps 3 and 4 by setting unneeded wire masks to 0 as in Sect. 4.3.

Lemma 6. *The protocol given in Fig. 9 securely computes a functionality f against malicious adversaries in the RO-$\mathcal{F}_{\mathsf{cp}}^{(C,\rho,\kappa)} - \mathcal{F}_{\mathsf{subVOLE}} - \mathcal{F}_{\mathsf{VOLE}}$-hybrid model, with $2\kappa + 3\rho$ bits of communication per AND gate, $\kappa + 1$ bits of communication per input gate, and 1 bit of communication per output gate.*

The key difficulty is protecting against a selective failure attack by A. Learning whether or not B aborts is equivalent to corrupting some subset of t table entries (by corrupting the messages $G_{i,j}$ or $G'_{i,j}$), and learning whether B opened *any* of those table entries during circuit evaluation. If the t table entries chosen correspond to rows of M_H that are linearly independent, then the labels $M_H\widetilde{b}$ are independent, and the probability of failure is $1 - 2^{-t}$.

We therefore give a simulator that aborts with probability $1-2^{-t}$, and restrict our attention to the case where the t entries correspond to linearly dependent rows of M_H. To treat this case, we recall the notion of (t, k)-independent sets (the concept was first introduced in [13], see [20] for a thorough treatment, and [8,9] for additional discussion). A (t, k)-independent set over $\mathbb{F}_q$ is a subset of $\mathbb{F}_q^k$ such that no $t + 1$ element subset is linearly dependent. For our purposes, it is sufficient to construct a $(\rho - 1, L)$-independent set $\mathbb{B} \subseteq \mathbb{F}_2^L$ such that $|\mathbb{B}| = n$ via a randomized algorithm. Then either the simulator gives the correct abort probability or the protocol aborts almost surely, with probability at least $1-2^{-\rho}$, and either way party A learns nothing. We give the full proof in the full version of this paper [12].

Proof of Theorem 2. We begin with $\mathcal{F}_{\mathsf{bVOLE}}$. We use Lemma 4 to construct $\mathcal{F}_{\mathsf{cp}}^{(C,\rho,\rho)}$, Lemma 5 to construct $\mathcal{F}_{\mathsf{cp}}^{(C,\rho,\kappa)}$ and prove the correctness of $\mathbf{\Pi}_{\mathsf{2pc}}^{\mathsf{VOLE}}$ in Lemma 6.

6 NISC from Garbled Circuits

6.1 Conditional Disclosure of Secrets from Programmable OLE

We construct a NISC protocol with A as sender and B as receiver. We generate our authenticated bits and the related conversion protocol to authenticated circuit wire labels using the programmable OLE functionality given in Fig. 10. This protocol allows us to the piece-wise product of any pair of vectors selected from a collection of p vectors from A and q vectors from B.

Two obstacles present themselves in the conversion from programmable OLE to authenticated circuit wire labels. First, we can no longer use $\mathbf{\Pi}_{\mathsf{LPZK}}$ to certify B's inputs, since this would violate non-interactivity. Instead, we use a specialized conditional disclosure of secrets (CDS) protocol that ensures that any future messages from A will be uniformly random if B cheats. The second obstacle is

Protocol $\mathbf{\Pi}_{\mathsf{2pc}}^{\mathsf{VOLE}}$

Inputs: Party A holds $x \in \{0,1\}^{|\mathcal{I}_1|}$ and B holds $y \in \{0,1\}^{|\mathcal{I}_2|}$. Both parties hold a circuit C for a function $f : \{0,1\}^{|\mathcal{I}_1|+|\mathcal{I}_2|} \to \{0,1\}^{|\mathcal{O}|}$.

1. A and B call $\mathcal{F}_{\mathsf{cp}}^{(C,\rho,\rho)}$ and then the compiler from $\mathcal{F}_{\mathsf{cp}}^{(C,\rho,\rho)}$ to $\mathcal{F}_{\mathsf{cp}}^{(C,\rho,\kappa)}$, so that A holds $\Delta_A, \mathbf{w}, \hat{\mathbf{w}}, \mathbf{a}, \hat{\mathbf{a}}, \mathbf{c}, \hat{\mathbf{c}}$ and B holds $\beta, , \mathbf{v}, \hat{\mathbf{v}}, \mathbf{b}, \hat{\mathbf{b}}, \mathbf{d}, \hat{\mathbf{d}}$. For each $i \in \mathcal{I}_1 \cup \mathcal{I}_2$, A also picks a uniform κ-bit string $L_{i,0}$. The parties jointly determine keys to hash functions $H : \mathbb{F}_{2^\kappa} \times \{1,\dots,n\} \to \mathbb{F}_{2^\kappa}$ and $H' : \mathbb{F}_{2^\kappa} \times \{1,\dots,n\} \to \mathbb{F}_{2^\rho}$.
2. Following the topological order of the circuit, for each gate $G = (i,j,k,T)$,
   - If $T = \oplus$, A computes $L_{k,0} := L_{i,0} \oplus L_{j,0}$
   - If $T = \wedge$, A computes $L_{i,1} := L_{i,0} \oplus \Delta_A$, $L_{j,1} := L_{j,0} \oplus \Delta_A$, and
     - $G_{k,0} := H(L_{i,0},k) \oplus H(L_{i,1},k) \oplus w_j \oplus a_j\Delta_A$
     - $G_{k,1} := H(L_{j,0},k) \oplus H(L_{j,1},k) \oplus w_i \oplus a_i\Delta_A \oplus L_{i,0}$
     - $L_{k,0} := H(L_{i,0},k) \oplus H(L_{j,0},k) \oplus (w_k \oplus \hat{w}_k) \oplus (a_k \oplus \hat{a}_k) \cdot \Delta_A$
     - $G'_{k,0} := H'(L_{i,0},k) \oplus H'(L_{j,0},k) \oplus c_k \oplus \hat{c}_k$
     - $G'_{k,1} := H'(L_{i,0},k) \oplus H'(L_{i,1},k) \oplus c_j$
     - $G'_{k,2} := H'(L_{j,0},k) \oplus H'(L_{j,1},k) \oplus c_i$

   A sends $G_{k,0}, G_{k,1}, G'_{k,0}, G'_{k,1}, G'_{k,2}$ to B.
3. For each $i \in \mathcal{I}_B$, B sends $y_i \oplus b_i$ to A. Then A sends $L_{i,y_i\oplus \mathsf{b}_i}$ to B.
4. For each $i \in \mathcal{I}_A$, A sends $x_i \oplus a_i$ and $L_{i,x_i\oplus a_i}$ to B.
5. B evaluates the circuit in topological order. For each gate $G = (i,j,k,T)$, B initially holds $(z_i \oplus \lambda_i, L_{i,z_i\oplus\lambda_i})$ and $(z_j \oplus \lambda_j, L_{j,z_j\oplus\lambda_j})$, where z_i, z_j are the underlying values of the wires.
   (a) If $T = \oplus$, B computes $z_k \oplus \lambda_k := (z_i \oplus \lambda_i) \oplus (z_j \oplus \lambda_j)$ and $L_{k,z_k\oplus\lambda_k} := L_{i,z_i\oplus\lambda_i} \oplus L_{j,z_j\oplus\lambda_j}$.
   (b) If $T = \wedge$, B computes $G_0 := G_{k,0} \oplus d_j$, $G_1 := G_{k,1} \oplus d_i$, and evaluates the garbled table (G_0, G_1) to obtain the output label

   $$\begin{aligned} L_{k,z_k\oplus\lambda_k} := & H\left((L_{i,z_i\oplus\lambda_i}),k\right) \oplus H\left((L_{j,z_j\oplus\lambda_j},k\right) \oplus (d_k \oplus \hat{d}_k) \\ & \oplus (z_i \oplus \lambda_i)G_0 \oplus (z_j \oplus \lambda_j)(G_1 \oplus L_{i,z_i\oplus\lambda_i}). \end{aligned}$$

   Then B computes

   $$\begin{aligned} & b_k \oplus \hat{b}_k \oplus (z_i \oplus \lambda_i)b_j \oplus (z_j \oplus \lambda_j)b_i \oplus (z_i \oplus \lambda_i) \wedge (z_j \oplus \lambda_j) \\ & \oplus \left((v_k \oplus \hat{v}_k \oplus (z_i \oplus \lambda_i)v_j \oplus (z_j \oplus \lambda_j)v_i\right)\beta^{-1} \\ & \oplus \left(H'(L_{i,z_{i\oplus\lambda_i}}) \oplus H'(L_{j,z_{j\oplus\lambda_j}}) \oplus G'_{k,0} \oplus (z_i \oplus \lambda_i)G'_{k,1} \oplus (z_j \oplus \lambda_j)G'_{k,2}\right)\beta^{-1} \\ & = \lambda_k \oplus \hat{\lambda}_k \oplus (z_i \oplus \lambda_i)\lambda_j \oplus (z_j \oplus \lambda_j)\lambda_i \oplus (z_i \oplus \lambda_i) \wedge (z_j \oplus \lambda_j) \\ & = \lambda_k \oplus z_k \end{aligned}$$

6. For each $i \in \mathcal{O}$, A sends a_i to B and calls $\mathbf{\Pi}_{\mathsf{LPZK}}$ to prove these values are correct. B computes $z_i := (\lambda_i \oplus z_i) \oplus a_i \oplus b_i$.

Fig. 9. Authenticated garbling protocol in the $\mathcal{F}_{\mathsf{cp}}$ hybrid model

Functionality $\mathcal{F}_{\mathsf{OLE}}^{(n,\kappa,p,q,Q)}$: Programmable OLE over a field $\mathbb{F}_{2^\kappa}$ and relations Q.

Parametrized by integers $n, p, q, \kappa \in \mathbb{N}$ and a set of relations $Q \subseteq \{1, \ldots, p\} \times \{1, \ldots, q\}$, i.e. elements $q \in Q$ are ordered pairs of integers.

- A chooses a collection of vectors $\mathbf{a}^1, \ldots, \mathbf{a}^p$ of length n and sends them to $\mathcal{F}_{\mathsf{OLE}}^{(n,\kappa,p,q,Q)}$.
- B chooses a collection of vectors $\mathbf{b}^1, \ldots, \mathbf{b}^q$ of length n and sends them to $\mathcal{F}_{\mathsf{OLE}}^{(n,\kappa,p,q,Q)}$.
- For each entry $q = (i, j) \in Q$, $\mathcal{F}_{\mathsf{OLE}}^{(n,\kappa,p,q,Q)}$ chooses vectors $\mathbf{v}^q$, $\mathbf{c}^q$ with $\mathbf{v}^q + \mathbf{c}^q = \mathbf{a}^i \cdot \mathbf{b}^j$.
- $\mathcal{F}_{\mathsf{OLE}}^{(n,\kappa,Q)}$ sends $\mathbf{v}^q$ to A and $\mathbf{c}^q$ to B, for all $q \in Q$.

Fig. 10. Programmable OLE

related to the task of minimizing p and q so that the protocol is concretely efficient, and we cover it in Sect. 6.2.

For CDS, informally, B sends a message to A that allows A to learn a secret value $\mathbf{s}_{\mathbf{B}}$ known to B if and only if B's message satisfies a desired set of relations. Otherwise, A will compute a guess $\mathbf{s}_A$, which on at least one entry will appear random to B. Then A appends $H(\mathbf{s}_A)$ to all future messages to B, so that B can recover the underlying message if and only if $\mathbf{s}_A = \mathbf{s}_B$. We give a formal definition of this functionality in Fig. 11.

We give a protocol realizing this functionality in Fig. 12, and prove its correctness in the full version of this paper [12]. Our protocol works by first proving that A and B each have one input vector that is constant, and using that to realize instances of subfield VOLE over A's input α and each of B's input vectors $\mathbf{b}^i$. Write $Q' := Q \cup \{(p+1, j)\} \cup \{(i, q+1)\}$, for $1 \leq j \leq q+1$ and $1 \leq i \leq p$, and $Q'' := Q' \cup \{(p+1, j\}$ for $j = q+2, q+3, q+4$.

It is possible to move Step 6 to Step 2, making the protocol non-interactive, since the values $\hat{c}_i^{(j,k)}$ used in Step 6 can be computed locally by B from the output of the random $\mathcal{F}_{\mathsf{OLE}}$ functionality and B's inputs. Step 6 is separated from Step 2 because the most complicated part of the protocol is in Steps 6 and 7, which are used to verify the relations in $\mathcal{R}_2$. Removing Steps 6 and 7 and using Q' instead of Q'' gives a warm-up CDS protocol for certifying the relations in $\mathcal{R}_1$ only.

Lemma 7. *The protocol in Fig. 12 realizes the functionality* $\mathcal{F}_{\mathsf{CDS}}^{(n,\kappa,p,q,Q,\mathcal{R})}$ *non-interactively in the RO-*$\mathcal{F}_{\mathsf{OLE}}^{(n,\kappa,p+1,q+4,Q'',\mathcal{R})}$*-hybrid model.*

Functionality $\mathcal{F}_{\mathsf{CDS}}^{(n,\kappa,p,q,Q,\mathcal{R})}$: CDS for $\mathcal{F}_{\mathsf{OLE}}^{(n,\kappa,p,q,Q)}$ over a field $\mathbb{F}_{2^\kappa}$ and relations $\mathcal{R}$.

Parametrized by integers $n, \kappa, p, q, \in \mathbb{N}$, a set of relations $Q \subseteq \{1,\ldots,p\} \times \{1,\ldots,q\}$ as above, and a set of relations $\mathcal{R} = \mathcal{R}_1 \cup \mathcal{R}_2$, where $\mathcal{R}_1$ is a collection of equality constraints $b_i^j = b_k^\ell$, and $\mathcal{R}_2$ is a collection of quadratic relations of the form $b_i^1 \cdot b_j^1 = b_k^1$. Additionally, let $\mathbf{m}$ be a message that A plans to send to B.

- A and B interact with $\mathcal{F}_{\mathsf{CDS}}$ playing the role of $\mathcal{F}_{\mathsf{OLE}}$ on B's input vectors $\mathbf{b}^i \in \mathbb{F}_2^n$ for $1 \leq i \leq q$ and A's input vectors $\mathbf{a}^i, \mathbf{v}^q \in \mathbb{F}_{2^\kappa}^n$ for $1 \leq i \leq p$ and $q \in Q$.
- If the vectors $\mathbf{b}^i$ satisfies the relations in $\mathcal{R}$, $\mathcal{F}_{\mathsf{CDS}}$ sends $\mathbf{m}$ to B.
- If any of the vectors $\mathbf{b}^i$ do not satisfy the relations in $\mathcal{R}$, $\mathcal{F}_{\mathsf{CDS}}$ sends a random vector to B.

Fig. 11. Programmable OLE with conditional disclosure of secrets

6.2 Non-interactive Authenticated Circuit Wires and Authenticated Garbling

The remainder of the construction is similar to the construction given in Sect. 5. We give a brief overview here, and a more detailed description in the appendices. As discussed in Sect. 1.1, the randomness computation time and the seed size grow with the number of piece-wise products required, i.e. with $|Q|$ using the notation in the functionality description. In order to minimize the numbers p, q required, we construct for A three vectors of inputs: $\mathbf{a}, \mathbf{a}^L, \mathbf{a}^R$, where $\mathbf{a}$, chosen randomly, represents authenticated bits for all wires, $\mathbf{a}^L$ represents only bit labels for wires used as labels for left inputs to multiplication gates, so that a_k^L is the left input to the kth multiplication gate, and $\mathbf{a}^R$ likewise represents only bit labels for wires used as labels for right inputs to multiplication gates. We similarly define $\mathbf{b}, \mathbf{b}^L, \mathbf{b}^R$. The full construction of the preprocessing functionality is similar to the protocol $\mathbf{\Pi}_{\mathsf{cp}}$. We give this protocol and a proof of its correctness in the full version of this paper [12].

The authenticated garbling functionality is also similar to the protocol $\mathbf{\Pi}_{\mathsf{2pc}}^{\mathsf{VOLE}}$ used in the VOLE-only case, replacing $\mathcal{F}_{\mathsf{cp}}$ with the NISC preprocessing functionality. Besides the first step of generating the preprocessing functionality, which is non-interactive by construction, the only message from B to A is given in Step 3, when B sends bit masks of its input values $y_i \oplus b_i$. This communication can be moved to Step 1 with no loss of security, making the entire protocol non-interactive, which we prove in the full version of this paper [12].

Protocol Π_{CDS}: Conditional disclosure of secrets over programmable OLE.

Parametrized by integers $n, \kappa, p, q, \in \mathbb{N}$, a set of relations $Q \subseteq \{1, \ldots, p\} \times \{1, \ldots, q\}$ as above, and a set of relations $\mathcal{R} = \mathcal{R}_1 \cup \mathcal{R}_2$ as above. Additionally, let $\mathbf{m}$ be a message that A plans to send to B.

1. A and B choose random values $\alpha, \beta \in \mathbb{F}_{2^\kappa}$ and define the vectors $\boldsymbol{\alpha} := (\alpha, \ldots, \alpha)$ and $\boldsymbol{\beta} := (\beta, \ldots, \beta)$.
2. A and B invoke $\mathcal{F}_{\mathsf{OLE}}^{(n,\kappa,p+1,q+1,Q')}$ with the additional inputs $\mathbf{a}^{p+1} := \boldsymbol{\alpha}$, $\mathbf{b}^{q+1} := \boldsymbol{\beta}$. Let $(\mathbf{m}_A^i)$ be the messages that A sends during the random-to-fixed OLE compiler, and let $\hat{\mathbf{c}}_i^{(j,k)}$ be the vectors held by B before receiving $(\mathbf{m}_A^i)$.
3. A computes $\mathbf{s}_A^1 := (v_1^{(p+1,q+1)} - v_2^{(p+1,q+1)}, \ldots, v_1^{(p+1,q+1)} - v_n^{(p+1,q+1)})$.
4. B computes $\mathbf{s}_B^1 := (c_1^{(p+1,q+1)} - c_2^{(p+1,q+1)}, \ldots, c_1^{(p+1,q+1)} - c_n^{(p+1,q+1)})$.
5. For each relation $b_i^j = b_k^\ell \in \mathcal{R}_1$, A appends $v_i^{(p+1,j)} - v_k^{(p+1,\ell)}$ to $\mathbf{s}_A^2$ and B appends $c_i^{(p+1,j)} - c_k^{(p+1,\ell)}$ to $\mathbf{s}_B^2$
6. B constructs three additional vectors, each of length equal to $|\mathcal{R}_2|$, with $\mathbf{b}^{q+2} = (b_i^1 \hat{c}_j^{(p+1,1)} + (b_j^1 \hat{c}_i^{(p+1,1)})$, $\mathbf{b}^{q+3} = (b_i^1 b_j^1)$, and $\mathbf{b}^{q+4} = \hat{c}_k^{(p+1,1)}$ for triples $(i, j, k) \in \mathcal{R}_2$, and both parties call $\mathsf{Extend}(\mathcal{F}_{\mathsf{OLE}})$,so that A and B now hold $\mathcal{F}_{\mathsf{OLE}}^{(n,\kappa,p+1,q+4,Q'')}$.
7. For each relation $b_i^1 \cdot b_j^1 = b_k^1 \in \mathcal{R}_2$, let r be the index of this relation in $\mathcal{R}_2$. A appends $v_i^{(p+1,1)} \cdot v_j^{(p+1,1)} - \alpha v_k^{(p+1,1)} - v_r^{(p+1,q+2)} - (v_r^{(p+1,q+3)}) \cdot (m_{A,i}^1 + m_{A,j}^1) - (v_r^{(p+1,q+4)}) m_{A,k}^1$ to $\mathbf{s}_A^3$, and B appends $c_i^{(p+1,1)} \cdot c_j^{(p+1,1)} - (c_r^{(p+1,q+3)}) \cdot (m_{A,i}^1 + m_{A,j}^1) - (c_r^{(p+1,q+4)}) m_{A,k}^1$ to $\mathbf{s}_B^3$.
8. Each party P computes $\mathbf{s}_P := \cup_i \mathbf{s}_P^i$.
9. A sends $\mathbf{m}_1 := \mathbf{m} + H(\mathbf{s}_A)$ to B.
10. B computes $\mathbf{m}_2 := \mathbf{m}_1 + H(\mathbf{s}_B)$ and outputs $\mathbf{m}_2$.

Fig. 12. Conditional disclosure of secrets

Acknowledgements. Supported in part by DARPA Contract No. HR001120C0087. Any opinions, findings and conclusions or recommendations expressed in this material are those of the author(s) and do not necessarily reflect the views of DARPA. Y. Ishai supported in part by ERC Project NTSC (742754), BSF grant 2018393, and ISF grant 2774/20.

References

1. Afshar, A., Mohassel, P., Pinkas, B., Riva, B.: Non-interactive secure computation based on cut-and-choose. In: Nguyen, P.Q., Oswald, E. (eds.) EUROCRYPT 2014. LNCS, vol. 8441, pp. 387–404. Springer, Heidelberg (2014). https://doi.org/10.1007/978-3-642-55220-5_22
2. Beaver, D.: Efficient multiparty protocols using circuit randomization. In: Feigenbaum, J. (ed.) CRYPTO 1991. LNCS, vol. 576, pp. 420–432. Springer, Heidelberg (1992). https://doi.org/10.1007/3-540-46766-1_34

3. Boyle, E., Couteau, G., Gilboa, N., Ishai, Y.: Compressing vector OLE. In: CCS 2018, pp. 896–912 (2018)
4. Boyle, E., et al.: Efficient two-round OT extension and silent non-interactive secure computation. In: CCS 2019, pp. 291–308 (2019)
5. Boyle, E., Couteau, G., Gilboa, N., Ishai, Y., Kohl, L., Scholl, P.: Efficient pseudorandom correlation generators: silent OT extension and more. In: Boldyreva, A., Micciancio, D. (eds.) CRYPTO 2019, Part III. LNCS, vol. 11694, pp. 489–518. Springer, Cham (2019). https://doi.org/10.1007/978-3-030-26954-8_16
6. Boyle, E., Couteau, G., Gilboa, N., Ishai, Y., Kohl, L., Scholl, P.: Efficient pseudorandom correlation generators from ring-LPN. In: Micciancio, D., Ristenpart, T. (eds.) CRYPTO 2020, Part II. LNCS, vol. 12171, pp. 387–416. Springer, Cham (2020). https://doi.org/10.1007/978-3-030-56880-1_14
7. Couteau, G., Rindal, P., Raghuraman, S.: Silver: silent VOLE and oblivious transfer from hardness of decoding structured LDPC codes. In: Malkin, T., Peikert, C. (eds.) CRYPTO 2021, Part III. LNCS, vol. 12827, pp. 502–534. Springer, Cham (2021). https://doi.org/10.1007/978-3-030-84252-9_17
8. Damelin, S.B., Michalski, G., Mullen, G.L.: The cardinality of sets of k-independent vectors over finite fields. Monatshefte für Mathematik **150**(4), 289–295 (2007)
9. Damelin, S.B., Michalski, G., Mullen, G.L., Stone, D.: The number of linearly independent binary vectors with applications to the construction of hypercubes and orthogonal arrays, pseudo (t, m, s)-nets and linear codes. Monatshefte für Mathematik **141**(4), 277–288 (2004)
10. Damgård, I., Pastro, V., Smart, N., Zakarias, S.: Multiparty computation from somewhat homomorphic encryption. In: Safavi-Naini, R., Canetti, R. (eds.) CRYPTO 2012. LNCS, vol. 7417, pp. 643–662. Springer, Heidelberg (2012). https://doi.org/10.1007/978-3-642-32009-5_38
11. Dittmer, S., Ishai, Y., Ostrovsky, R.: Line-point zero knowledge and its applications. In: ITC 2021 (2021). Full version: https://eprint.iacr.org/2020/1446
12. Dittmer, S., Ishai, Y., Lu, S., Ostrovsky, R.: Authenticated garbling from simple correlations. Cryptology ePrint Archive (2022)
13. Dodis, Y., Khanna, S.: Space-time tradeoffs for graph properties. In: Wiedermann, J., van Emde Boas, P., Nielsen, M. (eds.) ICALP 1999. LNCS, vol. 1644, pp. 291–300. Springer, Heidelberg (1999). https://doi.org/10.1007/3-540-48523-6_26
14. Ishai, Y., Kushilevitz, E., Ostrovsky, R., Prabhakaran, M., Sahai, A.: Efficient non-interactive secure computation. In: Paterson, K.G. (ed.) EUROCRYPT 2011. LNCS, vol. 6632, pp. 406–425. Springer, Heidelberg (2011). https://doi.org/10.1007/978-3-642-20465-4_23
15. Katz, J., Ranellucci, S., Rosulek, M., Wang, X.: Optimizing authenticated garbling for faster secure two-party computation. In: Shacham, H., Boldyreva, A. (eds.) CRYPTO 2018, Part III. LNCS, vol. 10993, pp. 365–391. Springer, Cham (2018). https://doi.org/10.1007/978-3-319-96878-0_13
16. Lindell, Y., Pinkas, B.: An efficient protocol for secure two-party computation in the presence of malicious adversaries. In: Naor, M. (ed.) EUROCRYPT 2007. LNCS, vol. 4515, pp. 52–78. Springer, Heidelberg (2007). https://doi.org/10.1007/978-3-540-72540-4_4
17. Mohassel, P., Franklin, M.: Efficiency tradeoffs for malicious two-party computation. In: Yung, M., Dodis, Y., Kiayias, A., Malkin, T. (eds.) PKC 2006. LNCS, vol. 3958, pp. 458–473. Springer, Heidelberg (2006). https://doi.org/10.1007/11745853_30

18. Rosulek, M., Roy, L.: Three halves make a whole? Beating the half-gates lower bound for garbled circuits. In: Malkin, T., Peikert, C. (eds.) CRYPTO 2021, Part I. LNCS, vol. 12825, pp. 94–124. Springer, Cham (2021). https://doi.org/10.1007/978-3-030-84242-0_5
19. Schoppmann, P., Gascón, A., Reichert, L., Raykova, M.: Distributed vector-OLE: improved constructions and implementation. In: CCS 2019, pp. 1055–1072 (2019)
20. Tassa, T., Villar, J.L.: On proper secrets, (t, k)-bases and linear codes. Designs Codes Cryptogr. **52**(2), 129–154 (2009)
21. Wang, X., Ranellucci, S., Katz, J.: Authenticated garbling and efficient maliciously secure two-party computation. In: CCS 2017, pp. 21–37 (2017)
22. Yang, K., Sarkar, P., Weng, C., Wang, X.: Quicksilver: efficient and affordable zero-knowledge proofs for circuits and polynomials over any field. In: CCS (2021). Full version: https://eprint.iacr.org/2021/076
23. Yang, K., Weng, C., Lan, X., Zhang, J., Wang, X.: Ferret: fast extension for correlated OT with small communication. In: CCS 2020, pp. 1607–1626 (2020)
24. Yao, A.C.-C.: How to generate and exchange secrets (extended abstract). In: FOCS, pp. 162–167 (1986)
25. Zahur, S., Rosulek, M., Evans, D.: Two halves make a whole. In: Oswald, E., Fischlin, M. (eds.) EUROCRYPT 2015, Part II. LNCS, vol. 9057, pp. 220–250. Springer, Heidelberg (2015). https://doi.org/10.1007/978-3-662-46803-6_8

Unique Topics

Dynamic Local Searchable Symmetric Encryption

Brice Minaud and Michael Reichle(✉)

DIENS, École normale supérieure, PSL University, CNRS, INRIA, 75005 Paris, France
michael.reichle@ens.fr

Abstract. In this article, we tackle for the first time the problem of *dynamic* memory-efficient Searchable Symmetric Encryption (SSE). In the term "memory-efficient" SSE, we encompass both the goals of *local* SSE, and *page-efficient* SSE. The centerpiece of our approach is a novel connection between those two goals. We introduce a map, called the Generic Local Transform, which takes as input a *page-efficient* SSE scheme with certain special features, and outputs an SSE scheme with strong *locality* properties. We obtain several results. (1) First, for page-efficient SSE with page size p, we build a *dynamic* scheme with storage efficiency $\mathcal{O}(1)$ and page efficiency $\widetilde{\mathcal{O}}(\log\log(N/p))$, called LayeredSSE. The main technical innovation behind LayeredSSE is a novel weighted extension of the two-choice allocation process, of independent interest. (2) Second, we introduce the Generic Local Transform, and combine it with LayeredSSE to build a *dynamic* SSE scheme with storage efficiency $\mathcal{O}(1)$, locality $\mathcal{O}(1)$, and read efficiency $\widetilde{\mathcal{O}}(\log\log N)$, under the condition that the longest list is of size $\mathcal{O}(N^{1-1/\log\log\lambda})$. This matches, in every respect, the purely *static* construction of Asharov et al. presented at STOC 2016: dynamism comes at no extra cost. (3) Finally, by applying the Generic Local Transform to a variant of the Tethys scheme by Bossuat et al. from Crypto 2021, we build an unconditional static SSE with storage efficiency $\mathcal{O}(1)$, locality $\mathcal{O}(1)$, and read efficiency $\mathcal{O}(\log^{\varepsilon} N)$, for an arbitrarily small constant $\varepsilon > 0$. To our knowledge, this is the construction that comes closest to the lower bound presented by Cash and Tessaro at Eurocrypt 2014.

1 Introduction

Searchable Symmetric Encryption. In Searchable Symmetric Encryption (SSE), a client outsources the storage of a set of documents to an untrusted server. The client wishes to retain the ability to search the documents, by issuing search queries to the server. In the setting of *dynamic* SSE, the client may also issue update queries, in order to modify the contents of the database, for instance by adding or removing entries. The server must be able to correctly process all queries, while learning as little information as possible about the client's data and queries. SSE is relevant in many cloud storage scenarios: for example, in cases such as outsourcing the storage of a sensitive database, or offering an encrypted messaging service, some form of search functionality may be highly desirable.

Y. Dodis and T. Shrimpton (Eds.): CRYPTO 2022, LNCS 13510, pp. 91–120, 2022.
https://doi.org/10.1007/978-3-031-15985-5_4

In theory, SSE is a special case of computation on encrypted data, and could be realized using generic solutions, such as Fully Homomorphic Encryption. In practice, such approaches incur a large performance penalty. Instead, SSE schemes typically aim for high-performance solutions, scalable to large real-world databases. Towards that end, SSE trades off security for efficiency. The server is allowed to learn some information about the client's data. For example, SSE schemes typically leak to the server the repetition of queries (*search pattern*), and the identifiers of the documents that match a query (*access pattern*). The security model of SSE is parametrized by a *leakage function*, which specifies the nature of the information leaked to the server.

Locality. In the case of single-keyword SSE, search queries ask for all documents that contain a given keyword. To realize that functionality, the server maintains an (encrypted) reverse index, where each keyword is mapped to the list of identifiers of documents that match the keyword. When the client wishes to search for the documents that match a given keyword, the client simply retrieves the corresponding list from the server. A subtle issue, however, is how the lists should be stored and accessed by the server.

The naive approach of storing one list after the other is unsatisfactory: indeed, the position of a given list in memory becomes dependent on the lengths of other lists, thereby leaking information about those lists. A common approach to address that issue is to store each list element at a random location in memory. In that case, when retrieving a list, the server must visit as many random memory locations as the number of elements in the list. This is also undesirable, for a different reason: for virtually all modern storage media, accessing many random memory locations is much more expensive than visiting one continuous region. Because SSE relies on fast symmetric cryptographic primitives, the cost of memory accesses becomes the performance bottleneck. To capture that cost, [CT14] introduces the notion of *locality*: in short, the locality of an SSE scheme is the number of discontinuous memory locations that the server must access to answer a query.

The two extreme solutions outlined above suggest a conflict between security and locality. At Eurocrypt 2014, Cash and Tessaro showed that this conflict is inherent [CT14]: if a secure SSE scheme has constant storage efficiency (the size of the encrypted database is linear in the size of the plaintext database), and constant read efficiency (the amount of data read by the server to answer a search query is linear in the size of the plaintext answer), then it cannot have constant locality.

Local SSE Constructions. Since then, many SSE schemes with constant locality have been proposed, typically at the cost of superconstant read efficiency. At STOC 2016, Asharov et al. presented a scheme with $\mathcal{O}(1)$ storage efficiency, $\mathcal{O}(1)$ locality, and $\widetilde{\mathcal{O}}(\log N)$ read efficiency, where N is the size of the database [ANSS16]. At Crypto 2018, Demertzis et al. improved the read efficiency to $\mathcal{O}(\log^{2/3+\varepsilon} N)$ [DPP18]. Several trade-offs with $\omega(1)$ storage efficiency were also proposed in [DP17]. When the size of the longest list in the database is bounded, stronger results are known. When such an upper bound is required, we will call the construction *conditional.* The first conditional SSE is due to Asharov et al., and achieves $\widetilde{\mathcal{O}}(\log\log N)$ read efficiency, on the condition that the size of the longest list is $\mathcal{O}(N^{1-1/\log\log N})$. This was later improved to $\widetilde{\mathcal{O}}(\log\log\log N)$ read efficiency, with a stronger condition of $\mathcal{O}(N^{1-1/\log\log\log N})$ on the size of the longest list.

Locality was introduced as a performance measure for memory accesses, assuming an implementation on Hard Disk Drives (HDDs). In [BBF+21], Bossuat et al. show that in the case of Solid State Drives (SSDs), such as flash disks, locality is no longer the relevant target. Instead, performance is mainly determined by the number of memory pages accessed, regardless of whether they are contiguous. In that setting the right performance metric is *page efficiency.* Page efficiency is defined as the number of pages read by the server to answer a query, divided by the number of pages needed to store the plaintext answer. The main construction of [BBF+21] achieves $\mathcal{O}(1)$ storage efficiency and $\mathcal{O}(1)$ page efficiency, assuming a client-side memory of $\omega(\log\lambda)$ pages.

To this day, a common point among all existing constructions, both local and page-efficient, is that they are purely *static*, as known techniques for sublogarithmic read efficiency and page efficiency do not apply to the dynamic setting. That may be because of the difficulty inherent in building local SSE, even in the static case (as evidenced, from the onset, by the impossibility result of Cash and Tessaro [CT14]). Nevertheless, many, if not most, applications of SSE require dynamism. This state of affairs significantly hinders the applicability of local and page-efficient SSE.

While one work [MM17] targets local SSE in a dynamic setting, and has constant storage efficiency and locality, it has read efficiency $\mathcal{O}(L\log W)$, where L is the maximum list size. Further, [MM17] employs an ORAM-variant which incurs a heavy computational overhead, in addition to the large read efficiency. When reinterpreting [MM17] in the context of page-efficiency, its guarantees improve to $\mathcal{O}(\log W)$ page efficiency and constant storage efficiency, but the heavy computational cost of ORAM remains.

1.1 Our Contributions

In this article, we consider the problem of dynamic memory-efficient SSE, by which we mean that we target both dynamic *page-efficient* SSE, and dynamic *local* SSE.

The centerpiece of our approach is a novel connection between these two goals. We introduce a map, called the Generic Local Transform, which takes as input a page-efficient SSE scheme with certain special features, and outputs a SSE scheme with strong locality properties. Our strategy will be to first build page-efficient schemes, then apply the Generic Local Transform to obtain local schemes. This approach turns out to be quite effective, and we present several results.

(1) **Dynamic page-efficient SSE.** We start by building a dynamic page-efficient SSE scheme, LayeredSSE. LayeredSSE achieves storage efficiency $\mathcal{O}(1)$, and

page efficiency $\widetilde{\mathcal{O}}\left(\log\log \frac{N}{p}\right)$, where p is the page size. In line with prior work on memory-efficient SSE, the technical core of LayeredSSE is a new dynamic allocation scheme, L2C. L2C is a weighted variant of the so-called "2-choice" algorithm, notorious in the resource allocation literature. L2C is of independent interest: the two-choice allocation process is ubiquitous in various areas of computer science, such as load balancing, hashing, job allocation, or circuit routing (a survey of applications may be found in [RMS01]). Weighted variants have been considered in the past, but have so far required a *distributional* assumption [TW07, TW14] or presorting [ANSS16]. What we show is that by slightly tweaking the two-choice process, a dynamic and distribution-free result can be obtained (Theorem 1). Such a distribution-free result is necessary for cryptographic applications, where the adversary may influence the weights (as in our case). Other uses beyond cryptography are discussed in the full version.

(2) **Generic Local Transform.** We introduce the Generic Local Transform. On input any page-efficient scheme PE-SSE with certain special features, called *page-length-hiding* SSE, the Generic Local Transform outputs a local SSE scheme Local[PE-SSE]. Roughly speaking, if PE-SSE has client storage $\mathcal{O}(1)$, storage efficiency $\mathcal{O}(1)$, and page efficiency $\mathcal{O}(P)$, then Local[PE-SSE] has storage efficiency $\mathcal{O}(1)$, and read efficiency $\mathcal{O}(P)$. Regarding locality, the key feature is that if PE-SSE has locality $\mathcal{O}(L)$ *when querying lists of size at most one page*, then Local[PE-SSE] has locality $\mathcal{O}(L + \log\log N)$ *when querying lists of any size*. Thus, the Local construction may be viewed as bootstrapping a scheme with weak locality properties into a scheme with much stronger locality properties.

The Generic Local Transform also highlights an interesting connection between the goals of page efficiency and locality. Originally, locality and page efficiency were introduced as distinct performance criterions, targeting the two most widespread storage media, HDDs and SSDs respectively. It was already observed in [BBF+21] that a scheme with locality L and read efficiency R must have page efficiency at most $R+2L$. In that sense, page efficiency is an "easier" goal. With the Generic Local Transform, surprisingly, we build a connection in the reverse direction: we use page-efficient schemes as building blocks to obtain local schemes. On a theoretical level, this shows a strong connection between the two goals. On a practical level, it provides a strategy to target both goals at once.

(3) **Dynamic local SSE.** By applying the Generic Local Transform to the LayeredSSE page-efficient scheme, we immediately obtain a dynamic SSE scheme Local[LayeredSSE], with storage efficiency $\mathcal{O}(1)$, locality $\mathcal{O}(1)$, and read efficiency $\widetilde{\mathcal{O}}(\log\log N)$. The construction is conditional: it requires that the longest list is of size $\mathcal{O}(N^{1-1/\log\log N})$. The asymptotic performance of Local[LayeredSSE] matches exactly the second *static* construction from [ANSS16], including the condition on maximum list size: dynamism comes at no extra cost. In particular, Local[LayeredSSE] matches the lower bound from [ASS21] for SSE schemes built using what [ASS21] refers to as "allocation schemes"—showing that the bound can be matched even in the dynamic setting.

(4) **Unconditional local SSE in the static setting.** The original 1-choice scheme from [ANSS16] achieves $\mathcal{O}(1)$ storage efficiency, $\mathcal{O}(1)$ locality, and $\widetilde{\mathcal{O}}(\log N)$ read efficiency, unconditionally. The read efficiency was improved to $\mathcal{O}(\log^{2/3+\varepsilon} N)$ in [DPP18], for any constant $\varepsilon > 0$. This was, until now, the only SSE construction to achieve sublogarithmic efficiency unconditionally. By applying the Generic Local Transform to a variant of Tethys [BBF+21], in combination with techniques inspired by [DPP18], we obtain an unconditional static SSE scheme with storage efficiency $\mathcal{O}(1)$, locality $\mathcal{O}(1)$, and read efficiency $\mathcal{O}(\log^{\varepsilon} N)$, for any constant $\varepsilon > 0$. To our knowledge, this is the construction that comes closest to the impossibility result of Cash and Tessaro, stating that $\mathcal{O}(1)$ locality, storage efficiency, and read efficiency simultaneously is impossible.

Table 1. Page-efficient SSE schemes. N denotes the total size of the database, W denotes the number of keywords, p is the number elements per page, $\varepsilon > 0$ is an arbitrarily small constant, and λ is the security parameter.

Schemes	Client st.	Page eff.	Storage eff.	Dynamism
$\Pi_{\text{pack}}, \Pi_{\text{2lev}}$ [CJJ+14]	$\mathcal{O}(1)$	$\mathcal{O}(1)$	$\mathcal{O}(p)$	Static
TCA [ANSS16]	$\mathcal{O}(1)$	$\widetilde{\mathcal{O}}(\log\log N)$	$\mathcal{O}(1)$	Static
Tethys [BBF+21]	$\mathcal{O}(p\log\lambda)$	3	$3+\varepsilon$	Static
IO-DSSE [MM17]	$\mathcal{O}(W)$	$\mathcal{O}(\log W)$	$\mathcal{O}(1)$	Dynamic
LayeredSSE	$\mathcal{O}(1)$	$\widetilde{\mathcal{O}}\left(\log\log\frac{N}{p}\right)$	$\mathcal{O}(1)$	Dynamic

Table 2. SSE schemes with constant locality and storage efficiency. N denotes the total size of the database, and $\varepsilon > 0$ is an arbitrarily small constant.

Schemes	Locality	Read eff.	St. eff.	Max list size	Dynamism
TCA [ANSS16]	$\mathcal{O}(1)$	$\widetilde{\mathcal{O}}(\log\log N)$	$\mathcal{O}(1)$	$\mathcal{O}(N^{1-1/\log\log N})$	Static
[ASS21]	$\mathcal{O}(1)$	$\widetilde{\mathcal{O}}(\log\log\log N)$	$\mathcal{O}(1)$	$\mathcal{O}(N^{1-1/\log\log\log N})$	Static
OCA [ANSS16]	$\mathcal{O}(1)$	$\widetilde{\mathcal{O}}(\log N)$	$\mathcal{O}(1)$	Unconditional	Static
[DPP18]	$\mathcal{O}(1)$	$\widetilde{\mathcal{O}}\left(\log^{2/3+\varepsilon} N\right)$	$\mathcal{O}(1)$	Unconditional	Static
Local[LayeredSSE]	$\mathcal{O}(1)$	$\widetilde{\mathcal{O}}(\log\log N)$	$\mathcal{O}(1)$	$\mathcal{O}(N^{1-1/\log\log N})$	Dynamic
UncondSSE	$\mathcal{O}(1)$	$\widetilde{\mathcal{O}}(\log^{\varepsilon} N)$	$\mathcal{O}(1)$	Unconditional	Static

Remark on Forward Security. The SSE schemes built in this work have a standard "minimal" leakage profile during Search: namely, searches leak the search pattern, the access pattern and the length of the retrieved list of document identifiers. For our dynamic schemes, Update operations importantly leak no information about unqueried keywords, but leak an identifier of the list being updated, as well as, in some cases, the length of the list. As a consequence, our dynamic schemes are not *forward-secure*. The underlying issue is that the goals of forward security and memory efficiency seem to be fundamentally at odds. Indeed, locality asks that identifiers associated to the same keywords must be stored close to each other; while forward-privacy requires that the location where a new identifier is inserted should be independent of the keyword it is associated with. That issue was already noted in [Bos16], who claims that "for dynamic schemes, locality and forward-privacy are two irreconcilable notions". We refer the reader to [Bos16] for more discussion of the problem and leave further analysis of this issue for future work.

Note that SSE has a very varied range of uses cases, for example private database services, online messaging and encrypted text search. In practice, its security requirements depend entirely on the use case. There are use cases where forward secrecy is crucial. The argument for forward security that is often given in the literature (e.g. [Bos16,BMO17,EKPE18,AKM19]) is to thwart file injection attacks in the style of [ZKP16]. Those attacks require injecting adversarially crafted entries into the target database. In an online messaging scenario, those attacks could be realistic, hence forward security is needed. In other cases, adversarial file injection is much less of a threat, and forward security can be reasonably dispensed with. For use cases where forward security is not required, we show that dynamism and memory efficiency are achievable at the same time.

Remark on the Focus on the Reverse Index. As most SSE literature, this work focuses on the (inverse) document index. The simplest usage scenario is to retrieve document indices from the index, then fetch those documents from a separate database. In reality, there are many other ways to use the index, for example by intersecting the document indices from several queries before fetching, fetching only some of the documents (see [MPC+18]), or building graph databases via several layers of inverse indices [CK10].

In most cases, the cost of fetching the actual documents is the same for the encrypted database as it is for the equivalent plaintext database: the efficiency overhead comes entirely from the inverse index. Schemes that hide access pattern or volume leakage are a possible exceptions but are out of the scope of this work.

2 Technical Overview

This work contains several results, tied together by the Generic Local Transform. As such, we believe it is beneficial to present them together within one paper. This requires introducing a number of different allocation mechanisms. We have endeavored to provide in this section a clear overview of those mechanisms. Formal specifications, theorems, and proofs will be presented in subsequent sections.

It is helpful to fist recall a few well-studied allocation mechanisms. In what follows, "with overwhelming probability" is synonymous with "except with negligible probability" (in the usual cryptographic sense), whereas "with high probability" simply means with probability close to 1 in some sense, but not necessarily overwhelming.

One-Choice Allocation. In one-choice allocation, n balls are thrown into n bins. Each ball is inserted into a bin chosen independently and uniformly at random (by hashing an identifier of the ball). A standard analysis using Chernoff bounds shows that, at the outcome of the insertion process, the most loaded bin contains $\mathcal{O}(\log n)$ balls with high probability [JK77]. (And at most $\mathcal{O}(f(n)\log n)$ balls with overwhelming probability, for any $f = \omega(1)$.)

Two-Choice Allocation. Once again, n balls are thrown into n bins. For each ball, two bins are chosen independently and uniformly at random (e.g. by hashing an identifier of the ball). The ball is inserted into whichever of the two bins contains the fewest balls at the time of insertion. A celebrated result by Azar et al. shows that, at the outcome of the insertion process, the most loaded bin contains $\mathcal{O}(\log\log n)$ balls with high probability [ABKU94]. (It was later shown that the result holds with overwhelming probability [RMS01].)

2.1 Layered 2-Choice Allocation

Our first goal is to build a dynamic page-efficient scheme. Let us summarize what this entails, starting with the static case. As explained in the introduction, to realize single-keyword SSE, we want to store lists of arbitrary sizes on an untrusted server. Hiding the contents of the lists can be achieved in a straightforward way using symmetric encryption. The main challenge is how to store the lists in the server memory, in such a way that accessing one list does not reveal information about the lengths of other lists.

In the case of page-efficient schemes, this challenge may be summarized as follows. We are given a set of lists, containing N items in total. We are also given a page size p, which represents the number of items that can fit within a physical memory page. The memory of the server is viewed as an array of pages. We want to store the lists in the server memory, with three goals in mind.

1. In order to store all lists, we use $S\lceil N/p\rceil$ pages of server memory in total, where S is called the *storage efficiency* of the allocation scheme. We want S to be as small as possible.
2. Any list of length ℓ can be retrieved by visiting at most $P\lceil \ell/p\rceil$ pages in server memory, where P is called the *page efficiency* of the allocation scheme. We want P to be as small as possible.
3. Finally, the pages visited by the server to retrieve a given list should not depend on the lengths of other lists.

The first two goals are precisely the aim of bin packing algorithms. The third goal is a security goal: it stipulates that the pattern of memory accesses performed by the server should not leak certain information. As such, the goal relates to oblivious or data-independent algorithms. In [BBF+21], a framework for realizing the three goals was formalized as *Data-Independent Packing* (DIP).

To ease presentation, we will focus on the case where all lists are of size at most one page. If a list is of length more than one page, the general idea is that it will be split into chunks of one page, plus one final chunk of size at most one page; each chunk will then be treated as a separate list by the allocation scheme. We assume from now on that lists are of length less than one page.

In a nutshell, the idea proposed by [BBF+21] to instantiate a DIP scheme is to use weighted variant of cuckoo hashing [PR04]. In more detail, for each list, two pages are chosen uniformly at random, by hashing an identifier of the list. Each element of the list will then be stored in one of the two designated pages, or a stash. The stash is stored on the client side. In order to choose how each list is split between its three possible destinations (the two chosen pages, or the stash), [BBF+21] uses a maximum flow algorithm. The details of this algorithm are not relevant for our purpose. The important point is that when retrieving a list, the server accesses two uniformly random pages. Clearly, this reveals no information to the server about the lengths of other lists. The resulting algorithm, called Tethys, achieves storage efficiency $\mathcal{O}(1)$, page efficiency $\mathcal{O}(1)$, with client storage $\omega(\log \lambda)$ pages (used to store the stash).

In this paper, we wish to build a dynamic SSE. For that purpose, the underlying allocation scheme needs to allow for a new *update* operation. An update operation allows the client to add a new item to a list, increasing its length by one. The security goal remains essentially the same as in the static case: the pages accessed by the algorithm in order to update a given list should not depend on the lengths of other lists.

Tethys is not a suitable basis for a dynamic scheme, because it does not allow for an efficient data-independent update procedure: when inserting an element into a cell, the update procedure requires running a max flow algorithm. This either requires accessing other cells, with an access pattern that is intrinsically data-dependent, or performing a prohibitively expensive data-oblivious max flow computation each update. Instead, a natural idea is to use a weighted variant of the two-choice allocation scheme. With two-choice allocation, the access pattern made during an update is simple: only the two destination buckets associated to the list being updated need to be read. The new item is then inserted into whichever of the two buckets currently contains less items.

Instantiating that approach would require a weighted *dynamic* variant of two-choice allocation, along the following lines: given a multiset of list sizes $\{\ell_i : 1 \leq i \leq k\}$ with $\ell_i \leq p$ and $\sum \ell_i = N$, at the outcome of a two-choice allocation process into $\mathcal{O}(N/p)$ buckets, the most loaded bucket contains $\mathcal{O}(p \log \log N)$ items with overwhelming probability, even if the weight of balls is updated during the process. However, a result of that form appears to be a long-standing open problem (some related partial results are discussed in [BFHM08]). The two-choice process with weighted items has been studied in the literature [TW07, TW14, ANSS16], but to our knowledge, all existing results assume that (1) either the weight of the balls are sampled identically and independently from a sufficiently smooth distribution or (2) the balls are sorted initially and then allocated in decreasing order. Even disregarding constraints on the distribution, in our setting, we cannot even afford to assume that list lengths are drawn independently: in the SSE security model, lists are chosen and updated *arbitrarily* by the adversary. Also, presorting the lists according to their length is not possible in a dynamic setting, as the list lengths can be changed via updates.

For our purpose, we require a *distribution-free* statement: we only know a bound p on the size of each list, and a bound N on the total size of all lists. We want an $\mathcal{O}(p \log\log N)$ upper bound on the size of the most loaded bucket that holds for *any* set of list sizes satisfying those constraints, even if list sizes are updated during the process. A result of that form is known for one-choice allocation processes [BFHM08] (with a $\mathcal{O}(p \log N)$ upper bound), but the same article shows that the same techniques cannot extend to the two-choice process.

To solve that problem, we introduce a *layered* weighted 2-choice allocation algorithm, L2C. L2C has the same basic behavior as a (weighted) two-choice algorithm: for each ball, two bins are chosen uniformly at random as possible destinations. The only difference is how the bin where the ball is actually inserted is selected among the two destination bins. The most natural choice would be to store the ball in whichever bin currently has the least load, where the *load* of a bin is a the sum of the weights of the balls it currently contains. Instead, we use a slightly more complex decision process. In a nutshell, we partition the possible weights of balls into $\mathcal{O}(\log\log \lambda)$ subintervals, and the decision process is performed independently for balls in each subinterval. For the first subinterval (holding the smallest weights), we use a weighted one-choice process, while for the other subintervals, we use an unweighted two-choice process.

The point of this construction is that its analysis reduces to the analysis of the weighted one-choice process, and the unweighted two-choice process, for which powerful analytical techniques are known. We leverage those techniques to show that L2C achieves the desired distribution-free guarantees on the load of the most loaded bin. In practice, what this means is that we have an allocation algorithm that, for most intents and purposes, behaves like a weighted variant of two-choice allocation, and for which updates and distribution-free guarantees can be obtained relatively painlessly.

The LayeredSSE scheme is obtained by adding a layer of encryption and key management on top of L2C, using standard techniques from the SSE literature, although some care is required for updates. We refer the reader to Sect. 5 for more details.

2.2 Generic Local Transform

At Crypto 2018, Asharov et al. identified two main paradigms for building local SSE [ASS18]. The first is the *allocation* paradigm, which typically uses variants of multiple-choice allocation schemes, or cuckoo hashing. The second is the *pad-and-split* approach. The main difficulty of memory-efficient SSE is to pack together lists of different sizes. The idea of the pad-and-split approach is to store lists separately according to their size, which circumvents the issue. The simplest way to realize this is to pad all lists length to the next power of 2. This yields

$\log N$ possible values for list lengths. All lists of a given length can be stored together using, for instance, a standard hash table. Since we do not want to reveal the number of lists of each length, the hash table at each level needs to be dimensioned to be able to receive the entire database. As a result, a basic pad-and-split scheme has storage efficiency $\mathcal{O}(\log N)$, but easily achieves $\mathcal{O}(1)$ locality and read efficiency.

For the Generic Local Transform, we introduce the notion of *Overflowing SSE* (OSSE). An OSSE behaves like an SSE scheme in all aspects, except that, during its setup and during updates, it may refuse to store some list elements. Such elements are called *overflowing*. An OSSE is intended to be used as a subcomponent within an overarching SSE construction. The OSSE scheme is used to store part of the database, while overflowing elements are stored using a separate mechanism. The notion of OSSE was not formalized before, but in hindsight, the use of OSSE may be viewed as implicit in several existing constructions [DPP18, ASS18, BBF+21]. We choose to introduce it explicitly here for ease of exposition.

We are now in a position to explain the Generic Local Transform. The chief limitation of the pad-and-split approach is that it creates a $\log N$ overhead in storage. The high-level idea of the Generic Local Transform, then, is to use an OSSE to store all but a fraction $1/\log N$ of the database. Then a pad-and-split variant is used to store the $N/\log N$ overflowing elements. The intent is to benefit from the high efficiency of the pad-and-split approach, without having to pay for the $\log N$ storage overhead.

There is, however, a subtle but important issue with that approach. A given list may be either entirely stored within the OSSE scheme, or only partially stored, or not stored at all. In the OSSE scheme that we will later use (as well as OSSEs that were implicit in prior work), those three situations should be indistinguishable to the server, or else security breaks down. To address that issue, we proceed as follows.

Let us assume all lists have been padded to the next power of 2. For the pad-and-split part of the construction, we create $\log N$ SSE instances, one for each possible list size. We call each of these instances a *layer*. The overflowing elements of a list of size ℓ will be stored in the layer that handles lists of size ℓ, regardless of how many elements did overflow from the OSSE for that list.

The OSSE guarantees that the total number of overflowing items is at most $n = \mathcal{O}(N/\log N)$. Thus, if we focus on the layer that handles lists of size ℓ, the layer will receive at most n elements. These elements will be split into lists of size at most ℓ (corresponding to the set of overflowing elements, for each list of size ℓ in the original database). To achieve storage efficiency $\mathcal{O}(S)$ overall, we want the layer to store those lists using $\mathcal{O}(Sn)$ storage. To achieve read efficiency R, the layer should also be able to retrieve a given list by visiting at most $R\ell$ memory locations. This is where everything comes together: an SSE scheme satisfying those conditions is precisely a page-efficient SSE scheme with page size ℓ, storage efficiency S, and page efficiency R.

The page-efficient scheme used for each layer is also required satisfy a few extra properties: first, when searching for a list of size at most one page, the length of the list should not be leaked. We call this property *page-length-hiding*. (We avoid the term *length-hiding* to avoid confusion with volume-hiding SSE, which fully hides lengths.) All existing page-efficient constructions have that property. Second, we require the page-efficient scheme to have $\mathcal{O}(1)$ client storage. All constructions in this article satisfy that property, but the construction from [BBF+21] does not. Finally, we require the scheme to have locality $\mathcal{O}(1)$ when fetching a single page. All existing page-efficient constructions have this property. (The last two properties could be relaxed, at the cost of more complex formulas and statements.) We call an SSE scheme satisfying those three properties *suitable*.

Putting everything together, the Generic Local Transform takes as input a suitable *page-efficient* scheme, with storage efficiency S and page efficiency P. It outputs a *local* scheme with storage efficiency $S + S'$, read efficiency $P + R'$, and locality L', where S', R', and L' are the storage efficiency, read efficiency, and locality of the underlying OSSE. It remains to explain how to build a local OSSE scheme with $\mathcal{O}(N/\log N)$ overflowing items, discussed next.

2.3 ClipOSSE: An OSSE Scheme with $\mathcal{O}(N/\log N)$ Overflowing Items

At STOC 2016, Asharov et al. introduced so-called "2-dimensional" variants of one-choice and two-choice allocation, for the purpose of building local SSE. The one-choice variant works as follows. Consider an SSE database with N elements. Allocate $m = \widetilde{\mathcal{O}}(N/\log N)$ buckets, initially empty. For each list of length ℓ in the database, choose one bucket uniformly at random. The first element of the list is inserted into that bucket. The second element of the list is inserted into the next bucket (assuming a fixed order of buckets, which wraps around when reaching the last bucket), the third one into the bucket after that, and so on, until all list elements have been inserted. Thus, assuming $\ell \leq m$, all list elements have been placed into ℓ consecutive buckets, one element in each. An analysis very similar to the usual analysis of the one-choice process shows that with overwhelming probability, the most loaded bucket receives at most $\tau = \widetilde{\mathcal{O}}(\log N)$ elements. To build a static SSE scheme from this allocation scheme, each bucket is padded to the maximal size τ and encrypted. Search queries proceed in the natural way.

Such a scheme yields storage efficiency $\mathcal{O}(1)$, locality $\mathcal{O}(1)$ (since retrieving a list amounts to reading consecutive buckets), and read efficiency $\widetilde{\mathcal{O}}(\log N)$ (since retrieving a list of length ℓ requires reading ℓ buckets, each of size $\tau = \widetilde{\mathcal{O}}(\log N)$). To build ClipOSSE, we start from the same premise, but "clip" buckets at the threshold $\tau = \widetilde{\mathcal{O}}(\log\log N)$. That is, each bucket can only receive up to τ elements. Elements that cannot fit are overflowing.

In the standard one-choice process, where n balls are thrown i.i.d. into n bins, it is not difficult to show that clipping bins at height $\tau = \mathcal{O}(\log\log n)$ results in at most $\mathcal{O}(n/\log n)$ overflowing elements with overwhelming probability. In fact, by adjusting the multiplicative constant in the choice of τ, the number of overflowing elements can be made $\mathcal{O}(n/\log^d n)$ for any given constant d. We show that a result of that form still holds for (a close variant of) the 2-dimensional one-choice process outlined earlier. The result is conditional: it requires that the maximum list size is $\mathcal{O}(N/\mathsf{polylog}\, N)$. (A condition of that form is necessary, insofar as the result fails when the maximum list size gets close to $N/\log N$.) The proof of the corresponding theorem is the most technically challenging part of this work, and relies on the combination of a convexity argument with a stochastic dominance argument. An overview of the proof is given in Sect. 6.5, so we omit more discussion here.

In the end, ClipOSSE achieves storage efficiency $\mathcal{O}(1)$, locality $\mathcal{O}(1)$, and read efficiency $\mathcal{O}(\log \log N)$, with $\mathcal{O}(N/\log^d N)$ overflowing elements (for any fixed constant d of our choice), under the condition that the maximum list size is $\mathcal{O}(N/\mathsf{polylog}\, N)$. All applications of the Generic Local Transform in this article use ClipOSSE as the underlying OSSE. (That is why we write Local[PE-SSE] for the Generic Local Transform applied to the page-efficient scheme PE-SSE, and do not put the underlying OSSE as an explicit parameter.)

2.4 Dynamic Local SSE with $\widetilde{\mathcal{O}}(\log \log N)$ Overhead

By using the Generic Local Transform with ClipOSSE as the underlying OSSE, and LayeredSSE as the page-efficient scheme, we obtain Local[LayeredSSE]. The Local[LayeredSSE] scheme has storage efficiency $\mathcal{O}(1)$, locality $\mathcal{O}(1)$, and read efficiency $\widetilde{\mathcal{O}}(\log \log N)$. This result follows from the main theorem regarding the Generic Local Transform, and does not require any new analysis.

Local[LayeredSSE] is a conditional scheme: it requires that the longest list is of length $\mathcal{O}(N^{1-1/\log \log \lambda})$. The reason is subtle. ClipOSSE by itself has a condition that the longest list is $\mathcal{O}(N/\mathsf{polylog}\, N)$, which is less demanding. The reason for the condition comes down to the fact that LayeredSSE only achieves a negligible probability of failure as long as the number of pages in the scheme is at least $\Omega(\lambda^{1/\log \log \lambda})$. More generally, the same holds for the number of bins in two-choice allocation processes in general, even the standard, unweighted process. The condition is optimal: [ASS21] shows that any sublogarithmic "allocation-based" scheme must be conditional, and gives a bound on the condition. Local[PE-SSE] matches that bound.

2.5 Unconditional Static Local SSE with $\mathcal{O}(\log^\varepsilon N)$ Overhead

The (static) Tethys scheme from [BBF+21] achieves storage efficiency $\mathcal{O}(1)$ and page efficiency $\mathcal{O}(1)$ simultaneously. It is also page-length-hiding. Since we have the Generic Local Transform at our disposal, it is tempting to apply it to Tethys. There is, however, one obstacle: Tethys uses $\omega(p\log \lambda)$ client memory, in order to store a stash on the client side. For the Generic Local Transform, we need $\mathcal{O}(1)$

client memory. To reduce the client memory of Tethys, a simple idea is to store the stash on the server side. Naively, reading the stash for every search would increase the page efficiency to $\omega(\log \lambda)$. To avoid this, we store the stash within an ORAM.

For that purpose, we need an ORAM with a failure probability of zero: indeed, since we may store as few as $\log \lambda$ elements in the ORAM, a correctness guarantee of the form $\mathsf{negl}(n)$, where $n = \log \lambda$ is the number items in the ORAM, fails to be sufficient (it is not $\mathsf{negl}(\lambda)$). We also need the ORAM to have $\mathcal{O}(1)$ locality. An ORAM with these characteristics was devised in [DPP18], motivated by the same problem. The ORAM from [DPP18] achieves read efficiency $\mathcal{O}(n^{1/3+\varepsilon})$, for any arbitrary constant $\varepsilon > 0$. It was already conjectured in [DPP18] that it could be improved to $\mathcal{O}(n^{\varepsilon})$. We build that variant explicitly, and name it LocORAM. Roughly speaking, LocORAM is a variant of the Goldreich-Ostrovsky hierarchical ORAM, with a constant number of levels.

By putting the stash of Tethys within LocORAM on the server side, we naturally obtain a page-efficient SSE scheme OramTethys, with $\mathcal{O}(\log^{\varepsilon} \lambda)$ read efficiency, suitable for use within the Generic Local Transform. This yields a static local SSE for lists of size at most $N/\mathsf{polylog}\, N$. To handle larger lists, borrowing some ideas from [DPP18], we group lists by size, and use again OramTethys to store them. In the end, we obtain an unconditional SSE with $\mathcal{O}(1)$ store efficiency, $\mathcal{O}(1)$ locality, and $\mathcal{O}(\log^{\varepsilon} \lambda)$ read efficiency.

Comparing with the $\mathcal{O}(\log^{2/3+\varepsilon} \lambda)$ construction from [DPP18], we note that the bottleneck of their construction comes from the allocation schemes the authors use for what they call "small" and "medium" lists. This is precisely the range where we use Local[OramTethys]. Our construction essentially removes that bottleneck, so that the $\mathcal{O}(\log^{\varepsilon} \lambda)$ read efficiency bottlneck now comes entirely from the ORAM component. A detailed description of the scheme is given in the full version.

3 Preliminaries

Let $\lambda \in \mathbb{N}$ be the security parameter. For a probability distribution X, we denote by $x \leftarrow X$ the process of sampling a value x from the distribution. Further, we say that x is We denote by $[a, b]_{\mathbb{R}}$ the interval $\{x \in \mathbb{R} \mid a \leq x \leq b\}$ and extend this naturally to intervals of the form $[a, b)_{\mathbb{R}}, (a, b]_{\mathbb{R}}, (a, b)_{\mathbb{R}}$.

3.1 Symmetric Searchable Encryption

A database $\mathsf{DB} = \{w_i, (\mathsf{id}_1, \ldots, \mathsf{id}_{\ell_i})\}_{i=1}^{W}$ is a set of keyword-identifier pairs with W keywords. We assume that each keyword w_i is represented by a machine word of $\mathcal{O}(\lambda)$ bits. We write $\mathsf{DB}(w_i) = (\mathsf{id}_1, \ldots, \mathsf{id}_{\ell_i})$ for the list of identifiers matching w_i. Throughout the article, we set $N = \sum_{i=1}^{W} \ell_i$ and define p as the page size (which we treat as a variable, independent of the size of the database N).

A dynamic searchable symmetric encryption scheme Σ is a 4-tuple of PPT algorithms (KeyGen, Setup, Search, Update) such that

- $\Sigma.\mathsf{KeyGen}(1^\lambda)$: Takes as input the security parameter λ and outputs client secret key K.
- $\Sigma.\mathsf{Setup}(\mathsf{K}, N, \mathsf{DB})$: Takes as input the client secret key K, an upper bound on the database size N and a database DB. Outputs encrypted database EDB and client state st.
- $\Sigma.\mathsf{Search}(\mathsf{K}, w, \mathsf{st}; \mathsf{EDB})$: The client receives as input the secret key K, keyword w and state st. The server receives as input the encrypted database EDB. Outputs some data d and updated state st' for the client. Outputs updated encrypted database EDB' for the server.
- $\Sigma.\mathsf{Update}(\mathsf{K}, (w, L), \mathsf{op}, \mathsf{st}; \mathsf{EDB})$: The client receives as input the secret key K, a pair (w, L) of keyword w and list L of identifiers, an operation $\mathsf{op} \in \{\mathsf{del}, \mathsf{add}\}$ and state st. The server receives as input the encrypted database EDB. Outputs updated state st' for the client. Outputs updated encrypted database EDB' for the server.

In the following, we omit the state st and assume that it is implicitly stored and updated by the client. We say that Σ is *static*, if it does not provide an Update algorithm. Further, we assume that the keyword w is preprocessed via a PRF by the client, whenever the client sends w to the server in either Search or Update. This ensures that the server never has access to w in plaintext and unqueried keywords are distributed uniformly random in the view of the server.

Intuitively, the client uses Setup to encrypt and outsource a database DB to the server. Then, the client can search keywords w using Search and receives the list of matching identifiers $\mathsf{DB}(w)$ from the server. The list $\mathsf{DB}(w)$ can be updated via Update, provided that the size of the database stays below N. Note that we allow the client to add (or delete) multiple identifiers at once for a single keyword (which is required for the Generic Local Transform Sect. 6).

Security. We now define correctness and semantic security of SSE. Intuitively, correctness guarantees that a search always retrieves all matching identifiers and semantic security guarantees that the server only learns limited information (quantified by a leakage function) from the client.

Definition 1 (Correctness). *A* SSE *scheme* Σ *is correct if for all databases* DB *and* $N \in \mathbb{N}$, *keys* $\mathsf{K} \leftarrow \Sigma.\mathsf{KeyGen}(1^\lambda)$, $\mathsf{EDB} \leftarrow \Sigma.\mathsf{Setup}(\mathsf{K}, \mathsf{DB})$ *and sequences of search, add or delete queries* S, *the search protocol returns the correct result for all queries of the sequence, if the size of the database remains at most* N.

We use the standard semantic security notion for SSE (see [CGKO06]). Security is parameterized by a leakage function $\mathcal{L} = (\mathcal{L}_{\mathsf{Stp}}, \mathcal{L}_{\mathsf{Srch}}, \mathcal{L}_{\mathsf{Updt}})$, composed of the setup leakage $\mathcal{L}_{\mathsf{Stp}}$, the search leakage $\mathcal{L}_{\mathsf{Srch}}$, and the update leakage $\mathcal{L}_{\mathsf{Updt}}$. We define two games, SSEREAL and SSEIDEAL. First, the adversary chooses a database DB. In SSEREAL, the encrypted database EDB is generated by $\mathsf{Setup}(\mathsf{K}, N, \mathsf{DB})$, whereas in SSEIDEAL the encrypted database is simulated by a (stateful) simulator Sim on input $\mathcal{L}_{\mathsf{Stp}}(\mathsf{DB}, N)$. After receiving EDB, the adversary issues search and update queries. All queries are answered honestly in

SSEREAL. In SSEIDEAL, the search queries on keyword w are simulated by Sim on input $\mathcal{L}_{\mathsf{Srch}}(w)$, and update queries for operation op, keyword w and identifier list L are simulated by Sim on input $\mathcal{L}_{\mathsf{Updt}}(\mathsf{op}, w, L)$. Finally, the adversary outputs a bit b.

We write SSEREAL^{adp} and SSEIDEAL^{adp} if the queries of the adversary were chosen adaptively, *i.e.* dependant on previous queries. Similarly, we write SSEREAL^{sel} and SSEIDEAL^{sel} if the queries are chosen selectively by the adversary, *i.e.* sent initially in conjunction with the database before receiving EDB.

Definition 2 (Semantic Security). *Let Σ be a* SSE *scheme and $\mathcal{L} = (\mathcal{L}_{\mathsf{Stp}}, \mathcal{L}_{\mathsf{Srch}}, \mathcal{L}_{\mathsf{Updt}})$ a leakage function. Scheme Σ is $\mathcal{L}$-adaptively secure if for all PPT adversaries $\mathcal{A}$, there exists a PPT simulator Sim such that*

$$|\Pr[\mathrm{SSEREAL}^{\mathsf{adp}}_{\Sigma,\mathcal{A}}(\lambda) = 1] - \Pr[\mathrm{SSEIDEAL}^{\mathsf{adp}}_{\Sigma,\mathit{Sim},\mathcal{L},\mathcal{A}}(\lambda) = 1]| = \mathsf{negl}(\lambda).$$

Similarly, scheme Σ is $\mathcal{L}$-selectively secure if for all PPT adversaries $\mathcal{A}$, there exists a PPT simulator Sim such that

$$|\Pr[\mathrm{SSEREAL}^{\mathsf{sel}}_{\Sigma,\mathcal{A}}(\lambda) = 1] - \Pr[\mathrm{SSEIDEAL}^{\mathsf{sel}}_{\Sigma,\mathit{Sim},\mathcal{L},\mathcal{A}}(\lambda) = 1]| = \mathsf{negl}(\lambda).$$

Intuitively, semantic security guarantees that the interaction between client and server reveals no information to the server, except the leakage of the given query. The schemes from this article have common leakage patterns. We use the standard notions of query pattern qp and history Hist from [Bos16] to formalize this leakage: (1) The query pattern $\mathsf{qp}(w)$ for a keyword w are the indices of previous search or update queries for keyword w. (3) The history $\mathsf{Hist}(w)$ is comprised of the list of identifiers matching keyword w that were inserted during setup and the history of updates on keyword w, that is each deleted and inserted identifier. We can retrieve the number ℓ_i of inserted identifiers and the number d_i of deleted identifiers from $\mathsf{Hist}(w)$ for each keyword.

We define two leakage patterns we use throughout the article. (1) We define *page-length hiding* leakage $\mathcal{L}_{\mathsf{len\text{-}hid}}$. We set $\mathcal{L}_{\mathsf{len\text{-}hid}} = (\mathcal{L}^{\mathsf{len\text{-}hid}}_{\mathsf{Stp}}, \mathcal{L}^{\mathsf{len\text{-}hid}}_{\mathsf{Srch}}, \mathcal{L}^{\mathsf{len\text{-}hid}}_{\mathsf{Updt}})$, where the setup leakage is $\mathcal{L}^{\mathsf{len\text{-}hid}}_{\mathsf{Stp}}(\mathsf{DB}, N) = N$ is the maximal size N of the database, the search leakage $\mathcal{L}^{\mathsf{len\text{-}hid}}_{\mathsf{Srch}}(w) = (\mathsf{qp}, \lceil \ell_i/p \rceil, \lceil d_i/p \rceil)$ is the query pattern and the number of pages required to store the inserted and deleted items, and the update leakage $\mathcal{L}^{\mathsf{len\text{-}hid}}_{\mathsf{Updt}}(\mathsf{op}, w, L) = (\mathsf{op}, \mathsf{qp}, \lceil (\ell_i + |L|)/p \rceil, \lceil (d_i + |L|)/p \rceil, \lceil \ell_i/p \rceil, \lceil d_i/p \rceil)$ is the operation, the query pattern and the number of pages required to store the inserted and deleted items (before and after the update)[1]. (2) Similarly, we define *length reveiling* leakage $\mathcal{L}_{\mathsf{len\text{-}rev}}$. We set $\mathcal{L}_{\mathsf{len\text{-}rev}} = (\mathcal{L}^{\mathsf{len\text{-}rev}}_{\mathsf{Stp}}, \mathcal{L}^{\mathsf{len\text{-}rev}}_{\mathsf{Srch}}, \mathcal{L}^{\mathsf{len\text{-}rev}}_{\mathsf{Updt}})$ with $\mathcal{L}^{\mathsf{len\text{-}rev}}_{\mathsf{Stp}}(\mathsf{DB}, N) = N$, $\mathcal{L}^{\mathsf{len\text{-}rev}}_{\mathsf{Srch}}(w) = (\mathsf{qp}, |L'|, \ell_i, d_i)$ and lastly $\mathcal{L}^{\mathsf{len\text{-}rev}}_{\mathsf{Updt}}(\mathsf{op}, w, L') = (\mathsf{op}, \mathsf{qp}, |L'|, \ell_i, d_i)$.

We will use $\mathcal{L}_{\mathsf{len\text{-}hid}}$ and $\mathcal{L}_{\mathsf{len\text{-}rev}}$ for both dynamic and static schemes. When we say that a static scheme is $\mathcal{L}$-semantically secure, for $\mathcal{L} \in \{\mathcal{L}_{\mathsf{len\text{-}hid}}, \mathcal{L}_{\mathsf{len\text{-}rev}}\}$, we

[1] Note that we allow for inserting more than one identifier per keyword in a single update operation in this work. Thus, the server will also learn (limited) information about the number $|L|$ of added or deleted identifiers.

simply ignore the update leakage. Note that both leakage patterns, $\mathcal{L}_{\text{len-hid}}$ and $\mathcal{L}_{\text{len-rev}}$, have standard setup and search leakage, common in most SSE schemes. The update leakage of $\mathcal{L}_{\text{len-hid}}$ and $\mathcal{L}_{\text{len-rev}}$ is similar to their search leakage, and reveals nothing about unqueried keywords. While the update leakage is not forward secure, similar leakage patterns are commonly considered in literature, for example [CJJ+14]. We hope our techniques pave the way for future work on dynamic schemes with forward security and memory efficiency.

Efficiency Measures. We recall the notions of locality, storage efficiency and read efficiency [CT14], and page efficiency [BBF+21] (and extend them to the dynamic SSE setting in a natural manner). In the following definitions, we set $\mathsf{K} \leftarrow \mathsf{KeyGen}(1^\lambda)$ and $\mathsf{EDB} \leftarrow \mathsf{Setup}(\mathsf{K}, N, \mathsf{DB})$ given database DB and upper bound N on the number of document identifiers. Also, $S = (\mathsf{op}_i, \mathsf{in}_i)_{i=1}^s$ is a sequence of search and update queries, where $\mathsf{op}_i \in \{\mathsf{add}, \mathsf{del}, \perp\}$ is a operation and $\mathsf{in}_i = (\mathsf{op}_i, w_i, L_i, \mathsf{st}_i, \mathsf{EDB}_i)$ its input. Here, w_i is a keyword and L_i is a (added or deleted) list of identifiers, and after executing all previous operations op_j for $j \leq i$, st_i is the client state and EDB_i the encrypted database. We denote by DB_i the database after i operations. We assume that the total number of identifiers never exceeds N. (If $\mathsf{op}_i = \perp$, the query is a search query and L_i is empty.)

Definition 3 (Read Pattern). *Regard server-side storage as an array of memory locations, containing the encrypted database* EDB. *When processing search query* $\mathsf{Search}(\mathsf{K}, w_i, \mathsf{st}_i; \mathsf{EDB}_i)$ *or update query* $\mathsf{Update}(\mathsf{K}, (w_i, L_i), \mathsf{op}_i, \mathsf{st}_i; \mathsf{EDB}_i)$, *the server accesses memory locations* $m_1, \ldots, m_h$. *We call these locations the* read pattern *and denote it with* $\mathsf{RdPat}(\mathsf{op}_i, \mathsf{in}_i)$.

Definition 4 (Locality). *A SSE scheme has locality L if for any λ,* DB, *N, sequence S, and any i,* $\mathsf{RdPat}(\mathsf{op}_i, \mathsf{in}_i)$ *consists of at most L disjoint intervals.*

Definition 5 (Read Efficiency). *A SSE scheme has read efficiency R if for any λ,* DB, *N, sequence S, and any i, $|\mathsf{RdPat}(\mathsf{op}_i, \mathsf{in}_i)| \leq R \cdot P$, where P is the number of memory locations needed to store all (added and deleted) document indices matching keyword w_i in plaintext (by concatenating indices).*

Definition 6 (Storage Efficiency). *A SSE scheme has storage efficiency E if for any λ,* DB, *N, sequence S, and any i, $|\mathsf{EDB}_i| \leq E \cdot |DB_i|$.*

Definition 7 (Page Pattern). *Regard server-side storage as an array of pages, containing the encrypted database* EDB. *When processing search query* $\mathsf{Search}(\mathsf{K}, w_i, \mathsf{st}_i; \mathsf{EDB}_i)$ *or update query* $\mathsf{Update}(\mathsf{K}, (w_i, L_i), \mathsf{op}_i, \mathsf{st}_i; \mathsf{EDB}_i)$, *the read pattern* $\mathsf{RdPat}(\mathsf{op}_i, \mathsf{in}_i)$ *induces a number of page accesses $p_1, \ldots, p_{h'}$. We call these pages the* page pattern, *denoted by* $\mathsf{PgPat}(\mathsf{op}_i, \mathsf{in}_i)$.

Definition 8 (Page Cost). *A SSE scheme has page cost $aX + b$, where a, b are real numbers, and X is a fixed symbol, if for any λ,* DB, *N, sequence S, and any i, $|\mathsf{PgPat}(\mathsf{op}_i, \mathsf{in}_i)| \leq aX + b$, where X is the number of pages needed to store document indices matching keyword w_i in plaintext.*

Definition 9 (Page Efficiency). *A SSE scheme has page efficiency P if for any λ, DB, N, sequence S, and any i, $|\mathsf{PgPat}(\mathsf{op}_i, \mathsf{in}_i)| \leq P \cdot X$, where X is the number of pages needed to store document indices matching keyword w_i in plaintext.*

4 Layered Two-Choice Allocation

In this section, we describe layered two-choice allocation ($\mathsf{L2C}$), a variant of two-choice allocation that allows to allocate n weighted balls (b_i, w_i) into m bins, where b_i is a unique identifier and $w_i \in [0,1]_{\mathbb{R}}$ is the weight of the ball. (We often write ball b_i for short.) First, let $1 \leq \delta(\lambda) \leq \log(\lambda)$ be a function. We denote by $w = \sum_{i=1}^{n} w_i$ the sum of all weights and set $m = w/(\delta(\lambda) \log\log w)$. We will later choose $\delta(\lambda) = o(\log\log\lambda)$ such that allocation has negligible failure probability. In the overview, we set $\delta(\lambda) = 1$ and assume that $m = \Omega(\lambda)$ for simplicity (which suffices for negligible failure probability).

Overview of $\mathsf{L2C}$. $\mathsf{L2C}$ is based on both *weighted* one-choice allocation ($\mathsf{1C}$) and *unweighted* two-choice allocation ($\mathsf{2C}$). On a high level, we split the set of possible weights $[0,1]_{\mathbb{R}}$ into $\log\log m$ subintervals

$$[0, 1/\log m]_{\mathbb{R}}, (1/\log m, 2/\log m]_{\mathbb{R}}, \ldots, (2^{\log\log m - 1}/\log m, 1]_{\mathbb{R}}.$$

In words, the first interval is of size $1/\log m$ and the boundaries between intervals grow by a factor 2 every time. We will allocate balls with weights in a given subinterval independently from the others.

Balls in the first subinterval have weights $w_i \leq \log m$ and are thus small enough to apply weighted $\mathsf{1C}$. Intuitively, this suffices because one-choice (provably) performs worst for uniform weights of maximal size $1/\log m$. In that case, there are at most $n' = w \log m$ balls and we expect a bin to contain $n'/m = \log m \cdot \log\log w$ balls of uniform weight, since $m = w/(\log\log w)$. As each ball has weight $1/\log m$, the expected load per bin is $\log\log w$. This translates to a $\mathcal{O}(\log\log w)$ bound with overwhelming probability after applying a Chernoff's bound.

For the other intervals, applying unweighted and independent $\mathsf{2C}$ per interval suffices, as the weights of balls differ at most by a factor 2 and there are only $\log\log m$ intervals. More concretely, let n_i be the number of balls in the i-th subinterval $A_i = (2^{i-1}/\log m, 2^i/\log m]_{\mathbb{R}}$ for $i \in \{1, \ldots, \log\log m\}$. Balls with weights in subinterval A_i fill the bins with at most $\mathcal{O}(n_i/m + \log\log m)$ balls, independent of other subintervals. Note that we are working with small weights, and thus potentially have $\omega(m)$ balls. Thus, we need to extend existing $\mathsf{2C}$ results to negligible failure probability in m for the heavily-loaded case. As there are only $\log\log m$ subintervals, and balls in interval A_i have weight at most $2^i/\log m$, we can just sum the load of each subinterval and receive a bound

$$\sum_{i=1}^{\log\log m} \frac{2^i}{\log m} \mathcal{O}(n_i/m + \log\log m) = \mathcal{O}(w/m + \log\log m).$$

In total, we have $\mathcal{O}(w/m + \log\log m) = \mathcal{O}(\log\log w)$ bounds for the first and the remaining intervals. Together, this shows that all bins have load at most $\mathcal{O}(\log\log w)$ after allocating all n items. This matches the bound of standard 2C with unweighted balls if $m = \Omega(\lambda)$. For our SSE application, we want to allow for negligible failure probability with the least number of bins possible. We can set $\delta(\lambda) = \log\log\log(\lambda)$ and obtain a bin size of $\widetilde{\mathcal{O}}(\log\log w)$ with overwhelming probability, if $m = \frac{w}{\delta(\lambda)\log\log w}$. The analysis is identical in this case.

Handling Updates. The described variant of L2C is static. That is, we have not shown a bound on the load of the most loaded bin if we add balls or update the weight of balls. Fortunately, inserts of new balls are trivially covered by the analysis sketched above, if m was chosen large enough initially in order to compensate for the added weight. Thus, we assume there is some upper bound w_{max} on the total weights of added balls which is used to initially set up the bins. We can also update weights if we proceed with care.

For this, let b_i be some ball with weight w_{old}. We want to update its weight to $w_{\mathsf{new}} > w_{\mathsf{old}}$. If w_{old} and w_{new} reside in the subinterval, we can directly update the weight of b_i, as L2C ignores the concrete weight of balls inside a given subinterval for the allocation. Indeed, in the first interval, the bin in which b_i is inserted is determined by a single random choice, and for the remaining subintervals, the 2C process only considers the number of balls inside the same subinterval, ignoring concrete weights.

When w_{new} is larger than the bounds of the current subinterval, we need to make sure that the ball is inserted into the correct bin of its two choices. For this, the ball b_i is inserted into the bin with the lowest number of balls with weights inside the new subinterval. Even though the bin of b_i might change in this process, we still need to consider b_i as a ball of weight w_{old} in the old bin for subsequent ball insertions in the old subinterval. Thus, we mark the ball as *residual* ball but do not remove it from its old bin. That is, we consider it as ball of weight w_{old} for the 2C process but assume it is not identified by b_i anymore. As there are only $\log\log m$ different subintervals, storing the residual balls has a constant overhead. The full algorithm L2C is given in Algorithm 1. We parameterize it by a hash function H mapping uniformly into $\{1, \ldots, m\}^2$. The random bin choices of a ball b_i are given by $\alpha_1, \alpha_2 \leftarrow \mathsf{H}(b_i)$.

Load Analysis of L2C. Let either $\delta(\lambda) = 1$ or $\delta(\lambda) = \log\log\log\lambda$ and m sufficiently large such that $m^{-\Omega(\delta(\lambda)\log\log w)} = \mathsf{negl}(\lambda)$. (Note that this is the probability that allocation of 1C and 2C fails.)

We need to show that after setup and during a (selective) sequence of operations, the most loaded bin has a load of at most $\mathcal{O}(\delta(\lambda)\log\log w_{\mathsf{max}})$, where w_{max} is an upper bound on the total weight of the inserted balls. We sketch the proof here and refer to the full version for further details. First, we modify the sequence S such that we can reduce the analysis to only (sufficiently independent) L2C.InsertBall operations, while only increasing the final bin load by a constant factor. This is constant factor of the load is due to the additional weight of residual balls. Then, we analyze the load of the most loaded bin for the

each subinterval independently. This boils down to an analysis of a 1C process in the first subinterval and a 2C process in the remaining subintervals as in the overview of L2C (see Sect. 4). Summing up the independent bounds yields the desired result.

Theorem 1. *Let either* $\delta(\lambda) = 1$ *or* $\delta(\lambda) = \log\log\log\lambda$*. Let* $w_{\mathsf{max}} = \mathsf{poly}(\lambda)$ *and* $m = w_{\mathsf{max}}/(\delta(\lambda)\log\log w_{\mathsf{max}})$*. We require that* $m = \Omega(\lambda^{\frac{1}{\log\log\lambda}})$ *if* $\delta(\lambda) = \log\log\log\lambda$ *or* $m = \Omega(\lambda)$ *otherwise. Let* $\{(b_i, w_i)_{i=1}^n\}$ *be balls with (pair-wise unique) identifier* b_i *and weight* $w_i \in [0,1]$*. Further, let* $S = (\mathsf{op}_i, \mathsf{in}_i)_{i=n+1}^{s+n}$ *be a sequence of* s *insert or update operations* $\mathsf{op}_i \in \{L2C.\mathsf{InsertBall}, L2C.\mathsf{UpdateBall}\}$ *with input* $\mathsf{in}_i = (b_i, w_i, B_{\alpha_{i,1}}, B_{\alpha_{i,2}})$ *for inserts and* $\mathsf{in}_i = (b_i, o_i, w_i, B_{\alpha_{i,1}}, B_{\alpha_{i,2}})$ *for updates. Here,* b_i *denotes the identifier of a ball with weight* w_i *and old weight* $o_i \leq w_i$ *before the execution of* op_i*. Also, the bins are chosen via* $\alpha_{i,1}, \alpha_{i,2} \leftarrow \mathsf{H}(b_i)$*.*

Execute $(B_i)_{i=1}^m \leftarrow L2C.\mathsf{Setup}(\{(b_i, w_i)_{i=1}^n\})$ *and the operations* $\mathsf{op}_i(\mathsf{in}_i)$ *for all* $i \in [n+1, n+s]$*. We require that* $\sum_{i=1}^{n+s} w_i - o_i \leq w_{\mathsf{max}}$*,* i.e. *the total weight after all operations is at most* w_{max}*.*

Then it holds that throughout the process, the most loaded bin of $B_1, \ldots, B_m$ *has at most load* $\mathcal{O}(\delta(\lambda)\log\log w_{\mathsf{max}})$ *except with negligible probability, if* H *is modeled as a random oracle.*

5 Dynamic Page Efficient SSE

We introduce the SSE scheme LayeredSSE based on L2C. Essentially, we interpret lists L_i of identifiers matching keyword w_i as balls of a certain weight. Then, we use L2C to manage the balls in m encrypted bins, where each bin corresponds to a memory page, yielding page efficiency $\widetilde{\mathcal{O}}(\log\log N/p)$ and constant storage efficiency. Let N be the maximal size of the database, $p \leq N^{1-1/\log\log\lambda}$ be the page size[2] and H be a hash function mapping into $\{1, \ldots, m\}^2$ for $m = \lceil w_{\mathsf{max}}/(\log\log\log\lambda \cdot \log\log w_{\mathsf{max}})\rceil$ and $w_{\mathsf{max}} = N/p$. Due to space limitations, we assume that each keyword has at most p associated keywords, and outline the scheme and its security analysis. We refer to the full version for details (without restrictions on the database[3]).

For convenience, we adapt the notation of L2C to lists of identifiers. A ball (w, L) of weight $|L|/p \in [0,1]_{\mathbb{R}}$ is a list of (at most p) identifiers matching keyword w. The 2 bin choices α_1, α_2 for ball (w, L) are given via $(\alpha_1, \alpha_2) \leftarrow \mathsf{H}(w)$. Now, L2C.Setup takes input balls $\{(w_i, L_i)\}_{i=1}^W$ and maximal weight w_{max}, and allocates them as before into m bins. L2C.InsertBall receives ball (w, L) and two bins $(B_{\alpha_1}, B_{\alpha_2})$, and inserts (w, L) into either bin B_{α_1} or bin B_{α_2} as before.

---

[2] This condition is needed for the requirement $m \geq \lambda^{1/\log\log\lambda}$ of L2C which guarantees negligible failure probability (see Theorem 1). In practice, we have $p \ll N$.

[3] For arbitrary lists sizes, we can split lists into sublists of size at most p and deal with each sublist separately as before. Some care has to be taken, for example with the random choices of the bins, but details are mostly straightforward.

Algorithm 1. Layered 2-Choice Allocation (L2C)

L2C.Setup($\{(b_i, w_i)\}_{i=1}^{n}, w_{\mathsf{max}}$)

Receive n balls (b_i, w_i), and maximal total weight w_{max}
Initialize $m = \lceil w_{\mathsf{max}}/(\delta(\lambda)\log\log w_{\mathsf{max}})\rceil$ empty bins $B_1, ..., B_m$
for all $i \in \{1, \ldots, n\}$ **do**
  Set $\alpha_1, \alpha_2 \leftarrow \mathsf{H}(b_i)$
  InsertBall($b_i, w_i, B_{\alpha_1}, B_{\alpha_2}$)
Return $B_1, ..., B_m$

L2C.InsertBall($b_{\mathsf{new}}, w_{\mathsf{new}}, B_{\alpha_1}, B_{\alpha_2}$)

Receive bins $B_{\alpha_1}, B_{\alpha_2}$, and ball $(b_{\mathsf{new}}, w_{\mathsf{new}})$
Assert that α_1, α_2 are the choices given by $\mathsf{H}(b_{\mathsf{new}})$
Split the set of possible weights $[0, 1]_{\mathbb{R}}$ into $\log\log m$ sub-intervals

$$[0, 1/\log m]_{\mathbb{R}}, (1/\log m, 2/\log m]_{\mathbb{R}}, ..., (2^{\log\log m - 1}/\log m, 1]_{\mathbb{R}}$$

Choose $k \in \mathbb{N}$ minimal such that $w_{\mathsf{new}} \leq 2^k/\log m$
if k = 1 **then**
  Set $\alpha \leftarrow \alpha_1$
else
  Let B_α be the bin with the least number of balls of weight in $\left(\frac{2^{k-1}}{\log m}, \frac{2^k}{\log m}\right]_{\mathbb{R}}$ among B_{α_1} and B_{α_2}
Insert ball b_{new} into bin B_α

L2C.UpdateBall($b_{\mathsf{old}}, w_{\mathsf{old}}, w_{\mathsf{new}}, B_{\alpha_1}, B_{\alpha_2}$)

Receive bins $B_{\alpha_1}, B_{\alpha_2}$ that contain ball $(b_{\mathsf{old}}, w_{\mathsf{old}})$, and new weight $w_{\mathsf{new}} \geq w_{\mathsf{old}}$
Assert that α_1, α_2 are the choices given by $\mathsf{H}(b_{\mathsf{old}})$
if $w_{\mathsf{old}}, w_{\mathsf{new}} \in \left(\frac{2^{k-1}}{\log m}, \frac{2^k}{\log m}\right]_{\mathbb{R}}$ for some k **then**
  Update the weight of b_{old} to w_{new} directly
else
  Mark b_{old} as residual ball (it is still considered as a ball of weight w_{old})
  InsertBall($b_{\mathsf{old}}, w_{\mathsf{new}}, B_{\alpha_1}, B_{\alpha_2}$)

L2C.UpdateBall receives old ball (w, L), identifiers L' and bins $(B_{\alpha_1}, B_{\alpha_2})$, and updates ball (w, L) to ball $(w, L \cup L')$ as before, while merging both identifier lists L and L'. (The weight of the updated ball is $|L \cup L'|/p \in [0, 1]_{\mathbb{R}}$.)

5.1 LayeredSSE

We describe LayeredSSE, focusing on insert operations. In the full version, we describe LayeredSSE in more detail, and show how to treat arbitrary list sizes, introduce delete operations and show how to obtain updates in 1 RTT. A detailed description of LayeredSSE is given in Algorithm 2.

Setup. To setup the initial database $\mathsf{DB} = (w, L_i)_{i=1}^{W}$, given upperbound N on the number of keyword-identifiers, allocate the balls (w, L_i) into m bins via L2C. Next, each bin is filled up to maximal size $p \cdot c\log\log\log(\lambda)\log\log(N/p)$, for some constant c. Finally, the encrypted bins are output.

Search. During a search operation on keyword w, the client retrieves encrypted bins $B_{\alpha_1}, B_{\alpha_2}$ for $(\alpha_1, \alpha_2) \leftarrow \mathsf{H}(w)$ from the server.

Update. During an update operation to add identifier list L' to keyword w, the client retrieves $B_{\alpha_1}, B_{\alpha_2}$, decrypts both bins and retrieves ball (w, L) from the corresponding bin $B_\alpha \in \{B_{\alpha_1}, B_{\alpha_2}\}$. Then, she calls L2C.UpdateBall with old ball (w, L), new identifiers L' and bins $B_{\alpha_1}, B_{\alpha_2}$ to insert the new identifiers L' into one of the bins. Finally, she reencrypts the bins and sends them to the server. The server then replaces the old bins with the updated bins.

Algorithm 2. LayeredSSE

Global parameters: constant $c \in \mathbb{N}$, page size p

LayeredSSE.KeyGen(1^λ)

- Sample $\mathsf{K_{Enc}}$ for Enc with input 1^λ
- **return** $K = \mathsf{K_{Enc}}$

LayeredSSE.Setup(K, N, DB)

- Set $\tau \leftarrow p \cdot c \log\log\log(\lambda) \log\log(N/p)$
- Sample bins $B_1, \ldots, B_m$ via L2C.Setup with input $(\{(w_i, \mathsf{DB}(w_i))\}_{i=1}^{W}, N/p)$
- Fill $B_1, \ldots, B_m$ up to size τ with zeros
- Set $B_i^{\mathsf{enc}} \leftarrow \mathsf{Enc}_{\mathsf{K_{Enc}}}(B_i)$ for $i \in [1, m]$
- **return** $\mathsf{EDB} = (B_1^{\mathsf{enc}}, \ldots, B_m^{\mathsf{enc}})$

LayeredSSE.Search(K, w; EDB)

Client:

- **return** w

Server:

- Set $\alpha_1, \alpha_2 \leftarrow \mathsf{H}(w)$
- **return** $B_{\alpha_1}^{\mathsf{enc}}, B_{\alpha_2}^{\mathsf{enc}}$

LayeredSSE.Update(K, (w, L'), add; EDB)

Client:

- **return** w

Server:

- Set $\alpha_1, \alpha_2 \leftarrow \mathsf{H}(w)$
- **return** $B_{\alpha_1}^{\mathsf{enc}}, B_{\alpha_2}^{\mathsf{enc}}$

Client:

- Set $B_{\alpha_i} \leftarrow \mathsf{Dec}_{\mathsf{K_{Enc}}}(B_{\alpha_i}^{\mathsf{enc}})$ for $i \in \{1, 2\}$
- Retrieve ball (w, L) from B_α for appropriate $\alpha \in \{\alpha_1, \alpha_2\}$
- Run L2C.UpdateBall($(w, L), L', B_{\alpha_1}, B_{\alpha_2}$)
- Set $B_{\alpha_i}^{\mathsf{new}} \leftarrow \mathsf{Enc}_{\mathsf{K_{Enc}}}(B_{\alpha_i})$ for $i \in \{1, 2\}$
- **return** $B_{\alpha_2}^{\mathsf{new}}, B_{\alpha_2}^{\mathsf{new}}$

Server:

- Replace $B_{\alpha_i}^{\mathsf{enc}}$ with $B_{\alpha_i}^{\mathsf{new}}$ for $i \in \{1, 2\}$

5.2 Security and Efficiency

Correctness. LayeredSSE is correct as each keyword has two bins that contain its identifiers associated to it (and these bins are consistently retrieved and updated with L2C). If the hash function is modeled as a random oracle, the bin choices are uniformly random and Theorem 1 guarantees that bins do not overflow.

Selective Security. LayeredSSE is selectively secure and has standard setup leakage N, such as search and update leakage qp, where qp is the query pattern[4]. This can be shown with a simple hybrid argument, sketched here. For setup, the simulator Sim receives N, recomputes m and initializes m empty bins $B_1, \ldots, B_m$ of size $p \cdot c \log\log\log(\lambda) \log\log(N/p)$ each. Sim then outputs $\mathsf{EDB}' = (\mathsf{Enc}_{\mathsf{K}'_{\mathsf{Enc}}}(B_i)_{i=1}^{m})$ for some sampled key $\mathsf{K}'_{\mathsf{Enc}}$. As Enc is IND-CPA secure (and bins do not overflow in the real experiment except with negligible probability), the output EDB' is indistinguishable from the output of Setup in the real

[4] This is equivalent to page length hiding leakage $\mathcal{L}_{\mathsf{len\text{-}hid}}$, as we only restrict ourselves to lists of size at most p.

experiment. For a search query on keyword w, Sim checks the query pattern qp whether w was already queried. If w was not queried before, Sim a new uniformly random keyword w'. Otherwise, Sim responds with the same keyword w' from the previous query. As we assume that keywords are preprocessed by the client via a PRF, the keywords w and w' are indistinguishable. For an update query on keyword w, the client output in the first flow is the same as in a search query and thus, Sim can proceed as in search. For the second flow, Sim receives two bins $B_{\alpha_1}, B_{\alpha_2}$ from the adversary, directly reencrypts them and sends them back to the adversary. This behaviour is indistinguishable, as the bins are encrypted and again, bins do not overflow except with negligible probability.

Adaptive Security. For adaptive security, the adversary can issue search and update queries that depend on previous queries. As Theorem 1 assumes selectively chosen InsertBall and UpdateBall operations, there is no guarantee that bins do not overflow anymore in the real game. Thus, the adversary can potentially distinguish update queries of the simulated game from real update queries if she manages to overflow a bin in the real game, as she would receive bins with increased size only in latter case. Fortunately, we can just add a check in Update whether one of the bins overflows after the L2C.UpdateBall operation. In that case, the client reverts the update and send back the (reencrypted) original bins. Now, Theorem 1 still guarantees that bins overflow only with negligible probability after Setup and we can show that the simulated game is indistinguishable from the real game as before. Note that LayeredSSE is still correct after this modification, since updates that lead to overflows cannot occur by accident, but only if the client systemically adapts the choice of updates to the random coins used during previous update operations (see Theorem 1).

Note that when the client remarks that a bin overflowed in an Update in a real world environment, this is due malicious Update operations. The client can adapt his reaction accordingly, whereas the server learns no information about the attack without being notified by the client. We can show that LayeredSSE with the adjustment of Update is correct and $\mathcal{L}_{\mathsf{len\text{-}hid}}$-adaptively secure. The same simulator Sim suffices and we omit the details.

Efficiency. LayeredSSE has constant storage efficiency, as the server stores $m = \left\lceil (N/p)/(\log\log\log\lambda \cdot \log\log\frac{N}{p})\right\rceil$ bins of $\mathcal{O}(p\log\log\log\lambda \cdot \log\log\frac{N}{p})$ identifiers each. There is no client stash required. Each search and update query, the server looks up 2 bins, and thus LayeredSSE has $\widetilde{\mathcal{O}}\left(\log\log\left(N/p\right)\right)$ page efficiency. Note that LayeredSSE has $\mathcal{O}(1)$ locality if only lists up to size p are inserted.

Extensions. With some care, LayeredSSE can handle deletes and arbitrary lists (without sacrificing security and efficiency). We refer to the full version for more details. The results are formalized in Theorem 2.

Theorem 2 (LayeredSSE). *Let N be an upper bound on the size of database* DB *and $p \leq N^{1-1/\log\log\lambda}$ be the page size. The scheme* LayeredSSE *is correct and* $\mathcal{L}_{\mathsf{len\text{-}hid}}$*-adaptively semantically secure if* Enc *is* IND-CPA *secure and* H *is modeled* *as a random oracle. It has constant storage efficiency and* $\widetilde{\mathcal{O}}(\log\log N/p)$ *page efficiency. If only lists up to size p are inserted,* LayeredSSE *has constant locality.*

6 The Generic Local Transform

In this section, we define the Generic Local Transform (GLT), creating a link between the two IO-efficiency goals of *locality* and *page efficiency.* Namely, the GLT builds an SSE scheme with good *locality* properties from an SSE scheme with good *page efficiency.* For a page-efficient scheme to be used within the GLT, it needs to have certain extra properties. We define such schemes as *suitable* page-efficient schemes in Sect. 6.1. Next, we introduce the useful notion of *overflowing* SSE. The GLT is then obtained by combining an overflowing SSE with a suitable page-efficient scheme. The OSSE we will use for that purpose, ClipOSSE, is presented in Sect. 6.2. Finally, the GLT is built from the previous components in Sect. 6.4. An overview of the correctness and security proofs is provided in section Sect. 6.5. Full proofs are available in the full version.

6.1 Preliminaries

Suitable Page-Efficient SSE. The GLT will create many instances of the underlying page-efficient scheme, each with a different page size. For that reason, for the purpose of the GLT, we slightly extend the standard SSE interface defined in Section Sect. 3: namely, $\mathsf{Setup}(\mathsf{K}, N, \mathsf{DB}, p)$ takes as an additional parameter the page size p. In addition, recall that, in Sect. 3, we have allowed the $\mathsf{Update}(\mathsf{K}, (w, L), \mathsf{op}, \mathsf{st}; \mathsf{EDB})$ procedure to add a *set* of matching documents K to a given keyword w in a single call. Note that S is allowed to be empty, in which case nothing is added.

If a scheme instantiates that interface, and, in addition, satisfies the following three conditions, we will call such as scheme a *suitable* page-efficient SSE.

- The scheme has client storage $\mathcal{O}(1)$.
- The scheme has locality $\mathcal{O}(1)$ during searches and updates *when accessing a list of length at most one page.*
- The leakage of the scheme is page-length-hiding.

Overflowing SSE. We introduce the notion of *Overflowing* SSE. An Overflowing SSE (OSSE) has the same interface and functionality as a standard SSE scheme, except that during a Setup or Update operation, it may refuse to store some document identifiers. Those identifiers are called *overflowing.* At the output of the Setup and Update operations, the client returns the set of overflowing elements. Compared to standard SSE, the correctness definition is relaxed in the following way: during a Search, only matching identifiers that were *not* overflowing need to be retrieved.

The intention of an Overflowing SSE is that it may be used as a component within a larger SSE scheme, which will store the overflowing identifiers using a separate mechanism. The use of an OSSE may be regarded as implicit in some prior SSE constructions. We have chosen to introduce the notion explicitly because it allows to cleanly split the presentation of the Generic Local Transform into two parts: an OSSE scheme that stores most of the database, and an array of page-efficient schemes that store the overflowing identifiers.

6.2 Dynamic Two-Dimensional One-Choice Allocation

The first component of the Generic Local Transform is an OSSE scheme, ClipOSSE. In line with prior work, we split the presentation of ClipOSSE into two parts: an allocation scheme, which specifies where elements should be stored; and the SSE scheme built on top of it, which adds a layer of encryption, key management, and other mechanisms needed to convert the allocation scheme into a full SSE.

The allocation scheme within ClipOSSE is called 1C-Alloc. Similar to [ANSS16], the allocation scheme is an abstract construct that defines the memory locations where items should be stored, but does not store anything itself. In the case of 1C-Alloc, items are stored within buckets, and the procedures return as output the indices of *buckets* where items should be stored. From the point of view of 1C-Alloc, each bucket has unlimited storage. In more detail, 1C-Alloc contains two procedures, Fetch and Add.

- Fetch(m, w, ℓ): given a number of buckets m, a keyword w, and a list length ℓ, Fetch returns (a superset of) the indices of buckets where elements matching keyword w may be stored, assuming there are ℓ such elements.
- Add(m, w, ℓ): given the same input, Add returns the index of the bucket where the *next* element matching keyword w should be inserted, assuming there are currently ℓ matching elements.

The intention is that Add is used during an SSE Update operation, in order to choose the bucket where the next list element is stored; while Fetch is used during a Search operation, in order to determine the buckets that need to be read to retrieve all list elements. 1C-Alloc will satisfy the correctness property given in Definition 10. Note that the number of buckets m is always assumed to be a power of 2.

Definition 10 (Correctness). *For all m, w, ℓ, if m is a power of 2, then*

$$\bigcup_{0 \leq i \leq \ell-1} \mathsf{Add}(m, w, i) \subseteq \mathsf{Fetch}(m, w, \ell).$$

To describe 1C-Alloc, it is convenient to conceptually group buckets into superbuckets. For $\ell = 2^i \leq m$, an *ℓ-superbucket* is a collection of ℓ consecutive buckets, with indices of the form $k \cdot \ell, k \cdot \ell + 1, \ldots, (k+1) \cdot \ell - 1$, for some $k \leq m/\ell$. A 1-superbucket is the same as a bucket. Notice that for a given ℓ, the ℓ-superbuckets do not overlap. They form a partition of the set of buckets. For $\ell > 1$, each ℓ-superbucket contains exactly two $\ell/2$-superbuckets.

Let H be a hash function, whose output is assumed to be uniformly random in $\{1, \ldots, m\}$. 1C-Alloc works as follows. Fix a keyword w and length $\ell \leq m$

(the case $\ell > m$ will be discussed later). Let $\ell' = 2^{\lceil \log \ell \rceil}$ be the smallest power of 2 larger than ℓ. On input w and ℓ, 1C-Alloc.Fetch returns the (unique) ℓ'-superbucket that contains $H(w)$.

Algorithm 3. Dynamic Two-Dimensional One-Choice Allocation (1C-Alloc)

1C-Alloc.Fetch(m, w, ℓ)

$\ell' \leftarrow 2^{\lceil \log \ell \rceil}$
if $\ell' \geq m$ **then**
    return $\{0, ..., m-1\}$
else
    $i \leftarrow \lfloor H(w)/\ell' \rfloor$
    return $\{\ell' \cdot i, ..., \ell' \cdot i + \ell' - 1\}$

1C-Alloc.Add(m, w, ℓ)

$\ell \leftarrow \ell \bmod m$
$\ell' \leftarrow 2^{\lceil \log (\ell+1) \rceil}$
$i \leftarrow \lfloor H(w)/\ell' \rfloor$
if $\lfloor 2H(w)/\ell' \rfloor \bmod 2 = 0$ **then**
    return $\ell' \cdot i + \ell$
else
    return $\ell' \cdot i + \ell - \ell'/2$

Meanwhile, 1C-Alloc.Add is designed in order to ensure that the first ℓ successive locations returned by Add for keyword w are in fact included within the ℓ'-superbucket above $H(w)$ (that is, in order to ensure correctness). For the first list element (when $\ell = 0$), Add returns the bucket $H(w)$; for the second element, it returns the other bucket contained inside the 2-superbucket above $H(w)$. More generally, if S is the smallest superbucket above $H(w)$ that contains at least $\ell+1$ buckets, Add returns the leftmost bucket within S that has not yet received an element. In practice, the index of that bucket can be computed easily based on ℓ and the binary decomposition of $H(w)$, as done in Algorithm 3. (In fact, the exact order in which buckets are selected by Add is irrelevant, as long as it selects distinct buckets, and correctness holds.)

When the size of the list ℓ grows above the number of buckets m, Fetch returns all buckets, while Add selects the same buckets as it did for $\ell \bmod m$.

6.3 Clipped One-Choice OSSE

ClipOSSE is the OSSE scheme obtained by storing lists according to 1C-Alloc, using $m = O(N/\log\log N)$ buckets, with each bucket containing up to $\tau = \lceil \alpha \log\log N \rceil$ items, for some constant α. Buckets are always padded to the threshold τ and encrypted before being stored on the server. Thus, from the server's point of view, they are completely opaque. A table T containing (in encrypted form) the length of the list matching each keyword w is also stored on the server.

Given 1C-Alloc, the details of ClipOSSE are straightforward. A short overview is given in text below. The encrypted database generated by Setup is essentially equivalent to starting from an empty database, and populating it by making repeated calls to Update, one for each keyword–document pair in the database. For that reason, we focus on Search and Update. The full specification for Setup, Search, and Update is given as pseudo-code in Algorithm 4.

Search. To retrieve the list of identifiers matching keyword w, ClipOSSE calls 1C-Alloc(m, w, ℓ) to get the set of bucket indices where the elements matching keyword w have been stored. The client retrieves those buckets from the server, and decrypts them to obtain the desired information.

Update. For simplicity, we focus on a the case where a single identifier is added. The case of a set of identifiers can be obtained by repeating the process for each identifier in the set. To add the new item to the list matching keyword w, ClipOSSE calls 1C-Alloc(m, w, ℓ) to determine the bucket where the new list item should be inserted. The client retrieves that bucket from the server, decrypts it, adds the new item, reencrypts the bucket, and sends it back to the server. If that bucket was already full, the item is overflowing, in the sense of Sect. 6.1.

Algorithm 4. Clipped One-Choice OSSE (ClipOSSE)

Global parameters: constants $d, \alpha \in \mathbb{N}^*$

ClipOSSE.KeyGen(1^λ)

Generate keys K, K_{PRF} for Enc, PRF
return $\mathsf{K} = (K, K_{\mathsf{PRF}})$

ClipOSSE.Setup$(\mathsf{K}, N, \mathsf{DB})$

$m \leftarrow 2^{\lceil \log (N/\log\log N)\rceil}$
$\tau \leftarrow \lceil \alpha \log\log N \rceil$
$B_0, \ldots, B_{m-1}, T, \mathsf{EDB}, \mathsf{clip} \leftarrow \varnothing$
for all each $(w, \{e_1, \ldots, e_\ell\})$ in DB **do**
  $K_w \leftarrow \mathsf{PRF}_{K_{\mathsf{PRF}}}(w)$
  $T[w] \leftarrow \mathsf{Enc}_{K_w}(\ell)$
  for all t from 1 to ℓ **do**
    $C \leftarrow \varnothing$
    $i \leftarrow$ 1C-Alloc.Add$(m, w, t-1)$
    if then$|B[i]| < \tau$
      $B[i] \leftarrow B[i] \cup \{e_i\}$
    else
      $C \leftarrow C \cup \{e_i\}$
    if $|S| > 0$ **then**
      $\mathsf{clip} \leftarrow \mathsf{clip} \cup (w, \ell, C)$
Let $B^{\mathsf{Enc}}[i] = \mathsf{Enc}_K(B_i)$ for each i
return $\mathsf{EDB} = (T, (B^{\mathsf{Enc}}[i])), \mathsf{clip}$

ClipOSSE.Search$(\mathsf{K}, w, \mathsf{st}; \mathsf{EDB})$

Client: *(search token)*
send $(w, K_w) = \mathsf{PRF}_{K_{\mathsf{PRF}}}(w)$

Server:
$\ell \leftarrow \mathsf{Dec}_{K_w}(T[w])$
$S \leftarrow$ 1C-Alloc.Fetch(m, w, ℓ)
return $\{B^{\mathsf{Enc}}[i] : i \in S\}$

ClipOSSE.Update$(\mathsf{K}, (w, \{e\}), \mathsf{op}, \mathsf{st}; \mathsf{EDB})$

Client: *(update token)*
send $(w, K_w = \mathsf{PRF}_{K_{\mathsf{PRF}}}(w))$

Server:
$\ell \leftarrow \mathsf{Dec}_{K_w}(T[w])$
$i \leftarrow$ 1C-Alloc.Add(m, w, ℓ)
send $B^{\mathsf{Enc}}[i]$

Client:
$B \leftarrow \mathsf{Dec}_K(B^{\mathsf{Enc}}[i])$
if $|B| < \tau$ **then**
  $\mathsf{clip} \leftarrow \varnothing$
  $B \leftarrow B \cup \{e\}$
else
  $\mathsf{clip} \leftarrow \{e\}$
send $B' = \mathsf{Enc}_K(B)$

Server:
$B^{\mathsf{Enc}}[i] \leftarrow B'$

Client:
return clip

6.4 The Generic Local Transform

The Generic Local Transform takes as input a page-length-hiding page-efficient SSE scheme PE-SSE. It outputs a local SSE scheme Local[PE-SSE].

To realize Local[PE-SSE], we use two structures. The first structure is an instance of ClipOSSE, which stores most of the database. The second structure is an array of n_{level} instances of PE-SSE. The i-th instance, denoted PE-SSE$_i$, has page size 2^i. The PE-SSE$_i$ instances are used to store elements that overflow from ClipOSSE. In addition, a table T stores (in encrypted form) the length of the list matching keyword w, for each keyword[5].

Fix a keyword w, matching ℓ elements. Let $\ell' = 2^{\lceil \log \ell \rceil}$ be the smallest power of 2 larger than ℓ. Let $i = \log \ell'$. At any point in time, the elements matching w are stored in two locations: ClipOSSE, and $\mathsf{PE\text{-}SSE}_i$. Each of these two locations stores part of the elements: ClipOSSE stores the elements that did not overflow, and $\mathsf{PE\text{-}SSE}_i$ stores the overflowing elements. Each element exists in only one of the two locations. Again, for simplicity, we define updates for adding a single identifier per keyword. The case of adding a set of identifiers at once can be deduced by repeating the same process for each identifier in the set.

Algorithm 5. Generic Local Transform (Local[PE-SSE])

Global parameters: constant $d \in \mathbb{N}^*$

Local[PE-SSE].KeyGen(1^λ)

Generate key K_{PRF} for PRF
return $\mathsf{K} = (K, K_{\mathsf{PRF}})$

Local[PE-SSE].Update($\mathsf{K}, (w, L)$; EDB)

Client: *(update token)*

send $(w, L, K_w = \mathsf{PRF}_{K_{\mathsf{PRF}}}(w))$

Server:

$C \leftarrow \mathsf{ClipOSSE.Update}(w, L)$
$\ell \leftarrow \mathsf{Dec}_{K_w}(T[w])$
$T[w] \leftarrow \mathsf{Enc}_{K_w}(\ell + 1)$
send ℓ

Client:

$i \leftarrow \lceil \log \ell \rceil$
if $\lceil \log \ell \rceil = \lceil \log (\ell + 1) \rceil$ **then**
    $\mathsf{PE\text{-}SSE}_i.\mathsf{Update}(w, C)$
else
    $S \leftarrow$ set of matches in $\mathsf{PE\text{-}SSE}_i.\mathsf{Search}(w)$
    $\mathsf{PE\text{-}SSE}_{i+1}.\mathsf{Update}(w, S \cup C)$

Local[PE-SSE].Setup(K, N, DB)

$n_{level} \leftarrow \lceil N / \log^d N \rceil$
for all $(w, S) \in \mathsf{DB}$ **do**
    $K_w \leftarrow \mathsf{PRF}_{K_{\mathsf{PRF}}}(w)$
    $T[w] \leftarrow \mathsf{Enc}_{K_w}(|S|)$
EDB, clip $\leftarrow$ ClipOSSE.Setup(DB)
for all i from 0 to n_{level} **do**
    $\mathsf{DB}_i \leftarrow \{(w, C) : (w, \ell, C) \in \mathsf{clip}$ and $2^{i-1} < \ell \leq 2^i\}$
    $\mathsf{PE\text{-}SSE}_i \leftarrow \mathsf{PE\text{-}SSE.Setup}(\lceil N/\log N \rceil, 2^i, \mathsf{DB}_i)$

Local[PE-SSE].Search(K, w, st; EDB)

Client: *(search token)*

send $(w, K_w = \mathsf{PRF}_{K_{\mathsf{PRF}}}(w))$

Server:

$i \leftarrow \lceil \log (\mathsf{Dec}_{K_w}(T[w])) \rceil$
return $\mathsf{ClipOSSE.Search}(w) \cup \mathsf{PE\text{-}SSE}_i.\mathsf{Search}(w)$

Search. During a search operation, Local[PE-SSE] queries both structures, and combines their output to retrieve all matching elements.

Update. During an update operation to add element e, Local[PE-SSE] forwards the update query to ClipOSSE, and gets as output $C = \varnothing$ if the element did not overflow, or $C = \{e\}$ if the element did overflow. For now, assume that $\lceil \log \ell \rceil = \lceil \log (\ell + 1) \rceil$, that is, the $\mathsf{PE\text{-}SSE}_i$ instance associated with the list remains the same during the update operation. In that case, $\mathsf{PE\text{-}SSE}_i$ is updated for the set C. (Recall from Sect. 6.1 that a length-hiding SSE such as PE-SSE accepts sets of elements as input in Update.) The length-hiding property is designed to guarantee that the content of C (including whether it is empty) is not leaked to the server. Now assume $\lceil \log \ell \rceil < \lceil \log (\ell + 1) \rceil$. In that

[5] The same table exists in ClipOSSE. In an actual implementation, they would be the same table, but using ClipOSSE in black box eases the presentation.

case, the PE-SSE instance associated with the list becomes $\mathsf{PE\text{-}SSE}_{i+1}$ instead of $\mathsf{PE\text{-}SSE}_i$. The client retrieves all current overflowing elements from $\mathsf{PE\text{-}SSE}_i$, adds the content of C, and stores the result in $\mathsf{PE\text{-}SSE}_{i+1}$.

6.5 Overflow of ClipOSSE

The main technical result in this section regards the number of overflowing items in ClipOSSE.

Theorem 3. *Suppose that* ClipOSSE *receives as input a database of size N, such that the size of the longest list is $\mathcal{O}(N/\log^d N)$ for some $d \geq 2$. Then for any constant c, there exists a choice of parameters of* ClipOSSE *such that the number of overflowing items is $\mathcal{O}(N/\log^c N)$.*

The proof of Theorem 3 is intricate. For space reasons, we only give a brief overview here. A detailed overview and the full proof is given in the full version.. First, we show that the result holds in the special case where all lists have length $N/\log^d N$. This uses a negative association argument, similar to the proof of [DPP18, Theorem 1]. The core of the proof is to then show that this special case implies the general case. This is done by iteratively merging short lists, while showing that this merging process can only have a limited effect on the number of overflowing elements. At the outcome of the merging process, all lists have length $N/\log^d N$, which reduces the problem to the special case. The main technique for the reduction is a stochastic dominance argument, combined with a convexity argument (similar to the proof of [BBF+21, Theorem 5]).

The Generic Local Transform itself uses standard SSE techniques, and its properties follow from previous discussions. We provide a formal statement below.

Theorem 4 (Generic Local Transform). *Let N be an upper bound on the size of database* DB. *Suppose that* PE-SSE *is a* suitable *page-efficient scheme with page efficiency P and storage efficiency S. Then* Local[PE-SSE] *is a correct and secure SSE scheme with storage efficiency $\mathcal{O}(S)$, locality $\mathcal{O}(1)$, and read efficiency $P + \widetilde{\mathcal{O}}(\log\log N)$.*

References

[ABKU94] Azar, Y., Broder, A.Z., Karlin, A.R., Upfal, E.: Balanced allocations. In: Proceedings of the Twenty-Sixth Annual ACM Symposium on Theory of Computing, pp. 593–602 (1994)

[AKM19] Amjad, G., Kamara, S., Moataz, T.: Breach-resistant structured encryption. In: Proceedings on Privacy Enhancing Technologies, vol. 2019, no. 1, pp. 245–265 (2019)

[ANSS16] Asharov, G., Naor, M., Segev, G., and Shahaf, I. Searchable symmetric encryption: optimal locality in linear space via two-dimensional balanced allocations. In: Wichs, D., Mansour, Y. (eds.) 48th Annual ACM Symposium on Theory of Computing, 18–21 June 2016, pp. 1101–1114. ACM Press, Cambridge (2016)

[ASS18] Asharov, G., Segev, G., Shahaf, I.: Tight tradeoffs in searchable symmetric encryption. In: Shacham, H., Boldyreva, A. (eds.) CRYPTO 2018, Part I. LNCS, vol. 10991, pp. 407–436. Springer, Cham (2018). https://doi.org/10.1007/978-3-319-96884-1_14

[ASS21] Asharov, G., Segev, G., Shahaf, I.: Tight tradeoffs in searchable symmetric encryption. J. Cryptol. **34**(2), 1–37 (2021)

[BBF+21] Bossuat, A., Bost, R., Fouque, P.-A., Minaud, B., Reichle, M.: SSE and SSD: page-efficient searchable symmetric encryption. In: Malkin, T., Peikert, C. (eds.) CRYPTO 2021, Part III. LNCS, vol. 12827, pp. 157–184. Springer, Cham (2021). https://doi.org/10.1007/978-3-030-84252-9_6

[BFHM08] Berenbrink, P., Friedetzky, T., Hu, Z., Martin, R.: On weighted balls-into-bins games. Theor. Comput. Sci. **409**(3), 511–520 (2008)

[BMO17] Bost, R., Minaud, B., Ohrimenko, O.: Forward and backward private searchable encryption from constrained cryptographic primitives. In: Thuraisingham, B.M., Evans, D., Malkin, T., Xu, D. (eds.) ACM CCS 2017: 24th Conference on Computer and Communications Security, 31 October–2 November 2017, pp. 1465–1482. ACM Press, Dallas (2017)

[Bos16] Bost, R.: $\Sigma o\phi o\varsigma$: forward secure searchable encryption. In: Weippl, E.R., Katzenbeisser, S., Kruegel, C., Myers, A.C., Halevi, S. (eds.) ACM CCS 2016: 23rd Conference on Computer and Communications Security, 24–28 October 2016, pp. 1143–1154. ACM Press, Vienna (2016)

[CGKO06] Curtmola, R., Garay, J.A., Kamara, S., Ostrovsky, R.: Searchable symmetric encryption: improved definitions and efficient constructions. In: Juels, A., Wright, R.N., De Capitani di Vimercati, S. (eds.) ACM CCS 2006: 13th Conference on Computer and Communications Security, 30 October–3 November 2006, pp. 79–88. ACM Press, Alexandria (2006)

[CJJ+14] Cash, D., et al.: Dynamic searchable encryption in very-large databases: Data structures and implementation. In: ISOC Network and Distributed System Security Symposium - NDSS 2014, 23–26 February 2014. The Internet Society, San Diego (2014)

[CK10] Chase, M., Kamara, S.: Structured encryption and controlled disclosure. In: Abe, M. (ed.) ASIACRYPT 2010. LNCS, vol. 6477, pp. 577–594. Springer, Heidelberg (2010). https://doi.org/10.1007/978-3-642-17373-8_33

[CT14] Cash, D., Tessaro, S.: The locality of searchable symmetric encryption. In: Nguyen, P.Q., Oswald, E. (eds.) EUROCRYPT 2014. LNCS, vol. 8441, pp. 351–368. Springer, Heidelberg (2014). https://doi.org/10.1007/978-3-642-55220-5_20

[DP17] Demertzis, I., Papamanthou, C.: Fast searchable encryption with tunable locality. In: Proceedings of the 2017 ACM International Conference on Management of Data, pp. 1053–1067 (2017)

[DPP18] Demertzis, I., Papadopoulos, D., Papamanthou, C.: Searchable encryption with optimal locality: achieving sublogarithmic read efficiency. In: Shacham, H., Boldyreva, A. (eds.) CRYPTO 2018, Part I. LNCS, vol. 10991, pp. 371–406. Springer, Cham (2018). https://doi.org/10.1007/978-3-319-96884-1_13

[EKPE18] Etemad, M., Küpçü, A., Papamanthou, C., Evans, D.: Efficient dynamic searchable encryption with forward privacy. In: Proceedings on Privacy Enhancing Technologies, vol. 2018, no. 1, pp. 5–20 (2018)

[JK77] Johnson, N.L., Kotz, S.: Urn Models and Their Application: An Approach to Modern Discrete Probability Theory. Wiley, New York (1977)

[MM17] Miers, I., Mohassel, P.: IO-DSSE: scaling dynamic searchable encryption to millions of indexes by improving locality. In: ISOC Network and Distributed System Security Symposium - NDSS 2017, 26 February–3 March 2017. The Internet Society, San Diego (2017)

[MPC+18] Mishra, P., Poddar, R., Chen, J., Chiesa, A., Popa, R.A.: Oblix: an efficient oblivious search index. In: 2018 IEEE Symposium on Security and Privacy, 21–23 May 2018, pp. 279–296. IEEE Computer Society Press, San Francisco (2018)

[PR04] Pagh, R., Rodler, F.F.: Cuckoo hashing. J. Algorithms **51**(2), 122–144 (2004)

[RMS01] Richa, A.W., Mitzenmacher, M., Sitaraman, R.: The power of two random choices: a survey of techniques and results. Comb. Optim. **9**, 255–304 (2001)

[TW07] Talwar, K., Wieder, U.: Balanced allocations: the weighted case. In: Proceedings of the Thirty-Ninth Annual ACM Symposium on Theory of Computing, pp. 256–265 (2007)

[TW14] Talwar, K., Wieder, U.: Balanced allocations: a simple proof for the heavily loaded case. In: Esparza, J., Fraigniaud, P., Husfeldt, T., Koutsoupias, E. (eds.) ICALP 2014. LNCS, vol. 8572, pp. 979–990. Springer, Heidelberg (2014). https://doi.org/10.1007/978-3-662-43948-7_81

[ZKP16] Zhang, Y., Katz, J., Papamanthou, C.: All your queries are belong to us: The power of file-injection attacks on searchable encryption. In: Holz, T., Savage, S. (eds.), USENIX Security 2016: 25th USENIX Security Symposium, 10–12 August 2016, pp. 707–720. USENIX Association, Austin (2016)

Programmable Distributed Point Functions

Elette Boyle[1,2], Niv Gilboa[3], Yuval Ishai[4], and Victor I. Kolobov[4(✉)]

[1] IDC Herzliya, Herzliya, Israel
elette.boyle@idc.ac.il
[2] NTT Research, Sunnyvale, USA
[3] Ben-Gurion University, Be'er Sheva, Israel
gilboan@bgu.ac.il
[4] Technion, Haifa, Israel
{yuvali,tkolobov}@cs.technion.ac.il

Abstract. A *distributed point function* (DPF) is a cryptographic primitive that enables compressed additive sharing of a secret unit vector across two or more parties. Despite growing ubiquity within applications and notable research efforts, the best 2-party DPF construction to date remains the tree-based construction from (Boyle et al., CCS'16), with no significantly new approaches since.

We present a new framework for 2-party DPF construction, which applies in the setting of feasible (polynomial-size) domains. This captures in particular all DPF applications in which the keys are expanded to the full domain. Our approach is motivated by a strengthened notion we put forth, of *programmable* DPF (PDPF): in which a short, input-independent "offline" key can be reused for sharing many point functions.

- *PDPF from OWF.* We construct a PDPF for feasible domains from the minimal assumption that one-way functions exist, where the second "online" key size is polylogarithmic in the domain size N.

Our approach offers multiple new efficiency features and applications:

- *Privately puncturable PRFs.* Our PDPF gives the first OWF-based *privately* puncturable PRFs (for feasible domains) with sublinear keys.
- $O(1)$*-round distributed DPF Gen.* We obtain a (standard) DPF with polylog-size keys that admits an analog of Doerner-shelat (CCS'17) distributed key generation, requiring only $O(1)$ rounds (versus $\log N$).
- *PCG with 1 short key.* Compressing useful correlations for secure computation, where one key is of minimal size. This provides up to exponential communication savings in some application scenarios.

Keywords: Distributed Point Function · Puncturable Psuedorandom Function

1 Introduction

A *distributed point function* (DPF) [12,27] is a cryptographic primitive that enables compressed sharing of a secret unit vector across two or more parties. More concretely, a two-party DPF allows one to split any *point function* f_α (i.e., for which $f_\alpha(x) = 1$ if $x = \alpha$, and 0 otherwise[1]) into succinctly described

[1] Slightly more generally, $f_{\alpha,\beta}$ with $f_{\alpha,\beta}(\alpha) = \beta$ for $\beta \in \{0, 1\}$.

Y. Dodis and T. Shrimpton (Eds.): CRYPTO 2022, LNCS 13510, pp. 121–151, 2022.
https://doi.org/10.1007/978-3-031-15985-5_5

functions f_0, f_1, that individually hide f_α, and which support a simple additive per-input reconstruction $f_\alpha(x) = f_0(x) + f_1(x)$.

DPFs with function share f_i size (sometimes referred to as "key size") comparable to the truth table of f_α are trivially achievable, by simply taking the function shares f_i to be an additive secret sharing of the full truth table itself. Efficient constructions with small key size, roughly logarithmic in the domain size of f_α, have been built from one-way functions [12,27].

The appealing compressing structure of DPF constructions has enabled a wide range of cryptographic applications, ranging from Private Information Retrieval (PIR) [18,27], to anonymous messaging systems [20], secure computation for RAM programs [25] and programs with mixed-mode operations [7,13], and recently Pseudorandom Correlation Generators [8,10,13] for expanding small correlated seeds into large pseudorandom instances of cryptographic correlations, with applications to secure computation and beyond.

In many (if not most) of these applications, the parties perform a full evaluation of the DPF function shares, on every input within the domain of the function f_α. This means that, in particular, the necessary DPF constructions are only relevant for relatively small, polynomial-size domains.

The growing list of applications has provided significant motivation for deeper study of the DPF primitive, including alternative constructions and careful fine-tuning of efficiency. However, despite notable research efforts, the best 2-party DPF construction to date (even concrete constants) remains the tree-based construction from [12]. In addition, no significantly new approaches toward construction have emerged since this time.

1.1 Our Results

We present a new approach of DPF construction, whose structure dramatically differs from existing DPFs, and which offers new efficiency features and applications in the setting of feasible (polynomial)-size domains.

Programmable DPF. Perhaps the primary downside of DPFs is that their security guarantees inherently require the existence of *two or more* non-colluding parties who receive shares f_0 and f_1 of the secret function. For example, DPFs yield solutions to the problem of *two*-server PIR, but seem useless for single-server PIR. Unfortunately, this non-collusion trust assumption is to some degree unavoidable for efficient solutions. For problems like PIR, for example, it is known that *single*-server cheap (symmetric-key) solutions simply cannot exist [24]. However, the two-server state of affairs has a further downside beyond the assumption of trust. Given two servers operating, DPF-based solutions incur twice as much computation, communication, and coordination costs between parties than if a single server could suffice.

Given the barrier of efficient single-server solutions, we consider a next best alternative: a form of *"1.5-server"* DPF, or what we will refer to as a *programmable* DPF. The idea is that participation and cost to one of the two servers will be pushed to minimum, thus incurring the burden of only "half" a server. Concretely, in a programmable DPF scheme, the share f_0 given to the first server is simply a random (i.e., "programmed") 128-bit string,[2] independent of the choice of—or in some cases, even the *parameters* of—the secret point function being shared. For example, one can execute the role of the first server across several applications via a public service.

Naive PDPF. As a baseline, consider a naive construction of PDPF: The offline key is a standard PRF key, and the online key is simply a domain-size string which together with the full-doman expansion of the PRF form additive secret shares of the desired truth table. The runtime of key generation is linear in the domain size N (which, looking ahead, will match that of our construction). However, the online key size is also linear in N, which we will succeed to compress exponentially. In addition, for the case of sharing a random point function, we will also obtain exponential improvement in the online key generation.

Related Notions. Our PDPF goal is related to two existing notions from the literature: privately puncturable PRFs [5], and two-server PIR in an offline/online model recently studied by Corrigan-Gibbs and Kogan [21].

Privately puncturable PRFs are pseudorandom functions (PRFs) that support generation of punctured keys which enable evaluation of the PRF on all but a single punctured input x^*, and which further *hide* the identity of x^*. (Single-key) privately puncturable PRFs are in fact implied by programmable DPFs, by taking the master PRF key to be the first-server DPF share, and generating a punctured key at x^* by computing a second-server DPF share for the function $f_{\alpha,\beta}$ with $\alpha = x^*$ and $\beta \leftarrow \{0,1\}$ selected at random. In turn, privately punctured PRF constructions can provide a direction toward programmable DPFs. However, the only existing instantiations of privately puncturable PRFs make use of heavy public-key cryptography machinery, and provide heavy costs for concrete applications [4,16,17,36]. There is also no clear way "scale down" these constructions to a polynomial-size domain in a way that circumvents these issues.

Analogous to the "half server" of programmable DPF, the offline/online 2-server PIR protocols of [21,38] consider a setting where first server's query and response (analogous to our first-server DPF key) can be computed *offline*, before the target input (analogous to the punctured point x^*) is specified. However, the resulting schemes do not yield the stronger target of a DPF. Indeed, the closest object they construct supports a nonlinear reconstruction procedure more complex than simple addition, which precludes a large subset of DPF applications requiring this structure (such as secure aggregation). In addition, [38] uses public-key cryptography.

Given the collective state of the art, no solutions exist for nontrivial programmable DPF without public-key cryptography, even for the restricted case of polynomial-size domains.

[2] Or rather, λ bits, where λ is the security parameter.

Programmable DPF on Small Domains from OWF. We present a 2-party programmable DPF (PDPF) construction for polynomial-size domains, relying on the minimal assumption that one-way functions exist.

We begin with a basic construction which has a non-negligible privacy error ϵ, which appears as a factor of $\log(1/\epsilon^2)$ in the key size and $1/\epsilon^2$ in full-domain evaluation, and which provides appealing concrete efficiency. For this reason, we express the result statement in terms of a length-doubling pseudorandom generator (whose existence is equivalent to one-way functions). We remark that small constant privacy error is motivated in many applications in the context of concrete efficiency, such as those anyway offering differential privacy guarantees (e.g., use of DPFs for private aggregate statistics in [3]).

For the final feasibility result, we then reduce this to negligible error via a nontrivial amplification procedure. Combining these two theorems provides a construction of PDPF with polylogarithmic online key size, from one-way functions.

Theorem 1 (1/poly-secure PDPF on small domains - Informal). *Given length doubling PRG* $G : \{0,1\}^\lambda \to \{0,1\}^{2\lambda}$, *there exists a computationally* ϵ-*secure Programmable DPF for point functions* $f_\alpha : [N] \to \{0,1\}$ *over output group* $\mathbb{G} = \mathbb{Z}$, *with online key size* $|k_1| = \lambda \log(/\epsilon^2)$.

- *Key generation makes* $(2N \log(N/\epsilon^2))/\lambda$ *invocations of* G, *and*
- *Full domain evaluation makes* $(2N \log N)/(\epsilon^2 \lambda)$ *invocations of* G.

Theorem 2 (Security amplification - Informal). *Suppose there exists a small-domain computationally* $1/p(N)$-*secure PDPF for any polynomial* p. *Then there exists a small-domain PDPF with negligible security error.*

Corollary 1 (PDPF from OWF - Informal). *Assuming the existence of OWF, there exists a PDPF for point functions* $f_\alpha : [N] \to \{0,1\}$ *where the runtime of key generation, single point evaluation, and full domain evaluation is quasilinear in* N, *and with online key size* $\mathrm{poly}(\lambda, \log N)$.

A few remarks are in order.

Small Domains: Applications and Non-applications. Note that the key generation and full evaluation algorithms of our construction run in time linear in N, and as such we are restricted to polynomial-sized domains in order to execute within polynomial time. As an additional point of interest, our techniques do not admit a more efficient single-point evaluation algorithm than a full-domain evaluation. An outstanding open problem in our work is to achieve a construction where the running time of key generation and a single point evaluation is only $\mathrm{poly}\log N$.

For many applications of DPFs, the required parameters are anyway on small (polynomial-size) domain. This captures a motivated range of applications and implemented systems, including:

1. *Private "reading"* applications, such as PIR, or private tag-based search for tag space of modest size. For example, the Popcorn system [29] ran 2-server PIR on $N = 8{,}000$ Netflix movies.

2. *Private "writing"* applications, such as secure distributed storage [35], voting, and aggregation. This includes Prio-style [19] applications for private collection of aggregate statistics, and Riposte [20], Blinder [1] and Spectrum [34] for anonymous messaging.
3. *Pseudorandom correlation generators (PCGs) for useful correlations.* Relevant correlation examples include "silent" generation of permuted one-time truth table correlations, oblivious linear evaluation (OLE), or authenticated multiplication triples [10] (for some simpler correlations the full power of DPF is not needed – see below).
4. *Mixed-mode secure computation with small-domain gates.* DPFs and their derivatives, most notably *distributed comparison functions* (DCF) (i.e. secret sharing functions of the form $f_{\alpha}^{\leq}$ that evaluate to 1 on all inputs $x \leq \alpha$), yield a method for highly efficient secure computation of certain types of non-arithmetic gates in the preprocessing model [13]. A DCF can be implemented by a logarithmic number of DPF invocations, one for each prefix of the shared point. However, in our small-domain construction the communication and computation for this DCF implementation essentially match those of a single DPF since both require full domain evaluation. Small-domain DPFs and DCFs suffice, e.g., for secure evaluation of zero-test, comparison/threshold, ReLU, splines, or finite-precision fixed-point arithmetic gates, on moderate-size inputs [7,13]. We remark that small domain sizes often arise naturally in settings such as privacy-preserving machine learning, where computations are frequently run in low precision.

Aside from the last (Item 4), each of the above application frameworks further requires the parties to perform a full-domain evaluation of the corresponding DPF function shares, *inherently* limiting the desired DPF tools to small domains.

The programmable feature of our PDPF, where the offline key is short and reusable, offers beneficial properties in the above settings. For example, for pseudorandom correlation generation, this enables a central server to have a *single short* PCG key for generating authenticated multiplication triples or truth-table correlations with many different users, requiring total storage of only 128 bits improving over present solutions that require the server to store approximately 1 MB *per user*. Such a "short-key PCG" can make a big difference in certain applications of secure two-party computation. For instance, this is the case when during a setup phase one of the two parties can be temporarily trusted. In this case, she can generate a pair of PCG seeds, send the short (128-bit) seed to the other party, and keep the longer one to herself. We discuss this application in more detail in Sect. 1.1.

There are, of course, application settings in which small-domain DPFs are not relevant. Prominent examples include:

1. *Private keyword search,* corresponding to PIR-type private queries where the space of possible inputs (e.g., universe of keywords) is large.
2. *Simpler pseudorandom correlation generators,* such as "silent" oblivious transfer, vector OLE, or (unauthenticated) multiplication triples, do not require the full 2-sided guarantees (so-called "puncturable PRFs" suffice).

3. *Mixed-mode secure computation with large-domain gates.* The above mixed-mode application is viable also for large domains, in which case our small-domain DPFs do not provide a solution. This includes instances of the above gates over large inputs.

Concrete Efficiency. In Table 1 we compare the efficiency of our programmable DPF construction to a "naive" construction with $O(N)$ key size, for domain size N (see Sect. 5 for more details). The comparison is done with output group $\mathbb{Z}$ and with payloads in $\{0, 1\}$, capturing a typical aggregation scenario. We compare these solutions with respect to key size, and estimate the running time of an AES-based implementation by using a standard benchmark of $1.8 \cdot 10^8$ length-doubling PRG calls per second on a single core.

To give one data point, for a domain of size $N = 100{,}000$ and security error $\epsilon = 2^{-8}$, the naive construction has 97.7 KB key size, and the running time for either key generation or full domain evaluation is 72.1 µs, while our construction achieves 0.5 KB key size, 548.3 µs running time for key generation, and 1.6 s running time for full domain evaluation[3]. In another data point, where $N = 20,000$ and $\epsilon = 2^{-6}$, the naive construction yields 14.7 KB key size and running time of 12.4 µs for both key generation and full domain evaluation, while our constructions has 0.4 KB key size, 68.7 µs running time for key generation, and 17.3 ms running time for full domain evaluation. Note that in applications that only require a random point α, the cost of Gen can be substantially smaller: 0.006 µs for a domain of size $N = 100{,}000$ and security error $\epsilon = 2^{-8}$, and 0.005 µs for $N = 20{,}000$ and $\epsilon = 2^{-6}$.

To conclude, for small input domains and small (but non-negligible) privacy levels ϵ, our construction offers a big advantage in key size, a moderate slowdown on the client side (running the key generation), and a more significant slowdown on the server side (running the full domain evaluation). Overall, we expect it to be attractive for applications where the client's communication is the most expensive resource.

Comparison to Standard DPF. Compared to a standard two-party DPF, our PDPF construction offers several qualitative advantages which can be appealing in the following settings:

- When simplifying the interaction pattern is important. For some DPF applications, the "1.5-server" feature means that online interaction only involves a single message from the client to the online server (and no interaction between servers). This offers several advantages for practical systems such as avoiding the dependence on two online, synchronised servers, reducing network latency, and also hiding the identity of the offline server, rendering the non-collusion assumption more realistic.

[3] In fact, the naive construction, as mentioned in Sect. 1.1, can provide a *negligible* privacy error for small output groups. Nevertheless, in aggregation-type applications, over output group $\mathbb{Z}$, we get a constant privacy error. See Remark 3 for more details.

- When the client can play the role of the online server, as in the "trusted-offline PCG" application discussed in Sect. 4.3. In such cases, a PDPF yields a near-exponential improvement in the *total* communication cost, since it only requires a one-time communication of an offline key which is reused many times without further interaction.
- When distributed key generation is carried out over a high-latency network, the constant-round black-box protocol from Sect. 4.2 can offer significant speedup.

All of the above advantages seem relevant for practical use cases. Our PDPF construction has a reasonable concrete overhead (to be discussed below) when settling for small but non-negligible values of ϵ, comparable to the acceptable practices for differential privacy.

Other than the application scenarios described above, our current PDPF construction is less practical than existing DPF constructions. First, it cannot offer negligible privacy error ϵ with good concrete efficiency; second, the running time of Gen and (single-point) Eval scale linearly (rather than logarithmically) with the domain size; finally, it has worse dependence (multiplicative rather than additive) on the size of the payload β. These gaps are smaller in applications that require a full-domain evaluation $\mathsf{EvalAll}$, or alternatively only require key generation for a random point α (see below).

Comparing the key size of the two constructions, note that the size of the keys in PDPF is $\log(N/\epsilon^2)$ PRG seeds for the online party and just a single PRG seed for the offline party, while the key size of both parties in standard DPF is roughly $\log(N)$ PRG seeds. Ignoring the qualitative advantages of PDPF over DPF, the total client communication, or total key size, of PDPF is smaller by almost a factor of two for concretely relevant parameters.

In the case of a *random-input* PDPF, the client computation becomes roughly equal to that of a standard DPF, i.e. dominated by $\log(N)$ calls to a PRG, since the client generates one key which is a seed of a GGM PRF and another key which is the same PRF punctured at a random point. A random-input PDPF is good enough for some applications, such as distributed key generation, on which we elaborate in Sect. 4.2. There, a random-input PDPF and can be converted to a chosen-input DPF by sending a $\log(N)$-bit offset to the offline server.

While our PDPF construction has higher overhead as the output size grows compared to a standard DPF, in Proposition 3 we provide an optimization to our construction for big payloads beyond the naive approach of executing a separate PDPF instance for every bit of the payload.

Applications. We explore three applications of our programmable DPF construction and associated techniques: (1) Privately Puncturable PRFs (on polynomial size domains); (2) (Standard) Distributed Point Functions that admit particularly efficient secure distributed key generation protocols; and (3) A new application regime of *trusted-offline* pseudorandom correlation generators. We additionally explore an optimization toward DPFs with larger payloads.

Privately Puncturable PRFs (on Small Domains). As discussed, our construction directly implies the first nontrivial *privately puncturable PRF* for domain size $N = \text{poly}(\lambda)$ under the minimal one-way function assumption. Here, non-triviality corresponds to requiring the key size of a (privately) punctured key that is sublinear in the truth table output size.

Even given the restriction to feasible domain sizes, this constitutes the first such construction without relying on structured public-key assumptions such as the Learning with Errors assumption or multi-linear maps [4,16,17,36].

Proposition 1 (Privately puncturable PRF - Informal). *Assuming the existence of OWF, there exist (selectively secure, 1-key) privately puncturable PRF (P-PPRF), where the runtime of punctured key generation and evaluation is quasilinear in the domain size M, and with punctured key size* $\text{poly}(\lambda, \log M)$.

DPF with Constant-Round Black-Box Distributed Key Generation. In any application of (standard) DPFs where the role of "client" is jointly executed across parties—including secure computation for RAM programs [25] or mixed-mode operations [7,13], use of pseudorandom correlation generators for secure computation preprocessing [8,10,13], and more—the Gen algorithm of the DPF must in turn be executed distributedly via a secure computation protocol. Minimizing the costs of this procedure is a highly desirable target.

This was highlighted by the work of Doerner and shelat [25], which identified that the low cost of distributed DPF Gen makes it a strong approach for secure computation of RAM programs. They presented a distributed DPF Gen protocol, which remains the most efficient to date, requiring computation time linear in the DPF domain size N, and runs in $\log N$ sequential communication rounds, but which crucially makes only *black-box* use of oblivious transfer and a pseudorandom generator. In contrast, alternative approaches each require the expensive secure evaluation of (many instances of) a circuit evaluating the PRG.

In particular, for any DPF with key size polylogarithmic in the domain size N,[4] no protocol exists for distributed Gen which is black-box in the underlying cryptographic tools and lower than $O(\log N)$ round complexity.

The techniques behind our PDPF give the first DPF (for feasible domains) which simultaneously achieves key size polylogarithmic in N, and admits a distributed Gen protocol that makes only black-box use of OT and a PRG, executing in *constant round complexity*. More concretely, we show that 5 rounds suffice.

Proposition 2 (Constant-round distributed Gen - Informal). *There exists a small-domain DPF* (Gen, Eval), *with key size* $\text{poly}(\lambda, \log N)$, *where* Gen *on secret-shared α, β can be implemented by a constant-round (5-round) protocol making only a black-box use of oblivious transfer and a pseudorandom generator.*

As with our PDPF constructions, the runtime of our DPF Eval algorithm will be linear in the domain size N. Note, however, that the application of DPF

[4] DPFs with significantly worse key size N^ϵ for constant $\epsilon > 0$ can be built with lower depth Gen, e.g. by "flattening" the tree structure of current best DPF constructions.

within secure computation of RAM programs anyway requires EvalAll as opposed to individual Eval operations (where we achieve the same linear complexity). In addition, our resulting DPF Gen procedure will only be logarithmic in N. This will be result of modifying the PDPF, adding a short second "offset" message to be added to the key k_0 after the choice of the secret point function $\hat{f}_{\alpha,\beta}$. This extra step adds minor cost in regard to computation and key size, but means the resulting construction is a DPF and not a *programmable* DPF which in particular requires the first key k_0 to be independent of the point function to be shared.

Compressing DPF Corelations. Standard DPFs have a variety of applications in the context of secure 2-party computation (2PC). For instance, they serve as crucial building blocks for concretely efficient 2PC of RAM programs [25] or for pseudorandom correlation generators (PCGs) of truth-table correlations [11] and (authenticated) multiplication triples [10]. Evaluating large circuits or multiple instances necessitates several DPF correlations. In particular, this strongly motivates the goal of generating many independent instances of a random DPF correlation with low communication cost. However, there are no known practical methods for achieving this.

We observe that PDPF inherently provides a solution for generating many such instances, where the size of one key scales with the number of instances, but *one key is short.*

In turn, our PDPF provides a solution to the above problem within a subset of interesting applications, captured by the following "trusted-offline" setting for 2PC. In an offline phase, Alice owns a long-term secret s (say, a secret key for encryption, identification, or signature). To eliminate a single point of failure, she splits s into two shares, s_A and s_B, sending s_B to Bob and keeping s_A to herself. She then erases all information except s_A. In the online phase, the parties receive online inputs P_i (resp., ciphertexts to decrypt, nonces for identification, or messages to sign) and wish to securely compute $f(s, P_i)$ for $i = 1, 2, \ldots, t$.

The key observation is that in the above setting, Alice can be fully trusted during the offline phase, since if she is corrupted at this phase (before erasing s) then the long-term secret is entirely compromised. In fact, if P_i is public, then s is the only secret in the system. For this reason, we can also trust Alice to generate pairs of DPF keys (k_0^j, k_1^j) in the offline phase, offload the keys k_0^j to Bob, and keep k_1^i to herself. However, when Alice wants to generate many DPF instances for the purpose of evaluating many g-gates, this has high communication cost.

A PDPF can provide a dramatic efficiency improvement in this scenario, where Alice needs only to send the single *short* PDPF key to Bob, and simply store the longer key locally. This reduces the communication requirements of existing solutions within this setting by an exponential factor.

Big Payload Optimization. Some applications of DPF explicitly require the point function payload to be larger than a single bit, e.g. an element in $\mathbb{Z}_{2^\ell}$, and to be random. A natural adaptation of our technique to this setting is to repeat the programmable DPF scheme with binary outputs ℓ times, once for each bit, and then locally map the outputs to elements in $\mathbb{Z}_{2^\ell}$. However, evaluation using this approach suffers from an $O(\ell^3)$ computational overhead compared to a binary programmable DPF achieving the same security[5].

We propose an optimization which maintains key size and reduces the computational overhead by $O(\ell)$ compared to the repetition method. In more detail, each PRF value is a pair of a point x in the input domain $[N]$ and a value $y \in \mathbb{Z}_{2^\ell}$. One key of the programmable DPF is again the short PRF key, while the second key is punctured at $O(\ell)$ points which evaluate to $(\alpha, y_i), i = 1, \ldots, O(\ell)$. The DPF evaluation at each point x is the sum of all y_i such that the PRF (or punctured PRF) evaluate to (x, y_i) at some point. This approach leads to the following:

Proposition 3 (Big payload optimization - Informal). *Given length doubling PRG $G : \{0,1\}^\lambda \rightarrow \{0,1\}^{2\lambda}$, there exists a computationally ϵ-secure PDPF for point functions $f_\alpha : [N] \rightarrow \mathbb{Z}_{2^\ell}$, with online key size $|k_1| = O\left(\lambda t \log \frac{tN}{\epsilon^2}\right)$ for $t = \ell + 2log\frac{1}{\epsilon}$. The number of invocations of G in the key generation algorithm is $O(tN \log \frac{t}{\epsilon^2})$, and in the full domain evaluation algorithm it is $O(\frac{Nt^2}{\epsilon^2})$.*

Due to space limitations, we defer the full treatment of this optimization to the full version of the paper.

1.2 Overview of Techniques

We now proceed to describe our techniques in greater detail. We focus here on the core construction of programmable DPF from OWF. We refer the reader to the main body for further detail on the related applications.

1/Poly-Secure PDPF. We begin by describing our construction of a computationally secure PDPF, which takes inspiration from the *puncturable pseudorandom sets* of Corrigan-Gibbs and Kogan [21].

Our construction relies on an underlying tool of Punctuarable Pseudorandom Functions (PPRF) [6,14,31]. Puncturable PRFs are an earlier-dating, weaker variant of privately puncturable PRFs discussed above, which similarly have the ability of generating *punctured* keys k_p from a master PRF key k enabling evaluation on all but a punctured input x_p. Even given the punctured key k_p, the output of the PRF at input x_p remains pseudorandom. Unlike privately puncturable PRFs, no hiding requirement is made for the identity of the punctured input x_p given the punctured key k_p, which makes the goal significantly easier to achieve. Such primitives can be constructed in a simple manner based on one-way functions via a GGM [28] tree [6,14,31].

Our construction proceeds roughly as follows. Consider the first party in the programmable DPF. The first (programmable) key of the DPF is simply the

5 In this approach, to get statistical error of ϵ we need to reduce the value of ϵ in each of the ℓ instances by a factor of ℓ. Since the computational cost per instance depends quadratically on $1/\epsilon$, this results in a total slowdown (compared to the 1-bit baseline) of $\ell \cdot \ell^2 = \ell^3$.

master key k for a PPRF whose output space is the *input* space for the DPF, $[N]$. The PRF input space D will be selected in the discussion following, as a function of the desired privacy error. (In particular, larger domain will yield smaller error, but higher complexity).

In order to expand its DPF key to a full-domain evaluation on the input domain $[N]$, the first party begins by evaluating its PRF tree on all inputs. Recall that each leaf of the PRF evaluation tree is now labeled by some element of $[N]$. For each $x \in [N]$, the corresponding DPF output evaluation $f_1(x)$ is defined to be the integer *number of occurrences* of the value x within the leaves of the PRF tree: i.e., the number of values ζ in the input space D of the PRF for which $PRF_k(\zeta) = x$.

Pictorially, each PRF leaf evaluation can be viewed as a "ball" thrown into one of N bins, labeled $1, \dots, N$. Evaluating on the complete PRF tree (given the master key k) results in a histogram, of number of balls per bin, which constitutes the evaluated DPF output share values.

The second key in the programmable DPF is generated given the target point function f_{α^*} we wish to share. Observe that (for payload $\beta = 1$) the goal is to recreate the same "balls in bins" histogram as above, but with 1 less ball in the $\alpha^* \in [N]$ bucket.[6] Indeed, if this can be achieved, then the parties' shares differ by 0 in all places apart from α^*, and precisely by 1 at α^*. To do so, the second server will be given the PRF key *punctured* at a random input x_p whose PRF output is α^*. In effect, one (random) ball is removed from the α^* bin.

Correctness of the construction holds as above. But, we find ourselves encountering a serious security challenge. While clearly the first party's share is independent of the secret function f_{α^*}, security against the second party must somehow rely on hiding the punctured PRF evaluation given access to a punctured key. However, in a puncturable PRF, pseudorandomness is only guaranteed when the punctured input is chosen *independently* of the PRF evaluation values. In contrast, the input we puncture is selected based on the PRF evaluations. In fact, the issue is even worse. Even the stronger notion of adaptive security of PPRF does not suffice, where the punctured input can be selected as function of the PRF evaluations on *other* inputs. In our construction the punctured input is chosen as function of *its own* evaluation—in general, one cannot hope to achieve this kind of security.

Indeed, the resulting construction does not provide negligible leakage in privacy. This corresponds to the (non-negligible, efficiently identifiable) statistical difference in the N histogram counts when throwing a polynomial number of balls and then removing a ball from one bin. This statistical difference can be decreased by increasing the total number of balls thrown: this corresponds directly to a larger choice of the puncturable PRF domain D. Roughly, increasing D by a factor of $c > 1$ cuts the error by a factor of $1/\sqrt{c}$.

[6] To account for the fact that the payload could be $\beta = 0$, we actually introduce dummy bucket $N + 1$ to the PRF output space; removing a ball from this bucket means that all $[N]$ buckets remain equal across parties.

We provide a tight analysis of privacy error via a careful sequence of hybrid experiments, where the α^*-output-punctured key is ultimately replaced by a key punctured at a random independent input. Each step within the proof introduces negligible error, aside from one: in which we move from a PRF key where we puncture an input with a random *output value* (i.e., the DPF construction for a random α^*, to one where we puncture a random *input.*

It is interesting to observe that the construction is sensitive to specific design choices. For example, slightly modifying the above procedure to instead puncture the *first* input whose output α^* (instead of a random such input) yields a serious attack: given the punctured PRF key, the second party can directly infer for all values $\alpha' \in [N]$ appearing as PRF evaluations *before* the punctured point that $f_{\alpha'}$ is *not* the secret shared point function.

Amplification. To amplify a DPF with 1/poly privacy error into one with negligible error, we apply a privacy amplification technique based on a locally random reduction. The idea is to lift the input domain to a codeword in a Reed-Muller code and decode along a random low-degree curve. This effectively reduces a single DPF with secret input α to a small number of instances of DPF with secret inputs α_i, where the α_i are λ-wise independent. By combining a "statistical-to-perfect" lemma from [26,32] with a computational hardcore lemma of [33], the 1/poly leakage on each α_i can be argued to be no worse than completely leaking each α_i with small probability, which by λ-wise independence suffices to hide α except with negligible probability.

2 Preliminaries

Notation. For $N \in \mathbb{N}$ we let $[N] = \{1, \ldots, N\}$. We denote the inner product of two vectors u and v of the same length by $\langle u, v\rangle = \sum_i u_i v_i$. We denote by negl a negligible function.

Probability. For two distributions D_1, D_2 we denote by $d(D_1, D_2) = \frac{1}{2}\sum_\omega |\Pr_{D_1}[\omega] - \Pr_{D_2}[\omega]|$ their statistical distance. We denote by U_ℓ uniformly distributed random strings of length ℓ.

Groups. We represent an Abelian group $\mathbb{G}$ of the form $\mathbb{G} = \mathbb{Z}_{q_1} \times \cdots \times \mathbb{Z}_{q_\ell}$, for prime powers $q_1, \ldots, q_\ell$ by $\hat{\mathbb{G}} = (q_1, \ldots, q_\ell)$ and represent a group element of $\mathbb{G}$ by a sequence of ℓ non-negative integers. Unlike previous DPF definitions, here we will also consider infinite groups, using $q_i = \infty$ for the group of integers $\mathbb{Z}$.

Point Functions. Given a domain size N and Abelian group $\mathbb{G}$, a *point function* $f_{\alpha,\beta} : [N] \to \mathbb{G}$ for $\alpha \in [N]$ and $\beta \in \mathbb{G}$ evaluates to β on input α and to $0 \in \mathbb{G}$ on all other inputs. Unlike previous DPF definitions, here we will also consider the case where the output β is guaranteed to be taken from a subset $\mathbb{G}' \subseteq \mathbb{G}$, where the subset $\mathbb{G}'$ can be leaked. This extension is especially useful where $\mathbb{G} = \mathbb{Z}$, in which we will typically let $\mathbb{G}' = \{0, 1\}$. When $\mathbb{G}'$ is omitted, we assume $\mathbb{G}' = \mathbb{G}$. We denote by $\hat{f}_{\alpha,\beta} = (N, \hat{\mathbb{G}}, \hat{\mathbb{G}}', \alpha, \beta)$ the representation of such a point function.

2.1 Distributed Point Functions

We begin by defining a slightly generalized notion of distributed point functions (DPFs), which accounts for the extra parameter $\mathbb{G}'$.

Definition 1 (DPF [12,27]). *A (2-party)* distributed point function (DPF) *is a triple of algorithms* $\Pi = (\mathsf{Gen}, \mathsf{Eval}_0, \mathsf{Eval}_1)$ *with the following syntax:*

- $\mathsf{Gen}(1^\lambda, \hat{f}_{\alpha,\beta}) \to (k_0, k_1)$: *On input security parameter* $\lambda \in \mathbb{N}$ *and point function description* $\hat{f}_{\alpha,\beta} = (N, \hat{\mathbb{G}}, \hat{\mathbb{G}}', \alpha, \beta)$, *the (randomized) key generation algorithm* Gen *returns a pair of keys* $k_0, k_1 \in \{0,1\}^*$. *We assume that* N *and* $\mathbb{G}$ *are determined by each key.*
- $\mathsf{Eval}_i(k_i, x) \to y_i$: *On input key* $k_i \in \{0,1\}^*$ *and input* $x \in [N]$ *the (deterministic) evaluation algorithm of server* i, Eval_i *returns* $y_i \in \mathbb{G}$.

We require Π *to satisfy the following requirements:*

- ***Correctness:*** *For every* λ, $\hat{f} = \hat{f}_{\alpha,\beta} = (N, \hat{\mathbb{G}}, \hat{\mathbb{G}}', \alpha, \beta)$ *such that* $\beta \in \mathbb{G}'$, *and* $x \in [N]$, *if* $(k_0, k_1) \leftarrow \mathsf{Gen}(1^\lambda, \hat{f})$, *then* $\Pr\left[\sum_{i=0}^{1} \mathsf{Eval}_i(k_i, x) = f_{\alpha,\beta}(x)\right] = 1$.
- ***Security:*** *Consider the following semantic security challenge experiment for corrupted server* $i \in \{0,1\}$:
  1. *The adversary produces two point function descriptions* $(\hat{f}^0 = (N, \hat{\mathbb{G}}, \hat{\mathbb{G}}', \alpha_0, \beta_0), \hat{f}^1 = (N, \hat{\mathbb{G}}, \hat{\mathbb{G}}', \alpha_1, \beta_1)) \leftarrow \mathcal{A}(1^\lambda)$, *where* $\alpha_i \in [N]$ *and* $\beta_i \in \mathbb{G}'$.
  2. *The challenger samples* $b \xleftarrow{\$} \{0,1\}$ *and* $(k_0, k_1) \leftarrow \mathsf{Gen}(1^\lambda, \hat{f}^b)$.
  3. *The adversary outputs a guess* $b' \leftarrow \mathcal{A}(k_i)$.

  Denote by $\mathrm{Adv}(1^\lambda, \mathcal{A}, i) = \Pr[b = b'] - 1/2$ *the advantage of* $\mathcal{A}$ *in guessing* b *in the above experiment. For circuit size bound* $S = S(\lambda)$ *and advantage bound* $\epsilon(\lambda)$, *we say that* Π *is* (S, ϵ)*-secure if for all* $i \in \{0,1\}$ *and all non-uniform adversaries* $\mathcal{A}$ *of size* $S(\lambda)$ *and sufficiently large* λ, *we have* $\mathrm{Adv}(1^\lambda, \mathcal{A}, i) \leq \epsilon(\lambda)$. *We say that* Π *is:*
  - Computationally ϵ-secure *if it is* (S, ϵ)*-secure for all polynomials* S.
  - Computationally secure *if it is* $(S, 1/S)$*-secure for all polynomials* S.

We will also be interested in applying the evaluation algorithm on *all* inputs. Given a DPF $(\mathsf{Gen}, \mathsf{Eval}_0, \mathsf{Eval}_1)$, we denote by $\mathsf{EvalAll}_i$ an algorithm which computes Eval_i on every input x. Hence, $\mathsf{EvalAll}_i$ receives only a key k_i as input.

DPF Efficieny Measures. We will pay attention to the following efficiency measures of a DPF:

- The key sizes $|k_0|, |k_1|$.
- The running time of $\mathsf{Gen}, \mathsf{Eval}_0, \mathsf{Eval}_1$.

Small-Domain and Large-Domain DPF. We say that a DPF is *small-domain* (resp., *large-domain*) if $\mathsf{Gen}, \mathsf{Eval}_0, \mathsf{Eval}_1$ have running time polynomial in N (resp., $\log N$) and their input length.

Next, we introduce our new notion of *programmable* DPF.

Definition 2 (PDPF). *We say that a small-domain DPF* $(\mathsf{Gen}, \mathsf{Eval}_0, \mathsf{Eval}_1)$ *is a* programmable DPF, *or PDPF for short, if* Gen *can be decomposed into a pair of algorithms* $\Pi = (\mathsf{Gen}_0, \mathsf{Gen}_1)$ *with the following syntax:*

- $\mathsf{Gen}_0(1^\lambda, N, \hat{\mathbb{G}}, \hat{\mathbb{G}}') \rightarrow k_0$*: On input security parameter* λ*, domain size* N *and output group description* $\hat{\mathbb{G}}$*, returns a key* $k_0 = (k_*, N, \hat{\mathbb{G}}, \hat{\mathbb{G}}')$ *where* $k_* \in \{0,1\}^\lambda$*.*
- $\mathsf{Gen}_1(k_0, \hat{f}_{\alpha,\beta}) \rightarrow k_1$*: On input key* $k_0 = (k_*, N, \hat{\mathbb{G}}, \hat{\mathbb{G}}')$ *and point function description* $\hat{f}_{\alpha,\beta} = (N, \hat{\mathbb{G}}, \hat{\mathbb{G}}', \alpha, \beta)$*, returns a key* $k_1 \in \{0,1\}^*$*.*

Moreover, we require that k_**, returned by* Gen_0 *as part of* k_0*, is a uniform random string, namely,* $k_* \xleftarrow{\$} \{0,1\}^\lambda$*.*

Since the operation of Gen_0 is fixed, in our PDPF constructions we will omit the description of Gen_0. Moreover, we will not be concerned with its running time or the key length of k_0. Finally, since our construction realizes $\mathsf{EvalAll}$ at essentially the same cost as Eval, we will directly describe the $\mathsf{EvalAll}$ algorithm.

In the full version of the paper we define the *reusability* feature for DPFs discussed in the Introduction, and show an easy construction of reusable DPF from PDPF (and vice versa).

Simulation Based Security. While for both DPF and PDPF we use a definition with indistinguishability-based security, there is an equivalent definition using simulation-based security [12]. There, the simulator is given "leakage" which is the description of the DPF function class. Simulation takes place by simply generating a key for an arbitrary function in the function class.

2.2 Pseudorandom Generators and Functions

We defer the definitions of PRG, PRF and puncturable PRF (PPRF) to the full version of the paper.

Theorem 3 ((P)PRF from OWFs [6,14,31]). *If OWFs exist, there exists a PPRF.*

More concretely, given a black-box access to a PRG $G : \{0,1\}^\lambda \rightarrow \{0,1\}^{2\lambda}$*, a PPRF,* $\mathit{PPRF} = (\mathsf{Eval}, \mathit{Punc}, \mathit{PuncEval})$*, with input domain* $[M]$ *and output domain* $[N]$*, can be implemented with punctured key length* $|k_p| = \lambda \log_2 M$*, such that* $\mathsf{Eval}, \mathit{Punc}, \mathit{PuncEval}$ *make* $(\log_2(M/N)\log_2 N)/2\lambda$ *calls to* G*.*

Furthermore, if Eval *or* $\mathit{PuncEval}$ *is computed on all points in* $[M]$*, it requires only* $((2M-1)\log_2 N)/2\lambda$ *calls to* G*.*

3 Small-Domain PDPF from One-Way Functions

In this section we construct small-domain PDPFs. We will first obtain a construction with inverse-polynomial security. Then, in Sect. 3.1, we will show how to amplify security and get negligible security error.

As was discussed in the introduction, our construction relies on analyzing the statistical distance between balls-and-bins experiments, where, after throwing M balls into N bins, we remove a single ball (randomly) from either bin i or bin j. The following lemma gives an exact expression for the statistical distance between these two distributions, and also provides an estimate which, numerically, is close up to a multiplicative factor of ≈ 0.564 (see Sect. 5).

Lemma 1. *For integers $M > N > 0$ and $i, j \in [N]$, let D_i and D_j be distributions over $\{1, \ldots, N, \perp\}^M$ of the locations of M balls independently and randomly thrown into N bins, such that we then change the position of a single ball, chosen randomly from bin i and bin j, respectively, to $\perp$ (this corresponds to the ball's "removal" from the bin). Then*

$$d(D_i, D_j) = \sum_{w=0}^{M} \binom{M}{w} \left(1 - \frac{2}{N}\right)^{M-w} \frac{\binom{w}{\lfloor w/2 \rfloor}}{N^w} \leq \sqrt{\frac{N}{M}}$$

We prove the lemma in the full version of the paper.

Next, we state Theorem 4, which constructs a PDPF (Fig. 1), restricted to output group $\mathbb{Z}$ and to payloads $\beta \in \{0, 1\}$. Later, we extend this PDPF in Theorem 5 to work over any finite Abelian group $\mathbb{G}$ and any payload $\beta \in \mathbb{G}$. The proof of the theorem below essentially mirrors that of Lemma 1 in the computational world by replacing the random configuration of M balls thrown into N bins by a pseudorandom configuration, using the truth table of a PPRF. Compared to Lemma 1, this yields an additive error term which is negligible in λ.

We defer the proofs of Theorem 4 and Theorem 5 to the full version of the paper.

Theorem 4 (Small-domain PDPF with $1/\text{poly}(\lambda, N)$ privacy error). *Suppose that $\mathsf{PPRF} = (\mathsf{PPRF.Eval}, \mathsf{PPRF.Punc}, \mathsf{PPRF.PuncEval})$ is a secure PPRF for input domain size M and output domain size N, with punctured key size $K_p(\lambda, M, N)$. In addition, let $G : \{0,1\}^\lambda \to [N+1] \times \{0,1\}^\lambda$ be a PRG. Then, the construction in Fig. 1 is a small-domain computationally ϵ-secure PDPF,*

$$\epsilon(\lambda, M, N) = \sqrt{\frac{(N+1)}{M}} + negl(\lambda)$$

for point functions with output group $\mathbb{G} = \mathbb{Z}$, $\mathbb{G}' = \{0, 1\}$, domain size N, and key size $|k_1| = K_p(\lambda, M, N+1)$. The number of invocations to PPRF in $\mathsf{Gen}_1, \mathsf{EvalAll}_0, \mathsf{EvalAll}_1$ is at most $O(M)$.

$\mathsf{Gen}_1(k_0 = (k_*, N, \hat{\mathbb{G}}, \hat{\mathbb{G}}'), \hat{f}_{\alpha,\beta} = (N, \hat{\mathbb{G}}, \alpha, \beta))$:

- Compute $(s, k_{\mathsf{PPRF}}) = G(k_*)$.
- If $\beta = 1$ then $\alpha' \leftarrow \alpha$, else $\alpha' \leftarrow N + 1$
- Find all indices

$$L \leftarrow \{\ell \in [M] : \mathsf{PPRF.Eval}(k_{\mathsf{PPRF}}, M, N+1, \ell) + s = \alpha'\}.$$

- Pick a random $\ell \in L$, compute $k_p \leftarrow \mathsf{PPRF.Punc}(k_{\mathsf{PPRF}}, M, N+1, \ell)$, and output $k_1 = (k_p, s)$.

$\mathsf{EvalAll}_0(k_0 = (k_{\mathsf{PPRF}}, N, \hat{\mathbb{G}}, \hat{\mathbb{G}}'))$:

- Compute $(s, k_{\mathsf{PPRF}}) = G(k_*)$.
- For every $\alpha \in [N]$, simultaneously compute

$$Y_\alpha \leftarrow |\{\ell \in [M] : \mathsf{PPRF.Eval}(k_{\mathsf{PPRF}}, M, N+1, \ell) + s = \alpha\}|.$$

- Output $Y = (Y_\alpha)_{\alpha \in [N]}$.

$\mathsf{EvalAll}_1(k_1 = (k_p, s))$:

- For every $\alpha \in [N]$, simultaneously compute

$$Y_\alpha \leftarrow (-|\{\ell \in [M] : \mathsf{PPRF.PuncEval}(k_p, \ell) + s = \alpha\}|).$$

- Output $Y = (Y_\alpha)_{\alpha \in [N]}$.

Fig. 1. Small-domain computationally $1/\text{poly}(\lambda, N)$-secure PDPF for point functions with output group $\mathbb{G} = \mathbb{Z}$, payload set $\mathbb{G}' = \{0, 1\}$, and domain size N. Here M is a parameter corresponding to the input space of the PPRF.

Theorem 5 (Small-domain PDPF over any payload set $\mathbb{G}'$). *If OWFs exists, there exists a small-domain computationally $\log|\mathbb{G}'|/\text{poly}(\lambda, N)$-secure PDPF for point functions with any allowed payload set $\mathbb{G}'$, Abelian output group $\mathbb{G} \supseteq \mathbb{G}'$, domain size N, and key size $|k_1| = O(\log|\mathbb{G}'|\lambda(\log\lambda + \log N))$.*

We finish this section with an optimization to Theorem 4.

Proposition 4 (Lazy Gen computation). *When instantiated with a PPRF from Theorem 3, the computation of Gen_1 in Fig. 1 can be done in just $((N+1)\log_2 M)/\lambda$ calls to a PRG, at the expense of an additional $2^{-(N+1)}$ error in correctness or privacy.*

Proof. Instead of having Gen_1 compute the entire set L and picking $\ell \in L$ at random, it is sufficient to keep trying values $\ell \in [M]$ at random until one is found such that $\mathsf{PPRF.Eval}(k_*, M, N+1, \ell) + s$ takes the correct value. This has a $1/(N+1)$ probability of success. By making T queries, the chance of failure is $1/(N+1)^T$. If we pick $T = (N+1)/\log_2(N+1)$, the failure chance becomes $2^{-(N+1)}$, which we can attribute to either correctness or privacy. Since each PPRF evaluation takes $(\log_2 M \log_2(N+1))/\lambda$ calls to the PRG, we are done.

3.1 Security Amplification

To amplify security we rely on Locally Decodable Codes (LDC). Theorem 4 gives us a PDPF with 1/poly leakage of α, which as we argue in the full version of the paper, is no worse than α leaking completely with probability 1/poly, and staying (computationally) hidden otherwise. By utilizing a locally decodable code with additive decoding we can essentially secret share α into shares $\alpha_1, \ldots, \alpha_q$ which are λ-wise independent. Since every α_i leaks independently with small probability, by using a Chernoff bound, α leaks with negligible probability.

To describe the main idea of the security amplification construction (Fig. 2) in more detail, note first that $f_\alpha(x) = \langle e_x, TT(f_\alpha)\rangle$, where e_x is a unit vector with 1 at index x, and $TT(f_\alpha)$ is the truth table of a point function f_α (also a unit vector). Now, we utilize a q-query LDC C with additive reconstruction and choose $\alpha_1, \ldots, \alpha_q$ to be the queries to C for coordinate α, which by the additive decoding of C yields

$$\langle C(e_x), TT(f_{\alpha_1}) + \ldots + TT(f_{\alpha_q})\rangle = \langle e_x, TT(f_\alpha)\rangle = f_\alpha(x).$$

Next, using the additive reconstruction of the PDPF, implying $TT(f_{\alpha_j}) = TT(f^0_{\alpha_j}) + TT(f^1_{\alpha_j})$, $j = 1, \ldots, q$, each server $i = 0, 1$ can locally compute $z_i = \langle C(e_x), TT(f^i_{\alpha_1}) + \ldots + TT(f^i_{\alpha_q})\rangle$ using $\mathsf{EvalAll}$ of each of the q PDPF keys, such that $z_0 + z_1 = f_\alpha(x)$ (hence yielding a PDPF). Here, the offline server will receive a *single* offline key, which it can expand to q offline keys using a PRF, while the online server will receive the q matching online keys.

The following lemma provides the locally decodable code (LDC) with the parameters we require (c.f. [15, Section 4]).

Lemma 2. *Fix integers $\lambda, w > 0$, a prime p, and let $r, N > 0$ be such that $N = \binom{r+w}{r}$ and $r = O(N^{1/w})$. There exist a deterministic mapping $C : \mathbb{Z}_p^N \to \mathbb{Z}_p^L$ and a randomized mapping $d : [N] \to [L]^q$, $L, q \in \mathbb{N}$, such that for every $z \in \mathbb{Z}_p^N$ and $\alpha \in [N]$ it holds that*

$$\Pr\left[\Delta \leftarrow d(\alpha) : \sum_{\ell=1}^{q} C(z)_{\Delta_\ell} = z_\alpha\right] = 1.$$

Moreover, the following properties hold:

1. $q = O(\lambda^2 N^{1/w})$ *and* $L = O(p^{w+1}\lambda^{w+1}N^{1+\frac{1}{w}})$.
2. C, d *are computable in polynomial time.*
3. *For every* $\alpha \in [N]$, *the random variables* $\Delta_1, \ldots, \Delta_q$ *are* λ*-wise independent.*

We prove this lemma in the full version of the paper. Intuitively, C corresponds to the LDC encoder taking N symbols to $L > N$, the randomized mapping d determines the set of q queried symbols of the codeword given a target index $\alpha \in [N]$ of the "message" vector $z \in \mathbb{Z}_p^N$, and the decoding procedure is simply the sum of the queried symbols $\sum_{\ell=1}^{q} C(z)_{\Delta_\ell} = z_\alpha$. For example, these requirements can be met by a form of Reed-Muller code, where the distribution of queried points $\Delta \leftarrow d(\alpha)$ corresponds to random λ-degree polynomial evaluations through the desired point (namely, Shamir secret sharing of α).

Next, we show that any small-domain computationally $1/\text{poly}(\lambda, N)$-secure PDPF can be transformed into a small-domain PDPF.

Theorem 6. *Fix integers* $\lambda, w > 0$, *let* $r, N > 0$ *be such that* $N = \binom{r+w}{r}$ *and* $r = O(N^{1/w})$, *and let* $p = \text{poly}(\lambda, N)$ *be a prime. Furthermore, let* $L = L(w, \lambda, N), q = q(w, \lambda, N)$ *be as in Lemma 2. Suppose there exists a small-domain computationally* $O(1/L{\cdot}q)$*-secure PDPF for point functions with Abelian output group* $\mathbb{Z}_p$, *domain size* L, *and key size* $|k_1| = K$. *Then, the construction in Fig. 2 gives a small-domain computationally secure PDPF for point functions with Abelian output group* $\mathbb{Z}_p$, *domain size* N, *and key size* $|k_1| = q \cdot K$.

We give the proof of Theorem 6 in the full version of the paper.

Remark 1. Via CRT we can handle any smooth integer characteristic. By introducing a small correctness error and converting it to privacy error we can handle any Abelian group.

Next, we prove the following corollary, in similar vein to how Theorem 5 was derived from Theorem 4. Note, however, that here $\mathbb{G}$ cannot be a general (finite) Abelian group, and we are restricted to $\mathbb{G}$ which is a product of $\mathbb{Z}_p$ for prime p.

Corollary 2. *Fix integers* $\lambda, w > 0$, *and let* $r, N > 0$ *be such that* $N = \binom{r+w}{r}$ *and* $r = O(N^{1/w})$. *If OWFs exist, there exists a* $\left(\log|\mathbb{G}| \cdot 2^{-\Omega(\lambda)}\right)$*-secure PDPF for point functions with Abelian output group* $\mathbb{G} = \prod_i \mathbb{Z}_{p_i}$, *where* p_i *are primes such that* $\sum_i p_i \leq \text{poly}(\lambda, N)$, *polynomial domain size* N, *and key size* $|k_1| = O(\log|\mathbb{G}|\lambda^3 N^{1/w}(\log\lambda + \log N))$.

Theorem 5 and Corollary 2 have the downside that their key length grows multiplicatively with $\log|\mathbb{G}|$. We show in the full version of the paper that this can be reduced to an additive term whenever $\log|\mathbb{G}| \gg \lambda$, at the cost of losing programmability, which still has the benefit of a DPF with one short $(\lambda{+}\log|\mathbb{G}|)$-length key.

Notation: Let $C : \mathbb{Z}_p^N \to \mathbb{Z}_p^L$ and $d : [N] \to [L]^q$ be the mappings from Lemma 2. In addition, let $(\mathsf{PDPF.Gen}_1, \mathsf{PDPF.EvalAll}_0, \mathsf{PDPF.EvalAll}_1)$ be a small-domain computationally $O(1/L \cdot q)$-secure PDPF for point functions with Abelian output group $\mathbb{Z}_p$, domain size L, and let $\mathsf{PRF.Eval}$ be a PRF.

$\mathsf{Gen}_1(k_0 = (k_*, N, \hat{\mathbb{G}}), \hat{f}_{\alpha,\beta} = (N, \hat{\mathbb{G}} = \widehat{\mathbb{Z}_p}, \alpha, \beta))$:
- Compute $\Delta \leftarrow d(\alpha)$.
- For $\ell = 1, \ldots, q$ let $k_*^\ell = \mathsf{PRF.Eval}(k_*, q, \lambda, \ell)$, $k_0^\ell = (k_*^\ell, L, \widehat{\mathbb{Z}_p})$, and

$$k_1^\ell \leftarrow \mathsf{PDPF.Gen}_1(k_0^\ell, (L, \widehat{\mathbb{Z}_p}, \Delta_\ell, \beta)).$$

- Output $k_1 = (k_1^1 \ldots, k_1^q)$.

$\mathsf{Eval}_0(k_0 = (k_*, N, \hat{\mathbb{G}} = \widehat{\mathbb{Z}_p}), x)$:

- For $\ell = 1, \ldots, q$ let $k_*^\ell = \mathsf{PRF.Eval}(k_*, q, \lambda, \ell)$ and $k_0^\ell = (k_*^\ell, L, \widehat{\mathbb{Z}_p})$.
- Compute and output

$$\left\langle C(e_x), \sum_{\ell=1}^{q} \mathsf{PDPF.EvalAll}_0(k_0^\ell) \right\rangle,$$

where $e_x \in \{0,1\}^L$ is a unit vector with 1 at index x.

$\mathsf{Eval}_1(k_1 = (k_1^1 \ldots, k_1^q), x)$:

- Compute and output

$$\left\langle C(e_x), \sum_{\ell=1}^{q} \mathsf{PDPF.EvalAll}_1(k_1^\ell) \right\rangle,$$

where $e_x \in \{0,1\}^L$ is a unit vector with 1 at index x.

Fig. 2. Security amplification via LDC

4 Applications

In this section, we present three applications of our programmable DPF construction and associated techniques: (1) Privately Puncturable PRFs (on polynomial-size domains) from the minimal assumption of one-way functions; (2) (Standard) Distributed Point Functions that admit particularly efficient secure distributed key generation protocols, namely the first to achieve constant round complexity while making only black-box use of oblivious transfer and a pseudorandom generator; and (3) A new application regime of *trusted-offline* pseudorandom correlation generators. We discuss each in turn within the following subsections.

4.1 Privately Puncturable PRFs

Our programmable DPF construction makes use of puncturable pseudorandom functions (PRFs); namely, PRFs supporting generation of punctured keys that enable evaluation of the PRF on all but a single punctured input x^*. Puncturable PRFs are lightweight objects, with simple constructions known from one-way functions [6,14,31] (for example, in a GGM-tree PRF on n-bit inputs, simply give the n co-path PRG evaluations). However, all such known simple constructions inherently *reveal* the identity of the punctured input x^*.

Interestingly, if one wishes to obtain the same functionality, while *hiding* the identity of x^*, the corresponding object becomes much more challenging to obtain. Such notion is known as a *privately* puncturable PRF [5]. In contrast to the simple puncturable PRF constructions, despite significant effort, the only known instantiations of privately puncturable PRFs make use of heavy public-key cryptography machinery, and rely on structured public-key assumptions such as the Learning with Errors assumption or multi-linear maps [4,16,17,36].

This challenging state of affairs remains the situation even for the case where the domain of the PRF is of feasible size. Indeed, there is no clear way "scale down" the constructions from above to a polynomial-size domain in a way that lessens the computational assumption, without reverting to trivial constructions where the key size grows to the entire truth table. Placing a requirement that the key size be sublinear in the domain size (or polylogarithmic, to more closely match the large-domain case), then the resulting notion falls in the same state of knowledge as in the general case: necessitating one-way functions, but only known to be achievable from the heavy public-key cryptography as above.

We observe that our notion of programmable DPF in fact directly *implies* privately puncturable PRFs with the same parameters. In turn, we provide the first construction of privately puncturable PRFs (on polynomial-size domains) from the minimal assumption of *one-way functions.*

We next present the definition of privately puncturable PRFs, together with our new feasibility result. We adapt the definition to mirror our PRF syntax, where Eval and Punc explicitly take the input domain size $M \in \mathbb{N}$ as input. For simplicity, we focus on the case of output space $\mathbb{Z}_2$, and thus omit output domain size from the syntax (we can, however, support more general output spaces as in Corollary 2). As with essentially all known constructions of privately constrained PRFs, we consider a setting of selective security, with security against 1 key query. We remark that in this setting, it was shown that indistinguishability-based and simulation-based definitions are equivalent [17].

Definition 3 (Privately Puncturable PRF (1-Key, Selective Security)). *A puncturable PRF* (Gen, Punc, Eval, $\mathit{PuncEval}$) *is a (selectively secure, 1-key)* privately puncturable PRF *family if for every non-uniform polynomial-time stateful adversary $\mathcal{A}$, there exists a polynomial-time simulator Sim such that the following are computationally indistinguishable:*

$$\{\mathsf{REAL}_{\mathcal{A}}(1^\lambda)\}_{\lambda \in \mathbb{N}} \overset{c}{\cong} \{\mathsf{IDEAL}_{\mathcal{A},\mathit{Sim}}(1^\lambda)\}_{\lambda \in \mathbb{N}},$$

where the real and ideal experiments are defined as follows:

Experiment $\mathsf{REAL}_{\mathcal{A}}(1^\lambda)$	*Experiment* $\mathsf{IDEAL}_{\mathcal{A},\mathit{Sim}}(1^\lambda)$
$x^* \leftarrow \mathcal{A}(1^\lambda)$	$x^* \leftarrow \mathcal{A}(1^\lambda)$
$k \leftarrow \mathsf{Gen}(1^\lambda)$	$k^* \leftarrow \mathit{Sim}(1^\lambda)$
$k^* \leftarrow \mathit{Punc}(k, M, x^*)$	$b \leftarrow \mathcal{A}(k^*)$; *Output* b
$b \leftarrow \mathcal{A}(k^*)$; *Output* b	

Intuitively, this notion of privately puncturable PRFs are directly implied by programmable DPFs, by taking the master PRF key to be the first-server DPF share, and generating a punctured key at x^* by computing a second-server DPF share for the function $f_{\alpha,\beta}$ with $\alpha = x^*$ and $\beta \leftarrow \{0,1\}$ selected at random.

Proposition 5 (Small-Domain Privately Puncturable PRF from OWF). *Assume the existence of a length-doubling PRG (implied by OWF). Then there exists a (selectively secure, 1-key) privately puncturable PRF* (Gen, Punc, Eval, $\mathit{PuncEval}$)*, with the following complexity properties:*

- $\mathsf{Gen}(1^\lambda)$ *outputs a master PRF key of size λ bits; $\mathit{PuncEval}$ on domain size M outputs a punctured key of size* $\mathrm{poly}(\lambda, \log(M))$ *bits.*
- *The runtime of Punc and $\mathit{PuncEval}$ on domain size M consists of $O(N)$ PRG evaluations. In particular, for polynomial-size domain $M = M(\lambda)$, then Punc and $\mathit{PuncEval}$ each run in probabilistic polynomial time.*

The proof appears in the full version of the paper.

Remark 2 (Privately Puncturable PRF $\Leftrightarrow$ PDPF). We note that in regard to feasibility, this implication in fact goes in both directions. That is, existence of a privately puncturable PRF (P-PPRF) additionally implies the existence of a PDPF. Intuitively, a P-PPRF is precisely a PDPF but with *random*, versus chosen, payload. For small output domains (such as $\mathbb{Z}_2$), however, this can be addressed, e.g., by rejection sampling.

Namely, given a P-PPRF, the corresponding $\mathsf{Gen}_0(1^\lambda, M, \hat{\mathbb{Z}}_2)$ will sample a random ("master") PRF key k_0. The algorithm $\mathsf{Gen}_1(k_0, \hat{f}_{\alpha,\beta})$ for a given point function $\hat{f}_{\alpha,\beta}$ will run independent executions of the randomized procedure $\mathsf{Punc}(k_0, M, \alpha)$ to generate a PRF key punctured at α, repeating until the resulting punctured key $k_1 \leftarrow \mathsf{Punc}(k_0, M, \alpha)$ yields the desired target offset $\mathsf{Eval}(k_0, M, \alpha) + \mathsf{PuncEval}(k_1, \alpha) = \beta$. The algorithms Eval_0 and Eval_1 of the PDPF then become the corresponding executions of Eval and $\mathsf{PuncEval}$ of the P-PPRF. Security follows from the privacy of the identity of the punctured input (intuitively, hiding α) together with pseudorandomness of the punctured evaluation on feasible output domain (intuitively, a punctured key for the real offset β is indistinguishable from a key for random $\beta' \leftarrow \mathbb{Z}_2$, since there are polynomially many possible offsets). And, since the output domain size is feasible, these algorithms remain polynomial time.

Overall, this close connection to P-PPRFs provides yet another motivation for the study of PDPFs.

4.2 DPF with Constant-Round Black-Box Distributed Gen

In this section we demonstrate that the techniques behind our PDPF construction can be used to give the first (standard) DPF construction (for feasible domain sizes) in which the key size is polylogarithmic in the domain size N, and whose key generation Gen admits a particularly efficient *secure distributed generation* procedure. Namely, the distributed Gen protocol makes only black-box use of OT and a PRG, and executes in a fixed *constant round complexity.* Concretely, we show that 5 rounds suffice.

As with the previous sections, the runtime of our DPF Eval algorithm (as well as EvalAll) will be linear in the domain size N. Note that in this section, however, our DPF Gen procedure will only be logarithmic in N.

Concretely, by "distributed Gen," we refer to a secure computation protocol between two parties. We consider only security against a semi-honest adversary (i.e., who follows the protocol as prescribed but attempts to extrapolate information beyond its own input and output). The input consists of the desired security parameter 1^λ and input/output domain descriptions of the desired point function as common input, as well as *secret shares* of the desired point function values α and β over the respective spaces. The output is a randomly sampled key pair $(k_0, k_1) \leftarrow \mathsf{Gen}(1^\lambda, \hat{f}_{\alpha,\beta})$, where each party learns its corresponding key.

Theorem 7 (Constant-round distributed Gen). *There exists a small-domain DPF* (Gen, Eval)*, with key size* $\mathrm{poly}(\lambda, \log N)$*, where* Gen *on secret-shared* α, β *can be implemented by a 5-round protocol making only a black-box use of oblivious transfer and a pseudorandom generator.*

The DPF is based on our PDPF construction from Corollary 2: Given a point function $\hat{f}_{\alpha,\beta}$, the DPF keys are formed via $\mathrm{poly}(\lambda, \log N)$ punctured PRFs, each serving as a ϵ-secure PDPF for some related $\hat{f}_{\alpha_i,\beta_i}$. The choice of the values (α_i, β_i) is computable via a small non-cryptographic randomized circuit as a function of α, β. For simplicity we present the results for fixed payload $\beta = 1$ and output space $\mathbb{Z}$; however, our construction extends naturally.

The main departure from our PDPF is that for each ϵ-secure DPF, instead of puncturing the corresponding PRF key k_i at a random input x_i^* *with the desired evaluation* $\mathsf{PRF.Eval}(k_i, x_i^*) = \alpha_i$, we will instead simply puncture the PRF at a completely random x_i^*, and provide both parties with the offset $\Delta_i = (\mathsf{PRF.Eval}(k_i, x_i^*) - \alpha_i)$. Recall that puncturing at x_i^* corresponds to an ϵ-secure DPF for $\alpha' = \mathsf{PRF.Eval}(k_i, x_i^*)$. Thus the parties will simply "shift" all evaluations by this offset Δ_i, effectively converting it to a DPF on α_i. This is possible due to the communication with *both* parties, which leads to computation being only logarithmic in N, as opposed to being linear in N in "1.5-server" regime, where we cannot afford online communication with both parties.

Consider the security of this modified scheme. Since the PPRF is now punctured at a random input, independent of any of its PRF evaluations, the punctured key (corresponding to DPF key k_1) now directly hides the punctured evaluation; thus, the offset Δ_i completely hides the secret value α_i. On the other hand, given the PRF key (corresponding to DPF key k_0), the evaluation of the

PRF on a random input has a close-to-uniform, but biased distribution, corresponding to the unequal representation of different output values. This will yield the inverse-polynomial ϵ security for the corresponding DPF (where α_i is masked by a biased one-time pad). Here the bias ϵ is precisely as in the statistical balls and bins analysis from Lemma 1 in the PDPF analysis.

Note that this offset-to-random simplifies the key generation procedure (e.g., the cost of Gen no longer scales with the full domain size N), and adds only minor cost in regard to computation and key size. The reason this was not used in the prior sections is because the resulting construction is no longer a *programmable* DPF, which in particular requires the first key k_0 to be completely independent of the point function to be shared. However, this intermediate version is also a compelling construction offering alternative complexity tradeoffs.

Given this modified DPF construction, the new Gen procedure takes the following form. We mark by (*) those steps whose computation requires evaluation of a cryptographic PRG; all other computations are non-cryptographic.

$\mathsf{Gen}(1^\lambda, \hat{f}_\alpha)$, where $\alpha \in [N]$:

1. Compute the randomized mapping $(\alpha_1, \ldots, \alpha_q) \leftarrow d(\alpha)$, where $d : [N] \to [L]^q$ is as in Lemma 2 (security amplification).[7]
2. Sample q random PPRF keys: $k_1, \ldots, k_q \leftarrow \{0,1\}^\lambda$.
3. For each $i \in [q]$:
   (a) (*) Generate a punctured key $k_i^* \leftarrow \mathsf{Punc}(k_i, x_i^*)$, for random input x_i^*.
   (b) (*) Compute the punctured evaluation $\alpha'_i = \mathsf{PRF.Eval}(k_i, x_i^*)$.
   (c) Compute offset $\Delta_i = \alpha'_i - \alpha_i$
4. Output DPF keys $K_0 = ((k_1, \Delta_1), \ldots, (k_q, \Delta_q))$ and $K_1 = ((k_1^*, \Delta_1), \ldots, (k_q^*, \Delta_q))$.

Consider now a protocol Π_{Gen} for securely evaluating distributed Gen, where parties know only secret shares of α and must learn only their own resulting DPF key. Note that each non-cryptographic computation step can be securely evaluated in constant rounds and making only black-box use of oblivious transfer by using generic secure computation techniques.

This leaves two additional steps to address: puncturing the PPRF keys, and computing (secret shares of) the evaluations of the PRFs at the punctured inputs. Note that the latter can be done directly if one party holds the full PRF key k_i and the other party holds the punctured PRF key k_i^*, by each simply computing the sum of all computable PRF output values, which differ precisely by the punctured output. For the former step, of puncturing the PPRF keys, we observe that a two-round protocol for *precisely* this task were presented in the works of [9,37] (within the context of an application of PPRFs to pseudorandom correlation generators for the OT correlation), applying the techniques of the Doerner-shelat protocol for DPFs [25] to the simpler setting of PPRFs. Intuitively, in order to puncture one

[7] Note that d is non-cryptographic. Concretely, for the case of Reed-Muller locally decodable codes, the mapping d corresponds to effectively generating Shamir secret shares of the input value α.

PPRF key, the protocol consists of a collection of string OTs executed in parallel, one for each level in the evaluation tree of the PPRF, where the selection bits correspond to the bits of the punctured input x^*, and the message strings are computable as a function of the partial PRF evaluations at the given level. In particular, the protocol supports direct secure parallel composition of multiple instances.

Theorem 8 ([9,37]). *Consider the GGM-based PPRF construction of [6, 14, 31]. There exists a two-round secure two-party protocol Π_{Punc} making only a black-box use of oblivious transfer and a pseudorandom generator, for evaluating the functionality with parties' inputs $((k_i)_{i\in[q]}, (x_i^*)_{i\in[q]})$ and outputs $(\bot, (k_i^*)_{i\in[q]})$, where each $k_i^* = \mathsf{Punc}(k_i, x_i^*)$.*

We next describe the constant-round distributed Gen protocol, making use of Π_{Punc} (and, in turn, the GGM-based PPRF). In the protocol description we refer to the two parties as P_0 and P_1.

Distributed Gen protocol, Π_{Gen}:
Inputs: Common: 1^λ, domain size N. P_0, P_1 hold secret shares α^0, α^1 of $\alpha \in [N]$.[8]

1. Party P_0 locally samples q random PPRF keys: $k_1, \ldots, k_q \leftarrow \{0,1\}^\lambda$.
2. Party P_1 locally samples q random PPRF inputs $x_1^*, \ldots, x_q^*$.
3. Parties P_0, P_1 jointly execute q parallel executions of protocol Π_{Punc}, on respective inputs $(k_i)_{i\in[q]}$ and $(x_i^*)_{i\in[q]}$. As output, party P_1 learns q punctured keys $(k_i^*)_{i\in[q]}$.
4. For each $i \in [q]$, each party locally computes the sum of all its computable PPRF evaluations: For P_0, this is $\sigma_i^0 = \sum_x \mathsf{PPRF.Eval}(k_i, x)$. For P_1, this is $\sigma_i^1 = \sum_{x\neq x_i^*} \mathsf{PPRF.PuncEval}(k_i^*, x)$, where sums are taken over $\mathbb{Z}_N$ (the domain space of the DPF).
5. The parties jointly perform a (generic) secure computation protocol for evaluating the following functionality:
   - Input: Each party P_b holds its original input share α^b and $(\sigma_i^b)_{i\in[q]}$.
   - Computation:
     (a) Evaluate the randomized mapping $(\alpha_1, \ldots, \alpha_q) \leftarrow d(\alpha^0 + \alpha^1) \in [L]^q$ from Lemma 2, where $\alpha^0 + \alpha^1$ represents the reconstructed value of the secret shared α (e.g., sum over $\mathbb{Z}_N$).
     (b) For each $i \in [q]$, compute $\Delta_i = (\sigma_i^0 - \sigma_i^1) - \alpha_i$. Recall σ_i^0 is equal to σ_i^1 plus the ith punctured evaluation.
   - Output: To both parties: $(\Delta_i)_{i\in[q]}$.

Security of the protocol Π_{Gen} follows by the security of the underlying Π_{Punc} and generic constant-round secure computation protocols. The round complexity of Π_{Gen} consists of (1) an execution of Π_{Punc}, in 2 rounds, followed by (2) the generic secure computation of a non-cryptographic functionality, in 3 rounds (note that both parties receive output). Thus, the combined round complexity is bounded by 5 rounds.

[8] This secret sharing can be over $\mathbb{Z}_N$, bitwise over $\mathbb{Z}_2$, or otherwise, with insignificant effect for the given protocol. We describe w.r.t. shares over $\mathbb{Z}_N$ for simplicity.

Comparison to Doerner-Shelat [25]. As stated, the round complexity of our DPF distributed generation protocol is constant (5 rounds), as opposed to $\log N$ as in [25]. The communication complexity of our distributed Gen is also better than [25], due to the roughly $2\times$ improvement in our key size and an additive communication overhead in [25]. To give some data points, for $N = 10^5$, and $2^{-10} \leq \epsilon \leq 2^{-4}$ the communication complexity of a single data access in our scheme is in the range of 48–122 KB, while in [25] it is ~240 KB.

The computational complexity of a data access is better than [25] for small values of N and large errors, but the situation is reversed as N grows and the linear scan of N data items in [25] vs. the M data items in our scheme dominates. In [25] the access time for $10^3 \leq N \leq 10^5$ is in the range 15–20 ms, while in our scheme the access time is lower for the pairs ($N = 10^3$, $\epsilon = 10^{-8}$), ($N = 20 \cdot 10^4$, $\epsilon = 2^{-6}$), and ($N = 10^5$, $\epsilon = 2^{-4}$), but is higher for each N when ϵ is lower than the quoted figure.

4.3 Compressing DPF Correlations

In this section we discuss an application of PDPFs for compressing correlated randomness in certain secure computation applications.

Standard DPFs have a variety of applications in the context of secure 2-party computation (2PC). For instance, they serve as crucial building blocks for concretely efficient 2PC of RAM programs [25] or for pseudorandom correlation generators (PCGs) of truth-table correlations [11] and (authenticated) multiplication triples [10].

As an example, suppose the two parties would like to securely evaluate a circuit which consists of arbitrary n-gates $g : \{0,1\}^n \rightarrow \{0,1\}$ (e.g., computing the AND or the majority of the n input bits). Using instances of a random OT correlation, the communication complexity of mapping a secret-shared input to a secret-shared output is linear in the circuit size of g and the round complexity is linear in the circuit depth. But given a random DPF correlation, this only requires n communication bits per party and a single communication round [23, 30]. Concretely, a random DPF correlation consists of secret-sharing of a random $\alpha \in \mathbb{Z}_N$, for $N = 2^n$, and a pair of keys $(k_0, k_1) \leftarrow \mathsf{Gen}(1^\lambda, \hat{f}_{\alpha,1})$ where $\hat{f}_{\alpha,1} : \mathbb{Z}_N \rightarrow \mathbb{Z}_2$. The idea is that the DPF correlation can be locally expanded into a truth-table correlation [11], which can in turn be used to evaluate a g-gate with minimal online communication and round complexity.

Given many independent instances of a DPF correlation, one can obtain a generic speedup for 2PC of Boolean circuits by grouping small sets of Boolean gates into bigger g-gates [22]. This strongly motivates the goal of generating many independent instances of a random DPF correlation with low communication cost. However, there are no known practical methods for achieving this.

We observe that PDPF can be used to solve this problem in the following "trusted-offline" setting for 2PC. In an offline phase, Alice owns a long-term secret s (say, a secret key for encryption, identification, or signature). To eliminate a single point of failure, she splits s into two shares, s_A and s_B, sending s_B to Bob and keeping s_A to herself. She then erases all information except

s_A. In the online phase, the parties receive online inputs P_i (resp., ciphertexts to decrypt, nonces for identification, or messages to sign) and wish to securely compute $f(s, P_i)$ for $i = 1, 2, \ldots, t$.

The key observation is that Alice can be fully trusted in the offline phase, since if she is corrupted before erasing s then the long-term secret is entirely compromised. In fact, if P_i is public, then s is the only secret in the system. Consequently, we trust Alice to generate pairs of DPF keys (k_0^j, k_1^j) in the offline phase, offload the keys k_0^j to Bob, and keep k_1^i. However, the communication cost of generating DPF instances for evaluating many g-gates is high.

A PDPF can provide a dramatic efficiency improvement in this scenario. To generate T independent instances of a DPF correlation, Alice generates and communicates only a single reusable offline key k_0 to Bob (128 communication bits in practice). Then, for each j, she generates an online key k_1^j for a point function $f_{\alpha^j,1}$ using the PDPF algorithm Gen_1. She also derives Bob's (fresh) $\mathbb{Z}_N$-share of α^j from the offline key and computes its own share α_1^j. In the end of the silent generation process, Alice erases all information except her DPF correlation entries (k_1^j, α_i^j). Now the two parties hold T compressed instances of a truth-table correlation that can be silently expanded just when needed.

Viewed more abstractly, the above PDPF-based solution yields a PCG for generating T instances of a size-N truth-table correlation, where one of the keys is of size λ and the other is of size $\approx T \cdot \lambda \log N$. Thus, if Alice acts as a PCG dealer (who is only trusted during the offline phase), the communication cost is constant in T and N and the storage cost grows logarithmically with N. This should be contrasted with two alternative solutions: (1) using a standard DPF, both PCG keys are of size $\approx T \cdot \lambda \log N$, and so the communication cost is high when T is large; (2) using a naive PDPF, with online key linear in the domain size, keeps Bob's key (communication) small, but requires Alice's key (storage) to grow linearly with $T \cdot N$ instead of $T \cdot \log N$. A similar improvement is relevant to other applications of DPF in 2PC, including silent generation of multiplication triples [10] or low-communication simulation of RAM programs [25].

Concrete Efficiency. We make a few remarks about the concrete efficiency of using PDPF to generate truth-table correlations. First, because the above applications only require *random* DPF instances (where α is chosen at random), the computational cost of the PDPF key generation is comparable to a standard DPF. Second, while the PDPF evaluation of our constructions is only concretely efficient for moderate values of N and ϵ (see Sect. 5), this can be good enough for applications. In particular, even a relatively high value of ϵ (say $\epsilon = 2^{-6}$) only amounts to a tiny (and easily quantifiable) leakage in the spirit of differential privacy, which is often considered tolerable. Functions with a small truth-table size N arise in many application scenarios, including S-box computations in distributed evaluation of block ciphers (cf. [23]) or nonlinear activation functions in low-precision Machine Learning algorithms (cf. [2]).

PDPF Correlations vs. FSS Correlations. The truth-table correlations we generate via PDPF are quite broadly applicable, since they effectively allow using a richer set of (small-domain) gates instead of just standard Boolean or arithmetic gates (see [22,23]). Their main disadvantage is the computational overhead inherited from the evaluation algorithm of our PDPF, which scales linearly with the truth-table size N. This should be contrasted with the recent use of FSS correlations for secure computation with preprocessing [7,13], in which the computation cost scales logarithmically with N. However, in applications where the value of N is moderate, this computation overhead may not form an efficiency bottleneck.

5 Concrete Efficiency

In this section we compare the concrete efficiency of our construction from Theorem 4 to a naive PDPF construction. For our comparison we will consider PDPFs over $\mathbb{G} = \mathbb{Z}$ and $\beta \in \mathbb{G}' = \{0, 1\}$. Throughout the section we model the PPRF as an ideal PPRF, see the full version of the paper for further analysis.

While Theorem 4 gives a $\epsilon \approx \sqrt{N/M}$ security bound, we empirically find that the real statistical distance in the statistical variant of the balls-and-bins experiment, as in Lemma 1 is $\epsilon \approx 0.564\sqrt{N/M}$, and we use this estimate in the tables below. For estimating the running time of $\mathsf{EvalAll}$ in our construction we use Theorem 3, by which $\mathsf{EvalAll}$ makes $(M \log_2(N+1)/\lambda$ PRG calls. In addition, by Proposition 4, Gen_1 makes $((N+1)\log_2 M)/\lambda$ PRG calls.

The naive PDPF construction is obtained by having $\mathsf{EvalAll}_0$ treat k_* (obtained by running Gen_0) as a PRF key, expanding it to a truth table of length N over $\{0, \dots, \lceil 1/\epsilon \rceil - 1\}$ for an integer $1/\epsilon$. Denote by $f^0 : [N] \to \mathbb{Z}$ the function with this truth table. Then, Gen_1 will generate k_1 by simply computing the truth table of the function $f^1 = f_{\alpha,\beta} - f^0$ (hence $|k_1| = N\lceil \log_2(1/\epsilon) \rceil$), and $\mathsf{EvalAll}_1$ will output the truth table it got. Note that this naive PDPF construction is ϵ-secure. Because both Gen and $\mathsf{EvalAll}$ compute the PRF on all points, by Theorem 3, they make $(2N-1)(\log N)/(2\lambda)$ PRG calls.

Remark 3 (Privacy and key length for the naive PDPF). The naive construction provides *negligible* privacy error and online key of $N \cdot \log |\mathbb{G}|$ for output group $\mathbb{G}$. In aggregation-type applications, one either needs to pick a very large finite $\mathbb{G}$ or use the group of integers $\mathbb{Z}$ with key size $N \cdot c$ and settle for 2^{-c}-privacy. To make the comparison meaningful, we went for the latter option with $\epsilon = 2^{-c}$.

In Table 1 we compare the key size and running time of Gen and $\mathsf{EvalAll}$ of our PDPF to the naive PDPF, for fixed $\lambda = 128$. Our time unit is PRG evaluations, assuming $1.8 \cdot 10^8$ evaluations per second of $G : \{0,1\}^{128} \to \{0,1\}^{256}$.

Table 1. Key size, running time of Gen_1 and $\mathsf{EvalAll}$ of our PDPF construction from Theorem 4 (left) compared to the naive one (right). For the PDPF from Theorem 4 there are two Gen_1 running times, the smaller one corresponding to time needed to generate a key for a *random point function*. Running times are based on an AES-based PRG implementation benchmarked at $1.8 \cdot 10^8$ PRG calls per second on a single core. For $M = 0.318 \cdot N/\epsilon^2$ and $\lambda = 128$, in our construction, the key size is $\lambda \log_2 M$, $\mathsf{EvalAll}$ makes $(2M-1)(\log N)/(2\lambda)$ calls to the PRG, and Gen_1 makes $(N+1)(\log(M/N))(\log N)/(2\lambda)$ calls to the PRG (and $(\log(N))^2/(2\lambda)$ PRG calls for the random point function). In the naive construction, the key size is $N \log_2(1/\epsilon)$, and $\mathsf{EvalAll}$ and Gen_1 both make $(2N-1)(\log N)/(2\lambda)$ calls to the PRG.

ϵ/N	1000	20000	100000
2^{-4}	**0.3 KB**/0.5 KB 1.5 µs, **0.002 µs**/0.4 µs 38.8 µs/0.4 µs	**0.3 KB**/9.8 KB 42.1 µs, **0.005 µs**/12.4 µs 1.1 ms/12.4 µs	**0.4 KB**/48.8 KB 242.6 µs, **0.006 µs**/72.1 µs 6.2 ms/72.1 µs
2^{-6}	**0.3 KB**/0.7 KB 2.5 µs, **0.002 µs**/0.4 µs 621.2 µs/0.4 µs	**0.4 KB**/14.7 KB 68.7 µs, **0.005 µs**/12.4 µs 17.3 ms/12.4 µs	**0.4 KB**/73.2 KB 395.5 µs, **0.006 µs**/72.1 µs 99.7 ms/72.1 µs
2^{-8}	**0.4 KB**/1.0 KB 3.4 µs, **0.002 µs**/0.4 µs 9.9 ms/0.4 µs	**0.5 KB**/19.5 KB 95.2 µs, **0.005 µs**/12.4 µs 276.8 ms/12.4 µs	**0.5 KB**/97.7 KB 548.3 µs, **0.006 µs**/72.1 µs 1.6 s/72.1 µs
2^{-10}	**0.4 KB**/1.2 KB 4.4 µs, **0.002 µs**/0.4 µs 159.0 ms/0.4 µs	**0.5 KB**/24.4 KB 121.8 µs, **0.005 µs**/12.4 µs 4.4 s/12.4 µs	**0.6 KB**/122.1 KB 701.2 µs, **0.006 µs**/72.1 µs 25.5 s/72.1 µs

Acknowledgements. We thank the CRYPTO reviewers for many useful comments and suggestions, including a simplification of the proof of Theorem 4. Elette Boyle was supported by AFOSR Award FA9550-21-1-0046, ERC Project HSS (852952), ERC Project NTSC (742754), and a Google Research Scholar Award. Niv Gilboa was supported by ISF grant 2951/20, ERC grant 876110, and a grant by the BGU Cyber Center. Yuval Ishai was supported by ERC Project NTSC (742754), BSF grant 2018393, and ISF grant 2774/20. Victor I. Kolobov was supported by ERC Project NTSC (742754) and ISF grant 2774/20.

References

1. Abraham, I., Pinkas, B., Yanai, A.: Blinder - scalable, robust anonymous committed broadcast. In: CCS 2020, pp. 1233–1252 (2020)
2. Agrawal, N., Shamsabadi, A.S., Kusner, M.J., Gascón, A.: QUOTIENT: two-party secure neural network training and prediction. In: ACM CCS 2019, pp. 1231–1247 (2019)
3. Boneh, D., Boyle, E., Corrigan-Gibbs, H., Gilboa, N., Ishai, Y.: Lightweight techniques for private heavy hitters, pp. 762–776 (2021)
4. Boneh, D., Kim, S., Montgomery, H.: Private puncturable PRFs from standard lattice assumptions. In: Coron, J.-S., Nielsen, J.B. (eds.) EUROCRYPT 2017, Part I. LNCS, vol. 10210, pp. 415–445. Springer, Cham (2017). https://doi.org/10.1007/978-3-319-56620-7_15

5. Boneh, D., Lewi, K., Wu, D.J.: Constraining pseudorandom functions privately. In: Fehr, S. (ed.) PKC 2017, Part II. LNCS, vol. 10175, pp. 494–524. Springer, Heidelberg (2017). https://doi.org/10.1007/978-3-662-54388-7_17
6. Boneh, D., Waters, B.: Constrained pseudorandom functions and their applications. In: Sako, K., Sarkar, P. (eds.) ASIACRYPT 2013, Part II. LNCS, vol. 8270, pp. 280–300. Springer, Heidelberg (2013). https://doi.org/10.1007/978-3-642-42045-0_15
7. Boyle, E., et al.: Function secret sharing for mixed-mode and fixed-point secure computation. In: Canteaut, A., Standaert, F.-X. (eds.) EUROCRYPT 2021, Part II. LNCS, vol. 12697, pp. 871–900. Springer, Cham (2021). https://doi.org/10.1007/978-3-030-77886-6_30
8. Boyle, E., Couteau, G., Gilboa, N., Ishai, Y.: Compressing vector OLE. In: Proceedings of the 2018 ACM SIGSAC Conference on Computer and Communications Security, pp. 896–912 (2018)
9. Boyle, E., et al.: Efficient two-round OT extension and silent non-interactive secure computation. In: Proceedings of the 2019 ACM SIGSAC Conference on Computer and Communications Security, CCS. ACM (2019)
10. Boyle, E., Couteau, G., Gilboa, N., Ishai, Y., Kohl, L., Scholl, P.: Efficient pseudorandom correlation generators from ring-LPN. In: Micciancio, D., Ristenpart, T. (eds.) CRYPTO 2020, Part II. LNCS, vol. 12171, pp. 387–416. Springer, Cham (2020). https://doi.org/10.1007/978-3-030-56880-1_14
11. Boyle, E., Couteau, G., Gilboa, N., Ishai, Y., Kohl, L., Scholl, P.: Efficient pseudorandom correlation generators: silent OT extension and more. In: Boldyreva, A., Micciancio, D. (eds.) CRYPTO 2019, Part III. LNCS, vol. 11694, pp. 489–518. Springer, Cham (2019). https://doi.org/10.1007/978-3-030-26954-8_16
12. Boyle, E., Gilboa, N., Ishai, Y.: Function secret sharing: improvements and extensions. In: CCS (2016)
13. Boyle, E., Gilboa, N., Ishai, Y.: Secure computation with preprocessing via function secret sharing. In: Hofheinz, D., Rosen, A. (eds.) TCC 2019, Part I. LNCS, vol. 11891, pp. 341–371. Springer, Cham (2019). https://doi.org/10.1007/978-3-030-36030-6_14
14. Boyle, E., Goldwasser, S., Ivan, I.: Functional signatures and pseudorandom functions. In: Krawczyk, H. (ed.) PKC 2014. LNCS, vol. 8383, pp. 501–519. Springer, Heidelberg (2014). https://doi.org/10.1007/978-3-642-54631-0_29
15. Boyle, E., Ishai, Y., Pass, R., Wootters, M.: Can we access a database both locally and privately? In: Kalai, Y., Reyzin, L. (eds.) TCC 2017, Part II. LNCS, vol. 10678, pp. 662–693. Springer, Cham (2017). https://doi.org/10.1007/978-3-319-70503-3_22
16. Brakerski, Z., Tsabary, R., Vaikuntanathan, V., Wee, H.: Private constrained PRFs (and more) from LWE. In: Kalai, Y., Reyzin, L. (eds.) TCC 2017, Part I. LNCS, vol. 10677, pp. 264–302. Springer, Cham (2017). https://doi.org/10.1007/978-3-319-70500-2_10
17. Canetti, R., Chen, Y.: Constraint-hiding constrained PRFs for NC^1 from LWE. In: Coron, J.-S., Nielsen, J.B. (eds.) EUROCRYPT 2017, Part I. LNCS, vol. 10210, pp. 446–476. Springer, Cham (2017). https://doi.org/10.1007/978-3-319-56620-7_16
18. Chor, B., Goldreich, O., Kushilevitz, E., Sudan, M.: Private information retrieval. In: Proceedings of IEEE 36th Annual Foundations of Computer Science, pp. 41–50. IEEE (1995)
19. Corrigan-Gibbs, H., Boneh, D.: Prio: private, robust, and scalable computation of aggregate statistics. In: 14th USENIX Symposium on Networked Systems Design and Implementation (NSDI 2017), pp. 259–282 (2017)

20. Corrigan-Gibbs, H., Boneh, D., Mazières, D.: Riposte: an anonymous messaging system handling millions of users. In: 2015 IEEE Symposium on Security and Privacy, pp. 321–338. IEEE (2015)
21. Corrigan-Gibbs, H., Kogan, D.: Private information retrieval with sublinear online time. In: Canteaut, A., Ishai, Y. (eds.) EUROCRYPT 2020, Part I. LNCS, vol. 12105, pp. 44–75. Springer, Cham (2020). https://doi.org/10.1007/978-3-030-45721-1_3
22. Couteau, G.: A note on the communication complexity of multiparty computation in the correlated randomness model. In: Ishai, Y., Rijmen, V. (eds.) EUROCRYPT 2019, Part II. LNCS, vol. 11477, pp. 473–503. Springer, Cham (2019). https://doi.org/10.1007/978-3-030-17656-3_17
23. Damgård, I., Nielsen, J.B., Nielsen, M., Ranellucci, S.: The TinyTable protocol for 2-party secure computation, or: gate-scrambling revisited. In: Katz, J., Shacham, H. (eds.) CRYPTO 2017, Part I. LNCS, vol. 10401, pp. 167–187. Springer, Cham (2017). https://doi.org/10.1007/978-3-319-63688-7_6
24. Di Crescenzo, G., Malkin, T., Ostrovsky, R.: Single database private information retrieval implies oblivious transfer. In: Preneel, B. (ed.) EUROCRYPT 2000. LNCS, vol. 1807, pp. 122–138. Springer, Heidelberg (2000). https://doi.org/10.1007/3-540-45539-6_10
25. Doerner, J., Shelat, A.: Scaling ORAM for secure computation. In: Proceedings of the 2017 ACM SIGSAC Conference on Computer and Communications Security, pp. 523–535 (2017)
26. Duc, A., Dziembowski, S., Faust, S.: Unifying leakage models: from probing attacks to noisy leakage. In: Nguyen, P.Q., Oswald, E. (eds.) EUROCRYPT 2014. LNCS, vol. 8441, pp. 423–440. Springer, Heidelberg (2014). https://doi.org/10.1007/978-3-642-55220-5_24
27. Gilboa, N., Ishai, Y.: Distributed point functions and their applications. In: Nguyen, P.Q., Oswald, E. (eds.) EUROCRYPT 2014. LNCS, vol. 8441, pp. 640–658. Springer, Heidelberg (2014). https://doi.org/10.1007/978-3-642-55220-5_35
28. Goldreich, O., Goldwasser, S., Micali, S.: How to construct random functions. J. ACM **33**(4), 792–807 (1986)
29. Gupta, T., Crooks, N., Mulhern, W., Setty, S.T.V., Alvisi, L., Walfish, M.: Scalable and private media consumption with Popcorn. In: USENIX (2016)
30. Ishai, Y., Kushilevitz, E., Meldgaard, S., Orlandi, C., Paskin-Cherniavsky, A.: On the power of correlated randomness in secure computation. In: Sahai, A. (ed.) TCC 2013. LNCS, vol. 7785, pp. 600–620. Springer, Heidelberg (2013). https://doi.org/10.1007/978-3-642-36594-2_34
31. Kiayias, A., Papadopoulos, S., Triandopoulos, N., Zacharias, T.: Delegatable pseudorandom functions and applications. In: CCS 2013, pp. 669–684
32. Maurer, U., Pietrzak, K., Renner, R.: Indistinguishability amplification. In: Menezes, A. (ed.) CRYPTO 2007. LNCS, vol. 4622, pp. 130–149. Springer, Heidelberg (2007). https://doi.org/10.1007/978-3-540-74143-5_8
33. Maurer, U., Tessaro, S.: A hardcore lemma for computational indistinguishability: security amplification for arbitrarily weak PRGs with optimal stretch. In: Micciancio, D. (ed.) TCC 2010. LNCS, vol. 5978, pp. 237–254. Springer, Heidelberg (2010). https://doi.org/10.1007/978-3-642-11799-2_15
34. Newman, Z., Servan-Schreiber, S., Devadas, S.: Spectrum: High-bandwidth anonymous broadcast with malicious security. IACR Cryptology ePrint Archive, p. 325 (2021)
35. Ostrovsky, R., Shoup, V.: Private information storage (extended abstract). In: STOC 1997, pp. 294–303 (1997)

36. Peikert, C., Shiehian, S.: Privately constraining and programming PRFs, the LWE way. In: Abdalla, M., Dahab, R. (eds.) PKC 2018, Part II. LNCS, vol. 10770, pp. 675–701. Springer, Cham (2018). https://doi.org/10.1007/978-3-319-76581-5_23
37. Schoppmann, P., Gascón, A., Reichert, L., Raykova, M.: Distributed vector-OLE: improved constructions and implementation. In: ACM CCS, pp. 1055–1072 (2019)
38. Shi, E., Aqeel, W., Chandrasekaran, B., Maggs, B.: Puncturable pseudorandom sets and private information retrieval with near-optimal online bandwidth and time. In: Malkin, T., Peikert, C. (eds.) CRYPTO 2021, Part IV. LNCS, vol. 12828, pp. 641–669. Springer, Cham (2021). https://doi.org/10.1007/978-3-030-84259-8_22

Snapshot-Oblivious RAMs: Sub-logarithmic Efficiency for Short Transcripts

Yang Du[1], Daniel Genkin[2], and Paul Grubbs[1](✉)

[1] University of Michigan, Ann Arbor, USA
{duyung,paulgrub}@umich.edu
[2] Georgia Tech, Atlanta, USA
genkin@gatech.edu

Abstract. Oblivious RAM (ORAM) is a powerful technique to prevent harmful data breaches. Despite tremendous progress in improving the concrete performance of ORAM, it remains too slow for use in many practical settings; recent breakthroughs in lower bounds indicate this inefficiency is inherent for ORAM and even some natural relaxations.

This work introduces snapshot-oblivious RAMs, a new secure memory access primitive. Snapshot-oblivious RAMs bypass lower bounds by providing security only for transcripts whose length (call it c) is fixed and known ahead of time. Intuitively, snapshot-oblivious RAMs provide strong security for attacks of short duration, such as the snapshot attacks targeted by many encrypted databases.

We give an ORAM-style definition of this new primitive, and present several constructions. The underlying design principle of our constructions is to store the history of recent operations in a data structure that can be accessed obliviously. We instantiate this paradigm with data structures that remain on the client, giving a snapshot-oblivious RAM with constant bandwidth overhead. We also show how these data structures can be stored on the server and accessed using oblivious memory primitives. Our most efficient instantiation achieves $\mathcal{O}(\log c)$ bandwidth overhead. By extending recent ORAM lower bounds, we show this performance is asymptotically optimal. Along the way, we define a new *hash queue* data structure—essentially, a dictionary whose elements can be modified in a first-in-first-out fashion—which may be of independent interest.

1 Introduction

Users of cloud computing services trust providers to store sensitive data. Encryption can protect the data itself, but cannot prevent information from being disclosed by attacks on metadata like the memory access patterns. A long line of work has conclusively demonstrated that access pattern attacks can be used to reveal sensitive information. In some settings, access patterns alone can be used to completely decrypt data [9,14,22–24,28,32,34,36,37].

Oblivious RAM (ORAM) is a technique that can hide memory access patterns and therefore prevent these kinds of harmful attacks. ORAM is quite useful, but its strong security guarantees come at a cost, both asymptotic and concrete. With the best known constructions [4] achieving $\mathcal{O}(\log n)$ overhead for an n-entry memory, and with a matching $\Omega(\log n)$ lower bound by [38], it seems impossible to have an ORAM scheme where the cost of each memory access does not depend on the total memory size.

Y. Dodis and T. Shrimpton (Eds.): CRYPTO 2022, LNCS 13510, pp. 152–181, 2022.
https://doi.org/10.1007/978-3-031-15985-5_6

Unfortunately, even relaxing security requirements does not allow bypassing the $\Omega(\log n)$ lower bound. Indeed, similar lower-bounds have been shown for differentially oblivious RAMs [42], or even when the memory access pattern is known ahead of time [6,19]. The attempt to gain efficiency in various settings has led to primitives such as structured/searchable encryption [11,13,48], which allows for fast database lookup at the cost of allowing attacks in some settings [9]. Alternatively, prior works have assumed the a-priori knowledge of a certain distribution of memory accesses [21], or provided an ORAM-based mechanisms for adjusting searchable encryption leakage [15].

Motivated by the goal of securing worst-case memory access patterns without dependence on the size of the entire memory, in this paper we tackle the following question:

How can we sidestep the $\Omega(\log n)$ lower bound, while providing a meaningful and general security guarantee for memory access patterns?

1.1 Our Contributions

We begin with the observation that many attacks on real systems follow a common pattern: an attacker gains access to an already-running system, is present in the system for a relatively short time, then either leaves or loses access because the attack was detected. The Verizon Data Breach Incident Report (DBIR) underscores the commonality of these kinds of attacks: for example, in 2021 it found nearly five thousand incidents of "Basic Web Application Attacks", simple attacks in which an attacker compromises the web application and quickly performs only a few actions, such as downloading emails. DBIR also found that roughly 50% of detected security incidents were detected within a few days [1]. A limiting case of this model is the so-called "snapshot" threat model targeted by many encrypted databases, where the attacker obtains only a one-time snapshot of the database system, giving it only the currently-running queries [23].

Thus, for encrypted memory primitives it makes sense to consider an attack model where the attacker sees only a "window" of memory access patterns of bounded size; however, the attacker cannot see the system's memory access pattern before the attack began, nor can it see the access pattern after the attack has concluded. Thus, we define the notion of c-Snapshot ORAM, which maintains ORAM-like security guarantees but against a weaker adversary which is limited to observing only c memory operations.

Definition 1 (informal). *We say a RAM emulator RE is c-snapshot oblivious in case the following holds. For any two sequences of operations $\overrightarrow{op}^1, \overrightarrow{op}^2$ of the same length, and for any subsequences of c operations: $\overrightarrow{op}_c^1 \subseteq \overrightarrow{op}^1, \overrightarrow{op}_c^2 \subseteq \overrightarrow{op}^2$, it holds that the access patterns seen while executing $\overrightarrow{op}_c^1$ and $\overrightarrow{op}_c^2$ are computationally indistinguishable.*

Next, with Definition 1 in hand, we then present our first c-Snapshot ORAM construction where the client's overhead is polylogarithmic in c but independent of n. More formally,

Theorem 1 (informal). *There exists a c-snapshot oblivious RAM emulator with $\mathcal{O}(\log^2 c)$ bandwidth overhead, using $\tilde{\mathcal{O}}(\log c)$ client storage.*

In particular, Theorem 1 offers the "best of both words" ORAM construction, as the client obtains a meaningful security guarantee against realistic adversaries while having its overhead not depend on n. Next, we proceed to reduce the client's storage to constant, while maintaining polylogarithmic (in c) overhead for the server. We achieve this in the amortized setting. See Theorem 2 below.

Theorem 2 (informal). *There exists a c-snapshot oblivious RAM emulator with $\mathcal{O}(\log c)$ amortized bandwidth overhead, using constant client storage.*

Finally, we proceed to find the lower bound for c-snapshot ORAMs. Here, we show that any c-snapshot secure construction with constant storage must have an $\Omega(\log c)$ amortized bandwidth overhead. In particular, this makes the construction in Theorem 2 asymptotically optimal.

Theorem 3. *Any c-snapshot oblivious RAM emulator using constant client storage, must have a lower bound of $\Omega(\log c)$ amortized bandwidth overhead.*

1.2 Technical Overview

Motivated by the challenge of bypassing the ORAM lower bound while still providing meaningful security guarantees in a natural setting, in Sect. 3 we begin by presenting our definition of a c-snapshot ORAM. Our aim is to provide security against an adversary that is capable of only seeing a window of at most c operations. We formalize this with an IND-CPA style game in which the adversary needs to distinguish which of two chosen transcripts were executed, given only the access patterns of the last c operations and the state of the memory before these operations. We also prove our definition has several desirable properties: notably, c-snapshot obliviousness implies security for smaller snapshots as well.

In this paper, we do not assume any encryption on the memory content and let adversary only see the accessed address. In practice, we can either use a standard "read, re-encrypt, write back" paradigm, or secret-sharing under multi-party setting.

A Folklore 1-Snapshot Oblivious Scheme. With the definition of c-snapshot ORAM in hand, we proceed to analyze a folklore RAM emulator which simply permutes memory addresses using a PRP, while hiding the operation type by performing a read and a write for both operation types. As we show in Sect. 4, this results in a 1-snapshot ORAM, as the adversary only sees an access to a single pseudorandom memory location.

Getting $c > 1$. Moving to the more general goal of c-snapshot obliviousness, we proceed to hide repeated accesses to the same memory locations by the client using a size-c queue. More specifically, we ask the ORAM client to maintain a queue of size $\mathcal{O}(c)$, which intuitively acts as a cache for the last c accesses. While addresses the are not present in the queue are fetched from the server's memory, we access a dummy element in case the address is present. Notably, as the attacker only sees a window of c, we do not need to re-shuffle, as any eviction of the queue is guaranteed to be touching an address which was last accessed more than c operations ago. This ensures that any address is accessed at most once in every size-c window, intuitively mimicking the 1-snapshot ORAM construction. See Sect. 5 for details.

Achieving Polylogarithmic Storage. Our next step is to reduce the storage required by the client from $O(c)$ to $\mathsf{polylog}(c)$. An intuitive approach will be to recursively delegate the client's storage to the server using an oblivious RAM. Because storage complexity of the construction in Sect. 5 in linear in c, such a recursive composition will result in reducing the client's storage overhead.

In Sects. 6 and 7.1 we present different constructions using a custom data structure we call an Oblivious Hash Queue (OHQ). More specifically, we begin by observing that obliviously delegating the client's queue to the server is simpler than general ORAM, as the queue only supports a limited set of operations. By efficiently solving the oblivious queue delegation problem, in Sect. 6 we are able to obtain c-snapshot oblivious construction with $\mathcal{O}(\log^2 c)$ bandwidth overhead, using $\tilde{\mathcal{O}}(\log c)$ client storage. Further refining our OHQ technique, in Sect. 7.1 we obtain a construction with $\mathcal{O}(\log c)$ amortized bandwidth and constant client overhead, albeit with a worse concrete efficiency compared to the construction in Sect. 6.

A Matching Lower Bound. Directly following from Larsen and Nielsen lower bound [38], in Sect. 7.3 we show a lower bound for obtaining c-snapshot ORAM, proving that every secure construction must have an $\Omega(\log c)$ amortized bandwidth overhead. We reuse Larsen and Nielsen's result in the c-snapshot security setting. This essentially proves the asymptotic optimality of the construction in Sect. 7.1, limiting future improvements to lower order terms.

1.3 Related Work

ORAM. There are two kinds of oblivious RAM: hierarchical ORAM, initially proposed in [19] and following works [4,19,20,35,41,43], and tree based ORAM, proposed by Shi et al. in [47] and followed by [12,17,44,47,49,51]. Computationally secure ORAM is optimized by [4] with an amortized bandwidth overhead of $\mathcal{O}(\log n)$, and de-amortized by [5]. These above ORAM constructions satisfies the most strict security definition (see Sect. 2.2). ORAM can be more efficient if it is designed for a specific usage, such as oblivious data structure [52] and zero-knowledge ORAM [26,27].

Variants of the basic ORAM model include the offline setting and the balls-in-bins model. Boyle and Naor [6] showed how to construct an ORAM scheme in the offline setting. Jafargholi et al. [30] gave a statistically secure offline ORAM with $\Omega(\log n)$ overhead, using an oblivious priority queue. Read only ORAM [53] supports only read operation in the online setting. If we remove the ball-in-bin model, ORAM efficiency can be enhanced given server computation ability [2,16,25,40]. Differentially private ORAM [50] further weakens the security requirement by requiring that the access patterns of adjacent transcripts (vs. any two transcripts) are statistically close.

Structured Encryption. Most of searchable encryption and structured encryption schemes [15,18,21,31] assumes a fully persistent adversary. But there are works assuming non-persistent adversary such as [3]. In their setting, adversary is only observing snapshots of database but not access pattern of queries. A line of works on leakage suppression [31] uses a cache to store most recent accessed queries, and retrieve from cache if queried again. However this does not allow writing things back to main memory unless a rebuild, which incurs an amortized $\Omega(\log n)$ overhead. Our schemes (Sect. 5, 6) allow writes back to main memory because we require security to hold only for a short operation sequence. A follow-up on leakage suppression [18] allows addition and deletion of keys in a multimap.

A recent line of work has studied intermediate security for persistent adversaries that is stronger than typical structured encryption but weaker than ORAM. For example, Pancake [21] shows how to do efficient key-value lookups with access pattern hiding in a setting where the distribution of queries is known a priori, and queries are independent. SEAL [15] combines structured encryption with ORAM, allowing more fine-grained tradeoffs between access pattern hiding (against persistent adversaries) and efficiency.

Lower Bounds. Larsen and Nielsen [38] gave the first cell-probe lower bound $\Omega(\log n)$ for online ORAM, answering the question asked in [6], which also reduced lower bound for offline ORAM to sorting circuits. A follow-up work from Jacob et al. [29] gave lower bounds for oblivious data structures. A recent work [33] generalized the overhead to both online and offline ORAM. Weiss and Wichs [53] showed lower bound for read only online ORAM, and Persiano and Yeo [42] gave a $\Omega(n)$ lower bound for differentially private RAM. Larsen et al. [39] gave an ORAM lower bound under multi-server setting. Recently, Patel et al. showed there is an inherent inefficiency in encrypted multi-maps with even decoupled key-equality pattern leakage, which leads to a $\Omega(\log n)$ overhead in the leakage cell probe model. Cash et al. gave lower bound for one-round ORAM [8], which requires either $\Omega(\sqrt{N})$ bandwidth overhead or $\Omega(\sqrt{N})$ client storage. Our snapshot oblivious RAM (Sect. 5.2) is also one-round but has constant overhead and needs $\Theta(c)$ client storage.

2 Preliminaries

2.1 Pseudorandom Permutation

Definition 2 ***(Pseudorandom permutation).*** *A Pseudorandom permutation (PRP) is a function family $E : \mathcal{K} \times \{0,1\}^n \rightarrow \{0,1\}^n$. We define the PRP security game $\mathbf{PRP}(E, \mathcal{A}, i)$. First, a key k is randomly generated from $\mathcal{K}$ and a random permutation π is randomly generated from all permutations of n elements $\mathsf{Perms}(n)$. The adversary has access to an oracle $\mathcal{O}_i^k$. When the adversary queries a string s, it receives either $E_k(s)$ in the case $i = 0$ or $\pi(s)$ in the case $i = 1$. Finally the adversary outputs a bit b. We say that E is a secure PRP if for all nuPPT adversaries $\mathcal{A}$ playing the PRP security game.*

$$\mathbf{Adv}_E^{prp}(\mathcal{A}) = \big|\Pr[\mathbf{PRP}(E, \mathcal{A}, 0) = 1] - \Pr[\mathbf{PRP}(E, \mathcal{A}, 1) = 1]\big|,$$

the advantage defined above is negligible.

2.2 ORAM

In this section, we describe the syntax of our execution model and RAM emulator. We then proceed to define the correctness requirements of RAM emulators, as well as their obliviousness security definitions.

Execution Model and Terminology. We define a random access memory (e.g., RAM) DB to be an array of M entries, where each entry contains at least $m \geq \lceil \log M \rceil$-bits. We define an operation to be a tuple (op, idx, val) where op is either read or write, idx is an integer between 0 and $M - 1$, and val is either a bit string of length m or the $\perp$ symbol. Finally, we define a transcript to be a sequence of operations.

A Note on "Blocks". Many works on ORAM [4,41,49] additionally define a "block" of memory to be a sequence of memory locations that can be accessed with unit cost. While we do not use blocks in this paper, and for simplicity assume that one operation

```
Run(RE, DB, T):
st_0 <-$ RE^{MemR,MemW}.init(DB)
For x = 1 to |T|:
  st_x, resp_i <-$ RE^{MemR,MemW}.exec(st_{i-1}, T[x])
respArr <- resp_1 || ... || resp_|T|
Return respArr

MemR(idx):
Return Mem[idx]

MemW(idx, val):
Mem[idx] <- val
Return ⊥
```

```
Execute(DB, T):
Mem <- empty array of length M
For x = 1 to |DB|:
  Mem[x] <- DB[x]
For x = 1 to |T|:
  op, idx, val <- T[x]
  If op = read:
    resp_x <- Mem[idx]
  If op = write:
    Mem[idx] <- val
    resp_x <- ⊥
respArr <- resp_1 || ... || resp_|T|
Return respArr
```

Fig. 1. RAM emulator correctness.

only reads or writes to a single memory location, we do note that our results can be easily extended to account for block memory accesses.

RAM Emulators. A RAM emulator RE is a pair of algorithms (init, exec) that simulates a RAM. Both init and exec have oracle access to two procedures—**MemR** and **MemW**—that allow reading and writing to an array Mem of size M. Below, we will mostly leave implicit the length of each array entry, and simply assume they are large enough. (To draw an analogy to encrypted databases, RE is the "client" and the array Mem it reads and writes through its oracles is the "server".)

The randomized initialization procedure RE.init(DB) takes an array of size N where each input is m bits long, representing the initial state of the memory, as input. It outputs an initial state st_0. The randomized execute procedure RE.exec(st, (op, idx, val)) takes as input a state st and an operation. It executes the operation and outputs the result and a new state. (Below, in cases where the result is not used, we will omit it.)

Access Pattern. We define an access pattern of an emulator RE on an array DB and transcript T to be the sequence of **MemR** and **MemW** oracle calls, and the first argument (accessed index) made by RE during init and while calling exec on each operation in the transcript. As an abuse of notation, we will sometimes use RE(DB, T) to refer to the access pattern corresponding to executing the operations in T on DB.

Correctness and Efficiency. Intuitively, a RAM emulator RE should always return the same results as the "canonical" RAM implementation Execute outlined in Fig. 1 (right). More formally, for a RAM emulator RE we define correctness using the pseudocode in Fig. 1 (left). That is, we say that RE is correct if for any database DB and transcript T, the output of Run(RE, DB, T) is equal to the output of Execute(DB, T) with probability 1 over the random choices made during init and exec.

Bandwidth Overhead. One of the main measures of efficiency for RAM emulators is bandwidth overhead, namely the increase in memory usage compared to the baseline of just executing the transcript directly. Formally, for an emulator RE, database DB, and transcript T, we define the bandwidth overhead as $\mathsf{Ex}[|\mathsf{RE}(DB, T)|/|T|]$ where the expectation is taken over the randomness of RE.

```
ObSec(RE, A, n, ℓ, i):
AP ← []
(DB_0, T_0), (DB_1, T_1) ←$ A_0(l)
If |DB_0| ≠ |DB_1| ∨ |T_0| ≠ ℓ ∨ |T_1| ≠ ℓ:
  Return ⊥
st_0 ←$ RE^{MemR,MemW}.init(DB_i)
For x = 1 to |T_i|:
  st_x ←$ RE^{MemR,MemW}.exec(st_{x-1}, T_i[x])
b ←$ A_1(AP).
Return b
```

```
MemR(idx):
AP ← AP || (r, idx)
Return Mem[idx]

MemW(idx, val):
Mem[idx] ← val
AP ← AP || (w, idx)
Return ⊥
```

Fig. 2. ORAM security game definition in pseudocode.

Oblivious RAM Emulators. Next we define the notion of obliviousness for RAM emulators, see Fig. 2. In this pseudocode, the adversary has two stages. The first stage adversary $\mathcal{A}_0$ chooses the arrays (databases) DB_0, DB_1 and the transcripts T_0, T_1. Next, the second stage adversary $\mathcal{A}_1$ tries to guess the bit b. We note that $\mathcal{A}_1$ is not given access to the contents of memory: all its input AP contains is the memory address accessed by each oracle call, and its type (r or w). This is make the definition agnostic to the way the memory contents are hidden—i.e., our definition can just as easily apply to a setting where the memory is encrypted as it can to one where RE is run in multi-party computation.

Definition 3 *(Oblivious RAM emulator security). We define the ObSec advantage of an adversary $\mathcal{A} = (\mathcal{A}_0, \mathcal{A}_1)$ against RAM emulator RE as*

$$\mathbf{Adv}^{obl}_{RE}(\mathcal{A}) = \left| \Pr[ObSec(RE, \mathcal{A}, n, \ell, 0) = 1] - \Pr[ObSec(RE, \mathcal{A}, n, \ell, 1) = 1] \right| .$$

We say the RAM emulator RE is computationally oblivious if for any nuPPT adversary $\mathcal{A}$, $\mathbf{Adv}^{obl}_{RE}(\mathcal{A}) = \mathrm{negl}(n)$.

Semi-honest Security. Finally, we note that because **MemR** and **MemW** read and write Mem, neither these ORAM definitions capture servers that modify memory contents or reply with stale values. Such attacks can be prevented using standard techniques [45].

2.3 Oblivious Maps

Below, we will use oblivious maps, which are oblivious data structures akin to ORAM but tailored for specific operation types (less generic than memory read/write).

As proposed in [52], we give oblivious map the following syntax. An oblivious map OM has an initialize function OM.init(N) which takes N as the maximum capacity and outputs an initial state. As with ORAMs, we view oblivious maps as having oracle access to **MemR** and **MemW** oracles to manipulate their memory. OM has an execution function that supports four operations: Find, Insert, Update, Delete. OM.Find(key) returns the value associated to key. OM.Insert(key, val) inserts the key value pair in to the map. OM.Update(key, val) replaces the value associated to key by val. OM.Delete(key) deletes the key value pair whose key is key. The execute function additionally inputs and outputs a state.

We require oblivious maps to satisfy a variant of the ORAM security definition defined above. Let OblivMapSec denote the security game. (We omit pseudocode since it is almost identical to ObSec.)

Definition 4 *(Oblivious map). We define the advantage of $\mathcal{A}$ against* OM *as*

$$\mathbf{Adv}_{\mathsf{OM}}^{OMap}(\mathcal{A}) = \big|\Pr[\mathit{OblivMapSec}(\mathsf{OM}, \mathcal{A}, N, \ell, 0) = 1] \\ - \Pr[\mathit{OblivMapSec}(\mathsf{OM}, \mathcal{A}, N, \ell, 1) = 1]\big|.$$

If this advantage is negligible for all nuPPT adversaries, we say OM *is an oblivious map.*

3 Snapshot-Oblivious RAM Emulators

In this section, we introduce our new primitive: c-snapshot oblivious RAM emulators. (We will usually shorten this to c-snapshot ORAMs.) The syntax of the new primitive is similar to ORAM, but with one important change: we allow the init procedure to take, in addition to the initial array DB, a natural number c denoting the number of operations' access patterns the adversary gets to see. The syntax is otherwise unchanged. The correctness notion for RAM emulators must change slightly as well: for a RAM emulator to be correct, the correctness condition defined in Sect. 2 must hold with probability 1 for every possible choice of c.

c-Snapshot Obliviousness. Next we explain our new security notion, c-snapshot obliviousness. Before formally stating the definition, we will briefly discuss the space of possible definitions, and identify some desirable properties of a snapshot-obliviousness definition. First, we expect snapshot-obliviousness should be *strictly* weaker than plain obliviousness. Namely, any ORAM should be c-snapshot oblivious for any c. Second, for any $c' < c$, it should be the case that c-snapshot obliviousness implies c'-snapshot obliviousness. Finally, to meaningfully capture snapshot attacks on real systems, we would like snapshot-obliviousness to allow the adversary to see any c operations of its choosing, without restricting the adversary to any particular locations.

Our Definition. We give the pseudocode of our definition in Fig. 3. Like plain obliviousness, the definition allows the adversary to specify two pairs of an array and transcript. The game runs RE.init on the ith pair using the oracles **MRH** and **MWH**, which allow the emulator to manipulate the memory Mem without recording the access patterns. Then the game runs RE.exec on all but the last c operations of T_i, again without recording the access patterns. Next, the game proceeds to execute final c operations of the transcript via RE.exec, but this time using **MemR** and **MemW** which record their access patterns in AP. Finally, the game runs the second adversary $\mathcal{A}_1$ on the recorded access patterns AP, and (implicitly) the state of $\mathcal{A}_0$. $\mathcal{A}_1$ in turn is expected to correctly guess i.

Definition 5 *(c-snapshot obliviousness). Let RE be a RAM emulator and c be a fixed number, the c-SnapObSec advantage of the adversary $\mathcal{A} = (\mathcal{A}_0, \mathcal{A}_1)$ against RE is*

$$\mathbf{Adv}_{RE}^{snap}(\mathcal{A}) = \big|\Pr[\mathit{SnapObSec}(RE, \mathcal{A}, n, c, 0) = 1] \\ - \Pr[\mathit{SnapObSec}(RE, \mathcal{A}, n, c, 1) = 1]\big|.$$

```
SnapObSec(RE, A, n, c, i):
  AP ← []
  (DB_0, T_0), (DB_1, T_1) ←$ A_0(n, c)
  If |DB_0| ≠ |DB_1| or |T_0| ≠ |T_1| then Return ⊥
  st_0 ←$ RE^{MRH,MWH}.init(DB_i, c)
  For x = 1 to |T_i| − c:
    st_x ←$ RE^{MRH,MWH}.exec(st_{x−1}, T_i[x])
  For x = |T_i| − c + 1 to |T_i|:
    st_x ←$ RE^{MemR,MemW}.exec(st_{x−1}, T_i[x])
  b ←$ A_1(AP).
  Return b
```

```
MemR(idx):
  AP ← AP || (r, idx)
  Return Mem[idx]

MemW(idx, val):
  Mem[idx] ← val
  AP ← AP || (w, idx)
  Return ⊥

MRH(idx):
  Return Mem[idx]

MWH(idx, val):
  Mem[idx] ← val
  Return ⊥
```

Fig. 3. SnapORAM security game.

The emulator RE *is said to be (computationally) c-snapshot oblivious if for any nuPPT adversary* $\mathcal{A}$, $\mathbf{Adv}^{snap}_{\mathsf{RE}}(\mathcal{A}) = \text{negl}(n)$.

Comparing to Obliviousness. We now argue that our c-snapshot obliviousness definition is a natural restriction of regular ORAM. In particular, if for a RAM emulator RE there exists a c and an adversary $\mathcal{A}$ with non-negligible c-SnapObSec advantage, we can build a reduction $\mathcal{B} = (\mathcal{B}_0, \mathcal{B}_1)$ that breaks ORAM security. The reduction $\mathcal{B}_0$ works by running $\mathcal{A}_0$ (with c as an argument) and outputting the two pairs it outputs. Then, $\mathcal{B}_1$ uses its access patterns AP to construct $\mathcal{A}_1$'s inputs. (Note that $\mathcal{A}_1$ takes the initial state of the memory Mem_0 as well as the access patterns of the last c operations; $\mathcal{B}_1$ can construct both with AP. Clearly, $\mathcal{A}$'s c-SnapObSec advantage is a lower bound on $\mathcal{B}$'s ORAM advantage.

Requiring Equal Length Transcripts. In the SnapObSec game, as in ObSec above, we require the adversary to output two equal length transcripts. This restriction is necessary in ObSec to prevent a trivial distinguishing attack based on the transcript length. However, astute readers may notice that since an adversary can only view the access pattern of c operations, specifying two differing-length transcripts does not give a SnapObSec adversary a trivial win. The c-snapshot obliviousness definition could conceivably be strengthened by removing the restriction that the transcripts are of equal length. However, the security analyses of some c-snapshot ORAM constructions below—e.g., UHQoram in Sect. 7—would require a non-standard transcript-length-hiding property of an underlying ORAM. Lifting the length restriction is a good question for future work.

Observing the Last c Operations. Our c-snapshot obliviousness definition allows the adversary to design the whole transcript but restricts the observing window to be the last c operations at the end of the transcript. We claim this setting is as strong as allowing to put the observing window anywhere in the middle of the transcript. For a typical ORAM not handling batching transcripts, the way to access one physical memory position, though randomized, does not depend on the remaining transcripts after that. This means any operation after the observing window will not change the distribution of access

```
FSO^{MemR,MemW}.init(DB, c):
  k_P <-$ K
  For idx = 0 to |DB| - 1:
    MemW(idx, DB[E^{-1}_{k_P}(idx)])
  Return k_P

FSO^{MemR,MemW}.exec(st, (op, idx, val)):
  k_P <- st
  If op = read:
    resp <- secure-read(k_P, idx)
  If op = write:
    resp <- secure-write(k_P, idx, val)
  Return st, resp
```

```
secure-read(k_P, idx):
  c <- MemR[E_{k_P}(idx)]
  MemW(E_{k_P}(idx), c)
  Return d

secure-write(k_P, idx, val):
  MemR[E_{k_P}(idx)]
  MemW(E_{k_P}(idx), val)
  Return ⊥
```

Fig. 4. The FSO RAM emulator, and the definition of *secure-read* and *secure-write*. (Note that both *secure-read* and *secure-write* implicitly have access to the same oracles as exec.)

patterns the adversary gets. Due to this independence, it is without loss of generality to put the c accesses at the end of the transcript.

c'-Snapshot Obliviousness for $c' < c$. The security definition immediately leads to a result that any snapshot-oblivious RAM emulator initialized with a DB and some number c is still secure if the adversary observes access pattern of c' operations and $c' < c$. We note, however, that this is different from saying any c-snapshot oblivious RAM emulator is c'-snapshot oblivious: this statement is not necessarily even correct. In SnapObSec game, the RE is initialized by a parameter c, so an adversary against a c-snapshot oblivious RAM emulator is getting access pattern from a RE is initialized by c. However, proving this would require building a reduction that wins the c-snapshot game given an adversary that wins the c'-snapshot game, and it's not clear if the adversary can simulate the view of a c'-snapshot adversary given its inputs (computed from a c-snapshot ORAM initialized with c fixed). We believe that for restricted classes of snapshot-oblivious RAMs, this statement is true, but we leave the details to future work.

4 FSO: A 1-Snapshot Oblivious RAM

Next we will give a "warm-up" analysis of a folklore snapshot-oblivious RAM, FSO, and show that it meets 1-snapshot obliviousness.

The Scheme. In Fig. 4, we give the pseudocode of FSO. It uses a pseudorandom permutation E. During init, FSO samples a PRP key, then loads the array into memory according to the permutation E. (The parameter c is ignored during init.) Then, it outputs the keys as its initial state.

During exec, the scheme performs either *secure-read* or *secure-write* depending on op. Both perform a *writeback* to hide the operation type: they first read index $E_{k_P}(idx)$ with **MemR**, and write it back to the same location with **MemW**. If the operation was a read, exec returns the value, else it returns nothing. Clearly, this scheme has both constant bandwidth overhead and constant client storage.

```
ICQoram^{MemR,MemW}.init(DB, c):
Q ← [ ]; f ← 0
k_P ←$ K
For idx = 0 to |DB| + 2c − 1:
  If E_{k_P}^{-1}(idx) < N:
    MemW(idx, DB[E_{k_P}^{-1}(idx)])
  Else: MemW(idx, 0^m)
Return (Q, k_P, k_E)

ICQoram^{MemR,MemW}.exec(st, (op, idx, val)):
Q, k_P ← st
If idx in Q:
  secure-read(k_P, |DB| + f)
  f ← (f + 1) mod 2c
Else:
(continue)
  d ← secure-read(k_P, idx)
  Q.push(idx, d)
 If op is read:
   resp ← Q[idx]
 If op is write:
   Q[idx] ← val
   resp ←⊥
If |Q| > c:
  idx, val ← Q.pop()
  secure-write(k_P, idx, val)
Else:
  secure-write(k_P, |DB| + f, ⊥)
  f ← (f + 1) mod 2c
Return (Q, k_P), resp
```

Fig. 5. ICQoram, an insecure queue-based scheme. The *secure-read* and *secure-write* procedures are as defined in Fig. 4. Three stages are in execution function, the second one is shaded.

Security of FSO**.** The security of FSO for restricted adversaries seems to be folklore—see, e.g., Cash [7]—but to our knowledge has never been formally proven. We validate this folklore by showing FSO is c-snapshot oblivious for $c = 1$.

Theorem 4. *If E is a secure PRP, then* FSO *RAM emulator is 1-snapshot oblivious.*

Proof. We define G_0 to be the case that FSO initializes on DB_0 and executes on T_0. In G_1 FSO initializes on DB_1 and executes on T_1. We want to show that both G_0 and G_1 are indistinguishable from G_{hybrid} where the adversary observes read and write a same but random idx in the access pattern.

In $G_0, G_1, G_{\mathsf{hybrid}}$, the adversary observes $\mathsf{AP} = (\mathsf{r}, idx')||(\mathsf{w}, idx')$. The first part of AP comes from *secure-read* and the second part comes from *secure-write*.

The difference between G_i and G_{hybrid} is that the idx' in AP is $E_{k_P}(idx)$ in G_i, which is computed by a PRP; while in G_{hybrid}, it is truly random, or we can say it is from a random permutation π, $idx' = \pi(idx)$ for fixed idx. If G_i and G_{hybrid} is distinguishable, we can tell difference between PRP and truly random permutation by a simple reduction, $|\Pr[G_{i,\mathsf{hybrid}} = 1] - \Pr[G_{\mathsf{hybrid}} = 1]| \leq \mathbf{Adv}_E^{\mathrm{prp}}(\mathcal{C}_i)$. Therefore, by the 2-step reduction, $|\Pr[G_0 = 1] - \Pr[G_1 = 1]| \leq 2\mathbf{Adv}_E^{\mathrm{prp}}(\mathcal{C})$.

5 The c-Queue Scheme

In the previous section, we showed a simple c-snapshot oblivious RAM. In this section we will show how to get $c > 1$. Before giving our construction, we will describe a natural approach that turns out to be insecure.

5.1 An Insecure Scheme

The FSO scheme in Sect. 4 is only 1-snapshot obliviousness because it leaks repetitions in accesses: reading the same "logical" address twice causes the scheme to make the same physical accesses. To make a secure scheme for general c we'd like the property that physical accesses are all distinct whether or not logical accesses are.

A natural way to ensure this is to augment FSO with a queue of recent accesses. It keeps track of which entries were accessed in the last c operations, along with their values. If any recently-accessed entries are accessed again within c operations, the scheme reads them from the queue instead of from the remote memory. To prevent the server from learning if the queue was used, the scheme can access a fake element.

The ICQoram scheme in Fig. 5 formalizes this idea. ICQoram.init works as in FSO, except it also adds $2c$ dummy elements. The procedure ICQoram.exec has three stages. First, it fetches address idx to the queue Q. If idx is already in the queue, it fetches a dummy element, otherwise reads idx into the queue. Second, it processes the operation (op, idx, val). If the operation is a write, it updates the value of idx in the queue; else, it stores val as the read's return value. Finally, ICQoram performs eviction. If the size of queue is greater than c, it writes the oldest element back to main memory, otherwise it writes a dummy element.

This scheme is fairly efficient: it requires $\mathcal{O}(c)$ additional storage in physical memory, $\mathcal{O}(c)$ additional client state, and has constant bandwidth overhead.

Security. The access pattern for each operation is one *secure-read* and one *secure-write*. If ICQoram could guarantee that for any c operations, the indices touched in the $2c$ *secure-read*s and *secure-write*s were different, it could be proven secure using a straightforward extension of the proof for FSO in Sect. 4.

However, this guarantee does not hold. ICQoram only makes sure the c *secure-read* have distinct indices; the c *secure-write* indices depend on what is residing in the queue in a way that can be exploited by an attacker to distinguish between two transcripts. We demonstrate this with a concrete example. (We remind the reader that although the attacker can only observe the access pattern of c operations, it can choose the entire transcript.) Let $c = 3$, $|DB| = 10$, and take the two transcripts

$$T_0 = \mathsf{read}(1), \mathsf{read}(2), \mathsf{read}(3), \mathsf{read}(4), \mathsf{read}(5),$$
$$T_1 = \mathsf{read}(1), \mathsf{read}(2), \mathsf{read}(3), \mathsf{read}(4), \mathsf{read}(1)\ .$$

At the end of the third operation, for both transcripts, there are three indices in the queue, $1, 2, 3$. Now we start the execution of the fourth and fifth operations. For T_0, the access pattern of last two operations is *secure-read*(4), *secure-write*(1), *secure-read*(5), *secure-write*(2). But access pattern of transcript T_1 is *secure-read*(4), *secure-write*(1), *secure-read*(1), *secure-write*(2). Since the adversary can see access pattern for the last three operations, it can tell T_0 or T_1 from whether the third to last *secure-write* touches the same address with the second to last *secure-read*.

5.2 CQoram: A c-Snapshot ORAM

Though ICQoram is insecure, the queue-based approach can be fixed. Fixing ICQoram is challenging because of a three-way tension between bounded state size, correctness, and security: to keep the queue's size bounded, elements in it must eventually be evicted. For correctness, the evicted element must be written back to its location in main memory; otherwise, an element updated while in the queue will not have the correct value in

```
CQoram^{MemR,MemW}.init(DB, c):
WQ ← [ ]; RQ ← [ ]; f ← 0
k_P ←$ K
For i = 0 to c − 1:
  WQ.push(⊥, ⊥)
  RQ.push(⊥, ⊥)
For idx = 0 to |DB| + 2c − 1:
  If E^{-1}_{k_P}(idx) < N:
    MemW(idx, DB[E^{-1}_{k_P}(idx)])
  Else: MemW(idx, 0^m)
Return (WQ, RQ, k_P)

CQoram^{MemR,MemW}.exec(st, (op, idx, val)):
WQ, RQ, k_P ← st
If idx in WQ:
  WQ.push(⊥, ⊥)
  secure-read(k_P, |DB| + f)
  f ← (f + 1) mod 2c
Else if idx in RQ:
  d ← RQ[idx]
(continue)
  WQ.push(idx, d)
  secure-read(k_P, |DB| + f)
  f ← (f + 1) mod 2c
Else:
  d ← secure-read(k_P, idx)
  WQ.push(idx, d)
If op = read:
  resp ← WQ[idx]
If op = write:
  WQ[idx] ← val
  resp ←⊥
(idx', val') ← WQ.pop()
RQ.push(idx', val')
If val' ≠⊥:
  secure-write(k_P, idx', val')
Else:
  secure-write(k_P, |DB| + f, ⊥)
  f ← (f + 1) mod 2c
RQ.pop()
Return (WQ, RQ, k_P), resp
```

Fig. 6. The CQoram scheme, a c-snapshot ORAM.

the future. But to maintain security—namely, the invariant that all $2c$ accesses are distinct—this location must not be touched again after eviction.

We begin with the simple observation that a second "read-only" queue could be used to keep track of the elements that were recently evicted from the main queue. This could be checked during exec to prevent duplicate accesses, preventing the attack above. Our CQoram scheme will use this idea; as we will see, there are several important subtleties that must be dealt with. Notably, care must be taken if an element is written while it is in this secondary read queue.

The CQoram **Scheme.** We give pseudocode of the scheme in Fig. 6. As with FSO, CQoram uses a PRP E with key space $\mathcal{K}$. The CQoram.init procedure is nearly identical to ICQoram's init, except it initializes two queues—the write queue WQ and the read queue RQ—instead of just one, and fills the queues with dummies. The invariant of this scheme is that at the beginning and end of CQoram.exec, both two queues have exactly c elements, either real or dummy, in them.

As with ICQoram, the CQoram.exec procedure has three main phases. First, it checks both WQ and RQ for the index idx to be accessed; like ICQoram, if either queue contains idx it reads a dummy, else it reads idx from main memory. One important new step is in the second branch, which checks RQ. Here, if idx is found in RQ, it will move it and its value back into WQ to maintain the invariant that WQ always contains the element. (We do not need to delete the element from RQ—the copy in RQ will always be deleted before the element is evicted from WQ.)

The second phase is executing the operation on the element. This phase is the same as in ICQoram. The third phase of CQoram.exec, eviction, is necessarily quite different than in ICQoram. It begins by popping the front (oldest) element from WQ and pushing it into RQ anyway. Then it checks if that element is a dummy; if not, writes the element back to main memory, otherwise writes a dummy. Finally, pop the front element from RQ and (implicitly) deletes it. Finally, we note that CQoram has the same asymptotic performance as ICQoram; concretely, CQoram requires twice as much client storage as ICQoram, but has identical bandwidth and storage overhead.

Security of CQoram. Next we prove that CQoram is a c-snapshot oblivious RAM emulator for any c. We begin with a lemma showing that any size-$2c$ subsequence of accesses made with CQoram are to distinct memory locations. Below, we will treat the pair of entries in AP made by our *secure-read* or *secure-write* procedures as one "access", since either procedure just performs a writeback—a read, then a write—on one memory location.

Lemma 1. *Let DB be an array of N m-bit strings, and T be a transcript of n operations. Let $x_1, x_2, \dots, x_{2n}$ be random variables denoting the sequence of indices in* Mem *accessed by* CQoram *while executing T on DB. For any $i \in [1, 2n]$ let $\{x_i, \dots, x_{i+2c-1}\}$ be the subsequence of at most $2c$ accesses starting with x_i. Then with probability 1 over the random coins of* CQoram, *all accesses in this subsequence are distinct.*

Proof. We prove this statement in two steps. First, we observe that it is sufficient to prove a weaker statement: namely that for any size-$2c$ sequence of physical accesses, the first access x_i occurs only once in that sequence. This implies all size-$2c$ subsequences are distinct because if there was a subsequence where this did not hold, there would also be a size-$2c$ subsequence where the first access occurred more than once in that subsequence.

Next we prove that the first access occurs only once. The $2c$ memory accesses are either "real" array values or dummies. We know that real values are at position $E_{k_P}(1), \dots, E_{k_P}(N)$, and dummies are at position $E_{k_P}(N+1), \dots, E_{k_P}(N+2c)$; thus, dummies cannot have the same address as real values, and so $x_i = x_{i+j}$ can only be the case if they are either both dummies or both real values.

Since the subsequence has $2c$ memory accesses there are at most $2c$ dummies being touched. During CQoram.init we add $2c$ dummies, and we use the counter f to make sure each dummy is accessed only once. Thus, if the accesses are both to dummy values, they must be distinct.

Now we only care about the case where x_i and x_{i+j} are both to real values, and let idx_i and idx_{i+j} be the corresponding real indices. First, we will state three facts about CQoram.exec. (1) Any access to a real value happens either because of *secure-read* or *secure-write*. (2) *secure-read*(idx_i) happens only if idx_i is neither in WQ or RQ. (3) *secure-write*(idx_i) happens only when idx_i is popped from WQ.

There are four cases to analyze.

- *secure-read*$(idx_i), \dots,$ *secure-read*(idx_{i+j}) After idx_i is read, it is pushed into WQ. idx_i is popped after c new elements are pushed into WQ. Each operation will push exactly 1 element into WQ. Therefore, in the next $c-1$ operations, idx_i is always in WQ, so $idx_i \neq idx_{i+j}$ and $x_i = x_{i+j}$ for all j.
- *secure-read*$(idx_i), \dots,$ *secure-write*(idx_{i+j}) After idx_i is read, it is pushed into WQ and it is written only when idx_i is popped out. Thus, in the next $c-1$ operations, idx_i is always in WQ, so $idx_i \neq idx_{i+j}$ for all j.
- *secure-write*$(idx_i), \dots,$ *secure-read*(idx_{i+j}). First, idx_i is pushed into RQ after being written. We read the index idx_i from the memory only if it is not in WQ or

RQ. idx_i is popped only after c new elements are pushed into RQ. Each operation will push 1 element into RQ. Therefore, in the next $c - 1$ operations, idx_i is always in RQ, and $idx_i \neq idx_{i+j}$ for all j. (Note that this is the case where ICQoram fails to prevent duplicate reads.)
- *secure-write*$(idx_i), \ldots,$ *secure-write*(idx_{i+j}). As above, idx_i is popped from WQ after being written. We write the index idx_i to the memory only if it is already in WQ. It takes one operation to read idx_i to WQ again and at least $c - 1$ operations before being popped out, so $idx_i \neq idx_{i+j}$ for all j.

Thus, we have proved that x_i is only accessed once, and we are done. ∎

Theorem 5. *The* CQoram *scheme is a c-snapshot oblivious RAM emulator, for any c.*

Proof. Each operation has one secure-read and one secure-write, which writes a $(\mathsf{r}, idx)||(\mathsf{w}, idx)$ to the access pattern AP. In c operations, the $2c$ read/write indices are distinct by Lemma 1. Call these $x_1, \ldots, x_{2c}$. Then AP has $2c$ copies of $(\mathsf{r}, idx^*)||(\mathsf{w}, idx^*)$ where the $2c$ $idx^* = E_{k_P}(x_i)$ are distinct and pseudorandom, which are indistinguishable from a hybrid game that idx^* are $\pi(1), \cdots, \pi(2c)$ where π is a random permutation. ∎

Discussion. The CQoram scheme has constant bandwidth overhead because each plaintext operation is done by one secure-read and one secure-write, each of which does two memory accesses. So $|\mathsf{CQoram}(DB, T)|/|T| = 4 = \mathcal{O}(1)$. But it needs $\mathcal{O}(c)$ client storage.

We can store the queue on the server, but during CQoram.exec, we need to check the queues' contents. This operation needs to iterate the entire queue, so it has to introduce a linear overhead in c. Therefore on each queue operation, we scan and update the entire queue, which gives us an $\mathcal{O}(c)$ bandwidth overhead and constant client storage. In the next section, we will present a much more efficient way to outsource the queue's storage to the server.

Readers may find that different from the ICQoram scheme, we pad the size of queues to c. Note that this does not fix the insecurity of ICQoram. Instead, if we choose to store the queues on the client's side, removing the paddings even enhances the efficiency. However, if we pop WQ only when $|\mathsf{WQ}| > c$, the latest version of some memory contents may be arbitrarily old. Suppose the transcript is repeatedly writing some values to address 1 to $c - 1$, then these updated values are never uploaded because the queue has size $c - 1$. Therefore if a client is shutdown unexpectedly, the "back-up" value on the server can be extremely out of date. Our CQoram scheme makes sure that every updated memory value will be uploaded to the server every c operations.

6 Oblivious Hash Queue Based c-SnapORAM

As we described above, for the CQoram scheme, the read and write queues can be stored on the server and simply streamed to the client during each CQoram.exec. This allows constant client-side storage but incurs $\mathcal{O}(c)$ bandwidth overhead, which may be prohibitive if c is large.

To reduce this overhead, we could instead store the queues in a smaller ORAM. Since the amount of storage needed for the queues is only $\mathcal{O}(c)$, this would in principle allow us to reduce the overhead of CQoram exponentially, to something like $\mathcal{O}(\log c)$.

However, making this strategy work is quite challenging. The read and write queues in CQoram are used in several different ways in CQoram.exec: searching for (idx, val) pairs, updating their values, and pushing and popping elements in a first-in, first-out fashion. Ultimately, no existing data structure efficiently provides the combination of dictionary and queue properties we need, so we invent our own novel data structure, which we term the *hash queue*.

In this section, we will introduce the syntax of hash queue and give an oblivious hash queue security definition. We show how to build a c-snapshot ORAM (PHQoram) using an oblivious hash queue, and how to use oblivious map to build an oblivious hash queue (OMOHQ). The PHQoram construction has polylogarithmic bandwidth overhead, which will be further reduced in Sect. 7.

Definition 6 ***(Hash queue).*** *A hash queue is a pair of algorithms: an initialization function* HQ.init(c) *and an execution function* HQ.exec$(op, args)$ *where* $args$ *is a tuple of arguments.*

A hash queue is initialized by calling its initialization function with argument c, which represents the maximum size of the hash queue. After initialization, the HQ.exec function takes a state as input and output, and supports the following four types of operation:

- $op =$ Find, $args = (key)$. The data structure searches on key and returns val if key is found, otherwise returns $\perp$.
- $op =$ Push, $args = (key, val)$. Insert the key value pair.
- $op =$ Access, $args = (op', key, val)$. If op' is read, searches for key and returns its value. If op' is write, searches on key and replaces its value by val and returns $\perp$. If key is not found, the data structure returns $\perp_0$, a reserved failure symbol distinct from $\perp$.
- $op =$ Pop, $args = ()$. Returns the oldest key-value pair and deletes it.

Below, we will abuse notation slightly and replace exec with the hash queue operation it executes. E.g., HQ.Find(key) instead of HQ.exec(Find, (key)).

6.1 Hash Queue Security

A natural security definition for hash queues is an ORAM-style notion that requires hiding everything except the operation count. This kind of definition is typical of other oblivious data structures [52]. However, such a definition is stronger than what we need: our goal is to replace the client-side queues in CQoram with hash queues; in CQoram (Fig. 6). Notice that no matter what the transcript is, for each CQoram.exec, we always search idx in WQ, then execute push, modify, and pop in the WQ. Likewise, we search in RQ at the beginning (not always, but we can do a dummy search), then push and pop. That is to say the sequence of operation executed on a queue which will be replaced by an oblivious hash queue, is always the same and publicly known in advance. Because of such observation, we propose our first obliviousness definition. We give the pseudocode for our *public operation obliviousness* security notion for hash queues in Fig. 7.

Similar to the security game of RAM emulators, we define both of init, exec as relative to a pair of oracles **MemR**, **MemW**. Cryptographic primitives like hash queue

```
PublicOpOblivHashSec(HQ, A, n, i):
AP ← []
st_0 ←$ HQ^{MemR,MemW}.init(n)
T_0, T_1 ←$ A_0(n)
For x = 1 to ℓ:
  If T_0[x].op ≠ T_1[x].op then Return ⊥
  op, args ← T_i[x]
  st_x ←$ HQ^{MemR,MemW}.exec(st_{x−1}, op, args)
b ←$ A_1(AP)
Return b
```

Fig. 7. Game defining public operation obliviousness for a hash queue. AP is modified by oracles **MemR**, **MemW** as defined in Fig. 2 during the execution of exec function.

use the same **MemR**, **MemW** oracles to access the entire physical memory. To make sure the primitives do not overwrite others' memory, each primitive is allocated a primitive identifier pid and memory space when calling init. **MemR**, **MemW** implicitly take pid as an argument and add a proper offset to get the physical memory address.

Definition 7 ***(Public-operation oblivious hash queue).*** *For a two-part adversary $\mathcal{A}$ playing game defined in Fig. 7, we define the public-operation obliviousness advantage of $\mathcal{A}$ against HQ as*

$$\mathbf{Adv}^{opo}_{HQ}(\mathcal{A}) = \Big| \Pr[PublicOpOblivHashSec(n, HQ, \mathcal{A}, 0) = 1] - PublicOpOblivHashSec(n, HQ, \mathcal{A}, 1) = 1\Big|.$$

If for a hash queue HQ, for any nuPPT adversary $\mathcal{A}$, the above advantage is negligible, we say that HQ is public-operation oblivious.

The game is similar to our obliviousness notion for RAM emulators in Sect. 2. It lets the adversary $\mathcal{A}_0$ output two pairs of transcripts with the same "operation pattern", executes the ith transcript, and gives the $\mathcal{A}_1$ the access patterns and outputs its guess b.

6.2 A c-Snapshot ORAM from Hash Queues

Next we describe a generic transformation that builds a c-snapshot ORAM from any hash queue meeting the public-operation obliviousness property defined above. (In the next subsection, we will construct a hash queue which enjoys this property.) We call our construction PHQoram, and give its pseudocode in Fig. 8. At a high level, PHQoram follows the strategy we outlined above of outsourcing CQoram's read and write queues to the server. PHQoram replaces RQ with a hash queue rOHQ, and likewise replaces WQ with a hash queue wOHQ. The procedure PHQoram.init initializes the two queues independently in non-overlapping regions of Mem (handled by **MemR**, **MemW** oracles), then samples a PRP key and fills the rest of Mem with DB entries and dummy elements. The procedure PHQoram.exec works similarly to CQoram.exec, with a few important differences. Most notably, it executes both wOHQ.Find and rOHQ.Find, whereas CQoram does not check RQ if the index is found in WQ. This prevents leaking the hash queue contents based on the number of accesses to each hash queue.

```
PHQoram^{MemR,MemW}.init(DB, c):
k_P <-$ K
st_wq <-$ wOHQ^{MemR,MemW}.init(c)
st_rq <-$ rOHQ^{MemR,MemW}.init(c)
f <- 0
For i = |DB| + 2c to |DB| + 3c - 1:
  st_wq <-$ wOHQ.Push(st_wq, i, ⊥)
  st_rq <-$ rOHQ.Push(st_rq, i, ⊥)
For i = 0 to |DB| + 2c - 1:
  If E^{-1}_{k_P}(i) < |DB|:
    MemW(i, DB[E^{-1}_{k_P}(i)])
  Else: MemW(i, 0^m)
Return k_P, st_wq, st_rq

PHQoram^{MemR,MemW}.exec(st, op, idx, val)):
k_P, st_wq, st_rq <- st
val_w, st_wq <-$ wOHQ^{MemR,MemW}.Find(st_wq, idx)
val_r, st_rq <-$ rOHQ^{MemR,MemW}.Find(st_rq, idx)
If val_w ≠ ⊥:
  secure-read(k_P, |DB| + f)
(continue)
  st_wq <-$ wOHQ^{MemR,MemW}.Push(st_wq, |DB| + f, ⊥)
  f <- (f + 1) mod 2c
Else If val_r ≠ ⊥:
  secure-read(k_P, |DB| + f)
  st_wq <-$ wOHQ^{MemR,MemW}.Push(st_wq, idx, val_r)
  f <- (f + 1) mod 2c
Else:
  d <- secure-read(k_P, idx)
  st_wq <- wOHQ^{MemR,MemW}.Push(st_wq, idx, d)
resp, st_wq <- wOHQ^{MemR,MemW}.Access(st_wq, op, idx, val)
(idx', val'), st_wq <-$ wOHQ.Pop(st_wq)
st_rq <-$ rOHQ^{MemR,MemW}.Push(st_rq, idx', val')
If val' ≠ ⊥:
  secure-write(k_P, idx', val')
Else:
  secure-write(k_P, |DB| + f, ⊥)
  f <- (f + 1) mod 2c
st_rq <-$ rOHQ^{MemR,MemW}.Pop(st_rq)
Return (k_P, st_wq, st_rq), resp
```

Fig. 8. Construction of PHQoram c-Snapshot ORAM emulator in pseudocode. The exec procedure starts on the left and continues on the right.

It is not too hard to see that if wOHQ, rOHQ has bandwidth overhead $g(c)$ for each operation, then PHQoram has bandwidth overhead $\mathcal{O}(g(c))$. Regardless of which branch is taken, PHQoram does the following things on each RAM operation:

wOHQ.Find, rOHQ.Find, *secure-read*, wOHQ.Push, wOHQ.Access,
wOHQ.Pop, rOHQ.Push, *secure-write*, rOHQ.Pop.

Since there are a constant number (7) of hash queue operations each with $g(c)$ overhead and a constant number (2) of accesses to the "main" memory with $\mathcal{O}(1)$ overhead, the overall bandwidth overhead is $\mathcal{O}(g(c))$.

Theorem 6. *Let E be a secure PRP and* wOHQ, rOHQ *be public-operation oblivious hash queues. Then the* PHQoram *scheme in Fig. 8 is a c-snapshot oblivious RAM emulator.*

Proof. We will prove c-snapshot obliviousness by reduction. The high-level strategy is as follows: first, we will perform two game hops to "decouple" the operations made against the two hash queues from the adversary's chosen transcripts in SnapObSec. (Specifically, we will simply execute the same operation sequence on wOHQ and rOHQ, but with dummy arguments.) In these hybrid games we will ensure the correctness of the distribution of accesses to the main memory using local queues; effectively, after these two game hops, the access pattern to the main memory will be distributed as in the CQoram scheme. Then, we can use a variant of the security argument for CQoram to perform one more game hop which changes the PRP's outputs to a random subset of the memory locations.

We now proceed more formally. Let $\mathcal{A}$ be a SnapObSec adversary. We will show that there exists adversaries $\mathcal{B}$, $\mathcal{C}$, and $\mathcal{D}$ such that

$$\mathbf{Adv}^{\text{snap}}_{\mathsf{PHQoram}}(\mathcal{A}) \leq 2\mathbf{Adv}^{\text{opo}}_{\mathsf{wOHQ}}(\mathcal{B}) + 2\mathbf{Adv}^{\text{opo}}_{\mathsf{rOHQ}}(\mathcal{C}) + 2\mathbf{Adv}^{\text{prp}}_{E}(\mathcal{D}) .$$

We do this via a sequence of games. Game G_0 is SnapObSec($\mathsf{PHQoram}, \mathcal{A}, c, 0$). Game G_1 is the same as G_0 except for two additional (local) queues, WQ and RQ, are added to PHQoram.exec that "mirror" (resp.) wOHQ and rOHQ: any modifications made to wOHQ or rOHQ are also made to their corresponding local queues, but the access pattern is otherwise unchanged. Clearly, this does not affect $\mathcal{A}$'s view, so $\Pr[G_0 = 1] = \Pr[G_1 = 1]$.

Next we define the game G_2. This game is identical to G_1, except the arguments to all wOHQ operations (except the state) are replaced with fixed values: all indices are replaced with zero. The local queue WQ is used in place of wOHQ. We can upper-bound the difference in advantage between G_1 and G_2 by building a reduction $\mathcal{B}_0$ to the public-operation obliviousness of wOHQ. The reduction $\mathcal{B}_0$ works as follows: first, it runs $\mathcal{A}_0$ to get $(DB_0, T_0), (DB_1, T_1)$. Then, it samples k_P and with its own simulated **MemR**, **MemW** oracles initializes rOHQ and executes PHQoram on (DB_0, T_0) as in G_1. However, $\mathcal{B}_0$ only uses WQ and does not perform wOHQ operations; instead, it marks the access patterns of these operations in AP with $\perp$ and records the operations that would have been executed against wOHQ. This is the "induced" transcript of operations on wOHQ in G_1. Call this transcript $\overrightarrow{op}_w^{G_1}$. Concretely, it consists of c Push operations made during init, then for each RAM operation, the transcript contains Find, Push, Access, Pop. (Note that the sequence of wOHQ operation *types* is fixed and does not depend on the RAM operation.) Then, $\mathcal{B}_0$ constructs the "dummy" transcript $\overrightarrow{op}_w^{G_2}$, containing the same operation types but with all-zero arguments; it then outputs $\overrightarrow{op}_w^{G_1}, \overrightarrow{op}_w^{G_2}$ as its chosen transcripts in its PublicOpOblivHashSec game. When $\mathcal{B}_0$ gets the array of access patterns in the second stage of the PublicOpOblivHashSec game, it uses them to fill in the entries of AP which were marked with $\perp$ previously.

At this point, $\mathcal{B}_0$ has an access pattern array AP which is distributed as in G_1 if $i = 0$ in PublicOpOblivHashSec, and distributed as in G_2 if $i = 1$. Thus, $\mathcal{B}_0$ can simply truncate AP to the last c operations, compute the state of Mem before these operations, run $\mathcal{A}_1$ as in SnapObSec, and return its output. By construction,

$$|\Pr[G_1 = 1] - \Pr[G_2 = 1]| \leq \mathbf{Adv}^{\text{opo}}_{\mathsf{wOHQ}}(\mathcal{B}_0) .$$

Next we define G_3, which is the same as G_2 except we also replace the arguments to rOHQ with "dummy" all-zeros strings. (Note that, like wOHQ, the operation types executed on rOHQ while PHQoram executes a RAM operation are fixed to Find, Push, Pop.) By an argument similar to the above, we can construct a reduction $\mathcal{C}_0$ to the public-operation obliviousness of rOHQ, giving us that $|\Pr[G_2 = 1] - \Pr[G_3 = 1]| \leq \mathbf{Adv}^{\text{opo}}_{\mathsf{rOHQ}}(\mathcal{C}_0)$.

In G_3, only the accesses to the "main" memory (i.e., the permuted array) depend on (DB_0, T_0). Dummy operations are made against wOHQ and rOHQ; the actual state of those queues is kept track of locally, as in the CQoram scheme in Sect. 5. Next, we construct game G_4, where the "main" memory consists of indices of the $2c$ accesses to the main memory (*secure-reads* and *secure-writes*) seen by $\mathcal{A}$ are chosen by sampling a

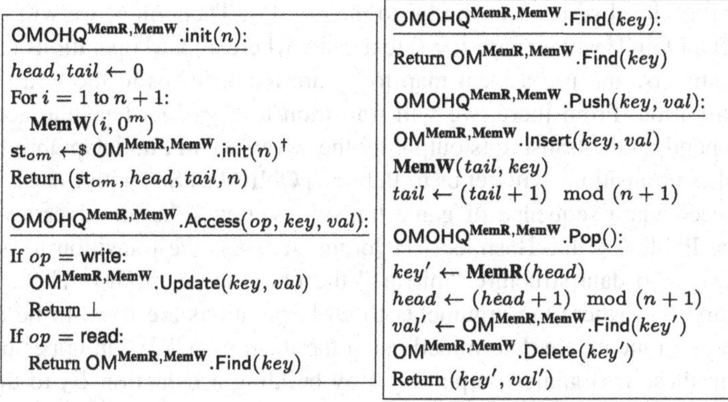

Fig. 9. The OMOHQ hash queue construction. All operations input and output the state returned from init; we leave this implicit for brevity. († We leave implicit the domain separation in these **MemR/MemW** oracles. See Sect. 6.)

subset of $[1, \ldots, |DB| + 2c]$ uniformly at random. By an argument very similar to the proof of Theorem 5, we can build $\mathcal{D}_0$ and $\mathcal{E}_0$ so that

$$|\Pr[G_3 = 1] - \Pr[G_4 = 1]| \leq \mathbf{Adv}_E^{\mathrm{prp}}(\mathcal{D}_0) .$$

In game G_4, $\mathcal{A}$'s view does not depend on either (DB_0, T_0) or (DB_1, T_1). Thus, we can perform the previous game transitions in reverse to get to SnapObSec(PHQoram, $\mathcal{A}$, c, 1). A standard argument lets us build $\mathcal{B}, \mathcal{C}, \mathcal{D}$ whose advantages are at most twice the right-hand sides of the above terms; applying the triangle inequality yields the result. ∎

6.3 Constructing Public-Operation Oblivious Hash Queues

Now that we have shown that c-snapshot ORAMs can be built from hash queues with public-operation obliviousness, we just need to construct a hash queue meeting this security notion. In this subsection we will give such a construction, which we call OMOHQ.

The OMOHQ **Construction.** In Fig. 9, we give the pseudocode of OMOHQ. It is built from an oblivious map which supports Insert, Find, Delete, Update, and an array which serves as a queue. The init function initializes OM, chooses a key k'_E, and writes an array of all-zeros to the memory. It also initializes two queue pointers *head*, *tail* to zero. The Find and Access procedures are essentially pass-throughs to their corresponding oblivious map operations, where Access branches on the *op* input. The Push and Pop procedures use both the array and OM. Push inserts *key*, *val* in the end of the hash queue, by storing it at the *tail* position and inserting the key/value pair in OM. Pop does the reverse—removing the key/value pair at the front of the hash queue. It does this by reading and decrypting the key stored at *head* and using two OM operations to read its value *val'* and delete it.

Theorem 7. *If* OM *is an oblivious map, then* OMOHQ *in Fig. 9 is a public operation oblivious hash queue.*

Proof. The high-level strategy is similar to the proof of Theorem 6: we will transition from PublicOpOblivHashSec with $i = 0$ to a game where all OM operations take fixed, dummy arguments, and use a local map to ensure the accesses to the array have the correct distribution. From there, we will transition to a game where the accesses in the array depend on the transcripts output by the adversary in PublicOpOblivHashSec. Reversing these transitions will get us to PublicOpOblivHashSec with $i = 0$.

We proceed via a sequence of game transitions. Let $\mathcal{A}$ be an adversary, and let game G_0 be PublicOpOblivHashSec$(\mathsf{PHQoram}, \mathcal{A}, n, 0)$. We transition to game G_1, where a local map data structure "mirrors" the oblivious map OM. Then, we transition to game G_2, where the arguments to OM operations are fixed to be all-zeros, and the array's contents are determined using the local map. We can upper-bound the difference in these two games outputting 1 by building a reduction $\mathcal{B}_0$ to the obliviousness of OM. The reduction $\mathcal{B}_0$ runs $\mathcal{A}$ to obtain T_0, T_1, then simulates OMOHQ on T_0 to determine the induced OM transcript. Then, $\mathcal{B}$ submits this along with the fixed all-zeros OM transcript as its chosen transcripts in the OblivMapSec game. It uses the access patterns it receives to simulate $\mathcal{A}$'s access pattern input. By construction, $|\Pr[G_1 = 1] - \Pr[G_2 = 1]| \leq \mathbf{Adv}^{\mathrm{om}}_{\mathsf{OM}}(\mathcal{B}_0)$.

We next move to game G_3, which is the same as G_2 except the array accesses depend only on the operation *type*, but not the arguments. The access pattern to the array is actually identically distributed in G_2 and G_3: observe that in OMOHQ, the way the array is accessed depends only on the operation type: init writes to it n times, Push writes to position $tail$, and Pop reads from $head$. Thus, for any pair of transcripts output by the adversary in PublicOpOblivHashSec, the access pattern to the array is fixed because the transcripts must have the same operation sequence. Thus, the game G_3 is identical to G_2, giving $\Pr[G_2 = 1] = \Pr[G_3 = 1]$.

In game G_3, the access patterns and the memory contents do not depend on either of $\mathcal{A}$'s output transcripts; thus, we can reverse these game transitions to get to PublicOpOblivHashSec with $i = 1$. By applying an argument similar to the one at the end of the proof of Theorem 6, the result follows. ∎

Asymptotic and Concrete Performance. The asymptotic performance of the c-snapshot ORAM PHQoram depends on how OM in OMOHQ is instantiated. A special-purpose oblivous map data structure (e.g. [52]) is likely to be the most efficient choice. The best-known oblivious maps achieve $\mathcal{O}(\log^2 n)$ bandwidth overhead for size-n memory. This implies that the bandwidth overhead of OMOHQ, and thus the PHQoram construction, is $\mathcal{O}(\log^2 c)$ for c-snapshot obliviousness.

The concrete performance of PHQoram is a more complex question, as it depends greatly on implementation specifics. The best-known oblivious map construction has good asymptotics, but its concrete bandwidth overhead is still quite large for small databases: for example, the evaluation of [46] shows that reading an eight-byte key/value pair requires communicating over 100 KBs to the client. Despite exponentially worse asymptotics, it may be the case that the CQoram scheme is more efficient than PHQoram for practical values of c, due to its small constants. It does not seem inherent that oblivious maps perform poorly for small memory sizes; we leave improving them in this parameter regime to future work.

```
UniqInsertOblivHashSec_op→(HQ, A, n, i):
AP ← []
st_0 ←$ HQ^{MemR,MemW}.init(n)
T_0, T_1 ←$ A_0(n, op→)
If !(UI(T_0) ∧ UI(T_1)) then Return ⊥
For x = 1 to ℓ:
  op_x, args^i_x ← T_i[x]
  st_x ←$ HQ^{MemR,MemW}.exec(st_{x−1}, op_x, args^i_x)
b ←$ A_1(AP).
Return b
```

Fig. 10. Unique insertion oblivious hash queue security definition. The function $\mathsf{UI}(T)$ returns 1 if the keys given to Push operations are all distinct, and 0 otherwise.

7 Asymptotically-Optimal c-Snapshot ORAM

In this section, we give tight upper and lower bounds on the asymptotic performance of c-snapshot ORAMs. Beginning with the upper bound, we propose a new oblivious hash queue security definition different from Sect. 6 and show the UHQoram construction in Sect. 7.1 using an instance (CCOHQ) of our new oblivious hash queue variant. UHQoram is a modification of PHQoram which guarantees an important unique-insertion property for the queues: namely, that duplicate keys are never Pushed. Though a seemingly small change, we show that guaranteeing unique insertions is crucial because it allows weakening the security requirements on UHQoram's hash queues, admitting more efficient instantiations.

We show CCOHQ, a hash queue construction meeting this weakened security requirement with $\mathcal{O}(\log n)$ bandwidth overhead for n items. Instantiating UHQoram with CCOHQ gives a c-snapshot ORAM with $\mathcal{O}(\log c)$ bandwidth overhead. Finally, in Sect. 7.3, we extend the seminal $\Omega(\log n)$ lower bound of [38]. Our lower bound implies that any c-snapshot ORAM must have $\Omega(\log c)$ bandwidth overhead, implying UHQoram is asymptotically optimal in terms of bandwidth overhead.

We first define the weakened hash queue security notion that UHQoram will use.

Definition 8 ***(Unique-insertion oblivious hash queue).*** *Let HQ be a hash queue, and let $\overrightarrow{op}$ be a sequence of hash queue operation types. Let UniqInsertOblivHashSec be the game in Fig. 10. We define the $\overrightarrow{op}$-unique insertion obliviousness advantage of an adversary $\mathcal{A}$ against HQ as*

$$\mathbf{Adv}^{uio}_{HQ,\overrightarrow{op}}(\mathcal{A}) = \big| \Pr[\mathit{UniqInsertOblivHashSec}_{\overrightarrow{op}}(\mathit{HQ}, \mathcal{A}, n, 0) = 1] - \Pr[\mathit{UniqInsertOblivHashSec}_{\overrightarrow{op}}(\mathit{HQ}, \mathcal{A}, n, 1) = 1] \big| .$$

We call HQ $\overrightarrow{op}$-unique-insertion oblivious if for all nuPPT adversaries $\mathcal{A}$, $\mathbf{Adv}^{uio}_{HQ}(\mathcal{A})$ is negligible. If HQ is $\overrightarrow{op}$-unique-insertion oblivious for all $\overrightarrow{op}$, we simply say it is unique-insertion oblivious.

Looking ahead, we will only analyze $\overrightarrow{op}$-unique-insertion oblivious for our CCOHQ hash queue construction for the fixed $\overrightarrow{op}$ induced by the UHQoram c-snapshot ORAM; thus, below we will always refer to $\overrightarrow{op}$-unique-insertion oblivious.

```
UHQoram^{MemR,MemW}.init(DB, c):
k_P ←$ K;  h, f ← 0
st_wq ←$ wOHQ^{MemR,MemW}.init(c)
st_rq ←$ rOHQ^{MemR,MemW}.init(c)
For i = |DB| + 2c to |DB| + 3c − 1:
  wOHQ.Push(−1||i, ⊥)
  rOHQ.Push(−1||i, ⊥)
For i = 0 to |DB| + 2c − 1:
  If E^{-1}_{k_P}(i) < |DB|:
    MemW(i, DB[E^{-1}_{k_P}(i)])
  Else: MemW(i, 0^m)
Return (k_P, st_wq, st_rq, h, f)

gvr(w_0, w_1, r_0, r_1, h'):
If w_0 ≠⊥:
  wqv ← w_0
  h'' ← h'
Else if w_1 ≠⊥:
  wqv ← w_1
  h'' ← h' − 1
Else:
  wqv ←⊥
  h'' ← h'
If r_0 ≠⊥:
  rqv ← r_0
Else if r_1 ≠⊥:
  rqv ← r_1
Else:
  rqv ←⊥
Return wqv, rqv, h''
```

```
UHQoram^{MemR,MemW}.exec(st, (op, idx, val)):
k_P, st_wq, st_rq, h, f ← st
h' ← ⌊h/c⌋
w_0 ← wOHQ.Find(h'||idx)
w_1 ← wOHQ.Find(h' − 1||idx)
r_0 ← rOHQ.Find(h' − 1||idx)
r_1 ← rOHQ.Find(h' − 2||idx)
wqv, rqv, h'' ← gvr(w_0, w_1, r_0, r_1, h')
If wqv ≠⊥:
  secure-read(k_P, |DB| + f)
  wOHQ.Push(h'|||DB| + f, ⊥)
  f ← (f + 1) mod 2c
Else if rqv ≠⊥:
  secure-read(k_P, |DB| + f)
  wOHQ.Push(h'||idx, rqv)
  f ← (f + 1) mod 2c
Else:
  d ← secure-read(k_P, idx)
  wOHQ.Push(h'||idx, d)
resp ← wOHQ.Access(op, h''||idx, val)
(h̃||idx', val') ← wOHQ.Pop()
rOHQ.Push(h̃||idx', val')
If val' ≠⊥:
  secure-write(k_P, idx', val')
Else:
  secure-write(k_P, |DB| + f, ⊥)
  f ← (f + 1) mod 2c
rOHQ.Pop()
h ← h + 1
Return resp, (k_P, st_wq, st_rq, h, f)
```

Fig. 11. Construction of UHQoram c-snapshot ORAM. The function gvr is a helper function used during exec. All hash queue operations in exec input and output a state. Oracles **MemR**, **MemW** are as defined in Fig. 2.

7.1 The UHQoram Construction

The UHQoram construction is depicted in pseudocode in Fig. 11. It is substantially similar to PHQoram above, with two important differences. First, in addition to the counter f, there is another counter h for the total number of operations executed. This counter is used to derive a "round" number, which is prepended to the index when it is written to either of the hash queues. This round number ensures all keys written to the hash queues are distinct (we will argue this more formally in Theorem 8). Another change from PHQoram is the addition of two calls to Find at the beginning of UHQoram.exec. Because each hash queue entry has a round number prepended, we need to check all possible round numbers to be sure to find an entry.

The final change is the use of a helper function gvr during exec. This helper function takes the result of the four Find operations, and outputs the correct value and the round number needed to modify the correct element in wOHQ.Access. The case logic in gvr looks complex, but it is just ensuring the newest copy of the element is always selected.

UHQoram has the same asymptotic overhead as the hash queue: if each hash queue operation takes $g(c)$ bandwidth, each UHQoram operation takes $\mathcal{O}(g(c))$ bandwidth.

Next we will state and prove a security theorem for UHQoram. This theorem will prove it is a c-snapshot ORAM by reduction to the PRP security, and the unique-insertion obliviousness of wOHQ, rOHQ.

We do not need unique-insertion obliviousness of wOHQ, rOHQ to hold for any operation sequences; for simplicity we instead focus on the two sequences induced by our UHQoram construction above. Specifically, define

$$\overrightarrow{op}_w = \mathsf{Push}, \ldots, \mathsf{Push}, \mathsf{Find}, \mathsf{Find}, \mathsf{Push}, \mathsf{Access}, \mathsf{Pop}, \ldots$$

where there are c Pushes, then copies of the Find, Find, Push, Access, Pop sequence. This is the sequence run on wOHQ by UHQoram above. Likewise, define

$$\overrightarrow{op}_r = \mathsf{Push}, \ldots, \mathsf{Push}, \mathsf{Find}, \mathsf{Find}, \mathsf{Push}, \mathsf{Pop}, \ldots .$$

This is the operation sequence for the rOHQ hash queue in UHQoram. The next theorem proves that as long as wOHQ and rOHQ are (resp.) $\overrightarrow{op}_w$ and $\overrightarrow{op}_r$-unique-insertion oblivious hash queues, UHQoram in Fig. 11 is a c-snapshot oblivious RAM emulator.

Theorem 8. *Let E be a secure PRP and wOHQ be $\overrightarrow{op}_w$-, and rOHQ be $\overrightarrow{op}_r$-unique-insertion oblivious hash queues. Then* UHQoram *in Fig. 11 is a c-snapshot oblivious RAM emulator.*

Proof. The proof is substantially similar to that of Theorem 6 above; the chief difference is that we reduce to a weaker security property of the hash queues (unique-insertion obliviousness for $\overrightarrow{op}_w$ and $\overrightarrow{op}_r$). Thus, we only need to extend our previous argument to explain why the unique-insertion property holds for wOHQ and rOHQ. First, define a "round" to be a group of c operations. We begin by proving there are no duplicate key insertions into wOHQ. An array entry idx, val can be inserted into wOHQ in only three places, namely the three branches of the first if-statement of UHQoram.exec. If it is inserted in the first branch, it is a dummy; since there are $2c$ dummies but the round counter h' increments every c operations, duplicate insertion is impossible there.

If it is inserted in the second branch, it is being re-added to wOHQ from rOHQ. In this case, the element had been in wOHQ previously; however, the round counter h' must be different from the one that was used in the previous insertion to wOHQ—this second branch can only happen c operations after the initial insertion.

If idx, val is inserted in the third branch, idx was neither in wOHQ nor rOHQ. Since the round counter for this insertion is always the current one, this insertion must be unique, since idx was last in wOHQ (with any round counter) at least c operations ago.

We've proven that wOHQ never sees a duplicate insertion, but still need to prove this holds for rOHQ. Observe that rOHQ contains exactly the same keys as wOHQ did c operations ago—essentially, rOHQ is an older replica of wOHQ. Thus, because wOHQ has the unique-insertion property, rOHQ does as well, and we are done. ∎

```
CKH^{MemR,MemW}.init(n):
A1 ← [], A2 ← []
h1, h2 ←$ H
For i = 1 to 3n:
  A1[i].key ← null
  A1[i].value ← null
  A2[i].key ← null
  A2[i].value ← null
Return (h1, h2)

CKH^{MemR,MemW}.Insert(k, v):
z.key ← k
z.value ← v
x ← 1
While x < 6n and z.key ≠ null:
  i ← x mod 2
  swap z and Ai[hi(z.key)]
  x ← x + 1
If x = 6n: REHASH
```

```
CKH^{MemR,MemW}.Find(k):
If A1[h1(k)].key = k:
  Return A1[h1(k)].value
Else if A2[h2(k)].key = k:
  Return A2[h2(k)].value
Else: Return ⊥

CKH^{MemR,MemW}.Delete(k):
If A1[h1(k)].key = k:
  A1[h1(k)].value ← null
If A2[h2(k)].key = k:
  A2[h2(k)].value ← null

CKH^{MemR,MemW}.Update(k, v):
If A1[h1(k)].key = k:
  A1[h1(k)].value ← v
If A2[h2(k)].key = k:
  A2[h2(k)].value ← v
```

Fig. 12. Pseudocode for cuckoo hashing algorithms. For space reasons we leave the definition of the rehashing procedure implicit.

7.2 Constructing Unique-Insertion Oblivious Hash Queues

Now, we give an oblivious hash queue called CCOHQ. Our pseudocode is in Fig. 13. As with OMOHQ, our construction consists of two parts: an array to maintain first-in-first-out order and a dictionary data structure. In CCOHQ, though, we do not use a generic oblivious map: instead, we use a specific construction, namely cuckoo hashing running on top of a generic ORAM. We give pseudocode for cuckoo hashing in Fig. 12. (Recall that cuckoo hashing supports $\mathcal{O}(1)$ time worst case lookup and delete, and expected $\mathcal{O}(1)$ time insert.) Note that to achieve bandwidth overhead $\mathcal{O}(\log c)$, we need to use an ORAM whose bandwidth overhead $\mathcal{O}(\log N)$, such as OptORAMa [4]. We depict this in the figure by having the cuckoo hash CKH use simulated memory read/write oracles built from ORAM, denoted **OMR** and **OMW**. We also apply a PRP to the keys before they are inserted into the cuckoo hash table. As we will see below, this is important to ensure security. We draw the reader's attention to the fact that this is different from oblivious cuckoo hashing in [4,10]. Their hash tables only support one-time lookups after being initialized but we need multiple time lookups and modifications.

Security of CCOHQ**.** Recall that UHQoram only needs hash queues that are unique-insertion oblivious for the two fixed operation sequences —$\overrightarrow{op}_w$ and $\overrightarrow{op}_r$—defined above. Thus, we only need to prove CCOHQ satisfies $\overrightarrow{op}_w$ and $\overrightarrow{op}_r$-unique-insertion obliviousness to conclude that UHQoram in Fig. 11 is a c-snapshot oblivious RAM emulator when instantiated with CCOHQ.

Theorem 9. *Let E be a secure PRP and* ORAM *be an oblivious RAM. Then* CCOHQ *in Fig. 13 is a $\overrightarrow{op}_w$- and $\overrightarrow{op}_r$-unique insertion oblivious hash queue.*

$\mathsf{CCOHQ}^{\mathbf{MemR},\mathbf{MemW}}.\mathsf{init}(n)$:	$\mathsf{CCOHQ}^{\mathbf{MemR},\mathbf{MemW}}.\mathsf{Find}(key)$:
$k_C \leftarrow\$ \mathcal{K}$; $head, tail \leftarrow 0$ For $i = 1$ to $n+1$: $\mathbf{MemW}(i, 0^m)$ $\mathsf{st}_o \leftarrow\$ \mathsf{ORAM}^{\mathbf{MemR},\mathbf{MemW}}.\mathsf{init}(2n)$ $\mathsf{st}_c \leftarrow\$ \mathsf{CKH}^{\mathbf{OMR},\mathbf{OMW}}.\mathsf{init}(n)$ Return $(\mathsf{st}_o, \mathsf{st}_c, k_C, head, tail, n)$	Return $\mathsf{CKH}^{\mathbf{OMR},\mathbf{OMW}}.\mathsf{Find}(E_{k_C}(key))$ $\mathsf{CCOHQ}^{\mathbf{MemR},\mathbf{MemW}}.\mathsf{Push}(key, val)$: $\mathsf{CKH}^{\mathbf{OMR},\mathbf{OMW}}.\mathsf{Insert}(E_{k_C}(key), val)$ $\mathbf{MemW}(tail, key)$ $tail \leftarrow (tail+1) \mod (n+1)$

$\mathsf{CCOHQ}^{\mathbf{MemR},\mathbf{MemW}}.\mathsf{Access}(op, key, val)$:
If $op = \mathsf{write}$:
  $\mathsf{CKH}^{\mathbf{OMR},\mathbf{OMW}}.\mathsf{Update}(E_{k_C}(key), val)$
  Return $\perp$
If $op = \mathsf{read}$:
  Return $\mathsf{CKH}^{\mathbf{OMR},\mathbf{OMW}}.\mathsf{Find}(E_{k_C}(key))$
	$\mathsf{CCOHQ}^{\mathbf{MemR},\mathbf{MemW}}.\mathsf{Pop}()$:
	$key' \leftarrow \mathbf{MemR}(head)$
	$head \leftarrow (head+1) \mod (n+1)$
	$val' \leftarrow \mathsf{CKH}^{\mathbf{OMR},\mathbf{OMW}}.\mathsf{Find}(E_{k_C}(key'))$
	$\mathsf{CKH}^{\mathbf{OMR},\mathbf{OMW}}.\mathsf{Delete}(E_{k_C}(key'))$
	Return (key', val')

Fig. 13. The CCOHQ hash queue. All operations take a state as input and output. All operations executed by the cuckoo hash table CKH are executed with *simulated* memory read/write oracles built from ORAM.

Before the proof we give an idea of why a simple combination of cuckoo hashing and an ORAM does not give us an oblivious data structure that supports arbitrary insertion, even if we do not hide operation type. This is because the number of memory accesses made during insertion depends on the number of swaps. Take these two transcripts:

$$T_1 = \mathsf{Insert}(1), \ldots, \mathsf{Insert}(100), \mathsf{Insert}(0), \mathsf{Delete}(0), \mathsf{Insert}(0), \mathsf{Delete}(0), \ldots$$
$$T_2 = \mathsf{Insert}(1), \ldots, \mathsf{Insert}(100), \mathsf{Insert}(101), \mathsf{Delete}(1), \mathsf{Insert}(102), \mathsf{Delete}(2), \ldots.$$

Both transcripts insert 1 to 100 at the beginning. Then the first one repeatedly inserts 0 and deletes 0, while the second one inserts new keys and deletes old keys. Now let's analyze the transcripts starting the first Delete operation. In the first transcript, since 0 is always deleted before being inserted, inserting 0 takes only one ORAM access. However, in the second transcript, inserting new keys such as 101, 102, ... is very likely to incur swaps, and therefore makes the access pattern longer than the previous one.

Proof. At a high level, the proof has the following steps. We will begin in game $\text{UniqInsertOblivHashSec}_{\overrightarrow{op}_w}$ with $i = 0$. Then, we move to a game where the array is replaced by all zeros, and the queue is stored locally. Then, we use the obliviousness of ORAM to make a series of changes to the transcript of cuckoo hash operations: in one game transition, we change all Update operations to Finds. Then, we change the arguments of all Finds to all-zeros, and all second arguments of Insert to zeros (keeping the indices the same). At this point, we are in a game where only the indices passed to CKH.Insert and CKH.Delete depend on the adversary's chosen transcript. However, since we can guarantee duplicate indices are never passed to CKH.Insert, we can apply the PRP security to swap the set of indices for a random subset of $[|DB|]$.

We now proceed formally. Let $\mathcal{A}$ be an adversary, and let game G_0 be $\text{UniqInsertOblivHashSec}_{\overrightarrow{op}_w}(\mathsf{CCOHQ}, \mathcal{A}, n, 0)$. Let T_0 be $\mathcal{A}$'s left transcript.

We build the game G_1, which is just like G_0 except in all CCOHQAccess operations, CKH.Find is always executed instead of choosing between Find and Update based on whether the operation is a read or a write. Again, the correctness of the values is maintained locally instead of by writing them to the cuckoo hash table. Note that this does not change the number of (oblivious) memory accesses made by CKH, since both Find and Update only access two locations. We can build a reduction $\mathcal{B}$ to the obliviousness of ORAM to get $|\Pr[G_1 = 1] - \Pr[G_0 = 1]| \le \mathbf{Adv}^{\mathrm{obl}}_{\mathsf{ORAM}}(\mathcal{B})$.

Next is game G_2, which is the same as G_1 except all CKH.Find operations have all-zeros arguments, and values written using CKH.Insert are replaced with zeros; correctness is ensured with local copies. Since this also does not change the number of operations executed, we can use a similar argument to build another reduction $\mathcal{C}$ to the obliviousness of ORAM, yielding $|\Pr[G_2 = 1] - \Pr[G_1 = 1]| \le \mathbf{Adv}^{\mathrm{obl}}_{\mathsf{ORAM}}(\mathcal{C})$.

In game G_2, only the indices passed to CKH.Insert and CKH.Delete depend on the adversary's transcript T_0. In game G_3, we replace the set of indices passed to CKH.Insert with a random subset of $[|DB|]$. This will change the number of memory accesses made by CKH.Insert, since a different number of swaps will be needed to insert the indices into the hash table. However, because of the unique-insertion property, in game G_2 the hash table contains the PRP evaluated on distinct keys; thus, by PRP security, the distribution of these inputs (and therefore of the swaps) is very similar in game G_3. We can build a reduction $\mathcal{D}$ to the PRP security of E to get $|\Pr[G_3 = 1] - \Pr[G_2 = 1]| \le \mathbf{Adv}^{\mathrm{prp}}_{E}(\mathcal{D})$.

Reversing these game transitions in a manner similar to the proofs above lets us transition to game $\mathrm{UniqInsertOblivHashSec}_{\overrightarrow{op}_w}(\mathsf{CCOHQ}, \mathcal{A}, n, 1)$, and we are done. Finally, the proof for $\overrightarrow{op}_r$-unique-insertion obliviousness is similar, so we omit it. ∎

7.3 Lower Bound

The lower bound for snapshot-oblivious RAM emulator follows from Larsen & Nielsen's lower bound [38]. In this subsection we first restate the main theorem of [38], then show that c-snapshot ORAM can simulate a normal ORAM in a parameter regime where the Larsen & Nielsen lower bound applies.

Theorem 10. *(Larsen & Nielsen lower bound [38]). Any online ORAM with n blocks of memory, consisting of $r \ge 1$ bits each, must have an expected amortized bandwidth overhead of $\Omega(\log(nr/m))$ on a sequence of $\Theta(n)$ operations. Here m denotes the client memory in bits.*

Applying this theorem to our setting where each block is only one address and the client memory is constant, which means r, m are constant, we obtain the following corollary.

Corollary 1. *Any RAM emulator defined in Sect. 2.2 initialized with a database of size N, executing on a sequence of N operations, with constant client storage, is secure only if it has an expected amortized bandwidth overhead of $\Omega(\log(N))$.*

The idea of our result is to use a snapshot-oblivious RAM emulator to simulate a full ORAM. Notice that if the transcript is of length c, and the memory is at least of size c, the c-snapshot-oblivious RAM emulator becomes a secure RAM emulator executing a sequence of c operations, and the corollary above applies. Thus, the lower bound of amortized bandwidth overhead is $\Omega(\log(c))$.

Theorem 11. *Let $c > 0$ be an integer. If* RE *is a c-snapshot oblivious RAM emulator, then* RE *must have $\Omega(\log c)$ expected amortized bandwidth overhead if the client has constant memory.*

Proof. Suppose for contradiction that RE is a c-snapshot oblivious RAM emulator, and it has $o(\log c)$ bandwidth overhead. We initialize RE on any database of size c. Given a transcript of c operations, RE can securely emulate the RAM by the definition of c-snapshot obliviousness, but its $o(\log c)$ bandwidth overhead contradicts Corollary 1. ∎

8 Conclusion

In this work, we initiated the study of snapshot-oblivious RAMs, a new oblivious memory primitive. There are many interesting open questions which we leave for future work.

First, while we prove that our UHQoram scheme is asymptotically optimal in terms of bandwidth overhead, its concrete performance is likely to be quite poor. Evaluating the concrete performance of c-snapshot ORAMs, and improving concretely upon the constructions of this paper, is a clear interesting question.

In this work we do not tackle the question of how system designers should choose c. This is a complex and highly contextual question; it is natural to imagine system designers choosing c by weighing the risks of different compromises in their systems. Which risks to consider, are questions we leave to future work.

For our security model to be an accurate characterization of real compromises, it should be the case in real systems that the amount of information about past operations is limited. If, for example, a system stored the history of every memory access on disk, the limited-time compromise model in this paper would be unrealistic.

Prior work found that existing systems do, in fact, store a great deal of information about past operations [23]. Realizing our security model in today's systems is indeed a challenge. We believe building systems with limited memories is ultimately tractable, and a fascinating research problem in its own right. In addition to being of theoretical interest today, our work builds a foundation for cryptography that can take advantage of these kinds of system-level guarantees in the future.

Finally, there are many interesting ways to extend and enrich our snapshot security model. One very clear open question is building schemes that remain secure even for multiple snapshot compromises that are separated in time. Real systems are sometimes compromised multiple times, so this extension is well-motivated practically. Another interesting enhancement is transcript-length-hiding: namely, requiring that the number of total operations executed is hidden by the snapshot-oblivious RAM.

Acknowledgments. The authors thank their shepherd Mark Simkin and the anonymous reviewers at CRYPTO 2022 for their helpful comments and suggestions. This work was partially supported by the Air Force Office of Scientific Research (AFOSR) under award number FA9550-20–1-0425; the National Science Foundation under grant CNS-1954712 and by a gift from Qualcomm.

References

1. Verizon Data Breach Incident Report (2021). https://www.verizon.com/business/resources/reports/2021-data-breach-investigations-report.pdfx

2. Abraham, I., Fletcher, C.W., Nayak, K., Pinkas, B., Ren, L.: Asymptotically tight bounds for composing ORAM with PIR. In: IACR PKC (2017)
3. Amjad, G., Kamara, S., Moataz, T.: Breach-resistant structured encryption. In: Proceedings on Privacy Enhancing Technologies (2019)
4. Asharov, G., Komargodski, I., Lin, W.K., Nayak, K., Peserico, E., Shi, E.: Optorama: optimal oblivious RAM. In: IACR EUROCRYPT (2020)
5. Asharov, G., Komargodski, I., Lin, W.K., Shi, E.: Oblivious RAM with worst-case logarithmic overhead. In: IACR CRYPTO (2021)
6. Boyle, E., Naor, M.: Is there an oblivious RAM lower bound? In: ITCS (2016)
7. Cash, D.: A survey of Oblivious RAMs (2012). https://cseweb.ucsd.edu/~cdcash/oram-slides.pdf
8. Cash, D., Drucker, A., Hoover, A.: A lower bound for one-round oblivious RAM. In: IACR TCC (2020)
9. Cash, D., Grubbs, P., Perry, J., Ristenpart, T.: Leakage-abuse attacks against searchable encryption. In: ACM CCS (2015)
10. Chan, T.H.H., Guo, Y., Lin, W.K., Shi, E.: Oblivious hashing revisited, and applications to asymptotically efficient ORAM and OPRAM. In: IACR ASIACRYPT (2017)
11. Chase, M., Kamara, S.: Structured encryption and controlled disclosure. In: IACR ASIACRYPT (2010)
12. Chung, K.M., Liu, Z., Pass, R.: Statistically-secure ORAM with $\tilde{O}(\log^2 n)$ overhead. In: IACR ASIACRYPT (2014)
13. Curtmola, R., Garay, J., Kamara, S., Ostrovsky, R.: Searchable symmetric encryption: improved definitions and efficient constructions. J. Comput. Secur. **19**(5), 895–934 (2011)
14. Dautrich, Jr., J.L., Ravishankar, C.V.: Compromising privacy in precise query protocols. In: EDBT (2013)
15. Demertzis, I., Papadopoulos, D., Papamanthou, C., Shintre, S.: SEAL: Attack mitigation for encrypted databases via adjustable leakage. In: Usenix Security (2020)
16. Devadas, S., Dijk, M.v., Fletcher, C.W., Ren, L., Shi, E., Wichs, D.: Onion ORAM: a constant bandwidth blowup oblivious RAM. In: IACR TCC (2016)
17. Gentry, C., Goldman, K.A., Halevi, S., Julta, C., Raykova, M., Wichs, D.: Optimizing ORAM and using it efficiently for secure computation. In: PETS (2013)
18. George, M., Kamara, S., Moataz, T.: Structured encryption and dynamic leakage suppression. In: IACR EUROCRYPT (2021)
19. Goldreich, O., Ostrovsky, R.: Software protection and simulation on oblivious RAMs. J. ACM **43**(3), 431–473 (1996)
20. Goodrich, M.T., Mitzenmacher, M.: Privacy-preserving access of outsourced data via oblivious RAM simulation. In: ICALP (2011)
21. Grubbs, P., Khandelwal, A., Lacharité, M.S., Brown, L., Li, L., Agarwal, R., Ristenpart, T.: Pancake: frequency smoothing for encrypted data stores. In: Usenix Security (2020)
22. Grubbs, P., McPherson, R., Naveed, M., Ristenpart, T., Shmatikov, V.: Breaking web applications built on top of encrypted data. In: ACM CCS (2016)
23. Grubbs, P., Ristenpart, T., Shmatikov, V.: Why your encrypted database is not secure. In: HotOS (2017)
24. Grubbs, P., Sekniqi, K., Bindschaedler, V., Naveed, M., Ristenpart, T.: Leakage-abuse attacks against order-revealing encryption. In: IEEE S&P (2017)
25. Hamlin, A., Varia, M.: Two-server distributed ORAM with sublinear computation and constant rounds. In: IACR PKC (2021)
26. Heath, D., Kolesnikov, V.: A 2.1 KHz zero-knowledge processor with BubbleRAM. In: ACM CCS (2020)
27. Heath, D., Kolesnikov, V.: PrORAM: fast $O(\log n)$ private coin ZK ORAM. Cryptology ePrint Archive (2021). https://eprint.iacr.org/2021/587

28. Islam, M.S., Kuzu, M., Kantarcioglu, M.: Access pattern disclosure on searchable encryption: Ramification, attack and mitigation. In: NDSS (2012)
29. Jacob, R., Larsen, K.G., Nielsen, J.B.: Lower bounds for oblivious data structures. In: ACM SODA (2019)
30. Jafargholi, Z., Larsen, K.G., Simkin, M.: Optimal oblivious priority queues. In: ACM SODA (2021)
31. Kamara, S., Moataz, T., Ohrimenko, O.: Structured encryption and leakage suppression. In: IACR CRYPTO (2018)
32. Kellaris, G., Kollios, G., Nissim, K., O'Neill, A.: Generic attacks on secure outsourced databases. In: ACM CCS (2016)
33. Komargodski, I., Lin, W.K.: A logarithmic lower bound for oblivious RAM (for all parameters). In: IACR CRYPTO (2021)
34. Kornaropoulos, E.M., Papamanthou, C., Tamassia, R.: Data recovery on encrypted databases with k-nearest neighbor query leakage. In: IEEE S&P (2019)
35. Kushilevitz, E., Lu, S., Ostrovsky, R.: On the (in) security of hash-based oblivious RAM and a new balancing scheme. In: ACM SODA (2012)
36. Lacharité, M.S., Minaud, B., Paterson, K.G.: Improved reconstruction attacks on encrypted data using range query leakage. In: IEEE S&P (2018)
37. Lacharité, M.S., Paterson, K.G.: A note on the optimality of frequency analysis vs. ℓ_p-optimization. IACR ePrint (2015). https://eprint.iacr.org/2015/1158
38. Larsen, K.G., Nielsen, J.B.: Yes, there is an oblivious RAM lower bound! In: IACR CRYPTO (2018)
39. Larsen, K.G., Simkin, M., Yeo, K.: Lower bounds for multi-server oblivious RAMs. In: IACR TCC (2020)
40. Moataz, T., Mayberry, T., Blass, E.O.: Constant communication ORAM with small blocksize. In: ACM CCS (2015)
41. Patel, S., Persiano, G., Raykova, M., Yeo, K.: PanORAMa: oblivious RAM with logarithmic overhead. In: IEEE FOCS (2018)
42. Persiano, G., Yeo, K.: Lower bounds for differentially private RAMs. In: IACR EUROCRYPT (2019)
43. Pinkas, B., Reinman, T.: Oblivious RAM revisited. In: IACR CRYPTO (2010)
44. Ren, L., Fletcher, C., Kwon, A., Stefanov, E., Shi, E., Van Dijk, M., Devadas, S.: Constants count: practical improvements to oblivious RAM. In: Usenix Security (2015)
45. Ren, L., Fletcher, C.W., Yu, X., Van Dijk, M., Devadas, S.: Integrity verification for path oblivious-ram. In: IEEE HPEC (2013)
46. Roche, D.S., Aviv, A., Choi, S.G.: A practical oblivious map data structure with secure deletion and history independence. In: IEEE S&P (2016)
47. Shi, E., Chan, T.H.H., Stefanov, E., Li, M.: Oblivious RAM with $O(\log^3 N)$ worst-case cost. In: IACR ASIACRYPT (2011)
48. Song, D.X., Wagner, D., Perrig, A.: Practical techniques for searches on encrypted data. In: IEEE S&P (2000)
49. Stefanov, E., et al.: Path ORAM: an extremely simple oblivious RAM protocol. In: ACM CCS (2013)
50. Wagh, S., Cuff, P., Mittal, P.: Differentially private oblivious RAM. In: Proceedings on Privacy Enhancing Technologies (2018)
51. Wang, X., Chan, H., Shi, E.: Circuit ORAM: on tightness of the goldreich-ostrovsky lower bound. In: ACM CCS (2015)
52. Wang, X., et al.: Oblivious data structures. In: ACM CCS (2014)
53. Weiss, M., Wichs, D.: Is there an oblivious RAM lower bound for online reads? J. Cryptology **34**(3), 1–44 (2021). https://doi.org/10.1007/s00145-021-09392-1

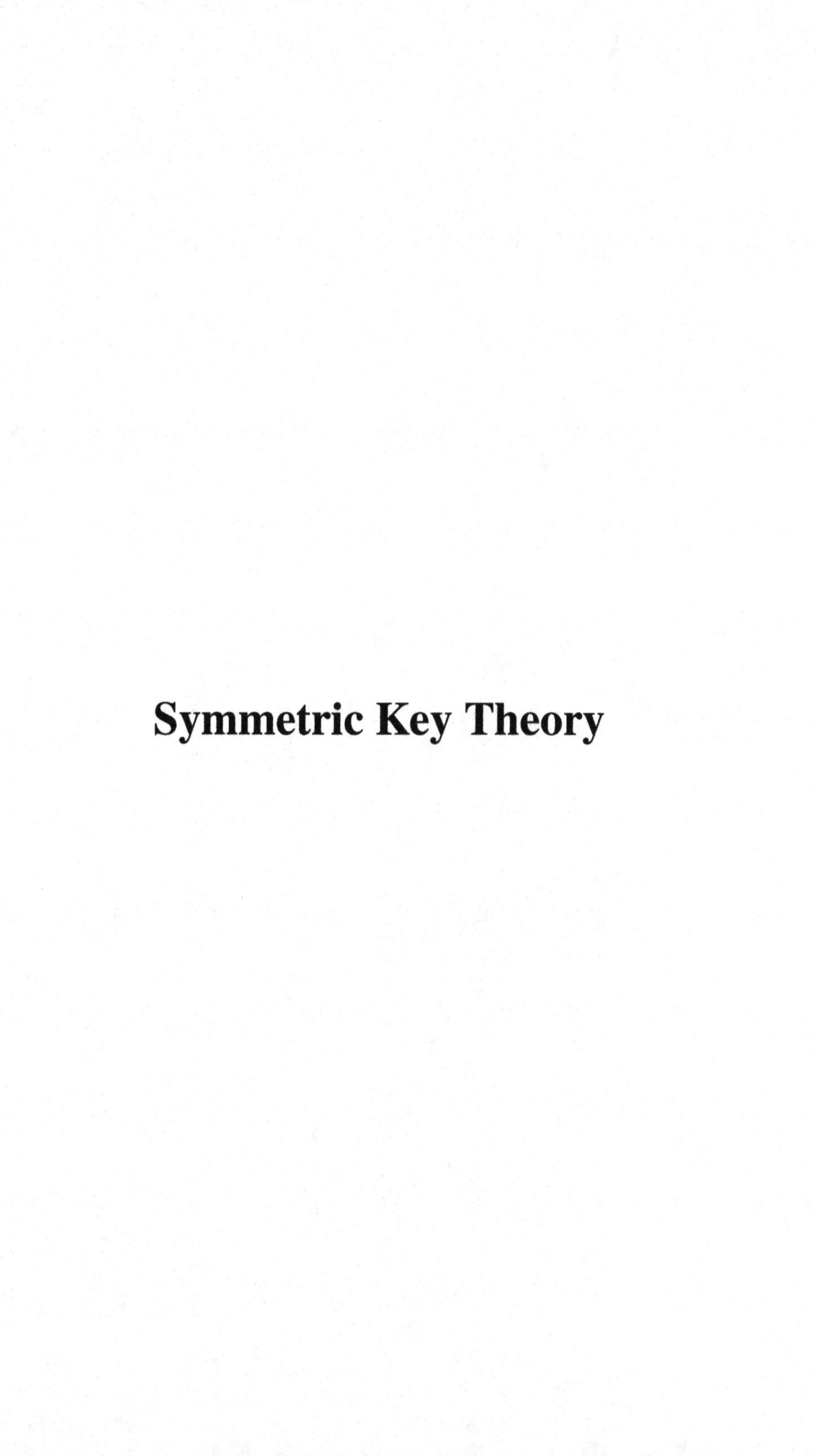

Symmetric Key Theory

Tight Preimage Resistance of the Sponge Construction

Charlotte Lefevre(✉) and Bart Mennink

Digital Security Group, Radboud University, Nijmegen, The Netherlands
charlotte.lefevre@ru.nl, b.mennink@cs.ru.nl

Abstract. The cryptographic sponge is a popular method for hash function design. The construction is in the ideal permutation model proven to be indifferentiable from a random oracle up to the birthday bound in the capacity of the sponge. This result in particular implies that, as long as the attack complexity does not exceed this bound, the sponge construction achieves a comparable level of collision, preimage, and second preimage resistance as a random oracle. We investigate these state-of-the-art bounds in detail, and observe that while the collision and second preimage security bounds are tight, the preimage bound *is not tight.* We derive an improved and tight preimage security bound for the cryptographic sponge construction.

The result has direct implications for various lightweight cryptographic hash functions. For example, the NIST Lightweight Cryptography finalist Ascon-Hash does not generically achieve 2^{128} preimage security as claimed, but even 2^{192} preimage security. Comparable improvements are obtained for the modes of Spongent, PHOTON, ACE, Subterranean 2.0, and QUARK, among others.

Keywords: sponge · hash function · preimage security · tightness

1 Introduction

The sponge construction of Bertoni et al. [9] is a popular approach for cryptographic hashing. At a high level, the sponge operates on a state of size b bits, which is split into an inner part of size c bits (the capacity) and an outer part of size r bits (the rate), where $b = c + r$. The sponge consists of an absorbing phase and a squeezing phase. In the absorbing phase, data is compressed into the state r bits at a time, interleaved with an evaluation of a b-bit permutation $\mathcal{P}$. In the squeezing phase, a digest is extracted from the state r bits at a time, again interleaved with an evaluation of $\mathcal{P}$. A slight relaxation of this approach, introduced by the developers of PHOTON [18], is to squeeze at a slightly larger rate $r' \geq r$. Throughout this work, we will in fact consider this generalized description of the sponge, as depicted in Fig. 1, but we will stick to calling it the “sponge”.

The sponge found quick adoption right after its introduction, and its popularity is ever-increasing. Most notably, the eventual winner of the NIST SHA-3

Y. Dodis and T. Shrimpton (Eds.): CRYPTO 2022, LNCS 13510, pp. 185–204, 2022.
https://doi.org/10.1007/978-3-031-15985-5_7

competition [22], Keccak [11], relies on the sponge methodology. It was quickly acknowledged that the sponge was particularly well-suited for lightweight hashing, see, e.g., QUARK [3], Spongent [12], and PHOTON [18], and in the ongoing NIST Lightweight Cryptography competition [23], no less than 22 submissions (including 5 finalists) offer hashing via the sponge construction or a derivative thereof.

Two causes for this quick adoption were the conceptual simplicity of the sponge, and its ability to offer variable output length digests (later, functions that facilitate this were dubbed extendable output functions (XOFs) [22]). Another main cause was that the developers [10] proved security of the sponge construction in the indifferentiability framework [13,20]. In a bit more detail, the authors proved that if $\mathcal{P}$ is assumed to be a random permutation, no adversary with an attack complexity less than $2^{c/2}$ can differentiate the sponge construction from a random oracle. (For the PHOTON construction with larger squeezing rate $r' \geq r$, a comparable bound was proven by Naito and Ohta [21].) The result, in words, implies that the sponge "behaves" like a random oracle and that it can be used in (most) applications that were proven secure in the random oracle model. This result also implies that, assuming that the query complexity is at most $2^{c/2}$, finding collisions, preimages, or second preimages for the sponge is not easier than for a random oracle. Andreeva et al. [2, Appendix A] made this implication explicit and demonstrated that for a sponge construction that outputs a digest of (fixed length) n bits, finding collisions requires at least

$$q \approx \min\{2^{c/2}, 2^{n/2}\} \tag{1}$$

work, and finding preimages or second preimages requires at least

$$q \approx \min\{2^{c/2}, 2^{n}\} \tag{2}$$

work (see also Sect. 3.1). These bounds have directly influenced the parameter choices of many sponge-based hash designs. Most notably, the SHA-3 hash function family consists of four functions: SHA3-n where $n \in \{224, 256, 384, 512\}$ defines the output size. Each of these four functions has its capacity c equal to *twice* the digest length n (see also Table 1).

It was clear from the start that the indifferentiability bound of Bertoni et al. [10] was tight. As a matter of fact, in around $2^{c/2}$ work, an adversary can find inner collisions, i.e., different sponge evaluations that collide on the c-bit inner part, and it can use these inner collisions to form a full collision for the sponge and this way distinguish it from random. Likewise, the collision security bound of (1) is tight, as a collision for a sponge with fixed n-bit output can be obtained either by finding a c-bit inner collision or an n-bit output collision. Finally, for second preimage resistance, tightness of the bound of (2) can be argued in a comparable way. Clearly, one approach the adversary can take to find a second preimage is an exhaustive search in 2^n work. Alternatively, given the first preimage, the attacker can recompute the sponge on input of this first preimage to determine the final state value *before* squeezing. Then, it computes the sponge forward from the initial value 0^b and backward from the state value *before* squeezing in order to find a collision on the c-bit inner part.

For preimage security, the situation is different, and it appears that *for certain values* c *and* n, the bound of (2) is *not tight.* This is mainly caused by the fact that, unlike for second preimage security, the final state *before* squeezing cannot always be easily found. Already in the original introduction of the sponge construction in 2007, it was claimed that a preimage attack can only be found in $\max\{2^{n-r'}, 2^{c/2}\}$ work [9, Section 5.3], where we recall that c is the capacity during absorbing and r' the rate during squeezing (in the original proposal, $r' = r$). In 2011, both the developers of PHOTON and Spongent made a comparable claim regarding the preimage security of their construction [12,18]. We discuss this generic attack in detail in Sect. 3.2. Here, we also elaborate a bit more on the generic collision and second preimage attacks, noting that they are de facto simplifications of the preimage attack. Unfortunately, *proving* tight preimage security of this level has remained an open problem since.

1.1 Tight Preimage Security

We solve this open problem and prove tight preimage security of the sponge construction. In detail, assuming that the underlying permutation $\mathcal{P}$ is random, we prove that the sponge achieves preimage security up to around

$$q \approx \min\left\{\max\left\{2^{n-r'}, 2^{c/2}\right\}, 2^n\right\} \tag{3}$$

work, where we recall that n is the digest size, c the capacity of the sponge (during absorption), and r' the rate (during squeezing). A detailed bound is given in Sect. 4, and the bound tightly matches the generic attack of Sect. 3.2 (up to constant). The security relies on a careful investigation of what events are needed to happen in order for a preimage to be found, and subsequently a detailed computation of the probability of these events to occur.

At a very high level, suppose the attacker aims to obtain a preimage for a digest Z consisting of ℓ r'-bit blocks $Z_1\|\cdots\|Z_\ell$, assuming $r' \mid n$ for the sake of simplicity. We assume, by definition, that the attacker is required to make all permutation queries that are required for the computation of its eventual preimage, and in particular, it must definitely obtain a cascaded evaluation of $\ell - 1$ permutation queries that correspond to outputs $Z_1, \ldots, Z_\ell$. In Fig. 1, these are the first permutation evaluation *after* outputting Z_1 up to and including the last permutation evaluation *before* outputting Z_ℓ. As we demonstrate in our proof, the attacker succeeds in finding such a path only after around $q \approx 2^{n-r'}$ queries.

However, the adversary is not done after just finding such cascade of permutation evaluations: the evaluations must also be *reached* from 0^b through the absorption of certain message blocks—these message blocks eventually constitute the preimage that the adversary would output. The adversary could succeed in this in two ways: either the last permutation query before squeezing is made in forward direction, or it is made in inverse direction. If it is made in forward direction, we have to go one step back in our reasoning, namely to the discussion of the squeezing cascade, and observe that in this case the cascade of ℓ permutation evaluations can only be found in $q \approx 2^n$ queries. If it is in inverse direction, this particular permutation query can be made *for free* from the cascade of above $\ell - 1$ evaluations, *but* in order to then connect the cascade to the initial value 0^b, the adversary must necessarily ever find a forward and an inverse permutation evaluation that collide on the inner part. This, in turn requires approximately $2^{c/2}$ work.

In summary, finding a preimage requires either around 2^n work, or the maximum of $2^{n-r'}$ and $2^{c/2}$ work, exactly as expressed in (3). Needless to say, the actual security analysis, and in particular the derivation of an upper bound on the probability of finding a matching cascaded permutation evaluation of length $\ell - 1$ or ℓ, is much more involved, among others as any permutation query of the adversary may appear at any position in this cascade.

1.2 Application

For hash functions with a large capacity, e.g., Keccak and eventually the SHA-3 hash function family, the old bound of (2) accurately described the preimage security. However, with the advent of lightweight cryptography, many sponge constructions with small permutation size b, small capacity c, and small squeezing rate r' have appeared. In many of these cases, our bound has immediate implications as it confirms higher preimage security.

The ISO/IEC standardized Spongent hash function of Bogdanov et al. [12] and the PHOTON hash function of Guo et al. [18] are two such cases. Spongent consists of five hash functions, all of which are sponges instantiated with a permutation of size $b \in \{88, 136, 176, 240, 272\}$ bits, a rate of $r = r' = 8$ bits for the smallest two versions and $r = r' = 16$ for the larger three, and a capacity $c = b - r$. The smallest version outputs $n = b = 88$ bits whereas the other versions output $n = c$ bits. The old bound of (2) implied that a preimage attack required at least $2^{c/2}$ work, whereas our new bound (3) implies that a preimage attack requires at least 2^{n-r} work. For the smallest version of Spongent, this is an improvement from 2^{40} to 2^{80}, and for the largest version, this is an improvement from 2^{128} to 2^{240}. PHOTON, likewise, consists of five sponge hash functions (with larger squeezing rate than absorbing rate), instantiated with a permutation of size $b \in \{100, 144, 196, 256, 288\}$, corresponding capacities $c \in \{80, 128, 160, 224, 256\}$, and with output size $n = c$. The squeezing rate differs for the five versions, but also here, a significant gain in the security bound is achieved: 2^{40} to 2^{64} for the smallest variant and 2^{128} to 2^{224} for the largest variant.

More recently, a notable example is Ascon-Hash, the hash function in the Ascon [17] finalist in the NIST Lightweight Cryptography competition [23]. Ascon-Hash is a plain sponge construction on top of a $b = 320$-bit permutation, with a capacity $c = 256$ and a rate $r' = 64$. It outputs digests of size $n = 256$ bits, which are thus generated in four squeezes. In this case, the old bound of (2) implied generic preimage security up to 2^{128} work, whereas our new bound (3) implies generic preimage security up to 2^{192} work. A similar effect is achieved for the modes of other second round and final candidates in the NIST Lightweight Cryptography competition, such as ACE [1], KNOT [25], SKINNY-HASH [6], Subterranean 2.0 [15], the hash proposal of Isap [16], and PHOTON-Beetle [4]. These sponge-based functions all have their parameters (c, r', n) satisfying $n - r' > c/2$.

In Table 1, we give a summary of these hash function constructions, and show how the new preimage security bound improves over the earlier bound. A more detailed evaluation of our new bound for SHA3-256, Spongent with $n = 256$, and Ascon-Hash with $n = 256$ is given in Sect. 5. We remark that in Table 1, we did not include hash functions that are sponge(-like) but squeeze digests in one round, such as Grindahl [19] and CubeHash [7], as our bound only improves over the state-of-the-art bound for sponge(-like) constructions that squeeze their digest in multiple rounds. Likewise, we did not include hash functions that squeeze digests over multiple rounds but that have a large enough c such that $n - r' \leq c/2$, such as Gimli [8], ESCH [5], and Xoodyak [14].

2 Preliminaries

2.1 Notation

We use $x := y$ to define x as being equal to y. For $b \in \mathbb{N}$, we denote by $\{0,1\}^b$ the set of binary strings of size b. Moreover, $\{0,1\}^*$ is defined to be $\bigcup_{b\in\mathbb{N}}\{0,1\}^b$. For a b-bit string s and $0 \leq x \leq y \leq b-1$, $s[x : y]$ denotes the substring containing the bits of s from position x to y. Moreover, $\mathrm{inner}_x(s) := s[b - x : b - 1]$, $\mathrm{outer}_x(s) := s[0 : x - 1]$. For a finite set $\mathcal{S}$, $x \xleftarrow{\$} \mathcal{S}$ means that x is sampled uniformly at random from $\mathcal{S}$. The set $\mathit{Perm}(b)$ denotes the set of permutations over $\{0,1\}^b$. For any $\mathcal{P} \in \mathit{Perm}(b)$ and $i \in \mathbb{N}^*$, $\mathcal{P}^0$ denotes the identity function and $\mathcal{P}^i$ is i iterations of $\mathcal{P}$. For $n, k \in \mathbb{N}$ such that $k \leq n$, we use $[n]_k$ to denote the falling factorial of n of depth k, i.e., the product $\prod_{i=0}^{k-1}(n-i)$. We remark that, provided $k^2 \leq n$, we have

$$
\begin{aligned}
[n]_k &= n^k \prod_{i=0}^{k-1} \frac{n-i}{n} \\
&\geq n^k e^{\sum_{i=0}^{k-1} \frac{-i}{n-i}} \\
&\geq n^k e^{\sum_{i=0}^{k-1} \frac{-i}{n-k}} \\
&= n^k e^{\frac{-k(k-1)}{2(n-k)}} \\
&\geq n^k e^{-1/2} \\
&\geq \frac{n^k}{2},
\end{aligned} \tag{4}
$$

where the first inequality uses $1 + x \leq e^x$ applied with $x = \frac{i}{n-i}$.

Table 1. Preimage security of the modes of SHA-3 (added for reference only, as our bound does not improve the state-of-the-art bound) and selected lightweight hash functions. Security bounds only hold under the assumption that the underlying permutations are ideal.

Scheme	Parameters						Security bound		Note
	b	c	r	r'	n	ℓ	Old (2)	New (3)	
SHA3-n	1600	448	1152	1152	224	1	2^{224}	2^{224}	SHA-3 standard [22]
	1600	512	1088	1088	256	1	2^{256}	2^{256}	(included for reference)
	1600	768	832	832	384	1	2^{384}	2^{384}	
	1600	1024	576	576	512	1	2^{512}	2^{512}	
Spongent	88	80	8	8	88	11	2^{40}	2^{80}	ISO/IEC standard [12]
	136	128	8	8	128	16	2^{64}	2^{120}	
	176	160	16	16	160	10	2^{80}	2^{144}	
	240	224	16	16	224	14	2^{112}	2^{208}	
	272	256	16	16	256	16	2^{128}	2^{240}	
PHOTON	100	80	20	16	80	5	2^{40}	2^{64}	ISO/IEC standard [18]
	144	128	16	16	128	8	2^{64}	2^{112}	
	196	160	36	36	160	5	2^{80}	2^{124}	
	256	224	32	32	224	7	2^{112}	2^{192}	
	288	256	32	32	256	8	2^{128}	2^{224}	
U-QUARK	136	128	8	8	128	16	2^{64}	2^{120}	[3]
D-QUARK	176	160	16	16	160	10	2^{80}	2^{144}	
T-QUARK	256	224	32	32	224	7	2^{112}	2^{192}	
ACE-Hash	320	256	64	64	256	4	2^{128}	2^{192}	NIST LWC round 2 [1]
KNOT Hash	256	224	32	128	256	2	2^{112}	2^{128}	NIST LWC round 2 [25]
	384	256	128	128	256	2	2^{128}	2^{128}	
	384	336	48	192	384	2	2^{168}	2^{192}	
	512	448	64	256	512	2	2^{224}	2^{256}	
SKINNY-tk2-Hash	256	224	32	128	256	2	2^{112}	2^{128}	NIST LWC round 2 [6]
Subterranean 2.0	257	248	9	32	256	8	2^{124}	2^{224}	NIST LWC round 2 [15]
Ascon-Hash	320	256	64	64	256	4	2^{128}	2^{192}	NIST LWC finalist [17]
PHOTON-Beetle-Hash	256	224	32	128	256	2	2^{112}	2^{128}	NIST LWC finalist [4]

2.2 Generalized Sponge Construction

Let $b, c, r, c', r', n \in \mathbb{N}$ with $b = c+r = c'+r'$. Let $\mathcal{P} \in Perm(b)$ be a cryptographic permutation. Let *pad* be an injective padding function that transforms a message M of arbitrary length into k blocks of r bits such that the last block is non-zero. A minimal example is the 10^*-padding that appends M with a one and $(-|M| - 1) \bmod r$ zeros. We will restrict our focus to the sponge construction with a fixed-length output of size n, and we define $\ell = \lceil n/r' \rceil$.

Let $M \in \{0,1\}^*$ be an input message. The sponge construction instantiated with the permutation $\mathcal{P}$, denoted by $\mathcal{H}^{\mathcal{P}} : \{0,1\}^* \to \{0,1\}^n$, is now defined as follows.

- M is first padded into k message blocks using *pad*: $M_1\|\cdots\|M_k \leftarrow pad(M)$;
- Absorbing phase: the state S is initialized as 0^b, and at the ith iteration, for $i = 1, \ldots, k$, the state is updated as $S \leftarrow \mathcal{P}(S \oplus (M_i\|0^c))$;
- Squeezing phase: at the ith iteration, for $i = 1, \ldots, \ell$, the outer r' bits of S are extracted as $Z_i \leftarrow \text{outer}_{r'}(S)$ and the state is updated as $S \leftarrow \mathcal{P}(S)$;
- The digest is computed as $Z \leftarrow (Z_1\|\cdots\|Z_\ell)[0 : n-1]$.

The sponge construction is illustrated in Fig. 1.

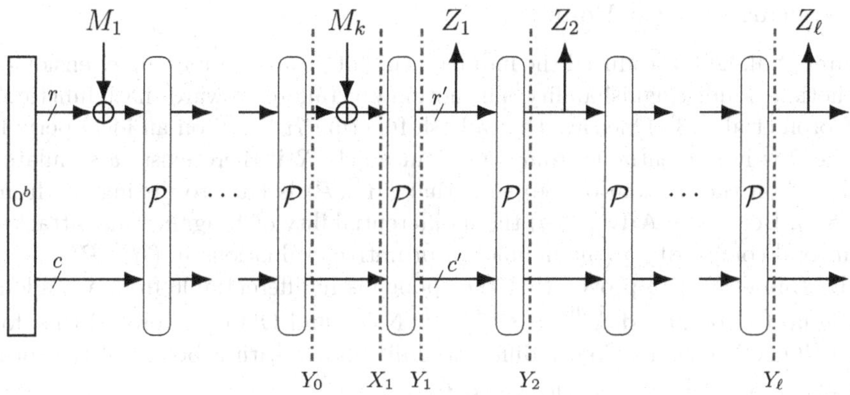

Fig. 1. Generalized sponge construction as described in Sect. 2.2. The values Y_i and X_i will be used in the proof in Sect. 4.

2.3 Security Model

An adversary $\mathcal{A}$ is a probabilistic algorithm. It has oracle access to a permutation $\mathcal{P}$ sampled uniformly at random. $\mathcal{A}$ is computationally restricted only by its number of evaluations of $\mathcal{P}$ and $\mathcal{P}^{-1}$, that we denote by q. We summarize all queries made by $\mathcal{A}$ in a query history $\mathcal{Q}$, an ordered list of tuples of the form $(X, Y, \text{d}) \in \{0,1\}^b \times \{0,1\}^b \times \{\text{fwd}, \text{inv}\}$, where $\mathcal{P}(X) = Y$ and where d denotes the query direction. We denote by $\mathcal{Q}_i$ the query history containing only the first i queries. Without loss of generality, we can assume that the adversary never makes a query that it already made before.

Preimage Resistance. We focus on everywhere preimage resistance [24]. In this model, we consider any image $Z \in \{0,1\}^n$ of length n and consider the adversary $\mathcal{A}$ that can query $\mathcal{P}$ and has as goal to eventually output a message M such that $\mathcal{H}^{\mathcal{P}}(M) = Z$. We require that the query history of $\mathcal{A}$ contains all evaluations of $\mathcal{P}$ required for the computation of $\mathcal{H}^{\mathcal{P}}(M)$.

Definition 1. *Let $b, n, q \in \mathbb{N}$, consider the sponge construction $\mathcal{H}$ of Sect. 2.2. For any adversary $\mathcal{A}$, we define its everywhere preimage advantage as*

$$\mathbf{Adv}^{\text{epre}}_{\mathcal{H}}(\mathcal{A}) = \max_{Z \in \{0,1\}^n} \mathbf{Pr}\left(\mathcal{P} \xleftarrow{\$} \mathit{Perm}(b),\ M \leftarrow \mathcal{A}^{\mathcal{P}}(Z) : \mathcal{H}^{\mathcal{P}}(M) = Z\right).$$

We define by $\mathbf{Adv}_{\mathcal{H}}^{\text{epre}}(q)$ *the supremum advantage over all adversaries making at most* q *queries.*

3 State-of-the-Art Generic Security Results

We will discuss the best known security lower bound in Sect. 3.1 and the best known generic attack in Sect. 3.2.

3.1 Security Lower Bound

Maurer et al. [20] introduced the indifferentiability framework as an extension of the notion of indistinguishability. The notion was tailored towards hash functions by Coron et al. [13]. One says that a hash function $\mathcal{H}$ based on an ideal permutation $\mathcal{P}$ is indifferentiable from a random oracle $\mathcal{R}$ if there exists a simulator $\mathcal{S}$ (based on the random oracle) such that $(\mathcal{H}^{\mathcal{P}}, \mathcal{P})$ is hard to distinguish from $(\mathcal{R}, \mathcal{S}^{\mathcal{R}})$. Denote by $\mathbf{Adv}_{\mathcal{H}}^{\text{indif}}(q)$ the indifferentiability of $\mathcal{H}$ against any attacker with total complexity q (the number of primitive evaluations in $(\mathcal{H}^{\mathcal{P}}, \mathcal{P})$).

Bertoni et al. [10] proved that the sponge is indifferentiable from a random oracle up to bound $\mathbf{Adv}_{\mathcal{H}}^{\text{indif}}(q) \leq \frac{q(q+1)}{2^{c+1}}$. Naito and Ohta [21] proved that for the PHOTON construction, indifferentiability holds with a bound of the form $\mathcal{O}\left(\frac{q}{2^{c/2}} + \frac{q}{2^{c'}}\right)$ (refer to [21] for the details).

Indifferentiability of a hash function $\mathcal{H}$ from a random oracle $\mathcal{R}$ in words means that the hash function "behaves" like a random oracle. In the context of preimage resistance, this means that [2, Appendix A]

$$\mathbf{Adv}_{\mathcal{H}}^{\text{epre}}(q) \leq \mathbf{Adv}_{\mathcal{H}}^{\text{indif}}(q) + \mathbf{Adv}_{\mathcal{R}}^{\text{epre}}(q),$$

where we are slightly abusing notation for the latter term: to be precise, for $\mathbf{Adv}_{\mathcal{R}}^{\text{epre}}(q)$ we consider the adversary to have query access to the random oracle $\mathcal{R}$ and its goal is to output a message M such that $\mathcal{R}(M) = Z$ for the predetermined Z. Clearly, $\mathbf{Adv}_{\mathcal{R}}^{\text{epre}}(q) = q/2^n$, and we thus obtain the state-of-the-art bound for preimage resistance of the sponge:

$$\mathbf{Adv}_{\mathcal{H}}^{\text{epre}}(q) \leq \frac{q(q+1)}{2^{c+1}} + \frac{q}{2^n}. \tag{5}$$

Note that this is the bound that supports the complexity estimation given in (2): generically finding a preimage for $\mathcal{H}^{\mathcal{P}}$ requires at least $\min\{2^{c/2}, 2^n\}$ evaluations. A comparable reasoning applies to the second preimage and collision resistance bounds.

3.2 Security Upper Bound

The best known attack, however, does not meet the first term of (5). In this section, we describe the best known preimage attack against the sponge construction. The attack de facto resembles the generic exhaustive preimage search attack and the attack that the sponge developers described in [9].

Let $Z \in \{0,1\}^n$ be any given image. W.l.o.g., we assume the minimal padding of Sect. 2.2. We make a case distinction depending on the values c, n. As we will focus on tightness up to constant, we will sometimes ignore the fact that any sponge evaluation of a message M of length k costs $k + \ell$ permutation calls, and simply count any such evaluation as 1 query.

- Case $n \le c/2$. The adversary fixes a message M and queries it to the construction. The query satisfies $\mathcal{H}^{\mathcal{P}}(M) = Z$ with probability around $1/2^n$. After $q \approx 2^n$ attempts, the adversary has with high probability found a preimage M.
- Case $c/2 < n$. The attack consists of two sequential parts.
  - First, the adversary fixes a state value Y_1 such that $Z_1 = \text{outer}_{r'}(Y_1)$. It queries $Y_2 = \mathcal{P}(Y_1)$, $Y_3 = \mathcal{P}^2(Y_1), \ldots, Y_\ell = \mathcal{P}^{\ell-1}(Y_1)$. The queries satisfy
  $$Z_i = \begin{cases} \text{outer}_{r'}(Y_i) & \text{for } i = 2, \ldots, \ell - 1, \\ \text{outer}_{n-(\ell-1)r'}(Y_i) & \text{for } i = \ell, \end{cases}$$
  with probability approximately
  $$\left(\frac{1}{2^{r'}}\right)^{\ell-2} \cdot \frac{1}{2^{n-(\ell-1)r'}} = \frac{1}{2^{n-r'}}.$$
  After $q \approx 2^{n-r'}$ attempts, the adversary has found a state value Y_1 such that ℓ squeezes result in Z.
  - Starting from 0^b, it computes $Y_0^{\rightarrow} := \mathcal{P}(M_1 \| 0^c)$ for q different values M_1. Starting from the value Y_1 found in the first part of the attack, it computes $Y_0^{\leftarrow} := \mathcal{P}^{-1}(\mathcal{P}^{-1}(Y_1) \oplus (M_3 \| 0^c))$ for q different non-zero values M_3. If $q \approx 2^{c/2}$, there will with high probability be two values M_1, M_3 such that
  $$\text{inner}_c(Y_0^{\rightarrow} \oplus Y_0^{\leftarrow}) = 0^c.$$
  Let $M_2 := \text{outer}_r(Y_0^{\rightarrow} \oplus Y_0^{\leftarrow})$. Define the preimage as the unique message M such that $\text{pad}(M) = M_1 \| M_2 \| M_3$. We remark that if $r \le c/2$ one will need multiple message blocks for both the forward and the inverse part in order to make $q \approx 2^{c/2}$ evaluations, but the attack works in a comparable way.

  In total, in this case the attack requires $q \approx 2^{n-r'} + 2^{c/2}$ evaluations.

In general, the attack thus has a complexity of around
$$q \approx \min\{2^{n-r'} + 2^{c/2}, 2^n\}$$
evaluations. We remark that the generic second preimage attack, as sketched in Sect. 1, is basically a simplification of above preimage attack, where in the case of $c/2 < n$, the attacker does not need to perform the first part of the attack but can rather compute Y_1 in a constant number of permutation evaluations from the first preimage. The generic collision attack, also as sketched in Sect. 1, in turn differs from this second preimage attack in the sense that for $n/2 \le c/2$ the attacker can perform exhaustive collision search in around $2^{n/2}$ evaluations (instead of 2^n).

4 Improved Preimage Resistance Lower Bound

In the following theorem, we state our main result.

Theorem 1. *Let $b, c, r, c', r', n, q \in \mathbb{N}$ with $b = c + r = c' + r'$, and let $\ell := \lceil \frac{n}{r'} \rceil$. If $q \leq 2^{c'-1}/3$ and $(\ell - 1)^2 \leq 2^b$ the sponge construction $\mathcal{H}$ of Sect. 2.2 satisfies the following bound:*

$$\mathbf{Adv}_{\mathcal{H}}^{\mathrm{epre}}(q) \leq \frac{4q}{2^n} + \min\left\{\frac{4\ell q}{2^{n-r'}}, \frac{q(q+1)}{2^c}\right\}. \tag{6}$$

The proof is given in the remainder of this section. We note that the bound indeed matches the generic attack of Sect. 3.2 up to constant. In Sect. 5, we will evaluate the bound of Theorem 1 more closely, and compare it with the generic attack of Sect. 3.2 and the state-of-the-art bound of Sect. 3.1.

4.1 Setup

Let $Z \in \{0,1\}^n$ be any image, and write $Z = Z_1 \| Z_2 \| \cdots \| Z_\ell$, where $|Z_i| = r'$ for $i \in \{1, \ldots, \ell - 1\}$ and $|Z_\ell| = s \leq r'$. Consider any adversary $\mathcal{A}$ as defined in Sect. 2.3. To represent its knowledge from the query history, we use a graph representation as done for example in [10,21]. Initially, the graph contains the nodes $\{0,1\}^b$, which represent all possible internal states of the sponge. For each query $(X, Y, \mathrm{d}) \in \mathcal{Q}$ with $d \in \{\mathrm{fwd}, \mathrm{inv}\}$, and for any $M \in \{0,1\}^r$, the edge $Y' \xrightarrow{M} Y$ is added, where $Y' := X \oplus (M \| 0^c)$. Note that in the squeezing phase, such edge must appear for a zero-block message. In this case, the label is omitted. Let $\boldsymbol{Z}_i$ be defined as follows:

$$\boldsymbol{Z}_i := \begin{cases} \{Y_i \in \{0,1\}^b \mid \mathrm{outer}_{r'}(Y_i) = Z_i\}, & \text{for } i \in \{1, \ldots, \ell - 1\}, \\ \{Y_i \in \{0,1\}^b \mid \mathrm{outer}_s(Y_i) = Z_i\}, & \text{for } i = \ell. \end{cases}$$

Then, the goal of $\mathcal{A}$ is to find a preimage of Z, which implies the following event $\mathsf{PRE}(\mathcal{Q})$:

$$\begin{aligned} \mathsf{PRE}(\mathcal{Q}) : \mathcal{Q} \text{ defines a path } & 0^b \xrightarrow{M_1} \cdots \xrightarrow{M_{k-1}} Y_0 \xrightarrow{M_k} Y_1 \rightarrow \cdots \rightarrow Y_\ell \\ & \text{such that } Y_i \in \boldsymbol{Z}_i \text{ for } i = 1, \ldots, \ell. \end{aligned}$$

We refer to Fig. 1 for a depiction of these parameters. In the case of the minimal injective padding presented in Sect. 2.2, finding a preimage corresponds to $\mathsf{PRE}(\mathcal{Q})$ with the restriction that the last message block is not zero. In such case, the preimage found by $\mathcal{A}$ is the unique message M such that $\mathrm{pad}(M) = M_1 \| \cdots \| M_k$.

4.2 Logic

We separate the event $\mathsf{PRE}(\mathcal{Q})$ as the disjoint union of the following two events:

$$\begin{aligned}\mathsf{PREFWD}(\mathcal{Q}) : &\ \mathsf{PRE}(\mathcal{Q}) \text{ with the restriction that the query} \\ &\ \text{linking } Y_0 \text{ and } Y_1 \text{ must be made in forward direction,} \\ \mathsf{PREINV}(\mathcal{Q}) : &\ \mathsf{PRE}(\mathcal{Q}) \text{ with the restriction that the query} \\ &\ \text{linking } Y_0 \text{ and } Y_1 \text{ must be made in inverse direction.}\end{aligned}$$

Clearly,

$$\mathsf{PRE}(\mathcal{Q}) \iff \mathsf{PREFWD}(\mathcal{Q}) \vee \mathsf{PREINV}(\mathcal{Q}). \tag{7}$$

We will consider dedicated trigger points for $\mathsf{PREFWD}(\mathcal{Q})$ and $\mathsf{PREINV}(\mathcal{Q})$. Let $\mathcal{S} = \{Y_1 \mid \mathcal{P}^{i-1}(Y_1) \in \boldsymbol{Z}_i \text{ for all } i \in \{1, \ldots, \ell\}\} \subseteq \boldsymbol{Z}_1$. We define the set $\mathcal{S}_{\text{fwd}}$ and the multiset $\mathcal{S}_{\text{inv}}$ as follows:

$$\begin{aligned}\mathcal{S}_{\text{fwd}} &= \{\mathcal{P}^{-1}(Y_1) \mid Y_1 \in \mathcal{S}\}, \\ \mathcal{S}_{\text{inv}} &= \{Y_1, \mathcal{P}(Y_1), \ldots, \mathcal{P}^{\ell-1}(Y_1) \mid Y_1 \in \mathcal{S}\}.\end{aligned}$$

Intuitively, $\mathcal{S}_{\text{inv}}$ includes all the nodes $Y_1, \ldots, Y_\ell$ appearing in paths which set $\mathsf{PRE}(\mathcal{Q})$ if discovered, while $\mathcal{S}_{\text{fwd}}$ captures all values X_1 from which such path $Y_1 \to \cdots \to Y_\ell$ starts. Looking ahead, $\mathcal{S}_{\text{fwd}}$ includes the set of trigger points for $\mathsf{PREFWD}(\mathcal{Q})$, and $\mathcal{S}_{\text{inv}}$, as a multiset, includes the set of trigger points for $\mathsf{PREINV}(\mathcal{Q})$. These trigger points can be repeated in $\mathcal{S}_{\text{inv}}$ when some values Z_i are colliding. (Based on this, we will typically simply refer to $\mathcal{S}_{\text{inv}}$ as a set.) We now introduce the following three events:

$$\begin{aligned}\mathsf{BADFWD}(\mathcal{Q}) : &\ \exists (X, Y, \text{fwd}) \in \mathcal{Q} \text{ such that } X \in \mathcal{S}_{\text{fwd}}, \\ \mathsf{BADINV}(\mathcal{Q}) : &\ \exists (X, Y, \text{fwd}) \in \mathcal{Q} \text{ such that } X \in \mathcal{S}_{\text{inv}} \text{ or} \\ &\ \exists (X, Y, \text{inv}) \in \mathcal{Q} \text{ such that } Y \in \mathcal{S}_{\text{inv}}, \\ \mathsf{INNER}(\mathcal{Q}) : &\ \exists (X, Y, \text{fwd}), (X', Y', \text{inv}) \in \mathcal{Q} \cup \{(, 0^b, \text{fwd})\} \\ &\ \text{such that } \text{inner}_c(Y) = \text{inner}_c(X').\end{aligned}$$

Note that for $\mathsf{INNER}(\mathcal{Q})$, the tuple $(, 0^b, \text{fwd})$ is explicitly added to cover the case where the adversary ever makes an inverse query that hits the initial state 0^b. Here, the first element of the tuple is irrelevant, and henceforth omitted.

Intuitively, for $\mathsf{PREFWD}(\mathcal{Q})$ to be set, the adversary must among others make a query $\mathcal{P}(X_1)$ with $X_1 \in \mathcal{S}_{\text{fwd}}$. Thus, $\mathsf{PREFWD}(\mathcal{Q})$ implies $\mathsf{BADFWD}(\mathcal{Q})$. Likewise, for $\mathsf{PREINV}(\mathcal{Q})$ to be set, the adversary must ever make *a* query that appears in *a* path $Y_1 \to \cdots \to Y_\ell$ in *a* query direction. In other words, it must ever query a value in $\mathcal{S}_{\text{inv}}$. Hence, $\mathsf{PREINV}(\mathcal{Q})$ implies $\mathsf{BADINV}(\mathcal{Q})$. Moreover, given that $\mathsf{PREINV}(\mathcal{Q})$ defines a path starting from 0^b that contains an edge between Y_0 and Y_1 corresponding to an inverse query, *somewhere* in this path from 0^b to Y_1 there must be a collision between an inverse query and a descendant of 0^b. This means that $\mathsf{PREINV}(\mathcal{Q})$ also implies $\mathsf{INNER}(\mathcal{Q})$. More formally:

$$\begin{aligned} \mathsf{PREFWD}(\mathcal{Q}) &\implies \mathsf{BADFWD}(\mathcal{Q}), &(8)\\ \mathsf{PREINV}(\mathcal{Q}) &\implies \mathsf{BADINV}(\mathcal{Q}) \wedge \mathsf{INNER}(\mathcal{Q}). &(9)\end{aligned}$$

From (7) to (9), we logically obtain

$$\mathsf{PRE}(\mathcal{Q}) \implies \mathsf{BADFWD}(\mathcal{Q}) \vee (\mathsf{BADINV}(\mathcal{Q}) \wedge \mathsf{INNER}(\mathcal{Q})), \tag{10}$$

and thus

$$\mathbf{Pr}\left(\mathsf{PRE}(\mathcal{Q})\right) \leq \mathbf{Pr}\left(\mathsf{BADFWD}(\mathcal{Q})\right) + \min\left\{\mathbf{Pr}\left(\mathsf{BADINV}(\mathcal{Q})\right), \mathbf{Pr}\left(\mathsf{INNER}(\mathcal{Q})\right)\right\}. \tag{11}$$

4.3 Probability Computation

We upper bound the three probabilities of (11), starting with $\mathbf{Pr}\left(\mathsf{INNER}(\mathcal{Q})\right)$ in Lemma 1, then $\mathbf{Pr}\left(\mathsf{BADFWD}(\mathcal{Q})\right)$ in Lemma 2, and finally $\mathbf{Pr}\left(\mathsf{BADINV}(\mathcal{Q})\right)$ in Lemma 3.

Lemma 1. *We have*

$$\mathbf{Pr}\left(\mathsf{INNER}(\mathcal{Q})\right) \leq \frac{q(q+1)}{2^c}. \tag{12}$$

Proof (Proof of Lemma 1). We index the queries by the query number, i.e., the ith query is denoted by (X^i, Y^i, d^i). $\mathsf{INNER}(\mathcal{Q})$ translates to the fact that either there is an inner collision between the set of forward and inverse queries, or that the output of an inverse query inner collides with 0^c. More formally, this implies that there exists $i \in \{1, \ldots, q\}$ such that one of the following two events happens:

$$\begin{aligned} \mathsf{HIT}_i^{\mathrm{fwd}}(\mathcal{Q}) &: (X^i, Y^i, \mathrm{fwd}) \in \mathcal{Q} \text{ and}\\ &\quad \mathrm{inner}_c(Y^i) \in \{\mathrm{inner}_c(X^1), \ldots, \mathrm{inner}_c(X^{i-1})\},\\ \mathsf{HIT}_i^{\mathrm{inv}}(\mathcal{Q}) &: (X^i, Y^i, \mathrm{inv}) \in \mathcal{Q} \text{ and}\\ &\quad \mathrm{inner}_c(X^i) \in \{\mathrm{inner}_c(Y^1), \ldots, \mathrm{inner}_c(Y^{i-1}), \mathrm{inner}_c(0^c)\}.\end{aligned}$$

By basic probability theory,

$$\begin{aligned} \mathbf{Pr}\left(\mathsf{INNER}(\mathcal{Q})\right) &\leq \sum_{i=1}^{q} \mathbf{Pr}\left(\mathsf{INNER}(\mathcal{Q}_i) \wedge \neg\mathsf{INNER}(\mathcal{Q}_{i-1})\right)\\ &\leq \sum_{i=1}^{q} \mathbf{Pr}\left(\mathsf{HIT}_i^{\mathrm{fwd}}(\mathcal{Q}_i) \vee \mathsf{HIT}_i^{\mathrm{inv}}(\mathcal{Q}_i) \;\middle|\; \neg\mathsf{INNER}(\mathcal{Q}_{i-1})\right).\end{aligned}$$

For any i, the query is either in forward direction or in inverse direction, so it can only set one of the two events. The response at the ith query is uniformly drawn from a set of size at least $2^b - q$, among which at most $i2^r$ elements set $\mathsf{HIT}_i^{\text{fwd}}(\mathcal{Q}_i)$ or $\mathsf{HIT}_i^{\text{inv}}(\mathcal{Q}_i)$. Thus:

$$\mathbf{Pr}\left(\mathsf{HIT}_i^{\text{fwd}}(\mathcal{Q}_i) \vee \mathsf{HIT}_i^{\text{inv}}(\mathcal{Q}_i) \,\middle|\, \neg\mathsf{INNER}(\mathcal{Q}_{i-1})\right) \leq \frac{i2^r}{2^b - q}.$$

Then, as $q \leq 2^{b-1}$,

$$\mathbf{Pr}\left(\mathsf{INNER}(\mathcal{Q})\right) \leq \sum_{i=1}^{q} \frac{2i}{2^c} \leq \frac{q(q+1)}{2^c}. \qquad \square$$

Remark 1. We remark that the PHOTON construction [18] in fact differs from the sponge construction [9] not only in the size of the squeezing blocks (as explained in Sect. 1), but also in the absorption of the *first* message block. To be precise, the PHOTON construction allows the first message block to be of size r'' bits. Extending our analysis, this would *only* affect the analysis of $\mathbf{Pr}\left(\mathsf{INNER}(\mathcal{Q})\right)$ in Lemma 1 above. In this case, the event $\mathsf{HIT}_i^{inv}(\mathcal{Q})$ would be triggered if $\text{inner}_c(X^i) \in \{\text{inner}_c(Y^1), \ldots, \text{inner}_c(Y^{i-1})\}$ or if $\text{inner}_{c''}(X^i) = 0^{c''}$, where $c'' := b - r''$. This change would eventually result in a bound of the form:

$$\mathbf{Pr}\left(\mathsf{INNER}(\mathcal{Q})\right) \leq \frac{q(q+1)}{2^c} + \frac{q}{2^{c''}}.$$

Lemma 2. *We have*

$$\mathbf{Pr}\left(\mathsf{BADFWD}(\mathcal{Q})\right) \leq \frac{4q}{2^n}. \tag{13}$$

Proof (Proof of Lemma 2). By basic probability theory,

$$\begin{aligned}&\mathbf{Pr}\left(\mathsf{BADFWD}(\mathcal{Q})\right)\\ &\qquad = \sum_{y=1}^{2^{c'}} \mathbf{Pr}\left(\mathsf{BADFWD}(\mathcal{Q}) \mid |\mathcal{S}_{\text{fwd}}| = y\right) \cdot \mathbf{Pr}\left(|\mathcal{S}_{\text{fwd}}| = y\right).\end{aligned} \tag{14}$$

We start by upper bounding the probability of the conditioned $\mathsf{BADFWD}(\mathcal{Q})$ event for any $y = 1, \ldots, 2^{c'}$, which is similar to a guessing game: in order to win, the adversary must guess $X_1 \in \mathcal{S}_{\text{fwd}}$ with a forward query. We start by remarking that $\mathcal{S}_{\text{fwd}}$ is defined via inverse $\mathcal{P}$-calls, and that the adversary has no a priori knowledge about those. Thus, one single query $\mathcal{P}(X)$ from the adversary succeeds with probability at most $\frac{y}{2^b}$. Moreover, one query eliminates at most one candidate: if the query (X, Y, d) does not set $\mathsf{BADFWD}(\mathcal{Q})$, then X can be removed from the set of candidates values to be in $\mathcal{S}_{\text{inv}}$. If additionally $\text{d} = \text{inv}$

and $X \in \mathcal{S}_{\text{fwd}}$, the adversary cannot guess this value anymore. Thus, defining $\mathsf{BADFWD}(\mathcal{Q}_0) := \bot$,

$$\begin{aligned}
\mathbf{Pr}\left(\mathsf{BADFWD}(\mathcal{Q}) \mid |\mathcal{S}_{\text{fwd}}| = y\right) &\leq \sum_{i=1}^{q} \mathbf{Pr}\left(\mathsf{BADFWD}(\mathcal{Q}_i) \mid |\mathcal{S}_{\text{fwd}}| = y \wedge \neg\mathsf{BADFWD}(\mathcal{Q}_{i-1})\right) \\
&\leq \sum_{i=1}^{q} \frac{y}{2^b - i + 1} \leq \frac{yq}{2^b - q} \leq 2\frac{yq}{2^b},
\end{aligned} \tag{15}$$

where in the last inequality, we used $q \leq 2^{b-1}$.

Plugging this bound into (14) gives

$$\begin{aligned}
\mathbf{Pr}\left(\mathsf{BADFWD}(\mathcal{Q})\right) &\leq \frac{2q}{2^b} \sum_{y=1}^{2^{c'}} y \cdot \mathbf{Pr}\left(|\mathcal{S}_{\text{fwd}}| = y\right) \\
&\leq \frac{2q}{2^b} \mathsf{E}\left(|\mathcal{S}_{\text{fwd}}|\right).
\end{aligned} \tag{16}$$

It remains to compute $\mathsf{E}\left(|\mathcal{S}_{\text{fwd}}|\right) = \mathsf{E}\left(|\mathcal{S}|\right)$. For any $Y \in \{0,1\}^b$, define Bernoulli variable I_Y as

$$I_Y = 1 \iff Y \in \mathcal{S}.$$

Note that $I_Y = 0$ whenever $Y \notin \boldsymbol{Z}_1$. We have

$$\begin{aligned}
\mathsf{E}\left(|\mathcal{S}|\right) &= \mathsf{E}\left(\sum_{Y \in \{0,1\}^b} I_Y\right) \\
&= \sum_{Y \in \boldsymbol{Z}_1} \mathsf{E}\left(I_Y\right) \\
&= \sum_{Y \in \boldsymbol{Z}_1} \mathbf{Pr}\left(Y \in \mathcal{S}\right) \\
&\leq \sum_{Y \in \boldsymbol{Z}_1} \frac{2^{c'}}{2^b} \frac{2^{c'}}{2^b - 1} \cdots \frac{2^{b-s}}{2^b - (\ell - 2)} \\
&= \frac{(2^{c'})^{\ell-1} \cdot 2^{b-s}}{[2^b]_{\ell-1}} \\
&\leq 2\frac{(2^{c'})^{\ell-1} \cdot 2^{b-s}}{(2^b)^{\ell-1}},
\end{aligned}$$

where the last inequality uses (4). Therefore,

$$\mathsf{E}\left(|\mathcal{S}|\right) \leq 2\frac{2^b}{2^n}. \tag{17}$$

Finally, from (16) and (17), we thus obtain

$$\mathbf{Pr}\left(\mathsf{BADFWD}(\mathcal{Q})\right) \leq \frac{4q}{2^n}, \tag{18}$$

which completes the proof. □

Lemma 3. *We have*

$$\mathbf{Pr}\left(\mathsf{BADINV}(\mathcal{Q})\right) \leq \frac{4\ell q}{2^{n-r'}}. \tag{19}$$

Proof (Proof of Lemma 3). We first note that if $\ell = 1$, $|\mathcal{S}_{\text{inv}}| = 2^{c'} \leq 2^{b-n}$, and the result will be meaningless as $\mathsf{BADINV}(\mathcal{Q})$ can be set with probability 1. We will henceforth focus on the case $\ell \geq 2$.

Similar to the proof of Lemma 2, by basic probability we obtain

$$\mathbf{Pr}\left(\mathsf{BADINV}(\mathcal{Q})\right) = \sum_{y=1}^{2^{c'}} \mathbf{Pr}\left(\mathsf{BADINV}(\mathcal{Q}) \mid |\mathcal{S}_{\text{inv}}| = \ell y\right) \cdot \mathbf{Pr}\left(|\mathcal{S}_{\text{inv}}| = \ell y\right), \tag{20}$$

where we used that $\mathcal{S}_{\text{inv}}$ is a multiset with a size multiple of ℓ. We start by investigating the conditioned $\mathsf{BADINV}(\mathcal{Q})$ event for any $y = 1, \ldots, 2^{c'}$, which is more involved than $\mathsf{BADFWD}(\mathcal{Q})$ studied in Lemma 2. Because of the condition $|\mathcal{S}_{\text{inv}}| = \ell y$, there are y paths $Y_1 \to \cdots \to Y_\ell$ with $Y_i \in \boldsymbol{Z}_i$ for $i = 1, \ldots, \ell$. The adversary wins if it ever queries a value that is on any of these paths. Note that this is different from the proof of Lemma 2, where the adversary had to guess any starting point of a path. In the current setting, the attacker learns additional information of failed attempts. For example, suppose that $Z_1 \neq Z_2$ and the adversary makes a forward query $\mathcal{P}(X) = Y$, where $X \in \boldsymbol{Z}_1$ and $Y \in \boldsymbol{Z}_2$ but which does *not* set $\mathsf{BADINV}(\mathcal{Q})$. As it does not set $\mathsf{BADINV}(\mathcal{Q})$, the adversary knows that querying $\mathcal{P}(Y)$ (i.e., guessing $Y \in \boldsymbol{Z}_2$ as candidate value for a chain) is fruitless.

To simplify our reasoning, we will be more generous to the adversary, and for each query input X that the adversary makes, it receives both the forward evaluation $\mathcal{P}(X)$ and the inverse evaluation $\mathcal{P}^{-1}(X)$. Stated differently, for the current game the query direction does not matter, and for each attempt X it learns $\mathcal{P}^{-1}(X) \to X \to \mathcal{P}(X)$. The adversary wins if this is a proper subpath of any of the y target paths $X_1 \to Y_1 \to \cdots \to Y_\ell \to Y_{\ell+1}$, where $X_1 = \mathcal{P}^{-1}(Y_1)$ and $Y_{\ell+1} = \mathcal{P}(Y_\ell)$.[1]

A visualization of this game is given in Fig. 2 for $\ell = 4$. For this example, recall that for $i = 1, 2, 3$, $\boldsymbol{Z}_i$ consists of all values $Y \in \{0,1\}^b$ such that $\text{outer}_{r'}(Y) = Z_i$, and that $\boldsymbol{Z}_4$ consists of all values $Y \in \{0,1\}^b$ such that $\text{outer}_s(Y) = Z_4$. By

[1] The usage of parameter X_1 in this path, as opposed to Y_0, appears illogical at first sight, but fits the parameter definitions as outlined in Fig. 1.

the conditioned event, there exist y paths through the sets $\boldsymbol{Z}_1, \ldots, \boldsymbol{Z}_4$. In the example, $y = 2$, hence there are two such paths. The adversary sets $\mathsf{BADINV}(\mathcal{Q})$ if and only if it ever queries one of the *at most* ℓy nodes on these lines (not including the ones on the outer shores $\{0,1\}^b$). It is noteworthy that these paths are disjoint: they never cross the same node in the same shore.

Now, suppose the adversary makes a query X, it thus results in a path $\mathcal{P}^{-1}(X) \to X \to \mathcal{P}(X)$. The query is considered a failed query if it is not a proper subpath of any of the y paths. In particular, a failed query either does not intersect with any of the y paths, *or* it intersects with one of the y paths at their very ends. In other words, a query is considered a failed one for path $X_1 \to Y_1 \to \cdots \to Y_\ell \to Y_{\ell+1}$ if and only if it intersects with either of $\varnothing, X_1, X_1 \to Y_1, Y_\ell \to Y_{\ell+1}, Y_\ell$, as illustrated in Fig. 2 (up to symmetry). Any other intersection of the failed query result with the path is impossible, as e.g., depicted in Fig. 2, due to the fact that $\mathcal{P}$ is a permutation.

We remark that for $0 \leq i < j \leq \ell + 1$, a query can be successful for one target path at position i, and failed for another target path at position j at the same time. In this case, the adversary is nevertheless successful. From this, we can conclude that any query attempt either is successful or it eliminates at most 3 possible values from further guessing.

In summary, to win, the adversary must make a query in $\mathcal{S}_{\text{inv}}$. This set is of size at most ℓy and is a subset of the set $\bigcup_{i=1}^{\ell} \boldsymbol{Z}_i$ of size at least $2^{c'}$.[2] Since one query eliminates at most 3 candidates and this is the only information available for the adversary, after $i-1$ unsuccessful attempts, the ith attempt succeeds with probability at most $\frac{\ell y}{2^{c'}-3(i-1)}$. Thus, defining $\mathsf{BADINV}(\mathcal{Q}_0) := \bot$,

$$
\begin{aligned}
&\mathbf{Pr}\left(\mathsf{BADINV}(\mathcal{Q}) \mid |\mathcal{S}_{\text{inv}}| = \ell y\right) \\
&\qquad = \sum_{i=1}^{q} \mathbf{Pr}\left(\mathsf{BADINV}(\mathcal{Q}_i) \mid |\mathcal{S}_{\text{inv}}| = \ell y \wedge \neg\mathsf{BADINV}(\mathcal{Q}_{i-1})\right) \\
&\qquad \leq \sum_{i=1}^{q} \frac{\ell y}{2^{c'} - 3(i-1)} \leq \frac{\ell y q}{2^{c'} - 3q} \leq 2\frac{\ell y q}{2^{c'}}, \qquad (21)
\end{aligned}
$$

where in the last inequality, we used $q \leq 2^{c'-1}/3$.

Now, it remains to plug the bound into (20). We can copy the analysis of Lemma 2 verbatim and obtain

$$
\begin{aligned}
\mathbf{Pr}\left(\mathsf{BADINV}(\mathcal{Q})\right) &\leq 2\frac{q}{2^{c'}} \sum_{y=1}^{2^{c'}} \ell y \cdot \mathbf{Pr}\left(|\mathcal{S}_{\text{inv}}| = \ell y\right) \\
&\leq 2\frac{q}{2^{c'}} \mathsf{E}\left(|\mathcal{S}_{\text{inv}}|\right) \\
&\leq \frac{4\ell q}{2^{n-r'}}, \qquad (22)
\end{aligned}
$$

[2] Note that this correctly captures the case $i = \ell$, as $|\boldsymbol{Z}_\ell| = 2^{n-s} \geq 2^{c'}$.

where the last inequality uses $|\mathcal{S}_{\text{inv}}| = \ell|\mathcal{S}|$ and (17). This completes the proof. $\square$

Remark 2. In the proof of Lemma 3, we bounded the probability that the ith query is successful by $\frac{y}{2^{c'}-3(i-1)}$. There is a small loss in this bound due to various simplifications we had to make. First note that as we provide the adversary both directions of the queries, we slightly increase its knowledge and thus success probability. In addition, each query attempt X has its leftmost r' bits $\text{outer}_{r'}(X)$ fixed, and the adversary thus commits itself to the value Z_i and thus to the position in Fig. 2 the query could occur. However, there is no way to make use of this property, as in the general case, the values $Z_1, \ldots, Z_\ell$ may be equal and the query can nevertheless occur at multiple positions. Finally, in the specific case where some values Z_i are mutually equal, this basically reduces the set of candidates to be in $\mathcal{S}$, thus also the set of possibly successful values, and possibly also the amount of information the adversary learns from a failed attempt.

4.4 Conclusion

From (11), Lemma 1, Lemma 2, and Lemma 3, we obtain

$$\mathbf{Pr}\left(\mathsf{PRE}(\mathcal{Q})\right) \leq \frac{4q}{2^n} + \min\left\{\frac{4\ell q}{2^{n-r'}}, \frac{q(q+1)}{2^c}\right\}, \tag{23}$$

and this completes the proof of Theorem 1.

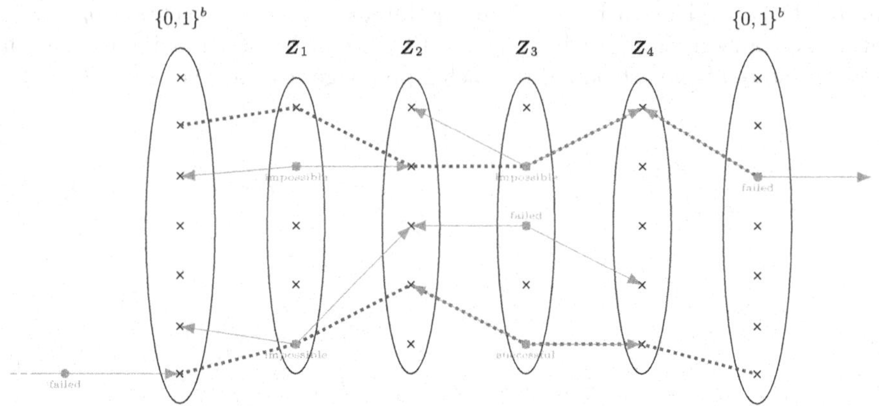

Fig. 2. Illustration of the conditioned $\mathsf{BADINV}(\mathcal{Q})$ event for $\ell = 4$ and $y = 2$. To win, the adversary must guess any node from $\bigcup_{i=1}^{4} \boldsymbol{Z}_i$ on any of the $y = 2$ dotted blue paths. A query attempt X is successful if and only if $\mathcal{P}^{-1}(X) \to X \to \mathcal{P}(X)$ (depicted solid red) is a proper subpath of any of the blue lines. As $\mathcal{P}$ is a permutation, a failed query attempt is either non-overlapping with any of the dotted blue paths, or it may partially overlap only at the ends of a blue line, the other cases are impossible and illustrated as such. (Color figure online)

5 Conclusion

In this section, we compare our result with the state-of-the-art bound of (5) (Sect. 3.1) and the best existing attack. Recall that in Theorem 1, we obtained the following bound:

$$\mathbf{Adv}_{\mathcal{H}}^{\mathrm{epre}}(q) \leq \frac{4q}{2^n} + \min\left\{\frac{4\ell q}{2^{n-r'}}, \frac{q(q+1)}{2^c}\right\}.$$

If $\ell = 1$, our security bound matches the state-of-the-art bound up to a factor of 4, while if $\ell > 1$, our bound improves the existing state of the art significantly. In both cases, the bound matches the best known attack outlined in Sect. 3.2 (up to constant). In the following, we show the improvement with the parameters used in the modes Ascon-Hash [17] and Spongent [12].

First consider the Ascon-Hash mode with parameters $(b, c, r, r', n) = (320, 256, 64, 64, 256)$. In this case, $\ell = n/r' = 4$. In Fig. 3, we compare the state-of-the-art bound of Sect. 3.1, our new bound of (6), and the best known attack of Sect. 3.2. We observe that our new bound *significantly* improves the state-of-the-art bound starting at a very low value of q. In detail, the adversarial advantage is approximately 1.5×10^{-36} for $q \approx 2^{69}$ at the intersection point as shown in Fig. 3b, i.e., at the point where the old bound starts to degenerate but our new bound stays low.

It is also interesting to consider the largest mode of Spongent, i.e., with parameters $(b, c, r, r', n) = (272, 256, 16, 16, 256)$. It has a small rate, and consequently a high value $\ell = n/r = 16$, but the same capacity and output size as the ones of Ascon-Hash. A comparison of the old bound, new bound, and best known attack is given in Fig. 4. Here, the intersection point occurs at $q \approx 2^{23}$, with an advantage of approximately 3×10^{-64}. Our bound thus improves even more the state-of-the-art bound to reach a preimage resistance close to 240 bits.

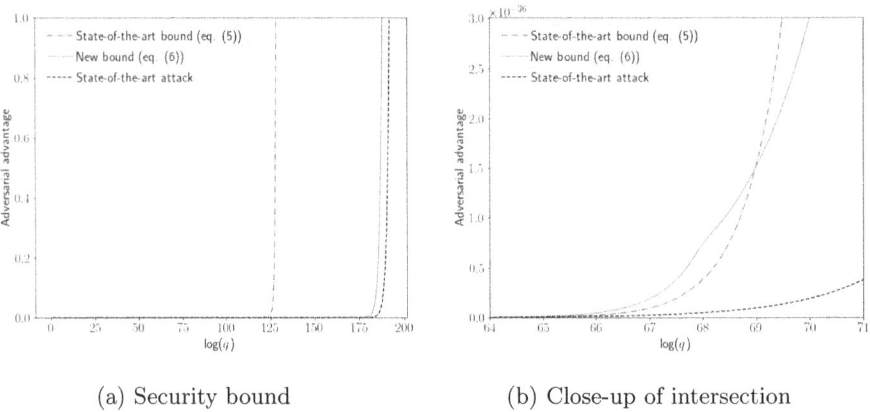

(a) Security bound (b) Close-up of intersection

Fig. 3. Comparison of the state-of-the-art security bound, new security bound, and best known attack for the Ascon-Hash mode with parameters $(b, c, r, r', n) = (320, 256, 64, 64, 256)$.

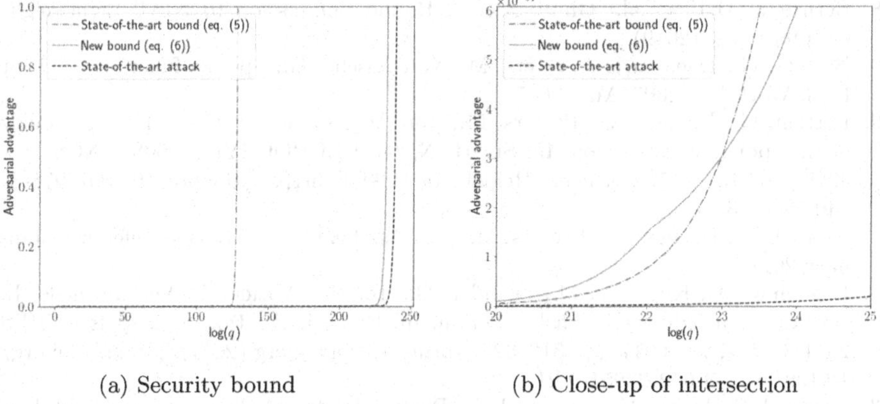

(a) Security bound (b) Close-up of intersection

Fig. 4. Comparison of the state-of-the-art security bound, new security bound, and best known attack for the Spongent mode with parameters $(b, c, r, r', n) = (272, 256, 16, 16, 256)$.

Acknowledgements. We would like to thank the anonymous reviewers for their valuable comments, and in particular the reviewer that proposed a fix to the square root loss that was present in an earlier version of the proof. Charlotte Lefevre is supported by the Netherlands Organisation for Scientific Research (NWO) under grant OCENW.KLEIN.435. Bart Mennink is supported by the Netherlands Organisation for Scientific Research (NWO) under grant VI.Vidi.203.099.

References

1. Aagaard, M., AlTawy, R., Gong, G., Mandal, K., Rohit, R.: ACE: an authenticated encryption and hash algorithm. Second Round Submission to NIST Lightweight Cryptography (2019)
2. Andreeva, E., Mennink, B., Preneel, B.: Security reductions of the second round SHA-3 candidates. In: Burmester, M., Tsudik, G., Magliveras, S., Ilić, I. (eds.) ISC 2010. LNCS, vol. 6531, pp. 39–53. Springer, Heidelberg (2011). https://doi.org/10.1007/978-3-642-18178-8_5
3. Aumasson, J.-P., Henzen, L., Meier, W., Naya-Plasencia, M.: Quark: a lightweight hash. In: Mangard, S., Standaert, F.-X. (eds.) CHES 2010. LNCS, vol. 6225, pp. 1–15. Springer, Heidelberg (2010). https://doi.org/10.1007/978-3-642-15031-9_1
4. Bao, Z., Chakraborti, A., Datta, N., Guo, J., Nandi, M., Peyrin, T., Yasuda, K.: PHOTON-Beetle. Final Round Submission to NIST Lightweight Cryptography (2019)
5. Beierle, C., et al.: Schwaemm and Esch: lightweight authenticated encryption and hashing using the sparkle permutation family. Final Round Submission to NIST Lightweight Cryptography (2019)
6. Beierle, C., et al.: SKINNY-AEAD and SKINNY-Hash v1.1. Second Round Submission to NIST Lightweight Cryptography (2019)
7. Bernstein, D.J.: CubeHash specification (2.B.1). Second Round Submission to NIST SHA-3 Competition (2009)

8. Bernstein, D.J., et al.: Gimli. Second Round Submission to NIST Lightweight Cryptography (2019)
9. Bertoni, G., Daemen, J., Peeters, M., Van Assche, G.: Sponge functions. Ecrypt Hash Workshop 2007, May 2007
10. Bertoni, G., Daemen, J., Peeters, M., Van Assche, G.: On the indifferentiability of the sponge construction. In: Smart, N. (ed.) EUROCRYPT 2008. LNCS, vol. 4965, pp. 181–197. Springer, Heidelberg (2008). https://doi.org/10.1007/978-3-540-78967-3_11
11. Bertoni, G., Daemen, J., Peeters, M., Van Assche, G.: The Keccak reference, January 2011
12. Bogdanov, A., Knežević, M., Leander, G., Toz, D., Varıcı, K., Verbauwhede, I.: SPONGENT: a lightweight hash function. In: Preneel, B., Takagi, T. (eds.) CHES 2011. LNCS, vol. 6917, pp. 312–325. Springer, Heidelberg (2011). https://doi.org/10.1007/978-3-642-23951-9_21
13. Coron, J.-S., Dodis, Y., Malinaud, C., Puniya, P.: Merkle-Damgård revisited: how to construct a hash function. In: Shoup, V. (ed.) CRYPTO 2005. LNCS, vol. 3621, pp. 430–448. Springer, Heidelberg (2005). https://doi.org/10.1007/11535218_26
14. Daemen, J., Hoffert, S., Peeters, M., Van Assche, G., Van Keer, R.: Xoodyak, a lightweight cryptographic scheme. Final Round Submission to NIST Lightweight Cryptography (2019)
15. Daemen, J., Massolino, P., Rotella, Y.: The Subterranean 2.0 cipher suite. Second Round Submission to NIST Lightweight Cryptography (2019)
16. Dobraunig, C., et al.: ISAP v2. Final Round Submission to NIST Lightweight Cryptography (2019)
17. Dobraunig, C., Eichlseder, M., Mendel, F., Schläffer, M.: Ascon v1.2. Final Round Submission to NIST Lightweight Cryptography (2019)
18. Guo, J., Peyrin, T., Poschmann, A.: The PHOTON family of lightweight hash functions. In: Rogaway, P. (ed.) CRYPTO 2011. LNCS, vol. 6841, pp. 222–239. Springer, Heidelberg (2011). https://doi.org/10.1007/978-3-642-22792-9_13
19. Knudsen, L.R., Rechberger, C., Thomsen, S.S.: The Grindahl hash functions. In: Biryukov, A. (ed.) FSE 2007. LNCS, vol. 4593, pp. 39–57. Springer, Heidelberg (2007). https://doi.org/10.1007/978-3-540-74619-5_3
20. Maurer, U., Renner, R., Holenstein, C.: Indifferentiability, impossibility results on reductions, and applications to the random oracle methodology. In: Naor, M. (ed.) TCC 2004. LNCS, vol. 2951, pp. 21–39. Springer, Heidelberg (2004). https://doi.org/10.1007/978-3-540-24638-1_2
21. Naito, Y., Ohta, K.: Improved indifferentiable security analysis of PHOTON. In: Abdalla, M., De Prisco, R. (eds.) SCN 2014. LNCS, vol. 8642, pp. 340–357. Springer, Cham (2014). https://doi.org/10.1007/978-3-319-10879-7_20
22. National Institute of Standards and Technology: FIPS PUB 202: SHA-3 Standard: Permutation-Based Hash and Extendable-Output Functions, August 2015. http://nvlpubs.nist.gov/nistpubs/FIPS/NIST.FIPS.202.pdf
23. NIST: Lightweight Cryptography, February 2019. https://csrc.nist.gov/Projects/Lightweight-Cryptography
24. Rogaway, P., Shrimpton, T.: Cryptographic hash-function basics: definitions, implications, and separations for preimage resistance, second-preimage resistance, and collision resistance. In: Roy, B., Meier, W. (eds.) FSE 2004. LNCS, vol. 3017, pp. 371–388. Springer, Heidelberg (2004). https://doi.org/10.1007/978-3-540-25937-4_24
25. Zhang, W., et al.: KNOT: algorithm specifications and supporting document. Second Round Submission to NIST Lightweight Cryptography (2019)

Block-Cipher-Based Tree Hashing

Aldo Gunsing(✉)

Digital Security Group, Radboud University, Nijmegen, The Netherlands
aldo.gunsing@ru.nl

Abstract. First of all we take a thorough look at an error in a paper by Daemen et al. (ToSC 2018) which looks at minimal requirements for tree-based hashing based on multiple primitives, including block ciphers. This reveals that the error is more fundamental than previously shown by Gunsing et al. (ToSC 2020), which is mainly interested in its effect on the security bounds. It turns out that the cause for the error is due to an essential oversight in the interaction between the different oracles used in the indifferentiability proofs. In essence, it reduces the claim from the normal indifferentiability setting to the weaker sequential indifferentiability one. As a matter of fact, this error appeared in multiple earlier indifferentiability papers, including the optimal indifferentiability of the sum of permutations (EUROCRYPT 2018) and the recent ABR$^+$ construction (EUROCRYPT 2021). We discuss in detail how this oversight is caused and how it can be avoided.

We next demonstrate how the negative effects on the security bound of the construction by Daemen et al. can be resolved. Instead of only allowing a truncated output, we generalize the construction to allow for *any* finalization function and investigate the security of this for five different types of finalization. Our findings, among others, show that the security of the SHA-2 mode does not degrade if the feed-forward is dropped and that the modern BLAKE3 construction is secure in principle but that its use of the extendable output requires its counter used for random access to be public. Finally, we introduce the tree sponge, a generalization of the sequential sponge construction with parallel absorbing and squeezing.

Keywords: Hash Functions · Block Ciphers · Tree Hashing · Indifferentiability

1 Introduction

1.1 Hash Functions

Hash functions, which are functions $H : \{0,1\}^* \to \{0,1\}^n$ that compress an arbitrarily-sized message M to a fixed sized output h, form a fundamental part of many cryptographic constructions. In practice they are not built directly, but from a smaller compression function that only takes a fixed sized input, for example $f : \{0,1\}^{2n} \to \{0,1\}^n$. A popular and simple method for this is the Merkle-Damgård construction [Mer89, Dam89], which uses a fixed-sized compression function in a sequential manner to obtain the hash digest. This construction

Y. Dodis and T. Shrimpton (Eds.): CRYPTO 2022, LNCS 13510, pp. 205–233, 2022.
https://doi.org/10.1007/978-3-031-15985-5_8

is sometimes 'strengthened' by appending an encoding of the length of the message to the end, giving a collision resistant hash function as long as the internal compression function is collision resistant, a fact proven by Merkle and Damgård independently.

However, it turned out that collision resistance is not strong enough for some situations. For example, strengthened Merkle-Damgård is susceptible to another attack, called the length extension attack: given the hash digest $H(M)$ of a message M and its length $|M|$ it is possible to compute $H(\text{pad}(M) \parallel M')$ for any M', without knowing the original message M. This is possible as the digest $H(M)$ leaks the internal state of the hash function when the blocks of $\text{pad}(M)$ are processed. By using this state as the initial value, it is straightforward to compute $H(\text{pad}(M) \parallel M')$ for any M'. This is especially troublesome when the function is used in the keyed fashion as $H(K \parallel M)$, noting it should be possible to build a MAC in this way, as the output of the hash should be unpredictable when K is unknown. The attack above shows that this construction is insecure when the hash function is instantiated with (strengthened) Merkle-Damgård, even when the internal compression function is secure. A remedy for this is the HMAC construction [KBC97,Bel06], but this is less efficient and unsatisfying.

This weakness asks for a more sophisticated security analysis for hash functions, namely one that guarantees that the hash function behaves like a random oracle, which gives an randomly generated and independent output for every input. The most general security notion we have is the one of indifferentiability introduced by Maurer et al. [MRH04], which is further applied to hash functions by Coron et al. [CDMP05].

1.2 Previous Work

Using this stronger security notion of indifferentiability, multiple constructions have been shown indifferentiable. For example, prefix-free Merkle-Damgård [CDMP05,LGD+09,LLG11] and Merkle-Damgård with truncation [CDMP05, CN08,LGD+09,LLG11] have been shown indifferentiable, all assuming that the underlying compression function is an ideal compression function. However, this is a very strong and unrealistic assumption: most constructions use a block-cipher-based design with commonly the Davies-Meyer transformation [PGV93] on top. This transformation defines the compression function $f : \{0,1\}^\kappa \times \{0,1\}^b \to \{0,1\}^b$ as $f(k,x) = \mathcal{E}_k(x) \oplus x$ for a block cipher $\mathcal{E} : \{0,1\}^\kappa \times \{0,1\}^b \to \{0,1\}^b$. This transformation does make it hard to find collisions or an inverse, but it is not indifferentiable from an ideal compression function and has some undesirable properties. For example, the computation of $\mathcal{E}_k^{-1}(0^b) = x$ for an arbitrary $k \in \{0,1\}^\kappa$ immediately gives a fixed point x where $f(k,x) = \mathcal{E}_k(x) \oplus x = 0^b \oplus x = x$, while finding such fixed point is very difficult for an ideal compression function. This means that one cannot directly use this compression function in a construction that expects an ideal compression function; additional analysis is required. In short, we cannot use constructions based on an ideal compression function to argue security of block-cipher-based constructions.

There have been some constructions shown to be indifferentiable from an ideal compression function [Men13, LMN16, GBK16], but these are very complex and inefficient. There is some work that have dedicated analysis of block-cipher-based constructions: for example, prefix-free Merkle-Damgård with Davies-Meyer [CLNY06, GLC08] or Merkle-Damgård with Davies-Meyer with truncation [GLC08], etc. Another approach for creating a hash function is by processing the message in parallel by using a tree hash, a direction looked at by for example Dodis et al. [DRRS09], where an ideal compression function is used as a primitive. They also show that one can use a truncated permutation to create a compression function that is indifferentiable from a random function, which is later improved upon [CLL19], however, this gives an unoptimized construction and inferior security bounds as the abstraction to an ideal compression function requires extra overhead.

The most promising work for this approach was by Daemen et al. [DMA18] who looked at general tree hashing based on, among others, block ciphers. This paper defined very general properties that a tree hash should satisfy in order to be indifferentiable from a random oracle. Importantly, it supposedly proved that truncation nor a feed-forward is not one of the required properties. However, Samuel Neves pointed out a critical error in the paper indicating that truncation should be required, which was also the formal fix used in the errata by Gunsing et al. [GDM20]. This still leaves us with an unsatisfactory situation as truncation is not always a desirable option when the size of the block cipher is small.

1.3 Our Contribution

1.3.1 Identification of the Flaw

In Sect. 3 we will discuss the nature of the error in more depth. It turns out that there is more to the error than the superficial correction of the bound in [GDM20] indicates. The original paper implicitly ignores some fundamental interaction between the primitive and construction oracles that appear in the definition of indifferentiability as they, after a transformation, incorrectly discard all queries made to the construction oracle. This can only be done when the construction queries are made after the primitive ones. In essence, one could reinterpret the proof to happen in the weaker sequential indifferentiability setting [MPS12] where all primitive queries happen before the construction queries, making this reasoning valid. The same reasoning error occurs in other papers as well [CN08, MPN10, MP15, Lee17, BN18, ABR21]. One [CN08] is about hash functions as well, but it does not make use of any invalid properties, which means that the bounds are not influenced at all and that the proof could be fixed in a straightforward manner. Most other ones [MPN10, MP15, Lee17, BN18] are about the indifferentiability of the sum of permutations and are all based on [MPN10] which contains the same error and the other papers copy the same faulty reasoning. At least the proof of the most recent work [BN18], claiming optimal indifferentiability of the sum of permutations, is significantly impacted. More recent work with the ABR^+ construction [ABR21] also contains the same error, although it should not influence its result.

1.3.2 Block-Cipher-Based Tree Hashing with General Finalization

We improve the state of the art by generalizing the the construction of Daemen et al. [DMA18], which only considers a truncated output. We generalize the construction to allow for *any* finalization function and analyze the security of this for five different types of finalization. These constructions and their security properties are summarized in Table 1. Section 4 contains the full security bounds.

Normal Truncation. First of all we re-prove the same construction as in [DMA18] but with more care where we take the error into account. This proves that the original properties are indeed sufficient when truncation is properly account for, as is also shown in the fixed version. Additionally, we generalize some properties slightly, allowing for a more flexible length of the initial value and digest size.

Truncation Without Subtree-Freeness. The most natural way to prevent the length extension attack is by requiring subtree-freeness, where the result of a hash can never be part of another hash. However, in order to prevent this situation, the mode has to use extra bits to mark, for example, the final node. This introduces extra overhead compared to a simpler mode. A different solution is to require more truncation, which was already done previously for the Merkle-Damgård mode specifically. We generalize this solution to tree hashes. It turns out that one can drop the subtree-freeness property by truncating to an even smaller digest, where the exact cost depends on the specific mode. In Sect. 5.1 we use this to prove the security of the mode used in truncated SHA-2 [SHA08], *without requiring any feed-forward.* This is a significant efficiency improvement, as SHA-2 uses a feed-forward in every compression call.

Chopping. Thirdly we look at chopping instead of truncating. Truncation keeps the first few bits of a string and drops the other bits, while chopping does the inverse: it drops the first few bits and keeps the remaining ones. At a first glance this should not make a difference, as the operations are symmetrical. However, as in our definition of tree hashes we assume that the chaining values are always the result of truncated outputs, it turns out that chopping the final value instead of truncating gives a superior security bound. It essentially voids the stronger requirement with respect to the digest size that the previous mode lost. In short, by using chopping as the finalization instead of truncation, we can drop the subtree-freeness requirement without compromising any security. In Sect. 5.3 we introduce the tree sponge, a generalization of the sponge construction allowing for parallel absorbing and squeezing, making full use of this result.

Enveloped. Fourthly we look at a generalized enveloped mode. This mode uses a fixed value in the data path of the final compression call, generalizing the Enveloped Merkle-Damgård construction [BR06]. Compared to normal Merkle-Damgård this switches the position of the chaining value from the data input to the key input. This simple change allows for a secure mode that does not require much overhead. We show that this approach generalizes from the sequential Merkle-Damgård mode to general tree-based hashes.

Feed-Forward. Fifthly we look at a feed-forward. We show that by having a feed-forward in the final compression call we do not need any truncation. The conventional approach, which has also been adopted in SHA-2, is that all compression calls use a feed-forward. However, we show that only the final one is required. More importantly, its use does not negate other conditions. For example, subtree-freeness is still required, which is not satisfied in SHA-2 and truncation is still required. In Sect. 5.2 we use this to analyze the security of the mode used in BLAKE3 [OANW20] when based on a block cipher. We show that the mode is secure in principle, but there is a non-negligible factor in the complexity of the simulator. As a consequence, the extendable output mode becomes insecure when a secret value is used for its offset.

Table 1. Summary of the indifferentiability bounds. The conditions MD, LA, RD, SF and FA stand for message-decodability, leaf-anchoring, radical-decodability, subtree-freeness and final-anchoring, respectively. The bits of security are with respect to the number of primitive queries either direct or indirect, where constant and logarithmic terms are ignored. b is the length of the data input of the block cipher, $c \leqslant b$ the capacity of the chaining values, $n \leqslant b$ the digest length and $m \leqslant c$ the length of IV_1 which is used for leaf-anchoring. For the finalization, x denotes the data input to the final block cipher call and y the output. The notations $\lfloor y \rfloor_n$ and $\lceil y \rceil_n$ denote truncation and chopping respectively (i.e. $x = \lfloor x \rfloor_n \parallel \lceil x \rceil_{|x|-n}$ for all n). Note that all chaining values are truncated block cipher outputs, hence the asymmetry between truncation and chopping. For the enveloped and feed-forward modes there is no truncation or similar hence $n = b$. The proofs are in the full version [Gun22].

mode	MD+LA+RD	SF	FA	finalization	bits of security
truncation	✓	✓	—	$\lfloor y \rfloor_n$	$\min(m, c/2, b-n)$
	✓	—	—	$\lfloor y \rfloor_n$	$\min(m, c/2, c-n)$
chopping	✓	—	—	$\lceil y \rceil_n$	$\min(m, c/2, b-n)$
enveloped	✓	✓	full	y	$\min(m, c/2)$
feed-forward	✓	✓	partial	$x \oplus y$	$\min(m, c/2)$

1.3.3 Comparison of the Variants

The different modes above all come with different trade-offs:

- Truncation/Chopping is useful when the block length b is sufficiently large. This is often the case for permutations (which is simply the special case $\kappa = 0$) or large block ciphers. The results show that chopping is basically superior to truncation, when the chaining values are constructed using truncation. If this is the other way around the same result holds by symmetry. The important observation is that dropping a different part of the output in the finalization compared to the internal chaining values is superior to doing the same operation twice. This is shown by the fact that an extra condition in the form of subtree-freeness can be dropped, or that the efficiency can be significantly improved: the change in the security term from $c - n$ to $b - n$ allows for a larger n with the same security level.

- If a large block size is not available, the enveloped mode is useful. This mode does not have any extra security terms and can achieve $b/2$ bits of security. The biggest disadvantage is that it requires one full extra block cipher call.
- The feed-forward mode is commonly used, but it does not reduce the required conditions compared to the other finalizations. For example, radical-decodability and subtree-freeness are still necessary. Its advantage compared to the enveloped mode is that it only requires partial final-anchoring, making it possible to process a larger message block in the final compression call, increasing its efficiency slightly.

2 Preliminaries

2.1 Notation

Our setup is in the ideal model and we denote $\mathcal{E} : \{0,1\}^\kappa \times \{0,1\}^b \to \{0,1\}^b$ for an ideal cipher with key length κ and block length b that is uniformly drawn from the set of all such block ciphers. For a bit string x of size at least n bits, we denote $\lfloor x \rfloor_n$ for the first n bits of x (truncation) and $\lceil x \rceil_n$ for the last n bits of x (chopping). Note that for any such x we have that $x = \lfloor x \rfloor_n \parallel \lceil x \rceil_{|x|-n}$, where $|x|$ denotes the length of a string x in bits and $\cdot \| \cdot$ concatenation. The uniform random drawing of an element x from a finite set X is denoted by $x \xleftarrow{\$} X$. We denote $n \leqslant b$ for the digest length, $c \leqslant b$ for the capacity, which is the size of the chaining values, and $m \leqslant c$ for the length of IV_1 which will be used for leaf-anchoring.

2.2 Tree Hashing

We follow the same tree hashing paradigm as in [DMA18], but specialized for block ciphers and with some small generalizations.

For our definition we use an explicit intermediate step of template generation in order to be able to reason about the hashing mode. It will consist of three steps: template construction, template execution and a finalization.

A block-cipher-based tree hashing mode $\mathcal{T} = (\mathcal{Z}, \zeta)$ consists of a template generating function $\mathcal{Z} : \mathbb{N} \times \mathcal{A} \to \mathcal{X}$ and a finalization function $\zeta : \{0,1\}^b \times \{0,1\}^b \to \{0,1\}^n$. Here, $\mathcal{A}$ is a set of parameters chosen by the mode and $\mathcal{X}$ is the set consisting of all possible templates and is independent of the mode. The resulting hash function $\mathcal{H}_\mathcal{T}[\mathcal{E}] : \{0,1\}^* \times \mathcal{A} \to \{0,1\}^n$ is based on an ideal cipher $\mathcal{E}$ and computes the hash digest of a message $M \in \{0,1\}^*$ with parameters $A \in \mathcal{A}$ in multiple steps:

- First it computes the tree template $Z = \mathcal{Z}(|M|, A)$ based on the message length $|M|$ and the parameters A. This step is elaborated on in Sect. 2.2.1.

- Then it executes the template based on an ideal cipher $\mathcal{E}$ to get the in- and output of the final node $(x, y) = \mathcal{Y}[\mathcal{E}](M, Z)$, with $\mathcal{Y}[\mathcal{E}] : \{0,1\}^* \times \mathcal{X} \to \{0,1\}^b \times \{0,1\}^b$. This function is the same for all modes and is elaborated on in Sect. 2.2.2.
- As the last step it applies the finalization function ζ to the in- and output to get the digest $h = \zeta_x(y)$. If the input x is not used we simply write $\zeta(y)$. This is a generalization compared to [DMA18], where only $\zeta(y) = \lfloor y \rfloor_n$ is considered. The major alternative is the feed-forward defined as $\zeta_x(y) = x \oplus y$. It has to be possible to randomly compute an inverse given some input x and digest h as $y \xleftarrow{\$} \zeta_x^{-1}(h)$.

2.2.1 Template Construction

Based on the message length $\mu \in \mathbb{N}$ and the parameters $A \in \mathcal{A}$ a tree template is constructed. The template consists of a number of block cipher calls called nodes, where the inputs of the block ciphers are already determined as virtual bits. These come in three flavors:

- Frame bits: these are fixed bits that are determined solely on the message length μ and the parameters A. For example, these can be used for domain separation or can encode the length of the message.
- Message pointer bits: these bits reference specific bits in M. For example, a bit can reference the 'fifth bit of M', but this bit is currently unknown.
- Chaining pointer bits: these bits refer to the result of another compression call. We require that all first c bits of every compression call are used exactly once (except the final one which is special) and consecutively, where $c \leqslant b$ is the *capacity*. For example, if c consecutive bits refer to the result of (k, x) it will equal $\lfloor \mathcal{E}_k(x) \rfloor_c$ when instantiated.

There is one special block cipher call whose output is not used in the tree. This is called the *final node* and is denoted by final(S) for an instantiation S. A *leaf node* is a node that does not contain any chaining pointer bits.

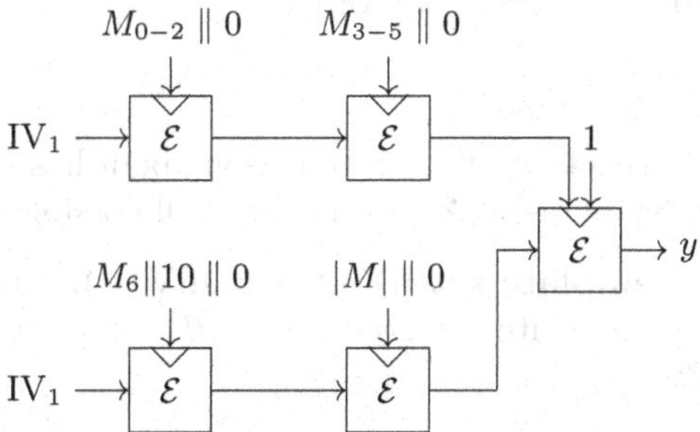

Fig. 1. Basic example of a block-cipher-based tree hashing mode with key size $\kappa = 4$, block size $b = 3$, capacity $c = 3$ and message length $\mu = 7$.

A basic example of a block-cipher-based tree hash is displayed in Fig. 1. The different kind of virtual bits in the example are:

- Frame bits: the two IV_1's, the 10 (padding), the four 0's, the 1 and the encoding of the message length $|M|$.
- Message pointer bits: the three blocks of M_{0-2}, M_{3-5} and M_6.
- Chaining pointer bits: the four outputs of a call to $\mathcal{E}$ that are fed into another block cipher call.

Note that the output of the final node is denoted by y, which is not necessarily the hash digest; there is an additional finalization function ζ applied to get the hash digest. In other words, $h = \zeta_x(y)$, with h the hash digest and x and y the in- and outputs of the final node. Furthermore, it is possible to have a capacity $c < b$, in which case the chaining values are truncated.

2.2.2 Template Execution

The procedure $\mathcal{Y}[\mathcal{E}](M, Z)$ executes the tree template Z on a message M with compatible length to get the hash digest $h \in \{0,1\}^n$. It uses the following procedure:

- It instantiates the template to get the corresponding tree S. This means that all message pointer bits are instantiated with their respective value of M and similarly for all chaining pointer bits, whose values depend on the block cipher $\mathcal{E}$.
- It gets the inputs of the final node $(k, x) = \mathrm{final}(S)$.
- It computes the output of the final node $y = \mathcal{E}_k(x)$.
- It returns the data input and output of the final node (x, y).

The tree S is represented as a list composed of values of the form (k, x, α), each representing one node. k and x are the key and data inputs to the block cipher and α denotes a different location in the tree. This value means that there is a block cipher call of the form $y = \mathcal{E}_k(x)$ and that the output $\lfloor y \rfloor_c$ is used in the position α. The output of the final node is not used in the tree, which is denoted by $\alpha = \perp$. An example is displayed in Table 2.

2.2.3 Definitions

Now we define a few terms that allow us to reason about hashing modes. First of all we define the tree template set $\mathcal{Z}_\mathcal{T}$ as the set of all possible tree templates.

Definition 1 (tree template set [DMA18,BDPV14]). *For a mode of operation $\mathcal{T}$ we define* tree template set $\mathcal{Z}_\mathcal{T} \subseteq \mathcal{X}$ *as the range of the template construction function $\mathcal{Z}$:*

$$\mathcal{Z}_\mathcal{T} = \{\mathcal{Z}(\mu, A) | \mu \in \mathbb{N}, A \in \mathcal{A}\},$$

where μ covers all message lengths and A all parameters.

Next, we define some useful subsets of trees that correspond to the tree templates.

Table 2. List representation of the example mode displayed in Fig. 1. The nodes are numbered **0** to **4**, with the key input denoted by $\mathbf{0}_0^k$ and data input denoted by $\mathbf{0}_0^x$ (for node **0**), where the subscript denotes the offset. The k, x and α denote the key input, the data input and the location the output is used ($\perp$ for the final node), respectively.

node	k	x	α
0	$\mathbf{1}_{0-2} \parallel 1$	$\mathbf{2}_0$	$\perp$
1	$M_{3-5} \parallel 0$	$\mathbf{3}_0$	$\mathbf{0}_0^k$
2	$\lvert M\rvert \parallel 0$	$\mathbf{4}_0$	$\mathbf{0}_0^x$
3	$M_{0-2} \parallel 0$	IV_1	$\mathbf{1}_0^x$
4	$M_6 \Vert 01 \parallel 0$	IV_1	$\mathbf{2}_0^x$

(a) List representation of the template of the example mode.

node	k	x	α
0	1101	101	$\perp$
1	0010	100	$\mathbf{0}_0^k$
2	1110	010	$\mathbf{0}_0^x$
3	0110	000	$\mathbf{1}_0^x$
4	1010	000	$\mathbf{2}_0^x$

(b) List representation of the instantiation of the example mode, with $\mathrm{IV}_1 = 000$, $M = 011\ 001\ 1$ and random block cipher outputs.

Definition 2 ((sub)tree set [DMA18,BDPV14]**).** *We say that a tree S complies with a template Z if it has the same tree topology and the frame bits in Z match those in S.*

For a mode of operation $\mathcal{T}$ we define the following sets:

- *$\mathcal{S}_\mathcal{T}$ is the set of all trees S such that there exists a $Z \in \mathcal{Z}_\mathcal{T}$ such that S complies with Z.*
- *$\mathcal{S}_\mathcal{T}^{\mathrm{sub}}$ is the set of trees S such that there exists a $S' \in \mathcal{S}_\mathcal{T}$ such that S is a proper subtree of S'.*
- *$\mathcal{S}_\mathcal{T}^{\mathrm{leaf}}$ is the subset of trees $S \in \mathcal{S}_\mathcal{T}^{\mathrm{sub}}$ such that there exists a $S' \in \mathcal{S}_\mathcal{T}$ such that S is a proper subtree of S' and S contains all its descendants in S'.*
- *$\mathcal{S}_\mathcal{T}^{\mathrm{final}}$ is the subset of trees $S \in \mathcal{S}_\mathcal{T}^{\mathrm{sub}}$ such that there exists a $S' \in \mathcal{S}_\mathcal{T}$ such that S is a proper subtree of S' and S contains the root node of S'.*

Intuitively, $\mathcal{S}_\mathcal{T}$ denotes the set of all possible trees, $\mathcal{S}_\mathcal{T}^{\mathrm{sub}}$ the set of all their proper subtrees, $\mathcal{S}_\mathcal{T}^{\mathrm{leaf}}$ the set of trees that cannot be extended backwards, i.e. ones that contain all necessary leafs and $\mathcal{S}_\mathcal{T}^{\mathrm{final}}$ the set of proper subtrees that contain the final node. Now we define the notion of a *radical*, which is an essential part of our requirements. Intuitively, a radical identifies bit positions which can only refer to a chaining value, but has no such value associated yet.

Definition 3 (radical [DMA18]**).** *A* radical *α in a tree instance $S \in \mathcal{S}_\mathcal{T}^{\mathrm{sub}}$ identifies c bit positions such that no node is attached to α in S, but in any $S' \in \mathcal{S}_\mathcal{T}$, with S a subtree of S', the value located by α is a chaining value (CV). This value is called the* radical CV *and is denoted as $S[\alpha]$.*

For example, take a Merkle-Damgård mode with the domain separation on the leaf node. That is, all templates are of the form displayed in Fig. 2. Given just the final two nodes (which is $\mathbf{0} : (\mathbf{1}, M_4 \Vert 0, \perp); \mathbf{1} : (x, M_3 \Vert 0, \mathbf{0}^x)$ in the list representation) with arbitrary M_3, M_4 and data input x for the node with key $M_3\|0$, this x will always be a chaining value. Only for leaf nodes the data input is not a chaining value, but we know that this is not a leaf node by the domain separation. This means that this position $(\mathbf{1}^x)$ is a radical.

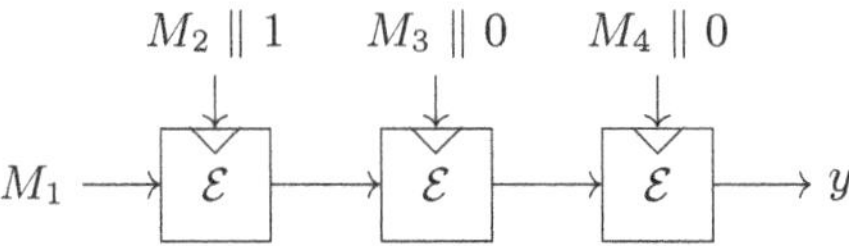

Fig. 2. A Merkle-Damgård mode with leaf-node separation. This means that data inputs are unambiguously either a chaining value or a message block, hence non-leaf subtrees have radicals.

Another example is displayed in Fig. 3. This mode is similar, but with domain separation on the final node instead of the leaf node. However, this does mean that the similar final two nodes as before (which is $\mathbf{0} : (\mathbf{1}, M_4\|1, \bot); \mathbf{1} : (x, M_3\|0, \mathbf{0}^x)$ in the list representation) with arbitrary M_3, M_4 and data input x for the node with key $M_3\|0$ do not have a radical. The data input x could be a chaining value, but it could also represent a message block, in which case the message would be $x\|M_3\|M_4$. As the role of this x is ambiguous its position $(\mathbf{1}^x)$ is not a radical, nor is any other position.

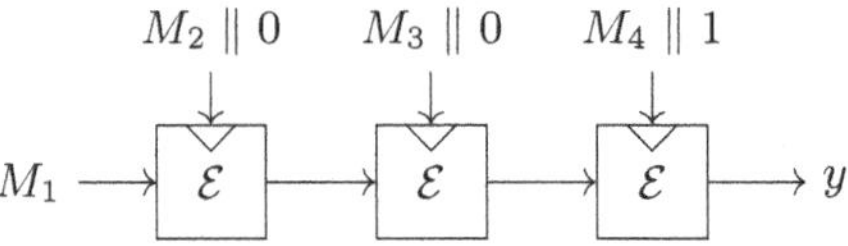

Fig. 3. A Merkle-Damgård mode with final-node separation. This means that data inputs are ambiguous and no radicals exist.

2.2.4 Conditions

We look at the conditions that a tree hashing mode has to satisfy in order to be secure. Message-decodability states that a message can be successfully extracted from a full tree, leaf-anchoring requires the first few bits of every node to either denote a fixed value or a chaining value and radical-decodability states that the previously defined radicals can efficiently be identified from chosen set $\mathcal{S}_T^{\mathrm{rad}}$. In general, message-decodability is trivially satisfied and leaf-anchoring is a straightforward property. Radical-decodability is a more tricky definition and sometimes requires more work to show.

Definition 4 (message-decodability [DMA18]**).** *A mode of operation $\mathcal{T}$ is* message-decodable *if there is an efficient function* extract() *that on input of $S \in \mathcal{S}_\mathcal{T}$ returns the template Z it complies with and the message M, and on input of $S \notin \mathcal{S}_\mathcal{T}$ returns $\perp$.*

Definition 5 (leaf-anchoring [DMA18]**).** *A mode of operation $\mathcal{T}$ is* leaf-anchored *if for every template $Z \in \mathcal{Z}_\mathcal{T}$, the first $m \leqslant c$ of every leaf node encode* $\mathrm{IV}_1 \in \{0,1\}^m$ *as frame bits and the first c bits of every non-leaf node are chaining pointer bits.*

Definition 5 is a minor generalization of the original definition in [DMA18] as it allows for a more flexible length of IV_1.

Definition 6 (radical-decodability [DMA18]**).** *A mode of operation $\mathcal{T}$ is* radical-decodable *if there exists a set $\mathcal{S}_\mathcal{T}^{\mathrm{rad}}$ such that all trees $S \in \mathcal{S}_\mathcal{T}^{\mathrm{rad}}$ have a radical, and there exists an efficient deterministic function* radical() *that returns a radical upon presentation of an $S \in \mathcal{S}_\mathcal{T}^{\mathrm{rad}}$, and $\perp$ otherwise. The set $\mathcal{S}_\mathcal{T}^{\mathrm{rad}}$ must satisfy $\mathcal{S}_\mathcal{T}^{\mathrm{final}} \subseteq \mathcal{S}_\mathcal{T}^{\mathrm{rad}} \subseteq \mathcal{S}_\mathcal{T}^{\mathrm{sub}} \setminus \mathcal{S}_\mathcal{T}^{\mathrm{leaf}}$.*

In essence, radical-decodability requires the existence of an efficient function radical() that finds chaining values in a tree such that:

1. it only finds radicals (so they are chaining values in every possible tree),
2. it always reconstructs the full tree when starting at the final node and extending the tree based on the found radicals.

Note that $\mathcal{S}_\mathcal{T}^{\mathrm{final}}$ and $\mathcal{S}_\mathcal{T}^{\mathrm{sub}}$ only contain *proper* subtrees, so if a full tree consists of a single node, i.e. it hashes a message consisting of a single block, it is not part of $\mathcal{S}_\mathcal{T}^{\mathrm{final}}$ or $\mathcal{S}_\mathcal{T}^{\mathrm{sub}}$ hence it should not be in $\mathcal{S}_\mathcal{T}^{\mathrm{rad}}$ as the tree is already complete.

As a first example we take a Merkle-Damgård mode with leaf-anchoring, depicted in Fig. 4. We take $\mathcal{S}_\mathcal{T}^{\mathrm{rad}} = \mathcal{S}_\mathcal{T}^{\mathrm{sub}} \setminus \mathcal{S}_\mathcal{T}^{\mathrm{leaf}}$, the largest possible set. This means that we have to identify a radical for any subtree that is not in $\mathcal{S}_\mathcal{T}^{\mathrm{leaf}}$. We do this by identifying radicals by the absence of IV_1. Our function radical() works as follows: first we identify the leftmost node (which exists as it is a sequential mode), then we return its data input if it is not equal to IV_1 and return $\perp$ otherwise. An implementation of radical() is illustrated in Algorithm 2. We check the two requirements for radical-decodability.

1. Radicals: indeed, by definition of the mode any data input that is not IV_1 has to be a chaining value.
2. Reconstruction: strictly speaking, it does not satisfy this property. If a chaining value is equal to IV_1 the function will stop too soon. However, this has a negligible probability of occurring and in fact our proof already takes it into account. This means that we can assume that no chaining value hits IV_1, hence our function will always reconstruct the message.

An implementation of extract() is also illustrated in Algorithm 3. It is similar to the procedure radical(), but it extracts the message instead of the radicals.

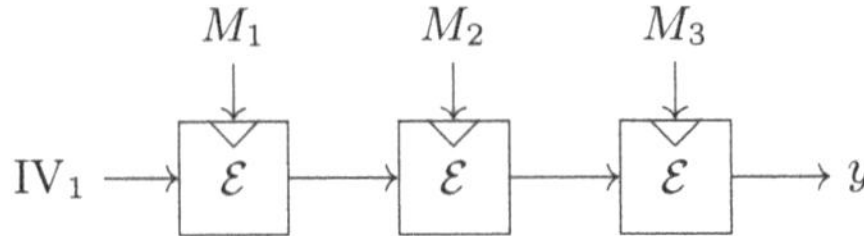

Fig. 4. A Merkle-Damgård mode with leaf-anchoring. Radical-decodability can be achieved by identifying radicals by the absence of IV_1 in the data input.

Algorithm 1. Helper function to lookup the node pointing to a location

```
Interface: lookup(S, α')
  for all i : (k, x, α) ∈ S do
    if α = α' then
      return i : (k, x, α)
    end if
  end for
  return ⊥
```

As a second example we take a Merkle-Damgård mode with final-node separation and length encoding, but without leaf anchoring, depicted in Fig. 5. This means that we cannot identify radicals by the absence of IV_1 anymore. However, we can make use of the other properties. We take $\mathcal{S}_{\mathcal{T}}^{\mathrm{rad}} = \mathcal{S}_{\mathcal{T}}^{\mathrm{final}}$, the smallest possible set. This means that we only have to identify a radical for any subtree that contains the final node. As we have final-node separation we can identify this. If the given tree does not contain a final node, we always return $\perp$ as we do not know how long the message is, which is allowed by the definition of radical-decodability as those trees are not in $\mathcal{S}_{\mathcal{T}}^{\mathrm{rad}}$. If a tree does contain a final node we can read the length of the message from it. Using this, we know the number of block cipher calls, from which we can deduce whether the data input is a chaining value or a message block, satisfying radical-decodability. An implementation of radical() is illustrated in Algorithm 4. The procedure extract() is not illustrated but is again very similar to radical(), but it extracts the message instead of the radicals.

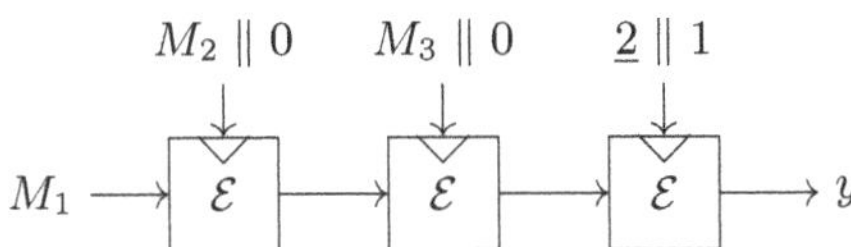

Fig. 5. A Merkle-Damgård mode with final-node separation and length encoding. Radical-decodability can be achieved by identifying the final node and using the length to know when to stop extending the tree.

Algorithm 2. Implementation of radical() for the mode pictured in Figure 4

```
Interface: radical(S)
  α' ← ⊥                                              ▷ initialize with the final node
  while lookup(S, α') ≠ ⊥ do
      i : (k, x, α) ← lookup(S, α')                   ▷ lookup the chaining value
      if x = IV₁ then                                  ▷ apply leaf-anchoring
          return ⊥                                     ▷ full tree
      end if
      α' ← i₀^x              ▷ the data input contains the next potential radical
  end while
  return α'                                            ▷ radical found
```

Algorithm 3. Implementation of extract() for the mode pictured in Figure 4

```
Interface: extract(S)
  M' ← ε                                       ▷ initialize with the empty string
  α' ← ⊥
  while lookup(S, α') ≠ ⊥ do
      i : (k, x, α) ← lookup(S, α')
      M' ← k || M'                      ▷ the key input contains a message block
      if x = IV₁ then
          return (M', ∅)           ▷ return the message and no parameters
      end if
      α' ← i₀^x
  end while
  return ⊥
```

Finally we may revisit the example in Fig. 3. We already noted that no radicals exist for this mode, meaning that only $\mathcal{S}_{\mathcal{T}}^{\mathrm{rad}} = \varnothing$ is possible. However, this contradicts the requirement that $\mathcal{S}_{\mathcal{T}}^{\mathrm{final}} \subseteq \mathcal{S}_{\mathcal{T}}^{\mathrm{rad}}$, hence this construction is not radical-decodable.

Now we define subtree-freeness, which is a generalization of the problem in length-extension attacks and states that a full tree can never be a subtree of a different tree.

Definition 7 (subtree-freeness [DMA18]). *A mode of operation $\mathcal{T}$ is* subtree-free *if*

$$\mathcal{S}_{\mathcal{T}} \cap \mathcal{S}_{\mathcal{T}}^{\mathrm{sub}} = \varnothing .$$

Next, we introduce some new conditions not present in [DMA18]. These are about full and partial final-anchoring. Full final-anchoring states that the full input of the final node should contain a fixed value, while partial final-anchoring additionally allows for a single chaining value to be present.

Definition 8 (full final-anchoring). *A mode of operation $\mathcal{T}$ that is leaf-anchored is* fully final-anchored *if for every template $Z \in \mathcal{Z}_{\mathcal{T}}$ the first b bits of the final node encode* $\mathrm{IV}_2 \in \{0,1\}^b$ *as frame bits.*

Algorithm 4. Implementation of radical() for the mode pictured in Figure 5

```
Interface: radical(S)
  i : (k, x, α) ← lookup(S, ⊥)
  ℓ ∥ s ← k                                          ▷ with |s| = 1
  if s = 0 then
      return ⊥                                       ▷ fail if it is not a final node
  end if
  α' ← i_0^x
  for j ← 0 to ℓ do                                  ▷ process ℓ blocks based on the length encoding
      if lookup(S, α') = ⊥ then
          return α'
      end if
      i : (k, x, α) ← lookup(S, α')
      α' ← i_0^x
  end for
  return ⊥
```

Strictly speaking, a mode cannot satisfy both leaf-anchoring and full final-anchoring as the definitions conflict on the first c bits of the final node. Leaf-anchoring requires these bits to be chaining pointer bits, while full final-anchoring requires them to encode IV_2. However, in our definition, we make an exception for this: the requirement of full final-anchoring overwrites the one of leaf-anchoring for the final node.

The final block cipher call of a mode with full final-anchoring will always look like the example in Fig. 6.

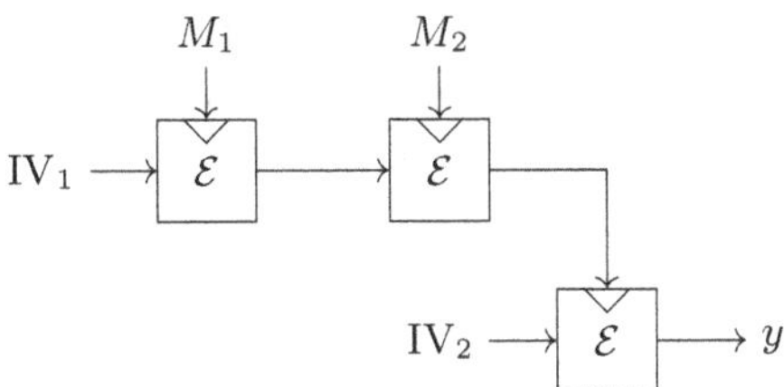

Fig. 6. Example mode using full final-anchoring.

Definition 9 (partial final-anchoring). *A mode of operation $\mathcal{T}$ that is leaf-anchored is* partially final-anchored *if for every template $Z \in \mathcal{Z}_\mathcal{T}$ the following holds for the final node:*

- *When it is a leaf node, it encodes IV'_1 as frame bits, where $\mathrm{IV}'_1 \in \{0,1\}^b$ with $\lfloor \mathrm{IV}'_1 \rfloor_m = \mathrm{IV}_1$.*
- *When it is a non-leaf node, the first c bits are chaining pointer bits and its last $b-c$ bits encode $\mathrm{IV}_2 \in \{0,1\}^{b-c}$ as frame bits.*

There may be P different possibilities for IV_2*, denoted by the set* $\mathcal{IV}_2$*.*

An example of a mode using partial final-anchoring is depicted in Fig. 7.

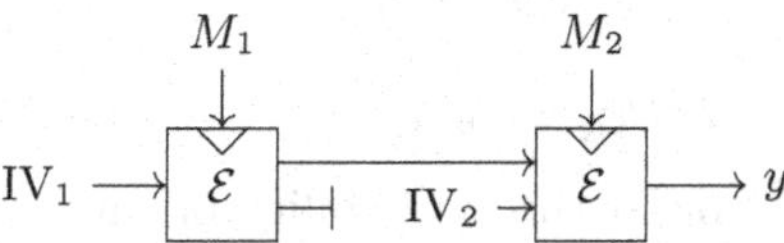

Fig. 7. Example mode using partial final-anchoring.

2.3 Indifferentiability

We use the indifferentiability framework introduced by Maurer et al. [MRH04] applied to hash functions by Coron et al. [CDMP05].

Definition 10. *Let* $\mathcal{T} = (\mathcal{Z}, \zeta)$ *be a hashing mode, with template generating function* $\mathcal{Z} : \mathbb{N} \times \mathcal{A} \to \mathcal{X}$ *and finalization function* $\zeta : \{0,1\}^b \times \{0,1\}^b \to \{0,1\}^n$*, based on an ideal cipher* $\mathcal{E} : \{0,1\}^\kappa \times \{0,1\}^b \to \{0,1\}^b$ *and let* $\mathcal{Y}[\mathcal{E}] : \{0,1\}^* \times \mathcal{X} \to \{0,1\}^b \times \{0,1\}^b$ *be the template execution function as described in Sect. 2.2.2. Let* $\mathcal{RO}$ *be a random oracle with the same domain and range as* $\zeta \circ \mathcal{Y}[\mathcal{E}]$ *and* $\mathcal{S}$ *be a simulator with oracle access to* $\mathcal{RO}$*. The indifferentiability advantage of a distinguisher* $\mathcal{D}$ *is defined as*

$$\mathsf{Adv}^{\mathrm{diff}}_{\mathcal{T}[\mathcal{E}],\mathcal{S}}(\mathcal{D}) = \left| \mathbb{P}\left[\mathcal{D}^{\zeta \circ \mathcal{Y}[\mathcal{E}],\mathcal{E},\mathcal{E}^{-1}} = 1\right] - \mathbb{P}\left[\mathcal{D}^{\mathcal{RO},\mathcal{S}[\mathcal{RO}],\mathcal{S}^{-1}[\mathcal{RO}]} = 1\right] \right| ,$$

where $\mathcal{D}$ *can only make construction queries* (M, Z) *such that* $Z = \mathcal{Z}(|M|, A)$ *for some* $A \in \mathcal{A}$*.*

2.4 Elementary Results

Our proof will rely on the H-coefficient technique introduced by Patarin [Pat08] and modernized by Chen and Steinberger [CS14]. Let $\mathcal{D}$ be a information-theoretic deterministic distinguisher trying to distinguish $\mathcal{O}_1 = (\zeta \circ \mathcal{Y}[\mathcal{E}], \mathcal{E}, \mathcal{E}^{-1})$ and $\mathcal{O}_2 = (\mathcal{RO}, \mathcal{S}[\mathcal{RO}], \mathcal{S}^{-1}[\mathcal{RO}])$. Let ν be the *view* of $\mathcal{D}$ after interacting with either oracle, consisting of a list of all its queries made. Let $\mathcal{D}_{\mathcal{O}_1}$ denote the probability distribution of views of $\mathcal{D}$ interacting with $\mathcal{O}_1$ and $\mathcal{D}_{\mathcal{O}_2}$ likewise for $\mathcal{O}_2$. A view ν is *attainable* if it can be observed by $\mathcal{D}$ in the ideal world, i.e. $\mathbb{P}[\mathcal{D}_{\mathcal{O}_2}] > 0$. We define $\mathcal{V}$ as the set of all attainable views. The H-coefficient technique states the following for $\mathsf{Adv}^{\mathrm{diff}}_{\mathcal{T}[\mathcal{E}],\mathcal{S}}(\mathcal{D})$.

Lemma 1 (H-coefficient Technique [Pat08, CS14]**).** *Let* $\mathcal{O}_1 = (\zeta \circ \mathcal{Y}[\mathcal{E}], \mathcal{E}, \mathcal{E}^{-1})$ *and* $\mathcal{O}_2 = (\mathcal{RO}, \mathcal{S}[\mathcal{RO}], \mathcal{S}^{-1}[\mathcal{RO}])$*. Let* $\mathcal{D}$ *be a deterministic* *distinguisher and* $\mathcal{V} = \mathcal{V}_{\text{good}} \cup \mathcal{V}_{\text{bad}}$ *be a partition of the set of views into good and bad views. Let* $\varepsilon \geqslant 0$ *be such that for all* $\nu \in \mathcal{V}_{\text{good}}$*:*

$$\frac{\mathbb{P}\left[\mathcal{D}_{\mathcal{O}_1} = \nu\right]}{\mathbb{P}\left[\mathcal{D}_{\mathcal{O}_2} = \nu\right]} \geqslant 1 - \varepsilon.$$

Then $\mathsf{Adv}^{\text{diff}}_{\mathcal{T}[\mathcal{E}],\mathcal{S}}(\mathcal{D}) \leqslant \varepsilon + \mathbb{P}\left[\mathcal{D}_{\mathcal{O}_2} \in \mathcal{V}_{\text{bad}}\right]$.

We will have to upper bound the probability of multi-collisions. We use the following result based on Choi et al. [CLL19] for this.

Lemma 2. *Suppose we have a sequence of* s *elements where every element is randomly chosen from* $\{0,1\}^a$ *and let* F_x *denote the number of elements that hit the value* $x \in \{0,1\}^a$*. Then we have that*

$$\mathbb{E}\left[\max_x F_x\right] \leqslant \frac{2s}{2^a} + \ln(s) + a + 1.$$

The proof is given in the full version [Gun22].

3 Errors

The faulty bounds in the original analysis in [DMA18] were superficially corrected in [GDM20]. Nevertheless, a more thorough investigation reveals that the root cause is more fundamental and applies to many earlier indifferentiability proofs.

3.1 Description of the Flaw

The main error is that the calls to the random oracle from the simulator are considered to be random. The output of the random oracle is indeed random. However, as the distinguisher also has access to this random oracle, it might know the output beforehand. Let us take a look at a simple example of this. Let $\mathcal{D}$ be a distinguisher that makes the following queries, where $\mathcal{T}$ is the construction oracle of a simple Merkle-Damgård-like mode and $\mathcal{E}$ the primitive oracle, with the message M consisting of one block:

- query $\mathcal{T}(M) = h$,
- query $\mathcal{E}_h(\text{IV}_1) = y$,
- query $\mathcal{E}_M(\text{IV}_1) = h$.

The final output needs to be h, as this computes the hash of M.

As the simulator simulates $\mathcal{E}$, the only queries that it sees are (h, IV_1) with output y and (M, IV_1) with output h. Although this h comes from the random oracle, its value is magically equal to the key input of the first query, from the simulator's point of view.

When presented in this way, it may be obvious that the output of (M, IV_1) cannot be considered random as it is part of the fundamental interaction between the oracles. However, it becomes more subtle when it is more abstractly presented and when some simplifications are made. It is very common to represent the queries to the oracle as two separate lists. In the above example we would get the list $\mathcal{M} = ((M, h))$ for the construction oracle and the list $\mathcal{L} = ((h, \mathrm{IV}_1, y), (M, \mathrm{IV}_1, h))$ for the primitive oracle. These lists contain duplicate information, as from either (M, h) or (M, IV_1, h) we can derive the fact that the hash of the message M is equal to h. In order to simplify the analysis we might be tempted to drop one of these queries. For example, we might drop all queries from $\mathcal{M}$ which can be derived from $\mathcal{L}$. In this case this means that $\mathcal{M}$ becomes empty and we would only have to consider $\mathcal{L} = ((h, \mathrm{IV}_1, y), (M, \mathrm{IV}_1, h))$. However, this is a faulty reasoning as the output of (M, IV_1) is always h and cannot be considered to be randomly generated.

3.2 Occurrence in Other Works

Besides [DMA18], where the error had a significant influence on the proven security bound, the same error appeared in multiple other papers as well [CN08, MPN10, MP15, Lee17, BN18, ABR21].

- In [CN08], the authors use the following reasoning in the Section 'Some Important Observations':
  "Thus, we assume that $\mathcal{A}$ do not make any $\mathcal{O}_1$-query which is computable from the previous query-responses of $\mathcal{O}_2$. More particularly, we can remove all those $\mathcal{O}_1$-queries from the final view which are computable from the query-responses of $\mathcal{O}_2$."
  Here, $\mathcal{A}$ denotes the distinguisher, $\mathcal{O}_1$ the construction oracle and $\mathcal{O}_2$ the primitive oracle. The first sentence is correct, but the second one is not. The error can be fixed in a straightforward manner by not removing those queries from the final view. The probabilities have to be computed in a slightly different way, as some output will be known. However, as the only way these known outputs are used is in upper bounding the probability of a mutlicollision, whose analysis remain exactly the same, this does not have any influence on the bound.
- The same error appeared in work on the indifferentiability of the sum of permutations [MPN10, MP15, Lee17, BN18]. In the original paper [MPN10] they apply a common transformation to the distinguisher $\mathcal{D}$. The new distinguisher $\mathcal{D}'$ is the same as $\mathcal{D}$, but it additionally verifies all the construction queries. This transformation is fine as it simplifies some analysis, we use this transformation as well. However, after this transformation they simply ignore the queries to the random oracle, which is not correct. The other papers [MP15, Lee17, BN18] are based on this and also copy the same error. As a matter of fact [DMA18] copied the approach from them as well.
  Looking at the most recent work with the best bound [BN18], the error does have a significant impact on the proof. The primitive queries are viewed as random variables, without taking possible construction queries into account. These queries influence the distributions, which has a significant effect on the

proof as these distributions are used in the χ^2-technique. This does not mean that the bound is necessarily incorrect, but the proof has to be significantly changed.

- The same error appeared in recent work of Andreeva et al. [ABR21]. In Sect. 5 the authors show that their ABR$^+$ mode is indifferentiable. However, again, after the common transformation to $\mathcal{D}'$ at the start of Sect. 5.3 the construction queries are incorrectly ignored. Nevertheless, in this case the error should not have an impact on the result. As the construction is fixed-length and uses a different random function (not permutation) in all locations, including the final one, the knowledge of the construction results will be independent and not influence other parts. In short, although the paper makes the same common error, the result should still be correct because of the specifics of the construction.

3.3 Possible Cause and Resolution

A possible cause for the error can be from the notations of the views. It is convenient to denote the interaction of the construction and primitive oracles separately. However, this notation can be misleading. It implies that the interaction between the two different oracles is somewhat disconnected, while this is not the case. The common error of dropping all the queries to the construction oracles is basically equivalent to changing the security model. Instead of always having access to both oracles, the adversary instead operates in two phases: first it is only allowed access to the primitive oracle and after it is done with this oracle, it is allowed to only query the construction oracle. This exact model does actually exist as sequential indifferentiability [MPS12]. In this setting the previously faulty transformation is valid, meaning that any proofs using it can be reinterpreted as occurring in the weaker sequential indifferentiability model, making them still proving a positive, but significantly weaker, result.

A way to prevent the faulty reasoning is to denote the view in one list. In our example we would denote the view as $\nu = ((M, h), (h, \mathrm{IV}_1, y), (M, \mathrm{IV}_1, h))$, where the final h contains no randomness. This can complicate the analysis, depending on the used mode. It can be easier to use this reasoning when there is truncation involved, as that means that there is still some randomness in the query that can be used. For example, the work [CLL19] does do this correctly: they denote the view as a single list and also have a mode using truncation.

4 Results

For all results stated below we consider a tree hashing mode based on a b-bit block cipher and with capacity c denoting the size of the chaining values. These results are also summarized in Table 1.

Theorem 1. *Let $\mathcal{T}$ be a mode that is subtree-free, radical-decodable, message-decodable, leaf-anchored with* IV_1*-length m and has finalization function*

$\zeta(y) = \lfloor y \rfloor_n$. *Then there exists a simulator $\mathcal{S}$ such that for any distinguisher $\mathcal{D}$ that makes q queries total and r queries to the construction oracle we have*

$$\mathsf{Adv}^{\mathsf{diff}}_{\mathcal{T}[\mathcal{E}],\mathcal{S}}(\mathcal{D}) \leqslant \frac{q}{2^m} + \frac{q^2}{2^c} + \frac{q^2+2qr}{2^b} + \frac{(\ln(r)+n+1)q}{2^{b-n}}.$$

The simulator $\mathcal{S}$ makes at most q queries to the random oracle.

Theorem 2. *Let $\mathcal{T}$ be a mode that is radical-decodable, message-decodable, leaf-anchored with IV_1-length m and has finalization function $\zeta(y) = \lfloor y \rfloor_n$. Then there exists a simulator $\mathcal{S}$ such that for any distinguisher $\mathcal{D}$ that makes q queries total and r queries to the construction oracle we have*

$$\mathsf{Adv}^{\mathsf{diff}}_{\mathcal{T}[\mathcal{E}],\mathcal{S}}(\mathcal{D}) \leqslant \frac{q+r}{2^m} + \frac{q^2+2qr}{2^c} + \frac{q^2+2qr}{2^b} + (\ln(r)+n+1)\left(\frac{q}{2^{c-n}} + \frac{q}{2^{b-n}}\right).$$

The simulator $\mathcal{S}$ makes at most q queries to the random oracle.

Theorem 3. *Let $\mathcal{T}$ be a mode that is radical-decodable, message-decodable, leaf-anchored with IV_1-length m and has finalization function $\zeta(y) = \lceil y \rceil_n$. Then there exists a simulator $\mathcal{S}$ such that for any distinguisher $\mathcal{D}$ that makes q queries total and r queries to the construction oracle we either have*

$$\mathsf{Adv}^{\mathsf{diff}}_{\mathcal{T}[\mathcal{E}],\mathcal{S}}(\mathcal{D}) \leqslant \frac{q}{2^m} + \frac{q^2}{2^c} + \frac{q^2}{2^{b-n}},$$

if $b - n \geqslant c$, and

$$\mathsf{Adv}^{\mathsf{diff}}_{\mathcal{T}[\mathcal{E}],\mathcal{S}}(\mathcal{D}) \leqslant \frac{q+r}{2^m} + \frac{q^2}{2^c} + \frac{q^2+2qr}{2^b} + \frac{(2\ln(r)+2n+2)q}{2^{b-n}}$$

otherwise. The simulator $\mathcal{S}$ makes at most q queries to the random oracle.

Theorem 4. *Let $\mathcal{T}$ be a mode that is subtree-free, radical-decodable, message-decodable, leaf-anchored with IV_1-length m, fully final-anchored and has finalization function $\zeta(y) = y$. Then there exists a simulator $\mathcal{S}$ such that for any distinguisher $\mathcal{D}$ that makes q queries total and r queries to the construction oracle we have*

$$\mathsf{Adv}^{\mathsf{diff}}_{\mathcal{T}[\mathcal{E}],\mathcal{S}}(\mathcal{D}) \leqslant \frac{q}{2^m} + \frac{3q^2+q}{2^c} + \frac{3q^2+2qr}{2^b}.$$

The simulator $\mathcal{S}$ makes at most q queries to the random oracle.

Theorem 5. *Let $\mathcal{T}$ be a mode that is subtree-free, radical-decodable, message-decodable, leaf-anchored with IV_1-length m, partially final-anchored with P possibilities for IV_2 and has finalization function $\zeta_x(y) = x \oplus y$. Then there exists a simulator $\mathcal{S}$ such that for any distinguisher $\mathcal{D}$ that makes q queries total and r queries to the construction oracle we have*

$$\mathsf{Adv}^{\mathsf{diff}}_{\mathcal{T}[\mathcal{E}],\mathcal{S}}(\mathcal{D}) \leqslant \frac{q}{2^m} + \frac{3q^2+4qr+4r^2+2r}{2^c} + \frac{3q^2+2Pqr}{2^b}.$$

The simulator $\mathcal{S}$ makes at most Pq^2 queries to the random oracle.

The proofs are given in the full version [Gun22].

5 Applications

5.1 Truncated SHA-2

SHA-2 [SHA08] uses a straightforward Merkle-Damgård mode based on a block cipher with the Davies-Meyer feed-forward on top of it. By using Theorem 2 we are able to prove this mode secure, *without requiring any feed-forward.* The mode is illustrated in Fig. 8.

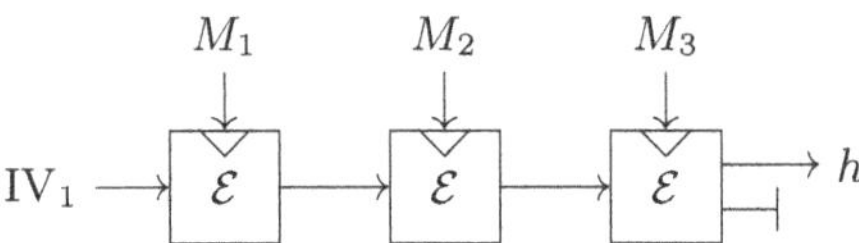

Fig. 8. Illustration of the Merkle-Damgård mode used in SHA-2, but without any feed-forward.

We show that this mode satisfies the required conditions. First of all, it is message-decodable as the message can be retrieved from the tree and it is also leaf-anchored by definition. For radical decodability we take $\mathcal{S}_T^{\mathrm{rad}} = \mathcal{S}_T^{\mathrm{sub}} \setminus \mathcal{S}_T^{\mathrm{leaf}}$ as the largest possible set and identify radicals by the absence of the IV_1. This means that we can apply Theorem 2 with $m = c = b \in \{256, 512\}$ the internal state size and $n \in \{224, 256, 384, 512\}$ (the latter two only for $b = 512$) the digest length. If n is close to b this gives an insecure bound, as then the mode is vulnerable to a length extension attack.

5.2 BLAKE3

BLAKE3 [OANW20] is a recently introduced tree hash that makes full use of the parallelism that it provides. We will not describe the hashing mode in detail, but we show that with our results we can analyze the security of the mode of operation of BLAKE3. The BLAKE3 paper cites the article by Daemen et al. [DMA18] in the security analysis and show that it satisfies the required conditions. This works for the truncated version, but a full-length output version is also used. For this they informally state that the feed-forward is sufficient for this. Using our Theorem 5 we are able to show that this informal reasoning is not completely correct, as the extendable output mode introduces new security considerations.

We succinctly describe what the final compression call looks like, as that one is relevant for the applicability of the feed-forward and the partial final-anchoring. The data input to the final call is of the for form $\mathrm{CV}\|\mathrm{IV}_2\|t\|b\|d$ with key a message $M \in \{0,1\}^{512}$, where $\mathrm{CV} \in \{0,1\}^{256}$ is the chaining value (or the initial value, if the block consists of one block), $\mathrm{IV}_2 \in \{0,1\}^{128}$ a fixed value used for every compression call, $t \in \{0,1\}^{64}$ a counter for extendable output,

$b \in \{0,1\}^{32}$ the number of bytes in the message M and $d \in \{0,1\}^{32}$ some flags. The output of the block cipher is $V_L \| V_H = \mathcal{E}_M(\mathrm{CV}\|\mathrm{IV}_2\|t\|b\|d)$, with $V_L, V_H \in \{0,1\}^{256}$. The final digest is $h = (V_L \oplus V_H) \parallel (V_H \oplus \mathrm{CV})$. This is also illustrated in Fig. 9.

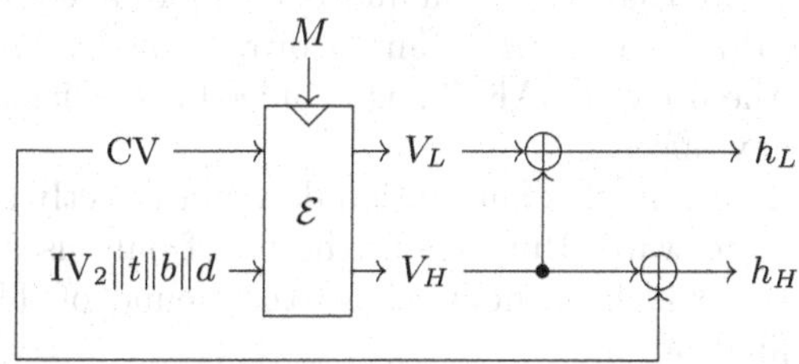

Fig. 9. Illustration of the final compression call of BLAKE3.

5.2.1 Fixed Output

In the fixed output mode of BLAKE3 the final digest h is truncated to 256 bits, which corresponds to $V_L \oplus V_H$, where $V_L\|V_H$ is the output of the final block cipher call. This means that no feed-forward with the previous chaining value is used. Although this finalization is different from truncation, which would be just V_L, this difference is not essential and the result could be easily modified for this finalization. Therefore, we do get an appropriate bound from Theorem 1 with $b = 512$, $m = 256$, $c = 256$ and $n = 256$.

5.2.2 Extendable Output

In addition to a fixed output mode, BLAKE3 also introduces an extendable output mode, allowing for an arbitrary number of output bits, similar to the sponge construction [BDPV07]. In contrast to the sponge construction, which uses a sequential output, BLAKE3 uses a counter for its extendable output. It behaves similar to the generic construction where the counter is appended to the message, which would result in the output $H(M\|0) \parallel H(M\|1) \parallel H(M\|2) \parallel \ldots$ for a generic hash function H. In contrast to this generic construction, the counter is placed in the final compression call, making computing successive outputs much more efficient, while still allowing efficient random access in contrast to the sponge. However, as we will see, this feature of allowing efficient random access comes with new security considerations which BLAKE3 does not adhere fully.

For the extendable output mode the full output $h = (V_L \oplus V_H) \parallel (V_H \oplus \mathrm{CV})$ of the compression function is used. To get an arbitrary number of output bits BLAKE3 uses a counter t that is part of the final compression call. Let h_t denote the output with size b stated above when a counter t is used. Then the full output is equal to $h_0\|h_1\|h_2\|\ldots$.

Our definition of a tree hashing mode does not directly include this extendable output, but it can be achieved by making use of the parameters. Recall that the tree template does not only depend on the length of the message $|M|$, but also on the parameters A which can be chosen freely from a custom defined set $\mathcal{A}$. In this case we choose $\mathcal{A} = \{0, 1, \ldots, \ell - 1\}$, where ℓ is the maximum number of allowed output blocks, to represent the value of the counter t. This means that the output can be computed by computing the hashes of (M, t) for all relevant counters t. Note that definition allows for more freedom than a sequential construction as this t can start at any arbitrary offset. This extra freedom does correspond to the use of BLAKE3, as it indeed can efficiently compute the output starting at any offset.

As with the fixed output, this finalization does not directly correspond to our definition of the feed-forward. But, again, the proof only uses the randomness of the chaining value, which is included, so the bound of Theorem 5 is still applicable for this finalization.

A more significant problem arises when we look at the other new requirement for a secure mode that uses feed-forwarding. The mode should also satisfy partial final-anchoring, which means that there should be a limited number of possibilities for the input of the final compression call other than the chaining value. As stated earlier, for BLAKE3 this consists of $\mathrm{IV}_2\|t\|b\|d$, where our main focus will be t, which is the counter that underlies the extendable output. This t has ℓ possible values, which is maximum number of allowed output blocks. As BLAKE3 allows for a maximum of 2^{64} output bytes we get $\ell = 2^{64}/64 = 2^{58}$, although the counter can in principle be any 64-bit value. The values b and d both have 2^6 possibilities, hence partial final-anchoring is satisfied with $P = \ell \cdot 2^{12}$, which is typically dominated by ℓ.

This means that we can apply Theorem 5 to this mode with $P = \ell \cdot 2^{12}$, $b = 512$, $m = 256$ and $c = 256$, with $\ell \leqslant 2^{58}$ the maximum number of output blocks in the extendable output mode. Although P is quite large, this still gives the expected security level as $P \cdot 2^c \leqslant 2^b$. There is a downside to the large P, though, as the simulator becomes quite inefficient with its query complexity of Pq^2. This is actually reflected in some non-ideal behavior of BLAKE3 that we describe next.

5.2.3 Computing the Counter

Suppose that a query of the form $h_L\|h_H = h = H(M, t)$ is performed, where M is the message and t the block offset in the extendable mode, which corresponds to the counter. Assume that M and h are known to an attacker, but t is not. Ideally, the only way to retrieve t is to try all possible $t' \leqslant \ell$ and check whether $H(M, t')$ equals h. However, in the case of BLAKE3 this t can be retrieved much more efficiently. Recall that digest is defined as $(V_L \oplus V_H) \parallel (V_H \oplus \mathrm{CV})$, with $V_L\|V_H$ the output of the final block cipher call. As M is known to the attacker, it can compute CV. Furthermore, $h_L = V_L \oplus V_H$ and $h_H = V_H \oplus \mathrm{CV}$ are also known, so it can compute $V_H = h_H \oplus \mathrm{CV}$ and $V_L = h_L \oplus V_H$. This means that it can perform the inverse of the final block cipher call as $\mathcal{E}_m^{-1}(V_L\|V_H) = \mathrm{CV}\|\mathrm{IV}_2\|t\|b\|d$, with m the message input to the final block, and retrieve t this way. This operation costs just one query to $\mathcal{E}$ (and some to compute CV), which is significantly less than the expected ℓ, which can be as high as 2^{58}.

This problem can be illustrated by the following example. Suppose that BLAKE3 is used as the following illustrative MAC. This MAC gets as input a key $K \in \{0,1\}^{128}$ and a message $M \in \{0,1\}^*$. It splits the key as $K = K_1 \| K_2$ with $K_1 \in \{0,1\}^{70}$ and $K_2 \in \{0,1\}^{58}$ and computes the MAC as $H(M\|K_1, t = K_2)$. For an ideal hash function this construction gives a secure MAC, as the offset can essentially be viewed as part of the input. However, when instantiated with BLAKE3 this is not the case. Given $h = H(M\|K_1, t = K_2)$ and M, but not K, an adversary can compute K in roughly 2^{70} queries, instead of the expected 2^{128}. This is done by first guessing an arbitrary $K_1 \in \{0,1\}^{70}$. Then the adversary can compute the offset K_2 from h and $M\|K_1$ as described above. If the guess of K_1 is correct, this computes the value of $K_2 \in \{0,1\}^{58}$ using a single query, performing a key-recovery attack. As there are 2^{70} possible values for K_1 this attack succeeds using roughly 2^{70} queries. Although BLAKE3 supports a dedicated keyed mode that is preferred, the previous example should still be secure. This shows that the counter in BLAKE3 can only contain public information.

5.2.4 Conclusion

BLAKE3 makes full use of tree hashing capabilities with an interesting way of generating extendable output by making use of a counter. Although its tree structure is secure, its use of a counter, which makes efficient random access possible, comes with new security considerations. In particular, from a usage perspective it behaves similar to an extra small efficient message input. However, its security properties do not align with this behavior as the counter can be efficiently computed by knowing the message and the hash output. This is not the case for a normal message input, making BLAKE3 in essence add an extra requirement in that the counter should always be public.

5.3 Tree Sponge

Here we introduce a tree generalization of the sponge construction [BDPV07]. The absorbing phase is generalized to have a tree structure, allowing for parallel compression. Additionally, the squeezing phase is modified to likewise allow for parallel expansion by making use of a counter. The construction requires a minimal number of frame bits: the only ones present are initial values required to prevent inverse queries from succeeding.

First of all we note that all our results also apply to permutations by simply setting $\kappa = 0$. The tree sponge makes use of the flexible conditions present in Theorem 3. The main observation is that subtree-freeness can be dropped without negative consequences when the chaining values and the hash digests originate from different parts of the output of the permutation. This is the same as in the original sponge construction, which has an inner part that outputs chaining values, which are secret, and an outer part that outputs hash digests, which are public.

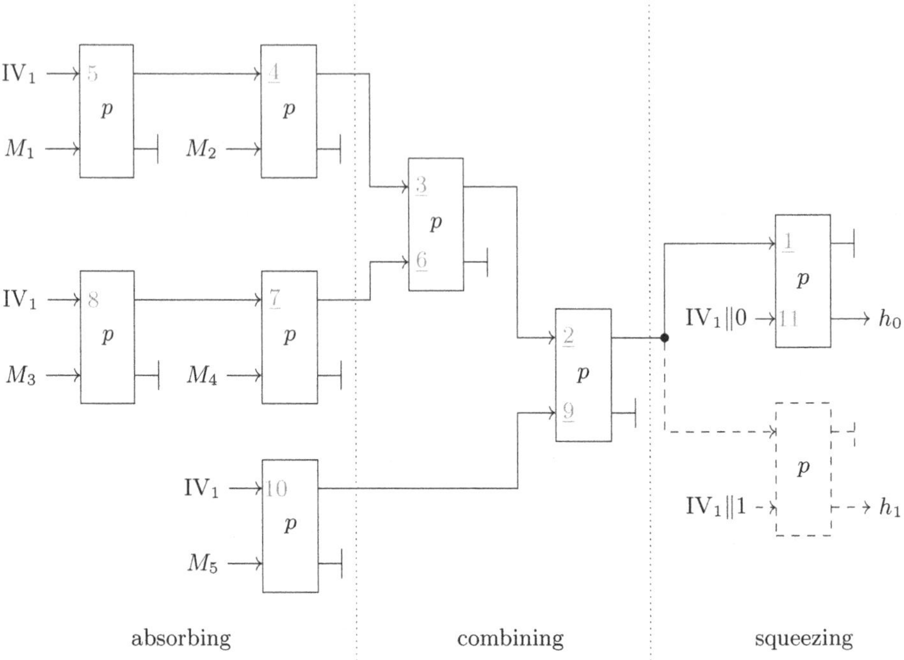

Fig. 10. Example of the minimal permutation-based tree hashing mode with $w = 2$ giving two blocks of output. The order in which the radicals are identified is indicated by the gray numbers 1–11, starting from the final permutation call resulting in h_0. Underlined numbers indicate a radical, while the other numbers indicate a different value: either a leaf or a counter value. The dashed permutation call resulting in h_1 is not part of the tree found by the radical finding algorithm.

5.3.1 Description

The tree sponge contains three different phases and depends on a fixed parameter $w \in \mathbb{N}_{>0}$ representing the width:

- Absorbing. In this phase the message is split such that every part can be absorbed by a sponge of width w. The final part may be smaller. All different parts are absorbed this way in parallel and each generate their own chaining value.
- Combining. The chaining values generated in the previous phase are combined by using a tree structure. The chaining values are split into two non-empty parts, with the first part the largest possible power of two. The two parts are recursively reduced to a single chaining value and combined using a permutation call.

Algorithm 5. Implementation of the tree sponge mode pictured in Figure 10

```
Interface: TreeSponge(M, t)
  CV ← combine(M)
  return ⌈p(CV ‖ IV_1 ‖ t)⌉_{3b/4}

Interface: combine(M)
  W ← w · b/2 + b/4                         ▷ maximum sequential absorption
  if |M| ⩽ W then
     return absorb(M)
  end if
  k ← ⌊log_2(|M|/W)⌋                        ▷ largest k such that W · 2^k ⩽ |M|
  M_L ‖ M_R ← M                             ▷ with |M_L| = W · 2^k
  CV_L ← combine(M_L)
  CV_R ← combine(M_R)
  return ⌊p(CV_L ‖ CV_R)⌋_{b/2}

Interface: absorb(M)
  M_0 ‖ M_1 ‖ ··· ‖ M_{ℓ−1} ← M             ▷ with |M_0| = 3b/4 and |M_i| = b/2
  x ← IV_1 ‖ M_0
  for i ← 1 to ℓ do
     x ← ⌊p(x)⌋_{b/2} ‖ M_i
  end for
  return ⌊p(x)⌋_{b/2}
```

- Squeezing. The resulting chaining value is fed into multiple final permutation calls appended by $\mathrm{IV}_1 \| t$, with $t = 0, 1, \ldots$ a counter for an arbitrary long output.

An example of this mode is pictured in Fig. 10 and an implementation is illustrated in Algorithm 5.

5.3.2 Security

We show that this mode satisfies the required conditions. Again, message-decodability and leaf-anchoring are satisfied in a straightforward way. Radical-decodability is more interesting for this mode.

We take $\mathcal{S}_T^{\mathrm{rad}} = \mathcal{S}_T^{\mathrm{sub}} \setminus \mathcal{S}_T^{\mathrm{leaf}}$ as the largest possible set and use leaf-anchoring to identify most radicals. We identify leaf nodes by the occurrence of IV_1, which do not have any radical. If we do not find a leaf node, we do not immediately know whether the node has one or two chaining values. However, we only have to find one radical at a time and we know that the first c bits will always point to a chaining value. We continue this process for the topmost chaining value until we hit a leaf node. Then we know that the first w calls after the leaf node are sequential and do not have any other chaining values. All the other nodes do have a chaining value in the bottom halve and we recursively continue the process on all those values. The only exception is the counter in the end, but we can recognize this again by the presence of IV_1. Furthermore, the fact that the final message block may have a width smaller than w does not matter as it is the final block the algorithm finds. An example of this process is pictured in Fig. 10 by the gray numbers and an implementation is illustrated in Algorithm 6.

Algorithm 6. Implementation of radical() for the tree sponge mode pictured in Figure 10

```
Interface: radical(S)
  (α, depth) ← radical′(S, ⊥)
  return α

Interface: radical′(S, α′)
  if lookup(S, α′) = ⊥ then
      return (α′, ⊥)
  end if
  i : (k, x, α) ← lookup(S, α′)
  if ⌊x⌋_{b/4} = IV_1 then
      return (⊥, 1)                          ▷ end of path by leaf-anchoring
  end if
  α′ ← i^x_0
  (α′, depth) ← radical′(S, α′)              ▷ scan the top half for radicals
  if α′ ≠ ⊥ then
      return (α′, ⊥)
  end if
  if depth ≠ ⊥ ∧ depth < w then
      return (⊥, depth + 1)                  ▷ absorb phase
  else
      x_1 || x_2 ← x                         ▷ with |x_1| = |x_2| = b/2
      if ⌊x_2⌋_{b/4} = IV_1 then
          return (⊥, ⊥)                      ▷ squeeze phase
      else
          α′ ← i^x_{b/2}                     ▷ combine phase
          return radical′(S, α′)             ▷ scan the bottom half for radicals
      end if
  end if
```

Given a permutation of size b we choose $c = b/2$ as we have a binary tree. This leads to a security level of at most $b/4$, which is inherently the maximum for a permutation-based tree hash. Given this security level we are additionally able to choose $m = b/4$ and $n = 3b/4$ to optimize the efficiency while keeping the same security level.

6 Proof Sketch

The full proof is given in the full version [Gun22], but the main ideas in it are the following:

- The simulator uses radical-decodability to reconstruct the tree corresponding to a (potential) message. Message-decodability is used to reconstruct the message in order to be consistent with the random oracle. Otherwise randomly generated values are used.
- Various bad events are defined to make sure the following properties hold for good views:
  - The simulator is consistent with the random oracle.
  - The simulator is consistent as a permutation, i.e. $\mathcal{S}_k(x_1) = \mathcal{S}_k(x_2)$ implies $x_1 = x_2$ and similar for the inverse.

  The main goal of the bad events is to prevent various collisions and to prevent inversions of the final compression call. This last property was not handled appropriate in [DMA18] and is solved by the various finalization functions:
  - Truncation/Chopping: by throwing away part of the input the inverse calls can only succeed by guessing the discarded bits, which is negligible for sufficient truncation.
  - Enveloped: as in the final compression call the message related can only be part of the key input, no information can be gained from an inverse call. The output contains the data input, which is constant. Notably, the inverse simulator has to modified to account for the possibility of making an unorthodox query by computing the hash normally, except for the final call for which the inverse is used.
  - Feed-forward: this case is similar to the enveloped case. A key difference is that the final inverse call does not necessarily correspond to a single message, making the inverse simulator having to loop over all possibilities.

  These bad events occur with negligible probability as all the values are randomly generated. Most of the difficulty comes from identifying the faulty queries. As the wrong simplification discussed in Sect. 3 cannot be applied, it becomes more tricky to identify the faulty queries, which become more varied. This is especially true for the feed-forward mode as the inverse queries can correspond to multiple messages.

Acknowledgments. Aldo Gunsing is supported by the Netherlands Organisation for Scientific Research (NWO) under TOP grant TOP1.18.002 SCALAR.

References

[ABR21] Andreeva, E., Bhattacharyya, R., Roy, A.: Compactness of hashing modes and efficiency beyond Merkle tree. In: Canteaut, A., Standaert, F.-X. (eds.) EUROCRYPT 2021. LNCS, vol. 12697, pp. 92–123. Springer, Cham (2021). https://doi.org/10.1007/978-3-030-77886-6_4

[BDPV07] Bertoni, G., Daemen, J., Peeters, M., Van Assche, G.: Sponge functions. In: Ecrypt Hash Workshop (2007). http://sponge.noekeon.org/SpongeFunctions.pdf

[BDPV14] Bertoni, G., Daemen, J., Peeters, M., Van Assche, G.: Sufficient conditions for sound tree and sequential hashing modes. Int. J. Inf. Secur. **13**(4), 335–353 (2013). https://doi.org/10.1007/s10207-013-0220-y

[Bel06] Bellare, M.: New proofs for NMAC and HMAC: security without collision-resistance. In: Dwork, C. (ed.) CRYPTO 2006. LNCS, vol. 4117, pp. 602–619. Springer, Heidelberg (2006). https://doi.org/10.1007/11818175_36

[BN18] Bhattacharya, S., Nandi, M.: Full indifferentiable security of the Xor of two or more random permutations using the χ^2 method. In: Nielsen, J.B., Rijmen, V. (eds.) EUROCRYPT 2018. LNCS, vol. 10820, pp. 387–412. Springer, Cham (2018). https://doi.org/10.1007/978-3-319-78381-9_15

[BR06] Bellare, M., Ristenpart, T.: Multi-property-preserving hash domain extension and the EMD transform. In: Lai, X., Chen, K. (eds.) ASIACRYPT 2006. LNCS, vol. 4284, pp. 299–314. Springer, Heidelberg (2006). https://doi.org/10.1007/11935230_20

[CDMP05] Coron, J.-S., Dodis, Y., Malinaud, C., Puniya, P.: Merkle-Damgård revisited: how to construct a hash function. In: Shoup, V. (ed.) CRYPTO 2005. LNCS, vol. 3621, pp. 430–448. Springer, Heidelberg (2005). https://doi.org/10.1007/11535218_26

[CLL19] Choi, W., Lee, B., Lee, J.: Indifferentiability of truncated random permutations. In: Galbraith, S.D., Moriai, S. (eds.) ASIACRYPT 2019. LNCS, vol. 11921, pp. 175–195. Springer, Cham (2019). https://doi.org/10.1007/978-3-030-34578-5_7

[CLNY06] Chang, D., Lee, S., Nandi, M., Yung, M.: Indifferentiable security analysis of popular hash functions with prefix-free padding. In: Lai, X., Chen, K. (eds.) ASIACRYPT 2006. LNCS, vol. 4284, pp. 283–298. Springer, Heidelberg (2006). https://doi.org/10.1007/11935230_19

[CN08] Chang, D., Nandi, M.: Improved indifferentiability security analysis of chopMD hash function. In: Nyberg, K. (ed.) FSE 2008. LNCS, vol. 5086, pp. 429–443. Springer, Heidelberg (2008). https://doi.org/10.1007/978-3-540-71039-4_27

[CS14] Chen, S., Steinberger, J.: Tight security bounds for key-alternating ciphers. In: Nguyen, P.Q., Oswald, E. (eds.) EUROCRYPT 2014. LNCS, vol. 8441, pp. 327–350. Springer, Heidelberg (2014). https://doi.org/10.1007/978-3-642-55220-5_19

[Dam89] Damgård, I.B.: A design principle for hash functions. In: Brassard, G. (ed.) CRYPTO 1989. LNCS, vol. 435, pp. 416–427. Springer, New York (1990). https://doi.org/10.1007/0-387-34805-0_39

[DMA18] Daemen, J., Mennink, B., Van Assche, G.: Sound hashing modes of arbitrary functions, permutations, and block ciphers. IACR Trans. Symmetric Cryptol. **2018**(4), 197–228 (2018)

[DRRS09] Dodis, Y., Reyzin, L., Rivest, R.L., Shen, E.: Indifferentiability of permutation-based compression functions and tree-based modes of operation, with applications to MD6. In: Dunkelman, O. (ed.) FSE 2009. LNCS, vol. 5665, pp. 104–121. Springer, Heidelberg (2009). https://doi.org/10.1007/978-3-642-03317-9_7

[GBK16] Gauravaram, P., Bagheri, N., Knudsen, L.R.: Building indifferentiable compression functions from the PGV compression functions. Des. Codes Crypt. **78**(2), 547–581 (2014). https://doi.org/10.1007/s10623-014-0020-z

[GDM20] Gunsing, A., Daemen, J., Mennink, B.: Errata to sound hashing modes of arbitrary functions, permutations, and block ciphers. IACR Trans. Symmetric Cryptol. **2020**(3), 362–366 (2020)

[GLC08] Gong, Z., Lai, X., Chen, K.: A synthetic indifferentiability analysis of some block-cipher-based hash functions. Des. Codes Cryptogr. **48**(3), 293–305 (2008)

[Gun22] Gunsing, A.: Block-Cipher-Based Tree Hashing. Cryptology ePrint Archive, Paper 2022/283 (2022). https://eprint.iacr.org/2022/283

[KBC97] Krawczyk, H., Bellare, M., Canetti, R.: HMAC: keyed-hashing for message authentication. RFC **2104**, 1–11 (1997)

[Lee17] Lee, J.: Indifferentiability of the sum of random permutations toward optimal security. IEEE Trans. Inf. Theory **63**(6), 4050–4054 (2017)

[LGD+09] Luo, Y., Gong, Z., Duan, M., Zhu, B., Lai, X.: Revisiting the Indifferentiability of PGV hash functions. IACR Cryptol. ePrint Arch. **2009**, 265 (2009)

[LLG11] Luo, Y., Lai, X., Gong, Z.: Indifferentiability of domain extension modes for hash functions. In: Chen, L., Yung, M., Zhu, L. (eds.) INTRUST 2011. LNCS, vol. 7222, pp. 138–155. Springer, Heidelberg (2012). https://doi.org/10.1007/978-3-642-32298-3_10

[LMN16] Luykx, A., Mennink, B., Neves, S.: Security analysis of BLAKE2's modes of operation. IACR Trans. Symmetric Cryptol. **2016**(1), 158–176 (2016)

[Men13] Mennink, B.: Indifferentiability of double length compression functions. In: Stam, M. (ed.) IMACC 2013. LNCS, vol. 8308, pp. 232–251. Springer, Heidelberg (2013). https://doi.org/10.1007/978-3-642-45239-0_14

[Mer89] Merkle, R.C.: One way hash functions and DES. In: Brassard, G. (ed.) CRYPTO 1989. LNCS, vol. 435, pp. 428–446. Springer, New York (1990). https://doi.org/10.1007/0-387-34805-0_40

[MP15] Mennink, B., Preneel, B.: On the XOR of multiple random permutations. In: Malkin, T., Kolesnikov, V., Lewko, A.B., Polychronakis, M. (eds.) ACNS 2015. LNCS, vol. 9092, pp. 619–634. Springer, Cham (2015). https://doi.org/10.1007/978-3-319-28166-7_30

[MPN10] Mandal, A., Patarin, J., Nachef, V.: Indifferentiability beyond the birthday bound for the Xor of two public random permutations. In: Gong, G., Gupta, K.C. (eds.) INDOCRYPT 2010. LNCS, vol. 6498, pp. 69–81. Springer, Heidelberg (2010). https://doi.org/10.1007/978-3-642-17401-8_6

[MPS12] Mandal, A., Patarin, J., Seurin, Y.: On the Public Indifferentiability and correlation intractability of the 6-round feistel construction. In: Cramer, R. (ed.) TCC 2012. LNCS, vol. 7194, pp. 285–302. Springer, Heidelberg (2012). https://doi.org/10.1007/978-3-642-28914-9_16

[MRH04] Maurer, U., Renner, R., Holenstein, C.: Indifferentiability, impossibility results on reductions, and applications to the random oracle methodology. In: Naor, M. (ed.) TCC 2004. LNCS, vol. 2951, pp. 21–39. Springer, Heidelberg (2004). https://doi.org/10.1007/978-3-540-24638-1_2

[OANW20] O'Connor, J., Aumasson, J.P., Neves, S., Wilcox-O'Hearn, Z.: BLAKE3. https://blake3.io (2020)

[Pat08] Patarin, J.: The coefficients H technique. In: Avanzi, R.M., Keliher, L., Sica, F. (eds.) SAC 2008. LNCS, vol. 5381, pp. 328–345. Springer, Heidelberg (2009). https://doi.org/10.1007/978-3-642-04159-4_21

[PGV93] Preneel, B., Govaerts, R., Vandewalle, J.: Hash functions based on block ciphers: a synthetic approach. In: Stinson, D.R. (ed.) CRYPTO 1993. LNCS, vol. 773, pp. 368–378. Springer, Heidelberg (1994). https://doi.org/10.1007/3-540-48329-2_31

[SHA08] National Institute of Standards and Technology. Secure Hash Standard (SHS). Federal Information Processing Standards Publication 180–3, October 2008

Provably Secure Reflection Ciphers

Tim Beyne(✉) and Yu Long Chen(✉)

imec-COSIC, KU Leuven, Leuven, Belgium
{tim.beyne,yulong.chen}@esat.kuleuven.be

Abstract. This paper provides the first analysis of reflection ciphers such as PRINCE from a provable security viewpoint.

As a first contribution, we initiate the study of key-alternating reflection ciphers in the ideal permutation model. Specifically, we prove the security of the two-round case and give matching attacks. The resulting security bound takes form $\mathcal{O}(qp^2/2^{2n} + q^2/2^n)$, where q is the number of construction evaluations and p is the number of direct adversarial queries to the underlying permutation. Since the two-round construction already achieves an interesting security lower bound, this result can also be of interest for the construction of reflection ciphers based on a single public permutation.

Our second contribution is a generic key-length extension method for reflection ciphers. It provides an attractive alternative to the FX construction, which is used by PRINCE and other concrete key-alternating reflection ciphers. We show that our construction leads to better security with minimal changes to existing designs. The security proof is in the ideal cipher model and relies on a reduction to the two-round Even-Mansour cipher with a single round key. In order to obtain the desired result, we sharpen the bad-transcript analysis and consequently improve the best-known bounds for the single-key Even-Mansour cipher with two rounds. This improvement is enabled by a new sum-capture theorem that is of independent interest.

Keywords: Reflection ciphers · Public random permutations · Ideal cipher model · Sum capture theorem · PRINCE

1 Introduction

Cryptographers have long been fascinated by self-inverse, or almost self-inverse, encryption schemes. For example, the Enigma rotor machine has the surprising property that its encryption and decryption operations are identical. This feature, enabled by the middle reflector or *Umkehrwalze*, made the encryption device considerably more compact.

Although the reflector ultimately contributed to the demise of Enigma, the use of self-inverse structures was not abandoned and persists in modern cryptography. Feistel ciphers such as the DES, for instance, are equal to their own inverse up to a reordering of the round keys. Despite this property, it was later

Y. Dodis and T. Shrimpton (Eds.): CRYPTO 2022, LNCS 13510, pp. 234–263, 2022.
https://doi.org/10.1007/978-3-031-15985-5_9

shown by Luby and Rackoff [28] and follow-up work that the generic Feistel construction is indeed sound.

Many traditional key-alternating ciphers also use involutions, i.e. self-inverse functions, as their components in order to keep the hardware implementation costs for encryption and decryption similar and to save area. The block ciphers ANUBIS [3], KHAZAD [4] and NOEKEON [16] are early examples of this strategy. Key-alternating ciphers have been extensively analyzed from the perspective of provable security [7,13,20,21,25], with results demonstrating their resistance against generic attacks. The provable security of key-alternating ciphers based on an involution instead of permutations has been studied by Lee [26].

At ASIACRYPT 2012, Borghoff et al. [8] introduced the block cipher PRINCE as an alternative approach to minimizing the overhead of supporting both efficient encryption and decryption. PRINCE has the following *reflection property*: decryption is the same as encryption using a related key. This feature is achieved by using the structure shown in Fig. 1, which we will call the *key-alternating reflection cipher*. Although the use of both permutations and their inverse risks increasing area requirements, this is not a concern for the low-latency use-case that PRINCE aims for. Indeed, PRINCE targets fully unrolled hardware implementations that encrypt a plaintext in a single cycle.

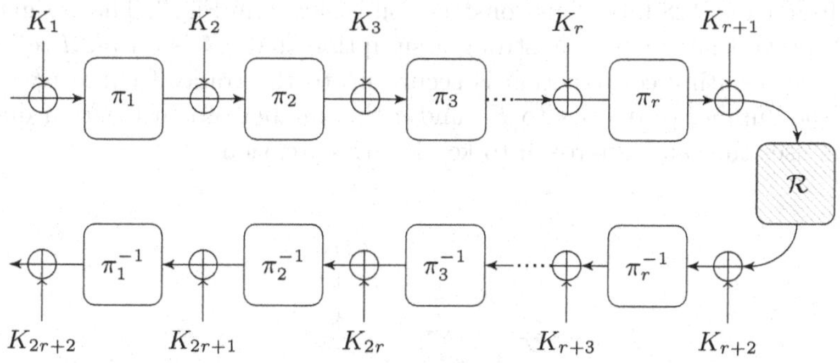

Fig. 1. A $2r$-round key-alternating reflection cipher based on r public permutations $\pi_1, \ldots, \pi_r$ and $2r+2$ keys $K_1, \ldots, K_{2r+2}$. Various key-schedules are possible. In the PRINCE core cipher $K_1 = \ldots = K_{r+1}$ and $K_{r+2} = \ldots = K_{2r+2} \oplus \alpha$ for some constant $\alpha \neq 0$. The reflector $\mathcal{R}$ is an involution.

Following increased interest in lightweight cryptography, and low-latency encryption in particular, several other key-alternating reflection ciphers were subsequently proposed. For example, PRINCESS [10] and PRINCE v2 [11] are variants of PRINCE. The tweakable block ciphers MANTIS [5] and QARMA [1] combine the key-alternating reflection cipher structure with involutive components and target applications such as memory encryption.

Despite their widespread use, the generic security of key-alternating reflection ciphers has not been analyzed from a provable security viewpoint. This stands in sharp contrast to Feistel ciphers and traditional key-alternating ciphers, which have been a regular subject of study in symmetric-key provably security. This is remarkable, since it is natural to wonder whether or not the additional structure of reflection ciphers leads to generic flaws.

Related Work. The block cipher PRINCE has been extensively analyzed from a cryptanalytic point of view, see for instance the results of the PRINCE cryptanalysis challenge which ran between 2014 and 2016 [9]. Boura et al. [10] discuss the choice of the reflector $\mathcal{R}$ and the key-schedule of general key-alternating reflection ciphers.

No results, for any number of rounds or any kind of key-schedule, are known about the provable security of key-alternating reflection ciphers. The study of traditional key-alternating ciphers, in contrast, goes back to Even and Mansour [20] for one round. The analysis of multiple rounds was initiated by Bogdanov et al. [7] and continued in [13,21,25]. Their results consider the case with independent round keys. For the two-round case, the security with three equal keys was shown by Chen et al. [12] at CRYPTO 2014.

Despite the lack of results about the provable security of key-alternating reflection ciphers, the design of PRINCE does rely on results from provable security for the purpose of key-length extension. Specifically, PRINCE uses a variant of the FX construction [24] to extend the key-length of its 64-bit core reflection cipher from 64 to 128 bits. This construction is shown in Fig. 2. The designers of PRINCE prove that, under the strong assumption that E^* is an *ideal reflection cipher*, the resulting construction is secure up to the tradeoff curve $pq = 2^{128}$ with p the number of queries to E^* and q the number of construction queries. MANTIS uses the same approach to key-length extension.

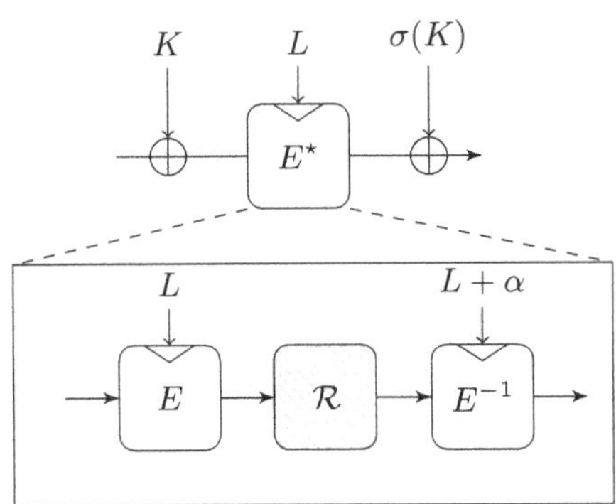

Fig. 2. The structure of PRINCE and MANTIS, with secret keys K and L, and E a block cipher. The map σ is an invertible linear map and $\mathcal{R}$ is a linear involution.

Although the construction in Fig. 2 can offer reasonable security when the number of construction queries q is limited, it has been observed that the security margin offered by the $pq = 2^{128}$ tradeoff may be less comfortable than expected.

In particular, at EUROCRYPT 2015, Dinur [18] proposed new time-memory-data tradeoff attacks against PRINCE. Recently, PRINCE v2 [11] was proposed with the explicit goal of obtaining improved security with minimal changes to the original design. The approach taken by PRINCE v2 is to use alternating round keys, i.e. $K_{2i-1} = K_1$ and $K_{2i} = K_2$ for $i = 1, \ldots, r$ in Fig. 1. They also slightly modify the reflector $\mathcal{R}$.

Contribution. The contribution of this paper is twofold. First, we initiate the study of the provable security of key-alternating reflection ciphers. Second, we provide a simple and generic key-extension method for reflection ciphers that achieves much better security than the FX construction.

For the first contribution, we analyze the security of the two-round variant of the general construction from Fig. 1 in the ideal permutation model. Specifically, our results focus on the case with a linear reflector $\mathcal{R}$ and two alternating round keys (i.e. $K_3 = K_1$, $K_4 = K_2$), similar to the PRINCE v2 construction. Decryption is then the same as encryption up to swapping of the keys K_1 and K_2. We denote this construction by KARC2. Our Theorem 1 shows that any adaptive distinguisher making p primitive queries and q construction queries to KARC2 achieves an advantage of at most $\mathcal{O}(p^2q/2^{2n} + q^2/2^n)$. In Sect. 3.2, alternative key-schedules are discussed, and we show that reducing the number of round keys is nontrivial and even results in insecure constructions for many natural choices of the key-schedule.

The KARC2 construction is the first generic reflection cipher construction with a security proof. This resolves the first case of a problem of intrinsic theoretical interest, similar to the study of key-alternating ciphers. From a more practical perspective, the result limits the power of generic attacks and motivates the general soundness of a widely used construction.

Although KARC2 achieves only birthday-bound security with respect to the number of construction queries q, the best tradeoff between primitive and construction queries satisfies $p^2q = 2^{2n}$. Since the amount of data q is often limited in practice, the latter tradeoff is usually dominant. Hence, we believe the KARC2 construction could also be instantiated directly with concrete reduced-round permutations to build an attractive reflection cipher. Although many permutations are only designed to be efficient in the forward direction, there are exceptions such as Friet [32].

In Sect. 4, we show that Theorem 1 is tight for general choices of the reflector $\mathcal{R}$, by providing two matching generic attacks. The first attack is information-theoretic and shows that the tradeoff curve $p^2q = 2^{2n}$ cannot be improved. The second attack is a variant of the mirror slide attack of Dunkelman, Keller and Shamir [19]. It uses $\mathcal{O}(2^{n/2})$ construction queries and has a similar time-complexity. The advantage achieved by the attack is lower bounded in Theorem 2, thereby showing that the $q^2/2^n$ term in Theorem 1 can not be avoided in general. Although this may suggest that the reflector $\mathcal{R}$ is not that important from a generic viewpoint, it is important from the viewpoint of dedicated cryptanalysis (when all permutations are instantiated). Another reason for considering $\mathcal{R}$ is simply that all practical reflection ciphers have such a layer, and we want our results to say something about their generic security.

The proof of Theorem 1 is given in Sect. 5. It relies on Patarin's H-coefficient technique [13,29]. The good transcript analysis resembles ideas of the first iteration of Patarin's mirror theory [30,31], but additional difficulties appear due to the fact that the underlying permutation can be queried by the distinguisher. Note that the framework of Chen et al. [14] relies on mirror theory for two independent permutations, so it cannot be applied to KARC2, which requires the single permutation variant of mirror theory. For the secret permutation case, different techniques can be used in order to obtain domain separation [17,30]. In our proof, the domain separation is covered by a bad event, which leads to the $q^2/2^n$ term in the final security bound. The proof, like many proofs in provable security, is in an idealized model. The assumption that the primitive is ideal will never be satisfied in practice. For this reason, it is good practice to complement the provable security analysis (which rules out generic attacks) with dedicated cryptanalysis when all components are instantiated.

Our second contribution is a general method to extend the key-length of reflections ciphers, similar to the FX construction shown in Fig. 2, but achieving much better security. Specifically, our proposal is to add the keys K and $\sigma(K)$ again before and after the reflector $\mathcal{R}$ respectively. For this construction, we model the block cipher E as an ideal cipher. Our Theorem 7 shows that any distinguisher making adaptively chosen plaintext and ciphertext queries to this construction achieves an advantage of at most $\widetilde{\mathcal{O}}(p\sqrt{q}/2^{n+k})$, with n the block size and k the key-length of the ideal cipher.

The proof of Theorem 7 is by a reduction to the security of the two-round Even-Mansour cipher with a single key. However, in order to be able to prove that $p^2q = 2^{2(n+k)}$ is the optimal tradeoff for our ideal cipher construction, we had to sharpen the analysis of two-round Even-Mansour by Chen et al. [12]. Hence, as a side-result that is of independent interest, we improve the best known bounds for the two-round Even-Mansour cipher with identical round keys. Figure 3 shows the difference between our new bound and the bound of Chen et al.. This result is presented in Theorem 3.

The proof of Theorem 3 is given in Sect. 6. Our improvement over the result of Chen et al. [12] is due to a sharpening of their bad-transcript analysis. This sharpening is made possible by an improved sum-capture theorem, which we present in Theorem 5 and prove in Sect. 6.1. Our sharpened sum-capture theorem is also of independent interest, as it is applicable to all other proofs relying on this result. In a nutshell, the new result removes the unnecessary discrepancy between the best-known sum-capture theorems for random functions and random permutations. Hence, we are able to avoid a term of order $p^2\sqrt{pq}/2^{2n}$ in the security bound. A detailed discussion of this result is given in Sect. 6.

Section 7 presents our ideal cipher construction and the proof of Theorem 7. When applied to PRINCE or MANTIS, we obtain a reflection cipher with an optimal tradeoff of $p^2q = 2^{256}$. This should be compared to the tradeoff curve $pq = 2^{128}$ for the FX construction. Hence, our construction can tolerate far more construction queries before becoming insecure. Compared to the dedicated

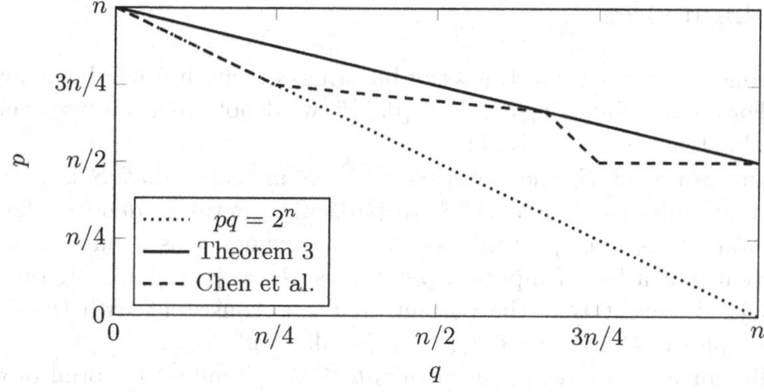

Fig. 3. Comparison between the result of Chen et al. [12] for 2-round Even-Mansour and Theorem 3. The lines correspond to an advantage upper bound equal to one.

construction PRINCE v2, it has the advantage of introducing a more minimalist change. In addition, PRINCE v2 does not completely preserve the reflection property of PRINCE due to the changes it introduces in the reflector $\mathcal{R}$.

Future Work. Our work opens up several directions for interesting future research. Currently, our results only apply when two independent keys are used. Several difficulties in using a single key are discussed in Sect. 3.2, but we believe that using a nonlinear involution σ could resolve these issues. However, this seems to require novel proof techniques, as the sum-capture theorem requires linear mappings. Likewise, it is an open question to categorize all strong linear key schedules using two independent master keys.

Another challenging problem is that the mirror slide attack from Sect. 4.2 suggests that a good choice of the reflector may improve the security of KARC2, in the sense that the birthday bound term $q^2/2^n$ can be avoided. However, proving this seems difficult with state-of-the-art techniques.

A third tantalizing open problem is to generalize our results to a larger number of rounds. Namely, for $r > 1$, can we find sufficient conditions on the key-schedule such that the $2r$-round key-alternating reflection cipher achieves tight security?

It would also be interesting to reduce the time complexity of attacks against the KARC2 construction (potentially down to $\widetilde{\mathcal{O}}(2^{2n/3})$). Note that the analogous problem for two-round Even-Mansour cipher is also open, with the best attack due to Leurent and Sibleyras [27] having a time-complexity of $\mathcal{O}(2^n/\sqrt{n})$.

Another possible future research direction is to design tweakable reflection ciphers from public random permutations. Finally, it could be interesting to study the related key security of KARC2 – apart from the intentional reflection relation, and to perform cryptanalysis of concrete instances of the KARC2 construction.

2 Preliminaries

For a non-negative integer n, the set of bitstrings of length n will be denoted by $\{0,1\}^n$. For any two bitstrings $X, Y \in \{0,1\}^n$, we denote their bitwise exclusive-or as the bitstring $X \oplus Y \in \{0,1\}^n$.

For any finite set $\mathcal{S}$, the notation $S \xleftarrow{\$} \mathcal{S}$ indicates that S is a random variable uniformly distributed on $\mathcal{S}$. In particular, $\mathrm{Perm}(n)$ denotes the set of all permutations on $\{0,1\}^n$ and $\pi \xleftarrow{\$} \mathrm{Perm}(n)$ defines π as a uniform random permutation. For a list of input-output tuples $\mathcal{Q}_\pi = \{(x_1, y_1), \dots\}$, we denote by $\pi \vdash \mathcal{Q}_\pi$ the event that the permutation π is consistent with the queries-response tuples in $\mathcal{Q}_\pi$, i.e. that $\pi(x) = y$ for all $(x, y) \in \mathcal{Q}_\pi$.

Finally, for any non-negative integers $b \leq a$, the falling factorial of a with respect to b will be denoted by $(a)_b$. The value $(a)_b$ is equal to the number of injections from a set of size b to a set of size a. In particular,

$$(a)_b = \begin{cases} 1 & \text{if } b = 0, \\ a(a-1)\dots(a-b+1) & \text{otherwise.} \end{cases}$$

2.1 Block Ciphers

For non-negative integers k and n, a block cipher is a function $F\colon \{0,1\}^k \times \{0,1\}^n \to \{0,1\}^n$, such that for every fixed key $K \in \{0,1\}^k$, the function $F_K(\cdot) = F(K, \cdot)$ is a permutation on $\{0,1\}^n$. The inverse of F_K will be denoted by $F_K^{-1}(\cdot) = F^{-1}(K, \cdot)$.

We will consider block ciphers F based on r public random permutations $\pi_1, \dots, \pi_r \xleftarrow{\$} \mathrm{Perm}(n)$. Our analysis of such constructions will use the strong pseudorandom permutation (sprp) security notion. Specifically, let $\mathcal{D}$ be a distinguisher with bi-directional access to either $(F_K[\pi_1, \dots, \pi_r], \pi_1, \dots, \pi_r)$ for secret key $K \xleftarrow{\$} \{0,1\}^k$, or $(\pi, \pi_1, \dots, \pi_r)$ for $\pi \xleftarrow{\$} \mathrm{Perm}(n)$. The goal of $\mathcal{D}$ is to determine which oracle it was given access to and its advantage with respect to this task is defined as

$$\mathbf{Adv}_F^{\mathrm{sprp}}(\mathcal{D}) = \left|\Pr\left[\mathcal{D}^{F_K^{\pm}[\pi_1,\dots,\pi_r], \pi_1^{\pm},\dots,\pi_r^{\pm}} = 1\right] - \Pr\left[\mathcal{D}^{\pi^{\pm}, \pi_1^{\pm},\dots,\pi_r^{\pm}} = 1\right]\right|.$$

It is possible to build a new block cipher F from an ideal cipher E. The sprp security notion carries over to this case, but the distinguisher $\mathcal{D}$ is given access to the ideal cipher E rather than to r random permutations. This means that $\mathcal{D}$ can query the random permutations $F(K, \cdot)$ or its inverse for any chosen key K. Formally, let $\mathcal{D}$ be a distinguisher with bi-directional access to either $(F_K[E], E)$ for a secret key $K \xleftarrow{\$} \{0,1\}^n$, or (π, E) with $\pi \xleftarrow{\$} \mathrm{Perm}(n)$. The sprp-advantage of $\mathcal{D}$ against F is defined as

$$\mathbf{Adv}_F^{\mathrm{sprp}}(\mathcal{D}) = \left|\Pr\left[\mathcal{D}^{F_K^{\pm}[E], E^{\pm}} = 1\right] - \Pr\left[\mathcal{D}^{\pi^{\pm}, E^{\pm}} = 1\right]\right|.$$

Here $\mathcal{D}^{\mathcal{O}}$ denotes the value returned by $\mathcal{D}$ when interacting with the oracle $\mathcal{O}$ and the superscript $\pm$ indicates that the distinguisher has bi-directional access.

2.2 Patarin's H-Coefficient Technique

We use the H-coefficient technique of Patarin [29], and our description of it follows the modernization of Chen and Steinberger [13].

Consider a deterministic distinguisher $\mathcal{D}$ that is given access to either a real world oracle $\mathcal{O}$ or an ideal world oracle $\mathcal{P}$. The distinguisher's goal is to determine which oracle it is given access to and we denote its advantage by

$$\mathbf{Adv}(\mathcal{D}) = \left|\Pr\left[\mathcal{D}^{\mathcal{O}} = 1\right] - \Pr\left[\mathcal{D}^{\mathcal{P}} = 1\right]\right|.$$

The query-response tuples learned by $\mathcal{D}$ during its interaction with the oracle $\mathcal{O}$ or $\mathcal{P}$ can be summarized in a transcript τ. Let $X_{\mathcal{O}}$ (respectively $X_{\mathcal{P}}$) be a random variable equal to transcript produced by the interaction between $\mathcal{D}$ and $\mathcal{O}$ (respectively $\mathcal{P}$). A particular transcript τ is called attainable if $\Pr[X_{\mathcal{P}} = \tau] > 0$ and the set of all attainable transcripts is denoted by $\mathcal{T}$.

Lemma 1 (H-coefficient technique). *Let $\mathcal{D}$ be any deterministic distinguisher. Define a partition $\mathcal{T} = \mathcal{T}_{\text{good}} \cup \mathcal{T}_{\text{bad}}$, where $\mathcal{T}_{\text{good}}$ is the subset of attainable transcripts $\mathcal{T}$ which contains all the "good" transcripts and $\mathcal{T}_{\text{bad}}$ is the subset with all the "bad" transcripts. If there exists an $\epsilon \geq 0$ such that for all attainable $\tau \in \mathcal{T}_{\text{good}}$,*

$$\frac{\Pr[X_{\mathcal{O}} = \tau]}{\Pr[X_{\mathcal{P}} = \tau]} \geq 1 - \epsilon,$$

then $\mathbf{Adv}(\mathcal{D}) \leq \epsilon + \Pr[X_{\mathcal{P}} \in \mathcal{T}_{\text{bad}}]$.

3 Construction Based on a Public Permutation

In this section, we consider the two-round variant of the general construction shown in Fig. 1. In particular, as shown in Fig. 4, we consider the case with $K_3 = K_1$ and $K_4 = K_2$ and a linear reflector $\mathcal{R}$. This case is of particular interest because it is both a natural choice for the key-schedule, and one which is used by concrete reflection ciphers such as PRINCE v2 [11]. A few alternative choices of the key-schedule are discussed in Sect. 3.2 below.

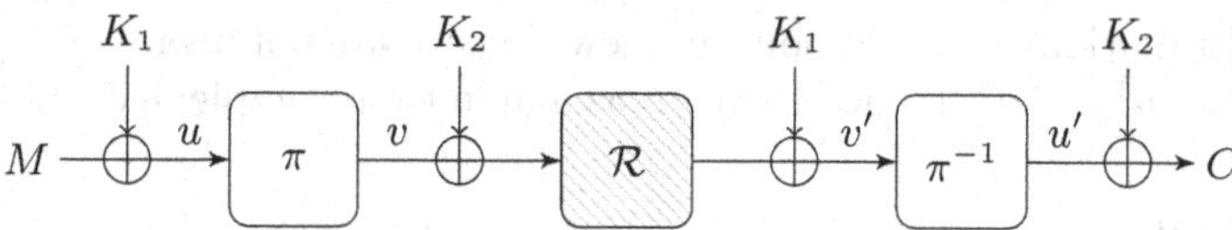

Fig. 4. The KARC2 construction based on a public permutation π and with secret keys K_1 and K_2.

The construction shown in Fig. 4 will be referred to as KARC2, for *key-alternating reflection cipher* with two rounds. Formally, let n be a positive integer, $\pi \in \mathrm{Perm}(n)$, and $\mathcal{R}\colon \{0,1\}^n \to \{0,1\}^n$ a linear involution. The generic construction $\mathsf{KARC2}\colon \{0,1\}^{2n} \times \{0,1\}^n \to \{0,1\}^n$ is defined as

$$\mathsf{KARC2}_{K_1,K_2}[\pi](M) = \pi^{-1}(\mathcal{R}(\pi(M \oplus K_1) \oplus K_2) \oplus K_1) \oplus K_2 \,.$$

The KARC2 construction has the following reflection property:

$$\left(\mathsf{KARC2}_{K_1,K_2}[\pi]\right)^{-1} = \mathsf{KARC2}_{K_2,K_1}[\pi]$$

The security of KARC2 is discussed in Sect. 3.1.

3.1 Security Lower Bound

In Sect. 5, we prove the following security bound for KARC2. As will be shown in Sect. 4, it is also the case that this bound is tight for general choices of the reflector $\mathcal{R}$, i.e., there are specific $\mathcal{R}$ (such as the identity) with a matching attack.

Theorem 1. *Let n be a positive integer, $\pi \xleftarrow{\$} \mathrm{Perm}(n)$ and $K_1, K_2 \xleftarrow{\$} \{0,1\}^n$. Let $\mathcal{R}$ be a linear involution on $\{0,1\}^n$. For any distinguisher $\mathcal{D}$ for $\mathsf{KARC2}_{K_1,K_2}[\pi]$ making at most q construction queries, and at most p primitive queries to $\pi^{\pm}$ such that $p + 2q < 2^{n-1}$, we have*

$$\mathbf{Adv}^{\mathsf{sprp}}_{\mathsf{KARC2}}(\mathcal{D}) \leq \frac{3qp^2}{2^{2n}} + \frac{q^2}{2^n} + \frac{4q^{3/2}}{2^n} + \frac{4q(p+2q)(p+2q+1)}{2^{2n}} \,.$$

On the one hand, Theorem 1 'only' shows that KARC2 achieves birthday-bound security with respect to the number of construction queries q. On the other hand, it also shows that the best possible tradeoff curve between construction and primitive queries is $p^2q = 2^{2n}$ up to a small constant. This is much better than the typical birthday-bound tradeoff $pq = 2^n$. This result is especially important since in practice the number of construction queries is usually limited by the application. The number of primitive queries, however, is only limited by the computational power of the adversary.

The attacks that will be presented in Sect. 4 show that the term $q^2/2^n$ cannot be avoided unless the reflector $\mathcal{R}$ is carefully chosen. However, for any *linear* involution $\mathcal{R}$, there is an attack with advantage approximately $2^{-n/2}$ using $q = 2^{n/2}$ construction queries and no primitive queries. Hence, some terms independent of p cannot be avoided. It will also be shown that the term $p^2q/2^{2n}$ is tight from an information-theoretic point of view, but we are not aware of any attacks achieving the $p^2q = 2^{2n}$ tradeoff with reasonable time complexity.

3.2 Variants

The choice of the key-schedule in Fig. 4 is not the only possibility. One tempting option is to further reduce the number keys by setting $K_2 = \sigma(K_1)$ for some involution σ. However, when σ is linear, this construction would not even be secure up to $q^2/2^n$ for general choices of $\mathcal{R}$. The reason is that $K_1 \oplus K_2 = K_1 \oplus \sigma(K_1)$ can then no longer be uniform random, and this significantly facilitates the attack presented in Sect. 4.2 below. Indeed, one has the following result.

Lemma 2. *Let n be a positive integer and $\sigma : \{0,1\}^n \to \{0,1\}^n$ a linear involution. Then σ has at least $2^{n/2}$ fixed points and the image of $\sigma \oplus \mathsf{id}$, where id is the identity function, contains at most $2^{n/2}$ distinct values.*

Proof. Since $f = \sigma \oplus \mathsf{id}$ is linear, the cardinality of its image is $2^{\dim(\mathrm{im} f)}$. Furthermore, $f^2 = 0$, so $\mathrm{im}(f) \subseteq \ker(f)$ and

$$\dim(\mathrm{im} f) \leq \dim(\ker f) = n - \dim(\mathrm{im} f)\,.$$

It follows that $\dim(\mathrm{im} f) \leq n/2$. The claim about the number of fixed points follows from the observation that the fixed points of σ are precisely the elements of $\ker f$. □

Due to the above issue, we focus on constructions with two keys. The case of one key, which necessarily requires either a special choice of $\mathcal{R}$ or a nonlinear σ, will be left as interesting (but likely challenging) future work. However, even with two keys, several constructions are possible. For example, Boura et al. [10] propose general key-schedules in which the third and fourth key-addition in Fig. 4 (counting from the left) are replaced by $F_2(K_1, K_2)$ and $F_1(K_1, K_2)$ respectively, where F_1 and F_2 are (possibly nonlinear) functions. The construction we analyze is arguably the simplest secure case: $F_1(K_1, K_2) = K_1$ and $F_2(K_1, K_2) = K_2$.

4 Attacks on the Public Permutation Construction

This section shows that the security bound in Theorem 1 is essentially tight by providing two matching generic attacks. The first attack is only information theoretic and has no practical significance: it shows that the tradeoff curve $p^2 q = 2^{2n}$ between the number of construction queries q and the number of primitive queries p can be achieved with a time-complexity of $\mathcal{O}(2^{2n})$. The second attack only uses construction queries and corresponds to the $q^2/2^n$ term in Theorem 1. Contrary to the first attack, the time-complexity of the second attack is limited to $\widetilde{\mathcal{O}}(2^{n/2})$ operations.

4.1 Information Theoretic Attack

Suppose the attacker makes $2q$ construction queries and p primitive queries with inputs-output pairs denoted by $(u_1, v_1), \ldots, (u_p, v_p)$. If $p^2 q = 2^{2n}$, then the expected number of plaintext-ciphertext pairs (M, C) and primitive query indices (i, j) such that

$$\begin{aligned} M \oplus K_1 &= u_i \\ C \oplus K_2 &= u_j\,, \end{aligned} \tag{1}$$

is equal to two. Whenever the above conditions hold, one also has $\mathcal{R}(v_i) \oplus v_j = K_1 \oplus \mathcal{R}(K_2)$. This suggests the following method for obtaining the keys K_1 and K_2. For each possible choice of K_1 and K_2, the adversary proceeds as follows:

(i) Identify the pairs (M, C) and (i, j) for which a collision of type (1) occurs.
(ii) For each of the cases identified in step i , check that $\mathcal{R}(v_i) \oplus v_j = K_1 \oplus \mathcal{R}(K_2)$. If this relation holds for all pairs that were identified, add (K_1, K_2) to a list of candidate keys.

Since the expected number of pairs satisfying (1) is equal to two, each incorrect key (K_1, K_2) has an average probability of $1/2^{2n}$ of being accepted. Hence, the adversary obtains a list of a constant number of candidate keys. These candidate keys can be checked using a few additional queries.

The attack sketched above is purely information theoretic and does not account for the computational cost of the procedure. Since the attack uses $\mathcal{O}(2^{2n})$ table lookups, it indeed has no practical significance. Nevertheless, it shows that the $p^2q/2^{2n}$ term in Theorem 1 cannot be avoided.

Finding attacks with lower computational cost is left for future work and we believe this is an interesting problem, as the situation for the two-round Even-Mansour cipher is similar. In that case, the best known attack is due to Leurent and Sibleyras [27] and has a time-complexity of $\mathcal{O}(2^n/\sqrt{n})$ [27]. Their attack is based on a reduction to the 3-XOR problem. However, since the KARC2 construction has two keys, this approach does not help to reduce the time-complexity below $\mathcal{O}(2^n)$.

4.2 Mirror Slide Attack

The second attack is a variant of the *mirror slide* attack of Dunkelman, Keller and Shamir [19]. The attack is applicable whenever $\mathcal{R}$ has many fixed points and recovers the value of $K_1 \oplus K_2$.

The original mirror slide attack is applicable to the one-round Even-Mansour cipher with an involutive permutation. To apply a similar technique to KARC2, we let

$$\mathcal{I}(x) = \pi^{-1}(K_1 \oplus \mathcal{R}(K_2) \oplus \mathcal{R}(\pi(x)))\,.$$

The KARC2 construction can then be written as $M \mapsto \mathcal{I}(x \oplus K_1) \oplus K_2$. In general, $\mathcal{I}$ is not an involution since

$$\mathcal{I}^{-1}(x) = \pi^{-1}(K_2 \oplus \mathcal{R}(K_1) \oplus \mathcal{R}(\pi(x)))\,.$$

Nevertheless, the equation above shows that $\mathcal{I}$ is an involution iff $K_1 \oplus K_2$ is a fixed point of the reflector $\mathcal{R}$. Since by Lemma 2 any linear involution has at least $2^{n/2}$ fixed points, the mirror slide attack is applicable for a fraction of at least $2^{-n/2}$ weak keys. However, if $\mathcal{R}$ is chosen as the identity map, then all keys are weak.

The attack is based on the following observation. Let (M, C) and (M^*, C^*) be two input-output pairs for the construction such that $M \oplus C^* = K_1 \oplus K_2$ with $K_1 \oplus K_2$ a fixed point of $\mathcal{R}$. Since $M \oplus K_1 = C^* \oplus K_2$, it then follows that

$$M^* = K_1 \oplus \mathcal{I}^{-1}(C^* \oplus K_2) = K_1 \oplus \mathcal{I}(M \oplus K_1) = K_1 \oplus K_2 \oplus C\,.$$

The attack itself is then simple: choose $\Theta(2^{n/2})$ distinct values $M_1, M_2, \ldots$ and $C_1, C_2, \ldots$. With high probability, there exist indices $i \neq j$ such that $M_i \oplus C_j = K_1 \oplus K_2 = M_j \oplus C_i$. Furthermore, since the expected number of collisions is small, one obtains a short list of candidates for $K_1 \oplus K_2$.

Theorem 2 gives a lower bound on the advantage of a distinguisher based on the same principle. Hence, the security lower bound in Theorem 1 is tight in the sense that the $\mathcal{O}(q^2/2^n)$ term cannot be avoided for some choices of $\mathcal{R}$. Finding matching attacks when $\mathcal{R}$ has only $2^{n/2}$ fixed points, or improving the security lower bound in this case, will be left as future work.

Theorem 2 (Mirror slide attack). *Let $n \geq 2$ be an even integer, $\pi \xleftarrow{\$} \mathrm{Perm}(n)$, and $K_1, K_2 \xleftarrow{\$} \{0,1\}^n$. Let $\mathcal{R}$ be a linear involution on $\{0,1\}^n$ with $\ell \geq 4$ fixed points. There exists a distinguisher $\mathcal{D}$ for $\mathsf{KARC2}_{K_1,K_2}[\pi]$ making $3 \cdot 2^{n/2} + 1$ construction queries such that*

$$\mathbf{Adv}^{\mathrm{sprp}}_{\mathsf{KARC2}}(\mathcal{D}) \geq \frac{\ell}{2^n} - \frac{4}{2^n}\,.$$

Proof. Let Δ be an arbitrary constant which is zero on the first $n/2$ bits, such as $\Delta = 0^{n-1} \| 1$. The distinguisher $\mathcal{D}$ follows the approach described above, but using a slightly different approach to make the attack deterministic in the real world (assuming $K_1 \oplus K_2$ is a fixed point of $\mathcal{R}$). Specifically, $\mathcal{D}$ operates as follows:

(i) For $i = 1, \ldots, 2^{n/2}$, query $M_i = \langle i \rangle_{n/2} \parallel 0^{n/2}$ to obtain its encryption C_i. Likewise, query $\widetilde{M}_i = M_i \oplus \Delta$ to obtain its encryption $\widetilde{C}_i$.
(ii) For $i = 1, \ldots, 2^{n/2}$, query $C_i^* = 0^{n/2} \parallel \langle i \rangle_{n/2}$ to obtain M_i^*. Likewise, define $\widetilde{C}_i^* = C_i \oplus \Delta$ and denote the corresponding plaintext by $\widetilde{M}_i^*$.
(iii) If there exists a pair of indices (i,j) such that $M_i \oplus C_j^* = M_i^* \oplus C_j$ and $\widetilde{M}_i \oplus \widetilde{C}_j^* = \widetilde{M}_i^* \oplus \widetilde{C}_j$, then output 1. Otherwise, output 0.

Since in step ii only $2^{n/2} + 1$ new queries are made, the total number of queries made is $3 \cdot 2^{n/2} + 1$. The distinguisher's advantage satisfies

$$\mathbf{Adv}^{\mathrm{sprp}}_{\mathsf{KARC2}}(\mathcal{D}) = \left| \Pr\left[\mathcal{D}^{\mathsf{KARC2}^{\pm}_{K_1,K_2}[\mathcal{R},\pi],\pi^{\pm}} = 1\right] - \Pr\left[\mathcal{D}^{\pi_I^{\pm},\pi^{\pm}} = 1\right] \right|.$$

Suppose that $K_1 \oplus K_2$ is a fixed point of $\mathcal{R}$. In the real world, there is a unique pair (i,j) such that $M_i \oplus C_j^* = K_1 \oplus K_2$. It then also holds that $(M_i \oplus \Delta) \oplus (C_j^* \oplus \Delta) = K_1 \oplus K_2$. Hence, as detailed in the explanation of the mirror slide attack above, the following two events then necessarily hold:

$$\begin{aligned} A_{i,j}: &\qquad M_i \oplus C_j^* = M_j^* \oplus C_i \\ B_{i,j}: &\qquad \widetilde{M}_i \oplus \widetilde{C}_j^* = \widetilde{M}_j^* \oplus \widetilde{C}_i\,. \end{aligned}$$

Thus, since the number of fixed points of $\mathcal{R}$ is ℓ,

$$\Pr\left[\mathcal{D}^{\mathsf{KARC2}^{\pm}_{K_1,K_2}[\mathcal{R},\pi],\pi^{\pm}} = 1\right] \geq \ell/2^n\,.$$

For the ideal world, we have

$$\Pr\left[\mathcal{D}^{\pi_I^\pm,\pi^\pm}=1\right]=\Pr\left[\bigvee_{i,j} A_{i,j}\wedge B_{i,j}\right]\le 2^n\Pr\left[A_{1,1}\wedge B_{1,1}\right]\le\frac{4}{2^n}\,.$$

Hence, the result follows provided that $\ell \geq 4$.

5 Security Proof for the Public Permutation Construction

In this section we prove Theorem 1. Let $K_1, K_2 \xleftarrow{\$} \{0,1\}^n$ and $\pi_I, \pi \xleftarrow{\$} \mathrm{Perm}(n)$. Consider any computationally unbounded and deterministic distinguisher $\mathcal{D}$ with access to the oracles $(\mathsf{KARC2}^{\pm}_{K_1,K_2}[\pi], \pi^{\pm})$ in the real world and $(\pi_I^{\pm}, \pi^{\pm})$ in the ideal world.

The distinguisher makes q construction queries to $\mathsf{KARC2}^{\pm}_{K_1,K_2}[\pi]$ or $\pi_I^{\pm}$, and these are summarized in a transcript of the form $\tau_0 = \{(M_1, C_1), \ldots, (M_q, C_q)\}$. It also makes p primitive queries to $\pi^{\pm}$, and these are summarized in the transcript $\tau_1 = \{(u_1, v_1), \ldots, (u_p, v_p)\}$. Without loss of generality, it can be assumed that the distinguisher does not make duplicate construction or primitive queries.

After $\mathcal{D}$'s interaction with the oracles, but before it outputs its decision, we disclose the keys K_1 and K_2 to the distinguisher. This can only increase its advantage. In the real world, these are the keys used in the construction. In the ideal world, K_1 and K_2 are dummy keys drawn uniformly at random. The complete view is denoted by $\tau = (\tau_0, \tau_1, K_1, K_2)$.

5.1 Bad Events

Throughout the proof, let $U = \{u \mid (u, v) \in \tau_1\}$ and $V = \{v \mid (u, v) \in \tau_1\}$. Recall that $\mathcal{R}\colon \{0,1\}^n \to \{0,1\}^n$ is an involution, i.e. $\mathcal{R}^{-1} = \mathcal{R}$. We say that $\tau \in \mathcal{T}_{\text{bad}}$ if and only if there exist construction queries $(M_i, C_i), (M_j, C_j) \in \tau_0$ and primitive queries $(u, v), (u', v') \in \tau_1$ such that one of the following conditions holds:

$$\text{bad}_1\colon M_j \oplus C_i = K_1 \oplus K_2\,, \tag{2}$$

$$\text{bad}_2\colon M_j \oplus u = K_1 \text{ and } C_j \oplus u' = K_2\,, \tag{3}$$

$$\text{bad}_3\colon M_j \oplus u = K_1 \text{ and } \mathcal{R}(v) \oplus v' = K_1 \oplus \mathcal{R}(K_2)\,, \tag{4}$$

$$\text{bad}_4\colon C_j \oplus u' = K_2 \text{ and } v \oplus \mathcal{R}(v') = \mathcal{R}(K_1) \oplus K_2\,, \tag{5}$$

When $p < q$, we also need the following two bad events for our good transcripts analysis:

$$\text{bad}_5\colon \alpha_1 = |\{(M_j, C_j) \in \tau_0 \mid M_j \oplus K_1 \in U\}| \geq \sqrt{q}\,, \tag{6}$$

$$\text{bad}_6\colon \alpha_2 = |\{(M_j, C_j) \in \tau_0 \mid C_j \oplus K_2 \in U\}| \geq \sqrt{q}\,. \tag{7}$$

Any attainable transcript τ for which $\tau \notin \mathcal{T}_{\text{bad}}$ will be called a good transcript.

We give an informal explanation of the definition of the first four bad events. The first bad event is necessary to exclude the mirror slide attack that was described in Sect. 4.2. The second bad event is exploited by the information-theoretic attack from Sect. 4.1. The motivation behind bad_3 and bad_4 is similar. In fact, note that $\mathcal{R}(v) \oplus v' = K_1 \oplus \mathcal{R}(K_2)$ in bad_3 and $v \oplus \mathcal{R}(v') = \mathcal{R}(K_1) \oplus K_2$ in bad_4 express the same equation. In the real world, if bad_1 does not hold, then every construction query j induces *exactly two* evaluations $(u, v), (u', v')$ of the underlying public permutation π, and these two pairs satisfy

$$\begin{aligned} M_j \oplus u &= K_1 \,, \\ C_j \oplus u' &= K_2 \,, \\ \mathcal{R}(v) \oplus v' &= K_1 \oplus \mathcal{R}(K_2) \,. \end{aligned}$$

Clearly, u and u' are fixed by M_j (if in the forward direction) or C_j (if in the inverse direction) and K_1, K_2, but there is "freedom" in the value $\mathcal{R}(v) \oplus v'$. If it happens to be that the distinguisher queried u, i.e., that $(u, v) \in \tau_1$, the construction query also fixes the input-output tuple (u', v'). However, in the ideal world, there is no such dependency. This means that if the adversary queries $u = M_j \oplus K_1$ and $u' = C_j \oplus K_2$ to π, with high probability the third equation would not hold. An identical reasoning applies for the case where the distinguisher happened to have set any other two out of three equations.

5.2 Probability of Bad Events in the Ideal World

We want to bound the probability $\Pr[X_\mathcal{P} \in \mathcal{T}_{\text{bad}}]$ that an ideal world transcript τ satisfies either of (2)–(7). Therefore, by the union bound, the probability that $X_\mathcal{P} \in \mathcal{T}_{\text{bad}}$ can be bounded as

$$\Pr[X_\mathcal{P} \in \mathcal{T}_{\text{bad}}] \le \sum_{i=1}^{6} \Pr[\text{bad}_i] \,.$$

1st Bad Event. We first consider the bad event bad_1. Here, we rely on the randomness of $K_1 \oplus K_2$. Since K_1 and K_2 are dummy keys generated independently of τ_0 and τ_1, the probability that (2) holds for fixed i and j is $1/2^n$. Summing over q^2 possible choices of the pair (i, j), we have

$$\Pr[\text{bad}_1] \le \frac{q^2}{2^n} \,.$$

2nd Bad Event. We now consider the event bad_2. For any construction query $(M_j, C_j) \in \tau_0$ and any primitive queries (u, v) and (u', v'), the only randomness in the first equation of (3) is K_1 and the only randomness in the second equation is K_2. This means that the event that one of the equations defining bad_2 holds is independent of the event that the other one holds. Since the keys $K_1, K_2 \xleftarrow{\$} \{0,1\}^n$ are dummy keys generated independently of τ_0 and τ_1, the probability that bad_2 holds for a fixed choice of j, (u, v), and (u', v') is $1/2^{2n}$. Summing over the q possible construction queries and p^2 possible pairs of primitive queries, we get

$$\Pr[\text{bad}_2] \le \frac{qp^2}{2^{2n}} \,.$$

3rd Bad Event. Next, we consider the bad event bad_3. Note that in the second equation of (4), we can replace K_1 by $M_j \oplus u$. Hence, the only randomness in the first equation is K_1 and the only randomness in the second equation (conditional on the first) is K_2. The events that one of the equations defining bad_2 holds is therefore independent of the other. Summed over q possible construction queries and p^2 possible pairs of primitive queries, we get

$$\Pr[\text{bad}_3] \leq \frac{qp^2}{2^{2n}}.$$

4th Bad Event. The same reasoning as in the case of bad_3 applies to bad_4. Hence, it also holds that $\Pr[\text{bad}_4] \leq qp^2/2^{2n}$.

5th Bad Event. Finally, if $p < q$, we also consider the bad event bad_5. Note that α_1 is a random variable over the random choice of K_1, and it is independent of K_2. Furthermore, by the uniformity of K_1,

$$\mathbb{E}[\alpha_1] = \sum_{j=1}^{q} \sum_{u \in U} \Pr[M_j \oplus K_1 = u] = \frac{qp}{2^n},$$

Hence, by Markov's inequality and because we only consider this event for $p < q$,

$$\Pr[\text{bad}_5] \leq \frac{\sqrt{q}p}{2^n} \leq \frac{q^{3/2}}{2^n}.$$

6th Bad Event. The analysis of the last bad event is similarly to that of bad_5. Hence, we also have $\Pr[\text{bad}_6] \leq q^{3/2}/2^n$.

Conclusion. Summing the probabilities of the bad events, we get

$$\Pr[X_{\mathcal{P}} \in \mathcal{T}_{\text{bad}}] \leq \frac{3qp^2}{2^{2n}} + \frac{q^2}{2^n} + \frac{2q^{3/2}}{2^n}. \tag{8}$$

This concludes the analysis of the bad transcripts in the ideal world.

5.3 Ratio for Good Transcripts

Before we continue with the proof, we present the following lemma, which will be useful in the good transcript analysis.

Lemma 3. *Let $a, b, c \geq 0$ and $N \geq 1$ be integers such that $2a + b \leq N/2$ and $2a + c + 1 \leq N/2$. Then*

$$\prod_{i=1}^{a} \frac{(N-i)(N-b-c-3i)}{(N-b-2i)(N-c-2i-1)} \geq 1 - \frac{4a(2a+b)(2a+c+1)}{N^2}$$

Proof. One has

$$\begin{aligned}
&\prod_{i=1}^{a} \frac{(N-i)(N-b-c-3i)}{(N-b-2i)(N-c-2i-1)} \\
&\quad \geq \prod_{i=1}^{a} \frac{N^2 - N(b+c+4i) - N}{N^2 - N(b+c+4i+1) + (b+2i)(c+2i+1)} \\
&\quad = \prod_{i=1}^{a} \left(1 - \frac{(b+2i)(c+2i+1)}{N^2 - N(b+c+4i+1) + (b+2i)(c+2i+1)}\right) \\
&\quad = \prod_{i=1}^{a} \left(1 - \frac{(b+2i)(c+2i+1)}{(N-b-2i)(N-c-2i-1)}\right) \\
&\quad \geq 1 - \frac{a(2a+b)(2a+c+1)}{(N-b-2a)(N-c-2a-1)} \\
&\quad \geq 1 - \frac{4a(2a+b)(2a+c+1)}{N^2},
\end{aligned}$$

where for the last inequality we used $2a+b \leq N/2$ and $2a+c+1 \leq N/2$. □

Consider an attainable transcript $\tau \in \mathcal{T}_{\text{good}}$. We now lower bound $\Pr[X_{\mathcal{O}} = \tau]$ and compute $\Pr[X_{\mathcal{P}} = \tau]$ in order to obtain a lower bound for the ratio of these probabilities. For the ideal world oracle $\mathcal{P}$, the probability of any good transcript τ is equal to

$$\begin{aligned}
\Pr[X_{\mathcal{P}} = \tau] &= \frac{1}{2^{2n}} \cdot \frac{(2^n - p)!}{2^n!} \cdot \frac{(2^n - q)!}{2^n!} \\
&= \frac{1}{2^{2n}} \cdot \frac{1}{(2^n)_p} \cdot \frac{1}{(2^n)_q}.
\end{aligned}$$

The first factor is due to the number of possible keys K_1 and K_2. The second and third factors correspond to the probability that the uniform random permutations π and π_I are consistent with the transcripts τ_1 and τ_0 respectively.

Similarly, the real world oracle $\mathcal{O}$ is compatible with a good transcript τ if and only if it is compatible with τ_0 and τ_1. Hence,

$$\Pr[X_{\mathcal{O}} = \tau] = \frac{1}{2^{2n}} \cdot \frac{1}{(2^n)_p} \cdot \Pr[\mathsf{KARC2}^{\pm}_{K_1,K_2}[\pi] \vdash \tau_0 \mid \pi \vdash \tau_1],$$

where the probability is taken with respect to $\pi \xleftarrow{\$} \mathrm{Perm}(n)$ and conditional on the keys. As before, the first factor corresponds to the number of possible keys K_1 and K_2. The second factor is the probability that π is consistent with τ_1. The third factor is the probability that the construction $\mathsf{KARC2}^{\pm}_{K_1,K_2}[\pi]$ is consistent with τ_0, given the keys K_1, K_2, and given that π is compliant with τ_1.

If we let $\rho(\tau) = \Pr[\mathsf{KARC2}^{\pm}_{K_1,K_2}[\pi] \vdash \tau_0 \mid \pi \vdash \tau_1]$, then from the above we obtain that

$$\frac{\Pr[X_{\mathcal{O}} = \tau]}{\Pr[X_{\mathcal{P}} = \tau]} = (2^n)_q\, \rho(\tau). \tag{9}$$

In order to bound $\rho(\tau)$, we re-group the construction queries in τ_0 according to their collisions with the primitive queries:

$$\begin{aligned} Q_{U_1} &= \{(M_j, C_j) \in \tau_0 \mid M_j \oplus K_1 \in U\}, \\ Q_{U_2} &= \{(M_j, C_j) \in \tau_0 \mid C_j \oplus K_2 \in U\}, \\ Q_0 &= \{(M_j, C_j) \in \tau_0 \mid M_j \oplus K_1, C_j \oplus K_2 \notin U\}. \end{aligned}$$

By definition, $\alpha_1 = |Q_{U_1}|$ and $\alpha_2 = |Q_{U_2}|$. Also note that $Q_{U_1} \cap Q_{U_2} = \emptyset$ by $\neg\text{bad}_2$, $Q_{U_1} \cap Q_0 = \emptyset$ and $Q_{U_2} \cap Q_0 = \emptyset$ by the definition of Q_{U_1}, Q_{U_2}, and Q_0. Denote respectively by E_1, E_2, and E_0 the events that $\mathsf{KARC2}^{\pm}_{K_1,K_2}[\pi] \vdash Q_{U_1}$, Q_{U_2}, and Q_0 such that

$$\rho(\tau) = \Pr[E_1 \wedge E_2 \mid \pi \vdash \tau_1] \Pr[E_0 \mid E_1 \wedge E_2 \wedge \pi \vdash \tau_1]. \tag{10}$$

Lower Bounding $\Pr[E_1 \wedge E_2 \mid \pi \vdash \tau_1]$. The consistency condition $\pi \vdash \tau_1$ already defines *exactly* p distinct input-output relations for π. We know that for each $(M_j, C_j) \in Q_{U_1}$, there is an unique $(u, v) \in \tau_1$ such that $M_j \oplus K_1 = u$, and $\pi(M_j \oplus K_1) = v$. We define

$$\begin{aligned} \tilde{V}_2 &= \{\mathcal{R}(\pi(M_j \oplus K_1) \oplus K_2) \oplus K_1 \colon (M_j, C_j) \in Q_{U_1}\}, \\ \tilde{U}_2 &= \{C_j \oplus K_2 \colon (M_j, C_j) \in Q_{U_1}\}. \end{aligned}$$

Similarly, for each $(M_j, C_j) \in Q_{U_2}$, there is a unique $(u, v) \in \tau_1$ such that $C_j \oplus K_2 = u$, and $\pi(C_j \oplus K_2) = v$. Again, define

$$\begin{aligned} \tilde{V}_1 &= \{\mathcal{R}(\pi(C_j \oplus K_2) \oplus K_1) \oplus K_2 \mid (M_j, C_j) \in Q_{U_2}\}, \\ \tilde{U}_1 &= \{M_j \oplus K_1 \mid (M_j, C_j) \in Q_{U_2}\}. \end{aligned}$$

Note that all values in $\tilde{U}_1$ and all values in $\tilde{V}_2$ are distinct since the M_j's are distinct, and all values in $\tilde{U}_2$ and all values in $\tilde{V}_1$ are distinct since the C_j's are distinct. We also have $\tilde{U}_1 \cap \tilde{U}_2 = \tilde{V}_1 \cap \tilde{V}_2 = \emptyset$ by $\neg\text{bad}_1$, $U \cap \tilde{U}_1 = U \cap \tilde{U}_2 = \emptyset$ by $\neg\text{bad}_2$, $V \cap \tilde{V}_2 = \emptyset$ by $\neg\text{bad}_3$, and $V \cap \tilde{V}_1 = \emptyset$ by $\neg\text{bad}_4$. Hence, the events E_1 and E_2 define *exactly* $\alpha = |Q_{U_1}| + |Q_{U_2}|$ new and distinct input-output pairs of π and it follows that

$$\Pr[E_1 \wedge E_2 \mid \pi \vdash \tau_1] = \frac{1}{(2^n - p)_\alpha}. \tag{11}$$

Lower Bounding $\Pr[E_0 \mid E_1 \wedge E_2 \wedge \pi \vdash \tau_1]$. The conditions $\pi \vdash \tau_1$, E_1 and E_2 now define *exactly* $p' = |U \cup \tilde{U}_1 \cup \tilde{U}_2| = |V \cup \tilde{V}_1 \cup \tilde{V}_2| = p + \alpha$ distinct input-output pairs of π. Our goal now is to count the number of new distinct input-output relations for π induced by the event E_0. Recall that the event E_0 holds if and only if the reflection cipher is consistent with the construction queries in Q_0, i.e. $\mathsf{KARC2}_{K_1,K_2}[\pi] \vdash Q_0$. The queries in Q_0 can be labeled as

$$Q_0 = \{(M_{l_1}, C_{l_1}), \ldots, (M_{l_{q'}}, C_{l_{q'}})\},$$

where $q' = |Q_0| = q - \alpha$ is the total number of these queries.

The event E_0 defines exactly $2q'$ relations for π of the form $\pi(\bar{u}_{2i-1}) = \bar{v}_{2i-1}$ and $\pi(\bar{u}_{2i}) = \bar{v}_{2i}$, where $\bar{u}_{2i-1} = M_{l_i} \oplus K_1$ and $\bar{u}_{2i} = C_{l_i} \oplus K_2$ for $i = 1, \ldots, q'$. By the definition of Q_0 and because bad_1 does not hold for good transcripts, it follows that

$$\{\bar{u}_1, \ldots, \bar{u}_{2q'}\} \not\subseteq U \cup \tilde{U}_1 \cup \tilde{U}_2 .$$

Hence, taking into account that π is a permutation, the values $\bar{v}_1, \ldots, \bar{v}_{2q'}$ must satisfy the following conditions (for $i = 1, \ldots, q'$) in the real world:

(1) $\mathcal{R}(\bar{v}_{2i-1}) \oplus \bar{v}_{2i} = K_1 \oplus \mathcal{R}(K_2)$.
(2) The variables $\bar{v}_{2i-1}$ additionally satisfy:
  (a) $\bar{v}_{2i-1} \notin V \cup \tilde{V}_1 \cup \tilde{V}_2$,
  (b) $\bar{v}_{2i-1} \notin \{\bar{v}_1, \ldots, \bar{v}_{2i-2}\}$ if $i > 1$.
(3) The variables $\bar{v}_{2i}$ additionally satisfy:
  (a) $\bar{v}_{2i} \notin V \cup \tilde{V}_1 \cup \tilde{V}_2$,
  (b) $\bar{v}_{2i} \notin \{\bar{v}_1, \bar{v}_3, \ldots, \bar{v}_{2i-1}\}$ if $i > 1$.

Observe that whenever conditions (1) and (2b) are satisfied, then it also holds that $\bar{v}_{2i} \notin \{\bar{v}_2, \bar{v}_4, \ldots, \bar{v}_{2i-2}\}$, since $K_1 \oplus \mathcal{R}(K_2)$ is a fixed value. It follows that conditions (1), (2b) and (3b) ensure that the values $\bar{v}_1, \ldots, \bar{v}_{2q'}$ are distinct.

For any positive integer $m \leq q'$, let N_m denote the number of distinct tuples $(\bar{v}_1, \ldots, \bar{v}_{2m})$ satisfying the conditions above for $i = 1, \ldots, m$. In particular, for each of the $N_{q'}$ possible consistent choices of $(\bar{v}_1, \ldots, \bar{v}_{2q'})$, the event E_0 is equivalent to exactly $2q'$ new input-output relations for π. Hence,

$$\Pr[E_0 \mid E_1 \wedge E_2 \wedge \pi \vdash \tau_1] = \frac{N_{q'}}{(2^n - p')_{2q'}} . \tag{12}$$

Below, a recursive formula for N_m in terms of N_{m-1} will be determined. This formula leads to a lower bound for N_m/N_{m-1}. Finally, in order to lower bound $N_{q'}$, the following telescoping product will be used ($N_0 = 1$):

$$N_{q'} = \prod_{m=1}^{q'} \frac{N_m}{N_{m-1}} . \tag{13}$$

Define R_m as the set of all tuples $(\bar{v}_1, \ldots, \bar{v}_{2m})$ that satisfy all conditions above for $i = 1, \ldots, m-1$ and satisfy condition (1) for $i = m$, but not (2) and (3) . It is easy to see that $|R_m| = 2^n N_{m-1}$.

Furthermore, let S_m be the set of values $(\bar{v}_1, \ldots, \bar{v}_{2m})$ also satisfying all conditions for $i = 1, \ldots, m-1$, and additionally satisfying (1) and (2) but *not* (3) for $i = m$. Define T_m analogously but with values satisfying (1) and (3) but *not* (2) for $i = m$. The set of complete solutions can then be written as $R_m \setminus (S_m \cup T_m)$. Hence, by the union bound,

$$N_{2m+2} = |R_m \setminus (S_m \cup T_m)| = |R_m| - |S_m \cup T_m| \geq |R_m| - |S_m| - |T_m| . \tag{14}$$

Since any $(\bar{v}_1, \ldots, \bar{v}_{2m}) \in S_m$ satisfies $\bar{v}_{2m-1} \in \{\bar{v}_1, \ldots, \bar{v}_{2m-2}\} \cup V_1 \cup \tilde{V}_1 \cup \tilde{V}_2$, one has that $|S_m| \leq (p' + 2m - 2)N_{m-1}$. Similarly, $|T_m| \leq (p' + m - 1)N_{m-1}$. Hence, substituting these inequalities and $|R_m| = 2^n N_{m-1}$ in (14) and dividing out N_{m-1} yields

$$\frac{N_m}{N_{m-1}} \geq 2^n - (p' + 2m - 2) - (p' + m - 1) = 2^n - 2p' - 3m + 3\,.$$

Using the telescoping product (13), it follows that

$$N_{q'} \geq \prod_{m=1}^{q'} (2^n - 2p' - 3m + 3) \geq \prod_{i=0}^{q'-1} (2^n - 2p' - 3i)\,.$$

Combining (10), (11) and (12), we obtain

$$\begin{aligned}\frac{\Pr[X_{\mathcal{O}} = \tau]}{\Pr[X_{\mathcal{P}} = \tau]} &\geq N_{q'} \frac{(2^n)_q}{(2^n - p')_{2q'}\,(2^n - p)_\alpha} \\ &\geq \underbrace{N_{q'} \frac{(2^n)_{q'}}{(2^n - p')_{2q'}}}_{A} \cdot \underbrace{\frac{(2^n - q')_\alpha}{(2^n - p)_\alpha}}_{B}\,. \end{aligned} \tag{15}$$

Plugging in the lower bound for $N_{q'}$ in A yields

$$\begin{aligned} A &\geq \frac{\prod_{i=0}^{q'-1} (2^n - i)(2^n - 2p' - 3i)}{(2^n - p')_{2q'}} \\ &\geq \prod_{i=0}^{q'-1} \frac{(2^n - i)(2^n - 2p' - 3i)}{(2^n - p' - 2i)(2^n - p' - 2i - 1)} \\ &\geq 1 - \frac{4q'(p' + 2q')(p' + 2q' + 1)}{2^{2n}} \\ &\geq 1 - \frac{4q(p + 2q)(p + 2q + 1)}{2^{2n}}\,, \end{aligned} \tag{16}$$

where we used Lemma 3 with $a = q'$ and $b = c = p'$, and the fact that $q' \leq q$ and $p' + 2q' + 1 \leq p + 2q + 1 \leq 2^n/2$.

Next, we consider the factor B in (15). Note that for $p \geq q \geq q'$ and using the fact that $q = q' + \alpha$, we have $B \geq 1$. For $p < q$, we have

$$B \geq \frac{(2^n - q')_\alpha}{2^{\alpha n}} \geq \left(\frac{2^n - q}{2^n}\right)^\alpha \geq 1 - \frac{2q^{3/2}}{2^n}\,, \tag{17}$$

where we used $\alpha = \alpha_1 + \alpha_2 \leq 2\sqrt{q}$, which is due to $\neg\mathrm{bad}_5$, and $\neg\mathrm{bad}_6$.

Conclusion. From (15), (16), and (17) we conclude that

$$\frac{\Pr[X_{\mathcal{O}} = \tau]}{\Pr[X_{\mathcal{P}} = \tau]} \geq 1 - \frac{4q(p + 2q)(p + 2q + 1)}{2^{2n}} - \frac{2q^{3/2}}{2^n} =: 1 - \epsilon\,,$$

using $(1 - x)(1 - y) \geq 1 - x - y$.

5.4 Conclusion

Using Patarin's H-Coefficient technique (Lemma 1), we obtain

$$\mathbf{Adv}^{\mathsf{sprp}}_{\mathsf{KARC2}}(\mathcal{D}) \leq \frac{3qp^2}{2^{2n+1}} + \frac{q^2}{2^n} + \frac{4q(p + 2q)(p + 2q + 1)}{2^{2n}} + \frac{4q^{3/2}}{2^n}\,.$$

6 Sharpened Analysis of Two-Round Even-Mansour

As an intermediate result that will be used to prove the security of our ideal cipher construction, we consider the following single-key variant of the 2-round Even-Mansour cipher. For any positive integer n, let $\pi_1, \pi_2 \in \text{Perm}(n)$, and let $\gamma_1, \gamma_2 \colon \{0,1\}^n \to \{0,1\}^n$ be arbitrary invertible linear maps on $\{0,1\}^n$ with respect to $\oplus$. Define the generic construction $\mathsf{EMIP2} \colon \{0,1\}^n \times \{0,1\}^n \to \{0,1\}^n$ as

$$\mathsf{EMIP2}_K[\pi_1, \pi_2](M) = \pi_2(\pi_1(M \oplus K) \oplus \gamma_1(K)) \oplus \gamma_2(K)\,.$$

Chen et al. [12] showed that for $\gamma_1 = \gamma_2 = \mathsf{id}$, EMIP2 is secure up to $\widetilde{\mathcal{O}}(2^{2n/3})$ queries. In this section, the following sharpened result will be shown. The result is sharper because, as explained below, our proof avoids the term $p^2\sqrt{qp}/2^{2n}$ in the bad transcript analysis. The latter term can play an important role when p is large. The difference between Theorem 3 and the result of Chen et al. is illustrated in Fig. 3 in the introduction.

Theorem 3. *Let $n \geq 4$ be an integer, let $K \xleftarrow{\$} \{0,1\}^n$ and $\pi_1, \pi_2 \xleftarrow{\$} \text{Perm}(n)$ independent and uniform random permutations. Let $\mathcal{D}$ be any distinguisher for $\mathsf{EMIP2}_K[\pi_1, \pi_2]$ making at most $q > 1$ construction queries, at most p primitive queries to $\pi_1^{\pm}$ and at most p primitive queries to $\pi_2^{\pm}$. For all $q < 2^{n-1}$ or $q = 2^n$, we have*

$$\mathbf{Adv}^{\mathrm{sprp}}_{\mathsf{EMIP2}}(\mathcal{D}) \leq \frac{12}{2^{2c-n}} + \frac{7qp^2}{2^{2n}} + \frac{6\sqrt{3cqp^2}}{2^n}\,,$$

with $c > 0$ an arbitrary real number.

We prove Theorem 3 in Sect. 6.2. The bad transcript analysis of Chen et al. [12] relies on a sum-capture theorem. The sharpened bound in Theorem 3 is due to a sharpening of this result. Several variants of the sum-capture theorem exist for different situations [12,15]. These results build on the work of Babai [2] and Steinberger [33]. Typically, a sum-capture theorem states that for a random subset Z of $\{0,1\}^n$ of size q, the quantity

$$\mu(Z, A, B) = |\{(z, a, b) \in Z \times A \times B \colon z = a \oplus b\}|$$

is not much larger than $q\,|A|\,|B|\,/2^n$ for any possible choice of A and B, except with negligible probability. In our setting, Z will consist of query-response tuples from a permutation, i.e. Z consists of values $u_i \oplus v_i$ where $\{(u_1, v_1), \ldots, (u_q, v_q)\}$ is a permutation transcript. For this case, Chen et al. [12] proved the following result.

Theorem 4 (Chen et al. [12]). *Let Γ be an invertible linear map on the $\mathbb{F}_2$-vector space $\{0,1\}^n$. Let $\pi \xleftarrow{\$} \text{Perm}(n)$, let $\mathcal{D}$ be some probabilistic algorithm making exactly q distinct two-sided adaptive queries to π. Let $Z = \{(u_1, v_1), \ldots, (u_q, v_q)\}$ be the transcript of the interaction of $\mathcal{D}$ with π, which consists of $q \geq 1$ pairs such that either $v_i = \pi(u_i)$ or $u_i = \pi(v_i)$ for all $i = 1, \ldots, q$. For any two subsets $A, B \subseteq \{0,1\}^n$, let*

$$\mu(Z, A, B) = |\{((u, v), a, b) \in Z \times A \times B \colon u \oplus a = \Gamma(v \oplus b)\}| \,.$$

Then, for $9n \leq q \leq 2^{n-1}$, we have

$$\Pr\left[\mu(Z, A, B) \geq \frac{q\,|A|\,|B|}{2^n} + \frac{2q^2\sqrt{|A|\,|B|}}{2^n} + 3\sqrt{nq\,|A|\,|B|}\right] \leq \frac{2}{2^n}\,.$$

In Sect. 6.1, we prove the following sharpened and simplified version of their result. For $c = n$, the bound in the theorem below is essentially identical to the one given in the sum-capture theorem of Cogliati et al. [15, Lemma 1] for the case where Z results from the interaction with a random *function*. Hence, our result removes the unnecessary discrepancy between the sum-capture theorems for random functions and random permutations.

Theorem 5 (Sum-capture theorem). *Let Γ be an invertible linear map on the $\mathbb{F}_2$-vector space $\{0,1\}^n$. Let $\pi \xleftarrow{\$} \mathrm{Perm}(n)$, and let $\mathcal{D}$ be some probabilistic algorithm making exactly q distinct two-sided adaptive queries to π. Let $Z = \{(u_1, v_1), \ldots, (u_q, v_q)\}$ be the transcript of the interaction of $\mathcal{D}$ with π, which consists of $q \geq 1$ pairs such that either $v_i = \pi(u_i)$ or $u_i = \pi(v_i)$ for all $i = 1, \ldots, q$. For any two subsets $A, B \subseteq \{0,1\}^n$, let*

$$\mu(Z, A, B) = |\{((u, v), a, b) \in Z \times A \times B \colon u \oplus a = \Gamma(v \oplus b)\}| \,.$$

For any real number $c > 0$, it then holds that

$$\Pr\left[\mu(Z, A, B) \geq \frac{q\,|A|\,|B|}{2^n} + 2\sqrt{3cq\,|A|\,|B|}\right] \leq \frac{4}{2^{2c-n}}\,.$$

As can be seen by comparing Theorem 4 and Theorem 5, our version of the sum-capture theorem does not contain the term $2q^2\sqrt{|A|\,|B|}/2^n$ and avoids the condition $9n \leq q \leq 2^{n-1}$. This eliminates the terms $2q^2 p/2^{2n}$ and $4p^2\sqrt{qp}/2^{2n}$ in our bad transcript analysis. The latter term can play an important role when p is large.

6.1 Proof of the Sharpened Sum-Capture Theorem

For a subset Z of $\{0,1\}^n \times \{0,1\}^n$ and an invertible linear map Γ of the $\mathbb{F}_2$-vector space $\{0,1\}^n$, we define the quantity

$$\Phi_\Gamma(Z) = \max_{\substack{\alpha \in \{0,1\}^n \\ \alpha \neq 0}} \left| \sum_{(x,y) \in Z} (-1)^{\langle \alpha, x\rangle \oplus \langle \alpha, \Gamma(y)\rangle} \right|.$$

In the expression above, $\langle \alpha, x\rangle = \oplus_{i=1}^n \alpha_i x_i$ denotes the standard dot product between bitstrings of length n. The following lemma was proven by Chen et al. [12], but in the statement of their result they replaced the smaller quantity $\Phi_\Gamma(Z)$ by the quantity

$$\Phi(Z) = \max_{\substack{\alpha, \beta \in \{0,1\}^n \\ \alpha, \beta \neq 0}} \left| \sum_{(x,y) \in Z} (-1)^{\langle \alpha, x\rangle \oplus \langle \beta, y\rangle} \right| \geq \Phi_\Gamma(Z)\,.$$

However, their proof carries over essentially completely.

Lemma 4 (Chen et al. [12]). *Let Γ be an automorphism of the $\mathbb{F}_2$-vector space $\{0,1\}^n$. For all sets $Z \subseteq \{0,1\}^n \times \{0,1\}^n$ and $A, B \subseteq \{0,1\}^n$, define*

$$\mu(Z, A, B) = |\{((u, v), a, b) \in Z \times A \times B \colon u \oplus a = \Gamma(v \oplus b)\}| .$$

Then it holds that

$$\mu(Z, A, B) \leq \frac{|Z|\,|A|\,|B|}{2^n} + \Phi_\Gamma(Z)\sqrt{|A|\,|B|} .$$

In order to obtain the simplified sum-capture theorem, it suffices to compute a tail bound for the quantity $\Phi_\Gamma(Z)$. Our improvement over the result of Chen et al. is enabled by the following theorem of Hoeffding [22], which is stated for the special case of zero-mean uniformly bounded populations below.

Theorem 6 (Hoeffding [22]). *If $x_1, x_2, \ldots, x_q$ is a random sample without replacement from a finite population (multiset) $\{\{c_1, c_2, \ldots, c_N\}\}$ such that $a \leq c_i \leq b$ for all $i = 1, \ldots, N$ and $\sum_{i=1}^N c_i = 0$, then for all $\delta > 0$, it holds that*

$$\Pr\left[\sum_{i=1}^q x_i \geq \sqrt{q}\delta\right] \leq \exp\left(\frac{-2\delta^2}{(b-a)^2}\right) .$$

Theorem 6 is precisely the same bound as the classical Hoeffding inequality for sampling *with* replacement [22, Theorem 2]. It is not surprising that the same result should be true for sampling without replacement, since the latter tends to decrease variability. To prove Theorem 6, Hoeffding first showed that the average of any continuous convex function of $\sum_{i=1}^q x_i$ is less than the same function of an equivalent sum involving random variables sampled with replacement. The result then follows by applying this argument for the exponential function (which is clearly convex) and by using Markov's inequality.

Lemma 5. *Let $\pi \xleftarrow{\$} \mathrm{Perm}(n)$ and let $\mathcal{D}$ be some probabilistic algorithm making exactly q distinct two-sided adaptive queries to π. Let $Z = \{(u_1, v_1), \ldots, (u_q, v_q)\}$ be the transcript of the interaction of $\mathcal{D}$ with π, which consists of $q \geq 1$ pairs such that $v_i = \pi(u_i)$ or $u_i = \pi(v_i)$. For any real number $c > 0$, the tail of $\Phi_\Gamma(Z)$ can be bounded as*

$$\Pr[\Phi_\Gamma(Z) \geq 2\sqrt{3cq}] \leq \frac{4}{2^{2c-n}} .$$

Proof. By swapping inputs and outputs where necessary for $i = 1, \ldots, q$, there exist pairs (x_i, y_i) such that $y_i = \pi(x_i)$ and

$$\Phi_\Gamma(Z) = \max_{\substack{\alpha \in \{0,1\}^n \\ \alpha \neq 0}} \left| \sum_{i=1}^q (-1)^{\langle \alpha, x_i \rangle \oplus \langle \alpha, \Gamma(y_i) \rangle} \right| .$$

For any $\alpha \neq 0$ the values $z_i = \langle \alpha, \Gamma(y_i) \rangle$ with $i = 1, \ldots, q$ are random samples *without replacement* from a population consisting of 2^{n-1} values 0 and 2^{n-1} values 1. Indeed, any nonzero linear combination of the output bits of a uniform random permutation is a uniform random balanced Boolean function and no queries to π can be repeated. Furthermore, due to the fact that π is a uniform random permutation, $z_1, \ldots, z_q$ are independent of $x_1, \ldots, x_q$. Hence, consider the sum

$$S_\alpha = \sum_{i=1}^{q} (-1)^{\langle \alpha, x_i \rangle} (-1)^{z_i} .$$

Note that S_α is a symmetric random variable and $\mathbb{E}[S_\alpha] = 0$. Applying the union bound[1] and Theorem 6 to the terms with positive and negative coefficients separately gives the tail bound

$$\Pr\left[|S_\alpha| \geq \delta\sqrt{q} \mid x_1, \ldots, x_q\right] \leq 4\, e^{-\delta^2/8} .$$

The law of total probability then directly yields the upper bound $\Pr\left[|S_\alpha| \geq \delta\sqrt{q}\right] \leq 4\, e^{-\delta^2/8}$. By the union bound,

$$\Pr\left[\Phi_\Gamma(Z) \geq \delta\sqrt{q}\right] = \Pr\left[\max_{\alpha \neq 0} |S_\alpha| \geq \delta\sqrt{q}\right] \leq 2^{n+2}\, e^{-\delta^2/8} .$$

Let $\delta = 2\sqrt{3c} > 4\sqrt{\ln 2^c}$ for $c > 0$, then

$$\Pr\left[\Phi_\Gamma(Z) \geq 2\sqrt{3cq}\right] \leq 2^{n+2}\, e^{-2\ln 2^c} = \frac{4}{2^{2c-n}} .$$

This concludes the proof. □

6.2 Proof of Theorem 3

In this section we prove Theorem 3. Let $K \xleftarrow{\$} \{0,1\}^n$ and $\pi_I, \pi_1, \pi_2 \xleftarrow{\$} \mathrm{Perm}(n)$. Consider any computationally unbounded and deterministic distinguisher $\mathcal{D}$ with access to the oracles $(\mathsf{EMIP2}^{\pm}_K[\pi_1, \pi_2], \pi_1^{\pm}, \pi_2^{\pm})$ in the real world and $(\pi_I^{\pm}, \pi_1^{\pm}, \pi_2^{\pm})$ in the ideal world.

The distinguisher makes q construction queries to $\mathsf{EMIP2}^{\pm}_K[\pi_1, \pi_2]$ or $\pi_I^{\pm}$, and these are summarized in a transcript of the form $\tau_0 = \{(M_1, C_1), \ldots, (M_q, C_q)\}$. It also makes p primitive queries to $\pi_1^{\pm}$, and p primitive queries to $\pi_2^{\pm}$, these are respectively summarized in the transcript $\tau_1 = \{(u_1, v_1), \ldots, (u_p, v_p)\}$ and $\tau_2 = \{(x_1, y_1), \ldots, (x_p, y_p)\}$. Without loss of generality, it can be assumed that the distinguisher does not make duplicate construction or primitive queries.

After $\mathcal{D}$'s interaction with the oracles, but before it outputs its decision, we disclose the key K to the distinguisher. In the real world, this is the key used in the construction. In the ideal world, K is a dummy key that is drawn uniformly at random. The complete view is denoted by $\tau = (\tau_0, \tau_1, \tau_2, K)$.

Bad Events. We say that $\tau \in \mathcal{T}_{\mathrm{bad}}$ if and only if there exist a construction query $(M_j, C_j) \in \tau_0$ and primitive queries $(u, v) \in \tau_1$ and $(x, y) \in \tau_2$ such that one of the following conditions holds:

[1] In the form $\Pr[X + Y \geq t] \leq \Pr[X \geq t/2] + \Pr[Y \geq t/2]$.

$$\text{bad}_1\colon M_j \oplus u = K \text{ and } C_j \oplus y = \gamma_2(K)\,, \tag{18}$$
$$\text{bad}_2\colon M_j \oplus u = K \text{ and } v \oplus x = \gamma_1(K)\,, \tag{19}$$
$$\text{bad}_3\colon C_j \oplus y = \gamma_2(K) \text{ and } v \oplus x = \gamma_1(K)\,. \tag{20}$$

Any attainable transcript τ for which $\tau \notin \mathcal{T}_{\text{bad}}$ will be called a good transcript.

Probability of Bad Events in the Ideal World. We want to bound the probability $\Pr[X_{\mathcal{P}} \in \mathcal{T}_{\text{bad}}]$ that an ideal world transcript τ satisfies either of (18)-(20). Therefore, the probability that $X_{\mathcal{P}} \in \mathcal{T}_{\text{bad}}$ is given by

$$\Pr[X_{\mathcal{P}} \in \mathcal{T}_{\text{bad}}] \leq \Pr[\text{bad}_1] + \Pr[\text{bad}_2] + \Pr[\text{bad}_3]\,.$$

Throughout the proof, let $U = \{u \mid (u,v) \in \tau_1\}$, $V = \{v \mid (u,v) \in \tau_1\}$, $X = \{x \mid (x,y) \in \tau_2\}$ and $Y = \{y \mid (x,y) \in \tau_2\}$. In addition, denote

$$\Omega_1 = \left|\left\{\left(j,(u,v),(x,y)\right) \mid M_j \oplus u = \gamma_2^{-1}(C_j \oplus y)\right\}\right|\,,$$
$$\Omega_2 = \left|\left\{\left(j,(u,v),(x,y)\right) \mid M_j \oplus u = \gamma_1^{-1}(v \oplus x)\right\}\right|\,,$$
$$\Omega_3 = \left|\left\{\left(j,(u,v),(x,y)\right) \mid C_j \oplus y = \gamma_2 \circ \gamma_1^{-1}(v \oplus x)\right\}\right|\,.$$

In the ideal world, Ω_1, Ω_2, and Ω_3 only depend on π_1, π_2 and π, and not on the key $K \xleftarrow{\$} \{0,1\}^n$, which is drawn uniformly at random at the end of the interaction. For any $i \in \{1,2,3\}$ and $\lambda_i > 0$ a real constant, we have

$$\Pr[\text{bad}_i] \leq \Pr[\Omega_i \geq \lambda_i] + \frac{\lambda_i}{2^n}\,.$$

To upper bound the first term above, the sharpened sum-capture theorem (Theorem 5) will be used. This application of the sum-capture theorem will also rely on the linearity of γ_1 and γ_2.

1st Bad Event. The first bad event can be rewritten as $M_j \oplus u = \gamma_2^{-1}(C_j) \oplus \gamma_2^{-1}(y) = K$. To apply the sum-capture lemma, define

$$Z_1 = \{M_j \oplus \gamma_2^{-1}(C_j) \mid (M_j, C_j) \in \tau_0\}\,,$$
$$A_1 = U\,,$$
$$B_1 = \{\gamma_2^{-1}(y) \mid y \in Y\}\,.$$

Since γ_2^{-1} is a permutation, Lemma 4 can be applied with $\Omega_1 = \mu(Z_1, A_1, B_1)$,

$$\Pr\left[\mu(Z_1, A_1, B_1) \geq \frac{qp^2}{2^n} + 2\sqrt{3cqp^2}\right] \leq \frac{4}{2^{2c-n}}\,.$$

We thus set $\lambda_1 = qp^2/2^n + 2\sqrt{3cqp^2}$ and obtain

$$\Pr[\text{bad}_1] \leq \frac{4}{2^{2c-n}} + \frac{qp^2}{2^{2n}} + \frac{2\sqrt{3cqp^2}}{2^n}\,.$$

2nd Bad Event. For $i = 2$, we rewrite bad_2 as $M_j \oplus u = \gamma_1^{-1}(v) \oplus \gamma_1^{-1}(x) = K$, and we define

$$Z_2 = \{u \oplus \gamma_1^{-1}(v) \mid (u,v) \in \tau_1\},$$
$$A_2 = \{M_j \mid (M_j, C_j) \in \tau_0\},$$
$$B_2 = \{\gamma_1^{-1}(x) \mid x \in X\}.$$

Then, since γ_1^{-1} is a permutation, we can apply Lemma 4 with $\Omega_2 = \mu(Z_2, A_2, B_2)$,

$$\Pr\left[\mu(Z_2, A_2, B_2) \geq \frac{qp^2}{2^n} + 2\sqrt{3cqp^2}\right] \leq \frac{4}{2^{2c-n}}.$$

We thus set $\lambda_2 = qp^2/2^n + 2\sqrt{3cqp^2}$ and obtain

$$\Pr[\text{bad}_2] \leq \frac{4}{2^{c-2n}} + \frac{qp^2}{2^{2n}} + \frac{2\sqrt{3cqp^2}}{2^n}.$$

3rd Bad Event. For $i = 3$, we rewrite bad_3 as $C_j \oplus y = \gamma_2 \circ \gamma_1^{-1}(v) \oplus \gamma_2 \circ \gamma_1^{-1}(x) = \gamma_2(K)$ and we define

$$Z_3 = \{\gamma_2 \circ \gamma_1^{-1}(x) \oplus y \mid (x,y) \in \tau_2\},$$
$$A_3 = \{C_j \mid (M_j, C_j) \in \tau_1\},$$
$$B_3 = \{\gamma_2 \circ \gamma_1^{-1}(v) \mid v \in V\}.$$

Then, since $\gamma_2 \circ \gamma_1^{-1}$ is a permutation, we can apply Lemma 4 with $\Omega_3 = \mu(Z_3, A_3, B_3)$,

$$\Pr\left[\mu(Z_3, A_3, B_3) \geq \frac{qp^2}{2^n} + 2\sqrt{3cqp^2}\right] \leq \frac{4}{2^{2c-n}}.$$

We thus set $\lambda_3 = qp^2/2^n + \sqrt{5nqp^2}$ and obtain

$$\Pr[\text{bad}_3] \leq \frac{4}{2^{2c-n}} + \frac{qp^2}{2^{2n}} + \frac{2\sqrt{3cqp^2}}{2^n}.$$

Conclusion. Summing the probabilities of the three bad events, we get

$$\Pr[X_{\mathcal{P}} \in \mathcal{T}_{\text{bad}}] \leq \frac{12}{2^{2c-n}} + \frac{3qp^2}{2^{2n}} + \frac{6\sqrt{3cqp^2}}{2^n}. \tag{21}$$

Probability Ratio for Good Transcripts. Since our bad events are the same as in the analysis of Chen et al. [12], their analysis of the good transcript ratio can be recycled. In particular, their Lemma 8 (i) implies that for any good transcript τ and any integers q and p such that $2q + 2p \leq 2^n$,

$$\frac{\Pr[X_{\mathcal{O}} = \tau]}{\Pr[X_{\mathcal{P}} \in \tau]} \geq 1 - \frac{4qp^2}{2^{2n}}.$$

However, the above bound is trivial whenever $p \geq 2^{n-1}/\sqrt{q}$. Hence, $2q + 2p \leq 2^n/\sqrt{q} + 2q$ and for $n \geq 4$ this is lower than 2^n whenever $q > 1$ and $q < 2^{n-1}$. Furthermore, by [12, Lemma 8 (ii)], the result also holds for $q = 2^n$.

Conclusion. Using Patarin's H-Coefficient technique (Lemma 1), we obtain

$$\mathbf{Adv}^{\text{sprp}}_{\text{EMIP2}}(\mathcal{D}) \leq \frac{12}{2^{2c-n}} + \frac{3qp^2}{2^{2n}} + \frac{6\sqrt{3cqp^2}}{2^n} + \frac{4qp^2}{2^{2n}}.$$

7 Construction Based on an Ideal Cipher

We now turn to our second reflection cipher construction, which is illustrated in Fig. 5 below. Theorem 7 will show that, for an n-bit ideal block cipher with a k-bit key, this construction achieves a $\widetilde{\mathcal{O}}(p\sqrt{q}/2^{n+k})$ security bound. The proof of this result is based on a reduction to our sharpened security bound for the two-round Even-Mansour cipher from Theorem 3.

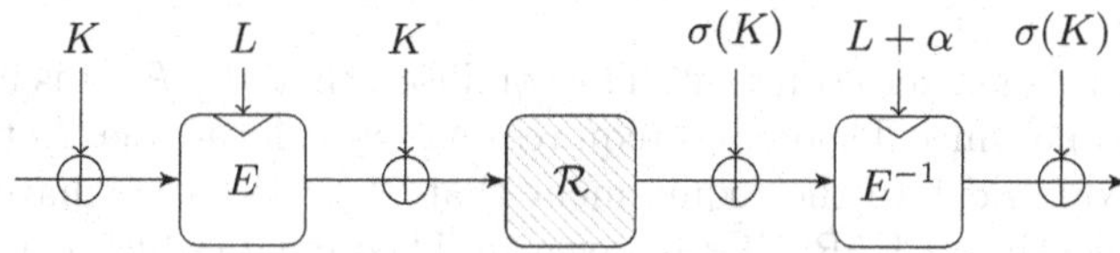

Fig. 5. The KARC-IC construction uses two secret keys K and L, and a block cipher E. The reflector $\mathcal{R}$ is a fixed linear involution and σ is an invertible linear map. To obtain a pure reflection property with respect to both keys, σ should be an involution.

Although the construction in Fig. 5 is based on the more powerful ideal cipher model, it is of considerable practical interest. Indeed, block-ciphers such as PRINCE [8], MANTIS [5] and QARMA [1] are designed to support a 64 bit block size with 128 bit keys (internally split into two 64 bit keys), and claim a security tradeoff of $pq = 2^{128}$.

In the case of PRINCE and MANTIS, this is achieved by instantiating the XEX-construction [23] with an ideal reflection cipher. Their construction is shown in Fig. 2 (in the introduction). Importantly, although this achieves the desired tradeoff, the construction of the ideal reflection cipher E^* in PRINCE and MANTIS closely follows our proposed construction: the only difference is the presence of key-additions in the middle layer of our construction. Hence, by minimally modifying PRINCE and MANTIS, our results show that an improved security tradeoff of $pq^2 = 2^{256}$ can be achieved. However, it should be stressed that our results only establish security against *generic* attacks. Careful analysis by cryptanalysts remains necessary, even for minor changes such as the one proposed by our construction. For instance, in the case of MANTIS, reduced-round nonlinear invariant attacks have been discovered [6]. The presence of key additions in the middle could provide additional flexibility to propagate the invariant property over more rounds. We believe a detailed analysis of this case would make for interesting future work.

The design of QARMA follows a very similar approach to our construction. In fact, Avanzi [1] remarks that the true security of the QARMA construction is likely to exceed the claimed $pq = 2^n$ trade-off. Our results corroborate this to some extent. However, our Theorem 7 is not directly applicable because QARMA uses a nonlinear reflector $\mathcal{R}$ between the middle key-additions. Analyzing the security of such construction would be possible if the sum-capture theorem could be extended to allow for nonlinearity. This is an interesting problem by itself.

Before giving Theorem 7 and its proof, we formalize our second construction. For any positive integers n and k, let E be a block cipher with key $L \in \{0,1\}^k$, and let $K \in \{0,1\}^n$ be a second construction key. Furthermore let $\mathcal{R}$ be a linear involution and σ an invertible linear map on $\{0,1\}^n$ such that $\mathrm{id} + \mathcal{R} \circ \sigma$ is invertible. The generic construction $\mathsf{KARC\text{-}IC2}\colon \{0,1\}^{n+k} \times \{0,1\}^n \to \{0,1\}^n$ is defined by

$$\mathsf{KARC\text{-}IC2}_{K,L}[E](M) = E^{-1}_{L+\alpha}(\mathcal{R}(E_L(M \oplus K) \oplus K) \oplus \sigma(K)) \oplus \sigma(K)\,, \quad (22)$$

with $\alpha \in \{0,1\}^k$ a nonzero constant. The condition that $\mathrm{id} + \mathcal{R} \circ \sigma$ is invertible is an important one, since Theorem 3 requires that γ_2 is invertible. Note that this condition is equivalent to the requirement that $\mathcal{R} \circ \sigma$ does not have any fixed points. The security of KARC-IC2 is given in Theorem 7, which can be proven by a reduction to the security of EMIP2.

Theorem 7. *For any positive integers $n \geq 2$ and k, let $K \xleftarrow{\$} \{0,1\}^n$ and $L \xleftarrow{\$} \{0,1\}^k$ be uniform random keys and E an ideal cipher. If $\mathcal{D}$ is any distinguisher for $\mathsf{KARC\text{-}IC2}_{K,L}[E]$ making at most $q > 1$ construction queries, and at most p primitive queries to $E^{\pm}$, then for all $q < 2^{n-1}$ or $q = 2^n$ it holds that:*

$$\mathbf{Adv}^{\mathrm{sprp}}_{\mathsf{KARC\text{-}IC2}}(\mathcal{D}) \leq \frac{12}{2^{n+k}} + 9\sqrt{2n+k}\,\frac{\sqrt{q}\,p}{2^{n+k}}\,.$$

Proof. Enumerate all $\ell = 2^k$ possible ideal cipher keys as $L_1, \ldots, L_\ell$. Suppose the distinguisher $\mathcal{D}$ makes $p_{1,i}$ queries to $E^{\pm 1}$ with key L_i. Likewise, let $p_{2,i}$ denote the number of queries to $E^{\pm 1}$ with key $L_i \oplus \alpha$. For convenience, let $p_i = \max\{p_{1,i}, p_{2,i}\}$ be the maximum number of queries made for either L_i or $L_i \oplus \alpha$. Since the total number of queries is equal to p, we have

$$\sum_{i=1}^{\ell} p_i \leq \sum_{i=1}^{\ell} p_{1,i} + p_{2,i} = 2p\,.$$

It follows from the law of total probability and the triangle inequality that

$$\mathbf{Adv}^{\mathrm{sprp}}_{\mathsf{KARC\text{-}IC2}}(\mathcal{D}) \leq \sum_{i=1}^{\ell} \frac{1}{\ell}\,\mathbf{Adv}^{\mathrm{sprp}}_{\mathsf{KARC\text{-}IC2}_{K,L_i}[E]}(\mathcal{D})\,.$$

Let $\mathcal{D}_i$ be a distinguisher running $\mathcal{D}$ to play the indistinguishability game against the $\mathsf{EMIP2}_K[\pi_1, \pi_2]$ construction with $\pi_1 = E_{L_i}$ and $\pi_2 = E^{-1}_{L_i \oplus \alpha}$ using $p_{1,i}$ primitive queries to π_1, $p_{2,i}$ primitive queries to π_2 and q construction queries.

In order to do this, $\mathcal{D}_i$ simulates $\mathcal{D}$'s queries to E whenever the key is different from L_i or $L_i \oplus \alpha$. A standard hybrid argument then shows that

$$\mathbf{Adv}^{\mathrm{sprp}}_{\mathsf{KARC\text{-}IC2}_{K,L_i}[E]}(\mathcal{D}) \leq \mathbf{Adv}^{\mathrm{sprp}}_{\mathsf{EMIP2}_K[E_{L_i}, E^{-1}_{L_i+\alpha}]}(\mathcal{D}_i)\,.$$

Since $L_i \neq L_i \oplus \alpha$, the permutations π_1 and π_2 are indeed independent and uniform random. Hence, Theorem 3 (with $c = n + k/2$) yields the upper bound

$$\begin{aligned}\mathbf{Adv}^{\mathrm{sprp}}_{\mathsf{EMIP2}_{K_1}[E_{L_i}, E^{-1}_{L_i+\alpha}]}(\mathcal{D}_i) &\leq \frac{12}{2^{n+k}} + \frac{7qp_i^2}{2^{2n}} + 6\sqrt{3(n+k/2)}\frac{\sqrt{q}\,p_i}{2^n} \\ &\leq \frac{12}{2^{n+k}} + (6\sqrt{3(n+k/2)} + \sqrt{7})\frac{\sqrt{q}\,p_i}{2^n} \\ &\leq \frac{12}{2^{n+k}} + 9\sqrt{2n+k}\,\frac{\sqrt{q}\,p_i}{2^n}\,,\end{aligned}$$

where the second inequality follows from $x^2 \leq x$ for all $x \in [0,1]$. Hence, it follows that

$$\mathbf{Adv}^{\mathrm{sprp}}_{\mathsf{KARC\text{-}IC2}}(\mathcal{D}) \leq \frac{12}{2^{n+k}} + 9\sqrt{2n+k}\,\frac{\sqrt{q}\,p}{2^{n+k}}\,.$$

This concludes the proof. □

To apply Theorem 7 to PRINCE, it remains to show that the linear map $\mathcal{R}\circ\sigma$ does not have any fixed points when $\mathcal{R}$ is the linear reflector and σ the whitening-key orthomorphism[2] of PRINCE. Specifically, $\sigma : \{0,1\}^n \to \{0,1\}^n$ is defined by

$$\sigma(x) = (x \ggg 1) \oplus (x \gg 63)\,. \qquad (23)$$

One can verify that $\operatorname{rank}(\mathrm{id} + \mathcal{R}\circ\sigma) = 64$. That is, $\mathcal{R}\circ\sigma$ does not have any fixed points.

Observe that the σ defined by (23) is not an involution. Hence, the PRINCE decryption algorithm is not the exactly same as the encryption algorithm: K and $\sigma(K)$ must also be swapped. Our construction preserves the same property, but we note that it is also possible to choose an involution σ such that $\mathcal{R}\circ\sigma$ does not have any fixed points. In this case, decryption and encryption are purely related by the coupling map $(K, L) \mapsto (\sigma(K), L \oplus \alpha)$.

However, since the block cipher E used in PRINCE starts by xoring L to the state, using an involution σ has the potential downside that $(K + L, \sigma(K) + L)$ is no longer jointly uniform for uniform random keys K and L. Indeed, for any linear involution σ, it holds that $\operatorname{rank}(\mathrm{id}+\sigma) \leq n/2$. This may facilitate partial key guessing. Again, this illustrates the importance of performing additional cryptanalysis when instantiating our (or, more generally, any) generic construction.

Acknowledgments. This work was supported in part by the Research Council KU Leuven: GOA TENSE (C16/15/058). Tim Beyne and Yu Long Chen are supported by a Ph.D. Fellowship from the Research Foundation - Flanders (FWO). The authors thank the reviewers for their valuable comments and suggestions.

[2] An orthomorphism such as σ is a linear map such that both σ and $\sigma\oplus\mathrm{id}$ are invertible.

References

1. Avanzi, R.: The QARMA block cipher family. IACR Trans. Symm. Cryptol. **2017**(1), 4–44 (2017)
2. Babai, L.: The Fourier transform and equations over finite Abelian groups: an introduction to the method of trigonometric sums. Lecture notes (1989)
3. Barreto, P., Rijmen, V.: The Anubis block cipher. Primitive submitted to NESSIE (2020)
4. Barreto, P., Rijmen, V.: The Khazad legacy-level block cipher. Primitive submitted to NESSIE (2020)
5. Beierle, C., et al.: The `SKINNY` family of block ciphers and its low-latency variant `MANTIS`. In: Robshaw, M., Katz, J. (eds.) CRYPTO 2016, Part II. LNCS, vol. 9815, pp. 123–153. Springer, Heidelberg (2016). https://doi.org/10.1007/978-3-662-53008-5_5
6. Beyne, T.: Block cipher invariants as eigenvectors of correlation matrices. In: Peyrin, T., Galbraith, S. (eds.) ASIACRYPT 2018. LNCS, vol. 11272, pp. 3–31. Springer, Cham (2018). https://doi.org/10.1007/978-3-030-03326-2_1
7. Bogdanov, A., Knudsen, L.R., Leander, G., Standaert, F.-X., Steinberger, J., Tischhauser, E.: Key-alternating ciphers in a provable setting: encryption using a small number of public permutations. In: Pointcheval, D., Johansson, T. (eds.) EUROCRYPT 2012. LNCS, vol. 7237, pp. 45–62. Springer, Heidelberg (2012). https://doi.org/10.1007/978-3-642-29011-4_5
8. Borghoff, J., et al.: PRINCE – a low-latency block cipher for pervasive computing applications. In: Wang, X., Sako, K. (eds.) ASIACRYPT 2012. LNCS, vol. 7658, pp. 208–225. Springer, Heidelberg (2012). https://doi.org/10.1007/978-3-642-34961-4_14
9. Borghoff, J., et al.: The PRINCE challenge (2014–2016). https://www.emsec.ruhr-uni-bochum.de/research/research_startseite/prince-challenge/
10. Boura, C., Canteaut, A., Knudsen, L.R., Leander, G.: Reflection ciphers. Des. Codes Cryptogr. **82**(1–2), 3–25 (2017)
11. Bozilov, D., et al.: PRINCEv2 - More security for (almost) no overhead. IACR Cryptol. ePrint Arch. 2020, 1269 (2020)
12. Chen, S., Lampe, R., Lee, J., Seurin, Y., Steinberger, J.: Minimizing the two-round even-mansour cipher. In: Garay, J.A., Gennaro, R. (eds.) CRYPTO 2014, Part I. LNCS, vol. 8616, pp. 39–56. Springer, Heidelberg (2014). https://doi.org/10.1007/978-3-662-44371-2_3
13. Chen, S., Steinberger, J.: Tight security bounds for key-alternating ciphers. In: Nguyen, P.Q., Oswald, E. (eds.) EUROCRYPT 2014. LNCS, vol. 8441, pp. 327–350. Springer, Heidelberg (2014). https://doi.org/10.1007/978-3-642-55220-5_19
14. Chen, Y.L., Lambooij, E., Mennink, B.: How to build pseudorandom functions from public random permutations. In: Boldyreva, A., Micciancio, D. (eds.) CRYPTO 2019, Part I. LNCS, vol. 11692, pp. 266–293. Springer, Cham (2019). https://doi.org/10.1007/978-3-030-26948-7_10
15. Cogliati, B., Seurin, Y.: Analysis of the single-permutation encrypted Davies-Meyer construction. Des. Codes Cryptogr. **86**(12), 2703–2723 (2018)
16. Daemen, J., Van Assche, G., Peeters, M., Rijmen, V.: Noekeon. Primitive submitted to NESSIE (2000)
17. Datta, N., Dutta, A., Nandi, M., Yasuda, K.: Encrypt or decrypt? to make a single-key beyond birthday secure nonce-based MAC. In: Shacham, H., Boldyreva, A. (eds.) CRYPTO 2018, Part I. LNCS, vol. 10991, pp. 631–661. Springer, Cham (2018). https://doi.org/10.1007/978-3-319-96884-1_21

18. Dinur, I.: Cryptanalytic time-memory-data tradeoffs for FX-constructions with applications to PRINCE and PRIDE. In: Oswald, E., Fischlin, M. (eds.) EUROCRYPT 2015, Part I. LNCS, vol. 9056, pp. 231–253. Springer, Heidelberg (2015). https://doi.org/10.1007/978-3-662-46800-5_10
19. Dunkelman, O., Keller, N., Shamir, A.: Minimalism in cryptography: the even-mansour scheme revisited. In: Pointcheval, D., Johansson, T. (eds.) EUROCRYPT 2012. LNCS, vol. 7237, pp. 336–354. Springer, Heidelberg (2012). https://doi.org/10.1007/978-3-642-29011-4_21
20. Even, S., Mansour, Y.: A construction of a cipher from a single pseudorandom permutation. In: Imai, H., Rivest, R.L., Matsumoto, T. (eds.) ASIACRYPT 1991. LNCS, vol. 739, pp. 210–224. Springer, Heidelberg (1993). https://doi.org/10.1007/3-540-57332-1_17
21. Hoang, V.T., Tessaro, S.: Key-alternating ciphers and key-length extension: exact bounds and multi-user security. In: Robshaw, M., Katz, J. (eds.) CRYPTO 2016, Part I. LNCS, vol. 9814, pp. 3–32. Springer, Heidelberg (2016). https://doi.org/10.1007/978-3-662-53018-4_1
22. Hoeffding, W.: Probability inequalities for sums of bounded random variables. In: Fisher, N.I., Sen, P.K. (eds.) The Collected Works of Wassily Hoeffding, pp. 409–426. Springer, Heidleberg (1994). https://doi.org/10.1007/978-1-4612-0865-5_26
23. Kilian, J., Rogaway, P.: How to protect DES against exhaustive key search. In: Koblitz, N. (ed.) CRYPTO 1996. LNCS, vol. 1109, pp. 252–267. Springer, Heidelberg (1996). https://doi.org/10.1007/3-540-68697-5_20
24. Kilian, J., Rogaway, P.: How to protect DES against exhaustive key search (an analysis of DESX). J. Cryptol. **14**(1), 17–35 (2001)
25. Lampe, R., Patarin, J., Seurin, Y.: An asymptotically tight security analysis of the iterated even-mansour cipher. In: Wang, X., Sako, K. (eds.) ASIACRYPT 2012. LNCS, vol. 7658, pp. 278–295. Springer, Heidelberg (2012). https://doi.org/10.1007/978-3-642-34961-4_18
26. Lee, J.: Key alternating ciphers based on involutions. Des. Codes Cryptogr. **86**(5), 955–988 (2018)
27. Leurent, G., Sibleyras, F.: Low-memory attacks against two-round even-mansour using the 3-XOR problem. In: Boldyreva, A., Micciancio, D. (eds.) CRYPTO 2019, Part II. LNCS, vol. 11693, pp. 210–235. Springer, Cham (2019). https://doi.org/10.1007/978-3-030-26951-7_8
28. Luby, M., Rackoff, C.: How to construct pseudo-random permutations from pseudo-random functions. In: Williams, H.C. (ed.) CRYPTO 1985. LNCS, vol. 218, pp. 447–447. Springer, Heidelberg (1986). https://doi.org/10.1007/3-540-39799-X_34
29. Patarin, J.: The "Coefficients H" Technique. In: Avanzi, R.M., Keliher, L., Sica, F. (eds.) SAC 2008. LNCS, vol. 5381, pp. 328–345. Springer, Heidelberg (2009). https://doi.org/10.1007/978-3-642-04159-4_21
30. Patarin, J.: Introduction to mirror theory: analysis of systems of linear equalities and linear non equalities for cryptography. IACR Cryptol. ePrint Arch. 2010, 287 (2010)
31. Patarin, J.: Mirror theory and cryptography. Appl. Algebra Eng. Commun. Comput. **28**(4), 321–338 (2017). https://doi.org/10.1007/s00200-017-0326-y
32. Simon, T., et al.: FRIET: an authenticated encryption scheme with built-in fault detection. In: Canteaut, A., Ishai, Y. (eds.) EUROCRYPT 2020, Part I. LNCS, vol. 12105, pp. 581–611. Springer, Cham (2020). https://doi.org/10.1007/978-3-030-45721-1_21
33. Steinberger, J.P.: The sum-capture problem for abelian groups. arXiv preprint arXiv:1309.5582 (2013)

Overloading the Nonce: Rugged PRPs, Nonce-Set AEAD, and Order-Resilient Channels

Jean Paul Degabriele[1,2](✉) and Vukašin Karadžić[2]

[1] Technology Innovation Institute, Abu Dhabi, UAE
jeanpaul.degabriele@tii.ae
[2] Technische Universität Darmstadt, Darmstadt, Germany
vukasin.karadzic@tu-darmstadt.de

Abstract. We introduce a new security notion that lies right in between pseudorandom permutations (PRPs) and strong pseudorandom permutations (SPRPs). We call this new security notion and any (tweakable) cipher that satisfies it a *rugged pseudorandom permutation* (RPRP). Rugged pseudorandom permutations lend themselves to some interesting applications, have practical benefits, and lead to novel cryptographic constructions. Our focus is on variable-length tweakable RPRPs, and analogous to the encode-then-encipher paradigm of Bellare and Rogaway, we can generically transform any such cipher into different AEAD schemes with varying security properties. However, the benefit of RPRPs is that they can be constructed more efficiently as they are weaker primitives than SPRPs (the notion traditionally required by the encode-then-encipher paradigm). We can construct RPRPs using only two layers of processing, whereas SPRPs typically require three layers of processing over the input data. We also identify a new transformation that yields RUP-secure AEAD schemes with more compact ciphertexts than previously known. Further extending this approach, we arrive at a new generalized notion of authenticated encryption and a matching construction, which we refer to as *nonce-set AEAD*. Nonce-set AEAD is particularly well-suited in the context of secure channels, like QUIC and DTLS, that operate over unreliable transports and employ a window mechanism at the receiver's end of the channel. We conclude by presenting a generic construction for transforming a nonce-set AEAD scheme into an order-resilient secure channel. Our channel construction sheds new light on order-resilient channels and additionally leads to more compact ciphertexts when instantiated from RPRPs.

Keywords: Rugged Pseudorandom Permutations · UIV · Authenticate with Nonce · QUIC · DTLS · Tweakable Ciphers

1 Introduction

The modern view of symmetric encryption follows a nonce-based syntax. At first, this may seem like a superficial detail but it has important ramifications

Y. Dodis and T. Shrimpton (Eds.): CRYPTO 2022, LNCS 13510, pp. 264–295, 2022.
https://doi.org/10.1007/978-3-031-15985-5_10

both practically and theoretically. When first conceived by Rogaway in [31], its primary motivation was to position the security of symmetric encryption on more solid ground by lifting its reliance on good sources of randomness. It thus replaced an initialization vector, required to be uniformly random, for a nonce that instead is only required to never repeat. Besides significantly reducing susceptibility to implementation errors, it added versatility by elegantly aligning the two main flavours of symmetric encryption—randomized and stateful—into a single unified syntax from which they can easily be realized. The resistance to misuse was later fortified in the strengthened security notion by Rogaway and Shrimpton in [32]. On the more theoretical side, this seemingly minor syntactical change has major consequences on how symmetric encryption and message authentication compose together to form authenticated encryption. In contrast to the traditional view that only encrypt-then-MAC results in a generically secure composition [7], all three composition paradigms become secure under the nonce-based syntax and the mild requirement of tidiness [26].

Secure Channels. A major application of nonce-based AEAD is to realize secure channels in protocols like TLS, SSH, and QUIC. Here, a number of options arise on how to handle the nonce, initialize it, update it, and communicate it to the other party. Typically, secure channels need to protect against the replay and reordering of ciphertexts, which in turn necessitates the receiver to be stateful [6]. Accordingly, a common approach is to initialize the nonce to a common value and each party increments it (independently) upon every encryption and decryption. This works well as long as the transport protocol, upon which the secure channel is realized, is reliable and order-preserving, meaning that ciphertexts are delivered in the same order as they were sent and without being lost. TLS and SSH operate over TCP, which is reliable and order-preserving, but at the same time introduces issues such as head-of-line blocking[1] which degrades performance. This motivated the emergence of protocols like DTLS and QUIC, which operate over UDP, thereby avoiding head-of-line blocking at the expense of having to deal with out-of-order delivery and dropped ciphertexts.

Operating secure channels over UDP means that the receiver cannot predict the nonce as ciphertexts may arrive out of order. Accordingly, the nonce has to be communicated together with each ciphertext. Moreover, if the nonce is set to be a message number, the receiver can use it to recover the correct ordering of the messages. In fact, because in nonce-based AEAD the nonce is implicitly authenticated, the above approach works even against adversarial reordering strategies. Indeed, this is roughly the approach adopted in DTLS 1.3 and QUIC. Thus, while the nonce was originally only intended to diversify ciphertexts, in these protocols it is 'overloaded' to additionally serve a secondary purpose for recovering the correct message ordering. This is yet another example of the beauty and versatility of a well-crafted definition like nonce-based AEAD. However, attaching the nonce to the ciphertext in the clear exposes metadata which can undermine privacy [13] and possibly confidentiality [8]. Accordingly QUIC

[1] https://en.wikipedia.org/wiki/Head-of-line_blocking.

and DTLS 1.3 separately encrypt the nonce before attaching it to the ciphertext. In turn this has led to the notion of nonce-hiding AEAD [8], an idea that can be traced back to Bernstein [10].

Encode-then-Encipher. A classical technique for constructing an authenticated encryption scheme is the encode-then-encipher paradigm by Bellare and Rogaway [9]. The technique builds an authenticated encryption scheme from a variable-input-length cipher by properly encoding the message with randomness and redundancy in order to obtain confidentiality and integrity. A more modern take on the encode-then-encipher paradigm was put forth by Shrimpton and Terashima in [34] where it was extended to obtain nonce-based authenticated encryption with associated data (AEAD) from tweakable variable-input-length ciphers. A noteworthy feature of the encode-then-encipher paradigm is that it yields AEAD schemes that satisfy the strongest possible security—misuse resistance [32] and release-of-unverified plaintext (RUP) security [1,3,21] simultaneously. Despite their strong security, such schemes are scarce in real-world systems. In all likelihood, this is due to tweakable ciphers generally being heavy primitives whose performance lags behind that of more efficient AEAD schemes. In this respect, one exception is AEZ [21] which offers competitive speeds although requiring three layers of processing. However its security relies on a non-standard heuristic analysis and, in addition, it is also a significantly complex scheme to implement.

1.1 Contribution

Rugged Pseudorandom Permutations. Our first contribution is a novel security definition for tweakable ciphers that sits between a pseudorandom permutation and a strong pseudorandom permutation. The security definition assumes a cipher defined over a 'split' domain, meaning that its inputs and outputs will typically consist of a pair of strings, possibly of different sizes, rather than a single string. A salient characteristic of our security definition is that it imposes stronger security requirements on the enciphering algorithm than on the deciphering algorithm. Intuitively, we will still require an adversary to distinguish between the cipher and a random permutation. However, while the adversary will have full access to the enciphering algorithm its access to the deciphering algorithm will be restricted, thereby giving rise to the asymmetric security between the two algorithms. Due to the uneven domain and the asymmetry in the cipher's security we choose to call such a cipher a rugged pseudorandom permutation (RPRP).

The benefit of this security definition is that it strikes a new balance in which security is sufficiently weakened to allow for more efficient cipher constructions while still being strong enough to be of use in practice. Our RPRP construction is inspired by the PIV construction by Terashima and Shrimpton [34] and the GCM-RUP construction by Ashur, Dunkelman, and Luykx [2]. Our construction, Unilaterally-Protected IV ($\mathtt{UIV}$), is directly obtained from the PIV construction by shaving off its last layer. GCM-RUP is similarly derived from PIV by shaving off the first layer and then augmenting it to obtain a nonce-based AEAD scheme that is RUP secure. Like GCM-RUP, UIV can be instantiated from GCM components and benefit from GCM's now-ubiquitous hardware support that enables its superior performance. The benefit of drawing the boundary around UIV is that firstly it is a length-preserving cipher which is advantageous in settings such as disk encryption. Secondly, it is a more versatile primitive which, as we shall see, can be easily augmented to yield different AEAD schemes. Indeed, one specific transformation recovers GCM-RUP, but our general treatment allows us to uncover several new AEAD schemes with differing properties and improvements.

Constructing AEAD from RPRPs. We revisit the encode-then-encipher paradigm in the context of RPRPs. The asymmetry in the RPRP security definition prompts us to consider two variations of this paradigm: Encode-then-Encipher (EtE) and Encode-then-Decipher (EtD), where the latter uses the deciphering algorithm to encrypt and the enciphering algorithm to decrypt. We show that EtE yields misuse-resistant AEAD and that EtD yields RUP-secure AEAD. A notable instantiation of the encode-then-encipher paradigm is to 'overload' the use of the nonce to additionally serve as the redundancy in the encoding that provides integrity. This approach appears to have been missed in prior works. For instance, GCM-RUP simultaneously encrypts the nonce and adds redundancy in the message, resulting in an unnecessary expansion in the ciphertext. On the other hand, when EtD is instantiated this way with UIV we obtain a RUP-secure scheme with more compact ciphertexts than GCM-RUP.

Nonce-Set AEAD and Its Construction from RPRPs. Taking this idea of overloading the nonce for integrity a step further, we arrive at a new AEAD construction with novel functionality. This functionality is motivated by the use case of AEAD in secure channels like QUIC and DTLS. We formalize this functionality as a new primitive that we call nonce-set AEAD, which extends and generalizes the standard definition of nonce-based AEAD. Nonce-set AEAD alters the decryption algorithm to additionally take a set of nonces instead of a single one. Intuitively decryption will succeed if the correct nonce is among this set. Moreover, the decryption algorithm will return the nonce in the supplied set that was deemed correct as part of its output. We show how to generically construct such a scheme from an RPRP through a construction we call Authenticate-with-Nonce (AwN) and show that it even achieves misuse-resistance AEAD security. The AwN construction requires a mechanism for representing nonce-sets compactly and efficiently testing for membership in this set. Of course, since any SPRP is automatically an RPRP, AwN can also be instantiated using other well-known SPRP constructions.

Order-Resilient Secure Channels from Nonce-Set AEAD. In order-resilient channels, the nonce is often overloaded to serve as a message number that can be used to recover the correct ordering of the decrypted messages.

Nonce-set AEAD facilitates such an approach and can be plugged in directly with the window mechanisms that are used in real-world protocols like QUIC and DTLS. Such window mechanisms can be fairly complex and hard to understand when presented as code. Moreover, they affect the security of the channel, and as a result, analyzing the security of these channels can become rather daunting at times. Our treatment based on nonce-set AEAD will help tame this complexity. The other reason for introducing nonce-set AEAD is that it will allow for more bandwidth-efficient constructions from RPRPs by additionally overloading the nonce to provide integrity in a way that is compatible with the window mechanisms in the channel.

Recent work by Fischlin, Günther, and Janson [18] introduces a formal framework for analyzing the security of order-resilient secure channels like QUIC and DTLS. Central to the framework is a support predicate that expresses the expected behaviour of such channels. Many possibilities exist here in terms of how much reordering should be tolerated, the specific window mechanism to use, and how to handle replays, but the support predicate neatly captures these variations in their full generality. We build on the framework in [18] to show how to generically transform any nonce-set AEAD scheme into a secure channel for any support predicate that may be required. Besides having practical value, that of offering order-resilient secure channels with more compact ciphertexts, our construction is also instructive in that it decomposes the structure of complex secure channels into a handful of much simpler and manageable components. It should be noted that nonce-set AEAD can also be realized through other constructions—such as the nonce-hiding schemes in [8]. As such, our approach is very general and versatile.

1.2 Relation to Counter Galois Onion

This work stemmed out from other work, concurrent to this one, on the design of Counter Galois Onion (CGO), a proposal for a new onion encryption scheme for Tor [15]. Under the hood, CGO employs an extended Rugged PRP to process each layer of encryption. In particular, the notion of a Rugged PRP was developed in both works in parallel and went through a number of iterations. It was initially conceived as an abstraction to facilitate the security proof of CGO, but we later realised that it had applications beyond onion encryption which motivated the research in this paper.

2 Preliminaries

Notation. For any non-negative integer $n \in \mathbb{N}$, $\{0,1\}^n$ denotes the set of bit strings of size n, $\{0,1\}^*$ denotes the set of all finite binary strings, and $\{0,1\}^{\geq n}$ denotes the set of all finite bit strings of size greater or equal to n. The empty string is denoted by ε. For any string X, $|X|$ denotes its length in bits. Then for any non-negative integer $n \leq |X|$, $\lfloor X \rfloor_n$ and $\lceil X \rceil_n$ denote respectively the substrings of the leftmost and rightmost n bits of X, and $X \ll n$ denotes the bit string of size $|X|$ obtained by truncating its leftmost n bits and appending n zeros to its right. For any two strings X and Y, of lengths $|X| = n$ and $|Y| = m$, where $n < m$, $X \oplus Y$ denotes the operation of appending $m - n$ zeros to the left of X, and then XORing the expanded string X with Y. For any pair of strings (X, Y) we define their combined length $|(X, Y)|$ as $|X| + |Y|$ and we use $\langle X, Y \rangle$ to denote an injective mapping from string pairs into single strings.

For any set $\mathcal{S}$, we use $|\mathcal{S}|$ to denote its cardinality, $\mathcal{P}(\mathcal{S})$ to denote its power set, i.e., the set of all its subsets, and $\text{Perm}[\mathcal{S}]$ to denote the set of all permutations over the elements of $\mathcal{S}$. The empty set is denoted by $\emptyset$. For any two sets $\mathcal{T}$ and $\mathcal{X}$, $\mathsf{IC}(\mathcal{T}, \mathcal{X})$ denotes the set of all ciphers over the domain $\mathcal{X}$ and key space $\mathcal{T}$, $\text{Func}(\mathcal{X}, \infty)$ denotes the set of all functions mapping elements in $\mathcal{X}$ to elements in $\{0,1\}^\infty$, and $\pm\text{Func}(\mathcal{T}, \mathcal{X})$ denotes the set of all functions mapping elements in $\{+, -\} \times \mathcal{T} \times \mathcal{X}$ to elements in $\mathcal{X}$. In our pseudocode we use lists as an abstract data type. We use $[\,]$ to denote the empty list, and for any two lists $\mathcal{L}_1$ and $\mathcal{L}_2$, we use $\mathcal{L}_1 \| \mathcal{L}_2$ to denote the list obtained by appending $\mathcal{L}_2$ to $\mathcal{L}_1$. Lists are indexed starting at position zero, and $\mathcal{L}_1[i]$ denotes the element in $\mathcal{L}_1$ at position i. For a string X and a list $\mathcal{L}$, the function $\text{index}(X, \mathcal{L})$ returns the smallest index in $\mathcal{L}$ in which X is located, if X is contained in $\mathcal{L}$, and returns $\perp$ otherwise.

For events E and F, we use $\neg E$ to denote the complement event of E, $\Pr[E]$ to denote the probability of E, and $\Pr[E \mid F]$ to denote the probability of E conditioned on F. Finally, $\Pr[P : E]$ denotes the probability of E occuring after executing some random process P.

Tweakable Ciphers. A tweakable cipher is an algorithm

$$\widetilde{\mathsf{EE}} : \mathcal{K} \times \mathcal{T} \times \mathcal{X} \to \mathcal{X}$$

such that for any $(K, T) \in \mathcal{K} \times \mathcal{T}$ the mapping $\widetilde{\mathsf{EE}}(K, T, \cdot)$ identifies a permutation over the elements in $\mathcal{X}$. We refer to $\mathcal{K}$ as the key space, $\mathcal{T}$ as the tweak space, and $\mathcal{X}$ as the domain. We use $\widetilde{\mathsf{EE}}_K(T, \cdot)$ as shorthand for $\widetilde{\mathsf{EE}}(K, T, \cdot)$ and $\widetilde{\mathsf{EE}}_K^{-1}(T, \cdot)$ to denote the corresponding inverse permutation. A tweakable cipher is required to be length preserving, meaning that for all $(K, T, X) \in \mathcal{K} \times \mathcal{T} \times \mathcal{X}$ it holds that $|\widetilde{\mathsf{EE}}_K(T, X)| = |X|$. We also refer to $\widetilde{\mathsf{EE}}$ and $\widetilde{\mathsf{EE}}^{-1}$ as the enciphering and deciphering algorithms of the tweakable cipher. In the special case where $\mathcal{X} = \{0,1\}^n$, for some positive integer n, we call the cipher a tweakable blockcipher and denote it by $\widetilde{\mathsf{E}}$. Thus we generally reserve $\widetilde{\mathsf{EE}}$ to denote a variable-input-length tweakable cipher, which may itself be constructed from an underlying tweakable blockcipher $\widetilde{\mathsf{E}}$.

Security. The typical security requirement for tweakable ciphers is the well-known (SPRP) notion. The formal definition can be found in the full version [16].

Nonce-Based AEAD. A nonce-based encryption scheme $\mathsf{SE} = (\mathsf{Enc}, \mathsf{Dec})$ is a pair of algorithms to which we associate a key space $\mathcal{K}$, a nonce space $\mathcal{N}$, a

$\mathsf{Ver}_K(N, H, C)$	$\$(N, H, M)$	$\bot(N, H, C)$
$M \leftarrow \mathsf{Dec}_K(N, H, C)$ **if** $M \in \mathcal{M}$ $\quad M \leftarrow \top$ **return** M	$C \leftarrow_\$ \{0,1\}^{\mathsf{clen}(\|N\|,\|H\|,\|M\|)}$ **return** C	**return** $\bot$

Fig. 1. Oracles used to define nAE, MRAE, and RUPAE security.

header (associated data) space $\mathcal{H}$, a message space $\mathcal{M}$ and a ciphertext space $\mathcal{C}$, all of which are subsets of $\{0,1\}^*$. The encryption algorithm Enc and the decryption algorithm Dec are both deterministic and their syntax is given by

$$\mathsf{Enc} : \mathcal{K} \times \mathcal{N} \times \mathcal{H} \times \mathcal{M} \to \mathcal{C} \text{ and } \mathsf{Dec} : \mathcal{K} \times \mathcal{N} \times \mathcal{H} \times \mathcal{C} \to \mathcal{M} \cup \{\bot\}.$$

The special symbol $\bot$ serves to indicate that the decryption algorithm deemed its input to be invalid. A nonce-based encryption scheme is required to be *correct* and *tidy* [26]. Correctness requires that for all $(K, N, H, M) \in \mathcal{K} \times \mathcal{N} \times \mathcal{H} \times \mathcal{M}$ it must hold that

$$\mathsf{Dec}_K(N, H, \mathsf{Enc}_K(N, H, M)) = M.$$

Tidiness, on the other hand, requires that for any $(K, N, H, C) \in \mathcal{K} \times \mathcal{N} \times \mathcal{H} \times \mathcal{C}$

$$\text{if } \mathsf{Dec}_K(N, H, C) \neq \bot \text{ then } \mathsf{Enc}_K(N, H, \mathsf{Dec}_K(N, H, C)) = C.$$

We further require that encryption be length-regular, meaning that the size of ciphertexts depend only on the *sizes* of N, H and M. Accordingly, we associate to every nonce-based AEAD scheme a ciphertext length function clen, mapping the triple $(|N|, |H|, |M|)$ to the ciphertext length in bits.

Security. A nonce-based encryption scheme is said to be AEAD if it additionally satisfies (nAE) security. We use a variant of nAE from [5] which is equivalent to the usual formulation. Namely we require that no efficient adversary be able to distinguish between oracle access to the real encryption algorithm $\mathsf{Enc}_K(\cdot,\cdot,\cdot)$ and the real *verification algorithm* $\mathsf{Ver}_K(\cdot,\cdot,\cdot)$ (defined in Fig. 1) from their corresponding idealisations $\$(\cdot,\cdot,\cdot)$ and $\bot(\cdot,\cdot,\cdot)$. Throughout this distinguishing game, the adversary is required to be *nonce-respecting*, meaning that it never repeats nonce values across encryption queries, and must not *forward* queries from the encryption oracle to the decryption oracle, meaning that it cannot make a query (N, H, C) if it previously queried (N, H, M) and got C in return.

Definition 1 (nAE **Advantage**). *Let* $\mathsf{SE} = (\mathsf{Enc}, \mathsf{Dec})$ *be a nonce-based encryption scheme and let* $\mathcal{A}$ *be a nonce-respecting adversary that does not make forwarding queries. Then the* nAE *advantage of* $\mathcal{A}$ *with respect to* SE *is defined as*

$$\mathbf{Adv}^{\mathrm{nae}}_{\mathsf{SE}}(\mathcal{A}) = \Big|\Pr\left[K \leftarrow_\$ \mathcal{K} : \mathcal{A}^{\mathsf{Enc}_K(\cdot,\cdot,\cdot), \mathsf{Ver}_K(\cdot,\cdot,\cdot)} \Rightarrow 1\right] - \Pr\left[\mathcal{A}^{\$(\cdot,\cdot,\cdot), \bot(\cdot,\cdot,\cdot)} \Rightarrow 1\right]\Big|.$$

The stronger notion of misuse-resistant AEAD MRAE is defined analogously by replacing the requirement on the adversary that it be nonce-respecting with the requirement that it never repeat an encryption query.

Definition 2 (MRAE **Advantage**). *Let* $\mathsf{SE} = (\mathsf{Enc}, \mathsf{Dec})$ *be a nonce-based encryption scheme and let* $\mathcal{A}$ *be an adversary that never repeats encryption queries and does not make forwarding queries. Then the* MRAE *advantage of* $\mathcal{A}$ *with respect to* SE *is defined as*

$$\mathbf{Adv}^{\mathrm{mrae}}_{\mathsf{SE}}(\mathcal{A}) = \left|\Pr\left[K \leftarrow\!\$\, \mathcal{K} : \mathcal{A}^{\mathsf{Enc}_K(\cdot,\cdot,\cdot),\mathsf{Ver}_K(\cdot,\cdot,\cdot)} \Rightarrow 1\right] - \Pr\left[\mathcal{A}^{\$(\cdot,\cdot,\cdot),\perp(\cdot,\cdot,\cdot)} \Rightarrow 1\right]\right|.$$

Release of Unverified Plaintext. In practice, in the event of a decryption failure, the decryption algorithm may leak more information than what is captured by the standard security notions. Prior works proposed strengthened notions which modelled such leakage as distinguishable decryption failures [11], release of unverified plaintexts (RUP) [1], and robust authenticated encryption [21]. Then in [3] Barwell et al. introduced *subtle* authenticated encryption to compare and unify these three security models. Here we will utilise the RUPAE security definition as defined by Barwell et al. through their subtle AE framework.

Subtle AE (*c.f.* [3]). A *subtle encryption scheme* $\mathsf{SSE} = (\mathsf{Enc}, \mathsf{Dec}, \Lambda)$ is a nonce-based encryption scheme $(\mathsf{Enc}, \mathsf{Dec})$ augmented with a (deterministic) decryption leakage function Λ intended to model the protocol leakage from decryption failures. The leakage function takes the same inputs as the decryption algorithm but instead returns either a leakage string or the special symbol $\top$. The symbol $\top$ indicates that decryption was successful, and thus for any subtle encryption scheme it must hold that for any K, N, H and C exactly one of the following be true:

$$\perp \leftarrow \mathsf{Dec}_K(N, H, C) \quad \text{or} \quad \top \leftarrow \Lambda_K(N, H, C).$$

That is, for any input either decryption returns $\perp$ and a leakage string is returned by Λ, or decryption succeeds thereby returning the full plaintext but Λ returns no leakage string. In practice the leakage depends on how the scheme is implemented, how it is integrated into the larger system, and the scheme itself. Thus a subtle encryption scheme aims to model any potential leakage, via Λ, in order to show that the underlying scheme remains secure even in the presence of this additional leakage. This is formalised through the following security notion.

Security. In rough terms, RUPAE security can be understood as extending nAE security by additionally giving the adversary oracle access to the decryption leakage function. For a subtle encryption scheme to be RUPAE secure we then require the existence of a corresponding leakage simulator S which can simulate this leakage in the ideal world for any adversary. Intuitively, if the leakage function can be simulated without the secret key it is of no use to the adversary.

Definition 3 (RUPAE **Advantage**). *Let* $\mathsf{SSE} = (\mathsf{Enc}, \mathsf{Dec}, \Lambda)$ *be a subtle AE encryption scheme and let* $\mathcal{A}$ *be a nonce-respecting adversary that does not forward encryption queries to the decryption and leakage oracles. Then the advantage of* $\mathcal{A}$ *with respect to* SSE *and the leakage simulator* S *is defined as*

$$\mathbf{Adv}^{\mathrm{rupae}}_{\mathsf{SSE}}(\mathcal{A}, \mathsf{S}) = \left| \Pr\left[K \leftarrow_{\$} \mathcal{K} : \mathcal{A}^{\mathsf{Enc}_K(\cdot,\cdot,\cdot),\mathsf{Dec}_K(\cdot,\cdot,\cdot),\Lambda_K(\cdot,\cdot,\cdot)} \Rightarrow 1\right] \right.$$
$$\left. - \Pr\left[\mathcal{A}^{\$(\cdot,\cdot,\cdot),\perp(\cdot,\cdot,\cdot),\mathsf{S}(\cdot,\cdot,\cdot)} \Rightarrow 1\right] \right| .$$

Nonce-Hiding AEAD. In the full version of this paper [16] we cover the syntax of nonce-hiding AEAD and how the security definitions covered so far adapt to that setting.

Encodings and Redundancy Functions. In the encode-then-encipher paradigm one typically requires some encoding scheme that maps messages to some sparse set of strings [9,34]. In our case, we will additionally require the ability to "localize" the redundancy within the encoding. Accordingly we will instead use a redundancy function for generating the redundancy which will then be joined to the message to form the encoded input to the tweakable cipher. More specifically, this redundancy function will satisfy one of the following two syntaxes:

$$\mathsf{Func}_2 : \mathcal{N} \times \mathcal{H} \rightarrow \mathcal{X}$$
or
$$\mathsf{Func}_3 : \mathcal{N} \times \mathcal{H} \times \mathcal{M} \rightarrow \mathcal{X}.$$

Furthermore, we will require Func_3 to be collision resistant over inputs with distinct nonces. We say that Func_3 is (δ, t)-*collision resistant* if for all efficient adversaries $\mathcal{A}$ running in time t it holds that:

$$\Pr\left[((N, H, M), (N', H', M')) \leftarrow \mathcal{A} : \mathsf{Func}_3(N, H, M) = \mathsf{Func}_3(N', H', M') \wedge N \neq N'\right] \leq \delta.$$

3 Rugged Pseudorandom Permutations

We now introduce a new security notion for tweakable ciphers that provides intermediate security. We call this notion, and by extension, any tweakable cipher that satisfies it a *rugged pseudorandom permutation* (RPRP). A distinctive characteristic of RPRPs is that they are tweakable ciphers over a split domain $\mathcal{X}_L \times \mathcal{X}_R$, where we refer to $\mathcal{X}_L$ as the *left set* and $\mathcal{X}_R$ as the *right set*. Note that the split domain is an implicit requirement of the security definition which would not make sense otherwise. We will typically let $\mathcal{X}_L = \{0,1\}^n$ and $\mathcal{X}_R = \{0,1\}^{\geq m}$ for some non-negative integers n and m, but other choices are possible. Furthemore, for ease of notation, we will simply write $\widetilde{\mathsf{EE}}_K(T, X_L, X_R)$ instead of $\widetilde{\mathsf{EE}}_K(T, (X_L, X_R))$ and apply the same rule to $\widetilde{\mathsf{EE}}^{-1}$.

For sufficiently large n, RPRP security sits right in between PRP security and SPRP security. This is achieved by giving the adversary only partial access to the decipher algorithm. This partial access is provided via two separate oracles, a partial *decipher* oracle and a *guess* oracle. Each oracle limits access to the decipher algorithm in a different way. The decipher oracle severely restricts the set of values on which it can be queried. In contrast, the guess oracle imposes no significant restrictions on the inputs, but it only returns a single bit of information. The combined effect of these restrictions is to relax the extent to which the decipher algorithm needs to be pseudorandom. As a result, there is an asymmetry between the encipher and decipher algorithms in that the former is required to be more pseudorandom than the latter. The term *rugged* in the name is meant to reflect this asymmetry in security and the uneven split in the domain.

The full formal security definition is presented in the next subsection. As we will show in later sections, this notion suffices to generically transform any tweakable cipher that satisfies it into an AEAD scheme with strong security properties. In Sects. 4 and 5.3 we present three such transformations. At the same time, the notion is significantly weaker than strong pseudorandom permutations as it allows for more efficient constructions. Strong pseudorandom permutations typically require three layers of processing, where each layer consists of processing the data through a block cipher or a universal hash, and both enciphering and deciphering are two-pass algorithms. In contrast, the `UIV` construction which we present in this section consists of two processing layers where enciphering is a two-pass algorithm but deciphering requires only a single pass over the data as the two layers can be processed in parallel. Admittedly some of the definitional choices, particularly the restrictions imposed on the decipher oracle and the introduction of the guess oracle, in the RPRP definition may seem arbitrary at first. Part of the rationale behind these definitional choices is to require the bare minimum from the tweakable cipher to make the generic transformations, shown in Sects. 4 and 5.3, go through.

3.1 RPRP Security

Let $\widetilde{\mathsf{EE}}$ be a tweakable cipher over a split domain $\mathcal{X}_L \times \mathcal{X}_R$ with an associated key space $\mathcal{K}$ and tweak space $\mathcal{T}$. Then for any cipher $\widetilde{\mathsf{EE}}$, RPRP security is defined via the RPRP game shown in Fig. 2. Here the adversary is given access to either the real tweakable cipher construction $\widetilde{\mathsf{EE}}$ or an ideal cipher $\widetilde{\Pi}$ and its task is to determine which of the two it is interacting with. It interacts with the cipher through three oracles: *encipher* (EN), *decipher* (DE), and *guess* (GU).

The EN oracle provides full access to the encipher algorithm, whereas DE provides only partial access to the decipher algorithm. In DE access is restricted by checking Y_L for membership in the sets $\mathcal{F}$ and $\mathcal{R}$ and then suppressing the output (via $\lightning$) when this is the case. This check translates to two types of decipher queries that the adversary cannot make. The first is a decipher query where the left value was previously output by the encipher oracle. That is, if an encipher

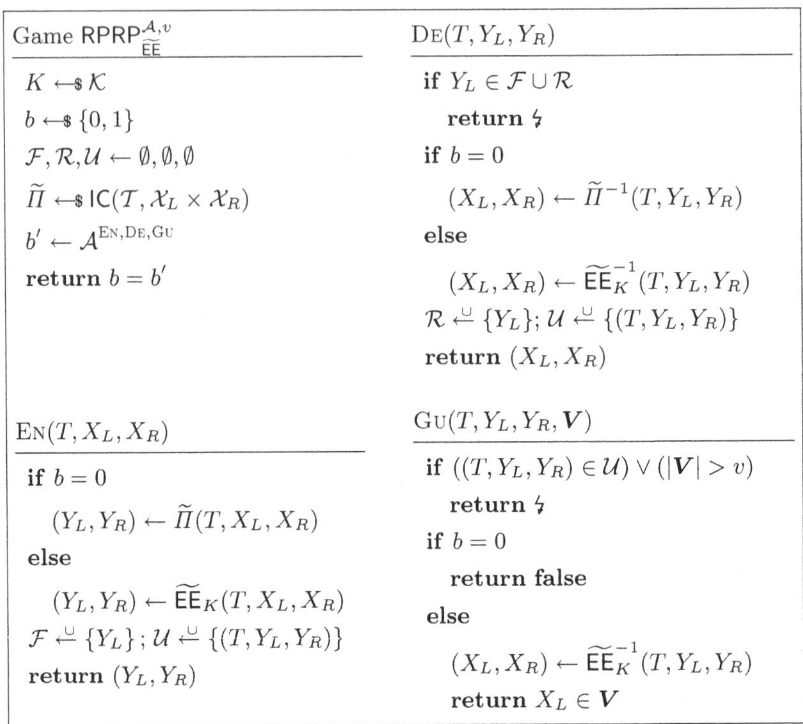

Fig. 2. The game used to define RPRP security for a tweakable cipher $\widetilde{\mathsf{EE}}$.

query was made such that $(Y_L, Y_R) \leftarrow \text{EN}(T, X_L, X_R)$, then no query of the form $\text{DE}(T', Y_L, Y'_R)$ is allowed for any values of T' and Y'_R. The second is a decipher query that repeats a left value from a prior decipher query. Namely, a query $\text{DE}(T, Y_L, Y_R)$ when a query of the form $\text{DE}(T', Y_L, Y'_R)$, for some T' and Y'_R, was already made.

The GU oracle provides an additional interface to the decipher algorithm. It takes an input to the decipher algorithm together with a set of guesses $\boldsymbol{V}$ for the corresponding left output. In the real world, GU returns a boolean value indicating whether any of the guesses is correct, whereas it always returns **false** in the ideal world. To avoid trivial-win conditions, we need to restrict the adversary to only make guess queries for which it does not already know the answer. Accordingly, guess queries are required to be "unused", meaning that they have not been already queried on DE or returned by EN. The set $\mathcal{U}$ serves to keep track of used triples (T, Y_L, Y_R) and suppress the output in GU when such a query is detected. Finally, the game is parametrized by a positive integer v, limiting the size of $\boldsymbol{V}$ in every query. We quantify the RPRP security of a tweakable cipher via the usual advantage measure shown below.

$\widetilde{\mathsf{EE}}_{K1,K2}(T, X_L, X_R)$	$\widetilde{\mathsf{EE}}^{-1}_{K1,K2}(T, Y_L, Y_R)$
$Y_L \leftarrow \widetilde{\mathsf{E}}_{K1}((T, X_R), X_L)$	$X_R \leftarrow \mathsf{F}_{K2}(Y_L, \lvert Y_R\rvert) \oplus Y_R$
$Y_R \leftarrow \mathsf{F}_{K2}(Y_L, \lvert X_R\rvert) \oplus X_R$	$X_L \leftarrow \widetilde{\mathsf{E}}^{-1}_{K1}((T, X_R), Y_L)$
return (Y_L, Y_R)	**return** (X_L, X_R)

Fig. 3. Pseudocode description of the UIV construction, a variable-input-length tweakable cipher realised from a tweakable blockcipher $\widetilde{\mathsf{E}}$ and a VOL-PRF F.

Definition 4 (RPRP Advantage). *Let $\widetilde{\mathsf{EE}}$ be a tweakable cipher over a split domain $(\mathcal{X}_L \times \mathcal{X}_R)$. Then for a positive integer v and an adversary $\mathcal{A}$ attacking the* RPRP *security of $\widetilde{\mathsf{EE}}$ the corresponding advantage is defined as*

$$\mathbf{Adv}^{\mathrm{rprp}}_{\widetilde{\mathsf{EE}}}(\mathcal{A}, v) = \left|2\Pr\left[\mathsf{RPRP}^{\mathcal{A},v}_{\widetilde{\mathsf{EE}}} \Rightarrow 1\right] - 1\right|.$$

3.2 Unilaterally-Protected IV (UIV)

We next present a variable-input-length tweakable cipher construction, called Unilaterally-Protected IV (UIV), that achieves RPRP security. It is easily derived from the three-round Protected IV construction from [34] by simply eliminating the last layer and using a slightly different abstraction. Shrimpton and Terashima noted that all three rounds are necessary for SPRP security, but as we show in Theorem 1, two rounds suffice for RPRP security. The construction is composed of a tweakable blockcipher $\widetilde{\mathsf{E}}$ over the domain $\mathcal{X}_L = \{0,1\}^n$ with tweak space $\mathcal{T} \times \mathcal{X}_R$ and a matching variable-output-length pseudorandom function F with domain $\mathcal{X}_L$ and range $\mathcal{X}_R$. The tweak space of the resulting UIV cipher is $\mathcal{T}$. A pseudocode description of the construction is given in Fig. 3 and Fig. 4 shows a graphical representation of its encipher algorithm. The RPRP security of the UIV construction is stated formally in Theorem 1, the proof of which can be found in the full version of this paper [16].

Theorem 1. *Let* UIV *be the construction defined in Fig. 3 over the domain $\{0,1\}^n \times \{0,1\}^{\geq m}$. For a positive integer v and an adversary $\mathcal{A}$ making q_{en} encipher queries, q_{de} decipher queries and q_{gu} guess queries under the constraint that $q_{\mathrm{gu}} v \leq 2^{n-1}$, there exist adversaries $\mathcal{B}$ and $\mathcal{C}$ such that*

$$\mathbf{Adv}^{\mathrm{rprp}}_{\mathtt{UIV}}(\mathcal{A}, v) \leq \mathbf{Adv}^{\mathrm{sprp}}_{\widetilde{\mathsf{E}}}(\mathcal{B}) + \mathbf{Adv}^{\mathrm{prf}}_{\mathsf{F}}(\mathcal{C}) + \frac{q_{\mathrm{gu}} v}{2^{n-1}} + \frac{q_1(q_1-1)}{2^{n+1}} + \frac{q_{\mathrm{en}}(q_{\mathrm{en}}-1)}{2^{n+1}} + \frac{q_2(q_2-1)}{2^{n+m+1}},$$

where $q_1 = q_{\mathrm{en}} + q_{\mathrm{de}} + q_{\mathrm{gu}}$ and $q_2 = q_{\mathrm{en}} + q_{\mathrm{de}}$. The SPRP *adversary $\mathcal{B}$ makes at most q_{en} encipher queries and $q_{\mathrm{de}} + q_{\mathrm{gu}}$ decipher queries, whereas the* PRF *adversary $\mathcal{C}$ makes at most $q_{\mathrm{en}} + q_{\mathrm{de}} + q_{\mathrm{gu}}$ queries.*

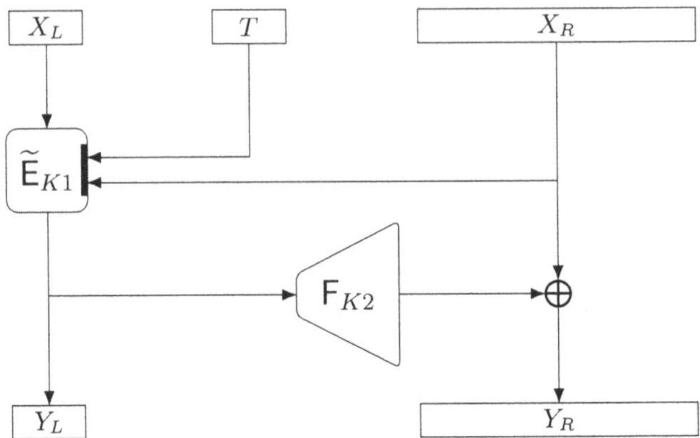

Fig. 4. Graphical representation of the `UIV` enciphering algorithm.

Concrete UIV Instantiations. We described the UIV construction generically in terms of a fixed-input-length tweakable cipher (FIL-TBC) with variable tweak length and a variable-output-length pseudorandom function (VOL-PRF). The tweakable cipher can be instantiated either via the LRW2 construction [24] using a blockcipher like AES and an Almost XOR-Universal (AXU) hash function like POLYVAL [20]. Alternatively one can use an off-the-shelf tweakable blockcipher with a fixed-size tweak, like Deoxys-TBC [23] or SKINNY [4] and augment it with an AXU hash via the XTX transform [25].

As for the VOL-PRF, it can be instantiated by a blockcipher operated in counter mode. In this case, the tricky part is to match the block size of the FIL-TBC with the input size of the VOL-PRF (equivalent to the IV in the counter mode instantiation). If counter mode uses a blockcipher with a block size equal to the block size of the FIL-TBC then the IV needs to be blinded with an additional key, acting as a universal hash, to avoid colliding counter values. Alternatively, if one is using an off-the-shelf tweakable blockcipher, the VOL-PRF can be instantiated using the Counter-in-Tweak mode of operation [28], circumventing this issue entirely.

Notably, UIV can be fully instantiated from AES and POLYVAL, using LRW2 and counter mode, which benefit from the native instruction sets on many modern-day processors. The corresponding instantiation, GCM-UIV, shares many similarities with GCM-SIV [20] (e.g. two-pass enciphering/encryption and one-pass deciphering/decryption), and its performance profile is also similar.

4 Encode-then-Encipher from Rugged PRPs

The encode-then-encipher paradigm is a generic approach, dating back to Bellare and Rogaway [9], for turning a variable-length cipher into an authenticated encryption scheme. Shrimpton and Terashima later extended this paradigm to cater for modern primitives such as tweakable ciphers and nonce-based AEAD [34]. However, both works require that the variable-length cipher satisfy SPRP security for the resulting authenticated encryption scheme to be secure. In this section, we show how to construct nonce-based AEAD from tweakable ciphers that are only RPRP secure. The asymmetric security properties of RPRPs prompt us to consider two schemes with complementary security properties, EtE and EtD, as well as nonce-hiding variants of each.

4.1 Encode-then-Encipher (EtE) Scheme

The first scheme, EtE, achieves *misuse-resistance* (MRAE) security and is the most natural as it uses the encipher algorithm to encrypt and the decipher algorithm to decrypt. It employs a rugged pseudorandom permutation $\widetilde{\mathsf{EE}}$ with domain $\{0,1\}^n \times \{0,1\}^{\geq m}$ and tweak space $\{0,1\}^*$, an injective mapping $\langle \cdot, \cdot \rangle$ from string pairs to single strings, and a function $\mathsf{Func}_2 : \{0,1\}^* \to \{0,1\}^n$. Its pseudocode is presented in Fig. 5. Note that since C_1 is of fixed size, C_1 and C_2 can be concatenated into a single-string ciphertext to fit the usual AEAD syntax, and any such ciphertext can easily be parsed back into such a pair.

Intuitively, the scheme is misuse resistant since altering any of N, H, or M results in an almost uniformly random ciphertext, by the pseudorandomness of the encipher algorithm. Authenticity is achieved via the function Func_2 under the sole assumption that it be deterministic. Namely, it can be instantiated through a hash function or more simply via truncation (assuming (N, H) is always at least n bits long), or by the constant function (e.g. $\mathsf{Func}_2(N, H) = 0^n$). Then, by RPRP security, it follows that altering either C_1 or C_2 will result in a value of Z' that is unpredictable. Accordingly, the condition $Z' = Z$ will only be satisfied with small probability, irrespective of the specific value of $Z \leftarrow \mathsf{Func}_2(N, H)$. It is worth noting that in reducing the MRAE security of EtE to the RPRP security of $\widetilde{\mathsf{EE}}$, the reduction only makes encipher and guess queries (with $v = 1$), i.e., the decipher oracle is not used at all. This is because in the EtE construction, the verification algorithm can be simulated entirely through the guess oracle. Below is the formal security theorem and its proof is presented in the full version of this paper [16].

Theorem 2. *Let* EtE *be the nonce-based AEAD scheme defined in Fig. 5 realized from a tweakable cipher over the domain* $\{0,1\}^n \times \{0,1\}^{\geq m}$*. Then for any adversary* $\mathcal{A}$ *making* q_{e} *encryption queries and* q_{v} *verification queries, there exists an adversary* $\mathcal{B}$ *such that*

$$\mathbf{Adv}^{\mathrm{mrae}}_{\mathtt{EtE}}(\mathcal{A}) \leq \mathbf{Adv}^{\mathrm{rprp}}_{\widetilde{\mathsf{EE}}}(\mathcal{B}, 1) + \frac{q_{\mathrm{e}}^2}{2^{n+m+1}},$$

where $\mathcal{B}$ *makes* q_{e} *encipher queries,* q_{v} *guess queries, and its runtime is similar to that of* $\mathcal{A}$*.*

$\mathsf{Enc}_K(N, H, M)$	$\mathsf{Dec}_K(N, H, C_1, C_2)$
$T \leftarrow \langle N, H \rangle$	$T \leftarrow \langle N, H \rangle$
$Z \leftarrow \mathsf{Func}_2(N, H)$	$Z \leftarrow \mathsf{Func}_2(N, H)$
$(C_1, C_2) \leftarrow \widetilde{\mathsf{EE}}_K(T, Z, M)$	$(Z', M') \leftarrow \widetilde{\mathsf{EE}}_K^{-1}(T, C_1, C_2)$
return (C_1, C_2)	**if** $Z' = Z$ **then**
	return M'
	else
	return $\perp$

Fig. 5. The EtE construction transforming a variable-length RPRP into a misuse-resistant nonce-based AEAD scheme.

4.2 Encode-then-Decipher (EtD) Scheme

In our second scheme, EtD, we switch the roles of the encipher and decipher algorithms, i.e., we decipher to encrypt and encipher to decrypt. By making this switch, we now obtain an AEAD scheme that is secure against the *release of unverified plaintext* (RUPAE). The EtD construction is presented in Fig. 6 together with the associated leakage function used to prove it RUPAE secure. In addition to the variable-length tweakable cipher, the construction makes use of an injective mapping $\langle \cdot, \cdot \rangle$ from string pairs to single strings and a (δ, t)-collision resistant deterministic function Func_3.

The full pseudorandomness of the encipher algorithm, which is now used for decryption, is what makes the scheme RUPAE secure. However, using the decipher algorithm to encrypt presents some new challenges in the security proof due to the constraints in the RPRP security definition. The requirement to never repeat Y_L values across decipher queries is easily satisfied by ensuring that distinct nonces result in distinct Z values. In our generic treatment we fulfill this condition by requiring that the function Func_3 be (δ, t)-collision resistant. On the other hand, the requirement to not forward Y_L values from the encipher oracle to the decipher oracle is a bit more challenging to address in the security proof. Finally, a peculiarity of the EtD construction is that the nonce is included both in the evaluation of Z as well as the tweak, which may seem unnecessary at first. However, its inclusion in the evaluation of Z is necessary to ensure that Y_L values do not repeat as it is the only AEAD input that is guaranteed to be distinct across encryption calls. At the same time its inclusion in the tweak is necessary for RUPAE security, as otherwise the adversary could forward a ciphertext from the encryption oracle to the leakage oracle with a different nonce and, in the real world, recover the original message. The security of EtD is formally stated below in Theorem 3 and its proof can be found in the full version of this paper [16].

Theorem 3. *Let* EtD *be the subtle AEAD scheme defined in Fig. 6 composed from a tweakable cipher over the domain* $\{0,1\}^n \times \{0,1\}^{\geq m}$, *and let* Func_3 *be a*

$\mathsf{Enc}_K(N, H, M)$	$\mathsf{Dec}_K(N, H, C_1, C_2)$	$\Lambda_K(N, H, C_1, C_2)$
$T \leftarrow \langle N, H\rangle$	$T \leftarrow \langle N, H\rangle$	$T \leftarrow \langle N, H\rangle$
$Z \leftarrow \mathsf{Func}_3(N, H, M)$	$(Z', M') \leftarrow \widetilde{\mathsf{EE}}_K(T, C_1, C_2)$	$(Z', M') \leftarrow \widetilde{\mathsf{EE}}_K(T, C_1, C_2)$
$(C_1, C_2) \leftarrow \widetilde{\mathsf{EE}}_K^{-1}(T, Z, M)$	$Z \leftarrow \mathsf{Func}_3(N, H, M')$	$Z \leftarrow \mathsf{Func}_3(N, H, M')$
return (C_1, C_2)	**if** $Z' = Z$ **then**	**if** $Z' = Z$ **then**
	return M'	**return** $\top$
	else	**else**
	return $\perp$	**return** M'

Fig. 6. The EtD construction, presented as a subtle AEAD scheme, transforming a variable-length RPRP into a RUPAE-secure AEAD scheme.

(δ, t)-collision resistant deterministic function. Then there exists a leakage simulator S*, such that for any adversary* $\mathcal{A}$ *making* $q_e \leq 2^{n-1}$ *encryption queries,* q_d *decryption queries,* q_l *queries to the leakage oracle and running in time* t*, there exist* RPRP *adversaries* $\mathcal{B}$ *and* $\mathcal{C}$ *such that*

$$\mathbf{Adv}^{\mathrm{rupae}}_{\mathtt{EtD}}(\mathcal{A}, \mathsf{S}) \leq \mathbf{Adv}^{\mathrm{rprp}}_{\widetilde{\mathsf{EE}}}(\mathcal{B}, 1) + \mathbf{Adv}^{\mathrm{rprp}}_{\widetilde{\mathsf{EE}}}(\mathcal{C}, 1) + \delta + \frac{(q_e+1)(q_d+q_l)}{2^{n-1}} + \frac{(q_e+q_d+q_l)^2}{2^{n+m}} + \frac{q_e(q_d+q_l)}{2^n}.$$

The adversary $\mathcal{B}$ *makes* q_e *queries to* En *oracle,* $q_d + q_l$ *queries to* De *oracle, and its runtime is similar to that of* $\mathcal{A}$*. The adversary* $\mathcal{C}$ *makes at most* q_e *queries to* En *oracle, at most* $q_d + q_l$ *queries to* De *oracle, and its runtime is similar to that of* $\mathcal{A}$*.*

4.3 Nonce-Hiding Variants of EtE and EtD

Up to this point our treatment has focused on the classical nonce-based syntax, but both constructions can be adapted to the nonce-hiding syntax while retaining analogous security properties. Intuitively, the main differences are that encryption now needs to embed the nonce in the ciphertext and the nonce is no longer available during decryption. We describe below how these differences affect each construction.

In the case of EtE, as before the redundancy Z must be located in the left input for security and consequently the nonce has to be embedded in the right input. As the nonce is not available to the decryption algorithm, Z can no longer depend on it. Furthermore Z cannot depend on any value contained in the right part. This is because in the security proof decryption is simulated through the Gu oracle, which does not return the right part, and thus the reduction would not be able to evaluate Z. As a result, the possibilities for instantiating the redundancy function are severely restricted here and we simply set $Z = 0^n$ instead.

In the case of EtD, since we are using the decipher algorithm to encrypt the left input must not repeat, and thus this makes it the natural choice of location for embedding the nonce. Accordingly the redundant value Z has to be moved to the right input, which is now possible in the case of EtD since the encipher algorithm is fully pseudorandom and non-malleable. Again, the nonce is not an input to the decryption algorithm, but in this case Z can depend on the nonce as the decryption algorithm can use the nonce that it recovers from the left part. However the nonce still cannot be included in the tweak. Interestingly, the attack that required us to include the nonce in the tweak for EtD is no longer applicable in the nonce-hiding setting, and thus this variant is also RUPAE secure. Note that for this construction Func_3 is only required to be a deterministic function and need not be collision resistant.

Pseudocode descriptions of the nonce-hiding variants of EtE and EtD are provided in the full version of this paper [16]. The security proofs for these variants proceed in a similar fashion to the original nonce-based schemes and we omit them to avoid tedious repetition.

4.4 Instantiations and Related Constructions

Compared to prior works [8,9,21,34], our treatment of the encode-then-encipher paradigm is the first to prove the security of the resulting AEAD by assuming a strictly weaker security notion than SPRP on the part of the cipher. In this light, our results on the MRAE security of EtE and its nonce-hiding variant are analogous to the construction in [34] and the HN5 construction in [8], respectively. Similarly, our result on the RUPAE security of nonce-based EtD is analogous to that in [21] for the closely-related notion of robust AEAD.

For generality, we specified the nonce-based constructions through the redundancy functions Func_2 and Func_3 which can be instantiated in a number of ways. Note that the redundancy functions are generally only required to be deterministic functions, except in nonce-based EtD, which additionally requires Func_3 to be (δ, t)-collision resistant. Thus, one could instantiate these with hash functions or, when applicable, more simply as constant functions that always return 0^n. Clearly, some instantiations are more advantageous in terms of efficiency, while others may prove to be beneficial in extended security models that we did not consider here. Instantiating the nonce-hiding variant of EtD with $\mathsf{Func}_3(N, H, M) := 0^n$ and GCM-UIV recovers the GCM-RUP scheme from [2]. However our treatment exposes other possibilities, such as $\mathsf{Func}_3(N, H, M) := N$, which is trivially $(0, \infty)$-collision resistant. In particular, instantiating the nonce-based variant of EtD with this redundancy function gives rise to a RUPAE-secure AEAD scheme with more compact ciphertexts than GCM-RUP or HN5, as it makes do without the extra n zero bits (assuming the nonce is also n bits long).

When instantiated with $\mathsf{Func}_3(N, H, M) := N$ the nonce-based variants of EtE and EtD will also conceal the nonce, even if decryption does not strictly fit the nonce-hiding syntax. Such a combination of nonce-concealing and compact ciphertexts is beneficial for constructing secure channels over a transmission protocol with out-of-order delivery, like UDP. Indeed, DTLS 1.3 and QUIC go through considerable efforts to achieve this. In Sect. 6 we will show how this approach, of employing an RPRP and overloading the use of the nonce for both authentication and message indexing, can be used to construct such secure channels more simply and in a more modular fashion. However, we first need to introduce a new type of authenticated encryption that better fits this purpose and allows the receiver to adopt different policies as to how to process ciphertexts that are delivered out of order. In the next section, we present this new and more general type of authenticated encryption and show how it can be realised generically from any nonce-hiding AEAD scheme or directly from an RPRP with the additional benefit of more compact ciphertexts.

5 Nonce-Set AEAD

A secure channel protocol operating over UDP, which may deliver ciphertexts out of order, requires some mechanism to recover the original ordering of the messages. Typically, such secure channels employ an AEAD scheme and overload the nonce to act as the *message number*. Here, nonce-hiding AEAD is advantageous because it attaches the nonce in encrypted form to the ciphertext, thereby making it available to the receiver for recovering the original ordering of messages without leaking the side information contained in the nonce. In Sect. 4.4 we showed how in the encode-then-encipher paradigm the nonce could be additionally overloaded to act as the redundant bits in the encoding that provide authenticity. This resulted in more compact ciphertexts, but it required that the nonce be already available to the receiver before decryption takes place. Thus, our technique of overloading the nonce for providing authentication is not compatible with a scenario where ciphertexts are delivered out of order, as the receiver is unable to determine the nonce associated with a ciphertext before decrypting it.

In practice, the amount of reordering that takes place over UDP will, on average, be limited. Accordingly, secure channel protocols will typically employ some form of window mechanism which determines which message numbers (and corresponding ciphertexts) can be accepted. If the message number of a ciphertext falls outside the window, it means that the ciphertext is either too old or too far ahead of the ones received and will be discarded. Such window mechanisms can take various forms and can implement a variety of different policies that determine how to deal with replays, when and how to change the window size, and when to advance the window ahead. Nevertheless, at an abstract level, they all specify a limited set of message numbers that can be accepted at that particular point in time.

We propose nonce-set AEAD as a new type of authenticated encryption that lends itself particularly well to this kind of scenario. The main change is that decryption will now additionally take a set of nonces as its input, and for it to succeed, the ciphertext has to be deemed valid with respect to that set of nonces. The motivation for introducing this primitive is twofold. The first is that it will enable the generic construction, which we present in the next section, for a secure channel operating over UDP that can support multiple different window policies. At a very high level, this construction combines a nonce-set AEAD scheme together with a tuple of algorithms that emulate the window mechanism by generating the nonce set for the decryption algorithm and updating it accordingly. This construction is appealing because although the security of the secure channel depends crucially on this tuple of algorithms, it turns out that they only need to satisfy a "functional" requirement and need not at all be cryptographic. In addition, this single construction can be tuned to realize various types of secure-channel behaviour. As such, nonce-set AEAD appears to be the right place for drawing the boundary between cryptographic and non-cryptographic processing. The second and complementary reason for introducing nonce-set AEAD is that we can realize it directly from an RPRP through an encode-then-encipher approach where authentication is achieved by overloading the nonce, thereby yielding more compact ciphertexts. Thus, by introducing nonce-set AEAD, we are now able to simultaneously accommodate these two mechanisms, which were otherwise incompatible. Below is the formal definition.

5.1 Formal Definition

Syntax. A nonce-set encryption scheme $\mathtt{NSE} = (\mathsf{Enc}, \mathsf{Dec})$ is a pair of algorithms with an associated key space $\mathcal{K}$, a nonce space $\mathcal{N} = \{0,1\}^t$ for some $t \in \mathbb{N}$, a nonce-set space $\mathcal{W} \subseteq \mathcal{P}(\mathcal{N})$, a header space $\mathcal{H}$, a message space $\mathcal{M}$ and a ciphertext space $\mathcal{C}$.

- The encryption algorithm follows the usual syntax, i.e.,

$$\mathsf{Enc} : \mathcal{K} \times \mathcal{N} \times \mathcal{H} \times \mathcal{M} \rightarrow \mathcal{C}.$$

  As before, encryption must be length-regular, thereby requiring the existence of a function clen, mapping the triple $(|N|, |H|, |M|)$ to the ciphertext length.
- The decryption algorithm works analogously to that in a nonce-hiding encryption scheme but additionally takes a set of nonces $\boldsymbol{W} \in \mathcal{W}$ as part of its input. That is, its syntax is given by

$$\mathsf{Dec} : \mathcal{K} \times \mathcal{W} \times \mathcal{H} \times \mathcal{C} \rightarrow (\mathcal{N} \times \mathcal{M}) \cup \{(\perp, \perp)\}.$$

  In addition, for all valid inputs $(K, \boldsymbol{W}, H, C)$ it must hold that:

$$\text{if } \mathsf{Dec}_K(\boldsymbol{W}, H, C) = (N', M') \neq (\perp, \perp) \text{ then } N' \in \boldsymbol{W}.$$

Correctness. For every nonce-set encryption scheme, it must hold that for all $(K, N, H, M) \in \mathcal{K} \times \mathcal{N} \times \mathcal{H} \times \mathcal{M}$ and every $\boldsymbol{W} \in \mathcal{W}$ such that $N \in \boldsymbol{W}$,

$$\text{if } C \leftarrow \mathsf{Enc}_K(N, H, M) \text{ then } (N, M) \leftarrow \mathsf{Dec}_K(\boldsymbol{W}, H, C).$$

Security. As before, security requires that no adversary can distinguish the real encryption and decryption algorithms $(\mathsf{Enc}(\cdot,\cdot,\cdot), \mathsf{Dec}(\cdot,\cdot,\cdot))$ from the ideal ones $(\$(\cdot,\cdot,\cdot), \bot(\cdot,\cdot,\cdot))$, under the condition that its encryption queries be nonce-respecting and it does not forward queries from the encryption oracle to the decryption oracle. The main difference to the classical nonce-based AEAD lies in how a forwarding query is defined. This is a query $(\boldsymbol{W}, H, C)$ to the decryption oracle where C was returned in a prior encryption query (N, H, M) and $N \in \boldsymbol{W}$. In other words, the adversary cannot query a ciphertext under a nonce-set containing the nonce with which it was produced. The security of a nonce-set encryption scheme is expressed through the following advantage measure.

Definition 5 (nsAE Advantage). *Let* $\mathtt{NSE} = (\mathsf{Enc}, \mathsf{Dec})$ *be a nonce-set based encryption scheme with associated spaces* $(\mathcal{K}, \mathcal{N}, \mathcal{W}, \mathcal{H}, \mathcal{M}, \mathcal{C})$*. Then for any nonce-respecting adversary* $\mathcal{A}$ *that does not make forwarding queries its advantage is defined as*

$$\mathbf{Adv}^{\mathrm{nsae}}_{\mathtt{NSE}}(\mathcal{A}) = \left|\Pr\left[K \leftarrow\!\!\$\, \mathcal{K} : \mathcal{A}^{\mathsf{Enc}_K(\cdot,\cdot,\cdot), \mathsf{Dec}_K(\cdot,\cdot,\cdot)} \Rightarrow 1\right] - \Pr\left[\mathcal{A}^{\$(\cdot,\cdot,\cdot), \bot(\cdot,\cdot,\cdot)} \Rightarrow 1\right]\right|.$$

Misuse Resistance. The above security notion can be strengthened to the misuse-resistance setting in the usual way. Namely by lifting the nonce-respecting requirement and simply requiring that the adversary never query the same triple (N, H, M) to the encryption more than once.

Unpacking the Definition. Note that if we set $\mathcal{W} = \{\{N\} : N \in \mathcal{N}\}$ then nonce-set AEAD effectively reduces to standard nonce-based AEAD with a nonce space $\mathcal{N}$. Thus, nonce-set AEAD can be seen as a natural extension of nonce-based AEAD. Our syntax requires that when decryption succeeds, it associates the decrypted ciphertext to a nonce in $\boldsymbol{W}$. Conversely, this means that if $\boldsymbol{W}$ is the empty set then decryption must fail. In addition, correctness guarantees that when $\boldsymbol{W}$ contains the nonce that was used to produce that ciphertext, decryption will recover the plaintext and will additionally recover that nonce. Finally, besides ruling out forgeries involving new ciphertexts, security also ensures that an adversary is unable to associate an honestly generated ciphertext to a different nonce. These features will come in handy in the next section where we show how to generically transform a nonce-set AEAD into an order-resilient channel.

A practical scheme must specify a format for representing $\boldsymbol{W}$ as a string. In general, this formatting must be concise for the scheme to be efficient. This will, in turn, impose heavy restrictions on the space $\mathcal{W}$ of all possible nonce sets that the decryption algorithm can accept. Thus, an important parameter of a nonce-set AEAD scheme is the maximum nonce set size w, defined as

$$w := \max_{\boldsymbol{W} \in \mathcal{W}} |\boldsymbol{W}|.$$

$\mathsf{Enc}_K(N, H, M)$	$\mathsf{Dec}_K(\boldsymbol{W}, H, C_1, C_2)$

$l \leftarrow \|M\|$
$(C_1, C_2) \leftarrow \widetilde{\mathsf{EE}}_K(H, N\|\lfloor M \rfloor_{n-t}, \lceil M \rceil_{l-n+t})$
return (C_1, C_2)
	$(X_L, X_R) \leftarrow \widetilde{\mathsf{EE}}_K^{-1}(H, C_1, C_2)$
	$N' \leftarrow \lfloor X_L \rfloor_t$
	$M' \leftarrow \lceil X_L \rceil_{n-t} \| X_R$
	if $N' \in \boldsymbol{W}$ **then**
	  return (N', M')
	else
	  return $(\bot, \bot)$

Fig. 7. The AwN construction, transforming an RPRP-secure cipher $\widetilde{\mathsf{EE}}$ over the domain $\{0,1\}^n \times \{0,1\}^{\geq m}$ into a nonce-set AEAD scheme that is MRAE secure. The scheme is parametrized by the nonce length t, where $t \leq n$.

The specific value of this parameter may be a result of the formatting used to represent $\boldsymbol{W}$, or it may need to be specifically restricted in order to guarantee a certain level of security. In addition, the formatting used to represent $\boldsymbol{W}$ will typically require an efficient means to do membership testing. This aspect of a nonce-set AEAD is beyond our scope. Still, it suffices to say that various instantiations exist that satisfy these requirements, including the formatting used in the window mechanisms employed by existing internet protocols.

5.2 Nonce-Set AEAD from Nonce-Hiding AEAD

Nonce-set AEAD can be easily realized from any nonce-hiding AEAD scheme simply by following decryption with a test verifying that the recovered nonce is in $\boldsymbol{W}$. This construction is described in the full version of this paper [16]. Thus the nonce-hiding constructions by Bellare, Ng, and Tackmann in [8] which are nonce-recovering, namely HN1, HN2, HN4, and HN5, can be readily transformed into nonce-set AEAD schemes. However, these constructions all incur a ciphertext expansion resulting from the underlying integrity mechanism as well as a second ciphertext expansion arising from the nonce encryption. In contrast, the construction we present next reduces this overhead by constructing a nonce-set AEAD scheme directly from a RPRP via the encode-then-encipher paradigm.

5.3 The Authenticate-with-Nonce (AwN) Construction

The Authenticate-with-Nonce (AwN) construction is similar in spirit to the EtE construction instantiated with $\mathsf{Func}_2(N, H) = N$, but it gives rise instead to a nonce-set AEAD scheme. A pseudocode description is provided in Fig. 7. Note that the integrity check is now done by verifying that $N' \in \boldsymbol{W}$, rather than an equality test as in EtE. By RPRP security, any mauled ciphertext will produce a left output that is hard to guess, thereby limiting the probability of this condition being satisfied, as long as $\boldsymbol{W}$ is not too large. As a result, the MRAE security of AwN depends on the maximum nonce set size w. Moreover, for added generality, we allow the nonce size t to be smaller or equal to the size of the left domain n. This too bears influence over the security of AwN. In combination, these two aspects give rise to the $w2^{n-t}$ term in the RPRP advantage term within the security bound. The MRAE security of AwN is formally stated in Theorem 4, the proof of which can be found in the full version of this paper [16].

Theorem 4. *Let* AwN *be the nonce-set AEAD scheme defined in Fig. 7, realized from a tweakable cipher over the domain* $\{0,1\}^n \times \{0,1\}^{\geq m}$, *with nonce size* t *and maximum nonce set size* w. *Then for any* MRAE *adversary* $\mathcal{A}$ *making* q_e *encryption queries and* q_v *verification queries, there exists an* RPRP *adversary* $\mathcal{B}$ *such that*

$$\mathbf{Adv}^{\mathrm{mrae}}_{\mathtt{AwN}}(\mathcal{A}) \leq \mathbf{Adv}^{\mathrm{rprp}}_{\widetilde{\mathsf{EE}}}(\mathcal{B}, w2^{n-t}) + \frac{q_e^2}{2^{n+m+1}}.$$

The adversary $\mathcal{B}$ *makes* q_e *queries to the* EN *oracle and* q_v *queries to the* GU *oracle, and runs in time similar to that of* $\mathcal{A}$.

6 Application to Order-Resilient Secure Channels

Equipped with the notion of nonce-set AEAD, we now turn our attention to constructing secure channels over an unreliable transport. QUIC [22,35] and DTLS [29,30], which operate over UDP, are two prime examples of order-resilient secure channels. Two recent works [17,18] have analyzed the security of QUIC. Here we will follow in large part the formal security model of Fischlin, Günther, and Janson [18] which builds on and improves over prior works [6,12,33] and is the most versatile.

As pointed out already in [12,13] several strategies are possible for dealing with out-of-order delivery and replay protection. However, their models fail to capture the more elaborate ones that rely on window mechanisms, as in the case of QUIC and DTLS. These window mechanisms can handle out-of-order delivery and replay protection without consuming too much memory and bandwidth. This comes, however, at the expense of added complexity that is harder to model mathematically. Even formulating correctness for such secure channels becomes rather challenging. To overcome the limitations of prior security models, Fischlin et al. replace the level-sets in [33] with a *support predicate*, which essentially serves to determine which ciphertexts should be accepted by the receiver. The point of this predicate is that it considers the receiver's perspective in making this determination. As is the case with QUIC and DTLS a ciphertext deemed invalid at a certain point in time (due to it falling outside the current window) may become valid later (when the window has shifted sufficiently ahead).

Our focus in this section is not to analyze the security of QUIC or DTLS. Instead, we take a fresh perspective on how such secure channels can be constructed differently and more simply through nonce-set AEAD. More specifically, we provide a generic construction for transforming any nonce-set AEAD scheme into a secure channel parametrized by a support predicate. Notably, the construction works for *any* desired support predicate by employing a quadruple of relatively simple algorithms. In turn, the security of the channel construction relies on the security of the nonce-set AEAD scheme and a mild requirement on the quadruple of algorithms with respect to the support predicate. We tame the complexity in constructions like QUIC and DTLS by introducing modularity into the picture and identifying the role of each component. Here the introduction of nonce-set AEAD plays a key role in glueing the different components together and permitting us to generically express the logic behind the support predicate by processing nonce values. We also strengthen the security definition from [18] to reflect the privacy requirement to conceal message numbers from eavesdroppers. In contrast, in [18] message numbers were required to be transmitted in the clear.

In addition, when the nonce-set AEAD scheme is instantiated with our RPRP-based construction, we end up with a secure channel construction that is competitive in comparison to QUIC and DTLS. To start with, it only requires a single key (instead of two) to process each ciphertext. Our nonce-set AEAD scheme can be realized with GCM components, leading to comparable performance to GCM-SIV and offering misuse-resistance. QUIC only transmits a partial nonce in the ciphertext in order to save bandwidth at the expense of an additional window mechanism to reconstruct it. In contrast, our construction transmits the full nonce, thereby simplifying the processing at the receiver's end, but saves bandwidth nonetheless from its overloaded use of the nonce (within the nonce-set AEAD construction) to provide integrity without a MAC tag.

6.1 Order-Resilient Channels

We start by defining the syntax of order-resilient channels. The definitions below are reproduced from [18] and we do not claim any novelty in them. We do, however, make some alterations in them which we point out along the way.

Definition 6 (Channel Syntax). *A channel consists of a triple of algorithms* $\mathtt{Ch} = (\mathsf{Init}, \mathsf{Send}, \mathsf{Recv})$ *with associated spaces* $\mathcal{ST}_S$, $\mathcal{ST}_R$, $\mathcal{MN}$, $\mathcal{A}$, $\mathcal{M}$ *and* $\mathcal{C}$ *such that:*

- $(\mathrm{st}_s, \mathrm{st}_r) \leftarrow\!\!\$\ \mathsf{Init}()$. *The probabilistic initialization algorithm that takes no input and returns an initial sender state* $\mathrm{st}_s \in \mathcal{ST}_S$ *and an initial receiver state* $\mathrm{st}_r \in \mathcal{ST}_R$.
- $(\mathrm{st}'_s, C) \leftarrow\!\!\$\ \mathsf{Send}(\mathrm{st}_s, A, M)$. *The send algorithm, may be probabilistic or stateful and takes as input a sender state* $\mathrm{st}_s \in \mathcal{ST}_S$, *associated data* $A \in \mathcal{A}$ *and a message* $M \in \mathcal{M}$, *and returns as output an updated sender state* $\mathrm{st}'_s \in \mathcal{ST}_S$ *and a ciphertext* $C \in \mathcal{C}$ *or the error symbol* $\bot$.
- $(\mathrm{st}'_r, mn, M) \leftarrow \mathsf{Recv}(\mathrm{st}_r, A, C)$. *The deterministic receive algorithm takes as input a receiver state* $\mathrm{st}_r \in \mathcal{ST}_R$, *associated data* $A \in \mathcal{A}$ *and a ciphertext* $C \in \mathcal{C}$. *It then returns an updated receiver state* $\mathrm{st}'_r \in \mathcal{ST}_R$ *together with, either a message number* $mn \in \mathcal{MN}$ *and a message* $M \in \mathcal{M}$, *or a pair of error symbols* $(\bot, \bot)$.

In comparison to [18] we augmented the Recv algorithm to return the message number together with the message. This reflects the real-world necessity that a higher layer needs such information to correctly position each message in the sequence in which it was sent. We also expanded Send with associated data A, and removed the auxiliary data and accompanying function as they are no longer needed in our setting.

The Support Predicate. There are varying degrees to which a channel may be order resilient. As explained in [18] the prior models by [12, 33] are not expressive enough to capture the order resilience of real-world protocols like QUIC and DTLS. To address this, they introduced the support predicate. In essence, the support predicate expresses the channel's tolerance to reordered, replayed, or dropped ciphertexts. It essentially captures the 'character' of the channel, which permeates into every aspect of it—from correctness to robustness (which we explain shortly) to security. Indeed, this conforms with and is reminiscent of the silencing approach in [33], but generalizes it further.

The support predicate takes three inputs: a list $\mathcal{C}_S$ of the sent ciphertexts, a list $\mathcal{DC}_R$ of the received ciphertexts together with a boolean value indicating whether each was deemed supported or not, and a candidate ciphertext C and returns a boolean indicating whether C is supported or not. Thus, whether a ciphertext is supported may depend on the ciphertexts sent, the ones received, and how the current ciphertext relates to them.

In conformance with [18], any ciphertext not in $\mathcal{C}_S$ must not be supported. However, whereas in [18] the list $\mathcal{C}_S$ is allowed to contain repeating ciphertexts, we specifically prohibit this. In particular, we require that every entry in $\mathcal{C}_S$ be identified uniquely. Whether two messages encrypt to the same ciphertext (a possibility with stateful schemes) or not depends on the scheme at hand. Thus allowing this to occur would render the support predicate scheme-specific, thereby introducing a circularity in the correctness and security definitions—which is why we avoid this possibility. Moreover, the representation of ciphertexts should not bear any weight on the predicate's value. Therefore, we allow ciphertexts to be identified by integers or other strings as long as the entries in $\mathcal{C}_S$ are unique.

There are two other minor points where we deviate from [18]. One is that we require that every support predicate accept perfectly-in-order delivery. The other is that we allow the support predicate to only return a boolean value, whereas in the formulation in [18] it could also return an integer. This seems to have been required due to the possibility of repeating ciphertexts in $\mathcal{C}_S$, which we specifically rule out.

An example support predicate, reflecting the required functionality of a typical real-world protocol, can be found in the full version of this paper [16]

Channel Correctness. Different support predicates identify different channel functionalities. Nevertheless, we can define channel correctness generically for *any* possible support predicate. Intuitively, correctness requires that for any supported (and thus honestly generated) ciphertext, the receiver must always be

Game $\mathsf{CORR}^{\mathcal{A}}_{\mathsf{Ch,supp}}$	Procedure $\textsc{Send}(A, M)$	Procedure $\textsc{Recv}(j)$

$(\mathsf{st}_s, \mathsf{st}_r) \leftarrow\$ \mathtt{Ch.Init}()$
$\mathcal{DC}_R, \mathcal{C}_S, \mathcal{T} \leftarrow [\,], [\,], [\,]$
$mn \leftarrow 0$
$\mathsf{win} \leftarrow \mathbf{false}$
$\mathcal{A}^{\textsc{Send},\textsc{Recv}}$
return win
	$(\mathsf{st}_s, C) \leftarrow\$ \mathtt{Ch.Send}(\mathsf{st}_s, A, M)$
	$\mathcal{C}_S \leftarrow \mathcal{C}_S \| C$
	$\mathcal{T} \leftarrow \mathcal{T} \| (mn, A, M, C)$
	$mn \leftarrow mn + 1$
	return C
		if $j > \|\mathcal{T}\|$ **then**
		  return $\lightning$
		$(mn, A, M, C) \leftarrow \mathcal{T}[j]$
		$\mathsf{d} \leftarrow \mathsf{supp}(\mathcal{C}_S, \mathcal{DC}_R, C)$
		if $\mathsf{d} = \mathbf{false}$ **then**
		  return $\lightning$
		$(\mathsf{st}_r, mn', M') \leftarrow \mathtt{Ch.Recv}(\mathsf{st}_r, A, C)$
		if $mn' \neq mn \vee M' \neq M$ **then**
		  $\mathsf{win} \leftarrow \mathbf{true}$
		$\mathcal{DC}_R \leftarrow \mathcal{DC}_R \| (\mathsf{d}, C)$
		return (mn', M')

Fig. 8. The game CORR used to define channel correctness.

able to recover the original message contained in that ciphertext together with its corresponding message number. Thus correctness ensures that the receiver is able to recover the original sequence of messages in the exact ordering in which they were sent. This is formally defined via the game in Fig. 8.

Definition 7 (Channel Correctness). *A channel* Ch *is said to be correct with respect to a support predicate* supp, *if for all possible adversaries* $\mathcal{A}$ *it holds that*

$$\Pr\left[\mathsf{CORR}^{\mathcal{A}}_{\mathsf{Ch,supp}} \Rightarrow 1\right] = 0.$$

6.2 The Robustness Property

Unlike TLS and similar protocols, where one invalid ciphertext typically results in the connection being torn down, order-resilient channels are inherently required to tolerate a significant amount of decryption failures during their operation. Such decryption failures may arise from the unreliable nature of the underlying protocol, or due to manipulation by a malicious adversary. Furthermore, the receiver will generally be unable to distinguish between these two cases. Thus, order-resilient channels must maintain their correct operation in the presence of adversarial manipulation. However, the above correctness requirement does not capture such a scenario as it considers only honestly-generated ciphertexts. Accordingly, [18] introduced the notion of *robustness* to capture this stronger requirement.

Robustness is formally defined through the ROB game located in the full version of this paper [16]. Here, the Recv oracle maintains internally two Recv instances, the *real* one, which is supplied with all queried ciphertexts, and the *correct* one, which is only supplied with supported ciphertexts. Then if at any point the adversary queries a supported ciphertext that causes the outputs of the two Recv instances to differ, it will constitute a win for the adversary. The advantage of an adversary is quantified as its probability of winning this game.

Definition 8 (ROB **Advantage**). *For a channel* $\mathsf{Ch} = (\mathsf{Init}, \mathsf{Send}, \mathsf{Recv})$ *and a support predicate* supp, *the corresponding robustness advantage of an adversary* $\mathcal{A}$ *is defined as:*

$$\mathbf{Adv}^{\mathrm{rob}}_{\mathsf{Ch},\mathsf{supp}}(\mathcal{A}) = \Pr\left[\mathsf{ROB}^{\mathcal{A}}_{\mathsf{Ch},\mathsf{supp}} \Rightarrow 1\right].$$

Note that in the ROB game both Recv instances are initialized with the same state. Thus, for the adversary to win, the states of the two instances must at some point diverge. On the other hand, only unsupported ciphertexts can cause such a divergence in their states. Therefore, a sufficient condition for satisfying robustness is that unsupported ciphertext do not change the state.

6.3 Channel Security

We use a single-game definition of channel security that combines confidentiality and integrity into one notion. It is heavily based on the security definitions from [18], without robustness, and adapted with some of the ideas from simulatable channels in [14]. Security is defined via the indistinguishability game INT-SIM-CCA shown in Fig. 9. Here, we essentially require the existence of a stateless algorithm S that can simulate the Send oracle to the adversary and that the adversary is unable to query an unsupported ciphertext to Recv that decrypts successfully, i.e., a forgery. Note that, as shown in [14], requiring the simulator S to be stateless results in a stronger security notion. Namely, it provides key privacy and ensures that ciphertexts do not leak the message number since the simulator cannot keep track of the number of messages that are sent. Below is the formal definition.

Definition 9 (INT-SIM-CCA **Advantage**). *Let* $\mathsf{Ch} = (\mathsf{Init}, \mathsf{Send}, \mathsf{Recv})$ *be a channel protocol realizing the functionality corresponding to the support predicate* supp. *Then,* Ch *is* INT-SIM-CCA *secure if there exists a stateless encryption simulator* S *such that for any adversary* $\mathcal{A}$ *the following quantity is small*

$$\mathbf{Adv}^{\mathrm{int\text{-}sim\text{-}cca}}_{\mathsf{Ch},\mathsf{supp}}(\mathcal{A}, \mathsf{S}) = \left|2\Pr\left[\mathsf{INT\text{-}SIM\text{-}CCA}^{\mathcal{A},\mathsf{S}}_{\mathsf{Ch},\mathsf{supp}} \Rightarrow 1\right] - 1\right|.$$

6.4 From Nonce-Set AEAD to Order-Resilient Secure Channels

We are now ready to present this section's main contribution - a generic construction for transforming any nonce-set AEAD scheme into an order-resilient channel. This construction consists of a nonce-set AEAD scheme combined with a tuple of four basic algorithms called the *nonce set processing scheme* algorithms. This construction has some notable features. Firstly, it works for *any* support predicate. This means that this template construction can be used to realize any channel functionality that can be expressed via the support predicate introduced by Fischlin et al. in [18]. In addition, any instantiation will automatically satisfy robustness and channel security for that support predicate. The main conditions for this to hold are that the underlying nonce-set AEAD be secure and that the

$\mathsf{INT\text{-}SIM\text{-}CCA}^{\mathcal{A},\mathsf{S}}_{\mathsf{Ch},\mathsf{supp}}$	Procedure $\textsc{Send}(A, M)$	Procedure $\textsc{Recv}(A, C)$
$(\mathrm{st}_s, \mathrm{st}_r) \leftarrow\$ \mathsf{Ch.Init}()$	**if** $b = 0$ **then** // ideal world	$(\mathrm{st}_r, mn, M) \leftarrow \mathsf{Ch.Recv}(\mathrm{st}_r, A, C)$
$\mathcal{C}_S, \mathcal{DC}_R \leftarrow [\,], [\,]$	$C \leftarrow\$ \mathsf{S}(A, \lvert M \rvert)$	**if** $b = 0$ **then** // ideal world
$b \leftarrow\$ \{0, 1\}$	**else** // real world	$(mn, M) \leftarrow (\perp, \perp)$
$b' \leftarrow \mathcal{A}^{\textsc{Send},\textsc{Recv}}$	$(\mathrm{st}_s, C) \leftarrow\$ \mathsf{Ch.Send}(\mathrm{st}_s, A, M)$	**else** // real world
return $b = b'$	$\mathcal{C}_S \leftarrow \mathcal{C}_S \Vert C$	$\mathsf{d} \leftarrow \mathsf{supp}(\mathcal{C}_S, \mathcal{DC}_R, C)$
	return C	**if** $\mathsf{d} = \mathbf{true}$ **then**
		$(mn, M) \leftarrow (\perp, \perp)$
		$\mathcal{DC}_R \leftarrow \mathcal{DC}_R \Vert (\mathsf{d}, C)$
		return (mn, M)

Fig. 9. The INT-SIM-CCA game used to define channel security.

nonce set processing scheme *faithfully* reproduce the functionality of the support predicate.

As the name implies, the nonce set processing scheme algorithms are primarily concerned with generating and updating the nonce-set that is fed to the nonce-set AEAD. The faithfulness property ensures that the nonce set processing scheme accurately reflects the channel behaviour corresponding to the support predicate. Recall that we required the support predicate to be defined over any possible way of identifying the ciphertexts as long as it uniquely represented each ciphertext in $\mathcal{C}_S$. This means that we can identify each ciphertext with the nonce it is assigned in the Send algorithm. Accordingly, the role of the nonce set processing algorithms is to identify the set of supported nonces at every stage of the Recv algorithm. Our channel construction will then use the set of supported nonces as the nonce set to be fed to the nonce-set AEAD. Thus our generic construction can be viewed as decomposing a channel into these constituent components, thereby adding to our understanding of order-resilient channels.

We start by describing the syntax of the nonce set processing scheme algorithms. A nonce set processing scheme NSP consists of the following constituent algorithms:

- $(\mathrm{st}_s, \mathrm{st}_r) \leftarrow\$ \mathsf{StInit}()$. A probabilistic initialization algorithm, that returns the initial sender state st_s and the initial receiver state st_r.
- $(\mathrm{st}'_s, N) \leftarrow \mathsf{NonceExtract}(\mathrm{st}_s)$. A deterministic nonce extraction algorithm, that takes as input the non-key component of the sender state and returns a (possibly) updated state together with a *unique* nonce N or the symbol $\perp$.
- $\boldsymbol{W} \leftarrow \mathsf{NonceSetPolicy}(\mathrm{st}_r)$. A deterministic nonce-set policy algorithm that takes as input the non-key component of the receiver state and returns a nonce set.
- $(\mathrm{st}'_r, mn) \leftarrow \mathsf{StUpdate}(\mathrm{st}_r, N)$. A deterministic state-update algorithm that takes as input the non-key component of the receiver state together with a nonce, and returns an updated state together with the message number corresponding to that nonce.

Game $\mathsf{FAITHFUL}^{\mathcal{A}}_{\mathsf{NSP},\mathsf{supp}}$	Procedure F-SEND()	Procedure F-RECV(N)

$(\mathsf{st}_s, \mathsf{st}_r) \leftarrow\!\$\ \mathsf{StInit}()$
$\mathcal{N}_S, \mathcal{DC}_R \leftarrow [\,], [\,]$
$\mathsf{win} \leftarrow \mathbf{false}$
$\mathcal{A}^{(\mathsf{st}_s, \mathsf{st}_r), \text{F-SEND}, \text{F-RECV}}$
return win
	$(\mathsf{st}_s, N) \leftarrow \mathsf{NonceExtract}(\mathsf{st}_s)$
	$\mathcal{N}_S \leftarrow \mathcal{N}_S \| N$
	return N
		if $N \notin \mathcal{N}_S$ **then**
		  return $\lightning$
		$\boldsymbol{W} \leftarrow \mathsf{NonceSetPolicy}(\mathsf{st}_r)$
		if $N \in \boldsymbol{W}$ **then**
		  $(\mathsf{st}_r, mn) \leftarrow \mathsf{StUpdate}(\mathsf{st}_r, N)$
		else
		  $mn \leftarrow \perp$
		$\mathsf{d} \leftarrow \mathsf{supp}(\mathcal{N}_S, \mathcal{DC}_R, N)$
		$\mathcal{DC}_R \leftarrow \mathcal{DC}_R \| (\mathsf{d}, N)$
		if $\mathsf{d} = \mathbf{true} \wedge$
		    $(N \notin \boldsymbol{W} \vee N \neq \mathcal{N}_S[mn])$ **then**
		  $\mathsf{win} \leftarrow \mathbf{true}$
		if $\mathsf{d} = \mathbf{false} \wedge N \in \boldsymbol{W}$ **then**
		  $\mathsf{win} \leftarrow \mathbf{true}$
		return (st_r, mn)

Fig. 10. The game FAITHFUL used to define faithfulness for a tuple of nonce set processing algorithms.

The Faithfulness Property. The only property that we require from a nonce set processing scheme is that it *faithfully* reproduces the functionality of the channel's support predicate. Note that none of the nonce set processing scheme algorithms makes use of a secret key. This is because faithfulness is a property that can be satisfied without cryptographic means. For any scheme, NSP and support predicate supp, faithfulness is defined via the game FAITHFUL shown in Fig. 10. The adversary's goal is to cause the nonce set processing algorithms and the support predicate to be misaligned or recover the wrong message number from a nonce. Note that the receiver is only allowed to query nonces to the F-RECV oracle that the F-SEND oracle has returned. A win occurs if the submitted nonce is supported, but not contained in the nonce set returned by NonceSetPolicy or the message number returned by StUpdate for that nonce is incorrect. Alternatively, if the nonce is not supported but the nonce set does contain that nonce, it is also a win for the adversary.

Definition 10 (FAITHFUL Advantage). *Let* NSP *be a nonce set processing scheme. Then for any adversary* $\mathcal{A}$ *and any support predicate* supp, *the corresponding advantage is defined as*

$$\mathbf{Adv}^{\mathrm{faithful}}_{\mathsf{NSP},\mathsf{supp}}(\mathcal{A}) = \Pr\left[\mathsf{FAITHFUL}^{\mathcal{A}}_{\mathsf{NSP},\mathsf{supp}} \Rightarrow 1\right].$$

We say that a nonce-set scheme NSP faithfully reproduces the support predicate supp, if for all possible adversaries $\mathcal{A}$ it holds that $\mathbf{Adv}^{\mathrm{faithful}}_{\mathsf{NSP},\mathsf{supp}}(\mathcal{A}) = 0$.

Generic Channel Construction. Our generic construction of an order-resilient secure channel $\mathsf{Ch}_{\mathsf{NS}} = (\mathsf{Init}, \mathsf{Send}, \mathsf{Recv})$ from a nonce-set AEAD scheme

$\mathsf{Init}()$	$\mathsf{Send}(\mathrm{stk}_s, A, M)$	$\mathsf{Recv}(\mathrm{stk}_r, A, C)$

$(\mathrm{st}_s, \mathrm{st}_r) \leftarrow\!\!\$\ \mathsf{StInit}()$
$K \leftarrow\!\!\$\ \{0,1\}^k$
$\mathrm{stk}_s \leftarrow (\mathrm{st}_s, K)$
$\mathrm{stk}_r \leftarrow (\mathrm{st}_r, K)$
return $(\mathrm{stk}_s, \mathrm{stk}_r)$
	$(\mathrm{st}_s, K) \leftarrow \mathrm{stk}_s$
	$(\mathrm{st}'_s, N) \leftarrow \mathsf{NonceExtract}(\mathrm{st}_s)$
	if $N = \bot$ **then**
	  return $(\mathrm{st}'_s, \bot)$
	$C \leftarrow \mathsf{Enc}(K, N, A, M)$
	$\mathrm{stk}'_s \leftarrow (\mathrm{st}'_s, K)$
	return (stk'_s, C)
		$(\mathrm{st}_r, K) \leftarrow \mathrm{stk}_r$
		$\boldsymbol{W} \leftarrow \mathsf{NonceSetPolicy}(\mathrm{st}_r)$
		$(N, M) \leftarrow \mathsf{Dec}(K, \boldsymbol{W}, A, C)$
		if $(N, M) = (\bot, \bot)$ **then**
		  $mn \leftarrow \bot$
		else
		  $(\mathrm{st}'_r, mn) \leftarrow \mathsf{StUpdate}(\mathrm{st}_r, N)$
		$\mathrm{stk}'_r \leftarrow (\mathrm{st}'_r, K)$
		return (stk'_r, mn, M)

Fig. 11. A generic construction of an order-resilient secure channel $\mathtt{Ch}_{\mathrm{NS}}$ from a nonce-set AEAD scheme and a nonce set processing scheme.

$\mathtt{NSE} = (\mathsf{Enc}, \mathsf{Dec})$ and a nonce set processing scheme $\mathtt{NSP} = (\mathsf{StInit}, \mathsf{NonceExtract}, \mathsf{NonceSetPolicy}, \mathsf{StUpdate})$ is presented in Fig. 11.

Channel Correctness. The proof of correctness for this generic construction is provided in the full version of this paper [16].

Theorem 5. *If the nonce-set AEAD scheme* $\mathtt{NSE}$ *is correct and the nonce set processing scheme* $\mathtt{NSP}$ *faithfully reproduces the support predicate* supp*, then the channel construction* $\mathtt{Ch}_{\mathrm{NS}}$ *presented in Fig. 11 is correct with respect to* supp.

Channel Robustness. We argue robustness based on our earlier observation that a sufficient condition for robustness is that unsupported ciphertexts never affect the channel state. The faithfulness of $\mathtt{NSP}$ guarantees that only the nonces used to generate supported ciphertexts will be included in the nonce set. Then, by the nsAE security of $\mathtt{NSE}$, decryption can only succeed as long as the ciphertext was produced by the sender under one of the nonces contained in the nonce set—otherwise, it would constitute a forgery. Thus decryption will always fail for unsupported ciphertexts, and by construction, the state is never updated ($\mathsf{StUpdate}$ is not called) when decryption fails.

Channel Security. The security of $\mathtt{Ch}_{\mathrm{NS}}$ is formally stated in the following theorem, the proof of which is presented in the full version of this paper [16].

Theorem 6 (Security of $\mathtt{Ch}_{\mathrm{NS}}$). *Let* $\mathtt{Ch}_{\mathrm{NS}}$ *be the generic channel construction described in Fig. 11, composed from a nonce-set AEAD scheme* $\mathtt{NSE}$ *with associated ciphertext space* $\{0,1\}^{\geq \ell}$ *and a nonce set processing scheme* $\mathtt{NSP}$*. Then, for any support predicate* supp *there exists a stateless simulator* S*, such that for every* INT-SIM-CCA *adversary* $\mathcal{A}$ *making* q_{s} *send queries and* q_{r} *receive queries, there exist adversaries* $\mathcal{B}$ *and* $\mathcal{C}$ *such that*

$$\mathbf{Adv}^{\text{int-sim-cca}}_{\mathtt{Ch}_{\mathrm{NS}},\mathsf{supp}}(\mathcal{A}, \mathsf{S}) \ \leq \mathbf{Adv}^{\mathrm{nsae}}_{\mathtt{NSE}}(\mathcal{B}) + \mathbf{Adv}^{\mathrm{faithful}}_{\mathtt{NSP},\mathsf{supp}}(\mathcal{C}) + \frac{q_{\mathrm{s}}(q_{\mathrm{s}}-1)}{2^{\ell}}.$$

Furthermore, $\mathcal{B}$ makes q_s encryption queries and at most q_r decryption queries, whereas $\mathcal{C}$ makes q_s send queries and at most q_r receive queries. Both adversaries run in time similar to that of $\mathcal{A}$.

Acknowledgments. We are grateful to Alessandro Melloni, Jean-Pierre Münch, and Martijn Stam for their collaboration in developing the RPRP security definition and other helpful discussions. We also thank the anonymous CRYPTO 2022 reviewers for their thorough reading and constructive comments. This research was supported by the German Federal Ministry of Education and Research and the Hessen State Ministry for Higher Education, Research and the Arts within their joint support of the National Research Center for Applied Cybersecurity ATHENE.

References

1. Andreeva, E., Bogdanov, A., Luykx, A., Mennink, B., Mouha, N., Yasuda, K.: How to securely release unverified plaintext in authenticated encryption. In: Sarkar, P., Iwata, T. (eds.) ASIACRYPT 2014, Part I. LNCS, vol. 8873, pp. 105–125. Springer, Heidelberg (2014). https://doi.org/10.1007/978-3-662-45611-8_6
2. Ashur, T., Dunkelman, O., Luykx, A.: Boosting authenticated encryption robustness with minimal modifications. In: Katz, J., Shacham, H. (eds.) CRYPTO 2017, Part III. LNCS, vol. 10403, pp. 3–33. Springer, Cham (2017). https://doi.org/10.1007/978-3-319-63697-9_1
3. Barwell, G., Page, D., Stam, M.: Rogue decryption failures: reconciling AE robustness notions. In: Groth, J. (ed.) IMACC 2015. LNCS, vol. 9496, pp. 94–111. Springer, Cham (2015). https://doi.org/10.1007/978-3-319-27239-9_6
4. Beierle, C., et al.: SKINNY-AEAD and SKINNY-hash. IACR Trans. Symm. Cryptol. **2020**(S1), 88–131 (2020)
5. Bellare, M., Keelveedhi, S.: Authenticated and misuse-resistant encryption of key-dependent data. In: Rogaway, P. (ed.) CRYPTO 2011. LNCS, vol. 6841, pp. 610–629. Springer, Heidelberg (2011). https://doi.org/10.1007/978-3-642-22792-9_35
6. Bellare, M., Kohno, T., Namprempre, C.: Authenticated encryption in SSH: Provably fixing the SSH binary packet protocol. In: Atluri, V. (ed.) ACM CCS 2002, pp. 1–11. ACM Press, Nov. (2002)
7. Bellare, M., Namprempre, C.: Authenticated encryption: relations among notions and analysis of the generic composition paradigm. In: Okamoto, T. (ed.) ASIACRYPT 2000. LNCS, vol. 1976, pp. 531–545. Springer, Heidelberg (2000). https://doi.org/10.1007/3-540-44448-3_41
8. Bellare, M., Ng, R., Tackmann, B.: Nonces are noticed: AEAD revisited. In: Boldyreva, A., Micciancio, D. (eds.) CRYPTO 2019, Part I. LNCS, vol. 11692, pp. 235–265. Springer, Cham (2019). https://doi.org/10.1007/978-3-030-26948-7_9
9. Bellare, M., Rogaway, P.: Encode-then-encipher encryption: how to exploit nonces or redundancy in plaintexts for efficient cryptography. In: Okamoto, T. (ed.) ASIACRYPT 2000. LNCS, vol. 1976, pp. 317–330. Springer, Heidelberg (2000). https://doi.org/10.1007/3-540-44448-3_24
10. Bernstein, D.J.: CAESAR competition call for submissions (2014). https://competitions.cr.yp.to/caesar-call.html

11. Boldyreva, A., Degabriele, J.P., Paterson, K.G., Stam, M.: On symmetric encryption with distinguishable decryption failures. In: Moriai, S. (ed.) FSE 2013. LNCS, vol. 8424, pp. 367–390. Springer, Heidelberg (2014). https://doi.org/10.1007/978-3-662-43933-3_19
12. Boyd, C., Hale, B., Mjølsnes, S.F., Stebila, D.: From stateless to stateful: generic authentication and authenticated encryption constructions with application to TLS. In: Sako, K. (ed.) CT-RSA 2016. LNCS, vol. 9610, pp. 55–71. Springer, Cham (2016). https://doi.org/10.1007/978-3-319-29485-8_4
13. Chan, J., Rogaway, P.: Anonymous AE. In: Galbraith, S.D., Moriai, S. (eds.) ASIACRYPT 2019, Part II. LNCS, vol. 11922, pp. 183–208. Springer, Cham (2019). https://doi.org/10.1007/978-3-030-34621-8_7
14. Degabriele, J.P., Fischlin, M.: Simulatable channels: extended security that is universally composable and easier to prove. In: Peyrin, T., Galbraith, S. (eds.) ASIACRYPT 2018, Part III. LNCS, vol. 11274, pp. 519–550. Springer, Cham (2018). https://doi.org/10.1007/978-3-030-03332-3_19
15. Degabriele, J.P., Karadžić, V., Melloni, A., Münch, J.-P., Stam, M.: Rugged pseudorandom permutations and their applications. In: The IACR Real World Crypto Symposium (2022)
16. Degabriele, J.P., Karadžić, V.: Overloading the nonce: rugged PRPs, nonce-set AEAD, and order-resilient channels. Cryptology ePrint Archive, Paper 2022/817 (2022). https://eprint.iacr.org/2022/817
17. Delignat-Lavaud, A., et al.: A security model and fully verified implementation for the IETF QUIC record layer. In: 2021 IEEE Symposium on Security and Privacy (SP), IEEE, May 2021
18. Fischlin, M., Günther, F., Janson, C.: Robust channels: handling unreliable networks in the record layers of QUIC and DTLS 1.3. Cryptology ePrint Archive, Report 2020/718 (2020). https://eprint.iacr.org/2020/718
19. Groth, J. (ed.): IMACC 2015. LNCS, vol. 9496. Springer, Cham (2015). https://doi.org/10.1007/978-3-319-27239-9
20. Gueron, S., Lindell, Y.: GCM-SIV: Full nonce misuse-resistant authenticated encryption at under one cycle per byte. In: Ray, I., Li, N., Kruegel, C. (eds.) ACM CCS 2015, pp. 109–119. ACM Press, New York (2015)
21. Hoang, V.T., Krovetz, T., Rogaway, P.: Robust authenticated-encryption AEZ and the problem that it solves. In: Oswald, E., Fischlin, M. (eds.) EUROCRYPT 2015, Part I. LNCS, vol. 9056, pp. 15–44. Springer, Heidelberg (2015). https://doi.org/10.1007/978-3-662-46800-5_2
22. Iyengar, J., Thomson, M.: RFC9000: QUIC: A UDP-based multiplexed and secure transport (2021). https://datatracker.ietf.org/doc/html/rfc9000
23. Jean, J., Nikolic, I., Peyrin, T., Seurin, Y.: The Deoxys AEAD family. J. Cryptology **34**(3), 31 (2021)
24. Liskov, M., Rivest, R.L., Wagner, D.: Tweakable block ciphers. In: Yung, M. (ed.) CRYPTO 2002. LNCS, vol. 2442, pp. 31–46. Springer, Heidelberg (2002). https://doi.org/10.1007/3-540-45708-9_3
25. Minematsu, K., Iwata, T.: Tweak-length extension for tweakable blockciphers. In: Groth, J. (ed.) IMACC 2015. LNCS, vol. 9496, pp. 77–93. Springer, Cham (2015). https://doi.org/10.1007/978-3-319-27239-9_5
26. Namprempre, C., Rogaway, P., Shrimpton, T.: Reconsidering generic composition. In: Nguyen, P.Q., Oswald, E. (eds.) EUROCRYPT 2014. LNCS, vol. 8441, pp. 257–274. Springer, Heidelberg (2014). https://doi.org/10.1007/978-3-642-55220-5_15

27. Okamoto, T. (ed.): ASIACRYPT 2000. LNCS, vol. 1976. Springer, Heidelberg (2000). https://doi.org/10.1007/3-540-44448-3
28. Peyrin, T., Seurin, Y.: Counter-in-tweak: authenticated encryption modes for tweakable block ciphers. In: Robshaw, M., Katz, J. (eds.) CRYPTO 2016, Part I. LNCS, vol. 9814, pp. 33–63. Springer, Heidelberg (2016). https://doi.org/10.1007/978-3-662-53018-4_2
29. Rescorla, E., Modadugu, N.: The datagram transport layer security version, 1 Feb 2012. https://datatracker.ietf.org/doc/html/rfc6347
30. Rescorla, E., Tschofenig, H., Modadugu, N.: The datagram transport layer security (DTLS) protocol version 1.3 IETF draft (2021). https://datatracker.ietf.org/doc/draft-ietf-tls-dtls13/
31. Rogaway, P.: Nonce-based symmetric encryption. In: Roy, B., Meier, W. (eds.) FSE 2004. LNCS, vol. 3017, pp. 348–358. Springer, Heidelberg (2004). https://doi.org/10.1007/978-3-540-25937-4_22
32. Rogaway, P., Shrimpton, T.: A provable-security treatment of the key-wrap problem. In: Vaudenay, S. (ed.) EUROCRYPT 2006. LNCS, vol. 4004, pp. 373–390. Springer, Heidelberg (2006). https://doi.org/10.1007/11761679_23
33. Rogaway, P., Zhang, Y.: Simplifying game-based definitions. In: Shacham, H., Boldyreva, A. (eds.) CRYPTO 2018, Part II. LNCS, vol. 10992, pp. 3–32. Springer, Cham (2018). https://doi.org/10.1007/978-3-319-96881-0_1
34. Shrimpton, T., Terashima, R.S.: A modular framework for building variable-input-length tweakable ciphers. In: Sako, K., Sarkar, P. (eds.) ASIACRYPT 2013, Part I. LNCS, vol. 8269, pp. 405–423. Springer, Heidelberg (2013). https://doi.org/10.1007/978-3-642-42033-7_21
35. Thomson, M., Turner, S.: RFC9001: Using TLS to secure QUIC (2021). https://datatracker.ietf.org/doc/html/rfc9001

Zero Knowledge

Orion: Zero Knowledge Proof with Linear Prover Time

Tiancheng Xie[1], Yupeng Zhang[2], and Dawn Song[1](✉)

[1] University of California, Berkeley, Berkeley, USA
{tianc.x,dawnsong}@berkeley.edu
[2] Texas A&M University, College Station, USA
zhangyp@tamu.edu

Abstract. Zero-knowledge proof is a powerful cryptographic primitive that has found various applications in the real world. However, existing schemes with succinct proof size suffer from a high overhead on the proof generation time that is super-linear in the size of the statement represented as an arithmetic circuit, limiting their efficiency and scalability in practice. In this paper, we present Orion, a new zero-knowledge argument system that achieves $O(N)$ prover time of field operations and hash functions and $O(\log^2 N)$ proof size. Orion is concretely efficient and our implementation shows that the prover time is 3.09 s and the proof size is 1.5 MB for a circuit with 2^{20} multiplication gates. The prover time is the fastest among all existing succinct proof systems, and the proof size is an order of magnitude smaller than a recent scheme proposed in Golovnev et al. 2021.

In particular, we develop two new techniques leading to the efficiency improvement. (1) We propose a new algorithm to test whether a random bipartite graph is a lossless expander graph or not based on the densest subgraph algorithm. It allows us to sample lossless expanders with an overwhelming probability. The technique improves the efficiency and/or security of all existing zero-knowledge argument schemes with a linear prover time. The testing algorithm based on densest subgraph may be of independent interest for other applications of expander graphs. (2) We develop an efficient proof composition scheme, code switching, to reduce the proof size from square root to polylogarithmic in the size of the computation. The scheme is built on the encoding circuit of a linear code and shows that the witness of a second zero-knowledge argument is the same as the message in the linear code. The proof composition only introduces a small overhead on the prover time.

1 Introduction

Zero-knowledge proof (ZKP) allows a *prover* to convince a *verifier* that a statement is valid, without revealing any additional information about the prover's secret witness of the statement. Since it was first introduced in the seminal paper by Goldwasser, Micali and Rackoff [GMR89], ZKP has evolved from a purely theoretical interest to a concretely efficient cryptographic primitive,

Y. Dodis and T. Shrimpton (Eds.): CRYPTO 2022, LNCS 13510, pp. 299–328, 2022.
https://doi.org/10.1007/978-3-031-15985-5_11

leading to many real-world applications in practice. It has been widely used in blockchains and cryptocurrencies to achieve privacy (Zcash [BCG+14, zca]) and to improve scalability (zkRollup [zkr]). More recently, it also found applications in zero-knowledge machine learning [ZFZS20, LKKO20, LXZ21, FQZ+21, WYX+21], zero-knowledge program analysis [FDNZ21], and zero-knowledge middlebox [GAZ+22].

There are three major efficiency measures in ZKP: the overhead of the prover to generate the proof, which is referred to as the *prover time*; the total communication between the prover and the verifier, which is called the *proof size*; and the time to verify the proof, which is called the *verifier time*. Despite its recent progress, the efficiency of ZKP is still not good enough for many applications. In particular, the prover time is one of the major bottlenecks preventing existing ZKP schemes from scaling to large statements. As pointed out by Golovnev et al. in [GLS+], to prove a statement that can be modeled as an arithmetic circuit with N gates, existing schemes with succinct proof size either perform a fast Fourier transform (FFT) due to the Reed-Solomon code encodings or polynomial interpolations, or a multi-scalar exponentiation due to the use of discrete-logarithm assumptions or bilinear maps, over a vector of size $O(N)$. The former takes $O(N \log N)$ field additions and multiplications and the latter takes $O(N \log |\mathbb{F}|)$ field multiplications, where $|\mathbb{F}|$ is the size of the finite field. With the Pippenger's algorithm [Pip], the complexity of the multi-scalar exponentiation can be improved to $O(N \log |\mathbb{F}| / \log N)$, which is still super-linear as $\log |\mathbb{F}| = \omega(\log N)$ to ensure security. These operations are indeed the dominating cost of the prover time both asymptotically and concretely. See Sect. 1.3 for more discussions about existing ZKP schemes categorized by the underlying cryptographic techniques.

The only exceptions in the literature are schemes in [BCG+17, BCG20, BCL22, GLS+]. Bootle et al. [BCG+17] proposed the first ZKP scheme with a prover time of $O(N)$ field operations and a proof size of $O(\sqrt{N})$ using a linear-time encodable error-correcting code. The proof size is later improved to $O(N^{1/c})$ for any constant c via a tensor code in [BCG20], and then to $\mathsf{polylog}(N)$ via a generic proof composition with a probabilistic checkable proof (PCP) in [BCL22]. These schemes are mainly for theoretical interests and do not have implementations with good concrete efficiency. Recently, Golovnev et al. [GLS+] proposed a ZKP scheme based on the techniques in [BCG20] by instantiating the linear-time encodable code with a randomized construction. However, the security guarantee (soundness error) is only inverse polynomial in the size of the circuit, instead of negligible. Moreover, the proof size of the implemented scheme is $O(\sqrt{N})$ (more details are presented in Sect. 1.3). Therefore, the following question still remains open:

Can we construct a concretely efficient ZKP scheme with $O(N)$ prover time and $\mathsf{polylog}(N)$ proof size?

Table 1. Comparison to existing ZKP schemes with linear prover time. N is the size of the circuit/R1CS and $c \geq 2$ is a constant.

	Prover time	Proof size	Verifier time	Soundness error	Concrete efficiency
[BCG+17]	$O(N)$	$O(\sqrt{N})$	$O(N)$	$\mathsf{negl}(N)$	✗
[BCG20]	$O(N)$	$O(N^{1/c})$	$O(N)$	$\mathsf{negl}(N)$	✗
[BCL22]	$O(N)$	$\mathsf{polylog}(N)$	$O(N)$	$\mathsf{negl}(N)$	✗
[GLS+]	$O(N)$	$O(\sqrt{N})$	$O(N)$	$O(\frac{1}{\mathsf{poly}(N)})$	✓
our scheme	$O(N)$	$O(\log^2 N)$	$O(N)$	$\mathsf{negl}(N)$	✓

1.1 Our Contributions

We answer the question above positively in this paper by proposing a new ZKP scheme. In particular, our contributions include:

- First, we propose a random construction of the linear-time encodable code that has a constant relative distance with overwhelming probability. Such a code was used in all existing linear-time ZKP schemes [BCG+17, BCG20, BCL22, GLS+] and thus our new construction also improves their efficiency. The key technique is a new algorithm to test whether a random graph is a good expander graph based on the densest sub-graph algorithm, which may be of independent interest for other applications of expander graphs [SZT02].
- Second, we propose a new reduction that achieves a proof size of $O(\log^2 N)$ efficiently. Our new technique is a proof composition named "code switching" that reduces the proof size of the schemes in [BCG20, GLS+] from $O(\sqrt{N})$ to $O(\log^2 N)$ with a small overhead on the prover time.
- Finally, we implement our new ZKP scheme, Orion, and evaluate it experimentally. On a circuit with 2^{20} gates (rank-1-constraint-system (R1CS) with 2^{20} constraints), the prover time is 3.09 s, the proof size is 1.5 MBs and the verifier time is 70 ms. Orion has the fastest prover time among all existing ZKP schemes in the literature. The proof size is 6.5× smaller than the system in [GLS+]. The scheme is plausibly post-quantum secure and can be made non-interactive via the Fiat-Shamir heuristic [FS86].

Table 1 shows the comparison between our scheme and existing schemes with linear prover time and succinct proof size.

1.2 Technical Overview

Testing Expander Graphs via Densest Sub-graph. All existing ZKP schemes with linear prover time and succinct proof size [BCG+17, BCG20, BCL22, GLS+] use linear-time encodable codes with a constant relative distance proposed in [Spi96, DI14, GLS+], which in turn all rely on the existence of good expander graphs. In a good expander graph, any subset of vertices expands to a large number of neighbors. Figure 1 shows an example of a bipartite graph where any subset of vertices on the left of size 2 expands to at least 5 vertices on the right. See Sect. 2.1 for formal definitions and constructions. However, how to

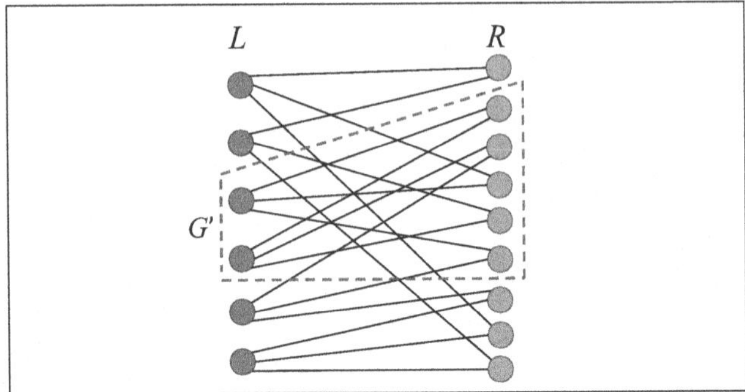

Fig. 1. An example of lossless expander. $k = 6, k' = 9, g = 3, \delta = 1, \epsilon = \frac{1}{6}$.

construct such good expanders remain unclear in practice. Explicit constructions [CRVW02] have large hidden constants in the complexity and thus are not practical. A random graph tends to have good expansion, but the probability that a random graph is not a good expander is inverse polynomial in the size of the graph. The code constructed from such a non-expanding graph does not have a good minimum distance, making the ZKP scheme insecure. Therefore, a randomly sampled graph is not good for cryptographic applications.

In this paper, we propose a new algorithm to efficiently test whether a random graph is a good expander or not. With the new testing algorithm, we are able to re-sample the random graph until it passes the test, obtaining a good expander with an overwhelming probability and boosting the soundness error of the ZKP scheme to be negligible. The testing algorithm is based on the densest sub-graph algorithm [Gol84]. The density of a graph $G = (V, E)$ is defined as the number of edges divided by the number of vertices $\frac{|E|}{|V|}$, and the densest sub-graph is simply the sub-graph in a graph with the maximum density. We observe that a good expander graph tends to have a small maximum density. This is because assuming the degree g of each vertex is a constant, e.g. $g = 3$ for all vertices on the left in Fig. 1, given any subset of vertices of size s in the graph, the total number of edges is fixed as $|E| = gs$ in the sub-graph defined by this subset and its neighbors. For example, any two vertices on the left in Fig. 1 as highlighted always have 6 outgoing edges. Then we differentiate two cases:

- In a good expander graph, any subset expands to a large number of neighbors, thus the total number of vertices in this sub-graph is large. Therefore, the density of any sub-graph is small;
- In contrast, if the graph is not a good expander, there is at least one subset that does not expand. Taking the sub-graph defined by this subset and its neighbors, again the number of edges is fixed, while the number of vertices is small. Therefore, the density of this sub-graph is large, which will be detected by the densest subgraph algorithm.

This observation gives us a way to differentiate good expanders. To the best of our knowledge, we are the first to make the connection between expander and the densest subgraph problem.

The real testing algorithm involves random sampling and repeating the densest sub-graph algorithm because of additional conditions of the expander. The formal algorithm, theorem and proofs are presented in Sect. 3.

Proof Composition via Code-Switching. With the expander graph sampled above and the corresponding linear code, we are able to build efficient ZKP schemes following the approaches in [BCG+17, BCG20, GLS+]. However, the proof size is $O(N^{1/c})$ instead of $\mathsf{polylog}(N)$. To reduce the proof size, a common technique in the literature is proof composition. Instead of sending the proof directly to the verifier, the prover uses a second ZKP scheme to show that the proof of the first ZKP is indeed valid. In particular, in [BCG+17, BCG20, GLS+], the proof is a codeword of the linear-time encodable code, and the checks can be represented as several inner products between the message in the codeword of the proof and some public vectors.

Unfortunately, we do not have a second ZKP scheme with a $\mathsf{polylog}(N)$ proof size to prove inner products. If we had it, we would already be able to build a ZKP scheme with $\mathsf{polylog}(N)$ proof size in the first place. Instead, we rely on the fact that the proof is a codeword of the linear code and construct the second ZKP scheme as follows. One component of the second ZKP scheme is the *encoding circuit* of the linear-time encodable code. It takes the witness of the second ZKP scheme, encodes it and outputs several random locations of the codeword. The verifier checks that these random locations are the same as the proof of the first ZKP scheme, without receiving the entire proof. By the distance of the linear-time encodable code, we show that the witness of the second ZKP must be the same as the message in the proof of the first ZKP with overwhelming probability. After that, the other component of the second ZKP checks the inner product relationship modeled as an arithmetic circuit.

With this idea, we can use any general-purpose ZKP scheme on arithmetic circuits with a $\mathsf{polylog}(N)$ proof size as the second ZKP scheme in the proof composition. The size of this circuit is only $O(\sqrt{N})$, thus the second ZKP does not introduce any overhead on the prover time as long as its prover time is no more than quadratic. In our construction, we use the ZKP scheme in [ZXZS20] as the second ZKP. The scheme is based on the interactive oracle proofs (IOP) and the witness is encoded using the Reed-Solomon code. Therefore, the technique is called code switching. The formal protocols are presented in Sect. 4.

1.3 Related Work

Zero-knowledge proof was introduced in [GMR89] and generic constructions based on PCPs were proposed by Kilian [Kil92] and Micali [Mic00] in the early days. Driven by various applications mentioned in the introduction, there has been significant progress in efficient ZKP protocols and systems. Categorized by their underlying techniques, there are ZKP systems based on bilinear maps [PHGR13, BSCG+13, BFR+13, BSCTV14, CFH+15, WSR+15, FFG+16, GKM+18, MBKM19, GWC19, CHM+20, KPPS20], MPC-in-the-head [GMO16, CDG+17, AHIV17, KKW18], interactive proofs [ZGK+17a, ZGK+17b, WTS+18,

ZGK+18, XZZ+19, ZLW+21], discrete logarithm [BBB+18, BFS20, Set20, SL20], interactive oracle proofs (IOP) [BSCR+19, BSBHR19, ZXZS20, BFH+20, COS20, BDFG20], and lattices [BBC+18, ESLL19, BLNS20, ISW21]. As mentioned in the introduction, these schemes perform either an FFT (such as schemes based on MPC-in-the-head and IOP) or a multi-scalar exponentiation (such as schemes based on discrete-log and bilinear pairing), making the complexity of the prover time super-linear in the size of the circuit.

With the techniques proposed in [XZZ+19, ZLW+21], the prover time of the schemes based on the interactive proofs (the GKR protocol [GKR08]) is linear if the size of the input is significantly smaller than the size of the circuit. However, the goal of this paper is to make the prover time strictly linear without such a requirement, and our polynomial commitment scheme can also be plugged into these schemes to improve their efficiency.

Schemes with Linear Prover Time. As mentioned before, schemes in [BCG+17, BCG20, BCL22, GLS+] are the only candidates in the literature with linear prover time and succinct proof size. They all use linear-time encodable codes based on expander graphs and our first contribution applies to all of them. Moreover, our ZKP scheme is based on the polynomial commitment in [GLS+] and the tensor IOP in [BCG20], and we improve the proof size to $O(\log^2 N)$ through a proof composition. In fact, the scheme in [BCL22] also proposes a proof composition with the PCP in [Mie09]. However, the complexity of the PCP is polynomial time. That is why the scheme in [BCL22] has to be built on the scheme in [BCG20] with a proof size of $O(N^{1/c})$ and is not concretely efficient, while our scheme can be built on top of the efficient scheme in [GLS+] with a proof size of $O(\sqrt{N})$. A similar proof composition with PCP was also used in [RZR20] for a different purpose. We view our approach using the encoding circuit as a variant of the proof composition that is efficient in practice, and we inherit the name "code switching" from [RZR20].

Finally, the scheme in [GLS+] samples a random graph to build the linear-time encodable code. The scheme achieves a soundness error of $O(\frac{1}{\mathsf{poly}(N)})$ and the authors spent great efforts to calculate parameters to achieve a concrete failure probability of 2^{-100} for large circuits in practice [GLS+, Claim 2 and Fig. 2]. Our sampling algorithm provides the provable security guarantee for a negligible soundness error for their scheme. Moreover, we improve the proof size from $O(\sqrt{N})$ to $O(\log^2 N)$ efficiently, solving an open problem left in [GLS+].

Schemes with Linear Proof Size. Recently, there is a line of work constructing ZKP based on secure multiparty computation (MPC) techniques [WYKW20, DIO21, BMRS21, YSWW21] and these schemes have demonstrated fast prover time in practice. If one treats a block cipher (e.g., AES) as a constant-time operation because of the CPU instruction, these schemes indeed have a linear time prover (we are using a similar CPU instruction for the hash function SHA-256 in our scheme to achieve linear prover time). However, they have linear proof size in the size of the circuit, are inherently interactive, and are not publicly verifiable, which are not desirable in many applications. We mainly focus on non-interactive ZKP with succinct proof size and public verifiability in this paper.

Expander Testing. Testing the properties of expander graphs is a deeply explored area in computer science. Many works [NS07,CS07,GR11] have proposed efficient testing algorithms without accessing the whole graph. However, these algorithms do not directly apply to our testing of lossless expander. For example, the algorithm in [NS07] based on random walks can differentiate good expanders from graphs that are far from expanders, while our scheme can differentiate whether a graph is a lossless expander or not with overwhelming probability. Of course our algorithm accesses the entire graph, which is fine in our application of linear-time encodable code. To the best of our knowledge, we are not aware of any testing algorithm with such properties.

There are also impossibility results on expander testing [KS16]. Due to different definitions of expansion, our testing algorithm cannot distinguish the cases in [KS16, Theorem 1.1] and thus it does not violate the impossibility results.

2 Preliminary

We use $[N]$ to denote the set $\{0, 1, 2, ..., N-1\}$. $\mathsf{poly}(N)$ means a function upper bounded by a polynomial in N with a constant degree. We use $\lambda = \omega(\log N)$ to denote the security parameter, and $\mathsf{negl}(N)$ to denote the negligible function in N, i.e. $\mathsf{negl}(N) \leq \frac{1}{\mathsf{poly}(N)}$ for all sufficiently large N and any polynomial. Some papers define $\mathsf{negl}(\lambda)$ as the negligible function. As λ is a function of N, they are essentially the same and $\mathsf{negl}(N) \leq \frac{1}{2^\lambda}$. "PPT" stands for probabilistic polynomial time. $\langle A(x), B(y)\rangle(z)$ denotes an interactive protocol between algorithms A, B with x as the input of A, y as the input of B and z as the common input.

2.1 Linear Time Encodable Linear Code

Definition 1 (Linear Code). *A linear error-correcting code with message length k and codeword length n is a linear subspace $C \in \mathbb{F}^n$, such that there exists an injective mapping from message to codeword $E_C : \mathbb{F}^k \to C$, which is called the encoder of the code. Any linear combination of codewords is also a codeword. The rate of the code is defined as $\frac{k}{n}$. The distance between two codewords u, v is the hamming distance denoted as $\Delta(u, v)$. The minimum distance is $d = \min_{u,v} \Delta(u, v)$. Such a code is denoted as $[n, k, d]$ linear code, and we also refer to $\frac{d}{n}$ as the relative distance of the code.*

Generalized Spielman Code. In our construction, we use a family of linear codes that can be encoded in linear time and has a constant relative distance [Spi96,DI14,GLS+]. The code was first proposed by Daniel Spielman in [Spi96] over the Boolean alphabet. Druk and Ishai [DI14] generalized it to a finite field $\mathbb{F}$, and introduced a distance boosting technique to achieve the Gilbert-Varshamov bound [Gil52, Var57]. We only use the basic construction over $\mathbb{F}$ without the distance boosting, and thus refer to it as the generalized Spielman code in this paper. The code relies on the existence of lossless expander graphs, which is defined below:

Definition 2 (Lossless Expander [Spi96]**).** *Let $G = (L, R, E)$ be a bipartite graph. $0 < \epsilon < 1$ and $0 < \delta$ be some constants. The vertex set consists of L and R, two disjoint subsets, henceforth the left and right vertex set. Let $\Gamma(S)$ be the neighbor set of some vertex set S. We say G is an $(k, k'; g)$-**lossless expander** if $|L| = k, |R| = k' = \alpha k$ for some constant α, and the following property hold:*

1. *Degree: The degree of every vertex in L is g.*
2. *Expansion: $|\Gamma(S)| \geq (1-\epsilon)g|S|$ for every $S \subseteq L$ with $|S| \leq \frac{\delta|L|}{g}$.*

Intuitively speaking, a lossless expander has very strong expansion. As the degree of each left vertex is g, a set of $|S|$ left vertices have at most $g|S|$ neighbors, while the second condition requires that every set expands to at least $(1-\epsilon)g|S|$ vertices for a small constant ϵ. Meanwhile, as the right vertext set has $|R| = \alpha k$ vertices, such an expansion is not possible if $|S| > \frac{\alpha k}{(1-\epsilon)g}$, thus there is a condition $|S| \leq \frac{\delta k}{g}$ bounding the size of S. An example is shown in Fig. 1.

Construction of Generalized Spielman Code. With the lossless expander, we give a brief description of the generalized Spielman code. Let $G = (L, R, E)$ be a lossless expander with $|L| = 2^t, |R| = 2^{t-1}$. Let A_t be a $2^t \times 2^{t-1}$ matrix where $A_t[i][j] = 1$ if there is an edge i, j in G for $i \in [2^t], j \in [2^{t-1}]$; otherwise $A_t[i][j] = 0$. The generalized Spielman code is constructed as follows:

1. Let $E_C^t(x)$ be the encoder function of input length $|x| = 2^t$, and its output will be a codeword of size 2^{t+2}. We use E_C to denote the encoder function when length is clear.
2. If $|x| \leq n_0$ then directly output x, for some constant n_0.
3. Compute $m_1 = xA_t$. Each entry of m_1 can be viewed as a vertex in R, and value of each vertex is the summation of its neighbors in L. The length of m_1 is 2^{t-1}.
4. Recursively apply the encoder E_C^{t-1} on m_1, let $c_1 = E_C^{t-1}(m_1)$.
5. Compute $c_2 = c_1 A_{t+1}$.
6. Output $x \odot c_1 \odot c_2$ as the codeword of size 2^{t+2}. $\odot$ denotes concatenation.

Lemma 1 (Generalized Spielman code, [DI14]**).** *Given a family of lossless expander, that achieves $(1-\epsilon)g|S|$ expansion with $|S| \leq \frac{\delta|L|}{g}$, for input size k, the generalized Spielman code is a $[4k, k, \frac{\delta}{8g}k]$ linear code over $\mathbb{F}$.*

The code in [GLS+] is a variant of generalized Spielman code. In their construction, random weights are assigned to each edge of lossless expander at line 3, 5. And randomize the output at line 6: $(x \otimes r) \odot c_1 \odot c_2$, here $\otimes$ is element-wise multiply, r is a random vector.

Definition 3 (Tensor code). *Let C be a $[n, k, d]$ linear code, the tensor code $C^{\otimes 2}$ of dimension 2 is the linear code in $\mathbb{F}^{n^2}$ with message length k^2, codeword length n^2, and distance nd. We can view the codeword as a $n \times n$ matrix. We define the encoding function below:*

1. *A message of length $k \times k$ is parsed as a $k \times k$ matrix. Each row of the matrix is encoded using E_C, resulting in a codeword C_1 of size $k \times n$.*
2. *Each column of C_1 is then encoded again using E_C. The result C_2 of size $n \times n$ is the codeword of the tensor code.*

2.2 Collision-Resistant Hash Functions and Merkle Tree

Let $H : \{0,1\}^{2\lambda} \to \{0,1\}^{\lambda}$ be a hash function. A Merkle Tree is a data structure that allows one to commit to $l = 2^{\mathsf{dep}}$ messages by a single hash value h, such that revealing any bit of the message require $\mathsf{dep} + 1$ hash values.

A Merkle hash tree is represented by a binary tree of depth dep where l messages elements $m_1, m_2, ..., m_l$ are assigned to the leaves of the tree. The values assigned to internal nodes are computed by hashing the value of its two child nodes. To reveal m_i, we need to reveal m_i together with the values on the path from m_i to the root. We denote the algorithm as follows:

1. $h \leftarrow \mathsf{Merkle.Commit}(m_1, ..., m_l)$.
2. $(m_i, \pi_{\mathsf{i}}) \leftarrow \mathsf{Merkle.Open}(m, i)$.
3. $\{\mathsf{accept}, \mathsf{reject}\} \leftarrow \mathsf{Merkle.Verify}(\pi_{\mathsf{i}}, m_i, h)$.

2.3 Zero-Knowledge Arguments

An argument system for an NP relation R is a protocol between a computationally bounded prover $\mathcal{P}$ and a verifier $\mathcal{V}$. At the end of the protocol $\mathcal{V}$ will be convinced that there exits a witness w such that $(x, w) \in R$ for some public input x. We focus on arguments of knowledge which require the prover know the witness w. We formally define zero-knowledge as follows:

Definition 4 (View). *We denote by $\mathsf{View}(\langle \mathcal{P}, \mathcal{V} \rangle(x))$ the view of $\mathcal{V}$ in an interactive protocol with $\mathcal{P}$. Namely, it is the random variable $(r, b_1, b_2, ..., b_n, v_1, v_2, ..., v_m)$ where r is $\mathcal{V}$'s randomness, $b_1, ..., b_n$ are messages from $\mathcal{V}$ to $\mathcal{P}$, and $v_1, ..., v_m$ are messages from $\mathcal{P}$ to $\mathcal{V}$.*

Definition 5. *Let $\mathcal{R}$ be an NP relation. A tuple of algorithm $(\mathcal{G}, \mathcal{P}, \mathcal{V})$ is a zero-knowledge argument of knowledge for $\mathcal{R}$ if the following holds.*

- ***Correctness***. *For every pp output by $\mathcal{G}(1^\lambda)$ and $(x, w) \in R$,*

$$\Pr[\langle \mathcal{P}(w), \mathcal{V}() \rangle(\mathsf{pp}, x) = \mathsf{accept}] = 1.$$

- ***Knowledge Soundness***. *For any PPT adversary $\mathcal{P}^*$, there exists a PPT extractor ε such that for every pp output by $\mathcal{G}(1^\lambda)$ and any x, the following probability is $\mathsf{negl}(N)$:*

$$\Pr[\langle \mathcal{P}^*(), \mathcal{V}() \rangle(\mathsf{pp}, x) = \mathsf{accept}, (x, w) \notin \mathcal{R} | w \leftarrow \varepsilon(\mathsf{pp}, x, \mathsf{View}(\langle \mathcal{P}^*(), \mathcal{V}() \rangle(\mathsf{pp}, x)))]$$

- ***Zero knowledge.*** *There exists a PPT simulator $\mathcal{S}$ such that for any PPT algorithm $\mathcal{V}^*$, $(x, w) \in R$, pp output by $\mathcal{G}(1^\lambda)$, it holds that*

$$\mathsf{View}(\langle \mathcal{P}(w), \mathcal{V}^*()\rangle(x)) \approx \mathcal{S}^{\mathcal{V}^*}(\mathsf{pp}, x)$$

Where $\mathcal{S}^{\mathcal{V}^*}(x)$ denotes that $\mathcal{S}$ is given oracle accesses to $\mathcal{V}^*$'s random tape.

We say that $(\mathcal{G}, \mathcal{P}, \mathcal{V})$ is a succinct *argument system if the total communication between $\mathcal{P}$ and $\mathcal{V}$ (proof size) is* $\mathsf{poly}(\lambda, |x|, \log |w|)$.

Definition 6 (Arithmetic circuit). *An arithmetic circuit C over $\mathbb{F}$ and a set of variables $x_1, ..., x_N$ is a directed acyclic graph as follows:*

1. *Each vertex is called a "gate". A gate with in-degree zero is an input gate and is labeled as a variable x_i or a constant field element in $\mathbb{F}$.*
2. *Other gates have 2 incoming edges. It calculates the addition or multiplication over the two inputs and output the result.*
3. *The size of the circuit is defined as the number of gates N.*

2.4 Polynomial Commitment

A polynomial commitment consists of three algorithms:

- $\mathsf{PC.Commit}(\phi(\cdot))$: the algorithm outputs a commitment $\mathcal{R}$ of the polynomial $\phi(\cdot)$.
- $\mathsf{PC.Prove}(\phi, \vec{x}, \mathcal{R})$: given an evaluation point $\phi(\vec{x})$, the algorithm outputs a tuple $\langle \vec{x}, \phi(\vec{x}), \pi_{\vec{x}} \rangle$, where $\pi_{\vec{x}}$ is the proof.
- $\mathsf{PC.VerifyEval}(\pi_{\vec{x}}, \vec{x}, \phi(\vec{x}), \mathcal{R})$: given $\pi_{\vec{x}}, \vec{x}, \phi(\vec{x}), \mathcal{R}$, the algorithm checks if $\phi(\vec{x})$ is the correct evaluation. The algorithm outputs accept or reject.

Definition 7 ((Multivariate) Polynomial commitment). *A polynomial commitment scheme has the following properties:*

- ***Correctness.*** *For every polynomial ϕ and evaluation point $\vec{x}$, the following probability holds:*

$$\Pr\left(\begin{array}{r} \mathsf{PC.Commit}(\phi) \to \mathcal{R} \\ \mathsf{PC.Prove}(\phi, \vec{x}, \mathcal{R}) \to \vec{x}, y, \pi \\ y = \phi(\vec{x}) \\ \mathsf{PC.VerifyEval}(\pi, \vec{x}, y, \mathcal{R}) \to \mathsf{accept} \end{array}\right) = 1$$

- ***Knowledge Soundness.*** *For any PPT adversary $\mathcal{P}^*$ with* $\mathsf{PC.Commit}^*$, $\mathsf{PC.Prove}^*$, *there exists a PPT extractor $\mathcal{E}$ such that the probability below is negligible:*

$$\Pr\left(\begin{array}{r|l} \mathsf{PC.Commit}^*(\phi^*) \to \mathcal{R}^* & \\ \mathsf{PC.Prove}^*(\phi^*, \vec{x}, \mathcal{R}^*) \to \vec{x}, y^*, \pi^* & \phi^* \leftarrow \mathcal{E}(\mathcal{R}^*, \vec{x}, \pi^*, y^*) \wedge y^* \neq \phi^*(\vec{x}) \\ \mathsf{PC.VerifyEval}(\pi^*, \vec{x}, y^*, \mathcal{R}^*) \to \mathsf{accept} & \end{array}\right)$$

- ***Zero-knowledge.*** *For security parameter λ, polynomial ϕ, any PPT adversary $\mathcal{A}$, there exists a simulator $\mathcal{S} = [\mathcal{S}_0, \mathcal{S}_1]$, we consider following two experiments:*

$\mathsf{Real}_{\mathcal{A},\phi}(\mathsf{pp})$:	$\mathsf{Ideal}_{\mathcal{A},\mathcal{S}^{\mathcal{A}}}(\mathsf{pp})$:
1. $\mathcal{R} \leftarrow \mathsf{Commit}(\mathsf{pp}, \phi)$	1. $\mathcal{R} \leftarrow \mathcal{S}_0(1^\lambda, \mathsf{pp})$
2. $\vec{x} \leftarrow \mathcal{A}(\mathcal{R}, \mathsf{pp})$	2. $\vec{x} \leftarrow \mathcal{A}(\mathcal{R}, \mathsf{pp})$
3. $(\vec{x}, y, \pi) \leftarrow \mathsf{Prove}(\phi, \vec{x}, \mathcal{R})$	3. $(\vec{x}, y, \pi) \leftarrow \mathcal{S}_1^{\mathcal{A}}(\vec{x}, \mathsf{pp})$, *given oracle access to* $y = \phi(\vec{x})$
4. $b \leftarrow \mathcal{A}(\pi, \vec{x}, y, \mathcal{R})$	4. $b \leftarrow \mathcal{A}(\pi, \vec{x}, y, \mathcal{R})$
5. *Output* b	5. *Output* b

For any PPT adversary $\mathcal{A}$, two experiments are identically distributed:

$$\Pr[|\mathsf{Real}_{\mathcal{A},f}(\mathsf{pp}) - \mathsf{Ideal}_{\mathcal{A},\mathcal{S}^{\mathcal{A}}}(\mathsf{pp})| = 1] \leq \mathsf{negl}(N)$$

3 Testing Algorithm for Lossless Expander

As explained above, the generalized Spielman code relies on the existence of lossless expanders. On one hand, there are explicit constructions of lossless expanders in the literature [CRVW02]. However, there are large hidden constants in the complexity and the constructions are not practical. On the other hand, a random bipartite graph is a lossless expander with a high probability of $1 - O(\frac{1}{\mathsf{poly}(k)})$, where k is the size of the left vertex set in the bipartite graph. However, this is not good enough for cryptographic applications.

In this section, we propose a new approach to sample a lossless expander with a negligible failure probability. The key ingredient of our approach is a new algorithm to test whether a randomly sampled bipartite graph is a lossless expander or not. We begin the section by introducing the classical randomized construction of a lossless expander and its analysis.

3.1 Random Construction of Lossless Expander

As defined in Definition 2, a lossless expander graph is a g-left-regular bipartite graph $G = (L, R, E)$. Wigderson et al. [HLW06, Lemma 1.9] showed that a random bipartite graph is a lossless expander with a high probability. In particular, we have the following lemma:

Lemma 2 ([HLW06]). *For fixed constant parameters $g, \delta, \alpha, \epsilon$, a random g-left-regular bipartite graph is a $(k, k'; g)$-lossless-expander with probability* $1 - O(\frac{1}{\mathsf{poly}(k)})$.

Proof. Let $G = (L, R, E)$ be a random bipartite graph with k vertices on the left and $k' = O(k)$ vertices on the right, where each left vertex connects to a randomly chosen set of g vertices on the right.

Let $s = |S|$ be the cardinality of a left subset of vertices $S \subseteq L$ such that $s \leq \frac{\delta k}{g}$, and let $t = |T|$ be the cardinality of a right subset of vertices $T \subseteq R$ such that $t \leq (1-\epsilon)gs$. Let $X_{S,T}$ be an indicator random variable for the event that all the edges from S connect to T. Then for a particular S, if $\sum_{T\in R} X_{S,T} = 0$, then the number of neighboring vertices of S must be larger than $(1-\epsilon)gs$. Otherwise, if there exists a $T \in R$ such that $X_{S,T} = 1$, i.e., all edges from S connect to T, the graph is not a lossless expander. As the edges are sampled randomly, the probability of this *non-expanding* event is $(\frac{t}{k'})^{sg}$. Therefore, summing over all S and by the union bound, the probability of a non-expanding graph is:

$$\Pr[(\sum_{S,T} X_{S,T}) > 0] \leq \sum_{S,T} Pr[X_{S,T} = 1] = \sum_{S,T} (\frac{t}{k'})^{sg}$$
$$\leq \sum_{s=2}^{\frac{\delta k}{g}} \binom{k}{s}\binom{k'}{t}(\frac{t}{k'})^{sg} \leq \sum_{s=2}^{\frac{\delta k}{g}} \binom{k}{s}\binom{k'}{(1-\epsilon)gs}(\frac{(1-\epsilon)gs}{k'})^{sg}$$

Using the inequality $\binom{k}{s} \leq (\frac{ke}{s})^s$, the probability above is

$$\leq \sum_{s=2}^{\frac{\delta k}{g}} (\frac{ke}{s})^s (\frac{k'e}{(1-\epsilon)gs})^{(1-\epsilon)gs} (\frac{(1-\epsilon)gs}{k'})^{sg}$$
$$= \sum_{s=2}^{\frac{\delta k}{g}} (\frac{ke}{s})^s e^{(1-\epsilon)gs} (\frac{(1-\epsilon)gs}{k'})^{\epsilon gs}$$
$$= \sum_{s=2}^{\frac{\delta k}{g}} e^{(1-\epsilon)gs+s} \cdot (\frac{k}{s})^s \cdot (\frac{(1-\epsilon)gs}{k'})^{\epsilon gs} \tag{1}$$

When s, ϵ, g are constants and $k' = O(k)$, $e^{(1-\epsilon)gs+s}$ is a constant, $(\frac{k}{s})^s$ is $O(\mathsf{poly}(k))$, and $(\frac{(1-\epsilon)gs}{k'})^{\epsilon gs}$ is $O(\frac{1}{\mathsf{poly}(k)})$. Therefore, the overall upper bound is at least $O(\frac{1}{\mathsf{poly}(k)})$.

The derivation above shows that the probability that a random graph is not a lossless expander is upper-bounded by $O(\frac{1}{\mathsf{poly}(k)})$, which is not negligible. Furthermore, we show that the lower-bound of the non-expanding probability is also not negligible through a simple argument here.

We focus on the case where s is a constant. The number of all possible subgraphs induced by a left subset of vertices S is at most $k'^{sg} = O(\mathsf{poly}(k))$. That is, the size of the entire probability space is bounded by a polynomial. The number of non-expanding graphs is at least 1 (e.g., all edges from S connect to a single vertex in R). Therefore, the non-expanding probability is at least $O(\frac{1}{\mathsf{poly}(k)})$.

Lossless Expander in [GLS+]. As explained in Sect. 2.1, in [GLS+], the authors extended the generalized Spielman code by adding random weights to the edges in the bipartite graph. However, the graph still needs to be a lossless expander in order to achieve a constant relative distance, and the same issue above applies to their construction. In particular, as shown by [GLS+, Claim 2], the probability of *not* sampling a lossless expander is

$$2^{kH(15/k)+\alpha kH(19.2/(\alpha k))-15g\log\frac{\alpha k}{19.2}},$$

where $H(x) = -x\log x - (1-x)\log(1-x)$. We show that the probability above is not negligible. First, for any constant const,

$$\begin{aligned} xH(\mathsf{const}/x) &= x(-\frac{\mathsf{const}}{x}\log\frac{\mathsf{const}}{x} - (1-\frac{\mathsf{const}}{x})\log(\frac{x-\mathsf{const}}{x}) \\ &= (\mathsf{const}\log(x) - \mathsf{const}\log\mathsf{const}) + (1-\frac{\mathsf{const}}{x})\log(\frac{x-\mathsf{const}}{x}). \end{aligned}$$

By taking the limit, we have $\lim_{x\to\infty} xH(\mathsf{const}/x) = (\mathsf{const}\log(x) - \mathsf{const}\log\mathsf{const}) + 1\times 0$. Therefore, $xH(\mathsf{const}/x) = O(\log x)$. Applying this fact to the equation above, $kH(15/k) + \alpha kH(19.2/(\alpha k)) = O(\log k)$, and $-15g\log\frac{\alpha k}{19.2} = -O(\log k)$. Therefore, $2^{kH(15/k)+\alpha kH(19.2/(\alpha k))-15g\log\frac{\alpha k}{19.2}}$ is at least $2^{-O(\log k)} = \frac{1}{\mathsf{poly}(k)}$. The failure probability is similar to the upper bound in Eq. 1.

3.2 Algorithm Based on Densest Sub-graph

To reduce the non-expanding probability of the random construction, we take a closer look at the equations above. Equation 1 shows that the probability that a random bipartite graph is a not lossless expander is upper bounded by $\frac{1}{\mathsf{poly}(k)}$. However, we observe that within the summation, the probability is actually negligible when s is large. In particular, if we decompose the summation in Eq. 1 into two sums, one for $2 \le s \le \log\log k$, and the other for $s \ge \log\log k$, the second part is

$$\sum_{s=\log\log k}^{\frac{\delta k}{g}} e^{(1-\epsilon)gs+s}\cdot(\frac{k}{s})^s\cdot(\frac{(1-\epsilon)gs}{k'})^{\epsilon gs}. \tag{2}$$

Lemma 3. *Equation 2 is negligible if the following conditions are met:*

1. $(1-\epsilon)\delta + \frac{\delta}{g} + \frac{\delta}{g}\log(\frac{g}{\delta}) + \log(\frac{\delta}{\alpha})\epsilon\delta < -0.001$,
2. $\epsilon d > 2$.

Here –0.001 is just any small constant that is less than 0. We give a proof in the full version of the paper. To provide an intuition on how these parameters are set, we give an example here: $\delta = \frac{1}{11}, \epsilon = \frac{7}{16}, g = 16, k' = \frac{1}{2}k$. We can verify the condition:

1. $\epsilon g = 7 > 2$.
2. $(1-\epsilon)\delta + \frac{\delta}{g} + \frac{\delta}{g}\log(\frac{g}{\delta}) + \log(\frac{\delta}{\alpha})\epsilon\delta = -0.009 < -0.001$.

Sampling Lossless Expander with Negligible Failure Probability. The observation above shows that the non-expanding probability is dominated by small sub-graphs with size $2 \leq s \leq \log\log k$. This actually matches our lower bound in Sect. 3.1, as there are only polynomially many such sub-graphs and there exist ones that do not expand. Therefore, in order to reduce the non-expanding probability, we propose a new algorithm that detects small sub-graphs of size $s \leq \log\log k$ that do not expand. The algorithm is based on the densest sub-graph problem, and we are the first to make the connection between the densest sub-graph and the lossless expander.

Definition 8 (Densest Sub-graph Problem). *Let $G = (V, E)$ be an undirected graph, and let $S = (E_S, V_S)$ be a subgraph of G. The density of S is defined to be $\mathsf{den}(S) = \frac{E_S}{V_S}$. The densest sub-graph problem is to find S such that it maximizes $\mathsf{den}(S)$. We denote the maximum density by $\mathsf{Den}(G)$.*

Theorem 1 *[Gol84]. For any graph $G = (V, E)$, there is a polynomial time algorithm that find the densest sub-graph $G' = (V', E')$ such that $V' \subseteq V$ and G' is the sub-graph. And $\frac{|E'|}{|V'|}$ is maximized. The running time of the algorithm is $O(|V||E| \log |E| \log |V|)$.*

We will use this algorithm as a building block of our testing algorithm. First, we define a notion of perfect expander, and then derive the density of a perfect expander.

Definition 9 (Perfect expander). *Let $G = (L, R, E)$ be a bipartite graph. We say G is an $(k^*, k'; g)$-**perfect expander** if $|L| = k^*, |R| = k'$, the following property holds (where $\Gamma(S)$ denotes the set of neighbors of a set S in G):*

1. *Degree: every vertex $a \in L$, it has constant degree g.*
2. *Expansion: $|\Gamma(S)| \geq (1 - \varepsilon)g|S|$ for every $S \subseteq L$.*

Compared to lossless expander, the perfect expander does not have the upper bound on $|S|$ in the expansion property. Therefore, k' has to be much larger than k^*, unlike the case of lossless expander where $k' = O(k)$. Now we show that the density of a perfect expander is low:

Theorem 2. *If a bipartite graph is a perfect expander, its density is at most $\frac{g}{1+(1-\epsilon)g}$; otherwise, the density of the graph is larger than $\frac{g}{1+(1-\epsilon)g}$.*

Proof. We first show that the density of a perfect expander is at most $\frac{g}{1+(1-\epsilon)g}$. For any subset $L' \subseteq L$, we prove that among all sub-graphs that L' is the left vertex set, the graph induced by $(L', \Gamma(L'))$ has the maximum density.

To see this, suppose $V' = (L', R'), R' \neq \Gamma(L')$ has density $\frac{|E'|}{|V'|}$ that is the densest sub-graph with L' as its left vertex set.

Case 1: If there exists a vertex $y \in R', y \notin \Gamma(L')$, then there is no edge between y and L'. We can increase the density by removing y from R', as $\frac{|E'|}{|V'|-1} > \frac{|E'|}{|V'|}$. This is a contradiction. Therefore, $R' \subseteq \Gamma(L')$.

Case 2: If there exists an element $y \in \Gamma(L'), y \notin R'$, let $c \geq 1$ be the number of edges between y and L', by adding y to R', the density becomes $\frac{|E'|+c}{|V'|+1} > \frac{|E'|}{|V'|}$. This is a contradiction again and thus $\Gamma(L') \subseteq R'$.

Therefore, we have $\Gamma(L') = R'$ and $V' = (L', \Gamma(L'))$ maximizes the density among all sub-graphs with L' as the left vertex set. Let that sub-graph be G'. By the expansion property of the perfect expander, $\mathsf{den}(G') = \frac{|E'|}{|V'|} \leq \frac{|L'|g}{|L'|+(1-\epsilon)g|L'|} = \frac{g}{1+(1-\epsilon)g}$. Therefore, the maximum density $\mathsf{Den}(G) = \max_{L' \subseteq L} \mathsf{den}(G') \leq \frac{g}{1+(1-\epsilon)g}$.

Next, we show that if a bipartite graph is not a perfect expander, its density is larger than $\frac{g}{1+(1-\epsilon)g}$. Let S^* be the set such that $|\Gamma(S^*)| < (1-\epsilon)g|S^*|$, then the density of the sub-graph $G' = (V' = (S^*, \Gamma(S^*)), E')$ is $\frac{|E'|}{|V'|} > \frac{g|S^*|}{|S^*|+(1-\epsilon)g|S^*|} = \frac{g}{1+(1-\epsilon)g}$, so $\mathsf{Den}(G) \geq \mathsf{den}(G') > \frac{g}{1+(1-\epsilon)g}$.

3.3 Testing Random Lossless Expander

Theorem 2 suggests a way to test whether a random graph is a lossless expander. As discussed in Lemma 3, when $s \geq \log\log k$ the non-expanding probability is negligible. Thus, it suffices to test whether there is a sub-graph of size $s < \log\log k$ that does not expand. In particular, we are trying to distinguish the following two cases:

1. **Yes case**: For $G = (L, R, E)$, $\forall S \subseteq L, |S| \leq \log\log k$, we have $|\Gamma(S)| \geq (1-\epsilon)g|S|$.
2. **No case**: For $G = (L, R, E)$, there exists a subset $S^* \subseteq L, |S^*| \leq \log\log k$, such that $|\Gamma(S^*)| < (1-\epsilon)g|S_0|$.

To distinguish these two cases, we cannot directly apply the densest sub-graph algorithm on the entire bipartite graph, because the expansion property only holds for $|S| \leq \frac{\delta k}{g}$ by Definition 2 of the lossless expander. The densest sub-graph algorithm would return a large sub-graph with $|S| > \frac{\delta k}{g}$ even if it is a lossless expander, as the density of the large sub-graph could be larger than $\frac{g}{1+(1-\epsilon)g}$ by Theorem 2.

Instead, we randomly sample sub-graphs $G^* = ((L', \Gamma(L')), E')$ with $\frac{\delta k}{g}$ vertexes in the left vertex set. If there exists a small non-expanding sub-graph with at most $\log\log k$ vertices on the left, the density of this small sub-graph is larger than $\frac{g}{1+(1-\epsilon)g}$ and the probability of it is in the sub-graph G^* is at least $(\frac{\delta}{g})^{\log\log k}$. Once it is contained in G', the densest-sub-graph algorithm will output a sub-graph with density larger than $\frac{g}{1+(1-\epsilon)}$. We will sample G^* $\frac{g}{\delta}^{\log\log k}$ times to amplify the probability. The formal algorithm is presented in Algorithm 1.

Theorem 3 (Distinguisher). *Algorithm 1 achieves the following properties:*

*1. If G is a **Yes case**, then the algorithm will return SUCC with probability* 1.

Algorithm 1. Distinguisher

Let $G = (L, R, E)$ be the random bipartite graph.

for $i \in [(\frac{g}{\delta})^{\log\log k}]$ **do**

  Sample a random set L', where $|L'| = \frac{\delta k}{g}$.

  Run densest graph algorithm in [Gol84] on the subgraph induced by L': $G^* = ((L', \Gamma(L')), E')$ to find its densest subgraph.

  if $\mathsf{Den}(G^*) > \frac{g}{1+(1-\varepsilon)g}$ **then**

    return FAIL

return SUCC

2. *If G is a* **No case**, *then the algorithm will return* FAIL *with probability at least* $1 - \frac{1}{e}$.

Proof. By Theorem 2, if the random graph is in **Yes case**, then the distinguisher will always return SUCC, since for every induced sub-graph G^*, it is a perfect expander. Otherwise, if the random graph contains a subset $S_0 \subseteq L, |S_0| \leq \log\log k$ such that $|\Gamma(S_0)| < (1-\epsilon)g|S_0|$, then with probability at least $(\frac{\frac{\delta k}{g}}{k})^{\log\log k} = (\frac{\delta}{g})^{\log\log k}$, S_0 will be a subset of L' sampled by the algorithm. In this case, L' is not a perfect expander graph and by Theorem 2, $\mathsf{Den}(G^*) > \frac{g}{1+(1-\epsilon)g}$ and the algorithm will return FAIL. Since we repeat it $\frac{g}{\delta}^{\log\log n}$ times, the probability that we did not successfully sample S_0 is $(1 - (\frac{\delta}{g})^{\log\log k})^{(\frac{g}{\delta})^{\log\log k}}$. By the inequality $(1-\frac{1}{n})^n \leq \frac{1}{e}$, we have $(1 - (\frac{\delta}{g})^{\log\log k})^{(\frac{g}{\delta})^{\log\log k}} \leq \frac{1}{e}$.

By repeating the distinguisher λ times, we can amplify the detection probability of the No case to $1 - \frac{1}{e^\lambda}$. Finally, we re-sample the random graph until the distinguisher returns SUCC. The successful probability of one sampling is $1 - O(\frac{1}{\mathsf{poly}(k)})$, so the expected number of sampling is a constant. The algorithm runs $\lambda(\frac{g}{\delta})^{\log\log k}$ instances of the densest sub-graph algorithm, and each instance involves a graph with at most $\delta\frac{k}{g}$ vertices and δk edges, so the total running time is $O(\lambda(\frac{g}{\delta})^{\log\log k} k^2 \log^2 k) = O(\lambda \mathsf{polylog}(k) k^2)$. The same algorithm can also apply to the lossless expander graph in [GLS+]. Our sampling algorithm is very efficient in practice. First, it does not involve any cryptographic operations and is done once. Second, $k = \sqrt{N}$ in our protocol of the polynomial commitment in the next section, so the complexity is actually quasi-linear in the size of the zero-knowledge argument instance. Finally, the complexity of the densest sub-graph algorithm in Theorem 1 is for arbitrary graphs. As observed in our experiments, the algorithm is faster on random bipartite graphs and we conjecture that there is a better complexity analysis, which is left as an interesting future work.

4 Our New Zero-Knowledge Argument

In this section, we present the construction of our zero-knowledge argument scheme. Many existing papers show that one can build zero-knowledge arguments from polynomial commitments [WTS+18, ZXZS20, CHM+20, Set20, GWC19, BFS20, GLS+]. We adopt the same technique and focus on constructing a polynomial commitment because of its simplicity and efficiency, but our approach can be applied directly to the zero-knowledge arguments for R1CS in [BCG20, BCL22] to improve the prover time and the proof size. We start the section by describing the polynomial commitment scheme in [GLS+] based on the tensor IOP protocol in [BCG20] with a proof size of $O(\sqrt{N})$.

4.1 Polynomial Commitment from Tensor Query

In [GLS+], Golovnev et al. observed that a polynomial evaluation can be expressed as a tensor product. Here we only consider multilinear polynomial commitments, which can be used to construct zero-knowledge arguments based on the approaches in [ZGK+17b, WTS+18, XZZ+19, ZXZS20, Set20], but our scheme can be extended to univariate polynomials. In particular, given a multilinear polynomial ϕ, its evaluation on input vector $x_0, x_1, ..., x_{\log N-1}$ is:

$$\phi(x_0, x_1, ..., x_{\log N-1}) = \sum_{i_0=0}^{1}\sum_{i_1=0}^{1} \cdots \sum_{i_{\log N-1}=0}^{1} w_{i_0 i_1 \ldots i_{\log N-1}} x_0^{i_0} x_1^{i_1} \ldots x_{\log N-1}^{i_{\log N-1}}.$$

The degree of each variable is either 0 or 1 by the definition of a multilinear polynomial, and thus there are N monomials and coefficients with $\log N$ variables. We let $i = \sum_{j=0}^{\log N-1} 2^j i_j$, that is, $i_0 i_1 \ldots i_{\log N-1}$ is the binary representation of number i. We use w to denote the coefficients where $w[i] = w_{i_0 i_1 \ldots i_{\log N-1}}$. Similarly we define $X_i = x_0^{i_0} x_1^{i_1} \ldots x_{\log N-1}^{i_{\log N-1}}$. Let $k = \sqrt{N}$, $r_0 = \{X_0, X_1, ..., X_{k-1}\}, r_1 = \{X_{0\times k}, X_{1\times k}, X_{2\times k}, ..., X_{(k-1)\times k}\}$. Then we have $X = r_0 \otimes r_1$. The polynomial evaluation is reduced to a tensor product $\phi(x_0, x_1, ..., x_{\log N-1}) = \langle w, r_0 \otimes r_1 \rangle$. Using the tensor IOP protocol in [BCG20], one can build a polynomial commitment [GLS+] and we present the protocol in Protocol 2 for completeness. Here we reuse the notation k as it is exactly the message length of the linear code.

As shown in the protocol, to commit to a polynomial, PC.Commit parses the coefficients w as a $k \times k$ matrix and encodes it using the tensor code with dimension 2 as defined in Definition 3. Then the algorithm constructs a Merkle tree commitment for every column $\mathsf{C}_2[:, i]$ of the $n \times n$ codeword C_2, and finally builds another Merkle tree on top of their roots as the final commitment.

To answer the tensor query, there are two checks in the protocol: a proximity check and a consistency check. The proximity check ensures that the matrix in the commitment is indeed close to a codeword of the tensor code. The consistency check ensures that $y = \langle r_0 \otimes r_1, w \rangle$ assuming $\mathcal{R}$ is a commitment of a codeword.

Proximity Check. The proximity heck has two steps. First, the verifier sends a random vector γ_0 to the prover, and the prover computes the linear combination of all rows of C_1 and w with γ_0, as in Step 8 in Protocol 2. Because of the property of a linear code, c_{γ_0} is a codeword with message y_{γ_0}, and this step is referred to as the "fold" operation in [BCG20]. Second, the prover shows that c_{γ_0} is indeed computed from the committed tensor codeword. To do so, the verifier randomly

Protocol 2. Polynomial commitment from [BCG20, GLS+]

Public input: The evaluation point $\vec{x}$, parsed as a tensor product $r = r_0 \otimes r_1$;
Private input: the polynomial ϕ, the coefficient of ϕ is denoted by w.
Let C be the $[n, k, d]$-linear code, $E_C : \mathbb{F}^k \to \mathbb{F}^n$ be the encoding function, $N = k \times k$. If N is not a perfect square, we can pad it to the next perfect square.
We use a python style notation to select the i-th column of a matrix $\mathsf{mat}[:, i]$.

1: **function** PC.COMMIT(ϕ)
2: Parse w as a $k \times k$ matrix. The prover computes the tensor code encoding $\mathsf{C}_1, \mathsf{C}_2$ locally as defined in Definition 3. Here C_1 is a $k \times n$ matrix and C_2 is a $n \times n$ matrix.
3: **for** $i \in [n]$ **do**
4: Compute the Merkle tree root $\mathsf{Root_i} = \mathsf{Merkle.Commit}(\mathsf{C}_2[:, \mathsf{i}])$.
5: Compute a Merkle tree root $\mathcal{R} = \mathsf{Merkle.Commit}([\mathsf{Root_0}, ..., \mathsf{Root_{n-1}}])$ and output $\mathcal{R}$ as the commitment.
6: **function** PC.PROVE($\phi, \vec{x}, \mathcal{R}$)
7: The prover receives a random vector $\gamma_0 \in \mathbb{F}^k$ from the verifier.
8: $c_{\gamma_0} = \sum_{i=0}^{k-1} \gamma_0[i]\mathsf{C}_1[i], y_{\gamma_0} = \sum_{i=0}^{k-1} \gamma_0[i]w[i]$. ▷ Proximity
9: $c_1 = \sum_{i=0}^{k-1} r_0[i]\mathsf{C}_1[i]$, $y_1 = \sum_{i=0}^{k-1} r_0[i]w[i]$. ▷ Consistency
10: Prover sends $c_1, y_1, c_{\gamma_0}, y_{\gamma_0}$ to the verifier.
11: Verifier randomly samples $t \in [n]$ indexes as an array $\hat{I}$ and send it to prover.
12: **for** $\mathsf{idx} \in \hat{I}$ **do**
13: Prover sends $\mathsf{C}_1[:, \mathsf{idx}]$ and the Merkle tree proof of $\mathsf{Root_{idx}}$ for $\mathsf{C}_2[:, \mathsf{idx}]$ under $\mathcal{R}$ to verifier
14: **function** PC.VERIFYEVAL($\pi_{\vec{x}}, \vec{x}, y = \phi(\vec{x}), \mathcal{R}$)
15: $\forall \mathsf{idx} \in \hat{I}, c_{\gamma_0}[\mathsf{idx}] == \langle \gamma_0, \mathsf{C}_1[:, \mathsf{idx}]\rangle$ and $E_C(y_{\gamma_0}) == c_{\gamma_0}$. ▷ Proximity
16: $\forall \mathsf{idx} \in \hat{I}, c_1[\mathsf{idx}] == \langle r_0, \mathsf{C}_1[:, \mathsf{idx}]\rangle$ and $E_C(y_1) == c_1$. ▷ Consistency
17: $y == \langle r_1, y_1 \rangle$. ▷ Tensor product
18: $\forall \mathsf{idx} \in \hat{I}$, $E_C(\mathsf{C}_1[:, \mathsf{idx}])$ is consistent with $\mathsf{Root_{idx}}$, and $\mathsf{Root_{idx}}$'s Merkle tree proof is valid.
19: Output accept if all conditions above holds. Otherwise output reject.

selects t columns and the prover opens them with their Merkle tree proofs. The verifier checks that the inner product between each column and the random vector γ_0 is equal to the corresponding element of c_{γ_0} (Step 15). As shown in [BCG+17, BCG20], if the linear code has a constant relative distance, the committed matrix is close to a tensor codeword with overwhelming probability.

Consistency Check. The consistency check follows exactly the same steps of the proximity check. Instead of using a random vector from the verifier, the linear combination is done with r_0 of the tensor query $r_0 \otimes r_1$. Similarly, c_1 is a codeword of the linear code with message y_1, and $\phi(x) = \langle y_1, r_1 \rangle$ by the definition of tensor product and polynomial evaluation. As shown in [BCG20], by the check in Step 16, if the committed matrix in $\mathcal{R}$ is close to a tensor codeword, then $y = \phi(x)$ with overwhelming probability. In particular, there exist an extractor to extract a polynomial ϕ from the commitment such that $y = \phi(x)$.

Theorem 4 (Polynomial commitment [BCG20, GLS+]**).** *Protocol 2 is a polynomial commitment that is correct and sound as defined in Definition 7.*

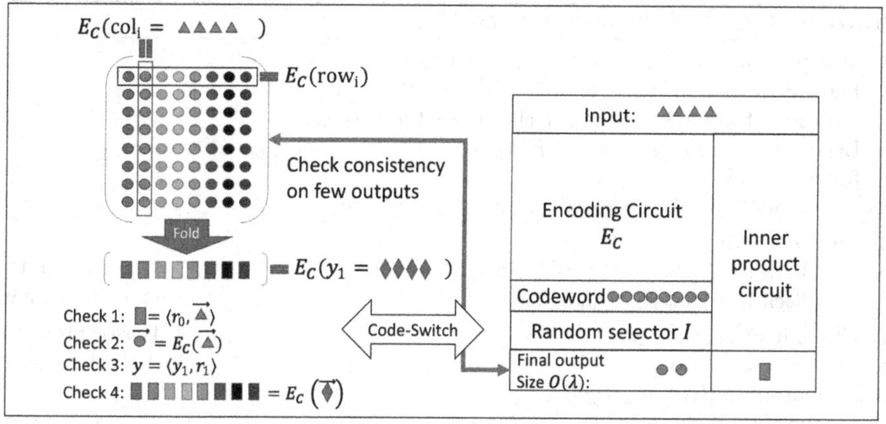

Fig. 2. An illustration of code switching. The circuit on the right for Check 1, 2 and Check 3, 4 are the same.

Efficiency. The prover's computation is dominated by encoding the tensor code, which takes $O(N)$ time using a linear-time encodable code such as the generalized Spielman code. The proof size is $O(t\sqrt{N})$, as the prover opens t random columns of size $\sqrt{N}$ to the verifier. The verifier time is also $O(t\sqrt{N})$ to check the inner products and to encode t columns.

4.2 Efficient Proof Composition via Code Switching

The proof size of the polynomial commitment in Protocol 2 is $O(\sqrt{N})$ (the complexity hides a security parameter t). There are three steps that incur $O(\sqrt{N})$ proof size in Protocol 2: Step 8, 9, and 13. In this section, we present a new protocol that reduces the proof size to $O(\log^2 N)$ via the technique of proof composition. The idea is to use a second proof system to prove that the checks of these three steps are satisfied, without sending the proofs of these steps to the verifier directly.

To design the second proof system efficiently, our key observation is that the values sent by the prover in these three steps are messages of the linear-time encodable code. That is, y_{γ_0} is the message of c_{γ_0} in Step 8, y_1 is the message of c_1 in Step 9 and $C_1[:, \mathsf{idx}]$ is the message of $C_2[:, \mathsf{idx}]$ for every idx in Step 13. Therefore, the second proof system takes y_{γ_0}, y_1 and $\mathsf{C}_1[:, \mathsf{idx}]$ for $\mathsf{idx} \in I$ as the witness, and performs the following computations:

1. It encodes the witness using the encoding circuit of the linear-time encodable code.
2. It outputs a subset of random indices of the codewords chosen by the verifier. By checking whether the values of these indices are consistent with the commitments by the prover via the Merkle tree, it guarantees that the witness is indeed the same as the messages specified above with overwhelming probability because of the minimum distance property of the code.

Protocol 3. Code Switching Statement C_{CS}

Witness: y_{γ_0}, y_1, $\mathsf{C}_1[:, \mathsf{idx}]\ \forall \mathsf{idx} \in \hat{I}$ in Protocol 2.
Public input: γ_0, r_0, r_1, y.
Public information: $\hat{I}$ and I chosen by the verifier.

Encode $c_{\gamma_0} := E_C(y_{\gamma_0})$, $c_1 := E_C(y_1)$.
for $\mathsf{idx} \in \hat{I}$ **do**
  Encode $\mathsf{C}_2[:, \mathsf{idx}] := E_C(\mathsf{C}_1[:, \mathsf{idx})$
for $\mathsf{idx} \in \hat{I}$ **do**
  Check if $c_{\gamma_0}[\mathsf{idx}] == \langle \gamma_0, \mathsf{C}_1[:, \mathsf{idx}] \rangle$. ▷ Proximity
  Check if $c_1[\mathsf{idx}] == \langle r_0, \mathsf{C}_1[:, \mathsf{idx}] \rangle$. ▷ Consistency
Check if $\langle r_1, y_1 \rangle == y$. ▷ Tensor product
for $0 \leq j < |I|$ **do** ▷ Encoder check
  Output $c_1[I[j]]$, $c_{\gamma_0}[I[j]]$.
  for $\mathsf{idx} \in \hat{I}$ **do**
    Output $\mathsf{C}_2[I[j], \mathsf{idx}]$

3. Finally, it checks that these messages and their codewords satisfy the conditions in line 15, 16 and 17 of Protocol 2.

The idea is illustrated in Fig. 2, and we formally present the statement of the second proof system in Protocol 3. Note that $\hat{I}$ is the random set chosen by the verifier in Protocol 2, and is only used as a notation for the subscripts in Protocol 3. I is the random set chosen by the verifier for the code switching. In this way, we switch the message encoded using the linear-time encodable code to the witness of the second proof system. In our implementation, we are using an IOP-based zero-knowledge argument with the Reed-Solomon code, we use the name "code switching" as in [RZR20].

We apply any zero-knowledge argument scheme $\mathcal{ZK}$ on the statement and then check the consistency between the output and the Merkle tree commitment $\mathcal{R}$ of the codeword of the linear-time encodable code. We present the new protocol in Protocol 4 and highlight the differences from Protocol 2 in blue. As shown in the protocol, instead of sending $c_1, y_1, c_{\gamma_0}, y_{\gamma_0}$, the prover commits to c_1 and c_{γ_0} in Step 8 and 9. The codeword C_2 was already committed column-wise in $\mathcal{R}$. The prover then proves the constraints of $c_1, y_1, c_{\gamma_0}, y_{\gamma_0}$ and $\mathsf{C}_1[:, \mathsf{idx}]$ using the code switching technique in Step 13. In this way, we are able to reduce the proof size and the verifier time of Protocol 2 to $O(\log^2 N)$.

Theorem 5. *Protocol 4 is a polynomial commitment as defined in Definition 7.*

The proof is presented in the full version of the paper.

Complexity of Protocol 4. The prover time remains $O(N)$. This is because in Step 8 and 9, the prover additionally commits to c_1, c_{γ_0}, which only takes $O(n) = O(\sqrt{N})$ time. In Step 13, the prover invokes another zero-knowledge argument on C_{CS}. C_{CS} consists of $t+2$ encoding circuits E_C of the linear-time encodable code and $t+2$ inner products. As the encoding circuit is of size $O(k)$, we will

Protocol 4. Polynomial commitment with code-switching

Public input: The evaluation point $\vec{x}$, parsed as a tensor product $r = r_0 \otimes r_1$;
Private input: the polynomial ϕ with coefficients w.

function COMMIT(ϕ)
    Parse w as a $k \times k$ matrix. The prover computes the tensor code encoding $\mathsf{C}_1, \mathsf{C}_2$ locally as defined in Definition 3.
    for $i \in [n]$ **do**
        Compute the Merkle tree root $\mathsf{Root_i} = \mathsf{Merkle.Commit}(\mathsf{C}_2[:, \mathsf{i}])$.
    Compute a Merkle tree root $\mathcal{R} = \mathsf{Merkle.Commit}([\mathsf{Root_0}, ..., \mathsf{Root_{n-1}}])$ and output $\mathcal{R}$ as the commitment.
function PROVE($\phi, \vec{x}, \mathcal{R}$)
    The prover receives a random vector $\gamma_0 \in \mathbb{F}^k$ from the verifier.
    $c_1 = \sum_{i=0}^{k-1} r_0[i]\mathsf{C}_1[i]$, $y_1 = \sum_{i=0}^{k-1} r_0[i]w[i]$, $\mathcal{R}_{c_1} = \mathsf{Merkle.Commit}(c_1)$
    $c_{\gamma_0} = \sum_{i=0}^{k-1} \gamma_0[i]\mathsf{C}_1[i], y_{\gamma_0} = \sum_{i=0}^{k-1} \gamma_0[i]w[i]$, $\mathcal{R}_{\gamma_0} = \mathsf{Merkle.Commit}(c_{\gamma_0})$
    The prover computes the answer $y := \langle y_0, r_1 \rangle$. Prover sends $\mathcal{R}_{c_1}, \mathcal{R}_{\gamma_0}, y$ to the verifier.
    The verifier randomly samples $t \in [n]$ indexes as an array $\hat{I}$ and send it to prover.
    The verifier randomly samples another index set $I \subseteq [k], |I| = t$ and sends it to the prover.
    The prover calls the zero-knowledge argument protocol $\mathcal{ZK}.\mathcal{P}$ on C_{CS}. Let π_{zk} be the proof of the zero-knowledge argument. The prover sends the output of C_{CS}: $\mathsf{C}_2[I[j], \mathsf{idx}]\ \forall \mathsf{idx} \in \hat{I}, c_1[I[j]], c_{\gamma_0}[I[j]]$ and π_{zk} to the verifier.
    The prover sends the Merkle tree proofs of $\mathsf{C}_2[I[j], \mathsf{idx}]\ \forall \mathsf{idx} \in \hat{I}$ under $\mathsf{Root_{idx}}$.
    The prover sends the Merkle tree proofs of $\mathsf{Root_{idx}}\ \forall \mathsf{idx} \in \hat{I}$ under $\mathcal{R}$.
    The prover sends the Merkle tree proofs of $c_1[I[j]], c_{\gamma_0}[I[j]]$ under $\mathcal{R}_{c_1}, \mathcal{R}_{c_{\gamma_0}}$.
function VERIFYEVAL($\pi_{\vec{x}}, \vec{x}, y = \phi(\vec{x}), \mathcal{R}$)
    The verifier calls the zero-knowledge argument protocol $\mathcal{ZK}.\mathcal{V}$ on C_{CS}.
    The verifier checks the Merkle tree proofs of $\mathsf{C}_2[I[j], \mathsf{idx}]\ \forall \mathsf{idx} \in \hat{I}$.
    The verifier checks the Merkle tree proofs of $\mathsf{Root_{idx}}\ \forall \mathsf{idx} \in \hat{I}$ using $\mathcal{R}$.
    The verifier checks the Merkle tree proofs of $c_1[I[j]], c_{\gamma_0}[I[j]]$ using $\mathcal{R}_{c_1}, \mathcal{R}_{c_{\gamma_0}}$.
Output accept if all checks pass. Otherwise output reject.

present the analysis in the full version of the paper, and the circuit to compute an inner product is of size $O(k)$, the overall circuit size is $O(t \cdot k)$. By using any zero-knowledge argument scheme with a quasi-linear prover time, such as [ZXZS20], the prover time of this step is $O(t \cdot k \log k)$. Since $k = \sqrt{N}$, the prover time is still $O(N)$ dominated by the encoding and the commitment of the $k \times k$ matrix in COMMIT(). With the code switching technique, the proof size and the verifier time becomes $O(t \log^2 k) = O(t \log^2 N)$.

4.3 Putting Everything Together

In this section, we show how to achieve zero-knowledge on top of our new polynomial commitment in Protocol 4, and sketch how to build a zero-knowledge argument using the polynomial commitment.

Protocol 5. zk-Polynomial commitment

Public input: The evaluation point $\vec{x}$, parsed as a tensor product $r = r_0 \otimes r_1$;
Private input: the polynomial ϕ with coefficients w.

```
function zkCommit(φ_w)
    The prover randomly samples m ∈ F^{|w|}.
    Output R_{w+m} = COMMIT(w + m), R_m = COMMIT(m).
function zkProve(φ, x⃗, R)
    Let φ_m be the masking polynomial, φ_{m+w} be the masked polynomial.
    Run Prove(φ_{m+w}, x⃗, R_{m+w}). Let the random index set used during the protocol
  be Î_0, I_0.
    Run Prove(φ_m, x⃗, R_m). In this step, the verifier samples the random index set
  Î_1, I_1. used during the protocol such that Î_0 ∩ Î_1 = ∅ ∧ I_0 ∩ I_1 = ∅.
function zkVerify(π_x⃗^{w+m}, π_x⃗^m, x⃗, y_{w+m}, y_m, R_{w+m}, R_m)
    The final polynomial evaluation φ(x⃗) should be y_{w+m} − y_m.
    Execute VerifyEval(π_{w+m}, x⃗, y_{w+m}, R_{w+m}).
    Execute VerifyEval(π_m, x⃗, y_m, R_m).
    Output accept if all checks above passes, otherwise output reject.
```

Achieving Zero-Knowledge. We apply a masking technique similar to the one in [BCG+17]. The codeword C_2 is masked by a codeword MSK of a masking polynomial with random coefficients m. We use our proof system to prove $y_{w+m} = \langle (w+m), r_0 \otimes r_1 \rangle$ and $y_m = \langle m, r_0 \otimes r_1 \rangle$ simultaneously, and the final answer of the polynomial evaluation is $y = y_{w+m} - y_m$. We present the protocol in Protocol 5.

Theorem 6. *Protocol 5 is a zero-knowledge polynomial commitment scheme by definition 7.*

We present the proof in the full version of the paper.

Zero-Knowledge Argument. Finally, we build our zero-knowledge argument system by combining the multivariate polynomial commitment with the sumcheck protocol as in [Set20, GLS+]. We state the theorem here and refer the readers to [Set20, GLS+] for the construction and the proof.

Theorem 7. *There exists a zero-knowledge argument scheme by definition 5 with $O(N)$ prover time, $O(\log^2 N)$ proof size and $O(N)$ verifier time.*

As we are using the IOP-based scheme in [ZXZS20] as the second zero-knowledge argument in the proof composition, our scheme is an IOP with a linear proof size and logarithmic query complexity. The scheme can be made non-interactive via the Fiat-Shamir [FS86] heuristic, and has plausible post-quantum security. Following the frameworks in [CHM+20, COS20, Set20, GLS+], our scheme can be turned into a holographic proof with a $\mathsf{polylog}(N)$ verifier time in a straight-forward way.

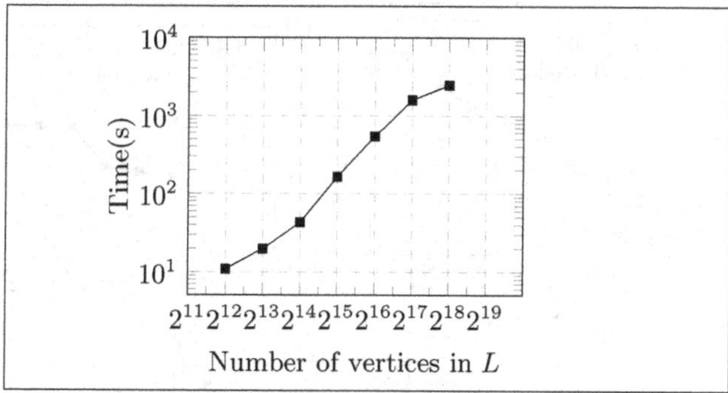

Fig. 3. Running time of our expander testing algorithm.

5 Experiments

We have implemented our scheme, Orion, and we present the evaluations of the system and the comparions to existing ZKP schemes in this section.

Settings and Parameters. Our polynomial commitment scheme is implemented in C++ with 6000 lines of code. The proof composition uses Virgo in [ZXZS20] and its open-source implementation. We combine the polynomial commitment with a sumcheck protocol to get our zero-knowledge argument following the approach in [Set20] and we implement our own code for this part.

Expander Graph used in Our Implementation. We use a modified version of generalized Spielman code in [GLS+]. The code assigns a random weight to each edge of the expander graph, achieving a better minimum distance. We take a step further and fine-tune the dimensions more aggressively. With our testing algorithm, the failure probability of the expander sampling remains negligible. There are two types of expander graph used in our construction and the parameters are G_1: $\alpha = 0.33, \delta = 0.6, \epsilon = 0.78, g = 6$; G_2: $\alpha = 0.337, g = 6, \delta = g, \epsilon = 0.88$.

Parameters of the our Linear Code. With expanders above, the final relative distance is 0.055. We set the security parameter $\lambda = 128$. This leads to opening $t = \frac{-128}{\log(1-0.055)} = 1568$ columns and locations in Protocol 4.

Hash Function and Finite Field. We use the SHA-256 hash function implemented by [arm]. We use the extension field of $\mathrm{GF}((2^{61}-1)^2)$ as our underlying field to be compatible with the zero-knowledge argument in [ZXZS20].

Environment and Method. We use an AWS m6i-32xlarge instance with Intel(R) Xeon(R) Platinum 8375C CPU @ 2.90 GHz CPU and 512 GB memory to execute all of our experiments. However, the largest instance in our experiment only utilize 16 GB of memory. All experiments are using a single thread except the expander testing algorithm. For each data point, we run the experiments 10 times and report the average.

5.1 Expander Testing

We first show the performance of our expander testing algorithm in Sect. 3. We implemented the densest sub-graph algorithm in [Gol84], which uses network-

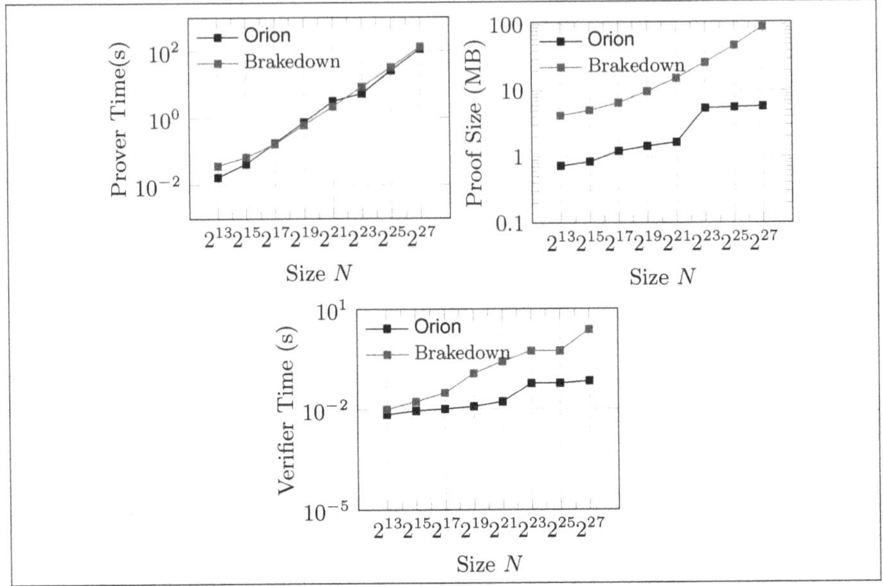

Fig. 4. Performance of polynomial commitments.

flow algorithm as a black-box. In our implementation, we use Dinic's algorithm [Din70], the complexity of which is $O(|V|^2|E|)$ on general graphs. However, on random bipartite graphs, the Dinic's algorithm runs significantly faster and as observed in our experiments, it scales almost linearly in the size of the graph.

Figure 3 shows the running time of the algorithm. We vary the size of left vertex set L in the random bipartite graph from 2^{12} to 2^{18}, and the size of R is set to be $|L| \times \alpha$. The implementation uses multi-threading utilizing all 128 CPU cores. As shown in the figure, it only takes 163 s to test whether a random bipartite graph with $|L| = 2^{15}$ vertices is a lossless expander with a failure probability $\mathsf{negl}(N) = 2^{-128}$. The running time almost grows linearly in $|L|$. As $k = \sqrt{N}$ in our zero-knowledge argument, this is enough for our experiments. As the sampling of the lossless expander is done once, our testing algorithm is very practical.

5.2 Polynomial Commitment

In this section, we report the performance of our polynomial commitment scheme and compare it with the scheme Brakedown in [GLS+], which is the only implemented polynomial commitment scheme with a linear prover time. We use the open-source implementation of Brakedown at [Wla] in the comparison. Our current implementation is for the plain version of the polynomial commitment without zero-knowledge, which is the same as Brakedown.

Figure 4 shows the performance of our polynomial commitment and the polynomial commitment in Brakedown. We vary the size of the polynomials from 2^{15}

to 2^{29} and measure the prover time, the proof size and the verifier time. As shown in the figure, our prover time is even slightly faster than Brakedown. It only takes 115 s for a polynomial with 2^{27} coefficients, while it is 132 s in Brakedown. This is because we use more aggressive parameters of the expander code, while still achieving 128-bit of security thanks to our expander testing algorithm. Moreover, the additional proof composition in our scheme involves a second zero-knowledge argument on a circuit of size $O(\sqrt{N})$. In our experiments, this extra zero-knowledge argument takes less than 20% of the total prover time, justifying that our code switching technique only introduces a small overhead on the prover time.

Our proof size and verifier time is significantly smaller than Brakedown. The proof size is only 6 MBs for a polynomial of size 2^{27}, 16× smaller than Brakedown. The verifier time is 70 ms for $N = 2^{27}$, 33× faster than Brakedown. The result shows the improvement of the $O(\log^2 N)$ proof size in our scheme.

Note that there is a jump from $N = 2^{21}$ to $N = 2^{23}$ in the proof size and verifier time. This is because in our implementation, instead of directly parsing the coefficients into $\sqrt{N} \times \sqrt{N}$ matrix, we optimize the dimensions for better performance. When $N < 2^{23}$, it is not meaningful to do code-switching on the columns. The prover only does the code-switching on the row (Protocol 4 Step 8 and 9), but opens the columns directly. We observe that this gives the best prover time and the proof size. When $N \geq 2^{23}$, the prover does the code-switching for both the row and the columns (Protocol 4, Step 8–13). Therefore, the proof size and the verifier time have a big increase because of the larger column size and the additional code-switching protocol.

5.3 Zero-Knowledge Arguments

Finally, we present the performance of our zero-knowledege argument scheme for R1CS as a whole in this section. We focus the comparison to existing schemes that work on R1CS and have transparent setup and plausible post-quantum security. They include Brakedown [GLS+], Aurora [BSCR+19] and Ligero [AHIV17]. We use the implementation of Brakedown at [Wla], and the open-source code of Ligero and Aurora at [aur] in the experiments.

We randomly generate the R1CS instances and vary the number of constraints from 2^{15} to 2^{20}. As shown in Fig. 5, Orion has the fastest prover among all schemes. It only takes 3.09 s to generate the proof for $N = 2^{20}$. This is slightly faster than Brakedown for the same reason as explained in Sect. 5.2. It is 20× faster than Ligero and 142× faster than Aurora because of the linear prover time and the simplified reduction via polynomial commitments.

The proof size of Orion is significantly smaller than Brakedown and Ligero. It is only 1.5 MB for $N = 2^{20}$, 6.5× smaller than Brakedown and 12.5× smaller than Ligero. The proof size is even comparable to Aurora, which has $O(\log^2 N)$ proof size and uses the Reed-Solomon code with a much better minimum distance than our linear code. The result justifies the improvement of our code switching.

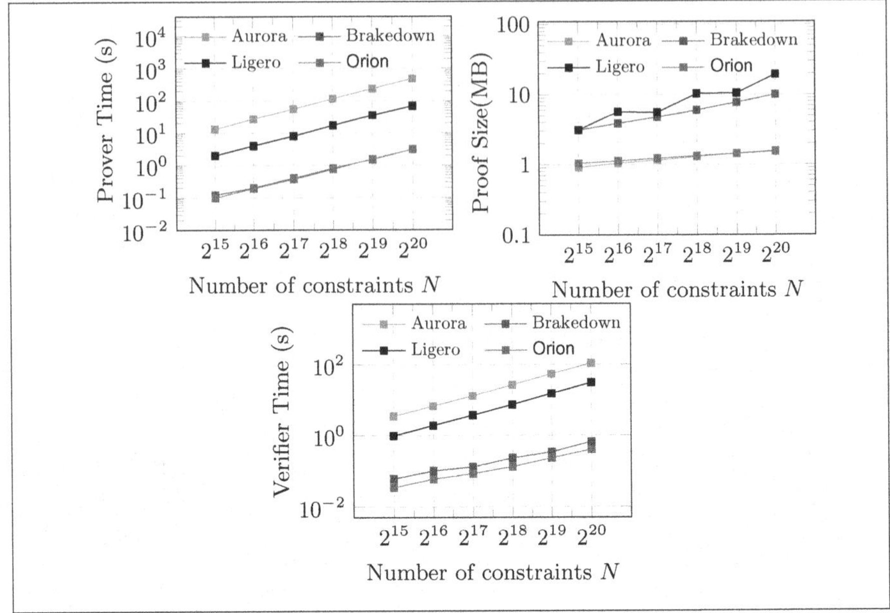

Fig. 5. Performance of zero-knowledge arguments on R1CS.

The verifier time of all schemes grow linearly with N and the comparisons are similar to the prover time. One can reduce the verifier time to sublinear in the holographic setting using the techniques in [CHM+20, COS20, Set20].

Other Related Schemes. There are several other existing transparent zero-knowledge argument schemes. Hyrax [WTS+18], Virgo [ZXZS20] and Virgo++ [ZLW+21] work on layered arithmetic circuits and STARK [BSBHR19] works on an algebraic intermediate representation that is close to a RAM program. It is hard to compare directly to R1CS, but we expect our prover time to be faster than these systems for similar computations based on the results shown in prior papers [ZXZS20, ZLW+21]. Spartan and schemes in [SL20] are using the same framework of polynomial commitment and sumcheck as in our scheme. However, they are based on discrete-log and bilinear pairing and thus are not post-quantum secure. As shown in [GLS+], their prover time is slower than Brakedown while the proof size is better (tens of KBs). Finally, Bulletproofs [BBB+18] and Supersonic [BFS20] are also based on discrete-log and group of unknown order. Their prover time is orders of magnitude slower than schemes mentioned above, while providing the smallest proof size (1–2 KBs) because of the underlying cryptographic techniques.

Acknowledgements. We thank Yuval Ishai for helpful discussions and valuable feedback on the paper. The material is supported by DARPA under Contract No. HR001120C0087, the NSF award #2144625 and the Center for Long-Term Cybersecurity

(CLTC). Any opinions, findings and conclusions or recommendations expressed in this material are those of the author(s) and do not necessarily reflect the views of DARPA, NSF or CLTC.

References

[AHIV17] Ames, S., Hazay, C., Ishai, Y., Venkitasubramaniam, M.: Lightweight sublinear arguments without a trusted setup. In: CCS, Ligero (2017)

[arm] armfazh. flo-shani-aesni. https://github.com/armfazh/flo-shani-aesni

[aur] libIOP. https://github.com/scipr-lab/libiop

[BBB+18] Bünz, B., Bootle, J., Boneh, D., Poelstra, A., Wuille, P., Maxwell, G.: Bulletproofs: short proofs for confidential transactions and more. In: IEEE S&P (2018)

[BBC+18] Baum, C., Bootle, J., Cerulli, A., Del Pino, R., Groth, J., Lyubashevsky, V.: Sub-linear lattice-based zero-knowledge arguments for arithmetic circuits. In: CRYPTO (2018)

[BCG+14] Ben-Sasson, E., Chiesa, A., Garman, C., Green, M., Miers, I., Tromer, E., Virza, M.: Decentralized anonymous payments from bitcoin. In: IEEE S&P, Zerocash (2014)

[BCG+17] Bootle, J., Cerulli, A., Ghadafi, E., Groth, J., Hajiabadi, M., Jakobsen, S.K.: Linear-time zero-knowledge proofs for arithmetic circuit satisfiability. In: Takagi, T., Peyrin, T. (eds.) ASIACRYPT 2017. LNCS, vol. 10626, pp. 336–365. Springer, Cham (2017). https://doi.org/10.1007/978-3-319-70700-6_12

[BCG20] Bootle, J., Chiesa, A., Groth, J.: Linear-time arguments with sublinear verification from tensor codes. In: TCC (2020)

[BCL22] Bootle, J., Chiesa, A., Liu, S.: Zero-knowledge IOPs with linear-time prover and polylogarithmic-time verifier. In: Dunkelman, O., Dziembowski, S. (eds.) Advances in Cryptology - EUROCRYPT 2022. EUROCRYPT 2022. Lecture Notes in Computer Science, vol. 13276, pp. 275–304. Springer, Cham (2022). https://doi.org/10.1007/978-3-031-07085-3_10

[BDFG20] Boneh, D., Drake, J., Fisch, B., Gabizon, A.: Halo infinite: Recursive zk-SNARKs from any additive polynomial commitment scheme. Cryptology ePrint Archive, Report 2020/1536 (2020)

[BFH+20] Bhadauria, R., Fang, Z., Hazay, C., Venkitasubramaniam, M., Xie, T., Zhang, Y.: Ligero++: a new optimized sublinear IOP. In: CCS (2020)

[BFR+13] Braun, B., Feldman, A.J., Ren, Z., Setty, S.T.V., Blumberg, A.J., Walfish, M.: Verifying computations with state. In: SOSP (2013)

[BFS20] Bünz, B., Fisch, B., Szepieniec, A.: Transparent SNARKs from DARK compilers. In: Eurocrypt (2020)

[BLNS20] Bootle, J., Lyubashevsky, V., Nguyen, N.K., Seiler, G.: A non-PCP approach to succinct quantum-safe zero-knowledge. In: CRYPTO (2020)

[BMRS21] Baum, C., Malozemoff, A.J., Rosen, M., Scholl, P.: Mac'n'cheese: zero-knowledge proofs for arithmetic circuits with nested disjunctions. In: CRYPTO (2021)

[BSBHR19] Ben-Sasson, E., Bentov, I., Horesh, Y., Riabzev, M.: Scalable zero knowledge with no trusted setup. In: CRYPTO (2019)

[BSCG+13] Ben-Sasson, E., Chiesa, A., Genkin, D., Tromer, E., Virza, M.: Verifying program executions succinctly and in zero knowledge. In: CRYPTO, SNARKs for C (2013)

[BSCR+19] Ben-Sasson, E., Chiesa, A., Riabzev, M., Spooner, N., Virza, M., Ward, N.P.: Aurora: transparent succinct arguments for R1CS. In: Eurocrypt (2019)

[BSCTV14] Ben-Sasson, E., Chiesa, A., Tromer, E., Virza, M.: Scalable zero knowledge via cycles of elliptic curves. In: CRYPTO (2014)

[CDG+17] Chase, M., et al.: Post-quantum zero-knowledge and signatures from symmetric-key primitives. In: CCS (2017)

[CFH+15] Costello, C., Zahur, S.: Versatile verifiable computation. In: IEEE S&P, Geppetto (2015)

[CHM+20] Chiesa, A., Yuncong, H., Maller, M., Mishra, P., Vesely, N., Ward, N.: Preprocessing zksnarks with universal and updatable SRS. In: Eurocrypt, Marlin (2020)

[COS20] Chiesa, A., Ojha, D., Spooner, N.: Post-quantum and transparent recursive proofs from holography. In: Eurocrypt, Fractal (2020)

[CRVW02] Capalbo, M., Reingold, O., Vadhan, S., Wigderson, A.: Randomness conductors and constant-degree lossless expanders. In: STOC (2002)

[CS07] Czumaj, A., Sohler, C.: Testing expansion in bounded-degree graphs. In: IEEE FOCS (2007)

[DI14] Druk, E., Ishai, Y.: Linear-time encodable codes meeting the gilbert-varshamov bound and their cryptographic applications. In: ITCS (2014)

[Din70] Dinic, E.A.: Algorithm for solution of a problem of maximum flow in networks with power estimation. In: Soviet Math. Doklady (1970)

[DIO21] Dittmer, S., Ishai, Y., Ostrovsky, R.: Line-point zero knowledge and its applications. In: ITC (2021)

[ESLL19] Esgin, M.F., Steinfeld, R., Liu, J.K., Liu, D.: Lattice-based zero-knowledge proofs: new techniques for shorter and faster constructions and applications. In: CRYPTO (2019)

[FDNZ21] Fang, Z., Darais, D., Near, J., Zhang, Y.: Zero knowledge static program analysis. In: CCS (2021)

[FFG+16] Fiore, D., Fournet, C., Ghosh, E., Kohlweiss, M., Ohrimenko, O., Parno, B.: Hash first, argue later: adaptive verifiable computations on outsourced data. In: CCS (2016)

[FQZ+21] Feng, B., Qin, L., Zhang, Z., Ding, Y., Chu, S.: ZEN: efficient zero-knowledge proofs for neural networks. Cryptology ePrint Archive, Report 2021/087 (2021)

[FS86] Fiat, A., Shamir, A.: How to prove yourself: practical solutions to identification and signature problems. In: CRYPTO (1986)

[GAZ+22] Grubbs, P., Arun, A., Bonneau, J., Walfish, M.: Zero-knowledge middleboxes. In: USENIX Security, Ye Zhang (2022)

[Gil52] Gilbert, E.N.: A comparison of signalling alphabets. Bell Syst. Tech. J. **31**(3), 504–522 (1952)

[GKM+18] Groth, J., Kohlweiss, M., Maller, M., Meiklejohn, S., Miers, I.: Updatable and universal common reference strings with applications to zk-SNARKs. In: CRYPTO (2018)

[GKR08] Goldwasser, S., Kalai, Y.T., Rothblum, G.: Delegating computation: interactive proofs for muggles. In: STOC (2008)

[GLS+] Golovnev, A., Lee, J., Setty, S., Thaler, J., Wahby, R.S.: Brakedown: linear-time and post-quantum snarks for r1cs. Cryptology ePrint Archive (2021). https://ia.cr/2021/1043

[GMO16] Giacomelli, I., Madsen, J., Orlandi, C.: Faster zero-knowledge for boolean circuits. In: USENIX Security, ZKBoo (2016)

[GMR89] Goldwasser, S., Micali, S., Rackoff, C.: The knowledge complexity of interactive proof systems. SIAM J. Comput. **18**(1), 186–208 (1989)

[Gol84] Goldberg, A.V.: Finding a maximum density subgraph. University of California Berkeley (1984)

[GR11] Goldreich, O., Ron, D.: On testing expansion in bounded-degree graphs. In: Goldreich, O. (ed.) Studies in Complexity and Cryptography. Miscellanea on the Interplay between Randomness and Computation. LNCS, vol. 6650, pp. 68–75. Springer, Heidelberg (2011). https://doi.org/10.1007/978-3-642-22670-0_9

[GWC19] Gabizon, A., Williamson, Z.J., Ciobotaru, O.: Plonk: Permutations over Lagrange-bases for oecumenical noninteractive arguments of knowledge. Cryptology ePrint Archive, Report 2019/953 (2019)

[HLW06] Hoory, S., Linial, N., Wigderson, A.: Expander graphs and their applications. Bull. Amer. Math. Soc. **43**(4), 439–561 (2006)

[ISW21] Ishai, Y., Su, H., Wu, D.J.: Shorter and faster post-quantum designated-verifier zksnarks from lattices. In: CCS (2021)

[Kil92] Kilian, J.: A note on efficient zero-knowledge proofs and arguments (extended abstract). In: STOC (1992)

[KKW18] Katz, J., Kolesnikov, V., Wang, X.: Improved non-interactive zero knowledge with applications to post-quantum signatures. In: CCS (2018)

[KPPS20] Kosba, A.E., Papadopoulos, D., Papamanthou, C., Song, D.: MIRAGE: succinct arguments for randomized algorithms with applications to universal zk-SNARKs. In: USENIX Security (2020)

[KS16] Khot, S., Saket, R.: Hardness of bipartite expansion. In: ESA (2016)

[LKKO20] Lee, S., Ko, H., Kim, J., Oh, H.: vCNN: Verifiable convolutional neural network based on zk-SNARKs. Cryptology ePrint Archive, Report 2020/584 (2020)

[LXZ21] Liu, T., Xie, X., Zhang, Y.: zkCNN: zero knowledge proofs for convolutional neural network predictions and accuracy. In: CCS (2021)

[MBKM19] Maller, M., Bowe, S., Kohlweiss, M., Meiklejohn, S.: Sonic: zero-knowledge snarks from linear-size universal and updatable structured reference strings. In: CCS (2019)

[Mic00] Micali, S.: Computationally sound proofs. SIAM J. Comput. **30**(4), 1253–1298 (2000)

[Mie09] Mie, T.: Short PCPPs verifiable in polylogarithmic time with O(1) queries. Ann. Math. Artif. Intell. **56**(3), 313–338 (2009)

[NS07] Nachmias, A., Shapira, A.: Testing the expansion of a graph. Electr. Colloquium Comput. Complex. (ECCC) **14**, 01 (2007)

[PHGR13] Parno, B., Howell, J., Gentry, C., Raykova, M.: Nearly practical verifiable computation. In: IEEE S&P, Pinocchio (2013)

[Pip] Pippenger, N.: On the evaluation of powers and related problems. In: SFCS, IEEE Computer Society (1976)

[RZR20] Ron-Zewi, N., Rothblum, R.D.: Local proofs approaching the witness length. In: FOCS (2020)

[Set20] Setty, S.: Spartan: Efficient and general-purpose zkSNARKs without trusted setup. In: CRYPTO (2020)

[SL20] Setty, S., Lee, J.: Quarks: quadruple-efficient transparent zkSNARKs. Cryptology ePrint Archive, Report 2020/1275 (2020)

[Spi96] Spielman, D.A.: Linear-time encodable and decodable error-correcting codes. IEEE Trans. Inf. Theor. **42**(6), 1723–1731 (1996)

[SZT02] Song, D., Zuckerman, D., Tygar, J.D.: Expander graphs for digital stream authentication and robust overlay networks. In: S&P, IEEE (2002)

[Var57] Varshamov, R.R.: Estimate of the number of signals in error correcting codes. Docklady Akad. Nauk, SSSR **117**, 739–741 (1957)

[Wla] Wahby, R.S.: lcpc authors. lcpc. https://github.com/conroi/lcpc

[WSR+15] Wahby, R.S., Setty, S.T.V., Ren, Z., Blumberg, A.J., Walfish, M.: Efficient RAM and control flow in verifiable outsourced computation. In: NDSS (2015)

[WTS+18] Wahby, R.S., Tzialla, I., Shelat, A., Thaler, J., Walfish, M.: Doubly-efficient zkSNARKs without trusted setup. In: S&P (2018)

[WYKW20] Weng, C/. Yang, K., Katz, J., Wang, X.: Wolverine: fast, scalable, and communication-efficient zero-knowledge proofs for boolean and arithmetic circuits. In: S&P (2020)

[WYX+21] Weng, C., Yang, K., Xie, X., Katz, J., Wang, X.: Mystique: efficient conversions for zero-knowledge proofs with applications to machine learning. In: USENIX Security (2021)

[XZZ+19] Xie, T., Zhang, J., Zhang, Y., Papamanthou, C., Song, D.: Succinct zero-knowledge proofs with optimal prover computation. In: CRYPTO, Libra (2019)

[YSWW21] Yang, K., Sarkar, P., Weng, C., Wang, X.: Quicksilver: efficient and affordable zero-knowledge proofs for circuits and polynomials over any field. In: CCS (2021)

[zca] Zcash. https://z.cash/

[ZFZS20] Zhang, J., Fang, Z., Zhang, Y., Song, D.: Zero knowledge proofs for decision tree predictions and accuracy. In: CCS (2020)

[ZGK+17a] Zhang, Y., Genkin, D., Katz, J., Papadopoulos, D., Papamanthou, C.: vSQL: verifying arbitrary SQL queries over dynamic outsourced databases. In: S&P (2017)

[ZGK+17b] Zhang, Y., Genkin, D., Katz, J., Papadopoulos, D., Papamanthou, C.: A zero-knowledge version of vSQL. Cryptology ePrint Archive: Report 2017/1146 (2017)

[ZGK+18] Zhang, Y., Genkin, D., Katz, J., Papadopoulos, D., Papamanthou, C.: vRAM: faster verifiable RAM with program-independent preprocessing. In: S&P (2018)

[zkr] An incomplete guide to rollups. https://vitalik.ca/general/2021/01/05/rollup.html

[ZLW+21] Zhang, J., et al.: Doubly efficient interactive proofs for general arithmetic circuits with linear prover time. In: CCS (2021)

[ZXZS20] Zhang, J., Xie, T., Zhang, Y., Song, D.: Transparent polynomial delegation and its applications to zero knowledge proof. In: S&P, IEEE (2020)

Moz$\mathbb{Z}_{2^k}$arella: Efficient Vector-OLE and Zero-Knowledge Proofs over $\mathbb{Z}_{2^k}$

Carsten Baum, Lennart Braun(✉), Alexander Munch-Hansen, and Peter Scholl

Aarhus University, Aarhus, Denmark
{cbaum,braun,almun,peter.scholl}@cs.au.dk

Abstract. Zero-knowledge proof systems are usually designed to support computations for circuits over $\mathbb{F}_2$ or $\mathbb{F}_p$ for large p, but not for computations over $\mathbb{Z}_{2^k}$, which all modern CPUs operate on. Although $\mathbb{Z}_{2^k}$-arithmetic can be emulated using prime moduli, this comes with an unavoidable overhead. Recently, Baum et al. (CCS 2021) suggested a candidate construction for a designated-verifier zero-knowledge proof system that natively runs over $\mathbb{Z}_{2^k}$. Unfortunately, their construction requires preprocessed random vector oblivious linear evaluation (VOLE) to be instantiated over $\mathbb{Z}_{2^k}$. Currently, it is not known how to efficiently generate such random VOLE in large quantities.

In this work, we present a maliciously secure, VOLE extension protocol that can turn a short seed-VOLE over $\mathbb{Z}_{2^k}$ into a much longer, pseudorandom VOLE over the same ring. Our construction borrows ideas from recent protocols over finite fields, which we non-trivially adapt to work over $\mathbb{Z}_{2^k}$. Moreover, we show that the approach taken by the QuickSilver zero-knowledge proof system (Yang et al. CCS 2021) can be generalized to support computations over $\mathbb{Z}_{2^k}$. This new VOLE-based proof system, which we call QuarkSilver, yields better efficiency than the previous zero-knowledge protocols suggested by Baum et al. Furthermore, we implement both our VOLE extension and our zero-knowledge proof system, and show that they can generate 13–50 million VOLEs per second for 64 bit to 256 bit rings, and evaluate 1.3 million 64 bit multiplications per second in zero-knowledge.

1 Introduction

Zero-knowledge (ZK) proofs allow a prover to convince a verifier that some statement is true, without revealing any additional information. They are a fundamental tool in cryptography with a wide range of applications. A common way of expressing statements used in ZK is with *circuit satisfiability*, where the prover and verifier hold some circuit $\mathcal{C}$, and the prover proves that she knows a witness w such that $\mathcal{C}(w) = 1$. Typically, $\mathcal{C}$ is an arithmetic circuit defined over a finite field such as $\mathbb{F}_2$ or $\mathbb{F}_p$ for a large prime p, but the same idea works for any finite ring.

Y. Dodis and T. Shrimpton (Eds.): CRYPTO 2022, LNCS 13510, pp. 329–358, 2022.
https://doi.org/10.1007/978-3-031-15985-5_12

A recent line of work [7,16,25,26] builds highly scalable zero-knowledge proofs based on vector oblivious linear evaluation, or VOLE. VOLE is a two-party protocol often used in secure computation settings, which allows a receiver holding Δ to learn a secret linear function $\mathbf{w} - \Delta \cdot \mathbf{u} = \mathbf{v}$ of a sender's private inputs $\mathbf{u}, \mathbf{w}$. VOLE-based ZK protocols have the key feature that the overhead of the prover is very small: compared with the cost of evaluating the circuit $\mathcal{C}$ in the clear, few additional computational or memory resources are needed. This allows proofs to scale to handle very large statements, such as proving properties of complex programs. On the other hand, potential drawbacks of using VOLE are that the communication complexity is typically linear in the size of $\mathcal{C}$ – unlike SNARKs (e.g. [8,22]) and MPC-in-the-head techniques (e.g. [2]), which can be sublinear – and proofs are only verifiable by a single, designated verifier.

VOLE Constructions. In a length-n VOLE protocol over some ring R, the sender has input two vectors $\mathbf{u}, \mathbf{w} \in R^n$, while the receiver has input $\Delta \in R$, and receives as output $\mathbf{v} \in R^n$ as defined above. In applications such as ZK proofs, it is actually enough to construct *random VOLEs*, or VOLE correlations, where both parties' inputs are chosen at random. The most efficient approaches for generating random VOLE are based on the method of Boyle et al. [11], which relies on an arithmetic variant of the learning parity with noise (LPN) assumption. The protocol has the key feature that the communication cost is *sublinear* in the output length, n.

The original protocol of [11] has only semi-honest security (or malicious security using expensive, generic 2-PC techniques). Later, dedicated maliciously secure protocols over fields were developed [12,25], which essentially match the cost of the underlying semi-honest protocols, by using lightweight consistency checks for verifying honest behavior. In general, these protocols assume that R is a finite field.

ZK Based on VOLE. The state-of-the-art, VOLE-based protocol for proving circuit satisfiability in zero-knowledge is the QuickSilver protocol. QuickSilver, which builds upon the previous Line-Point ZK [16] protocol, works for circuits over any finite field $\mathbb{F}_q$, and has a communication cost of essentially 1 field element per multiplication gate. Concretely, QuickSilver achieves a throughput of up to 15.8 million AND gates per second for a Boolean circuit, or 8.9 million multiplication gates for an arithmetic circuit over the 61-bit Mersenne prime field. Another approach is the Mac'n'Cheese protocol [7], which can also achieve an amortized cost as small as 1 field element, but with slightly worse computational costs and round complexity.

ZK Over Rings. While most ZK protocols are based on circuits over fields, it can in certain applications be more desirable to work with circuits over a finite ring such as $\mathbb{Z}_{2^k}$. For instance, to prove a property of an existing program (such as proving a program contains a bug, or does not violate some safety property) the program logic and computations must all be emulated using a circuit. Since

CPUs perform arithmetic in $\mathbb{Z}_{2^k}$, this is a natural choice of ring that leads to a simpler translation of program code into a satisfiable circuit $\mathcal{C}$.

Unfortunately, not many existing ZK proof systems can natively support computations over rings. The recent work of [5] gave the first ZK protocol over $\mathbb{Z}_{2^k}$ based on VOLE over $\mathbb{Z}_{2^k}$, obtaining a proof system with a communication cost of $O(1)$ ring elements per multiplication gate (for large rings), asymptotically matching QuickSilver over large fields. However, a major drawback of their protocols is that they require maliciously secure VOLE over $\mathbb{Z}_{2^k}$, which is much more expensive to build: the only known instantiation of this [23] would increase the concrete communication of their ZK protocol by 1–2 orders of magnitude. Finally, another approach to zero-knowledge proof systems over rings has been proposed based on SNARKs [17]. When using $\mathbb{Z}_{2^k}$, this work obtains a designated-verifier SNARK, however, the scheme has not been implemented, and suffers from a dependency on expensive, public-key cryptography, as in many field-based SNARKs.

1.1 Contributions

In this work, we address the question of building efficient protocols for VOLE and zero-knowledge proofs over $\mathbb{Z}_{2^k}$. Firstly, we show how to build a maliciously secure VOLE protocol over $\mathbb{Z}_{2^k}$, with efficiency comparable to state-of-the-art protocols over finite fields [12,25]. Our protocol introduces new consistency checks for verifying correctness of VOLE extension, which are tailored to overcome the difficulties of working with the ring $\mathbb{Z}_{2^k}$. Secondly, using our VOLE over $\mathbb{Z}_{2^k}$, we show how to adapt the QuickSilver protocol [26] to the ring setting, obtaining an efficient ZK protocol called QuarkSilver that is dedicated to proving circuit satisfiability over $\mathbb{Z}_{2^k}$. Here, we extend techniques from the MPC world [15] to be suitable for our ZK proof. Finally, we implemented and benchmarked both our VOLE and ZK protocols to demonstrate their performance. In a high-bandwidth, low-latency setting, our implementation achieves a throughput of 13–50 million VOLEs per second for 64 bit to 256 bit rings with 40 bit statistical security while transmitting only ≈1 bit per VOLE. Our QuarkSilver implementation is able to compute and verify 1.3 million 64 bit multiplications per second.

1.2 Our Techniques

Below, we expand on our contributions, the techniques involved and some more relevant background.

Challenge of Working in $\mathbb{Z}_{2^k}$. Before delving into our protocols, we first briefly recap the main challenges when working with rings like $\mathbb{Z}_{2^k}$, compared with finite fields. When using VOLE for zero-knowledge, VOLE is used to *commit* the prover to its inputs and intermediate wire values in the circuit. This is possible by viewing each VOLE output $M[x] = \Delta \cdot x + K[x]$ as an information-theoretic homomorphic MAC in the input x.

When working over a finite field, it's easy to see that if a malicious prover can come up with a valid MAC $M[\overline{x}]$ on an input $\overline{x} \neq x$, for the same key $K[x]$, then the prover can recover the MAC key Δ from the relation:

$$M[x] - M[\overline{x}] = \Delta \cdot (x - \overline{x})$$

However, this relies on $x - \overline{x}$ being invertible, which is usually not the case when working over a ring such as $\mathbb{Z}_{2^k}$. Indeed, if $x - \overline{x} = 2^{k-1}$, then the prover can forge a MAC $M[\overline{x}]$ with probability 1/2, since $M[x] - M[\overline{x}] \bmod 2^k$ now only depends on the least significant bit of Δ.

The SPD$\mathbb{Z}_{2^k}$ protocol [15] for multi-party computation showed how to work around this issue by extending the modulus to 2^{k+s}, for some statistical security parameter s. This way, it can be shown that the lower s bits of the key Δ are still enough to protect the integrity of the lower k bits of the message x.

Indeed, this was exactly the type of MAC scheme used in the recent work on conversions and ZK over rings [5]. However, as in the SPD$\mathbb{Z}_{2^k}$ protocols, further challenges arise when handling more complex protocols for verifying computation on MACed values.

Maliciously Secure VOLE Extension in $\mathbb{Z}_{2^k}$. Current state-of-the-art VOLE protocols all stem from the approach of Boyle et al. [11], which builds a *pseudorandom correlation generator* based on (variants of) the *learning parity with noise* (LPN) assumption. This approach exploits the fact that sparse LPN errors can be used to compress secret-sharings of pseudorandom vectors, allowing the two parties to generate a long, pseudorandom instance of a VOLE correlation in a succinct manner.

These protocols proceed by first constructing a protocol for *single-point* VOLE, where the sender's input vector has only a single non-zero entry. Then, the single-point VOLE protocol is repeated t times, to obtain a t-point VOLE where the sender's input is viewed as a long, sparse, LPN error vector. Finally, by combining t-point VOLE and the LPN assumption, the parties can locally transform this into pseudorandom VOLE by applying a linear mapping.

Using this blueprint leads to (random) VOLE protocols with communication much smaller than the output length. This can be seen as a form of *VOLE extension*, where in the first step, a small "seed" VOLE of length $m \ll n$ is used to create the single-point VOLEs, and then extended into a longer VOLE of length n. In the Wolverine protocol [25], it was additionally observed that when repeating this process, it can greatly help communication if m of the n extended outputs are reserved and used to bootstrap the next iteration of the protocol, saving generation of fresh seed VOLEs.

With semi-honest security, the above approach can easily be instantiated over rings, following the protocols of [12,24]. When adapting this protocol to malicious security, our main technical challenge is that previous works over fields [12,25] used a consistency check to verify correctness of the outputs, which involved taking random linear combinations over the field. Due to the existence of zero divisors, this technique does not directly translate to $\mathbb{Z}_{2^k}$. One possible approach, similarly to the MAC scheme described above, is to increase the size of the ring to, say, $\mathbb{Z}_{2^{k+s}}$, and use computations in the larger ring to ensure that the VOLEs are correct modulo 2^k. However, the problem is, it would then no longer be compatible with the bootstrapping technique of [25]: to check consistency, the seed VOLE must be in the larger ring $\mathbb{Z}_{2^{k+s}}$, however, since the outputs are only in $\mathbb{Z}_{2^k}$, they can't then be used as a seed for the next execution! One solution would be to start with an even larger ring ($\mathbb{Z}_{2^{k+2s}}$), and keep decreasing the ring size after each iteration, but this would be far too expensive when done repeatedly.

Instead, we take a different approach. First, we adopt a hash-based check from [12], which verifies correctness of a puncturable pseudorandom function based on a GGM tree, created during the protocol. This hash check (which we optimize by using universal hashing instead of a cryptographic hash function) works over rings as well as fields, however, it does not suffice to ensure consistency of the entire protocol. On top of this, we incorporate a linear combination check, however, one with binary coefficients instead of coefficients in the large ring. This type of check can be used over a ring, but allows a cheating prover to try to bypass the check and cheat successfully with probability 1/2. Nevertheless, we show that by allowing some additional leakage in the single-point VOLE functionality, we can still simulate the protocol with this check. For our final VOLE protocol, this leakage implies that a few noise coordinates of the LPN error vector may have leaked.

While previous protocols also allowed a limited form of leakage [12,25], in this case, ours is more serious since entire noise coordinates can be leaked with probability 1/2. To counter this, we analyze the state-of-the-art attacks on LPN, and show how to adjust the parameters and increase the noise rate accordingly.

Similarly to [25], we focus on using the "primal" form of LPN, which was also used for semi-honest VOLE over $\mathbb{Z}_{2^k}$ in [24]. While the "dual" form of LPN, as considered in [11,12,14], achieves lower communication costs (and does not rely on bootstrapping), it involves a more costly matrix multiplication, which is expensive to implement. In [12], dual-LPN was instantiated using quasi-cyclic codes to achieve $\tilde{O}(n)$ complexity, but this approach does not readily adapt to rings instead of fields; it is plausible that the fast, LDPC-based dual-LPN variant proposed in [14] can be adapted to work over rings, but the security of this assumption has not been analyzed thoroughly.

Efficient Zero-Knowledge via QuarkSilver in $\mathbb{Z}_{2^k}$. Given VOLE, the standard approach to obtaining a ZK proof is using the homomorphic MAC scheme described above. There, the prover first commits to the input $\mathbf{w}$ as well as all intermediate circuit wire values of $\mathcal{C}(\mathbf{w})$. Then, the prover must show consistency of all the wire values and that the output wire indeed contains 1. Since the MACs are linearly homomorphic, the main challenge is verifying multiplications. In QuickSilver [26], to verify that committed values x, y, z satisfy $x \cdot y = z$, the parties locally compute a quadratic function on their MACs and MAC keys, obtaining a new value which has a consistent MAC only if the multiplication is correct.

The catch is that this new MAC relation being checked leads to a quadratic equation in the secret key Δ, instead of linear as before, which is chosen by a possibly dishonest prover. If this quadratic equation has a root in Δ, then the check passes. In the field case, this is not a problem as there are no more than two solutions to a quadratic equation, so we obtain a soundness error of $2/|\mathbb{F}|$. However, with rings, there can be many solutions. For instance, with

$$f(X) = aX^2 + bX + c \pmod{2^k},$$

if $a = 2^{k/2}$ and $b = c = 0$ then any multiple of $2^{k/4}$ is a possible choice for X, i.e. the check would erroneously pass for $2^{3k/4}$ choices of Δ. To remedy this, we reduce the number of valid solutions by working modulo 2^ℓ for some $\ell > k$, and adding the constraint on the solution that $\Delta \in \{0, \ldots, 2^s - 1\}$, where s is a statistical security parameter.

An additional challenge is that when checking a batch of multiplications, we actually check a random linear combination of a large number of these equations, which again leads to complications with zero divisors. By carefully analyzing the number of bounded solutions to equations of this type, and extending techniques from SPD$\mathbb{Z}_{2^k}$ [15] for handling linear combinations over rings, we show that it suffices to choose $\ell \approx k + 2(\sigma + \log \sigma)$ to achieve $2^{-\sigma}$ failure probability in the check. Overall, we obtain a communication complexity of ℓ bits per input and multiplication gate in the circuit.

2 Preliminaries

2.1 Notation

We use lower case, bold symbols for vectors $\mathbf{x}$ and upper case, bold symbols for matrices $\mathbf{A}$. We use κ as the computational and σ as the statistical security parameter. In our UC functionalities and proofs, $\mathcal{Z}$ denotes the environment, and $\mathcal{S}$ is the simulator, while $\mathcal{A}$ will refer to the adversary.

2.2 Vector OLE

Vector OLE (VOLE) is a two party functionality between a sender $\mathsf{P_S}$ and a receiver $\mathsf{P_R}$ to obtain correlated random vectors of the following form: $\mathsf{P_S}$ obtains two vectors $\mathbf{u}, \mathbf{w}$, and $\mathsf{P_R}$ gets a random scalar Δ and a random vector $\mathbf{v}$ so that $\mathbf{w} = \Delta \cdot \mathbf{u} + \mathbf{v}$ holds.

We parameterize the functionality with two values ℓ and s such that $s \leq \ell$. The scalar Δ is sampled from $\mathbb{Z}_{2^s}$, and the vectors $\mathbf{u}, \mathbf{v}, \mathbf{w}$ are sampled from $\mathbb{Z}_{2^\ell}^n$ where n denotes the size of the correlation. We require that the equation $\mathbf{w} = \Delta \cdot \mathbf{u} + \mathbf{v}$ holds modulo 2^ℓ. The ideal functionality is described in Fig. 1.

As in SPD$\mathbb{Z}_{2^k}$ [15], we can implement $\mathcal{F}_{\mathsf{vole2k}}^{\ell,s}$ using the oblivious transfer protocol (OT) of [23]. Basing VOLE on OT has the drawback of quadratic communication costs in the ring size, since it requires one OT of size ℓ bit for each of the ℓ bits of a ring element. Hence, we would use this approach only once to create a set of base VOLEs. Then we can use the more efficient protocol presented in Sect. 4 to repeatedly generate large batches to VOLEs.

VOLE for $\mathbb{Z}_{2^k}$: $\mathcal{F}^{\ell,s}_{\mathsf{vole2k}}$

Let $\ell \geq s$.

Init This method is the first to be called by the parties. On input (Init) from both parties proceed as follows:

1. If $\mathsf{P_R}$ is honest, sample $\Delta \in_R \mathbb{Z}_{2^s}$ and send Δ to $\mathsf{P_R}$.
2. If $\mathsf{P_R}$ is corrupt, receive $\Delta \in \mathbb{Z}_{2^s}$ from $\mathcal{S}$.
3. Δ is stored by the functionality.

All further (Init) queries are ignored.

Extend On input (Extend, n) from both parties proceed as follows:

1. If $\mathsf{P_R}$ is honest, sample $\mathbf{v} \in_R \mathbb{Z}^n_{2^\ell}$. Otherwise receive $\mathbf{v} \in_R \mathbb{Z}^n_{2^\ell}$ from $\mathcal{S}$.
2. If $\mathsf{P_S}$ is honest, sample $\mathbf{u} \in_R \mathbb{Z}^n_{2^\ell}$ and compute $\mathbf{w} := \Delta \cdot \mathbf{u} + \mathbf{v} \in \mathbb{Z}_{2^\ell}$. Otherwise receive $\mathbf{u} \in \mathbb{Z}^n_{2^\ell}$ and $\mathbf{w} \in \mathbb{Z}^n_{2^\ell}$ from $\mathcal{S}$ and then recompute $\mathbf{v} := \mathbf{w} - \Delta \cdot \mathbf{u} \in \mathbb{Z}^n_{2^\ell}$
3. Send $(\mathbf{u}, \mathbf{w})$ to $\mathsf{P_S}$ and $\mathbf{v}$ to $\mathsf{P_R}$.

Global-key Query If $\mathsf{P_S}$ is corrupted, receive (Guess, Δ') from $\mathcal{S}$ with $\Delta' \in \mathbb{Z}_{2^s}$. If $\Delta' = \Delta$, send success to $\mathsf{P_S}$ and ignore subsequent global-key queries. Otherwise, send abort to both parties and abort.

Fig. 1. Ideal functionality VOLE over $\mathbb{Z}_{2^k}$.

2.3 Equality Test

In our work, we use an equality test functionality $\mathcal{F}_{\mathsf{EQ}}$ (Fig. 2) between two parties $\mathcal{P}, \mathcal{V}$ where $\mathcal{V}$ learns the input of $\mathcal{P}$. The equality check functionality can be implemented using a simple commit-and-open protocol, see e.g. [25]. When using a hash function with 2κ bit output (modeled as random oracle) to implement the commitment scheme, the equality check of ℓ bit values can be implemented with $\ell + 3\kappa$ bit of communication.

2.4 Zero-Knowledge Proofs of Knowledge

In Fig. 3 we provide an ideal functionality for zero-knowledge proofs. The functionality implies the standard definition of a ZKPoK as it is complete, knowledge sound and zero-knowledge.

Equality Test: $\mathcal{F}_{\mathsf{EQ}}$

On input $V_{\mathcal{P}}$ from $\mathcal{P}$ and $V_{\mathcal{V}}$ from $\mathcal{V}$:

1. Send $V_{\mathcal{P}}$ and $(V_{\mathcal{P}} \stackrel{?}{=} V_{\mathcal{V}})$ to $\mathcal{V}$.
2. If $\mathcal{V}$ is honest and $V_{\mathcal{P}} = V_{\mathcal{V}}$, or $\mathcal{V}$ is corrupted and sends continue, then send $(V_{\mathcal{P}} \stackrel{?}{=} V_{\mathcal{V}})$ to $\mathcal{P}$
3. If $\mathcal{V}$ is honest and $V_{\mathcal{P}} \neq V_{\mathcal{V}}$, or $\mathcal{V}$ is corrupted and sends abort, then send abort to $\mathcal{P}$.

Fig. 2. Ideal functionality for equality tests.

Zero-Knowledge Functionality $\mathcal{F}^k_{\mathsf{ZK}}$

Prove: On input (prove, $\mathcal{C}$, $\mathbf{w}$) from $\mathcal{P}$ and (verify, $\mathcal{C}$) from $\mathcal{V}$ where $\mathcal{C}$ is a circuit over $\mathbb{Z}_{2^k}$ and $\mathbf{w} \in \mathbb{Z}^n_{2^k}$ for some $n \in \mathbb{N}$: Send true to $\mathcal{V}$ iff $\mathcal{C}(\mathbf{w}) = 1$, and false otherwise.

Fig. 3. Ideal functionality for zero-knowledge proofs for circuit satisfiability.

2.5 The LPN Assumption over Rings

The *Learning Parity with Noise* (LPN) assumption [9] states that, given the noisy dot product of many public vectors $\mathbf{a}_i$ with a secret vector $\mathbf{s}$, the result is indistinguishable from a vector of random values. Adding noise to indices is done by adding a noise vector $\mathbf{e}$ at the end, consisting of random values.

We rely on the following arithmetic variant of LPN over a ring $\mathbb{Z}_M$, as also considered in [11,24].

Definition 1 (LPN). *Let $\mathcal{D}^M_{n,t}$ be a distribution over $\mathbb{Z}^n_M$ such that for any $t, n, M \in \mathbb{N}$, $\mathrm{Im}(\mathcal{D}^M_{n,t}) \in \mathbb{Z}^n_M$. Let G be a probabilistic code generation algorithm such that $\mathsf{G}(m, n, M)$ outputs a matrix $\mathbf{A} \in \mathbb{Z}^{m\times n}_M$. Let parameters m, n, t be implicit functions of security parameter κ. The $\mathsf{LPN}^{\mathsf{G}}_{m,n,t,M}$ assumptions states that:*

$$\{(\mathbf{A}, \mathbf{x}) \mid \mathbf{A} \leftarrow \mathsf{G}(m, n, M), \mathbf{s} \in_R \mathbb{Z}^m_M, \mathbf{e} \leftarrow \mathcal{D}^M_{n,t}, \mathbf{x} := \mathbf{s}\cdot\mathbf{A} + \mathbf{e}\}$$
$$\approx_C \{(\mathbf{A}, \mathbf{x}) \mid \mathbf{A} \leftarrow \mathsf{G}(m, n, M), \mathbf{x} \in_R \mathbb{Z}^n_M\}.$$

There exists two flavours of the LPN assumption; the primal (Definition 1) and the dual (see e.g. [12]).

Informally, the main advantage of the *primal* version of LPN is that there exist practical (and implemented) constructions of the LPN-friendly codes required for this. Specifically, one can choose the code matrix $\mathbf{A}$ from a family of codes G supporting *linear-time* matrix-vector multiplication, such as *d-local linear codes* so that each column of $\mathbf{A}$ has exactly d non-zero entries. According to [1], the hardness of LPN for local linear codes is well-established. Its main disadvantage however, is that its output size can be at most quadratic in the size of the seed, as intuitively, a higher stretch would make it significantly easier for an adversarial verifier to guess enough noiseless coordinates to allow efficient decoding via Gaussian Elimination [4].

The main advantage of the *dual* variant is that it allows for an arbitrary polynomial stretch. However, the compressive mapping used within the dual variant cannot have constant locality and is more challenging to instantiate. Recently, Silver [14] proposed an instantiation of dual-LPN based on structured LDPC codes, which have been practically implemented over finite fields, and may plausibly also work over rings.

Dealing with Reduction Attacks over Rings. When working over a ring $\mathbb{Z}_M$ instead of a finite field, we must take care that the presence of zero divisors does not weaken security. For instance, a simple reduction attack was pointed out in [21], where noise values can become zero after reducing modulo a factor of M (for instance, in $\mathbb{Z}_{2^k}$, reducing the LPN sample modulo 2 cuts the number of noisy coordinates in half, significantly reducing security). To mitigate this attack, we always sample non-zero entries of the error vector $\mathbf{e}$ and matrix $\mathbf{A}$ to be in $\mathbb{Z}_M^*$, that is, invertible mod M.[1] While [21] did not consider the effect on the matrix $\mathbf{A}$, we observe that if $\mathbf{A}$ is sparse then its important to ensure that its sparsity cannot also be decreased through reduction.[2] With these countermeasures, we are not aware of any attacks on LPN in $\mathbb{Z}_M$ that perform better than the field case.

We elaborate below on our choice of primal-LPN distribution.

Choice of Matrix over $\mathbb{Z}_M$. We choose a random, sparse matrix $\mathbf{A}$ with d non-zero entries per column. We choose each non-zero entry randomly from $\mathbb{Z}_M^*$, to ensure that it remains non-zero after reduction modulo any factor of M. We fix the sparsity to $d = 10$, as in previous works [11,24,25], which according to [3,28] suffices to ensure that $\mathbf{A}$ has a large dual distance, which implies the LPN samples are unbiased [14].

Noise Distribution in $\mathbb{Z}_M$. The noise distribution $\mathcal{D}_{n,t}^M$ is chosen to have t expected non-zero coordinates. This can be done on expectation with a Bernoulli distribution, where each coordinate is either zero, or non-zero (and uniform otherwise) with probability t/n. In our applications, we instead use an exact noise weight, where $\mathcal{D}_{n,t}^M$ fixes t non-zero coordinates in the length-n vector.

[1] This countermeasure was missing from the original version of this paper, before [21] was available.

[2] On the other hand, the LPN secret $\mathbf{s}$ must *not* be chosen over $\mathbb{Z}_M^*$, but instead uniformly over $\mathbb{Z}_M$, since if e.g. $\mathbf{s}$ was known to be odd over $\mathbb{Z}_{2^k}$ then solving the reduced instance modulo 2 would be trivial.

Invertible Noise Terms. When working over a ring $\mathbb{Z}_M$, we sample the non-zero noise values to be in $\mathbb{Z}_M^*$, that is, invertible mod M. This prevents the reduction attack mentioned above, which would otherwise reduce the expected noise weight by a factor of two for $M = 2^k$.

Uniform vs Regular Noise Patterns. For fixed-weight noise, we speak of *two types* of error; *regular* or *uniform*. We call uniform errors the case where $\mathcal{D}_{n,t}^M$ is the uniform distribution over all weight-t vectors of $\mathbb{Z}_M^n$ with non-zero values in $\mathbb{Z}_M^*$. Implementing LPN-based PCGs with uniform errors has previously been investigated by [24,27]. It is commonly implemented by utilising a sub-protocol to place a single non-zero value within a vector of length $n' \ll n$ and then using Cuckoo hashing to generate a uniform distribution over n from several of these smaller vectors, ending up with the t points distributed randomly across the n coordinates.

Our construction uses a *regular* noise distribution for the primal-LPN instance. Here, the noise vector in $\mathbb{Z}_M^n$ is divided into t blocks of length $\lfloor n/t \rfloor$, such that each block has exactly one non-zero coordinate. Generally, using LPN with regular errors is practically more efficient than for uniform errors [25,27].

3 Single-Point Vector OLE

Single-point VOLE is a specialized functionality that generates a VOLE correlation $\mathbf{w} = \Delta \cdot \mathbf{u} + \mathbf{v}$ (see Sect. 2.2) where $\mathbf{u}$ has only one non-zero coordinate $\alpha \in [n]$. We consider a variant where u_α is not only non-zero, but additionally also required to be invertible.

We present an ideal functionality for single-point VOLE $\mathcal{F}_{\mathsf{sp\text{-}vole2k}}^{\ell,s}$ in Fig. 4. In the functionality, $\mathsf{P_S}$ obtains $\mathbf{u}, \mathbf{w} \in \mathbb{Z}_{2^\ell}^n \times \mathbb{Z}_{2^\ell}^n$, and $\mathsf{P_R}$ gets $\Delta, \mathbf{v} \in \mathbb{Z}_{2^s} \times \mathbb{Z}_{2^\ell}^n$. As in the full VOLE functionality $\mathcal{F}_{\mathsf{vole2k}}^{\ell,s}$ we allow $\mathsf{P_S}$ to attempt to guess Δ. Additionally, $\mathcal{F}_{\mathsf{sp\text{-}vole2k}}^{\ell,s}$ also allows $\mathsf{P_R}$ to obtain leakage on the non-zero index:

1. $\mathsf{P_R}$ is allowed to guess a set $I \subseteq [n]$ that should contain the index α. Upon correct guess, if $|I| = 1$ then it learns $\mathbf{u}_\alpha$ while if $|I| > 1$ the functionality continues. If $\alpha \notin I$ then the functionality aborts.
2. $\mathsf{P_R}$ is also allowed a second query for a set $J \subset [n]$ that might contain α where $|J| = n/2$. If $\mathsf{P_R}$ guesses correctly then the functionality outputs α, while it aborts otherwise.

The leakage is somewhat inherent to our protocol which we use to realize $\mathcal{F}_{\mathsf{sp\text{-}vole2k}}^{\ell,s}$.

Protocol Overview. Our protocol $\Pi_{\mathsf{sp\text{-}vole2k}}^{\ell,s}$ (Fig. 5) achieves active security using consistency checks inspired by the constructions from [12] and [25]. We now give a high-level overview.

As a setup, we assume functionalities $\mathcal{F}_{\mathsf{vole2k}}^{\ell,s}$, $\mathcal{F}_{\mathsf{OT}}$ and $\mathcal{F}_{\mathsf{EQ}}$. For $\mathcal{F}_{\mathsf{vole2k}}^{\ell,s}$ we assume that $\mathsf{P_R}$ called (Init) already, thus setting Δ. Additionally, we require two pseudorandom generators (PRGs; with certain extra properties that we clarify

Single-Point VOLE for $\mathbb{Z}_{2^\ell}$: $\mathcal{F}^{\ell,s}_{\text{sp-vole2k}}$

This functionality extends the functionality $\mathcal{F}^{\ell,s}_{\text{vole2k}}$ (Fig. 1). In addition to the methods (Init) and (Extend), it also provides the method (SP-Extend) and a modified global-key query.

SP-Extend On input (SP-Extend, n) with $n \in \mathbb{N}$ from both parties the functionality proceeds as follows:

1. Sample $\mathbf{u} \in_R \mathbb{Z}^n_{2^\ell}$ with a single entry invertible modulo 2^ℓ and zeros everywhere else, $\mathbf{v} \in_R \mathbb{Z}^n_{2^\ell}$, and compute $\mathbf{w} := \Delta \cdot \mathbf{u} + \mathbf{v} \in \mathbb{Z}^n_{2^\ell}$.
2. If $\mathsf{P_S}$ is corrupted, receive $\mathbf{u} \in \mathbb{Z}^n_{2^\ell}$ with at most one non-zero entry and $\mathbf{w} \in \mathbb{Z}^n_{2^\ell}$ from $\mathcal{S}$, and recompute $\mathbf{v} := \mathbf{w} - \Delta \cdot \mathbf{u}$.
3. If $\mathsf{P_R}$ is corrupted:
   (a) Receive a set $I \subseteq [n]$ from $\mathcal{S}$. Let $\alpha \in [n]$ be the index of the non-zero entry $\mathbf{u}$, and let $\beta := u_\alpha$. If $I = \{\alpha\}$, then send (success, β) to $\mathsf{P_R}$. If $\alpha \in I$ and $|I| > 1$, then send success to $\mathsf{P_R}$ and continue. Otherwise send abort to both parties and abort.
   (b) Receive either (continue) or (query, J) from $\mathcal{S}$. If (continue) was received, continue with Step 3c. If (query, J) with $J \subset [n]$ and $|J| = \frac{n}{2}$ was received and $\alpha \in J$, then send α to $\mathcal{S}$. Otherwise, send abort to all parties, and abort.
   (c) Receive $\mathbf{v} \in \mathbb{Z}^n_{2^\ell}$ from $\mathcal{S}$, and recompute $\mathbf{w} := \Delta \cdot \mathbf{u} + \mathbf{v}$.
4. Send $(\mathbf{u}, \mathbf{w})$ to $\mathsf{P_S}$ and $\mathbf{v}$ to $\mathsf{P_R}$.

Global-key Query If $\mathsf{P_S}$ is corrupted, receive (Guess, Δ', s') from $\mathcal{S}$ with $s' \leq s$ and $\Delta' \in \mathbb{Z}_{2^{s'}}$. If $\Delta' = \Delta \pmod{2^{s'}}$, send success to $\mathsf{P_S}$. Otherwise, send abort to both parties and abort.

Fig. 4. Ideal functionality for a leaky single-point VOLE.

in Sect. 3.1) to create a GGM tree. Recall, the GGM construction [18] builds a PRF from a length-doubling PRG, by recursively expanding a PRG seed into 2 seeds, defining a complete binary tree where each of the n leaves is one evaluation of the PRF. We use this to build a puncturable PRF, where a subset of intermediate tree nodes is given out, enabling evaluating the PRF at all-but-one of the points in the domain.

The sender $\mathsf{P_S}$ begins by picking a random index α from $[n]$, and β randomly from $\mathbb{Z}^*_{2^\ell}$. This defines the vector $\mathbf{u}$ where $\mathbf{u}_\alpha = \beta$ and every other index is 0. $\mathsf{P_S}$ and $\mathsf{P_R}$ use a single VOLE from $\mathcal{F}^{\ell,s}_{\text{vole2k}}$ to authenticate β, resulting in the receiver holding γ and the sender holding δ, β such that $\delta = \Delta \cdot \beta + \gamma$.

To extend this correlation to the whole vector $\mathbf{u}$, $\mathsf{P_R}$ computes a GGM tree with $2n$ leaves. We consider all n leaves that are "left children" of their parent as comprising the vector $\mathbf{v}$. Using $\log_2(n)$ instances of $\mathcal{F}_{\mathsf{OT}}$, $\mathsf{P_S}$ learns all "right children" as well as all of the "left children" except the one at position α –

meaning that the sender learns $\mathbf{v}$ for all indices except α. $\mathsf{P_S}$ now sets $\mathbf{w}_i = \mathbf{v}_i$ for $i \neq \alpha$. This gives a valid correlation on these $n-1$ positions, because since $\mathbf{u}_i = 0$ for $i \neq \alpha$, we have that $\mathbf{w}_i = \Delta \cdot \mathbf{u}_i + \mathbf{v}_i$.

What remains in the protocol is for $\mathsf{P_S}$ to learn $\mathbf{w}_\alpha = \Delta \cdot \mathbf{u}_\alpha + \mathbf{v}_\alpha$ without revealing α and β to $\mathsf{P_R}$. Using the output of the VOLE instance, if $\mathsf{P_R}$ computes $d \leftarrow \gamma - \sum_{j=1}^{n} \mathbf{v}_j$ and sends d to $\mathsf{P_S}$, then $\mathsf{P_S}$ can compute

$$\begin{aligned}\mathbf{w}_\alpha &= \delta - d - \sum_{j\in[n]\setminus\{\alpha\}} \mathbf{w}_j \\ &= \delta - \Big(\gamma - \sum_{i\in[n]} \mathbf{v}_i\Big) - \sum_{j\in[n]\setminus\{\alpha\}} \mathbf{w}_j \\ &= \delta - \gamma + \mathbf{v}_\alpha = \Delta \cdot \beta + \mathbf{v}_\alpha\end{aligned}$$

which is exactly the missing value for the correlation. While this protocol can somewhat easily be proven secure against a dishonest $\mathsf{P_S}$ (assuming that the hybrid functionalities are actively secure), a corrupted $\mathsf{P_R}$ can cheat in two ways:

1. It can provide inconsistent GGM tree values to the $\mathcal{F}_{\mathsf{OT}}$ instances, thus leading to unpredictable protocol behavior.
2. It can construct d incorrectly.

To ensure a "somewhat consistent" GGM tree (and inputs to $\mathcal{F}_{\mathsf{OT}}$) we use a check that sacrifices all the leaves that are "right children". Here, $\mathsf{P_R}$ has to send a random linear combination of these, over a binary extension field, with $\mathsf{P_S}$ choosing the coefficients. The check makes sure that if it passes, then the "left children" are consistent for every choice of α that would have made $\mathsf{P_S}$ not abort. This reduces arbitrary leakage to an essentially unavoidable selective failure attack (due to the use of $\mathcal{F}_{\mathsf{OT}}$).

To prevent the second attack, the sender and receiver use an additional VOLE from $\mathcal{F}_{\mathsf{vole2k}}^{\ell,s}$ and perform a random linear combination check to ensure correctness of the value d. Due to the binary coefficients used in the linear combination over $\mathbb{Z}_{2^\ell}$, our check only has soundness 1/2. This, however, suffices to prove security if we relax the functionality by allowing a corrupt receiver to learn α with probability 1/2. This way, in the simulation in our security proof, if the challenge vector $\boldsymbol{\chi}$ is such that the receiver passes the check despite cheating, the simulator can still extract a valid input using its knowledge of α.

The full protocol is presented in Fig. 5. Before proving security of it, we first recap the Puncturable PRF from GGM construction and its security properties.

3.1 Checking Consistency of the GGM Construction

We use the GGM [19] construction to implement a puncturable PRF F with domain $[n]$ and range $\{0,1\}^\kappa$.

In a puncturable PRF (PPRF), one party $\mathsf{P_1}$ generates a PRF key k, and then both parties engage in a protocol where the second party $\mathsf{P_2}$ obtains a punctured key $k\{\alpha\}$ for an index $\alpha \in [n]$ of its choice. With $k\{\alpha\}$, it is possible

Single-Point VOLE for $\mathbb{Z}_{2^\ell}$: $\Pi^{\ell,s}_{\text{sp-vole2k}}$

For the (Init) and (Extend) operations, the parties simply query $\mathcal{F}^{\ell,s}_{\text{vole2k}}$.

SP-Extend For (SP-Extend, n): Let $h := \lceil \log n \rceil$ and $\sigma' := \sigma + 2h$.

1. The parties send (Extend, 1) to $\mathcal{F}^{\ell,s}_{\text{vole2k}}$. $\mathsf{P_S}$ receives $a, c \in \mathbb{Z}_{2^\ell}$ and $\mathsf{P_R}$ receives $b \in \mathbb{Z}_{2^\ell}$ such that $c = \Delta \cdot a + b \pmod{2^\ell}$ holds.
2. $\mathsf{P_S}$ samples $\alpha \in_R [n], \beta \in_R \mathbb{Z}^*_{2^\ell}$ and lets $\mathbf{u} \in \mathbb{Z}^n_{2^\ell}$ be the vector with $u_\alpha = \beta$ and $u_i = 0$ for all $i \neq \alpha$.
3. $\mathsf{P_S}$ sets $\delta := c$ and sends $a' := \beta - a \in \mathbb{Z}_{2^\ell}$ to $\mathsf{P_R}$. $\mathsf{P_R}$ computes $\gamma := b - \Delta \cdot a' \in \mathbb{Z}_{2^\ell}$. Now, $\delta = \Delta \cdot \beta + \gamma \pmod{2^\ell}$.
4. $\mathsf{P_R}$ computes $k \leftarrow \mathsf{GGM.KeyGen}(1^\kappa)$, runs $(\mathbf{v}, \mathbf{t}, (\overline{K}^i_0, \overline{K}^i_1)_{i\in[h]}, \overline{K}^{h+1}_1) \leftarrow \mathsf{GGM.Gen}(n, k)$, and sends $\overline{K}^{h+1} := \overline{K}^{h+1}_1 \in \mathbb{F}_{2^{\sigma'}}$ to $\mathsf{P_S}$.
5. Write $\alpha = \sum_{i=0}^{h-1} 2^i \cdot \alpha_{h-i}$, for $\alpha_i \in \{0,1\}$. For $i \in [h]$, the parties call $\mathcal{F}_{\mathsf{OT}}$ where $\mathsf{P_S}$, acting as the receiver, inputs $\overline{\alpha}_i$ and $\mathsf{P_R}$ inputs $(\overline{K}^i_0, \overline{K}^i_1)_{i\in[h]}$ to $\mathcal{F}_{\mathsf{OT}}$. $\mathsf{P_S}$ receives $\overline{K}^i := \overline{K}^i_{\overline{\alpha}_i}$.
6. *Check the GGM tree:*
   (a) $\mathsf{P_S}$ samples $\boldsymbol{\xi} \in_R \mathbb{F}^n_{2^{\sigma'}}$ and sends $\boldsymbol{\xi}$ to $\mathsf{P_R}$.[a]
   (b) $\mathsf{P_R}$ computes $\Gamma := \langle \boldsymbol{\xi}, \mathbf{t} \rangle \in \mathbb{F}_{2^{\sigma'}}$ and sends Γ to $\mathsf{P_S}$.
   (c) $\mathsf{P_S}$ runs $\mathbf{v}^\alpha \leftarrow \mathsf{GGM.PuncEval}(n, \alpha, (\overline{K}^i)_{i\in[h+1]})$ followed by $\mathsf{GGM.Check}(n, \alpha, (\overline{K}^i)_{i\in[h+1]}, \boldsymbol{\xi}, \Gamma)$. If the latter returns $\bot$, $\mathsf{P_S}$ aborts. Otherwise it has obtained $(v_j)_{j\in[n]\setminus\{\alpha\}}$.
7. $\mathsf{P_R}$ sends $d := \gamma - \sum_{j=1}^n v_j \in \mathbb{Z}_{2^\ell}$ to $\mathsf{P_S}$. $\mathsf{P_S}$ defines $\mathbf{w} \in \mathbb{Z}^n_{2^\ell}$ such that $w_j := v_j$ for $j \in [n]\setminus\{\alpha\}$ and $w_\alpha := \delta - d - \sum_{1\le j\le n, j\neq\alpha} w_j$. Then $\mathbf{w} = \Delta \cdot \mathbf{u} + \mathbf{v}$.
8. *Check consistency of d:*
   (a) The parties send (Extend, 1) to $\mathcal{F}^{\ell,s}_{\text{vole2k}}$. $\mathsf{P_S}$ receives $x, z \in \mathbb{Z}_{2^\ell}$ and $\mathsf{P_R}$ receives $y^* \in \mathbb{Z}_{2^\ell}$ such that $z = \Delta \cdot x + y^* \pmod{2^\ell}$ holds.
   (b) $\mathsf{P_S}$ samples $\boldsymbol{\chi} \in_R \{0,1\}^n$ with $\mathrm{HW}(\boldsymbol{\chi}) = \frac{n}{2}$ and sends it to $\mathsf{P_R}$.[b]
   (c) $\mathsf{P_S}$ computes $x^* := \chi_\alpha \cdot \beta - x \in \mathbb{Z}_{2^\ell}$ and sends x^* to $\mathsf{P_R}$. $\mathsf{P_R}$ computes $y := y^* - \Delta \cdot x^* \in \mathbb{Z}_{2^\ell}$. Then $z = y + \Delta \cdot \chi_\alpha \cdot \beta$.
   (d) $\mathsf{P_S}$ computes $V_{\mathsf{P_S}} := \sum_{i=1}^n \chi_i \cdot w_i - z$, and $\mathsf{P_R}$ computes $V_{\mathsf{P_R}} := \sum_{i=1}^n \chi_i \cdot v_i - y$. They send $V_{\mathsf{P_S}}, V_{\mathsf{P_R}}$ to $\mathcal{F}_{\mathsf{EQ}}$. If it returns (abort), then abort.
9. $\mathsf{P_S}$ outputs $(\mathbf{u}, \mathbf{w})$, and $\mathsf{P_R}$ outputs $\mathbf{v}$.

[a] Instead of sending the whole vector $\boldsymbol{\xi}$, $\mathsf{P_S}$ can send a κ bit random seed which is then expanded with a PRG to obtain $\boldsymbol{\xi}$.

[b] Again, $\mathsf{P_S}$ can send a short seed instead of $\boldsymbol{\chi}$.

Fig. 5. Protocol instantiating $\mathcal{F}^{\ell,s}_{\text{sp-vole2k}}$ in the $(\mathcal{F}^{\ell,s}_{\text{vole2k}}, \mathcal{F}_{\mathsf{OT}}, \mathcal{F}_{\mathsf{EQ}})$-hybrid model.

for P_2 to evaluate F at all points $[n] \setminus \{\alpha\}$ so that $F(k, i) = F(k\{\alpha\}, i)$ for $i \neq \alpha$, while nothing about $F(k, \alpha)$ is revealed. More formally:

Definition 2 (Adapted from [12]). *A puncturable pseudorandom function (PPRF) with keyspace $\mathcal{K}$, domain $[n]$ and range $\{0,1\}^\kappa$ is a pseudorandom function F with an additional keyspace $\mathcal{K}_p$ and 3 PPT algorithms* KeyGen, Gen, PuncEval *such that*

KeyGen *on input 1^κ outputs a random key $k \in \mathcal{K}$.*
Gen *on input n, k outputs $\{F(k, i), k\{i\}\}_{i \in [n]}$ where $k\{i\} \in \mathcal{K}_p$.*
PuncEval *on input $n, \alpha, k\{\alpha\}$ outputs $\mathbf{v}^\alpha$ such that $\mathbf{v}^\alpha \in (\{0,1\}^\kappa)^n$.*

where $F(k, i) = \mathbf{v}_i^\alpha$ for all $i \neq \alpha$ and no PPT adversary $\mathcal{A}$, given $n, \alpha, k\{\alpha\}$ as input, can distinguish $F(k, \alpha)$ from a uniformly random value in $\{0,1\}^\kappa$ except with probability $\mathsf{negl}(\kappa)$.

For simplicity, we describe the algorithms for domains of size $n = 2^h$ for some $h \in \mathbb{N}$. By pruning the tree appropriately, the procedures can be adapted to support domain sizes that are not powers of two. Throughout the coming sections, we let $\alpha_1, \ldots, \alpha_h$ be the bit decomposition of $\alpha = \sum_{i=0}^{h-1} 2^i \cdot \alpha_{h-i}$, and let $\overline{\alpha}_i$ denote the complement. Let κ be a computational and σ be a statistical security parameter. Define $\sigma' := \sigma + 2\log n$ and let $\mathsf{G}\colon \{0,1\}^\kappa \to \{0,1\}^{2\kappa}$ and $\mathsf{G}'\colon \{0,1\}^\kappa \to \mathbb{Z}_{2^\ell} \times \mathbb{F}_{2^{\sigma'}}$ be two PRGs.

Recall that to achieve malicious security when generating a PPRF key in our protocol, we use the redundancy introduced from extending the domain to size $2n$, and check consistency by letting the receiver provide a hash of all the right leaves of the GGM tree. In order for the right leaves of the GGM tree to fix a unique tree, we require the PRG used for the final layer $\mathsf{G}'\colon \{0,1\}^\kappa \to \mathbb{Z}_{2^\ell} \times \mathbb{F}_{2^{\sigma'}}$ to satisfy the *right-half injectivity* property[3] as defined below.

Definition 3. *We say that a function $f = (f_0, f_1)\colon \{0,1\}^\kappa \to \mathbb{Z}_{2^\ell} \times \mathbb{F}_{2^{\sigma'}}, x \mapsto (f_0(x), f_1(x))$ is* right-half injective, *if its restriction to the right-half of the output space $f_1\colon \{0,1\}^\kappa \to \mathbb{F}_{2^{\sigma'}}$ is injective.*

In order to achieve active security of our construction, we provide an additional algorithm Check, together with a finite challenge set Ξ. This algorithm, on input $n, \alpha, k\{\alpha\}$, a challenge ξ and a checking value Γ outputs $\top$ or $\bot$.

Definition 4 (PPRF consistency). *Let F be a PPRF and let Ξ be a challenge set whose size depends on a statistical security parameter σ. Consider the following game for* Check*:*

1. $(k\{1\}, \ldots, k\{n\}, \mathsf{state}) \leftarrow \mathcal{A}(1^\kappa, n)$.
2. $\xi \in_R \Xi$
3. $\Gamma \leftarrow \mathcal{A}(1^\kappa, \mathsf{state}, \xi)$
4. *For all $\alpha \in [n]$, let* $\mathbf{v}^\alpha \leftarrow \mathsf{PuncEval}(1^\kappa, \alpha, k\{\alpha\})$.

[3] As noted in [12], this can be replaced with a weaker notion of right-half collision resistance, which is easier to achieve in practice.

5. *Define* $I := \{\alpha \in [n] \mid \top = \mathsf{Check}(n, \alpha, k\{\alpha\}, \xi, \Gamma)\}$.
6. *We say* $\mathcal{A}$ *wins the game if there exists* $\alpha \neq \alpha' \in I$ *such that there is an index* $i \in [n] \setminus \{\alpha, \alpha'\}$ *with* $v_i^{\alpha} \neq v_i^{\alpha'}$.

We say that F has consistency *if no algorithm* $\mathcal{A}$ *wins the above game with probability more than* $2^{-\sigma}$.

Our algorithms $\mathsf{GGM.KeyGen}$, $\mathsf{GGM.Gen}$, $\mathsf{GGM.PuncEval}$, $\mathsf{GGM.Check}$, which are used to generate the key, set up the punctured keys, evaluate and check consistency of the punctured keys in our protocol are then as follows:

1. $\mathsf{GGM.KeyGen}(1^\kappa)$ samples $k \in \{0,1\}^\kappa$ uniformly at random and outputs it.
2. $\mathsf{GGM.Gen}(n, k)$ where $n = 2^h$ and $k \in \{0,1\}^\kappa$ is a key:
   (a) Set $K_0^0 \leftarrow k$.
   (b) For each level $i \in [h]$, and for $j \in \{0, \ldots, 2^{i-1} - 1\}$ compute $(K_{2j}^i, K_{2j+1}^i) \leftarrow \mathsf{G}(K_j^{i-1})$.
   (c) For $i \in [h]$, set $\overline{K}_0^i \leftarrow \bigoplus_{j=0}^{2^{i-1}-1} K_{2j}^i$ and $\overline{K}_1^i \leftarrow \bigoplus_{j=0}^{2^{i-1}-1} K_{2j+1}^i$.
   (d) For $j \in [2^h]$ compute $v_j, t_j \leftarrow \mathsf{G}'(K_{j-1}^h)$, and set $\mathbf{v} := (v_1, \ldots, v_{2^h})$ and $\mathbf{t} := (t_1, \ldots, t_{2^h})$.
   (e) Compute $\overline{K}_1^{h+1} \leftarrow \sum_{j \in [2^h]} t_i$.
   (f) Output $(\mathbf{v}, \mathbf{t}, (\overline{K}_0^i, \overline{K}_1^i)_{i \in [h]}, \overline{K}_1^{h+1})$.
3. $\mathsf{GGM.PuncEval}(n, \alpha, (\overline{K}^i)_{i \in [h+1]})$ where $n = 2^h$, $\alpha \in [n]$, and $\overline{K}^i \in \{0,1\}^\kappa$:
   (a) Set $K_{\overline{\alpha}_1}^1 \leftarrow \overline{K}^1$.
   (b) For each level $i \in \{2, \ldots, h\}$:
      i. Let $x := \sum_{j=1}^{i-1} 2^{j-1} \cdot \alpha_{i-j}$
      ii. For $j \in \{0, \ldots, 2^{i-1} - 1\} \setminus \{x\}$, compute $(K_{2j}^i, K_{2j+1}^i) \leftarrow \mathsf{G}(K_j^{i-1})$.
      iii. Compute $K_{2x+\overline{\alpha}_i}^i \leftarrow \overline{K}^i \oplus \bigoplus_{\substack{0 \le j < 2^{i-1} \\ j \neq x}} K_{2j+\overline{\alpha}_i}^i$.
   (c) For the last level $h+1$:
      i. For $j \in [2^h] \setminus \{\alpha\}$ compute $(v_j, t_j) \leftarrow \mathsf{G}'(K_{j-1}^h)$
   (d) Output $(v_j)_{j \in [2^h] \setminus \{\alpha\}}$.
4. $\mathsf{GGM.Check}(n, \alpha, (\overline{K}^i)_{i \in [h+1]}, (\xi_i)_{i \in [n]}, \Gamma)$ where $n = 2^h$, and $\overline{K}^i \in \{0,1\}^\kappa$, $\xi_i \in \mathbb{F}_{2^{\sigma'}}$, and $\Gamma \in \mathbb{F}_{2^{\sigma'}}$:
   (a) For $j \in [2^h] \setminus \{\alpha\}$ recompute t_j as in $\mathsf{GGM.PuncEval}$.
   (b) Compute $t_\alpha \leftarrow \overline{K}^{h+1} - \sum_{j \in [2^h] \setminus \{\alpha\}} t_j$.
   (c) If $\Gamma = \sum_{i \in [n]} \xi_i \cdot t_i$, output $\top$. Otherwise, output $\perp$.

In comparison to Definition 2 $\mathsf{GGM.Gen}$ computes a compressed version of all keys. The pseudorandomness for GGM, as defined in Definition 2, follows from the standard pseudorandomness argument of the GGM construction [10,13,20].

The following theorem shows that the check ensures that a corrupted P_1 cannot create an inconsistent GGM tree, where P_2 obtains different values depending on α. We give the proof in the full version [6].

Theorem 5 (Consistency of the GGM Tree). *Let* $n = 2^h \in \mathbb{N}$, $\sigma' = \sigma + 2h$, *and* G, G' *as above, and let* $\mathcal{A}$ *be any time adversary. If* G' *is right-half injective, then* $\mathcal{A}$ *can win the game in Definition 4 with probability at most* $2^{-(\sigma+1)}$.

3.2 Security of $\Pi^{\ell,s}_{\mathsf{sp\text{-}vole2k}}$

Theorem 6. *The protocol* $\Pi^{\ell,s}_{\mathsf{sp\text{-}vole2k}}$ *(Fig. 5) securely realizes the functionality* $\mathcal{F}^{\ell,s}_{\mathsf{sp\text{-}vole2k}}$ *in the* $(\mathcal{F}^{\ell,s}_{\mathsf{vole2k}}, \mathcal{F}_{\mathsf{OT}}, \mathcal{F}_{\mathsf{EQ}})$*-hybrid model: No PPT environment* $\mathcal{Z}$ *can distinguish the real execution of the protocol from a simulated one except with probability* $2^{-(\sigma+1)} + \mathsf{negl}(\kappa)$.

In the proof, we construct simulators for a corrupted sender and receiver. For the corrupted sender, the simulator follows the protocol by behaving like an honest receiver, but additionally extracts α from the interactions of the dishonest sender with $\mathcal{F}_{\mathsf{OT}}$ and β from the VOLE. Its choice of GGM tree as well as other messages are used to define a consistent vector $\mathbf{w}$ that it sends to the functionality. A subtlety here is simulating the equality check in Step 8d of the protocol, as a corrupt sender can pass this with an ill-formed x^* if it can guess a portion of Δ used in the VOLE-functionality correctly. The simulator must make a key query to $\mathcal{F}^{\ell,s}_{\mathsf{sp\text{-}vole2k}}$ to simulate the success event correctly. Another issue is that d sent by an honest receiver has a different distribution than how it is chosen in the simulation, but we show that any distinguisher can break the pseudorandomness of the GGM PPRF.

In the simulation for the corrupted receiver, the simulator first translates $\mathcal{F}_{\mathsf{OT}}$ inputs into leakage queries to the functionality. For this, we know that due to Step 6c any adversarial choice leads to consistent GGM tree leaves, so the simulator chooses the set of indices where the check in this Step would pass as leakage input to the functionality $\mathcal{F}^{\ell,s}_{\mathsf{sp\text{-}vole2k}}$. This query then allows the simulator to create a valid transcript: if the attacker guessed α exactly correct (the set is of size 1), then the simulator obtains β from the functionality and can directly follow the protocol with the honest inputs. If the adversary instead guessed a set of size > 1 correctly that contains the secret α, then the simulator can reconstruct the whole GGM tree and thus a potential input $\mathbf{v}$. This furthermore allows the simulator to detect an inconsistent d that is sent by the corrupt receiver. An inconsistent d can be shown to translate into a selective failure attack on the equality check in Step 8d of the protocol, which requires the simulator to make the second leakage query. If it succeeds, then it obtains α and can adjust $\mathbf{v}_\alpha$ accordingly.

The full proof of Theorem 6, together with a summary of the protocol complexity, can be found in the full version [6].

4 Vector OLE Construction

Given our single-point VOLE protocol, we build a protocol for random VOLE extension over $\mathbb{Z}_{2^\ell}$ by running t single-point instances of length n/t, and concatenating their outputs to obtain a weight t VOLE correlation of length n. Then, these (together with some additional VOLEs) can be extended into pseudorandom VOLEs by applying the primal LPN assumption over $\mathbb{Z}_{2^\ell}$ with regular noise vectors of weight t. Since our single-point protocol introduces some leakage on the hidden point, we need to rely on a variant of LPN with some leakage on the regular noise coordinates.

4.1 Leaky Regular LPN Assumption

The assumption, below, translates the leakage from the single-point VOLE functionality (Fig. 4) into leakage on the LPN error vector. Note that there are two separate leakage queries: the first of these allows the adversary to try and guess a single predicate on the entire noise vector, and aborts if this guess is incorrect. This is similar to previous works [12,25], and essentially only leaks 1 bit of information on average on the position of the non-zero entries. The second query, in Step 5 is more powerful, since for each query made by the adversary, the exact position of one noise coordinate is leaked with probability 1/2. Intuitively, this means that up to c coordinates of the error vector can be leaked with probability 2^{-c}.

Definition 7. *Let $\mathbf{A} \leftarrow \mathsf{G}(m, n, 2^\ell) \in \mathbb{Z}_{2^\ell}^{m \times n}$ be a primal-LPN matrix, and consider the following game $G_b(\kappa)$ with a PPT adversary $\mathcal{A}$, parameterized by a bit b and security parameter κ:*

1. *Sample $\mathbf{e} = (\mathbf{e}_1, \dots, \mathbf{e}_t) \leftarrow \mathbb{Z}_{2^\ell}^n$, where each sub-vector $\mathbf{e}_i \in \mathbb{Z}_{2^\ell}^{n/t}$ has exactly one non-zero entry in $\mathbb{Z}_{2^\ell}^*$, in position α_i, and sample $\mathbf{s} \leftarrow \mathbb{Z}_{2^\ell}^m$ uniformly*
2. *$\mathcal{A}$ sends sets $I_1, \dots, I_t \subset [n/t]$*
3. *If $\alpha_j \in I_j$ for all $j \in [t]$, send OK to $\mathcal{A}$, otherwise abort. Additionally, for any j where $|I_j| = 1$, send $\mathbf{e}_j$ to $\mathcal{A}$*
4. *$\mathcal{A}$ sends sets $J_1, \dots, J_t \subset [n/t]$*
5. *For each J_i where $|J_i| = n/(2t)$: if $\alpha_i \in J_i$, send α_i to $\mathcal{A}$, otherwise abort*
6. *Let $\mathbf{y}_0 = \mathbf{s} \cdot \mathbf{A} + \mathbf{e}$ and sample $\mathbf{y}_1 \leftarrow \mathbb{Z}_{2^\ell}^n$*
7. *Send $\mathbf{y}_b$ to $\mathcal{A}$*
8. *$\mathcal{A}$ outputs a bit b' (if the game aborted, set the output to $\perp$)*

The assumption is that $|\Pr[\mathcal{A}^{G_0(\kappa)} = 1] - \Pr[\mathcal{A}^{G_1(\kappa)} = 1]|$ is negligible in κ.

4.2 Vector OLE Protocol

Our complete VOLE protocol is given in Fig. 6. It realises the functionality $\mathcal{F}_{\mathsf{vole2k}}^{\ell,s}$ (Fig. 1), which is the same functionality used for base VOLEs in our single-point protocol. This allows us to use the same kind of "bootstrapping" mechanism as [25], where a portion of the produced VOLE outputs is reserved to be used as the base VOLEs in the next iteration of the protocol.

In the Init phase of the protocol, the parties create a base VOLE of length m, defining the random LPN secret $\mathbf{u}$, given to the sender, and the scalar Δ, given to the receiver. Then, in each call to Extend, the parties run t instances of $\mathcal{F}_{\mathsf{sp\text{-}vole2k}}^{\ell,s}$ to generate $\mathbf{c} = (c_1, \dots, c_t)$ and $\mathbf{e} = (e_1, \dots, e_t)$ for the sender and $\mathbf{b} = (b_1, \dots, b_t)$ for the receiver. The sender then simply computes $\mathbf{x} \leftarrow \mathbf{u} \cdot \mathbf{A} + \mathbf{e} \in \mathbb{Z}_{2^r}^n$ and $\mathbf{z} \leftarrow \mathbf{w} \cdot \mathbf{A} + \mathbf{c} \in \mathbb{Z}_{2^r}^n$ and the receiver computes $\mathbf{y} = \mathbf{v} \cdot \mathbf{A} + \mathbf{b} \in \mathbb{Z}_{2^r}^n$. This results in the sender holding $\mathbf{x}, \mathbf{z}$ and the receiver holding $\mathbf{y}$ such that $\mathbf{z} = \mathbf{x} \cdot \Delta + \mathbf{y}$. The first m entries of these are reserved to define a fresh LPN secret for the next call to Extend, while the remainder are output by the parties.[4]

VOLE for $\mathbb{Z}_{2^k}$: $\Pi^{\ell,s}_{\mathsf{vole2k}}$

Parameters Fix some parameters:
- n: LPN output size
- m: LPN secret size
- t: number of error coordinates for LPN (assume that $t \mid n$)
- n/t: size of a block in regular LPN
- $\mathbf{A} \in \mathbb{Z}_{2^\ell}^{m \times n}$ is the generator matrix used in primal-LPN

Init This must be called by the parties first and is executed once.
1. $\mathsf{P_S}$ and $\mathsf{P_R}$ send (Init) to $\mathcal{F}^{\ell,s}_{\mathsf{sp\text{-}vole2k}}$, and $\mathsf{P_R}$ receives $\Delta \in \mathbb{Z}_{2^s}$.
2. $\mathsf{P_S}$ and $\mathsf{P_R}$ send (Extend, m) to $\mathcal{F}^{\ell,s}_{\mathsf{sp\text{-}vole2k}}$. $\mathsf{P_S}$ receives $\mathbf{u}, \mathbf{w} \in \mathbb{Z}_{2^\ell}^m$, and $\mathsf{P_R}$ receives $\mathbf{v} \in \mathbb{Z}_{2^\ell}^m$, such that $\mathbf{w} = \Delta \cdot \mathbf{u} + \mathbf{v}$ over $\mathbb{Z}_{2^\ell}$.

Extend This protocol can be executed multiple times.
1. For $i \in [t]$, $\mathsf{P_S}$ and $\mathsf{P_R}$ send $(\mathsf{SP\text{-}Extend}, n/t)$ to $\mathcal{F}^{\ell,s}_{\mathsf{sp\text{-}vole2k}}$ which returns $\mathbf{e}_i, \mathbf{c}_i$ to $\mathsf{P_S}$ and $\mathbf{b}_i$ to $\mathsf{P_R}$ such that $\mathbf{c}_i = \Delta \cdot \mathbf{e}_i + \mathbf{b}_i$ over $\mathbb{Z}_{2^\ell}^{n/t}$, and $\mathbf{e}_i \in \mathbb{Z}_{2^\ell}^{n/t}$ has exactly one entry invertible modulo 2^ℓ and zeros everywhere else.
2. Define $\mathbf{e} := (\mathbf{e}_1, \ldots, \mathbf{e}_t) \in \mathbb{Z}_{2^\ell}^n$, $\mathbf{c} := (\mathbf{c}_1, \ldots, \mathbf{c}_t) \in \mathbb{Z}_{2^\ell}^n$, and $\mathbf{b} := (\mathbf{b}_1, \ldots, \mathbf{b}_t) \in \mathbb{Z}_{2^\ell}^n$. Then $\mathsf{P_S}$ computes $\mathbf{x} := \mathbf{u} \cdot \mathbf{A} + \mathbf{e} \in \mathbb{Z}_{2^\ell}^n$, and $\mathbf{z} := \mathbf{w} \cdot \mathbf{A} + \mathbf{c} \in \mathbb{Z}_{2^\ell}^n$. $\mathsf{P_R}$ computes $\mathbf{y} := \mathbf{v} \cdot \mathbf{A} + \mathbf{b} \in \mathbb{Z}_{2^\ell}^n$.
3. $\mathsf{P_S}$ updates $\mathbf{u}, \mathbf{w}$ by setting $\mathbf{u} := \mathbf{x}[0 : m) \in \mathbb{Z}_{2^\ell}^m$ and $\mathbf{w} := \mathbf{z}[0 : m) \in \mathbb{Z}_{2^\ell}^m$, and outputs $(\mathbf{x}[m : n), \mathbf{z}[m : n)) \in \mathbb{Z}_{2^\ell}^\ell \times \mathbb{Z}_{2^\ell}^\ell$. $\mathsf{P_R}$ updates $\mathbf{v}$ by setting $\mathbf{v} := \mathbf{y}[0 : m) \in \mathbb{Z}_{2^\ell}^m$ and outputs $\mathbf{y}[m : n) \in \mathbb{Z}_{2^\ell}^\ell$.

Fig. 6. Protocol for VOLE over $\mathbb{Z}_{2^k}$ in the $\mathcal{F}^{\ell,s}_{\mathsf{sp\text{-}vole2k}}$-hybrid model. Based on [25].

Theorem 8. *The protocol $\Pi^{\ell,s}_{\mathsf{vole2k}}$ in Fig. 6 securely realizes the functionality $\mathcal{F}^{\ell,s}_{\mathsf{vole2k}}$ in the $\mathcal{F}^{\ell,s}_{\mathsf{sp\text{-}vole2k}}$-hybrid model, under the leaky regular LPN assumption.*

The proof, given in the full version [6], is straightforward for the malicious sender, and for the malicious receiver we translate the protocol into an instance of primal LPN from Definition 1, which yields indistinguishability.

Communication Complexity. When we instantiate the single-point VOLE with our protocol $\Pi^{\ell,s}_{\mathsf{sp\text{-}vole2k}}$ from Sect. 3, use the equality test sketched in Sect. 2.3, and Silent OT [12,14,27], our VOLE extension protocol $\Pi^{\ell,s}_{\mathsf{vole2k}}$ with

[4] In our implementation, we actually reserve $m + 2t$ of the outputs, since we need 2 extra VOLEs for each execution of the protocol for $\mathcal{F}^{\ell,s}_{\mathsf{sp\text{-}vole2k}}$.

LPN parameters, (m, t, n) requires $m + 2t$ base VOLEs and $4t\ell + 2t\sigma + 4t\lceil \log n/t \rceil + (5 + 2\lceil \log n/t \rceil)t\kappa$ bit of communication. The costs for the single-point VOLE protocol are broken down in the full version [6].

5 QuarkSilver: QuickSilver Modulo 2^k

We now construct the QuarkSilver zero-knowledge proof system, which is based on a similar principle as the QuickSilver protocol. The main technique to achieve soundness in QuickSilver [26], similar to LPZK [16], is that a dishonest prover can only cheat in multiplication checks if it can come up with a quadratic polynomial of a certain form, which has a root Δ unknown to the prover. This is straightforward over fields, but over $\mathbb{Z}_{2^k}$ there might be many more than just two roots for a polynomial. Before constructing the zero-knowledge protocol, we therefore give upper-bounds on the number of roots of certain quadratic polynomials over $\mathbb{Z}_{2^k}$.

5.1 Bounding the Number of Solutions to Quadratic Equations

In the following theorem, we analyze a security game that corresponds to our amortized check for verifying t multiplications. At the core of this, we need to upper bound the number of solutions to quadratic equations in $\mathbb{Z}_{2^\ell}$, where both the coefficients and solutions are bounded in certain ways.

Theorem 9. *Let $\ell, s, k \in \mathbb{N}^+$ so that $\ell \geq k+2s$ and consider the following game between a challenger $\mathcal{C}$ and an adversary $\mathcal{A}$:*

1. *$\mathcal{C}$ chooses $\Delta \in \mathbb{Z}_{2^s}$ uniformly at random.*
2. *$\mathcal{A}$ sends $\delta_0, \ldots, \delta_t \in \mathbb{Z}$ such that not all δ_i for $i > 0$ are $0 \bmod 2^k$.*
3. *$\mathcal{C}$ chooses $\chi_1, \ldots, \chi_t \leftarrow \mathbb{Z}_{2^s}$ uniformly at random and sends these to $\mathcal{A}$.*
4. *$\mathcal{A}$ sends $b, c \in \mathbb{Z}$.*
5. *$\mathcal{A}$ wins iff $(\delta_0 + \sum_i \chi_i \delta_i)\Delta^2 + b\Delta + c = 0 \bmod 2^\ell$.*

Then $\mathcal{A}$ can win with probability at most $(\ell - k + 2) \cdot 2^{-s+1}$.

The proof of Theorem 9 follows a similar way as Lemma 1 of [15]. The key observation is that Step 3 determines an upper-bound on r, the largest number such that 2^r divides all coefficients of the polynomial. This is because no choice of b, c can increase r as it also must divide the leading coefficient, which is randomized. By the random choice of the χ_i, one can show that the larger r is, the smaller the chance that it divides $\delta_0 + \sum_i \chi_i \delta_i$.

Since a larger r leads to more roots of the polynomial, we can then bound the overall attack success for each possible r. The full proof can be found in the full version [6], where we also show the following corollary.

Corollary 10. *Let $\sigma \geq 7$ be a statistical security parameter. By setting $s := \sigma + \log \sigma + 3$ and $\ell := k + 2s$, any adversary $\mathcal{A}$ can win the game from Theorem 9 with probability at most $2^{-\sigma}$.*

5.2 QuarkSilver

We now construct the QuarkSilver zero-knowledge proof system. Its main building block are linearly homomorphic commitments instantiated from VOLEs over $\mathbb{Z}_{2^\ell}$.

Linearly Homomorphic Commitments. As in the A2B [5] zero-knowledge protocols, we use linearly homomorphic commitments from VOLE to authenticate values in $\mathbb{Z}_{2^k}$: Define a commitment $[x]$ to a value $x \in \mathbb{Z}_{2^k}$ known to the prover by a global key $\Delta \in_R \mathbb{Z}_{2^s}$ and values $K[x], M[x] \in_R \mathbb{Z}_{2^\ell}$ with $\ell \geq k + s$ so that

$$K[x] = M[x] + \widetilde{x} \cdot \Delta \pmod{2^\ell} \tag{1}$$

holds for $\widetilde{x} = x \pmod{2^k}$. Here the prover knows $\widetilde{x}$ and $M[x]$, and the verifier knows Δ and $K[x]$. To open the commitment, the prover reveals $\widetilde{x}, K[x]$ to the verifier who checks that the aforementioned equalities hold.

The commitment scheme is linearly homomorphic, as no interaction is needed to compute $[a \cdot x + b]$ from $[x]$ for publicly known $a, b \in \mathbb{Z}_{2^k}$: $\mathcal{P}, \mathcal{V}$ simply update $\widetilde{x}, K[x]$ and $M[x]$ in the appropriate way modulo 2^ℓ. The same linearity also holds when adding commitments. Unfortunately, the upper $\ell - k$ bits of $\widetilde{x}$ may not be uniformly random when opening a commitment. To resolve this, the prover instead opens $[x + 2^k y]$ using a random commitment $[y]$.

How QuarkSilver Works. QuarkSilver follows the established commit-and-prove paradigm for zero-knowledge proofs. For the commitments, we use the linearly homomorphic commitments described above. For a circuit with n inputs and t multiplications, we start by generating $n + t + 2$ authenticated random values $[r_1], \ldots, [r_{n+t+2}]$ with $\widetilde{r}_i \in_R \mathbb{Z}_{2^\ell}$ for $i \in [n + t + 2]$, i.e. commitments to random values. For this, $\mathcal{P}$ and $\mathcal{V}$ call (Extend, $n + t + 2$) to $\mathcal{F}_{\mathsf{vole2k}}^{\ell,s}$. $\mathcal{P}$ then commits to $\mathbf{w}$ using the first n random commitments. Next, the parties evaluate the circuit topologically, computing commitments to the outputs of linear gates using the homomorphism of $[\cdot]$. For each multiplication gate, $\mathcal{P}$ commits to the output using another unused random commitment. It then remains to show that the commitment to the output of the circuit is a commitment to 1 and that all committed outputs of multiplication gates are indeed consistent with the committed inputs.

To verify the committed output wire, QuarkSilver uses the "blinded opening" procedure that was introduced above. This procedure will consume another random commitment. To check validity of a multiplication, observe that for 3 commitments $[w_\alpha], [w_\beta], [w_\gamma]$ with $\gamma = \alpha \cdot \beta \bmod 2^k$ it holds that

$$\underbrace{K[w_\alpha] \cdot K[w_\beta] - \Delta \cdot K[w_\gamma]}_{B} =$$

$$\underbrace{M[w_\alpha] \cdot M[w_\beta]}_{A_0} + \Delta \cdot \underbrace{(\tilde{w}_\alpha \cdot M[w_\beta] + \tilde{w}_\beta \cdot M[w_\alpha] - M[w_\gamma])}_{A_1},$$

QuarkSilver Π^k_{QS}

The prover $\mathcal{P}$ and the verifier $\mathcal{V}$ have agreed on a circuit $\mathcal{C}$ over $\mathbb{Z}_{2^k}$ with n inputs and t multiplication gates, and $\mathcal{P}$ holds a witness $\mathbf{w} \in \mathbb{Z}^n_{2^k}$ so that $\mathcal{C}(\mathbf{w}) = 1$.

Preprocessing phase The preprocessing phase is independent of $\mathcal{C}$ and just needs upper bounds on the number of inputs and multiplication gates of $\mathcal{C}$ as input.

1. $\mathcal{P}$ and $\mathcal{V}$ send (Init) to $\mathcal{F}^{\ell,s}_{\mathsf{vole2k}}$, and $\mathcal{V}$ receives $\Delta \in \mathbb{Z}_{2^s}$.
2. $\mathcal{P}$ and $\mathcal{V}$ send (Extend, n + t + 2) to $\mathcal{F}^{\ell,s}_{\mathsf{vole2k}}$, which returns authenticated values $([\mu_i])_{i\in[n]}$, $([\nu_i])_{i\in[t]}$, $[o]$, and $[\pi]$, where all $\widetilde{\mu}_i, \widetilde{\nu}_i, \widetilde{o}, \widetilde{\pi} \in_R \mathbb{Z}_{2^\ell}$.

Online phase

1. For each input w_i, $i \in [n]$, $\mathcal{P}$ sends $\delta_i := w_i - \widetilde{\mu}_i$ to $\mathcal{V}$, and both parties locally compute $[w_i] := [\mu_i] + \delta_i$.
2. For each gate $(\alpha, \beta, \gamma, T) \in \mathcal{C}$, in topological order:
   - If $T =$ Add, then $\mathcal{P}$ and $\mathcal{V}$ locally compute $[w_\gamma] := [w_\alpha] + [w_\beta]$.
   - If $T =$ Mul and this is the ith multiplication gate, then $\mathcal{P}$ sends $d_i := w_\alpha \cdot w_\beta - \widetilde{\nu}_i$, and both parties locally compute $[w_\gamma] := [\nu_i] + d_i$.
3. For the ith multiplication gate, the parties hold $([w_\alpha], [w_\beta], [w_\gamma])$ with $K[w_i] = M[w_i] + \widetilde{w}_i \cdot \Delta$ for $i \in \{\alpha, \beta, \gamma\}$.
   - $\mathcal{P}$ computes $A_{0,i} := M[w_\alpha] \cdot M[w_\beta] \in \mathbb{Z}_{2^\ell}$ and $A_{1,i} := \widetilde{w}_\alpha \cdot M[w_\beta] + \widetilde{w}_\beta \cdot M[w_\alpha] - M[w_\gamma] \in \mathbb{Z}_{2^\ell}$.
   - $\mathcal{V}$ computes $B_i := K[w_\alpha] \cdot K[w_\beta] - \Delta \cdot K[w_\gamma] \in \mathbb{Z}_{2^\ell}$.
4. $\mathcal{P}$ and $\mathcal{V}$ run the following check:
   (a) Set $A^*_0 := M[o]$, $A^*_1 := \widetilde{o}$, and $B^* := K[o]$ so that $B^* = A^*_0 + A^*_1 \cdot \Delta$.
   (b) $\mathcal{V}$ samples $\chi \in_R \mathbb{Z}^t_{2^s}$ and sends it to $\mathcal{P}$.
   (c) $\mathcal{P}$ computes $U := \sum_{i\in[t]} \chi_i \cdot A_{0,i} + A^*_0 \in \mathbb{Z}_{2^\ell}$ and $V := \sum_{i\in[t]} \chi_i \cdot A_{1,i} + A^*_1 \in \mathbb{Z}_{2^\ell}$, and sends (U, V) to $\mathcal{V}$.
   (d) $\mathcal{V}$ computes $W := \sum_{i\in[t]} \chi_i \cdot B_i + B^* \in \mathbb{Z}_{2^\ell}$, and checks that $W = U + V \cdot \Delta \pmod{2^\ell}$. If the check fails, $\mathcal{V}$ outputs false and aborts.
5. For the single output wire w_h, both parties hold $[w_h]$. They first compute $[z] := [w_h] + 2^k \cdot [\pi]$. Then $\mathcal{P}$ sends $\widetilde{z}$ and $M[z]$ to $\mathcal{V}$ who checks that $\widetilde{z} = 1 \pmod{2^k}$ and $K[z] = M[z] + \widetilde{z} \cdot \Delta$. $\mathcal{V}$ outputs true iff the check passes, and false otherwise.

Fig. 7. Zero-knowledge protocol for circuit satisfiability in the $\mathcal{F}^{\ell,s}_{\mathsf{vole2k}}$-hybrid model with $s := \sigma + \log(\sigma) + 3$ and $\ell := k + 2s$ for statistical security parameter σ.

where $\mathcal{P}$ can compute A_0, A_1 while $\mathcal{V}$ can compute B. Hence, by sending A_0, A_1 to $\mathcal{V}$ the latter can check that the relation on B, Δ holds. Instead of sending these for every multiplication, we check all t relations simultaneously by having $\mathcal{V}$

choose a string $\chi \leftarrow \mathbb{Z}_{2^s}^t$, so that the prover instead sends $(\sum_i \chi_i A_{0,i}, \sum_i \chi_i A_{1,i})$ while the verifier checks the relation on $\sum_i \chi_i B_i$ and Δ. Since revealing these linear combinations directly might leak information, $\mathcal{P}$ will first blind the opening with the remaining random commitment from the preprocessing.

While the completeness and zero-knowledge of the aforementioned protocol follows directly, we will explain the soundness in more detail in the security proof. The full protocol is presented in Fig. 7.

Security of the QuarkSilver Protocol

Theorem 11. *The protocol Π_{QS}^k (Fig. 7) securely realizes the functionality $\mathcal{F}_{\mathsf{ZK}}^k$ in the $\mathcal{F}_{\mathsf{vole2k}}^{\ell,s}$-hybrid model when instantiated with the parameters $s := \sigma + \log(\sigma) + 3$ and $\ell := k + 2s$: No unbounded environment $\mathcal{Z}$ can distinguish the real execution of the protocol from a simulated one except with probability $2^{-\sigma+1}$.*

As our protocol is an adaption of QuickSilver [26], the structure of our proof is also similar. The main difference, lies in the proof of soundness of the multiplication check. We will sketch the argument briefly, while the full proof of Theorem 11 can be found in the full version [6].

For the ith multiplication gate (α, β, γ), let $\widetilde{w}_\gamma = \widetilde{w}_\alpha \cdot \widetilde{w}_\beta + e_i \pmod{2^\ell}$, where $\widetilde{w}_\alpha, \widetilde{w}_\beta, \widetilde{w}_\gamma \in \mathbb{Z}_{2^\ell}$ are the committed values in $[w_\alpha], [w_\beta], [w_\gamma]$ and $e_i \in \mathbb{Z}_{2^\ell}$ is a possible error. Suppose that not all $e_i = 0 \pmod{2^k}$ for $i \in [t]$. Then

$$K[w_\gamma] = M[w_\gamma] + \widetilde{w}_\gamma \cdot \Delta = M[w_\gamma] + (\widetilde{w}_\alpha \cdot \widetilde{w}_\beta) \cdot \Delta + e_i \cdot \Delta \pmod{2^\ell}$$

and (also modulo 2^ℓ)

$$\begin{aligned} B_i &= K[w_\alpha] \cdot K[w_\beta] - \Delta \cdot K[w_\gamma] \\ &= (M[w_\alpha] \cdot M[w_\beta]) + (\widetilde{w}_\alpha \cdot M[w_\beta] + M[w_\alpha] \cdot \widetilde{w}_\beta - M[w_\gamma]) \cdot \Delta - e_i \cdot \Delta^2 \\ &= A_{i,0} + A_{i,1} \cdot \Delta - e_i \cdot \Delta^2 \end{aligned}$$

where $A_{i,0}$ and $A_{i,1}$ are as above the values that an honest $\mathcal{P}$ would send. The equations for all gates are aggregated using a random linear combination:

$$\begin{aligned} W &= \sum\nolimits_{i \in [t]} \chi_i \cdot B_i + B^* \\ &= \underbrace{\sum_{i \in [t]} \chi_i \cdot A_{i,0} + A_0^*}_{U} + (\underbrace{\sum_{i \in [t]} \chi_i \cdot A_{i,1} + A_1^*}_{V}) \cdot \Delta - (\sum_{i \in [t]} \chi_i \cdot e_i) \cdot \Delta^2 \end{aligned} \tag{2}$$

Here, U, V denote the values that an honest $\mathcal{P}$ would send. The corrupted $\mathcal{P}^*$ may choose to send $U' := U + e_U$ and $V' := V + e_V$ instead, and $\mathcal{V}$ accepts if $W = U' + V' \cdot \Delta$ holds. Rearranging Eq. 2, we get that $\mathcal{V}$ accepts if

$$0 = e_U + e_V \cdot \Delta + \left(\sum\nolimits_{i \in [t]} \chi_i \cdot e_i\right) \cdot \Delta^2 \pmod{2^\ell} \tag{3}$$

holds. The key observation is that the steps in the protocol correspond exactly to the game defined in Theorem 9 and the dishonest prover wins the game, i.e., cheats successfully, if Equation (3) holds. By Corollary 10 the probability that this happens is at most $2^{-\sigma}$.

General Degree-2 Checks. Yang et al. [26] also provide zero-knowledge proofs for sets of t polynomials of degree d in n variables (in total), where the communication consists of $n + d$ field element – independent of t. With the results proved in Sect. 5.1, we can directly instantiate this protocol with $d = 2$. This allows us to verify arbitrary degree-2 relations including the important use case of inner products. Extending the check for higher-degree relations is principally possible. However, the number of roots of the corresponding polynomials grows exponentially with increasing degree. Hence, to achieve the same soundness, we would need to increase the ring size further, which reduces the efficiency. We give the full protocol and its security proof in the full version [6].

6 Experiments

In this section we report on the performance of our VOLE protocol $\Pi^{r,s}_{\mathsf{vole2k}}$ (Sect. 4) and our zero-knowledge proof system QuarkSilver (Sect. 5). We implemented the protocols in the Rust programming language using the *swanky* framework[5]. Our implementation is open source and available on GitHub under https://github.com/AarhusCrypto/Mozzarella.

Our implementation is generic, it allows to plugin any ring type that implements certain interfaces. We implement $\mathbb{Z}_{2^\ell}$ based on 64, 128, 192 and 256 bit integers. Depending on the size of ℓ, we choose the smallest of these types. Hence, running the protocol with, e.g., $\ell = 129$ and $\ell = 192$ has exactly the same computational and communication costs. In our experiments, we choose one representative ring for each considered size. It is possible to further optimize the communication cost of the implementation by transmitting exactly ℓ bits instead of the complete underlying integer value at the additional cost for the (un)packing operations.

6.1 Benchmarking Environment

All benchmarks were run on two servers with Intel Core i9-7960X processors that have 16 cores and 32 threads. Each server has 128 GiB memory available. They are connected via 10 Gigabit Ethernet with an average RTT of 0.25 ms.

We consider different network settings: For the *LAN* setting, we use the network as described above without further restrictions. To emulate a *WAN* setting, we configure Traffic Control in the Linux kernel via the `tc (8)` tool to artificially restrict the bandwidth to 100 Mbit/s, and increase the RTT to 100 ms. Finally, to explore the bandwidth dependence of our VOLE protocol, we consider a set of network settings with 20, 50, 100 and 500 Mbit/s as well as 1 and 10 Gbit/s bandwidth, and an RTT of 1 ms.

6.2 VOLE Experiments

In this section, we evaluate the performance of our VOLE protocol $\Pi^{\ell,s}_{\mathsf{vole2k}}$ (Sect. 4). We consider the setting of batch-wise VOLE extension: Given set of n_b

[5] swanky: https://github.com/GaloisInc/swanky.

base VOLEs, we use our protocols to expand them to $n_o + n_b$ VOLEs to obtain a batch of n_o VOLEs plus n_b VOLEs that can be used as base VOLEs to generate the next batch. We do not consider here how the initial set of base VOLEs are created. As performance measure we use the run-time and communication per generated VOLE correlation in one iteration of the protocol.

LPN Parameter Selection. For a triple of LPN parameters (m, t, n), our protocol extends $n_b = m + 2 \cdot t$ base VOLEs to n new ones. Hence, for a target batch size n_o, we need to find (m, t, n) such that $n \geq n_o + n_b$ and the corresponding LPN problem is still considered infeasible w.r.t. the security parameters.

As suggested in prior work [24,25,27], we pick the public LPN matrix $\mathbf{A} \in \mathbb{Z}_{2^\ell}^{m \times n}$ as a generator of a 10-local linear code (i.e. each column of $\mathbf{A}$ contains exactly 10 uniform non-zero entries). As discussed in Sect. 2.5, each non-zero entry is picked randomly from $\mathbb{Z}_{2^\ell}^*$ (i.e. odd), to ensure that reduction modulo 2 does not reduce sparsity. This results in fast computation of the expansion $\mathbf{u} \cdot \mathbf{A}$ (for some $\mathbf{u} \in \mathbb{Z}_{2^\ell}$), as each entry involves only 10 positions of $\mathbf{u}$. We then pick (m, t, n) such that all known attacks on the LPN problem require at least 2^κ operations [12,25] (see also full version [6]). Note that, as our variant of the regular LPN assumption (Definition 7) leaks blocks of the noise vector, we must pick t such that our protocols are secure in advent of leaking up to $\sigma \in \{40, 80\}$ blocks. To do this, we assume that leaking the noisy index within a single block of $\Pi_{\text{sp-vole2k}}^{\ell,s}$ directly gives an index of the secret and then subtract the leaked block from the noise vector as well as the corresponding index from the secret and make sure that the new problem is still infeasible to solve.

For a given n_o we experimentally find the LPN parameter set (m, t, n) that gives us the best performance while satisfying the above conditions.

We chose LPN parameters targeting a level of $\kappa = 128$ bits of computational security, and used the approach of Boyle et al. [11] to estimate the hardness of the LPN problem. Recently, Liu et al. [21] noted that this significantly underestimates the hardness of the LPN problem. Using their estimation, our parameters yield about 153–158 bits of security. Hence, we could reduce the parameters to get a more efficient instantiation of our protocol. We chose to use LPN with odd noise values in $\mathbb{Z}_{2^k}$ to resist the reduction attack of Liu et al. [21], which otherwise reduces the effective noise rate by half. In case of a potential future attack on LPN with odd noise, with the same impact, we would still achieve 103–109 bits of security.

For more details regarding the choice of LPN parameters and how we estimate the hardness of the leaky LPN problem, we refer to the full version [6].

General Benchmarks. For each statistical security level $\sigma \in \{40, 80\}$, we selected two LPN parameter sets (m, t, n) targeting VOLE batch sizes of $n_o \in \{10^7, 10^8\}$. We execute the protocol in two different network settings with four different ring sizes $\ell \in \{64, 104, 144, 244\}$ (one representative for each of the underlying integer types) for each of the parameter sets. Table 1 contains the results of our experiments.

With increasing ring size ℓ the costs increase as the arithmetic becomes more costly and more data needs to be transferred. Moreover, with a larger batch size the costs per VOLE decrease. In terms of run-time and communication costs, it is more efficient to generate a larger amount of VOLEs at once. However, the required resources, e.g., memory consumption, also increase with the batch size. In the WAN setting, a larger batch size is especially more efficient, since the effect of the higher latency is less pronounced on the amortized run-times.

Although the chosen LPN parameter sets worked well in our case, other combinations of m and t can yield a similar performance with same security, while influencing the computation and communication cost slightly. Such an effect can be noticed in the first parameter sets, where the communication cost decreases when going from $\sigma = 40$ to $\sigma = 80$. It is a trade-off, and we deem experimental verification necessary to choose the best-performing parameter set.

Table 1. Benchmark results of our VOLE protocol. We measure the run-time of the Extend operation in ns per VOLE and the communication cost in bit per VOLE. The benchmarks are parametrized by the ring size ℓ (i.e., using $\mathbb{Z}_{2^\ell}$). The computational security parameter is set to $\kappa = 128$. For statistical security $\sigma \in \{40, 80\}$, we target batch sizes of $n_o = 10^7$ and $n_o = 10^8$, and use the stated LPN parameters (m, t, n).

σ	ℓ	Run-time		Communication		
		LAN	WAN	$P_S \to P_R$	$P_R \to P_S$	total
	$m = 553\,600$, $t = 2\,186$, $n = 10\,558\,380$					
	64	27.3	190.8	0.467	0.927	1.394
	104	40.7	186.7	0.509	0.955	1.464
	144	55.2	212.6	0.551	0.983	1.534
40	244	80.7	255.0	0.593	1.011	1.604
	$m = 773\,200$, $t = 15\,045$, $n = 100\,816\,545$					
	64	20.1	46.0	0.318	0.636	0.954
	104	33.2	58.9	0.347	0.655	1.002
	144	46.7	75.1	0.376	0.674	1.050
	244	76.7	102.8	0.405	0.694	1.098
	$m = 830\,800$, $t = 2\,013$, $n = 10\,835\,979$					
	64	27.6	171.9	0.431	0.853	1.284
	104	42.6	194.1	0.469	0.879	1.349
	144	59.4	217.1	0.508	0.905	1.413
80	244	89.3	277.4	0.547	0.931	1.477
	$m = 866\,800$, $t = 18\,114$, $n = 100\,913\,094$					
	64	21.4	48.2	0.383	0.765	1.148
	104	34.3	61.0	0.418	0.789	1.206
	144	49.2	76.0	0.453	0.812	1.264
	244	79.8	106.8	0.487	0.835	1.322

Comparison with Wolverine. We compare the efficiency of our VOLE extension protocol with that of Wolverine [25]. While we use different hardware, we try to replicate their benchmarking setup by restricting our benchmark to maximal 5 threads and up to 64 GiB memory, and select LPN parameters to generate $n_o \approx 10^7$ VOLEs. The results are given in Table 2, where we list our run-times in different bandwidth settings with the corresponding numbers given in [25]. Note that Wolverine uses the prime field $\mathbb{F}_{2^{61}-1}$, whereas we instantiate our protocol with different larger rings $\mathbb{Z}_{2^\ell}$. In network settings with at least 50 Mbit/s bandwidth, we achieve similar or better performance for the ring sizes up to 128 bit.

Table 2. Run-times in ns per VOLE in different bandwidth settings, when generating ca. 10^7 VOLEs with 5 threads and statistical security $\sigma \geq 40$. The parameter ℓ denotes the size of a ring or field element. The numbers for Wolverine are taken from [25].

	ℓ	20 Mbit/s	50 Mbit/s	100 Mbit/s	500 Mbit/s	1 Gbit/s	10 Gbit/s
this work	64	110.0	68.7	55.0	50.2	50.6	50.4
	104	142.0	95.2	80.1	73.2	71.5	73.6
	144	178.6	134.7	119.3	111.6	112.6	113.3
	244	266.3	219.1	201.7	194.5	193.7	196.5
Wolverine	61	101	87	85	85	85	—

Bandwidth Dependence. Table 2 also shows how the available bandwidth affects the performance of our protocol. We observe that increasing the network bandwidth beyond 100 Mbit/s does not improve the run-time significantly. This indicates that the required computation is the bottleneck above this point.

6.3 Zero-Knowledge Experiments

We explore at what rate our QuarkSilver protocol (Sect. 5) is able to verify the correctness of multiplications. In our experiments we check for $N \approx 10^7$ triples of the form $([w_{i,\alpha}], [w_{i,\beta}], [w_{i,\gamma}])$ for $i \in [N]$ that $w_{i,\alpha} \cdot w_{i,\beta} = w_{i,\gamma} \pmod{2^k}$ holds. Assuming the prover has already committed to $2N$ values $([w_{i,\alpha}], [w_{i,\beta}])$, we execute the following three steps:

1. vole: Perform the Extend operation of $\Pi^{s,\ell}_{\mathsf{vole2k}}$ to create the necessary amount of VOLEs (at least $N+1$).
2. mult: Step 2 of Π^k_{QS} (Fig. 7) to commit to the results $w_{i,\gamma} := w_{i,\alpha} \cdot w_{i,\beta}$ of the multiplications.
3. check: Steps 3 and 4 of Π^k_{QS} to verify that the multiplications are correct modulo 2^k.

While the execution of $\Pi^{s,\ell}_{\mathsf{vole2k}}$ in Step 1 is parallelized, the further steps are executed in a single thread, and there is still room for optimizations, e.g., using smaller integers for the coefficients of the random linear combination and better interleaving computation and communication.

For statistical security levels of $\sigma = 40$ and $\sigma = 80$, we run the protocol with ring sizes $\ell = 162$ and $\ell = 244$, respectively. This corresponds to the required ring size ℓ to enable zero-knowledge proof over $\mathbb{Z}_{2^k}$ with $k = 64$. It also covers the $k = 32$ setting, since the corresponding rings (with $\ell \in \{130, 212\}$) are implemented in the same way.

In Table 3 we list the achieved run-times and communication costs per multiplication and show how they are distributed over the three steps of the protocol. We clearly see that the costs are dominated by Step 2, where the majority of the communication happens (one $\mathbb{Z}_{2^\ell}$ element per multiplication). Additional benchmarks show that increasing the bandwidth to more than 500 Mbit/s does not increase the performance.

Table 3. Benchmark results of our QuarkSilver protocol. We measure the run-time of a batch of $\approx 10^7$ multiplications and their verification in ns per multiplication and the communication cost in bit per multiplication. The benchmarks are parametrized by the statistical security parameter σ, and the computational security parameter is set to $\kappa = 128$. For $\sigma = 40$, we use the ring of size $\ell = 162$, for $\sigma = 80$, we use $\ell = 244$.

σ		Run-time		Communication		
		LAN	WAN	$P_S \to P_R$	$P_R \to P_S$	total
40	vole	78.5	265.5	0.5	1.0	1.5
	mult	663.2	2101.5	192.0	0.0	192.0
	check	28.2	38.2	0.0	0.0	0.0
	total	769.9	2405.2	192.5	1.0	193.5
80	vole	125.3	345.5	0.5	0.9	1.5
	mult	680.7	2767.2	256.0	0.0	256.0
	check	42.3	52.4	0.0	0.0	0.0
	total	848.3	3165.2	256.5	0.9	257.5

With a completely single-threaded implementation (including single-threaded VOLEs), we can verify about 0.9 million multiplications per second for statistical security parameter $\sigma = 40$ and ring $\mathbb{Z}_{2^{162}}$, compared to (single-threaded) QuickSilver's up to 4.8 million multiplications per second over the field $\mathbb{F}_{2^{61}-1}$, as reported by Yang et al. [26]. This is a factor 5.3 difference.

When looking at the performance of $\mathbb{Z}_{2^{162}}$ compared to $\mathbb{F}_{2^{61}-1}$, we see that $\mathbb{Z}_{2^{162}}$ ring elements are represented by three 64 bit integers compared to $\mathbb{F}_{2^{61}-1}$ field elements which fit into a single integer. While this results in $3\times$ more communication, the computational costs are also higher: In microbenchmarks, arithmetic operations in $\mathbb{Z}_{2^{162}}$ are $2.1-2.5\times$ slower compared to the corresponding operations in $\mathbb{F}_{2^{61}-1}$ (e.g., $\mathbb{Z}_{2^{162}}$ multiplications require 6 IMUL/MULX instructions, $\mathbb{F}_{2^{61}-1}$ multiplications need one MULX instruction). Moreover, the compiler can automatically vectorize element-wise computations on vectors of field elements with AVX instruction due to the smaller element size, but this is (at least currently) not possible with the larger ring. Computation on rings also results in a slightly higher rate of cache misses, which we attribute to the fact that more field elements than ring elements fit in a cache line, simply due to their size.

We want to stress that this direct comparison is not necessarily fair, though: The Mersenne prime modulus $p = 2^{61} - 1$ has been chosen because it allows to implement the field arithmetic very efficiently. The plaintext space has roughly the same size in both settings (64 vs. 61 bit), but the arithmetic on the secrets is entirely different which is the main difference of our work to the field-based approach of QuickSilver. While QuarkSilver supports 64 bit arithmetic natively (which is one of the main points of considering $\mathbb{Z}_{2^k}$ protocols), things are more complicated with fields. To emulate 64 bit arithmetic in a prime field, the prime modulus has to have size ≥ 128 bit (so no modular wraparound occurs during multiplications) which means more communication and more complicated arithmetic. Then, one also has to commit to the correct reduction modulo 2^{64} and prove that the reduction is computed correctly, e.g., with range proofs or using the truncation protocols of Baum et al. [5] – both are not cheap, in particular given they are needed for each multiplication mod 2^{64} (and possibly additions, too). Moreover, with a prime modulus of this size one cannot take advantage of a Mersenne prime (the nearest Mersenne primes would be $p = 2^{127} - 1$ (too small) and $p = 2^{521} - 1$ (much larger)) to increase computational efficiency.

Acknowledgements. This work is supported by the European Research Council (ERC) under the European Unions's Horizon 2020 research and innovation programme under grant agreement No. 803096 (SPEC), the Carlsberg Foundation under the Semper Ardens Research Project CF18-112 (BCM), the Independent Research Fund Denmark (DFF) under project number 0165-00107B (C3PO), the Aarhus University Research Foundation, and the Defense Advanced Research Projects Agency (DARPA) under Contract No. HR001120C0085. Any opinions, findings and conclusions or recommendations expressed in this material are those of the author(s) and do not necessarily reflect the views of the Defense Advanced Research Projects Agency (DARPA). Distribution Statement "A" (Approved for Public Release, Distribution Unlimited). We thank the ENCRYPTO group at TU Darmstadt for allowing us to use their servers for our experiments.

References

1. Alekhnovich, M.: More on average case vs approximation complexity. In: 44th FOCS, pp. 298–307. IEEE Computer Society Press, October 2003. https://doi.org/10.1109/SFCS.2003.1238204

2. Ames, S., Hazay, C., Ishai, Y., Venkitasubramaniam, M.: Ligero: lightweight sublinear arguments without a trusted setup. In: Thuraisingham, B.M., Evans, D., Malkin, T., Xu, D. (eds.) ACM CCS 2017, pp. 2087–2104. ACM Press, October/November 2017. https://doi.org/10.1145/3133956.3134104
3. Applebaum, B., Damgård, I., Ishai, Y., Nielsen, M., Zichron, L.: Secure arithmetic computation with constant computational overhead. In: Katz, J., Shacham, H. (eds.) CRYPTO 2017, Part I. LNCS, vol. 10401, pp. 223–254. Springer, Cham (2017). https://doi.org/10.1007/978-3-319-63688-7_8
4. Arora, S., Ge, R.: New algorithms for learning in presence of errors. In: Aceto, L., Henzinger, M., Sgall, J. (eds.) ICALP 2011, Part I. LNCS, vol. 6755, pp. 403–415. Springer, Heidelberg (2011). https://doi.org/10.1007/978-3-642-22006-7_34
5. Baum, C., Braun, L., Munch-Hansen, A., Razet, B., Scholl, P.: Appenzeller to brie: efficient zero-knowledge proofs for mixed-mode arithmetic and Z2k. In: Vigna, G., Shi, E. (eds.) ACM CCS 2021, pp. 192–211. ACM Press, November 2021. https://doi.org/10.1145/3460120.3484812
6. Baum, C., Braun, L., Munch-Hansen, A., Scholl, P.: MozZ$_{2^k}$arella: efficient vector-OLE and zero-knowledge proofs over $\mathbb{Z}_{2^k}$. Cryptology ePrint Archive, Paper 2022/819 (2022). https://eprint.iacr.org/2022/819, Full Version
7. Baum, C., Malozemoff, A.J., Rosen, M.B., Scholl, P.: Mac′*n′Cheese*: zero-knowledge proofs for boolean and arithmetic circuits with nested disjunctions. In: Malkin, T., Peikert, C. (eds.) CRYPTO 2021. LNCS, vol. 12828, pp. 92–122. Springer, Cham (2021). https://doi.org/10.1007/978-3-030-84259-8_4
8. Ben-Sasson, E., Bentov, I., Horesh, Y., Riabzev, M.: Scalable zero knowledge with no trusted setup. In: Boldyreva, A., Micciancio, D. (eds.) CRYPTO 2019, Part III. LNCS, vol. 11694, pp. 701–732. Springer, Cham (2019). https://doi.org/10.1007/978-3-030-26954-8_23
9. Blum, A., Furst, M., Kearns, M., Lipton, R.J.: Cryptographic primitives based on hard learning problems. In: Stinson, D.R. (ed.) CRYPTO 1993. LNCS, vol. 773, pp. 278–291. Springer, Heidelberg (1994). https://doi.org/10.1007/3-540-48329-2_24
10. Boneh, D., Waters, B.: Constrained pseudorandom functions and their applications. In: Sako, K., Sarkar, P. (eds.) ASIACRYPT 2013, Part II. LNCS, vol. 8270, pp. 280–300. Springer, Heidelberg (2013). https://doi.org/10.1007/978-3-642-42045-0_15
11. Boyle, E., Couteau, G., Gilboa, N., Ishai, Y.: Compressing vector OLE. In: Lie, D., Mannan, M., Backes, M., Wang, X. (eds.) ACM CCS 2018, pp. 896–912. ACM Press, October 2018. https://doi.org/10.1145/3243734.3243868
12. Boyle, E., et al.: Efficient two-round OT extension and silent non-interactive secure computation. In: Cavallaro, L., Kinder, J., Wang, X., Katz, J. (eds.) ACM CCS 2019, pp. 291–308. ACM Press, November 2019. https://doi.org/10.1145/3319535.3354255
13. Boyle, E., Goldwasser, S., Ivan, I.: Functional signatures and pseudorandom functions. In: Krawczyk, H. (ed.) PKC 2014. LNCS, vol. 8383, pp. 501–519. Springer, Heidelberg (2014). https://doi.org/10.1007/978-3-642-54631-0_29
14. Couteau, G., Rindal, P., Raghuraman, S.: Silver: silent VOLE and oblivious transfer from hardness of decoding structured LDPC codes. In: Malkin, T., Peikert, C. (eds.) CRYPTO 2021, Part III. LNCS, vol. 12827, pp. 502–534. Springer, Cham (2021). https://doi.org/10.1007/978-3-030-84252-9_17
15. Cramer, R., Damgård, I., Escudero, D., Scholl, P., Xing, C.: SPDZ$_{2^k}$: efficient MPC mod 2^k for dishonest majority. In: Shacham, H., Boldyreva, A. (eds.) CRYPTO 2018, Part II. LNCS, vol. 10992, pp. 769–798. Springer, Cham (2018). https://doi.org/10.1007/978-3-319-96881-0_26

16. Dittmer, S., Ishai, Y., Ostrovsky, R.: Line-point zero knowledge and its applications. In: 2nd Conference on Information-Theoretic Cryptography (ITC 2021). Schloss Dagstuhl-Leibniz-Zentrum für Informatik (2021)
17. Ganesh, C., Nitulescu, A., Soria-Vazquez, E.: Rinocchio: SNARKs for ring arithmetic. Cryptology ePrint Archive, Report 2021/322 (2021). https://eprint.iacr.org/2021/322
18. Goldreich, O., Goldwasser, S., Micali, S.: How to construct random functions (extended abstract). In: 25th FOCS, pp. 464–479. IEEE Computer Society Press, October 1984. https://doi.org/10.1109/SFCS.1984.715949
19. Goldreich, O., Goldwasser, S., Micali, S.: How to construct random functions. J. ACM (JACM) **33**(4), 792–807 (1986)
20. Kiayias, A., Papadopoulos, S., Triandopoulos, N., Zacharias, T.: Delegatable pseudorandom functions and applications. In: Sadeghi, A.R., Gligor, V.D., Yung, M. (eds.) ACM CCS 2013, pp. 669–684. ACM Press, November 2013. https://doi.org/10.1145/2508859.2516668
21. Liu, H., Wang, X., Yang, K., Yu, Y.: The hardness of LPN over any integer ring and field for PCG applications. Cryptology ePrint Archive, Paper 2022/712 (2022). https://eprint.iacr.org/2022/712
22. Maller, M., Bowe, S., Kohlweiss, M., Meiklejohn, S.: Sonic: zero-knowledge SNARKs from linear-size universal and updatable structured reference strings. In: Cavallaro, L., Kinder, J., Wang, X., Katz, J. (eds.) ACM CCS 2019, pp. 2111–2128. ACM Press, November 2019. https://doi.org/10.1145/3319535.3339817
23. Scholl, P.: Extending oblivious transfer with low communication via key-homomorphic PRFs. In: Abdalla, M., Dahab, R. (eds.) PKC 2018, Part I. LNCS, vol. 10769, pp. 554–583. Springer, Cham (2018). https://doi.org/10.1007/978-3-319-76578-5_19
24. Schoppmann, P., Gascón, A., Reichert, L., Raykova, M.: Distributed vector-OLE: improved constructions and implementation. In: Cavallaro, L., Kinder, J., Wang, X., Katz, J. (eds.) ACM CCS 2019, pp. 1055–1072. ACM Press, November 2019. https://doi.org/10.1145/3319535.3363228
25. Weng, C., Yang, K., Katz, J., Wang, X.: Wolverine: fast, scalable, and communication-efficient zero-knowledge proofs for boolean and arithmetic circuits. In: 2021 IEEE Symposium on Security and Privacy, pp. 1074–1091. IEEE Computer Society Press, May 2021. https://doi.org/10.1109/SP40001.2021.00056
26. Yang, K., Sarkar, P., Weng, C., Wang, X.: QuickSilver: efficient and affordable zero-knowledge proofs for circuits and polynomials over any field. In: Vigna, G., Shi, E. (eds.) ACM CCS 2021, pp. 2986–3001. ACM Press, November 2021. https://doi.org/10.1145/3460120.3484556
27. Yang, K., Weng, C., Lan, X., Zhang, J., Wang, X.: Ferret: fast extension for correlated OT with small communication. In: Ligatti, J., Ou, X., Katz, J., Vigna, G. (eds.) ACM CCS 2020, pp. 1607–1626. ACM Press, November 2020. https://doi.org/10.1145/3372297.3417276
28. Zichron, L.: Locally computable arithmetic pseudorandom generators. Master's thesis, School of Electrical Engineering, Tel Aviv University (2017). http://www.eng.tau.ac.il/~bennyap/pubs/Zichron.pdf

Nova: Recursive Zero-Knowledge Arguments from Folding Schemes

Abhiram Kothapalli[1(✉)], Srinath Setty[2(✉)], and Ioanna Tzialla[3]

[1] Carnegie Mellon University, Pittsburgh, USA
akothapa@andrew.cmu.edu

[2] Microsoft Research, Redmond, USA
srinath@microsoft.com

[3] New York University, New York, USA

Abstract. We introduce a new approach to realize incrementally verifiable computation (IVC), in which the prover recursively proves the correct execution of incremental computations of the form $y = F^{(\ell)}(x)$, where F is a (potentially non-deterministic) computation, x is the input, y is the output, and $\ell > 0$. Unlike prior approaches to realize IVC, our approach avoids succinct non-interactive arguments of knowledge (SNARKs) entirely and arguments of knowledge in general. Instead, we introduce and employ *folding schemes*, a weaker, simpler, and more efficiently-realizable primitive, which reduces the task of checking two instances in some relation to the task of checking a single instance. We construct a folding scheme for a characterization of NP and show that it implies an IVC scheme with improved efficiency characteristics: (1) the "recursion overhead" (i.e., the number of steps that the prover proves in addition to proving the execution of F) is a constant and it is dominated by two group scalar multiplications expressed as a circuit (this is the smallest recursion overhead in the literature), and (2) the prover's work at each step is dominated by two multiexponentiations of size $O(|F|)$, providing the fastest prover in the literature. The size of a proof is $O(|F|)$ group elements, but we show that using a variant of an existing zkSNARK, the prover can prove the knowledge of a valid proof succinctly and in zero-knowledge with $O(\log |F|)$ group elements. Finally, our approach neither requires a trusted setup nor FFTs, so it can be instantiated efficiently with any cycles of elliptic curves where DLOG is hard.

1 Introduction

We revisit the problem of realizing *incrementally-verifiable computation (IVC)* [43]: a cryptographic primitive that enables producing proofs of correct execution of "long running" computations such that a verifier can efficiently verify the correct execution of any prefix of the computation. IVC enables a wide variety of applications including verifiable delay functions [9,45], succinct blockchains [13,31], and incrementally-verifiable versions of verifiable state machines [33,39].

A well-known approach to construct IVC is to use succinct non-interactive arguments of knowledge (SNARKs) for NP [23,24,29,36]: at each incremental step i, the prover produces a SNARK proving that it has applied F correctly to the output of step $i-1$ and that the SNARK verifier *represented as a circuit* has accepted

Y. Dodis and T. Shrimpton (Eds.): CRYPTO 2022, LNCS 13510, pp. 359–388, 2022.
https://doi.org/10.1007/978-3-031-15985-5_13

the SNARK from step $i-1$ [6,8]. However, it is well-known that this approach is impractical [6,19]. Alternatively, one can use SNARKs without trusted setup [17, 21,38,41] but their verifiers are more expensive than those of SNARKs with trusted setup, both asymptotically and concretely. Recent works [10,12,15,16] aim to address the inefficiency of SNARK-based IVC, with an innovative approach: at each step, the verifier circuit "defers" expensive steps in verifying a SNARK for NP instances (e.g., verifying polynomial evaluation proofs) by accumulating those steps into a single instance that is later checked efficiently. However, these works still require the prover to produce a SNARK at each step and the verifier circuit to partially verify that SNARK.

We introduce a new approach that avoids SNARKs (and more generally arguments of knowledge) entirely and relies purely on deferral to realize IVC. In a nutshell, instead of accumulating expensive steps of verifying a SNARK for NP instances, the verifier circuit in our approach accumulates the NP instances themselves. We formalize this technique as a new and minimal primitive, which we refer to as a *folding scheme*. A folding scheme is weaker, simpler, and far more efficient compared to arguments of knowledge including SNARKs. Indeed, realizing IVC via folding schemes results in improved efficiency over prior work (Fig. 3): (1) the verifier circuit is constant-sized and its size is dominated by two group scalar multiplications; this is the smallest verifier circuit in the literature (in the context of recursive proof composition); and (2) the prover's work at each step is dominated by two multiexponentiations of size $O(|F|)$, providing the fastest prover in the literature, both asymptotically and concretely. Section 1.4 provides a detailed comparison between our approach and prior work.

1.1 Folding Schemes

A folding scheme is defined with respect to an NP relation, and it is a protocol between an untrusted *prover* and a *verifier*. Both entities hold two N-sized NP instances, and the prover in addition holds purported witnesses for both instances. The protocol enables the prover and the verifier to output a single N-sized NP instance, which we refer to as a *folded instance*. Furthermore, the prover privately outputs a purported witness to the folded instance using purported witnesses for the original instances. Informally, a folding scheme guarantees that the folded instance is satisfiable only if the original instances are satisfiable. A folding scheme is said to be *non-trivial* if the verifier's costs and the communication are lower in the case where the verifier participates in the folding scheme and then verifies a purported NP witness for the folded instance than the case where the verifier verifies purported NP witnesses for each of the original instances.

Several existing techniques exhibit the two-to-one reduction pattern of folding schemes. Examples include the sumcheck protocol [35] and the split-and-fold techniques in inner product arguments [11]. [30, App. A] provides further details.

Remark 1 (Folding Schemes vs. SNARKs). SNARKs for NP [7,23,24,29,36] trivially imply a folding scheme for NP: given two NP instances u_1 and u_2 and the corresponding witnesses, the prover proves u_1 by producing a SNARK. The verifier checks that SNARK and then sets u_2 to be the folded instance. However, we construct a folding scheme for NP without relying on SNARKs (or more generally arguments of knowledge). Specifically, our folding scheme is weaker than any argument of knowledge (succinct or otherwise) because it merely *reduces* the satisfiability of two NP instances to the satisfiability of a single NP instance.[1]

To design a folding scheme for NP, we start with a popular NP-complete language that generalizes arithmetic circuit satisfiability: R1CS (Definition 10). As we illustrate later, it is difficult to devise a folding scheme for R1CS. To address this, we introduce a variant of R1CS, called *relaxed R1CS*, which, like R1CS, not only characterizes NP, but, unlike R1CS, can support a folding scheme. The following theorem captures the cryptographic and efficiency characteristics of our folding scheme for relaxed R1CS.

Theorem 1. *There exists a constant-round, public-coin, zero-knowledge folding scheme for relaxed R1CS where for N-sized relaxed R1CS instances over a finite field $\mathbb{F}$ with the same "structure" (i.e., R1CS coefficient matrices), the prover's work is $O_\lambda(N)$, and the verifier's work and the communication are both $O_\lambda(1)$, assuming the existence of any additively-homomorphic commitment scheme that provides $O_\lambda(1)$-sized commitments to N-sized vectors over $\mathbb{F}$ (e.g., Pedersen's commitments), where λ is the security parameter.*

Because our folding scheme is public coin, it can be made non-interactive in the random oracle model using the Fiat-Shamir transform [22], and be instantiated (heuristically) in the standard model using a concrete hash function. We rely on such a non-interactive folding scheme to construct IVC.

1.2 IVC from Non-interactive Folding Schemes

We show how to realize IVC using a non-interactive version of our folding scheme for relaxed R1CS. We refer to our construction as Nova.

Recall that an IVC is an argument of knowledge [29,36][2] for incremental computations of the form $y = F^{(\ell)}(x)$, where F is a (possibly non-deterministic) computation, $\ell > 0$, x is a public input, and y is the public output. At each incremental step, the IVC prover produces a proof that the step was computed correctly *and* it has verified a proof for the prior step. In other words, at each incremental step, the IVC prover produces a proof of satisfiability for an augmented circuit that augments the circuit for F with a "verifier circuit" that verifies the proof of the prior step. Recursively, the final proof proves the correctness of the entire incremental computation. A key aspect of IVC is that neither the IVC verifier's work nor the IVC proof size depends on the number of

[1] This work realizes IVC using our folding scheme. As IVC implies SNARKs (e.g., see [6]), one might wonder whether folding schemes are in general weaker than SNARKs. However, existing constructions of IVC (including our own) rely on additional assumptions (§4.2), which the resulting IVC-based SNARK inherits.

[2] An *argument of knowledge* for circuit satisfiability enables an untrusted polynomial-time prover to prove to a verifier the knowledge of a witness w such that $C(w, x) = y$, where C is a circuit, x is some public input, and y is some public output.

steps in the incremental computation. In particular, the IVC verifier only verifies the proof produced at the last step of the incremental computation.

In Nova, we consider incremental computations, where each step of the incremental computation is expressed with R1CS (all the steps in the incremental computation share the same R1CS coefficient matrices). At step i of the incremental computation, as in other approaches to IVC, Nova's prover proves that the step i was computed correctly. Furthermore, at step i, instead of verifying a proof for step $i-1$ (as in traditional approaches to IVC), Nova's approach treats the computation at step $i-1$ as an R1CS instance and folds that into a running relaxed R1CS instance. Specifically, at each step, Nova's prover proves that it has performed the step's computation and has folded its prior step represented as an R1CS instance into a running relaxed R1CS instance. In other words, the circuit satisfiability instance that the prover proves at each incremental step computes a step of the incremental computation and includes a circuit for the computation of the verifier in the non-interactive folding scheme for relaxed R1CS.

A distinctive aspect of Nova's approach to IVC is that it achieves the smallest "verifier circuit" in the literature. Since the verifier's costs in the non-interactive version of the folding scheme for relaxed R1CS is $O_\lambda(1)$, the size of the computation that Nova's prover proves at each incremental step is $\approx|F|$, assuming N-sized vectors are committed with an $O_\lambda(1)$-sized commitments (e.g., Pedersen's commitments). In particular, the verifier circuit in Nova is constant-sized and its size is dominated by two *group scalar multiplications*. Furthermore, Nova's prover's work at each step is dominated by two multiexponentiations of size $\approx|F|$. Note that Nova's prover does not perform any FFTs, so it can be instantiated efficiently using *any* cycles of elliptic curves where DLOG is hard.

With the description thus far, the size of an IVC proof (which is a purported witness for the running relaxed R1CS instance) is $O_\lambda(|F|)$. Instead of sending such a proof to a verifier, at any point in the incremental computation, Nova's prover can prove the knowledge of a satisfying witness to the running relaxed R1CS instance in zero-knowledge with an $O_\lambda(\log|F|)$-sized succinct proof using a zkSNARK that we design by adapting Spartan [38]. The following theorem summarizes our key result.

Theorem 2. *For any incremental function where each step of the incremental function applies a (non-deterministic) function F, there exists an IVC scheme with the following efficiency characteristics, assuming N-sized vectors are committed with an $O_\lambda(1)$-sized commitments.*

- *IVC proof sizes are $O(|F|)$ and the verifier's work to verify them is $O_\lambda(|F|)$. The prover's work at each incremental step is $\approx|F|$. Specifically, the prover's work at each step is dominated by two multiexponentiations of size $\approx|F|$.*
- *Succinct zero-knowledge proofs of valid IVC proofs are size $O_\lambda(\log|F|)$, and the verifier's work to verify them is either $O_\lambda(\log|F|)$ or $O_\lambda(|F|)$ depending on the commitment scheme for vectors. The prover's work to produce this succinct zero-knowledge proof is $O_\lambda(|F|)$.*

1.3 Implementation and Performance Evaluation

We implement Nova as a library in about 6,000 lines of Rust [3]. The library is generic over a cycle of elliptic curves and a hash function (used internally as the random oracle). The library provides candidate implementations with the Pasta cycle of elliptic curves [4] and Poseidon [2,26]. Finally, the library accepts F (i.e., a step of the incremental computation) as a bellperson gadget [1].

Recursion Overheads. We measure the size of Nova's verifier circuit, as it determines the *recursion overhead*: the number of additional constraints that the prover must prove at each incremental step besides proving an invocation of F.

We find that Nova's verifier circuit is ≈20,000 R1CS constraints. This is the smallest verifier circuit in the literature and hence Nova incurs the lowest recursion overhead. Specifically, Nova's recursion overhead is >10× lower than in SNARK-based IVC [6] with state-of-the-art per-circuit trusted setup SNARK [27], and over 100× smaller than with a SNARK without trusted setup [21]. Compared to recent works, Nova's recursion overhead is over 7× lower than Halo's [12], and over 2× lower than the scheme of Bunz et al. [15] (Fig. 1).

	Primary Curve	Secondary Curve
Scalar multiplications	12,362	12,362
Random oracle call	1,431	1,434
Collision-resistant hash	2,300	2,306
Non-native arithmetic	3,240	3,240
Glue code	1,251	1,782
Total	20,584	21,124

Fig. 1. A detailed breakdown of sub-routines in Nova's verifier's circuit and the associated number of R1CS constraints. The verifier circuit on each of the curves in the cycle are not identical as they have slightly different base cases. We find that a majority of constraints in the verifier circuit step from the group scalar multiplications.

Performance of Nova. We experiment with Nova on an Azure Standard F32s_v2 VM (16 physical CPUs, 2.70 GHz Intel(R) Xeon(R) Platinum 8168, and 64 GB memory). In our experiments, we vary the number of constraints in F. Our performance metrics are: the prover time, the verifier time, and proof sizes. We measure these for Nova's IVC scheme as well as its Spartan-based zkSNARK to compress IVC proofs. Figure 2 depicts our results, and we find the following.

- The prover's per-step cost to produce an IVC proof and compress it scale sub-linearly with the size of F (since the cost is dominated by two multiexponentiations, which scale sub-linearly due to the Pippenger algorithm and parallelize better at larger sizes). When $|F| \approx 2^{20}$ constraints, the prover's per-step cost to produce an IVC proof is ≈1 µs/constraint. For the same F, the cost to produce a compressed IVC proof is ≈24 µs/constraint.[3]

[3] If the prover produces a compressed IVC proof every ≈24 steps, the prover incurs at most 2× overhead to compress IVC proofs. Similarly, if the prover compresses its IVC proof every ≈240 steps, the overhead drops to ≈20%.

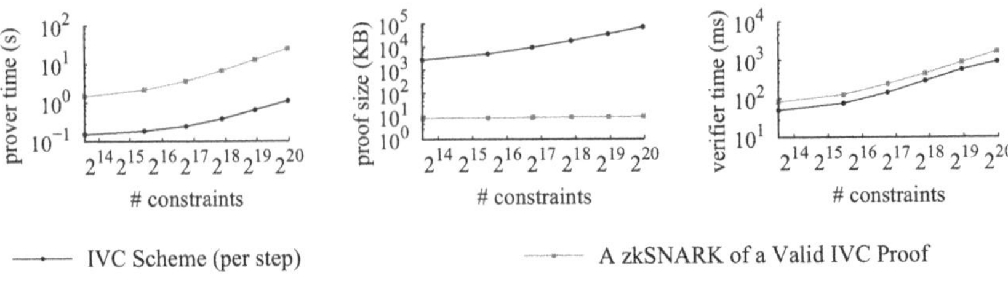

Fig. 2. Performance of Nova as a function of $|F|$. See the text for details.

- Compressed IVC proofs are ≈8–9 KB and are significantly shorter than IVC proofs (e.g., they are ≈7,400× shorter when $|F| \approx 2^{20}$ constraints).
- Verifying a compressed proof is only ≈2× higher costs than verifying a significantly longer IVC proof.

1.4 A More Detailed Comparison with Prior Work

Figure 3 compares Nova with prior approaches. Nova's approach can be viewed as taking Halo's approach to the extreme. Specifically:

- At each incremental step, Halo's verifier circuit verifies a "partial" SNARK. This still requires Halo's prover to perform $|F|$-sized FFTs and $O(|F|)$ exponentiations (i.e., *not* an $|F|$-sized multiexponentiation). Whereas, in Nova, the verifier circuit folds an entire NP instance representing computation at the prior step into a running relaxed R1CS instance. This only requires Nova's prover to commit to a satisfying assignment of an $\approx|F|$-sized circuit (which computes F and performs the verifier's computation in a folding scheme for relaxed R1CS), so at each step, Nova's prover only computes an $O(|F|)$-sized multiexponentiation and does not compute any FFTs. So, Nova's prover incurs lower costs than Halo's prover, both asymptotically and concretely.
- The verifier circuit in Halo is of size $O_\lambda(\log|F|)$ whereas in Nova, it is $O_\lambda(1)$. Concretely, the dominant operations in Halo's circuit is $O(\log|F|)$ group scalar multiplications, whereas in Nova, it is two group scalar multiplications.
- Halo and Nova have the same proof sizes $O_\lambda(\log|F|)$ and verifier time $O_\lambda(|F|)$.

Bünz et al. [16] apply Halo's approach to other polynomial commitment schemes. Halo Infinite [10] generalizes the approach in Halo [12] to any homomorphic polynomial commitment scheme; they also obtain PCD (and hence IVC) even when polynomial commitment schemes do not satisfy succinctness.

Bünz et al. [15] propose a variant of the approach in Halo, where they realize PCD (and hence IVC) without relying on succinct arguments. Specifically, they first devise a non-interactive argument of knowledge (NARK) for R1CS with $O_\lambda(N)$-sized proofs and $O_\lambda(N)$ verification times for N-sized R1CS instances. Then, they show that most of the NARK's verifier's computation can be deferred by performing $O_\lambda(1)$ work in the verifier circuit. For zero-knowledge, Nova relies

	"Verifier circuit" (dominant ops)	Prover (each step)	Proof size	Verifier	assumptions
BCTV14 [6] with [27][†]	3 $\mathbb{P}$	$O(C)$ FFT $O(C)$ MSM	$O_\lambda(1)$	$O_\lambda(1)$	q-type
Spartan [38]-based IVC	$O(\sqrt{C})$ $\mathbb{G}$	$O(C)$ MSM	$O_\lambda(\sqrt{C})$	$O_\lambda(\sqrt{C})$	DLOG, RO
Fractal [21]	$O_\lambda(\log^2 C)$ $\mathbb{F}$ $O(\log^2 C)$ $\mathbb{H}$	$O(C)$ FFT $O(C)$ MHT	$O_\lambda(\log^2 C)$	$O_\lambda(\log^2 C)$	RO
Halo [12]	$O(\log C)$ $\mathbb{G}$	$O(C)$ FFT $O(C)$ EXP	$O_\lambda(\log C)$	$O_\lambda(C)$	DLOG, RO
BCLMS [15]*	8 $\mathbb{G}$	$O(C)$ FFT $O(C)$ MSM	$O_\lambda(C)$	$O_\lambda(C)$	DLOG, RO
Nova (this work)	2 $\mathbb{G}$	$O(C)$ MSM	$O_\lambda(\log C)$	$O_\lambda(C)$	DLOG, RO
Nova (this work)	2 $\mathbb{G}_T$	$O(C)$ MSM	$O_\lambda(\log C)$	$O_\lambda(\log C)$	SXDH, RO

[†] Requires per-circuit trusted setup and is undesirable in practice
$O(C)$ FFT: FFT over an $O(C)$-sized vector costing $O(C \log C)$ operations over $\mathbb{F}$
$O(C)$ MHT: Merkle tree over an $O(C)$-sized vector costing $O(C)$ hash computations
$O(C)$ EXP: $O(C)$ exponentiations in a cryptographic group
$O(C)$ MSM: $O(C)$-sized multi-exponentiation in a cryptographic group

Fig. 3. Asymptotic costs of Nova and its baselines to produce and verify a proof for an incremental computation where each incremental step applies a function F. C denotes the size of the computation at each incremental step, i.e., $|F| + |\mathcal{C}_\mathcal{V}|$, where $\mathcal{C}_\mathcal{V}$ is the "verifier circuit" in IVC. The "verifier circuit" column depicts the number of dominant operations in $\mathcal{C}_\mathcal{V}$, where $\mathbb{P}$ denotes a pairing in a pairing-friendly group, $\mathbb{F}$ denotes the number of finite field operations, $\mathbb{H}$ denotes a hash computation, and $\mathbb{G}$ denotes a scalar multiplication in a cryptographic group. The prover column depicts the cost to the prover for each step of the incremental computation, and proof sizes and verifier times refer respectively to the size of the proof of the incremental computation and the associated verification times. For Nova's proof sizes and verification times, we depict the compressed proof sizes (otherwise, they are $O_\lambda(C)$) and the time to verify a compressed proof (otherwise, they are $O_\lambda(C)$). Rows with RO require heuristically instantiating the random oracle with a concrete hash function in the standard model.

on zero-knowledge arguments with succinct proofs, whereas their approach does not rely on succinct arguments. However, Nova's approach has several conceptual and efficiency advantages over the work of Bünz et al. [15]:

- Nova introduces a new primitive called a folding scheme, which is conceptually simpler and is easier to realize than prior notions such as (split) accumulation schemes used in prior work [15,16]. Furthermore, a folding scheme for NP directly leads to IVC and is again easier to analyze than with prior notions.
- At each step, their prover performs an $O(|F|)$-sized FFT (which costs $O(|F| \log |F|)$ operations over $\mathbb{F}$). Whereas, Nova does not perform any FFTs.
- Their prover's work for multiexponentitions at each step and the size of their verifier circuit are both higher than in Nova by $\approx 4\times$.
- Proof sizes are $O_\lambda(|F|)$ in their work, whereas in Nova, they are $O_\lambda(\log |F|)$. We believe, in theory, they can also compress their proofs, using a succinct argument, but unlike Nova, they do not specify how to do so in a concretely efficient manner. Furthermore, using succinct arguments is inconsistent with their goal of not employing them.

Concurrent Work. In an update concurrent with this work, Bünz et al. [15] provide an improved construction of their NARK for R1CS, which leads to an IVC that, like Nova, avoids FFTs. Furthermore, they improve the size of the verifier circuit by $\approx 2\times$, which is still larger than Nova's verifier circuit by $\approx 2\times$. The per-step computation of the prover remains $4\times$ higher than Nova.

1.5 An Overview of the Rest of the Paper

Section 2 provides the necessary background. Section 3 formally defines folding schemes and their properties. In Sect. 4, we introduce a variant of R1CS called relaxed R1CS for which we provide a folding scheme satisfying Theorem 1. Then, in Sect. 5, we use a non-interactive version of the folding scheme (§4.2) to construct an IVC scheme and a scheme to compress IVC proofs satisfying Theorem 2 by assuming the existence of a zkSNARK for relaxed R1CS with logarithmic-sized proofs. Finally, in Sect. 6, we construct such a zkSNARK.

2 Preliminaries

Let $\mathbb{F}$ denote a finite field with $|\mathbb{F}| = 2^{\Theta(\lambda)}$, where λ is the security parameter. Let $\cong$ denote computational indistinguishability with respect to a PPT adversary. We globally assume that generator algorithms that produce public parameters are additionally provided appropriate size bounds.

2.1 A Commitment Scheme for Vectors over $\mathbb{F}$

We require a commitment scheme for vectors over $\mathbb{F}$ that is additively homomorphic and succinct. We formally define these two properties and others noted below in [30, App. F]. Below, we define the syntax for commitment schemes.

Definition 1 (A Commitment Scheme for Vectors). *A commitment scheme for $\mathbb{F}^m$ is a tuple of three protocols with the following interface.*

- $\mathsf{Gen}(1^\lambda, m) \to \mathsf{pp}$*: takes length parameter m; produces public parameters* pp.
- $\mathsf{Com}(\mathsf{pp}, v, r) \to C$*: takes vector $v \in \mathbb{F}^m$ and $r \in \mathbb{F}$; produces commitment C.*
- $\mathsf{Open}(\mathsf{pp}, C, v, r) \to \{0,1\}$*: verifies the opening of commitment C to $v \in \mathbb{F}^m$.*

A commitment scheme satisfies hiding (the commitment reveals no information), binding (a PPT adversary cannot open a commitment to two different values), and succinctness (the commitment size is logarithmic in the opening size).

2.2 Non-interactive Arguments of Knowledge

Definition 2 (Non-Interactive Argument of Knowledge). *Consider a relation $\mathcal{R}$ over public parameters, structure, instance, and witness tuples. A non-interactive argument of knowledge for $\mathcal{R}$ consists of PPT algorithms $(\mathcal{G}, \mathcal{P}, \mathcal{V})$ and deterministic $\mathcal{K}$, denoting the generator, the prover, the verifier and the encoder respectively with the following interface.*

- $\mathcal{G}(1^\lambda) \rightarrow \mathsf{pp}$: *On input security parameter* λ, *samples public parameters* pp.
- $\mathcal{K}(\mathsf{pp}, \mathsf{s}) \rightarrow (\mathsf{pk}, \mathsf{vk})$: *On input structure* s, *representing common structure among instances, outputs the prover key* pk *and verifier key* vk.
- $\mathcal{P}(\mathsf{pk}, u, w) \rightarrow \pi$: *On input instance* u *and witness* w, *outputs a proof* π *proving that* $(\mathsf{pp}, \mathsf{s}, u, w) \in \mathcal{R}$.
- $\mathcal{V}(\mathsf{vk}, u, \pi) \rightarrow \{0, 1\}$: *Checks instance* u *given proof* π.

An argument of knowledge satisfies completeness if for any PPT adversary $\mathcal{A}$

$$\Pr\left[\mathcal{V}(\mathsf{vk}, u, \pi) = 1 \;\middle|\; \begin{array}{l} \mathsf{pp} \leftarrow \mathcal{G}(1^\lambda), \\ (\mathsf{s}, (u, w)) \leftarrow \mathcal{A}(\mathsf{pp}), \\ (\mathsf{pp}, \mathsf{s}, u, w) \in \mathcal{R}, \\ (\mathsf{pk}, \mathsf{vk}) \leftarrow \mathcal{K}(\mathsf{pp}, \mathsf{s}), \\ \pi \leftarrow \mathcal{P}(\mathsf{pk}, u, w) \end{array}\right] = 1.$$

An argument of knowledge satisfies knowledge soundness if for all PPT adversaries $\mathcal{A}$ *there exists a PPT extractor* $\mathcal{E}$ *such that for all randomness* ρ

$$\Pr\left[\begin{array}{l} \mathcal{V}(\mathsf{vk}, u, \pi) = 1, \\ (\mathsf{pp}, \mathsf{s}, u, w) \notin \mathcal{R} \end{array} \;\middle|\; \begin{array}{l} \mathsf{pp} \leftarrow \mathcal{G}(1^\lambda), \\ (\mathsf{s}, u, \pi) \leftarrow \mathcal{A}(\mathsf{pp}; \rho), \\ (\mathsf{pk}, \mathsf{vk}) \leftarrow \mathcal{K}(\mathsf{pp}, \mathsf{s}), \\ w \leftarrow \mathcal{E}(\mathsf{pp}, \rho) \end{array}\right] = \mathsf{negl}(\lambda).$$

Definition 3 (Zero-Knowledge). *An argument of knowledge* $(\mathcal{G}, \mathcal{K}, \mathcal{P}, \mathcal{V})$ *for relation* $\mathcal{R}$ *satisfies zero-knowledge if there exists PPT simulator* $\mathcal{S}$ *such that for all PPT adversaries* $\mathcal{A}$

$$\left\{ (\mathsf{pp}, \mathsf{s}, u, \pi) \;\middle|\; \begin{array}{l} \mathsf{pp} \leftarrow \mathcal{G}(1^\lambda), \\ (\mathsf{s}, (u, w)) \leftarrow \mathcal{A}(\mathsf{pp}), \\ (\mathsf{pp}, \mathsf{s}, u, w) \in \mathcal{R}, \\ (\mathsf{pk}, \mathsf{vk}) \leftarrow \mathcal{K}(\mathsf{pp}, \mathsf{s}), \\ \pi \leftarrow \mathcal{P}(\mathsf{pk}, u, w) \end{array} \right\} \cong \left\{ (\mathsf{pp}, \mathsf{s}, u, \pi) \;\middle|\; \begin{array}{l} (\mathsf{pp}, \tau) \leftarrow \mathcal{S}(1^\lambda), \\ (\mathsf{s}, (u, w)) \leftarrow \mathcal{A}(\mathsf{pp}), \\ (\mathsf{pp}, \mathsf{s}, u, w) \in \mathcal{R}, \\ (\mathsf{pk}, \mathsf{vk}) \leftarrow \mathcal{K}(\mathsf{pp}, \mathsf{s}), \\ \pi \leftarrow \mathcal{S}(\mathsf{pp}, u, \tau) \end{array} \right\}$$

Definition 4 (Succinctness). *A non-interactive argument system is succinct if the size of the proof* π *is polylogarithmic in the size of the witness* w.

2.3 Incrementally Verifiable Computation

Incrementally verifiable computation (IVC) [43] enables verifiable computation for repeated function application. Intuitively, for a function F, with initial input z_0, an IVC scheme allows a prover to produce a proof Π_i for the statement $z_i = F^{(i)}(z_0)$ (i.e., i applications of F on input z_0) given a proof Π_{i-1} for the statement $z_{i-1} = F^{(i-1)}(z_0)$. Formally, IVC schemes additionally permit F to take auxiliary input ω. We recall the definition of IVC using notational conventions of modern argument systems.

Definition 5 (IVC). *An incrementally verifiable computation (IVC) scheme is defined by PPT algorithms* $(\mathcal{G}, \mathcal{P}, \mathcal{V})$ *and deterministic* $\mathcal{K}$ *denoting the generator,* *the prover, the verifier, and the encoder respectively. An IVC scheme* $(\mathcal{G}, \mathcal{K}, \mathcal{P}, \mathcal{V})$ *satisfies perfect completeness if for any PPT adversary* $\mathcal{A}$

$$\Pr\left[\mathcal{V}(\mathsf{vk}, i, z_0, z_i, \Pi_i) = 1 \middle| \begin{array}{l} \mathsf{pp} \leftarrow \mathcal{G}(1^\lambda), \\ F, (i, z_0, z_i, z_{i-1}, \omega_{i-1}, \Pi_{i-1}) \leftarrow \mathcal{A}(\mathsf{pp}), \\ (\mathsf{pk}, \mathsf{vk}) \leftarrow \mathcal{K}(\mathsf{pp}, F), \\ z_i = F(z_{i-1}, \omega_{i-1}), \\ \mathcal{V}(\mathsf{vk}, i-1, z_0, z_{i-1}, \Pi_{i-1}) = 1, \\ \Pi_i \leftarrow \mathcal{P}(\mathsf{pk}, i, z_0, z_i; z_{i-1}, \omega_{i-1}, \Pi_{i-1}) \end{array}\right] = 1$$

where F *is a polynomial time computable function. Likewise, an IVC scheme satisfies knowledge-soundness if for any constant* $n \in \mathbb{N}$*, and expected polynomial time adversaries* $\mathcal{P}^*$ *there exists expected polynomial-time extractor* $\mathcal{E}$ *such that for any input randomness* ρ

$$\Pr\left[\begin{array}{l} z_n \neq z, \\ \mathcal{V}(\mathsf{vk}, n, z_0, z, \Pi) = 1 \end{array} \middle| \begin{array}{l} \mathsf{pp} \leftarrow \mathcal{G}(1^\lambda), \\ F, (z_0, z, \Pi) \leftarrow \mathcal{P}^*(\mathsf{pp}; \rho), \\ (\mathsf{pk}, \mathsf{vk}) \leftarrow \mathcal{K}(\mathsf{pp}, F), \\ (\omega_0, \ldots, \omega_{n-1}) \leftarrow \mathcal{E}(\mathsf{pp}, z_0, z; \rho), \\ z_i \leftarrow F(z_{i-1}, \omega_{i-1}) \quad \forall i \in \{1, \ldots, n\} \end{array}\right] \leq \mathsf{negl}(\lambda).$$

An IVC scheme satisfies succinctness if the size of the IVC proof Π *does not grow with the number of applications* n.

We note that in the definition above, the number of steps n is treated as a fixed environment variable that characterizes the extractor. This model is required for all known general recursive techniques as they rely on recursive extractors that blowup polynomially for each additional recursive step [10,13, 15,16,21]. Bitansky et al. [8] avoid such a restriction by making non-blackbox assumptions about the extractors runtime with respect to that of the malicious prover. In any case, there are no known attacks on arbitrary depth recursion.

3 Folding Schemes

This section formally defines folding schemes. Intuitively, a folding scheme for a relation $\mathcal{R}$ is a protocol that reduces the task of checking two instances in $\mathcal{R}$ to the task of checking a single instance in $\mathcal{R}$.

Definition 6 (Folding Scheme). *Consider a relation* $\mathcal{R}$ *over public parameters, structure, instance, and witness tuples. A folding scheme for* $\mathcal{R}$ *consists of a PPT generator algorithm* $\mathcal{G}$*, a deterministic encoder algorithm* $\mathcal{K}$*, and a pair of PPT algorithms* $\mathcal{P}$ *and* $\mathcal{V}$ *denoting the prover and verifier respectively, with the following interface:*

- $\mathcal{G}(1^\lambda) \rightarrow \mathsf{pp}$*: On input security parameter* λ*, samples public parameters* pp.
- $\mathcal{K}(\mathsf{pp}, \mathsf{s}) \rightarrow (\mathsf{pk}, \mathsf{vk})$*: On input* pp*, and a common structure* s *between instances to be folded, outputs a prover key* pk *and a verifier key* vk.

- $\mathcal{P}(\mathsf{pk}, (u_1, w_1), (u_2, w_2)) \rightarrow (u, w)$: *On input instance-witness tuples* (u_1, w_1) *and* (u_2, w_2) *outputs a new instance-witness tuple* (u, w) *of the same size.*
- $\mathcal{V}(\mathsf{vk}, u_1, u_2) \rightarrow u$: *On input instances* u_1 *and* u_2*, outputs a new instance* u*.*

Let

$$(u, w) \leftarrow \langle \mathcal{P}(\mathsf{pk}, w_1, w_2), \mathcal{V}(\mathsf{vk}) \rangle (u_1, u_2)$$

denote the the verifier's output instance u *and the prover's output witness* w *from the interaction of* $\mathcal{P}$ *and* $\mathcal{V}$ *on witnesses* (w_1, w_2)*, prover key* pk*, verifier key* vk *and instances* (u_1, u_2)*. Likewise, let*

$$\mathsf{tr} = \langle \mathcal{P}(\mathsf{pk}, w_1, w_2), \mathcal{V}(\mathsf{vk}) \rangle (u_1, u_2)$$

denote the corresponding interaction transcript. A folding scheme satisfies perfect completeness if for all PPT adversaries $\mathcal{A}$

$$\Pr\left[(\mathsf{pp}, \mathsf{s}, u, w) \in \mathcal{R} \;\middle|\; \begin{array}{l} \mathsf{pp} \leftarrow \mathcal{G}(1^\lambda), \\ (\mathsf{s}, (u_1, w_1), (u_2, w_2)) \leftarrow \mathcal{A}(\mathsf{pp}), \\ (\mathsf{pp}, \mathsf{s}, u_1, w_1), (\mathsf{pp}, \mathsf{s}, u_2, w_2) \in \mathcal{R}, \\ (\mathsf{pk}, \mathsf{vk}) \leftarrow \mathcal{K}(\mathsf{pp}, \mathsf{s}), \\ (u, w) \leftarrow \langle \mathcal{P}(\mathsf{pk}, w_1, w_2), \mathcal{V}(\mathsf{vk}) \rangle (u_1, u_2) \end{array} \right] = 1.$$

A folding scheme satisfies knowledge soundness if for any expected polynomial-time adversary $\mathcal{P}^*$ *there is an expected polynomial-time extractor* $\mathcal{E}$ *such that*

$$\Pr\left[\begin{array}{l} (\mathsf{pp}, \mathsf{s}, u_1, w_1) \in \mathcal{R}, \\ (\mathsf{pp}, \mathsf{s}, u_2, w_2) \in \mathcal{R} \end{array} \;\middle|\; \begin{array}{l} \mathsf{pp} \leftarrow \mathcal{G}(1^\lambda), \\ (\mathsf{s}, (u_1, u_2)) \leftarrow \mathcal{P}^*(\mathsf{pp}, \rho), \\ (w_1, w_2) \leftarrow \mathcal{E}(\mathsf{pp}, \rho) \end{array} \right] \geq$$

$$\Pr\left[(\mathsf{pp}, \mathsf{s}, u, w) \in \mathcal{R} \;\middle|\; \begin{array}{l} \mathsf{pp} \leftarrow \mathcal{G}(1^\lambda), \\ (\mathsf{s}, (u_1, u_2)) \leftarrow \mathcal{P}^*(\mathsf{pp}, \rho), \\ (\mathsf{pk}, \mathsf{vk}) \leftarrow \mathcal{K}(\mathsf{pp}, \mathsf{s}), \\ (u, w) \leftarrow \langle \mathcal{P}^*(\mathsf{pk}, \rho), \mathcal{V}(\mathsf{vk}) \rangle (u_1, u_2) \end{array} \right] - \mathsf{negl}(\lambda)$$

where ρ *denotes arbitrary input randomness for* $\mathcal{P}^*$*. We call a transcript an accepting transcript if* $\mathcal{P}$ *outputs a satisfying folded witness* w *for the folded instance* u*. We consider a folding scheme non-trivial if the communication costs and* $\mathcal{V}$*'s computation are lower in the case where* $\mathcal{V}$ *participates in the folding scheme and then checks a witness sent by* $\mathcal{P}$ *for the folded instance than the case where* $\mathcal{V}$ *checks witnesses sent by* $\mathcal{P}$ *for each of the original instances.*

Definition 7 (Non-Interactive). *A folding scheme* $(\mathcal{G}, \mathcal{K}, \mathcal{P}, \mathcal{V})$ *is non-interactive if the interaction between* $\mathcal{P}$ *and* $\mathcal{V}$ *consists of a single message from* $\mathcal{P}$ *to* $\mathcal{V}$*. This single message is denoted as an output of* $\mathcal{P}$*, and an input to* $\mathcal{V}$*.*

Definition 8 (Zero-Knowledge). *A folding scheme* $(\mathcal{G}, \mathcal{K}, \mathcal{P}, \mathcal{V})$ *satisfies zero-knowledge for relation* $\mathcal{R}$ *if there exists a PPT simulator* $\mathcal{S}$ *such that for all*

PPT adversaries $\mathcal{A}$, and $\mathcal{V}^*$, and input randomness ρ

$$\left\{ \text{tr} \left| \begin{array}{l} \mathsf{pp} \leftarrow \mathcal{G}(1^\lambda), \\ (\mathsf{s}, (u_1, w_1), (u_2, w_2)) \leftarrow \mathcal{A}(\mathsf{pp}), \\ (\mathsf{pk}, \mathsf{vk}) \leftarrow \mathcal{K}(\mathsf{pp}, \mathsf{s}), \\ (\mathsf{pp}, \mathsf{s}, u_1, w_1), (\mathsf{pp}, \mathsf{s}, u_2, w_2) \in \mathcal{R}, \\ \mathsf{tr} = \langle \mathcal{P}(\mathsf{pk}, w_1, w_2), \mathcal{V}^*(\mathsf{vk}, \rho) \rangle (u_1, u_2) \end{array} \right. \right\} \cong$$

$$\left\{ \text{tr} \left| \begin{array}{l} \mathsf{pp} \leftarrow \mathcal{G}(1^\lambda), \\ (\mathsf{s}, (u_1, w_1), (u_2, w_2)) \leftarrow \mathcal{A}(\mathsf{pp}), \\ (\mathsf{pp}, \mathsf{s}, u_1, w_1), (\mathsf{pp}, \mathsf{s}, u_2, w_2) \in \mathcal{R}, \\ (\mathsf{pk}, \mathsf{vk}) \leftarrow \mathcal{K}(\mathsf{pp}, \mathsf{s}), \\ \mathsf{tr} \leftarrow \mathcal{S}^{\mathcal{V}^*(\mathsf{vk}, \rho)}(\mathsf{pk}, u_1, u_2) \end{array} \right. \right\}$$

Definition 9 (Public Coin). *A folding scheme $(\mathcal{G}, \mathcal{K}, \mathcal{P}, \mathcal{V})$ is called public coin if all the messages sent from $\mathcal{V}$ to $\mathcal{P}$ are sampled from a uniform distribution.*

Typically, knowledge soundness is difficult to prove directly. To assist these proofs, prior works employ the forking lemma [11], which abstracts away much of the probabilistic reasoning. The original forking lemma shows that to prove knowledge soundness it is sufficient to construct a PPT extractor that takes as input a "tree" of accepting transcripts and outputs a satisfying witness. However, in our setting, this extractor must *additionally* take as input the prover's output (i.e., the folded instance and witness) for each of these transcripts, which contains information needed to reconstruct the original witness. So, we introduce a small variant of the forking lemma that captures this modification.

Lemma 1 (Forking Lemma for Folding Schemes). *Consider a $(2\mu + 1)$-move folding scheme $\Pi = (\mathcal{G}, \mathcal{K}, \mathcal{P}, \mathcal{V})$. Π satisfies knowledge soundness if there exists a PPT $\mathcal{X}$ such that for all input instance pairs u_1, u_2, outputs satisfying witnesses w_1, w_2 with probability $1 - \mathsf{negl}(\lambda)$, given public parameters pp, structure s, and an $(n_1, \ldots, n_\mu)$-tree of accepting transcripts and corresponding folded instance-witness pairs (u, w). This tree comprises n_1 transcripts (and corresponding instance-witness pairs) with fresh randomness in $\mathcal{V}$'s first message; and for each such transcript, n_2 transcripts (and corresponding instance-witness pairs) with fresh randomness in $\mathcal{V}$'s second message; etc., for a total of $\prod_{i=1}^{\mu} n_i$ leaves bounded by $\mathsf{poly}(\lambda)$.*

Proof Intuition. A proof for our variant of the forking lemma is similar to that of Bootle et al. [11]. We present a formal proof in [30, App. F]. □

4 A Folding Scheme for NP

In this section, we describe a public-coin, zero-knowledge interactive folding scheme for NP. We additionally discuss how to make it non-interactive. We leverage the non-interactivity property to realize IVC in the next section, and the zero-knowledge property to achieve zero-knowledge IVC proof compression.

4.1 A Public-Coin, Zero-Knowledge Folding Scheme

To design a folding scheme for NP, we need an NP-complete language. While theoretically any NP-complete language is a viable candidate, we focus on R1CS,[4] a popular algebraic representation that generalizes arithmetic circuit satisfiability.

Definition 10 (R1CS). *Consider a finite field $\mathbb{F}$. Let the public parameters consist of size bounds $m, n, \ell \in \mathbb{N}$ where $m > \ell$. The R1CS structure consists of sparse matrices $A, B, C \in \mathbb{F}^{m \times m}$ with at most $n = \Omega(m)$ non-zero entries in each matrix. An instance $\mathsf{x} \in \mathbb{F}^{\ell}$ consists of public inputs and outputs and is satisfied by a witness $W \in \mathbb{F}^{m-\ell-1}$ if $(A \cdot Z) \circ (B \cdot Z) = C \cdot Z$, where $Z = (W, \mathsf{x}, 1)$.*

As we show in the next section, to realize IVC, we only need a folding scheme that can fold two R1CS instances with the same R1CS matrices (A, B, C). Specifically, given R1CS matrices (A, B, C), and two corresponding instance-witness pairs (x_1, W_1) and (x_2, W_2), we would like to devise a scheme that reduces the task of checking both instances into the task of checking a single new instance-witness pair (x, W) against the same R1CS matrices (A, B, C). Unfortunately, as we illustrate now, it is difficult to devise a folding scheme for R1CS such that it satisfies completeness, let alone knowledge soundness.

First Attempt. As R1CS is an algebraic system, the most direct approach would be to take a random linear combination. Ignoring efficiency concerns, suppose that the prover sends witnesses W_1 and W_2 in the first step. The verifier responds with a random $r \in \mathbb{F}$; the prover and the verifier both compute

$$\begin{aligned} \mathsf{x} &\leftarrow \mathsf{x}_1 + r \cdot \mathsf{x}_2 \\ W &\leftarrow W_1 + r \cdot W_2, \end{aligned}$$

and set the new instance-witness pair to be (x, W). However, for non-trivial $Z_1 = (W_1, \mathsf{x}_1, 1)$ and $Z_2 = (W_2, \mathsf{x}_2, 1)$, and $Z = (W, \mathsf{x}, 1)$, we *roughly* have that

$$\begin{aligned} AZ \circ BZ &= A(Z_1 + r \cdot Z_2) \circ B(Z_1 + r \cdot Z_2) \\ &= AZ_1 \circ BZ_1 + r \cdot (AZ_1 \circ BZ_2 + AZ_2 \circ BZ_1) + r^2 \cdot (AZ_2 \circ BZ_2) \\ &\neq CZ. \end{aligned}$$

The failed attempt exposes three issues. First, we must account for an additional cross-term, $r \cdot (AZ_1 \circ BZ_2 + AZ_2 \circ BZ_1)$. Second, the terms excluding the cross-term combine to produce a term that does not equal CZ:

$$AZ_1 \circ BZ_1 + r^2 \cdot (AZ_2 \circ BZ_2) = CZ_1 + r^2 \cdot CZ_2 \neq CZ_1 + r \cdot CZ_2 = CZ.$$

Third, we do not even have that $Z = Z_1 + r \cdot Z_2$ because $Z_1 + r \cdot Z_2 = (W, \mathsf{x}, 1 + r \cdot 1)$.

[4] R1CS is implicit in the QAPs formalism of GGPR [23], but it was made explicit in subsequent work [40]; they refer to it as a "constraint system in quadratic form".

Second Attempt. To handle the first issue, we introduce a "slack" (or error) vector $E \in \mathbb{F}^m$ which absorbs the cross terms generated by folding. To handle the second and third issues, we introduce a scalar u, which absorbs an extra factor of r in $CZ_1 + r^2 \cdot CZ_2$ and in $Z = (W, \mathsf{x}, 1 + r \cdot 1)$. We refer to a variant of R1CS with these additional terms as *relaxed* R1CS.

Definition 11 (Relaxed R1CS). *Consider a finite field $\mathbb{F}$. Let the public parameters consist of size bounds $m, n, \ell \in \mathbb{N}$ where $m > \ell$. The relaxed R1CS structure consists of sparse matrices $A, B, C \in \mathbb{F}^{m \times m}$ with at most $n = \Omega(m)$ non-zero entries in each matrix. A relaxed R1CS instance consists of an error vector $E \in \mathbb{F}^m$, a scalar $u \in \mathbb{F}$, and public inputs and outputs $\mathsf{x} \in \mathbb{F}^\ell$. An instance (E, u, x) is satisfied by a witness $W \in \mathbb{F}^{m-\ell-1}$ if $(A \cdot Z) \circ (B \cdot Z) = u \cdot (C \cdot Z) + E$, where $Z = (W, \mathsf{x}, u)$.*

Note that any R1CS instance can be expressed as a relaxed R1CS instance by augmenting it with $u = 1$ and $E = 0$, so relaxed R1CS retains NP-completeness.

Building on the first attempt, the prover and verifier can now use E to accumulate the cross-terms. In particular, for $Z_i = (W_i, \mathsf{x}_i, u_i)$, the prover and verifier additionally compute

$$\begin{aligned} &u \leftarrow u_1 + r \cdot u_2 \\ &E \leftarrow E_1 + r \cdot (AZ_1 \circ BZ_2 + AZ_2 \circ BZ_1 - u_1 CZ_2 - u_2 CZ_1) + r^2 \cdot E_2, \end{aligned}$$

and set the new instance-witness pair to be $((E, u, \mathsf{x}), W)$. Conveniently, updating u in this manner also keeps track of how the constant term in Z should be updated, which motivates our choice to use u in $Z = (W, \mathsf{x}, u)$ rather than introducing a new variable. Now, for $Z = (W, \mathsf{x}, u)$, and for random $r \in \mathbb{F}$,

$$\begin{aligned} AZ \circ BZ &= AZ_1 \circ BZ_1 + r \cdot (AZ_1 \circ BZ_2 + AZ_2 \circ BZ_1) + r^2 \cdot (AZ_2 \circ BZ_2) \\ &= (u_1 CZ_1 + E_1) + r \cdot (AZ_1 \circ BZ_2 + AZ_2 \circ BZ_1) + r^2 \cdot (u_2 CZ_2 + E_2) \\ &= (u_1 + r \cdot u_2) \cdot C(Z_1 + rZ_2) + E \\ &= uCZ + E. \end{aligned}$$

This implies that, for R1CS matrices (A, B, C), the folded witness W is a satisfying witness for the folded instance (E, u, x) as promised. A few issues remain: in the above scheme, the prover sends witnesses (W_1, W_2) for the verifier to compute E. As a result, the folding scheme is *not* non-trivial; it is also not zero-knowledge.

Final Protocol. To circumvent these issues, we use succinct and hiding additively homomorphic commitments to W and E in the instance, and treat both W and E as the witness. We refer to this variant of relaxed R1CS as *committed relaxed R1CS*. Below, we describe a folding scheme for committed relaxed R1CS, where the prover sends a single commitment to aid the verifier in computing commitments to the folded witness (W, E).

Definition 12 (Committed Relaxed R1CS). *Consider a finite field* $\mathbb{F}$ *and a commitment scheme* Com *over* $\mathbb{F}$. *Let the public parameters consist of size bounds* $m, n, \ell \in \mathbb{N}$ *where* $m > \ell$, *and commitment parameters* pp_W *and* pp_E *for vectors of size* m *and* $m - \ell - 1$ *respectively. The committed relaxed R1CS structure consists of sparse matrices* $A, B, C \in \mathbb{F}^{m \times m}$ *with at most* $n = \Omega(m)$ *non-zero entries in each matrix. A committed relaxed R1CS instance is a tuple* $(\overline{E}, u, \overline{W}, \mathsf{x})$, *where* $\overline{E}$ *and* $\overline{W}$ *are commitments,* $u \in \mathbb{F}$, *and* $\mathsf{x} \in \mathbb{F}^{\ell}$ *are public inputs and outputs. An instance* $(\overline{E}, u, \overline{W}, \mathsf{x})$ *is satisfied by a witness* $(E, r_E, W, r_W) \in (\mathbb{F}^m, \mathbb{F}, \mathbb{F}^{m-\ell-1}, \mathbb{F})$ *if* $\overline{E} = \mathsf{Com}(\mathsf{pp}_E, E, r_E)$, $\overline{W} = \mathsf{Com}(\mathsf{pp}_W, W, r_W)$, *and* $(A \cdot Z) \circ (B \cdot Z) = u \cdot (C \cdot Z) + E$, *where* $Z = (W, \mathsf{x}, u)$.

Construction 1 (A Folding Scheme for Committed Relaxed R1CS). Consider a finite field $\mathbb{F}$ and a succinct, hiding, and homomorphic commitment scheme Com over $\mathbb{F}$. We define the generator and the encoder as follows.

- $\mathcal{G}(1^\lambda) \to \mathsf{pp}$: output size bounds $m, n, \ell \in \mathbb{N}$, and commitment parameters pp_W and pp_E for vectors of size m and $m - \ell - 1$ respectively.
- $\mathcal{K}(\mathsf{pp}, (A, B, C)) \to (\mathsf{pk}, \mathsf{vk})$: output $\mathsf{pk} \leftarrow (\mathsf{pp}, (A, B, C))$ and $\mathsf{vk} \leftarrow \bot$.

The verifier $\mathcal{V}$ takes two committed relaxed R1CS instances $(\overline{E}_1, u_1, \overline{W}_1, \mathsf{x}_1)$ and $(\overline{E}_2, u_2, \overline{W}_2, \mathsf{x}_2)$. The prover $\mathcal{P}$, in addition to the two instances, takes witnesses to both instances, $(E_1, r_{E_1}, W_1, r_{W_1})$ and $(E_2, r_{E_2}, W_2, r_{W_2})$. Let $Z_1 = (W_1, \mathsf{x}_1, u_1)$ and $Z_2 = (W_2, \mathsf{x}_2, u_2)$. The prover and the verifier proceed as follows.

1. $\mathcal{P}$: Send $\overline{T} := \mathsf{Com}(\mathsf{pp}_E, T, r_T)$, where $r_T \leftarrow_R \mathbb{F}$ and with cross term

$$T = AZ_1 \circ BZ_2 + AZ_2 \circ BZ_1 - u_1 \cdot CZ_2 - u_2 \cdot CZ_1.$$

2. $\mathcal{V}$: Sample and send challenge $r \leftarrow_R \mathbb{F}$.
3. $\mathcal{V}, \mathcal{P}$: Output the folded instance $(\overline{E}, u, \overline{W}, \mathsf{x})$ where

$$\begin{aligned} \overline{E} &\leftarrow \overline{E}_1 + r \cdot \overline{T} + r^2 \cdot \overline{E}_2 \\ u &\leftarrow u_1 + r \cdot u_2 \\ \overline{W} &\leftarrow \overline{W}_1 + r \cdot \overline{W}_2 \\ \mathsf{x} &\leftarrow \mathsf{x}_1 + r \cdot \mathsf{x}_2 \end{aligned}$$

4. $\mathcal{P}$: Output the folded witness (E, r_E, W, r_W), where

$$\begin{aligned} E &\leftarrow E_1 + r \cdot T + r^2 \cdot E_2 \\ r_E &\leftarrow r_{E_1} + r \cdot r_T + r^2 \cdot r_{E_2} \\ W &\leftarrow W_1 + r \cdot W_2 \\ r_W &\leftarrow r_{W_1} + r \cdot r_{W_2} \end{aligned}$$

Theorem 3 (A Folding Scheme for Committed Relaxed R1CS). *Construction 1 is a public-coin folding scheme for committed relaxed R1CS with perfect completeness, knowledge soundness, and zero-knowledge.*

Proof Intuition. With textbook algebra, we can show that if witnesses $(E_1, r_{E_1}, W_1, r_{W_1})$ and $(E_2, r_{E_2}, W_2, r_{W_2})$ are satisfying witnesses, then the folded witness (E, r_E, W, r_W) must be a satisfying witness. We prove knowledge soundness via the forking lemma (Lemma 1) by showing that the extractor can produce the initial witnesses given three accepting transcripts and the corresponding folded witnesses. Specifically, the extractor uses all three transcripts to compute E_i and r_{E_i}, and any two transcripts to compute W_i and r_{W_i} for $i \in \{1, 2\}$. The choice of which two transcripts does not matter due to the binding property of the commitment scheme. We present a formal proof in [30, App. B]. □

4.2 Achieving Non-interactivity via the Fiat-Shamir Transform

To design Nova's IVC scheme, we require our folding scheme for committed relaxed R1CS to be non-interactive in the standard model. To do so we first achieve non-interactivity in the random oracle model using the (strong) Fiat-Shamir transform [22]. Next, we heuristically instantiate the random oracle using a cryptographic hash function. As a result, we can only heuristically argue the security of the resulting non-interactive folding scheme. Note that all existing IVC constructions in the standard model require instantiating the random oracle with a cryptographic hash function [12,15,21,43].

Construction 2 (A Non-Interactive Folding Scheme). We achieve non-interactivity in the random oracle model using the strong Fiat-Shamir transform [22]. Let ρ denote a random oracle sampled during parameter generation and provided to all parties. Let $(\mathsf{G}, \mathsf{K}, \mathsf{P}, \mathsf{V})$ represent our interactive folding scheme (Construction 1). We construct a non-interactive folding scheme $(\mathcal{G}, \mathcal{K}, \mathcal{P}, \mathcal{V})$ as follows:

- $\mathcal{G}(1^\lambda)$: output $\mathsf{pp} \leftarrow \mathsf{G}(1^\lambda)$.
- $\mathcal{K}(\mathsf{pp}, (A, B, C))$: $\mathsf{vk} \leftarrow \rho(\mathsf{pp}, \mathsf{s})$ and $\mathsf{pk} \leftarrow (\mathsf{pp}, (A, B, C), \mathsf{vk})$; output $(\mathsf{vk}, \mathsf{pk})$.
- $\mathcal{P}(\mathsf{pk}, (u_1, w_1), (u_2, w_2))$: runs $\mathsf{P}((\mathsf{pk.pp}, \mathsf{pk}.(A, B, C))$ to retrieve its first message $\overline{T}$, and sends $\overline{T}$ to $\mathcal{V}$; computes $r \leftarrow \rho(\mathsf{vk}, u_1, u_2, \overline{T})$, forwards this to P, and outputs the resulting output.
- $\mathcal{V}(\mathsf{vk}, u_1, u_2, \overline{T})$: runs V with $\overline{T}$ as the message from the prover and with randomness $r \leftarrow \rho(\mathsf{vk}, u_1, u_2, \overline{T})$, and outputs the resulting output.

Assumption 1 (RO instantiation). Construction 2 is a non-interactive folding scheme that satisfies completeness, knowledge soundness, and zero-knowledge in the standard model when ρ is instantiated with a cryptographic hash function.

5 Nova: An IVC Scheme with Proof Compression

This section describes Nova, an IVC scheme designed from a non-interactive folding scheme, which when instantiated with any additively-homomorphic commitment scheme with succinct commitments achieves the claimed efficiency (Lemma 4). In addition, Nova incorporates an efficient zkSNARK to prove the knowledge of valid IVC proofs succinctly and in zero-knowledge, providing a succinct, zero-knowledge proof of knowledge of a valid IVC proof.

In Nova, at each incremental step, the prover folds a particular step of the incremental computation (represented as a committed relaxed R1CS instance-witness pair) into a running committed relaxed R1CS instance-witness pair. At any step in the incremental computation, a valid "IVC proof", in a nutshell, is a satisfying witness of the running committed relaxed R1CS instance (which an honest prover can compute by folding witnesses associated with each step of the incremental computation) along with the running committed relaxed R1CS instance. Furthermore, at any incremental step, Nova's prover can prove in zero-knowledge and with a succinct proof—using a variant of an existing zkSNARK [38] (Sect. 6)—that it knows a valid IVC proof (i.e., a satisfying witness) to the running committed relaxed R1CS instance (Construction 4).

Note that Nova is *not* a zero-knowledge IVC scheme, as that would additionally require an IVC proof to be zero-knowledge (in Nova's case, an IVC proof does *not* hide witnesses associated with steps of the incremental computation). This difference is immaterial in the context of a single prover since it can use Nova's auxiliary zkSNARK to provide a zero-knowledge proof of knowledge of a valid IVC proof; we leave it to future work to achieve zero-knowledge IVC.

5.1 Constructing IVC from a Folding Scheme for NP

Recall that an IVC scheme allows a prover to show that $z_n = F^{(n)}(z_0)$ for some count n, initial input z_0, and output z_n. We now show how to construct an IVC scheme for a non-deterministic, polynomial-time computable function F using our non-interactive folding scheme for committed relaxed R1CS (Construction 2).[5]

In our construction, as in a SNARK-based IVC, the prover uses an augmented function F' (Fig. 4), which, in addition to invoking F, performs additional book-keeping to fold proofs of prior invocations of itself.

We first describe a simplified version of F', to provide intuition. F' takes as non-deterministic advice two committed relaxed R1CS instances u_i and U_i. Suppose that U_i represents the correct execution of invocations $1, \ldots, i-1$ of F' so long as u_i represents the correct execution of invocation i of F'. F' performs two tasks. First, it executes a step of the incremental computation: instance u_i contains z_i which F' uses to output $z_{i+1} = F(z_i)$. Second, F' invokes the verifier of the non-interactive folding scheme to fold the task of checking u_i and U_i into the task of checking a single instance U_{i+1}. The IVC prover then computes a new instance u_{i+1} which attests to the correct execution of invocation $i+1$ of F', thereby attesting that $z_{i+1} = F(z_i)$ and U_{i+1} is the result of folding u_i and U_i. Now, we have that U_{i+1} represents the correct execution of invocations $1, \ldots, i$ of F' so long as u_{i+1} represents the correct execution of invocation $i+1$ of F'.

The above description glossed over a subtle discrepancy: Because F' must output the running instance U_{i+1} for the next invocation to use, it is contained

[5] While, in theory, we can use any folding scheme for NP, we specifically invoke our construction for committed relaxed R1CS for a simpler presentation.

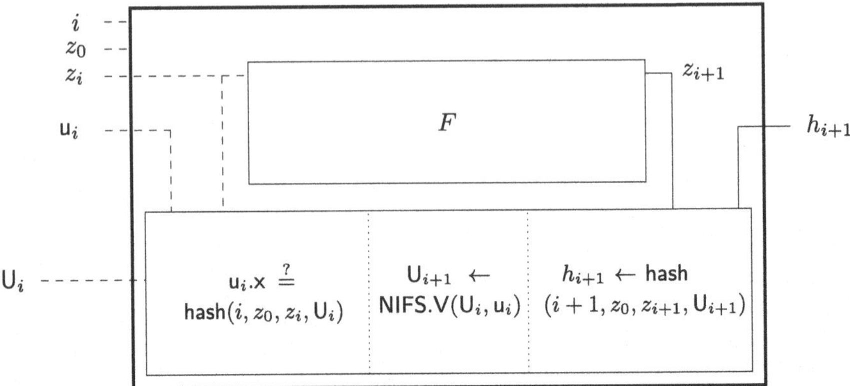

Fig. 4. Overview of F'. F' represented as a committed relaxed R1CS instance u_{i+1} encodes the statement that there exists $((i, z_0, z_i, u_i, U_i), U_{i+1}, \overline{T})$ such that $u_i.x = \mathsf{hash}(\mathsf{vk}, i, z_0, z_i, U_i)$, $h_{i+1} = \mathsf{hash}(\mathsf{vk}, i+1, z_0, F(z_i), U_{i+1})$, $U_{i+1} = \mathsf{NIFS}.V(\mathsf{vk}, U_i, u_i, \overline{T})$, and that F' outputs h_{i+1}. The diagram omits depicting vk, ω, and $\overline{T}$.

in $u_{i+1}.x$ (i.e., the public IO of u_{i+1}). But, in the next iteration, F' must fold $u_{i+1}.x$ into $U_{i+1}.x$, meaning that F' is stuck trying to squeeze U_{i+1} into $U_{i+1}.x$. To handle this inconsistency, we modify F' to output a *collision-resistant hash* of its public IO rather than producing it directly (this ensures that the public IO of F' is a constant number of finite field elements). The next invocation of F' then additionally takes the preimage of this hash as non-deterministic advice. We assume that the hash function takes an additional random input (which provides hiding) but for notational convenience we do not explicitly depict this.

Producing IVC Proofs. Let $(u_\perp, w_\perp)$ be the trivially satisfying instance-witness pair, where E, W, and x are appropriately-sized zero vectors, $r_E = 0$, $r_W = 0$, and $\overline{E}$ and $\overline{W}$ are commitments of E and W respectively.

Now, in iteration $i+1$, the IVC prover runs F' and computes u_{i+1} and U_{i+1} as well as the corresponding witnesses w_{i+1} and W_{i+1}. Because u_{i+1} and U_{i+1} together attest to the correctness of $i+1$ invocations of F' (which indirectly attests to $i+1$ invocations of F) the IVC proof Π_{i+1} is $((U_{i+1}, W_{i+1}), (u_{i+1}, w_{i+1}))$. Moreover, succinctness is maintained by the properties of the underlying folding scheme. We formally describe our construction below.

Construction 3 (IVC). Let NIFS $= (\mathsf{G}, \mathsf{K}, \mathsf{P}, \mathsf{V})$ be the non-interactive folding scheme for committed relaxed R1CS (Construction 2). Consider a polynomial-time function F that takes non-deterministic input, and a cryptographic hash function hash. We define our augmented function F' as follows (all arguments to F' are taken as non-deterministic advice):

$F'(\mathsf{vk}, U_i, u_i, (i, z_0, z_i), \omega_i, \overline{T}) \rightarrow \mathsf{x}$:

If i is 0, output $\mathsf{hash}(\mathsf{vk}, 1, z_0, F(z_0, \omega_i), u_\perp)$;

otherwise,

(1) check that $\mathsf{u}_i.\mathsf{x} = \mathsf{hash}(\mathsf{vk}, i, z_0, z_i, \mathsf{U}_i)$, where $\mathsf{u}_i.\mathsf{x}$ is the public IO of u_i,
(2) check that $(\mathsf{u}_i.\overline{E}, \mathsf{u}_i.u) = (\mathsf{u}_\perp.\overline{E}, 1)$,
(3) compute $\mathsf{U}_{i+1} \leftarrow \mathsf{NIFS.V}(\mathsf{vk}, \mathsf{U}, \mathsf{u}, \overline{T})$, and
(4) output $\mathsf{hash}(\mathsf{vk}, i+1, z_0, F(z_i, \omega_i), \mathsf{U}_{i+1})$.

Because F' can be computed in polynomial time, it can be represented as a committed relaxed R1CS structure $\mathsf{s}_{F'}$. Let

$$(\mathsf{u}_{i+1}, \mathsf{w}_{i+1}) \leftarrow \mathsf{trace}(F', (\mathsf{vk}, \mathsf{U}_i, \mathsf{u}_i, (i, z_0, z_i), \omega_i, \overline{T}))$$

denote the satisfying committed relaxed R1CS instance-witness pair $(\mathsf{u}_{i+1}, \mathsf{w}_{i+1})$ for the execution of F' on non-deterministic advice $(\mathsf{vk}, \mathsf{U}_i, \mathsf{u}_i, (i, z_0, z_i), \omega_i, \overline{T})$.

We define the IVC scheme $(\mathcal{G}, \mathcal{K}, \mathcal{P}, \mathcal{V})$ as follows.

$\mathcal{G}(1^\lambda) \rightarrow \mathsf{pp}$: Output $\mathsf{NIFS.G}(1^\lambda)$.

$\mathcal{K}(\mathsf{pp}, F) \rightarrow (\mathsf{pk}, \mathsf{vk})$:

Compute $(\mathsf{pk}_{\mathsf{fs}}, \mathsf{vk}_{\mathsf{fs}}) \leftarrow \mathsf{NIFS.K}(\mathsf{pp}, \mathsf{s}_{F'})$ and output $(\mathsf{pk}, \mathsf{vk}) \leftarrow ((F, \mathsf{pk}_{\mathsf{fs}}), (F, \mathsf{vk}_{\mathsf{fs}}))$.

$\mathcal{P}(\mathsf{pk}, (i, z_0, z_i), \omega_i, \Pi_i) \rightarrow \Pi_{i+1}$:

Parse Π_i as $((\mathsf{U}_i, \mathsf{W}_i), (\mathsf{u}_i, \mathsf{w}_i))$ and then
(1) if i is 0, compute $(\mathsf{U}_{i+1}, \mathsf{W}_{i+1}, \overline{T}) \leftarrow (\mathsf{u}_\perp, \mathsf{w}_\perp, \mathsf{u}_\perp.\overline{E})$;
otherwise, compute $(\mathsf{U}_{i+1}, \mathsf{W}_{i+1}, \overline{T}) \leftarrow \mathsf{NIFS.P}(\mathsf{pk}, (\mathsf{U}_i, \mathsf{W}_i), (\mathsf{u}_i, \mathsf{w}_i))$,
(2) compute $(\mathsf{u}_{i+1}, \mathsf{w}_{i+1}) \leftarrow \mathsf{trace}(F', (\mathsf{vk}, \mathsf{U}_i, \mathsf{u}_i, (i, z_0, z_i), \omega_i, \overline{T}))$, and
(3) output $\Pi_{i+1} \leftarrow ((\mathsf{U}_{i+1}, \mathsf{W}_{i+1}), (\mathsf{u}_{i+1}, \mathsf{w}_{i+1}))$.

$\mathcal{V}(\mathsf{vk}, (i, z_0, z_i), \Pi_i) \rightarrow \{0, 1\}$:

If i is 0, check that $z_i = z_0$;
otherwise,

(1) parse Π_i as $((\mathsf{U}_i, \mathsf{W}_i), (\mathsf{u}_i, \mathsf{w}_i))$,
(2) check that $\mathsf{u}_i.\mathsf{x} = \mathsf{hash}(\mathsf{vk}, i, z_0, z_i, \mathsf{U}_i)$,
(3) check that $(\mathsf{u}_i.\overline{E}, \mathsf{u}.u) = (\mathsf{u}_\perp.\overline{E}, 1)$, and
(4) check that W_i and w_i are satisfying witnesses to U_i and u_i respectively.

Lemma 2 (Completeness). *Construction 3 is an IVC scheme that satisfies completeness.*

Proof Intuition. Given a satisfying IVC proof $\Pi_i = ((\mathsf{U}_i, \mathsf{W}_i), (\mathsf{u}_i, \mathsf{w}_i))$ suppose that $\mathcal{P}$ outputs $\Pi_{i+1} = ((\mathsf{U}_{i+1}, \mathsf{W}_{i+1}), (\mathsf{u}_{i+1}, \mathsf{w}_{i+1}))$. Because Π_i is a valid IVC proof, $(\mathsf{u}_i, \mathsf{w}_i)$ and $(\mathsf{U}_i, \mathsf{W}_i)$ are satisfying instance-witness pairs. Because $(\mathsf{U}_{i+1}, \mathsf{W}_{i+1})$ is obtained by folding $(\mathsf{u}_i, \mathsf{w}_i)$ and $(\mathsf{U}_i, \mathsf{W}_i)$, it must be satisfying by the folding scheme's completeness. By construction, $(\mathsf{u}_{i+1}, \mathsf{w}_{i+1})$ is satisfying instance-witness pair that satisfies the IVC verifier's auxiliary checks. Thus, Π_{i+1} is satisfying. [30, App. C] provides a formal proof. □

Lemma 3 (Knowledge Soundness). *Construction 3 is an IVC scheme that satisfies knowledge soundness.*

Proof Intuition. For function F, constant n, $\mathsf{pp} \leftarrow \mathcal{G}(1^\lambda)$, and $(\mathsf{pk}, \mathsf{vk}) \leftarrow \mathcal{K}(\mathsf{pp}, F)$, consider an adversary $\mathcal{P}^*$ that outputs (z_0, z, Π) such that $\mathcal{V}(\mathsf{vk}, (n, z_0, z), \Pi) = 1$ with probability ϵ. We construct an extractor $\mathcal{E}$ that with input (pp, z_0, z), outputs $(\omega_0, \ldots, \omega_{n-1})$ such that by computing $z_i \leftarrow F(z_{i-1}, \omega_{i-1})$ for all $i \in \{1, \ldots, n\}$ we have that $z_n = z$ with probability $\epsilon - \mathsf{negl}(\lambda)$. We show inductively that $\mathcal{E}$ can construct an extractor $\mathcal{E}_i$ that outputs $(z_i, \ldots, z_{n-1})$, $(\omega_i, \ldots, \omega_{n-1})$, and Π_i such that for all $j \in \{i+1, \ldots, n\}$, $z_j = F(z_{j-1}, \omega_{j-1})$, $\mathcal{V}(\mathsf{vk}, i, z_0, z_i, \Pi_i) = 1$, and $z_n = z$ with probability $\epsilon - \mathsf{negl}(\lambda)$. Then, because in the base case when $i = 0$, $\mathcal{V}$ checks that $z_0 = z_i$, it is sufficient for $\mathcal{E}$ to run $\mathcal{E}_0$ to retrieve values $(\omega_0, \ldots, \omega_{n-1})$. Initially, $\mathcal{E}_n$ simply runs the assumed $\mathcal{P}^*$ to get a satisfying Π_n. Given extractor $\mathcal{E}_i$ that satisfies the inductive hypothesis, we can construct extractor $\mathcal{E}_{i-1}$. [30, App. C] provides a formal proof. □

Lemma 4 (Efficiency). *When instantiated with the Pedersen commitment scheme, we have that* $|F'| = |F| + o(2 \cdot \mathsf{G} + 2 \cdot \mathsf{H} + \mathsf{R})$, *where* $|F|$ *denotes the number of R1CS constraints to encode a function* F, G *is the number of constraints required to encode a group scalar multiplication,* H *is the number of constraints required to encode* hash, *and* R *is the number of constraints to encode the RO* ρ.

Proof. On input instances U and u, $\mathsf{NIFS.V}$ computes $\overline{E} \leftarrow \mathsf{U}.\overline{E} + r \cdot \overline{T} + r^2 \cdot \mathsf{u}.\overline{E}$ and $\overline{W} \leftarrow \mathsf{U}.\overline{W} + r \cdot \mathsf{u}.\overline{W}$. However, by construction, $\mathsf{u}.\overline{E} = \mathsf{u}_\perp.\overline{E} = \overline{0}$. So, $\mathsf{NIFS.V}$ computes two group scalar multiplications, as it does not need to compute $r^2 \cdot \mathsf{u}.\overline{E}$. $\mathsf{NIFS.V}$ additionally invokes the RO once to obtain a random scalar. Finally, F' makes two additional calls to hash (details are in the description of F'). □

5.2 Compressing IVC Proofs with zkSNARKs

To prove a statement about an incremental computation, the prover can produce an IVC proof using the construction in the prior section and send the IVC proof to the verifier. However, this does not satisfy zero-knowledge (as the IVC proof described in the prior section does not hide the prover's non-deterministic inputs) and succinctness (as the IVC proof size is linear in the size F). In theory, one can address this problem with any zkSNARK for NP. Specifically, $\overline{\mathcal{P}}$ can produce a zkSNARK proving that it knows Π_i such that IVC verifier $\mathcal{V}$ accepts for statement (i, z_0, z_i). Naturally, the proof sent to the verifier is succinct and zero-knowledge due to the corresponding properties of the zkSNARK.

Unfortunately, employing an off-the-shelf zkSNARK makes the overall solution impractical as the zkSNARK prover must prove, among other things, the knowledge of vectors whose commitments equal a particular value; this requires encoding a linear number of group scalar multiplications in the programming model of zkSNARKs (e.g., R1CS or circuits). To address this, we design a zkSNARK tailored for our particular purpose and we describe it in Sect. 6. Below, we describe how to use a zkSNARK to prove the knowledge of a valid IVC proof.

Construction 4 (A zkSNARK of a Valid IVC Proof). Let IVC denote the IVC scheme in Construction 3, let NIFS denote the non-interactive folding scheme in Construction 2, and let hash denote a randomized cryptographic hash function. Assume a zero-knowledge succinct non-interactive argument of knowledge (Definition 2), $\mathsf{zkSNARK}$, for committed relaxed R1CS. That is, given public parameters pp, structure s, and instance u, $\mathsf{zkSNARK.P}$ can convince $\mathsf{zkSNARK.V}$ in zero-knowledge and with a succinct proof (e.g., $O_\lambda(\log N)$-sized proof) that it knows a corresponding witness w such that $(\mathsf{pp}, \mathsf{s}, \mathsf{u}, \mathsf{w})$ is a satisfying committed relaxed R1CS tuple.

Consider a polynomial-time computable function F. Suppose $\mathsf{pp} \leftarrow \mathsf{IVC.G}(1^\lambda)$ and $(\mathsf{pk}, \mathsf{vk}) \leftarrow \mathsf{IVC.K}(\mathsf{pp}, F)$. Suppose the prover $\mathcal{P}$ and verifier $\mathcal{V}$ are provided an instance (i, z_0, z_i). We construct a zkSNARK that allows the prover to show that it knows an IVC proof Π_i such that $\mathsf{IVC.V}(\mathsf{vk}, i, z_0, z_i, \Pi_i) = 1$.

In a nutshell, we leverage the fact that Π is two committed relaxed R1CS instance-witness pairs. So, $\mathcal{P}$ first folds instance-witness pairs (u, w) and (U, W) to produce a folded instance-witness pair $(\mathsf{U}', \mathsf{W}')$, using $\mathsf{NIFS.P}$. Next, $\mathcal{P}$ runs $\mathsf{zkSNARK.P}$ to prove that it knows a valid witness for U'. In more detail, for polynomial-time computable function F and corresponding function F' as defined in Construction 3 (and instantiated with hash), we define $(\mathcal{G}, \mathcal{K}, \mathcal{P}, \mathcal{V})$ as follows.

$\mathcal{G}(1^\lambda) \rightarrow \mathsf{pp}$:

(1) Compute $\mathsf{pp}_{\mathsf{NIFS}} \leftarrow \mathsf{NIFS.G}(1^\lambda)$
(2) Compute $\mathsf{pp}_{\mathsf{zkSNARK}} \leftarrow \mathsf{zkSNARK.G}(1^\lambda)$
(3) Output $(\mathsf{pp}_{\mathsf{NIFS}}, \mathsf{pp}_{\mathsf{zkSNARK}})$

$\mathcal{K}(\mathsf{pp}, F) \rightarrow (\mathsf{pk}, \mathsf{vk})$:

(1) Compute $(\mathsf{pk}_{\mathsf{NIFS}}, \mathsf{vk}_{\mathsf{NIFS}}) \leftarrow \mathsf{NIFS.K}(\mathsf{pp}.\mathsf{pp}_{\mathsf{NIFS}}, \mathsf{s}_{F'})$.
(2) Compute $(\mathsf{pk}_{\mathsf{zkSNARK}}, \mathsf{vk}_{\mathsf{zkSNARK}}) \leftarrow \mathsf{zkSNARK.K}(\mathsf{pp}.\mathsf{pp}_{\mathsf{zkSNARK}}, \mathsf{s}_{F'})$.
(3) Output $((\mathsf{pk}_{\mathsf{NIFS}}, \mathsf{pk}_{\mathsf{zkSNARK}}), (\mathsf{vk}_{\mathsf{NIFS}}, \mathsf{vk}_{\mathsf{zkSNARK}}))$.

$\mathcal{P}(\mathsf{pk}, (i, z_0, z_i), \Pi) \rightarrow \pi$:

If i is 0, output $\perp$;
otherwise,

(1) parse Π as $((\mathsf{U}, \mathsf{W}), (\mathsf{u}, \mathsf{w}))$
(2) compute $(\mathsf{U}', \mathsf{W}', \overline{T}) \leftarrow \mathsf{NIFS.P}(\mathsf{pk}_{\mathsf{NIFS}}, (\mathsf{U}, \mathsf{W}), (\mathsf{u}, \mathsf{w}))$
(3) compute $\pi_{\mathsf{U}'} \leftarrow \mathsf{zkSNARK.P}(\mathsf{pk}_{\mathsf{zkSNARK}}, \mathsf{U}', \mathsf{W}')$
(4) output $(\mathsf{U}, \mathsf{u}, \overline{T}, \pi_{\mathsf{U}'})$.

$\mathcal{V}(\mathsf{vk}, (i, z_0, z_i), \pi) \rightarrow \{0, 1\}$:

If i is 0, check that $z_0 = z_i$;
otherwise,

(1) parse π as $(\mathsf{U}, \mathsf{u}, \overline{T}, \pi_{\mathsf{U}'})$,
(2) check that $\mathsf{u}.\mathsf{x} = \mathsf{hash}(\mathsf{vk}_{\mathsf{NIFS}}, i, z_0, z_i, \mathsf{U})$,
(3) check that $(\mathsf{u}.\overline{E}, \mathsf{u}.u) = (\mathsf{u}_{\perp}.\overline{E}, 1)$,
(4) compute $\mathsf{U}' \leftarrow \mathsf{NIFS.V}(\mathsf{vk}_{\mathsf{NIFS}}, \mathsf{U}, \mathsf{u}, \overline{T})$, and
(5) check that $\mathsf{zkSNARK.V}(\mathsf{vk}_{\mathsf{zkSNARK}}, \mathsf{U}', \pi_{\mathsf{U}'}) = 1$.

Theorem 4. *Construction 4 is a zkSNARK of a valid IVC proof produced by Construction 3.*

Proof Intuition. Completeness and knowledge soundness hold due to the completeness and knowledge soundness of the underlying zkSNARK and the non-interactive folding scheme. Assuming the non-interactive folding scheme satisfies succinctness (e.g., by using the Pedersen commitment scheme), succinctness holds due to the fact that u, U, and $\overline{T}$ are succinct, and due to the succinctness of the underling zkSNARK.

To prove zero-knowledge, we construct a simulator $\mathcal{S}$ that first iteratively simulates $(\mathsf{U}_i, \mathsf{u}_i)$ for all $i \in \{1, \ldots, n\}$. Specifically, given a simulated proof $(\mathsf{U}_i, \mathsf{u}_i)$, $\mathcal{S}$ first uses the simulator of the non-interactive folding scheme to simulate $\overline{T}_i$. $\mathcal{S}$ then folds U_i and u_i using $\overline{T}_i$ to produce U_{i+1}. $\mathcal{S}$ simulates u_i using the observation that all terms are randomized. In the final round, $\mathcal{S}$ folds u_n and U_n (again using a simulated $\overline{T}_n$) to produce an instance U', and then uses the simulator of the zkSNARK to produce $\pi_{\mathsf{U}'}$. $\mathcal{S}$ outputs $(\mathsf{U}_n, \mathsf{u}_n, \overline{T}_n, \pi_{\mathsf{U}'})$. We provide a formal proof in [30, App. D]. □

6 A zkSNARK for Committed Relaxed R1CS

As described in Sect. 5.2, Nova needs a zkSNARK for committed relaxed R1CS to prove the knowledge of a valid IVC proof succinctly and in zero-knowledge. This section presents such a zkSNARK by adapting Spartan [38]. We build on Spartan [38] to avoid FFTs and a trusted setup.

6.1 Background

We assume familiarity with polynomials. We provide background in [30, App. G].

Definition 13 (Polynomial Extension). *Suppose $f : \{0,1\}^\ell \rightarrow \mathbb{F}$ is a function that maps ℓ-bit strings to an element of $\mathbb{F}$. A polynomial extension of f is a low-degree ℓ-variate polynomial $\widetilde{f} : \mathbb{F}^\ell \rightarrow \mathbb{F}$ such that $\widetilde{f}(x) = f(x)$ for all $x \in \{0,1\}^\ell$. A multilinear extension (MLE) of a function $f : \{0,1\}^\ell \rightarrow \mathbb{F}$ is a low-degree polynomial extension where the extension is a multilinear polynomial.*

Every function $f : \{0,1\}^\ell \rightarrow \mathbb{F}$ has a unique MLE, and conversely every ℓ-variate multilinear polynomial over $\mathbb{F}$ extends a unique function mapping $\{0,1\}^\ell \rightarrow \mathbb{F}$. Below, we use $\widetilde{f}$ to denote the unique MLE of f.

Lemma 5 (The Sum-Check Protocol [35]**).** *For ℓ-variate polynomial G over $\mathbb{F}$ with degree at most μ in each variable, there exists a public-coin interactive proof protocol (known as the sum-check protocol) to reduce the task of checking $\sum_{x\in\{0,1\}^\ell} G(x) = T$ to the task of checking $G(r) = e$ for $r \in \mathbb{F}^\ell$. The interaction consists of a total of ℓ rounds, where in each round the verifier sends a single element of $\mathbb{F}$ and the prover responds with $\mu + 1$ elements of $\mathbb{F}$.*

6.2 A Polynomial IOP for Idealized Relaxed R1CS

Our exposition below is based on Spartan [38] and its recent recapitulation [34]. The theorem below and its proof is a verbatim adaptation of Spartan's polynomial IOP for R1CS to relaxed R1CS.

Recall that an interactive proof (IP) [25] for a relation $\mathcal{R}$ is an interactive protocol between a prover and a verifier where the prover proves the knowledge of a witness w for a prescribed instance u such that $(u, w) \in \mathcal{R}$. An interactive oracle proof (IOP) [5,37] generalizes interactive proofs where in each round the prover may send an oracle (e.g., a string) and the verifier may query a previously-sent oracle during the remainder of the protocol. A polynomial IOP [17] is an IOP in which the oracle sent by the prover is a polynomial and the verifier may query for an evaluation of the polynomial at a point in its domain. We consider a (minor) variant of polynomial IOPs, where the verifier has oracle access to polynomials in the R1CS structure and instance.

We first construct a polynomial IOP for an idealized version of relaxed R1CS (Definition 14) where the instance contains a purported witness. We then compile it into a zkSNARK for committed relaxed R1CS (Definition 12).

Definition 14 (Idealized Relaxed R1CS). *Consider a finite field $\mathbb{F}$. Let the public parameters consist of size bounds $m, n, \ell \in \mathbb{N}$ where $m > \ell$. The idealized relaxed R1CS structure consists of sparse matrices $A, B, C \in \mathbb{F}^{m\times m}$ with at most $n = \Omega(m)$ non-zero entries in each matrix. A idealized relaxed R1CS instance consists of an error vector $E \in \mathbb{F}^m$, a scalar $u \in \mathbb{F}$, witness vector $W \in \mathbb{F}^m$, and public inputs and outputs $\mathsf{x} \in \mathbb{F}^\ell$. An instance (E, u, W, x) is satisfying if $(A \cdot Z) \circ (B \cdot Z) = u \cdot (C \cdot Z) + E$, where $Z = (W, \mathsf{x}, u)$.*

Construction 5 (Polynomial IOP for Idealized Relaxed R1CS). Consider an idealized relaxed R1CS statement φ consisting of public parameters (m, n, ℓ), structure (A, B, C), and instance (E, u, W, x), Without loss of generality, we assume that m and n are powers of 2 and that $m = 2 \cdot (\ell + 1)$.

Let $s = \log m$. We interpret the matrices A, B, C as functions with signature $\{0,1\}^{\log m} \times \{0,1\}^{\log m} \to \mathbb{F}$ in a natural manner. In particular, an input in $\{0,1\}^{\log m} \times \{0,1\}^{\log m}$ is interpreted as the binary representation of an index $(i, j) \in [m] \times [m]$, where $[m] := \{1, \dots, m\}$ and the function outputs (i, j)th entry of the matrix. As such, let $\widetilde{A}$, $\widetilde{B}$, and $\widetilde{C}$ denote multilinear extensions of A, B, and C interpreted as functions, so they are $2\log m$-variate sparse multilinear polynomials of size n. Similarly, we interpret E and W as functions with respective signatures $\{0,1\}^{\log m} \to \mathbb{F}$ and $\{0,1\}^{\log m-1} \to \mathbb{F}$. Furthermore, let $\widetilde{E}$

and $\widetilde{W}$ denote the multilinear extensions of E and W interpreted as functions, so they are multilinear polynomials in $\log m$ and $\log m - 1$ variables respectively.

As noted earlier, the verifier has an oracle access to the following polynomials: $\widetilde{A}$, $\widetilde{B}$, $\widetilde{C}$, $\widetilde{E}$, and $\widetilde{W}$. Additionally, the verifier reads u and x in entirety.

Let $Z = (W, \mathsf{x}, u)$. Similar to how we interpret matrices as functions, we interpret Z and (x, u) as functions with the following respective signatures: $\{0,1\}^s \to \mathbb{F}$ and $\{0,1\}^{s-1} \to \mathbb{F}$. Observe that the MLE $\widetilde{Z}$ of Z satisfies

$$\widetilde{Z}(X_1, \ldots, X_s) = (1 - X_1) \cdot \widetilde{W}(X_2, \ldots, X_s) + X_1 \cdot \widetilde{(\mathsf{x}, u)}(X_2, \ldots, X_s) \quad (1)$$

Similar to [38, Theorem 4.1], checking if φ is satisfiable is equivalent, except for a soundness error of $\log m/|\mathbb{F}|$ over the choice of $\tau \in \mathbb{F}^s$, to checking if the following identity holds:

$$0 \stackrel{?}{=} \sum_{x \in \{0,1\}^s} \widetilde{\mathsf{eq}}(\tau, x) \cdot F(x), \quad (2)$$

where

$$F(x) = \left(\sum_{y \in \{0,1\}^s} \widetilde{A}(x, y) \cdot \widetilde{Z}(y) \right) \cdot \left(\sum_{y \in \{0,1\}^s} \widetilde{B}(x, y) \cdot \widetilde{Z}(y) \right) - \left(u \cdot \sum_{y \in \{0,1\}^s} \widetilde{C}(x, y) \cdot \widetilde{Z}(y) + \widetilde{E}(x) \right),$$

and $\widetilde{\mathsf{eq}}$ is the multilinear extension of $\mathsf{eq} : \{0,1\}^s \times \{0,1\}^s \to \mathbb{F}$ where $\mathsf{eq}(x, e) = 1$ if $x = e$ and 0 otherwise.

That is, if φ is satisfiable, then Eq. (2) holds with probability 1 over the choice of τ, and if not, then Eq. (2) holds with probability at most $O(\log m/|\mathbb{F}|)$ over the random choice of τ.

To compute the right-hand side in Eq. (2), the prover and the verifier apply the sum-check protocol to the following polynomial: $g(x) := \widetilde{\mathsf{eq}}(\tau, x) \cdot F(x)$ From the verifier's perspective, this reduces the task of computing the right-hand side of Eq. (2) to the task of evaluating g at a random input $r_x \in \mathbb{F}^s$. Note that the verifier can locally evaluate $\widetilde{\mathsf{eq}}(\tau, r_x)$ in $O(\log m)$ field operations via $\widetilde{\mathsf{eq}}(\tau, r_x) = \prod_{i=1}^{s} (\tau_i r_{x,i} + (1 - \tau_i)(1 - r_{x,i}))$. With $\widetilde{\mathsf{eq}}(\tau, r_x)$ in hand, $g(r_x)$ can be computed in $O(1)$ time given the four quantities: $\sum_{y \in \{0,1\}^s} \widetilde{A}(r_x, y) \cdot \widetilde{Z}(y)$, $\sum_{y \in \{0,1\}^s} \widetilde{B}(r_x, y) \cdot \widetilde{Z}(y)$, $\sum_{y \in \{0,1\}^s} \widetilde{C}(r_x, y) \cdot \widetilde{Z}(y)$, and $\widetilde{E}(r_x)$.

The last quantity can be computed with a single query to polynomial $\widetilde{E}$. Furthermore, the first three quantities can be computed by applying the sum-check protocol three more times in parallel, once to each of the following three polynomials (using the same random vector of field elements, $r_y \in \mathbb{F}^s$, in each of the three invocations): $\widetilde{A}(r_x, y) \cdot \widetilde{Z}(y)$, $\widetilde{B}(r_x, y) \cdot \widetilde{Z}(y)$, and $\widetilde{C}(r_x, y) \cdot \widetilde{Z}(y)$.

To perform the verifier's final check in each of these three invocations of the sum-check protocol, it suffices for the verifier to evaluate each of the above three polynomials at the random vector r_y, which means it suffices for the verifier to evaluate $\widetilde{A}(r_x, r_y)$, $\widetilde{B}(r_x, r_y)$, $\widetilde{C}(r_x, r_y)$, and $\widetilde{Z}(r_y)$. The first three evaluations can be obtained via the verifier's assumed query access to $(\widetilde{A}, \widetilde{B}, \widetilde{C})$. $\widetilde{Z}(r_y)$ can be computed (via Eq. (1)) from a query to $\widetilde{W}$ and from computing $\widetilde{(\mathsf{x}, u)}$.

In summary, we have the following polynomial IOP.

1. $\mathcal{V} \rightarrow \mathcal{P}$: $\tau \in_R \mathbb{F}^s$
2. $\mathcal{V} \leftrightarrow \mathcal{P}$: run the sum-check protocol to reduce the check in Eq. (2) to checking if the following hold, where r_x, r_y are vectors in $\mathbb{F}^s$ chosen at random by the verifier over the course of the sum-check protocol:
   - $\widetilde{A}(r_x, r_y) \stackrel{?}{=} v_A$, $\widetilde{B}(r_x, r_y) \stackrel{?}{=} v_B$, and $\widetilde{C}(r_x, r_y) \stackrel{?}{=} v_C$;
   - $\widetilde{E}(r_x) \stackrel{?}{=} v_E$; and
   - $\widetilde{Z}(r_y) \stackrel{?}{=} v_Z$.
3. $\mathcal{V}$:
   - check if $\widetilde{A}(r_x, r_y) \stackrel{?}{=} v_A$, $\widetilde{B}(r_x, r_y) \stackrel{?}{=} v_B$, and $\widetilde{C}(r_x, r_y) \stackrel{?}{=} v_C$, with a query to $\widetilde{A}, \widetilde{B}, \widetilde{C}$ at (r_x, r_y);
   - check if $\widetilde{E}(r_x) \stackrel{?}{=} v_E$ with an oracle query to $\widetilde{E}$; and
   - check if $\widetilde{Z}(r_y) \stackrel{?}{=} v_Z$ by checking if: $v_Z = (1 - r_y[1]) \cdot v_W + r_y[1] \cdot \widetilde{(\mathsf{x}, u)}(r_y[2..])$, where $r_y[2..]$ refers to a slice of r_y without the first element of r_y, and $v_W \leftarrow \widetilde{W}(r_y[2..])$ via an oracle query (see Eq. (1)).

Theorem 5. *Construction 5 is a polynomial IOP for idealized relaxed R1CS defined over a finite field $\mathbb{F}$, with the following parameters, where m denotes the dimension of the R1CS matrices, and n denotes the number of non-zero entries in the matrices: Soundness error is $O(\log m)/|\mathbb{F}|$; round complexity is $O(\log m)$; The verifier has query access to $2\log m$-variate multilinear polynomials $\widetilde{A}, \widetilde{B}, \widetilde{C}$ in the structure, and $(\log m)$-variate multilinear polynomial $\widetilde{E}$, and $(\log m - 1)$-variate multilinear polynomial $\widetilde{W}$ in the instance; the verifier issues a single query to polynomials $\widetilde{A}$, $\widetilde{B}$, $\widetilde{C}$, and $\widetilde{W}$, $\widetilde{E}$, and otherwise performs $O(\log m)$ operations over $\mathbb{F}$; the prover performs $O(n)$ operations over $\mathbb{F}$ to compute its messages in the polynomial IOP and to respond to the verifier's queries to $(\widetilde{W}, \widetilde{E}, \widetilde{A}, \widetilde{B}, \widetilde{C})$.*

Proof. Perfect completeness follows from perfect completeness of the sum-check protocol and the fact that Eq. (2) holds with probability 1 over the choice of τ if φ is satisfiable. Applying a standard union bound to the soundness error introduced by probabilistic check in Eq. (2) with the soundness error of the sum-check protocol [35], we conclude that the soundness error for the depicted polynomial IOP as at most $O(\log m)/|\mathbb{F}|$.

The sum-check protocol is applied four times (although three of the invocations occur in parallel and in practice combined into one [38]). In each invocation, the polynomial to which the sum-check protocol is applied has degree at most 3 in each variable, and the number of variables is $s = \log m$. Hence, the round complexity of the polynomial IOP is $O(\log m)$. Since each polynomial has degree at most 3 in each variable, the total communication cost is $O(\log m)$ field elements.

The claimed verifier runtime is immediate from the verifier's runtime in the sum-check protocol, and the fact that $\widetilde{\mathsf{eq}}$ can be evaluated at any input $(\tau, r_x) \in \mathbb{F}^{2s}$ in $O(\log m)$ field operations. As in Spartan [38], the prover's work in the polynomial IOP in $O(n)$ operations over $\mathbb{F}$ using prior techniques [42,46]. □

6.3 Compiling Polynomial IOPs to zkSNARKs

As in prior works [17,20,38], we compile our polynomial IOP into a zkSNARK using a polynomial commitment scheme [28] and the Fiat-Shamir transform [22].

Interpreting Commitments to Vectors as Polynomial Commitments. It is well known that commitments to m-sized vectors over $\mathbb{F}$ are commitments to $\log m$-variate multilinear polynomials represented with evaluations over $\{0,1\}^m$ [32,38,44,47]. Furthermore, there is a polynomial commitment scheme for $\log m$-variate multilinear polynomials if there exists an argument protocol to prove an inner product computation between a committed vector and an m-sized public vector $((r_1, 1 - r_1) \otimes \ldots \otimes (r_{\log m}, 1 - r_{\log m}))$, where $r \in \mathbb{F}^{\log m}$ is an evaluation point. There are two candidate constructions in the literature. Note that the primary difference between two schemes is in the verifier's time.

1. $\mathsf{PC_{BP}}$. If the commitment scheme for vectors over $\mathbb{F}$ is Pedersen's commitments, as in prior work [44], Bulletproofs [14] provides a suitable inner product argument protocol. The polynomial commitment scheme here achieves the following efficiency characteristics, assuming the hardness of the discrete logarithm problem. For a $\log m$-variate multilinear polynomial, committing takes $O_\lambda(m)$ time to produce an $O_\lambda(1)$-sized commitment; the prover incurs $O_\lambda(m)$ costs to produce an evaluation proof of size $O_\lambda(\log m)$ that can be verified in $O_\lambda(m)$. Note that $\mathsf{PC_{BP}}$ is a special case of Hyrax's polynomial commitment scheme [44].
2. $\mathsf{PC_{Dory}}$. If vectors over $\mathbb{F}$ are committed with a two-tiered "matrix" commitment (see for example, [18,32]), which provides $O_\lambda(1)$-sized commitments to m-sized vectors under the SXDH assumption. With this commitment scheme, Dory [32] provides the necessary inner product argument. The polynomial commitment here achieves the following efficiency characteristics, assuming the hardness of SXDH. For a $\log m$-variate multilinear polynomial, committing takes $O_\lambda(m)$ time to produce an $O_\lambda(1)$-sized commitment; the prover incurs $O_\lambda(m)$ costs to produce an evaluation proof of size $O_\lambda(\log m)$ that can be verified in $O_\lambda(\log m)$.

Polynomial Commitments for Sparse Multilinear Polynomials. In our constructions below, we require polynomial commitment schemes that can efficiently handle sparse multilinear polynomials. Spartan [38, §7] (and its optimization [41, §6]) provides a generic compiler to transform existing polynomial commitment schemes for multilinear polynomials into those that can efficiently handle sparse multilinear polynomials. Specifically, we apply [34, Theorem 5]) (which captures Spartan's compiler in a generic manner) to $\mathsf{PC_{BP}}$ and $\mathsf{PC_{Dory}}$ to obtain their variants that can efficiently handle sparse multilinear polynomials; we refer to them as "Sparse-$\mathsf{PC_{BP}}$" and "Sparse-$\mathsf{PC_{Dory}}$" respectively.

Theorem 6 (A zkSNARK from $\mathsf{PC_{BP}}$). *Assuming the hardness of the discrete logarithm problem, there exists a zkSNARK in the random oracle model for committed relaxed R1CS with the following efficiency characteristics, where m denotes the dimensions of R1CS matrices and n denotes the number of non-zero entries in the matrices: The encoder runs in time $O_\lambda(n)$; The prover runs in time $O_\lambda(n)$; The proof length is $O_\lambda(\log n)$; and the verifier runs in time $O_\lambda(n)$.*[6]

Proof. For R1CS structure (A, B, C), we first have the encoder directly provide $(\widetilde{A}, \widetilde{B}, \widetilde{C})$ in the prover key, and additionally provide sparse polynomial commitments to $\widetilde{A}, \widetilde{B}, \widetilde{C}$ using Sparse-$\mathsf{PC_{BP}}$ in both the prover and verifier keys. Next, we apply the compiler of [17] using $\mathsf{PC_{BP}}$ to the polynomial IOP from Construction 5. At a high level, this replaces all of the oracles provided to the verifier with $\mathsf{PC_{BP}}$ commitments, which the prover and verifier then use to simulate ideal queries to a committed oracle. By [17, Theorem 6] this provides a public-coin honest-verifier zero-knowledge interactive argument of knowledge. In particular, we can treat the resulting protocol as an argument for committed relaxed R1CS because the verifier is now provided with (polynomial) commitments to E and W. Applying the Fiat-Shamir transform [22] achieves non-interactivity and zero-knowledge in the random oracle model.

The claimed efficiency follows from the efficiency of the polynomial IOP, $\mathsf{PC_{BP}}$, and Sparse-$\mathsf{PC_{BP}}$. In more detail, using Sparse-$\mathsf{PC_{BP}}$, the encoder takes $O_\lambda(n)$ time to create commitments $2 \log m$-variate sparse multilinear polynomials $\widetilde{A}, \widetilde{B}, \widetilde{C}$. The prover's costs in the polynomial IOP is $O(n)$. Furthermore, proving the evaluations of two $O(\log m)$-variate multilinear polynomials using $\mathsf{PC_{BP}}$, it takes $O_\lambda(m)$ time. And, to prove the evaluations of three $2 \log m$-variate sparse multilinear polynomials of size n, using Sparse-$\mathsf{PC_{BP}}$, it takes $O_\lambda(n)$ time. In total, the prover time is $O_\lambda(n)$. The proof length in the polynomial IOP is $O(\log m)$, and the proof sizes in the polynomial evaluation proofs is $O_\lambda(\log n)$, so the proof length is $O_\lambda(\log n)$. The verifier's time in the polynomial IOP is $O(\log m)$. In addition, it verifies five polynomial evaluations, which costs $O_\lambda(n)$ time: the two polynomial in the instance take $O_\lambda(m)$ time using $\mathsf{PC_{BP}}$, and the three polynomials in the structure takes $O_\lambda(n)$ time using Sparse-$\mathsf{PC_{BP}}$. So, in total, the verifier time is $O_\lambda(n)$. □

Corollary 1 (A zkSNARK from $\mathsf{PC_{Dory}}$). *Assuming the hardness of the SXDH problem, there exists a zkSNARK in the random oracle model for committed relaxed R1CS with the following efficiency characteristics, where m denotes the dimensions of R1CS matrices and n denotes the number of non-zero entries in the matrices: The encoder runs in time $O_\lambda(n)$; The prover runs in time $O_\lambda(n)$; The proof length is $O_\lambda(\log n)$; and the verifier runs in time $O_\lambda(\log n)$.*

[6] [30, App. H] describes a minor optimization and a corresponding Corollary.

References

1. bellperson. https://github.com/filecoin-project/bellperson
2. neptune. https://github.com/filecoin-project/neptune
3. Nova: Recursive SNARKs without trusted setup. https://github.com/Microsoft/Nova
4. Pasta curves. https://github.com/zcash/pasta
5. Ben-Sasson, E., Chiesa, A., Spooner, N.: Interactive Oracle Proofs. In: TCC (2016)
6. Ben-Sasson, E., Chiesa, A., Tromer, E., Virza, M.: Scalable zero knowledge via cycles of elliptic curves. In: Garay, J.A., Gennaro, R. (eds.) CRYPTO 2014. LNCS, vol. 8617, pp. 276–294. Springer, Heidelberg (2014). https://doi.org/10.1007/978-3-662-44381-1_16
7. Bitansky, N., Canetti, R., Chiesa, A., Tromer, E.: From extractable collision resistance to succinct non-interactive arguments of knowledge, and back again. In: ITCS (2012)
8. Bitansky, N., Canetti, R., Chiesa, A., Tromer, E.: Recursive composition and bootstrapping for SNARKs and proof-carrying data. In: STOC (2013)
9. Boneh, D., Bünz, B., Fisch, B.: A survey of two verifiable delay functions. Cryptology ePrint Archive, Report 2018/712 (2018)
10. Boneh, D., Drake, J., Fisch, B., Gabizon, A.: Halo infinite: recursive zk-SNARKs from any additive polynomial commitment scheme. Cryptology ePrint Archive, Report 2020/1536 (2020)
11. Bootle, J., Cerulli, A., Chaidos, P., Groth, J., Petit, C.: Efficient zero-knowledge arguments for arithmetic circuits in the discrete log setting. In: Fischlin, M., Coron, J.-S. (eds.) EUROCRYPT 2016. LNCS, vol. 9666, pp. 327–357. Springer, Heidelberg (2016). https://doi.org/10.1007/978-3-662-49896-5_12
12. Bowe, S., Grigg, J., Hopwood, D.: Halo: recursive proof composition without a trusted setup. Cryptology ePrint Archive, Report 2019/1021 (2019)
13. Bowe, S., Grigg, J., Hopwood, D.: Halo2 (2020). https://github.com/zcash/halo2
14. Bünz, B., Bootle, J., Boneh, D., Poelstra, A., Wuille, P., Maxwell, G.: Bulletproofs: short proofs for confidential transactions and more. In: S&P (2018)
15. Bünz, B., Chiesa, A., Lin, W., Mishra, P., Spooner, N.: Proof-carrying data without succinct arguments. Cryptology ePrint Archive, Report 2020/1618 (2020)
16. Bünz, B., Chiesa, A., Mishra, P., Spooner, N.: Proof-carrying data from accumulation schemes. In: TCC (2020)
17. Bünz, B., Fisch, B., Szepieniec, A.: Transparent SNARKs from DARK compilers. In: Canteaut, A., Ishai, Y. (eds.) EUROCRYPT 2020. LNCS, vol. 12105, pp. 677–706. Springer, Cham (2020). https://doi.org/10.1007/978-3-030-45721-1_24
18. Bünz, B., Maller, M., Mishra, P., Vesely, N.: Proofs for inner pairing products and applications. Cryptology ePrint Archive, Report 2019/1177 (2019)
19. Chen, W., Chiesa, A., Dauterman, E., Ward, N.P.: Reducing participation costs via incremental verification for ledger systems. Cryptology ePrint Archive, Report 2020/1522 (2020)
20. Chiesa, A., Hu, Y., Maller, M., Mishra, P., Vesely, N., Ward, N.: Marlin: preprocessing zkSNARKs with universal and updatable SRS. In: Canteaut, A., Ishai, Y. (eds.) EUROCRYPT 2020. LNCS, vol. 12105, pp. 738–768. Springer, Cham (2020). https://doi.org/10.1007/978-3-030-45721-1_26
21. Chiesa, A., Ojha, D., Spooner, N.: Fractal: post-quantum and transparent recursive proofs from holography. In: Canteaut, A., Ishai, Y. (eds.) EUROCRYPT 2020. LNCS, vol. 12105, pp. 769–793. Springer, Cham (2020). https://doi.org/10.1007/978-3-030-45721-1_27

22. Fiat, A., Shamir, A.: How to prove yourself: practical solutions to identification and signature problems. In: Odlyzko, A.M. (ed.) CRYPTO 1986. LNCS, vol. 263, pp. 186–194. Springer, Heidelberg (1987). https://doi.org/10.1007/3-540-47721-7_12
23. Gennaro, R., Gentry, C., Parno, B., Raykova, M.: Quadratic span programs and succinct NIZKs without PCPs. In: Johansson, T., Nguyen, P.Q. (eds.) EUROCRYPT 2013. LNCS, vol. 7881, pp. 626–645. Springer, Heidelberg (2013). https://doi.org/10.1007/978-3-642-38348-9_37
24. Gentry, C., Wichs, D.: Separating succinct non-interactive arguments from all falsifiable assumptions. In: STOC, pp. 99–108 (2011)
25. Goldwasser, S., Micali, S., Rackoff, C.: The knowledge complexity of interactive proof-systems. In: STOC (1985)
26. Grassi, L., Khovratovich, D., Rechberger, C., Roy, A., Schofnegger, M.: Poseidon: a new hash function for zero-knowledge proof systems. Cryptology ePrint Archive, Paper 2019/458 (2019)
27. Groth, J.: On the size of pairing-based non-interactive arguments. In: Fischlin, M., Coron, J.-S. (eds.) EUROCRYPT 2016. LNCS, vol. 9666, pp. 305–326. Springer, Heidelberg (2016). https://doi.org/10.1007/978-3-662-49896-5_11
28. Kate, A., Zaverucha, G.M., Goldberg, I.: Constant-size commitments to polynomials and their applications. In: ASIACRYPT, pp. 177–194 (2010)
29. Kilian, J.: A note on efficient zero-knowledge proofs and arguments (extended abstract). In: STOC (1992)
30. Kothapalli, A., Setty, S., Tzialla, I.: Nova: recursive zero-knowledge arguments from folding schemes. Cryptology ePrint Archive, Paper 2021/370 (2021)
31. Labs, O.: Mina cryptocurrency (2020). https://minaprotocol.com
32. Lee, J.: Dory: efficient, transparent arguments for generalised inner products and polynomial commitments. Cryptology ePrint Archive, Report 2020/1274 (2020)
33. Lee, J., Nikitin, K., Setty, S.: Replicated state machines without replicated execution. In: S&P (2020)
34. Lee, J., Setty, S., Thaler, J., Wahby, R.: Linear-time zero-knowledge SNARKs for R1CS. Cryptology ePrint Archive, Report 2021/030 (2021)
35. Lund, C., Fortnow, L., Karloff, H., Nisan, N.: Algebraic methods for interactive proof systems. In: FOCS, October 1990
36. Micali, S.: CS proofs. In: FOCS (1994)
37. Reingold, O., Rothblum, G.N., Rothblum, R.D.: Constant-round interactive proofs for delegating computation. In: STOC, pp. 49–62 (2016)
38. Setty, S.: Spartan: efficient and general-purpose zkSNARKs without trusted setup. In: Micciancio, D., Ristenpart, T. (eds.) CRYPTO 2020. LNCS, vol. 12172, pp. 704–737. Springer, Cham (2020). https://doi.org/10.1007/978-3-030-56877-1_25
39. Setty, S., Angel, S., Gupta, T., Lee, J.: Proving the correct execution of concurrent services in zero-knowledge. In: OSDI, October 2018
40. Setty, S., Braun, B., Vu, V., Blumberg, A.J., Parno, B., Walfish, M.: Resolving the conflict between generality and plausibility in verified computation. In: EuroSys, April 2013
41. Setty, S., Lee, J.: Quarks: quadruple-efficient transparent zkSNARKs. Cryptology ePrint Archive, Report 2020/1275 (2020)
42. Thaler, J.: Time-optimal interactive proofs for circuit evaluation. In: Canetti, R., Garay, J.A. (eds.) CRYPTO 2013. LNCS, vol. 8043, pp. 71–89. Springer, Heidelberg (2013). https://doi.org/10.1007/978-3-642-40084-1_5
43. Valiant, P.: Incrementally verifiable computation or proofs of knowledge imply time/space efficiency. In: Canetti, R. (ed.) TCC 2008. LNCS, vol. 4948, pp. 1–18. Springer, Heidelberg (2008). https://doi.org/10.1007/978-3-540-78524-8_1

44. Wahby, R.S., Tzialla, I., Shelat, A., Thaler, J., Walfish, M.: Doubly-efficient zkSNARKs without trusted setup. In: S&P (2018)
45. Wesolowski, B.: Efficient verifiable delay functions. In: Ishai, Y., Rijmen, V. (eds.) EUROCRYPT 2019. LNCS, vol. 11478, pp. 379–407. Springer, Cham (2019). https://doi.org/10.1007/978-3-030-17659-4_13
46. Xie, T., Zhang, J., Zhang, Y., Papamanthou, C., Song, D.: Libra: succinct zero-knowledge proofs with optimal prover computation. In: Boldyreva, A., Micciancio, D. (eds.) CRYPTO 2019. LNCS, vol. 11694, pp. 733–764. Springer, Cham (2019). https://doi.org/10.1007/978-3-030-26954-8_24
47. Zhang, Y., Genkin, D., Katz, J., Papadopoulos, D., Papamanthou, C.: vSQL: verifying arbitrary SQL queries over dynamic outsourced databases. In: S&P (2017)

A New Approach to Efficient Non-Malleable Zero-Knowledge

Allen Kim, Xiao Liang(✉), and Omkant Pandey

Stony Brook University, Stony Brook, USA
{allekim,omkant}@cs.stonybrook.edu, xiao.crypto@gmail.com

Abstract. Non-malleable zero-knowledge, originally introduced in the context of man-in-the-middle attacks, serves as an important building block to protect against concurrent attacks where different protocols may coexist and interleave. While this primitive admits almost optimal constructions in the plain model, they are *several* orders of magnitude slower in practice than standalone zero-knowledge. This is in sharp contrast to non-malleable *commitments* where practical constructions (under the DDH assumption) have been known for a while.

We present a new approach for constructing efficient non-malleable zero-knowledge for all languages in $\mathcal{NP}$, based on a new primitive called *instance-based non-malleable commitment* (IB-NMC). We show how to construct practical IB-NMC by leveraging the fact that *simulators* of *sub-linear* zero-knowledge protocols can be much faster than the honest prover algorithm. With an efficient implementation of IB-NMC, our approach yields the first general-purpose non-malleable zero-knowledge protocol that achieves practical efficiency *in the plain model.*

All of our protocols can be instantiated from symmetric primitives such as block-ciphers and collision-resistant hash functions, have reasonable efficiency in practice, and are general-purpose. Our techniques also yield the first efficient non-malleable commitment scheme *without public-key assumptions.*

Keywords: Non-malleability · Efficiency · Symmetric assumptions

1 Introduction

Non-Malleable Zero-Knowledge. Dolev, Dwork, and Naor [27] introduced the notion on non-malleable cryptography. They also provided constructions of non-malleable zero-knowledge and non-malleable commitments in the *plain*

This material is based upon work supported in part by DARPA SIEVE Award HR00112020026, NSF CAREER Award 2144303, NSF grants 1907908, 2028920, 2106263, and 2128187. Any opinions, findings and conclusions or recommendations expressed in this material are those of the author(s) and do not necessarily reflect the views of the United States Government, DARPA, or NSF.

Y. Dodis and T. Shrimpton (Eds.): CRYPTO 2022, LNCS 13510, pp. 389–418, 2022.
https://doi.org/10.1007/978-3-031-15985-5_14

model assuming only the existence of *one-way functions* (OWFs). While these primitives were originally introduced in the context of "man-in-the-middle" attacks, they were soon used as a *building block* for constructing secure computation protocols. For example, non-malleable commitments were used extensively to improve their round-efficiency [3,20,33,41,49,69,81], and non-malleable zero-knowledge played a central role in protecting them against concurrent attacks [12–14,19,62,71,76].

A long line of research has since focused on several aspects of these primitives, including their round-complexity [5,21,27,41,50,55,57,60,74,81], black-box usage of underlying primitives [42,45], and even concrete efficiency [11] without assuming any trusted setup. Notably, constant-round non-malleable commitments assuming only OWFs were first constructed in independent and concurrent works of Goyal [41] and Lin and Pass [57]. Finally, four-round non-malleable *zero-knowledge* assuming only OWFs was first achieved by Goyal et al. [45] for all of $\mathcal{NP}$; and three-round non-malleable commitments assuming injective OWFs were constructed by Goyal, Pandey, and Richelson [43,44]. Under falsifiable assumptions [34,65], these rounds are optimal for commitments [72], and likely to be optimal for zero-knowledge as well [32,39]. Stronger forms of this notion such as *concurrent* non-malleability, eventually achieved optimally in a series of works [21,60,73], are not considered in this work. We note that non-malleability has been explored in several other contexts as well [10,26,27,30].

Efficient Constructions. While the aforementioned results are almost optimal for non-malleable zero-knowledge, their focus is primarily on *feasibility* as opposed to actual efficiency. To the best of our knowledge, the actual efficiency of non-malleable zero-knowledge has never been explicitly addressed before. This is in sharp contrast to non-malleable *commitments*, for which efficient plain-model constructions are known (under the DDH assumption) [11].

We therefore consider the efficiency of some of the main approaches for non-malleable zero-knowledge. Unless stated otherwise, we are concerned with *general-purpose* protocols (that work for all languages in $\mathcal{NP}$) *in the plain model.*

- The most common approach for non-malleable zero-knowledge is "commit-and-prove." At a high level, the prover first sends a *non-malleable* commitment to the witness, and then uses (ordinary) zero-knowledge to prove that the committed value is a valid witness [7,21,27,45]. If the commitment supports k-bit identities and has λ-bit security, the circuit corresponding to the state-of-the-art non-malleable commitment [11] is at least $16k^2\lambda^2$, or over 100 million gates for $k = 32, \lambda = 80$. Zero-knowledge proofs for such circuits would take more than one minute using state-of-the-art (plain-model) protocols such as Ligero [2] (even taking advantage of the amortization admitted by Ligero). This is true even if the actual statement, say proving $y = \text{SHA256}(x)$, requires less than a second [2] in the standalone case.[1]

[1] Although details may vary, known protocols in this paradigm generally require some form of non-algebraic consistency proof over a non-malleable commitment supporting large identities and message spaces.

It is worth noting that using state-of-the-art commitments [11] additionally requires assuming DDH, whereas "symmetric assumptions" such as OWFs are sufficient in theory. Efficient non-malleable commitments *without* relying on public-key assumptions such as DDH are therefore also not known. One option here is to implement the consistency proofs in [11] with Ligero to avoid DDH. However, this also results in large circuits.[2] Jumping ahead, our techniques offer new results for efficient non-malleable commitments, too.

- Non-malleable zero-knowledge *without* relying on non-malleable commitments was first constructed by Barak [5], and by Pass and Rosen [74] under improved assumptions. Both of these constructions were based on Barak's non-black-box simulation [4]. A critical component of these protocols is a universal argument [6], which consists of a Merkle tree commitment to a *Probabilistically Checkable Proof* (PCP), parts of which are opened later in the protocol. Unfortunately, as shown by Ben-Sasson et al. [9], the underlying PCP proof in the universal argument can be astronomically large even for moderate parameters. To the best of our knowledge, the true efficiency of non-black-box simulation based constructions is currently not well understood.
- A third approach, due to Ostrovsky, Pandey, and Visconti [68], relies on the DDH assumption, and efficiently converts any public-coin honest-verifier statistical zero-knowledge argument into a (concurrent) non-malleable one [7]. While this approach uses non-malleable commitments, it avoids general-purpose proofs over them using ideas from the "simulatable commitment" of Micciancio and Petrank [63]. Though efficient, this transformation quickly becomes pretty slow. For example, for the standalone setting, it requires roughly $20k\lambda \log \lambda$ group exponentiations to support k bit identities at $2^{-\lambda}$ security level;[3] this is roughly 0.32 million exponentiations for $k = 32, \lambda = 80$. In addition, it requires efficient non-malleable commitments as well as efficient (and compatible) simulatable commitments, both of which are only known from DDH. Ideally, we would like to use only symmetric assumptions.

Constructions in the Random Oracle Model (ROM). The protocols we seek are straightforward to construct in the ROM [8] (see, e.g., [31,70]). Briefly, a random oracle (RO) is non-malleable by design, which completely sidesteps this issue. Furthermore, zero-knowledge is also trivial since the simulator and the reduction are allowed to see adversary's queries to the oracle and control the

---

[2] We remark that for non-malleable commitments based on non-malleable codes such as [43], it is hard to estimate the overall complexity; the asymptotic analysis of underlying codes such as [1] has astronomically large constants, making them unsuitable in practice.

[3] The analysis in [68] does not separate identity lengths from security levels; it further provides only asymptotic analysis which hides multiplicative constants and does not specify the exact negligible and super-logarithmic functions. This makes it difficult to assess the security level supported by their protocol. If the analysis is performed to support λ-bit security and k-bit identities, the overhead is at least $20k\lambda \log \lambda$ group exponentiations.

responses. In the real world, a cryptographic hash function is used to replace the RO, thus providing a concrete construction. This is an attractive methodology that often leads to practical constructions. That being so, there are several reasons to pursue constructions in the plain model, *even if efficient constructions are already known in the ROM*. We highlight some of them here.

- A protocol such as a zero-knowledge proof in the ROM can be particularly troublesome when it is used as a sub-protocol in a larger protocol. If the RO is shared by other parts of the larger protocol, the security is jeopardized since the security reduction for the sub-protocol does not hold when a particular RO has already been selected by the larger protocol (see, e.g., [15,70,79]). In addition, security proofs in this model often *program* the oracle, resulting in loss of properties such as *deniability* which are otherwise implied by zero-knowledge (see [70,80]). Deniability is a natural and useful property that has been explored in other contexts as well [16,29,67,78].
- Using random oracles often sidesteps the main difficulty in achieving a particular task, such as CCA secure encryption or non-malleable commitments from standard assumption. Therefore, a construction or security proof in the ROM, while valuable, is usually not as *insightful* as its plain-model counterparts.
- Finally, while security proofs in the ROM are valuable, it requires a leap of faith to believe that instantiating the random oracle with a real world hash function maintains claimed security. Indeed, this is not always the case [17,28,40,66]. It stands to reason that whenever possible the ROM should be avoided.

Improved constructions can be achieved in other trusted setup models as well. Di Crescendo, Isiah, and Ostrovsky [24] construct non-interactive non-malleable commitments in the CRS model, and Di Crescenzo et al. [25] do so efficiently under DDH. Lower rounds can also be achieved in the plain model under non-falsifiable assumptions [51,58,69,72].

1.1 Our Results

We present a new approach for constructing *efficient* and *general-purpose* non-malleable zero-knowledge *in the plain model*. Our protocols can be viewed as a transformation which takes as input an efficient general-purpose zero-knowledge protocol, such as Ligero [2], and yields a *non-malleable* zero-knowledge protocol of (less but still) comparable efficiency. To the best of our knowledge, this is the first construction of general-purpose non-malleable zero-knowledge that achieves practical efficiency in the plain model. Our approach has the additional benefit of requiring only *symmetric* assumptions (in addition to the assumptions of the given proof system). Specifically, it suffices to assume collision-resistant hash functions.

Table 1. Performance of our protocols for λ-bit security and k-bit identities. NMZK proves a witness for SHA256.

Param	NMZK			NMCom		
(k, λ)	P time (s)	V time (s)	Comm. (MB)	P time (s)	V time (s)	Comm. (MB)
(32, 40)	1.68	0.74	19.68	2.52	1.12	19.74
(32, 80)	3.56	1.49	24.88	4.68	2.06	24.97
(64, 80)	5.04	2.23	28.84	6.72	3.09	28.93

While our primary focus is on non-malleable zero-knowledge, we also get new results for non-malleable *commitments*. Specifically, we get the first efficient construction of non-malleable commitments with large identities and message space *under symmetric assumptions*. Though this improves upon the DDH assumption required by the state-of-the-art construction [11], our construction is somewhat slower in comparison.

Even though our focus is on efficiency, our results are theoretical in nature. Our transformation makes use of non-malleable commitments in a fundamentally new way. We define and construct a new primitive called *instance-based non-malleable commitments* (IB-NMC), which admit more efficient modes than a traditional non-malleable commitment. We show how IB-NMC can be used in conjunction with the *OR-Composition* technique from [22,23] to obtain efficient *simulation-sound* protocols, which in turn yields efficient non-malleable protocols for both zero-knowledge and commitments. This primitive may be useful in other contexts as well.

The overhead of our transformation is within reach of practical computing. Table 1 shows the running times and communication for our non-malleable protocols for some sample parameters. Due to space constraints, a detailed analysis of the empirical results is postponed to the full version [53].

1.2 Overview of Techniques

We start by recalling the central efficiency bottleneck in constructing non-malleable zero-knowledge for $\mathcal{NP}$. We assume that efficient *standalone* zero-knowledge (ZK) proofs already exist for all languages $L \in \mathcal{NP}$ in the plain model such as [2,35]. For concreteness, we will use Ligero [2].

The main inefficiency of non-malleable zero-knowledge stems from the fact that almost all known constructions [7,56,59] make a non-black-box use of non-malleable commitments. More specifically, the prover commits to a witness or a trapdoor string using a non-malleable commitment and later relies on expensive $\mathcal{NP}$ reductions to prove that it either committed a valid witness *or* a trapdoor (i.e., an OR-statement); the latter is shown difficult to do for the man-in-the-middle adversary M by relying on the non-malleability of the commitment. The $\mathcal{NP}$ reduction corresponding to the OR-statement typically results in a circuit description of formidable size since the non-malleable commitment usually contains many calls to cryptographic functions such as block-ciphers. The resulting protocols are prohibitively inefficient even with state-of-the-art ZK constructions. Other approaches (based on non-black-box simulation or DDH outlined earlier) are irrelevant to our construction.

The starting point of our work is the observation that the use of non-malleable commitments in these protocols is merely *a means to an end*. In particular, the honest prover generally commits to a random or an all-zero string in these commitments; it is the simulator who makes real use of their non-malleable properties. Therefore, if we can create a situation in our protocols where the honest prover *does not have to execute even a single full non-malleable commitment*, we can improve the computational efficiency of these protocols. Let us briefly highlight why achieving this property is extremely important for our goals: As noted above, efficient non-malleable commitments in the plain model are based on DDH [11,68]. One option to avoid public-key assumptions is to instantiate the scheme in [11] with Ligero; However, the running time of the resulting commitment scheme *alone* (under moderate parameters) will run in more than one minute. The actual non-malleable zero-knowledge protocol which depends on these commitments in a non-black-box way will be much worse. We therefore seek to avoid even *one* full execution of a non-malleable commitment in our ZK protocol.

It is worthwhile to note that *black-box* constructions of non-malleable ZK from non-malleable commitments are (surprisingly) not known. The closest work in this regard is by Jain and Pandey [48], who construct simulation-sound ZK from a stronger version of non-malleable commitments (called *1-1 CCA* [18,54]) in black-box. Currently, it is unclear if their approach can yield an efficient protocol that avoids even one execution of the non-malleable commitment.

Instance-Based Non-Malleable Commitments. Returning back to our goal of avoiding even one execution of full non-malleable commitment during the proof, we consider a new relaxation of such commitments which we call *instance-based* non-malleable commitments (IB-NMCs). Roughly speaking, an IB-NMC is just like an ordinary non-malleable commitment except that it takes as input a statement y (from an implicit $\mathcal{NP}$ language Y). The commitment has two modes: if $y \notin Y$, then it is an ordinary non-malleable commitment, and the committer commits to any desired value v by following the actual commitment algorithm C. Otherwise, if $y \in Y$, then the commitment is not guaranteed to have any non-malleability property. However, in this case, there exists a much faster algorithm C^* that, with the help of a witness for $y \in Y$, can *fake* (or simulate) an execution that looks indistinguishable from the real execution with C for any value v.

To construct IB-NMC, we combine the following key ideas:

- The simulator of a general-purpose zero-knowledge proof can be much faster than the real prover algorithm. This is best seen by considering the sublinear zero-knowledge arguments based on PCPs [52,61]. In such protocols,

a prover commits to a full Merkle tree over the PCP proof; but note that the simulator does not have to construct the whole tree. Instead, the simulator can simply prepare the nodes of the opened paths in a consistent manner, which is much faster. In particular, this is true for our chosen ZK system Ligero.
- The well-known OR-Composition technique developed for Σ-protocols [22,23] can be applied in our setting to give proofs for statements of the type "either $x \in L$ or $y \in Y$." Recall that under this technique, a prover with a witness for x constructs proofs correctly for the "$x \in L$" part, but uses the *simulator* of the Σ-protocol for the "$y \in Y$" part. Observe that if the simulator for the "$y \in Y$" part is fast (as discussed in the previous item), then the composed proofs can be almost as fast as a proof *only* for $x \in L$.
- Finally, we apply the aforementioned observations to a suitable non-malleable commitment scheme to get an efficient IB-NMC. In particular, we apply it to a modification of the BGRRV protocol [11], leading to a construction based solely on symmetric-key (or Minicrypt) assumptions (referred to as $\Pi^{\mathsf{Mini}}_{\mathrm{BGRRV}}$). More specifically, $\Pi^{\mathsf{Mini}}_{\mathrm{BGRRV}}$ has a *commit phase* and a *proof phase* where the latter proves the "consistency" of the former. To get IB-NMC, we simply change the proof phase to prove that either the first phase is consistent or $y \in Y$ (where y is an additional input to the committer); this proof is done using the OR-composition of two Ligero protocols as described above.

We remark that this approach runs into several other issues that are not discussed here, e.g., OR-composition in general applies only to Σ-protocols but Ligero is not a Σ-protocol, the role of Y and how to choose it, etc. We will handle them in Sect. 5. The use of a honest-verifier simulator to protect against malicious attacks first appears in the work of Cramer, Damgård, and Schoenmakers [22].

Non-Malleability via Simulation Soundness. While IB-NMC is an interesting primitive, it is not clear how to use it at all to construct non-malleable zero knowledge. Instead, we show that IB-NMC can be used successfully to construct a fast *simulation-sound* ZK protocol [48,77]. Constructing this protocol requires repeated applications of the OR composition and the fake-proof technique discussed above. The simulation-sound protocol can be directly useful in larger protocols since this notion suffices for typical applications of non-malleability. Finally, we show how to use this protocol to get an efficient and full-fledged non-malleable ZK as well as an efficient non-malleable commitment. In both cases, the transformation inherits the assumptions of the underlying zero-knowledge and IB-NMC, which in our case, are symmetric primitives only.

2 Preliminaries

We use $\lambda \in \mathbb{N}$ to denote the security parameter. Symbols $\overset{\mathrm{c}}{\approx}$, $\overset{\mathrm{s}}{\approx}$, and $\overset{\mathrm{id}}{=}$ are used to denote computational, statistical, and perfect indistinguishability respectively. Let $\mathsf{negl}(\lambda)$ denote negligible functions. Familiarity with basic definitions including commitments, witness indistinguishability, zero-knowledge, arguments of knowledge, etc. is assumed; we refer to [36,37] for formal treatment of these notions. We also recall the definitions of CRHFs, extractable commitments, and statistically-hiding commitments in [53, Appendix A].

Non-Malleable Interactive Proofs. We work with identity-based (or "tag-based") definitions of non-malleability and follow the definitions and conventions from [74]. Let $\mathcal{A}$ be a (non-uniform) probabilistic Turing machine, specifying a man-in-the-middle strategy. $\mathcal{A}$ runs in time polynomial in the security parameter λ. Let $z \in \{0,1\}^*$ be an arbitrary string (denoting the non-uniform "advice" for $\mathcal{A}$). Let $\langle P, V, \rangle$ be an interactive proof system for an $\mathcal{NP}$ complete language L. Let $x \in L$ be a statement of length λ; we assume that P is PPT and receives a witness $w \in R_L(x)$ as its auxiliary input. The definition is based on the comparison between a *man-in-the-middle* execution and a *stand-alone* execution among the above parties.

The man-in-the-middle experiment begins by selecting uniform randomness for $\mathcal{A}$, and honest parties P and V. $\mathcal{A}(x, z)$ interacts with $P(x, w)$ on left acting as a verifier in the proof for $x \in L$; $\mathcal{A}$ simultaneously participates in a right proof with V, proving a related statement $\widetilde{x}$, supposedly in L.[4] Let the tag (or "identity") strings on left and right be id and $\widetilde{\mathsf{id}}$ respectively with $|\mathsf{id}| = |\widetilde{\mathsf{id}}| = \lambda$. We let $\mathsf{mim}_V^{\mathcal{A}}(\mathsf{id}, \widetilde{\mathsf{id}}, x, \widetilde{x}, w, z)$ be a random variable describing the output of V in the man-in-the-middle execution.

In the stand-alone execution, a machine S interacts with the honest verifier V. As in the man-in-the-middle execution, V receives as input an instance $\widetilde{x}$ and the identity $\widetilde{\mathsf{id}}$. S receives x, an auxiliary input z and id as input. We let $\mathsf{sta}_V^S(\mathsf{id}, \widetilde{\mathsf{id}}, x, \widetilde{x}, z)$ be a random variable describing the output of V in the stand-alone execution.

Definition 1 (Non-Malleable Interactive Proof). *An interactive proof $\langle P, V \rangle$ for language L is said to be non-malleable w.r.t. tags of length m if for every* PPT *man-in-the-middle adversary $\mathcal{A}$, there exists a* PPT *stand-alone prover S and a negligible function* negl *such that for every $x \in L$, every $w \in R_L(x)$, every $\widetilde{x} \in \{0,1\}^{|x|}$, every $\mathsf{id}, \widetilde{\mathsf{id}} \in \{0,1\}^m$ so that $\mathsf{id} \neq \widetilde{\mathsf{id}}$, and every $z \in \{0,1\}^*$, it holds that*

$$\Pr[\mathsf{mim}_V^{\mathcal{A}}(\mathsf{id}, \widetilde{\mathsf{id}}, x, \widetilde{x}, w, z) = 1] < \Pr[\mathsf{sta}_V^S(\mathsf{id}, \widetilde{\mathsf{id}}, x, \widetilde{x}, z) = 1] + \mathsf{negl}(|x|).$$

We will refer to *synchronizing* adversaries: they are the man-in-the-middle attackers who, upon receiving a message in one session, immediately respond with the corresponding message in the other session. An adversary is said to be *non-synchronizing* if it is not synchronizing.

Definition 2 (Non-Malleable Zero Knowledge). *An interactive proof between prover P and verifier V is said to be non-malleable zero knowledge if it is a non-malleable interactive proof that also has the zero-knowledge property.*

[4] We remark that statement $\widetilde{x}$ may be chosen either adaptively depending on the left execution, or statically by announcing it before the left execution begins.

Simulation Soundness. The notion of *simulation soundness* [77] is a form of non-malleable ZK. Typically it is all one needs when building higher-level constructs using non-malleable ZK. In the non-interactive setting, it requires that a man-in-the-middle adversary cannot generate convincing proofs for false statements, even given access to a simulator who can generate false proofs.

The definition for the interactive setting appears in [48]. It requires a *single* machine S—the simulator—which guarantees indistinguishability of the view for true statements (to capture ZK), and the soundness for statements on the *right hand side* even in the presence of simulated false proofs *on the left hand side.* We use $\mathsf{MIM}^{\mathcal{A}}_{\langle P,V\rangle}(x,w,z,\mathsf{id})$ to denote the joint view of the adversary $\mathcal{A}$ in the same man-in-the-middle execution described above.

Definition 3 (Simulation-Sound Zero-Knowledge). *An interactive argument $\langle P, V\rangle$ for a language L is said to be a* simulation-sound zero-knowledge argument *if for every* PPT *man-in-the-middle algorithm $\mathcal{A}$, there exists a expected PPT algorithm S (the simulator) such that:*

- **(Indistinguishable Simulation)** *For every $x \in L$, every $w \in R_L(x)$, every $\mathsf{id} \in \{0,1\}^\lambda$, and every (auxiliary input) $z \in \{0,1\}^*$:*

$$S(x,z,\mathsf{id}) \overset{c}{\approx} \mathsf{MIM}^{\mathcal{A}}_{\langle P,V\rangle}(x,w,z,\mathsf{id})$$

- **(Simulation Soundness)** *There exists a negligible function $\mathsf{negl}(\cdot)$ such that for every $x \in \{0,1\}^\lambda$, every $\mathsf{id} \in \{0,1\}^\lambda$, and every $z \in \{0,1\}^*$:*

$$\Pr\left[\nu \leftarrow S(x,z,\mathsf{id}) : \widetilde{x} \notin L \wedge \widetilde{\mathsf{id}} \neq \mathsf{id} \wedge \widetilde{b} = 1\right] \leq \mathsf{negl}(\lambda)$$

where $\widetilde{x}, \widetilde{\mathsf{id}}$ and $\widetilde{b}$ denote the statement, identity, and verifier's decision in the right-side view of the simulated joint-view ν.

Non-Malleable Commitments. We use the tag-based definition from [43, 60]. Specifically, we compare an ideal interaction with a real one. In the ideal interaction, a man-in-the-middle adversary $\mathcal{A}$ interacting with a committer C in the *left* session, and a receiver R in the *right.* We denote the relevant entities used in the right interaction as "tilde'd" version of the corresponding entities on the left. In particular, suppose that C commits to v in the left interaction, and $\mathcal{A}$ commits to $\widetilde{v}$ on the right. Let MIM_v denote the random variable that is the pair $(\mathsf{View}, \widetilde{v})$, consisting of the adversary's entire view of the man-in-the-middle execution as well as the value committed to by $\mathcal{A}$ on the right (assuming C commits to v on the left). The *ideal* interaction is similar, except that C commits to some arbitrary fixed value (say $0^{|v|}$, i.e. an all-zero string of length $|v|$) on the left. Let MIM_0 denote the pair $(\mathsf{View}, \widetilde{v})$ in the ideal interaction. We ensure that $\mathcal{A}$ uses a distinct identity (or "tag") $\widetilde{\mathsf{id}}$ on the right from the identity id it uses on the left. This is done by stipulating that MIM_v and MIM_0 both output a special value $\perp_{id}$ when $\mathcal{A}$ uses the same identity in both the left and right executions. Let $\mathsf{MIM}_v(z)$ and $\mathsf{MIM}_0(z)$ denote real and ideal interactions resp., when $\mathcal{A}$'s auxiliary input is z.

Definition 4 (Non-Malleable Commitments). *A tag-based statistically binding commitment scheme* $\langle C, R\rangle$ *is* non-malleable *if* $\forall$ *PPT* $\mathcal{A}$*, and* $\forall v \in \{0,1\}^\lambda$*, it holds that* $\{\mathsf{MIM}_v(z)\}_{\lambda\in\mathbb{N},z\in\{0,1\}^*} \stackrel{c}{\approx} \{\mathsf{MIM}_0(z)\}_{\lambda\in\mathbb{N},z\in\{0,1\}^*}$.

3 Preparatory Work

In this section, we prepare the ingredients for use in the construction of our non-malleable zero-knowledge protocol. More specifically, we recall how Ligero's ZK simulator works (from [2]). Also, we show a slightly-modified version of the non-malleable commitment from [11]. We will recall related notation/techniques only to the extent that is adequate to understand our construction. See the full version of the current paper for a more detailed review of Ligero [53].

On Notation. In [2], the authors first built a public-coin *zero-knowledge interactive PCP* (ZKIPCP) scheme. They then converted the ZKIPCP to a 6-round *honest-verifier* ZK protocol relying on Kilian's transformation [52,61]. Finally, they further converted it to a 7-round (fully) zero-knowledge protocol using the techniques from [46,47][5]. Henceforth, we will use Ligero to denote their *honest-verifier* ZK protocol, and use Ligero′ to denote their *fully* ZK construction.

Simulator HVSim for Ligero. We will use the fact that simulating a Ligero (i.e., the honest-verifier version of [2]) proof is *much faster* than the real prover algorithm if the challenge of the verifier is known. The simulator's algorithm will be denoted by HVSim (HV for "honest-verifier"). There are two parts to be simulated: the first one is simulating the ZKIPCP interaction (a.k.a. the challenge-response slot); and the second one is simulating paths of the Merkle tree that are consistent with opened parts of the ZKIPCP proof string π (a.k.a. the oracle query-answer slot). The full description of HVSim is presented in Algorithm 1.

Algorithm 1: HVSim: Honest-Verifier Zero-Knowledge Simulator for Ligero

Input: a statement x, a collision-resistant hash function h, and a ZKIPCP query b:

1. Run the honest-verifier simulator algorithm corresponding to the ZKIPCP system for statement x and verifier randomness (h, b) to obtain a (perfectly) simulated ZKIPCP transcript. By definition, the transcript contains simulated parts of the "proof string" π. Let $L = \{(i, \pi_i)\}$ denote these simulated parts where $i \in [|\pi|]$ denotes position in the proof. Thus, L is simply the list of opened leaves in a Merkle tree (constructed below). Note that $n = |\pi|$ is the total number of leaves and known in advance. The simulated transcript also contains the honest verfier's challenge, which is simuilated as a random string b, and the corresponding (simulated) response c
2. Generate the paths of the Merkle tree that are consistent with $L = \{(i, \pi_i)\}$. This is straightforward, we provide the steps below for completeness:

[5] We remark that [2] also presented another approach—applying Fiat-Shamir transformation to their ZKIPCP will give a (fully) ZK protocol directly; moreover, the resulting protocol will be non-interactive. But this approach is irrelevant in the current paper as we are interested in constructions in the plain model (without random oracles).

(a) For every element $z = (i, \pi_i)$ in L, let i' represent the index corresponding to the sibling of z in the Merkle tree (note that i' exists for every i by definition). We first check if the sibling of z exists in L by checking if any element in L contains index i'. If no sibling for z exists in L, we add a new element $z' = (i', r_i)$ into L, where r_i is a random string with length equal to the output length of h.

(b) Let L^* be the empty set. For every z, along with its sibling z', in L, we let $z^* = h(z||z')$. We add z^* to L^*. In the end, the cardinality of L^* is equal to $|L|/2$.

(c) Set $L = L^*$ and $L^* = \emptyset$. Repeat Steps 2a to 2c while $|L| > 1$.

(d) The remaining element in L is the root of the Merkle tree.

Instantiating BGRRV with Symmetric Primitives. We will need an extractable non-malleable commitment (ENMC) that is fast and, preferably, based only on symmetric-key primitives. We work with a modified version of Brenner et al.'s protocol [11] (which is in turn based on [45]). This modified version uses Ligero′ (the malicious-verifier version of Ligero) as the ZK proof system in the consistency-proof stage of the protocol. For concreteness, this instantiation is completely specified in Protocol 1. We refer to it as $\Pi^{\mathsf{Mini}}_{\mathrm{BGRRV}}$.

Protocol 1: $\Pi^{\mathsf{Mini}}_{\mathrm{BGRRV}}$: Extractable Non-Malleable Commitment in Minicrypt

Public Input: an identity id $\in \{0,1\}^k$, a large prime q, an integer ℓ, and vector spaces $V_1, \ldots, V_n \subset \mathbb{Z}_q^\ell$ which are derived from id. These parameters satisfy the following relation: $\ell = 2(k+1)$ and $n = k+1$. (For the meanings of these parameters, we refer the readers to [11].)
Private Input: commiter C takes $\mathbf{m} \in \mathbb{Z}_q^{\ell-1}$ as its private input (the value to be committed).
Committing Stage. The committing stage consists of the following steps.

1. $R \to C$: Send the first message ρ of the Naor's commitment scheme [64].
2. $C \to R$: C chooses random values $r_1, \ldots, r_n \in \mathbb{Z}_q$. This defines vectors $\mathbf{z}_1, \ldots, \mathbf{z}_n \in \mathbb{Z}_q^\ell$ where $\mathbf{z}_i = (r_i, \mathbf{m})$. C sends commitments $(\widehat{\mathbf{m}}, \widehat{\mathbf{r}})$ where:
$$\widehat{\mathbf{m}} = (\mathsf{Com}_\rho(m_1; s_1), \ldots, \mathsf{Com}_\rho(m_{\ell-1}; s_{\ell-1})),\ \ \widehat{\mathbf{r}} = (\mathsf{Com}_\rho(r_1; s_1'), \ldots, \mathsf{Com}_\rho(r_n; s_n')),$$
where Com_ρ denotes the second round of Naor's commitment w.r.t. first message ρ. Note that this commits C to every coordinate of $\mathbf{z}_i$. For future reference, define the following language which contains valid commitment and message pairs:
$$L_{\mathsf{Com}_\rho} := \{(c, a) : \exists b \text{ s.t. } c = \mathsf{Com}_\rho(a; b)\}.$$
3. $R \to C$: Send random challenge vectors $\{\mathbf{v}_i\}_{i=1,\ldots,n}$ where each $\mathbf{v}_i \in V_i \subset \mathbb{Z}_q^\ell$.
4. $C \to R$: C sends evaluations $\{w_i\}$, where each $w_i = \langle \mathbf{v}_i, \mathbf{z}_i \rangle \in \mathbb{Z}_q$.

Consistency Proof. Using Ligero′, C proves that the preamble was executed correctly. That is, C proves the following statement: $\exists((m_1, s_1), \ldots, (m_{\ell-1}, s_{\ell-1}), (r_1, s_1'), \ldots, (r_n, s_n'))$ such that

- $\widehat{\mathbf{m}} = (\mathsf{Com}_\rho(m_1; s_1), \ldots, \mathsf{Com}_\rho(m_{\ell-1}; s_{\ell-1}))$, **and**
- $\widehat{\mathbf{r}} = (\mathsf{Com}_\rho(r_1; s_1'), \ldots, \mathsf{Com}_\rho(r_n; s_n'))$, **and**
- $w_i = \langle \mathbf{z}_i, \mathbf{v}_i \rangle\ \forall i \in [n]$ where $\mathbf{z}_i = (r_i, m_1, \ldots, m_{\ell-1})$.

Notation: Henceforth, we denote the above language as L^ρ_{consis}. We say that the above **Consistency Proof** stage is proving that $(\widehat{\mathbf{m}}, \widehat{\mathbf{r}}, \{w_i\}_{i\in[n]})$ is in language L^ρ_{consis}.

Observe that each message from the $\Pi^{\mathsf{Mini}}_{\mathrm{BGRRV}}$ receiver, informally speaking, is *efficiently simulatable* during "rewindings" given all prior information. That is, each message must be of one of the following three types: (i) it is a public random string; (ii) it can be sampled from scratch; *or* (iii) it is simply a complete opening of a previous commitment (and thus repeatable in rewind threads if needed). This observation will play an important role later when we prove the non-malleability of our ZK protocol (more specifically, in Claim 1). But we also emphasize that this observation is crucial *only* in the non-synchronous setting (but not in the synchronous setting).

Extractability of BGRRV. We remark that BGRRV is an extractable commitment scheme. Extraction can be performed from the preamble stage by simply rewinding to the second message, obtaining a valid answer for a different challenge, and then solving two equations in $\mathbb{Z}_p$.

4 Our Non-Malleable Zero Knowledge Protocol

In this section, we present the generic framework of our non-malleable zero-knowledge. Later in Sect. 5, we will instantiate each component of this protocol in special ways so that the final protocol admits an efficient implementation using only symmetric-key primitives. We use the following ingredients:

1. An extractable commitment scheme ExtCom. We will use the standard 3-round scheme from [75]. Note that the first committer message of this scheme is statistically-binding.
2. A tag-based commitment scheme ENMC that is both *non-malleable* and *extractable*; for concreteness, we will use scheme $\Pi^{\mathsf{Mini}}_{\mathrm{BGRRV}}$ specified in Protocol 1. We assume for convenience that the commitments are generated using Naor's scheme [64] w.r.t. an implicit first string ρ chosen by the receiver of the commitment (and dropped from the notation henceforth).
   We assume that the first *committer* message of ENMC is statistically binding. For concreteness, we say that a string c is an **honest ENMCcommitment to a value v with tag** id if there exists randomness r such that c is the first committer message of ENMC produced by the honest committer algorithm on input value v, tag id, and randomness r.
3. A *statistically* witness-indistinguishable argument of knowledge sWIAoK.

Our construction is shown in Protocol 2 below. At a high level, the protocol is as follows: V starts by committing to a random string σ. P then uses an extractable non-malleable commitment ENMC to commit to an all-zero string. Then V decommits to its commitment made at the beginning of the protocol. Finally, P and V execute a sWIAoK protocol, where P proves to V that *either* it knows a witness to x, *or* that the commitment in ENMC equals σ.

Protocol 2: $\langle P, V\rangle_{\mathsf{NMZK}}$: Non-Malleable Zero-Knowledge

Public input: Security parameter λ, statement x (supposedly in an $\mathcal{NP}$ language L), and a tag $\mathsf{id} \in \{0,1\}^{\leq\lambda}$.
Private input: P takes the witness w as its private input.

1. V commits to a random string $\sigma \leftarrow \{0,1\}^\lambda$, using the extractable commitment scheme ExtCom. We denote the first committer message by com_1.
2. P commits to $\sigma' = 0^\lambda$ using the extractable non-malleable commitment ENMC with tag id. We denote the first committer message of this stage by com_2.
3. V sends σ along with decommitment information for com_1.
4. If Step 3 decommitment is valid, P proves the following compound statement to V using a *statistical* witness-indistinguishable argument of knowledge sWIAoK:
   - there exists a w such that $R(x, w) = 1$; **or**
   - com_2 is an honest ENMC commitment to σ with tag id.

For future reference (σ', r) is called the trapdoor witness for statement $(\mathsf{com}_2, \mathsf{id})$ if r is s.t. com_2 is the 1st committer message of ENMC on input σ', tag id, and randomness r.

Theorem 1. *The protocol $\langle P, V\rangle_{\mathsf{NMZK}}$ (shown in Protocol 2) is a non-malleable zero-knowledge argument of knowledge for $\mathcal{NP}$.*

To prove Theorem 1, we first need to prove that $\langle P, V\rangle_{\mathsf{NMZK}}$ is a zero-knowledge argument of knowledge. This follows from standard techniques. Due to space constraints, we postpone it to the full version [53]. In the following, we show the non-malleability of $\langle P, V\rangle_{\mathsf{NMZK}}$.

Lemma 1. *$\langle P, V\rangle_{\mathsf{NMZK}}$ is non-malleable.*

We prove Lemma 1 in subsequent subsections. We first present in Sect. 4.1 the proof regarding synchronous adversaries (who send their right messages as soon as they receive the corresponding left message). Then, we deal with the general case of non-synchronous adversaries in Sect. 4.2.

When reading the proofs in the synchronous setting, it would be helpful to keep in mind also the non-synchronous case. We add remarks at the end of each hybrid to address this. We hope it can improve the readability when we talk about the non-synchronous setting later.

4.1 Non-Malleability Against Synchronous Adversaries

To prove non-malleability, we need to build a simulator which can convince V with roughly the same probability as a man-in-the-middle adversary $\mathcal{A}_{\mathsf{mim}}$ (up to some negligible difference), but without the help of the left interaction. We first define the following invariant condition.

Definition 5 (Invariant Condition). *The probability that the value $\widetilde{\sigma}'$ committed in com_2 by $\mathcal{A}_{\mathsf{mim}}$ is equal to $\widetilde{\sigma}$ committed in com_1 by the honest verifier is negligible.*

Note that if the invariant condition holds and $\mathcal{A}_{\mathsf{mim}}$ gives a convincing proof, we can extract the witness $\widetilde{w}$ for $\widetilde{x}$ by running the sWIAoK extractor.

At a high level, our proof goes in the following way. We start with the man-in-the-middle setting, where an honest prover $P(x, w)$ interacts with $\mathcal{A}_{\mathsf{mim}}$ in the left interaction, and $\mathcal{A}_{\mathsf{mim}}$ proves to an honest verifier V for a statement $\widetilde{x} \neq x$ in the right. We will build a sequence of hybrids, where we gradually substitute $P(x, w)$ and $V(\widetilde{x})$ with our simulator. Between each pair of adjacent hybrids, we show that the view of $\mathcal{A}_{\mathsf{mim}}$ does not change *and* that the invariant condition holds. In the last hybrid, we do not need the real witness w in the left interaction, and we can extract $\mathcal{A}_{\mathsf{mim}}$'s witness $\widetilde{w}$ via the sWIAoK extractor (we are guaranteed to extract $\widetilde{w}$ because of the invariant condition). With the extracted $\widetilde{w}$, our simulator can give a "straight-line" proof for the statement $\widetilde{x}$ to V, which completes the proof of non-malleability. Next, we describe the hybrids.

Hybrid H_0. This is the real execution of the MIM game. Specifically, H_0 sets up the left and right executions for $\mathcal{A}_{\mathsf{mim}}$ with $P(x, w)$ and V, respectively. H_0 outputs the joint view of $\mathcal{A}_{\mathsf{mim}}$ containing both left and right executions.

Invariant Condition. If the invariant condition does not hold, then consider the prover machine P^* which behaves identically to H_0 except that it forwards the right ExtCom to an external committer. Using this P^* we can violate the hiding of ExtCom by extracting the value committed in the right ENMC.

Hybrid H_1. This hybrid is identical to H_0, except that whenever the left ExtCom is accepting, H_1 extracts the committed value σ in the left ExtCom. If the extractor fails ($\sigma = \perp$), H_1 outputs $\perp$ and halts; otherwise it continues as H_0.

$H_0 \overset{\text{s}}{\approx} H_1$. The outputs of H_0 and H_1 differ only when $\sigma = \perp$; and due to the extractability of ExtCom, that happens with only negligible probability.

Invariant Condition. The invariant condition holds in H_1 since it holds in H_0 and the two hybrids are statistically close.

Remark 1. Note that the above proofs for both indistinguishability and invariant condition are independent of $\mathcal{A}_{\mathsf{mim}}$'s scheduling of the messages. Thus, they also hold in the non-synchronous scenario.

Hybrid H_2. This hybrid is identical to H_1, except that H_2 sets $\sigma' = \sigma$ in **Stage-2** ENMC on left.

$H_1 \overset{\text{c}}{\approx} H_2$ follows immediately from the computational-hiding property of ENMC.

Invariant Condition. The fact that the invariant condition holds can be reduced to the *non-malleability* of ENMC. Specifically, we consider a man-in-the-middle adversary $\mathcal{A}_{\mathsf{ENMC}}$ for ENMC that acts as follows: $\mathcal{A}_{\mathsf{ENMC}}$ internally runs H_2 except that it obtains the left ENMC execution from an outsider committer on the left and forwards the right ENMC interaction to an external receiver. Furthermore, the external committer commits as follows: recall that H_2 already has the extracted value σ before the left ENMC begins; $\mathcal{A}_{\mathsf{ENMC}}$ forwards $\sigma'_0 = 0^\lambda$ and $\sigma'_1 = \sigma$ to the external committer who then commits to one of them at random. $\mathcal{A}_{\mathsf{ENMC}}$ halts when H_2 halts. Now consider a distinguisher D (that incorporates the above adversary $\mathcal{A}_{\mathsf{ENMC}}$), and by definition of non-malleability, receives the value $\mathcal{A}_{\mathsf{ENMC}}$ commits to in the right interaction, say $\widetilde{\sigma}$. Clearly, if the invariant condition does not hold in H_2 then the distribution of $\widetilde{\sigma}$ is different depending on whether $\mathcal{A}_{\mathsf{ENMC}}$ receives commitment to σ'_0 or σ'_1. This condition can be tested by D (which incorporates $\mathcal{A}_{\mathsf{ENMC}}$), thus violating the non-malleability of ENMC.

Remark 2. Observe that in the non-synchronous case, the proof of indistinguishability will go through, but the proof of invariant condition will not. This is because the extraction of α on left from ExtCom may rewind some parts of ENMC on right, and this is not allowed by the non-malleability definition. We will deal with this issue in Sect. 4.2.

Hybrid H_3. Identical to H_2 except that it switches from real witness w to the trapdoor witness (i.e., values and randomness corresponding to $\sigma' = \sigma$) in the **Stage-4** sWIAoK on left.

$H_3 \overset{\text{s}}{\approx} H_2$ follows directly from the statistical WI property of sWIAoK.

Invariant Condition. Since we are in the synchronous setting, the invariant condition holds since the executions in the two hybrids are identical up to the end of **Stage-2**, at which point the invariant condition is already determined; any changes after that stage have no effect on the invariant condition.

Remark 3. As in Remark 2, in the non-synchronous case, the argument for indistinguishability still holds, but the argument for the invariant condition will require extra caution. This is because the left sWIAoK may get aligned with the right ENMC so that the switch of witness may affect the invariant condition. We will deal with this issue in Sect. 4.2.

Simulator for Non-Malleability. The indistinguishability among the above hybrids implies that: if $\mathcal{A}_{\mathsf{mim}}$ gives a convincing proof in the right interaction of H_0, it should also give a convincing proof in the right interaction of H_3. We construct a simulator Sim in the following way. Given a man-in-the-middle adversary $\mathcal{A}_{\mathsf{mim}}$, Sim first invokes H_3 with $\mathcal{A}_{\mathsf{mim}}$. If $\mathcal{A}_{\mathsf{mim}}$ indeed gives a convincing proof in the right interaction, Sim extracts $\mathcal{A}_{\mathsf{mim}}$'s witness $\widetilde{w}$ from sWIAoK on the right execution; otherwise, Sim aborts. The invariant condition in H_3 guarantees that Sim can extract such a $\widetilde{w}$. With $\widetilde{w}$, Sim then executes protocol $\langle P, V \rangle_{\mathsf{NMZK}}$ (in "straight-line") with an honest verifier. It convinces the honest verifier with roughly the same probability as $\mathcal{A}_{\mathsf{mim}}$ (except for negligible difference due to Sim's failure in extracting $\widetilde{w}$). This finishes the proof of non-malleability *against synchronous adversaries.*

4.2 Non-Malleability Against Non-Synchronous Adversaries

As mentioned in Remarks 1 to 3, the proofs for indistinguishability among *all* hybrids, as well as the invariant condition for H_0 and H_1, remain unchanged in the non-synchronous setting. Therefore, we only need to prove the invariant conditions for H_2 and H_3, which will be done in the sequel. (We first show the proof for H_3 since it is simpler.)

The Invariant Condition for H_3. Recall that the witness indistinguishability of the sWIAoK is *statistical.* It follows that the invariant condition must hold in H_3 for non-synchronous adversaries as well. If not, an exponential time distinguisher can recover the value committed by $\mathcal{A}_{\mathsf{mim}}$, thus breaks the statistical WI by testing whether the invariant condition.

The Invariant Condition for H_2. Before giving the formal lemma and proof, we provide the high-level idea. As mentioned in Remark 2, the problem happens if the $\mathcal{A}_{\mathsf{mim}}$ interleaves the left ExtCom messages with the right ENMC messages. In such a schedule, we cannot reduce the invariant condition to the non-malleability of ENMC without rewinding the outside challenger in ENMC's man-in-the-middle game. Recall that both H_1 and H_2 rewind the left ExtCom to extract the committed value σ.

We first note that if the reduction can simulate the receiver-to-committer messages in ENMC, then there is no issue during rewinding since in the right interaction, the reduction can forward messages between $\mathcal{A}_{\mathsf{mim}}$ and the outside challenger to the "main thread" and simply simulate them in "rewinding" threads. This (informally-explained) property is indeed satisfied by our $\Pi^{\mathsf{Mini}}_{\mathrm{BGRRV}}$ commitment (Protocol 1).

In the following, we show the formal claim and its proof.

Claim 1. *The invariant condition holds in Hybrid H_2 described in Sect. 4.1 for non-synchronous adversaries.*

Proof. This proof relies on the special structure of ENMC (when instantiated as the $\Pi^{\mathsf{Mini}}_{\mathrm{BGRRV}}$ protocol shown in Protocol 1). We will refer to different rounds of $\Pi^{\mathsf{Mini}}_{\mathrm{BGRRV}}$, which are recalled below for convenience (see and compare with Protocol 1):

- **(1):** R sends the first message for Naor's commitment, which consists of public coins only.
- **(2):** C sends the second message of Naor's commitment.
- **(3):** R sends some (public) random vectors as his challenge.
- **(4):** C responds to R's challenges. C also sends the first message (which consists of some public coins that specifies a CRHF) of a Ligero$'$ instance, which is used for consistency proof.
- **(5)-(10):** These are rounds 2 to 7 of Ligero$'$ between C and R. Note that **(5)** is the (statistically-hiding) commitments to verifier's random challenge Γ_1 and Γ_2; **(7)** is R's decommitment to Γ_1 and **(9)** is R's decommitment to Γ_2.

With the structure of ENMC in mind, we now start to prove Claim 1. First, observe that ExtCom has only one "slot" that is rewound to extract σ. Therefore, we only need to worry about the schedule where some messages of the right ENMC are "nested" in this slot. In the following, we show that the invariant condition hold for all schedules.

In the following, we use (i) $(i \in [10])$ to denote the i-th step of the right ENMC (as recalled above). We denote the first message of the rewindable slot in the left ExtCom as top, and the last message as bottom. See Fig. 1 for an illustration of these notations. Note that in Fig. 1, no messages can appear between "adjacent messages" of the right ENMC, for example, message **(2)**-**(3)**, **(6)**-**(7)** etc. This is because honest parties send their next message as soon as they receive the previous message.

Easy Cases. First, note that if bottom happens before **(1)**, we can rewind the slot without rewinding the right ENMC. Therefore, the same proof for the invariant condition in H_2 in the synchronous setting also applies here. Also, it is an easy case when **(10)** happens before bottom. In this case, $\mathcal{A}_{\mathsf{mim}}$ cannot generate the right ENMC messages based on the left ENMC interactions, since the left ENMC has not started yet. Therefore, the invariant condition holds automatically. Another easy case is when **(1)** gets nested in the slot. In such a case, rewinding the slot will cause a fresh execution of the right ENMC, so it will not cause any problem when we try to reduce the invariant condition to the non-malleability of ENMC. At a high level, this is because we can always forward the messages when we do the last rewinding to the outside non-malleability challenger in the reduction. But we suppress the details here since we will provide a formal argument of such type when we handle the hard cases next.

Hard Cases. We now focus on the remaining schedules (beyond those discussed in **Easy cases**). These schedules consist of the situations where

- **(1)** happens before top, *and*
- **(10)** happens after bottom.

There are 10 such cases in total. Since these 10 schedules can be handled via similar arguments, in the following, we will use the one in Fig. 1 as a representative to present a full proof, and then discuss how to extend the same proof to the remaining 9 cases in the full version [53].

For the schedule shown in Fig. 1, we build a man-in-the-middle adversary $\mathcal{A}_{\mathsf{ENMC}}$ attacking the non-malleability of ENMC. Recall that in the non-malleability game, the man-in-the-middle adversary $\mathcal{A}_{\mathsf{ENMC}}$ talks to an honest committer in the left, and to an honest receiver in the right. We will refer to them as the left challenger and right challenger respectively. Our $\mathcal{A}_{\mathsf{ENMC}}$ acts in the following way:

1. $\mathcal{A}_{\mathsf{ENMC}}$ starts by running the hybrid experiment H_2 *internally* with $\mathcal{A}_{\mathsf{mim}}$ up to the step right before **(1)**. It then invokes the right challenger for the non-malleability game of ENMC, and forwards the messages between the

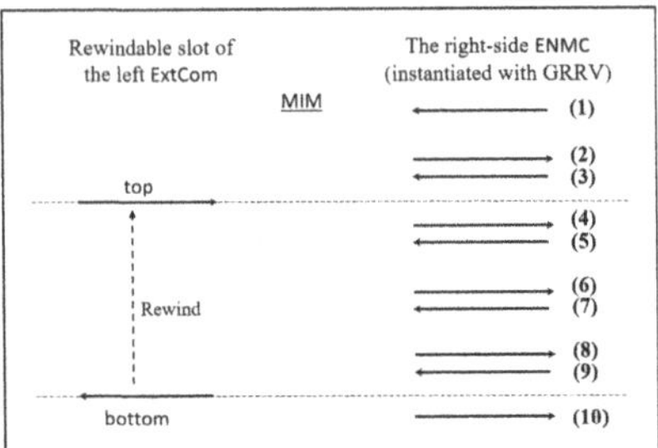

Fig. 1. Special Schedules in the Non-Synchronous Scenario

challenger and $\mathcal{A}_{\mathsf{mim}}$ as the right interaction. It plays the left interaction in the same way as the simulator in H_2, until the execution reaches top for the first time.

2. $\mathcal{A}_{\mathsf{ENMC}}$ now needs to execute the slot $(\mathsf{top}, \mathsf{bottom})$ in the "main-thread", and then rewind this slot for (w.l.o.g.) $k = \mathsf{poly}(\lambda)$ times to extract the σ value in the left interaction. To do that, $\mathcal{A}_{\mathsf{ENMC}}$ proceeds as follows:
   (a) For the main-thread execution, $\mathcal{A}_{\mathsf{ENMC}}$ plays the right interaction by forwarding messages between $\mathcal{A}_{\mathsf{mim}}$ and the outside right challenger.
   (b) From the 1st to the k-th rewinding, $\mathcal{A}_{\mathsf{ENMC}}$ will prepare the right ENMC incoming messages (i.e. **(5)**, **(7)**, and **(9)**) *by himself*, instead of forwarding them between $\mathcal{A}_{\mathsf{mim}}$ and the outside right challenger. To do that, $\mathcal{A}_{\mathsf{ENMC}}$ samples *fresh* Γ_1 and Γ_2, and commits to them as message **(5)**; it sends the honest decommitments to (the fresh) Γ_1 as message **(7)**; similarly, it sends the honest decommitments to (the fresh) Γ_2 as message **(9)**. We emphasize that $\mathcal{A}_{\mathsf{ENMC}}$ can indeed decommit to them because the commitments in **(5)** (in these rewinding threads) are generated by himself.

   Note that the simulated messages during rewinding have identical distribution as the main-thread **(5)**, **(7)**, and **(9)**, which guarantees that $\mathcal{A}_{\mathsf{mim}}$'s view does not change. Thus, after the above rewindings, σ can be extracted except for negligible probability, for which $\mathcal{A}_{\mathsf{ENMC}}$ just halts outputting $\perp$.
3. $\mathcal{A}_{\mathsf{ENMC}}$ continues the internal (main-thread) interaction until the left ENMC starts. He then invokes the outside left challenger by sending the values $\sigma'_0 = 0^\lambda$ and $\sigma'_1 = \sigma$. Then, ENMC forwards the messages between $\mathcal{A}_{\mathsf{mim}}$ and the outside left challenger and $\mathcal{A}_{\mathsf{mim}}$ as the left ENMC interaction. In the right interaction, ENMC acts as the simulator in H_2 except that when $\mathcal{A}_{\mathsf{mim}}$ sends the message **(10)**, it forwards the message to the outside right challenger.
4. $\mathcal{A}_{\mathsf{ENMC}}$ continues to finish the internal interaction with $\mathcal{A}_{\mathsf{mim}}$ as in H_2 for the remaining parts of the protocol.

Now consider a distinguisher D (that incorporates the above adversary $\mathcal{A}_{\mathsf{ENMC}}$), and by definition of non-malleability, receives the value $\mathcal{A}_{\mathsf{ENMC}}$ commits to in the right interaction, say $\widetilde{\sigma}$. Clearly, if the invariant condition does not hold in H_2 then the distribution of $\widetilde{\sigma}$ is different depending on whether $\mathcal{A}_{\mathsf{ENMC}}$ receives commitment to σ'_0 or σ'_1. This condition can be easily tested by D (since it incorporates $\mathcal{A}_{\mathsf{ENMC}}$), thus violating the non-malleability of ENMC.

The above argument proves Claim 1 for the special scheduling shown in Fig. 1. Due to space constraints, we postpone the discussion for the other 9 schedules to the full version [53]. □

4.3 Generalization to "Almost Public-Coin" Statistically ZK

In this part, we take another look at the proof in Sect. 4.2 with the following purpose: in Sect. 4.2, we proved the invariant condition in H_2, relying on the special structure of $\Pi^{\mathsf{Mini}}_{\mathrm{BGRRV}}$. In particular, we assumed that the **Consistency Proof** stage of $\Pi^{\mathsf{Mini}}_{\mathrm{BGRRV}}$ is conducted by Ligero′. However, we argue that Ligero′ can be replaced by any "almost public-coin" (explained below) statistically zero-knowledge argument.

Motivation. Before delving into the details, let us first explain why we want to generalize the proof to almost public-coin ZK protocols: While Ligero′ is efficient, using it directly in the **Consistency Proof** stage of $\Pi^{\mathsf{Mini}}_{\mathrm{BGRRV}}$ results in unacceptable running time. This is because the language $L^{\rho}_{\mathsf{consis}}$ (defined toward the end of Protocol 1) has a huge circuit size. As mentioned in Sect. 1.2, we will (in Sect. 5.3) introduce the new idea of converting $\Pi^{\mathsf{Mini}}_{\mathrm{BGRRV}}$ to an *instance-based* non-malleable commitment to achieve better efficiency. Looking ahead, the instance-based $\Pi^{\mathsf{Mini}}_{\mathrm{BGRRV}}$ shares the same structure of the original $\Pi^{\mathsf{Mini}}_{\mathrm{BGRRV}}$, with the only difference being that the **Consistency Proof** stage is not conducted by Ligero′ anymore. Instead, it will be done using a customized statistical ZK protocol called Π'_{OR}, which we construct by applying (a modified version of) the OR-composition technique [22] on Ligero (i.e., the honest-verifier version of Ligero′). We need to show that the same proof in Sect. 4.2 will still go through when we replace (the original) $\Pi^{\mathsf{Mini}}_{\mathrm{BGRRV}}$ with this instance-based $\Pi^{\mathsf{Mini}}_{\mathrm{BGRRV}}$ (i.e., when we replace Ligero′ in the **Consistency Proof** stage with Π'_{OR}). Fortunately, this is possible because Π'_{OR} shares the same structure as Ligero′, in terms of the application in Sect. 4.2. In particular, Π'_{OR} also enjoys the same "almost public-coin" property of Ligero′, and this is exactly why the same proof in Sect. 4.2 can be applied when we replace Ligero′ with Π'_{OR}. The purpose of this subsection is to distill this "almost public-coin" property and explain how it helps in the proof in Sect. 4.2.

Almost Public-Coin Protocols. Let us summarize how the proof in Sect. 4.2 makes use of the structure of $\Pi^{\mathsf{Mini}}_{\mathrm{BGRRV}}$. As we mentioned in the beginning of Sect. 4.2, $\Pi^{\mathsf{Mini}}_{\mathrm{BGRRV}}$ has 10 rounds that can be understood as two stages:

1. **Commit Stage:** This includes rounds **(1)** to **(4)**, and

2. **Consistency Proof:** This includes rounds **(4)** to **(10)**, which is exactly the statistically ZK protocol Ligero'.

We emphasize that all the receiver's messages are public coins except for rounds **(5)** and **(7)**, which constitute the commitment and corresponding decommitment to some random coins. This public-coin property is the main reason that $\mathcal{A}_{\mathsf{ENMC}}$ works properly: in Step 2, $\mathcal{A}_{\mathsf{ENMC}}$ needs to simulate the receiver's message in rewinding threads; because all the receiver's messages (except for rounds **(5)** and **(7)**) are public-coin, $\mathcal{A}_{\mathsf{ENMC}}$ can simply sample them freshly for each rewinding; moreover, round **(5)** (resp. **(7)**) is a commitment (resp. the corresponding decommitment) to random coins, so $\mathcal{A}_{\mathsf{ENMC}}$ can also sample and commit to (resp. decommit honestly to) random coins itself. Therefore, the rewinding threads can be shown to be identically distributed as the main thread.

In light of the above, it is clear that the $\Pi^{\mathsf{Mini}}_{\mathrm{BGRRV}}$ can be replaced with any ENMC that enjoys the above public-coin property. In particular, the **Commit Stage** of $\Pi^{\mathsf{Mini}}_{\mathrm{BGRRV}}$ is public-coin by design; the **Consistency Proof** stage, when implemented with Ligero', is public-coin (again, except for **(5)** and **(7)** as discussed above) because Ligero' is obtained in a special way: it is obtained by applying the Goldreich-Kahan transform on the honest-verifier version Ligero, which is a public-coin protocol.

Looking ahead, our Π'_{OR} enjoys the above public-coin property. As we will show in Sect. 5.3, Π'_{OR} is obtained by applying Goldreich-Kahan transform on a protocol Π_{OR} (which will appear in Sect. 5.2), which is also a public-coin honest-verifier ZK argument. Therefore, the above argument applies.

In summary, when we replace $\Pi^{\mathsf{Mini}}_{\mathrm{BGRRV}}$ with its instance-based version, the same proof in Sect. 4.2 will still go through.

5 Improving Efficiency Through Fake Executions

5.1 Road Map of This Section

In this section, we describe how to instantiate our NMZK protocol $\langle P, V\rangle_{\mathsf{NMZK}}$ (shown in Protocol 2) to achieve concrete efficiency. The major bottlenecks are:

1. Step 4 of $\langle P, V\rangle_{\mathsf{NMZK}}$ is a statistical WIAoK on the OR-composition of the statement x and a trapdoor statement (let us denote it as $(x \vee x_{\mathsf{tr}})$). This proof is non-black-box on the Step 2 commitments and involves expensive $\mathcal{NP}$ reduction.
2. Step 2 of $\langle P, V\rangle_{\mathsf{NMZK}}$ is instantiated with $\Pi^{\mathsf{Mini}}_{\mathrm{BGRRV}}$ (Protocol 1), whose **Consistency Proof** step involves an expensive ZK proof.

To address Item 1, we want to employ the OR-composition technique in [22] to construct the desired sWIAoK from Ligero. This will allow the prover to finish the proof for $(x \vee x_{\mathsf{tr}})$ by conducting a (light) proof for x, and running the fast Ligero simulator HVSim for the x_{tr} part. This will be much more efficient than running Ligero on $(x \vee x_{\mathsf{tr}})$ directly. However, this approach encounters obstacles:

Ligero does not have the properties required by [22]. We show how to solve related problems in Sect. 5.2.

To address Item 2, we wish to reuse the OR-composition technique described above. But it does not immediately apply because the target statement of the **Consistency Proof** does not have the $(x \vee x_{\mathsf{tr}})$ structure; instead, it is a single statement $x_{\mathsf{com}} \in L^{\rho}_{\mathsf{consis}}$, which is related to some vector of commitments[6]. Running Ligero for x_{com} is prohibitively expensive. To handle this issue, observe that this $\Pi^{\mathsf{Mini}}_{\mathrm{BGRRV}}$ protocol is executed as a part of our $\langle P, V\rangle_{\mathsf{NMZK}}$ protocol on some statement x_{zk}. Therefore, we change the statement of **Consistency Proof** to $(x_{\mathsf{zk}} \vee x_{\mathsf{com}})$, and then use the above OR-composition technique to boost the efficiency. We denote this extended non-malleable commitments as *instance-based non-malleable commitments* (IB-NMC). We elaborate on the above idea in Sect. 5.3.

Non-Malleability from Simulation-Soundness. Unfortunately, the above strategy induces an extra problem—replacing the Step 2 ENMC by the above instance-based version (i.e. the IB-NMC) jeopardizes the security of $\langle P, V\rangle_{\mathsf{NMZK}}$ (Protocol 2). Specifically, it is not clear whether the resulting protocol is still non-malleable. However, we will be able to prove that it is a *simulation-sound* ZK protocol (which is already sufficient for many applications). Finally, we show in Sect. 5.4 (resp. Sect. 5.5) how to use this simulation-sound ZK protocol to obtain non-malleable ZK protocols (resp. non-malleable commitments), with (almost) no efficiency overhead.

5.2 OR-Composition of Ligero

The OR-composition [22] was originally designed for Σ protocols, i.e., 3-round public-coin HVZK protocols with *special soundness*, which requires that a witness can be extracted from two convincing transcripts with distinct challenges. To prove an OR statement $x \vee x'$, the OR-composition invokes a parallel execution of two Σ-protocol instances: (a_1, b_1, c_1) for proving x and (a_2, b_2, c_2) for proving x', which are called the left and right execution respectively. But the verifier sends only a single round-2 challenge b; the prover has the freedom to "decompose" it as $b = b_1 \oplus b_2$ to finish the two parallel executions. The prover may only have a witness for, say, the x part; since it can always "equivocate" one share of b, it will first "finish" (in other words, fake) the left execution by running the HVZK simulator for the Σ-protocol by setting b_2 in advance; it can answer any $b_1 = b \oplus b_2$ as it has the witness for x.

We want to apply the above OR-composition to Ligero. However, Ligero is not a Σ-protocol—it has six rounds (i.e., two challenge-response slots). Indeed, it is known that straightforward generalization of OR-composition to multi-slots protocols (i.e., the original OR-composition is applied on each slot separately) will yield an *unsound* protocol.

The First Attempt. In more detail, recall that Ligero's messages are denoted as $(h, a, b, c, \widetilde{b}, \widetilde{c})$, where $(h, b, \widetilde{b})$ are nothing but public random coins. If we do

[6] Recall that the language $L^{\rho}_{\mathsf{consis}}$ is defined toward the end of $\Pi^{\mathsf{Mini}}_{\mathrm{BGRRV}}$ (Protocol 1).

the straightforward generalization of the above OR-composition (to prove an OR statement $x \vee x'$), it will work as follows: assuming P knows witness w for x, P uses $\mathsf{HVSim}(x')$ to simulate a proof $(h_2, a_2, b_2, c_2, \widetilde{b}_2, \widetilde{c}_2)$ for the x' part (because P does not have witness for it). Meanwhile, P generates the proof for x honestly, in the following manner: V sends h and P derives h_1 as $h_1 = h \oplus h_2$; P runs the honest Ligero prover's algorithm on input (x, w) to generate a_1, assuming the first Ligero verifier's message is h_1. Similarly, when V sends b (resp. $\widetilde{b}$), P will set $b_1 = b \oplus b_2$ (resp. $\widetilde{b}_1 = \widetilde{b} \oplus \widetilde{b}_2$), and compute the response c_1 (resp. $\widetilde{c}_1$) using the honest Ligero prover's algorithm (as it has witness w for x).

However, the above approach suffers from the following "cross attack": Since P^* has the opportunity to decide how to decompose h, b, and $\widetilde{b}$, it can pick a bad b_1 and a bad $\widetilde{b}_2$. That is, a cheating prover can choose malicious challenges in the first slot of the *left* execution and the second slot of the *right* execution, and there is no soundness guarantee for Ligero when a malicious prover can control (even) one challenge out of the two slots.

Solution. To resolve this problem, we ask P to commit to its decomposition in advance. More accurately, we ask P to generate $\mathsf{com} = \mathsf{SHCom}(h_2 \| b_2 \| \widetilde{b}_2; r)$ at the very beginning of the protocol, where SHCom is a statistically-hiding commitment. Then, we continue as the above. At the end of the execution, we ask P to give a statistical WI argument of knowledge sWIAoK for the following statement:

- com is committing to either $(h_1, b_1, \widetilde{b}_1)$ or $(h_2, b_2, \widetilde{b}_2)$.[7]

Intuitively, due to the (knowledge) soundness of sWIAoK, P^* cannot conduct the above "cross attack" anymore.

We denote this protocol as Π_{OR}. Due to space constraints, we put the formal description of Π_{OR} in the full version [53], where we also provide the complete security proof. Here, we want to emphasize that this approach invokes very small efficiency overhead compared with the plain OR-composition described in **The First Attempt**: what we add is simply a statistically-hiding commitment and a sWIAoK for its consistency. Using a modified version of Ligero as the underlying sWIAoK (see [53, Appendix C.3]), this only adds an extra computation cost of 32 milliseconds and an extra communication cost of 6.4MB. See [53, Appendix C.2] for more details.

Regarding Malicious-Verifiers ZK. It is not hard to see that the above Π_{OR} is also an honest-verifier ZK argument (of knowledge). Using the Goldreich-Kahan technique [38] (as done in [2,46]), we can convert it to a fully-secure ZK argument, i.e., against malicious verifiers. We denote the resulting protocol as Π'_{OR}, and present the full description of it in [53, Protocol 11]. Looking ahead, Π'_{OR} will be used in the instance-based non-malleable commitment in the next subsection (in Protocol 3).

[7] Note that $(h_1, b_1, \widetilde{b}_1)$ and $(h_2, b_2, \widetilde{b}_2)$ will be known to V when the protocol reaches the final sWIAoK stage.

5.3 Instance-Based Non-Malleability

Recall that we use $\Pi^{\mathsf{Mini}}_{\mathrm{BGRRV}}$ (Protocol 1) as our ENMC. The primary efficiency bottleneck in $\Pi^{\mathsf{Mini}}_{\mathrm{BGRRV}}$ is the consistency proof, which is done using Ligero'. Since an honest committer is never cheating, our goal is to provide the prover an easier way to get through this proof. Toward this goal, we first show an *instance-based* version of $\Pi^{\mathsf{Mini}}_{\mathrm{BGRRV}}$, denoted as $\langle C_L, R_L\rangle$. The instance-based version simply gives the option of using a witness for a true statement in the consistency proof phase of $\Pi^{\mathsf{Mini}}_{\mathrm{BGRRV}}$. At a high level, the parties get a statement x as input which may or may not be true. If x is true, the committer can additionally take as input a witness $w \in \mathcal{R}_L(x)$ and succeed in the proof phase by using w instead of completing the consistency proof for any message m. This allows the honest prover to fake the ENMC execution using a faster simulator thanks to the OR-composition. If x is false, the committer commits to a valid value m. It is also possible to do both: commit to m properly and execute consistency proof as well as proof for x. We present the full construction in Protocol 3,[8] and establish its security in Lemmas 2 and 3.

Protocol 3: $\langle C_L, R_L\rangle(x)$: Instance-Based Non-Malleable Commitment

Instance-based $\Pi^{\mathsf{Mini}}_{\mathrm{BGRRV}}$ is the following commitment scheme, denoted as $\langle C_L, R_L\rangle$, defined for an arbitrary $\mathcal{NP}$ language L: the common input to both algorithms is a statement x; in addition, C_L takes a (private) auxiliary input that is either of the form $(m, \bot)$ or $(\bot, w)$ where w is a witness for $x \in L$. Recall that $\Pi^{\mathsf{Mini}}_{\mathrm{BGRRV}}$ is denoted by $\langle C, R\rangle$ and depicted in Prot. 1. The protocol proceeds in two phases:

- **Commit Stage:** In this stage R_L proceeds identically to algorithm R of $\Pi^{\mathsf{Mini}}_{\mathrm{BGRRV}}$ and let ρ be its first message. For input $(m, \bot)$, C_L proceeds exactly as C proceeds in the commit stage on input m. For input $(\bot, w)$, C_L simply sends *random* values of appropriate size as the second and fourth messages of the commit stage (when interacting with R_L). Recall that the execution of the **Commit Stage** of $\Pi^{\mathsf{Mini}}_{\mathrm{BGRRV}}$ will yield messages $\widehat{\mathbf{m}}$, $\widehat{\mathbf{r}}$, and $\{w_i\}_{i\in[n]}$) (see Prot. 1). We denote $\mathsf{st} := (\widehat{\mathbf{m}}, \widehat{\mathbf{r}}, \{w_i\}_{i\in[n]})$.
- **Proof Stage:** In this stage, C_L proves that $(x, \mathsf{st}) \in L \vee L^{\rho}_{\mathsf{consis}}$ using Π'_{OR}, i.e., the fully ZK version of Π_{OR} (see [53, Protocol 11]). For input $(m, \bot)$, C_L uses the simulator HVSim for the left part (i.e., for x), and completes right part (i.e., for st) honestly by using the witness for st (from the first phase). For input $(\bot, w)$ it uses w to succeed in the left part of the proof and simulator HVSim to succeed in the right part.

If the common statement is fixed to x, we denote the instance-based $\Pi^{\mathsf{Mini}}_{\mathrm{BGRRV}}$ by $\langle C_L, R_L\rangle(x)$. The executions corresponding to inputs $(m, \bot)$ will be called **real or honest executions**, and those corresponding to $(\bot, w)$, **fake or simulated executions** of $\Pi^{\mathsf{Mini}}_{\mathrm{BGRRV}}$ (or ENMC).

Lemma 2. *Let L be an $\mathcal{NP}$ language. For every $x \notin L$ protocol $\langle C_L, R_L\rangle(x)$ (Protocol 3) is an extractable non-malleable commitment scheme.*

Proof. We observe that for every $x \notin L$, the **Proof Stage** of the protocol is a ZK argument for $\mathsf{st} \in L^{\rho}_{\mathsf{consis}}$ (i.e., consistent execution of the commit stage). In this case, $\langle C_L, R_L\rangle(x)$ is simply an instantiation of the original $\Pi^{\mathsf{Mini}}_{\mathrm{BGRRV}}$ protocol. The claim then follows from the security of $\Pi^{\mathsf{Mini}}_{\mathrm{BGRRV}}$. □

[8] We warn that this version cannot be used in our NMZK protocol yet. See Sect. 5.4.

Lemma 3. *Let L be an $\mathcal{NP}$ language with witness relation $\mathcal{R}_L$. For every message m and every $(x, w) \in \mathcal{R}_L$, the following holds:*

$$\{\mathsf{view}_0 \leftarrow \langle C_L((m, \bot)), R_L\rangle(x) : \mathsf{view}_0\} \overset{c}{\approx} \{\mathsf{view}_1 \leftarrow \langle C_L((\bot, w)), R_L\rangle(x) : \mathsf{view}_1\}.$$

Proof. This lemma follows from the following two observations: (i) committer's messages in the commit stage are *pseudorandom* (since second message of Naor's commitment is pseudorandom), and (ii) the proof stage is WI (it is indeed ZK). Since the proof follows from a standard hybrid argument, we omit the details. □

Remark 4 (On Efficiency). It is worth noting that if x admits a fast Ligero proof, then fake executions are faster than the real executions since the simulator for Ligero for the right part (i.e., the real consistency proof for st) is much faster than the prover. As mentioned in Sect. 1.2, this is how we manage to obtain significant improvement on the efficiency.

5.4 Efficient Simulation-Sound Zero-Knowledge

The main benefit of the instance-based $\Pi^{\mathsf{Mini}}_{\mathrm{BGRRV}}$ in Protocol 3 is that if $x \in L$ admits fast proofs, it can be used in place of standard $\Pi^{\mathsf{Mini}}_{\mathrm{BGRRV}}$ in our NMZK protocol. Unfortunately, the resulting protocol is not a NMZK for true x! Nevertheless, the resulting protocol is *simulation-sound* (as per Definition 3), and equally importantly, *efficient*. We refer to this protocol by Π_{SS} and specify it in Protocol 4.

Protocol 4: Π_{SS}: Simulation-Sound ZKAoK
The common input is x and prover's input is a witness w for $x \in L$, where L is the desired $\mathcal{NP}$ language. This protocol is identical to protocol $\langle P, V\rangle_{\mathsf{NMZK}}$ (Prot. 2) except that the Step 2 ENMC is replaced with the instance-based non-malleable commitment (Prot. 3) with the following inputs: the common input is x and committer's auxiliary input in the **Proof Stage** of the commitment is $(\bot, w)$. Observe that the honest prover only performs a simulated execution of the non-malleable commitment.

Theorem 2. *Protocol Π_{SS} (Protocol 4) is a simulation-sound zero-knowledge argument of knowledge.*

Due to space constraints, we postpone the proof of Theorem 2 to the full version [53].

5.5 Putting It All Together: Fast NMZK and NMCom

Now we show how to get efficient and full-fledged non-malleable zero-knowledge and commitment protocols with the help of our efficient simulation-sound ZKAoK protocol Π_{SS} and the statistically WIAoK protocol Π_{OR}.

Fast NMZKProtocol. We present our final NMZK protocol in Protocol 5. At a high level, the prover in Protocol 5 sets up a "trapdoor statement" in the form of a commitment cm, and proves using Π_{SS} that cm is a commitment to 0. Later, the prover proves using protocol Π_{OR} that either the statement is true or that cm is a commitment to 1. The honest prover always commits to 0 and thus remains fast. The simulator commits to 1 instead. The security of Protocol 5 can be proven Following a similar proof as that of Lemma 1. Due to space constraints, we postpone the proof to the full version [53].

Protocol 5: $\langle P, V\rangle_{\mathsf{final}}$: Non-Malleable ZKAoK

The common inputs are statement x, tag id, and security parameter λ. Prover's private input is a witness $w \in R_L(x)$, where L is the desired $\mathcal{NP}$ language. The protocol proceeds as follows:

1. P commits to 0^λ using 2-round Naor commitment; let ρ be the first message of this commitment and $\mathsf{cm} = \mathsf{Com}_\rho(0^\lambda)$ the second message.
2. P and V execute Π_{SS} with tag id, where P proves that cm is a valid commitment to 0^λ.
3. P and V execute Π_{OR}, where P proves that:
   - $x \in L$, **or**
   - cm is a valid commitment to 1^λ, i.e., $(\mathsf{cm}, 1^\lambda) \in L_{\mathsf{Com}_\rho}$.

Fast NMCom Protocol. Our non-malleable commitment protocol is presented in Protocol 6. At a high level, Protocol 6 works in the same way as the non-malleable zero-knowledge protocol above, except that x is replaced with a commitment to the desired value. Its security proof follows closely from the proof Lemma 1. The details are omitted.

Protocol 6: $\langle C, R\rangle_{\mathsf{final}}$: Non-Malleable Commitment

The common input is a tag id and the security parameter λ. Private input of the committer is a value $v \in \{0,1\}^\lambda$. The protocol proceeds as follows:

1. C commits to v using two-round Naor commitment; let R's first message be ρ, and $c = \mathsf{Com}_\rho(v)$ denote the second message.
2. C further commits to 0^λ using ρ as first message. Let $\mathsf{cm} = \mathsf{Com}_\rho(0^\lambda)$.
3. C proves that cm is valid commitment to 0^λ using Π_{SS} with tag id.
4. C proves using Π_{OR} that:
   - there exists v such that c is a valid commitment to v, i.e., $(c, v) \in L_{\mathsf{Com}_\rho}$, **or**
   - cm is a valid commitment to 1^λ, i.e., $(\mathsf{cm}, 1^\lambda) \in L_{\mathsf{Com}_\rho}$.

References

1. Aggarwal, D., Dodis, Y., Lovett, S.: Non-malleable codes from additive combinatorics. In: Shmoys, D.B. (ed.) 46th ACM STOC, pp. 774–783. ACM Press, May/June 2014. https://doi.org/10.1145/2591796.2591804
2. Ames, S., Hazay, C., Ishai, Y., Venkitasubramaniam, M.: Ligero: Lightweight sublinear arguments without a trusted setup. In: Thuraisingham, B.M., Evans, D., Malkin, T., Xu, D. (eds.) ACM CCS 2017, pp. 2087–2104. ACM Press, October/November 2017. https://doi.org/10.1145/3133956.3134104

3. Badrinarayanan, S., Goyal, V., Jain, A., Kalai, Y.T., Khurana, D., Sahai, A.: Promise zero knowledge and its applications to round optimal MPC. In: Shacham, H., Boldyreva, A. (eds.) CRYPTO 2018, Part II. LNCS, vol. 10992, pp. 459–487. Springer, Cham (2018). https://doi.org/10.1007/978-3-319-96881-0_16
4. Barak, B.: How to go beyond the black-box simulation barrier. In: 42nd FOCS, pp. 106–115. IEEE Computer Society Press, October 2001. https://doi.org/10.1109/SFCS.2001.959885
5. Barak, B.: Constant-round coin-tossing with a man in the middle or realizing the shared random string model. In: 43rd FOCS, pp. 345–355. IEEE Computer Society Press, November 2002. https://doi.org/10.1109/SFCS.2002.1181957
6. Barak, B., Goldreich, O.: Universal arguments and their applications. SIAM J. Comput. **38**(5), 1661–1694 (2008)
7. Barak, B., Prabhakaran, M., Sahai, A.: Concurrent non-malleable zero knowledge. In: 47th FOCS, pp. 345–354. IEEE Computer Society Press, October 2006. https://doi.org/10.1109/FOCS.2006.21
8. Bellare, M., Rogaway, P.: Random oracles are practical: A paradigm for designing efficient protocols. In: Denning, D.E., Pyle, R., Ganesan, R., Sandhu, R.S., Ashby, V. (eds.) ACM CCS 93, pp. 62–73. ACM Press, November 1993. https://doi.org/10.1145/168588.168596
9. Ben-Sasson, E., Chiesa, A., Genkin, D., Tromer, E.: On the concrete efficiency of probabilistically-checkable proofs. In: Boneh, D., Roughgarden, T., Feigenbaum, J. (eds.) 45th ACM STOC, pp. 585–594. ACM Press, June 2013. https://doi.org/10.1145/2488608.2488681
10. Boldyreva, A., Cash, D., Fischlin, M., Warinschi, B.: Foundations of non-malleable hash and one-way functions. In: Matsui, M. (ed.) ASIACRYPT 2009. LNCS, vol. 5912, pp. 524–541. Springer, Heidelberg (2009). https://doi.org/10.1007/978-3-642-10366-7_31
11. Brenner, H., Goyal, V., Richelson, S., Rosen, A., Vald, M.: Fast non-malleable commitments. In: Ray, I., Li, N., Kruegel, C. (eds.) ACM CCS 2015, pp. 1048–1057. ACM Press, October 2015. https://doi.org/10.1145/2810103.2813721
12. Broadnax, B., Döttling, N., Hartung, G., Müller-Quade, J., Nagel, M.: Concurrently composable security with shielded super-polynomial simulators. In: Coron, J.-S., Nielsen, J.B. (eds.) EUROCRYPT 2017, Part II. LNCS, vol. 10210, pp. 351–381. Springer, Cham (2017). https://doi.org/10.1007/978-3-319-56620-7_13
13. Canetti, R.: Security and composition of multiparty cryptographic protocols. J. Cryptol. **13**(1), 143–202 (2000). https://doi.org/10.1007/s001459910006
14. Canetti, R.: Universally composable security: a new paradigm for cryptographic protocols. In: 42nd FOCS, pp. 136–145. IEEE Computer Society Press, October 2001. https://doi.org/10.1109/SFCS.2001.959888
15. Canetti, R., Dodis, Y., Pass, R., Walfish, S.: Universally composable security with global setup. In: Vadhan, S.P. (ed.) TCC 2007. LNCS, vol. 4392, pp. 61–85. Springer, Heidelberg (2007). https://doi.org/10.1007/978-3-540-70936-7_4
16. Canetti, R., Dwork, C., Naor, M., Ostrovsky, R.: Deniable encryption. In: Kaliski, B.S. (ed.) CRYPTO 1997. LNCS, vol. 1294, pp. 90–104. Springer, Heidelberg (1997). https://doi.org/10.1007/BFb0052229
17. Canetti, R., Goldreich, O., Halevi, S.: The random oracle methodology, revisited (preliminary version). In: 30th ACM STOC, pp. 209–218. ACM Press, May 1998. https://doi.org/10.1145/276698.276741
18. Canetti, R., Lin, H., Pass, R.: Adaptive hardness and composable security in the plain model from standard assumptions. In: 51st FOCS, pp. 541–550. IEEE Computer Society Press, October 2010. https://doi.org/10.1109/FOCS.2010.86

19. Canetti, R., Lindell, Y., Ostrovsky, R., Sahai, A.: Universally composable two-party and multi-party secure computation. In: 34th ACM STOC, pp. 494–503. ACM Press, May 2002. https://doi.org/10.1145/509907.509980
20. Rai Choudhuri, A., Ciampi, M., Goyal, V., Jain, A., Ostrovsky, R.: Round optimal secure multiparty computation from minimal assumptions. In: Pass, R., Pietrzak, K. (eds.) TCC 2020, Part II. LNCS, vol. 12551, pp. 291–319. Springer, Cham (2020). https://doi.org/10.1007/978-3-030-64378-2_11
21. Ciampi, M., Ostrovsky, R., Siniscalchi, L., Visconti, I.: Four-round concurrent non-malleable commitments from one-way functions. In: Katz, J., Shacham, H. (eds.) CRYPTO 2017, Part II. LNCS, vol. 10402, pp. 127–157. Springer, Cham (2017). https://doi.org/10.1007/978-3-319-63715-0_5
22. Cramer, R., Damgård, I., Schoenmakers, B.: Proofs of partial knowledge and simplified design of witness hiding protocols. In: Desmedt, Y.G. (ed.) CRYPTO 1994. LNCS, vol. 839, pp. 174–187. Springer, Heidelberg (1994). https://doi.org/10.1007/3-540-48658-5_19
23. Damgård, I.: On σ-protocols (2002). http://www.cs.au.dk/~ivan/Sigma.pdf
24. Di Crescenzo, G., Ishai, Y., Ostrovsky, R.: Non-interactive and non-malleable commitment. In: 30th ACM STOC, pp. 141–150. ACM Press, May 1998. https://doi.org/10.1145/276698.276722
25. Di Crescenzo, G., Katz, J., Ostrovsky, R., Smith, A.: Efficient and non-interactive non-malleable commitment. In: Pfitzmann, B. (ed.) EUROCRYPT 2001. LNCS, vol. 2045, pp. 40–59. Springer, Heidelberg (2001). https://doi.org/10.1007/3-540-44987-6_4
26. Dodis, Y., Wichs, D.: Non-malleable extractors and symmetric key cryptography from weak secrets. In: Mitzenmacher, M. (ed.) 41st ACM STOC, pp. 601–610. ACM Press, May/June 2009. https://doi.org/10.1145/1536414.1536496
27. Dolev, D., Dwork, C., Naor, M.: Non-malleable cryptography (extended abstract). In: 23rd ACM STOC, pp. 542–552. ACM Press, May 1991. https://doi.org/10.1145/103418.103474
28. Dwork, C., Naor, M., Reingold, O., Stockmeyer, L.J.: Magic functions. In: 40th FOCS, pp. 523–534. IEEE Computer Society Press, October 1999. https://doi.org/10.1109/SFFCS.1999.814626
29. Dwork, C., Sahai, A.: Concurrent zero-knowledge: reducing the need for timing constraints. In: Krawczyk, H. (ed.) CRYPTO 1998. LNCS, vol. 1462, pp. 442–457. Springer, Heidelberg (1998). https://doi.org/10.1007/BFb0055746
30. Dziembowski, S., Pietrzak, K., Wichs, D.: Non-malleable codes. ICS, pp. 434–452 (2010)
31. Faust, S., Kohlweiss, M., Marson, G.A., Venturi, D.: On the non-malleability of the fiat-shamir transform. In: Galbraith, S., Nandi, M. (eds.) INDOCRYPT 2012. LNCS, vol. 7668, pp. 60–79. Springer, Heidelberg (2012). https://doi.org/10.1007/978-3-642-34931-7_5
32. Fleischhacker, N., Goyal, V., Jain, A.: On the existence of three round zero-knowledge proofs. In: Nielsen, J.B., Rijmen, V. (eds.) EUROCRYPT 2018, Part III. LNCS, vol. 10822, pp. 3–33. Springer, Cham (2018). https://doi.org/10.1007/978-3-319-78372-7_1
33. Garg, S., Mukherjee, P., Pandey, O., Polychroniadou, A.: The exact round complexity of secure computation. In: Fischlin, M., Coron, J.-S. (eds.) EUROCRYPT 2016, Part II. LNCS, vol. 9666, pp. 448–476. Springer, Heidelberg (2016). https://doi.org/10.1007/978-3-662-49896-5_16

34. Gentry, C., Wichs, D.: Separating succinct non-interactive arguments from all falsifiable assumptions. In: Fortnow, L., Vadhan, S.P. (eds.) 43rd ACM STOC, pp. 99–108. ACM Press, June 2011. https://doi.org/10.1145/1993636.1993651
35. Giacomelli, I., Madsen, J., Orlandi, C.: ZKBoo: faster zero-knowledge for boolean circuits. In: 25th USENIX Security Symposium (USENIX Security 2016), pp. 1069–1083 (2016)
36. Goldreich, O.: Foundations of Cryptography: Basic Tools, vol. 1. Cambridge University Press, Cambridge (2001)
37. Goldreich, O.: Foundations of Cryptography: Basic Applications, vol. 2. Cambridge University Press, Cambridge (2004)
38. Goldreich, O., Kahan, A.: How to construct constant-round zero-knowledge proof systems for NP. J. Cryptol. **9**(3), 167–189 (1996). https://doi.org/10.1007/BF00208001
39. Goldreich, O., Oren, Y.: Definitions and properties of zero-knowledge proof systems. J. Cryptol. **7**(1), 1–32 (1994). https://doi.org/10.1007/BF00195207
40. Goldwasser, S., Kalai, Y.T.: On the (in)security of the Fiat-Shamir paradigm. In: 44th FOCS, pp. 102–115. IEEE Computer Society Press, October 2003. https://doi.org/10.1109/SFCS.2003.1238185
41. Goyal, V.: Constant round non-malleable protocols using one way functions. In: Fortnow, L., Vadhan, S.P. (eds.) 43rd ACM STOC, pp. 695–704. ACM Press, June 2011. https://doi.org/10.1145/1993636.1993729
42. Goyal, V., Lee, C.K., Ostrovsky, R., Visconti, I.: Constructing non-malleable commitments: a black-box approach. In: 53rd FOCS, pp. 51–60. IEEE Computer Society Press, October 2012. https://doi.org/10.1109/FOCS.2012.47
43. Goyal, V., Pandey, O., Richelson, S.: Textbook non-malleable commitments. In: Wichs, D., Mansour, Y. (eds.) 48th ACM STOC, pp. 1128–1141. ACM Press, June 2016. https://doi.org/10.1145/2897518.2897657
44. Goyal, V., Richelson, S.: Non-malleable commitments using goldreich-levin list decoding. In: 2019 IEEE 60th Annual Symposium on Foundations of Computer Science (FOCS), pp. 686–699. IEEE (2019)
45. Goyal, V., Richelson, S., Rosen, A., Vald, M.: An algebraic approach to non-malleability. In: 55th FOCS, pp. 41–50. IEEE Computer Society Press, October 2014. https://doi.org/10.1109/FOCS.2014.13
46. Ishai, Y., Mahmoody, M., Sahai, A.: On efficient zero-knowledge PCPs. In: Cramer, R. (ed.) TCC 2012. LNCS, vol. 7194, pp. 151–168. Springer, Heidelberg (2012). https://doi.org/10.1007/978-3-642-28914-9_9
47. Ishai, Y., Weiss, M.: Probabilistically checkable proofs of proximity with zero-knowledge. In: Lindell, Y. (ed.) TCC 2014. LNCS, vol. 8349, pp. 121–145. Springer, Heidelberg (2014). https://doi.org/10.1007/978-3-642-54242-8_6
48. Jain, A., Pandey, O.: Non-malleable zero knowledge: black-box constructions and definitional relationships. In: Abdalla, M., De Prisco, R. (eds.) SCN 2014. LNCS, vol. 8642, pp. 435–454. Springer, Cham (2014). https://doi.org/10.1007/978-3-319-10879-7_25
49. Katz, J., Ostrovsky, R., Smith, A.: Round efficiency of multi-party computation with a dishonest majority. In: Biham, E. (ed.) EUROCRYPT 2003. LNCS, vol. 2656, pp. 578–595. Springer, Heidelberg (2003). https://doi.org/10.1007/3-540-39200-9_36
50. Khurana, D.: Round optimal concurrent non-malleability from polynomial hardness. In: Kalai, Y., Reyzin, L. (eds.) TCC 2017, Part II. LNCS, vol. 10678, pp. 139–171. Springer, Cham (2017). https://doi.org/10.1007/978-3-319-70503-3_5

51. Khurana, D., Sahai, A.: How to achieve non-malleability in one or two rounds. In: Umans, C. (ed.) 58th FOCS, pp. 564–575. IEEE Computer Society Press, October 2017. https://doi.org/10.1109/FOCS.2017.58
52. Kilian, J.: A note on efficient zero-knowledge proofs and arguments (extended abstract). In: 24th ACM STOC, pp. 723–732. ACM Press, May 1992. https://doi.org/10.1145/129712.129782
53. Kim, A., Liang, X., Pandey, O.: A new approach to efficient non-malleable zero-knowledge. Cryptology ePrint Archive, Paper 2022/767 (2022). https://eprint.iacr.org/2022/767
54. Kiyoshima, S.: Round-efficient black-box construction of composable multi-party computation. In: Garay, J.A., Gennaro, R. (eds.) CRYPTO 2014, Part II. LNCS, vol. 8617, pp. 351–368. Springer, Heidelberg (2014). https://doi.org/10.1007/978-3-662-44381-1_20
55. Lin, H., Pass, R.: Non-malleability amplification. In: Mitzenmacher, M. (ed.) 41st ACM STOC, pp. 189–198. ACM Press, May/June 2009. https://doi.org/10.1145/1536414.1536442
56. Lin, H., Pass, R.: Concurrent non-malleable zero knowledge with adaptive inputs. In: Ishai, Y. (ed.) TCC 2011. LNCS, vol. 6597, pp. 274–292. Springer, Heidelberg (2011). https://doi.org/10.1007/978-3-642-19571-6_17
57. Lin, H., Pass, R.: Constant-round non-malleable commitments from any one-way function. In: Fortnow, L., Vadhan, S.P. (eds.) 43rd ACM STOC, pp. 705–714. ACM Press, June 2011. https://doi.org/10.1145/1993636.1993730
58. Lin, H., Pass, R., Soni, P.: Two-round and non-interactive concurrent non-malleable commitments from time-lock puzzles. In: Umans, C. (ed.) 58th FOCS, pp. 576–587. IEEE Computer Society Press, October 2017. https://doi.org/10.1109/FOCS.2017.59
59. Lin, H., Pass, R., Tseng, W.-L.D., Venkitasubramaniam, M.: Concurrent non-malleable zero knowledge proofs. In: Rabin, T. (ed.) CRYPTO 2010. LNCS, vol. 6223, pp. 429–446. Springer, Heidelberg (2010). https://doi.org/10.1007/978-3-642-14623-7_23
60. Lin, H., Pass, R., Venkitasubramaniam, M.: Concurrent non-malleable commitments from any one-way function. In: Canetti, R. (ed.) TCC 2008. LNCS, vol. 4948, pp. 571–588. Springer, Heidelberg (2008). https://doi.org/10.1007/978-3-540-78524-8_31
61. Micali, S.: CS proofs (extended abstracts). In: 35th FOCS, pp. 436–453. IEEE Computer Society Press, November 1994. https://doi.org/10.1109/SFCS.1994.365746
62. Micali, S., Pass, R., Rosen, A.: Input-indistinguishable computation. In: 47th FOCS, pp. 367–378. IEEE Computer Society Press, October 2006. https://doi.org/10.1109/FOCS.2006.43
63. Micciancio, D., Petrank, E.: Simulatable commitments and efficient concurrent zero-knowledge. In: Biham, E. (ed.) EUROCRYPT 2003. LNCS, vol. 2656, pp. 140–159. Springer, Heidelberg (2003). https://doi.org/10.1007/3-540-39200-9_9
64. Naor, M.: Bit commitment using pseudo-randomness. In: Brassard, G. (ed.) CRYPTO 1989. LNCS, vol. 435, pp. 128–136. Springer, New York (1990). https://doi.org/10.1007/0-387-34805-0_13
65. Naor, M.: On cryptographic assumptions and challenges. In: Boneh, D. (ed.) CRYPTO 2003. LNCS, vol. 2729, pp. 96–109. Springer, Heidelberg (2003). https://doi.org/10.1007/978-3-540-45146-4_6

66. Nielsen, J.B.: Separating random oracle proofs from complexity theoretic proofs: the non-committing encryption case. In: Yung, M. (ed.) CRYPTO 2002. LNCS, vol. 2442, pp. 111–126. Springer, Heidelberg (2002). https://doi.org/10.1007/3-540-45708-9_8
67. O'Neill, A., Peikert, C., Waters, B.: Bi-deniable public-key encryption. In: Rogaway, P. (ed.) CRYPTO 2011. LNCS, vol. 6841, pp. 525–542. Springer, Heidelberg (2011). https://doi.org/10.1007/978-3-642-22792-9_30
68. Ostrovsky, R., Pandey, O., Visconti, I.: Efficiency preserving transformations for concurrent non-malleable zero knowledge. In: Micciancio, D. (ed.) TCC 2010. LNCS, vol. 5978, pp. 535–552. Springer, Heidelberg (2010). https://doi.org/10.1007/978-3-642-11799-2_32
69. Pandey, O., Pass, R., Vaikuntanathan, V.: Adaptive One-Way Functions and Applications. In: Wagner, D. (ed.) CRYPTO 2008. LNCS, vol. 5157, pp. 57–74. Springer, Heidelberg (2008). https://doi.org/10.1007/978-3-540-85174-5_4
70. Pass, R.: On deniability in the common reference string and random oracle model. In: Boneh, D. (ed.) CRYPTO 2003. LNCS, vol. 2729, pp. 316–337. Springer, Heidelberg (2003). https://doi.org/10.1007/978-3-540-45146-4_19
71. Pass, R.: Simulation in quasi-polynomial time, and its application to protocol composition. In: Biham, E. (ed.) EUROCRYPT 2003. LNCS, vol. 2656, pp. 160–176. Springer, Heidelberg (2003). https://doi.org/10.1007/3-540-39200-9_10
72. Pass, R.: Concurrent security and non-malleability. In: Ishai, Y. (ed.) TCC 2011. LNCS, vol. 6597, pp. 540–540. Springer, Heidelberg (2011). https://doi.org/10.1007/978-3-642-19571-6_32
73. Pass, R., Rosen, A.: Concurrent non-malleable commitments. In: 46th FOCS, pp. 563–572. IEEE Computer Society Press, October 2005. https://doi.org/10.1109/SFCS.2005.27
74. Pass, R., Rosen, A.: New and improved constructions of non-malleable cryptographic protocols. In: Gabow, H.N., Fagin, R. (eds.) 37th ACM STOC, pp. 533–542. ACM Press, May 2005. https://doi.org/10.1145/1060590.1060670
75. Pass, R., Wee, H.: Black-box constructions of two-party protocols from one-way functions. In: Reingold, O. (ed.) TCC 2009. LNCS, vol. 5444, pp. 403–418. Springer, Heidelberg (2009). https://doi.org/10.1007/978-3-642-00457-5_24
76. Prabhakaran, M., Sahai, A.: New notions of security: achieving universal composability without trusted setup. In: Babai, L. (ed.) 36th ACM STOC. pp. 242–251. ACM Press, June 2004. https://doi.org/10.1145/1007352.1007394
77. Sahai, A.: Non-malleable non-interactive zero knowledge and adaptive chosen-ciphertext security. In: 40th FOCS, pp. 543–553. IEEE Computer Society Press, October 1999. https://doi.org/10.1109/SFFCS.1999.814628
78. Sahai, A., Waters, B.: How to use indistinguishability obfuscation: deniable encryption, and more. In: Shmoys, D.B. (ed.) 46th ACM STOC, pp. 475–484. ACM Press, May/June 2014. https://doi.org/10.1145/2591796.2591825
79. Unruh, D.: Random Oracles and auxiliary input. In: Menezes, A. (ed.) CRYPTO 2007. LNCS, vol. 4622, pp. 205–223. Springer, Heidelberg (2007). https://doi.org/10.1007/978-3-540-74143-5_12
80. Wee, H.: Zero knowledge in the random Oracle model, revisited. In: Matsui, M. (ed.) ASIACRYPT 2009. LNCS, vol. 5912, pp. 417–434. Springer, Heidelberg (2009). https://doi.org/10.1007/978-3-642-10366-7_25
81. Wee, H.: Black-box, round-efficient secure computation via non-malleability amplification. In: 51st FOCS, pp. 531–540. IEEE Computer Society Press, October 2010. https://doi.org/10.1109/FOCS.2010.87

Secure Multiparty Computation III

An Algebraic Framework for Silent Preprocessing with Trustless Setup and Active Security

Damiano Abram(✉), Ivan Damgård, Claudio Orlandi, and Peter Scholl

Aarhus University, Aarhus, Denmark
damiano.abram@cs.au.dk

Abstract. Recently, number-theoretic assumptions including DDH, DCR and QR have been used to build powerful tools for secure computation, in the form of *homomorphic secret-sharing* (HSS), which leads to secure two-party computation protocols with succinct communication, and *pseudorandom correlation functions* (PCFs), which allow non-interactive generation of a large quantity of correlated randomness. In this work, we present a group-theoretic framework for these classes of constructions, which unifies their approach to computing distributed discrete logarithms in various groups. We cast existing constructions in our framework, and also present new constructions, including one based on class groups of imaginary quadratic fields. This leads to the first construction of two-party homomorphic secret sharing for branching programs from class group assumptions.

Using our framework, we also obtain pseudorandom correlation functions for generating oblivious transfer and vector-OLE correlations from number-theoretic assumptions. These have a *trustless, public-key setup* when instantiating our framework using class groups. Previously, such constructions either needed a trusted setup in the form of an RSA modulus with unknown factorisation, or relied on multi-key fully homomorphic encryption from the learning with errors assumption.

We also show how to upgrade our constructions to achieve active security using appropriate zero-knowledge proofs. In the random oracle model, this leads to a one-round, actively secure protocol for setting up the PCF, as well as a 3-round, actively secure HSS-based protocol for secure two-party computation of branching programs with succinct communication.

1 Introduction

Homomorphic secret sharing (HSS) [BGI16] can be seen as a relaxed form of fully-homomorphic encryption (FHE), where two non-colluding servers evaluate a function on private inputs without interaction. At the end of the computation, the servers each obtain a secret share, and these can be combined to obtain the result. At the core of existing HSS constructions is a procedure for *distributed discrete log*, where two parties are given group elements g_0, g_1 such that $g_1 = g_0 \cdot g^x$ for some fixed base g, and want to convert these multiplicative shares into additive shares x_0, x_1, where $x_1 = x_0 + x$ over the integers. The

Y. Dodis and T. Shrimpton (Eds.): CRYPTO 2022, LNCS 13510, pp. 421–452, 2022.
https://doi.org/10.1007/978-3-031-15985-5_15

method from [BGI16], which is based on the decisional Diffie-Hellman (DDH) assumption, allows doing this conversion without interaction, however, there is an inherent correctness error. This results in significant extra work to ensure that the magnitude of the error is small. Moreover, the error cannot be made negligible. This limitation carries over to the final HSS construction, which has a non-negligible probability that the result of the computation is incorrect.

Recently, it was shown that the non-negligible correctness error of the DDH construction can be overcome, when switching to the Paillier [Pai99] or Damgård-Jurik [DJ01] cryptosystems based on the decisional composite residuosity (DCR) assumption. With these encryption schemes, which work over $\mathbb{Z}_{N^2}^*$ for an RSA modulus N, discrete logarithms can be computed in a distributed manner with a very simple and perfectly correct algorithm [OSY21,RS21]. This avoids the challenges of the DDH setting, by exploiting the fact that the messages in these schemes lie in a subgroup where solving discrete log is easy.

In [OSY21], the same distributed discrete log technique was used for several other applications in secure computation. In particular, they constructed *pseudorandom correlation functions* based on the Paillier and quadratic residuosity assumptions. A pseudorandom correlation function (PCF) is a way of generating two short, correlated keys, such that when evaluating the function on each of the keys, the two outputs are correlated in some secret manner. This generalizes the notion of a pseudorandom correlation generator [BCG+19], which only supports a bounded number of outputs. Examples of useful correlations for PCFs and PCGs are random oblivious transfer correlations, or secret-shared multiplication triples, which can be used in GMW-style multi-party computation protocols [GMW87] with very lightweight online computation.

An appealing feature of the PCFs from [OSY21] is that the PCF keys can be generated in a *public-key* manner, where after publishing just a single, short message, each party can locally derive their PCF key and compute the correlated randomness. However, a major drawback is that to achieve this public-key setup, the parties first need to have a trusted setup in the form of a public RSA modulus with unknown factorisation.

1.1 Our Contributions

It may seem from the previous work in [OSY21,RS21] that their efficient approach to distributed discrete log depends on very specific properties of Paillier, or more generally Damgård-Jurik encryption.

However, we show that this is not the case: in Sect. 3 we present a general framework, where we demonstrate that the approach from previous works can be phrased in terms of abstract group-theoretic properties. Naturally, the known methods based on Paillier and Damgård-Jurik become special cases of our framework, but we also show instantiations under different assumptions in Sect. 4.

Below, we describe the main applications of our framework to secure two-party computation, and the results obtained from our new instantiations.

Homomorphic Secret Sharing. We show in Sect. 5 that any instantiation of our framework that supports superpolynomially large plaintexts can be used to build homomorphic secret sharing for the class of polynomial size branching programs. This construction follows the same blueprint as previous works that obtain HSS for branching programs [BGI16, BKS19, OSY21, RS21]. Using this, two new instantiations of our framework imply two new constructions of HSS based on a flavour of the decisional Diffie-Hellman assumption for short exponents.

Firstly, we obtain HSS from a variant of the Joye-Libert cryptosystem [JL13, BHJL17], modified to work over a modulus that is a product of many small, distinct primes; compared with the analogous constructions based on Paillier, this has the advantage that ciphertexts are only a single element of $\mathbb{Z}_N$, and we can be more flexible in our choice of plaintext space, which is limited to $\mathbb{Z}_{N^s}$ otherwise. For a plaintext space modulo Q, we need to choose N such that $p-1, q-1$ are divisible by Q, so when Q is large we should clearly increase p, q to compensate, however, for reasonable sizes of Q the resulting ciphertext size should still be smaller than Paillier, which is an element of $\mathbb{Z}_{N^2}$.

Secondly, we obtain HSS from the DDH assumption in class groups of imaginary quadratic fields, based on the CL cryptosystem [CL15]. Class groups have recently seen many cryptographic applications, since they offer a way to generate a group of unknown order, without relying on any trusted setup to create the group parameters. Using class groups in HSS, we avoid the need for a setup with an RSA modulus where no party knows the factorization, instead only relying on a CRS that can be sampled with public randomness. For security, we rely on the DDH assumption with short exponents, where the short exponents are used to ensure that the secret key fits in the message space of the scheme, which allows us to easily encrypt functions of the secret key without introducing a circular security assumption.

Public-Key Pseudorandom Correlation Functions with Trustless Setup. Our starting point here is the PCFs from Paillier and quadratic residuosity from [OSY21], which give PCFs for generating vector-OLE and OT correlations, respectively.

PCFs, by definition, involve a setup procedure where a trusted dealer distributes a pair of short keys to the two parties. In [OSY21], it was shown that given a 1-round protocol for vector-OLE, where each party sends one parallel message, the PCF setup procedure can be replaced with a simple *public-key setup*, where each party publishes one message, which is then used to derive a PCF key. To realize the 1-round vector-OLE protocol, they give a dedicated construction based on distributed discrete log from Paillier, however, this still relies on a trusted setup in the form of an RSA modulus with unknown factorisation. We show in Sect. 6 that this construction can be generalised to work under any instantiation of our framework; with our class groups instantiation, we then obtain vector-OLE with a trustless setup. Put together with the PCFs from [OSY21], this leads to a public-key PCF with trustless setup for vector-

OLE based on the combination of class group assumptions and DCR, or one for OT by combining class groups and quadratic residuosity.

Active Security. Given a public-key PCF, where after exchanging public keys, two parties can compute as much correlated randomness as they need, it is natural to ask, can this type of protocol be made actively secure? Although there are many ways of generically compiling passively secure protocols into active ones [GMW86, IPS08], we want to achieve something reasonably practical, in particular, to avoid using generic zero-knowledge techniques that require expressing group operations as circuits or similar. We show in Sect. 7 how to upgrade our PCFs to achieve active security, while preserving their public-nature by using Fiat-Shamir based NIZKs in the random oracle model. We do this via a careful combination of sigma protocols, which all make black-box use of the group, so avoid the complications of generic techniques. One challenge is that to build the public-key PCF, we need one party to prove that their input to the vector-OLE protocol corresponds to a secret key for an RSA modulus used in the PCF. As an essential tool, we use an integer commitment scheme which we show can be built from class groups and a trustless set-up. Thus, even our actively secure PCF does not need a trusted dealer. See the next section for details on the assumption required for this.

Finally, in the full version of the paper [ADOS22, Section 8], we also show how to add active security to our HSS construction. In the random oracle model, this gives a 3-round protocol for actively secure two-party computation of branching programs, which makes black-box use of the operations needed by our group-theoretic framework. Here, as well as proving that ciphertexts used to the secret-share HSS inputs are well-formed, we also need range proofs to ensure that the inputs are bounded in size.

A Comparison to [OSY21] and [RS21]. As summarised above, previous work focuses its analysis on Paillier and Goldwasser-Micali [OSY21], and Damgård-Jurik [RS21]. Both [OSY21] and [RS21] describe how to solve distributed discrete log in the setting they study and use the techniques to build HSS for branching programs. In [OSY21], the authors also explain how to build public-key PCFs for OT and VOLE using the distributed discrete log techniques. All the constructions presented in [OSY21] and [RS21] rely on a trusted setup for the generation of a public RSA modulo of unknown factorisation.

The main contribution of this work is to generalise the techniques of [OSY21] and [RS21] to an abstract algebraic framework. We characterise the assumptions that the framework needs to satisfy to solve distributed discrete log, build HSS for branching programs and public-key PCFs for OT and VOLE. We present also new instantiations of the framework in addition to Paillier, Goldwasser-Micali and Damgård-Jurik, namely variants of the Joye-Libert cryptosystem and class groups. The latter allows us to build HSS and public-key PCFs that do not need trusted setups. Finally, while [OSY21] and [RS21] limit their study to passive security only, this work explains how to upgrade the constructions to active security obtaining implementable solutions that make black-box use of the underlying group.

1.2 An Overview of the Framework

In a nutshell, our framework consists of a large, finite group G, where $G = F \times H$. In the subgroup F, which is cyclic with generator f, discrete log is easy, and the order of F is public (whereas this is not the case for H). In the distributed discrete logarithm problem, two parties are given group elements $g_0, g_1 \in G$, with the condition that $g_0/g_1 = f^m$ for some message m. The goal is for the parties to convert this into shares m_0, m_1, where $m_0 + m_1 = m$ modulo the order of F. The crucial ingredient we need for distributed discrete log is a function we call a *coset labelling function*, which, for each coset C of F in G, maps all elements in C to a specific element in C. Existence of a coset labelling function turns out to be enough to solve distributed discrete log assuming that the two parties start from elements in the same coset, and it further turns out that this is sufficient to implement all our constructions, as long as some appropriate computational assumptions hold in G.

Instantiations. This framework easily encompasses previous constructions where distributed discrete logs are computed with Paillier, Damgård-Jurik, or Goldwasser-Micali ciphertexts. We also show that a natural variant of the Joye-Libert cryptosystem can be used (although it remains open to find a coset labelling function for the original Joye-Libert scheme, with plaintexts modulo 2^k). Finally, we give an instantiation based on class groups over imaginary quadratic fields. Here, we essentially apply the framework of the CL cryptosystem [CL15] for linearly homomorphic encryption, and combine it with the observation that the coset labelling function can be obtained via a special surjective map, which was previously used in the NICE cryptosystem [PT00] and its cryptanalysis [CJLN09].

Trustless Setup and the DXDH Assumption. For all applications of our framework, we rely on the standard DDH assumption in the group G. In settings where we need a trustless setup, we sometimes use a new assumption we call the *decisional cross-group Diffie-Hellman*, or DXDH, assumption. This states that for group elements $g, h \leftarrow G$ sampled with random coins ρ_g, ρ_h, and random exponents r, s,

$$(\rho_g, \rho_h, g, h, g^r, h^r) \cong (\rho_g, \rho_h, g, h, g^r, g^s)$$

This assumption arises in settings where we have a CRS with two group elements g, h, and we want the CRS to be public-coin. Having a public-coin CRS implies a trustless setup, since in practice the parties can derive randomness using e.g. a random oracle, and use this to sample the group elements. Note that in a standard cyclic DDH group (such as with elliptic curves), DXDH and DDH are equivalent because g, h always generate the same group, and furthermore, given a group element g it is easy to find some random coins that 'explain' it.

With class groups, however, this is not the case, since we are not aware of any invertible sampling algorithm, nor any method for sampling g and h such that they lie in the same subgroup.

Thus, when aiming for a trustless setup, we need DXDH. An additional complication of this setting is that the assumption makes it harder to use a CRS in security proofs: there is no way to introduce a trapdoor in the CRS by picking $h = g^t$ in the simulation, as we do not know how to explain the random coins used to sample h (without leaking t).

We note that recently, [CKLR21] presented zero-knowledge proofs built using integer commitments from class groups, which require a CRS (g, h) and the assumption that (g, h) is indistinguishable from (g, g^s). Note that this assumption is incompatible with a trustless setup: if the CRS contains the random coins used to sample g and h, then the assumption doesn't hold as it is hard for the simulator to come up with the random coins needed to explain sampling $h = g^s$.[1] However, in Sect. 7 we show that the same commitment scheme *does* permit a trustless setup under the DXDH assumption, and we use this in our zero-knowledge proofs to obtain active security.

Recap of the Framework. We now summarise the description of our framework. Our setting is an finite, Abelian group

$$G \cong F \times H \qquad \text{where} \qquad F = \langle f \rangle.$$

The group G needs to satisfy these properties:

1. The discrete log function over F is efficiently computable.
2. There exists an efficiently computable coset labelling function π.
3. There exists an efficiently computable function δ (the lifting function) such that $\pi\big(\delta(x)\big) = x$ for every input x.

In order to build HSS for branching programs and public-key PCFs for OT and VOLE, the group needs to satisfy additional computational assumption which are summarised in Table 1.

Table 1. Computational assumptions needed by our constructions. Elements written in between brackets are needed only for active security.

Construction	*Assumptions and Model*
HSS for branching programs	DDH, small exponent (DXDH, weak hidden order + RO)
Public-Key PCF for VOLE	DCR, DXDH, DDH (weak hidden order, QR) + RO
Public-Key PCF for OT	QR, DXDH, DDH (weak hidden order) + RO

[1] The authors of [CKLR21] have acknowledged. They claim to have found a solution and are going to update their work.

2 Notation and Preliminaries

Let λ denote the security parameter. Our constructions are restricted to the two-party setting and we denote them P_0 and P_1. For any $a, b \in \mathbb{Z}$ with $a < b$, we represent the set of integers $\{a, a+1, \ldots, b\}$ by $[a, b]$. We use $[b]$ to represent $[0, b-1]$. We assume that by reducing an element modulo $t \in \mathbb{N}$, we obtain a value in $[t]$.

Given a deterministic algorithm Alg, we denote its evaluation on an input x and the assignment of the result to a variable y by $y \leftarrow \mathsf{Alg}(x)$. If Alg is instead probabilistic, we write $y \overset{R}{\leftarrow} \mathsf{Alg}(x)$. The operation assumes that the random bits used by the algorithm are sampled uniformly. When we want to use a specific random string r, we write instead $y \leftarrow \mathsf{Alg}(x; r)$. Finally, if the element y is uniformly sampled from a set $\mathcal{X}$, we write $y \overset{R}{\leftarrow} \mathcal{X}$.

We denote vectorial elements using the bold font, the i-th entry of a vector $\boldsymbol{v}$ is denoted by v_i or by $\boldsymbol{v}[i]$. The cyclic subgroup generated by a group element g is represented by $\langle g \rangle$. Finally, we denote secret-shared elements y using the y-in-a-box notation, i.e. $[y]$. It will be clear from the context if that denotes a secret-sharing or the set $\{0, 1, \ldots, y-1\}$.

In the full version of the paper [ADOS22, Section 2], we provide an overview on homomorphic secret-sharing (HSS) and pseudorandom correlation functions (PCFs).

3 A Group-Theoretic Framework

We will assume we have a probabilistic polynomial time algorithm Gen that takes $1\!\!1^\lambda$ as input where λ is a security parameter. When running Gen, we get output

$$\mathsf{par} \overset{R}{\leftarrow} \mathsf{Gen}(1\!\!1^\lambda), \text{ where } \mathsf{par} = (G, F, H, f, t, \ell, \mathsf{aux}).$$

Here, G is a finite Abelian group with subgroups F, H such that $G = F \times H$, f is a generator of F and t is the order of F. We assume we can compute the group operation and inverses in time polynomial in λ. The natural number ℓ will be used in the following: when we select a random exponent r and compute g^r where $g \in G$, r will usually be chosen uniformly between 0 and ℓ.[2] Finally, we say that Gen is *public-coin* if the random coins used by Gen appear in the string aux.

We also assume a probabilistic polynomial time algorithm $\mathcal{D}$ for sampling random elements in G. We will use the notation $(g, \rho) \overset{R}{\leftarrow} \mathcal{D}(1\!\!1^\lambda, \mathsf{par})$, where $g \in G$ is the sampled element and ρ contains the random coins used in the sampling (i.e., the sampling of g is always *public-coin*). We do not require that g is uniform in G, but we do require f is in the subgroup generated by g, except perhaps with negligible probability.

[2] We will always choose ℓ large enough so that g^r is statistically indistinguishable from uniform in $\langle g \rangle$. This is possible, even if $|H|$ is sometimes not known by anyone, since an upper bound is always known.

We assume that discrete log base f is easy, that is, given f^a for any $a \in \mathbb{Z}_t$, a can be computed in polynomial time in λ.

In the following sections, we will specify a number of computational problems that we need to assume are hard to solve, given par and various elements sampled by $\mathcal{D}$. Loosely speaking, the most basic one is that the order of the subgroup H is hard to compute, and that the DDH assumption holds in the subgroup generated by g where g is sampled by $\mathcal{D}$. More details will be given in Sect. 3.1.

The main problem we want to solve in the context of the framework is the following, which we call Non-Interactive Discrete Log Sharing (NIDLS). This is defined as follows:

Definition 1. *The NIDLS problem involves two parties, A and B. A gets as input $\alpha \in G$, while B gets $\beta \in G$. It is promised that $\alpha\beta^{-1} \in F$, so that $\alpha\beta^{-1} = f^m$ for some $m \in \mathbb{Z}_t$. A and B now do only local computation and A outputs a number a, while B outputs b. The goal is that $a + b \equiv m \bmod t$.*

It will be convenient to introduce the following notation: for $g \in G$, we denote by C_g be the coset of F in G that contains g. As we explain in a moment, the NIDLS problem can be solved using the following tool:

Definition 2. *A* coset labelling function for F in G *is an efficiently computable function $\phi : G \mapsto G$ with the following property: for any $g \in G$ we have $\phi(g) \in C_g$ and furthermore, for any $h \in C_g$ we have $\phi(h) = \phi(g)$.*

In other words, for every coset C_g, ϕ defines a fixed element $c \in C_g$ and c can be efficiently computed given any element in C_g.

Given a coset labelling function the NIDLS problem can be solved using the following protocol:

1. A computes $\phi(\alpha)^{-1} \cdot \alpha$ which is in F since α and $\phi(\alpha)$ are in the same coset. Using that discrete log in F is easy, A computes a such that $\phi(\alpha)^{-1} \cdot \alpha = f^a$, and outputs a.
2. B computes $\phi(\beta) \cdot \beta^{-1}$ which is in F since β and $\phi(\beta)$ are in the same coset. Using that discrete log in F is easy, B computes b such that $\phi(\beta) \cdot \beta^{-1} = f^b$, and outputs b.

This works because the property of ϕ guarantees that $\phi(\alpha) = \phi(\beta)$. Therefore

$$f^a \cdot f^b = \phi(\alpha)^{-1} \cdot \alpha \cdot \phi(\beta) \cdot \beta^{-1} = \alpha \cdot \beta^{-1} = f^m,$$

from which it follows immediately that $a + b \equiv m \bmod t$.

It turns out that if F is small, then a coset labelling function always exists:

Lemma 1. *Let $G = F \times H$ be groups as described above, where the order t of F is polynomial. Then a coset labelling function for F in G always exists.*

Proof. We define the desired function ϕ as follows: on input g, compute a list of all elements in C_g by multiplying g by all powers of f. This is feasible since t is polynomial. Sort the elements in lexicographical order and output the first element. As the content of the list is the same no matter which element in the coset we start from, this function has the desired property. □

There is also a different approach to constructing a coset labelling function which, as we shall see, sometimes works for superpolynomial size F.

Namely, assume that for every G that Gen can produce, there exists an efficiently computable and surjective homomorphism $\pi : G \mapsto G'$ (for some group G'), where $ker(\pi) = F$. This implies that for each coset of F in G, π maps all elements of the coset to a single element in G', and that distinct cosets are mapped to distinct elements.

Note that $\pi(g)$ is actually a unique "label" for the coset C_g, the only problem is that it is in G' and not in G.

To get around this, we assume that outputs from π can be "lifted" deterministically to G such that we land in the coset we came from. That is, we assume there exists an efficiently computable function $\delta : G' \mapsto G$ such that for any $x \in G'$ we have that $\delta(x)$ is in the coset of F in G that is mapped to x by π. Put slightly differently, what we want is that $\pi(\delta(x)) = x$ for all $x \in G'$.

Now, observe that $\delta(\pi(g))$ only depends on which coset g belongs to, since $\pi(g)$ already has this property. Therefore, the following lemma is immediate:

Lemma 2. *Let $G = F \times H$, G' be groups as described above and π, δ be functions as described above, with $\pi(\delta(x)) = x$ for all $x \in G'$. Then ϕ defined by $\phi(g) = \delta(\pi(g))$ is a coset labelling function for F in G.*

3.1 Assumptions

In this section we list the computational assumptions we need in order to prove our constructions secure.

Definition 3 (Weak Hidden Order Assumption). *We say that the weak hidden order assumption holds in the NIDLS framework if for any PPT adversary $\mathcal{A}$:*

$$\Pr[\mathcal{A}(\mathsf{par}, g, \rho) = x \text{ and } g^x = 1] = \mathsf{negl}(\lambda)$$

when $\mathsf{par} := (G, F, H, f, t, \ell, \mathsf{aux}) \stackrel{R}{\leftarrow} \mathsf{Gen}(1\!\!1^\lambda)$ *and* $(g, \rho) \stackrel{R}{\leftarrow} \mathcal{D}(1\!\!1^\lambda, \mathsf{par})$.

Notice that in the standard hidden order assumption [Tuc20], the adversary is let free to choose any $g \neq 1$. We rely instead on a *weaker* assumption in which g is sampled according to $\mathcal{D}$.

Definition 4 (DDH Assumption). *We say that the DDH assumption holds in the NIDLS framework if for any PPT adversary $\mathcal{A}$ the following quantity is negligible:*

$$|\Pr[\mathcal{A}(\mathsf{par}, \rho, g, g^x, g^y, g^{xy}) = 1] - \Pr[\mathcal{A}(\mathsf{par}, \rho, g, g^x, g^y, g^z) = 1]| = \mathsf{negl}(\lambda)$$

when $\mathsf{par} := (G, F, H, f, t, \ell, \mathsf{aux}) \xleftarrow{R} \mathsf{Gen}(1\!\!1^\lambda), (g, \rho) \xleftarrow{R} \mathcal{D}(1\!\!1^\lambda, \mathsf{par}), (x, y, z) \xleftarrow{R} [\ell]^3$.

We introduce a new variant of the DDH assumption that allows us to infer the security of our protocols that use two generators g, C which are generated with a trustless setup i.e., the adversary is allowed to see the random coins used for their generation. In some settings, this assumption is equivalent to DDH but this does not cover all our instantiations of the framework[3].

Definition 5 (Decisional Cross-Group DH Assumption (DXDH)). *We say that the DXDH assumption holds in the NIDLS framework if for any PPT adversary* $\mathcal{A}$*:*

$$|\Pr[\mathcal{A}(\mathsf{par}, g, \rho_0, C, \rho_1, g^r, C^r) = 1] - \Pr[\mathcal{A}(\mathsf{par}, g, \rho_0, C, \rho_1, C^s, C^r) = 1]| = \mathsf{negl}(\lambda)$$

when $\mathsf{par} := (G, F, H, f, t, \ell, \mathsf{aux}) \xleftarrow{R} \mathsf{Gen}(1\!\!1^\lambda)$, $(g, \rho_0) \xleftarrow{R} \mathcal{D}(1\!\!1^\lambda, \mathsf{par})$, $(C, \rho_1) \xleftarrow{R} \mathcal{D}(1\!\!1^\lambda, \mathsf{par})$, $C \neq g$ *and* $(r, s) \xleftarrow{R} [\ell]^2$.

Finally, in our HSS constructions, we would like to have ElGamal-style secret keys bounded by $\ell_{\mathsf{sk}} < t$, which may be significantly smaller than ℓ. This allows to encrypt the private key under its public counterpart without worrying about wrap-arounds. In order for security to hold in these conditions, we rely on the small exponent assumption defined below.

Definition 6 (Small Exponent Assumption). *We say that the small-exponent assumption with length* $\ell_{\mathsf{sk}}(\lambda)$ *holds in the NIDLS framework if for any PPT adversary* $\mathcal{A}$*:*

$$|\Pr[\mathcal{A}(\mathsf{par}, \ell_{\mathsf{sk}}, g, \rho, g^x) = 1] - \Pr[\mathcal{A}(\mathsf{par}, \ell_{\mathsf{sk}}, g, \rho, g^y) = 1]| = \mathsf{negl}(\lambda)$$

when $\mathsf{par} := (G, F, H, f, t, \ell, \mathsf{aux}) \xleftarrow{R} \mathsf{Gen}(1\!\!1^\lambda)$, $(g, \rho) \xleftarrow{R} \mathcal{D}(1\!\!1^\lambda, \mathsf{par})$, $x \xleftarrow{R} [\ell]$ *and* $y \xleftarrow{R} [\ell_{\mathsf{sk}}]$.

4 Instantiations of the Framework

In this section, we give a number of concrete instantiations of the framework we just discussed. Some were already known, and some are new.

4.1 Paillier and Damgård-Jurik

This example was already known from [OSY21] who presented a NIDLS protocol based on Paillier encryption and independent work from [RS21] who did it from Damgård-Jurik encryption.

[3] For equivalence, it is needed that g and C are random generators of the same subgroup and that $\mathcal{D}$ is invertible, i.e., that given any group element h in the output domain, one can efficiently compute random coins that would cause $\mathcal{D}$ to output h.

These instantiations are closely related and we cover them in one go as follows: we let $\mathsf{Gen}(1\!\!1^\lambda)$ output an RSA modulus $n = pq$ of bit length λ, where $p' = (p-1)/2$ and $q' = (q-1)/2$ are also prime and where $gcd(n, \phi(n)) = 1$. We set $G = \mathbb{Z}^*_{n^s}$, for some constant natural number $s \geq 2$ and it now holds that $G = F \times H$ where F is the subgroup of order n^{s-1}, and H is the subgroup of order $(p-1)(q-1)$. Discrete log in F is easy in this case (see [DJ01] for details). This generator is not public-coin, as the prime factors of n must remain secret.

To get a coset labelling function for this example, we use Lemma 2: we set $G' = \mathbb{Z}^*_n$ and $\pi(g) = g \bmod n$. Since n divides n^s, it is clear that π is a surjective homomorphism from G to G'. Therefore its kernel has order $|G|/|G'| = n^{s-1}$. Note that all non-trivial elements in F must have orders relatively prime to $\phi(n) = |G'|$ and hence the homomorphism into G' must send all these elements to 1. It follows that F is contained in the kernel and so is in fact equal to the kernel because $|F| = n^{s-1}$. We define the function $\delta : G' \mapsto G$ by $\delta(x) = x$, that is, δ just returns its input, but now understood as a number modulo n^s (instead of n).

With these definitions, it is clear that $\pi(\delta(x)) = x$, so by Lemma 2, $\phi(g) = \delta(\pi(g))$ is a coset labelling function.

The sampling algorithm $\mathcal{D}$ will output a random $g \in \mathbb{Z}^*_{n^s}$, such that the Jacobi symbol of g modulo n is 1. Note that because $|F| = n^{s-1}$ contains only large prime factors, a random g will contain F in the subgroup it generates except with negligible probability. Similarly, reducing modulo n, we see that $g \bmod n$ has order divisible by $p'q'$ except with negligible probability since p', q' are prime.

As for the assumptions, computing the order is trivially equivalent to factoring n. The DDH assumption was introduced in [DJ03] and used there for an "El-Gamal style" variant of Paillier encryption. In this setting, we can claim that if you can break the DXDH assumption, you can also break DDH. This is because g (or C) sampled as above have order $n^{s-1}p'q'$ or $2n^{s-1}p'q'$ except with negligible probability. Whether 2 divides the order cannot be efficiently determined (by the standard quadratic residuosity assumption). Further, the sampling algorithm is clearly invertible. All this means that, given an element g^x from a DDH challenge, we can claim it was instead sampled by $\mathcal{D}$ and let it play the role of C in the DXDH setting.

Finally, the small exponent assumption is reasonable in a setting where discrete log and DDH are hard, as we do assume here, as long as the domain from which the exponent is chosen is exponentially large. Also, this type of assumption has been used several times before, for instance in [BCG+17] to optimize an HSS construction.

4.2 Joye-Libert Variants

Small Order F. In this example, the generator outputs an RSA modulus $n = pq$ where 2^ℓ is the maximal 2-power that divides $p - 1$, and $q - 1$. It also outputs an element $f \in \mathbb{Z}^*_n$ of order 2^ℓ modulo both p and q (and so it also has order 2^ℓ modulo n). Let $p' = (p-1)/2^\ell, q' = (q-1)/2^\ell$, where we assume that p', q'

are prime. Then we let $F = \langle f \rangle$, we let $H \leq \mathbb{Z}_n^*$ be the subgroup of order $p'q'$, and we set $G = F \times H$. The group G is actually not all of $\mathbb{Z}_n^*$, but this is of no consequence in the following. Discrete log in F is easy by the Pohlig-Hellman algorithm.

For this variant, as long as 2^ℓ is polynomial, we can use Lemma 1 to get a coset labelling function. Doing it for larger values of 2^ℓ is an open problem. When $\ell = 1$, we can set $f = -1$ and we get a setting closely related to the Goldwasser-Micali cryptosystem, as observed in [OSY21].

Large Order *F*. We now construct a different variant of the Joye-Libert case where we are able to accommodate an exponentially large order subgroup F. Once again, the generator outputs an RSA modulus $n = pq$. This time, both $p-1$ and $q-1$ are divisible by the product of the first ℓ primes q_ℓ, that is $q_\ell = \prod_{i=1}^{\ell} p_i$ where p_i is the i'th prime.

We let $f \in \mathbb{Z}_n^*$ be an element of order q_ℓ modulo both p and q. Let $p' = (p-1)/q_\ell, q' = (q-1)/q_\ell$. As before, we let $F = \langle f \rangle$, we let $H \leq \mathbb{Z}_n^*$ be the subgroup of order $p'q'$, and we set $G = F \times H$.

It is not hard to see that since the i'th prime is approximately $i \ln i$, we can arrange for q_ℓ to be exponentially large, while each prime in the product is only polynomial.

We now show that if all primes in the product q_ℓ are polynomial size, we can solve the NIDLS problem in this setting, basically by using Lemma 1 for each p_i and then assembling a complete solution using the Chinese remainder theorem (CRT).

Some notation: we have $F = F_1 \times ... \times F_\ell$, where F_i is of order p_i. So it follows from Lemma 1 that we have a coset labelling function ϕ_i for the group $G_i = F_i \times H$. Also, if we let $u_i = q_\ell / p_i$, then $f_i = f^{u_i}$ is a generator of F_i. Now observe that if α, β is an instance of the NIDLS problem in $G = F \times H$, then $\alpha^{u_i}, \beta^{u_i}$ is an instance of the NIDLS problem in $G_i = F_i \times H$. This is simply because $\alpha \cdot \beta^{-1} = f^m$ implies $\alpha^{u_i} \cdot (\beta^{u_i})^{-1} = (f^{u_i})^m = f_i^{m \bmod p_i}$. Using this notation, the protocol works as follows:

1. For each $i = 1...\ell$, A uses ϕ_i to compute a solution a_i to the NIDLS problem in G_i. Finally, using CRT, A computes and outputs $a \in \mathbb{Z}_t$ such that $a \bmod p_i = a_i$ for all i.
2. For each $i = 1...\ell$, B uses ϕ_i to compute a solution b_i to the NIDLS problem in G_i. Finally, using CRT, B computes and outputs $b \in \mathbb{Z}_t$ such that $b \bmod p_i = b_i$ for all i.

This works because $(a+b) \bmod p_i = (a_i + b_i) \bmod p_i$ by definition of a, b, and since a_i, b_i solves the NIDLS problem in G_i we further have

$$(a+b) \bmod p_i = (a_i + b_i) \bmod p_i = m \bmod p_i.$$

Since this holds for all i, CRT implies that $a + b \bmod q_\ell = m$.

For this instantiation, the sampling algorithm $\mathcal{D}$ will choose a random $r \in \mathbb{Z}_n^*$ and output $g = f \cdot r^{q_\ell} \bmod n$. Note that $r^{q_\ell} \bmod n$ has order $p'q'$ except with negligible probability, in particular, the order is prime to q_ℓ so g has order $q_\ell p'q'$, and hence f is in the group generated by g.

The assumptions for this instantiation can be motivated similarly to what was done for Paillier above, as also here we rely on factoring to hide the order of the group. For this to be reasonable, we need, of course, that q_ℓ is much smaller than n so that enough uncertainty remains about p, q even given q_ℓ. The exception is that in this case, $\mathcal{D}$ is not invertible, so we cannot claim that DDH implies DXDH. The assumptions are also closely related to what Joye and Libert [JL13] assumed for their cryptosystem, but one should note that our assumptions are stronger because we need to make an element of order exactly 2^ℓ (or q_ℓ) public, while they just needed an element of order divisible by 2^ℓ. When 2^ℓ is small, such an element can be guessed with good probability while it is not clear how to efficiently compute an element of order exactly 2^ℓ given only n.

4.3 Class Groups

We explain here how to instantiate our framework on top of the CL framework [CL15] (see also [Tuc20] for an excellent introduction to class groups). Basically, we take the CL framework, and combine this with the observation that a coset-labelling function can be obtained from a surjective homomorphism used previously in the NICE cryptosystem [PT00, CJLN09].

Let $\mathsf{Gen}(1\!\!1^\lambda)$ output two primes p and q such that $pq \equiv 3 \pmod 4$ and $(p/q) = -1$. This generator is public-coin, p and q will be public. We set $\Delta_K = -pq$ and $\Delta_q = -pq^3$. We set $G = Cl(\Delta_q)$, the class group of the quadratic order $\mathcal{O}_{\Delta_q}$ of discriminant Δ_q and $G' = Cl(\Delta_K)$ the class group of the maximal order $\mathcal{O}_{\Delta_K}$. The size of pq is chosen such that computing the class number $|G'|$ is intractable.

Let $f \in G$ be the class of the ideal $q^2\mathbb{Z} + (-q + \sqrt{\Delta_q})/2\mathbb{Z}$ then f has order q and the discrete logarithm problem in F, generated by f, is easy.

If q has λ bits then q is prime to $|G'|$ except with negligible probability by the Cohen-Lenstra heuristics. Then $G \simeq F \times H$ where H is a subgroup of order $|G'|$.

We denote by $I(\mathcal{O}_{\Delta_q}, q)$ (resp. $I(\mathcal{O}_{\Delta_K}, q)$) the subgroup of fractional ideals generated by $\mathcal{O}_{\Delta_q}$-ideals prime to q (resp. of $\mathcal{O}_{\Delta_K}$-ideals prime to q). Then, the map $\varphi_q : I(\mathcal{O}_{\Delta_q}, q) \to I(\mathcal{O}_{\Delta_K}, q)$, $\mathfrak{a} \mapsto \mathfrak{a}\mathcal{O}_{\Delta_K}$ is an isomorphism. The reverse map is $\varphi_q^{-1} : I(\mathcal{O}_{\Delta_K}, q) \to I(\mathcal{O}_{\Delta_q}, q)$, $\mathfrak{a} \mapsto \mathfrak{a} \cap \mathcal{O}_{\Delta_q}$. Both maps are efficiently computable knowing q. The map φ_q induces a surjective homomorphism from G to G'. This will be the surjection π of the framework. The kernel of π is F.

We then define the function $\delta : G' \mapsto G$ by $\delta(x) = [\varphi_q^{-1}(\mathfrak{a})]$ where $\mathfrak{a}$ is an ideal in the class of x prime to q (it can also be found efficiently).

We then have $\pi(\delta(x)) = x$ by construction, so by Lemma 2, $\phi(g) = \delta(\pi(g))$ is a coset labelling function.

As sampling algorithm $\mathcal{D}$ we use the one introduced in [CL15], and also described in [Tuc20], Sect. 3.1.2. It outputs g of large order such that f is guaranteed to be in the subgroup generated by g. Very briefly, it works by selecting a small prime r such that Δ_K is a square modulo r. From this r, we can construct an element in G' by considering the ideal that lies "above r" and the class of this ideal squared. We then lift this element to G as explained above, to get a group element h. Finally, we output $g = f \cdot h^t$.

With this sampling algorithm, the DDH assumption is the same that has been used before in the CL framework, sometimes known as the DDH-CL assumption. The DXDH assumption in this setting is not implied by DDH, since elements sampled from different randomness do not necessarily generate the same group. Nevertheless, we can argue that the assumption is reasonable: to break it, one needs to decide, for given g, C if a pair of group elements is of form g^r, C^r. The natural approach to this is to use index calculus type methods to find a relation of form $g^a = C^b$ which, for a pair of the form mentioned would imply $(g^r)^a = (C^r)^b$. However, once such an attack succeeds one would also be in a position to find orders of elements and hence break the (much more standard) hidden order assumption.

5 HSS Constructions

In this section, we explain how any instantiation of the framework can be used to build a cryptosystem and a homomorphic secret-sharing scheme (HSS) for restricted multiplication straight-line programs (RMS). Note that given the NIDLS-ElGamal encryption and a distributed DDLOG procedure, constructing an HSS follows in a more or less direct way by following the blueprint of the HSS in [OSY21]. However, since upcoming sections build on top of the HSS we provide the full description of the HSS anyway to make the paper self-contained.

5.1 NIDLS ElGamal

Our HSS construction is based on an ElGamal-style encryption scheme instantiated over our group-theoretic framework. We refer to the construction by *NIDLS ElGamal*, the cryptosystem is formally described in Fig. 1. Correctness of the construction follows immediately as for standard ElGamal.

CPA Security. Similarly to [CL15], the security of NIDLS ElGamal is implied by the DDH assumption, which states that random tuples (g, g^x, g^y, g^{xy}) are indistinguishable from (g, g^x, g^y, g^z). Since $\mathcal{D}$ outputs elements g for which $f \in \langle g \rangle$, we can use g^z to hide f^x.

Generating Encryptions of the Secret Key. Note that in addition to the standard algorithms $(\mathsf{Gen}, \mathsf{Enc}, \mathsf{Dec})$, we have included an additional algorithm SkEnc which encrypts the message "in the wrong place". It turns out that this results in a valid encryption of the value $s \cdot x \bmod t$ i.e., an encryption of the secret key s times the input value x. In particular

$$c_1 \cdot c_0^{-s} = h^r \cdot (g^r \cdot f^{-x})^{-s} = (g^{rs} \cdot g^{-rs}) \cdot f^{sx}$$

This will be useful in our HSS construction. Formal proofs of the security of the scheme are in the full version of the paper [ADOS22, Section 5.1].

ElGamal Cryptosystem

$\mathsf{EG.Gen}(1^\lambda)$:

1. Sample $\mathsf{par} := (G, F, H, f, t, \ell, \mathsf{aux}) \xleftarrow{R} \mathsf{Gen}(\mathbb{1}^\lambda)$
2. Sample a random $(g, \rho) \xleftarrow{R} \mathcal{D}(\mathbb{1}^\lambda, \mathsf{par})$
3. Sample a random $s \xleftarrow{R} [\ell]$, and let $h = g^s$
4. Output $\mathsf{pk} = (\mathsf{par}, g, \rho, h)$ and $\mathsf{sk} = s$.

$\mathsf{EG.Enc}(\mathsf{pk}, x)$:

1. Sample a random $r \xleftarrow{R} [\ell]$
2. Output $\mathsf{ct} = (g^r, h^r \cdot f^x)$

$\mathsf{EG.Dec}(\mathsf{sk}, \mathsf{ct} = (c_0, c_1))$:

1. Output $x = \mathsf{DLog}_f(c_1 \cdot c_0^{-s})$

$\mathsf{EG.SkEnc}(\mathsf{pk}, x)$:

1. Sample a random $r \xleftarrow{R} [\ell]$
2. Output $\mathsf{ct} = (g^r \cdot f^{-x}, h^r)$

Fig. 1. A description of the ElGamal cryptosystem in the NIDLS framework.

5.2 Public-Key HSS

We now present a homomorphic secret-sharing scheme (HSS) for RMS programs based on the NIDLS framework. The main advantage of our NIDLS-based HSS compared to the Paillier-based HSS of [OSY21] is that we remove any need for trusted setups when instantiating the NIDLS over class groups, while previous constructions had to rely on a trusted dealer for the generation of an RSA modulus.

RMS Programs. Restricted multiplications straight-line (RMS) programs are arithmetic circuits over $\mathbb{Z}$ that never compute multiplications between two intermediate value of the computation: at least one of the two factors must be an input. Intermediate values of the computation are often referred to as memory values. This class includes also branching programs, which likewise contains NC^1.

Definition 7 (RMS Programs). *An RMS program consists of a bound $B \in \mathbb{N}$, a modulo $n_{\mathsf{out}} \in \mathbb{N}$ and a polynomial-sized circuit in which the only gate types allowed are the following.*

- $\mathsf{ConvertInput}(\mathsf{I}_x) \to \mathsf{M}_x$. *Load the value of the input wire I_x to the memory wire M_x.*

- $\mathsf{Add}(\mathsf{M}_x, \mathsf{M}_y) \to \mathsf{M}_z$. *Add the values of the memory wires* M_x *and* M_y *and assign the result to the memory wire* M_z.
- $\mathsf{Mult}(\mathsf{I}_x, \mathsf{M}_y) \to \mathsf{M}_z$. *Multiply the value of the input wire* I_x *by the value of the memory wire* M_y. *Assign the result to the memory wire* M_z.
- $\mathsf{Output}(\mathsf{M}_z) \to z$. *Output the value of the memory wire* M_z *reducing it modulo* n_{out}.

The circuit accepts only integral inputs. Whenever the absolute value $|x|$ *of any wire exceeds the bound* B, *the output of the execution is* $\perp$.

The Public-Key HSS Scheme. We are now ready to present our construction, which is formally described in Fig. 2. We discuss the main ideas.

Our HSS scheme allows two parties to non-interactively apply an RMS program C on secret-shared inputs, obtaining additively secret-shared outputs. The scheme relies on a setup procedure[4] that provides the parties with a PRF key k, a NIDLS ElGamal public key pk, and a subtractive secret-sharing over the integers of the private counterpart $s = s_1 - s_0$. We assume that the length $\mathsf{len}_{\mathsf{sk}}$ of the private key is sufficiently small, so that $s < t$. If this condition is not satisfied, we need to proceed as in [OSY21], splitting the private key into small blocks and providing the parties with an encryption of each of them.

Input Wires and Memory Wires. During the evaluation of the circuit C, each input wire I_x is associated with two NIDLS ElGamal ciphertexts: an encryption of the value of the wire x and an encryption of the product between x and the ElGamal secret key s. Such ciphertexts are produced and broadcast by the party providing the input. Remember that one does not need to know s in order to encrypt $x \cdot s$. Indeed, the algorithm SkEnc described in Sect. 5.1 can be used instead. Each memory wire M_x is instead associated with two subtractive secret-sharings over the integers: a secret-sharing of the value of the wire x and a secret-sharing of $x' := x \cdot s$.

Linear Operations. Performing additions between memory values is straightforward due to the linearity of subtractive secret-sharing, i.e. to add M_x and M_y, it is sufficient to compute $[z] \leftarrow [x]+[y]$ and $[z'] \leftarrow [x']+[y'] = [x \cdot s]+[y \cdot s]$. Observe that additions allow us to model also multiplications by public constants in $\mathbb{Z}$.

Multiplications Between Input Wires and Memory Wires. Multiplications between input wires and memory wires require more interesting techniques based on DDLOG. Let $\mathsf{ct}_x = (c_0, c_1)$ be the ElGamal encryption of x, the value of the input wire I_x. Moreover, let $[y]$ and $[y' = y \cdot s]$ be the subtractive secret-sharings associated with the memory wire M_y. In particular, the parties P_0 and P_1 own integers y_0, y_0' and y_1, y_1' such that $y_1 = y_0 + y$ and $y_1' = y_0' + y \cdot s$. Now, observe that $c_1^{y_0} \cdot c_0^{-y_0'}$ and $c_1^{y_1} \cdot c_0^{-y_1'}$ are a divisive secret-sharing of f^{xy}. Indeed,

$$c_1^{y_1} \cdot c_0^{-y_1'} = c_1^{y_0+y} \cdot c_0^{-(y_0'+y \cdot s)} = (c_1 \cdot c_0^{-s})^y \cdot c_1^{y_0} \cdot c_0^{-y_0'} = f^{xy} \cdot c_1^{y_0} \cdot c_0^{-y_0'}.$$

[4] Following the blueprint of [OSY21], it is possible to substitute the setup with a one-round protocol.

HSS Scheme

Setup($1\!\!1^\lambda$):

1. Let $\mathsf{par} := (G, F, H, f, t, \ell, \mathsf{aux}) \xleftarrow{R} \mathsf{Gen}(1\!\!1^\lambda)$ and ℓ_{sk} be the parameter for the small-exponent assumption.
2. $(g, \rho) \xleftarrow{R} \mathcal{D}(1\!\!1^\lambda, \mathsf{par})$
3. $s_0, s_1 \xleftarrow{R} [\ell_{\mathsf{sk}}]$
4. $\mathsf{pk} \leftarrow g^{s_1} \cdot g^{-s_0}$
5. $k \xleftarrow{R} \{0,1\}^\lambda$
6. Output $\big(\mathsf{par}, g, \rho, \ell_{\mathsf{sk}}, \mathsf{pk}, k, (s_0, s_1)\big)$.

Input(pk, x):

1. $\mathsf{ct}_x \xleftarrow{R} \mathsf{EG.Enc}(\mathsf{pk}, x)$
2. $\mathsf{ct}_{xs} \xleftarrow{R} \mathsf{EG.SkEnc}(\mathsf{pk}, x)$
3. Output $\mathsf{I}_x \leftarrow (\mathsf{ct}_x, \mathsf{ct}_{xs})$.

Eval$\big(i, s_i, (\mathsf{I}^1, \mathsf{I}^2, \ldots, \mathsf{I}^n), P\big)$:

Party P_i evaluates the RMS program P gate by gate as follows.

- $\mathsf{M}_x \leftarrow \mathsf{ConvertInput}(\mathsf{I}_x)$:
  Compute $\mathsf{M}_x \leftarrow \mathsf{Mult}\big(\mathsf{I}_x, \mathsf{M}_1 := (i, s_i)\big)$.
- $\mathsf{M}_z \leftarrow \mathsf{Add}(\mathsf{M}_x, \mathsf{M}_y)$:
  Compute $z_i \leftarrow x_i + y_i$ and $z'_i \leftarrow x'_i + y'_i$ and set $\mathsf{M}_z \leftarrow (z_i, z'_i)$.
- $\mathsf{M}_z \leftarrow \mathsf{Mult}(\mathsf{I}_x, \mathsf{M}_y)$:
  Let $\mathsf{ct}_x = (c_0, c_1)$ and $\mathsf{ct}_{xs} = (d_0, d_1)$. Let id be the label of the gate.
  1. $z_i \leftarrow (-1)^{1-i} \cdot \mathsf{DDLog}\big(c_1^{y_i} \cdot c_0^{-y'_i}\big) + \mathsf{F}_k(\mathsf{id}, 0) \bmod t$
  2. $z'_i \leftarrow (-1)^{1-i} \cdot \mathsf{DDLog}\big(d_1^{y_i} \cdot d_0^{-y'_i}\big) + \mathsf{F}_k(\mathsf{id}, 1) \bmod t$
  3. $\mathsf{M}_z \leftarrow (z_i, z'_i)$
- $\mathsf{Output}(\mathsf{M}_z)$:
  1. Output $(-1)^{1-i} \cdot z_i \bmod n_{\mathsf{out}}$

Fig. 2. The HSS scheme for RMS programs based on the NIDLS framework.

By applying DDLOG on the respective divisive shares, the parties are therefore able to obtain a secret-sharing of the product $x \cdot y$ over $\mathbb{Z}_t$ (we recall that $t := \mathsf{ord}(f)$). By repeating the procedure for the other ciphertext associated with the input wire I_x, namely the encryption of $x \cdot s$, the parties can non-interactively obtain also a secret-sharing of $x \cdot y \cdot s$. Observe that the additive secret-sharings over $\mathbb{Z}_t$ can be easily converted into subtractive ones by simply changing the signs of the shares of P_0. In order to be sure that the shares are random over $\mathbb{Z}_t$, we rerandomise them using the PRF key k. As a consequence, as long as $|x \cdot y \cdot s| \ll t$, with overwhelming probability, the difference of the shares does not wrap around t, so the parties actually obtain a subtractive secret-sharing over $\mathbb{Z}$.

Input Conversions and Outputs. It remains to explain how to perform the input conversions and how to retrieve the outputs. Both operations are now rather straightforward. In order to convert an input to a memory element, it is indeed sufficient to multiply it by a memory value containing 1. The latter corresponds to a subtractive secret-sharing of 1, e.g. $y_1 = 1$ and $y_0 = 0$ and a subtractive secret-sharing of s, which was provided to the parties by the initial setup. Outputting the value of a memory wire M_z is even simpler, the parties just broadcast their share of z reducing it modulo n_{out}. By subtracting the two messages modulo n_{out}, the players can obtain the final result of the computation.

On the Bound on the Values of the Wires. The correctness of the HSS scheme described above relies on the assumption that $|x \cdot y \cdot s| \ll t$ for every multiplication. If this condition is not satisfied, there is a non-negligible probability that the secret-sharing over $\mathbb{Z}_t$ obtained as result cannot be converted into an integer secret-sharing of the same value. Observe, anyway, that denoting by B the bound of the RMS circuit, $|x \cdot y \cdot s| \leq B \cdot 2^{\mathsf{len}_{\mathsf{sk}}}$, so, in order to circumvent the problem, we can choose the parameters of the NIDLS framework so that $B \cdot 2^{\mathsf{len}_{\mathsf{sk}}} \cdot 2^{\lambda} < t$.

Theorem 1. *If the DDH assumption and the small exponent assumption hold in the NIDLS framework and* F *is a secure PRF outputting values in* $\mathbb{Z}_t$*, the construction in Fig. 2 is a correct and secure HSS scheme for RMS circuits with bound* $B < t/2^{\mathsf{len}_{\mathsf{sk}}+\lambda}$*. The ring where the computation takes place is* $R = \mathbb{Z}_{n_{\mathsf{out}}}$*. Assuming* $n_{\mathsf{out}} < B$*, the input space is* $\mathcal{I} = R$*.*

We prove Theorem 1 in the full version of the paper [ADOS22, Section 5.2].

5.3 Implementing the Setup Using One Round

The HSS scheme described in Fig. 2 relies on a setup producing a NIDLS ElGamal public key and a subtractive secret-sharing over the integers of the private counterpart. One of the main goals of this work is to improve upon the results of [OSY21] by removing the need for trusted dealers. In this section, we therefore explain how the parties can setup the HSS material in one round. The protocol, which is formally described in Fig. 3, relies on a CRS providing the parties with the parameters of the NIDLS framework and a PRF key k. When the framework is instantiated over class groups, the generation of the CRS does not need any trusted dealer. Indeed, the parties just need to produce public, random coins and input them into the algorithm producing the CRS. In the random oracle model, this procedure can be performed non-interactively. In [OSY21], the HSS scheme was based on Paillier. Since the associated group is described by an RSA modulo N where $\varphi(N)$ needs to remain secret, designing an efficient setup for the HSS scheme without relying on trusted dealers is a challenging task in that case.

Our setup protocol is very simple. Each party just generates a NIDLS ElGamal key pair, publishing the public counterpart. The parties then output the quotient between the two public keys and their respective secret key.

Function $\mathcal{F}_{\mathsf{HSS\text{-}Setup}}$

1. Compute $(\mathsf{par}, g, \rho, \ell_{\mathsf{sk}}, \mathsf{pk}, k, (s_0, s_1)) \xleftarrow{R} \mathsf{Setup}(\mathbb{1}^\lambda)$
2. Output $(\mathsf{par}, g, \rho, \ell_{\mathsf{sk}}, \mathsf{pk}, s_i, k)$ to every party P_i.

Protocol $\Pi_{\mathsf{HSS\text{-}Setup}}$

CRS:

1. Let $\mathsf{par} := (G, F, H, f, t, \ell, \mathsf{aux}) \xleftarrow{R} \mathsf{Gen}(\mathbb{1}^\lambda)$ and ℓ_{sk} be the parameter for the small-exponent assumption.
2. $(g, \rho) \xleftarrow{R} \mathcal{D}(\mathbb{1}^\lambda, \mathsf{par})$
3. $k \xleftarrow{R} \{0,1\}^\lambda$
4. Output $(\mathsf{par}, \ell_{\mathsf{sk}}, g, \rho, k)$

PROCEDURE:

1. Every party P_i samples $s_i \xleftarrow{R} [\ell_{\mathsf{sk}}]$
2. Every party P_i sends $\mathsf{pk}_i \leftarrow g^{s_i}$ to P_{1-i}
3. Every party P_i outputs $\mathsf{pk} \leftarrow \mathsf{pk}_1/\mathsf{pk}_0$, s_i and k.

Fig. 3. The HSS setup functionality and a one-round protocol implementing it.

Theorem 2. *The protocol $\Pi_{\mathsf{HSS\text{-}Setup}}$ implements the functionality $\mathcal{F}_{\mathsf{HSS\text{-}Setup}}$ against a semi-honest adversary with perfect security.*

Proof. Suppose that P_i is corrupted. The simulator receives $(\mathsf{par}, g, \rho, \ell_{\mathsf{sk}}, \mathsf{pk}, s_i, k)$ from the functionality. It can then simulate the CRS by providing the adversary with $(\mathsf{par}, \ell_{\mathsf{sk}}, g, \rho, k)$. The view of P_i is perfectly simulated by sending s_i and $\mathsf{pk} \cdot g^{s_i}$ if $i = 0$ or g^{s_i}/pk if $i = 1$. Observe that the output of P_{1-i} is consistent with the elements sent to the adversary. □

6 Public-Key PCFs and One-Round VOLE Protocol Without Trusted Setup

In [OSY21], the authors designed a one-round VOLE protocol based on the Paillier cryptosystem and the NIDLS problem on the underlying group. A VOLE protocol involves two parties, the input of the first one is a element in a ring R, the input of the second party is a R-vector $\boldsymbol{a}$. The output of the protocol consists of an additive secret-sharing of the product $x \cdot \boldsymbol{a}$.

We now present a version of such protocol in the NIDLS framework (see Fig. 5). By generalising the techniques to a more abstract setting, we are able to

Function $\mathcal{F}_{\mathsf{VOLE}}$

INITIALISATION: The functionality waits for a value $t \in \mathbb{N}$ from the adversary.
EVALUATION: On input $x \in \mathbb{Z}_t$ from P_0 and $\boldsymbol{a} \in \mathbb{Z}_t^m$ from P_1, the functionality sends m to the adversary.

- If both parties are honest, $\mathcal{F}_{\mathsf{VOLE}}$ samples $\boldsymbol{y}_0 \stackrel{R}{\leftarrow} \mathbb{Z}_t^m$ and sets $\boldsymbol{y}_1 \leftarrow \boldsymbol{a} \cdot x - \boldsymbol{y}_0$. Then, it outputs $\boldsymbol{y}_i$ to P_i for every $i \in \{0, 1\}$.
- If P_i is corrupt, $\mathcal{F}_{\mathsf{VOLE}}$ waits for $\boldsymbol{y}_i \in \mathbb{Z}_t^m$ from the adversary and sets $\boldsymbol{y}_{1-i} \leftarrow \boldsymbol{a} \cdot x - \boldsymbol{y}_i$. Then, it outputs $\boldsymbol{y}_{1-i}$ to P_{1-i}.

Function $\mathcal{F}_{\mathsf{NIKE}}$

If both parties are honest, sample $k \stackrel{R}{\leftarrow} \{0, 1\}^\lambda$ and output it to all the parties. If one party is corrupted, wait for $k \in \{0, 1\}^\lambda$ from the adversary and output it to the other party.

Fig. 4. The NIKE and vector-OLE functionalities

leverage the properties of the various instantiations. In the case of class groups, that allows us to not rely on any trusted setup. In order to achieve this goal, we had to slightly modify the CRS used by the protocol. In [OSY21], the latter consisted of a pair of group elements (g, C) where $C = g^r$ for some unknown r. In order to avoid trusted setups, we now need to provide the parties with the randomness used for the generation of the CRS. Unfortunately, in class groups, such randomness would leak the value of r to the adversary, compromising security. In order to circumvent the problem, in this work, g and C are sampled independently using $\mathcal{D}(\mathbb{1}^\lambda)$, so with high probability $C \notin \langle g \rangle$. We prove security by relying on the DXDH assumption.

The construction makes use of a non-interactive key exchange functionality $\mathcal{F}_{\mathsf{NIKE}}$ (see Fig. 4). The latter provides the parties with a random PRF key $k \in \{0, 1\}^\lambda$. When one of the parties is corrupt, the functionality lets the adversary choose k, forwarding it to the honest party. It is possible to implement $\mathcal{F}_{\mathsf{NIKE}}$ in one round using NIKE constructions such as Diffie-Hellman.

Correctness. To understand why the protocol works, observe that

$$D^{r_1^i} \cdot E^{a_i} = g^{r_0 \cdot r_1^i} \cdot f^{x \cdot a_i} \cdot C^{r_0 \cdot a_i} = f^{x \cdot a_i} \cdot A_i^{r_0}.$$

In other words, for every index i, the elements $D^{r_1^i} \cdot E^{a_i}$ and $A_i^{-r_0}$ are a multiplicative secret-sharing of $f^{x \cdot a_i}$. Using DDLog for every $i \in [m]$, the parties are therefore able to obtain an additive secret-sharing of $x \cdot \boldsymbol{a}$ without any additional interaction.

Protocol Π_{VOLE}

INPUTS: The first party P_0 has input $x \in \mathbb{Z}_t$. The other party P_1 has input $\boldsymbol{a} \in \mathbb{Z}_t^m$ for some $m \in \mathbb{N}$.

SETUP $\mathsf{Setup}(1\!\!1^\lambda)$:

1. $\mathsf{par} := (G, F, H, f, t, \ell, \mathsf{aux}) \xleftarrow{R} \mathsf{Gen}(1\!\!1^\lambda)$
2. $(g, \rho_0) \xleftarrow{R} \mathcal{D}(1\!\!1^\lambda, \mathsf{par})$
3. $(C, \rho_1) \xleftarrow{R} \mathcal{D}(1\!\!1^\lambda, \mathsf{par})$
4. If $g = C$, go to step 3.
5. Output $(\mathsf{par}, g, \rho_0, C, \rho_1)$

PROCEDURE:

1. The parties call $\mathcal{F}_{\mathsf{NIKE}}$ to obtain a key $k \in \{0,1\}^\lambda$.
2. $\forall i \in [m]:\quad P_1$ sends $A_i \leftarrow g^{r_1^i} \cdot C^{a_i}$ where $r_1^i \xleftarrow{R} [\ell]$.
3. P_0 sends $(D, E) \leftarrow (g^{r_0}, f^x \cdot C^{r_0})$ where $r_0 \xleftarrow{R} [\ell]$.
4. P_1 outputs $\boldsymbol{y}_1$ where $\boldsymbol{y}_1[i] \leftarrow \mathsf{DDLog}_{\mathsf{par}}(D^{r_1^i} \cdot E^{a_i}) + \mathsf{F}_k(i)$ for every $i \in [m]$.
5. P_0 outputs $\boldsymbol{y}_0$ where $\boldsymbol{y}_0[i] \leftarrow \mathsf{DDLog}_{\mathsf{par}}(A_i^{r_0}) - \mathsf{F}_k(i)$

Fig. 5. A one-round VOLE protocol based on the NIDLS framework.

Security. At first glance, it might seem that the security of the protocol follows from the fact that the A_i's are Pedersen commitments with respect to (g, C). However, note that the element C is *not guaranteed to be* in the cyclic group generated by g. As a consequence, A_i does not hide the input a_i with information-theoretic security and we need instead to rely on a computational assumption. The same happens also in step 3, where C plays the role of the public key in an NIDLS ElGamal encryption. However, again, C is not guaranteed to belong to $\langle g \rangle$. Therefore, we need to argue for security in a different way. To solve both issues, we use the DXDH assumption (see Definition 5).

Observe that under the DXDH assumption, g^r looks like C^s even when the randomness used for the generation of the CRS is known. As a consequence, no adversary can distinguish $A_i = g^{r_1^i} \cdot C^{a_i}$ from $C^s \cdot C^{a_i}$. The latter contains no information about a_i. The privacy of x is instead preserved as $(D, E) = (g^{r_0}, f^x \cdot C^{r_0})$ is indistinguishable, under our assumption, from $(C^s, f^x \cdot C^r)$. Since the distribution $\mathcal{D}$ outputs an element C such that $f \in \langle C \rangle$, the pair $(C^s, f^x \cdot C^r)$ hides all the information about x. The proof of the next theorem is omitted, as it easily follows from the arguments sketched above.

Theorem 3. *If the DXDH assumption holds and* F *is a secure PRF outputting pseudorandom elements in* $\mathbb{Z}_t$*, the protocol* Π_{VOLE} *UC implements the functionality* $\mathcal{F}_{\mathsf{VOLE}}$ *against a semi-honest adversary in the* $\mathcal{F}_{\mathsf{NIKE}}$*-hybrid model.*

6.1 Public-Key PCFs Without Trusted Setup

In [OSY21], Orlandi *et al.* present PCFs for vector-OLE and OT based on Paillier and the Goldwasser-Micali cryptosystem respectively (see the full version of the paper [ADOS22, Fig. 8–9]). The interesting property of both constructions is that, thanks to the one-round VOLE protocol of [OSY21], the PCF keys can be set up using only one round of interaction and low-communication in the output size. For this reason, the authors introduced the notion of public-key PCF to refer to them.

On the downside, as we mentioned in the previous subsection, the one-round VOLE protocol of [OSY21] needs a trusted setup. The issue is immediately inherited by the public-key PCFs. Now, by plugging our new VOLE protocol, we obtain public-key PCFs with no need for trusted setups. We describe the resulting protocols in the full version of the paper [ADOS22, Section 6.1].

On the Need for the Hardness of Factoring. The security of both our public-key PCFs still relies on the hardness of factoring. This requirement is inherited from the original PCFs of [OSY21]. At first, it may seem possible to generalise the two constructions to the NIDLS framework, potentially obtaining public-key PCFs based on class groups only. Unfortunately, this turns out to be false.

Indeed, in the public-key PCFs for VOLE and OT, we need to non-interactively sample random ciphertexts without leaking any information about the plaintext to P_1. For Paillier, this is not a problem as any element in $\mathbb{Z}_{N^2}^{\times}$ is a valid encryption. For Goldwasser-Micali instead, it is sufficient to sample a random element in $\mathbb{Z}_N$ with Jacobi symbol 1. Now, if we try to move the constructions to class groups, we need to use the ElGamal cryptosystem. By modifying the PCF keys and using techniques as in the HSS scheme (see Sect. 5), it is still possible for the parties to non-interactively obtain an additive secret-sharing of $a \cdot x$ given the encryption of a random a. The issue is that the only known way to sample such encryption is to directly encrypt a (not every pair of elements in the class group is an ElGamal ciphertext). That would leak the value of a to P_1.

7 Actively Secure Public-Key PCFs

In addition to requiring a trusted setup, the public key PCFs in [OSY21] achieve security in the semi-honest setting only. In this section, we explain how to upgrade the constructions described in Sect. 6 to active security, while preserving, at the same time, their round-complexity properties, namely that the parties need to speak only once. When the NIDLS framework is instantiated over class groups, the constructions do not need any trusted setup.

The particular interaction pattern limits the techniques we can rely on. For instance, we cannot perform checks that verify the correctness of the outputs, as that would require an additional round of interaction after the outputs are derived. For this reason, we develop NIZKs for our framework which might be of independent interest. We start presenting some building blocks (commitments in Sect. 7.1 and ZK proofs in Sect. 7.2). Then, we describe an actively secure public-key PCF for vector-OLE (Sect. 7.3). In the full version of the paper [ADOS22, Section 7.4], we also present an active public-key PCF for OT.

7.1 An Integer Commitment Scheme in the NIDLS Framework

Our NIZKs follow a commit-and-prove approach. Notice that in order to achieve active security, party P_0 has to prove that its input to the one-round vector-OLE protocol is the private key associated with the RSA modulo N. For this reason, we need to prove particular number-theoretic relations for which commitment schemes based on modular rings such as $\mathbb{Z}_t$ are not really suited.

Recall that, in the NIDLS framework, determining the order of the group from its parameters is assumed to be hard. This property crucially allows us to design integer commitment schemes. This fact was already noticed for class groups by Couteau *et al.* [CKLR21]. In this work, we adopt a generalisation of their construction to the NIDLS framework (see Fig. 6), basing however its security on the DXDH assumption. As we discuss at the end of this section, despite the claims in [CKLR21], their construction is not compatible with trustless setup.

Integer commitment scheme

CRS:

1. $\mathsf{par}' := (G, F, H, f, t, \ell, \mathsf{aux}) \xleftarrow{R} \mathsf{Gen}(1\!\!1^\lambda)$
2. $(g, \rho_0) \xleftarrow{R} \mathcal{D}(1\!\!1^\lambda, \mathsf{par})$
3. $(C, \rho_1) \xleftarrow{R} \mathcal{D}(1\!\!1^\lambda, \mathsf{par})$
4. If $C = g$, go to step 3.
5. Output $\mathsf{par} := (\mathsf{par}', g, \rho_0, C, \rho_1)$

COMMITMENT: $\mathsf{Commit}(\mathsf{par}, x)$

1. $r \xleftarrow{R} [\ell]$
2. Output the commitment $X \leftarrow C^x \cdot g^r$ and the opening information r.

VERIFICATION: $\mathsf{Verify}(\mathsf{par}, X, x, r)$

1. If $X = C^x \cdot g^r$ output 1 otherwise output 0.

Fig. 6. Integer commitment scheme in the NIDLS framework.

Theorem 4. *If the DXDH assumption and the weak hidden order assumption hold, the construction in Fig. 6 is a hiding and binding integer commitment scheme. Moreover, the scheme is linearly homomorphic.*

Proof. It is straightforward to see that the construction is correct and linearly homomorphic.

Binding. The proof for binding is made interesting by the fact that C is not (necessarily) an element in the group generated by g. Suppose that we have an adversary that breaks binding e.g., after being provided with the parameters, the adversary returns (x, r) and (y, s) with $x \neq y$ such that $C^x g^r = C^y g^s$, and therefore $C^{x-y} = g^{s-r}$. Let $\alpha := x - y \neq 0$ and $\beta = s - r$. Since the order of the group is unknown we cannot invert these elements. Instead, we resort to the DXDH assumption, which implies the following claim:

Claim. Assume there exists an adversary $\mathcal{A}$ that, on input (g, C), returns (α, β) with $C^\alpha = g^\beta$ and $\alpha \neq 0$. Then, with overwhelming probability over $u, v \stackrel{R}{\leftarrow} [\ell]$, it holds that:

$$(g^u)^\alpha = (g^v)^\beta \tag{1}$$

Proof (of claim). The reduction is given a DXDH tuple (g, C, g^u, T) where T is either C^u or g^v for random $u, v \stackrel{R}{\leftarrow} [\ell]$, and feeds (g, C) to $\mathcal{A}$. Now the reduction concludes that $T = C^u$ when

$$(T)^\alpha = (g^v)^\beta \tag{2}$$

or $T = g^v$ otherwise. Note that if $T = C^u$ then Eq. 2 is trivially true. Thus if $(g^u)^\alpha \neq (g^v)^\beta$ the reduction correctly distinguished between DXDH tuple and non-DXDH tuples. □

We now go back to the proof of the binding property and argue that under the weak hidden order assumption, no adversary can output α, β such that Eq. 1 holds for random (u, v). We first rewrite $(g^u)^\alpha = (g^v)^\beta$ as $u \cdot \alpha \equiv v \cdot \beta \bmod \mathsf{ord}(g)$. We argue the following:

Claim. Let α, β be such that

$$u \cdot \alpha \equiv v \cdot \beta \bmod \mathsf{ord}(g)$$

with overwhelming probability for uniform $u, v \stackrel{R}{\leftarrow} [\ell]$. Then $\mathsf{ord}(g) | \alpha$.

Proof (of claim). For the sake of contradiction assume that this is not the case, e.g., $\mathsf{ord}(g) \nmid \alpha$. Then there is a non-negligible probability that $u \cdot \alpha \not\equiv v \cdot \beta \bmod \mathsf{ord}(g)$. Indeed, let p be a prime that divides $\mathsf{ord}(g)$ but not α, it must hold that $u \equiv v \cdot \beta \cdot \alpha^{-1} \bmod p$. This happens with probability $1/p < 1/2$, so it must be that α is a multiple of $\mathsf{ord}(g)$. □

We have reached a contradiction. Indeed, under the weak hidden order assumption, no adversary can output α such that $g^\alpha = 1$.

Hiding. We show that no adversary can distinguish a commitment to x_0 from a commitment to x_1. Indeed by the DXDH assumption, (g, C, g^r, C^r) with r uniform in $[\ell]$, is indistinguishable from (g, C, C^s, C^r) with s again uniform in $[\ell]$. Thus $C^{x_b} \cdot g^r$ is indistinguishable from $C^{x_b} \cdot C^s$. From the way ℓ is chosen, C^s is statistically close to the uniform distribution over $\langle C \rangle$. So, as commitments to both x_0, x_1 are indistinguishable from random elements in $\langle C \rangle$, no adversary can distinguish between a commitment to x_0 and a commitment to x_1. □

In [CKLR21], the authors proved the security of this commitment scheme in the class group setting by relying on the *subgroup indistinguishability* assumption. The latter states that no PPT adversary can distinguish between a pair of random elements (g, C) both sampled according to $\mathcal{D}$ and a pair (g, g^s) where s is uniform over $[\ell]$. Despite what the authors claim, this assumption is not sufficient to prove security when we do not rely on a trusted dealer for the generation of the CRS. Indeed, in order to remove trusted setups, we need to provide the parties with the random coins used for the generation of the CRS. That prevents us from substituting C with g^s in the security proofs. The reason is that the distribution $\mathcal{D}$ is, surprisingly, not invertible over class groups. Specifically, given $C \in \mathsf{Supp}(\mathcal{D})$, it is hard to find a bit string r such that $\mathcal{D}(1\!\!1^\lambda; r) = C$.

7.2 Zero-Knowledge Proofs in the NIDLS Framework

We describe how to build useful ZK-proofs in the NIDLS framework such as: range proofs, multiplication proofs, proofs of knowledge of openings and proofs of commitment to the plaintext. In particular, we build sigma protocols that use the NIDLS framework in a black-box way, independently of its instantiation. Thus, our proofs do not need to express operations in the NIDLS framework as circuits. Since these tools are all based on fairly standard techniques, we will only give a brief overview and direct the reader to the full version of the paper [ADOS22, Appendix A] for more details.

Proof of Knowledge of Openings. Π_{com} allows to convince a verifier holding a commitment X that the prover knows integers x and r such that $X = C^x \cdot g^r$.

Compared to standard Σ-protocols for proving knowledge of a (Pedersen) commitment in a prime order group, we need two major changes: First, all the computation between scalars is done over the integers (since the order of the group is unknown) and therefore, the random strings chosen in the first round must be larger than an upper bound on the witness (x, r). Second, we can only use binary challenges: this is due to the fact that, again, the order of the group is unknown and therefore, we cannot invert the challenge when extracting the witness in the special soundness property. Thus, we need to repeat the proofs λ times. Note that for most of our instantiations there usually are ways around this issue, mostly relying on instantiation-dependent assumptions (such as the strong root problem and the low order assumption for class groups). However, those do not carry over to our general framework.

Multiplication Proofs. Π_{mult} allows to convince a verifier with commitments X, Y and Z, that the prover knows $x, y, z \in \mathbb{Z}$ and $r_1, r_2, r_3 \in \mathbb{Z}$ such that $X = C^x \cdot g^{r_1}$, $Y = C^y \cdot g^{r_2}$, $Z = C^z \cdot g^{r_3}$ and $z = x \cdot y$. We construct Π_{mult} by adapting the protocol of [DF02] to our framework, similarly to what we did for Π_{com}.

Range Proofs. Π_{range} allows to convince a verifier holding a commitment X and a bound $B \in \mathbb{N}$ that the prover knows $x, r \in \mathbb{Z}$ such that $x \in [0, B]$ and $X = C^x \cdot g^r$. Our protocol is based on a technique by Groth [Gro05], who observed that

$$x \in [0, B] \quad \Longleftrightarrow \quad \exists x_1, x_2, x_3 \in \mathbb{Z} \quad \text{s.t. } 1 + 4x \cdot (B - x) = x_1^2 + x_2^2 + x_3^2.$$

The protocol can be therefore constructed exploiting multiplication proofs just introduced and the linearity of the commitment.

We remark that in [CKLR21], the authors designed a range proof for our commitment scheme in the class group setting. Their solution never relies on binary challenges, so its efficiency is better by a factor of λ. However, their construction is only proven secure when the CRS is generated by a trusted dealer. This is due to the issue described at the end of Sect. 7.1.

Proof of Commitment to the Plaintext. Π_{plain} can be used to convince a verifier holding group elements D, E, X that the prover knows $x, r, s \in \mathbb{Z}$ such that $X = C^x \cdot g^s$, $D = g^r$ and $E = f^x \cdot C^r$. The protocol uses standard techniques adapted to our framework as sketched for Π_{com}.

7.3 Actively Secure Public-Key PCF for Vector-OLE

In the semi-honest public-key PCF for vector-OLE (Fig. 5 and [ADOS22, Fig. 8]), the only message sent by party P_0 consists of an RSA modulo N and a pair of groups elements D, E where $D = g^{r_0}$ and $E = f^d \cdot C^{r_0}$. Here, the exponent d represents the Paillier private key associated with the RSA modulo N, whereas g and C are groups elements described in the CRS. We recall that d is the only element in $[0, N \cdot \varphi(N) - 1]$ satisfying $d \equiv 0 \bmod \varphi(N)$ and $d \equiv 1 \bmod N$.

The only message sent by party P_1 is instead $A := C^x \cdot g^{r_1}$. In order for the construction to be correct, the value of x needs to be smaller than $2^\lambda \cdot 2^{\mathsf{len}_N}$.

An active adversary can always deviate from the protocol and send malformed material. For this reason, it is fundamental that our NIZKs prove the well-formedness of the messages of the parties. In the case of P_1, the task is rather simple. Using the Fiat-Shamir heuristic, we can indeed convert Π_{range} into the NIZK we are looking for. Proving the well-formedness of P_0's message is however more challenging.

Proving the Well-Formedness of P_0's Message. As usual we first design a public coin honest-verifier zero-knowledge proof and then convert it into a NIZK by applying the Fiat-Shamir heuristic. Our protocol makes use of a public-coin HVZK $\Pi_{\mathsf{semiprime}}$ for proving that the RSA modulo N is the product of two distinct primes p and q. Moreover, $\Pi_{\mathsf{semiprime}}$ proves that $\gcd(N, \varphi(N)) = 1$. Such protocol can be found e.g., in [GRSB19].

The main idea of our protocol is as follows: the prover commits to d, the primes p and q and integers k_1 and k_2 satisfying $d = k_1 \cdot \varphi(N)$ and $d = k_2 \cdot N + 1$. We denote the five commitments by Z, X_1, X_2, Y_1 and Y_2 respectively. The parties run $\Pi_{\mathsf{semiprime}}$ to verify that N is semiprime. By relying on Π_{mult}, the prover also shows that X_1 and X_2 are commitments to a factorisation of N. Furthermore, using Π_{range}, the verifier checks that the value committed in X_1 belongs to $[2, N-1]$ (this is done by showing that $C^{-2} \cdot X_1$ is a commitment to a value in $[0, N-3]$). In this way, it is sure that the prover committed to a proper factorisation and not just $N \cdot 1$. Now, the verifier is also certain that $W := C^N \cdot X_1^{-1} \cdot X_2^{-1} \cdot C$ is a commitment to $N - p - q + 1 = \varphi(N)$. Next, using Π_{range}, the prover shows that the value committed in Y_1 belongs to $[0, N-1]$. Using Π_{com}, it also proves the knowledge of opening for Y_2. The verifier also checks that Y_1 is a commitment to $d/\varphi(N)$. This is done by running Π_{mult} on Y_1, W and Z. If the check passes, the verifier is also sure that the value committed in Z belongs to $[0, N \cdot \varphi(N) - 1]$. In the end, the prover shows that Y_2 is a commitment to $(d-1)/N$ by proving that $Z \cdot C^{-1} \cdot Y_2^{-N}$ opens to 0. Finally, the prover uses Π_{plain} to convince the verifier that the values hidden in Z and in (D, E) coincide. The formal description of the protocol, which we call Π_{Paillier}, and the proof of the following theorem are in the full version of the paper [ADOS22, Section 7.3].

Theorem 5. *Let $\Pi_{\mathsf{semiprime}}$ be a honest-verifier zero-knowledge public-coin proof proving that N is the product of two distinct primes and $\gcd(N, \varphi(N)) = 1$. If the commitment scheme in Fig. 6 is hiding and binding, the construction Π_{Paillier} (see [ADOS22, Fig. 11]) is a complete, special-sound public-coin proof for the relation*

$$\mathcal{R}_{\mathsf{Paillier}} := \left\{ (D, E, N), (d, p, q, r) \;\middle|\; \begin{array}{l} N = p \cdot q, \text{ where } p, q \text{ are positive primes} \\ \gcd(N, \varphi(N)) = 1 \\ D = g^r, E = f^d \cdot C^r \\ d \equiv 0 \bmod \varphi(N) \\ d \equiv 1 \bmod N \\ 0 \le d < N \cdot \varphi(N) \end{array} \right\}$$

Moreover, when $r \in [\ell]$, the proof is honest-verifier zero-knowledge.

Deploying the NIZKs to Obtain Active Security. We can finally present our active public key PCF for vector-OLE. The construction, called $\Pi_{\mathsf{VOLE}}^{\mathsf{Active}}$, is described in Fig. 7.

We prove that the pk-PCF protocol implements the random vector-OLE functionality $\mathcal{F}_{\mathsf{r\text{-}VOLE}}$ (see Fig. 8) in the UC model. $\mathcal{F}_{\mathsf{r\text{-}VOLE}}$ is a functionality that, during the initialisation, samples a random RSA modulo N and a value $x \in \mathbb{Z}_N$, which outputs to P_1. Upon any request for a vector-OLE tuple, the

Active PK-PCF for VOLE $\Pi_{\mathsf{VOLE}}^{\mathsf{Active}}$

Let F be a PRF. Let len_N denote the length of the Paillier modulo and let t, the order of the NIDLS group, be greater than $2^\lambda \cdot 2^{2\mathsf{len}_N} \cdot 2^{\lambda+\mathsf{len}_N}$.

INITIALISATION:

1. The parties initialise $\mathcal{F}_{\mathsf{NIDLS\text{-}ZK}}$ obtaining $\mathsf{par} := (\mathsf{par}', g, \rho_0, C, \rho_1)$.
2. The parties call $\mathcal{F}_{\mathsf{NIKE}}$ to obtain a PRF key k.
3. P_0 computes $(N, d) \xleftarrow{R} \mathsf{Paillier.Gen}(\mathbb{1}^\lambda)$ where $N = p \cdot q$.
4. P_1 samples $x \xleftarrow{R} [B]$ where $B := 2^{\lambda+\mathsf{len}_N}$.
5. P_0 samples $r_0 \xleftarrow{R} [\ell]$ and sets $D \leftarrow g^{r_0}$, $E \leftarrow f^d \cdot C^{r_0}$.
6. P_0 sends N, D, E.
7. P_1 samples $r_1 \xleftarrow{R} [\ell]$ and computes $A \leftarrow C^x \cdot g^{r_1}$
8. P_1 sends A.
9. The parties call $\mathcal{F}_{\mathsf{NIDLS\text{-}ZK}}$ with input $(\mathsf{Paillier}, D, E, N)$. P_0 inputs also (p, q, r_0). The parties abort if the functionality outputs 0 or if $N > 2^{\mathsf{len}_N}$.
10. The parties call $\mathcal{F}_{\mathsf{NIDLS\text{-}ZK}}$ with input (range, A, B). P_1 inputs also (x, r_1). The parties abort if the functionality outputs 0.
11. The parties query (A, D, E, N) to the random oracle and obtain a random $u \in \mathbb{Z}_t$ as a reply.
12. P_0 computes $v_0 \leftarrow \mathsf{DDLog}_{\mathsf{par}}(A^{r_0}) - u \bmod t$
13. P_1 computes $v_1 \leftarrow \mathsf{DDLog}_{\mathsf{par}}(D^{r_1} \cdot E^x) + u \bmod t$
14. P_0 stores $\mathsf{k}_0 \leftarrow (N, k, y_0 := -v_0, d)$.
15. P_1 stores $\mathsf{k}_1 \leftarrow (N, k, y_1 := v_1, x \bmod N)$.

EVALUATION: Query the label id to the oracle. Let $\mathsf{ct} \in \mathbb{Z}_{N^2}^\times$ be the response:

1. P_0 computes $a \leftarrow \mathsf{Paillier.Dec}(d, \mathsf{ct}) \bmod N$.
2. Each P_i computes $z_i \leftarrow (-1)^{1-i} \cdot \mathsf{DDLog}_{\mathsf{Paillier}}(\mathsf{ct}^{y_i}) + \mathsf{F}_k(\mathsf{ct}) \bmod N$.
3. P_0 outputs (a, z_0), P_1 outputs $(x \bmod N, z_1)$.

Fig. 7. Active public-key PCF for vector-OLE

functionality samples a random $a \in \mathbb{Z}_N$ and computes a subtractive secret-sharing of $z_1 - z_0 = a \cdot x$ over $\mathbb{Z}_N$. Then, $\mathcal{F}_{\mathsf{r\text{-}VOLE}}$ outputs (a, z_0) to P_0 and z_1 to P_1. If one of the parties is corrupted, the functionality let the adversary choose the outputs of the corrupt player, then it samples the outputs of the honest party at random conditioned on $z_1 = z_0 + a \cdot x$. Moreover, if P_0 is corrupted, the functionality lets the adversary select the RSA modulo N. When P_1 is corrupt, instead, $\mathcal{F}_{\mathsf{r\text{-}VOLE}}$ lets the adversary choose x after providing it with N.

The Resources. The protocol $\Pi_{\mathsf{VOLE}}^{\mathsf{Active}}$ relies on the non-interactive key-exchange functionality $\mathcal{F}_{\mathsf{NIKE}}$ (see Fig. 4) and a ZK functionality $\mathcal{F}_{\mathsf{NIDLS\text{-}ZK}}$ (see Fig. 9). The former provides the parties with a random PRF key $k \in \{0,1\}^\lambda$. When one of the parties is corrupt, the functionality lets the adversary choose k, forwarding

Function $\mathcal{F}_{\text{r-VOLE}}$

INITIALISATION:

- If both parties are honest, generate $(N, p, q) \xleftarrow{R} \mathsf{Paillier.Gen}(\mathbb{1}^\lambda)$ and sample $x \xleftarrow{R} \mathbb{Z}_N$.
- If P_0 is corrupt, wait for N from the adversary and sample $x \xleftarrow{R} \mathbb{Z}_N$. If the adversary sends $\perp$, abort.
- If P_1 is corrupt, generate $(N, p, q) \xleftarrow{R} \mathsf{Paillier.Gen}(\mathbb{1}^\lambda)$, send N to the adversary to the adversary and wait for $x \in \mathbb{Z}_N$ as a reply. If the adversary sends $\perp$, abort.

EVALUATION: On input a fresh label id from an honest party P_i.

- If both parties are honest, the functionality samples $a, z_0 \xleftarrow{R} \mathbb{Z}_N$ and sets $z_1 \leftarrow a \cdot x - z_0$. Then, it sets $R_0 \leftarrow (a, z_0)$ and $R_1 \leftarrow (x, z_1)$. $\mathcal{F}_{\text{r-VOLE}}$ outputs R_i to P_i and stores $(\mathsf{id}, 1-i, R_{1-i})$.
- If $i = 1$ and P_0 is corrupted, the functionality waits for $a, z_0 \in \mathbb{Z}_N$ from the adversary and sets $z_1 \leftarrow a \cdot x - z_0$. Then, it outputs (x, z_1) to P_i.
- If $i = 0$ and P_1 is corrupted, the functionality waits for $z_1 \in \mathbb{Z}_N$ from the adversary, samples $a \xleftarrow{R} \mathbb{Z}_N$ and computes $z_0 \leftarrow a \cdot x - z_1$. Then, it outputs (a, z_0) to P_i.

If id is not fresh, retrieve the triple (id, i, R_i) and output R_i to P_i.

Fig. 8. The random vector-OLE functionality

it to the honest party. It is possible to implement $\mathcal{F}_{\mathsf{NIKE}}$ in one round using NIKE constructions such as Diffie-Hellman, augmenting them with NIZKs to achieve security against an active adversary.

The functionality $\mathcal{F}_{\mathsf{NIDLS\text{-}ZK}}$ is instead used to prove statements for a fixed set of NP relations. We can assume that this set includes range proofs and $\mathcal{R}_{\mathsf{Paillier}}$. Upon initialisation, $\mathcal{F}_{\mathsf{NIDLS\text{-}ZK}}$ outputs the parameters of the NIDLS framework, including the random coins used for their generation. When $\mathcal{F}_{\mathsf{NIDLS\text{-}ZK}}$ is provided with a statement x for one of the supported NP relations, the functionality waits for the prover to provide the corresponding witness w. If the verification fails, $\mathcal{F}_{\mathsf{NIDLS\text{-}ZK}}$ outputs 0 to both parties, otherwise, it outputs 1. The functionality $\mathcal{F}_{\mathsf{NIDLS\text{-}ZK}}$ is also equipped with a different predicate for each supported NP-relation. Such predicate makes sure that the witness satisfies the properties for zero-knowledge. If that is not the case, the w is leaked to the adversary.

Note that Fiat-Shamir NIZKs, including the ones we designed, do not implement the functionality $\mathcal{F}_{\mathsf{NIDLS\text{-}ZK}}$ in the UC model. Indeed, in order to extract the witness w, we need to rewind the adversary and this operation is incompatible with UC. Using Fiat-Shamir NIZKs to implement $\mathcal{F}_{\mathsf{NIDLS\text{-}ZK}}$ is, however, a common practice, which is considered secure. Moreover, the resulting protocols

Function $\mathcal{F}_{\mathsf{NIDLS\text{-}ZK}}$

Let $\mathcal{U}$ be a finite set of NP relations. Let P_{L} be a predicate corresponding to the relation $\mathcal{R}_{\mathsf{L}} \in \mathcal{U}$.

INITIALISATION:

1. $\mathsf{par}' := (G, F, H, f, t, \ell, \mathsf{aux}) \xleftarrow{R} \mathsf{Gen}(1\!\!1^\lambda)$
2. $(g, \rho_0) \xleftarrow{R} \mathcal{D}(1\!\!1^\lambda, \mathsf{par})$
3. $(C, \rho_1) \xleftarrow{R} \mathcal{D}(1\!\!1^\lambda, \mathsf{par})$
4. If $C = g$, go to step 3.
5. Output $\mathsf{par} := (\mathsf{par}', g, \rho_0, C, \rho_1)$ to all the parties.

VERIFY:

On input an NP relation $\mathcal{R}_{\mathsf{L}} \in \mathcal{U}$ and a statement st from both parties and a witness w from only one of the parties, $\mathcal{F}_{\mathsf{NIDLS\text{-}ZK}}$ checks whether $(\mathsf{st}, w) \in \mathcal{R}_{\mathsf{L}}$. If that is the case, $\mathcal{F}_{\mathsf{NIDLS\text{-}ZK}}$ outputs 1 to all the parties, otherwise it outputs 0. If $P_{\mathsf{L}}(\mathsf{par}, w) = 0$, the functionality leaks w to the adversary.

Fig. 9. The NIDLS ZK functionality

can be proven secure in weaker models that allow sequential composability only. Finally, using standard techniques [DP92], it is still possible to adapt our NIZKs so that they implement $\mathcal{F}_{\mathsf{NIDLS\text{-}ZK}}$ in the UC model. The proof of the following theorem is in the full version of the paper [ADOS22, Section 7.3].

Theorem 6. *Let $\mathsf{len}_N(\lambda)$ be the length of the RSA modulo and assume that $t > 2^{2\lambda+3\mathsf{len}_N}$. Let F be a secure PRF outputting pseudorandom elements in $[2^{\lambda+\mathsf{len}_N}]$. If the DXDH assumption holds, the protocol $\Pi_{\mathsf{VOLE}}^{\mathsf{Active}}$ UC-implements the functionality $\mathcal{F}_{\mathsf{r\text{-}VOLE}}$ against an active adversary in the $(\mathcal{F}_{\mathsf{NIDLS\text{-}ZK}}, \mathcal{F}_{\mathsf{NIKE}})$-hybrid model with random oracle.*

Acknowledgments. The authors would like to thank Guilhem Castagnos and Fabien Laguillaumie for their crucial clarifications about the CL framework and class groups, Lasse Rønne Møller for important observations on the DXDH assumption and the anonymous reviewers for their feedback.

Research supported by: the Concordium Blockhain Research Center, Aarhus University, Denmark; the Carlsberg Foundation under the Semper Ardens Research Project CF18-112 (BCM); the European Research Council (ERC) under the European Unions's Horizon 2020 research and innovation programme under grant agreement No 803096 (SPEC); the Independent Research Fund Denmark (DFF) under project number 0165-00107B (C3PO); the Aarhus University Research Foundation; and the Defense Advanced Research Projects Agency (DARPA) under Contract No. HR001120C0085. Any opinions, findings and conclusions or recommendations expressed in this material are those of the author(s) and do not necessarily reflect the views of the Defense Advanced Research Projects Agency (DARPA). Distribution Statement "A" (Approved for Public Release, Distribution Unlimited).

References

[ADOS22] Abram, D., Damgård, I., Orlandi, C., Scholl, P.: An algebraic framework for silent preprocessing with trustless setup and active security. Cryptology ePrint Archive, Report 2022/363 (2022). https://eprint.iacr.org/2022/363

[BCG+17] Boyle, E., Couteau, G., Gilboa, N., Ishai, Y., Orrù, M.: Homomorphic secret sharing: optimizations and applications. In: ACM CCS 2017. ACM Press, October/November 2017

[BCG+19] Boyle, E., Couteau, G., Gilboa, N., Ishai, Y., Kohl, L., Scholl, P.: Efficient pseudorandom correlation generators: silent OT extension and more. In: Boldyreva, A., Micciancio, D. (eds.) CRYPTO 2019, Part III. LNCS, vol. 11694, pp. 489–518. Springer, Cham (2019). https://doi.org/10.1007/978-3-030-26954-8_16

[BGI16] Boyle, E., Gilboa, N., Ishai, Y.: Breaking the circuit size barrier for secure computation under DDH. In: Robshaw, M., Katz, J. (eds.) CRYPTO 2016, Part I. LNCS, vol. 9814, pp. 509–539. Springer, Heidelberg (2016). https://doi.org/10.1007/978-3-662-53018-4_19

[BHJL17] Benhamouda, F., Herranz, J., Joye, M., Libert, B.: Efficient cryptosystems from 2^k-th power residue symbols. J. Cryptol. **30**(2), 519–549 (2016). https://doi.org/10.1007/s00145-016-9229-5

[BKS19] Boyle, E., Kohl, L., Scholl, P.: Homomorphic secret sharing from lattices without FHE. In: Ishai, Y., Rijmen, V. (eds.) EUROCRYPT 2019, Part II. LNCS, vol. 11477, pp. 3–33. Springer, Cham (2019). https://doi.org/10.1007/978-3-030-17656-3_1

[CJLN09] Castagnos, G., Joux, A., Laguillaumie, F., Nguyen, P.Q.: Factoring pq^2 with quadratic forms: nice cryptanalyses. In: Matsui, M. (ed.) ASIACRYPT 2009. LNCS, vol. 5912, pp. 469–486. Springer, Heidelberg (2009). https://doi.org/10.1007/978-3-642-10366-7_28

[CKLR21] Couteau, G., Klooß, M., Lin, H., Reichle, M.: Efficient range proofs with transparent setup from bounded integer commitments. In: Canteaut, A., Standaert, F.-X. (eds.) EUROCRYPT 2021, Part III. LNCS, vol. 12698, pp. 247–277. Springer, Cham (2021). https://doi.org/10.1007/978-3-030-77883-5_9

[CL15] Castagnos, G., Laguillaumie, F.: Linearly homomorphic encryption from DDH. In: Nyberg, K. (ed.) CT-RSA 2015. LNCS, vol. 9048, pp. 487–505. Springer, Cham (2015). https://doi.org/10.1007/978-3-319-16715-2_26

[DF02] Damgård, I., Fujisaki, E.: A statistically-hiding integer commitment scheme based on groups with hidden order. In: Zheng, Y. (ed.) ASIACRYPT 2002. LNCS, vol. 2501, pp. 125–142. Springer, Heidelberg (2002). https://doi.org/10.1007/3-540-36178-2_8

[DJ01] Damgård, I., Jurik, M.: A generalisation, a simplification and some applications of Paillier's probabilistic public-key system. In: Kim, K. (ed.) PKC 2001. LNCS, vol. 1992, pp. 119–136. Springer, Heidelberg (2001). https://doi.org/10.1007/3-540-44586-2_9

[DJ03] Damgård, I., Jurik, M.: A length-flexible threshold cryptosystem with applications. In: Safavi-Naini, R., Seberry, J. (eds.) ACISP 2003. LNCS, vol. 2727, pp. 350–364. Springer, Heidelberg (2003). https://doi.org/10.1007/3-540-45067-X_30

[DP92] Santis, A.D., Persiano, G.: Zero-knowledge proofs of knowledge without interaction (extended abstract). In: 33rd FOCS. IEEE Computer Society Press, October 1992

[GMW86] Goldreich, O., Micali, S., Wigderson, A.: Proofs that yield nothing but their validity and a methodology of cryptographic protocol design (extended abstract). In: 27th FOCS. IEEE Computer Society Press, October 1986

[GMW87] Goldreich, O., Micali, S., Wigderson, A.: How to play any mental game or A completeness theorem for protocols with honest majority. In: 19th ACM STOC. ACM Press, May 1987

[Gro05] Groth, J.: Non-interactive zero-knowledge arguments for voting. In: Ioannidis, J., Keromytis, A., Yung, M. (eds.) ACNS 2005. LNCS, vol. 3531, pp. 467–482. Springer, Heidelberg (2005). https://doi.org/10.1007/11496137_32

[GRSB19] Goldberg, S., Reyzin, L., Sagga, O., Baldimtsi, F.: Efficient noninteractive certification of RSA moduli and beyond. In: Galbraith, S.D., Moriai, S. (eds.) ASIACRYPT 2019, Part III. LNCS, vol. 11923, pp. 700–727. Springer, Cham (2019). https://doi.org/10.1007/978-3-030-34618-8_24

[IPS08] Ishai, Y., Prabhakaran, M., Sahai, A.: Founding cryptography on oblivious transfer – efficiently. In: Wagner, D. (ed.) CRYPTO 2008. LNCS, vol. 5157, pp. 572–591. Springer, Heidelberg (2008). https://doi.org/10.1007/978-3-540-85174-5_32

[JL13] Joye, M., Libert, B.: Efficient cryptosystems from 2^k-th power residue symbols. In: Johansson, T., Nguyen, P.Q. (eds.) EUROCRYPT 2013. LNCS, vol. 7881, pp. 76–92. Springer, Heidelberg (2013). https://doi.org/10.1007/978-3-642-38348-9_5

[OSY21] Orlandi, C., Scholl, P., Yakoubov, S.: The Rise of Paillier: homomorphic secret sharing and public-key silent OT. In: Canteaut, A., Standaert, F.-X. (eds.) EUROCRYPT 2021, Part I. LNCS, vol. 12696, pp. 678–708. Springer, Cham (2021). https://doi.org/10.1007/978-3-030-77870-5_24

[Pai99] Paillier, P.: Public-key cryptosystems based on composite degree residuosity classes. In: Stern, J. (ed.) EUROCRYPT 1999. LNCS, vol. 1592, pp. 223–238. Springer, Heidelberg (1999). https://doi.org/10.1007/3-540-48910-X_16

[PT00] Paulus, S., Takagi, T.: A new public-key cryptosystem over a quadratic order with quadratic decryption time. J. Cryptol. **13**(2), 263–272 (2000). https://doi.org/10.1007/s001459910010

[RS21] Roy, L., Singh, J.: Large message homomorphic secret sharing from DCR and applications. In: Malkin, T., Peikert, C. (eds.) CRYPTO 2021, Part III. LNCS, vol. 12827, pp. 687–717. Springer, Cham (2021). https://doi.org/10.1007/978-3-030-84252-9_23

[Tuc20] Tucker, I.: Functional encryption and distributed signatures based on projective hash functions, the benefit of class groups. (Chiffrement fonctionnel et signatures distribuées fondés sur des fonctions de hachage à projection, l'apport des groupes de classe). Ph.D thesis, University of Lyon, France (2020)

Quadratic Multiparty Randomized Encodings Beyond Honest Majority and Their Applications

Benny Applebaum[1(✉)], Yuval Ishai[2], Or Karni[1], and Arpita Patra[3]

[1] Tel Aviv University, Tel Aviv, Israel
bennyap@post.tau.ac.il
[2] Technion, Haifa, Israel
yuvali@cs.technion.ac.il
[3] Indian Institute of Science, Bangalore, India
arpita@iisc.ac.in

Abstract. Multiparty randomized encodings (Applebaum, Brakerski, and Tsabary, SICOMP 2021) reduce the task of securely computing a complicated multiparty functionality f to the task of securely computing a simpler functionality g. The reduction is non-interactive and preserves information-theoretic security against a passive (semi-honest) adversary, also referred to as *privacy*. The special case of a degree-2 encoding g (2MPRE) has recently found several applications to secure multiparty computation (MPC) with either information-theoretic security or making black-box access to cryptographic primitives. Unfortunately, as all known constructions are based on information-theoretic MPC protocols in the plain model, they can only be private with an honest majority.

In this paper, we break the honest-majority barrier and present the first construction of general 2MPRE that remains secure in the presence of a dishonest majority. Our construction encodes every n-party functionality f by a 2MPRE that tolerates at most $t = \lfloor 2n/3 \rfloor$ passive corruptions.

We derive several applications including: (1) The first non-interactive client-server MPC protocol with perfect privacy against any coalition of a minority of the servers and up to t of the n clients; (2) Completeness of 3-party functionalities under non-interactive t-private reductions; and (3) A single-round t-private reduction from general-MPC to an ideal oblivious transfer (OT). These positive results partially resolve open questions that were posed in several previous works. We also show that t-private 2MPREs are necessary for solving (2) and (3), thus establishing new equivalence theorems between these three notions.

Finally, we present a new approach for constructing fully-private 2MPREs based on multi-round protocols in the OT-hybrid model that achieve *perfect privacy* against active attacks. Moreover, by slightly restricting the power of the active adversary, we derive an equivalence between these notions. This forms a surprising, and quite unique, connection between a non-interactive passively-private primitive to an interactive actively-private primitive.

Y. Dodis and T. Shrimpton (Eds.): CRYPTO 2022, LNCS 13510, pp. 453–482, 2022.
https://doi.org/10.1007/978-3-031-15985-5_16

1 Introduction

Information-theoretic secure multiparty computation (IT-MPC) deals with the problem of jointly computing a function over distributed inputs while providing information-theoretic privacy against an adversary that may corrupt a subset of the parties. IT-MPC has several important features. It does not rely on unproven intractability assumptions and does not depend on the computational power of the adversary. This notion also tends to provide clean frameworks (e.g., in the form of idealized models) for studying more complicated cryptographic questions without facing our ignorance regarding the nature of efficient computation. Moreover, apart from being a playground for basic theoretical feasibility results, IT-based solutions often lead to highly efficient protocols with a good concrete computational complexity. Finally, IT-MPC solutions typically form the basis for efficient computational MPC solutions that make a black-box use of cryptographic primitives.

In this paper, we consider several basic questions in the domain of IT-MPC and reveal new connections between them. By default, we consider n parties and assume that at most t of them can be passively corrupted by a (semi-honest) computationally unbounded adversary.[1] We refer to this as *t-privacy*. The following questions are open for any $t \geq n/2$.

MPC in the Client-Server Model. Suppose that $n \geq 2$ parties, called *clients*, wish to employ $m \geq 3$ external parties, called *servers*, in order to securely compute some (possibly complex) function of their inputs. We would like to obtain a non-interactive protocol in which each client sends a single message to each server, depending on its input and its local randomness, and gets a single message from each server in return without any additional interaction.

Question 1. Is there a non-interactive client-server MPC protocol with privacy against any (semi-honest) adversary who corrupts a minority of the m servers and up to t of the n clients?

This question dates back to the work of Barkol, Ishai and Weinreb [6], who noted that even the 3-server case is open. Earlier client-server protocols [15,22] only apply to the settings where less than *one third* of the servers (and $t < n$ clients) can be corrupted. The work of Applebaum, Brakerski and Tsabary [4] presented a client-server protocol that can tolerate any minority of corrupted servers,

[1] For simplicity, here and throughout the paper, we think of functionalities as finite objects and accordingly derive protocols and simulators with finite fixed complexity. All our statements carry over to the asymptotic setting (possibly with a tiny loss of the privacy threshold) and yield constructions whose complexity is polynomial in the size of the formulas (or branching program) of the underlying functionality. Furthermore, if one is willing to make a black-box use of a PRG and relax privacy to computational, these results also extend to size-s *circuits*, where the complexity is linear in s [8,15,32]. In fact, all these "liftings" can be done automatically by using appropriate completeness results from [2–4,22]. See the full version for details.

but at the expense of tolerating only $t < n/2$ corrupted clients. The case $t \geq n/2$ remains open. In this context, even a computationally-private solution with good concrete efficiency would be useful. However, the only known computationally-secure solution (which is in fact secure against an arbitrary strict subset of servers) makes a non-black-box use of OT. This solution is obtained by applying a general transformation from [19] to the 2-round (non-black-box) OT-based MPC protocols from [11,20].

Completeness of 3PC Under Non-interactive Reductions. Let us move to the standard model where no servers are available. Classical completeness results, by Yao [32] and Goldreich, Micali and Wigderson [21], show that, for an arbitrary corruption threshold $t \leq n$, the problem of securely computing a general n-party functionality t-privately reduces to the problem of securely computing the elementary finite 2-party *Oblivious Transfer* (OT) functionality [18,31]. The OT functionality takes a bit x from the Receiver and a pair of bits (m_0, m_1) from the Sender, and delivers to the Receiver the message m_x while hiding m_{1-x} from the Receiver and x from the Sender. In the 2-party setting, Yao's reduction [32] is completely non-interactive and makes only parallel invocations of an ideal OT-oracle without any further interaction. In the multiparty setting, known reductions are either interactive (i.e., make sequential calls to the OT) [21] or make a non-black-box use of the underlying OT [20], leading to computational security and to a large, typically impractical, computational overhead. In [3] it was shown that this limitation is inherent: No 2-party functionality can be complete under *round-preserving black-box* (RPBB) reductions. The same paper also established the completeness of 4-party functionalities, and stated the case of 3-party functionalities as an open question:

Question 2. What is the minimal primitive that is non-interactively complete for t-private MPC? Are 3-party functionalities complete?

The Round Complexity of Protocols Based on Ideal-OT. Let us move back to OT-based protocols. In light of the negative result of [3], it is natural to ask what is the best achievable round complexity given a black-box access to an OT oracle. A partial answer was recently given by Patra and Srinivasan [30] who showed that, given a black-box access to a 2-round OT protocol, general secure multiparty computation with full computational privacy ($t \leq n$) can be realized in 3 rounds. This result falls short of providing information-theoretic security and, more importantly, it strongly relies on an access to an OT *protocol.* Consequently, we do not know whether a 3-round protocol can be based on other realizations of 2-round OT such as ones that are based on physical means such as noisy channels or secure hardware, or on some limited form of a trusted party (e.g., [13,14,16,17,27,29]).[2] To capture such scenarios, we consider a refined version of the OT-hybrid model in which the OT takes 2 rounds. That is, if

[2] More generally, one may ask whether $k+1$ round protocols can be based on k-round OT, i.e., is it possible to obtain a *single-round reduction.* We focus on the minimal case of $k = 2$ for simplicity, though all our results actually hold for the general case.

both parties send their inputs to an OT in round i, the output is delivered to the receiver at the *end* of round $i + 1$. In addition, the parties are allowed to exchange messages via standard point-to-point private channels. We refer to this model as the *2-round OT hybrid* model.[3] (See Remark 10 for further discussion about the model). Refining an open question from [3], we ask

Question 3. What is the minimal number of rounds that are needed for t-private MPC in the 2-round OT hybrid model? Are 3-rounds achievable?

MPC with Active Perfect Privacy in the OT-hybrid Model. Let us change gears and move to the problem of perfect privacy under active attacks in the (standard) OT-hybrid model without putting any limitation on the round complexity. The results of Kilian [26] and Ishai, Prabhakaran, and Sahai [25] show that in this model one can achieve information-theoretic security with abort against a computationally unbounded adversary that corrupts an arbitrary subset of the parties. However, unlike the passive case, where one can achieve perfect simulation, current constructions suffer from a negligible statistical simulation error. It is known that one cannot simultaneously achieve perfect correctness and perfect privacy (aka perfect security) unless NP is contained in BPP (see, e.g., [23]). Still one can hope for a protocol that achieves *perfect privacy* against active attacks (i.e., a perfect simulation of the adversary's view) together with some weak form of correctness. Partial positive results are known for special classes of functionalities either in the correlated randomness setting [23] or in the 2-party setting [1]. Remarkably, for general functionalities the following basic question is wide open:

Question 4. Is general MPC feasible in the OT-hybrid model with perfect passive correctness and perfect active t-privacy feasible?

The difference between prefect privacy to statistical privacy is analogous to the difference between perfect zero-knowledge and statistical zero-knowledge. Furthermore, since the communication complexity grows logarithmically with the inverse error, perfectly-private protocols may lead to more economical solutions.

2MPREs Beyond Honest Majority. In the honest-majority setting ($t < n/2$), Questions 1–3 can be settled in the affirmative based on the existence of t-private

[3] In the terminology of [3] the reduction of Patra and Srinivasan [30] is a "free Black-Box" reduction, whereas the (2-round) OT hybrid model corresponds to so-called "strict Black-box reduction". To illustrate the distinction between the two notions, note that in a free-BB reduction, party A can, for example, generate several different "first messages" of the OT protocol, manipulate them (e.g., encrypt them) and deliver them to B or to a third party. Moreover, the 2nd part of these OT invocations can be later continued or withdrawn based on additional information (e.g., the inputs of B). In a strict BB reduction there is no notion of "first message" and the parties can only feed their inputs into the OT functionality and obtain the output. Thus a strict-BB reduction implies a free-BB reduction. See further discussion in [30].

quadratic *multiparty randomized encoding* (MPRE).[4] The MPRE notion was introduced in [4] as a multiparty generalization of the notion of randomized encoding of functions from [2,22]. Roughly speaking, a functionality f has a t-private quadratic-MPRE (2MPRE) if the task of securely-computing f non-interactively reduces to a single call to a degree-2 functionality g via a t-private information-theoretic reduction. In [4] it was shown that every functionality can be realized by an honest-majority 2MPREs. Other constructions were also given in [19,28]. All these constructions are essentially based on plain-model MPC protocols and are therefore limited to the honest-majority setting. In an attempt to understand whether this limitation is inherent, we ask:

Question 5 ([4]). Is t-private 2MPRE feasible with $t > n/2$?

2 Our Results

We construct new 2MPREs and derive new connections between Questions 1–5.

2.1 New 2MPREs Beyond Honest-Majority

We present the first construction of perfect 2MPRE that achieves privacy against coalitions of size at most $\lfloor 2n/3 \rfloor$.

Theorem 1 (main theorem). *Every n-party functionality can be perfectly realized by $\lfloor 2n/3 \rfloor$-private 2MPRE.*

The theorem "separates" the model of 2MPRE from plain-model MPC, demonstrating the power of the former. We will later discuss the implications of Theorem 1. For now observe that for 3-party functionalities the theorem provides privacy against coalitions of size at most 2. Since privacy against 3-party functionalities vacuously hold, we derive the following corollary.

Corollary 1 (2MPRE for 3PC). *Every 3-party functionality can be perfectly realized by a 3-private 2MPRE.*

Note that any tiny improvement to Theorem 1, e.g., from $\lfloor 2n/3 \rfloor$-privacy to $\lceil 2n/3 \rceil$-privacy would allow us to obtain fully-private MPRE for 4-party functionalities. Since 4-party functionalities are known to be complete under non-interactive reductions [3], such an improvement would immediately yield n-private 2MPREs for any n-party functionality! Thus, the $\lfloor 2n/3 \rfloor$ bound is a natural intermediate point between the case of full corruption $t = n$ and the honest-majority setting $t < n/2$. This puts 2MPRE somewhere between the OT-hybrid model, in which n-privacy can be achieved, to the plain model that is restricted to $(n-1)/2$-privacy.

[4] To the best of our knowledge, for Question 4, no solution is known beyond the trivial case of $t < n/3$ in which perfect active security can be achieved in the plain model [10].

Indeed, while proving Theorem 1, we show that 2MPREs are equivalent to an MPC model where the parties are allowed to communicate via private point-to-point channels for an arbitrary number of rounds and at the end are allowed to make a single call to a degree-2 functionality. If we remove this last round, we get the standard plain model and if we allow to call degree-2 functionalities in every round we get the standard OT-hybrid model. In fact, by preprocessing OTs [7], the OT-hybrid model is equivalent to a model where all the OT-calls are performed in the first round and all other rounds use private point-to-point channels. Thus, the "only difference" between the 2MPRE model and the OT-hybrid model is whether the degree-2 functionality is being invoked before the plain-model sub-protocol or after it.

2.2 Equivalences and Implications

Theorem 1 implies affirmative answers to Questions 2 and 3 with $t = \lfloor 2n/3 \rfloor$. We prove that 2MPREs are also necessary for the resolution of these questions.

Theorem 2 (Necessity of 2MPRE). *The following holds for every n-party functionality f and privacy threshold $1 \leq t \leq n$.*

1. *If f non-interactively t-privately reduces to some 3-party functionality, then f has a t-private 2MPRE.*
2. *If f can be t-privately computed in 3 rounds in the 2-round OT hybrid model, then f has a t-private 2MPRE.*

The results of [3] imply that if f has t-private 2MPREs then it non-interactively t-privately reduces to the following 3-party variant of OT (hereafter referred to as TOT). Given a pair of bits (x_1, y_1) from Alice, and a pair of bits (x_2, y_2) from Bob, the functionality delivers to Carol the value $x_1x_2 + y_1 + y_2$ where addition and multiplication are computed over the binary field. Alice and Bob receive no output.[5] TOT takes its input from only 2 parties and deliver it to the third party and so it can be seen as an extremely simple variant of a 3-party functionality. Nevertheless, by combining Theorem 2 with the above implication, we conclude that TOT is complete for 3-party functionalities. Finally, we observe that TOT can be easily computed in 3 rounds in the 2-round OT hybrid model (see Sect. 6). We therefore derive the following equivalence.

Corollary 2. *Let f be an n-party functionality and let $1 \leq t \leq n$ be some integers. The following statements are equivalent:*

1. *f can be realized by t-private 2MPRE.*
2. *f non-interactively t-privately reduces to TOT.*
3. *f non-interactively t-privately reduces to some 3-party functionality.*
4. *f can be t-privately computed in 3 rounds in the 2-round OT hybrid model.*

[5] We refer to this as "3-party OT" since the 2-party version of this functionality, where the output is delivered to, say, Alice, is essentially equivalent to the standard 1-out-of-2 OT.

The theorem yields an equivalence between Questions 2, 3 and 5. This equivalence is fairly strong: it holds for each functionality separately and carries to the statistical setting as well while preserving correctness and privacy errors.

The Client-Server Model. Let us get back to the client-server model (Question 1). It was shown in [4] that t-private 2MPREs imply non-interactive t-private client-server protocols. As an immediate corollary of Theorem 1, we derive the following statement.

Corollary 3. *Every n-party functionality has a non-interactive client-server MPC with privacy against any coalition that consists of a minority of the m servers and up to $\lfloor 2n/3 \rfloor$ of the n clients. For the case of 3 clients, we derive privacy against an arbitrary (mixed) coalition of clients and a minority of the servers.*

Being an information-theoretic protocol, our construction is fairly efficient and may turn to be useful in 3PC applications.

2.3 2MPREs vs Active Perfect-Privacy

In an attempt to obtain better 2MPREs with privacy threshold larger than $\lfloor 2n/3 \rfloor$, we reveal a new connection to the problem of achieving perfect-privacy under active attacks (Question 4). Specifically, we show that any protocol in the OT-hybrid model with perfect t-privacy under active attacks and passive perfect (or statistical) correctness can be turned into a t-private 2MPRE with statistical correctness error. We find this implication quite surprising; the protocol is an actively-secure primitive with no round-complexity requirements, whereas the 2MPRE is a passively-secure object whose main feature is low interaction. In fact, by weakening the notion of active attacks we derive a surprising equivalence between these 2 objects. Loosely speaking, we consider a *weakly-active* adversary that corrupts a subset T of the parties and deviates from the protocol as follows: For every OT-call between two corrupted parties, the adversary is allowed to replace the receiver's received message m with some arbitrary value m'. Once this value is replaced, the adversary must consistently use this fake value according to the instructions of the protocol. For example, if the protocol instructs the receiver to pass m to all the parties, then the adversary passes m' to all the parties. (See Sect. 7 for a formal definition.)

We prove the following theorem.

Theorem 3. *Let f be an n-party public-output functionality and let $0 \leq t \leq n$ be an arbitrary privacy threshold. The functionality f has a protocol in the OT-hybrid model with statistical (passive) correctness and t-perfect privacy against weakly-active adversaries if and only if f has a t-private 2MPRE with statistical correctness error.*

The error can be reduced to an arbitrarily small ϵ with $O(\log(1/\epsilon))$ overhead via standard error-reduction techniques. A public-output functionality is a functionality that delivers the same output to all the parties; it is known that general functionalities can be reduced to public-output functionalities via a non-interactive reduction.

Note that in the honest-majority setting, any protocol with perfect passive t-privacy is also t-perfectly private against a weakly-active adversary (since there are no calls to OT). In this setting, Theorem 3 yields a new alternative construction of 2MPREs. In fact, as a by-product, we derive a new completeness result in the honest-majority setting.

Theorem 4 (completeness of $\mathsf{AND} \circ \mathsf{EQ}$ for honest majority). *In the honest majority setting, every n-party functionality f non-interactively reduces to multiple parallel calls to $\mathsf{AND} \circ \mathsf{EQ}$ functionality. The reduction has perfect privacy and an arbitrarily small 1-sided statistical correctness error.*

For parameters ℓ and k, the predicate $\mathsf{AND} \circ \mathsf{EQ}$ takes ℓ pairs of k-bit strings, computes for each pair an equality bit v_i that determines whether the ith pair is equal, and outputs the logical AND of all the bits $v_1, \ldots, v_\ell$. Specifically, we allocate a single equality for each pair of parties (i.e., $\ell = \binom{n}{2}$).

Features of the $\mathsf{AND} \circ \mathsf{EQ}$ *Predicate.* Since $\mathsf{EQ}(x, y) = \bigwedge_i (x_i \oplus \bar{y}_i)$, the $\mathsf{AND} \circ \mathsf{EQ}$ predicate can be replaced by a conjunction of *parities* of *pairs* of bits. Another feature of this predicate is the following physical implementation: suppose each pair of parties are connected by pipes (alternatively, electrical wires), one for each comparison of two bits held by these parties. For each pipe (wire), one can ensure that water (electricity) flows through only if equality holds. For instance, an input bit may determine the position of a switch, where the two switches need to be aligned to enable flow. Finally, connecting all pipes via an Euler path, the output of the $\mathsf{AND} \circ \mathsf{EQ}$ predicate corresponds to whether or not the flow gets through the system.

2.4 Techniques

To illustrate some of our techniques, let us focus on the 2MPRE construction and on the implications of protocols that achieve perfect-privacy under active attacks.

Constructing 2MPREs. Our new construction (Theorem 1) is based on two components. First, we introduce a new round-collapsing lemma that turns a 2-round protocol that satisfies some "nice" form into a 2MPRE. Then, we design a nice protocol with $\lceil 2n/3 \rceil$-privacy and collapse it into a 2MPRE. Let us elaborate on these steps.

Round-Collapsing Lemma. Recall that a 2MPRE can be viewed as a non-interactive protocol that makes only parallel calls to some degree-2 functionalities (WLOG, we may use only TOT calls). Consider the seemingly more liberal model where the parties are allowed to make a single round of communication over private point-to-point channels before calling the TOT functionalities. We prove that such a *nice* protocol π can be turned into a 2MPRE. To explain the high-level idea, let us assume that the protocol π makes a single call to TOT where A and B are the senders with inputs f and g, respectively, and C receives $\mathsf{TOT}(f, g)$. The messages f and g are computed based on first-round messages that were sent to A and B during the first round by all the parties $P_1, \ldots, P_n$. Denote by $a = (a_1, \ldots, a_n)$ and $b = (b_1, \ldots, b_n)$ the vectors of these first-round messages. Our goal is to replace the second-round call to TOT with many first-round calls to TOT. All these TOTs are delivered to the receiver C and the pair of senders range over all possible pairs of the form (A, B), (A, P_i) or (B, P_i). Let us imagine, for a moment, that the original TOT computation $\mathsf{TOT}(f, g)$ is replaced with some multi-output function $H(f, g)$ in which each output depends on a single bit either of f or of g. Moreover, let us assume that each bit of $f = f(a)$ and $g = g(b)$ depends on a single bit of the input. In this case, each output of H depends on some message, a_i or b_i, that some P_i have sent in the first round. Therefore, the corresponding bit of H could be delivered to C directly at the first round by some party P_i. Of course, we cannot really hope for such single-bit dependencies. Instead, we replace each of the above computation with a fully-decomposable randomized encoding [2,22]. Such an encoding preserves the original information while maintaining privacy, at the expense of using some secret randomness. The crucial observation is that in our case the randomness can be chosen either jointly by A and B (for randomizing the TOT part), or solely by A (for randomizing the f part) or solely by B (for randomizing the g part). This is due to the fact that we do not need to hide f (resp., g) from A (resp., B). Overall, this allows us to collapse the computation to first-round calls to multiple 2-party functionalities.[6] The latter can be trivially encoded by 2MPRE, which, by a proper form of composition, leads to 2MPRE for the entire computation. For full details see Lemma 1 and its proof. By applying the reduction repeatedly, one can turn a multi-round plain-model protocol whose last round makes calls to degree-2 ideal functionalities into a 2MPRE, establishing the equivalence of these 2 models. The round-preserving lemma plays a central role in our constructions as well as in our negative results about the necessity of 2MPREs.

Nice Protocols. Equipped with the round-collapsing lemma, we explore the power of nice protocols. To illustrate the power of the model, let us start by observing

[6] A related observation is in the heart of other recent round reduction techniques [4,11,20], though we do not see a way to obtain our result based on their techniques. Specifically, [11,20] makes a non-black-box use of OTs and [4] exploit the specific properties of Yao's based randomized encodings. In particular, the latter result does not seem to extend to arithmetic protocols while our result does.

that for degree-3 computation (which is known to be complete [22]), the passive honest-majority version of the BGW protocol [10] gives rise to a nice protocol! In the standard description of the protocol, in (R1) the parties secret share their inputs, then the parties multiply their shares locally and (R2) apply a round of degree-reduction, then the parties apply another local multiplication and (R3) publish the randomized shares. Since degree reduction is a linear operation one can replace the last 2 rounds (including the second local multiplication) with a call to a degree-2 functionality, and derive a "nice" protocol. The resulting construction can be viewed as an abstract version of a recent algebraic construction of honest-majority arithmetic 2MPREs [28]. The round-collapsing lemma allows us to derive this result immediately in a conceptually clean way.

Observe that the BGW-based 2MPRE works even if the ideal degree-2 functionality is only private against a corrupted minority. Put differently, we did not use the full power of the degree-2 oracle that provides *privacy against an arbitrary coalition*. Our result for $t = \lfloor 2n/3 \rfloor$ is derived by making a stronger use of this resource. Following BGW, we dedicate the first round to input sharing, except that this time we use a CNF-based secret sharing scheme. That is, we additively share each input into $\binom{n}{t}$ shares where each share corresponds to some "unauthorized" t-subset T of the parties, and hand the corresponding share to all parties outside T. Now a degree-3 computation boils down to a sum of degree-3 monomials over the additive shares. A threshold of $t = \lfloor 2n/3 \rfloor - 1$ guarantees that for each monomial there must exists a party who holds 2 variables of the monomials. (A slightly modified version yields $t = \lfloor 2n/3 \rfloor$). By locally computing these values, we can realize the remaining parts via a call to a degree-2 functionality. See Sect. 5. We note that a similar degree-reduction technique was previously used in the contexts of communication complexity [5] and information-theoretic private information retrieval [9]. The current application is unique in that it applies this technique in the context of *feasibility* rather than *efficiency*.

2MPREs from Perfect Active Privacy. Consider the following MPC-in-the-head type approach [24,25] for transforming a plain-model (passively) t-private protocol π to a t-private 2MPRE. Each party P_i samples locally a random tape and guesses randomly a sequence of incoming messages. Then P_i computes, based on this random view, the vector of outgoing messages that should be sent in π given this view. Finally, P_i sends her guesses for the incoming messages together with the computed outgoing messages to an ideal functionality V. The functionality V checks that the local views match; namely, that each guessed incoming message is equal to the corresponding outgoing message. If all these tests pass, V returns the output of the protocol (assume wlog that this output appears in the transcript), say to all the parties. Otherwise, V outputs zero.

It can be shown that the resulting protocol σ is perfectly private. Correctness holds when all the guesses succeed which happens with probability 2^{-c} where c is the communication complexity of π. Since privacy is perfect we can arbitrarily reduce the correctness error via repetition. The ideal functionality V can be written as a conjunction of Equality tests. Since Equality of two bits is a linear function over $\mathbb{F}_2$, and since AND has a degree-2 RE (with statistical correctness error), V can be replaced with a degree-2 functionality. By instantiating π with a perfect plain-model honest majority protocol (e.g., BGW) we obtain another construction of honest-majority 2MPRE, this time with a statistical correctness error. (Note that so far π is only required to be passively private).

In order to obtain an MPRE in the honest-minority setting, we start with a protocol π that operates in the OT-hybrid model and add pair-wise consistency checks over OT values. That is, each party guesses the incoming messages and incoming OT messages and computes the corresponding outgoing messages and OT-inputs. Now V verifies that the local views are pair-wise consistent. Unfortunately, an OT consistency check corresponds to a quadratic relation. Since these tests are being fed into a degree-2 function (the randomized encoding of AND), we get a degree-3 encoding of V. We bypass the problem by letting the pair of parties that use the OT call to locally sample part of the randomness of the RE. This allows us to reduce the degree at the expense of leaking some information about the inputs of V. We show that this leakage can still be simulated if the original protocol π is weakly-active perfectly private. See Sect. 7 for more details.

Organization. Following some preliminaries in Sect. 3, we relate 2MPREs to non-interactive protocols in the TOT-hybrid model and prove the round-collapsing lemma in Sect. 4. We present our main construction in Sect. 5, and dedicate Sect. 6 to the equivalence between 2MPREs and protocols in the 2-round-OT hybrid model. Finally, in Sect. 7, we establish the equivalence between 2MPREs and perfect privacy under weakly-active attacks. Due to space limitations some of the proofs are deferred to the full version.

3 Preliminaries

We assume familiarity with standard MPC definitions. Some background is omitted and can be found in the full version. We will extensively use randomized encoding (RE) of functions and multiparty randomized encoding as means for transforming and manipulating protocols.

Definition 1 (Randomized Encoding of functions [22]**).** *Let $f : X \to Y$ be a function. We say that a function $\widehat{f} : X \times R \to Z$ is a δ-correct and ϵ-private* randomized encoding *(RE) of f if the following holds:*

- *(δ-correctness) There exists a randomized algorithm* Dec *such that for every input $x \in X$,*

$$\Pr_{r \leftarrow R}\left[\mathsf{Dec}(\widehat{f}(x;r)) \neq f(x)\right] \leq \delta$$

- *(ϵ-privacy) There exists a randomized algorithm* Sim *such that for every $x \in X$, the distributions*

$$\mathsf{Sim}\left(f(x)\right) \quad \text{and} \quad \widehat{f}(x;r), \qquad \text{where } r \leftarrow R,$$

are ϵ-close in statistical distance.

By default, we assume that both correctness and privacy are perfect, *i.e.,* ϵ *and* δ *are both zero.*

By default, the set X (resp., R, Z) is a set of strings of some fixed length. An RE, $\widehat{f}$, is *fully decomposable* if each of its outputs $\widehat{f}_i(x;r)$ depends on at most a single input bit of x. The encoding $\widehat{f}$ has degree d if each of its outputs can be written as a degree-d polynomial over a field $\mathbb{F}$ (by default the binary field). If $X = \mathbb{F}^n, R = \mathbb{F}^\rho$ and $Z = \mathbb{F}^s$, then each output $\widehat{f}_i(x,r)$ can be written as a degree-d polynomial in the inputs $(x_1, \ldots, x_n, r_1, \ldots, r_\rho)$. The encoding is d-local if each output depends on at most d inputs $(x_1, \ldots, x_n, r_1, \ldots, r_\rho)$. The *complexity* of an encoding $\widehat{f}$ is s if the encoding can be computed, simulated, and decoded by s-size circuits. In the asymptotic setting, when f is treated as a polynomial-time uniform family of circuits, s is required to be polynomial-time bounded and the circuits for encoding, decoding and simulating should all be uniform. All known RE constructions satisfy these properties.

Functionalities. An n-party functionality is a function that maps the inputs of n parties to a vector of outputs that are distributed among the parties. Without loss of generality, we assume that the inputs and outputs of each party are taken from some fixed input and output domains X and Y (e.g., bit strings of fixed length). We will also make use of *randomized functionalities.* In this case, we let f take an additional random input r_0 that is chosen uniformly from some finite domain R, and view r_0 as an internal source of randomness that does not belong to any party. We typically write $f(x_1, \ldots, x_n; r_0)$ and use semicolon to separate the inputs of the parties from the internal randomness of the functionality.

Definition 2 (Multiparty Randomized Encoding (MPRE) [4]**).** *Let* $f : X^n \rightarrow Y^n$ *be an* n*-party functionality. We say that an* n*-party randomized functionality* $\widehat{f} : (X \times R)^n \times R \rightarrow Z^n$ *is a* multiparty randomized encoding *of* f *if the following holds:*

- *(δ-correctness): There exists a decoder* Dec *such that for every party* $i \in [n]$*, and every input* $x = (x_1, \ldots, x_n)$ *it holds that*

$$\Pr_{(r_0,r_1,\ldots,r_n)\leftarrow R^{n+1}} [\mathsf{Dec}(i, \widehat{y}[i], x_i, r_i) = y[i]] \leq \delta,$$

  where $y = f(x_1, \ldots, x_n), \widehat{y} = \widehat{f}((x_1, r_1), \ldots, (x_n, r_n); r_0)$*, and* $y[i]$ *and* $\widehat{y}[i]$ *are the restrictions of* y *and* $\widehat{y}$ *to the coordinates delivered to party* i *by* f *and* $\widehat{f}$*, respectively.*
- *((t, ϵ)-privacy): There exists a randomized simulator* Sim *such that for every* t*-subset* $T \subseteq [n]$ *of parties and every set of inputs* $x = (x_1, \ldots, x_n)$ *it holds that the distributions*

$$\mathsf{Sim}(T, x[T], y[T]), \quad \textit{where } y = f(x_1, \ldots, x_n)$$

and the distributions

$$(x[T], r[T], \widehat{y}[T])$$

where

$$\widehat{y} = \widehat{f}((x_1, r_1), \ldots, (x_n, r_n); r_0), \text{ and } (r_0, r_1, \ldots, r_n) \leftarrow R^{n+1}$$

are ϵ-close in statistical distance.

We say that $\widehat{f}$ is perfectly correct *if it has δ-correctness for $\delta = 0$, and* perfectly t-private *if it has (t, ϵ)-privacy for $\epsilon = 0$. We say that $\widehat{f}$ is* t-private *if it is both perfectly correct and perfectly t-private.*

Definition 3 (Effective degree and 2MPRE). *A (possibly randomized) n-party functionality $f : X^n \times R \to \{0,1\}^m$ has effective degree d if there exist a tuple of local preprocessing functions $(h_1, \ldots, h_n)$ and a degree-d function h such that*

$$h\,(h_1(x_1), \ldots, h_n(x_n); r) = f(x_1, \ldots, x_n; r),$$

for every input $x_1, \ldots, x_n$ and internal randomness r.

A functionality f has a t-private quadratic MPRE (2MPRE) if it has a t-private MPRE with an effective degree of 2. Unless stated otherwise, we assume, by default, that the privacy and correctness errors are zero.

If f has a t-private 2MPRE $h\,(h_1(x_1), \ldots, h_n(x_n); r)$ then it can be computed by a non-interactive t-private reduction: First, the ith party locally computes h_i on her input and random tape; then she sends the result to the degree-2 functionality h; and finally she locally computes her output by using the MPRE decoder. In fact, the converse direction also holds, and so f has a t-private 2MPRE if and only if it reduces to a degree 2 functionality g via a non-interactive t-private reduction that makes a single call to g.[7] Despite this equivalence, the MPRE abstraction will be useful as it will allow us to conveniently manipulate protocols and gradually turn them into 2MPREs. Specifically, we will often use the composition lemma [4, Lemma 3.3] that asserts that if f is encoded by an MPRE g, and g is encoded by an MPRE h then h encodes f. Finally, let us make the following simple, yet useful, observation. (The proof appears in the full version).

Observation 5. *Let f be a 3-party functionality that takes its input from only 2 parties (aka 2-input functionality). Then, f has a 3-private 2MPRE.*

4 2MPRE and TOT-hybrid Model

The TOT-hybrid Model. A protocol in the TOT-hybrid model consists of black-box calls to the TOT functionality. We assume that each 3-tuple of parties

[7] The requirement for a single call is without loss of generality in the semi-honest setting, since multiple parallel calls can be packed in a single call.

(A, B, C) can make a call to an ideal TOT functionality $\mathsf{TOT} : \{0,1\}^2 \times \{0,1\}^2 \times \{\bot\} \to \{\bot\} \times \{\bot\} \times \{0,1\}$ where

$$\mathsf{TOT}\big((x_1, y_1), (x_2, y_2), \bot\big) = (\bot, \bot, x_1 x_2 + y_1 + y_2).$$

By letting $A = C$ or $A = B$ respectively, TOT calls can emulate OT calls as well as 2-wise private channels. Still, it will be sometimes convenient to make explicit use of private point-to-point channels. We will mainly be interested in non-interactive protocols in this model where the parties make a single round of parallel calls to the TOT functionality.

The following claim can be derived from [3] who studied a close variant of TOT known as (2, 3)-MULTPlus. (See the full version for a proof).

Claim 6. *If a functionality F has a t-private 2MPRE then it has a t-private non-interactive protocol in the TOT-hybrid model.*

The converse direction trivially holds since by definition, a non-interactive protocol in the TOT-hybrid model is also a non-interactive reduction to a degree-2 functionality. The following lemma provides a stronger converse: It shows that a 2MPRE can be derived even if we start from a 2-round protocol in the TOT-hybrid model whose first round only consists of private messages (carried over private point-to-point channels) and its second rounds consists of parallel calls to the TOT functionality.

Lemma 1 (Collapsing a round in TOT-hybrid model). *Suppose that the n-party functionality f can be realized by a t-private protocol π in the TOT-hybrid model whose first round only consists of private messages (carried over private point-to-point channels) and its second round consists of parallel calls to the TOT functionality. Then f has a t-private 2MPRE f'. Moreover, f can be realized by a t-private non-interactive protocol σ in the TOT-hybrid model. The transformation holds even if π has a correctness error or a privacy error while preserving these errors.*

Before proving the lemma, we note that once we can collapse a single plain-model round, we can also collapse multiple plain-model rounds. Specifically,

Corollary 4 (Collapsing multiple rounds in TOT-hybrid model). *Suppose that the n-party functionality f can be realized by a t-private multi-round protocol π in the TOT-hybrid model that makes TOT calls only in the last round (all other rounds are in the plain model). Then f has a t-private 2MPRE f'. Moreover, f can be realized by a t-private non-interactive protocol σ in the TOT-hybrid model. The transformation holds even if π has a correctness error or a privacy error while preserving these errors.*

The proof is deferred to the full version. We move on and prove Lemma 1.

Proof (Proof of Lemma 1). Let $f : X^n \to \{0,1\}^m$ be an n-party functionality, and let π be δ-correct (t, ϵ)-private protocol in the TOT-hybrid model whose first-round only consists of private messages and its second-round consists of parallel calls to the TOT functionality. For each call to the TOT functionality with parties $A \in \mathcal{P}$ and $B \in \mathcal{P}$ and receiver $C \in \mathcal{P}$, the protocol π can be viewed as computing the following functionality o:

- Each party P_i locally computes messages a_i and b_i based on its private input and randomness and sends a_i to A and b_i to B. As part of this step, A (resp., B) sends her private input/randomness to herself.
- The receiver C gets the TOT output
$$\mathsf{TOT}((f_0(a), f_1(a)), (g_0(b), g_1(b))),$$
where $a = (a_i)_{i \in [n]}$ and $b = (b_i)_{i \in [n]}$ and f_0, f_1, g_0, g_1 are some Boolean functions. (In π the party A computes f_0 and f_1 locally and the party B locally computes the functions g_0, g_1).

To prove the lemma it suffices to encode the functionality o by a perfect MPRE of effective degree-2. To gain some intuition, imagine the case where a and b are selected by A and B, respectively. Then the output that is delivered to C is a 2-party functionality that depends only on values that can be computed by either A or B. Such a function trivially has an effective degree of 2 as per Observation 5. Our setting is slightly more involved: While some inputs are neither chosen by A nor by B, each of these inputs is being leaked either to A or to B. We show that in this case one can still obtain a 2MPRE.

As our first step, we construct an MPRE for o based on degree-3 RE as follows. Let $\widehat{o}(a, b; r)$ be the standard degree-3 fully-decomposable RE from [2,22] where $r = (r_1, \dots, r_m)$ is the internal randomness of the RE. Consider the functionality $\widehat{o}_1$ in which party A randomly samples $\alpha = (\alpha_i)_{i \in [m]}$, party B randomly samples $\beta = (\beta_i)_{i \in [m]}$, and party P_i locally computes a_i and b_i as before. The functionality $\widehat{o}_1$ delivers the value
$$\widehat{o}(a, b; \alpha + \beta)$$
to C and the vector a to A and b to B. We claim that $\widehat{o}_1$ is an MPRE of o. Indeed, correctness follows from the correctness of the RE. As for privacy, fix a set $T \subseteq [n]$ that contains the receiver C (if $C \notin T$ simulation is trivial). Observe that if A or B are not in T, then privacy follows from the privacy of the RE (since, conditioned on the view of the parties in T, the distribution of C's output in $\widehat{o}_1$ is identical to the distribution of $\widehat{o}(a, b; \alpha + \beta)$). Finally, if both A and B are in T, then simulating C's output is trivial since we have both a and b as part of T's view in o.

Next, our goal is to construct a 2MPRE for $\widehat{o}_1$. First, let us take a step backward and recall that the degree-3 RE $\widehat{o}(a, b; r)$ is so-called *fully-decomposable* RE, which means that each of its outputs is either a degree-2 function (of the form $r_i + r_j + r_k$ or $r_i r_j + r_k$ or $x_i r_i + r_j$) or an expression of the form
$$x r_j r_k + r_\ell$$
where x is either a_i, b_i or r_i and r_i, r_j, r_k, r_ℓ are part of the internal random bits $r = (r_1, \dots, r_m)$ of the RE. Recalling that $r = \alpha + \beta$, observe that each output bit that $\widehat{o}_1$ delivers to C is of the form

$$x(\alpha_j+\beta_j)(\alpha_k+\beta_k)+(\alpha_\ell+\beta_\ell) = x\alpha_j\alpha_k+x\alpha_j\beta_k+x\beta_j\alpha_k+x\beta_j\beta_k+(\alpha_\ell+\beta_\ell) \quad (1)$$

where x is either a_i, b_i or $\alpha_i + \beta_i$. Let us start by breaking this sum to separate monomials. That is, we define the functionality $\widehat{o}_2$ that operates identically to $\widehat{o}_1$ except that each bit in (1) that $\widehat{o}_1$ delivers to C is replaced with the tuple

$$(x\alpha_j\alpha_k + s_1, x\alpha_j\beta_k + s_2, x\beta_j\alpha_k + s_3, x\beta_j\beta_k + (\alpha_\ell + \beta_\ell) - (s_1 + s_2 + s_3)) \quad (2)$$

where s_1, s_2 and s_3 are uniform bits that are sampled as part of the internal randomness of the functionality $\widehat{o}_2$.[8] The tuple in (2) is a tuple of 4 random bits whose sum equals to (1). Therefore, (2) perfectly encodes (1) and so $\widehat{o}_2$ perfectly encodes $\widehat{o}_1$.

Observe that the first entry of (2) has an effective degree of 2 since A can precompute $\alpha_j \cdot \alpha_k$. Similarly, the last entry has an effective degree 2 since B can precompute $\beta_j \cdot \beta_k$. Moreover if $x = \alpha_i + \beta_i$ then the second and third entries of (2) have also an effective degree of 2. It remains to handle the second and third entries in the case where x is either a_i or b_i. Let us focus on the second entry and assume that $x = a_i$ (the other cases are handled similarly). Consider the functionality $\widehat{o}_3$ that is identical to $\widehat{o}_2$ except that instead of delivering the second entry of (2) to C we deliver to C the tuple

$$(a_i + \alpha', \alpha_j\beta_k + s', a_i s' + \alpha'\alpha_j\beta_k + \alpha' s' - s_2)\,. \quad (3)$$

Here s' is sampled as part of the internal randomness of the functionality, and, crucially, α' is sampled uniformly by A. Therefore, (3) has an effective degree of 2. We claim that $\widehat{o}_3$ perfectly encodes $\widehat{o}_2$. Indeed, given an output (y_1, y_2, y_3) of (3), we can decode the second entry of (2) by outputting the value $y_1 y_2 - y_3$. As for privacy, consider a set $T \subsetneq [n]$ and assume that $C \in T$ (again the other case is trivial). If $A \notin T$, then simulation is simple: given y, the second entry of (2), sample y_1, y_2 uniformly at random and set $y_3 = y_1 y_2 - y$. If $A \in T$, then the simulator is given y,a_i and α' as part of A's private tape, accordingly we set $y_1 = a_i + \alpha'$, sample y_2 uniformly and set $y_3 = y_1 y_2 - y$. It is not hard to verify that the simulation is perfect.

By handling the third entry of (2) similarly, we derive an MPRE of effective degree 2 that encodes $\widehat{o}_2$. By the MPRE composition lemma [4, Lemma 3.3],we conclude that the functionality o admits a perfect 2MPRE. Overall, we encoded f by a a δ-correct (t, ϵ)-private f'.

To prove the "Moreover" part, observe that, by Claim 6, f' can be perfectly realized by a non-interactive protocol π' in the TOT-hybrid model. By [4, Prop. 3.1],π' admits a non-interactive protocol σ in the TOT-Hybrid model that realizes f with δ-correctness and (t, ϵ)-privacy, as required. □

[8] In fact, we could take s_i to be the sum of a random bit that is sampled by A and a random bit that is sampled by B.

5 New 2MPRE Construction

In this section we present our main construction and prove Theorem 1.

5.1 2MPREs for 3-party Functionalities

We begin with the following simple observation that deals with a degree-3 function whose output is delivered to one of the parties who owns one of the multiplicands as an input.

Claim 7. *The Boolean n-party functionality*

$$f\left((x_1, y_1), (x_2, y_2), (x_3, y_3), y_4, \ldots, y_n\right) = \left(x_1 x_2 x_3 + \sum_{i=1}^{n} y_i, \bot, \ldots, \bot\right)$$

(where additions and multiplications are in $\mathbb{F}_2$) that delivers the output to P_1 admits a 2MPRE with perfect correctness and perfect privacy against arbitrary coalitions.

Proof. The MPRE $\widehat{f}$ employs private randomness r that is sampled internally by the functionality. (By [4, Prop. 3.2], one can always replace it by the sum $\sum r_i$ where r_i is sampled locally by P_i). The output of $\widehat{f}$ is delivered to P_1 and it consists of two entries:

$$\left(x_1 r + \sum_i y_i, \quad (1 - x_1)r + x_2 x_3 + \sum_i y_i\right).$$

Given the output (z_0, z_1), party P_1 decodes the value of f by outputting z_{x_1}. Indeed, if $x_1 = 0$ then the output z_0 is $\sum_i y_i$ and if $x_1 = 1$ then the output z_1 is $x_2 x_3 + \sum_i y_i$, as required. To prove privacy, consider a set of corrupted parties $T \subsetneq [n]$ and assume that $P_1 \in T$ (the other case is trivial). Given the output y, the inputs x_1, y_1 and possibly the inputs of other parties, the simulator samples a random bit b and outputs the value (z_0, z_1) where $z_{x_1} = y$ and $z_{1-x_1} = b$. It is not hard to verify that this is a perfect simulator. □

As an immediate corollary we derive the following theorem which implies Corollary 1.

Theorem 8 (Corollary 1 restated). *Every 3-party functionality f admits a 2MPRE with perfect correctness and perfect privacy against arbitrary coalitions.*

Proof. By the completeness of degree-3 REs [22], f can be perfectly encoded by a degree-3 RE f' where each of its outputs is of the form $x_1 x_2 x_3 + r_1 + r_2 + r_3$ where x_i is an input of P_i and r_i is a linear combination of the random inputs of P_i. Therefore, by composition [4, Lemma 3.3], the theorem follows from Claim 7. □

5.2 $\lfloor \frac{2n}{3} \rfloor$-private2MPRE

Theorem 9 (Theorem 1 restated). *Let n and t be positive integers for which $t < \frac{2n+1}{3}$. Then, every n-party functionality admits a t-private 2MPRE.*

Unfortunately, the complexity of the resulting MPRE is exponential in n. (This is the only result in this paper that suffers from this drawback). However, by using "player virtualization", one can derive an efficient poly(n)-time version of the 2MPRE at the expense of reducing the privacy threshold to $\frac{2}{3} - \epsilon$ for an arbitrary small constant $\epsilon > 0$. In fact, we can even take $\epsilon = o_n(1)$. (See the full version for details).

Proof. Consider the n-party functionality f that takes a pair of bits (a, α) from P_1, (b, β) from P_2 and (c, γ) from P_3 and delivers the value

$$abc + \alpha + \beta + \gamma$$

to some designated receiver $R \in \{P_1, \ldots, P_n\}$. Since this functionality is known to be complete under non-interactive reductions [2,12,22] (for an arbitrary privacy threshold), it suffices to focus on f. Observe that if $R \in \{P_1, P_2, P_3\}$ the theorem follows from Claim 7, hence we will focus on the case where $R \notin \{P_1, P_2, P_3\}$. For concreteness, set $R = P_n$.

We will construct a t-perfect 2-round protocol π for f whose first round makes use of only private point-to-point channels and its second round makes parallel calls to TOT. By Lemma 1, such a protocol can be compiled back into an MPRE with an effective degree of 2.

Before presenting the protocol π, let us start with the following simple protocol π_0:

- At the first round, P_1 shares its input a via a t-private CNF secret sharing among the parties $\mathcal{P}$. That is, for each t-subset $S \subset \mathcal{P}$, party P_1 samples a random bit a_S conditioned on $a = \sum_S a_S$ and delivers a_S to all the parties $P_i, i \notin S$. Similarly, P_2 shares b into $b = \sum_{T \subset \mathcal{P}, |T|=t} b_T$ and sends b_T to every party $P_i, i \notin T$ and P_3 shares c into $c = \sum_{U \subset \mathcal{P}, |U|=t} c_U$ and sends c_U to every party $P_i, i \notin U$.
- At the second round, the parties make a call to an ideal functionality g that delivers the value

$$\left(\sum_{S \subset \mathcal{P}, |S|=t} a_S \right) \cdot \left(\sum_{T \subset \mathcal{P}, |T|=t} b_T \right) \cdot \left(\sum_{U \subset \mathcal{P}, |U|=t} c_U \right) + \alpha + \beta + \gamma$$

to P_n.

It is not hard to verify that the protocol π_0 achieves perfect correctness and perfect t-privacy.

Our next protocol, π_1 is obtained by replacing the call to g by a call to a perfect MPRE for g (with full privacy) and by letting P_n apply the MPRE decoder. Specifically, the MPRE $\widehat{g}$ is defined via

$$(a_S \cdot b_T \cdot c_U + r_{S,T,U})_{S,T,U}, \qquad \alpha + \beta + \gamma - \sum_{S,T,U} r_{S,T,U},$$

where S, T, U range over all t-subsets of $\mathcal{P}$, and where each random bit $r_{S,T,U}$ is taken to the sum of random bits $r_{S,T,U,1}, \ldots, r_{S,T,U,n}$ that are sampled locally by $P_1, \ldots, P_n$, respectively. By [4, Prop. 3.1],the privacy and correctness of π_1 are inherited from π_0.

Next, we claim that each output of $\widehat{g}$ can be perfectly encoded by a functionality of effective degree-2 (with full privacy). Fix some S, T and U, and let us focus on the output $y = a_S \cdot b_T \cdot c_U + r_{S,T,U}$. Define the complement sets by

$$\overline{S} := \mathcal{P} \setminus S, \qquad \overline{T} := \mathcal{P} \setminus T, \qquad \overline{U} := \mathcal{P} \setminus U,$$

and let $V = \overline{S} \cup \overline{T} \cup \overline{U}$. Recall that a_S (resp., b_T, c_U) is known to all the parties in $\overline{S}$ (resp., $\overline{T}, \overline{U}$). We distinguish between two cases.

If $P_n \in V$, then the output y can be perfectly encoded by an MPRE of effective degree 2 by Claim 7. Next, suppose that $P_n \notin V$. We claim that in this case there must exist a party that owns at least 2 out of the 3 elements a_S, b_T, c_U, and so the effective degree is 2. Indeed, assume towards a contradiction, that such a party does not exist. That is, the sets $\overline{S}, \overline{T}, \overline{U}$ are pairwise disjoint. Since $|\overline{S}| = |\overline{T}| = |\overline{U}| = (n-t)$, it follows that $|V| = 3(n-t)$. Since $t < \frac{2n+1}{3}$, $|V| > n-1$. But $V \subset \{P_1, \ldots, P_{n-1}\}$ and so $|V| \leq n-1$, a contradiction.

Overall, the second round of π_1 can be realized by a call to a functionality $\widehat{g}$ of effective degree 2. Hence, by Claim 6, the second round can be replaced by parallel calls to TOT, and by Lemma 1, the resulting protocol can be compiled back into an MPRE with an effective degree of 2, as required. □

6 2MPREs vs. 2-round-OT-hybrid Model

The equivalence between t-private 2MPREs and the completeness of 3-party functionalities under non-interactive t-private reductions follows from Corollary 1 and Claim 6. In this section we establish an equivalence between 2MPREs and 3-round protocols in the 2-round-OT-hybrid Model. Recall that in the 2-round OT hybrid model we assume that OT takes 2 rounds. That is, if both parties send their inputs to an OT in round i, the output is delivered to the receiver at the *end* of round $i+1$. In addition, the parties are allowed to exchange messages via standard point-to-point private channels.

Remark 1 (On the 2-round-OT-hybrid Model). The 2-round-OT-hybrid Model attempts to capture an information-theoretic reduction to OT with the minimal possible interaction. (Recall that a single-round reduction in which the parties exchange messages over private channels and make parallel calls to OT was shown to be impossible in [3]). A natural suggestion is to consider a 2-round reduction that is allowed to make oracle calls to OT. However, this allows the reduction to make calls to OT both in the first round and in the second round, which leads to an actual round complexity of 4 when the OT is realized via a 2-round protocol. Our refined notion of 2-round-OT-hybrid Model is therefore stronger than 2-round reduction to OT. One could also consider a seemingly stronger model in which the reduction has 2 rounds but only the first round is allowed to make calls to an ideal OT. Our theorem shows that such a 2-round "OT-then-plain" reduction is actually equivalent to the 2-round-OT-hybrid Model.

Theorem 10. *The following holds for every n-party functionality f and every privacy threshold* $1 \leq t \leq n$. *The functionality f can be t-privately computed by a 3-round protocol* π *in the 2-round OT hybrid model if and only if it has a t-private 2MPRE. Furthermore, for the "if" direction the resulting protocol makes OT calls only at the first round and no private messages are exchanged in the second round and so derive a 2-round "OT-then-plain" reduction. The transformation preserves the privacy and correctness errors.*

The "only if" direction establishes the second item of Theorem 2 (whose first item follows from Corollary 1).

Proof. We begin with the easy "if" direction. It suffices to realize the TOT functionality with a 2-round protocol π' in the OT-hybrid model with perfect correctness and perfect privacy against any coalition, in which only the first round consists of OT calls. Consider a TOT between the parties, Alice, Bob and Carol, where Alice holds the inputs (x_1, y_1), Bob holds the inputs (x_2, y_2), and Carol should receive $z = x_1x_2 + y_1 + y_2$. The protocol proceeds as follows:

1. (Round 1) Alice samples a random bit α, she sends to Carol the value $a = y_1 - \alpha$ and initiates an OT with Bob.[9] In this invocation, Alice plays the Sender with inputs $(\alpha, x_1 + \alpha)$ and Bob uses x_2 as the selection bit.
2. (Round 3) Given the output $m = x_1x_2 + \alpha$ of the OT, Bob sends to Carol the value $b = m + y_2$.
3. (Output) Carol outputs the sum $a + b$.

Clearly, the protocol can be realized in 3 rounds in the 2-round OT-hybrid model . Correctness can be easily verified. For privacy, consider any coalition that contains Carol and either Alice or Bob (all other cases are trivial). Given $z = x_1x_2 + y_1 + y_2$, sample a random bit a and set Carol's view to $(a, b = z - a)$. A corrupted Alice adds nothing to the view (except for her inputs). If Bob is corrupted, then we are also given the inputs (x_2, y_2) and we can simulate m by $b - y_2$. It is not hard to verify that the simulation is perfect.

We move on to prove the more interesting "only if" direction. We show that any 3-round protocol in the 2-round OT-hybrid model can be transformed into a protocol in which the party first exchanges private messages and then makes parallel calls to 3-party functionalities. These functionalities can be replaced

[9] Despite the equivalence of addition and subtraction over the binary field, we use both signs to indicate that the construction generalizes to general fields.

by 2MPREs (based on Corollary 1) and the resulting 2-round protocol can be compiled into a 2MPRE via the aid of the round-collapsing lemma (Lemma 1). Details follow.

Consider the protocol π. For any round number $1 \leq R \leq 3$ and parties P_i, P_j, let $m_{i,j}^R$ be the private message sent from P_i to P_j on round R. Without loss of generality, we further assume that in each round each party P_i sends to herself her entire private view, including the input x_i and the private random tape ρ_i. Since the protocol has only 3 rounds and the OT takes 2 rounds, we may assume that OT calls are performed either on the first round or on the second round. Let us further assume that, both in round 1 and in round 2, each pair of parties (P_i, P_j) performs exactly ℓ OT-calls in which P_i is the sender and P_j is the receiver. Denote by $o_{i,j}^2 = (o_{i,j,1}^2, \dots, o_{i,j,\ell}^2)$ and $o_{i,j}^3 = (o_{i,j,1}^3, \dots, o_{i,j,\ell}^3)$ the vector of OT-outputs of the first-round calls and the second-round calls, respectively. Observe that $o_{i,j}^R$ arrives at the end of round R. For every round $R \in [3]$ and party i, let

$$m_i^R = (m_{1,i}^R, \dots, m_{n,i}^1) \quad \text{and} \quad o_i^R = (o_{1,i}^R, \dots, o_{n,i}^R).$$

By definition, for $R \in [3]$ and $i, j \in [n]$ there exist functions $f_{i,j}^R, g_{i,j}^R$ such that

$$\begin{aligned} m_{i,j}^1 &= f_{i,j}^1(x_j, \rho_i), & & \\ m_{i,j}^2 &= f_{i,j}^2(m_i^1), & o_{i,j}^2 &= g_{i,j}^2(m_{i,i}^1, m_{j,j}^1), \\ m_{i,j}^3 &= f_{i,j}^3(m_i^2, o_i^2), & o_{i,j}^3 &= g_{i,j}^3(m_i^1, m_j^1). \end{aligned}$$

Note that the g functions "merge" together the OT computation with the local computation that is being used in order to generate the input to the OT. To prove the lemma it suffices to securely compute each of these values by a non-interactive TOT-hybrid protocol with perfect correctness and perfect privacy against an arbitrary coalition. In fact, by Lemma 1, it suffices to obtain a 2-round protocol π' that makes TOT calls only in the second round. First observe that the values $m_{i,j}^1, m_{i,j}^2$ can be easily computed by a 2-round protocol via private point-point channels in which $m_{i,j}^2$ can be transferred using a TOT call in the round 2. Moreover, since the messages $o_{i,j}^2 = g_{i,j}^2(m_{ii}^1, m_{jj}^1)$ and $o_{i,j}^3 = g_{i,j}^3(m_i^1, m_j^1)$ depend only on values that are known to P_i and P_j after the first round, we can use Observation 5, and deliver them to P_j by making parallel calls to TOT in the second round (where P_i is the sender and P_j is the selector and receiver). It is left to deliver the value $m_{i,j}^3$.

Fix some $i, j \in [n]$, and let $\widehat{f}$ be a fully decomposable RE of $f_{i,j}^3$, e.g., from [2]. Observe that it suffices to deliver the value of $\widehat{f}(m_i^2, o_i^2; w)$ to P_j where the randomness w is chosen *solely* by P_i. (Indeed, privacy for coalitions that do not contain P_i follows from the RE privacy and privacy for coalitions that contain P_i vacuously holds, since m_i^2 and o_i^2 are given to the simulator). Being fully-decomposable, each output of $\widehat{f}$ depends on the randomness w, selected by P_i, and on at most a single input bit y of m_i^2 or o_i^2. Thus, after some reordering of the outputs, we can write $\widehat{f}(m_i^2, o_i^2; w)$ as

$$\widehat{f}_1(m^2_{1,i}, o^2_{1,i}, w), \ldots, \widehat{f}_n(m^2_{n,i}, o^2_{n,i}, w)$$

where the functions $\widehat{f}_1, \ldots, \widehat{f}_n$ are multi-output functions. Note that $o^2_{k,i}$ itself is the result of $g^2_{k,i}(m^1_{k,k}, m^1_{i,i})$. Therefore there exist functions $h_1, \ldots, h_n$ such that for all $k \in [n]$ we can write $\widehat{f}_k(m^2_{k,i}, o^2_{k,i}, w) = h_k(m^1_{k,i}, m^1_{k,k}, m^1_{i,i}, w)$. Since the input to h_k is being held by only two parties, P_i and P_j, and is available at the end of the first round, it can be encoded by a 2MPRE (Observation 5). It follows, by Claim 6, that h_k can be computed by making parallel calls to TOT at the second round. The theorem follows. □

7 2MPREs vs Perfect Privacy Under Active Attacks

In this section we will prove Theorem 3. Most of the work will be devoted to the construction of 2MPREs, the converse direction will be proved in Sect. 7.3. Along the way, we will also prove Theorem 4.

Recall that a public-output functionality is a function that delivers the same output to all the parties. We begin with the following basic construction.

Construction 11. *Let π be a protocol that realizes some Boolean public-output functionality $f(x_1, \ldots, x_n)$. The protocol π may have an arbitrary number of rounds, and may use OT calls as well as private channels. We construct a non-interactive protocol σ that realizes f and makes use of an ideal functionality V as follows.*

1. *(Local pre-computation) First, each party P_i uniformly samples a local view of π. That is, P_i samples a private random tape r_i, and randomly "guesses" a vector of incoming private messages, and a vector of incoming OT messages corresponding to all the OT calls in which P_i plays the receiver. Then, P_i appends her input x_i to the sampled view, and computes the corresponding outgoing messages that she would send in π either over private channels or as inputs to the OT functionality.*
2. *(Calling V) The parties send their sampled views and the computed outgoing messages to an ideal functionality V. We further assume that P_1 sends to V her final π-output. The functionality V verifies that for every pair of parties, (P_i, P_j), the sampled views are* consistent *in the following sense:*
   - *For every message m that is delivered from P_i to P_j it holds that the guess of P_j for m is equal to the value of the outgoing message m as computed by P_i.*
   - *For every OT-call in which the sender P_i computes her inputs as (a_0, a_1) and the receiver P_j computes her input as s, it holds that the value a' that is guessed by the receiver equals to a_0 if $s = 0$ and to a_1 if $s = 1$.*

   If all these pair-wise tests succeed and P_1's output is 1, the functionality V outputs 1 to all the parties. Else, it outputs 0.
3. *(Output) The parties terminate with the output that V passes.*

Lemma 2. *If π realizes f with perfect correctness, perfect privacy against a coalition T, and a total communication of c bits (where each OT call is counted as a single bit), then the protocol σ defined in Construction 11 realizes f with perfect privacy against T, and a 1-sided correctness error of $1-2^{-c}$.*

Proof. Fix an input $x=(x_1,\dots,x_n)$ for f. It is not hard to see that if $f(x)=0$, the protocol σ always outputs 0. On the other hand, when $f(x)=1$ the protocol σ outputs the correct result only when the sampled views are consistent. Fix the local random tapes $r=(r_1,\dots,r_n)$ in π. Under this fixing, all the communication in a real execution of π is fully determined, and can be represented by a *transcript string* $C_{x,r}\in\{0,1\}^c$ whose ith bit corresponds to the ith bit that is delivered in π from party $A=A(i)$ to party $B=B(i)$ either via OT or via a private channel. (We assume, wlog, that the communication in π is ordered in some canonical way). Since each bit of communication is being guessed by the receiving party uniformly and independently, the parties submit the consistent transcript $C_{x,r}$ with probability exactly 2^{-c}.

We move on to privacy. Fix some coalition T. Syntactically, the view of T in π consists of the input $x_T=(x_i)_{i\in T}$ the local random tapes $r_T=(r_i)_{i\in T}$ and all the incoming messages that a party in T receives. Let I_T denote the set of all indices $i\in[c]$, such that the ith message in π is received by a party in T. Given a full transcript $C\in\{0,1\}^c$, we denote by $C[I_T]$ the restriction of C to the messages that are delivered to members in the coalition T. For convenience, let us further assume that the final output of the protocol, y, appears as part of the view. Similarly, the view of T in σ consists of $(x_T,r_T,C'[I_T],v)$ where $C'[I_T]$ are the *guessed* incoming messages, and v is the bit that V delivers.

Consider the following randomized mapping g that maps a T-view $(x_T,r_T,C[I_T],y)$ under π to a T-view $(x_T,r_T,C'[I_T],v)$ under σ: First, uniformly sample a sequence $e=(e_1,\dots,e_c)$ of random bits (where $e_i=1$ indicates an "incorrect" guess for the ith bit in the full transcript). Then, copy $C[T]$ to $C'[T]$ and flip the value of the ith entry if $i\in I_T$ and $e_i=1$. Finally, set v to zero if some e_i is' one, and otherwise set $v=y$.

We can define a simulator Sim' for σ as follows. Given x_T and an output y, use the simulator Sim of π to sample a view $(x_T,r_T,C[I_T],y)$ under π, apply the mapping g and output the resulting σ view $(x_T,r_T,C'[I_T],v)$. To analyze the simulator, fix an input x to all the parties. By the privacy of π, the distribution generated by $\mathsf{Sim}'(x_T,f(x))$ is identically distributed to the distribution $g(x_T,r_T,C_{x,r}[I_T],f(x))$ where $C_{x,r}[I_T]$ is the vector of incoming messages to T in a *real execution* of π over the input x and fresh randomness $r=(r_1,\dots,r_n)$, and $r_T=(r_i)_{i\in T}$.

We complete the argument by showing that $g(x_T,r_T,C_{x,r}[I_T],f(x))$ is distributed identically to the real execution of σ. We prove that this is the case for every fixing of r. Indeed, in σ the entire vector of guesses $C'\in\{0,1\}^c$ is chosen uniformly at random, and the coalition T receives the restricted transcript $C'[I_T]$ together with a bit v which is equal to 0 if $C'\neq C_{x,r}$ and to $f(x)$ otherwise. Equivalently, we could sample an error vector $e\leftarrow\{0,1\}^c$, set $C'=C_{x,r}\oplus e$ and deliver to T the restricted vector $C'[I_T]$ with the bit v which is set to 0 if some bit of e is 1, and otherwise takes the value $f(x)$. The resulting distribution is exactly the one that is sampled by g. The lemma follows. □

Remark 2 (Handling protocols with imperfect correctness). One can use a variant of Construction 11 in which V outputs an additional consistency bit b that indicates whether the views were consistent. (Our simulator can simulate this additional information). At the post-processing stage, the parties output a special "I do not know", $\perp$, symbol when $b = 0$ and otherwise output the main output v of V. Assuming that the original protocol π is perfectly correct, the resulting protocol never errs and outputs a non-$\perp$ symbol with probability 2^{-c}.

This variant also allows us to handle protocols that have imperfect correctness. Specifically, if the original protocol π suffers from some correctness error of $\delta < 0.5$ we get a protocol with similar correctness error (conditioned on not outputting $\perp$). Such an error can be reduced to an arbitrary ϵ by taking a majority vote over $k = O(\log(1/\epsilon)2^c/(1-2\delta))$ independent parallel copies of the new protocol. This new protocol σ_k is syntactically similar to σ except that it makes k calls to (the extended version of) V. This allows us to extend the above lemma (and all the subsequent results) to the case where π has a correctness error of $\delta < 0.5$. For simplicity, we omit these extensions from the current version.

7.1 2MPRE for Protocols Without OT Calls

Observation 12. *If π does not use OT calls then the functionality V can be written as $\bigwedge_{i,j\in[n]} z_{i,j}$ where $z_{i,j}$ is computed by taking the equality between a string $a_{i,j}$, computed locally by P_i, and a string $b_{i,j}$ computed locally by P_j. The length of $a_{i,j}$ and $b_{i,j}$ equals to the number of bits that P_i delivers to P_j in π.*

Indeed, $a_{i,j}$ is the vector of messages that P_i should deliver to P_j according to her local computation (under the sampled view) and $b_{i,j}$ is vector of incoming messages that P_j receives from P_i according to her guesses.

Corollary 5 (Theorem 4 restated). *In the honest majority setting, every n-party functionality f non-interactively reduces to multiple parallel calls to $\mathsf{AND} \circ \mathsf{EQ}$ functionality. The reduction has perfect privacy and an arbitrarily small 1-sided statistical correctness error of ϵ. The complexity of the protocol is $O(\log(m/\epsilon))$ where m is the number of outputs of f and the hidden constant in the O-notation depends on the complexity of f.*

Proof. Every n-party functionality f has a protocol in the plain model (i.e. does not use OT calls) that is perfectly correct and perfectly $\lfloor \frac{n-1}{2} \rfloor$-private [10]. Assuming that f is a Boolean public-output functionality, we can use Lemma 2 and Observation 12 to non-interactively reduce f to $\mathsf{AND} \circ \mathsf{EQ}$ with perfect privacy and a constant 1-sided correctness error δ against minority coalitions. (The constant δ depends on the description of f). We can reduce the error to ϵ' by executing the reduction $\ell = O(\frac{\log(1/\epsilon')}{1-\delta})$ times in parallel and outputting 1 if and only if at least one of these executions outputs 1. (The latter step is computed locally, i.e., by the decoder). Since σ has perfect privacy, repeating it in parallel does not affect privacy. Finally, since every m-output functionality non-interactively reduces to m parallel calls to Boolean public-output functionalities, the statement extends to such functionalities as well, while the error grows to $\epsilon = m\epsilon'$ where m is the number of outputs. □

Remark 3 (The complexity of the construction). Recall that every n-party multi-output functionality f that is computable by s-size formula (or even s-size branching program) non-interactively n-privately reduces to a functionality g with $\mathrm{poly}(s)$ outputs and each of its output is a constant-size deterministic public-output functionality (that takes a constant number of input bits from a constant number of parties) [2,3,22]. Therefore, by Corollary 5, f reduces to $\mathrm{poly}(s)\log(1/\epsilon)$ calls to $\mathsf{AND} \circ \mathsf{EQ}$ over constant fan-in.

Observe that the equality function over k-bit strings, $\mathsf{EQ}(x, y)$ can be written as a linear function $L(x, y) = (x_i - y_i + 1)_{i\in[k]}$ over an arbitrary finite field $\mathbb{F}$ such that $L(x, y) = 1^k$ iff $x = y$. In addition, the AND predicate admits a degree-2 statistical randomized encoding as follows.

Fact 13 (Encoding AND by Inner-Products [22]**).** *Fix an arbitrary finite field $\mathbb{F}$. Let $v = (v_1, \ldots, v_\ell)$ be a vector of 0–1 values. Consider the randomized function*

$$g(v; \rho) := \sum_{i\in[\ell]} \rho_i \cdot (1 - v_i),$$

where $\rho \leftarrow \mathbb{F}^\ell$ and the addition and multiplication are taken over $\mathbb{F}$. Then, g is a randomized encoding of $\bigwedge_{i\in[\ell]} v_i$ with perfect privacy and correctness error of $1/|\mathbb{F}|$. When all v_is are 1, we get 0 from g. So the output is decoded as (a) 1 when g outputs 0 and (b) 0 otherwise. Note that when we output 0, this is always correct. But when we output 1, it may not be correct, since the sum of ρ_i's can lead to zero. Since the sum is random, the probability that it can be 0 is $1/|\mathbb{F}|$. Lastly, in this case g is a degree-2 function over the binary field. By default, we let $\mathbb{F}$ be a binary extension field. In this case, g can be written as a degree-2 function over the binary field, and it can be computed by a Boolean circuit of size $\ell \log |\mathbb{F}|$. Unless stated otherwise, we assume that $\mathbb{F}$ is the field of size $2^{\ell+1}$.[10]

It follows that $\mathsf{AND} \circ \mathsf{EQ}$ reduces non-interactively to a degree-2 functionality (with statistical correctness error) and so Corollary 5 yields a new alternative construction of honest-majority 2MPRE, alas with statistical correctness.

7.2 2MPRE for Protocols with OT Calls

Note that when the underlying protocol is the OT-hybrid channel, the functionality (also a predicate) V has a slightly more complicated form. In particular,

[10] Alternatively, one can instantiate g over the binary field, and reduce the error to ϵ by repeating the encoding $\log(1/\epsilon)$ times with fresh independent randomness. See [22].

it computes an AND over degree-2 functions. As a result, we cannot use Fact 13 directly to derive a 2MPRE. We bypass the problem by letting the pair of parties that use the ith OT call, to locally select the ith randomizer ρ_i of the AND in the inner-product based RE of Fact 13. (Note that previously we treated the randomizers as being part of the internal randomness of the MPRE). Unfortunately, this leads to a "leaky" 2MPRE of V. We show that this leakage can still be simulated if the original protocol π is weakly-active private. Details follow.

Definition 4 (Weakly-active adversaries). *Let π be an n-party protocol in the OT-hybrid model. A* weakly-active *adversary $\mathcal{A}$ that corrupts a subset T is defined by deviating from the protocol π as follows. For every OT-call between two* corrupted *parties, a sender S with values $(a_0, a_1) \in \{0,1\}^2$ and a receiver R with selector bit $s \in \{0,1\}$, the adversary sets the received value to be some fixed value $a' \in \{0,1\}$. After these modifications, the adversary honestly follows the protocol where a' is used as the received value of the OT instance with inputs (a_0, a_1) and s. Such a deviation can be fully specified by a vector $a' = (a'_i)_{i \in O_T}$ where $i \in O_T$ if the ith bit that is exchanged in π is delivered via an OT between 2 corrupted parties. We write $\pi_{a'}$ to denote the protocol that is obtained for a given fixing of a'.*

*A protocol π in the OT-hybrid model computes a (deterministic) functionality f with t-*perfect privacy against weakly-active adversaries *if for every t-bounded subset T, and every vector $a' = (a'_i)_{i \in O_T}$, it holds that*

$$\mathsf{Sim}(T, a', x_T, f_T(x)) \equiv \mathsf{View}_{T,\pi_{a'}}(x, r),$$

where $r = (r_1, \ldots, r_n)$ are chosen uniformly at random and $\mathsf{View}_{T,\pi_{a'}}(x, r)$ denotes the view of coalition T when running the protocol $\pi_{a'}$ with input $x = (x_1, \ldots, x_n)$ and randomness $r = (r_1, \ldots, r_n)$.

We also require either statistical or perfect correctness against a passive adversary, i.e.,

$$\Pr_{r_1, \ldots, r_n}[\pi(x_1, \ldots, x_n; r_1, \ldots, r_n) \neq f(x_1, \ldots, x_n)] \leq \delta,$$

where r_i is the randomness used by the ith party in π.

A Leaky Version of Construction 11. Before introducing the leaky 2MPRE of V, it will be useful to consider an intermediate case where V itself is leaky. Let $\widetilde{V}$ denote the corruption-aware predicate that takes the same input as V in Construction 11, delivers the same output as V to all the honest parties, but leaks some additional information to the adversary. Specifically, $\widetilde{V}$ leaks to the adversary the consistency bit that verifies consistency of the transcript without taking into account the OT-messages that are exchanged between pairs of corrupted parties. Formally, for a set of corrupted parties $T \subset [n]$, the functionality $\widetilde{V}$ is defined as follows.

- Input: For each index $i \in [c]$, (a) if the ith bit in π is a private-channel message from a sender $A(i)$ to a receiver $B(i)$, then $\widetilde{V}$ receives a bit m_i from $A(i)$ and

m'_i from $B(i)$; (b) if the ith bit in π is transferred over an OT-channel then $\widetilde{V}$ receives $(a_{i,0}, a_{i,1})$ from the sender $A(i)$ and (s_i, a'_i) from the receiver $B(i)$. In addition, the functionality $\widetilde{V}$ receives from the first party P_1 her output v_{c+1} (computed based on her guesses).

- Output: The parties receive the output

$$V = \bigwedge_{i \in [c+1]} v_i$$

where for v_i is defined as follows. If the ith communication bit of π is delivered over a private-channel then $v_i = 1$ if and only if $m_i = m'_i$. If the ith communication bit of π is delivered over an OT-channel then $v_i = 1$ if and only if $a'_i = s_i \cdot a_{i,1} + (1 - s_i) \cdot a_{i,0}$. Lastly, recall that $v_{c+1} = 1$ if and only if the output of P_1 is 1. In addition, the adversary receives the value

$$V_T = \bigwedge_{i \notin O_T} v_i$$

where $i \in O_T$ if the ith communication bit in π is an OT-message that is delivered between a pair of corrupted parties $A(i), B(i) \in T$.

Claim 14. *Suppose that π realizes f with perfect passive correctness and t-perfect privacy against weakly-active adversaries. Let $\tilde{\sigma}$ denote the protocol that is obtained by instantiating Construction 11 with the functionality (predicate) $\widetilde{V}$ instead of V. Then, $\tilde{\sigma}$ realizes f with perfect t-privacy and 1-sided correctness error of $1 - 2^{-c}$.*

The proof is deferred to the full version.

In order to obtain a 2MPRE we will need the following extension to the inner-product encoding from Fact 13.

Fact 15 (leaky inner products). *Under the notation of Fact 13, the following holds. For every set $S \subseteq [\ell]$, let $\rho_S = (\rho_i)_{i \in S}$ and $v_S = (v_i)_{i \in S}$. There exists a simulator Sim_S that, for every $v \in \{0,1\}^\ell$, perfectly samples the distribution*

$$(g(v; \rho), \rho_S, v_S) \qquad \textit{where } \rho \leftarrow \mathbb{F}^\ell$$

given ρ_S, v_S and $\bigwedge_{i \notin S} v_i$.

Lemma 3 (2MPRE from weak-active privacy). *Suppose that the functionality f can be realized in the OT-hybrid model by a protocol π with t-perfect privacy against weakly-active adversaries and perfect passive correctness. Then f can be realized by t-private 2MPRE with an arbitrarily small correctness error of ϵ and with complexity of $\log(1/\epsilon)(n + T_\pi)2^{O(c)}$ where n is the number of parties and T_π is the computational complexity of π.*

The proof is deferred to the full version.

7.3 2MPRE Implies Weak-Active Perfect Privacy

We prove the converse of Theorem 3.

Lemma 4. *If the functionality f has t-private 2MPRE, then it can be realized in the OT-hybrid model with perfect (passive) correctness and t-perfect privacy against weakly active adversaries. The transformation carries to the statistical setting while preserving the error.*

Proof. Suppose that f has t-private 2MPRE. By Theorem 10, f can be computed by a protocol in which the result of OT messages only affect the last-round messages of the parties. This means that a deviation of a weakly-active adversary can only affect the view of an honest party after the last round of messages. Put differently, at the beginning of the last round the view of all honest parties is consistent with an honest execution of the protocol. Consequently, all the messages that are being sent to the adversary (including the last round messages) are consistent with an honest execution of the protocol, and so weak-active perfect privacy follows from passive perfect privacy, as required. □

Acknowledgements. B. Applebaum and O. Karni are supported by the Israel Science Foundation grant no. 2805/21. Y. Ishai is supported by ERC Project NTSC (742754), BSF grant 2018393, and ISF grant 2774/20. A. Patra is supported by DST National Mission on Interdisciplinary Cyber-Physical Systems (NM-CPS) 2020–2025 and SERB MATRICS (Theoretical Sciences) Grant 2020-2023.

References

1. Alon, B., Paskin-Cherniavsky, A.: On perfectly secure 2PC in the OT-hybrid model. Theor. Comput. Sci. **891**, 166–188 (2021)
2. Applebaum, B., Ishai, Y., Kushilevitz, E.: Cryptography in NC^0. In: 45th Annual IEEE Symposium on Foundations of Computer Science, pp. 166–175 (2004)
3. Applebaum, B., Brakerski, Z., Garg, S., Ishai, Y., Srinivasan, A.: Separating two-round secure computation from oblivious transfer. In: 11th Innovations in Theoretical Computer Science Conference, ITCS. LIPIcs, vol. 151, pp. 71:1–71:18. Schloss Dagstuhl - Leibniz-Zentrum für Informatik (2020)
4. Applebaum, B., Brakerski, Z., Tsabary, R.: Perfect secure computation in two rounds. SIAM J. Comput. **50**(1), 68–97 (2021)
5. Babai, L., Gál, A., Kimmel, P.G., Lokam, S.V.: Communication complexity of simultaneous messages. SIAM J. Comput. **33**(1), 137–166 (2003)
6. Barkol, O., Ishai, Y., Weinreb, E.: On d-multiplicative secret sharing. J. Cryptol. **23**(4), 580–593 (2010)
7. Beaver, D.: Precomputing oblivious transfer. In: Coppersmith, D. (ed.) CRYPTO 1995. LNCS, vol. 963, pp. 97–109. Springer, Heidelberg (1995). https://doi.org/10.1007/3-540-44750-4_8
8. Beaver, D., Micali, S., Rogaway, P.: The round complexity of secure protocols (extended abstract). In: Proceedings of the 22nd Annual ACM Symposium on Theory of Computing, Baltimore, Maryland, USA, 13–17 May 1990, pp. 503–513 (1990)

9. Beimel, A., Ishai, Y., Kushilevitz, E.: General constructions for information-theoretic private information retrieval. J. Comput. Syst. Sci. **71**(2), 213–247 (2005)
10. Ben-Or, M., Goldwasser, S., Wigderson, A.: Completeness theorems for non-cryptographic fault-tolerant distributed computation. In: Proceedings of the 20th Annual ACM Symposium on Theory of Computing, pp. 1–10 (1988)
11. Benhamouda, F., Lin, H.: k-round multiparty computation from k-round oblivious transfer via garbled interactive circuits. In: Nielsen, J.B., Rijmen, V. (eds.) EUROCRYPT 2018. LNCS, vol. 10821, pp. 500–532. Springer, Cham (2018). https://doi.org/10.1007/978-3-319-78375-8_17
12. Boyle, E., Gilboa, N., Ishai, Y., Lin, H., Tessaro, S.: Foundations of homomorphic secret sharing. In: ITCS 2018, vol. 94, pp. 21:1–21:21 (2018)
13. Crépeau, C.: Efficient cryptographic protocols based on noisy channels. In: Fumy, W. (ed.) EUROCRYPT 1997. LNCS, vol. 1233, pp. 306–317. Springer, Heidelberg (1997). https://doi.org/10.1007/3-540-69053-0_21
14. Crépeau, C., Kilian, J.: Achieving oblivious transfer using weakened security assumptions (extended abstract). In: 29th Annual Symposium on Foundations of Computer Science, White Plains, New York, USA, 24–26 October 1988, pp. 42–52. IEEE Computer Society (1988)
15. Damgård, I., Ishai, Y.: Constant-round multiparty computation using a black-box pseudorandom generator. In: Shoup, V. (ed.) CRYPTO 2005. LNCS, vol. 3621, pp. 378–394. Springer, Heidelberg (2005). https://doi.org/10.1007/11535218_23
16. Döttling, N., Kraschewski, D., Müller-Quade, J.: Unconditional and composable security using a single stateful tamper-proof hardware token. In: Ishai, Y. (ed.) TCC 2011. LNCS, vol. 6597, pp. 164–181. Springer, Heidelberg (2011). https://doi.org/10.1007/978-3-642-19571-6_11
17. Dubovitskaya, M., Scafuro, A., Visconti, I.: On efficient non-interactive oblivious transfer with tamper-proof hardware. IACR Cryptol. ePrint Arch., p. 509 (2010), http://eprint.iacr.org/2010/509
18. Even, S., Goldreich, O., Lempel, A.: A randomized protocol for signing contracts. Commun. ACM **28**(6), 637–647 (1985)
19. Garg, S., Ishai, Y., Srinivasan, A.: Two-round MPC: information-theoretic and black-box. In: TCC 2018, pp. 123–151 (2018)
20. Garg, S., Srinivasan, A.: Two-round multiparty secure computation from minimal assumptions. In: Nielsen, J.B., Rijmen, V. (eds.) EUROCRYPT 2018. LNCS, vol. 10821, pp. 468–499. Springer, Cham (2018). https://doi.org/10.1007/978-3-319-78375-8_16
21. Goldreich, O., Micali, S., Wigderson, A.: How to play any mental game, or a completeness theorem for protocols with honest majority. In: Providing Sound Foundations for Cryptography: On the Work of Shafi Goldwasser and Silvio Micali, pp. 307–328 (2019)
22. Ishai, Y., Kushilevitz, E.: Randomizing polynomials: a new representation with applications to round-efficient secure computation. In: Proceedings 41st Annual Symposium on Foundations of Computer Science, pp. 294–304 (2000)
23. Ishai, Y., Kushilevitz, E., Meldgaard, S., Orlandi, C., Paskin-Cherniavsky, A.: On the power of correlated randomness in secure computation. In: Sahai, A. (ed.) TCC 2013. LNCS, vol. 7785, pp. 600–620. Springer, Heidelberg (2013). https://doi.org/10.1007/978-3-642-36594-2_34
24. Ishai, Y., Kushilevitz, E., Ostrovsky, R., Sahai, A.: Zero-knowledge from secure multiparty computation. In: Proceedings of the 39th Annual ACM Symposium on Theory of Computing, San Diego, California, USA, 11–13 June 2007, pp. 21–30 (2007)

25. Ishai, Y., Prabhakaran, M., Sahai, A.: Founding cryptography on oblivious transfer – efficiently. In: Wagner, D. (ed.) CRYPTO 2008. LNCS, vol. 5157, pp. 572–591. Springer, Heidelberg (2008). https://doi.org/10.1007/978-3-540-85174-5_32
26. Kilian, J.: Founding cryptography on oblivious transfer. In: Proceedings of the 20th Annual ACM Symposium on Theory of Computing, Chicago, Illinois, USA, 2–4 May 1988, pp. 20–31. ACM (1988)
27. Kolesnikov, V.: Truly efficient string oblivious transfer using resettable tamper-proof tokens. In: Micciancio, D. (ed.) TCC 2010. LNCS, vol. 5978, pp. 327–342. Springer, Heidelberg (2010). https://doi.org/10.1007/978-3-642-11799-2_20
28. Lin, H., Liu, T., Wee, H.: Information-theoretic 2-round mpc without round collapsing: adaptive security, and more. In: Pass, R., Pietrzak, K. (eds.) TCC 2020. LNCS, vol. 12551, pp. 502–531. Springer, Cham (2020). https://doi.org/10.1007/978-3-030-64378-2_18
29. Nascimento, A.C.A., Winter, A.J.: On the oblivious transfer capacity of noisy correlations. In: Proceedings 2006 IEEE International Symposium on Information Theory, ISIT 2006, The Westin Seattle, Seattle, Washington, USA, 9–14 July 2006, pp. 1871–1875. IEEE (2006)
30. Patra, A., Srinivasan, A.: Three-round secure multiparty computation from black-box two-round oblivious transfer. In: Malkin, T., Peikert, C. (eds.) CRYPTO 2021. LNCS, vol. 12826, pp. 185–213. Springer, Cham (2021). https://doi.org/10.1007/978-3-030-84245-1_7
31. Rabin, M.O.: How to exchange secrets with oblivious transfer. Technical report TR-81, Aiken Computation Lab, Harvard University (1981)
32. Yao, A.C.C.: How to generate and exchange secrets. In: 27th Annual Symposium on Foundations of Computer Science, pp. 162–167 (1986)

Tight Bounds on the Randomness Complexity of Secure Multiparty Computation

Vipul Goyal[1,2], Yuval Ishai[3(✉)], and Yifan Song[1]

[1] Carnegie Mellon University, Pittsburgh, USA
vipul@cmu.edu, yifans2@andrew.cmu.edu
[2] NTT Research, Sunnyvale, USA
[3] Technion, Haifa, Israel
yuvali@cs.technion.ac.il

Abstract. We revisit the question of minimizing the *randomness complexity* of protocols for secure multiparty computation (MPC) in the setting of perfect information-theoretic security. Kushilevitz and Mansour (*SIAM J. Discret. Math.*, 1997) studied the case of n-party semi-honest MPC for the XOR function with security threshold $t < n$, showing that $O(t^2 \log(n/t))$ random bits are sufficient and $\Omega(t)$ random bits are necessary. Their positive result was obtained via a non-explicit protocol, whose existence was proved using the probabilistic method.

We essentially close the question by proving an $\Omega(t^2)$ lower bound on the randomness complexity of XOR, matching the previous upper bound up to a logarithmic factor (or constant factor when $t = \Omega(n)$). We also obtain an *explicit* protocol that uses $O(t^2 \cdot \log^2 n)$ random bits, matching our lower bound up to a polylogarithmic factor. We extend these results from XOR to general *symmetric* Boolean functions and to addition over a finite Abelian group, showing how to amortize the randomness complexity over multiple additions.

Finally, combining our techniques with recent randomness-efficient constructions of private circuits, we obtain an explicit protocol for evaluating a general circuit C using only $O(t^2 \cdot \log |C|)$ random bits, by employing additional "helper parties" who do not contribute any inputs. This upper bound too matches our lower bound up to a logarithmic factor.

1 Introduction

The *randomness complexity* of probabilistic algorithms and distributed protocols is an important complexity measure that has been the subject of a large body of research. From a practical point of view, the design of algorithms and protocols that use a minimal amount of randomness is motivated by the difficulty of generating high-quality randomness from physical sources. While pseudorandomness provides a generic way of reducing the amount of randomness in a computational setting, this solution (besides requiring unproven cryptographic assumptions) is not always practical, especially in a distributed setting or when parties may be subject to resetting attacks. This motivated a line of work on minimizing the amount of randomness used by secure cryptographic

Y. Dodis and T. Shrimpton (Eds.): CRYPTO 2022, LNCS 13510, pp. 483–513, 2022.
https://doi.org/10.1007/978-3-031-15985-5_17

hardware [2,3,14,17,19,22,24]. From a theoretical perspective, the goal of minimizing the use of randomness is a fundamental challenge that has driven many important developments in computer science, including a rich theory of pseudorandomness and randomness extraction.

This work studies the randomness complexity of *secure multiparty computation* (MPC) in the simplest setting of *perfect* security against a *passive* (semi-honest) adversary who may corrupt up to t parties. Such an MPC protocol allows n parties, each holding a local input $x_i \in D_i$, to jointly compute a function $f : D_1 \times D_2 \times \ldots \times D_n \to Z$ of their inputs by exchanging messages over secure point-to-point channels. At the end of the protocol, all parties should learn $f(x_1, x_2, \ldots, x_n)$. We say that the protocol is t*-secure* if every set of at most t parties jointly learn nothing beyond what follows from their inputs and the output. To achieve this goal, the parties may toss random coins at any time during the protocol's execution, possibly depending on their inputs and the messages they receive. The randomness complexity of the protocol is the total number of random bits used by all parties.

Classical MPC protocols for this setting [4,11] can compute every function f with randomness complexity $\tilde{O}(s \cdot t^2)$, where s is the Boolean circuit size of f, as long as $t < n/2$. (For bigger thresholds t, most functions cannot be realized at all in the information-theoretic setting.) In the useful special case of the XOR function, where $f(x_1, x_2, \ldots, x_n) = x_1 \oplus x_2 \oplus \cdots \oplus x_n$ (or more generally, addition over a finite Abelian group), the "textbook" protocol from [5,13] requires $O(nt)$ random bits for any $t < n$.

The question of minimizing the randomness complexity of MPC has been the topic of a fairly large body of work [6,7,9,16,18,21,22,25,27–31]. While some of these works focus on the minimal security thresholds of $t = 1$ or $t = 2$, here we are interested in how the randomness complexity grows with t.

We will be mainly interested in the simple special case of computing the XOR function and, more generally, addition over finite Abelian groups, but will also consider other classes of functions f, including symmetric functions and even general functions. The case of addition is particularly well motivated because of its usefulness for many applications, including secure voting [5], anonymous communication [10], linear sketching [23], privacy-preserving analytics [15], federated learning [8], and more.

The randomness complexity of XOR was studied by Kushilevitz and Mansour [27], who proved that $O(t^2 \log(n/t))$ random bits are sufficient and $\Omega(t)$ random bits are necessary. This leaves a quadratic gap between the two bounds. Another question left open by [27] is the existence of an *explicit* protocol meeting the upper bound. The positive result was obtained via a non-explicit protocol, relying on a combinatorial object that can either be generated by an efficient probabilistic construction (with small but nonzero failure probability) or generated deterministically in super-polynomial time. Blundo et al. [6] obtain a lower bound of $\Omega(t^2/(n-t))$, which is asymptotically matched by the upper bound of [5,13] when $t = n - \Omega(1)$, but still leaves a quadratic gap when $t \leq (1-\epsilon)n$.

1.1 Our Contribution

In this work, we settle the main open questions about the randomness complexity of t-secure MPC for XOR and addition over finite Abelian groups, and obtain similar results for other functions. Concretely, we obtain the following results.

Lower Bounds. We prove an $\Omega(t^2)$ lower bound on the randomness complexity of XOR, matching the previous upper bound of Kushilevitz and Mansour [27] up to a logarithmic factor (or even a constant factor when $t = \Omega(n)$). Our lower bound extends to arbitrary symmetric Boolean functions, including AND and majority. It applies also when the output is revealed to a strict subset of the parties and even in the case where there are additional participating parties who do not hold an input.

Our lower bounds do *not* apply to statistically private (let alone computationally private) MPC for the following inherent reason: in the setting of statistical privacy, one of the parties can pick a random committee $\mathcal{P}$ of σ parties, for a statistical security parameter σ, and the parties can securely add their inputs by secret-sharing them among the parties in $\mathcal{P}$. This folklore protocol, which is statistically $2^{-\Omega(\sigma)}$-secure against any (non-adaptive) adversary corrupting $t = 0.99n$ parties, has randomness complexity $O(n \cdot \sigma)$, which beats our $\Omega(n^2)$ lower bound when $\sigma = o(n)$. This explains the quick deterioration of the information-theoretic lower bound technique from [6], which is robust to small statistical deviations, when t gets farther away from n. Indeed, our lower bound proof relies on combinatorial rather than information-theoretic methods.

Explicit Upper Bounds for XOR and Addition. To complement our lower bounds, we obtain an *explicit* protocol for XOR that uses $O(t^2 \cdot \log^2 n)$ random bits, matching our lower bound up to a polylogarithmic factor and at most a polylog-factor worse than the non-explicit protocol from [27]. We extend the protocol from XOR to general symmetric Boolean functions as well as addition over any finite Abelian group, and show that t additions can be performed using only $\tilde{O}(t^2)$ random bits, namely essentially for the same price as one.

Upper Bounds for General Functions. Finally, building on the techniques with recent randomness-efficient constructions of private circuits [19], we obtain an explicit protocol for evaluating a general circuit C using only $O(t^2 \cdot \log |C|)$ random bits, but in an easier setting that allows for additional "helper parties" who do not contribute any inputs but still participate in the protocol. This upper bound too matches our lower bound up to the logarithmic factor, and gives at least a factor $\Omega(t)$ improvement over previous randomness-efficient MPC protocols from [9,22].

We leave open the question of characterizing the randomness complexity of general MPC without helper parties, as well as closing the remaining (polylogarithmic) gaps between our lower bounds and upper bounds. Evidence for the difficulty of these questions in some parameter regimes was given by Kushilevitz et al. [29], who showed a two-way relation between the randomness complexity of f for $t = 1$ and its circuit complexity. We refer the readers to the full version of this paper [20] for discussion about other related directions.

2 Technical Overview

In this section, we give an overview of the technical ideas behind the main results.

2.1 Background: Secure Multiparty Computation

We consider the standard model of information-theoretic MPC: a set of n parties $\{P_1, P_2, \ldots, P_n\}$, each holding an input x_i from a finite domain D_i, jointly run a protocol Π to compute a function $f : D_1 \times D_2 \times \ldots \times D_n \to Z$. At the end of the protocol, all parties will receive the function output $f(x_1, x_2, \ldots, x_n)$.

During the protocol execution, when needed, each party can toss a random coin and use this random bit in the computation. The randomness complexity of the protocol Π is measured by the total number of random bits that are used during the protocol execution.

In the following, we will use $\boldsymbol{x} = (x_1, x_2, \ldots, x_n)$ to denote the input, and $\boldsymbol{r} = (r_1, r_2, \ldots, r_n)$ to denote the random tapes of all parties. The function output is denoted by $f(\boldsymbol{x})$, and an execution of the protocol Π with input $\boldsymbol{x}$ and random tapes $\boldsymbol{r}$ is denoted by $\Pi(\boldsymbol{x}, \boldsymbol{r})$.

We consider the standard definition of correctness and semi-honest security.

- The correctness of the protocol Π requires that, when all parties honestly follow the protocol, they will finally output $f(\boldsymbol{x})$ at the end of the protocol.
- Let t be the number of corrupted parties. The semi-honest security of the protocol Π requires that the joint view of any set of t parties can be perfectly simulated by their inputs and the function output.

Note that the semi-honest security implies that, for any set T of t parties, and for all $\boldsymbol{x}, \boldsymbol{x}'$ such that $f(\boldsymbol{x}) = f(\boldsymbol{x}')$ and $x_i = x_i'$ for all $i \in T$, the distribution of the joint view of parties in T of a random execution with input $\boldsymbol{x}$ is identical to that of a random execution with input $\boldsymbol{x}'$.

2.2 Randomness Lower Bound for XOR and Symmetric Functions

To better exhibit our idea, we begin with an n-ary XOR function for simplicity. Concretely, we consider the function $f : (\{0,1\})^n \to \{0,1\}$ defined by

$$f(x_1, x_2, \ldots, x_n) = x_1 \oplus x_2 \oplus \ldots \oplus x_n.$$

Suppose Π is an MPC protocol that computes f. Our result shows that any such protocol must use $\Omega(t^2)$ random bits, improving the previous $\Omega(t)$ lower bound from [27] and matching their $O(t^2 \log(n/t))$ upper bound up to at most a logarithmic factor.

We start with the following known fact:

Fact 1. For every P_i, the messages exchanged with P_i together with $f(\boldsymbol{x})$ fully determine its input x_i.

A similar fact was proved and used in [13] to show a lower bound on the communication complexity of the XOR function, and in [6] to show a lower bound on the randomness complexity of the XOR function.[1]

Ideas Behind Fact 1. To see why this fact is true, suppose that there are two executions, $\Pi(\boldsymbol{x},\boldsymbol{r})$ and $\Pi(\boldsymbol{x}',\boldsymbol{r}')$, such that x_i and x_i' are different, but the messages exchanged with P_i and the function output are identical. Now consider a third execution $\Pi(\tilde{\boldsymbol{x}},\tilde{\boldsymbol{r}})$ where $\tilde{\boldsymbol{x}}=\boldsymbol{x}$ except that $\tilde{x}_i=x_i'$, and $\tilde{\boldsymbol{r}}=\boldsymbol{r}$ except that $\tilde{r}_i=r_i'$. I.e., the third execution $\Pi(\tilde{\boldsymbol{x}},\tilde{\boldsymbol{r}})$ is the first execution $\Pi(\boldsymbol{x},\boldsymbol{r})$ except that we replace P_i's input and random tape by those in the second execution $\Pi(\boldsymbol{x}',\boldsymbol{r}')$. Consider the messages exchanged with P_i in these three executions:

- From the point of view of the party P_i, P_i uses the same input and random tape in $\Pi(\boldsymbol{x}',\boldsymbol{r}')$ and $\Pi(\tilde{\boldsymbol{x}},\tilde{\boldsymbol{r}})$. Therefore, if P_i always receives the same messages from other parties in these two executions, he cannot distinguish these two executions, and thus will always send the same messages to other parties.
- Similarly, from the point of view of all other parties $\{P_j\}_{j\neq i}$, they use the same input and random tapes in $\Pi(\boldsymbol{x},\boldsymbol{r})$ and $\Pi(\tilde{\boldsymbol{x}},\tilde{\boldsymbol{r}})$. Therefore, if $\{P_j\}_{j\neq i}$ always receive the same messages from P_i in these two executions, they cannot distinguish these two executions, and thus will always send the same messages to P_i.

Note that before the first message exchanged with P_i, P_i cannot distinguish $\Pi(\boldsymbol{x}',\boldsymbol{r}')$ and $\Pi(\tilde{\boldsymbol{x}},\tilde{\boldsymbol{r}})$, and all other parties $\{P_j\}_{j\neq i}$ cannot distinguish $\Pi(\boldsymbol{x},\boldsymbol{r})$ and $\Pi(\tilde{\boldsymbol{x}},\tilde{\boldsymbol{r}})$. It implies that the first message exchanged with P_i is always the same in these three executions. Thus, by induction, the messages exchanged with P_i are identical in these three executions.

It follows that parties other than P_i cannot distinguish between $\Pi(\boldsymbol{x},\boldsymbol{r})$ and $\Pi(\tilde{\boldsymbol{x}},\tilde{\boldsymbol{r}})$ at the end of the protocol, which means that they will output the same value in both executions. However, since $\boldsymbol{x}$ and $\tilde{\boldsymbol{x}}$ only differ in the i-th input, for the XOR function f, we must have $f(\boldsymbol{x})\neq f(\tilde{\boldsymbol{x}})$. It means that at least one of $\Pi(\boldsymbol{x},\boldsymbol{r})$ and $\Pi(\tilde{\boldsymbol{x}},\tilde{\boldsymbol{r}})$ outputs an incorrect result, which contradicts with the correctness of Π. Thus, Fact 1 holds.

With Fact 1, we can view the messages exchanged with P_i together with the function output as an *encoding* of P_i's input x_i. Moreover, we observe that this encoding is t-private, i.e., the distribution of any t messages in a random codeword of x_i is independent of x_i.

Fact 2. For every P_i, the messages exchanged with P_i together with $f(\boldsymbol{x})$ form a t-private encoding of x_i.

[1] [6] focuses on a broader class of functions which they refer to as functions with sensitivity n. The XOR function is a concrete instance in this class.

Ideas Behind Fact 2. Intuitively, it follows from the semi-honest security of Π: for any t messages, the joint view of the senders and the receivers (other than P_i) of these t messages should not reveal the input of P_i. To formally argue it, we consider the following encoding scheme:

- Let $\boldsymbol{x} = (0, 0, \ldots, 0, 1)$, i.e., all inputs are 0 except the last input is 1. And let $\boldsymbol{x}'$ be the input subject to $x'_i = 1$ and $x'_j = 0$ for all $j \neq i$. Then $f(\boldsymbol{x}) = f(\boldsymbol{x}') = 1$ but $x_i \neq x'_i$.
- The encoding of 0 is the messages exchanged with P_i in a random execution with input $\boldsymbol{x}$. And the encoding of 1 is the messages exchanged with P_i of a random execution with input $\boldsymbol{x}'$.

For $t \leq n-2$ and any t messages, we want to show that the distribution of these t messages in a random codeword of 0 is identical to that in a random codeword of 1. To this end, we consider the set T of t parties which are senders or receivers (other than P_i) of these t messages.

If $P_n \notin T$, then we have $x_j = x'_j = 0$ for all $j \in T$. Since $f(\boldsymbol{x}) = f(\boldsymbol{x}')$, by the semi-honest security of Π, the distribution of the joint view of parties in T of a random execution with input $\boldsymbol{x}$ is identical to that of a random execution with input $\boldsymbol{x}'$. Note that these t messages are in the joint view of parties in T. Therefore, the distribution of these t messages in a random execution with input $\boldsymbol{x}$ is identical to that in a random execution with input $\boldsymbol{x}'$.

When $P_n \in T$, the above argument fails because $x_n = 1$ while $x'_n = 0$. To fix it, we consider another input $\tilde{\boldsymbol{x}}$ as an intermediate step towards proving the t-privacy. Since $t \leq n-2$, there is a party $P_{i^\star}$ which is not in $T \bigcup \{P_i\}$. We choose $\tilde{\boldsymbol{x}}$ subject to $\tilde{x}_{i^\star} = 1$ and $\tilde{x}_j = 0$ for all $j \neq i^\star$. Then $f(\boldsymbol{x}) = f(\boldsymbol{x}') = f(\tilde{\boldsymbol{x}}) = 1$.

On one hand, since $x_i = \tilde{x}_i = 0$ and $f(\boldsymbol{x}) = f(\tilde{\boldsymbol{x}})$, by the semi-honest security of Π, P_i cannot distinguish a random execution with input $\boldsymbol{x}$ from a random execution with input $\tilde{\boldsymbol{x}}$. Note that these t messages are in the view of P_i. Therefore, the distribution of these t messages in a random execution with input $\boldsymbol{x}$ is identical to that in a random execution with input $\tilde{\boldsymbol{x}}$.

On the other hand, since $x'_j = \tilde{x}_j = 0$ for all $j \in T$ and $f(\boldsymbol{x}') = f(\tilde{\boldsymbol{x}})$, by the semi-honest security of Π, $\{P_j\}_{j \in T}$ cannot distinguish a random execution with input $\boldsymbol{x}'$ from a random execution with input $\tilde{\boldsymbol{x}}$. Note that these t messages are also in the joint view of parties in T. Therefore, the distribution of these t messages in a random execution with input $\boldsymbol{x}'$ is identical to that in a random execution with input $\tilde{\boldsymbol{x}}$.

Combining these two parts together, we have shown that the above encoding scheme is t-private.

With Fact 2, we are interested in the randomness complexity of a t-private encoding scheme. In our work, we show that for any t-private encoding scheme for a single bit, the support of 0 (i.e., the set of all possible codewords of 0) is of size at least 2^t. In Sect. 2.2, we will discuss how we prove this result. Jumping ahead, this implies that when the input is $\boldsymbol{x}$, the view of each party P_i has at least 2^t possibilities.

Connection to Randomness Complexity. In [21,31], it has been shown that for a fixed input $\boldsymbol{x}$, if the protocol execution with input $\boldsymbol{x}$ has 2^d different transcripts (i.e., the joint view of all parties), then the protocol uses at least d random bits. Thus, the result that the view of P_i has at least 2^t possibilities implies that the protocol requires at least t random bits.

Final Piece. Indeed, the above result is when we *only* consider the view of a *single* party. We note that, if we fix the view of the first party P_1 (by corrupting P_1), the protocol Π effectively computes the XOR function for the rest of $n-1$ parties that is secure against $t-1$ parties. In particular, we show that the above argument continues to work for the view of the second party: given the view of P_1, the view of P_2 has at least 2^{t-1} possibilities. In general, we show the following:

Fact 3. For all $i \in \{1, 2, \ldots, t\}$, for a fixed input $\boldsymbol{x}$ and given the views of the first $i-1$ parties, the view of P_i has at least 2^{t-i+1} different possibilities.

Thus, for a fixed input $\boldsymbol{x}$, the joint view of the first t parties has at least $\prod_{i=1}^{t} 2^{t-i+1} = 2^{t(t+1)/2}$ different possibilities. It implies that the protocol Π requires $\Omega(t^2)$ random bits.

We note that this lower bound argument holds even if the output is only given to a strict (nonempty) subset of the parties and even if there is an arbitrary number of additional "helper" parties who do not have an input.

Extending to Symmetric Functions. We generalize the previous lower bound to an arbitrary (nontrivial) symmetric Boolean function. For this, it suffices to prove that the above three facts still hold.

- For Fact 1, the main task is to find two executions $\Pi(\boldsymbol{x}, \boldsymbol{r})$ and $\Pi(\boldsymbol{x}', \boldsymbol{r}')$ such that (1) $x_i \neq x_i'$ but the messages exchanged with P_i together with the function output in $\Pi(\boldsymbol{x}, \boldsymbol{r})$ are identical to those in $\Pi(\boldsymbol{x}', \boldsymbol{r}')$, and (2) $f(x_1, \ldots, x_{i-1}, x_i', x_{i+1}, \ldots, x_n) \neq f(\boldsymbol{x}')$. We show that such two executions exist for any symmetric function that outputs a single bit.
- For Fact 2, it relies on Fact 1 and the semi-honest security of the protocol. Beyond that, we also need to find proper inputs $\boldsymbol{x}, \boldsymbol{x}'$ for the encoding scheme and $\tilde{\boldsymbol{x}}$ that is used to prove the t-privacy of the encoding scheme. We observe that for a symmetric function, we can continue to use the inputs we construct above.
- For Fact 3, it follows from Fact 2 and the randomness complexity of t-private encoding schemes.

Thus, we show that for any non-constant n-ary symmetric function that outputs a single bit, any MPC protocol requires $\Omega(t^2)$ random bits.

Randomness Complexity of t-Private Encoding Schemes. Let $(\mathtt{Enc}, \mathtt{Dec})$ be a t-private encoding scheme for a single bit. Here t-privacy means that the distribution of any t bits in a random codeword is independent of the input bit.

Our goal is to show that the support of 0 (i.e., the set of all possible codewords of 0) is of size at least 2^t. Let $\mathsf{supp}(m)$ denote the support of $m \in \{0,1\}$. The lower bound is proved using the following simple inductive argument:

1. When $t = 1$, we show that the support of 0 is of size at least 2. Let c be a codeword of 0 and c' be a codeword of 1. By the correctness of the encoding scheme, $c \neq c'$. Without loss of generality, assume the first bits of c and c' are different. Since the encoding scheme is 1-private, the distribution of the first bit in a random codeword of 0 is identical to that in a random codeword of 1. Then the first bit in a random codeword of 0 is not a constant bit. Otherwise, the first bit in a random codeword of 1 should be the same constant bit, which contradicts with the assumption that the first bits of c and c' are different. Since the first bit can take both 0 and 1, there are at least two codewords of 0. The statement holds for $t = 1$.
2. Suppose the statement holds for $t - 1$. With the same argument as above, there exists a bit in a random codeword of 0 which is not a constant bit. Without loss of generality, assume that it is the first bit.
   Since the encoding scheme is t-private, the distribution of any t bits in a random codeword of 0 is identical to that in a random codeword of 1. Then, given the first bit, the encoding scheme is $(t-1)$-private. Thus, according to the induction hypothesis, there are at least 2^{t-1} codewords of 0 given the first bit. Note that the first bit can take both 0 and 1, and in each case, there are at least 2^{t-1} codewords of 0 given the first bit. Thus, there are at least 2^t codewords of 0. The statement holds for t.
3. By induction, we conclude that $|\mathsf{supp}(0)| \geq 2^t$.

In the full version of this paper [20], we provide an alternative proof (due to Yuval Filmus) of a slightly weaker lower bound using Fourier analysis. This alternative proof also applies to t-private encodings with imperfect correctness.

2.3 Explicit Randomness Upper Bounds for XOR and Addition

In [27], Kushilevitz and Mansour gave an n-party MPC protocol for the XOR function with semi-honest security against t corrupted parties, which uses $O(t^2 \cdot \log(n/t))$ random bits. This upper bound matches our lower bound, $\Omega(t^2)$ random bits, up to (at most) a logarithmic factor. However, the construction in [27] is non-explicit, relying on a combinatorial object that can either be generated by a probabilistic construction (with small but nonzero failure probability) or generated deterministically in time $(n/t)^{O(t)}$. In this part, we introduce our techniques towards constructing an explicit n-party computation protocol for the XOR function, which uses $O(t^2 \cdot \log^2 n)$ random bits, and where the running time of all parties is polynomial in n.

Basic Protocol. We start with describing the construction in [27]. Following [27], we first assume that there is an ideal functionality $\mathcal{F}_{\text{rand}}$ that generates correlated random bits for all parties. The protocol is as follows:

1. $\mathcal{F}_{\text{rand}}$ first prepare n random bits $r_1, r_2, \ldots, r_n$ subject to $\oplus_{i=1}^n r_i = 0$. We will specify the distribution of these n bits later. Then $\mathcal{F}_{\text{rand}}$ sends r_i to P_i.
2. Each party P_i uses r_i to mask its input x_i by computing $g_i = x_i \oplus r_i$. Note that $\oplus_{i=1}^n g_i = (\oplus_{i=1}^n x_i) \oplus (\oplus_{i=1}^n r_i) = \oplus_{i=1}^n x_i$. Therefore, the task becomes to compute the XOR of $g_1, g_2, \ldots, g_n$.
3. From $i = 2$ to n, the party P_i receives the partial result $G_{i-1} = \oplus_{j=1}^{i-1} g_j$ from P_{i-1} and computes the partial result $G_i = G_{i-1} \oplus g_i$. Then this result is sent to P_{i+1}. Thus, the last party P_n learns $G_n = \oplus_{i=1}^n g_i = \oplus_{i=1}^n x_i$ and distributes the function output to all other parties.

The correctness of the protocol follows from the description. As for security, note that when $(r_1, r_2, \ldots, r_n)$ are uniformly random subject to $\oplus_{i=1}^n r_i = 0$, $(g_1, g_2, \ldots, g_n)$ are also uniformly random subject to $\oplus_{i=1}^n g_i = f(\boldsymbol{x})$, where $f(\boldsymbol{x})$ is the function output. Thus, even learning all $\{g_i\}_{i=1}^n$ reveals no information about honest parties' inputs. Therefore, the protocol is secure when $(r_1, r_2, \ldots, r_n)$ are uniformly random subject to $\oplus_{i=1}^n r_i = 0$.

Kushilevitz and Mansour [27] noted that, as long as the distribution of the joint view of corrupted parties remains unchanged, we can relax the requirement of the distribution of $\boldsymbol{r} = (r_1, r_2, \ldots, r_n)$ without breaking the security. Concretely, let $\tilde{\boldsymbol{r}} = (\tilde{r}_1, \tilde{r}_2, \ldots, \tilde{r}_n)$ be uniformly random bits subject to $\oplus_{i=1}^n \tilde{r}_i = 0$. Let $\texttt{View}(P_i, \boldsymbol{x}, \boldsymbol{r})$ denote the view of P_i in an execution with input $\boldsymbol{x}$ and random bits $\boldsymbol{r}$. A sufficient condition of maintaining the protocol security is that, for all $\boldsymbol{x}$ and for all set T of t parties, the random variables $\boldsymbol{r}$ satisfy that

$$\{\texttt{View}(P_i, \boldsymbol{x}, \boldsymbol{r})\}_{i \in T} \equiv \{\texttt{View}(P_i, \boldsymbol{x}, \tilde{\boldsymbol{r}})\}_{i \in T}.$$

Note that $\texttt{View}(P_i, \boldsymbol{x}, \boldsymbol{r})$ contains (x_i, r_i, G_{i-1}, G_n) (Here G_n is the value received from P_n). Recall that $g_i = x_i \oplus r_i$ for all $i \in \{1, 2, \ldots, n\}$. Given $\boldsymbol{x}$, we are interested in $(r_i, \oplus_{j=1}^{i-1} r_j, \oplus_{j=1}^n r_j)$. Let $W = \{r_i, \oplus_{j=1}^{i-1} r_j\}_{i \in T} \bigcup \{\oplus_{j=1}^n r_j\}$. Then the above condition can be interpreted as

$$\mathcal{D}(\boldsymbol{r}, W) \equiv \mathcal{D}(\tilde{\boldsymbol{r}}, W),$$

where $\mathcal{D}(\boldsymbol{r}, W)$ and $\mathcal{D}(\tilde{\boldsymbol{r}}, W)$ refer to the distributions of the variables in W instantiated by $\boldsymbol{r}$ and $\tilde{\boldsymbol{r}}$ respectively.[2]

Based on this observation, Kushilevitz and Mansour [27] showed the existence of a sampling space of $\boldsymbol{r}$ of size $(n/t)^{O(t)}$. Therefore, sampling a random $\boldsymbol{r}$ requires $O(t \cdot \log(n/t))$ random bits. Finally, to obtain a protocol in the standard model, it is sufficient to realize $\mathcal{F}_{\text{rand}}$. This is done by letting each of the first $t+1$ parties sample a fresh copy of the random string $\boldsymbol{r}$. Then all parties use the XOR of all random strings in the protocol. Intuitively, since there are at most t corrupted parties, at least one copy of the random string is generated by an honest party, which is unknown to the corrupted parties. Therefore, given the random strings generated by corrupted parties, the XOR of all random strings has the same distribution as that generated by $\mathcal{F}_{\text{rand}}$. In this way, Kushilevitz and Mansour [27] obtained an MPC protocol for XOR with randomness complexity $O(t^2 \cdot \log(n/t))$.

---

[2] This formalization is from [19].

Parity Sharing Generator [19]. In [19], Goyal et al. generalized the approach of Kushilevitz and Mansour [27] to support any order of computing the XOR of $g_1, g_2, \ldots, g_n$.[3] Similarly to [19], our protocol is based on a tree $\mathtt{Tr}$ with n leaf nodes that represents a possible way of computing the parity of n bits. However, unlike [19], for our explicit construction it is crucial that $\mathtt{Tr}$ be a low-depth *full* binary tree (i.e., each node has either two children or no child). Then $\mathtt{Tr}$ has exactly $n-1$ internal nodes and logarithmic depth. The tree $\mathtt{Tr}$ defines the following order of computing the XOR of n bits: All parties start with n bits $g_1, g_2, \ldots, g_n$ associated with all leaf nodes. Each time, P_i is responsible to compute the bit associated with the i-th internal node by querying from other parties the bits associated with the two children of the i-th internal node and XORing these two bits. Finally, P_{n-1} computes the bit associated with the root node, which is equal to $\sum_{i=1}^{n} g_i$.

For a node $v \in \mathtt{Tr}$, let g_v denote the value associated with v, and S_v denote the set of all leaf nodes that are descendants of v. Then $\{g_v\}_{v \in \mathtt{Tr}}$ satisfy that for all internal node v, $g_v = \sum_{i \in S_v} g_i$. For a set T of t corrupted parties, let V be the set of nodes such that for all $v \in V$, g_v is in the joint view of all corrupted parties. Note that the view of each party only contains g_v's for a constant number of nodes v. We have $|V| = O(t)$. Consider the set $W := \{\oplus_{i \in S_v} r_i \mid v \in V\}$. With a similar argument, a sufficient condition of proving security is that, the random variables $\boldsymbol{r}$ satisfy that

$$\mathcal{D}(\boldsymbol{r}, W) \equiv \mathcal{D}(\tilde{\boldsymbol{r}}, W),$$

where $\tilde{\boldsymbol{r}} = (\tilde{r}_1, \tilde{r}_2, \ldots, \tilde{r}_n)$ are uniformly random subject to $\oplus_{i=1}^{n} \tilde{r}_i = 0$.

To generate such random bits $\boldsymbol{r}$, Goyal et al. [19] introduced the notion of *parity sharing generators.*[4]

Definition 1 (Access Set [19]**).** *An access set $\mathcal{A}$ of a set of random variables $\{r_1, r_2, \ldots, r_n\}$ is a set of jointly distributed random variables satisfying the following requirements:*

1. *For all $i \in \{1, 2, \ldots, n\}$, $r_i \in \mathcal{A}$.*
2. *Every variable in $\mathcal{A}$ is a linear combination of $r_1, r_2, \ldots, r_n$.*

Definition 2 (Parity Sharing Generators [19]**).** *Let $G : \{0,1\}^m \to \{0,1\}^n$ be a function, $\boldsymbol{u} = (u_1, u_2, \ldots, u_m)$ be a vector of random variables in $\{0,1\}^m$ that are uniformly distributed, and $\boldsymbol{r} = (r_1, r_2, \ldots, r_n) = G(\boldsymbol{u})$. Let $\mathcal{A}$ be an access set of the random variables $\{r_1, r_2, \ldots, r_n\}$. The function G is a t-resilient parity sharing generator with respect to $\mathcal{A}$ if the following holds:*

1. *The output $\boldsymbol{r} = (r_1, r_2, \ldots, r_n)$ satisfies that $r_1 \oplus r_2 \oplus \ldots \oplus r_n = 0$.*

[3] The work [19] focuses on the private circuits model of [24]. However, it can be transformed to the setting of MPC.

[4] In fact, Goyal et al. [19] introduced the stronger notion of *robust* parity sharing generators, but only gave a probabilistic construction. See more discussion in the full version of this paper [20].

2. *Let $\tilde{\boldsymbol{r}} = (\tilde{r}_1, \tilde{r}_2, \dots, \tilde{r}_n)$ be a vector of random variables in $\{0,1\}^n$ which are uniformly distributed subject to $\tilde{r}_1 \oplus \tilde{r}_2 \oplus \dots \oplus \tilde{r}_n = 0$. For any set W of t variables in $\mathcal{A}$, the output $\boldsymbol{r}$ satisfies that*

$$\mathcal{D}(\boldsymbol{r}, W) \equiv \mathcal{D}(\tilde{\boldsymbol{r}}, W),$$

where $\mathcal{D}(\boldsymbol{r}, W)$ and $\mathcal{D}(\tilde{\boldsymbol{r}}, W)$ denote the distributions of the variables in W when they are instantiated by $\boldsymbol{r}$ and $\tilde{\boldsymbol{r}}$ respectively.

Note that when we choose the access set $\mathcal{A} = \{\oplus_{i \in S_v} r_i \mid v \in \mathtt{Tr}\}$, the output of an $O(t)$-resilient parity sharing generator with respect to $\mathcal{A}$ satisfies the sufficient condition. Thus, to obtain an explicit MPC protocol for the XOR function, it is sufficient to construct an explicit parity sharing generator with respect to $\mathcal{A}$.

Explicit Construction of Parity Sharing Generators. For a set of random variables $\{r_1, r_2, \dots, r_n\}$ and a full binary tree $\mathtt{Tr}$ with n leaf nodes, an access set $\mathcal{A}$ with respect to $\mathtt{Tr}$ is defined by $\mathcal{A} = \{\oplus_{i \in S_v} r_i \mid v \in \mathtt{Tr}\}$. We are interested in access sets that are based on full binary trees. Our construction uses a t-wise independent pseudo-random generator in a black box way.

Our idea is to assign a bit to each node in $\mathtt{Tr}$ such that for all internal node v and its two children c_0, c_1, the bit assigned to v is equal to the XOR of the bits assigned to c_0 and c_1. Then the bits associated with the leaf nodes are the output. Note that the access set $\mathcal{A}$ consists of the bits associated with all nodes in $\mathtt{Tr}$. For a node $v \in \mathtt{Tr}$, we use $\mathsf{val}(v)$ to denote the bit associated with v.

Let D be the depth of $\mathtt{Tr}$. Our construction works as follows:

1. We start with the root node. We set $\mathsf{val}(\mathtt{rt}) = 0$. This ensures that the XOR of the bits associated with all leaf nodes is equal to 0.
2. From $d = 2$ to D, assume that we have assigned bits to nodes of depth $d-1$. Let ℓ_d denote the number of nodes of depth d. Since $\mathtt{Tr}$ is a full binary tree, ℓ_d is even. We use $c_1, c_1, \dots, c_{\ell_d}$ to denote the nodes of depth d such that for all $i \in \{1, 2, \dots, \ell_d/2\}$, (c_{2i-1}, c_{2i}) are the two children of a node v_i of depth $d-1$. Since $\mathsf{val}(c_{2i}) = \mathsf{val}(c_{2i-1}) \oplus \mathsf{val}(v_i)$, we only need to assign a bit to the node c_{2i-1} and then compute the bit associated with c_{2i} accordingly. For $\{c_{2i-1}\}_{i=1}^{\ell_d/2}$, we use the output of a t-wise independent PRG.

Consider a set W of t bits in $\mathcal{A}$. Let $V = \{v \mid \mathsf{val}(v) \in W\}$. Then $|V| = t$. We want to prove that

$$\mathcal{D}(\boldsymbol{r}, \{\mathsf{val}(v)\}_{v \in V}) \equiv \mathcal{D}(\tilde{\boldsymbol{r}}, \{\mathsf{val}(v)\}_{v \in V}).$$

For a node v in $\mathtt{Tr}$, we say v is a *left node* if v is a left child of some node in $\mathtt{Tr}$. Similarly, we say v is a *right node* if v is a right child of some node in $\mathtt{Tr}$. Effectively, we only assign bits to all left nodes in $\mathtt{Tr}$. For each depth $d \geq 2$, the bits associated with all left nodes of depth d are t-wise independent. Thus, we want to find a set $V' \subset \mathtt{Tr}$ such that V' only contains left nodes and the bits in V' fully determine the bits in V.

Consider the following process:

- For each right node in V, since the bit associated with this node is determined by the bits associated with its left sibling and its parent, we can remove this right node from V and add its left sibling and its parent in V. We repeat the same step for its parent until the parent node is a left node or a root node.
- Note that the bit associated with the root node is a constant 0. We can always remove the root node from V.

In this way, we obtain the set V' that only contains left nodes such that the bits in V' fully determine the bits in V. Thus, it is sufficient to prove that

$$\mathcal{D}(\boldsymbol{r}, \{\mathsf{val}(v)\}_{v\in V'}) \equiv \mathcal{D}(\tilde{\boldsymbol{r}}, \{\mathsf{val}(v)\}_{v\in V'}).$$

We observe that, to remove a right node in V, we may need to insert a left node of each depth. In other words, for all $d \geq 2$, removing a right node in V may insert at most 1 left node of depth d. Therefore, the number of left nodes in V' is bounded by $|V| = t$. Recall that in our construction, we use t-wise independent random bits for all left nodes of each depth. It means that the bits associated with nodes in V' are uniformly random. Thus $\mathcal{D}(\boldsymbol{r}, \{\mathsf{val}(v)\}_{v\in V'})$ is identical to the distribution of $|V'|$ random bits.

We can show that $\mathcal{D}(\tilde{\boldsymbol{r}}, \{\mathsf{val}(v)\}_{v\in V'})$ is also identical to the distribution of $|V'|$ random bits. Intuitively, this is because $\tilde{\boldsymbol{r}}$ is already the most uniform output we can hope. Since $\{\mathsf{val}(v)\}_{v\in V'}$ are uniformly random bits when instantiated by $\boldsymbol{r}$, they should also be uniformly random when instantiated by $\tilde{\boldsymbol{r}}$. Thus, our construction yields a t-resilient parity sharing generator.

Regarding the input size of our construction (i.e., the number of random bits), we need to invoke a t-wise independent PRG for each depth. Therefore, the input size of our construction is D times the input size of a t-wise independent PRG. It is well-known that when the output size is n, there is an explicit t-wise independent PRG with input size $O(t \cdot \log n)$. Also, we can choose to use a full binary tree of depth $\log n$. Therefore, we obtain an explicit construction of a t-resilient parity sharing generator that uses $O(t \cdot \log^2 n)$ random bits. When we use our explicit construction to instantiate the MPC protocol for XOR from [19,27], we obtain an MPC protocol that uses $O(t^2 \cdot \log^2 n)$ random bits.

From a Single Parity to Multiple Additions. All of the above techniques (including the techniques from [19,27] and our techniques of constructing parity sharing generators) can be naturally extended to addition over any Abelian group $\mathbb{G}$, increasing the randomness complexity by a $\log |\mathbb{G}|$ factor. We show that one can in fact do better in the *amortized* setting of computing many additions. Concretely, the asymptotic randomness cost of computing t additions is essentially the same computing a single addition. We outline the techniques below.

First, we naturally extend the notion of a parity sharing generator to a general Abelian group $\mathbb{G}$, referring to the generalized notion as a *zero sharing generator*. We show that our technique also yields an explicit construction of zero-sharing generator. We then amortize the randomness complexity by using the following natural randomness extraction approach. Consider the case of $\mathbb{Z}_2$ for simplicity. Suppose all parties want to compute the XOR function ℓ times. We can first prepare the random strings $\boldsymbol{r}^{(1)}, \boldsymbol{r}^{(2)}, \ldots, \boldsymbol{r}^{(\ell)}$ in a batch way, and then use one fresh copy in each execution. Finally, we use a t-resilient randomness extractor $\texttt{Ext} : \{0,1\}^m \rightarrow \{0,1\}^\ell$ for bit-fixing sources [12], guaranteeing that when the input is randomly sampled from $\{0,1\}^m$, the output is uniformly random even when conditioned on any t input bits.

To prepare the random strings $\boldsymbol{r}^{(1)}, \boldsymbol{r}^{(2)}, \ldots, \boldsymbol{r}^{(\ell)}$, we will let each P_i of the first m parties distribute a fresh copy of the random string, denoted by $\boldsymbol{\tau}^{(i)}$. Then all parties use Ext to extract ℓ random strings. By the property of a t-resilient randomness extractor, the output strings $\{\boldsymbol{r}^{(i)}\}_{i=1}^{\ell}$ are random given the random strings $\{\boldsymbol{\tau}^{(i)}\}_{i\in T}$ generated by corrupted parties.

It is known that there is a t-resilient randomness extractor based on Vandermonde matrices with input size $m = \ell + t \cdot \log(\ell + t)$. Thus, we obtain an MPC protocol for ℓ XOR computations that uses $O((\ell+t\cdot\log(\ell+t))\cdot t\cdot\log^2 n)$ random bits, giving an amortized cost of only $O(t \cdot \log^2 n)$ random bits per XOR.

2.4 Upper Bounds Beyond Linear Functions

The previous upper bounds apply only to linear functions over an Abelian group. Building on these results, we obtain near-optimal upper bounds for general symmetric functions, or even general circuits if additional "helper parties" are allowed.

Upper Bound for Symmetric Functions. For any symmetric function $f : \{0,1\}^n \rightarrow \{0,1\}$, we show that there is an explicit MPC protocol that uses $O(t^2 \cdot \log^3 n)$ random bits. This includes useful functions such as majority or threshold, and matches the previous lower bound for nontrivial symmetric functions up to a polylogarithmic term. Our protocol uses the standard Shamir secret sharing scheme and the BGW protocol [4,11]. We will use $[r]_t$ to denote a degree-t Shamir sharing of r. Our idea works for all $t < \frac{n}{\lceil \log n \rceil}$:

1. For a symmetric function f, the output only depends on the number of 1s in the input bits. Let p be a prime such that $n < p < 2n$. Consider the finite field $\mathbb{F}_p$. All parties will first compute a degree-t Shamir secret sharing of the summation of all input bits in $\mathbb{F}_p$, denoted by $[s]_t$. This is achieved by the following steps:
   (a) All parties first prepare a random degree-t Shamir sharing $[r]_t$ by letting each of the first $t+1$ parties distributes a random degree-t Shamir sharing and using the summation of these $t+1$ sharings. They transform $[r]_t$ to a random additive sharing by locally multiplying proper Lagrange coefficients with their shares.
   (b) All parties compute the summation of all input bits together with all shares of the random additive sharing by using our protocol for addition over $\mathbb{F}_p$ (recall that we extend the protocol for XOR to addition over any Abelian group). Then the output is equal to $s + r$, where s is the summation of all input bits.
   (c) Finally, all parties locally compute $[s]_t = (s + r) - [r]_t$.

2. Note that s is the number of 1s in the input bits, and $s \in \{0,1,\ldots,n\}$. Therefore, there exists a function $g : \{0,1,\ldots,n\} \rightarrow \{0,1\}$ such that $f(\boldsymbol{x}) = g(s)$, where $s = \sum_{i=1}^{n} x_i$. We note that g can be represented by a degree-n polynomial in $\mathbb{F}_p$. Our idea is to compute a Shamir sharing of the output $g(s)$.
   (a) All parties first use the BGW protocol to compute $[s^{2^i}]_t$ for all $i \in \{0,1,\ldots,\lceil \log n \rceil - 1\}$. This step requires $O(\log n)$ multiplications.
   (b) Then, all parties can use $\{[s^{2^i}]_t\}_{i=0}^{\lceil \log n \rceil - 1}$ to locally compute a Shamir sharing of s^j for all $j \in \{1,2,\ldots,n\}$. In particular, the resulting sharing has degree at most $t \cdot \lceil \log n \rceil < n$. Therefore, the resulting sharing can still be reconstructed by all parties. Thus, they can locally compute a Shamir sharing of the output $g(s)$ of degree at most $t \cdot \lceil \log n \rceil < n$.
3. Finally, all parties reconstruct the Shamir sharing of $g(s)$. This is achieved by first transforming it to an additive sharing of $g(s)$ and then using our protocol for addition over $\mathbb{F}_p$.

In summary, we need 2 invocations of the addition protocol over $\mathbb{F}_p$ and $O(\log n)$ multiplications using the BGW protocol [4] (the preparation of a degree-t Shamir sharing costs the same amount of randomness as doing 1 multiplication in [4]). In [4], doing $O(\log n)$ multiplications require $O(t^2 \cdot \log n)$ random field elements. Our addition protocol over $\mathbb{F}_p$ requires $O(t^2 \cdot \log^2 n)$ random field elements. Since each element in $\mathbb{F}_p$ is of size $O(\log n)$, for any symmetric function, we obtain an explicit construct that uses $O(t^2 \cdot \log^3 n)$ random bits. We refer the readers to the full version of this paper [20] for more details.

Upper Bound for General Circuits with Helper Parties. Finally, we consider the goal of evaluating general functions in a relaxed setting where there are extra helper parties that can participate in the protocol but do not have inputs nor receive the output. In this model, we give an explicit MPC protocol for a general circuit C that uses $O(t^2 \cdot \log |C|)$ random bits, where $|C|$ is the circuit size. Since our lower bound for XOR extends to the setting of helper parties, this upper bound is essentially optimal.

Our construction uses a variant of the private circuits model from [24] referred to as a *leakage-tolerant* private circuit [1,22], building on the recent randomness-efficient construction from [19].[5] Informally, a leakage-tolerant private circuit with (unprotected) input x and output y is a randomized circuit such that the values of any t internal wire values can be simulated by probing t input and output wires. Letting each party simulate a single gate in such a tolerant circuit, we obtain an MPC protocol with helper parties in which corrupting t parties reveals at most t inputs and outputs. Note that it does *not* directly give us an

[5] In the current context, one could plausibly use the explicit construction of a private circuit with quadratic randomness complexity in [14] as a substitute for the quasilinar-randomness construction from [19]. However, the analysis of [14] only considers standard leakage-resilience whereas here we need the stronger leakage-tolerance property analyzed in [19].

MPC protocol in the usual sense, since the revealed inputs and outputs may belong to honest parties.

Our idea is to first let all parties secret-share their inputs among the helper parties. Then all helper parties together emulate a leakage-tolerant private circuit to compute a secret-sharing of the function output. Finally, the output is reconstructed to the parties who should receive it. To make this idea work, we need to design an efficient protocol that allows parties to secret-share their inputs:

1. We note that, for each party P_i, it is sufficient to use a t-private encoding of its input. This is because corrupting any t helper parties reveals at most t input and output values, which are independent of P_i's input. We borrow the encoding scheme from [19], which is based on a strong t-wise independent PRG. It requires $O(t \cdot \log m)$ random bits to encode m bits.
2. However, we cannot afford the cost of allowing each party to use fresh random seeds to encode their inputs, since it requires $O(t \cdot n \cdot \log m)$ random bits. We observe that all parties can actually use t-wise independent random seeds. This is because each corrupted party who holds an input only observes its own random seed, and each corrupted helper party receives at most one bit of the encoding of some input. Thus, the joint view of corrupted parties depends on the encoding of at most t inputs, which in turn depend on at most t random seeds. Therefore, t-wise independent random seeds are sufficient. Generating these random seeds (via a trusted party) require $O(t^2 \cdot \log m)$ random bits.
3. Finally, note that we *cannot* use the same method as that in [27] to generate these random seeds in a distributed way because the random seeds have size $O(t^2 \cdot \log m)$. If we ask each of the first $t+1$ parties to generate a fresh copy of the random seeds, we would need $O(t^3 \cdot \log m)$ random bits. Our idea is to use a t-resilient randomness extractor. We ask each of the first $2t$ parties to generate t-wise independent random seeds of size $O(t \cdot \log m)$. Then, all parties use a t-resilient randomness extractor to extract t copies of fresh random seeds. Finally, each party concatenates its t copies and obtains a random seed of length $O(t^2 \cdot \log m)$.

We use the construction of a leakage-tolerant private circuit from [19], which uses $O(t \cdot \log t|C|)$ random bits. Since the input size m is upper bounded by the circuit size, we obtain an MPC protocol for a general circuit that uses only $O(t^2 \cdot \log |C|)$ random bits.

As a final challenge, note that the leakage-tolerant private circuit in [19] is not explicit. In the full version of this paper [20], we show that our technique allows us to obtain an explicit multi-phase parity sharing generator, which outputs multiple additive sharings of 0. Then, we show how to use our explicit construction of multi-phase parity sharing generators to instantiate the private circuit in [19]. The instantiation only requires $O(t^2 \cdot \log^2 t|C|)$ random bits. We use it to obtain an *explicit* construction of an MPC protocol (with helper parties) for a general circuit C that uses $O(t^2 \cdot \log^2 t|C|)$ random bits.

3 Preliminaries

3.1 Secure Multiparty Computation

In this work, we consider the setting where a set of n parties, $\{P_1, P_2, \ldots, P_n\}$, each holding an input x_i from a finite domain D_i, jointly run a protocol to compute a function $f : D_1 \times \ldots \times D_n \to Z$. At the end of the protocol, all parties receive the function output $f(x_1, \ldots, x_n)$.

Each party has a private random tape which contains uniformly random bits. We use $\boldsymbol{x} = (x_1, x_2, \ldots, x_n)$ to denote the inputs of all parties and $\boldsymbol{r} = (r_1, r_2, \ldots, r_n)$ to denote the random tapes of all parties. For a party P_i, we use $\texttt{View}(P_i, \boldsymbol{x}, \boldsymbol{r})$ to denote the information that is observed by P_i in an execution with inputs $\boldsymbol{x}$ and random tapes $\boldsymbol{r}$, which includes his input, random tape, messages received from other parties, and the function output. We use $\texttt{View}(P_i, \boldsymbol{x})$ to denote the random variable over the distribution induced by $\texttt{View}(P_i, \boldsymbol{x}, \boldsymbol{r})$ when $\boldsymbol{r}$ is sampled uniformly.

In this work, we consider perfect correctness and semi-honest security with perfect privacy, defined as follows.

Definition 3 (Correctness and Security). *Let $f : D_1 \times \ldots \times D_n \to Z$ be an n-ary function. For an n-party computation protocol Π that computes f,*

- *(Correctness). We say Π achieves perfect correctness if for all input $\boldsymbol{x}$, when all parties honestly follow the protocol Π, they will finally output $f(\boldsymbol{x})$.*
- *(Security). We say Π achieves semi-honest security with perfect privacy if for all set T of at most t parties, and for all input $\boldsymbol{x}$, there is a probabilistic algorithm $\mathcal{S}$, which takes as input the inputs of parties in T and the function output, and outputs the views of parties in T, such that the following two distributions are identical:*

$$\{\mathcal{S}(\{x_i\}_{i\in T}, f(\boldsymbol{x})), f(\boldsymbol{x})\} \equiv \{\{\texttt{View}(P_i, \boldsymbol{x})\}_{i\in T}, f(\boldsymbol{x})\}.$$

If Π achieves both perfect correctness and semi-honest security with perfect privacy, we say Π achieves perfect semi-honest security.

Intuitively, the security requires that the joint view of all corrupted parties only depends on their inputs and the function output. We have the following property of a protocol Π with semi-honest security and perfect privacy.

Property 1. Let $f : D_1 \times \ldots D_n \to Z$ be an n-ary function. Let Π be an n-party protocol that computes f with semi-honest security and perfect privacy against t corrupted parties. Then for all set T of at most t parties, and for all $\boldsymbol{x}, \boldsymbol{x}' \in D_1 \times \ldots \times D_n$ such that $f(\boldsymbol{x}) = f(\boldsymbol{x}')$ and $x_i = x'_i$ for all $i \in T$, the following two distributions are identical:

$$\{\texttt{View}(P_i, \boldsymbol{x})\}_{i\in T} \equiv \{\texttt{View}(P_i, \boldsymbol{x}')\}_{i\in T}.$$

Randomness Complexity of a Protocol. We follow the definition of randomness complexity from [27]. At the beginning of the protocol, each party has a private random tape that contains uniformly random bits. Each time a party needs to use a random bit, he reads the rightmost unused bit on his random tape. Note that each party may use different number of random bits in different executions. The number of random bits that is used by the protocol is the total number of random bits used by all parties. The randomness complexity is the worst case (over all inputs and all executions) number of random bits. The same model for randomness complexity is also used in [21,29,31].

We will use the following lemma from [21,31].

Lemma 1 ([21,31]). *For a given input $\boldsymbol{x}$, let d be the maximum, over all protocol executions on $\boldsymbol{x}$, of the number of random bits used by all parties during a given execution. Then, the number of different transcripts (i.e., the joint view of all parties) of the protocol execution on $\boldsymbol{x}$ is at most 2^d.*

For some of our positive results, it is convenient to use a natural generalization of this model where parties can sample a uniform value from $\{1, 2, \ldots, p\}$ for any choice of integer $p > 1$. We assume that $\lceil p \rceil = O(\log p)$ random bits are consumed. This can be justified by either entropy considerations, or by the fact that $O(\log p)$ random bits are sufficient to generate a uniform value from $\{1, 2, \ldots, p\}$ in expectation [9,26].

We note that our lower bound also applies to the generalized model with the help of Lemma 1 in the generalized model, of which we provide a proof in the full version of this paper [20].

Helper Parties. We also consider a general model where there are extra k parties $\{P_{n+1}, P_{n+2}, \ldots, P_{n+k}\}$. These parties can participate in the computation but do not have inputs, nor receive the output. We refer to these parties as *helper parties.* The randomness complexity of a protocol in the general model also counts the random bits used by helper parties. The perfect semi-honest security in the general model is defined similarly.

Functions with Minimal Input Domain. For a party P_i, and two distinct inputs $x_i \neq x_i'$, we say a function f is sensitive to (P_i, x_i, x_i') if there exists $\{x_j\}_{j \neq i}$ such that

$$f(x_1, \ldots, x_{i-1}, x_i, x_{i+1}, \ldots, x_n) \neq f(x_1, \ldots, x_{i-1}, x_i', x_{i+1}, \ldots, x_n).$$

We say a function f has minimal input domain if f is sensitive to all possible (P_i, x_i, x_i').

Note that if f is not sensitive to (P_i, x_i, x_i'), it means that the function behaves identically on input x_i and x_i'. Then, P_i can always use x_i when his input is x_i' without changing the output of the function, which reduces the size of P_i's input domain. Thus, for a function f that is *not* sensitive to all (P_i, x_i, x_i'), we can repeat the above step and reduce the input domain of f. Therefore, without loss of generality, it is sufficient to only consider functions with minimal input domain.

Symmetric Functions. We say a function f is a symmetric function if it satisfies that:

- All inputs have the same input domain. I.e., $D_1 = D_2 = \ldots = D_n$.
- The output of the function f is independent of the order of the inputs. I.e., for all $\boldsymbol{x} = (x_1, x_2, \ldots, x_n)$ and $\boldsymbol{x}' = (x'_1, x'_2, \ldots, x'_n)$, where $\boldsymbol{x}'$ is a permutation of $\boldsymbol{x}$, $f(\boldsymbol{x}) = f(\boldsymbol{x}')$.

3.2 t-Private Encoding Schemes

Definition 4 (Encoding Scheme). *Let ℓ, n be positive integers. Let $\mathcal{M} \subset \{0,1\}^\ell$ be the message space and $\mathcal{C} \subset \{0,1\}^n$ be the codeword space. An* encoding scheme *consists of a pair of algorithms* $(\mathtt{Enc}, \mathtt{Dec})$ *where:*

- $\mathtt{Enc}$ *is a randomized algorithm which takes as input a message $m \in \mathcal{M}$ and a random tape $r \in \mathcal{R}$, and outputs a codeword $c \in \mathcal{C}$, denoted by $c = \mathtt{Enc}(m; r)$. When r is not important in the context, we will omit r and simply write $c = \mathtt{Enc}(m)$.*
- $\mathtt{Dec}$ *is a deterministic algorithm which takes as input a codeword $c \in \mathcal{C}$ and outputs a message $m \in \mathcal{M}$.*

The correctness of an encoding scheme requires that for all $m \in \mathcal{M}$, the following holds:

$$\Pr[\mathtt{Dec}(\mathtt{Enc}(m)) = m] = 1$$

Definition 5 (t-Private Encoding Scheme). *We say an encoding scheme* $(\mathtt{Enc}, \mathtt{Dec})$ *is t-private, if for all $m, m' \in M$ and for all t indices $i_1, i_2, ..., i_t \in \{1, 2, \ldots, n\}$, the following two distributions are identical:*

$$\{c \leftarrow \mathtt{Enc}(m) : c[i_1], c[i_2], \ldots, c[i_t]\} \equiv \{c' \leftarrow \mathtt{Enc}(m') : c'[i_1], c'[i_2], \ldots, c'[i_t]\},$$

where $c[i]$ (resp., $c'[i]$) is the i-th bit of c (resp., c').

Strong t-wise Independent Pseudo-random Generators. Our work will use the standard notion of (strong) t-wise independent pseudo-random generators.

Definition 6 ((Strong) t-wise Independent PRG). *Let $\mathbb{G}$ be a finite Abelian group. A function $G : \mathbb{G}^\ell \to \mathbb{G}^n$ is a t-wise independent pseudo-random generator (or t-wise independent PRG for short) if any subset of t group elements of $G(x)$ are uniformly random and independently distributed when x is uniformly sampled from $\mathbb{G}^\ell$.*

If any subset of t group elements of $(x, G(x))$ are uniformly random and independently distributed when x is uniformly sampled from $\mathbb{G}^\ell$, then we say G is a strong t-wise independent PRG.

We say that a (strong) t-wise independent PRG G is linear *if every output group element is a linear combination of the input group elements. In particular, a linear (strong) t-wise independent PRG G satisfies that for all $x, x' \in \mathbb{G}^\ell$, $G(x) + G(x') = G(x + x')$.*

For a finite field $\mathbb{F}$, it is well known that there is a linear and strong t-wise independent PRG $G : \mathbb{F}^\ell \to \mathbb{F}^n$ based on Reed-Solomon codes with input size $\ell = O(t \cdot \log n)$. (See [19] for a construction over binary field, which can be extended to any finite field.)

Theorem 1. *Let $\mathbb{F}$ be a finite field and n, t be positive integers. Then there is a linear and strong t-wise independent PRG $G : \mathbb{F}^\ell \to \mathbb{F}^n$ with input size $\ell = O(t \cdot \log n)$.*

Randomness Efficient t-Private Encoding Scheme. We borrow the following linear t-private encoding scheme from [19].

Let $G : \{0,1\}^\ell \to \{0,1\}^n$ be a linear and strong t-wise independent PRG. The encoding scheme $(\mathtt{Enc}, \mathtt{Dec})$ works as follows:

- The message space is $\mathcal{M} = \{0,1\}^n$ and the codeword space is $\mathcal{C} = \{0,1\}^{\ell+n}$.
- The encoder $\mathtt{Enc}$ takes $\boldsymbol{x} \in \{0,1\}^n$ as input and $\boldsymbol{\rho} \in \{0,1\}^\ell$ as random tape. Then
$$\mathtt{Enc}(\boldsymbol{x}; \boldsymbol{\rho}) = (\boldsymbol{\rho}, G(\boldsymbol{\rho}) \oplus \boldsymbol{x}).$$
- The decoder $\mathtt{Dec}$ takes $(\boldsymbol{c}_1, \boldsymbol{c}_2) \in \{0,1\}^\ell \times \{0,1\}^n$ as input and outputs
$$\mathtt{Dec}(\boldsymbol{c}_1, \boldsymbol{c}_2) = G(\boldsymbol{c}_1) \oplus \boldsymbol{c}_2.$$

The linearity follows from that the t-wise independent PRG G is linear. As for t-privacy, since G is a strong t-wise independent PRG, any t bits of $(\boldsymbol{\rho}, G(\boldsymbol{\rho}))$ are uniformly random when $\boldsymbol{\rho}$ is uniformly sampled from $\{0,1\}^\ell$. Therefore, any t bits of $(\boldsymbol{\rho}, G(\boldsymbol{\rho}) \oplus \boldsymbol{x})$ are also uniformly random and thus, independent of $\boldsymbol{x}$.

3.3 Zero Sharing Generators

We first define the notion of access set of a set of random variables $\{r_1, r_2, \ldots, r_n\}$.

Definition 1 (Access Set [19]). *An access set $\mathcal{A}$ of a set of random variables $\{r_1, r_2, \ldots, r_n\}$ is a set of jointly distributed random variables satisfying the following requirements:*

1. *For all $i \in \{1, 2, \ldots, n\}$, $r_i \in \mathcal{A}$.*
2. *Every variable in $\mathcal{A}$ is a linear combination of $r_1, r_2, \ldots, r_n$.*

Let $\boldsymbol{r} = (r_1, r_2, \ldots, r_n)$. For a set $W \subset \mathcal{A}$, we use $\mathcal{D}(\boldsymbol{r}, W)$ to denote the distribution of the variables in W when they are instantiated by $\boldsymbol{r}$.

We follow [19] and define the notion of zero sharing generators. In [19], Goyal, et al. focuses on the binary field. We extend this notion to any finite Abelian group $\mathbb{G}$.

Definition 7 (Zero Sharing Generators [19]). *Let $\mathbb{G}$ be a finite Abelian group. Let $G : \mathbb{G}^m \to \mathbb{G}^n$ be a function, $\boldsymbol{u} = (u_1, u_2, \ldots, u_m)$ be a vector of random variables in $\mathbb{G}^m$ that are uniformly distributed, and $\boldsymbol{r} = (r_1, r_2, \ldots, r_n) = G(\boldsymbol{u})$. Let $\mathcal{A}$ be an access set of the random variables $\{r_1, r_2, \ldots, r_n\}$. The function G is a t-resilient zero sharing generator with respect to $\mathcal{A}$ if the following holds:*

1. *The output* $\boldsymbol{r} = (r_1, r_2, \ldots, r_n)$ *satisfies that* $r_1 + r_2 + \ldots + r_n = 0$.
2. *Let* $\tilde{\boldsymbol{r}} = (\tilde{r}_1, \tilde{r}_2, \ldots, \tilde{r}_n)$ *be a vector of random variables in* $\mathbb{G}^n$ *which are uniformly distributed subject to* $\tilde{r}_1 + \tilde{r}_2 + \ldots + \tilde{r}_n = 0$. *For any set* W *of* t *variables in* $\mathcal{A}$, *the output* $\boldsymbol{r}$ *satisfies that*

$$\mathcal{D}(\boldsymbol{r}, W) \equiv \mathcal{D}(\tilde{\boldsymbol{r}}, W),$$

where $\mathcal{D}(\boldsymbol{r}, W)$ *and* $\mathcal{D}(\tilde{\boldsymbol{r}}, W)$ *denote the distributions of the variables in* W *when they are instantiated by* $\boldsymbol{r}$ *and* $\tilde{\boldsymbol{r}}$ *respectively.*

One can view a t-resilient zero sharing generator as a generalization of a t-wise independent PRG in the following two ways:

- First, the output vector should satisfies that the summation of all entries is equal to 0.
- Second, for a t-wise independent PRG, one may think that there is an adversary which can access any t entries in the output vector. A t-resilient zero sharing generator allows an adversary to access any t variables in the access set $\mathcal{A}$ which contains all entries of the output vector.

We can extend a t-resilient zero sharing generator to generating multiple zero sharings with different number of shares as follows.

Definition 8 (Multi-Phase Zero Sharing Generators [19]**).** *Let* $\mathbb{G}$ *be a finite Abelian group. Let* p *and* $n_1, n_2, \ldots, n_p$ *be positive integers,* $G : \mathbb{G}^m \rightarrow \mathbb{G}^{n_1} \times \mathbb{G}^{n_2} \times \ldots \times \mathbb{G}^{n_p}$ *be a function,* $\boldsymbol{u} = (u_1, u_2, \ldots, u_m)$ *be a vector of random variables in* $\mathbb{G}^m$ *that are uniformly distributed, and* $\boldsymbol{r} = (\boldsymbol{r}^{(1)}, \ldots, \boldsymbol{r}^{(p)}) = G(\boldsymbol{u})$ *where* $\boldsymbol{r}^{(j)} = (r_1^{(j)}, \ldots, r_{n_j}^{(j)})$ *for all* $j \in \{1, 2, \ldots, p\}$. *For each* $\boldsymbol{r}^{(j)}$, *let* $\mathcal{A}_j$ *be an access set of the random variables* $\{r_1^{(j)}, \ldots, r_{n_j}^{(j)}\}$, *and* $\mathcal{A} = \bigcup_{j=1}^{p} \mathcal{A}_j$. *The function* G *is a multi-phase* t*-resilient zero sharing generator with respect to* $\mathcal{A}$ *if the following holds:*

1. *For all* $j = \{1, 2, \ldots, p\}$, *the output vector* $\boldsymbol{r}^{(j)} = (r_1^{(j)}, \ldots, r_{n_j}^{(j)})$ *satisfies* $r_1^{(j)} + \ldots + r_{n_j}^{(j)} = 0$.
2. *Let* $\tilde{\boldsymbol{r}} = (\tilde{\boldsymbol{r}}^{(1)}, \ldots, \tilde{\boldsymbol{r}}^{(p)}) \in \mathbb{G}^{n_1} \times \ldots \times \mathbb{G}^{n_p}$ *be uniformly random variables such that for all* $j = \{1, 2, \ldots, p\}$, *the vector* $\tilde{\boldsymbol{r}}^{(j)} = (\tilde{r}_1^{(j)}, \ldots, \tilde{r}_{n_j}^{(j)})$ *satisfies* $\tilde{r}_1^{(j)} + \ldots + \tilde{r}_{n_j}^{(j)} = 0$. *For any set* W *of* t *variables in* $\mathcal{A}$, *the output* $\boldsymbol{r}$ *satisfies*

$$\mathcal{D}(\boldsymbol{r}, W) \equiv \mathcal{D}(\tilde{\boldsymbol{r}}, W),$$

where $\mathcal{D}(\boldsymbol{r}, W)$ *and* $\mathcal{D}(\tilde{\boldsymbol{r}}, W)$ *denote the distributions of the variables in* W *when instantiated by* $\boldsymbol{r}$ *and* $\tilde{\boldsymbol{r}}$ *respectively.*

We say a (multi-phase) t-resilient zero sharing generator G is linear if every output group element is a linear combination of the input group elements. In particular, a linear (multi-phase) t-resilient zero sharing generator G satisfies that for all $\boldsymbol{u}, \boldsymbol{u}' \in \mathbb{G}^m$, $G(\boldsymbol{u}) + G(\boldsymbol{u}') = G(\boldsymbol{u} + \boldsymbol{u}')$.

Tree Based Access Sets. In our work, we are interested in access sets that are based on full binary trees. A full binary tree $\mathtt{Tr}$ satisfies that every node has either no children (i.e., a leaf node) or 2 children. For a set of random variables $\{r_1, r_2, \ldots, r_n\}$ and a full binary tree $\mathtt{Tr}$ with n leaf nodes, an access set $\mathcal{A}$ with respect to $\mathtt{Tr}$ is defined as follows: We first associate the i-th leaf node with the random variable r_i. Then, each internal node is associated with a random variable which is equal to the sum of the random variables associated with its two children. The set $\mathcal{A}$ contains the random variables associated with all nodes in $\mathtt{Tr}$.

4 Lower Bound for Symmetric Functions

In this section we prove our main lower bound, improving over the previous lower bound of [27]. We start with a technical lemma about the randomness complexity of a t-private encoding scheme and then use it to obtain the lower bound.

4.1 Lower Bound for t-private Encoding Schemes

In this section, we discuss the randomness complexity of a t-private encoding scheme. We focus on t-private encoding schemes that encode a single bit. We will show that, for any t-private encoding scheme and any input bit $m \in \{0, 1\}$, the number of codewords of m is at least 2^t. Note that it implies that any such a t-private encoding scheme requires at least t random bits. This result will be used to prove the lower bound of the randomness complexity of secure multiparty computation in the next section.

Lemma 2. *For any t-private encoding scheme* $(\mathtt{Enc}, \mathtt{Dec})$ *and any bit* $m \in \{0, 1\}$, $|\mathsf{supp}(m)| \geq 2^t$.

Proof. We prove the lemma by induction.

When $t = 1$, we show that the support of 0 is of size at least 2. Let c be a codeword of 0 and c' be a codeword of 1. By the correctness of the encoding scheme, $c \neq c'$. Without loss of generality, assume the first bits of c and c' are different. Since the encoding scheme is 1-private, the distribution of the first bit in a random codeword of 0 is identical to that in a random codeword of 1. Then the first bit in a random codeword of 0 is not a constant bit. Otherwise, the first bit in a random codeword of 1 should be the same constant bit, which contradicts with the assumption that the first bits of c and c' are different. Since the first bit can take both 0 and 1, there are at least two codewords of 0. The statement holds for $t = 1$.

Now suppose the statement holds for $t-1$, i.e., for any $(t-1)$-private encoding scheme $(\mathtt{Enc}, \mathtt{Dec})$ and any bit $m \in \{0, 1\}$, $|\mathsf{supp}(m)| \geq 2^{t-1}$. Consider a t-private encoding scheme $(\mathtt{Enc}, \mathtt{Dec})$. With the same argument as above, there exists a bit in a random codeword of 0 which is not a constant bit. Without loss of generality, assume that it is the first bit.

Consider the following encoding scheme $(\mathtt{Enc}', \mathtt{Dec}')$:

- For $m \in \{0,1\}$, $\mathtt{Enc}'(m)$ outputs a random codeword $c = \mathtt{Enc}(m)$ subject to $c[1] = 0$. Here $c[1]$ refers to the first bit of the codeword c.
- $\mathtt{Dec}' = \mathtt{Dec}$.

We show that $(\mathtt{Enc}', \mathtt{Dec}')$ is a $(t-1)$-private encoding scheme. Let $\mathtt{supp}'(m)$ denote the set of codewords of m defined by $(\mathtt{Enc}', \mathtt{Dec}')$.

The correctness of $(\mathtt{Enc}', \mathtt{Dec}')$ follows from the correctness of $(\mathtt{Enc}, \mathtt{Dec})$: if there exists a codeword $c \in \mathtt{supp}'(m)$ such that $\mathtt{Dec}'(c) \neq m$, since $\mathtt{supp}'(m)$ is a subset of $\mathtt{supp}(m)$ and $\mathtt{Dec}' = \mathtt{Dec}$, we have $c \in \mathtt{supp}(m)$ and $\mathtt{Dec}(c) \neq m$, which contradicts with the correctness of $(\mathtt{Enc}, \mathtt{Dec})$.

As for $(t-1)$-privacy, recall that $(\mathtt{Enc}, \mathtt{Dec})$ is t-private. Therefore, for any t bits, the distribution of these t bits in $c = \mathtt{Enc}(0)$ is identical to the distribution of these t bits in $c' = \mathtt{Enc}(1)$. Then, fixing the first bit to be 0, for any $t-1$ bits, the distribution of these $t-1$ bits in $c = \mathtt{Enc}(0)$ subject to $c[1] = 0$ is identical to the distribution of these $t-1$ bits in $c' = \mathtt{Enc}(1)$ subject to $c'[1] = 0$. Recall that $\mathtt{Enc}'(m)$ outputs a random codeword $c = \mathtt{Enc}(m)$ subject to $c[1] = 0$. Therefore $(\mathtt{Enc}', \mathtt{Dec}')$ is $(t-1)$-private.

According to the induction hypothesis, $|\mathtt{supp}'(0)| \geq 2^{t-1}$. I.e., there are 2^{t-1} different codewords in $\mathtt{supp}(0)$ whose first bit is 0. By the same argument, there are 2^{t-1} different codewords in $\mathtt{supp}(0)$ whose first bit is 1. Therefore, $|\mathtt{supp}(0)| \geq 2^t$.

By induction, we conclude that the lemma holds for all t.

We note the following direct corollary.

Corollary 1. *Any t-private encoding scheme* $(\mathtt{Enc}, \mathtt{Dec})$ *uses at least t random bits.*

Proof. According to Lemma 2, $|\mathtt{supp}(0)| \geq 2^t$. Therefore, $\mathtt{Enc}(0)$ has at least 2^t different output. Thus the random seed has length at least t.

In the full version of this paper [20], we give an alternative proof (due to Yuval Filmus) of a variant of Lemma 2 by relying on Fourier analysis of Boolean functions and a known bound on the number of roots of a low-degree polynomial over the Boolean hypercube. This variant applies also to t-private encoding with imperfect correctness, to which the above simple combinatorial argument does not apply.

4.2 Randomness Lower Bound for Symmetric Functions

In this section we prove a lower bound on the randomness complexity of secure multiparty computation protocols that compute symmetric functions with a single output bit. This includes parity and threshold functions (including AND, OR, majority) as special cases.

Theorem 2. *For all $n \geq 3$ and $t \leq n-2$, and for all non-constant symmetric functions f that outputs a single bit, any n-party protocol Π that computes f with perfect semi-honest security against t corrupted parties requires at least $\frac{t^2}{2}$ random bits. Moreover, this holds even with an arbitrary number k of helper parties.*

Proof. Recall that, without loss of generality, it is sufficient to only consider functions with minimal input domain. In the following, we assume that f is a non-constant symmetric function with minimal input domain. Without loss of generality, we assume that in every round, each party sends a message in $\{0, 1, \perp\}$ to every other party. This can be achieved by requiring that in each round, every party P_i sends a $\perp$ to every party P_j if P_i does not need to send any bit to P_j in this round, which does not change the randomness complexity of the protocol.

Note that an execution is determined by the inputs and random tapes of all parties. For an execution with inputs $\boldsymbol{x}$ and random tapes $\boldsymbol{r}$, we use $M_{P_i}(\boldsymbol{x}, \boldsymbol{r})$ to denote the messages that P_i receives from or sends to other parties. We use $M_{P_i}(\boldsymbol{x})$ to denote the random variable over the distribution induced by $M_{P_i}(\boldsymbol{x}, \boldsymbol{r})$ when $\boldsymbol{r}$ is sampled uniformly.

By the definition of symmetric functions, all parties have the same input domain. Recall that we have assumed that f is a non-constant symmetric function with minimal input domain. Also recall that f outputs a single bit.

We first prove the following lemma:

Lemma 3. *For all $P_i \in \{P_1, P_2, \ldots, P_n\}$, and for all $(\boldsymbol{x}, \boldsymbol{r})$ and $(\boldsymbol{x}', \boldsymbol{r}')$ such that $x_i \neq x_i'$,*

$$(M_{P_i}(\boldsymbol{x}, \boldsymbol{r}), f(\boldsymbol{x})) \neq (M_{P_i}(\boldsymbol{x}', \boldsymbol{r}'), f(\boldsymbol{x}'))$$

Proof. For the sake of contradiction, assume that this lemma is not true. Then there exists two executions, one with inputs $\boldsymbol{x}$ and random tapes $\boldsymbol{r}$ and the other one with inputs $\boldsymbol{x}'$ and random tapes $\boldsymbol{r}'$, such that $x_i \neq x_i'$ but

$$(M_{P_i}(\boldsymbol{x}, \boldsymbol{r}), f(\boldsymbol{x})) = (M_{P_i}(\boldsymbol{x}', \boldsymbol{r}'), f(\boldsymbol{x}'))$$

Since f has minimal input domain, f is sensitive to (P_i, x_i, x_i'), which means that there exists $\{\tilde{x}_j\}_{j \neq i}$ such that

$$f(\tilde{x}_1, \ldots, \tilde{x}_{i-1}, x_i, \tilde{x}_{i+1}, \ldots, \tilde{x}_n) \neq f(\tilde{x}_1, \ldots, \tilde{x}_{i-1}, x_i', \tilde{x}_{i+1}, \ldots, \tilde{x}_n).$$

Let $\tilde{\boldsymbol{x}} = (\tilde{x}_1, \ldots, \tilde{x}_{i-1}, x_i, \tilde{x}_{i+1}, \ldots, \tilde{x}_n)$ and $\tilde{\boldsymbol{x}}' = (\tilde{x}_1, \ldots, \tilde{x}_{i-1}, x_i', \tilde{x}_{i+1}, \ldots, \tilde{x}_n)$. Then $\tilde{x}_i = x_i$, $\tilde{x}_i' = x_i'$, $\tilde{x}_j = \tilde{x}_j'$ for all $j \neq i$, but $f(\tilde{\boldsymbol{x}}) \neq f(\tilde{\boldsymbol{x}}')$. Since f outputs a single bit, either $f(\boldsymbol{x}) = f(\boldsymbol{x}') = f(\tilde{\boldsymbol{x}})$ or $f(\boldsymbol{x}) = f(\boldsymbol{x}') = f(\tilde{\boldsymbol{x}}')$. Without loss of generality, assume that $f(\boldsymbol{x}) = f(\boldsymbol{x}') = f(\tilde{\boldsymbol{x}})$.

We first show that there exists $\tilde{\boldsymbol{r}}$ such that $(M_{P_i}(\boldsymbol{x}, \boldsymbol{r}), f(\boldsymbol{x})) = (M_{P_i}(\tilde{\boldsymbol{x}}, \tilde{\boldsymbol{r}}), f(\tilde{\boldsymbol{x}}))$. Since $\boldsymbol{x}, \tilde{\boldsymbol{x}}$ satisfy that $x_i = \tilde{x}_i$ and $f(\boldsymbol{x}) = f(\tilde{\boldsymbol{x}})$, by Property 1, the following two distributions are identical:

$$\{\texttt{View}(P_i, \boldsymbol{x})\} \equiv \{\texttt{View}(P_i, \tilde{\boldsymbol{x}})\}$$

Thus, there exists $\tilde{\boldsymbol{r}}$ such that $\texttt{View}(P_i, \boldsymbol{x}, \boldsymbol{r}) = \texttt{View}(P_i, \tilde{\boldsymbol{x}}, \tilde{\boldsymbol{r}})$. Since $(M_{P_i}(\boldsymbol{x}, \boldsymbol{r}), f(\boldsymbol{x}))$ is determined by P_i's view, we have $(M_{P_i}(\boldsymbol{x}, \boldsymbol{r}), f(\boldsymbol{x})) = (M_{P_i}(\tilde{\boldsymbol{x}}, \tilde{\boldsymbol{r}}), f(\tilde{\boldsymbol{x}}))$. Recall that $(M_{P_i}(\boldsymbol{x}, \boldsymbol{r}), f(\boldsymbol{x})) = (M_{P_i}(\boldsymbol{x}', \boldsymbol{r}'), f(\boldsymbol{x}'))$. Therefore, $(M_{P_i}(\tilde{\boldsymbol{x}}, \tilde{\boldsymbol{r}}), f(\tilde{\boldsymbol{x}})) = (M_{P_i}(\boldsymbol{x}', \boldsymbol{r}'), f(\boldsymbol{x}'))$.

Let $\tilde{\boldsymbol{r}}' = (\tilde{r}_1, \dots, \tilde{r}_{i-1}, r'_i, \tilde{r}_{i+1}, \dots, \tilde{r}_n)$, i.e., $\tilde{\boldsymbol{r}}' = \tilde{\boldsymbol{r}}$ except $\tilde{r}'_i = r'_i$. We will prove that $M_{P_i}(\tilde{\boldsymbol{x}}', \tilde{\boldsymbol{r}}') = M_{P_i}(\tilde{\boldsymbol{x}}, \tilde{\boldsymbol{r}}) = M_{P_i}(\boldsymbol{x}', \boldsymbol{r}')$ by induction:

- Consider the first message in $M_{P_i}(\tilde{\boldsymbol{x}}', \tilde{\boldsymbol{r}}')$. If it is a message sent from P_i to another party, then this message is fully determined by $\tilde{x}'_i = x'_i$ and $\tilde{r}'_i = r'_i$ since P_i does not receive any message from other parties. Thus, this message is identical to the first message in $M_{P_i}(\boldsymbol{x}', \boldsymbol{r}')$. Since $M_{P_i}(\tilde{\boldsymbol{x}}, \tilde{\boldsymbol{r}}) = M_{P_i}(\boldsymbol{x}', \boldsymbol{r}')$, the statement holds for the first message.
  If the first message in $M_{P_i}(\tilde{\boldsymbol{x}}', \tilde{\boldsymbol{r}}')$ is received from another party, then this message is fully determined by $\{\tilde{x}'_j, \tilde{r}'_j\}_{j \neq i}$ since P_i does not send any message to other parties. Note that $\{\tilde{x}'_j, \tilde{r}'_j\}_{j \neq i} = \{\tilde{x}_j, \tilde{r}_j\}_{j \neq i}$. Thus this message is identical to the first message in $M_{P_i}(\tilde{\boldsymbol{x}}, \tilde{\boldsymbol{r}})$. Since $M_{P_i}(\tilde{\boldsymbol{x}}, \tilde{\boldsymbol{r}}) = M_{P_i}(\boldsymbol{x}', \boldsymbol{r}')$, the statement holds for the first message.
- Assume the statement holds for the first $\ell - 1$ messages. For the ℓ-th message, if it is a message sent from P_i to another party, then this message is determined by $\tilde{x}'_i = x'_i, \tilde{r}'_i = r'_i$ and the first $\ell - 1$ messages in $M_{P_i}(\tilde{\boldsymbol{x}}', \tilde{\boldsymbol{r}}')$. According to the induction hypothesis, the first $\ell - 1$ messages in $M_{P_i}(\tilde{\boldsymbol{x}}', \tilde{\boldsymbol{r}}')$ are identical to the first $\ell - 1$ messages in $M_{P_i}(\boldsymbol{x}', \boldsymbol{r}')$. We also have $(\tilde{x}'_i, \tilde{r}'_i) = (x'_i, r'_i)$. Thus, the ℓ-th message in $M_{P_i}(\tilde{\boldsymbol{x}}', \tilde{\boldsymbol{r}}')$ is identical to the ℓ-th message in $M_{P_i}(\boldsymbol{x}', \boldsymbol{r}')$ as well. Since $M_{P_i}(\tilde{\boldsymbol{x}}, \tilde{\boldsymbol{r}}) = M_{P_i}(\boldsymbol{x}', \boldsymbol{r}')$, the statement holds for the first ℓ messages.
  If the ℓ-th message of P_i is received from another party, then this message is fully determined by $\{\tilde{x}'_j, \tilde{r}'_j\}_{j \neq i}$ and the first $\ell - 1$ messages in $M_{P_i}(\tilde{\boldsymbol{x}}', \tilde{\boldsymbol{r}}')$. According to the induction hypothesis, the first $\ell - 1$ messages in $M_{P_i}(\tilde{\boldsymbol{x}}', \tilde{\boldsymbol{r}}')$ are identical to the first $\ell - 1$ messages in $M_{P_i}(\tilde{\boldsymbol{x}}, \tilde{\boldsymbol{r}})$. We also have $\{\tilde{x}'_j, \tilde{r}'_j\}_{j \neq i} = \{\tilde{x}_j, \tilde{r}_j\}_{j \neq i}$. Thus, the ℓ-th message in $M_{P_i}(\tilde{\boldsymbol{x}}', \tilde{\boldsymbol{r}}')$ is identical to the ℓ-th message in $M_{P_i}(\tilde{\boldsymbol{x}}, \tilde{\boldsymbol{r}})$ as well. Since $M_{P_i}(\tilde{\boldsymbol{x}}, \tilde{\boldsymbol{r}}) = M_{P_i}(\boldsymbol{x}', \boldsymbol{r}')$, the statement holds for the first ℓ messages.
- Therefore, by induction, the statement holds for all ℓ. We have $M_{P_i}(\tilde{\boldsymbol{x}}', \tilde{\boldsymbol{r}}') = M_{P_i}(\tilde{\boldsymbol{x}}, \tilde{\boldsymbol{r}}) = M_{P_i}(\boldsymbol{x}', \boldsymbol{r}')$.

Recall that $f(\tilde{\boldsymbol{x}}') \neq f(\tilde{\boldsymbol{x}})$. On the other hand, for parties in $\{P_j\}_{j \neq i}$, their views are determined by $\{\tilde{x}'_j, \tilde{r}'_j\}_{j \neq i}$ and $M_{P_i}(\tilde{\boldsymbol{x}}', \tilde{\boldsymbol{r}}')$. Since $\{\tilde{x}'_j, \tilde{r}'_j\}_{j \neq i} = \{\tilde{x}_j, \tilde{r}_j\}_{j \neq i}$ and $M_{P_i}(\tilde{\boldsymbol{x}}', \tilde{\boldsymbol{r}}') = M_{P_i}(\tilde{\boldsymbol{x}}, \tilde{\boldsymbol{r}})$, parties in $\{P_j\}_{j \neq i, j \leq n}$ will obtain the same output in both the execution with $(\tilde{\boldsymbol{x}}', \tilde{\boldsymbol{r}}')$ and the execution with $(\tilde{\boldsymbol{x}}, \tilde{\boldsymbol{r}})$, which contradicts with $f(\tilde{\boldsymbol{x}}') \neq f(\tilde{\boldsymbol{x}})$.

Lemma 3 shows that the messages a party (of the first n parties) receives or sends together with the output can determine his input. Without loss of generality, assume that $0, 1$ are in the input domain. Now consider the first t parties $P_1, P_2, \dots, P_t$. For all $1 \leq i \leq t$, and for all vectors V subject to

$$\Pr[(\texttt{View}(P_1, \boldsymbol{x}), \dots, \texttt{View}(P_{i-1}, \boldsymbol{x})) = V] \neq 0,$$

we define an encoding scheme $(\texttt{Enc}, \texttt{Dec})$ for the message space $\{0, 1\}$ as follows:

- Let $\boldsymbol{x} = (0, 0, ..., 0, 1)$ (i.e., all inputs are 0 except the last input is 1) and $\boldsymbol{x}' \in \{0,1\}^n$ subject to $x'_i = 1$ and $x'_j = 0$ for all $j \neq i$. Since f is a symmetric function, we have $f(\boldsymbol{x}) = f(\boldsymbol{x}')$ but $x_i \neq x'_i$.
  $\mathtt{Enc}(0)$ samples $\boldsymbol{r}$ uniformly subject to $\{\mathtt{View}(P_j, \boldsymbol{x}, \boldsymbol{r})\}_{j=1}^{i-1} = V$ and outputs $M_{P_i}(\boldsymbol{x}, \boldsymbol{r})$.
  $\mathtt{Enc}(1)$ samples $\boldsymbol{r}'$ uniformly subject to $\{\mathtt{View}(P_j, \boldsymbol{x}', \boldsymbol{r}')\}_{j=1}^{i-1} = V$ and outputs $M_{P_i}(\boldsymbol{x}', \boldsymbol{r}')$.
- The decoding algorithm takes as input a codeword $c = M_{P_i}(\tilde{\boldsymbol{x}}, \tilde{\boldsymbol{r}})$, where $\tilde{\boldsymbol{x}} \in \{\boldsymbol{x}, \boldsymbol{x}'\}$. Recall that $f(\boldsymbol{x}) = f(\boldsymbol{x}')$. Therefore, $f(\tilde{\boldsymbol{x}}) = f(\boldsymbol{x}) = f(\boldsymbol{x}')$. According to Lemma 3, $(M_{P_i}(\tilde{\boldsymbol{x}}, \tilde{\boldsymbol{r}}), f(\tilde{\boldsymbol{x}}))$ can determine the input $\tilde{x}_i$. $\mathtt{Dec}(c)$ outputs the input determined by $(c, f(\boldsymbol{x}))$.

We first show that $\mathtt{supp}(0)$ and $\mathtt{supp}(1)$ of the encoding scheme are not empty. It is sufficient to show that there exist $\boldsymbol{r}$ and $\boldsymbol{r}'$ such that

$$(\mathtt{View}(P_1, \boldsymbol{x}, \boldsymbol{r}), \ldots, \mathtt{View}(P_{i-1}, \boldsymbol{x}, \boldsymbol{r})) = V$$

and

$$(\mathtt{View}(P_1, \boldsymbol{x}', \boldsymbol{r}'), \ldots, \mathtt{View}(P_{i-1}, \boldsymbol{x}', \boldsymbol{r}')) = V.$$

Recall that V satisfies that $\Pr[(\mathtt{View}(P_1, \boldsymbol{x}), \ldots, \mathtt{View}(P_{i-1}, \boldsymbol{x})) = V] \neq 0$. Therefore, the existence of $\boldsymbol{r}$ follows. Recall that $f(\boldsymbol{x}) = f(\boldsymbol{x}')$ and $x_j = x'_j$ for all $j \in \{1, 2, \ldots, i-1\}$, by Property 1, we have

$$\{\mathtt{View}(P_1, \boldsymbol{x}), \ldots, \mathtt{View}(P_{i-1}, \boldsymbol{x})\} \equiv \{\mathtt{View}(P_1, \boldsymbol{x}'), \ldots, \mathtt{View}(P_{i-1}, \boldsymbol{x}')\}.$$

Thus,

$$\begin{aligned} &\Pr[(\mathtt{View}(P_1, \boldsymbol{x}), \ldots, \mathtt{View}(P_{i-1}, \boldsymbol{x})) = V] \\ =\ &\Pr[(\mathtt{View}(P_1, \boldsymbol{x}'), \ldots, \mathtt{View}(P_{i-1}, \boldsymbol{x}')) = V] \neq 0. \end{aligned}$$

The existence of $\boldsymbol{r}'$ follows. This implies that the encoding scheme $(\mathtt{Enc}, \mathtt{Dec})$ is well defined.

Lemma 4. *The encoding scheme* $(\mathtt{Enc}, \mathtt{Dec})$ *constructed above is* $(t - i + 1)$*-private.*

We refer the readers to the full version of this paper [20] for the proof of Lemma 4.

According to Lemma 2, $|\mathtt{supp}(0)| \geq 2^{t-i+1}$. That is, for inputs $\boldsymbol{x} = (0, 0, \ldots, 0, 1)$, when fixing the views of the first $i-1$ parties, the view of the i-th party has at least 2^{t-i+1} different possibilities. Consider the joint view of the first t parties when the inputs are $\boldsymbol{x}$. It has at least $\prod_{i=1}^{t} 2^{t-i+1} = 2^{t(t+1)/2}$ different views. It implies that the number of random bits required by the protocol in the worst case is at least $t(t+1)/2 \geq t^2/2$. Therefore, the randomness complexity of the protocol is at least $t^2/2$.

Remark 1. We note that Theorem 2 holds even if the output is only given to a strict (nonempty) subset of the parties.

To see it, note that for Lemma 3, the statement holds for P_i as long as there is a party $P_j \neq P_i$ that receives the function output. Therefore, if there are at least two parties that receive the output, Lemma 3 holds. If only one party receives output, say P_n, then the statement holds for all parties other than P_n. Then in the rest of the proof, we can continue to focus on the number of views of the first t parties. With the same argument, we can show that the randomness complexity is at least $t^2/2$.

5 Explicit Construction of Zero Sharing Generators

In this section, we will give an explicit construction of a *linear* (multi-phase) t-resilient zero sharing generator by using a linear t-wise independent PRG in a black box way.

Theorem 3. *Let $\mathbb{G}$ be a finite Abelian group. Let p and $n_1, n_2, \ldots, n_p$ be positive integers, and $\mathtt{Tr}_1, \mathtt{Tr}_2, \ldots, \mathtt{Tr}_p$ be full binary trees such that $\mathtt{Tr}_j$ has n_j leaf nodes for all $j \in \{1, 2, \ldots, p\}$. For each tree $\mathtt{Tr}_j$, let $\mathcal{A}_j$ denote the access set determined by $\mathtt{Tr}_j$. Set $n = n_1 + n_2 + \ldots + n_p$, $\mathcal{A} = \bigcup_{j=1}^{p} \mathcal{A}_j$, and D to be the largest depth of $\mathtt{Tr}_1, \mathtt{Tr}_2, \ldots, \mathtt{Tr}_p$. Suppose $F : \mathbb{G}^m \rightarrow \mathbb{G}^n$ is a linear t-wise independent PRG. Then there exists an explicit linear multi-phase t-resilient zero sharing generator with respect to the access set $\mathcal{A}$ that uses $(D-1) \cdot m$ random group elements in $\mathbb{G}$.*

Proof. For every tree $\mathtt{Tr}_j$ and every node $v \in \mathtt{Tr}_j$, the depth of v is the length of the path towards the root of $\mathtt{Tr}_j$ plus 1. I.e., the root node of $\mathtt{Tr}_j$ has depth 1, the two children of the root node of $\mathtt{Tr}_j$ have depth 2, and so on. Note that leaf nodes of $\mathtt{Tr}_j$ do not necessarily have the same depth.

Let $\mathtt{Fr}$ denote the collection of the trees $\mathtt{Tr}_1, \mathtt{Tr}_2, \ldots, \mathtt{Tr}_p$. $\mathtt{Fr}$ is also referred to as a forest. Recall that $F : \mathbb{G}^m \rightarrow \mathbb{G}^n$ is a linear t-wise independent PRG. To construct a linear multi-phase t-resilient zero sharing generator G, we will assign to each node v in $\mathtt{Fr}$ a linear combination of the outputs of F, denoted by $\mathsf{val}(v)$, such that for all internal node v and its two children c_0, c_1, $\mathsf{val}(v) = \mathsf{val}(c_0) + \mathsf{val}(c_1)$. Then the values associated with the leaf nodes in $\mathtt{Fr}$ represent the output of G.

Explicit Construction of Linear Multi-Phase Zero Sharing Generator. The construction works as follows:

1. Let $\boldsymbol{u} = (\boldsymbol{u}^{(1)}, \boldsymbol{u}^{(2)}, \ldots, \boldsymbol{u}^{(D-1)}) \in \mathbb{G}^{(D-1)\times m}$ be the input of G, where D is the largest depth of $\mathtt{Tr}_1, \mathtt{Tr}_2, \ldots, \mathtt{Tr}_p$.
2. For all root node $\mathtt{rt}_j$, we set $\mathsf{val}(\mathtt{rt}_j) = 0$.
3. From $d = 2$ to D, we will assign values to all nodes of depth d in $\mathtt{Fr}$. Let ℓ_d denote the number of nodes of depth d. Since $\mathtt{Tr}_1, \mathtt{Tr}_2, \ldots, \mathtt{Tr}_p$ are full binary trees, ℓ_d is even. We use $c_1, c_1, \ldots, c_{\ell_d}$ to denote the nodes of depth

d such that for all $i \in \{1, 2, \ldots, \ell_d/2\}$, (c_{2i-1}, c_{2i}) are the two children of a node v_i of depth $d-1$.
Suppose we have assigned values to all nodes of depth $d-1$ in $\texttt{Fr}$. We compute $\boldsymbol{y}^{(d)} = F(\boldsymbol{u}^{(d-1)})$. Then for all $i \in \{1, 2, \ldots, \ell_d/2\}$, we set $\mathsf{val}(c_{2i-1}) = y_i^{(d)}$ and $\mathsf{val}(c_{2i}) = \mathsf{val}(v_i) - y_i^{(d)}$. In this way, for the node v_i and its two children c_{2i-1}, c_{2i}, we have $\mathsf{val}(v_i) = \mathsf{val}(c_{2i-1}) + \mathsf{val}(c_{2i})$.

4. The output of G are the values associated with the leaf nodes in $\texttt{Fr}$. In particular, for all $j \in \{1, 2, \ldots, p\}$, $\boldsymbol{r}^{(j)} = (r_1^{(j)}, \ldots, r_{n_j}^{(j)})$ are the values associated with the leaf nodes of $\texttt{Tr}_j$.

Lemma 5. *The above construction is a linear multi-phase t-resilient zero sharing generator.*

We refer the readers to the full version of this paper [20] for the proof of Lemma 5.

When $\mathbb{G}$ is a finite field $\mathbb{F}$, by Theorem 1, we can instantiate the linear t-wise independent PRG $F : \mathbb{F}^m \to \mathbb{F}^n$ with input size $m = O(t \cdot \log n)$. For all $j \in \{1, 2, \ldots, p\}$, we can use a full binary tree $\texttt{Tr}_j$ with n_j leaf nodes of depth $O(\log n_j) = O(\log n)$. Thus, we have the following corollary.

Corollary 2. *Let $\mathbb{F}$ be a finite field. Let p and $n_1, n_2, \ldots, n_p$ be positive integers, and $\texttt{Tr}_1, \texttt{Tr}_2, \ldots, \texttt{Tr}_p$ be full binary trees such that $\texttt{Tr}_j$ has n_j leaf nodes of depth $O(\log n_j)$ for all $j \in \{1, 2, \ldots, p\}$. For each tree $\texttt{Tr}_j$, let $\mathcal{A}_j$ denote the access set determined by $\texttt{Tr}_j$. Set $n = n_1 + n_2 + \ldots + n_p$ and $\mathcal{A} = \bigcup_{j=1}^{p} \mathcal{A}_j$. Then there exists an explicit linear multi-phase t-resilient zero sharing generator that uses $O(t \cdot \log^2 n)$ random elements in $\mathbb{F}$.*

6 Upper Bound for Addition

In this section we prove our main new upper bounds, obtaining an explicit version of the previous upper bound for XOR from [27] and extending it to Abelian group addition. In the full version of this paper [20], we show (1) how to amortize randomness complexity over multiple executions, (2) how to construct an explicit protocol for any symmetric Boolean functions with $O(t^2 \cdot \log^3 n)$ random bits, and (3) how to construct an explicit protocol for general circuits with helper parties, which uses $O(t^2 \cdot \log s)$ random bits, where s is the circuit size.

We start by considering a function f that computes addition of n elements in a finite Abelian group $\mathbb{G}$. Concretely, f takes $x_i \in \mathbb{G}$ from the party P_i and computes $\sum_{i=1}^{n} x_i$. Assuming the existence of a linear t-resilient zero sharing generator $G : \mathbb{G}^m \to \mathbb{G}^n$, we construct an n-party computation protocol for f against t corrupted parties with perfect semi-honest security.

Theorem 4. *Let m, n, t be positive integers, $\texttt{Tr}$ be a full binary tree with n leaf nodes, and $\mathbb{G}$ be a finite Abelian group. Let $f : \mathbb{G}^n \to \mathbb{G}$ be the addition function which is defined by $f(x_1, x_2, \ldots, x_n) = \sum_{i=1}^{n} x_i$. Assume that $G : \mathbb{G}^m \to \mathbb{G}^n$ is a linear $(4t+1)$-resilient zero sharing generator with respect to the access set*

$\mathcal{A}$ determined by Tr. *There is an n-party computation protocol for f against t corrupted parties with perfect semi-honest security, which uses $(t+1)\cdot m$ random group elements in $\mathbb{G}$.*

Proof. We first construct a protocol for f assuming the existence of an ideal functionality $\mathcal{F}_{\text{rand}}$ that distributes correlated randomness to all parties. For a full binary tree $\texttt{Tr}$ with n leaf nodes, it has exactly $n-1$ internal nodes. We use $\{1, 2, \ldots, n\}$ to label the leaf nodes in $\texttt{Tr}$, and $\{n+1, n+2, \ldots, 2n-1\}$ to label the internal nodes in $\texttt{Tr}$. We also use $\texttt{rt}$ to denote the root of $\texttt{Tr}$.

Protocol with Ideal Functionality $\mathcal{F}_{\text{rand}}$. Consider an ideal functionality $\mathcal{F}_{\text{rand}}$ that samples $\boldsymbol{u} \in \mathbb{G}^m$ uniformly, computes $\boldsymbol{r} = (r_1, r_2, \ldots, r_n) = G(\boldsymbol{u})$, and distributes r_i to the party P_i for all $i \in \{1, 2, \ldots, n\}$. All parties run the following steps:

1. Each party P_i locally computes $g_i = x_i + r_i$.
2. For each node v in $\texttt{Tr}$, let S_v be the set of indices of leaf nodes that are descendants of v. We will ask a single party to compute $g_v := \sum_{i\in S_v} g_i$. Note that for all leaf nodes $v \in \{1, 2, \ldots, n\}$, we have already computed $g_v = x_v + r_v$ in Step 1. Now we describe how parties compute g_v for all internal nodes. Recall that $\texttt{Tr}$ has $n-1$ internal nodes. From $i = 1$ to $n-1$, all parties run the following steps:
   (a) Let v be the first internal node in $\texttt{Tr}$ such that g_v has not been computed but g_{c_0}, g_{c_1} have been computed, where c_0, c_1 are the two children of v. Suppose that g_{c_0} is computed by P_{j_0}, and g_{c_1} is computed by P_{j_1}.
   (b) P_i receives g_{c_0} from P_{j_0} and receives g_{c_1} from P_{j_1}. Then P_i computes $g_v = g_{c_0} + g_{c_1}$.
3. Note that in the last iteration of Step 2, P_{n-1} computes $g_{\texttt{rt}}$ for the root node $\texttt{rt}$. Then
$$g_{\texttt{rt}} = \sum_{i=1}^{n} g_i = \sum_{i=1}^{n} x_i + \sum_{i=1}^{n} r_i.$$
Since G is a zero sharing generator and $\boldsymbol{r} = (r_1, r_2, \ldots, r_n)$ is the output of G, we have $\sum_{i=1}^{n} r_i = 0$. Therefore, $g_{\texttt{rt}} = \sum_{i=1}^{n} x_i$. Thus, P_{n-1} learns $f(\boldsymbol{x})$. P_{n-1} sends the result to all other parties.

The correctness of our construction follows from the description. we show that our construction is secure in the full version of this paper [20].

Realizing $\mathcal{F}_{\text{rand}}$. To obtain an n-party computation protocol for f in the plain model, it is sufficient to realize $\mathcal{F}_{\text{rand}}$. We simply follow the approach in [27]: Recall that G is a linear zero sharing generator. To realize $\mathcal{F}_{\text{rand}}$, we ask each party P_i of the first $t+1$ parties randomly samples $\boldsymbol{u}^{(i)} \in \mathbb{G}^m$, computes $\boldsymbol{r}^{(i)} = G(\boldsymbol{u}^{(i)})$, and distributes $r_j^{(i)}$ to P_j for all $j \neq i$. Then all parties locally set $\boldsymbol{r} = \boldsymbol{r}^{(1)} + \ldots + \boldsymbol{r}^{(t+1)} = G(\boldsymbol{u}^{(1)} + \ldots + \boldsymbol{u}^{(t+1)})$. The security follows from the fact that at least one of the first $t+1$ parties is not corrupted. Therefore,

$\boldsymbol{u} = \sum_{i=1}^{t+1} \boldsymbol{u}^{(i)}$ is uniformly random and $\boldsymbol{r} = G(\boldsymbol{u})$ has the same distribution as that generated by $\mathcal{F}_{\text{rand}}$.

In summary, the whole protocol uses $(t+1) \cdot m$ random elements in $\mathbb{G}$.

When $\mathbb{G}$ is a finite field $\mathbb{F}$, and when we use a full binary tree $\mathtt{Tr}$ with n leaf nodes of depth $O(\log n)$, by Corollary 2, there is an explicit linear $(4t+1)$-resilient zero sharing generator $G : \mathbb{F}^m \to \mathbb{F}^n$ with input size $m = O(t \cdot \log^2 n)$. We have the following corollary.

Corollary 3. *Let n, t be positive integers, $\mathbb{F}$ be a finite field, and $f : \mathbb{F}^n \to \mathbb{F}$ be the addition function which is defined by $f(x_1, x_2, \ldots, x_n) = \sum_{i=1}^{n} x_i$. There is an n-party computation protocol for f against t corrupted parties with perfect semi-honest security, which uses $O(t^2 \cdot \log^2 n)$ random field elements in $\mathbb{F}$.*

Acknowledgements. Y. Ishai was supported by ERC Project NTSC (742754), BSF grant 2018393, and ISF grant 2774/20. V. Goyal and Y. Song were supported by the NSF award 1916939, DARPA SIEVE program under Agreement No. HR00112020025, a gift from Ripple, a DoE NETL award, a JP Morgan Faculty Fellowship, a PNC center for financial services innovation award, and a Cylab seed funding award. Y. Song was also supported by a Cylab Presidential Fellowship.

References

1. Ananth, P., Ishai, Y., Sahai, A.: Private circuits: a modular approach. In: Shacham, H., Boldyreva, A. (eds.) CRYPTO 2018. LNCS, vol. 10993, pp. 427–455. Springer, Cham (2018). https://doi.org/10.1007/978-3-319-96878-0_15
2. Andrychowicz, M., Dziembowski, S., Faust, S.: Circuit compilers with $O(1/\log(n))$ leakage rate. In: Fischlin, M., Coron, J.-S. (eds.) EUROCRYPT 2016. LNCS, vol. 9666, pp. 586–615. Springer, Heidelberg (2016). https://doi.org/10.1007/978-3-662-49896-5_21
3. Barthe, G., et al.: Strong non-interference and type-directed higher-order masking. In: ACM CCS 2016, pp. 116–129 (2016)
4. Ben-Or, M., Goldwasser, S., Wigderson, A.: Completeness theorems for non-cryptographic fault-tolerant distributed computation. In: STOC 1988, pp. 1–10 (1988)
5. Benaloh, J.C.: Secret sharing homomorphisms: keeping shares of a secret secret (extended abstract). In: Odlyzko, A.M. (ed.) CRYPTO 1986. LNCS, vol. 263, pp. 251–260. Springer, Heidelberg (1987). https://doi.org/10.1007/3-540-47721-7_19
6. Blundo, C., De Santis, A., Persiano, G., Vaccaro, U.: Randomness complexity of private computation. Comput. Complex. **8**(2), 145–168 (1999)
7. Blundo, C., Galdi, C., Persiano, G.: Low-randomness constant-round private XOR computations. Int. J. Inf. Sec. **6**(1), 15–26 (2007)
8. Bonawitz, K.A., et al.: Practical secure aggregation for privacy-preserving machine learning. In: CCS 2017, pp. 1175–1191 (2017)
9. Canetti, R., Kushilevitz, E., Ostrovsky, R., Rosén, A.: Randomness versus fault-tolerance. J. Cryptol. **13**(1), 107–142 (2000). https://doi.org/10.1007/s001459910005
10. Chaum, D.: The dining cryptographers problem: Unconditional sender and recipient untraceability. J. Cryptol. **1**(1), 65–75 (1988)

11. Chaum, D., Crépeau, C., Damgard, I.: Multiparty unconditionally secure protocols. In: STOC 1988, pp. 11–19 (1988)
12. Chor, B., Goldreich, O., Hasted, J., Freidmann, J., Rudich, S., Smolensky, R.: The bit extraction problem or t-resilient functions. In: FOCS 1985, pp. 396–407 (1985)
13. Chor, B., Kushilevitz, E.: A communication-privacy tradeoff for modular addition. Inf. Process. Lett. **45**(4), 205–210 (1993)
14. Coron, J.-S., Greuet, A., Zeitoun, R.: Side-channel masking with pseudo-random generator. In: Canteaut, A., Ishai, Y. (eds.) EUROCRYPT 2020. LNCS, vol. 12107, pp. 342–375. Springer, Cham (2020). https://doi.org/10.1007/978-3-030-45727-3_12
15. Corrigan-Gibbs, H., Boneh, D.: Prio: private, robust, and scalable computation of aggregate statistics. In: USENIX NSDI 2017, pp. 259–282 (2017)
16. Data, D., Prabhakaran, V.M., Prabhakaran, M.M.: Communication and randomness lower bounds for secure computation. IEEE Trans. Inf. Theor. **62**(7), 3901–3929 (2016)
17. Faust, S., Paglialonga, C., Schneider, T.: Amortizing randomness complexity in private circuits. In: Takagi, T., Peyrin, T. (eds.) ASIACRYPT 2017. LNCS, vol. 10624, pp. 781–810. Springer, Cham (2017). https://doi.org/10.1007/978-3-319-70694-8_27
18. Gál, A., Rosén, A.: A theorem on sensitivity and applications in private computation. SIAM J. Comput. **31**(5), 1424–1437 (2002)
19. Goyal, V., Ishai, Y., Song, Y.: Private circuits with quasilinear randomness. In: Dunkelman, O., Dziembowski, S. (eds.) EUROCRYPT 2022. LNCS, vol. 13277, pp. 192–221. Springer, Cham (2022). https://doi.org/10.1007/978-3-031-07082-2_8
20. Goyal, V., Ishai, Y., Song, Y.: Tight bounds on the randomness complexity of secure multiparty computation. Cryptology ePrint Archive, Paper 2022/799 (2022). https://eprint.iacr.org/2022/799
21. Gál, A., Rosén, A.: $\Omega(\log n)$ lower bounds on the amount of randomness in 2-private computation. SIAM J. Comput. **34**(4), 946–959 (2005). Earlier version in STOC 2003
22. Ishai, Y., et al.: Robust pseudorandom generators. In: Fomin, F.V., Freivalds, R., Kwiatkowska, M., Peleg, D. (eds.) ICALP 2013. LNCS, vol. 7965, pp. 576–588. Springer, Heidelberg (2013). https://doi.org/10.1007/978-3-642-39206-1_49
23. Ishai, Y., Malkin, T., Strauss, M.J., Wright, R.N.: Private multiparty sampling and approximation of vector combinations. Theor. Comput. Sci. **410**(18), 1730–1745 (2009)
24. Ishai, Y., Sahai, A., Wagner, D.: Private circuits: securing hardware against probing attacks. In: Boneh, D. (ed.) CRYPTO 2003. LNCS, vol. 2729, pp. 463–481. Springer, Heidelberg (2003). https://doi.org/10.1007/978-3-540-45146-4_27
25. Jakoby, A., Liśkiewicz, M., Reischuk, R.: Private computations in networks: topology versus randomness. In: Alt, H., Habib, M. (eds.) STACS 2003. LNCS, vol. 2607, pp. 121–132. Springer, Heidelberg (2003). https://doi.org/10.1007/3-540-36494-3_12
26. Knuth, D., Yao, A.: The complexity of nonuniform random number generation. In: Algorithms and Complexity: New Directions and Recent Results. Academic Press (1976)
27. Kushilevitz, E., Mansour, Y.: Randomness in Private Computations. SIAM J. Discrete Math. **10**(4), 647–661 (1997). Earlier version in PODC 1996

28. Kushilevitz, E., Ostrovsky, R., Prouff, E., Rosén, A., Thillard, A., Vergnaud, D.: Lower and upper bounds on the randomness complexity of private computations of AND. SIAM J. Discret. Math. **35**(1), 465–484 (2021). Earlier version in TCC 2019
29. Kushilevitz, E., Ostrovsky, R., Rosén, A.: Characterizing linear size circuits in terms of privacy. In: STOC 1996, pp. 541–550 (1996)
30. Kushilevitz, E., Ostrovsky, R., Rosén, A.: Amortizing randomness in private multiparty computations. SIAM J. Discrete Math. **16**(4), 533–544 (2003)
31. Kushilevitz, E., Rosén, A.: A randomness-rounds tradeoff in private computation. SIAM J. Discrete Math. **11**(1), 61–80 (1998)

Threshold Signatures

Better than Advertised Security for Non-interactive Threshold Signatures

Mihir Bellare[1], Elizabeth Crites[2(✉)], Chelsea Komlo[3], Mary Maller[4], Stefano Tessaro[5], and Chenzhi Zhu[5(✉)]

[1] Department of Computer Science and Engineering, University of California San Diego, La Jolla, USA
mihir@eng.ucsd.edu

[2] University of Edinburgh, Edinburgh, UK
ecrites@ed.ac.uk

[3] University of Waterloo, Zcash Foundation, Waterloo, Canada
ckomlo@uwaterloo.ca

[4] Ethereum Foundation, London, UK
mary.maller@ethereum.org

[5] Paul G. Allen School of Computer Science & Engineering, University of Washington, Seattle, USA
{tessaro,zhucz20}@cs.washington.edu

Abstract. We give a unified syntax, and a hierarchy of definitions of security of increasing strength, for non-interactive threshold signature schemes. These are schemes having a single-round signing protocol, possibly with one prior round of message-independent pre-processing. We fit FROST1 and BLS, which are leading practical schemes, into our hierarchy, in particular showing they meet stronger security definitions than they have been shown to meet so far. We also fit in our hierarchy a more efficient version FROST2 of FROST1 that we give. These definitions and results, for simplicity, all assume trusted key generation. Finally, we prove the security of FROST2 with key generation performed by an efficient distributed key generation protocol.

1 Introduction

Threshold signatures, which originated in the late 1980s [17,18], are seeing renewed attention, driven in particular by an interest in using them to secure digital wallets in the cryptocurrencies ecosystem [22]. Parallel IETF [32] and NIST [35] standardization efforts are evidence as to the speed at which the area is moving into practice.

Whether securing a user's digital wallet, or being used by a CA to create a certificate, forgery of a digital signature is costly. The rising tide of system breaches and phishing attacks makes exposure of a signing key too plausible to ignore. The idea of a threshold signature scheme is to distribute the secret signing key across multiple parties who then interact to produce a signature, the intent being to retain security even in the face of compromise of up to a threshold number of these parties. Over the years, threshold versions of many schemes have been presented, including RSA [16,26,37], DSA/ECDSA [9,13,21–23,25,34], Schnorr signatures [24,30,39] and BLS signatures [8].

Y. Dodis and T. Shrimpton (Eds.): CRYPTO 2022, LNCS 13510, pp. 517–550, 2022.
https://doi.org/10.1007/978-3-031-15985-5_18

Today, we see interest converging on schemes that are non-interactive. The representative examples are BLS [8,12], and FROST [30]. FROST is a partially non-interactive threshold signature scheme, consisting of a message-independent pre-processing round and one round of signing. Threshold BLS is fully non-interactive, i.e., consists of a single round, but it does require pairings.

OUR CONTRIBUTIONS. We advance the area of non-interactive threshold signature schemes via the following contributions.

1. Framework and Stronger Security. We contend that schemes like FROST and BLS are *better than advertised*, meeting definitions of security that are *stronger* than ones that have been previously defined, or that these schemes have been shown to meet in existing literature. Furthermore, these definitions capture natural strengths of the schemes that may be valuable for applications.

The classical development paradigm in theoretical cryptography is to ask what security we would like, define it, and then seek schemes that meet it. Yet if we look back, there has been another path alongside: canonical, reference schemes guided a choice of definitions that modeled them, and, once made, these definitions went on to be influential targets for future schemes. (The formal definition of trapdoor permutations [27], for example, was crafted to model RSA). We are inspired by the latter path. BLS [11] yields a threshold scheme [8] so natural and simple that it is hard to not see it as canonical, and, within the space of Schnorr threshold schemes, FROST [30] has a similarly appealing minimality. Examining them, we see strengths not captured by current definitions or results. We step back to create corresponding abstractions, including a unified syntax and a hierarchy of definitions of security for non-interactive threshold signature schemes. We then return to ask where in this hierarchy we can fit the starting schemes, giving proofs that fit BLS and FROST as high as possible. The proofs this requires, and that we provide, turn out to be challenging and technically interesting.

Although inspired by specific schemes, our definitional development, once begun, unfolds in a logical way, and yields definitions that go beyond even what BLS and FROST achieve. These make intriguing new targets. We show how to achieve them, with minimal modifications to the existing schemes.

2. FROST2 and its Security with DKG. We introduce FROST2, a variant of the original FROST scheme (we hereafter refer to the original as FROST1) that reduces the number of exponentiations required for signing and verification from *linear* in the number of signers to *constant*. We analyze the security of FROST2 in our above security framework, and highlight subtle differences between it and FROST1.

The above-discussed results are all in a setting with (ideal) trusted key generation. In practice however it is desirable that key generation itself be done via a threshold, distributed key generation protocol (DKG). Accordingly, we prove the security of FROST2 with a DKG, namely an efficient variant of Pedersen's DKG (PedPoP) introduced in conjunction with FROST1 [30]. Unlike prior proofs that modeled key generation using Pedersen's DKG [24], our security proof allows concurrent executions of the signing protocol once key generation has completed, and generalizes which honest parties are assumed to participate. We demonstrate that FROST2 instantiated with PedPoP is secure in the random oracle model (ROM) [5] assuming extractable proofs of possession and the one-more discrete logarithm (OMDL) assumption of [2]. The assumption of extractable proofs of possession is required *only* for the simulation of PedPoP. Indeed, our proofs for FROST1 and FROST2 without ideal key generation only rely on the OMDL assumption, along with random oracles.

Our proofs here fill a gap towards demonstrating security with respect to well-understood assumptions. We have a complete implementation of our security proof in python[1] in which we see that our reduction accurately outputs a valid OMDL solution and that our simulated outputs pass verification.

NON-INTERACTIVE THRESHOLD SCHEMES. We consider schemes where the signing operations involve a leader and a set of ns nodes, which we refer to as servers, with server i holding a secret share sk_i of the secret signing key sk. Signing is done via an interactive protocol that begins with a leader request to some set of at least t number of servers and culminates with the leader holding the signature, where $t \leq \mathsf{ns}$, the threshold, is a protocol parameter.

In a *fully non-interactive* threshold signature scheme, this protocol is a simple, one-round one. The leader sends a leader request lr, which specifies a message M and possibly other things, to any server i and obtains in response a *partial signature*, $psig_i$, that i computes as a function of sk_i and M. The leader can request partial signatures asynchronously, at any time, and independently for each server, and there is no server-to-server communication. Once it has enough partial signatures, the leader aggregates them into a signature sig of M under the verification key vk corresponding to sk. The canonical example is the threshold BLS scheme [8,12], where $sk, sk_1, \ldots, sk_{\mathsf{ns}} \in \mathbb{Z}_p$ for a public prime p, and $psig_i \leftarrow \mathsf{h}(M)^{sk_i}$ where $\mathsf{h} : \{0,1\}^* \rightarrow \mathbb{G}$ is a public hash function with range a group $\mathbb{G}$ of order p. Aggregation produces sig as a weighted product of the partial signatures.

A *partially non-interactive* threshold signature scheme adds to the above a message-independent pre-processing round in which, pinged by the leader at any point, a server i returns a pre-processing token pp_i. The leader's request for partial signatures will now depend on tokens it has received. The canonical example is FROST [30]. This understanding of a non-interactive scheme encompasses what FROST calls flexibility: obtaining $psig_i$ from *any* $\geq t$ servers allows reconstruction of the signature.

WHICH FORGERIES ARE NON-TRIVIAL? For a regular (non-threshold) signature scheme, the first and most basic notion of security is un-forgeability (UF) [27]. The adversary (given access to a signing oracle) outputs a forgery consisting of a message M and a valid signature for it. To win, the forgery must be *non-trivial*, meaning not obtained legitimately. This is naturally captured, in this context, as meaning that M was not a signing query.

[1] https://github.com/mmaller/multi_and_threshold_signature_reductions.

Turning to define un-forgeability for a non-interactive threshold signature scheme, we assume the adversary has corrupted the leader and up to $t-1$ servers, where $1 \le t \le \mathsf{ns}$ is the threshold. Furthermore, it has access to the honest servers. Again, it outputs a forgery consisting of a message M and valid signature for it, and, to win, the forgery must be *non-trivial*, meaning not obtained legitimately. Deciding what "non-trivial" means, however, is now a good deal more delicate, and interesting, than it was for regular signatures.

In this regard, we suggest that many prior works have set a low bar, being more generous than necessary in declaring a forgery trivial, leading to definitions that are weaker than one can desire, and weaker even than what their own schemes seem to meet. The definitions we formulate rectify this by considering five non-triviality conditions of increasing stringency, yielding a corresponding hierarchy TS-UF-0 $\leftarrow$ TS-UF-1 $\leftarrow$ TS-UF-2 $\leftarrow$ TS-UF-3 $\leftarrow$ TS-UF-4 of notions of un-forgeability of increasing strength. (Here an arrow B $\leftarrow$ A means A implies B: any scheme that is A-secure is also B-secure). TS-UF-0, the lowest in the hierarchy, is the notion currently in the literature.

Returning to regular (non-threshold) signature schemes, *strong* unforgeability (SUF) has the same template as UF, but makes the non-triviality condition more strict, asking that there has been no signing query M that returned sig. We ask if SUF has any analogue in the threshold setting. For non-interactive schemes, we suggest it does and give a hierarchy of three definitions of strong unforgeability TS-SUF-2 $\leftarrow$ TS-SUF-3 $\leftarrow$ TS-SUF-4. The numbering reflects that TS-UF-i $\leftarrow$ TS-SUF-i for $i = 2, 3, 4$.

<u>THE CASE OF BLS.</u> Boldyreva's analysis of threshold BLS [8] adopts the formalism of Gennaro, Jarecki, Krawczyk, and Rabin [23,25,26]. The non-triviality condition here is that *no* server was asked to issue a partial signature on the forgery message M. This is TS-UF-0 in our hierarchy. But allowing asynchronous requests is a feature of this scheme and model. A corrupted leader could ask one honest server i for a partial signature. No other server would even be aware of this request, but the adversary would now have $psig_i$. Under TS-UF-0, the forgery is now trivial, and the adversary does not win. Yet (assuming a threshold $t \ge 2$), there is no reason possession of just $psig_i$ should allow creation of a signature, and indeed for threshold BLS there is no attack that seems able to create such a signature, indicating the scheme is achieving more than TS-UF-0. This leads to the next level of our hierarchy, TS-UF-1, where the non-triviality condition is that a partial signature of M was requested from at most $t-1-c$ honest servers, where c is the number of corrupted servers. Does threshold BLS achieve this TS-UF-1 definition? As we will see, proving this presents challenges, but we will succeed in showing that the answer is yes, under a variant of the computational Diffie-Hellman (CDH) assumption. (The proof is deferred to [7] for lack of space). Yet, TS-UF-1 was not considered in the literature, and only TS-UF-0 is proved for many other non-interactive schemes [10,29,37,40]. The only exceptions are the work of Libert, Joye, and Yung [33] and recent concurrent work by Groth [28], which comes to a similar conclusion/result on BLS. (We discuss the relation below). We note that Shoup [37] implicitly tackles a

similar technical challenge by dealing with differing corruption and reconstruction thresholds, but the resulting security notion is not TS-UF-1.

The distinction between TS-UF-1 and TS-UF-0 is not just academic. Implicit in applications of threshold signing in wallets is the fact that servers also perform well-formedness checks of what is being signed (typically, as part of a transaction). TS-UF-1 guarantees that every issued signature has been inspected by sufficiently many servers, but TS-UF-0 does not.

THE CASE OF FROST. Yet the hierarchy needs to go higher, and this becomes apparent when looking at partially non-interactive schemes like FROST1 [30], and its optimized version, FROST2, which we introduce. Here, the discussion becomes more subtle, and interesting.

In more detail, a FROST1 pre-processing token takes the form of a pair $pp_i = (g^{r_i}, g^{s_i})$ of group elements for one-time use. (A server will ensure that the pre-processing token in its name in the leader request is one it has previously sent, and will never use it again). An honest request lr includes, along with the message M to be signed, a sufficiently large server set $lr.\mathsf{SS} \subseteq [1..\mathsf{ns}]$, and, for each i in this set, a pre-processing token pp_i that i previously sent. Each server $i \in lr.\mathsf{SS}$ will then generate a signature share $psig_i = (R, z_i)$, where R is a value which can be computed (publicly) from the tokens included in lr, whereas z_i depends on the discrete logarithms of the server's token and its own key share sk_i. The z_i's can then be aggregated into a value z such that (R, z) is a valid Schnorr signature for M.

In terms of our framework, we show that FROST1 achieves TS-SUF-3 security. This considers a signature trivial even if some of the honest servers in $lr.\mathsf{SS}$ do not respond to a (malicious) leader request, as long as the tokens associated with these servers are not honestly generated. In particular, the honest servers may not respond because they recognize these tokens as invalid, or because the malicious leader did not submit the request to them. We show that, while FROST2 fails to achieve TS-SUF-3, it achieves the next step down in our hierarchy, TS-SUF-2. This is still stronger than the notions lower in the hierarchy. Our proofs for FROST1 and FROST2 signing operations rely on the OMDL assumption and the ROM.

STRONGER GOALS. A stronger security goal (TS-UF-4 in our hierarchy) is to expect that the *only* way to obtain a signature for a message M is to follow the above blueprint, i.e., to issue the same honest leader request lr to all servers in $lr.\mathsf{SS}$. In fact, we may even ask for more, in terms of *strong* unforgeability—the value R is uniquely defined by lr, and, along with the message M, it defines a *unique* signature (although not efficiently computable given the verification key alone). An ideal goal, which corresponds to our strongest security goal, is to ensure that the *only* way to generate the signature associated with lr is to obtain a signature share for lr from every honest server whose tokens are included in lr. This is a notion we refer to as TS-SUF-4.

We will however show that neither FROST1 nor FROST2 meet TS-SUF-4. To overcome this, we will show a general transformation which can boost the security of a TS-SUF-3-secure scheme like FROST1 to achieve TS-SUF-4.

Our framework allows schemes more general than the FROST ones, and also leaves the question open of better and more efficient designs achieving the stronger notions. Moreover, we provide simple reference schemes for all of our notions, which, while inefficient, guide us in understanding the subtle differences among notions and baseline requirements. In particular, these schemes will enable us to separate the proposed notions.

A SUMMARY FOR OUR NOTIONS. In summary, our unforgeabilty notions declare a signature for a message M trivial in the following cases:

- TS-UF-0: A partial signature for the message M was generated by at least one honest server.
- TS-UF-1: A partial signature for the message M was generated by at least $t - c$ honest servers, where c is the number of corrupted servers.
- TS-UF-2: There exists a leader request lr for the message M which was answered by at least $t - c$ honest servers.
- TS-UF-3: There exists a leader request lr for the message M such that every honest server $i \in lr.\mathsf{SS}$ either answered lr or the token pp_i associated with i in lr is maliciously generated.
- TS-UF-4: There exists a leader request lr for the message M such that every honest server $i \in lr.\mathsf{SS}$ answered lr.

Analogous notions of strong unforgeability are obtained by further associating a request lr to a (unique) signature, in addition to a message M.

We stress that it is not clear which scenarios demand which notions in our hierarchy. This is especially true because we are still lacking formal analyses of full-fledged systems using threshold signatures, but it is not hard to envision a potential mismatch between natural expectations from such schemes and what they actually achieve. In both FROST variants, for example, it is natural to expect that a signature can only be generated by a sufficient number of honest servers answering the *same* request, a property which we show is actually achieved. Further, one may also expect that all honest servers that generated these honest tokens need to be involved in the generation of a valid signature, but this stronger property is actually not achieved by either of the FROST variants.

FROST2 WITH DKG. Our syntax above assumes key generation is carried out by a trusted algorithm, which allows us to focus on the signing protocol. However, security in practice is enhanced when the key generation itself is a distributed threshold protocol, so that the key is never in the clear in any one location, even ephemerally. In this setting, we prove the security of $\mathsf{FROST2}$ with the distributed key generation protocol (DKG) originally proposed in [30], which we refer to as PedPoP. Our proof for the combination of $\mathsf{FROST2}$ and PedPoP relies on the ROM, the OMDL assumption, and a new knowledge-type assumption. However, we stress that the latter assumption is only necessary to handle PedPoP, as indeed we give *stronger* proofs of security without this assumption in a setting with ideal key generation.

WHAT WE DO NOT DO. Our framework does not handle adaptive corruptions, i.e., we demand instead that the adversary declares its corruption set initially. We could extend our definitions to adaptive corruptions rather easily, but our concrete bounds would be impacted. In particular, we would resort to a generic reduction guessing the corrupted set beforehand, with a multiplicative loss of 2^{ns}, which is acceptable for the smaller values of the number ns of parties that we consider common in practice.

Our framework cannot cover recent protocols, like that of Canetti et al. [13], which combine a *multi-round* message-independent pre-processing phase with a final, message-dependent, round. (Conversely, their UC security analysis does not give definitions which help our fine-grained framework).

Many prior works also consider *robustness*, i.e., the guarantee that a signature is always produced. Here, we follow the same viewpoint as in FROST, and do not focus on robustness explicitly. This allows us to prevent imposing a small t (relative to ns) just for the sake of ensuring it. However, our schemes all implicitly give verification keys vk_i for each server, and it is not hard to verify individual partial signatures $psig_i$. Any t valid partial signatures will always aggregate into a valid signature.

<u>RELATED AND CONCURRENT WORK.</u> A recent preprint by Groth [28] presents a general definition for fully non-interactive schemes in a setting with a (non-interactive) DKG. His definition implies TS-UF-1, and he also provides a proof sketch that BLS (with his newly proposed non-interactive DKG) is secure under a variant of the OMCDH assumption, which is closely related to our variant of the CDH assumption and which we also show to be hard in the GGM. Groth's framework is not suitable for partially non-interactive schemes like FROST, which are the main focus of our work.

<u>HISTORY OF THIS PAPER.</u> This paper is the result of a (hard) merge imposed by the Crypto 2022 PC on two submissions. CKM [14] introduces $\mathsf{FROST2}$. BTZ [7] introduces the framework and definitions for non-interactive schemes with trusted key generation and proofs for BLS, $\mathsf{FROST1}$ and $\mathsf{FROST2}$ in this framework. CKM [14] provides a proof of security for $\mathsf{FROST2}$ that includes distributed key generation. Most security proofs have been deferred to the respective full versions. We see each group of authors as responsible for the contribution relevant to their part of the work.

2 Preliminaries

<u>NOTATION.</u> If $b \geq a \geq 1$ are positive integers, then $\mathbb{Z}_a$ denotes the set $\{0, \ldots, a-1\}$ and $[a..b]$ denotes the set $\{a, \ldots, b\}$. If $\boldsymbol{x}$ is a vector then $|\boldsymbol{x}|$ is its length (the number of its coordinates), $\boldsymbol{x}[i]$ is its i-th coordinate and $[\boldsymbol{x}] = \{ \boldsymbol{x}[i] : 1 \leq i \leq |\boldsymbol{x}| \}$ is the set of all its coordinates. A string is identified with a vector over $\{0, 1\}$, so that if x is a string then $x[i]$ is its i-th bit and $|x|$ is its length. By ε we denote the empty vector or string. The size of a set S is denoted $|S|$. For sets D, R let $\mathrm{FNS}(D, R)$ denote the set of all functions $f : D \to R$.

Let S be a finite set. We let $x \leftarrow\!\!\$\ S$ denote sampling an element uniformly at random from S and assigning it to x. We let $y \leftarrow A^{\mathrm{O}_1, \ldots}(x_1, \ldots; r)$ denote executing algorithm A on inputs $x_1, \ldots$ and coins r with access to oracles $\mathrm{O}_1, \ldots$ and letting y be the result. We let $y \leftarrow\!\!\$\ A^{\mathrm{O}_1, \ldots}(x_1, \ldots)$ be the result of picking r

at random and letting $y \leftarrow A^{\mathrm{O}_1,\cdots}(x_1,\ldots;r)$. Algorithms are randomized unless otherwise indicated. Running time is worst case.

GAMES. We use the code-based game playing framework of [6]. (See Fig. 2 for an example). Games have procedures, also called oracles. Among the oracles are INIT (Initialize) and FIN (Finalize). In executing an adversary $\mathcal{A}$ with a game Gm, the adversary may query the oracles at will, with the restriction that its first query must be to INIT (if present), its last to FIN, and it can query these oracles at most once. The value returned by the FIN procedure is taken as the game output. By $\mathrm{Gm}(\mathcal{A}) \Rightarrow y$ we denote the event that the execution of game Gm with adversary $\mathcal{A}$ results in output y. We write $\Pr[\mathrm{Gm}(\mathcal{A})]$ as shorthand for $\Pr[\mathrm{Gm}(\mathcal{A}) \Rightarrow \mathsf{true}]$, the probability that the game returns true.

In writing game or adversary pseudocode, it is assumed that Boolean variables are initialized to false, integer variables are initialized to 0 and set-valued variables are initialized to the empty set $\emptyset$.

GROUPS. Let $\mathbb{G}$ be a group of order p. We will use multiplicative notation for the group operation, and we let $1_{\mathbb{G}}$ denote the identity element of $\mathbb{G}$. We let $\mathbb{G}^* = \mathbb{G} \setminus \{1_{\mathbb{G}}\}$ denote the set of non-identity elements, which is the set of generators of $\mathbb{G}$ if the latter has prime order. If $g \in \mathbb{G}^*$ is a generator and $X \in \mathbb{G}$, the discrete logarithm base g of X is denoted $\mathsf{DL}_{\mathbb{G},g}(X)$, and it is in the set $\mathbb{Z}_{|\mathbb{G}|}$.

3 A Framework for Non-interactive Threshold Signatures

We present our hierarchy of definitions of security for non-interactive threshold schemes, formalizing both unforgeability (UF) and strong unforgeability (SUF) in several ways. We provide relations between all notions considered.

3.1 Syntax and Correctness

MAINTAINING STATE. Parties as implemented in protocols would maintain state. When activated with some inputs (which include messages from other parties), they would apply some algorithm Alg to these and their current state to get outputs (including outgoing messages) and an updated state. To model this, we do not change our definition of algorithms, but make the state an explicit input and output that will, in definitions, be maintained by the overlying game. Thus, we would write something like $(\cdots, \mathsf{st}) \leftarrow\$ \mathsf{Alg}(\cdots, \mathsf{st})$.

SYNTAX. A non-interactive threshold signature scheme TS specifies a number $\mathsf{ns} \geq 1$ of servers, a reconstruction threshold t, a set HF of functions from which the random oracle is drawn, a key generation algorithm Kg, a server pre-processing algorithm SPP, a leader pre-processing algorithm LPP, a leader signing-request algorithm LR, a server partial-signature algorithm PS, a leader partial-signature aggregation algorithm Agg and a verification algorithm Vf. If disambiguation is needed, we write $\mathsf{TS.ns}, \mathsf{TS}.t, \mathsf{TS.HF}, \mathsf{TS.Kg}, \mathsf{TS.SPP}, \mathsf{TS.LPP}$, $\mathsf{TS.LR}, \mathsf{TS.PS}, \mathsf{TS.Agg}, \mathsf{TS.Vf}$, respectively. We now explain the operation and

Game $\mathbf{G}_{\mathsf{TS}}^{\text{ts-cor}}$

INIT:

1 $\mathsf{h} \leftarrow_\$ \mathsf{TS.HF}$; $sk_0 \leftarrow \bot$; $(vk, aux, sk_1, \ldots, sk_{\mathsf{ns}}) \leftarrow_\$ \mathsf{Kg}[\mathsf{h}]$
2 For $i = [0..\mathsf{ns}]$ do // Initialize party states with keys
3    $\mathsf{st}_i.\mathsf{sk} \leftarrow sk_i$; $\mathsf{st}_i.\mathsf{vk} \leftarrow vk$; $\mathsf{st}_i.\mathsf{aux} \leftarrow aux$
4 Return $vk, aux, sk_1, \ldots, sk_{\mathsf{ns}}$

PPO(i): // $i \in [1..\mathsf{ns}]$

5 $(pp, \mathsf{st}_i) \leftarrow_\$ \mathsf{SPP}[\mathsf{h}](\mathsf{st}_i)$; $\mathsf{st}_0 \leftarrow \mathsf{LPP}[\mathsf{h}](pp, \mathsf{st}_0)$
6 Require: $pp \neq \bot$
7 Return pp

PPO(M, SS):

8 Require: $SS \subseteq [1..\mathsf{ns}]$ and $|SS| \geq t$ // Set of signers
9 $(lr, \mathsf{st}_0) \leftarrow_\$ \mathsf{LR}[\mathsf{h}](M, SS, \mathsf{st}_0)$
10 Require: $lr \neq \bot$ // Leader accepts request
11 If ($lr.\mathsf{msg} \neq M$ or $lr.\mathsf{SS} \neq SS$) then $\mathsf{win} \leftarrow \mathsf{true}$
12 For $i \in SS$ do
13    $(psig_i, \mathsf{st}_i) \leftarrow_\$ \mathsf{PS}[\mathsf{h}](lr, i, \mathsf{st}_i)$ // Server partial signatures
14 $(sig, \mathsf{st}_0) \leftarrow_\$ \mathsf{Agg}[\mathsf{h}](lr, \{psig_i\}_{i \in SS}, \mathsf{st}_0)$
15 If $\mathsf{Vf}[\mathsf{h}](vk, M, sig) = \mathsf{false}$ then $\mathsf{win} \leftarrow \mathsf{true}$

RO(x): // Random oracle

16 Return $\mathsf{h}(x)$

FIN:

17 Return win

Fig. 1. Game used to define correctness of threshold signature scheme TS with threshold t.

use of these components, the understanding of which may be aided by already looking at the correctness game $\mathbf{G}_{\mathsf{TS}}^{\text{ts-cor}}$ of Fig. 1.

Parties involved are a leader (numbered 0, implicit in some prior works, but made explicit here) and servers numbered $1, \ldots, \mathsf{ns}$, for a total of $\mathsf{ns}+1$ parties. Algorithms have oracle access to a function h that is drawn at random from HF in games (line 1 Fig. 1) and plays the role of the random oracle. Specifying HF as part of the scheme allows the domain and range of the random oracle to be scheme dependent.

The key generation algorithm Kg, run once at the beginning (line 1 of Fig. 1), creates a public signature-verification key vk, associated public auxiliary information aux and an individual secret signing key sk_i for each server $i \in [1..\mathsf{ns}]$. (Usually, $sk_1, \ldots, sk_{\mathsf{ns}}$ will be shares of a global secret key sk, but the definitions do not need to make sk explicit. The leader does not hold any secrets associated to vk). While key generation may in practice be performed by a distributed key generation protocol, our syntax assumes it done by a trusted algorithm to allow a modular treatment. Keys are held by parties in their state, encoded into dedicated fields of the latter as shown at line 3 of Fig. 1. For specific scheme, we will typically use aux to model additional information that can be leaked by key generation step without violating security (e.g., the values g^{sk_i} in most cases).

The signing protocol can be seen as having two rounds, which we think as a pre-processing and online stage. In a pre-processing round, any server i can run $(pp, \mathsf{st}_i) \leftarrow\$ \mathsf{SPP}[\mathsf{h}](\mathsf{st}_i)$ to get a *pre-processing token pp* which it sends to the leader. (Here st_i is the state of i.) Via $\mathsf{st}_0 \leftarrow \mathsf{LPP}[\mathsf{h}](pp, \mathsf{st}_0)$, the leader updates its state st_0 to incorporate token pp. (In Fig. 1, this is reflected in lines 5–7).

In a signing round the leader begins with a message and a choice of a signer set $SS \subseteq [1..\mathsf{ns}]$ of size at least t. Via $(lr, \mathsf{st}_0) \leftarrow\$ \mathsf{LR}[\mathsf{h}](M, SS, \mathsf{st}_0)$ it generates a leader request lr that, through st_0, implicitly depends on a choice of pre-processing tokens. (Lines 8,9 of Fig. 1). The leader request is sent to each $i \in SS$, who, via $(psig_i, \mathsf{st}_i) \leftarrow\$ \mathsf{PS}[\mathsf{h}](lr, \mathsf{st}_i)$, computes a partial signature $psig_i$ and returns it to the leader. Via $(sig, \mathsf{st}_0) \leftarrow\$ \mathsf{Agg}[\mathsf{h}](lr, \{psig_i\}_{i \in SS}, \mathsf{st}_0)$, the leader aggregates the partial signatures into a signature sig of M, the desired output of the protocol. (Lines 12–14 of Fig. 1).

The verification algorithm, like in a standard signature scheme, takes vk, a message M and a candidate signature, and returns a boolean validity decision.

ECHO SCHEMES. We define a sub-class of non-interactive threshold schemes that we call *echo schemes*. Recall that a leader request lr is mandated to specify a message $lr.\mathsf{msg}$ and a set $lr.\mathsf{SS} \subseteq [1..\mathsf{ns}]$ of servers from whom partial signatures are being requested. In an echo scheme, lr additionally specifies a function $lr.\mathsf{PP} : lr.\mathsf{SS} \rightarrow \{0,1\}^*$. If the leader is honest, $lr.\mathsf{PP}(i)$ is a token pp that i had previously sent to the leader. That is, the leader is echoing tokens back to the servers, whence the name. In considering security, of course, $lr.\mathsf{PP}(i)$ is picked by the adversary and may not be a prior token. As we will discuss in Sect. 4.1, FROST is a typical example of an echo scheme.

CORRECTNESS OF A TS SCHEME. The game of Fig. 1 defines correctness, and serves also to detail the above. Recall that TS specifies a threshold $t \in [1..\mathsf{ns}]$. The adversary will make the leader's pre-processing requests, via oracle PPO. It will likewise make signing requests via oracle PPO. If any condition listed under Require: fails the adversary is understood as losing, the game automatically returning false. We let $\mathbf{Adv}^{\text{ts-corr}}_{\mathsf{TS}}(\mathcal{A}) = \Pr[\mathbf{G}^{\text{ts-cor}}_{\mathsf{TS}}(\mathcal{A})]$ be the advantage of an adversary $\mathcal{A}$. The default requirement is perfect correctness, which means that $\mathbf{Adv}^{\text{ts-corr}}_{\mathsf{TS}}(\mathcal{A}) = 0$ for all $\mathcal{A}$, regardless of computing time and number of oracle queries, but this can be relaxed, as may be necessary for lattice-based protocols.

The way in which we are supposed to interpret the correctness definition is that a request lr is associated with a set SS and a message M, and if such a request is issued successfully by the leader (i.e., $lr \neq \bot$), then the servers in SS would all accept lr producing partial signatures which aggregate into a

Games $\mathbf{G}_{\mathsf{TS}}^{\text{ts-uf-}i}$ ($i = 0, 1, 2, 3, 4$) and $\mathbf{G}_{\mathsf{TS}}^{\text{ts-suf-}i}$ ($i = 2, 3, 4$)

$\textsc{Init}(CS)$:

1 Require: $CS \subseteq [1..\mathsf{ns}]$ and $|CS| < t$ // Set of corrupted parties
2 $\mathsf{h} \leftarrow\$ \mathsf{TS.HF}$; $(vk, aux, sk_1, \ldots, sk_{\mathsf{ns}}) \leftarrow\$ \mathsf{Kg}[\mathsf{h}]$
3 $HS \leftarrow [1..\mathsf{ns}] \setminus CS$ // Set of honest parties
4 For $i \in HS$ do
5 $\quad \mathsf{st}_i.\mathsf{sk} \leftarrow sk_i$; $\mathsf{st}_i.\mathsf{vk} \leftarrow vk$; $\mathsf{st}_i.\mathsf{aux} \leftarrow aux$
6 Return $vk, aux, \{sk_i\}_{i \in CS}$

$\mathrm{PPO}(i)$:

7 Require: $i \in HS$
8 $(pp, \mathsf{st}_i) \leftarrow\$ \mathsf{SPP}[\mathsf{h}](\mathsf{st}_i)$; $\mathrm{PP}_i \leftarrow \mathrm{PP}_i \cup \{pp\}$; Return pp

$\textsc{PSignO}(i, lr)$:

9 $M \leftarrow lr.\mathsf{msg}$
10 Require: $lr.\mathsf{SS} \subseteq [1..\mathsf{ns}]$ and $M \in \{0,1\}^*$ and $i \in HS$
11 $\mathrm{L} \leftarrow \mathrm{L} \cup \{lr\}$; $(psig, \mathsf{st}_i) \leftarrow\$ \mathsf{PS}[\mathsf{h}](lr, i, \mathsf{st}_i)$
12 If $(psig \neq \perp)$ then
13 $\quad \mathrm{S}_1(M) \leftarrow \mathrm{S}_1(M) \cup \{i\}$; $\mathrm{S}_2(lr) \leftarrow \mathrm{S}_2(lr) \cup \{i\}$
14 Return $psig$

$\mathrm{RO}(x)$: // Random oracle

15 Return $\mathsf{h}(x)$

$\textsc{Fin}(M, sig)$:

16 For all $lr \in \mathrm{L}$ do
17 $\quad \mathrm{S}_3(lr) \leftarrow \{\, i \in HS \cap lr.\mathsf{SS} : lr.\mathsf{PP}(i) \in \mathrm{PP}_i \,\}$; $\mathrm{S}_4(lr) \leftarrow HS \cap lr.\mathsf{SS}$
18 If (not $\mathsf{Vf}[\mathsf{h}](vk, M, sig)$) then return false
19 Return (not $\mathtt{tf}_i(M)$) // Game $\mathbf{G}_{\mathsf{TS}}^{\text{ts-uf-}i}$ for $i = 0, 1$
20 Return (not $\exists\, lr$ ($lr.\mathsf{msg} = M$ and $\mathtt{tf}_i(lr)$)) // Game $\mathbf{G}_{\mathsf{TS}}^{\text{ts-uf-}i}$ for $i = 2, 3, 4$
21 Return (not $\exists\, lr$ ($lr.\mathsf{msg} = M$ and $\mathtt{tsf}_i(lr, vk, sig)$)) // Game $\mathbf{G}_{\mathsf{TS}}^{\text{ts-suf-}i}$

Fig. 2. Games used to define TS-UF-i and TS-SUF-i unforgeability of threshold signature scheme TS. Line 20 is included only in game $\mathbf{G}_{\mathsf{TS}}^{\text{ts-uf-}i}$ and line 21 only in game $\mathbf{G}_{\mathsf{TS}}^{\text{ts-suf-}i}$. These lines refer to the trivial-forgery predicates $\mathtt{tf}_i(lr)$ and trivial-strong-forgery predicates $\mathtt{tsf}_i(lr, vk, sig)$ from Figure 3. In particular, the set $\mathrm{S}_3(lr)$ and, thus, TS-UF-3 and TS-SUF-3 unforgeability are defined only if TS is an echo scheme.

valid signature for M. We note that this definition assumes that we submit requests to all servers in the same order. One can give a stronger (but more complex) definition which ensures correctness even when servers process requests in different orders, but note that for all schemes we discuss below they will be equivalent, and we hence omit the more cumbersome game to define it.

3.2 Unforgeability and Strong Unforgeability

UNFORGEABILITY. Unforgeability as usual asks that the adversary be unable to produce a valid signature *sig* on some message M of its choice except in a trivial way. The question is what "trivial" means. For regular signatures, it means that the adversary did not obtain a signature of M from the signing oracle [27]. For threshold signatures, it is more subtle. We will give several definitions.

Figure 2 simultaneously describes several games, $\mathbf{G}^{\text{ts-uf-}i}_{\mathsf{TS}}$ for $i = 0, 1, 2, 3, 4$, where $\mathbf{G}^{\text{ts-uf-3}}_{\mathsf{TS}}$ is only defined if TS is an echo scheme. (We will get to the second set of games later). They are almost the same, differing only at line 20. The corresponding advantages of an adversary $\mathcal{A}$ are $\mathbf{Adv}^{\text{ts-uf-i}}_{\mathsf{TS}}(\mathcal{A}) = \Pr[\mathbf{G}^{\text{ts-uf-}i}_{\mathsf{TS}}(\mathcal{A})]$. The adversary calls INIT with a choice of a set of servers to corrupt. It is also viewed as having corrupted the leader. Playing the leader role, it can request pre-processing tokens via oracle PPO. It can provide a server with a leader-request lr of its choice to obtain a partial signature *psig*. At the end, it outputs to FIN its forgery message M and signature *sig*. If the signature is not valid, line 18 ensures that the adversary does not win. Now, to win, the signature must be non-trivial. It is in how this is defined that the games differ. Associated to i is a *trivial-forgery* predicate $\mathtt{tf}_i$ that is invoked at line 20. The choices for these predicates are shown in the table in Fig. 3, and the notion corresponding to game $\mathtt{tf}_i$ is denoted TS-UF-i. When $i = 0$ we have the usual notion from the literature, used in particular in [8,23,25]. As i increases, we get more stringent (less generous) in declaring a forgery trivial, and the notion gets stronger.

Concretely, TS-UF-0 considers a signature for a message M trivial if a request lr with $lr.\mathsf{msg}$ was answered by server with a partial signature. Moving on, TS-UF-1 strengthens this by declaring a signature trivial only if at least $t - |CS|$ servers have responded to some request for message M, where these requests could have been different. In turn, TS-UF-2 strengthens this even further by requiring that there was a single prior request lr for M which was answered by $t - |CS|$ servers.

The notion TS-UF-3 only deals with echo schemes. Recall that for these schemes, a request lr contains a map $lr.\mathsf{PP} : lr.\mathsf{SS} \to \{0,1\}^*$, where $lr.\mathsf{PP}(i)$ is meant to be a token issued by server i. Here, we consider a signature for message M trivial if there exists a request lr for M which is answered by all honest servers i for which $lr.\mathsf{PP}(i)$ is a valid token previously output by i, and this set consists of at least $t - |CS|$ servers. Finally, our strongest notion, TS-UF-4 simply considers a signature trivial if there exists a request lr for M which is answered by all honest servers in $i \in lr.\mathsf{SS}$.

It is natural to expect TS-UF-3 and TS-UF-4 to be similar, but as we will see below, they are actually not equivalent. (Although we will give a transformation that boosts an TS-UF-3-secure scheme into an TS-UF-4-secure one).

STRONG UNFORGEABILITY. For standard signatures, strong unforgeability asks, in addition to unforgeability, that the adversary be unable to produce a new signature on any message, where new means different from any obtained legitimately for that message. We ask, does this have any counterpart in threshold

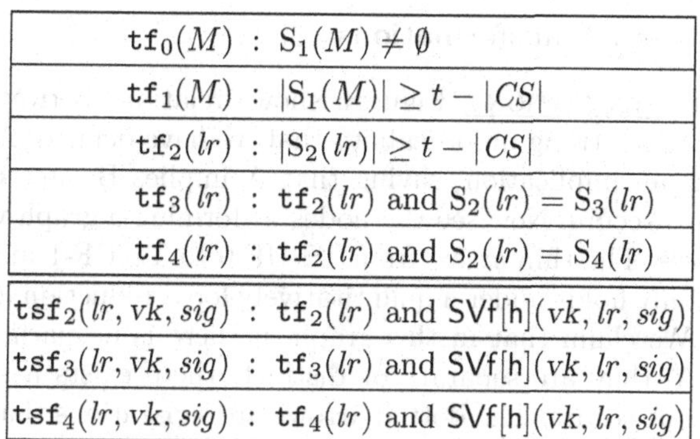

$\mathtt{tf}_0(M)$	: $\mathrm{S}_1(M) \neq \emptyset$
$\mathtt{tf}_1(M)$	: $\lvert \mathrm{S}_1(M) \rvert \geq t - \lvert CS \rvert$
$\mathtt{tf}_2(lr)$	: $\lvert \mathrm{S}_2(lr) \rvert \geq t - \lvert CS \rvert$
$\mathtt{tf}_3(lr)$	: $\mathtt{tf}_2(lr)$ and $\mathrm{S}_2(lr) = \mathrm{S}_3(lr)$
$\mathtt{tf}_4(lr)$	: $\mathtt{tf}_2(lr)$ and $\mathrm{S}_2(lr) = \mathrm{S}_4(lr)$
$\mathtt{tsf}_2(lr, vk, sig)$	: $\mathtt{tf}_2(lr)$ and $\mathsf{SVf}[\mathsf{h}](vk, lr, sig)$
$\mathtt{tsf}_3(lr, vk, sig)$	: $\mathtt{tf}_3(lr)$ and $\mathsf{SVf}[\mathsf{h}](vk, lr, sig)$
$\mathtt{tsf}_4(lr, vk, sig)$	: $\mathtt{tf}_4(lr)$ and $\mathsf{SVf}[\mathsf{h}](vk, lr, sig)$

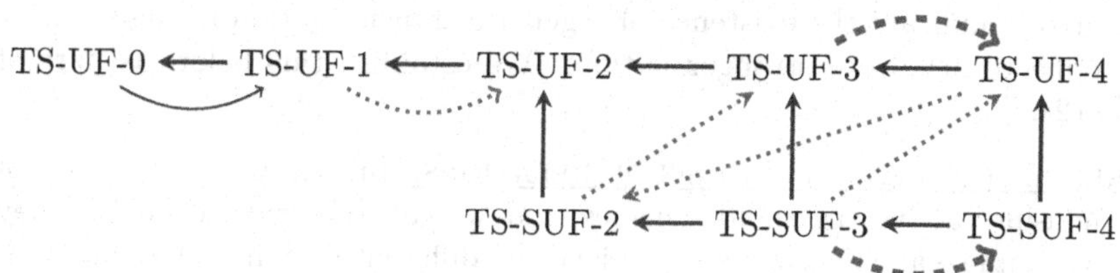

Fig. 3. Top: Trivial-forgery conditions $\mathtt{tf}_i(lr)$ $(i = 0, 1, 2, 3, 4)$ and trivial-strong-forgery conditions $\mathtt{tsf}_i(lr, vk, sig)$ $(i = 1, 2, 3, 4)$ used to define TS-SUF-i and TS-SUF-i security in games $\mathbf{G}^{\text{ts-uf-}i}_{\mathsf{TS}}$ and $\mathbf{G}^{\text{ts-suf-}i}_{\mathsf{TS}}$, respectively. **Bottom:** Relations between notions of security.

---

signatures? In fact, FROST seems to have such a property. We now provide formalisms to capture such properties.

It turns out that giving a general definition of strong unforgeability is rather complex, and we will restrict ourselves to a natural sub-class of schemes (which includes FROST). Concretely, we ask that there is an algorithm SVf, called a *strong verification algorithm*, that takes a public key vk, a leader request lr, and a signature sig as inputs and outputs true or false. We require that for any vk, lr there exists at most one signature sig such that $\mathsf{SVf}(vk, lr, sig) = \mathsf{true}$. Also, TS is asked to satisfy a strong correctness property which is defined using the same game as $\mathbf{G}^{\text{ts-cor}}_{\mathsf{TS}}$ except the condition $\mathsf{Vf}[\mathsf{h}](vk, M, sig) = \mathsf{false}$ in line 15 is replaced with $\mathsf{SVf}[\mathsf{h}](vk, lr, sig) = \mathsf{false}$.

For a scheme TS with a strong verification algorithm, we consider the $\mathbf{G}^{\text{ts-suf-}i}_{\mathsf{TS}}$ $(i = 2, 3, 4)$ games in Fig. 2, where $\mathbf{G}^{\text{ts-suf-3}}_{\mathsf{TS}}$ is only defined if TS additionally is an echo scheme. The differences (across the different values of i) are only in the trivial-strong forgery predicates $\mathtt{tsf}_i$ used at line 21, and the choices are again shown in the table in Fig. 3. The corresponding advantage of an adversary $\mathcal{A}$ is $\mathbf{Adv}^{\text{ts-suf-i}}_{\mathsf{TS}}(\mathcal{A}) = \Pr[\mathbf{G}^{\text{ts-suf-}i}_{\mathsf{TS}}(\mathcal{A})]$. The ensuing notion is called TS-SUF-i.

3.3 Relations and Transformations

Relations between notions. Figure 3 shows relations between the notions of unforgeability and strong unforgeabilty that we have defined. A (non-dotted) arrow A $\rightarrow$ B is an implication, saying that A implies B: any scheme that is A-secure is also B-secure. Now see the nodes as forming a graph with edges the non-dotted arrows. The thin arrow from TS-UF-0 to TS-UF-1 indicates us that the implication only holds under a quantitatively loose reduction. (We prove this in Theorem 1). We claim that in this graph, if there is no path from a notion B to a notion A, they are separate or distinct: there exists a scheme that is B-secure but not A-secure. The dotted arrows are separations that we explicitly prove. These, together with the full arrows, prove the claim just made. The thick dotted arrows indicate the existence of a generic transformation lifting security of a scheme to achieve a stronger notion. (We establish this below as part of Theorem 2).

Reference schemes and proofs of relations. In [7], we give a set of (fully) non-interactive threshold schemes that we call reference schemes. They represent simple, canonical ways to achieve the different notions. They may not be of practical interest, because they have key and signature sizes proportional to ns, but the point is to embody notions in a representative way. A few things emanate from these schemes. One is that we use them to establish the separations given by the dotted lines in Fig. 3, thereby showing that any notions between which there is no path, in the graph given by the full arrows, are indeed separate. Second, we get a scheme that achieves our strongest notion, TS-SUF-4, which neither FROST nor BLS achieve. (Although we can get such a scheme by applying our transformation from Theorem 2 to $\mathsf{FROST1}$). Finally, reference schemes, as canonical examples, are ways to understand the notions.

From TS-UF-0 to TS-UF-1, loosely. The following theorem shows TS-UF-1 security is implied by TS-UF-0 security, although with an exponential loss in t, which is acceptable in settings where t is expected to be constant.

Theorem 1. *Let* TS *be a threshold signature scheme. For any TS-UF-1 adversary* $\mathcal{A}$ *there exists a TS-UF-0 adversary* $\mathcal{B}$ *such that* $\mathbf{Adv}^{\text{ts-uf-1}}_{\mathsf{TS}}(\mathcal{A}) \leq \binom{\mathsf{ns}}{t-1} \cdot \mathbf{Adv}^{\text{ts-uf-0}}_{\mathsf{TS}}(\mathcal{B})$. *Moreover,* $\mathcal{B}$ *runs in time roughly equal that of* $\mathcal{A}$*, and the number of* $\mathcal{B}$*'s queries to each oracle is at most that of* $\mathcal{A}$.

If the adversary always corrupts $t-1$ parties, it is clear that TS-UF-0 and TS-UF-1 are equivalent. Otherwise, in general, for an adversary that breaks TS-UF-1 security and corrupts a subset CS of servers with size less than $t-1$, if the adversary wins the game $\mathbf{G}^{\text{ts-uf-1}}_{\mathsf{TS}}$ by outputting (M^*, sig^*), we know $|\mathrm{S}_1(M^*)| < t - |CS|$. Therefore, we can modify the adversary to initially guess a subset $ECS \subseteq [1..\mathsf{ns}] \setminus CS$ with size $t - |CS| - 1$ and corrupt all parties in ECS. If ECS happens to contain $\mathrm{S}_1(M^*)$, the adversary actually wins. It is not hard to see that the probability that this is true is $1/\binom{\mathsf{ns}-|CS|}{t-|CS|-1} \geq 1/\binom{\mathsf{ns}}{t-1}$. We give a formal proof in [7].

```
Protocol ATS[TS, DS]

Kg[h]:
  vk, taux, {tsk_i}_{i∈[1..ns]} ← TS.Kg
  For i ∈ [1..ns] do
    (svk_i, ssk_i) ←$ DS.Kg
    sk_i ← (tsk_i, ssk_i)
  aux ← (taux, svk_1, ..., svk_ns)
  Return vk, aux, {sk_i}_{i∈[1..ns]}

SPP[h](st_i):
  (tpp, st_i) ←$ SPP[h](st_i)
  (tsk_i, ssk_i) ← st_i.sk
  tsig ←$ DS.Sig(ssk_i, tpp)
  Return ((tpp, tsig), st_i)

LPP[h](i, pp, st_O):
  (tpp, tsig) ← pp
  st_O.SigMap(i, tpp) ← tsig
  Return TS.LPP[h](i, tpp, st_O)

OriginLR(lr):
  For i ∈ lr.SS do
    (tpp, tsig) ← lr.PP(i)
    lr.PP(i) ← tpp
  Return lr

LR[h](M, SS, st_O):
  (lr, st_O) ← TS.LR[h](M, SS, st_O)
  For i ∈ SS do
    tpp_i ← lr.PP(i)
    lr.PP(i) ← (tpp_i, st_O.SigMap(i, tpp_i))
  Return (lr, st_O)

PS[h](lr, i, st_i):
  (taux, svk_1, ..., svk_ns) ← st_i.aux
  For i ∈ lr.SS do
    (tpp_i, tsig_i) ← lr.PP(i)
    If DS.Vf(svk_i, tpp_i, tsig_i) = false then
      Return ⊥
  Return TS.PS[h](OriginLR(lr), i, st_i)

Agg[h](PS, st_O):
  Return TS.Agg[h](PS, st_O)

Vf[h](vk, M, sig):
  Return TS.Vf[h](vk, M, sig)

SVf[h](vk, lr, sig):
  Return TS.SVf[h](vk, OriginLR(lr), sig)
```

Fig. 4. The threshold signature ATS[TS, DS] constructed from an echo scheme TS and a digital signature scheme DS such that ATS.ns = TS.ns and ATS.t = TS.t. The algorithm OriginLR transforms a well-formed leader request lr for ATS to a well-formed leader request in TS. st_{O}.SigMap is a table that stores the signature corresponding to each token generated by honest servers, which is initially set to empty. PS denotes a set of partial signatures.

FROM TS-(S)UF-3 TO TS-(S)UF-4. Figure 4 gives a general transformation from TS-(S)UF-3 security to TS-(S)UF-4 security. Concretely, we give a construction ATS from any TS-(S)UF-3-secure echo scheme TS and a digital signature scheme DS. The size of signatures produced by ATS and the verification algorithm Vf are exactly the same as TS. The main idea is to use signatures to authenticate each token contained in a leader request lr from TS, so that an honest server only answers the request if all the authentications are valid. The rest of the protocol remains the same.

In the game $\mathbf{G}^{\text{ts-(s)uf-4}}_{\mathsf{ATS}}$, we can show that as long as the adversary does not break the strong unforgeability of DS, for any leader request lr such that

Game $\mathbf{G}_{\mathsf{DS}}^{\text{suf-cma}}$	$\text{FIN}(M, sig)$:
INIT:	If $\mathsf{DS.Vf}(vk, M, sig)$ and $(M, sig) \notin Q$ then
$(vk, sk) \leftarrow\!\!\$\ \mathsf{DS.Kg}$	Return true
Return vk	Return false
PPO(M):	
$sig \leftarrow\!\!\$\ \mathsf{DS.Sig}(sk, M)$	
$Q \leftarrow Q \cup \{(M, sig)\}$	
Return sig	

Fig. 5. The game $\mathbf{G}_{\mathsf{DS}}^{\text{suf-cma}}$, where DS is a digital signature scheme.

$\mathrm{S}_2(lr) > 0$, it holds that $\mathrm{S}_3(lr) = \mathrm{S}_4(lr)$, which implies the conditions $\mathtt{tf}_3$ and $\mathtt{tf}_4$ are equivalent. Therefore, we can reduce TS-(S)UF-4 security of ATS to TS-(S)UF-3 security of TS and SUF-CMA security of DS. (The latter notion is formally defined via the game in Fig. 5). This is captured by the following theorem. (The proof is in [7]).

Theorem 2. *Let $XX \in \{SUF, UF\}$. Let* TS *be an echo scheme and* DS *be a digital signature scheme. For any TS-XX-4 adversary $\mathcal{A}$ there exists a TS-XX-3 adversary $\mathcal{B}$ and a SUF-CMA adversary $\mathcal{C}$ such that*

$$\mathbf{Adv}_{\mathsf{ATS[TS,DS]}}^{\text{ts-xx-4}}(\mathcal{A}) \leq \mathbf{Adv}_{\mathsf{TS}}^{\text{ts-xx-3}}(\mathcal{B}) + \mathsf{ns} \cdot \mathbf{Adv}_{\mathsf{DS}}^{\text{suf-cma}}(\mathcal{C}).$$

Moreover, $\mathcal{B}$ and $\mathcal{C}$ run in time roughly equal that of $\mathcal{A}$. The number of $\mathcal{B}$'s queries to each oracle is at most that of $\mathcal{A}$. The number of $\mathcal{C}$'s PPO *queries is at most the number of* PPO *queries made by $\mathcal{A}$.*

4 The Security of FROST

4.1 The FROST1 and FROST2 Schemes

SCHEME DESCRIPTIONS. This section revisits the security of FROST, first proposed in [31] by Komlo and Goldberg, as a (partially) non-interactive threshold signature scheme.

First, we consider the original scheme, which we refer to as FROST1. We then present FROST2, an optimized version that reduces the number of exponentiations required for signing and verification from $|lr.\mathsf{SS}|$ to one. We give a detailed description of both schemes in Fig. 6. The leader state st_0 contains a set curPP_i for each server i representing the set of tokens generated by server i that has not yet been used in a signing request. The state st_i for server i contains a function mapPP that maps each token pp to the randomness that is used to generate pp and $\mathsf{st}_i.\mathrm{mapPP}(pp) = \bot$ if pp is not generated by server i yet or has already

```
Protocol [FROST1], [FROST2][G]

Kg[h]:
For i ∈ [0..t − 1] do
    a_i ←$ Z_p
For i ∈ [1..ns] do
    sk_i ←$ Σ_{j=0}^{t−1} i^j · a_j ; vk_i ← g^{sk_i}
vk ← g^{a_0}
aux ← (vk_1, ..., vk_ns)
Return vk, aux, {sk_i}_{i∈[1..ns]}

SPP[h](st_i):
r ← Z_p ; s ← Z_p
pp ← (g^r, g^s)
st_i.mapPP(pp) ← (r, s)
Return (pp, st_i)

LPP[h](i, pp, st_O):
st_O.curPP_i ← st_O.curPP_i ∪ {pp}
Return st_O

LR[h](M, SS, st_O):
If ∃ i ∈ SS : st_O.curPP_i = ∅ then
    Return ⊥
lr.msg ← M ; lr.SS ← SS
For i ∈ SS do
    Pick pp_i from st_O.curPP_i
    lr.PP(i) ← pp_i
    st_O.curPP_i ← st_O.curPP_i \ {pp_i}
Return (lr, st_O)

Vf[h](vk, M, sig):
(R, z) ← sig
c ← h_2(vk, M, R)
Return (g^z = R · vk^c)

CompPar[h](vk, lr):
M ← lr.msg
For i ∈ lr.SS do
    [d_i ← h_1(vk, lr, i)]        (solid box)
    [d_i ← h_1(vk, lr)]           (dashed box)
    (R_i, S_i) ← lr.PP(i)
R ← Π_{i∈lr.SS} R_i S_i^{d_i}
c ← h_2(vk, M, R)
Return (R, c, {d_i}_{i∈lr.SS})

PS[h](lr, i, st_i):
pp_i ← lr.PP(i)
If st_i.mapPP(pp_i) = ⊥ then
    Return (⊥, st_i)
(r_i, s_i) ← st_i.mapPP(pp_i)
st_i.mapPP(pp_i) ← ⊥
(R, c, {d_j}_{j∈lr.SS})
    ← CompPar[h](st_i.vk, lr)
z_i ← r_i + d_i · s_i + c · λ_i^{lr.SS} · st_i.sk
Return ((R, z_i), st_i)

Agg[h](PS, st_O):
R ← ⊥ ; z ← 0
For (R', z') ∈ PS do
    If R = ⊥ then R ← R'
    If R ≠ R' then return (⊥, st_O)
    z ← z + z'
Return ((R, z), st_O)

SVf[h](vk, lr, sig):
(R*, z*) ← sig
(R, c, {d_j}_{j∈lr.SS})
    ← CompPar[h](vk, lr)
Return (R = R*) ∧ (g^{z*} = R · vk^c)
```

Fig. 6. The protocol $\mathsf{FROST1}[\mathbb{G}]$ and $\mathsf{FROST2}[\mathbb{G}]$, where $\mathbb{G}$ is a cyclic group with prime order p and generator g. Further, ns is the number of parties, and t is the threshold of the schemes. We require $t \leq \mathsf{ns} \leq p-1$. The protocol $\mathsf{FROST1}$ contains all but the dashed box, and the protocol $\mathsf{FROST2}$ contains all but the solid box. The function $\mathsf{h}_i(\cdot)$ is computed as $\mathsf{h}(i, \cdot)$ for $i = 1, 2$. PS denotes a set of partial signatures.

Game $\mathbf{G}_{\mathbb{G}}^{\mathrm{omdl}}$

INIT:

$\mathrm{cid} \leftarrow 0;\ \ell \leftarrow 0;\ T \leftarrow ()$

CHAL():

$\mathrm{cid} \leftarrow \mathrm{cid} + 1;\ x_{\mathrm{cid}} \leftarrow\!\!\$\ \mathbb{Z}_p$

Return $g^{x_{\mathrm{cid}}}$

DLOG(X):

If $T(X) \neq \bot$ then return $T(X)$

$\ell \leftarrow \ell + 1;\ T(X) \leftarrow \mathsf{DL}_{\mathbb{G},g}(X)$

Return $T(X)$

FIN($\{y_i\}_{i \in [\mathrm{cid}]}$):

If $\ell \geq \mathrm{cid}$ then return false

If $\forall\, i \in [\mathrm{cid}] : y_i = x_i$ then

  Return true

Return false

Fig. 7. The OMDL game, where $\mathbb{G}$ is a cyclic group with prime order p and generator g.

been used in a signing request. The coefficient $\lambda_i^{lr.\mathsf{SS}}$ in line 39 is the Lagrange coefficient for the set $lr.\mathsf{SS}$, which is defined (for any set $S \subseteq [1..\mathsf{ns}]$) as

$$\lambda_i^S := \prod_{j \in S, i \neq j} \frac{j}{j-i}.$$

The algorithm $\mathsf{CompPar}$ is a helper algorithm that computes the parameters $R, c, \{d_i\}_{i \in lr.\mathsf{SS}}$ used during signing. The difference between $\mathsf{FROST1}$ and $\mathsf{FROST2}$ is the way d_i is computed in $\mathsf{CompPar}$. In $\mathsf{FROST1}$, each d_i is a different hash value for each server i, while in $\mathsf{FROST2}$, d_i's are the same hash value for all servers.

It is not hard to verify that both schemes satisfy perfect correctness.

OVERVIEW OF OUR RESULTS. We begin by showing that $\mathsf{FROST2}$ is TS-SUF-2-secure (under OMDL) but not TS-UF-3-secure. We then show that $\mathsf{FROST1}$ is TS-SUF-3-secure but not TS-UF-4-secure. Theoretically, our results imply the separations between TS-(S)UF-2 and TS-(S)UF-3 and between TS-(S)UF-3 and TS-(S)UF-4. Practically speaking, our results indicate a separation between the security of $\mathsf{FROST1}$ and $\mathsf{FROST2}$. To complete the picture, a TS-SUF-4-secure variant of $\mathsf{FROST1}$ can be obtained via the general transformation from Theorem 2, although it is an interesting open question whether a more efficient variant exists.

4.2 TS-SUF-2 Security of FROST2

We first show that $\mathsf{FROST2}$ is TS-SUF-2-secure in the ROM under the OMDL assumption, which is formally defined in Fig. 7. Formally, we show the following theorem.

Theorem 3. *For any TS-SUF-2 adversary $\mathcal{A}$ making at most q_s queries to* PPO *and at most q_h queries to* RO*, there exists an OMDL adversary $\mathcal{B}$ making at most $2q_s + \mathsf{ns}$ queries to* CHAL *such that*

$$\mathbf{Adv}^{\text{ts-suf-2}}_{\mathsf{FROST2}[\mathbb{G}]}(\mathcal{A}) \leq \sqrt{q \cdot (\mathbf{Adv}^{\mathrm{omdl}}_{\mathbb{G}}(\mathcal{B}) + 3q^2/p)}\ ,$$

where $q = q_s + q_h + 1$. *Moreover,* $\mathcal{B}$ *runs in time roughly equal two times that of* $\mathcal{A}$*, plus the time to perform at most* $(4\mathsf{ns}+2) \cdot q + 2q_s + 2\mathsf{ns}^2$ *exponentiations and group operations.*

The core of the proof is a reduction from OMDL [2], which will need to use rewinding (via a variant of the Forking Lemma). The main challenge is to ensure that the reduction can simulate properly with a number of queries to DLOG which is smaller than the number of DL challenges. Further below, we are going to show that FROST2 is not TS-UF-3 secure, thus showing the above result is optimal with respect to our hierarchy.

Proof (of Theorem 3). Let $\mathcal{A}$ be an adversary as described in the theorem. Denote the output message-signature pair of $\mathcal{A}$ as $(M^*, sig^* = (R^*, z^*))$. Without loss of generality, we assume $\mathcal{A}$ always queries RO on $\mathsf{h}_2(vk, M^*, R^*)$ before $\mathcal{A}$ returns and always queries RO on $\mathsf{h}_1(vk, lr)$ prior to the query PSIGNO(i, lr) for some i and lr. (This adds up to q_s additional RO queries, and we let $q = q_h + q_s + 1$). Denote lr^* as the leader query such that $\mathsf{h}_1(vk, lr^*)$ is the first query prior to the query $\mathsf{h}_2(vk, M^*, R^*)$ satisfying $\mathsf{SVf}[\mathsf{h}](vk, lr^*, sig^*) = \mathsf{true}$. If such lr^* does not exists, lr^* is set to $\perp$. Denote the event E_1 as

$$\mathsf{Vf}[\mathsf{h}](vk, M^*, sig^*) \wedge (lr^* = \perp \vee \mathrm{S}_2(lr^*) < t - |CS|).$$

It is clear that if $\mathcal{A}$ wins the game $\mathbf{G}^{\text{ts-suf-2}}_{\mathsf{FROST2}}$, then E_1 must occur, which implies $\Pr[E_1] \geq \mathbf{Adv}^{\text{ts-suf-2}}_{\mathsf{FROST2}[\mathbb{G}]}(\mathcal{A})$. Therefore, the theorem will follow from the following lemma. (We isolate this statement as its own lemma also because it will be helpful in the proof of Theorem 5 below). □

Lemma 4. *There exists an OMDL adversary* $\mathcal{B}$ *making at most* $2q_s + t$ *queries to* CHAL *such that*

$$\Pr[E_1] \leq \sqrt{q \cdot (\mathbf{Adv}^{\mathrm{omdl}}_{\mathbb{G}}(\mathcal{B}) + 3q^2/p)}.$$

Moreover, $\mathcal{B}$ *runs in time roughly twice that of* $\mathcal{A}$*, plus the time to perform at most* $(4\mathsf{ns}+2) \cdot q + 2q_s + 2\mathsf{ns}^2$ *exponentiations and group operations.*

The proof of Lemma 4 is in [7]. It uses a variant of the general Forking Lemma of [3], also given in 4, that allows us to get better bounds in our analysis.

4.3 TS-SUF-3 Security of FROST1

In this section, we show that FROST1 is TS-SUF-3-secure in the ROM under the OMDL assumption. Formally, we show the following theorem.

Theorem 5. *For any TS-SUF-3 adversary* $\mathcal{A}$ *making at most* q_s *queries to* PPO *and at most* q_h *queries to* RO*, there exists an OMDL adversary* $\mathcal{B}$ *making at most* $2q_s + t$ *queries to* CHAL *such that*

$$\mathbf{Adv}^{\text{ts-suf-3}}_{\mathsf{FROST1}[\mathbb{G}]}(\mathcal{A}) \leq 4\mathsf{ns} \cdot q \cdot \sqrt{\mathbf{Adv}^{\mathrm{omdl}}_{\mathbb{G}}(\mathcal{B}) + 6q/p}\ ,$$

where $q = q_s + q_h + 1$. *Moreover,* $\mathcal{B}$ *runs in time roughly equal two times that of* $\mathcal{A}$*, plus the time to perform at most* $6\mathsf{ns} \cdot q + 4q_s + 2\mathsf{ns}^2$ *exponentiations and group operations.*

The proof here follows a similar pattern than that of Theorem 3, but will be more complex. In particular, the lesser tight bound is due to the fact that we need to consider an additional bad event, which we upper bound via a different reduction from OMDL. As we explain in detail below, this reduction will make use of a looser Forking Lemma, which is a variant of the "Local Forking Lemma" [1], which only resamples a single random oracle output when rewinding. The extra looseness is due to needing to ensure an extra condition when rewinding.

Proof (of Theorem 5). Let $\mathcal{A}$ be the adversary described in the theorem. Denote the output message-signature pair of $\mathcal{A}$ as $(M^*, sig^* = (R^*, z^*))$. Without loss of generality, we assume $\mathcal{A}$ always queries RO on $\mathsf{h}_2(vk, M^*, R^*)$ before $\mathcal{A}$ returns and always queries RO on $\mathsf{h}_1(vk, lr, i)$ prior to the query PSIGNO(i, lr) for some i and lr. (This adds up to q_s additional RO queries, and we let $q = q_h + q_s + 1$). Denote lr^* as the leader query such that $\mathsf{h}_1(vk, lr^*, i)$ is the first RO query prior to the $\mathsf{h}_2(vk, M^*, R^*)$ query for some i satisfying $\mathsf{SVf}[\mathsf{h}](vk, lr^*, sig^*) = \mathsf{true}$. If such lr^* does not exist, lr^* is set to $\perp$. Denote the event E_1 as

$$\mathsf{Vf}[\mathsf{h}](vk, M^*, sig^*) \ \wedge\ (lr^* = \perp \ \vee\ \mathrm{S}_2(lr^*) < t - |CS|).$$

Denote the event E_2 as

$$\mathsf{Vf}[\mathsf{h}](vk, M^*, sig^*) \ \wedge\ lr^* \neq \perp \ \wedge\ \mathrm{S}_2(lr^*) \neq \mathrm{S}_3(lr^*).$$

If $\mathcal{A}$ wins the game $\mathbf{G}^{\text{ts-suf-3}}_{\mathsf{FROST2}}$ and $lr^* \neq \perp$, we know either $\mathrm{S}_2(lr^*) < t - |CS|$ or $\mathrm{S}_2(lr^*) \neq \mathrm{S}_3(lr^*)$. Therefore, if $\mathcal{A}$ wins the game $\mathbf{G}^{\text{ts-suf-3}}_{\mathsf{FROST2}}$, then either E_1 or E_2 occurs, which implies

$$\mathbf{Adv}^{\text{ts-suf-3}}_{\mathsf{FROST1}[\mathbb{G}]}(\mathcal{A}) \leq \Pr[E_1] + \Pr[E_2] \leq 2\max\{\Pr[E_1], \Pr[E_2]\}.$$

Thus, we conclude the theorem with the following two lemmas.

Lemma 6. *There exists an OMDL adversary $\mathcal{B}$ making at most $2q_s + t$ queries to* CHAL *such that*

$$\Pr[E_1] \leq \sqrt{q \cdot (\mathbf{Adv}^{\mathrm{omdl}}_{\mathbb{G}}(\mathcal{B}) + 3q^2(\mathsf{ns}+1)^2/p)}\ ,$$

Moreover, $\mathcal{B}$ runs in time roughly equal two times that of $\mathcal{A}$, plus the time to perform at most $6\mathsf{ns} \cdot q + 4q_s + 2\mathsf{ns}^2$ exponentiations and group operations.

Lemma 7. *There exists an OMDL adversary $\mathcal{B}$ making at most $2q_s$ queries to* CHAL *such that*

$$\Pr[E_2] \leq \mathsf{ns} \cdot q\sqrt{2(\mathbf{Adv}^{\mathrm{omdl}}_{\mathbb{G}}(\mathcal{B}) + 1/p)}.$$

Moreover, $\mathcal{B}$ runs in time roughly equal two times that of $\mathcal{A}$, plus the time to perform at most $6\mathsf{ns} \cdot q + 4q_s + 2\mathsf{ns}^2$ exponentiations and group operations.

The proof of Lemma 6 is almost the same as Lemma 4, so we omit the full proof. The only difference is that $\mathcal{C}$ takes as input $h_1, \ldots, h_{(\mathsf{ns}+1)q}$ in order to simulate all RO queries. For a RO query $\mathsf{h}_1(vk, lr, i)$, $\mathcal{C}$ first enumerates all $i' \in [\mathsf{ns}]$ and assigns $h_{(\mathrm{ctr}_h - 1)(\mathsf{ns}+1)+i'}$ to $\mathsf{h}_1(vk, lr, i')$. Then, $\mathcal{C}$ computes the nonce R for lr and assigns $h_{\mathrm{ctr}_h(\mathsf{ns}+1)}$ to $\mathsf{h}_2(vk, lr.\mathsf{msg}, R)$ if it is not assigned any value yet. Similarly, for a new RO query $\mathsf{h}_1(vk, M, R)$, its value is set to $h_{\mathrm{ctr}_h(\mathsf{ns}+1)}$. The rest follows by similar analysis.

Adversary $\mathcal{A}^{\text{INIT,PPO,PSIGNO,RO}}$:

$CS \leftarrow \{3,4\}$; $(vk, aux, \{sk_3, sk_4\}) \leftarrow\!\!\$\ \text{INIT}(CS)$
$(R_1, S_1) \leftarrow\!\!\$\ \text{PPO}(1)$; $(R_2, S_2) \leftarrow\!\!\$\ \text{PPO}(2)$; $\gamma \leftarrow \lambda_1^{\{1,3,4\}}/\lambda_1^{\{1,2,3\}}$
$lr.\mathsf{msg} \leftarrow M$; $lr.\mathsf{SS} \leftarrow \{1,2,3\}$
$lr.\mathsf{PP}(1) \leftarrow (R_1, S_1)$; $lr.\mathsf{PP}(2) \leftarrow (R_2, S_2)$
$lr.\mathsf{PP}(3) \leftarrow (R_1^{\gamma-1}R_2^{-1}, S_1^{\gamma-1}S_2^{-1})$
$z_1 \leftarrow \text{PSIGNO}(1, lr)$
$d \leftarrow \text{RO}(1, vk, lr)$; $R \leftarrow R_1^{\gamma}S_1^{\gamma\cdot d}$; $c \leftarrow \text{RO}(2, vk, R, M)$
$z \leftarrow \gamma \cdot z_1 + c(\lambda_3^{\{1,3,4\}} \cdot sk_3 + \lambda_4^{\{1,3,4\}} \cdot sk_4)$
Return $(M, (R, z))$

Fig. 8. Adversary $\mathcal{A}$ that wins the game $\mathbf{G}^{\text{ts-uf-3}}_{\mathsf{FROST2}}$, where M is a fixed message.

Adversary $\mathcal{A}^{\text{INIT,PPO,PSIGNO,RO}}$:

$CS \leftarrow \{5,10\}$; $(vk, aux, \{sk_5, sk_{10}\}) \leftarrow\!\!\$\ \text{INIT}(CS)$
$(R_1, S_1) \leftarrow\!\!\$\ \text{PPO}(11)$; $s_2, r_2, s_3, r_3 \leftarrow\!\!\$\ \mathbb{Z}_p$
$lr.\mathsf{msg} \leftarrow M$; $lr.\mathsf{SS} \leftarrow \{11,15,20\}$
$lr.\mathsf{PP}(11) \leftarrow (R_1, S_1)$; $lr.\mathsf{PP}(15) \leftarrow (g^{r_2}, g^{s_2})$; $lr.\mathsf{PP}(20) \leftarrow (g^{r_3}, g^{s_3})$
$z_1 \leftarrow \text{PSIGNO}(11, lr)$
For $i \in \{11,15,20\}$ do $d_i \leftarrow \text{RO}(1, vk, lr, i)$
$R \leftarrow R_1 S_1^{d_{11}} g^{r_2+r_3+s_2\cdot d_{15}+s_3\cdot d_{20}}$; $c \leftarrow \text{RO}(2, vk, R, M)$
$z \leftarrow z_1 + r_2 + r_3 + s_2 \cdot d_{15} + s_3 \cdot d_{20} + c(\lambda_5^{\{5,10,11\}} \cdot sk_5 + \lambda_{10}^{\{5,10,11\}} \cdot sk_{10})$
Return $(M, (R, z))$

Fig. 9. Adversary $\mathcal{A}$ that wins the game $\mathbf{G}^{\text{ts-uf-4}}_{\mathsf{FROST1}}$, where M is a fixed message.

To prove Lemma 7, we need a variant of the Local Forking Lemma of [1], which is given in [7] along with the proof of Lemma 7 itself.

4.4 Attacks for FROST1 and FROST2

<u>FROST2 IS NOT TS-UF-3 SECURE.</u> Consider the setting where $\mathsf{ns} = 4$ and $t = 3$ and the adversary $\mathcal{A}$ for the game $\mathbf{G}^{\text{ts-uf-3}}_{\mathsf{FROST2}}$ described in Fig. 8. We now show that $\mathbf{Adv}^{\text{ts-uf-3}}_{\mathsf{FROST2}}(\mathcal{A}) = 1$. From the execution of PSIGNO, we know $g^{z_1} = R_1 S_1^d vk_1^{\lambda_1^{\{1,2,3\}}\cdot c}$. Therefore,

$$
\begin{aligned}
g^z &= R_1^{\gamma} S_1^{d\cdot\gamma} vk_1^{\gamma\cdot\lambda_1^{\{1,2,3\}}\cdot c} vk_3^{\lambda_3^{\{1,3,4\}}\cdot c} vk_4^{\lambda_4^{\{1,3,4\}}\cdot c} \\
&= R g^{c\cdot\sum_{i\in\{1,3,4\}}\lambda_i^{\{1,3,4\}}\cdot sk_i} = R \cdot vk^c ,
\end{aligned}
$$

which implies $(M, (R, z))$ is valid for vk. Also, it is clear that $\mathrm{S}_2(lr) = \{1\}$ and $\mathrm{S}_3(lr) = \{1,2\}$, which implies the condition $\mathtt{tf}_3(lr)$ does not hold. Therefore, $\mathcal{A}$ wins the game $\mathbf{G}^{\text{ts-uf-3}}_{\mathsf{FROST2}}$ with probability 1.

FROST1 IS NOT TS-UF-4 SECURE. Consider the setting where $\mathsf{ns} = 20$ and $t = 3$ and the adversary $\mathcal{A}$ for the game $\mathbf{G}^{\text{ts-uf-4}}_{\mathsf{FROST1}}$ described in Fig. 9. We now show that $\mathbf{Adv}^{\text{ts-uf-4}}_{\mathsf{FROST1}}(\mathcal{A}) = 1$. From the execution of PSIGNO, we know $g^{z_1} = R_1 S_1^{d_{11}} vk_{11}^{\lambda_{11}^{\{11,15,20\}} \cdot c}$. The key observation here is that $\lambda_{11}^{\{11,15,20\}} = \frac{15 \cdot 20}{(15-11)(20-11)} = \frac{25}{3} = \frac{5 \cdot 10}{(5-11)(10-11)} = \lambda_{11}^{\{5,10,11\}}$. Therefore,

$$g^z = R_1 S_1^{d_{11}} g^{r_2+r_3+s_2 \cdot d_{15}+s_3 \cdot d_{20}} vk_{11}^{\lambda_{11}^{\{11,15,20\}} \cdot c} vk_5^{\lambda_5^{\{5,10,11\}} \cdot c} vk_{10}^{\lambda_{10}^{\{5,10,11\}} \cdot c}$$

$$= R g^{c \cdot \sum_{i \in \{5,10,11\}} \lambda_i^{\{5,10,11\}} \cdot sk_i} = R \cdot vk^c ,$$

which implies $(M, (R, z))$ is valid for vk. Also, it is clear that $\mathrm{S}_2(lr) = \{11\}$ and $\mathrm{S}_4(lr) = \{11, 15, 20\}$, which implies the condition $\mathtt{tf}_4(lr)$ does not hold. Therefore, $\mathcal{A}$ wins the game $\mathbf{G}^{\text{ts-uf-4}}_{\mathsf{FROST1}}$ with probability 1.

The reason why the attack is possible for FROST1 is because the honest server 11 replies to the leader request lr with tokens $lr.\mathsf{PP}(15)$ and $lr.\mathsf{PP}(20)$ not generated by the honest servers 15 and 20 but by the adversary instead. Therefore, the attack is prevented by the general transformation from TS-SUF-3 security to TS-SUF-4 security described in Fig. 4 since after the transformation, an honest server replies to a leader request only when all the tokens within the request are authenticated by the corresponding servers, and thus the adversary cannot generate tokens on behalf of honest servers anymore.

5 FROST2 with Distributed Key Generation

In this section, we prove the security of FROST2 together with distributed key generation (DKG). In particular, we prove the security of FROST2 with the variant of the Pedersen DKG protocol [24] with proofs of possession originally proposed in combination with FROST1 [30]. We call this protocol PedPoP and provide a description in Fig. 10.

Throughout this section, we denote public keys by X, instead of vk, and corresponding secret keys by x, instead of sk. We also denote the joint public key by $\tilde{X}$ and aggregated nonce by $\tilde{R}$. Hash function $\mathsf{h}_i(\cdot)$ is computed as $\mathsf{h}_i(\cdot)$ for $i = 0, 1, 2$.

EFFICIENT DISTRIBUTED KEY GENERATION. The Pedersen DKG can be viewed as ns parallel instantiations of Feldman verifiable secret sharing (VSS) [19], which itself is derived from Shamir secret sharing [36] but additionally requires each participant to provide a vector commitment $\vec{C}$ to ensure their received share is consistent with all other participants' shares. In addition, PedPoP requires each participant to provide a Schnorr proof of knowledge of the secret corresponding to the first term of their commitment. This is to ensure that unforgeability (but not liveness) holds even if more than half of the participants are dishonest.

SCHNORR KNOWLEDGE OF EXPONENT ASSUMPTION. We introduce the Schnorr knowledge of exponent assumption (Schnorr-KoE), which we show is true under the discrete logarithm (DL) assumption in the algebraic group model

PedPoP.KeyGen(t, ns)

1. Each party P_i chooses a random polynomial $f_i(Z)$ over $\mathbb{Z}_p$ of degree $t-1$

$$f_i(Z) = a_{i,0} + a_{i,1}Z + \cdots + a_{i,t-1}Z^{t-1}$$

and computes $A_{i,k} = g^{a_{i,k}}$ for $k =\in [0..t-1]$. Denote $x_i = a_{i,0}$ and $X_{i,0} = A_{i,0}$. Each P_i computes a proof of possession of $X_{i,0}$ as a Schnorr signature on $X_{i,0}$ as follows. They sample $\bar{r}_i \leftarrow\!\!\$\ \mathbb{Z}_p$ and set $\bar{R}_i \leftarrow g^{\bar{r}_i}$. They compute $\bar{c}_i \leftarrow \mathsf{h}_0(X_{i,0}, X_{i,0}, \bar{R}_i)$ and set $\bar{z}_i \leftarrow \bar{r}_i + \bar{c}_i \cdot x_i$. They then derive a commitment $\vec{C}_i = (A_{i,0}, ..., A_{i,t-1})$ and broadcast $((\bar{R}_i, \bar{z}_i), \vec{C}_i)$.
2. After receiving commitments from all other parties, each participant verifies the Schnorr signatures by computing $\bar{c}_j \leftarrow \mathsf{h}_0(A_{j,0}, A_{j,0}, \bar{R}_j)$ and checking that

$$g^{\bar{z}_j} = \bar{R}_j A_{j,0}{}^{\bar{c}_j} \text{ for } j \in [1..\mathsf{ns}]$$

If any checks fail, they disqualify the corresponding participant.
3. Each P_i computes secret shares $\bar{x}_{i,j} = f_i(\mathsf{id}_j)$ for $j \in [1..\mathsf{ns}]$, where id_j is the participant identifier, and sends $\bar{x}_{i,j}$ secretly to party P_j.
4. Each party P_j verifies the shares they received from the other parties by checking that

$$g^{\bar{x}_{i,j}} = \prod_{k=0}^{t-1} A_{i,k}^{\mathsf{id}_j^k}$$

If the check fails for an index i, P_j broadcasts a complaint against P_i.
5. For each of the complaining parties P_j against P_i, P_i broadcasts the share $\bar{x}_{i,j}$. If any of the revealed shares fails to satisfy the equation, or should P_i not broadcast anything for a complaining player, then P_i is disqualified. The share of a disqualified party P_i is set to 0.
6. The secret share for each P_j is $\bar{x}_j = \sum_{i=1}^{\mathsf{ns}} \bar{x}_{i,j}$.
7. If $X_{i,0} = X_{j,0}$ for any $i \neq j$, then abort. Else, the output is the joint public key $\tilde{X} = \prod_{i=1}^{\mathsf{ns}} X_{i,0}$.

Fig. 10. PedPoP: The Pedersen distributed key generation protocol with proofs of possession.

(AGM) without any tightness loss. The purpose of the Schnorr-KoE assumption is to ensure that the Pedersen DKG can be run in the honest minority setting, where we assume the existence of at least a single honest party and up to $t-1$ corrupt parties. The Schnorr-KoE assumption can be avoided if we assume an honest majority in the DKG. However, we prefer to allow more corruptions with the tradeoff of a stronger assumption.

Game $\mathbf{G}^{\text{sch-koe}}_{\mathbb{G},\mathsf{Ext}}(\mathcal{A})$

INIT:

$\omega \leftarrow_{\$} \{0,1\}^{\mathsf{rl}_{\mathcal{A}}}$ // Coins given to $\mathcal{A}$
Return ω

FSIGNO:

$x, \bar{r} \leftarrow_{\$} \mathbb{Z}_p$
$X \leftarrow g^x$; $\bar{R} \leftarrow g^{\bar{r}}$
$\bar{c} \leftarrow \tilde{\mathsf{h}}_0(X, X, \bar{R})$
$\bar{z} \leftarrow \bar{r} + \bar{c} \cdot x$
$Q_{\text{FSIGNO}} \leftarrow Q_{\text{FSIGNO}} \cup \{(X, \bar{R}, \bar{z})\}$
Return $(X, \bar{R}, \bar{z})$

CHAL$(X, \bar{R}, \bar{z})$:

$\bar{c} \leftarrow \tilde{\mathsf{h}}_0(X, X, \bar{R})$
If $(X, \bar{R}, \bar{z}) \in Q_{\text{FSIGNO}}$ or $g^{\bar{z}} \neq \bar{R}X^{\bar{c}}$
  Return $\bot$
$\alpha \leftarrow_{\$} \mathsf{Ext}(\mathbb{G}, \omega, Q_{\text{FSIGNO}}, \mathsf{Q}_{\tilde{\mathsf{h}}_0})$
If $g^{\alpha} \neq X$ then win $\leftarrow$ true
Return α

RO(θ): // Random oracle

If $\tilde{\mathsf{h}}(\theta) = \bot$ then $\tilde{\mathsf{h}}(\theta) \leftarrow_{\$} \mathbb{Z}_p$
Return $\tilde{\mathsf{h}}(\theta)$

FIN$(\{0,1\}^*)$: // $\mathcal{A}$ outputs a bit string

Return win

Fig. 11. Game used to define the Schnorr knowledge of exponent (Schnorr-KoE) assumption, where $\mathbb{G}$ is a cyclic group of order p with generator g. By $\mathsf{rl}_{\mathcal{A}}$ we denote the randomness length of $\mathcal{A}$. $\tilde{\mathsf{h}}$ is initialized to be an empty table.

The Schnorr-KoE assumption allows us to prove the security of multi-party signatures in the setting where each participant is required to provide a proof of possession of their secret key during a key generation and registration phase. By formatting our desired security property directly as an assumption, we avoid the complexity of rewinding adversaries, which is required when proving security of Schnorr signatures in the ROM only, and which may result in a loss of tightness exponential in the number of parties that the adversary controls [38]. The Schnorr-KoE assumption implies that if an adversary can forge a Schnorr signature for some public key, then it must know the corresponding secret key. It is a non-falsifiable assumption.

Our proof for Schnorr-KoE extends a result by Fuchsbauer et al. [20], which showed that the security of Schnorr signatures can be tightly reduced to the DL assumption in the AGM. We improve on their result by considering extraction rather than forgeability and by allowing extraction even when the adversary chooses their own public key. While new to the setting of multi-party signatures, Schnorr-KoE is reminiscent of prior knowledge of exponent assumptions [4,15] employed to prove the security of Succinct NIZK arguments (SNARKs).

For the definition, consider the game in Fig. 11 associated to group $\mathbb{G}$, adversary $\mathcal{A}$, and an algorithm Ext, called an extractor. The adversary $\mathcal{A}$ is run with coins ω. $\mathcal{A}$ has access to a signing oracle FSIGNO that outputs a Schnorr signature under a randomly sampled key X on the message X. (The name, Full Sign Oracle, reflects that the oracle samples a fresh public key with each invocation). It can call its challenge oracle CHAL with a triple $(X, \bar{R}, \bar{z})$. If this is not a triple returned by the full signing oracle, yet verifies as a Schnorr signature under public key X, the extractor is asked to find the discrete logarithm α of X, and the adversary wins (the game sets win to true) if the extractor fails. The inputs to the extractor are the coins of the adversary, the description of the group $\mathbb{G}$, the set Q_{FSIGNO} and a list $\mathsf{Q}_{\tilde{\mathsf{h}}_0}$. The latter, for every query $(X, X, \bar{R})$ that $\mathcal{A}$ made to random oracle $\tilde{\mathsf{h}}_0$, stores the response of the oracle. (The length of the list is thus the number of $\tilde{\mathsf{h}}_0$ queries made by $\mathcal{A}$). Note that multiple queries to CHAL are allowed, so that this captures the ability to perform multiple extractions.

Asymptotically, we would say that the Schnorr-KoE assumption holds with respect to $\mathbb{G}$ if for all PPT adversaries $\mathcal{A}$, there exists a PPT extractor Ext such that $\mathbf{Adv}^{\text{sch-koe}}_{\mathbb{G},\mathsf{Ext}}(\mathcal{A})$, which would now be a function of the security parameter, is negligible.

The proof of the following can be found in [14]. For convenience, the statement is asymptotic. Note that the random oracle model is implicit through $\tilde{\mathsf{h}}_0$ being a random oracle in the game of Fig. 11.

Theorem 8 (DL $\Rightarrow$ Schnorr-KoE). *The* Schnorr-KoE *assumption with respect to the group* $\mathbb{G}$ *is implied by the DL assumption with respect to* $\mathbb{G}$ *in the AGM.*

TS-UF-0 SECURITY. In terms of our framework, our proof of FROST2 + PedPoP considers a single honest player and so aligns with the notion of TS-UF-0 security defined in Fig. 2. Since we now consider distributed key generation instead of trusted key generation, the initialization oracle INIT is replaced with a single execution of PedPoP.KeyGen as defined in Fig. 10. The proofs of possession required by PedPoP.KeyGen ensure that the simulator in our security reduction is able to extract sufficient information (via the Schnorr-KoE assumption) to simulate signing as in the TS-UF-0 definition, in which all secret key material is generated by the simulator directly. The signing oracles PPO and PSIGNO remain identical to Fig. 2. We have not currently investigated whether TS-UF-2 security holds.

5.1 Security of FROST2 + PedPoP

We now prove the security of FROST2 with distributed key generation protocol PedPoP under the Schnorr-KoE assumption and OMDL assumption in the ROM.

Theorem 9 (FROST2+PedPoP). FROST2 *with distributed key generation protocol* PedPoP *is* TS-UF-0 *secure under the* Schnorr-KoE *assumption and the OMDL assumption in the ROM.*

We make use of an intermediary assumption, the binonce Schnorr computational (Bischnorr) assumption, which we define and prove secure under the OMDL assumption in the ROM (Fig. 12).

Equipped with this assumption, our proof proceeds as follows. Let $\mathcal{A}$ be a PPT adversary attempting to break the TS-UF-0 security of FROST2. We construct a PPT adversary $\mathcal{B}_1$ playing game $\mathbf{G}^{\text{sch-koe}}_{\mathbb{G},\mathsf{Ext}}(\mathcal{B}_1)$ and thence, from the

Game $\mathbf{G}_{\mathbb{G}}^{\text{bi-sch}}$:

INIT:

$\dot{x} \leftarrow\!\!\$\ \mathbb{Z}_p$
$\dot{X} \leftarrow g^{\dot{x}}$
Return $\dot{X}$

BINONCEO():

$r, s \leftarrow\!\!\$\ \mathbb{Z}_p$
$(R, S) \leftarrow (g^r, g^s)$
$Q_{\text{BIN}} \leftarrow Q_{\text{BIN}} \cup \{(R, S, r, s)\}$
Return (R, S)

BISIGNO$(k, M, \{(\gamma_i, R_i, S_i)\}_{i \in SS})$:

If $(R_k, S_k, r_k, s_k) \notin Q_{\text{BIN}}$ or $(R_k, S_k) \in Q_{\text{USED}}$
  Return false
$Q_{\text{USED}} \leftarrow Q_{\text{USED}} \cup \{(R_k, S_k)\}$
$d \leftarrow \hat{\mathsf{h}}_1(\dot{X}, M, \{(\gamma_i, R_i, S_i)\}_{i \in SS})$
$\tilde{R} \leftarrow \prod_{i \in SS} R_i S_i^d$
$c \leftarrow \hat{\mathsf{h}}_2(\dot{X}, M, \tilde{R})$
$z_k \leftarrow r_k + d \cdot s_k + c \cdot \gamma_k \cdot \dot{x}$
$Q_{\text{BIS}} \leftarrow Q_{\text{BIS}} \cup \{(M, \tilde{R})\}$
Return z_k

RO(θ): // Random oracle

If $\hat{\mathsf{h}}(\theta) = \perp$ then $\hat{\mathsf{h}}(\theta) \leftarrow\!\!\$\ \mathbb{Z}_p$
Return $\hat{\mathsf{h}}(\theta)$

FIN(M^*, R^*, z^*):

If $g^{z^*} = R^* \dot{X}^{\hat{\mathsf{h}}_2(\dot{X}, M^*, R^*)}$ and $(M^*, R^*) \notin Q_{\text{BIS}}$
  Return true
Else return false

Fig. 12. Game used to define the binonce Schnorr computational (Bischnorr) assumption, where $\mathbb{G}$ is a cyclic group of order p with generator g. $\hat{\mathsf{h}}$ is initialized to be an empty table.

Schnorr-KoE assumption, obtain an extractor Ext for it. We construct a PPT adversary $\mathcal{B}_2$ playing game $\mathbf{G}_{\mathbb{G}}^{\text{bi-sch}}(\mathcal{B}_2)$ such that whenever $\mathcal{A}$ outputs a valid forgery, either $\mathcal{B}_1$ breaks the Schnorr-KoE assumption or $\mathcal{B}_2$ breaks the Bischnorr assumption. Formally, for security parameter κ, we have

$$\mathbf{Adv}_{\mathsf{FROST2}}^{\text{ts-uf-0}}(\mathcal{A}) \leq \mathbf{Adv}_{\mathbb{G},\mathsf{Ext}}^{\text{sch-koe}}(\mathcal{B}_1) + \mathbf{Adv}_{\mathbb{G}}^{\text{bi-sch}}(\mathcal{B}_2) + \mathsf{negl}(\kappa)$$

BINONCE SCHNORR ASSUMPTION. The Bischnorr assumption equips an adversary with two oracles, BINONCEO and BISIGNO, and two hash functions, $\hat{\mathsf{h}}_1$ and $\hat{\mathsf{h}}_2$, and asks it to forge a new Schnorr signature with respect to a challenge public key $\dot{X}$. The BINONCEO oracle takes no input and responds with two random nonces (R, S). The BISIGNO oracle takes as input an index k, a message M, and a set of nonces and scalars $\{(\gamma_i, R_i, S_i)\}_{i \in SS}$. It checks that (R_k, S_k) is a BINONCEO response and that it has not been queried on (R_k, S_k) before. It returns an error if not. It then computes an aggregated randomized nonce $\tilde{R} = \prod_{i \in SS} R_i S_i^d$, where $d = \hat{\mathsf{h}}_1(\dot{X}, M, \{(\gamma_i, R_i, S_i)\}_{i \in SS})$. BISIGNO then returns z such that $(\tilde{R}, z)$ is a valid Schnorr signature with respect to $\hat{\mathsf{h}}_2$. The adversary wins if it can output a verifying (M^*, R^*, z^*) that was not output by BISIGNO.

The oracle BISIGNO can only be queried once for each pair of nonces (R, S) output by BINONCEO. The index k denotes which (γ_k, R_k, S_k) out of the list $\{(\gamma_i, R_i, S_i)\}_{i \in SS}$ is being queried; the remaining scalars and nonces appear only to inform BINONCEO what to include as input to $\hat{\mathsf{h}}_1$. The scalar γ_k allows the response z_k to be given as $z_k = r_k + d \cdot s_k + c \cdot \gamma_k \cdot \dot{x}$, as opposed to $r_k + d \cdot s_k + c \cdot \dot{x}$. This is useful for threshold signatures, where γ_k corresponds to the Lagrange coefficient. Note that $\{\gamma_i\}_{i \in SS}$ (in addition to the nonces) must be included as input to $\hat{\mathsf{h}}_1$ or else there is an attack.

Asymptotically, we would say that the Bischnorr assumption holds with respect to $\mathbb{G}$ if for all PPT adversaries $\mathcal{A}$, we have that $\mathbf{Adv}_{\mathbb{G}}^{\text{bi-sch}}(\mathcal{A})$, which would now be a function of the security parameter, is negligible.

The proof of the following can be found in [14]. For convenience, the statement is asymptotic.

Lemma 10 (OMDL $\Rightarrow$ Bischnorr). *Let $\hat{\mathsf{h}}_1, \hat{\mathsf{h}}_2$ be random oracles. The* Bischnorr *assumption is implied by the OMDL assumption with respect to the group $\mathbb{G}$ and $\hat{\mathsf{h}}_1, \hat{\mathsf{h}}_2$.*

Equipped with this assumption, we are now ready to prove Theorem 9.

Proof (of Theorem 9). Let $\mathcal{A}$ be a PPT adversary attempting to break the TS-UF-0 security of FROST2. We construct a PPT adversary $\mathcal{B}_1$ playing game $\mathbf{G}_{\mathbb{G},\mathsf{Ext}}^{\text{sch-koe}}(\mathcal{B}_1)$ and thence, from the Schnorr-KoE assumption, obtain an extractor Ext for it. We construct a PPT adversary $\mathcal{B}_2$ playing game $\mathbf{G}_{\mathbb{G}}^{\text{bi-sch}}(\mathcal{B}_2)$ such that whenever $\mathcal{A}$ outputs a valid forgery, either $\mathcal{B}_1$ breaks the Schnorr-KoE assumption or $\mathcal{B}_2$ breaks the Bischnorr assumption. Formally, for security parameter κ, we have

$$\mathbf{Adv}_{\mathsf{FROST2}}^{\text{ts-uf-0}}(\mathcal{A}) \leq \mathbf{Adv}_{\mathbb{G},\mathsf{Ext}}^{\text{sch-koe}}(\mathcal{B}_1) + \mathbf{Adv}_{\mathbb{G}}^{\text{bi-sch}}(\mathcal{B}_2) + \mathsf{negl}(\kappa)$$

<u>**The Reduction $\mathcal{B}_1$:**</u> We first define the reduction $\mathcal{B}_1$ against Schnorr-KoE. Let $CS = \{\mathsf{id}_j\}$ be the set of corrupt parties, and let $HS = \{\mathsf{id}_k\}$ be the set of honest parties. Assume that $|CS| = t-1$ and $|HS| = \mathsf{ns} - (t-1)$. We will show that when PedPoP outputs public key share $\tilde{X}_k = g^{\bar{x}_k}$ for each honest party $\mathsf{id}_k \in HS$, $\mathcal{B}_1$ returns (α_k, β_k) such that $\tilde{X}_k = \dot{X}^{\alpha_k} g^{\beta_k}$. $\mathcal{B}_1$ is responsible for simulating honest parties in PedPoP (Fig. 10) and queries to h_0, h_1, and h_2. $\mathcal{B}_1$ receives as input a group $\mathbb{G}$ and random coins ω. It can query the random oracle RO from Schnorr-KoE. It can also query FSIGNO to receive signatures under $\tilde{\mathsf{h}}_0$ and CHAL on inputs $(X, \bar{R}, \bar{z})$ to challenge the extractor Ext to output a discrete logarithm α for X.

<u>**Initialization.**</u> $\mathcal{B}_1$ may program $\mathsf{h}_0, \mathsf{h}_1$, and h_2, but not $\tilde{\mathsf{h}}_0$ (because it is part of $\mathcal{B}_1$'s challenge). Let $\mathsf{Q}_{\mathsf{h}_0}$ be the set of h_0 queries and their responses. $\mathcal{B}_1$ first queries FSIGNO and receives $(\dot{X}, \bar{R}, \bar{z})$. $\mathcal{B}_1$ computes α_k for each honest party $\mathsf{id}_k \in HS$ as follows. First, $\mathcal{B}_1$ computes the t Lagrange polynomials $\{L'_k(Z), \{L'_j(Z)\}_{\mathsf{id}_j \in CS}\}$ relating to the set $\mathsf{id}_k \cup CS$. Then, $\mathcal{B}_1$ sets $\alpha_k \leftarrow L'_k(0)^{-1}$. (It will become clear why α_k is computed this way).

<u>**Hash Queries.**</u> $\mathcal{B}_1$ handles $\mathcal{A}$'s hash queries throughout the DKG protocol as follows.

<u>h_0:</u> When $\mathcal{A}$ queries h_0 on $(X, X, \bar{R})$, $\mathcal{B}_1$ checks whether $(X, X, \bar{R}, \bar{c}) \in \mathsf{Q}_{\mathsf{h}_0}$ and, if so, returns $\bar{c}$. Else, $\mathcal{B}_1$ queries $\bar{c} \leftarrow \tilde{\mathsf{h}}_0(X, X, \bar{R})$, appends $(X, X, \bar{R}, \bar{c})$ to $\mathsf{Q}_{\mathsf{h}_0}$, and returns $\bar{c}$.

$\underline{\mathsf{h}_1}$: When $\mathcal{A}$ queries h_1 on $(X, lr) = (X, M, \{(\mathsf{id}_i, R_i, S_i)\}_{i \in SS})$, $\mathcal{B}_1$ queries $\hat{d} \leftarrow \tilde{\mathsf{h}}_1(X, M, \{(\mathsf{id}_i, R_i, S_i)\}_{i \in SS})$ and returns $\hat{d}$.

$\underline{\mathsf{h}_2}$: When $\mathcal{A}$ queries h_2 on (X, M, R), $\mathcal{B}_1$ queries $\hat{c} \leftarrow \tilde{\mathsf{h}}_2(X, M, R)$ and returns $\hat{c}$.

Simulating the DKG. $\mathcal{B}_1$ runs $\mathcal{A}$ on input coins ω and simulates PedPoP as follows. $\mathcal{B}_1$ embeds $\dot{X}$ as the public key of the honest party that the adversary queries first. Let this first honest party be id_τ. $\mathcal{B}_1$ simulates the public view of id_τ but follows the PedPoP protocol for all other honest parties $\{\mathsf{id}_k\}_{k \neq \tau}$ as prescribed. Note that $\mathcal{A}$ can choose the order in which it interacts with honest parties, so $\mathcal{B}_1$ must be able to simulate any of them.

Honest Party id_τ. $\mathcal{B}_1$ is required to output

$$(\bar{R}_\tau, \bar{z}_\tau), \vec{C}_\tau = (A_{\tau,0} = X_{\tau,0}, A_{\tau,1}, ..., A_{\tau,t-1})$$

that are indistinguishable from valid outputs as well as $t-1$ shares $f_\tau(\mathsf{id}_j) = \bar{x}_{\tau,j}$, one to be sent to each corrupt party $\mathsf{id}_j \in CS$. Here, $(\bar{R}_\tau, \bar{z}_\tau)$ is a Schnorr signature proving knowledge of the discrete logarithm of $X_{\tau,0}$, and $\vec{C}_\tau$ is a commitment to the coefficients that represent f_τ. $\mathcal{B}_1$ simulates honest party id_τ as follows.

1. $\mathcal{B}_1$ sets the public key $X_{\tau,0} \leftarrow \dot{X}$.
2. $\mathcal{B}_1$ simulates a verifiable Shamir secret sharing of the discrete logarithm of $\dot{X}$ by performing the following steps.
   (a) $\mathcal{B}_1$ samples $t-1$ random values $\bar{x}_{\tau,j} \leftarrow\!\!\$\ \mathbb{Z}_p$ for $\mathsf{id}_j \in CS$.
   (b) Let f_τ be the polynomial whose constant term is the challenge $f_\tau(0) = \dot{x}$ and for which $f_\tau(\mathsf{id}_j) = \bar{x}_{\tau,j}$ for all $\mathsf{id}_j \in CS$. $\mathcal{B}_1$ computes the t Lagrange polynomials $\{L'_0(Z), \{L'_j(Z)\}_{\mathsf{id}_j \in CS}\}$ relating to the set $0 \cup CS$.
   (c) For $1 \leq i \leq t-1$, $\mathcal{B}_1$ computes
   $$A_{\tau,i} = \dot{X}^{L'_{0,i}} \prod_{\mathsf{id}_j \in CS} g^{\bar{x}_{\tau,j} \cdot L'_{j,i}} \tag{1}$$
   where $L'_{j,i}$ is the ith coefficient of $L'_j(Z) = L'_{j,0} + L'_{j,1}Z + \cdots + L'_{j,t-1}Z^{t-1}$.
   (d) $\mathcal{B}_1$ outputs $(\bar{R}_\tau, \bar{z}_\tau), \vec{C}_\tau = (A_{\tau,0} = X_{\tau,0}, A_{\tau,1}, ..., A_{\tau,t-1})$ for the broadcast round, and then sends shares $\bar{x}_{\tau,j}$ for each $\mathsf{id}_j \in CS$.
3. $\mathcal{B}_1$ simulates private shares $f_\tau(\mathsf{id}_k) = \bar{x}_{\tau,k}$ for honest parties $\mathsf{id}_k \in HS$ by computing α'_k, β'_k such that $g^{\bar{x}_{\tau,k}} = \dot{X}^{\alpha'_k} g^{\beta'_k}$. First, $\mathcal{B}_1$ computes the t Lagrange polynomials $\{L'_k(Z), \{L'_j(Z)\}_{\mathsf{id}_j \in CS}\}$ relating to the set $\mathsf{id}_k \cup CS$. Then, implicitly,
   $$f_\tau(0) = \dot{x} = \bar{x}_{\tau,k} \cdot L'_k(0) + \sum_{\mathsf{id}_j \in CS} \bar{x}_{\tau,j} \cdot L'_j(0)$$
   Solving for $\bar{x}_{\tau,k}$, $\mathcal{B}_1$ sets $\alpha'_k = L'_k(0)^{-1}$ and $\beta'_k = -\alpha'_k \sum_{\mathsf{id}_j \in CS} \bar{x}_{\tau,j} \cdot L'_j(0)$.

All Other Honest Parties. For all other honest parties $\mathsf{id}_k \in HS, k \neq \tau$, $\mathcal{B}_1$ follows the protocol. $\mathcal{B}_1$ samples $f_k(Z) = a_{k,0} + a_{k,1}Z + ... + a_{k,t-1}Z^{t-1} \leftarrow\!\!\$\ \mathbb{Z}_p[Z]$ and sets $A_{k,i} \leftarrow g^{a_{k,i}}$ for all $i \in [0..t-1]$. $\mathcal{B}_1$ provides a proof of possession $(\bar{R}_k, \bar{z}_k)$ of the public key $X_{k,0} = A_{k,0}$ and computes the private shares $\bar{x}_{k,i} = f_k(\mathsf{id}_i)$.

Adversarial Contributions. When $\mathcal{A}$ returns a contribution

$$(\bar{R}_j, \bar{z}_j), \vec{C}_j = (A_{j,0} = X_{j,0}, A_{j,1}, ..., A_{j,t-1})$$

if $(X_{j,0}, \bar{R}_j, \bar{z}_j)$ verifies (i.e., $g^{\bar{z}_j} = \bar{R}_j X_{j,0}^{\tilde{\mathsf{h}}_0(X_{j,0},X_{j,0},\bar{R}_j)}$) and $X_{j,0} \neq \dot{X}$, then $\mathcal{B}_1$ queries $\text{CHAL}(X_{j,0}, \bar{R}_j, \bar{z}_j)$ from the Schnorr-KoE game.

Complaints. If $\mathcal{A}$ broadcasts a complaint, $\mathcal{B}_1$ reveals the relevant $\bar{x}_{k,j}$. If $\mathcal{A}$ does not send verifying $\bar{x}_{j,k}$ to party $\mathsf{id}_k \in HS$, then $\mathcal{B}_1$ broadcasts a complaint. If $\bar{x}_{j,k}$ fails to satisfy the equation, or should $\mathcal{A}$ not broadcast a share at all, then id_j is disqualified.

DKG Termination. When PedPoP terminates, the output is the joint public key $\tilde{X} = \prod_{i=0}^{\mathsf{ns}} X_{i,0}$. $\mathcal{B}_1$ simulates private shares $\bar{x}_k$ for honest parties $\mathsf{id}_k \in HS$ by computing α_k, β_k such that $\tilde{X}_k = g^{\bar{x}_k} = \dot{X}^{\alpha_k} g^{\beta_k}$. Implicitly, $\bar{x}_k = \bar{x}_{\tau,k} + \sum_{i=1,i\neq\tau}^{\mathsf{ns}} \bar{x}_{i,k}$ and $\bar{x}_{\tau,k} = \dot{x} \cdot \alpha'_k + \beta'_k$ from Step 3 above, so $\alpha_k = \alpha'_k$ and $\beta_k = \beta'_k + \sum_{i=1,i\neq\tau}^{\mathsf{ns}} \bar{x}_{i,k}$. $\mathcal{B}_1$ returns $\{a_k\}_{\mathsf{id}_k \in HS, k\neq\tau}, \{(\alpha_k, \beta_k)\}_{\mathsf{id}_k \in HS}$.

We now argue that: (1) $\mathcal{A}$ cannot distinguish between a real run of the DKG protocol and its interaction with $\mathcal{B}_1$; and (2) $\mathsf{Ext}(\mathbb{G}, \omega, Q_{\text{FSIGNO}}, \mathsf{Q}_{\tilde{\mathsf{h}}_0})$ outputs $a_{j,0}$ such that $X_{j,0} = g^{a_{j,0}}$ whenever $\mathcal{B}_1$ queries $\text{CHAL}(X_{j,0}, \bar{R}_j, \bar{z}_j)$.

(1) See that $\mathcal{B}_1$'s simulation of PedPoP is perfect, as performing validation of each player's share (Step 4 in Fig. 10) holds, and by Eq. 1, interpolation in the exponent correctly evaluates to the challenge $\dot{X}$.

(2) See that $\mathsf{h}_0(X_{j,0}, X_{j,0}, \bar{R}_j) = \tilde{\mathsf{h}}_0(X_{j,0}, X_{j,0}, \bar{R}_j)$ unless $(X_{j,0}, \bar{R}_j) = (\dot{X}, \bar{R}_\tau)$. The latter happens only if $X_{j,0} = X_{\tau,0}$, but in this case PedPoP will not terminate. We thus have that $(X_{j,0}, \bar{R}_j, \bar{z}_j)$ is a verifying signature under $\tilde{\mathsf{h}}_0$ and either Ext succeeds, or $\mathcal{B}_1$ breaks the Schnorr-KoE assumption. Therefore, the probability of the event occurring where Ext fails to outputs $a_{j,0}$ is bounded by $\mathbf{Adv}_{\mathbb{G},\mathsf{Ext}}^{\text{sch-koe}}(\mathcal{B}_1)$.

<u>**The Reduction $\mathcal{B}_2$**</u>: We next define the reduction $\mathcal{B}_2$ against Bischnorr. We will show that when PedPoP outputs the joint public key $\tilde{X}$, $\mathcal{B}_2$ returns y such that $\tilde{X} = \dot{X} g^y$. Together with the (α_k, β_k) returned by $\mathcal{B}_1$ such that $\tilde{X}_k = \dot{X}^{\alpha_k} g^{\beta_k}$, this representation allows $\mathcal{B}_2$ to simulate FROST2 signing under each $\tilde{X}_k$. $\mathcal{B}_2$ is responsible for simulating honest parties during signing and queries to h_0, h_1, and h_2. $\mathcal{B}_2$ receives as input a group $\mathbb{G}$ and a challenge public key $\dot{X}$. It can query RO, BINONCEO, BISIGNO from the Bischnorr game.

<u>**Initialization.**</u> $\mathcal{B}_2$ may program $\mathsf{h}_0, \mathsf{h}_1$, and h_2, but not $\hat{\mathsf{h}}_1$ or $\hat{\mathsf{h}}_2$ (because they are part of $\mathcal{B}_2$'s challenge). Let Q_{PPO} be the set of PPO queries and responses in the pre-processing round, and let Q_{PSIGNO} be the set of PSIGNO queries and responses in the signing round.

<u>**DKG Extraction.**</u> $\mathcal{B}_2$ first simulates a Schnorr proof of possession of $\dot{X}$ as follows. $\mathcal{B}_2$ samples $\bar{c}_\tau, \bar{z}_\tau \leftarrow\$ \mathbb{Z}_p$, computes $\bar{R}_\tau \leftarrow g^{\bar{z}_\tau} \dot{X}^{-\bar{c}_\tau}$, and appends $(\dot{X}, \dot{X}, \bar{R}_\tau, \bar{c}_\tau)$ to $\mathsf{Q}_{\mathsf{h}_0}$. Then, $\mathcal{B}_2$ runs

$$\{a_{k,0}\}_{\mathsf{id}_k \in HS, k\neq\tau}, \{(\alpha_k, \beta_k)\}_{\mathsf{id}_k \in HS} \leftarrow \mathcal{B}_1(\mathbb{G}; \omega)$$

on coins ω. $\mathcal{B}_2$ handles $\mathcal{B}_1$'s queries as follows. When $\mathcal{B}_1$ queries $\tilde{\mathsf{h}}_0$ on $(X, X, \bar{R})$, $\mathcal{B}_2$ checks whether $(X, X, \bar{R}, \bar{c}) \in \mathsf{Q}_{\tilde{\mathsf{h}}_0}$ and, if so, returns $\bar{c}$. Else, $\mathcal{B}_2$ queries $\bar{c} \leftarrow \hat{\mathsf{h}}_0(X, X, \bar{R})$, appends $(X, X, \bar{R}, \bar{c})$ to $\mathsf{Q}_{\tilde{\mathsf{h}}_0}$, and returns $\bar{c}$. When $\mathcal{B}_1$ queries $\tilde{\mathsf{h}}_1, \tilde{\mathsf{h}}_2$, $\mathcal{B}_2$ handles them the same way it handles $\mathcal{A}$'s $\mathsf{h}_1, \mathsf{h}_2$ queries, described below. The first time $\mathcal{B}_1$ queries its FSIGNO oracle, $\mathcal{B}_2$ returns $(\dot{X}, \bar{R}_\tau, \bar{z}_\tau)$. When

$\mathcal{B}_1$ queries $\text{CHAL}(X_{j,0}, \bar{R}_j, \bar{z}_j)$, $\mathcal{B}_2$ runs $a_{j,0} \leftarrow \mathsf{Ext}(\mathbb{G}, \omega, Q_{\text{FSIGNO}}, \mathsf{Q}_{\tilde{\mathsf{h}}_0})$ to obtain $a_{j,0}$ such that $X_{j,0} = g^{a_{j,0}}$ and aborts otherwise. Then $y = \sum_{i=1, i \neq \tau}^{\mathsf{ns}} a_{i,0}$ such that $\tilde{X} = \dot{X} g^y$.

$\mathcal{A}$'s Hash Queries. $\mathcal{B}_2$ handles $\mathcal{A}$'s hash queries throughout the signing protocol as follows.

h_0: When $\mathcal{A}$ queries h_0 on $(X, X, \bar{R})$, $\mathcal{B}_2$ checks whether $(X, X, \bar{R}, \bar{c}) \in \mathsf{Q}_{\mathsf{h}_0}$ and, if so, returns $\bar{c}$. Else, $\mathcal{B}_2$ queries $\bar{c} \leftarrow \hat{\mathsf{h}}_0(X, X, \bar{R})$, appends $(X, X, \bar{R}, \bar{c})$ to $\mathsf{Q}_{\mathsf{h}_0}$, and returns $\bar{c}$. Note that $\mathcal{B}_1$ and $\mathcal{B}_2$ share the state of $\mathsf{Q}_{\mathsf{h}_0}$.

h_1: When $\mathcal{A}$ queries h_1 on $(X, lr) = (X, M, \{(\mathsf{id}_i, R_i, S_i)\}_{i \in SS})$, $\mathcal{B}_2$ checks whether $(X, M, \{(\mathsf{id}_i, R_i, S_i)\}_{i \in SS}, \hat{M}, \hat{d}) \in \mathsf{Q}_{\mathsf{h}_1}$ and, if so, returns $\hat{d}$. Else, $\mathcal{B}_2$ checks whether there exists some $k' \in SS$ such that $(\mathsf{id}_{k'}, R_{k'}, S_{k'}) \in Q_{\text{PPO}}$. If not, $\mathcal{B}_2$ samples a random message $\hat{M}$ and a random value $\hat{d}$, appends $(X, M, \{(\mathsf{id}_i, R_i, S_i)\}_{i \in SS}, \hat{M}, \hat{d})$ to $\mathsf{Q}_{\mathsf{h}_1}$, and returns $\hat{d}$.

If there does exist some $k' \in SS$ such that $(\mathsf{id}_{k'}, R_{k'}, S_{k'}) \in Q_{\text{PPO}}$, $\mathcal{B}_2$ computes the Lagrange coefficients $\{\lambda_i\}_{i \in SS}$, where $\lambda_i = L_i(0)$ and $\{L_i(Z)\}_{i \in SS}$ are the Lagrange polynomials relating to the set $\{\mathsf{id}_i\}_{i \in SS}$. $\mathcal{B}_2$ sets $\gamma_k = \lambda_k \cdot \alpha_k$ for all $\mathsf{id}_k \in HS$ and $\gamma_j = \lambda_j$ for all $\mathsf{id}_j \in CS$ in the set SS. $\mathcal{B}_2$ then samples a random message $\hat{M}$ (to prevent trivial collisions), queries $\hat{d} \leftarrow \hat{\mathsf{h}}_1(\dot{X}, \hat{M}, \{(\gamma_i, R_i, S_i)\}_{i \in SS})$, and appends $(X, M, \{(\mathsf{id}_i, R_i, S_i)\}_{i \in SS}, \hat{M}, \hat{d})$ to $\mathsf{Q}_{\mathsf{h}_1}$. $\mathcal{B}_2$ computes $\hat{R} = \prod_{i \in SS} R_i S_i^{\hat{d}}$ and checks if there exists a record $(X, M, \hat{R}, \hat{M}, \hat{c}) \in \mathsf{Q}_{\mathsf{h}_2}$. If so, $\mathcal{B}_2$ aborts. Else, $\mathcal{B}_2$ queries $\hat{c} \leftarrow \hat{\mathsf{h}}_2(\dot{X}, \hat{M}, \hat{R})$ and appends $(\tilde{X}, M, \hat{R}, \hat{M}, \hat{c})$ to $\mathsf{Q}_{\mathsf{h}_2}$. Finally, $\mathcal{B}_2$ returns $\hat{d}$.

h_2: When $\mathcal{A}$ queries h_2 on (X, M, R), $\mathcal{B}_2$ checks whether $(X, M, R, \hat{M}, \hat{c}) \in \mathsf{Q}_{\mathsf{h}_2}$ and, if so, returns $\hat{c}$. Else, $\mathcal{B}_2$ samples a random message $\hat{M}$, queries $\hat{c} \leftarrow \hat{\mathsf{h}}_2(\dot{X}, \hat{M}, R)$, appends $(X, M, R, \hat{M}, \hat{c})$ to $\mathsf{Q}_{\mathsf{h}_2}$, and returns $\hat{c}$.

Simulating FROST2 Signing. After $\mathcal{B}_1$ completes the simulation of PedPoP, $\mathcal{B}_2$ then simulates honest parties in the FROST2 signing protocol.

Pre-processing Round. When $\mathcal{A}$ queries PPO on $\mathsf{id}_k \in HS$, $\mathcal{B}_2$ queries BINONCEO to get (R_k, S_k), appends $(\mathsf{id}_k, R_k, S_k)$ to Q_{PPO}, and returns (R_k, S_k).

Signing Round. When $\mathcal{A}$ queries PSIGNO on $(k', lr) = (k', M, \{(\mathsf{id}_i, R_i, S_i)\}_{i \in SS})$, $\mathcal{B}_2$ first checks whether $(\mathsf{id}_{k'}, R_{k'}, S_{k'}) \in Q_{\text{PPO}}$ and, if not, returns $\perp$. Then, $\mathcal{B}$ checks whether $(R_{k'}, S_{k'}) \in Q_{\text{PSIGNO}}$ and, if so, returns $\perp$.

If all checks pass, $\mathcal{B}_2$ internally queries $\hat{\mathsf{h}}_1$ on $(\tilde{X}, M, \{(\mathsf{id}_i, R_i, S_i)\}_{i \in SS})$ to get $\hat{d}'$ and looks up $\hat{M}'$ such that $(\tilde{X}, M, \{(\mathsf{id}_i, R_i, S_i)\}_{i \in SS}), \hat{M}', \hat{d}') \in \mathsf{Q}_{\mathsf{h}_1}$. $\mathcal{B}_2$ computes $\hat{R}' = \prod_{i \in SS} R_i S_i^{\hat{d}'}$ and internally queries $\hat{\mathsf{h}}_2$ on $(\tilde{X}, M, \hat{R}')$ to get $\hat{c}'$.

Next, $\mathcal{B}_2$ computes the Lagrange coefficients $\{\lambda_i\}_{i \in SS}$, where $\lambda_i = L_i(0)$ and $\{L_i(Z)\}_{i \in SS}$ are the Lagrange polynomials relating to the set $\{\mathsf{id}_i\}_{i \in SS}$. $\mathcal{B}_2$ sets $\gamma_k = \lambda_k \cdot \alpha_k$ for all $\mathsf{id}_k \in HS$ and $\gamma_j = \lambda_j$ for all $\mathsf{id}_j \in CS$ in the set SS. Then, $\mathcal{B}_2$ queries BISIGNO on $(k', \hat{M}', \{(\gamma_i, R_i, S_i)\}_{i \in SS})$ to get $z_{k'}$. Finally, $\mathcal{B}_2$ computes

$$\tilde{z}_{k'} = z_{k'} + \hat{c}' \cdot \lambda_{k'} \cdot \beta_{k'} \tag{2}$$

For $\mathcal{A}$'s query to PSIGNO, $\mathcal{B}_2$ returns $\tilde{z}_{k'}$.

Output. When $\mathcal{A}$ returns $(\tilde{X}, M^*, sig^*)$ such that $sig^* = (\tilde{R}^*, z^*)$ and $\mathsf{Vf}(\tilde{X}, M^*, sig^*) = 1$, $\mathcal{B}_2$ computes its output as follows. $\mathcal{B}_2$ looks up $\hat{M}^*$ such that $(\tilde{X}, M^*, \tilde{R}^*, \hat{M}^*, \hat{c}^*) \in \mathsf{Q}_{\mathsf{h}_2}$ and outputs $(\hat{M}^*, \tilde{R}^*, z^* - \hat{c}^* \cdot y)$.

To complete the proof, we must argue that: (1) $\mathcal{B}_2$ only aborts with negligible probability; (2) $\mathcal{A}$ cannot distinguish between a real run of the protocol and its interaction with $\mathcal{B}_2$; and (3) whenever $\mathcal{A}$ succeeds, $\mathcal{B}_2$ succeeds.

(1) $\mathcal{B}_2$ aborts if Ext fails to return $a_{j,0}$ such that $X_{j,0} = g^{a_{j,0}}$ for some j. This happens with maximum probability $\mathbf{Adv}^{\text{sch-koe}}_{\mathbb{G},\mathsf{Ext}}(\mathcal{B}_1)$.

$\mathcal{B}_2$ aborts if $\mathcal{A}$ queries h_2 on $(\tilde{X}, M, \prod_{i \in SS} R_i S_i^{\hat{d}})$ before having first queried h_1 on $(\tilde{X}, M, \{(\mathsf{id}_i, R_i, S_i)\}_{i \in SS})$. This requires $\mathcal{A}$ to have guessed $\hat{d}$ ahead of time, which occurs with negligible probability q_H/p.

(2) As long as $\mathcal{B}_2$ does not abort, $\mathcal{B}_2$ is able to simulate the appropriate responses to $\mathcal{A}$'s oracle queries so that $\mathcal{A}$ cannot distinguish between a real run of the protocol and its interaction with $\mathcal{B}_2$.

Indeed, $\mathcal{B}_1$'s simulation of PedPoP is perfect.

When $\mathcal{A}$ queries h_2 on (X, M, R), $\mathcal{B}_2$ queries $\hat{c} \leftarrow \hat{\mathsf{h}}_2(\dot{X}, \hat{M}, R)$ on a random message $\hat{M}$. The random message prevents trivial collisions; for example, if $\mathcal{A}$ were to query h_2 on (X, M, R) and (X', M, R), where $X' \neq X$, $\mathcal{A}$ would receive the same value $c \leftarrow \hat{\mathsf{h}}_2(\dot{X}, M, R)$ for both and would know it was operating inside a reduction. Random messages ensure that the outputs are random, so $\mathcal{A}$'s view is correct. $\mathcal{B}_2$ also ensures that $\mathcal{A}$ receives h_1 values that are consistent with h_2 queries.

After the signing rounds have been completed, $\mathcal{A}$ may verify the signature share $\tilde{z}_{k'}$ on M as follows. $\mathcal{A}$ checks if

$$g^{\tilde{z}_{k'}} = R_{k'} S_{k'}^{\mathsf{h}_1(\tilde{X}, M, \{(\mathsf{id}_i, R_i, S_i)\}_{i \in SS})} \tilde{X}_{k'}^{\lambda_{k'} \mathsf{h}_2(\tilde{X}, M, \prod_{i \in SS} R_i S_i^{\mathsf{h}_1(\tilde{X}, M, \{(\mathsf{id}_i, R_i, S_i)\}_{i \in SS})})} \quad (3)$$

When $\mathcal{B}_2$ queried BISIGNO on $(k', \hat{M}', \{(\gamma_i, R_i, S_i)\}_{i \in SS})$ in the Signing Round, the signature share $z_{k'}$ was computed such that

$$g^{z_{k'}} = R_{k'} S_{k'}^{\hat{\mathsf{h}}_1(\dot{X}, \hat{M}', \{(\gamma_i, R_i, S_i)\}_{i \in SS})} \dot{X}^{\gamma_{k'} \hat{\mathsf{h}}_2(\dot{X}, \hat{M}', \prod_{i \in SS} R_i S_i^{\hat{\mathsf{h}}_1(\dot{X}, \hat{M}', \{(\gamma_i, R_i, S_i)\}_{i \in SS})})}$$

$\mathcal{B}$ computed the signature share $\tilde{z}_{k'}$ (Eq. 2) as

$$\begin{aligned} \tilde{z}_{k'} = z_{k'} + \hat{c}' \cdot \lambda_{k'} \cdot \beta_{k'} &= r_{k'} + d \cdot s_{k'} + \hat{c}' \cdot \gamma_{k'} \cdot \dot{x} + \hat{c}' \cdot \lambda_{k'} \cdot \beta_{k'} \\ &= r_{k'} + d \cdot s_{k'} + \hat{c}' \cdot \lambda_{k'} (\alpha_{k'} \cdot \dot{x} + \beta_{k'}) \end{aligned}$$

where $\hat{c}' = \hat{\mathsf{h}}_2(\dot{X}, \hat{M}', \prod_{i \in SS} R_i S_i^{\hat{\mathsf{h}}_1(\dot{X}, \hat{M}', \{(\gamma_i, R_i, S_i)\}_{i \in SS})})$. Thus, $\tilde{z}_{k'}$ satisfies

$$g^{\tilde{z}_{k'}} = R_{k'} S_{k'}^{\hat{\mathsf{h}}_1(\dot{X}, \hat{M}', \{(\gamma_i, R_i, S_i)\}_{i \in SS})} \tilde{X}_{k'}^{\lambda_{k'} \hat{\mathsf{h}}_2(\dot{X}, \hat{M}', \prod_{i \in SS} R_i S_i^{\hat{\mathsf{h}}_1(\dot{X}, \hat{M}', \{(\gamma_i, R_i, S_i)\}_{i \in SS})})} \quad (4)$$

$\mathcal{B}_2$ has programmed the hash values in Eqs. 3 and 4 to be equal and therefore simulates $\tilde{z}_{k'}$ correctly.

(3) $\mathcal{A}$'s forgery satisfies $\mathsf{Vf}(\tilde{X}, M^*, sig^*) = 1$, which implies:

$$\begin{aligned} g^{z^*} &= \tilde{R}^* (\tilde{X})^{\mathsf{h}_2(\tilde{X}, M^*, \tilde{R}^*)} = \tilde{R}^* (\dot{X} g^y)^{\mathsf{h}_2(\tilde{X}, M^*, \tilde{R}^*)} \\ g^{z^* - \mathsf{h}_2(\tilde{X}, M^*, \tilde{R}^*) \cdot y} &= \tilde{R}^* \dot{X}^{\mathsf{h}_2(\tilde{X}, M^*, \tilde{R}^*)} \end{aligned}$$

At some point, $\mathcal{A}$ queried h_2 on $(\tilde{X}, M^*, \tilde{R}^*)$ and received one of two values: (1) $\hat{c}^* \leftarrow \hat{\mathsf{h}}_2(\dot{X}, \hat{M}^*, \prod_{i \in SS^*} R_i^*(S_i^*)^{\hat{d}^*})$ related to a query $\mathcal{A}$ made to h_1 on $(M^*, \{(\mathsf{id}_i^*, R_i^*, S_i^*)\}_{i \in SS^*})$, where it received $\hat{d}^* \leftarrow \hat{\mathsf{h}}_1(\dot{X}, \hat{M}^*, (\gamma_i^*, R_i^*, S_i^*)_{i \in SS^*})$, or (2) $\hat{c}^* \leftarrow \hat{\mathsf{h}}_2(\dot{X}, \hat{M}^*, \tilde{R}^*)$ without having queried h_1 first. In either case, $\mathcal{B}_2$ has a record $(\tilde{X}, M^*, \tilde{R}^*, \hat{M}^*, \hat{c}^*) \in \mathsf{Q}_{\mathsf{h}_2}$ such that $\hat{c}^* \leftarrow \hat{\mathsf{h}}_2(\dot{X}, \hat{M}^*, \tilde{R}^*)$. (Note that $\mathcal{B}_2$ can check which case occurred by looking for $\hat{M}^*$ in its $\mathsf{Q}_{\mathsf{h}_1}$ records). Thus, $\mathcal{A}$'s forgery satisfies

$$g^{z^* - \hat{\mathsf{h}}_2(\dot{X}, \hat{M}^*, \tilde{R}^*) \cdot y} = \tilde{R}^* \dot{X}^{\hat{\mathsf{h}}_2(\dot{X}, \hat{M}^*, \tilde{R}^*)}$$

and $\mathcal{B}_2$'s output $(\hat{M}^*, \tilde{R}^*, z^* - \hat{c}^* \cdot y)$ under $\dot{X}$ is correct.

Acknowledgements. Bellare was supported in part by NSF grant CNS-2154272 and a gift from Microsoft. Elizabeth Crites was supported by Input Output through their funding of the Edinburgh Blockchain Technology Lab. Tessaro and Zhu are supported in part by NSF grants CNS-1930117 (CAREER), CNS-2026774, CNS-2154174, a JP Morgan Faculty Award, a CISCO Faculty Award, and a gift from Microsoft.

References

1. Bellare, M., Dai, W., Li, L.: The local forking lemma and its application to deterministic encryption. In: Galbraith, S.D., Moriai, S. (eds.) ASIACRYPT 2019, Part III. LNCS, vol. 11923, pp. 607–636. Springer, Cham (2019). https://doi.org/10.1007/978-3-030-34618-8_21
2. Bellare, M., Namprempre, C., Pointcheval, D., Semanko, M.: The one-more-RSA-inversion problems and the security of Chaum's blind signature scheme. J. Cryptol. **16**(3), 185–215 (2003)
3. Bellare, M., Neven, G.: Multi-signatures in the plain public-key model and a general forking lemma. In: Juels, A., Wright, R.N., De Capitani di Vimercati, S. (eds.) ACM CCS 2006, pp. 390–399. ACM Press, October/November 2006
4. Bellare, M., Palacio, A.: The knowledge-of-exponent assumptions and 3-round zero-knowledge protocols. In: Franklin, M. (ed.) CRYPTO 2004. LNCS, vol. 3152, pp. 273–289. Springer, Heidelberg (2004). https://doi.org/10.1007/978-3-540-28628-8_17
5. Bellare, M., Rogaway, P.: Random oracles are practical: a paradigm for designing efficient protocols. In: Denning, D.E., Pyle, R., Ganesan, R., Sandhu, R.S., Ashby, V. (eds.) ACM CCS 1993, pp. 62–73. ACM Press, November 1993
6. Bellare, M., Rogaway, P.: The security of triple encryption and a framework for code-based game-playing proofs. In: Vaudenay, S. (ed.) EUROCRYPT 2006. LNCS, vol. 4004, pp. 409–426. Springer, Heidelberg (2006). https://doi.org/10.1007/11761679_25
7. Bellare, M., Tessaro, S., Zhu, C.: Stronger security for non-interactive threshold signatures: BLS and FROST. Cryptology ePrint Archive, Report 2022/833 (2022). https://eprint.iacr.org/2022/833
8. Boldyreva, A.: Threshold signatures, multisignatures and blind signatures based on the Gap-Diffie-Hellman-Group signature scheme. In: Desmedt, Y.G. (ed.) PKC 2003. LNCS, vol. 2567, pp. 31–46. Springer, Heidelberg (2003). https://doi.org/10.1007/3-540-36288-6_3

9. Boneh, D., Gennaro, R., Goldfeder, S.: Using level-1 homomorphic encryption to improve threshold DSA signatures for bitcoin wallet security. In: Lange, T., Dunkelman, O. (eds.) LATINCRYPT 2017. LNCS, vol. 11368, pp. 352–377. Springer, Cham (2019). https://doi.org/10.1007/978-3-030-25283-0_19
10. Boneh, D., et al.: Threshold cryptosystems from threshold fully homomorphic encryption. In: Shacham, H., Boldyreva, A. (eds.) CRYPTO 2018, Part I. LNCS, vol. 10991, pp. 565–596. Springer, Cham (2018). https://doi.org/10.1007/978-3-319-96884-1_19
11. Boneh, D., Lynn, B., Shacham, H.: Short signatures from the Weil pairing. In: Boyd, C. (ed.) ASIACRYPT 2001. LNCS, vol. 2248, pp. 514–532. Springer, Heidelberg (2001). https://doi.org/10.1007/3-540-45682-1_30
12. Boneh, D., Lynn, B., Shacham, H.: Short signatures from the Weil pairing. J. Cryptol. **17**(4), 297–319 (2004)
13. Canetti, R., Gennaro, R., Goldfeder, S., Makriyannis, N., Peled, U.: UC non-interactive, proactive, threshold ECDSA with identifiable aborts. In: Ligatti, J., Ou, X., Katz, J., Vigna, G. (eds.) ACM CCS 2020, pp. 1769–1787. ACM Press, November 2020
14. Crites, E., Komlo, C., Maller, M.: How to prove Schnorr assuming Schnorr: security of multi- and threshold signatures. Cryptology ePrint Archive, Report 2021/1375 (2021). https://eprint.iacr.org/2021/1375
15. Damgård, I.: Towards practical public key systems secure against chosen ciphertext attacks. In: Feigenbaum, J. (ed.) CRYPTO 1991. LNCS, vol. 576, pp. 445–456. Springer, Heidelberg (1992). https://doi.org/10.1007/3-540-46766-1_36
16. De Santis, A., Desmedt, Y., Frankel, Y., Yung, M.: How to share a function securely. In: 26th ACM STOC, pp. 522–533. ACM Press, May 1994
17. Desmedt, Y.: Society and group oriented cryptography: a new concept. In: Pomerance, C. (ed.) CRYPTO 1987. LNCS, vol. 293, pp. 120–127. Springer, Heidelberg (1988). https://doi.org/10.1007/3-540-48184-2_8
18. Desmedt, Y., Frankel, Y.: Threshold cryptosystems. In: Brassard, G. (ed.) CRYPTO 1989. LNCS, vol. 435, pp. 307–315. Springer, New York (1990). https://doi.org/10.1007/0-387-34805-0_28
19. Feldman, P.: A practical scheme for non-interactive verifiable secret sharing. In: 28th FOCS, pp. 427–437. IEEE Computer Society Press, October 1987
20. Fuchsbauer, G., Kiltz, E., Loss, J.: The algebraic group model and its applications. In: Shacham, H., Boldyreva, A. (eds.) CRYPTO 2018, Part II. LNCS, vol. 10992, pp. 33–62. Springer, Cham (2018). https://doi.org/10.1007/978-3-319-96881-0_2
21. Gennaro, R., Goldfeder, S.: Fast multiparty threshold ECDSA with fast trustless setup. In: Lie, D., Mannan, M., Backes, M., Wang, X. (eds.) ACM CCS 2018, pp. 1179–1194. ACM Press, October 2018
22. Gennaro, R., Goldfeder, S., Narayanan, A.: Threshold-optimal DSA/ECDSA signatures and an application to bitcoin wallet security. In: Manulis, M., Sadeghi, A.-R., Schneider, S. (eds.) ACNS 2016. LNCS, vol. 9696, pp. 156–174. Springer, Cham (2016). https://doi.org/10.1007/978-3-319-39555-5_9
23. Gennaro, R., Jarecki, S., Krawczyk, H., Rabin, T.: Robust threshold DSS signatures. In: Maurer, U. (ed.) EUROCRYPT 1996. LNCS, vol. 1070, pp. 354–371. Springer, Heidelberg (1996). https://doi.org/10.1007/3-540-68339-9_31
24. Gennaro, R., Jarecki, S., Krawczyk, H., Rabin, T.: Secure applications of Pedersen's distributed key generation protocol. In: Joye, M. (ed.) CT-RSA 2003. LNCS, vol. 2612, pp. 373–390. Springer, Heidelberg (2003)
25. Gennaro, R., Jarecki, S., Krawczyk, H., Rabin, T.: Secure distributed key generation for discrete-log based cryptosystems. J. Cryptol. **20**(1), 51–83 (2007)

26. Gennaro, R., Rabin, T., Jarecki, S., Krawczyk, H.: Robust and efficient sharing of RSA functions. J. Cryptol. **13**(2), 273–300 (2000)
27. Goldwasser, S., Micali, S., Rivest, R.L.: A digital signature scheme secure against adaptive chosen-message attacks. SIAM J. Comput. **17**(2), 281–308 (1988)
28. Groth, J.: Non-interactive distributed key generation and key resharing. Cryptology ePrint Archive, Report 2021/339 (2021). https://eprint.iacr.org/2021/339
29. Katz, J., Yung, M.: Threshold cryptosystems based on factoring. In: Zheng, Y. (ed.) ASIACRYPT 2002. LNCS, vol. 2501, pp. 192–205. Springer, Heidelberg (2002). https://doi.org/10.1007/3-540-36178-2_12
30. Komlo, C., Goldberg, I.: FROST: flexible round-optimized Schnorr threshold signatures. In: Dunkelman, O., Jacobson, Jr., M.J., O'Flynn, C. (eds.) SAC 2020. LNCS, vol. 12804, pp. 34–65. Springer, Cham (2021). https://doi.org/10.1007/978-3-030-81652-0_2
31. Komlo, C., Goldberg, I.: FROST: flexible round-optimized Schnorr threshold signatures. Cryptology ePrint Archive, Report 2020/852 (2020). https://eprint.iacr.org/2020/852
32. Komlo, C., Goldberg, I., Wilson-Brown, T.: Two-Round Threshold Signatures with FROST. Internet-Draft draft-irtf-cfrg-frost-01, Internet Engineering Task Force, August 2021. Work in Progress
33. Libert, B., Joye, M., Yung, M.: Born and raised distributively: fully distributed non-interactive adaptively-secure threshold signatures with short shares. In: Halldórsson, M.M., Dolev, S. (eds.) 33rd ACM PODC, pp. 303–312. ACM, July 2014
34. Lindell, Y., Nof, A., Ranellucci, S.: Fast secure multiparty ECDSA with practical distributed key generation and applications to cryptocurrency custody. Cryptology ePrint Archive, Report 2018/987 (2018). https://eprint.iacr.org/2018/987
35. National Institute of Standards and Technology: Multi-Party Threshold Cryptography (2018-Present). https://csrc.nist.gov/Projects/threshold-cryptography
36. Shamir, A.: How to share a secret. Commun. Assoc. Comput. Mach. **22**(11), 612–613 (1979)
37. Shoup, V.: Practical threshold signatures. In: Preneel, B. (ed.) EUROCRYPT 2000. LNCS, vol. 1807, pp. 207–220. Springer, Heidelberg (2000). https://doi.org/10.1007/3-540-45539-6_15
38. Shoup, V., Gennaro, R.: Securing threshold cryptosystems against chosen ciphertext attack. In: Nyberg, K. (ed.) EUROCRYPT 1998. LNCS, vol. 1403, pp. 1–16. Springer, Heidelberg (1998). https://doi.org/10.1007/BFb0054113
39. Stinson, D.R., Strobl, R.: Provably secure distributed Schnorr signatures and a (t, n) threshold scheme for implicit certificates. In: Varadharajan, V., Mu, Y. (eds.) ACISP 2001. LNCS, vol. 2119, pp. 417–434. Springer, Heidelberg (2001). https://doi.org/10.1007/3-540-47719-5_33
40. Wee, H.: Threshold and revocation cryptosystems via extractable hash proofs. In: Paterson, K.G. (ed.) EUROCRYPT 2011. LNCS, vol. 6632, pp. 589–609. Springer, Heidelberg (2011). https://doi.org/10.1007/978-3-642-20465-4_32

Threshold Signatures with Private Accountability

Dan Boneh[1] and Chelsea Komlo[2(✉)]

[1] Stanford University, Stanford, USA
[2] University of Waterloo, Waterloo, Canada
ckomlo@uwaterloo.ca

Abstract. Existing threshold signature schemes come in two flavors: (i) *fully private*, where the signature reveals nothing about the set of signers that generated the signature, and (ii) *accountable*, where the signature completely identifies the set of signers. In this paper we propose a new type of threshold signature, called TAPS, that is a hybrid of privacy and accountability. A TAPS signature is fully private from the public's point of view. However, an entity that has a secret tracing key can trace a signature to the threshold of signers that generated it. A TAPS makes it possible for an organization to keep its inner workings private, while ensuring that signers are accountable for their actions. We construct a number of TAPS schemes. First, we present a generic construction that builds a TAPS from any accountable threshold signature. This generic construction is not efficient, and we next focus on efficient schemes based on standard assumptions. We build two efficient TAPS schemes (in the random oracle model) based on the Schnorr signature scheme. We conclude with a number of open problems relating to efficient TAPS.

1 Introduction

A threshold signature scheme [30] enables a group of n parties to sign a message only if t or more of the parties participate in the signing process. There are two types of threshold signature schemes:

- *A private threshold signature (PTS) scheme:* A signature σ on a message m reveals nothing about the threshold t, and reveals nothing about the quorum of t parties that generated the signature. The same holds even if the adversary sees a sequence of signatures on messages of its choice. Examples of PTS schemes include [15,26,34,38,45,56,57] and many others.
- *An accountable threshold signature (ATS) scheme:* A signature σ on a message m reveals the identity of all t parties who participated in generating the signature (and hence also reveals t). Moreover, it is not feasible for a quorum of t parties to frame another quorum. An ATS scheme is closely related to the notion of an *accountable subgroup multisignature* (ASM) [5,9,17,44,50,53]. However, we prefer the term ATS to contrast the two flavors of threshold signatures: ATS vs. PTS. An ATS has also been described as Traceable Secret Sharing (TSS) [42].

Y. Dodis and T. Shrimpton (Eds.): CRYPTO 2022, LNCS 13510, pp. 551–581, 2022.
https://doi.org/10.1007/978-3-031-15985-5_19

We will define these concepts more precisely in the next section.

A private threshold signature (PTS) scheme is used when there is a need to hide the inner-workings of an organization. For example, an organization that runs a web server may choose to split the server's secret TLS key among n machines so that at least t are needed to generate a signature and complete a TLS handshake. By using a PTS, the organization can hide the threshold t from the public, to avoid leaking the number of machines that an attacker needs to compromise in order to forge a signature. Similarly, a signature should reveal nothing about the set of t machines that participated in generating the signature so that nothing is revealed about which machines are currently online.

In contrast, an accountable threshold signature (ATS) scheme is often used in financial applications where there is a need for accountability. For example, if three of five bank executives are needed to authorize a banking transfer, then one wants full accountability in case a fraudulent transfer is approved. When using an ATS scheme, the signature on a fraudulent transaction will identify the three bank executives who authorized it.

The trivial t-out-of-n ATS scheme is one where every signing party locally generates a public-private key pair. The complete public key is defined as the concatenation of all n local public keys. When t parties need to sign a message m, they each sign the message using their local secret key, and the final signature is the concatenation of all t signatures. The verifier accepts such an ATS signature if it contains t valid signatures. This trivial ATS is used widely in practice, for example in Bitcoin multisig transactions [1]. While the scheme has many benefits, its downside is that signature size and verification time are at least linear in $t\lambda$, where λ is the security parameter. Several ATS constructions achieve much smaller signature size and verification time [9,17,50,53].

In summary, existing threshold signatures offer either complete privacy or complete accountability for the signing quorum, but cannot do both.

A New Type of Threshold Signature. In this work we introduce a new type of threshold signature scheme, called TAPS, that provides full accountability while maintaining privacy for the signing quorum.

A **Threshold, Accountable, and Private Signature** scheme, or simply a **TAPS**, works as follows: (i) a key generation procedure generates the public key pk and the n private keys $sk_1, \ldots, sk_n$ for the signers, (ii) a signing protocol among some t signers is used to generate a signature σ on a message m, and (iii) a signature verification algorithm takes as input pk, m, and σ and outputs accept or reject. Signatures generated by the signing protocol reveal nothing to the public about t or the quorum that generated the signature. In addition, the key generation procedure outputs a **tracing key** sk_{t}. Anyone in possession of sk_{t} can reliably trace a signature to the quorum that generated it. For security we require that a set of signers should be unable to frame some other set of signers by fooling the tracing procedure. We define the precise syntax for a TAPS scheme, and the security requirements, in Sect. 3.

If the tracing key sk_t is made public to all, then a TAPS is no different than an ATS scheme. Similarly, if sk_t is destroyed, then a TAPS is no different than a PTS scheme. However, if sk_t is known to a trusted tracing party (or secret shared among several parties), then the tracing party can provide accountability in case of a fraudulent transaction, while keeping all other information about the inner-workings of the organization private.

Applications. Consider an organization that holds digital assets that are managed on a public ledger (e.g., a blockchain). A digital signature must be recorded on the ledger in order to transfer an asset. The organization can protect the assets by requiring t-out-of-n trustees to sign a transfer request. It can use an ATS scheme, but then the threshold t and the set of signers will be public for the world to see. Or it can use a PTS scheme to secret share a single signing key among the n trustees, but then there is no accountability for the trustees.

A TAPS provides a better solution: the organization can hold on to the tracing key sk_t so that the threshold and the set of signers remain private, but the trustees are accountable in case of a fraudulent transfer. The value of n and t are typically relatively small, say less than twenty.

The same applies in the web server setting. The web server's TLS secret signing key could be shared among t-out-of-n machines so that t machines are needed to complete a TLS handshake. The tracing key would be kept in offline storage. If at some point it is discovered that the web server's secret key has been compromised, and is being used by a rogue web server, then the tracing key could be applied to the rogue server's signatures to identify the set of machines that were compromised by the attacker.

Constructing TAPS. We provide a number of constructions for TAPS schemes. In Sect. 4 we present a generic construction that shows how to construct a TAPS from any ATS scheme. The construction is quite inefficient since it makes use of general zero knowledge. While there are several important details that are needed to obtain a secure construction, the high level approach for generating a TAPS signature is as follows: (i) the signing parties generate an ATS signature σ on a message m, (ii) they encrypt σ using a public key encryption scheme to obtain a ciphertext ct, and (iii) the final TAPS signature is $\sigma' = (ct, \pi)$, where π is a non-interactive zero knowledge proof that the decryption of ct is a valid ATS signature on m. To verify a signature, one verifies that π is valid. The tracing key sk_t is the decryption key that lets one decrypt ct. Then, using sk_t one can decrypt ct, and run the ATS tracing algorithm on the resulting ATS signature σ. The description here is only meant as an outline, and is not secure as is. The complete construction is provided in Sect. 4.

Next, we turn to constructing a practical TAPS scheme. In Sect. 5 we build two efficient TAPS schemes from Schnorr signatures [55]. To do so, we modify the generic construction so that the statement that needs to be proved in zero knowledge is as simple as possible. We then use either a Sigma protocol [27] or Bulletproofs [20,22] to prove the statement. The resulting public key and signature sizes are summarized in Table 1. For small n, both schemes have reasonable performance. As n grows, signatures produced by the Bulletproofs scheme are about 40 times shorter.

Table 1. An n-party TAPS based on the Schnorr signature scheme in a group $\mathbb{G}$ of order q. The construction uses either a Sigma protocol or Bulletproofs. The Bulletproofs TAPS signature is shorter by a factor of about e, but tracing time is higher. Taking $e := 40$ is a reasonable choice.

	Public Key Size		Signature Size		Verify Time (group ops)	Trace Time (group ops)
	$\mathbb{G}$	$\mathbb{Z}_q$	$\mathbb{G}$	$\mathbb{Z}_q$		
Sigma	$2n+4$	0	$n+4$	$2n+5$	$O(n)$	$O(n)$
Bulletproofs	$n+\frac{n}{e}+O(1)$	0	$\frac{n}{e}+O(\log n)$	4	$O(n)$	$O(n \cdot 2^{e/2})$

We note that due to the traceability and privacy requirements, a TAPS signature must encode the signing quorum while hiding the threshold t, and therefore must be at least n bits long. In Sect. 6 we discuss relaxing the *full tracing* requirement with a weaker tracing property we call *quorum confirmation*. Here the tracing algorithm takes as input sk_t and a suspect quorum set $C \subseteq [n]$, and confirms if C is indeed the quorum set that generated a given signature. If this weaker confirmation property is sufficient, then our Bulletproofs approach can lead to a logarithmic size TAPS signature. Note that when n is small, confirmation can lead to full tracing by testing all possible quorum sets until one is confirmed.

A Different Perspective. A TAPS system can be described as a group signature scheme where t signers are needed to sign on behalf of the group. Recall that in a group signature scheme [25] a group manager provisions every member in the group with a secret signing key. Any group member can sign on behalf of the group without revealing the identity of the signer. In addition, there is a tracing key that lets an entity that holds that key trace a given group signature to the single member that issued that signature. A TAPS can be viewed as a generalization of this mechanism. In a TAPS scheme, at least t members of the group are needed to generate a group signature. The signature reveals nothing to the public about the identity of the signers or t. However, the tracing key enables one to trace the signature back to some t members that participated in generating the signature.

In the literature, the term *threshold group signature* refers to a scheme where the role of the group manager is distributed among a set of authorities with a threshold access structure [14,24]. A TAPS is quite different. Here the threshold refers to the number of parties needed to generate a signature on behalf of the group. See also our discussion of related work below.

1.1 Additional Related Work

Ring Signatures. Ring signatures [11,52,54] allow a signer to sign a message on behalf of an ad-hoc ring of signers. The signature reveals nothing about which ring member generated the signature. As such, anyone can gather a set of public keys, and produce a ring signature over some message without interacting with the owners of those keys. Our notion of TAPS signatures requires a threshold of t signers to generate a signature, where t is hidden from the public. In the basic group or ring setting the threshold t is not secret, it is always set to $t = 1$.

While accountable (traceable) ring signatures with a tracing authority have been defined in the literature [19,35,36,59], these schemes are limited to a *single* signer, as opposed to a threshold of signers within the ring. Dodis et al. [31] defined a multi-party ring signature that builds upon one-way cryptographic accumulators and supports an identity escrow extension. However, the scheme does not enforce a threshold number of signers to anyone other than the designated tracing authority (by recovering the identities of the signers). In contrast, TAPS requires that anyone be able to verify that a threshold number of signers participated in generating a signature.

Threshold ring signatures, called *thring signatures*, were studied in a number of works [21,43,47,51,58]. Here the ring signature represents some t-out-of-n set of signers. However, these schemes provide no tracing, and therefore do not fulfill the notions of accountability required by TAPS. Similarly, linkable threshold ring signatures [4,32] only require that any two ring signatures produced by the same signers can be linked, but not traced.

A ring signature by Bootle et al. [19] combines Camenisch's group signature scheme [23] with a one-out-of-many proof of knowledge. This construction uses similar techniques as our Schnorr TAPS construction, but supports only a single signer, rather than a threshold, so provides quite a different functionality.

Group Signatures. First introduced by Chaum and van Heyst [25], group signatures [12,16,18,29,37,46,48] enable a group member to sign a message such that the verifier can determine that a member generated the signature, but not *which* member. If needed, a tracing authority can trace a signature to its signer. A group manager is trusted to manage the group's membership. The security notions for a group signatures were defined by Bellare et al. [8], but focus on a single signer who is signing on behalf of the group. Traditionally *threshold group signatures* refers to the ability to distribute the roles of the group manager [14,24], as opposed to requiring a threshold number of participants to issue a signature.

2 Preliminaries

Notation: We use $\lambda \in \mathbb{Z}$ to denote the security parameter in unary. We use $x \leftarrow y$ to denote the assignment of the value of y to x. We write $x \xleftarrow{\$} S$to denote sampling an element from the set S independently and uniformly at random. For a randomized algorithm $\mathcal{A}$ we write $y \xleftarrow{\$} \mathcal{A}(x)$ to denote the random variable that is the output of $\mathcal{A}(x)$. We use $[n]$ for the set $\{1,\ldots,n\}$. Throughout the paper $\mathbb{G}$ is a cyclic group of prime order q, and $\mathbb{Z}_q$ is the ring $\mathbb{Z}/q\mathbb{Z}$. We let g be a generator of $\mathbb{G}$. We denote vectors in bold font: $\mathbf{u} \in \mathbb{Z}_q^m$ is a vector of length m whose elements are each in $\mathbb{Z}_q$. We write $\mathbf{g}^{\mathbf{a}} = \prod_{i=1}^{n} {g_i}^{a_i} \in \mathbb{G}$, for a vector $\mathbf{g} = (g_1,\ldots,g_n) \in \mathbb{G}^n$ and $\mathbf{a} = (a_1,\ldots,a_n) \in \mathbb{Z}_q^n$.

Our construction make use of a few standard primitives. We define these briefly here.

Definition 1. *A* **public key encryption scheme** $\mathcal{PKE}$ *for a message space* $\mathcal{M} = \{\mathcal{M}_\lambda\}_{\lambda\in\mathbb{N}}$ *is a triple of PPT algorithms (KeyGen, Encrypt, Decrypt) invoked as*

$$(pk, sk) \xleftarrow{\$} KeyGen(1^\lambda), \quad ct \xleftarrow{\$} Encrypt(pk, m), \quad m \leftarrow Decrypt(sk, ct).$$

The only security requirement is that $\mathcal{PKE}$ *be* **semantically secure**, *namely, for every PPT adversary* $\mathcal{A}$ *the following function is negligible*

$$\mathbf{Adv}^{\text{indcpa}}_{\mathcal{A},\mathcal{PKE}}(\lambda) := \left|\Pr\left[\mathcal{A}^{\text{ENC}(0,\cdot,\cdot)}(pk) = 1\right] - \Pr\left[\mathcal{A}^{\text{ENC}(1,\cdot,\cdot)}(pk) = 1\right]\right|,$$

where $(pk, sk) \xleftarrow{\$} KeyGen(1^\lambda)$, *and for* $b \in \{0,1\}$ *and* $m_0, m_1 \in \mathcal{M}_\lambda$, *the oracle* $\text{ENC}(b, m_0, m_1)$ *returns* $ct \xleftarrow{\$} Encrypt(pk, m_b)$.

When $\mathcal{M}_\lambda \subseteq \{0,1\}^{\leq \ell_\lambda}$, for some ℓ_λ, our definition of semantic security requires that the encryption scheme be *length hiding*: an adversary cannot distinguish the encryption of $m_0 \in \mathcal{M}_\lambda$ from $m_1 \in \mathcal{M}_\lambda$ even if m_0 and m_1 are different lengths. This can be achieved by having the encryption algorithm pad the plaintext to a fixed maximum length using an injective pad (e.g., $100\ldots00$), and having the decryption algorithm remove the pad.

Definition 2. *Let* $\mathcal{R} := \{\mathcal{R}_\lambda\}_{\lambda\in\mathbb{N}}$. *A* **commitment** *scheme* $\mathcal{COM}$ *is a pair of PPT algorithms (Commit, Verify) invoked with* $r \in \mathcal{R}_\lambda$ *as*

$$\mathsf{com} \leftarrow Commit(x, r) \quad and \quad Verify(x, r, \mathsf{com}) \in \{0,1\}.$$

The scheme is **secure** *if it is unconditionally hiding and computationally binding. In particular, for all* x, x' *the distributions* $\{\mathcal{COM}(x,r)\}$ *and* $\{\mathcal{COM}(x',r')\}$ *have negligible statistical distance* $\epsilon(\lambda)$ *when* $r, r' \xleftarrow{\$} \mathcal{R}_\lambda$. *In addition, for every PPT adversary* $\mathcal{A}$ *the following function is negligible*

$$\mathbf{Adv}^{\text{bind}}_{\mathcal{A},\mathcal{COM}}(\lambda) := \Pr\left[\begin{array}{l} x \neq x', \quad r, r' \in \mathcal{R}_\lambda, \\ Verify(x, r, \mathsf{com}) = 1 \\ Verify(x', r', \mathsf{com}) = 1 \end{array} : \ (\mathsf{com}, x, r, x', r') \xleftarrow{\$} \mathcal{A}(\lambda)\right].$$

Definition 3. *A* **signature scheme** $\mathcal{SIG}$ *is a triple of PPT algorithms (KeyGen, Sign, Verify) invoked as*

$$(pk, sk) \xleftarrow{\$} KeyGen(1^\lambda), \quad \sigma \xleftarrow{\$} Sign(sk, m), \quad Verify(pk, m, \sigma) \in \{0,1\}.$$

The scheme is **strongly unforgeable** *if the following function is negligible*

$$\mathbf{Adv}^{\mathrm{eufcma}}_{\mathcal{A},\mathcal{SIG}}(\lambda) := \Pr\left[\begin{matrix} \mathit{Verify}(pk, m, \sigma) = 1 \\ (m,\sigma) \notin \{(m_i,\sigma_i)\}_{i=1}^{q} \end{matrix} : \begin{matrix} (pk, sk) \xleftarrow{\$} \mathit{KeyGen}(1^\lambda) \\ (m,\sigma) \xleftarrow{\$} \mathcal{A}^{\mathrm{SIGN}(\cdot)}(pk) \end{matrix}\right]$$

where $\mathrm{SIGN}(m_i)$ *returns* $\sigma_i \xleftarrow{\$} \mathit{Sign}(sk, m_i)$ *for* $i = 1, \ldots, q$.

Definition 4. *A* **proof system** *for a relation* $\mathcal{R} := \{\mathcal{R}_\lambda \subseteq \mathcal{X}_\lambda \times \mathcal{W}_\lambda\}_{\lambda\in\mathbb{N}}$ *is a pair of interactive machines* $(\mathcal{P}, \mathcal{V})$*, where for* $x \in \mathcal{X}_\lambda$ *and* $w \in \mathcal{W}_\lambda$*, the prover is invoked as* $\mathcal{P}(x, w)$ *and the verifier is invoked as* $\mathcal{V}(x)$*. We let* $\langle\mathcal{P}(x, w); \mathcal{V}(x)\rangle$ *be a random variable that is the verifier's output at the end of the interaction. We let* $\mathsf{trans}(\mathcal{P}(x, w); \mathcal{V}(x))$ *denote a random variable that is the transcript of the interaction.*

- *The proof system* $(\mathcal{P}, \mathcal{V})$ *has* **perfect completeness** *if for all* $(x, w) \in \mathcal{R}_\lambda$ *we have* $\Pr[\langle\mathcal{P}(x, w); \mathcal{V}(x)\rangle = 1] = 1$.
- *The proof system* $(\mathcal{P}, \mathcal{V})$ *is* **honest verifier zero knowledge**, *or HVZK, if there is a PPT Sim such that for all* $(x, w) \in \mathcal{R}_\lambda$ *the two distributions*

$$\{\mathit{Sim}(x)\} \quad \text{and} \quad \{\mathsf{trans}(\mathcal{P}(x, w); \mathcal{V}(x))\}$$

are computational indistinguishable. In particular, let $\mathbf{Adv}^{\mathrm{hvzk}}_{\mathcal{A},(\mathcal{P},\mathcal{V})}(\lambda)$ *be the distinguishing advantage for an adversary* $\mathcal{A}$*. Then this function is negligible for all PPT adversaries* $\mathcal{A}$.
- *The proof system* $(\mathcal{P}, \mathcal{V})$ *is an* **argument of knowledge** *if it is perfectly complete, and for every PPT* $\mathcal{P} = (\mathcal{P}_1, \mathcal{P}_2)$ *there is an expected polynomial time extractor Ext so that the functions*

$$\epsilon_1(\lambda) := \Pr\left[\langle\mathcal{P}_2(\mathtt{state}); \mathcal{V}(x)\rangle = 1 \;:\; (x, \mathtt{state}) \xleftarrow{\$} \mathcal{P}_1(1^\lambda)\right]$$
$$\epsilon_2(\lambda) := Pr\left[(x, w) \in \mathcal{R}_\lambda \;:\; (x, \mathtt{state}) \xleftarrow{\$} \mathcal{P}_1(1^\lambda),\; w \xleftarrow{\$} \mathit{Ext}^{\mathcal{P}_2(\mathtt{state})}(x)\right]$$

satisfy

$$\epsilon_2(\lambda) \geq (\epsilon_1(\lambda) - \kappa(\lambda))/q(\lambda), \tag{1}$$

for some negligible function κ *called the* **knowledge error**, *and a polynomial function* q *called the* **extraction tightness**. *Here* $\mathtt{state}$ *is state data output by* $\mathcal{P}_1$*, and* $\mathit{Ext}^{\mathcal{P}_2(\mathtt{state})}$ *denotes that Ext has oracle access to* $\mathcal{P}_2(\mathtt{state})$ *which is modeled as an "interactive function" [7]. We refer to* $\mathcal{P}_1$ *as an* **instance generator**.
- *We say that a proof system* $(\mathcal{P}, \mathcal{V})$ *is* **non-interactive** *if the only interaction is a single message* π *from the prover* $\mathcal{P}$ *to the verifier* $\mathcal{V}$.
- *We say that the proof system* $(\mathcal{P}, \mathcal{V})$ *is a non-interactive HVZK argument of knowledge in the* **random oracle model** *if* $(\mathcal{P}^H, \mathcal{V}^H)$ *is a proof system that is non-interactive, HVZK, and an argument of knowledge, where* H *is a random oracle.*

A public coin proof system can be made non-interactive using the Fiat-Shamir transform [33]. For some proof systems, this transformation retains the argument of knowledge and HVZK properties in the random oracle model [3]. Implementing the Fiat-Shamir transform in practice is error-prone and it is recommended to use an established implementation to do it (e.g., [28]).

3 Threshold, Accountable, and Private Signatures

In this section, we formalize the notion of threshold, accountable, and private signatures (TAPS). We use n for the total number of allowed signers, and t for the threshold number of required users. We let $\mathcal{M}$ denote the message space.

The Combiner. When t parties wish to generate a signature on some message m, they send their signature shares to a *Combiner* who uses the t shares to generate a complete signature. Notice that the Combiner will learn the threshold t, which is secret information in our settings. Since the Combiner must be trusted with this private information, we also allow the Combiner to hold a secret key denoted sk_c. Secrecy of the Combiner's key is only needed for privacy of the signing quorum. It is not needed for security: if sk_c becomes public, an adversary cannot use it to defeat the unforgeability or accountability properties of the scheme. As we will see, we model this by giving sk_c to the adversary in the unforgeability and accountability security games, but we keep this key hidden in the privacy game.

The Tracer. A tracing entity is trusted to hold a secret tracing key sk_t that allows one to trace a valid signature to the quorum of signers who generated it. Without knowledge of sk_t, recovering the quorum should be difficult.

With these parties in mind, let us define the syntax for a TAPS.

Definition 5. *A* **private and accountable threshold signature** *scheme, or* **TAPS**, *is a tuple of five polynomial time algorithms*

$$\mathcal{S} = (\mathit{KeyGen}, \mathit{Sign}, \mathit{Combine}, \mathit{Verify}, \mathit{Trace})$$

where:

- $\mathit{KeyGen}(1^\lambda, n, t) \rightarrow (pk, (sk_1, \ldots, sk_n), sk_c, sk_t)$: *a probabilistic algorithm that takes as input a security parameter* λ, *the number of parties* n *and threshold* t. *It outputs a public key* pk, *signer keys* $\{sk_1, \ldots, sk_n\}$, *a combiner secret key* sk_c, *and a tracing secret key* sk_t.
- $\mathit{Sign}(sk_i, m, C) \rightarrow \delta_i$: *a probabilistic algorithm performed by* one *signer who uses its secret key* sk_i *to generate a signature "share"* δ_i *on a message* m *in* $\mathcal{M}$. *In some constructions it is convenient to allow the signer to know the identity of the members of the signing quorum* $C \subseteq [n]$. *We provide it as an optional input to Sign.*
- $\mathit{Combine}(sk_c, m, C, \{\delta_i\}_{i \in C}) \rightarrow \sigma$: *a probabilistic algorithm that takes as input the Combiner's secret key, a message* m, *a description of the signing quorum* $C \subseteq [n]$, *where* $|C| = t$, *and* t *valid signature shares by members of* C. *If the input is valid, the algorithm outputs a* TAPS *signature* σ.

- *Verify*$(pk, m, \sigma) \to 0/1$: *a deterministic algorithm that verifies the signature* σ *on a message* m *with respect to the public key* pk.
- *Trace*$(sk_t, m, \sigma) \to C/\textsf{fail}$: *a deterministic algorithm that takes as input the tracer's secret key* sk_t, *along with a message and a signature. The algorithm outputs a set* $C \subseteq [n]$, *where* $|C| \geq t$, *or a special message* fail. *If the algorithm outputs a set* C, *then the set is intended to be a set of signers whose keys must have been used to generate* σ. *We refer to the entity performing Trace as the* Tracer.
- *For correctness we require that for all allowable* $1 \leq t \leq n$, *for all* t*-size sets* $C \subseteq [n]$, *all* $m \in \mathcal{M}$, *and for* $(pk, (sk_1, \ldots, sk_n), sk_c, sk_t) \xleftarrow{\$} KeyGen(1^\lambda, n, t)$ *the following two conditions hold:*

$$\Pr\big[\, Verify(pk, m, Combine(sk_c, m, C, \{Sign(sk_i, m, C)\}_{i \in C})) = 1\big] = 1$$
$$\Pr\big[\, Trace(sk_t, m, Combine(sk_c, m, C, \{Sign(sk_i, m, C)\}_{i \in C})) = C\big] = 1. \quad (2)$$

Remark 1 (signing algorithm vs. signing protocol). In this paper we treat *Sign*() as an algorithm that is run locally by each of the signing parties. However, in some schemes, *Sign* is an interactive protocol between each signing party and the Combiner. Either way, the end result is that the Combiner obtains a list of signature shares $\{\delta_i\}_{i \in C}$, one share from each signer. The distinction between a local non-interactive signing algorithm vs. an interactive signing protocol is not relevant to the constructions in this paper.

Remark 2 (distributed key generation). Our syntax assumes a centralized setup algorithm *KeyGen* to generate the signing key shares. However, all our schemes can be adapted to use a decentralized key generation protocol among the signers, the Combiner, and the Tracer. At the end of the protocol every signer knows its secret key, the Combiner knows sk_c, the Tracer knows sk_t, and pk is public. No other information is known to any party.

Remark 3 (Why use a Tracer?). The Combiner knows which parties contributed signature shares to create a particular signature. A badly designed tracing system could operate as follows: whenever the Combiner constructs a signature, it records the quorum that was used to generate that signature in its database. Later, when a signature needs to be traced, the Combiner could look up the signature in its database and reveal the quorum that generated that signature. If the signature scheme is strongly unforgeable, then one could hope that the only valid signatures in existence are ones generated by an honest Combiner, so that every valid signature can be easily traced with the help of the Combiner. The problem, of course, is that a malicious quorum of signers could collude with the Combiner to generate a valid signature that cannot be traced because the data is not recorded in the database. Or a malicious quorum might delete the relevant entry from the Combiner's database and prevent tracing.

Instead, we require that every valid signature can be traced to the quorum that generated it using the secret tracing key sk_t. The tracing key sk_t can be kept in a "safety deposit box" and only accessed when tracing is required. The Combiner in a TAPS is *stateless*.

Unforgeability and accountability attack game:

$(n, t, C, \mathsf{state}) \xleftarrow{\$} \mathcal{A}_0(1^\lambda)$; where $t \in [n]$ and $C \subseteq [n]$	// $\mathcal{A}_0$ outputs n, t and C (no size bound on C)
$(pk, \{sk_1, \ldots, sk_n\}, sk_c, pk_t) \xleftarrow{\$} KeyGen(1^\lambda, n, t)$	// generate keys using n and t
$(m', \sigma') \xleftarrow{\$} \mathcal{A}_1^{\mathcal{O}(\cdot,\cdot)}(pk, \{sk_i\}_{i \in C}, sk_c, sk_t, \mathsf{state})$	// $\mathcal{A}_1$ receives secret keys for all of C, // as well as the tracing and combiner's secret keys
where $\mathcal{O}(C_j, m_j)$ returns the sig. shares $\{Sign(sk_i, m_j, C_j)\}_{i \in C_j}$	// $\mathcal{A}_1$ can request signature shares for m_j
winning condition: let $(C_1, m_1), (C_2, m_2), \ldots$ be $\mathcal{A}_1$'s queries to $\mathcal{O}$	
let $C' \leftarrow \bigcup C_j$, union over all queries to $\mathcal{O}(C_j, m')$,	// collect all signers that signed m'
if no such queries, set $C' \leftarrow \emptyset$	// if no $\mathcal{O}$-queries for m', then $C' = \emptyset$
let $C_t \leftarrow Trace(sk_t, m', \sigma')$	// trace the forgery (m', σ')
output 1 if $Verify(pk, m', \sigma') = 1$ and either	// $\mathcal{A}$ wins if someone outside of $(C \cup C')$ is blamed,
$C_t \not\subseteq (C \cup C')$ or $C_t = \mathsf{fail}$	// or if tracing fails

Fig. 1. Game defining the advantage of an adversary $\mathcal{A} = (\mathcal{A}_0, \mathcal{A}_1)$ to produce a valid forgery against a TAPS scheme $\mathcal{S} = (KeyGen, Sign, Combine, Verify, Trace)$ with respect to a security parameter λ.

In the next two subsections we define security, privacy, and accountability for a TAPS. The scheme has to satisfy the standard notion of existential unforgeability under a chosen messages attack (EUF-CMA) [41]. In addition, the scheme has to be private and accountable. It is convenient to define unforgeability and accountability in a single game. We define privacy as an additional requirement.

3.1 Unforgeability and Accountability

Like any signature scheme, a TAPS must satisfy the standard notion of unforgeability against a chosen message attack (EUF-CMA). Further, a TAPS scheme should be *accountable*. Informally, this means that a tracer that has the tracing key sk_t should output the correct quorum set $C \subseteq [n]$ of signers for a given message-signature pair.

We refer to these simultaneous notions of unforgeability and accountability as *Existential Unforgeability under a Chosen Message Attack with Traceability*. Informally, this notion captures the following unforgeability and accountability properties, subject to restrictions of the chosen message attack:

- Unforgeability: an adversary that controls fewer than t participants cannot construct a valid message-signature pair; and
- Accountability: an adversary that controls t or more corrupt participants cannot construct a valid message-signature pair that traces to at least one honest participant.

We formalize this in the attack game in Fig. 1. Let $\mathbf{Adv}^{\mathrm{forg}}_{\mathcal{A},\mathcal{S}}(\lambda)$ be the probability that adversary $\mathcal{A}$ wins the game of Fig. 1 against the TAPS scheme $\mathcal{S}$.

Definition 6 (accountable TAPS). *A TAPS scheme $\mathcal{S}$ is* ***unforgeable and accountable*** *if for all probabilistic polynomial time adversaries $\mathcal{A} = (\mathcal{A}_0, \mathcal{A}_1)$, the function $\mathbf{Adv}^{\mathrm{forg}}_{\mathcal{A},\mathcal{S}}(\lambda)$ is a negligible function of λ.*

Our game in Fig. 1 captures both unforgeability (EUF-CMA) for a threshold signature scheme as well as accountability. During the game the adversary obtains the secret keys of parties in C and obtains signature shares for m' from parties in C'. The adversary should be unable to produce a valid signature σ' that causes the tracing algorithm to fail, or causes the tracing algorithm to blame a signing party outside of $C \cup C'$. This captures the accountability property. To see why this implies unforgeability, suppose the adversary $\mathcal{A}$ obtains fewer than threshold t signature shares for m', meaning that $|C \cup C'| < t$. Yet, the adversary is able to produce a valid signature σ' that causes the tracing algorithm to blame some quorum C_t. By definition of *Trace* we know that $|C_t| \geq t$ and therefore C_t cannot be contained in $C \cup C'$. Therefore the adversary succeeds in blaming an honest party, and consequently $\mathcal{A}$ wins the game. Hence, if the adversary cannot win the game, the scheme must be unforgeable.

Remark 4. Definition 6 captures unforgeability, but not strong unforgeability, where the adversary should be unable to generate a new signature on a previously signed message. If needed, one can enhance the definition to require strong unforgeability. Moreover, any unforgeable scheme can be made strongly unforgeable by adapting to the setting of threshold signatures a general transformation from an unforgeable signature scheme to a strongly unforgeable signature scheme [10].

3.2 Privacy

Next, we define privacy for a TAPS. Privacy for a threshold signature scheme is often defined by requiring that a threshold signature on a message m be indistinguishable from a signature on m generated by some standard (non-threshold) signature scheme [39]. This property ensures that a threshold signature reveals nothing about the threshold and the quorum that produced the signature.

A TAPS may not be derived from a non-threshold signature scheme, so this definitional approach does not work well in our setting. Instead, we define privacy as an intrinsic property of the TAPS. Our definition of privacy applies equally well to a private threshold signature (PTS) scheme.

We impose two privacy requirements:

- **Privacy against the public:** A party who only has *pk* and sees a sequence of message-signature pairs, learns nothing about the threshold t or the set of signers that contributed to the creation of those signatures.
- **Privacy against signers:** The set of all signers working together, who also have *pk* (but not sk_{c} or sk_{t}), and see a sequence of message-signature pairs, cannot determine which signers contributed to the creation of those signatures. Note that t is not hidden in this case since the set of all signers knows the threshold.

The game defining privacy against the public:

$b \xleftarrow{\$} \{0,1\}$

$(n, t_0, t_1, \texttt{state}) \xleftarrow{\$} \mathcal{A}_0(1^\lambda)$ where $t_0, t_1 \in [n]$ // $\mathcal{A}_0$ outputs n and two thresholds t_0, t_1

$(pk, \{sk_1, \ldots, sk_n\}, sk_c, sk_t) \xleftarrow{\$} KeyGen(1^\lambda, n, t_b)$ // generate keys using n and t_b

$b' \leftarrow \mathcal{A}_1^{\mathcal{O}_1(\cdot,\cdot,\cdot),\, \mathcal{O}_2(\cdot,\cdot)}(pk, \texttt{state})$

output $(b = b')$

where $\mathcal{O}_1(C_0, C_1, m)$ returns $\sigma \xleftarrow{\$} Combine(sk_c, m, C_b, \{Sign(sk_i, m, C_b)\}_{i \in C_b})$ // sign using C_b

for $C_0, C_1 \subseteq [n]$ with $|C_0| = t_0$ and $|C_1| = t_1$,

and where $\mathcal{O}_2(m, \sigma)$ returns $Trace(sk_t, m, \sigma)$. // trace (m, σ)

Restriction: if σ is obtained from a query $\mathcal{O}_1(\cdot, \cdot, m)$, then $\mathcal{O}_2$ is never queried at (m, σ).

Fig. 2. The game used to define privacy against the public for an adversary $\mathcal{A} = (\mathcal{A}_0, \mathcal{A}_1)$ against a TAPS scheme $\mathcal{S}$ = (*KeyGen*, *Sign*, *Combine*, *Verify*, *Trace*) with respect to a security parameter λ.

These properties are captured by the games in Fig. 2 and Fig. 3 respectively.

Let W be the event that the game in Fig. 2 outputs 1. Similarly, let W' be the event that the game in Fig. 3 outputs 1. We define the two advantage functions for an adversary $\mathcal{A}$ against the scheme $\mathcal{S}$, as a function of the security parameter λ:

$$\mathbf{Adv}^{\text{priv1}}_{\mathcal{A},\mathcal{S}}(\lambda) = \bigl|2\Pr[W] - 1\bigr| \quad \text{and} \quad \mathbf{Adv}^{\text{priv2}}_{\mathcal{A},\mathcal{S}}(\lambda) = \bigl|2\Pr[W'] - 1\bigr|.$$

Definition 7 (Privacy for a TAPS scheme). *A TAPS scheme is* ***private*** *if for all probabilistic polynomial time public adversaries $\mathcal{A} = (\mathcal{A}_0, \mathcal{A}_1)$, the functions $\mathbf{Adv}^{\text{priv1}}_{\mathcal{A},\mathcal{S}}(\lambda)$ and $\mathbf{Adv}^{\text{priv2}}_{\mathcal{A},\mathcal{S}}(\lambda)$ are negligible functions of λ.*

To give some intuition, privacy against the public for a TAPS is defined using the game in Fig. 2. The adversary chooses two thresholds t_0 and t_1 in $[n]$ and is given a public key pk for one of these thresholds. The adversary then issues a sequence of signature queries to a signing oracle $\mathcal{O}_1$, where each signature query includes a message m and two quorums C_0 and C_1. The adversary gets back a signature generated using either the left or the right quorum. We also give the adversary access to a restricted tracing oracle $\mathcal{O}_2$ that will trace a valid message-signature pair. The adversary should be unable to determine whether the sequence of signatures it saw were with respect to the left or the right sequence of quorums.

Our definition of privacy ensures that the threshold t is hidden, but we do not try to hide the number of signers n because there is no need to: one can covertly inflate n to some upper bound by generating superfluous signing keys.

Privacy against signers is defined using the game in Fig. 3. This game is the same as in Fig. 2, however here the adversary chooses the threshold t, and is given *all* the signing keys. Again, the adversary should be unable to determine if a signing oracle $\mathcal{O}_1$ that takes two quorums C_0 and C_1, responds using the

The game defining privacy against signers:

$b \xleftarrow{\$} \{0,1\}$

$(n, t, \text{state}) \xleftarrow{\$} \mathcal{A}_0(1^\lambda)$ where $t \in [n]$ // $\mathcal{A}_0$ outputs n and t

$(pk, \{sk_1, \ldots, sk_n\}, sk_c, sk_t) \xleftarrow{\$} KeyGen(1^\lambda, n, t)$ // generate keys using n and t

$b' \leftarrow \mathcal{A}_1^{\mathcal{O}_1(\cdot,\cdot,\cdot),\, \mathcal{O}_2(\cdot,\cdot)}(pk, \{sk_1, \ldots, sk_n\}, \text{state})$ // $\mathcal{A}_1$ issues signature and trace queries

output $(b = b')$

where $\mathcal{O}_1(C_0, C_1, m)$ returns $\sigma \xleftarrow{\$} Combine(sk_c, m, C_b, \{Sign(sk_i, m, C_b)\}_{i \in C_b})$ // sign using C_b

for $C_0, C_1 \subseteq [n]$ with $|C_0| = |C_1| = t$,

and where $\mathcal{O}_2(m, \sigma)$ returns $Trace(sk_t, m, \sigma)$. // trace (m, σ)

Restriction: if σ is obtained from a query $\mathcal{O}_1(\cdot, \cdot, m)$, then $\mathcal{O}_2$ is never queried at (m, σ).

Fig. 3. The game used to define privacy against signers for an adversary $\mathcal{A} = (\mathcal{A}_0, \mathcal{A}_1)$ against a TAPS scheme $\mathcal{S} = (KeyGen, Sign, Combine, Verify, Trace)$ with respect to a security parameter λ. Here, $\mathcal{A}_1$ is granted knowledge of all signing keys $sk_1, \ldots, sk_n$.

left or the right quorum. As before, the adversary has access to a restricted tracing oracle $\mathcal{O}_2$. As in private threshold signatures (PTS), we do not aim to prevent signers from recognizing a signature that was generated with their help, as discussed in Sect. 6.

Remark 5 (Randomized signing). The privacy games in Figs. 2 and 3 require that signature generation be a randomized process: calling

$$Combine(sk_c, m, C, \{Sign(sk_i, m, C)\}_{i \in C})$$

with the same arguments m and C twice must result in different signatures, with high probability. Otherwise, the adversary could trivially win these games: it would query $\mathcal{O}_1$ twice, once as $\mathcal{O}_1(C_0, C_1, m)$ and again as $\mathcal{O}_1(C_0, C_1', m)$, for suitable quorums C_0, C_1, C_1' where $C_1 \neq C_1'$. It would then check if the resulting signatures are the same. If so, it learns that $b = 0$, and if not it learns that $b = 1$. For this reason, if a scheme satisfies Definition 7, then the output of $Combine(sk_c, m, C, \{Sign(sk_i, m, C)\}_{i \in C})$ must be sampled from some high entropy distribution.

3.3 Accountable Threshold Schemes (ATS)

For completeness, we note that the standard notions of private threshold signatures (PTS) and accountable threshold signatures (ATS) are special cases of a TAPS. We review these concepts in the next two definitions.

To obtain an ATS we impose two syntactic requirements on a TAPS scheme:

- In an ATS, the tracing key is publicly known, meaning that anyone can trace a valid message-signature pair to the quorum that participated in generating it. We capture this by requiring that the TAPS tracing key sk_t is equal to the public key pk.

- In an ATS, the Combiner is not a trusted party and cannot hold secrets. We capture this by requiring that the Combiner's secret key sk_c is also equal to the public key pk.

For clarity, whenever we make use of an ATS, we will drop sk_t and sk_c as explicit inputs and outputs to the relevant TAPS algorithms.

Definition 8. *An* **accountable threshold signature scheme**, *or an* **ATS**, *is a special case of a* TAPS, *where the tracing key* sk_t *and the Combiner key* sk_c *are both equal to the public key* pk. *The scheme is said to be* **secure** *if it is accountable and unforgeable as in Definition 6.*

Notice that there is no privacy requirement in Definition 8.

Remark 6. As mentioned in the introduction, an ATS scheme is closely related to the concept of an *accountable multi-signature scheme* (ASM) [9]. One can construct an ATS from an ASM by including a threshold t in the ASM public key. The ASM verification algorithm is modified to ensure that at least t signers represented in pk signed the message.

Next, we define a private threshold signature scheme, or a PTS. In the literature, a private threshold signature scheme is simply called a *threshold signature scheme*. However, ATS and PTS are equally important concepts, and we therefore add an explicit adjective to clarify which threshold signature concept we are using.

Definition 9. *A* **private threshold signature scheme**, *or a* **PTS**, *is a special case of a* TAPS, *where the Trace algorithm always returns* fail, *and the correctness requirement for a* TAPS *in Definition 5 is modified to remove the requirement on Trace in Eq.* (2). *The scheme is said to be* **secure** *if it is private as in Definition 7, and unforgeable as in Definition 6 with one modification: the adversary wins if the forgery is valid and* $|C \cup C'| < t$.

The modification of Definition 6 reduces the accountability and unforgeability game in Definition 6 to a pure unforgeability game under a chosen message attack, ignoring accountability. Interestingly, this game captures a security notion related to *dual-parameter* threshold security [56]. If one puts a further bound requiring $|C| < t' < t$ in Fig. 1, for some parameter t', then one obtains the usual definition of dual-parameter threshold security from [56].

4 A Generic Construction via an Encrypted ATS

We next turn to constructing a TAPS scheme. In this section we present a generic construction from a secure ATS scheme. The generic TAPS construction makes use of five building blocks:

- a secure accountable threshold signature (ATS) scheme as in Definition 8, namely $\mathcal{ATS} = (KeyGen, Sign, Combine, Verify, Trace)$;

- a semantically secure public-key encryption scheme as in Definition 1, namely $\mathcal{PKE} = (KeyGen, Encrypt, Decrypt)$, whose message space is the space of signatures output by the ATS signing algorithm;
- a binding and hiding commitment scheme $\mathcal{COM} = (Commit, Verify)$, where algorithm $Commit(m, r)$ outputs a commitment to a message m using a random nonce $r \xleftarrow{\$} \mathcal{R}$;
- a strongly unforgeable signature scheme $\mathcal{SIG} = (KeyGen, Sign, Verify)$;
- a non-interactive zero knowledge argument of knowledge (P, V), possibly constructed in the random oracle model using the Fiat-Shamir transform.

Recall that our definition of semantic security in Sect. 2 ensures that the encryption scheme $\mathcal{PKE}$ is length-hiding: the encryption of messages m_0 and m_1 of different lengths are indistinguishable.

The Generic TAPS **Scheme.** The generic TAPS scheme $\mathcal{S}$ is shown in Fig. 4. In our construction, a TAPS signature on a message m is a triple $\sigma = (ct, \pi, tg)$, where (i) ct is a public key encryption of an ATS signature σ_{m} on m, encrypted using the tracing public key pk_{t}, (ii) π is a zero-knowledge proof that the decryption of ct is a valid ATS signature on m, and (iii) tg is the Combiner's signature on (m, ct, π). The reason for the Combiner's signature is explained in Remark 7.

Recall that an ATS public key can reveal the threshold t in the clear, which would violate the TAPS privacy requirements. As such, the TAPS public key cannot include the ATS public key in the clear. Instead, the TAPS public key only contains a hiding *commitment* to the ATS public key.

Correctness. The scheme is correct if the underlying ATS scheme, commitment scheme, encryption scheme, signature scheme, and proof system are correct.

Efficiency. When using a succinct commitment scheme, the public key is quite short; its length depends only on the security parameter. When using a zk-SNARK [13] for the proof system, the signature overhead over the underlying ATS signature is quite short; its length depends only on the security parameter. Moreover, signature verification time is dominated by the SNARK proof verification, which is at most logarithmic in the total number of signing parties n.

However, the Combiner's work in this scheme is substantial because it needs to generate a zk-SNARK proof for a fairly complex statement. In addition, zk-SNARK proof systems rely on strong complexity assumptions for security [40]. To address these issues, we construct in the next section more efficient TAPS schemes whose security relies on DDH in the random oracle model, a much simpler assumption.

Security, Privacy, and Accountability. We next turn to proving that the generic scheme is secure, private, and accountable.

Theorem 1. *The generic* TAPS *scheme $\mathcal{S}$ in Fig. 4 is unforgeable, accountable, and private, assuming that the underlying accountable threshold scheme $\mathcal{ATS}$ is secure, the encryption scheme $\mathcal{PKE}$ is semantically secure, the non-interactive*

- $\underline{\mathcal{S}.KeyGen(1^\lambda, n, t)}$:

  $(pk',\ (sk_1, \ldots, sk_n)) \xleftarrow{\$} \mathcal{ATS}.KeyGen(1^\lambda, n, t)$

  $r_{pk} \xleftarrow{\$} \mathcal{R}_\lambda$ and $\mathsf{com}_{pk} \leftarrow \mathcal{COM}.Commit(pk', r_{pk})$

  $(pk_\mathrm{t}, sk'_\mathrm{t}) \xleftarrow{\$} \mathcal{PKE}.KeyGen(1^\lambda)$

  $(pk_\mathrm{cs}, sk_\mathrm{cs}) \xleftarrow{\$} \mathcal{SIG}.KeyGen(1^\lambda)$ // Combiner's signing key

  $sk_\mathrm{t} \leftarrow (pk', sk'_\mathrm{t}, pk_\mathrm{cs})$ // the secret tracing key

  $sk_\mathrm{c} \leftarrow (pk', pk_\mathrm{t}, sk_\mathrm{cs}, t, \mathsf{com}_{pk}, r_{pk})$ // Combiner's secret key

  $pk \leftarrow (\mathsf{com}_{pk},\ pk_\mathrm{t},\ pk_\mathrm{cs})$

  output $(pk,\ (sk_1, \ldots, sk_n),\ sk_\mathrm{c},\ sk_\mathrm{t}))$

- $\underline{\mathcal{S}.Sign}(sk_i, m, C) \rightarrow \delta_i$: output $\delta_i \xleftarrow{\$} \mathcal{ATS}.Sign(sk_i, m, C)$.

  Here $C \subseteq [n]$ is a set of size t of participating signers. Recall that in some schemes $\mathcal{ATS}.Sign$ is an algorithm run by the signing parties, while in other schemes $\mathcal{ATS}.Sign$ is an interactive protocol between the Combiner and the signing parties. Either way, the end result in that the Combiner obtains signature shares $\{\delta_i\}_{i \in C}$.

- $\underline{\mathcal{S}.Combine}(sk_\mathrm{c}, m, C, \{\delta_i\}_{i \in C}) \rightarrow \sigma$: with $sk_\mathrm{c} = (pk', pk_\mathrm{t}, sk_\mathrm{cs}, t, \mathsf{com}_{pk}, r_{pk})$, the Combiner does

  $\sigma_\mathrm{m} \xleftarrow{\$} \mathcal{ATS}.Combine(pk', m, C, \{\delta_i\}_{i \in C})$

  $ct \leftarrow \mathcal{PKE}.Encrypt(pk_\mathrm{t}, \sigma_\mathrm{m}; r)$, where r is a fresh nonce

  use the prover P to generate a proof π for the relation:

$$\mathcal{R}\Big((\mathsf{com}_{pk}, pk_\mathrm{t}, m, ct)\ ;\ (\sigma_\mathrm{m}, r, r_{pk}, pk')\Big) = \text{true} \quad \text{iff} \quad \left\{ \begin{array}{l} ct = \mathcal{PKE}.Encrypt(pk_\mathrm{t}, \sigma_\mathrm{m}; r), \\ \mathcal{ATS}.Verify(pk', m, \sigma_\mathrm{m}) = 1, \\ \mathcal{COM}.Verify(pk', r_{pk}, \mathsf{com}_{pk}) = 1 \end{array} \right\} \tag{3}$$

  $tg \xleftarrow{\$} \mathcal{SIG}.Sign(sk_\mathrm{cs}, (m, ct, \pi))$ // sign with Combiner's signing key

  output the TAPS signature $\sigma \leftarrow (ct, \pi, tg)$

- $\underline{\mathcal{S}.Verify}\Big(pk = (\mathsf{com}_{pk}, pk_\mathrm{t}, pk_\mathrm{cs}),\ m,\ \sigma = (ct, \pi, tg)\Big) \rightarrow \{0, 1\}$: accept if
  - π is a valid proof for the relation $\mathcal{R}$ in (3) with respect to the statement $(\mathsf{com}_{pk}, pk_\mathrm{t}, m, ct)$, and
  - $\mathcal{SIG}.Verify(pk_\mathrm{cs},\ (m, ct, \pi),\ tg) = 1$.

- $\underline{\mathcal{S}.Trace}\Big(sk_\mathrm{t} = (pk', sk'_\mathrm{t}, pk_\mathrm{cs}),\ m,\ \sigma = (ct, \pi, tg)\Big) \rightarrow C$:

  if $\mathcal{SIG}.Verify(pk_\mathrm{cs}, (m, ct, \pi), tg) \neq 1$, output fail and stop

  set $\sigma_\mathrm{m} \leftarrow \mathcal{PKE}.Decrypt(sk'_\mathrm{t}, ct)$, if fail then output fail and stop

  otherwise, output $\mathcal{ATS}.Trace(pk', m, \sigma_\mathrm{m})$

Fig. 4. The generic TAPS scheme $\mathcal{S}$

proof system (P, V) *is an argument of knowledge and HVZK, the commitment scheme* $\mathcal{COM}$ *is hiding and binding, and the signature scheme* $\mathcal{SIG}$ *is strongly unforgeable.*

We provide concrete security bounds in the lemmas below. First, let us explain the need for the Combiner's signature in Step 4 of $\mathcal{S}$.*Combine.*

Remark 7. Observe that the privacy games in Figs. 2 and 3 give the adversary a tracing oracle for any message-signature pair of its choice. In the context of our construction this enables the adversary to mount a chosen ciphertext attack on the encryption scheme $\mathcal{PKE}$. Yet, Theorem 1 only requires that $\mathcal{PKE}$ be semantically secure, not chosen ciphertext secure. The need for a weak security requirement on $\mathcal{PKE}$ will become important in the next section where we construct more efficient TAPS schemes. To secure against the chosen ciphertext attack, we rely on the Combiner's signature included in every TAPS signature. It ensures that the adversary cannot call the tracing oracle with anything other than a TAPS signature output by the Combiner.

We now prove Theorem 1. The proof is captured in the following three lemmas.

Lemma 1. *The generic* TAPS *scheme* $\mathcal{S}$ *is unforgeable and accountable, as in Definition 6, assuming the accountable threshold scheme* $\mathcal{ATS}$ *is secure, the non-interactive proof system* (P, V) *is an argument of knowledge, and the commitment scheme is binding. Concretely, for every adversary* $\mathcal{A}$ *that attacks* $\mathcal{S}$ *there exists adversaries* $\mathcal{B}_1, \mathcal{B}_2$*, that run in about the same time as* $\mathcal{A}$*, such that*

$$\mathbf{Adv}^{\mathrm{forg}}_{\mathcal{A},\mathcal{S}}(\lambda) \leq \left(\mathbf{Adv}^{\mathrm{forg}}_{\mathcal{B}_1,\mathcal{ATS}}(\lambda) + \mathbf{Adv}^{\mathrm{bind}}_{\mathcal{B}_2,\mathcal{COM}}(\lambda)\right) \cdot q(\lambda) + \kappa(\lambda) \tag{4}$$

where κ *and* q *are the knowledge error and tightness of the proof system from Definition 4.*

We provide the proof of Lemma 1 in the full version of the paper.

Lemma 2. *The generic* TAPS *scheme* $\mathcal{S}$ *is private against the public assuming the non-interactive proof system* (P, V) *is HVZK, the public-key encryption scheme* $\mathcal{PKE}$ *is semantically secure, the commitment scheme* $\mathcal{COM}$ *is hiding, and the signature scheme* $\mathcal{SIG}$ *is strongly unforgeable. Concretely, for every adversary* $\mathcal{A}$ *that attacks* $\mathcal{S}$ *there exist adversaries* $\mathcal{B}_1, \mathcal{B}_2, \mathcal{B}_3$*, that run in about the same time as* $\mathcal{A}$*, such that*

$$\mathbf{Adv}^{\mathrm{priv1}}_{\mathcal{A},\mathcal{S}}(\lambda) \leq 2\Big(\mathbf{Adv}^{\mathrm{eufcma}}_{\mathcal{B}_1,\mathcal{SIG}}(\lambda) + \mathbf{Adv}^{\mathrm{indcpa}}_{\mathcal{B}_2,\mathcal{PKE}}(\lambda) + Q \cdot \mathbf{Adv}^{\mathrm{hvzk}}_{\mathcal{B}_3,(P,V)}(\lambda) + \epsilon(\lambda)\Big) \tag{5}$$

where $\epsilon(\lambda)$ *is the hiding statistical distance of the commitment scheme* $\mathcal{COM}$ *and* Q *is the number of signature queries from* $\mathcal{A}$*.*

We provide the proof of Lemma 2 in the full version of the paper.

Lemma 3. *The generic* TAPS *scheme $\mathcal{S}$ is private against signers assuming the non-interactive proof system (P, V) is HVZK, the public-key encryption scheme $\mathcal{PKE}$ is semantically secure, and the signature scheme $\mathcal{SIG}$ is strongly unforgeable. Concretely, for every adversary $\mathcal{A}$ that attacks $\mathcal{S}$ there exist adversaries $\mathcal{B}_1, \mathcal{B}_2, \mathcal{B}_3$, that run in about the same time as $\mathcal{A}$, such that*

$$\mathbf{Adv}^{\mathrm{priv2}}_{\mathcal{A},\mathcal{S}}(\lambda) \le 2\Big(\mathbf{Adv}^{\mathrm{eufcma}}_{\mathcal{B}_1,\mathcal{SIG}}(\lambda) + \mathbf{Adv}^{\mathrm{indcpa}}_{\mathcal{B}_2,\mathcal{PKE}}(\lambda) + Q \cdot \mathbf{Adv}^{\mathrm{hvzk}}_{\mathcal{B}_3,(P,V)}(\lambda)\Big). \quad (6)$$

The proof of Lemma 3 is almost identical to the proof of Lemma 2.

5 An Efficient TAPS from Schnorr Signatures

In this section we construct a secure TAPS in the random oracle model, based on the Schnorr signature scheme. The construction is far more efficient than applying the generic construction from the previous section to a Schnorr ATS. We obtain this improvement by taking advantage of the algebraic properties of the Schnorr signature scheme to vastly simplify the zero knowledge statement that the Combiner needs to prove when making a signature.

The construction makes use of a group $\mathbb{G}$ of prime order q in which the Decision Diffie-Hellman problem is hard. Let g, h be independent generators of $\mathbb{G}$. We also require a hash function $H : \mathcal{PK} \times \mathbb{G} \times \mathcal{M} \to \mathbb{Z}_q$ that will be modeled as a random oracle, where $\mathcal{PK}$ is a space of public keys.

5.1 A Review of the Schnorr ATS Schemes

Let us first review the (uncompressed) Schnorr signature scheme [55]:

- *KeyGen*(λ): $sk \xleftarrow{\$} \mathbb{Z}_q$, $pk \leftarrow g^{sk}$, output (sk, pk).
- *Sign*(sk, m): $r \xleftarrow{\$} \mathbb{Z}_q$, $R \leftarrow g^r$, $c \leftarrow H(pk, R, m) \in \mathbb{Z}_q$, $z \leftarrow r + sk \cdot c \in \mathbb{Z}_q$, output $\sigma \leftarrow (R, z)$.
- *Verify*(pk, m, σ): compute $c \leftarrow H(pk, R, m) \in \mathbb{Z}_q$ and accept if $g^z = pk^c \cdot R$.

Our Schnorr TAPS builds upon an existing Schnorr accountable threshold signature (ATS), such as [49,50,53][1]. Using our terminology, these ATS schemes operate as follows:

- *KeyGen*(λ, n, t): Choose $sk_1, \ldots, sk_n \xleftarrow{\$} \mathbb{Z}_q$ and set $pk_i \leftarrow g^{sk_i}$ for $i \in [n]$. Set $pk \leftarrow (t, pk_1, \ldots, pk_n)$ and $sk \leftarrow (sk_1, \ldots, sk_n)$. Output (pk, sk).
  In an ATS, the Combiner key sk_{c} and the tracing key sk_{t} are equal to pk.
- *Sign*(sk_i, m, C): An interactive protocol between the Combiner and signer i. At the end of the protocol the Combiner has $\delta_i = (R_i, z_i) \in \mathbb{G} \times \mathbb{Z}_q$, where

[1] Technically, these are multisignature schemes, but as noted in Remark 6, they can easily be made into an ATS.

(R_i, z_i) satisfies $g^{z_i} = pk_i^c \cdot R_i$ for $c \leftarrow H(pk, R, m) \in \mathbb{Z}_q$. Here $R \in \mathbb{G}$ is defined[2] as $R := \prod_{i \in C} R_i$. This R is obtained from the Combiner's interaction with all the signers participating in the current signature process.

- *Combine*$(pk, m, C, \{\delta_i\}_{i \in C})$: Abort if $|C| \neq t$. Parse δ_i as $\delta_i = (R_i, z_i)$, set $z \leftarrow \sum_{i \in C} z_i \in \mathbb{Z}_q$ and $R \leftarrow \prod_{i \in C} R_i$. Output $\sigma \leftarrow (R, z, C)$.

  One can confirm that (R, z) is a valid Schnorr signature on m with respect to the public key $pk_C \leftarrow \prod_{i \in C} pk_i$.
- *Verify*(pk, m, σ): parse $pk = (t, pk_1, \ldots, pk_n)$ and $\sigma = (R, z, C)$. Accept if $|C| = t$ and the Schnorr verification algorithm accepts the triple (pk_C, m, σ') where $\sigma' \leftarrow (R, z)$ and $pk_C \leftarrow \prod_{i \in C} pk_i$. Here the challenge c is computed as $c \leftarrow H(pk, R, m) \in \mathbb{Z}_q$ and the algorithm accepts if $|C| = t$ and $g^z = pk_C^c \cdot R$.
- *Trace*(pk, m, σ): parse $\sigma = (R, z, C)$, run *Verify*(pk, m, σ), the verification algorithm from the previous bullet, and if valid, output C; else output fail.

The Schnorr ATS papers [49,50,53] describe different ways to instantiate the *Sign* protocol. They prove security of the resulting Schnorr ATS scheme using differing security models. Here we treat the *Sign* protocol as a black box, and rely on the following assumption.

Assumption 1. *The Schnorr ATS outlined above is a secure ATS scheme, as in Definition 8.*

5.2 An Efficient Schnorr TAPS

We next construct our Schnorr-based TAPS scheme. If we were to follow the generic construction from Sect. 4, the combiner would encrypt the entire Schnorr signature (R, z), and would need to produce a zero knowledge proof for a complicated relation. In particular, it would need to prove that an encrypted Schnorr signature is valid, which is difficult to prove in zero knowledge efficiently. However, observe that in the public's view, R is a product of random elements in $\mathbb{G}$, and as such, is independent of the quorum set C. Therefore, R can be revealed in the TAPS signature in the clear without compromising the privacy of C in the public's view. Even an adversary who has all the signing keys learns nothing about C from R. We only need to encrypt the quantity $z \in \mathbb{Z}_q$. The challenge then is to develop an efficient zero knowledge proof that the cleartext R and an encrypted z are a valid Schnorr signature with respect to an encrypted quorum set C.

The Scheme. Our Schnorr TAPS is built from any Schnorr ATS that operates as described in Sect. 5.1 and satisfies Assumption 1. In addition, we use a single-party (non-threshold) signature scheme $\mathcal{SIG} = (KeyGen, Sign, Verify)$.

[2] In some Schnorr ATS schemes (e.g., [53]) this R is defined as $R := \prod_{i \in C} R_i^{\gamma_i}$, for public scalars $\{\gamma_i \in \mathbb{Z}_q\}_{i \in C}$. We assume that all these scalars are set to 1, but our constructions can easily accommodate any scalars.

The complete TAPS scheme is presented in Fig. 5. The combine algorithm in Step 4 generates a zero-knowledge proof for the relation $\mathcal{R}_S$ in Fig. 6. We present two efficient proof systems for this relation in Sects. 5.3 and 5.4.

In Step 4 of the tracing algorithm there is a need to find a set $C \subseteq [n]$ of size t that satisfies a certain property. If n is logarithmic in the security parameter, then this set C can be found by exhaustive search over all t-size subsets of $[n]$. For larger n, we explain how to find C efficiently in Sects. 5.3 and 5.4.

Correctness. The scheme is correct assuming the Schnorr ATS scheme, the signature scheme $\mathcal{SIG}$, and proof system for $\mathcal{R}_S$ are correct.

Security. We next prove security, privacy, and accountability.

Theorem 2. *The Schnorr* TAPS *scheme is unforgeable, accountable, and private, assuming that the underlying Schnorr ATS is secure (Assumption 1), the signature scheme $\mathcal{SIG}$ is strongly unforgeable, DDH holds in $\mathbb{G}$, and the non-interactive proof system (P, V) for $\mathcal{R}_S$ is an HVZK argument of knowledge.*

The proof of Theorem 2 is presented in the following three lemmas, where we also provide concrete security bounds.

Lemma 4. *The Schnorr* TAPS *scheme is unforgeable and accountable, as in Definition 6, assuming the underlying Schnorr ATS is secure, as in Definition 8, and the non-interactive proof system (P, V) for $\mathcal{R}_S$ is an argument of knowledge. Concretely, for every adversary $\mathcal{A}$ that attacks* TAPS, *there exists an adversary $\mathcal{B}$ that runs in about the same time as $\mathcal{A}$ such that*

$$\mathbf{Adv}^{\text{forg}}_{\mathcal{A},\mathcal{S}}(\lambda) \leq \left(\mathbf{Adv}^{\text{forg}}_{\mathcal{B},\mathcal{ATS}}(\lambda)\right) \cdot q(\lambda) + \kappa(\lambda) \tag{7}$$

where κ and q are the knowledge error and tightness of the proof system.

We provide the proof of Lemma 4 in the full version of the paper.

Lemma 5. *The Schnorr* TAPS *scheme is private against the public, as in Definition 7, assuming DDH holds in $\mathbb{G}$, the non-interactive proof system (P, V) for $\mathcal{R}_S$ is HVZK, and the signature scheme $\mathcal{SIG}$ is strongly unforgeable. Concretely, for every adversary $\mathcal{A}$ that attacks $\mathcal{S}$ there exist adversaries $\mathcal{B}_1, \mathcal{B}_2, \mathcal{B}_3$ that run in about the same time as $\mathcal{A}$ such that*

$$\mathbf{Adv}^{\text{priv1}}_{\mathcal{A},\mathcal{S}}(\lambda) \leq 2\Big(\mathbf{Adv}^{\text{eufcma}}_{\mathcal{B}_1,\mathcal{SIG}}(\lambda) + Q \cdot \mathbf{Adv}^{\text{hvzk}}_{\mathcal{B}_2,(P,V)}(\lambda) \; + (Q+1) \cdot \mathbf{Adv}^{\text{ddh}}_{\mathcal{B}_3,\mathbb{G}}(\lambda)\Big) \tag{8}$$

where Q is the number of signature queries from $\mathcal{A}$.

We provide the proof of Lemma 5 in the full version of the paper.

Lemma 6. *The Schnorr scheme is private against signers, as in Definition 7, assuming DDH holds in $\mathbb{G}$, the non-interactive proof system (P, V) for $\mathcal{R}_S$ is HVZK, and the signature scheme $\mathcal{SIG}$ is strongly unforgeable.*

The proof of Lemma 6 is mostly the same as the proof of Lemma 5.

- $\mathcal{S}.KeyGen(\lambda, n, t)$: using the independent generators g and h of $\mathbb{G}$ do:
  1: Run the Schnorr ATS *KeyGen* procedure from Section 5.1. That is, choose $sk_1, \ldots, sk_n \xleftarrow{\$} \mathbb{Z}_q$ and set $pk_i \leftarrow g^{sk_i}$ for $i \in [n]$.
  Set $pk' \leftarrow (pk_1, \ldots, pk_n)$
  2: Encrypt t with ElGamal: $\psi \xleftarrow{\$} \mathbb{Z}_q$ and $(T_0, T_1) \leftarrow (g^{\psi},\ g^t h^{\psi})$
  3: Generate $(sk_{\text{cs}}, pk_{\text{cs}}) \xleftarrow{\$} \mathcal{SIG}.KeyGen(\lambda)$ and $sk_{\text{e}} \xleftarrow{\$} \mathbb{Z}_q$
  4: $sk_{\text{t}} \leftarrow (pk', sk_{\text{e}}, pk_{\text{cs}})$ and $pk_{\text{t}} \leftarrow g^{sk_{\text{e}}} \in \mathbb{G}$ // the tracing secret key
  5: $sk_{\text{c}} \leftarrow (pk', pk_{\text{t}}, sk_{\text{cs}}, t, \psi)$ // the combiner's secret key
  6: $pk \leftarrow (pk', pk_{\text{t}}, pk_{\text{cs}}, T_0, T_1)$ // the verifier's public key
  7: Output $(pk,\ (sk_1, \ldots, sk_n),\ sk_{\text{c}},\ sk_{\text{t}}))$
- $\underline{\mathcal{S}.Sign}(sk_i, m, C)$: Run the Schnorr ATS *Sign* procedure from Section 5.1 so that the Combiner obtains a signature share $\delta_i \xleftarrow{\$} (R_i, z_i) \in \mathbb{G} \times \mathbb{Z}_q$.
- $\underline{\mathcal{S}.Combine}(sk_{\text{c}}, m, C, \{\delta_i\}_{i \in C})$: With $\delta_i = (R_i, z_i)$, the coordinator does:
  1: $R \leftarrow \prod_{i \in C} R_i, \quad z \leftarrow \sum_{i \in C} z_i \in \mathbb{Z}_q, \quad c \leftarrow H(pk, R, m) \in \mathbb{Z}_q$
  // we know that $g^z = \left[\prod_{i \in C} pk_i\right]^c \cdot R$.
  2: Encrypt z with ElGamal: $\rho \xleftarrow{\$} \mathbb{Z}_q, \quad ct := (c_0, c_1) \leftarrow (g^{\rho},\ g^z pk_{\text{t}}^{\rho})$.
  3: Set $(b_1, \ldots, b_n) \in \{0,1\}^n$, such that $b_i = 1$ iff $i \in C$
  // then $g^z = \left[\prod_{i=1}^{n} (pk_i)^{b_i}\right]^c \cdot R$.
  4: Generate a zero knowledge proof π for the relation $\mathcal{R}_S$ listed in Figure 6. We present two efficient non-interactive proof systems for this relation in Sections 5.3 and 5.4.
  5: $tg \xleftarrow{\$} \mathcal{SIG}.Sign(sk_{\text{cs}}, (m, R, ct, \pi))$ // sign with Combiner's key
  6: Output the TAPS signature $\sigma \leftarrow (R, ct, \pi, tg)$.
- $\underline{\mathcal{S}.Verify}(pk,\ m,\ \sigma)$: Let $\sigma = (R, ct, \pi, tg)$ where $ct = (c_0, c_1)$.
  Parse $pk = (pk', pk_{\text{t}}, pk_{\text{cs}}, T_0, T_1)$ and set $c \leftarrow H(pk, R, m)$. Accept if:
  - $\mathcal{SIG}.Verify(pk_{\text{cs}}, (m, R, ct, \pi), tg) = 1$, and
  - π is a valid proof for the relation $\mathcal{R}_S$ in Figure 6 with respect to the statement $(g, h, pk', pk_{\text{t}}, T_0, T_1, R, c, ct = (c_0, c_1))$.
- $\underline{\mathcal{S}.Trace}(sk_{\text{t}}, m, \sigma)$: Parse $sk_{\text{t}} = \left(pk' = (pk_1, \ldots, pk_n), sk_{\text{e}}, pk_{\text{cs}}\right)$ and do:
  1: Parse σ as (R, ct, π, tg) and $ct = (c_0, c_1)$. Set $c \leftarrow H(pk, R, m)$.
  2: If $\mathcal{SIG}.Verify(pk_{\text{cs}}, (m, R, ct, \pi), tg) \neq 1$, output fail and stop.
  3: ElGamal decrypt $ct = (c_0, c_1)$ as $g^{(z')} \leftarrow c_1 / c_0{}^{sk_{\text{e}}} \in \mathbb{G}$.
  4: Find a set $C \subseteq [n]$, where $|C| = t$ and $g^{(z')} = R \cdot (\prod_{i \in C} pk_i)^c$.
  This equality implies that (R, z') is a valid Schnorr signature on m with respect to the public key $pk_C \leftarrow \prod_{i \in C} pk_i$.
  5: If such a set $C \subseteq [n]$ is found, output C. Otherwise, output fail.

Fig. 5. The Schnorr TAPS scheme

$$\mathcal{R}_S = \Big\{(g, h, pk' = (pk_1, \dots, pk_n), pk_t, T_0, T_1, R, c, ct = (c_0, c_1)) \ ; \ (z, \rho, \psi, b_1, \dots, b_n)\Big\}$$

$$\begin{aligned}
\text{iff} \quad &(1) \quad g^z = \Big[\prod_{i=1}^{n} (pk_i)^{b_i}\Big]^c \cdot R, \\
&(2) \quad c_0 = g^\rho \quad \text{and} \quad c_1 = g^z \cdot pk_t^\rho, \\
&(3) \quad T_0 = g^\psi \quad \text{and} \quad T_1 = g^{\sum_{i=1}^n b_i} \cdot h^\psi, \\
&(4) \quad b_i(1 - b_i) = 0 \qquad \text{for } i = 1, \dots, n \qquad (\text{i.e. } b_i \in \{0, 1\}).
\end{aligned}$$

Fig. 6. The relation $\mathcal{R}_S$ used in the *Combine* algorithm of the Schnorr TAPS. Condition (1) verifies that (R, z) is a valid signature for m assuming $c = H(pk, R, m)$; (2) verifies that (c_0, c_1) is an ElGamal encryption of z using the tracing public key pk_t; (3) verifies that the quorum C contains t signers; and (4) verifies that each b_i is in $\{0, 1\}$. Here g and h are public random generators of $\mathbb{G}$.

5.3 A Sigma Protocol Proof for $\mathcal{R}_S$

It remains to construct an efficient non-interactive zero knowledge argument of knowledge for the relation $\mathcal{R}_S$ from Fig. 6. In this section we construct a Sigma protocol, and in the next section we construct a protocol using Bulletproofs. We describe these as interactive protocols, but they can be made non-interactive using the Fiat-Shamir transform [3,33].

Let $g, h, h_1, \dots, h_n \in \mathbb{G}$ be independent random generators of $\mathbb{G}$. To prove knowledge of a witness for the relation $\mathcal{R}_S$ from Fig. 6 we use the following approach:

Protocol $S1$:

1: The prover chooses $\gamma \xleftarrow{\$} \mathbb{Z}_q$ and commits to its bits $(b_1, \dots, b_n) \in \{0, 1\}^n$ as

$$\big(\ v_0 \leftarrow g^\gamma, \quad v_1 \leftarrow g^{b_1} h_1^\gamma, \quad \dots, \quad v_n \leftarrow g^{b_n} h_n^\gamma\ \big) \in \mathbb{G}^{n+1}$$

It sends $(v_0, v_1, \dots, v_n)$ to the verifier. Observe that for $i \in [n]$ the pair (v_0, v_i) is an ElGamal encryption of b_i with respect to the public key h_i. The term v_0 will be used for efficient tracing.

2: The verifier samples a challenge $\alpha \xleftarrow{\$} \mathbb{Z}_q$ and sends α to the prover.

3: The prover computes $\phi_i \leftarrow \alpha^i \gamma (1 - b_i) \in \mathbb{Z}_q$ for $i \in [n]$.

4: Finally, the prover uses a Sigma protocol to prove knowledge of a witness $(z, \rho, \psi, \gamma, b_1, \dots, b_n, \phi_1, \dots, \phi_n)$ for the relation $\mathcal{R}_{S1}$ in Fig. 7.

We present the concrete steps for the 3-round Sigma protocol for the relation $\mathcal{R}_{S1}$ used in Step 4 in the full version, where we also show the TAPS signature obtained from this protocol. After applying the Fiat-Shamir transform to Protocol $S1$, the resulting proof π for the relation $\mathcal{R}_S$ from Fig. 6 contains $n + 1$ group elements and $2n + 5$ elements in $\mathbb{Z}_q$.

$$\mathcal{R}_{S1} := \Big\{(g, h, h_1, \ldots, h_n, pk_1, \ldots, pk_n, pk_t, T_0, T_1, R, c, ct = (c_0, c_1), v_0, v_1, \ldots, v_n, \alpha) \; ;$$
$$(z, \rho, \psi, \gamma, b_1, \ldots, b_n, \phi_1, \ldots, \phi_n)\Big\} \text{ where}$$

$$(1) \quad g^z = R \cdot \prod_{i=1}^{n} (pk_i)^{c \cdot b_i}$$

$$(2) \quad c_0 = g^\rho \quad \text{and} \quad c_1 = pk_t^\rho \cdot g^z$$

$$(3) \quad T_0 = g^\psi \quad \text{and} \quad T_1 = g^{\sum_{i=1}^n b_i} \cdot h^\psi$$

$$(4) \quad v_0 = g^\gamma \quad \text{and} \quad v_i = g^{b_i} h_i^\gamma \text{ for } i \in [n] \quad \text{and} \quad \prod_{i=1}^{n} v_i^{\alpha^i(1-b_i)} = \prod_{i=1}^{n} h_i^{\phi_i}$$

Fig. 7. The relation $\mathcal{R}_{S1}$. Equations (1), (2), and (3) are the same as in the relation $\mathcal{R}_S$ in Figure 6. Equation (4) proves that $b_i(1-b_i) = 0$ for $i \in [n]$. As usual, both the prover and verifier have $c \leftarrow H(pk, R, m)$. The prover computes the witness element $\phi_1, \ldots, \phi_n \in \mathbb{Z}_q$ on its own as $\phi_i \leftarrow \alpha^i \gamma(1-b_i)$.

Theorem 3. *Let $\mathbb{G}$ be a group of prime order q. If the Decision Diffie-Hellman (DDH) assumption holds in $\mathbb{G}$, and n/q is negligible, then Protocol $S1$ is an HVZK argument of knowledge for the relation $\mathcal{R}_S$ from Fig. 6.*

We provide the proof for Theorem 3 in the full version.

Remark 8 (***Efficient tracing***). Recall that the tracing algorithm in Fig. 5 requires the tracer to find a set $C \subseteq [n]$ of size t such that $g^{(z')} = (\prod_{i \in C} pk_i)^c \cdot R$. When using Protocol $S1$, the tracing algorithm can efficiently find this set $C \subseteq [n]$ by decrypting the Combiner's ElGamal commitment $(v_0, v_1, \ldots, v_n) \in \mathbb{G}^{n+1}$ to the bits $b_1, \ldots, b_n \in \{0, 1\}$ that define C. To see how, let us extend algorithm *KeyGen* in Fig. 5 by adding the following steps:

- choose $\tau_i \xleftarrow{\$} \mathbb{Z}_q$ and set $h_i \leftarrow g^{\tau_i}$ for $i \in [n]$
- $aug\text{-}sk_t \leftarrow (sk_t,\ \tau_1, \ldots, \tau_n)$ // augmented tracing key
- $aug\text{-}sk_c \leftarrow (sk_c,\ h_1, \ldots, h_n)$ // augmented Combiner's key
- $aug\text{-}pk \leftarrow (pk,\ h_1, \ldots, h_n)$ // augmented public key

The Combiner and verifier use $h_1, \ldots, h_n$ in their augmented keys to produce and verify the proof for the relation $\mathcal{R}_S$ using Protocol $S1$. The proof contains an ElGamal commitment $(v_0, v_1, \ldots, v_n)$ to the bits $b_1, \ldots, b_n$. The tracing algorithm can obtain $b_1, \ldots, b_n \in \{0, 1\}$ by decrypting the ElGamal ciphertexts (v_0, v_i) for $i \in [n]$ using the secret keys $\tau_1, \ldots, \tau_n \in \mathbb{Z}_q$. Soundness of Protocol $S1$ ensures that the resulting bits define the correct quorum set C. Note that *aug-pk* contains a total of $2n + 4$ group elements.

5.4 A Bulletproofs Protocol Proof for $\mathcal{R}_S$

The Sigma protocol for the relation $\mathcal{R}_S$ from Fig. 6 may be adequate for many real-world settings where the number of allowed signers is small. However, if a large number of parties n is used, then the resulting proof size may be too large. We can shrink the proof using an argument system that produces shorter proofs (e.g., using a zk-SNARK). This approach raises two difficulties. First, computing the proof will be slow because the exponentiations in Fig. 6 would need to be implemented explicitly in the zk-SNARK relation. Second, we would lose the efficient tracing algorithm from Remark 8.

We can avoid both issues using the Bulletproofs proof system [20,22] or its treatment as a compressed Sigma protocol in [2]. First, the exponentiations in Fig. 6 are handled efficiently. Second, we can retain efficient tracing with a much shorter TAPS signature compared to the Sigma protocol in Sect. 5.3.

Let $\mathbb{G}$ be a group of prime order q, let $a_1, \ldots, a_n$ be generators of $\mathbb{G}$, and $\mathbf{a} := (a_1, \ldots, a_n) \in \mathbb{G}^n$. For $\mathbf{w} \in \mathbb{Z}_q^n$ we write $\mathbf{a}^{\mathbf{w}} := \prod_{i=1}^{n} a_i^{w_i} \in \mathbb{G}$.

Recall that bulletproofs is an HVZK proof system that can prove knowledge of a satisfying witness $\mathbf{w} \in \mathbb{Z}_q^n$ for the relation

$$\mathcal{R}_{\mathrm{BP}} := \big\{(P,\ \mathbf{a} \in \mathbb{G}^n,\ u \in \mathbb{G})\ ;\ \mathbf{w} \in \mathbb{Z}_q^n\big\} \qquad \text{iff } P(\mathbf{w}) = 1 \text{ and } \mathbf{a}^{\mathbf{w}} = u,$$

where P is a *rank one constraint system* (R1CS), meaning that P is a triple of matrices $A, B, C \in \mathbb{Z}_q^{\ell \times n}$ and $P(\mathbf{w}) = 1$ iff $(A\mathbf{w}) \circ (B\mathbf{w}) = C\mathbf{w}$. The $\circ$ operator denotes the Hadamard product (component-wise product) of two vectors in $\mathbb{Z}_q^n$. The program P is said to have ℓ constraints over n variables. We represent the program P in $\mathcal{R}_{\mathrm{BP}}$ using R1CS instead of an arithmetic circuit because R1CS is more convenient in our settings: it more directly captures the relations we need to prove.

The Bulletproofs proof is succinct, containing only $2\lceil \log_2(n + \ell) \rceil$ group elements and two elements in $\mathbb{Z}_q$. For a convincing prover P^*, the Bulletproofs extractor outputs some $\mathbf{w} \in \mathbb{Z}_q^n$ such that either (i) $\mathbf{w}$ is a valid witness for $\mathcal{R}_{\mathrm{BP}}$, or (ii) $\mathbf{w}$ is a non-trivial relation among the generators[3] $\mathbf{a} \in \mathbb{G}^n$, namely $\mathbf{a}^{\mathbf{w}} = 1$. If the discrete log problem in $\mathbb{G}$ is difficult, and $\mathbf{a}$ are random generators of $\mathbb{G}$, then an efficient prover cannot cause (ii) to happen. Then bulletproofs is an argument of knowledge for $\mathcal{R}_{\mathrm{BP}}$.

Shorter Proofs with Efficient Tracing. In the full version of the paper we show that Bullerptoofs gives an efficient *logarithmic size* proof for the relation $\mathcal{R}_S$ from Fig. 6. However, in doing so we lose the ability to efficiently trace a signature using the tracing key. Recall that the tracing algorithm in Fig. 5 needs to find a set $C \subseteq [n]$ of size t such that $g^{(z')} = (\prod_{i \in C} pk_i)^c \cdot R$. This can be done, in principal, by trying all sets $C \subseteq [n]$ of size t, assuming $\binom{n}{t}$ is polynomial in the security parameter λ. However, we want a more efficient tracing algorithm.

We can restore efficient tracing for larger n and t in a way similar to Remark 8. Let $(b_1, \ldots, b_n) \in \{0,1\}^n$ be the characteristic vector of the quorum of signers $C \subseteq [n]$. In Sect. 5.3 we encrypted every bit b_i on its own, and added the $n+1$ group elements $(v_0, \ldots, v_n)$ to the signature. The tracing algorithm could then

[3] This relation might include additional random generators of $\mathbb{G}$.

decrypt each of the n ElGamal ciphertexts (v_0, v_i), for $i \in [n]$, and efficiently recover the quorum set C.

Using Bulletproofs we can compress the commitment to the bits $(b_1, \ldots, b_n)$ by committing to a *batch* of bits at a time using a single ElGamal ciphertext. We will then need to extend the Bulletproofs relation to verify that every batch commitment is well formed.

To see how, let us fix a batch size e, say $e := 40$. For simplicity suppose that e divides n. We extend algorithm *KeyGen* in Fig. 5 by adding the following steps:

- for $i \in [n/e]$: choose $\tau_i \xleftarrow{\$} \mathbb{Z}_q$ and set $h_i \leftarrow g^{\tau_i} \in \mathbb{G}$
- $\textit{aug-sk}_t \leftarrow (sk_t,\ \tau_1, \ldots, \tau_{n/e})$ // augmented tracing key
- $\textit{aug-sk}_c \leftarrow (sk_c,\ h_1, \ldots, h_{n/e})$ // augmented Combiner's key
- $\textit{aug-pk} \leftarrow (pk,\ h_1, \ldots, h_{n/e})$ // augmented public key

Next, we augment the prover for the relation $\mathcal{R}_S$ from Fig. 6 by adding a step 0 where the prover does:

- step (i): Divide the n bits into (n/e) buckets $0 \le B_1, \ldots, B_{n/e} < 2^e$ as:

$$\begin{cases} B_1 \leftarrow b_1 + 2b_2 + 4b_3 + \ldots + 2^e b_e \in \mathbb{Z}_q, \\ B_2 \leftarrow b_{e+1} + 2b_{e+2} + \ldots + 2^e b_{2e} \in \mathbb{Z}_q, \\ \vdots \\ B_{n/e} \leftarrow b_{n-e+1} + 2b_{n-e+2} + \ldots + 2^e b_n \in \mathbb{Z}_q. \end{cases}$$

- step (ii): Choose a random $\gamma \xleftarrow{\$} \mathbb{Z}_q$ and compute

$$\left(\ v_0 \leftarrow g^{\gamma},\quad v_1 \leftarrow g^{B_1} h_1^{\gamma},\quad \ldots,\quad v_{n/e} \leftarrow g^{B_{n/e}} h_{n/e}^{\gamma}\ \right) \in \mathbb{G}^{(n/e)+1}.$$

Send $(v_0, v_1, \ldots, v_{n/e})$ to the verifier. Observe that for $i \in [n/e]$ the pair (v_0, v_i) is an ElGamal encryption of g^{B_i} with respect to the public key h_i.

Finally, we augment the relation $\mathcal{R}_S$ to verify that $(v_0, v_1, \ldots, v_{n/e})$ were constructed correctly, but this has only a small impact on the size of the proof. The final TAPS signature is expanded by $(n/e)+1$ group elements $(v_0, v_1, \ldots, v_{n/e})$.

When the tracing algorithm is given a signature to trace, it can obtain $g^{B_1}, \ldots, g^{B_{n/e}} \in \mathbb{G}$ by decrypting the ElGamal ciphertexts (v_0, v_i) for $i \in [n/e]$ using the secret keys $\tau_1, \ldots, \tau_{n/e} \in \mathbb{Z}_q$ in the tracing key $\textit{aug-sk}_t$. Next, the tracing algorithm computes the discrete log base g of these group elements to obtain $B_1, \ldots, B_{n/e} \in \mathbb{Z}_q$. Since each B_i is in $\{0, 1, \ldots, 2^e - 1\}$, each discrete log computation can be done with about $2^{e/2}$ group operations.

Taking $e := 40$ gives a reasonable amount of time for computing all of $B_1, \ldots, B_{n/e} \in \mathbb{Z}_q$ from $g^{B_1}, \ldots, g^{B_{n/e}}$. The tracing algorithm then computes $b_1, \ldots, b_n \in \{0, 1\}$ from $B_1, \ldots, B_{n/e}$, and this reveals the required quorum set C. Soundness of the argument system for the relation $\mathcal{R}_S$ ensures that the resulting bits $b_1, \ldots, b_n$ define the correct quorum set $C \subseteq [n]$.

6 Extensions

Shorter Public Keys. While the size of the public key in our Schnorr construction grows linearly in n, there are several ways to shrink the public key. First, the public key can be replaced by a short binding commitment to the linear-size public key, and the full public key could be included in every signature. This shrinks the public key at the cost of expanding the signature. Alternatively, both the public key and signature can be kept short by making the public key a witness in the zero-knowledge proof statement, as is done in the generic construction (Fig. 4). However, doing so comes at the cost of increased complexity of the statement that the Combiner needs to prove.

Shorter Signatures Using Tracing Confirmation. The need to trace a TAPS signature to the signing quorum implies that a TAPS signature must encode the signing set, and therefore must be at least $\log_2 \binom{n}{t}$ bits long. We can design shorter TAPS signatures by relaxing this requirement: replace the tracing algorithm by a *quorum confirmation* algorithm. The confirmation algorithm takes the signing quorum set C as input, along with the secret tracing key sk_{t}, and a pair (m, σ). It outputs 1 if the set C is the set that generated σ. The security definitions in Sect. 3 can be adapted to support quorum confirmation instead of tracing. Since a signature no longer needs to encode the quorum set, this lets us construct TAPS where signature size in independent of the number of parties, for example by using a constant-size zk-SNARK for the relation $\mathcal{R}_S$ in Fig. 6. Our bulletproofs construction can be made to directly achieve a TAPS with quorum confirmation and logarithmic size signatures.

Stronger Privacy Against Signers. Our privacy against signers game in Fig. 3 ensures that the signer's private keys cannot be used to link a TAPS signature to the quorum that created it. However, it is possible that the quorum of signers that helped create a TAPS signature σ, can later recognize σ, using its knowledge of the random bits used during the signing process. The same is true for many Schnorr private threshold signature (PTS) schemes: the quorum that creates a signature can recognize that signature. If needed, our Schnorr TAPS construction can be strengthened so that the Combiner can ensure that a TAPS signature cannot be recognized by the quorum of signers that helped create it. The Combiner need only blind the quantity $R \in \mathbb{G}$ in the signature by a random group element, and adjust the relation in Fig. 6 accordingly. We leave this variation for future work.

A Construction from the BLS Signature Scheme. In this paper we focused on a TAPS from the Schnorr signature scheme. A TAPS can also be constructed from the BLS signature scheme [17] as the underlying ATS. We leave this for future work.

Beyond Threshold: Supporting Monotone Access Structures. While threshold access structures are widely used in practice, our constructions generalize to support more general monotone access structures. For example, one can require that a quorum of signers contain t_1 parties from one set of signers and t_2 from another set of signers. More generally, standard techniques [6] can be used to generalize our construction to support any access structure derived from a polynomial size monotone formula.

7 Conclusion and Future Work

In this work, we present TAPS, a new threshold signature primitive that ensures both accountability and privacy. While notions of accountable threshold schemes and private threshold schemes exist in the literature, our work takes a step towards defining a primitive with both properties simultaneously.

We hope that future work can lead to TAPS schemes with shorter signatures and public keys. Our generic construction has a short public key: the public key is simply a commitment to an ATS public key, and so its size is independent of the number of parties n. However, our Schnorr-based systems with efficient tracing require a linear size public key. An important research direction is to design an efficient TAPS that relies on standard assumptions where the size of the public key is independent of n. One possible avenue for a more efficient TAPS is for pk to be the root of a Merkle tree whose leaves are the n signers' public keys. The zero-knowledge proof output by the Combiner will then be a succinct non-interactive zero-knowledge argument of knowledge (a zk-SNARK) demonstrating that t of the n signers participated in signing. A related direction is to employ the approach of Dodis et al. [31], by defining the public key via an accumulator scheme. The signature is then a proof that the t signers know the corresponding secret keys to t public keys in the accumulator. However, it remains an open problem to design such a scheme that fulfills our notion of accountability.

Another direction for future work is to improve the efficiency of verification in our Schnorr TAPS. In settings where n is small, such as financial transactions, the linear-time cost of verification of the Schnorr construction is acceptable. For large n the cost may be prohibitive. Future work could consider other constructions that support full tracing, but with a faster verifier.

Acknowledgments. This work was funded by NSF, DARPA, a grant from ONR, and the Simons Foundation. Opinions, findings, and conclusions or recommendations expressed in this material are those of the authors and do not necessarily reflect the views of DARPA.

References

1. Andresen, G.: Bitcoin m-of-n standard transactions (2011). BIP-0011
2. Attema, T., Cramer, R.: Compressed Σ-protocol theory and practical application to plug & play secure algorithmics. In: Micciancio, D., Ristenpart, T. (eds.) CRYPTO 2020. LNCS, vol. 12172, pp. 513–543. Springer, Cham (2020). https://doi.org/10.1007/978-3-030-56877-1_18

3. Attema, T., Fehr, S., Klooß, M.: Fiat-shamir transformation of multi-round interactive proofs. Cryptology ePrint Archive, Report 2021/1377 (2021). https://ia.cr/2021/1377
4. Au, M.H., Chow, S.S.M., Susilo, W., Tsang, P.P.: Short linkable ring signatures revisited. In: Atzeni, A.S., Lioy, A. (eds.) EuroPKI 2006. LNCS, vol. 4043, pp. 101–115. Springer, Heidelberg (2006). https://doi.org/10.1007/11774716_9
5. Bagherzandi, A., Cheon, J.H., Jarecki, S.: Multisignatures secure under the discrete logarithm assumption and a generalized forking lemma. In: Conference on Computer and Communications Security (2008)
6. Beimel, A.: Secret-sharing schemes: a survey. In: Chee, Y.M., et al. (eds.) IWCC 2011. LNCS, vol. 6639, pp. 11–46. Springer, Heidelberg (2011). https://doi.org/10.1007/978-3-642-20901-7_2
7. Bellare, M., Goldreich, O.: On defining proofs of knowledge. In: Brickell, E.F. (ed.) CRYPTO 1992. LNCS, vol. 740, pp. 390–420. Springer, Heidelberg (1993). https://doi.org/10.1007/3-540-48071-4_28
8. Bellare, M., Micciancio, D., Warinschi, B.: Foundations of group signatures: formal definitions, simplified requirements, and a construction based on general assumptions. In: Biham, E. (ed.) EUROCRYPT 2003. LNCS, vol. 2656, pp. 614–629. Springer, Heidelberg (2003). https://doi.org/10.1007/3-540-39200-9_38
9. Bellare, M., Neven, G.: Multi-signatures in the plain public-key model and a general forking lemma. In: Juels, A., Wright, R.N., di Vimercati, S.D.C. (eds.) CCS 2006, pp. 390–399. ACM (2006)
10. Bellare, M., Shoup, S.: Two-tier signatures from the fiat-shamir transform, with applications to strongly unforgeable and one-time signatures. IET Inf. Secur. **2**(2), 47–63 (2008)
11. Bender, A., Katz, J., Morselli, R.: Ring signatures: stronger definitions, and constructions without random oracles. J. Cryptol. **22**(1), 114–138 (2009)
12. Bichsel, P., Camenisch, J., Neven, G., Smart, N.P., Warinschi, B.: Get shorty via group signatures without encryption. In: Garay, J.A., De Prisco, R. (eds.) SCN 2010. LNCS, vol. 6280, pp. 381–398. Springer, Heidelberg (2010). https://doi.org/10.1007/978-3-642-15317-4_24
13. Bitansky, N., Canetti, R., Chiesa, A., Tromer, E.: From extractable collision resistance to succinct non-interactive arguments of knowledge, and back again. In: ITCS 2012, pp. 326–349. ACM (2012)
14. Blömer, J., Juhnke, J., Löken, N.: Short group signatures with distributed traceability. In: Kotsireas, I.S., Rump, S.M., Yap, C.K. (eds.) MACIS 2015. LNCS, vol. 9582, pp. 166–180. Springer, Cham (2016). https://doi.org/10.1007/978-3-319-32859-1_14
15. Boldyreva, A.: Threshold signatures, multisignatures and blind signatures based on the gap-diffie-hellman-group signature scheme. In: Desmedt, Y.G. (ed.) PKC 2003. LNCS, vol. 2567, pp. 31–46. Springer, Heidelberg (2003). https://doi.org/10.1007/3-540-36288-6_3
16. Boneh, D., Boyen, X., Shacham, H.: Short group signatures. In: Franklin, M. (ed.) CRYPTO 2004. LNCS, vol. 3152, pp. 41–55. Springer, Heidelberg (2004). https://doi.org/10.1007/978-3-540-28628-8_3
17. Boneh, D., Lynn, B., Shacham, H.: Short signatures from the Weil pairing. In: Boyd, C. (ed.) ASIACRYPT 2001. LNCS, vol. 2248, pp. 514–532. Springer, Heidelberg (2001). https://doi.org/10.1007/3-540-45682-1_30
18. Bootle, J., Cerulli, A., Chaidos, P., Ghadafi, E., Groth, J.: Foundations of fully dynamic group signatures. J. Cryptol. **33**(4), 1822–1870 (2020)

19. Bootle, J., Cerulli, A., Chaidos, P., Ghadafi, E., Groth, J., Petit, C.: Short accountable ring signatures based on DDH. In: Pernul, G., Ryan, P.Y.A., Weippl, E. (eds.) ESORICS 2015. LNCS, vol. 9326, pp. 243–265. Springer, Cham (2015). https://doi.org/10.1007/978-3-319-24174-6_13
20. Bootle, J., Cerulli, A., Chaidos, P., Groth, J., Petit, C.: Efficient zero-knowledge arguments for arithmetic circuits in the discrete log setting. In: Fischlin, M., Coron, J.-S. (eds.) EUROCRYPT 2016. LNCS, vol. 9666, pp. 327–357. Springer, Heidelberg (2016). https://doi.org/10.1007/978-3-662-49896-5_12
21. Bresson, E., Stern, J., Szydlo, M.: Threshold ring signatures and applications to ad-hoc groups. In: Yung, M. (ed.) CRYPTO 2002. LNCS, vol. 2442, pp. 465–480. Springer, Heidelberg (2002). https://doi.org/10.1007/3-540-45708-9_30
22. Bünz, B., Bootle, J., Boneh, D., Poelstra, A., Wuille, P., Maxwell, G.: Bulletproofs: short proofs for confidential transactions and more. In: IEEE S&P, pp. 315–334 (2018)
23. Camenisch, J.: Efficient and generalized group signatures. In: Fumy, W. (ed.) EUROCRYPT 1997. LNCS, vol. 1233, pp. 465–479. Springer, Heidelberg (1997). https://doi.org/10.1007/3-540-69053-0_32
24. Camenisch, J., Drijvers, M., Lehmann, A., Neven, G., Towa, P.: Short threshold dynamic group signatures. In: Galdi, C., Kolesnikov, V. (eds.) SCN 2020. LNCS, vol. 12238, pp. 401–423. Springer, Cham (2020). https://doi.org/10.1007/978-3-030-57990-6_20
25. Chaum, D., van Heyst, E.: Group signatures. In: Davies, D.W. (ed.) EUROCRYPT 1991. LNCS, vol. 547, pp. 257–265. Springer, Heidelberg (1991). https://doi.org/10.1007/3-540-46416-6_22
26. Damgård, I., Koprowski, M.: Practical threshold RSA signatures without a trusted dealer. In: Pfitzmann, B. (ed.) EUROCRYPT 2001. LNCS, vol. 2045, pp. 152–165. Springer, Heidelberg (2001). https://doi.org/10.1007/3-540-44987-6_10
27. Damgård, I.: On Σ Protocols (2010)
28. de Valence, H.: Merlin transcripts. https://merlin.cool
29. Derler, D., Slamanig, D.: Highly-efficient fully-anonymous dynamic group signatures. In: AsiaCCS 2018 (2018)
30. Desmedt, Y., Frankel, Y.: Threshold cryptosystems. In: Brassard, G. (ed.) CRYPTO 1989. LNCS, vol. 435, pp. 307–315. Springer, New York (1990). https://doi.org/10.1007/0-387-34805-0_28
31. Dodis, Y., Kiayias, A., Nicolosi, A., Shoup, V.: Anonymous Identification in *Ad Hoc* Groups. In: Cachin, C., Camenisch, J.L. (eds.) EUROCRYPT 2004. LNCS, vol. 3027, pp. 609–626. Springer, Heidelberg (2004). https://doi.org/10.1007/978-3-540-24676-3_36
32. Feng, H., Liu, J., Li, D., Li, Y.-N., Wu, Q.: Traceable ring signatures: general framework and post-quantum security. Des. Codes Crypt. **89**(6), 1111–1145 (2021). https://doi.org/10.1007/s10623-021-00863-x
33. Fiat, A., Shamir, A.: How to prove yourself: practical solutions to identification and signature problems. In: Odlyzko, A.M. (ed.) CRYPTO 1986. LNCS, vol. 263, pp. 186–194. Springer, Heidelberg (1987). https://doi.org/10.1007/3-540-47721-7_12
34. Fouque, P.-A., Stern, J.: Fully distributed threshold RSA under standard assumptions. In: Boyd, C. (ed.) ASIACRYPT 2001. LNCS, vol. 2248, pp. 310–330. Springer, Heidelberg (2001). https://doi.org/10.1007/3-540-45682-1_19
35. Fujisaki, E.: Sub-linear size traceable ring signatures without random oracles. In: Kiayias, A. (ed.) CT-RSA 2011. LNCS, vol. 6558, pp. 393–415. Springer, Heidelberg (2011). https://doi.org/10.1007/978-3-642-19074-2_25

36. Fujisaki, E., Suzuki, K.: Traceable ring signature. In: Okamoto, T., Wang, X. (eds.) PKC 2007. LNCS, vol. 4450, pp. 181–200. Springer, Heidelberg (2007). https://doi.org/10.1007/978-3-540-71677-8_13
37. Furukawa, J., Imai, H.: An efficient group signature scheme from bilinear maps. IEICE Tran. Fundam. Electron. Commun. Comput. Sci. **89–A**(5), 1328–1338 (2006)
38. Gennaro, R., Goldfeder, S.: One round threshold ECDSA with identifiable abort. IACR Cryptol. ePrint Arch. (2020)
39. Gennaro, R., Jarecki, S., Krawczyk, H., Rabin, T.: Robust threshold DSS signatures. Inf. Comput. **164**(1), 54–84 (2001)
40. Gentry, C., Wichs, D.: Separating succinct non-interactive arguments from all falsifiable assumptions. In: STOC 2011, pp. 99–108. ACM (2011)
41. Goldwasser, S., Micali, S., Yao, A.C.: Strong signature schemes. In: FOCS 1983, pp. 431–439. ACM (1983)
42. Goyal, V., Song, Y., Srinivasan, A.: Traceable secret sharing and applications. In: Malkin, T., Peikert, C. (eds.) CRYPTO 2021. LNCS, vol. 12827, pp. 718–747. Springer, Cham (2021). https://doi.org/10.1007/978-3-030-84252-9_24
43. Haque, A., Scafuro, A.: Threshold ring signatures: new definitions and post-quantum security. In: Kiayias, A., Kohlweiss, M., Wallden, P., Zikas, V. (eds.) PKC 2020. LNCS, vol. 12111, pp. 423–452. Springer, Cham (2020). https://doi.org/10.1007/978-3-030-45388-6_15
44. Itakura, K., Nakamura, K.: A public-key cryptosystem suitable for digital multisignatures. NEC Res. Dev. **71**, 1–8 (1983)
45. Komlo, C., Goldberg, I.: FROST: flexible round-optimized Schnorr threshold signatures. In: Dunkelman, O., Jacobson, Jr., M.J., O'Flynn, C. (eds.) SAC 2020. LNCS, vol. 12804, pp. 34–65. Springer, Cham (2021). https://doi.org/10.1007/978-3-030-81652-0_2
46. Libert, B., Yung, M.: Dynamic fully forward-secure group signatures. In: AsiaCCS 2010 (2010)
47. Liu, J.K., Wei, V.K., Wong, D.S.: A separable threshold ring signature scheme. In: Lim, J.-I., Lee, D.-H. (eds.) ICISC 2003. LNCS, vol. 2971, pp. 12–26. Springer, Heidelberg (2004). https://doi.org/10.1007/978-3-540-24691-6_2
48. Manulis, M., Fleischhacker, N., Günther, F., Kiefer, F., Poettrering, B.: Group signatures: authentication with privacy. Bundesamt fur Sicherheit in der Informationstechnik (2012)
49. Maxwell, G., Poelstra, A., Seurin, Y., Wuille, P.: Simple Schnorr multi-signatures with applications to bitcoin. Des. Codes Crypt. **87**(9), 2139–2164 (2019)
50. Micali, S., Ohta, K., Reyzin, L.: Accountable-subgroup multisignatures: extended abstract. In: CCS 2001, pp. 245–254. ACM (2001)
51. Munch-Hansen, A., Orlandi, C., Yakoubov, S.: Stronger notions and a more efficient construction of threshold ring signatures. In: Longa, P., Ràfols, C. (eds.) LATINCRYPT 2021. LNCS, vol. 12912, pp. 363–381. Springer, Cham (2021). https://doi.org/10.1007/978-3-030-88238-9_18
52. Naor, M.: Deniable ring authentication. In: Yung, M. (ed.) CRYPTO 2002. LNCS, vol. 2442, pp. 481–498. Springer, Heidelberg (2002). https://doi.org/10.1007/3-540-45708-9_31
53. Nick, J., Ruffing, T., Seurin, Y.: MuSig2: simple two-round Schnorr multi-signatures. In: Malkin, T., Peikert, C. (eds.) CRYPTO 2021. LNCS, vol. 12825, pp. 189–221. Springer, Cham (2021). https://doi.org/10.1007/978-3-030-84242-0_8

54. Rivest, R.L., Shamir, A., Tauman, Y.: How to leak a secret. In: Boyd, C. (ed.) ASIACRYPT 2001. LNCS, vol. 2248, pp. 552–565. Springer, Heidelberg (2001). https://doi.org/10.1007/3-540-45682-1_32
55. Schnorr, C.P.: Efficient identification and signatures for smart cards. In: Brassard, G. (ed.) CRYPTO 1989. LNCS, vol. 435, pp. 239–252. Springer, New York (1990). https://doi.org/10.1007/0-387-34805-0_22
56. Shoup, V.: Practical threshold signatures. In: Preneel, B. (ed.) EUROCRYPT 2000. LNCS, vol. 1807, pp. 207–220. Springer, Heidelberg (2000). https://doi.org/10.1007/3-540-45539-6_15
57. Stinson, D.R., Strobl, R.: Provably secure distributed Schnorr signatures and a (t, n) threshold scheme for implicit certificates. In: Varadharajan, V., Mu, Y. (eds.) ACISP 2001. LNCS, vol. 2119, pp. 417–434. Springer, Heidelberg (2001). https://doi.org/10.1007/3-540-47719-5_33
58. Tsang, P.P., Wei, V.K., Chan, T.K., Au, M.H., Liu, J.K., Wong, D.S.: Separable linkable threshold ring signatures. In: Canteaut, A., Viswanathan, K. (eds.) INDOCRYPT 2004. LNCS, vol. 3348, pp. 384–398. Springer, Heidelberg (2004). https://doi.org/10.1007/978-3-540-30556-9_30
59. Xu, S., Yung, M.: Accountable ring signatures: a smart card approach. In: Quisquater, J.-J., Paradinas, P., Deswarte, Y., El Kalam, A.A. (eds.) CARDIS 2004. IIFIP, vol. 153, pp. 271–286. Springer, Boston (2004). https://doi.org/10.1007/1-4020-8147-2_18

Author Index